THE NEUROSES

THE NEUROSES

Henry P. Laughlin

Practicing Psychiatrist in Bethesda, Maryland

Past President, American College of Psychiatrists

WASHINGTON

BUTTERWORTHS

1967

U. S. A.:   BUTTERWORTH INC.
                   WASHINGTON, D. C.: 7300 Pearl Street, 20014

ENGLAND: BUTTERWORTH & CO. (PUBLISHERS) LTD.
                   LONDON: 88 Kingsway, W.C.2

AUSTRALIA: BUTTERWORTH & CO. (AUSTRALIA) LTD.
                   SYDNEY: 20 Loftus Street
                   MELBOURNE: 473 Bourke Street
                   BRISBANE: 240 Queen Street

CANADA: BUTTERWORTH & CO. (CANADA) LTD.
                   TORONTO: 1367 Danforth Avenue, 6

NEW ZEALAND: BUTTERWORTH & CO. (NEW ZEALAND) LTD.
                   WELLINGTON: 49/51 Ballance Street
                   AUCKLAND: 35 High Street

SOUTH AFRICA: BUTTERWORTH & CO. (SOUTH AFRICA) LTD.
                   DURBAN: 33/35 Beach Grove

LIBRARY OF CONGRESS CATALOGUE CARD NO. 65-12909

LITHOGRAPHED IN THE UNITED STATES OF AMERICA
BY MAHONY & ROESE INC.

Dedicated to

Marion, our children John, Robert, Barbara,
Deborah and Constance, and her husband
Clifford Kuhn . . .

And to each who opens these pages.

PREFACE

I have written THE NEUROSES for everyone who is concerned with emotions, motivation, and behavior. It is especially oriented toward the private practice of medicine and psychiatry. Psychodynamics and therapy, and their correlation with today's clinical findings, are stressed. This represents the textbook in extra-mural psychiatry which I very much wanted in my own student days.

I hope that every student, resident, colleague, and in particular the Board Candidate in Psychiatry, will find something of value in THE NEUROSES. Each has been most carefully borne in mind throughout its preparation.

THE NEUROSES succeeds THE NEUROSES IN CLINICAL PRACTICE, orginally published in 1956. The clinical studies and research required have been a strictly personal endeavor, and have received no outside subsidy.

I appreciate very much the helpful comments of all those who have encouraged me during the course of this work. As with the "blue book" of MENTAL MECHANISMS (published by Butterworths in 1963), all the royalties from THE NEUROSES have been assigned in advance to worthy causes.

Bethesda and Mount Airy, Maryland,
December 16, 1966.

Henry P. Laughlin, M.D.

CONTENTS

Chapter

1. THE NATURE AND ORIGINS OF ANXIETY / 1
  . . . *Fear in the absence of a known cause*

2. THE ILLUSORY GAINS OF EMOTIONAL
  ILLNESS / 55
  . . . *Defensively-motivated reactions self-defeating*

3. THE ANXIETY REACTIONS / 81
  . . . *The more direct expression of anxiety and its effects*

4. THE DEPRESSIVE REACTIONS / 135
  . . . *Pathologically lowered spirits, sadness, and dejection*

5. THE CHARACTER REACTIONS / 227
  . . . *Character trait defenses, their constellations and hypertrophy*

6. THE OBSESSIVE-COMPULSIVE REACTIONS / 307
  . . . *Defensively elaborated patterns of reaction marked by the
  intrusion of insistent, repetitive, and unwelcome thoughts and urges*

7. THE FATIGUE REACTIONS / 379
  . . . *Fatigue incident to emotional stress, tension and psychic conflict*

8. THE HYGEIAPHRONTIC REACTIONS / 441
  . . . *Anxious concern about health; non-organic symptomatology*

9. FEAR AND ITS AVOIDANCE / 515
  . . . *An introduction to the phobic and soterial patterns of reaction*

10. THE PHOBIC REACTIONS / 545
  . . . *Avoidance through displacement and substitution*

11. THE SOTERIAL REACTIONS / 607
  . . . *Security from an external object-source*

12. THE CONVERSION REACTIONS / 639

> *... Emotional conflicts are converted so as to secure symbolic external expression via somatic and physiologic routes*

13. THE DISSOCIATIVE REACTIONS / 721

> *... Dissociative concepts, dreams, somnambulism, depersonalization, fainting, amnesia, fugue states, alternating personality, automatic behavior, and hypnosis*

14. THE NEUROSES FOLLOWING TRAUMA / 831

> *... A group of neurotic reactions the onset of which follows trauma*

15. MILITARY REACTIONS AND PRISONER PROCESSING / 899

> *... Emotional reactions incident to military operations and psychologic conditioning*

APPENDIX: EMOTIONAL AND MENTAL ILLNESS: AN OUTLINE CLASSIFICATION / 951

A GLOSSARY OF PSYCHIATRIC CONCEPTS AND TERMS / 957

INDEX / 1031

TABLES

1. The Manifestations of Anxiety / 20
2. The Sources of Anxiety / 30
3. Diagnostic Trends in the Neuroses / 46
4. The Epigain / 65
5. The Endogain / 69
6. The "Gains" of Emotional Illness / 77
7. The Emotional Illnesses / 87
8. Anxiety Neurosis and Its Clinical Manifestations / 113
9. Sound Bases for Assisting Depressed Persons;
   Why Therapy is Worthwhile / 139
10. Features in Distinguishing Neurotic from
    Psychotic Depression / 147
11. The Clinical and Personal Experience of Groups of
    Physicians and Students with Suicidal Tendencies / 152
12. Incidence and Relative Importance of Emotional
    Depression as Found in 108 Consecutive Persons
    Studied in a Private Psychiatric Practice / 154
13. The Potential-For-Suicide Index / 163
14. The Depressive Endogain / 178
15. Three Major Groups of Character Defenses / 239
16. The Relative Incidence of Types of Neurotic Reactions / 243
17. The Obsessive Character Defenses / 247
18. The Character Defenses Associated with the
    Conversion (hysterical) Personality / 259
19. Twelve Factors Which Predispose to the Development
    of Obsessive Patterns of Defense / 342
20. Clinical and Personal Experience of Groups of Physicians
    and Students with the Symptom of Emotional Fatigue / 395
21. Emotional Fatigue and Depression / 407
22. Conscious Secondary Gain and Epigain of Emotional
    Fatigue / 409
23. The Principal Features of Neurasthenia / 428
24. The Clinical and Personal Experience of Groups of
    Physicians and Students with Hygeiaphrontis / 459

25. Indications for Psychiatric Consultation and Therapy
      in Hygeiaphrontis / 502
26. Hygeiaphrontic Endogain and Epigain / 511
27. The More Common Phobic Reactions / 553
28. Selection of the Phobic Object / 583
29. Seven Goals of Psychotherapy / 593
30. The Soteria and the Phobia / 628
31. Terms in the Diagnosis of the Physiologic Conversions / 655
32. The Psychologic Purposes of the Conversion Reactions;
      The Conversion Endogain / 690
33. Important Factors (Determinants) in Symptom
      Choice and Location / 697
34. Major Types of Dissociation / 729
35. The Dissociative Reactions: Comparative Data / 738
36. The Sources and Stimuli of Depersonalization / 764
37. Types of Amnesia / 777
38. Clinical Types of Fugue States / 796
39. Psychic Pressures in Inducing Confessions / 818
40. Compensation and Neuroses; Bases for Problems in
      Management / 877
41. Instances of Emotional Disability Following Trauma / 881
42. Goals of Psychotherapy / 890
43. Diagnoses Accorded Combat Reactions / 904
44. Diagnoses of Neurotic Reactions Accorded Servicemen
      Overseas / 905
45. The Diagnoses Given 470 Consecutive Combat Reactions / 906
46. The Symptoms of Combat Reactions / 908
47. Individual Factors in Susceptibility to Combat Stress / 920
48. Individual Factors in "Success" of Prisoner Processing / 937

CHAPTER 1

THE NATURE AND ORIGINS OF ANXIETY

.... Fear in the Absence of a Known Cause

I. CRUCIAL ROLE OF ANXIETY
  A. Law of Relativity in Emotional Health
    1. Problems are Universal; 2. Relativity in Diagnosis and Classification; 3. Value of Separate Categories in Neuroses
  B. Man Seeks to Avoid Anxiety
    1. Fundamental Conceptions in Dynamic Psychiatry; 2. Bases of Symptoms; 3. Anxiety Manifested Directly and Indirectly; 4. Anxiety a New Concept of Universal Application
  C. Yardstick for Measuring Emotional Health
    1. Interpersonal Relationships have Vital Importance in Emotional Development; 2. Neurosis vs. Maturity; 3. Important "Whys" and "Hows"
  D. Incidence in Private Practice
    1. Neuroses Constitute Majority; 2. Areas to be Considered

II. THE NATURE OF ANXIETY
  A. Major Role in Development and History of Man
    1. Powerful Influence in Maturation; 2. Principle of Universality; 3. Interest in Anxiety Recent; 4. Anxiety a Stimulus to Seeking Therapeutic Help; Inverse Ratio Concept; 5. Possible Restrictive Forces in Study of Anxiety
  B. Anxiety Normal or Pathologic?
  C. Anxiety Defined
    1. Fear vs. Anxiety; 2. Anxiety vs. Fear
  D. Apprehensive Anticipation
  E. Discharge of Anxiety Into Activity
    1. Energy Potential Released; 2. Transformed into Anger as Anxiety-Equivalent

  F. Direct and Indirect Manifestations of Anxiety
    1. Condensed Tabulation; 2. Psychogenesis of Emotional Manifestations; 3. Applications for Childhood, as for Adults

III. EMOTIONAL CONFLICT
  A. Clash Between Two Opposing Emotional Forces
    1. "Instinctual" Drives vs. Prohibiting Personal and Social Standards; 2. Goal of Equanimity Concept
  B. Conflict→Anxiety→ Repression→Symptoms
    1. Conflicts over Aggressive and Sexual Drives More Basic and Important: Derepression; 2. Emotional Conflict Defined; Vital Sequence of Events
  C. Instincts and Acculturation: First Tenet of Parental Role
  D. Psychologic "Fight or Flight" Responses
    1. Analogous to Physical Responses to External Threat or Danger; 2. Central Dynamic Concept; Attempted Defenses Against Anxiety
  E. To Secure Benefits through Psychotherapy, Patient Must Help
    1. Unique Kind of Collaborative Relationship between Doctor and Patient; Joint Endeavor Principle; 2. Psychotherapy Encounters Resistances; 3. In Therapy Understanding Meaning of Symptoms Sought

IV. THE ORIGINS OF ANXIETY
  A. Development of Theory
  B. The Primary Sources of Anxiety
    1. Theory of Antecedent Conflicts; 2. Helplessness; 3. Separation; 4. Privation and Loss; 5. Frustration; 6. "Emotional Contagion" of Anxiety; 7. Disapproval or Fear of

Disapproval from Significant Adults; 8. Physical Threats; 9. Specific Emotional Hazards of Childhood; 10. Conditioned Responses

C. The Secondary Sources of Anxiety
1. Influences of Antecedent Prototypes and Maturation Level Important; 2. Superego Conflict (Conflicts with Conscience); 3. Disapproval, or Fear of Disapproval, Especially from Significant Persons; 4. Social Conflict; 5. Threats to Self-Preservation; 6. Threats to Racial Preservation; Conditioned Responses; 8. Frustration and Hostility; 9. Infantile Carry-overs, and Miscellaneous Sources; 10. Apprehensive Anticipation; 11. Specific Emotional Hazards of Adulthood

V. ANXIETY AND SLEEP
A. Role of Sleep in Emotional Health
1. Principle of Trend Toward Emotional Health; Sleep Refurbishes One's Psychologic Strength; 2. Widespread Recognition; 3. Hypothesis of Dream's Contribution to Emotional Health
B. Sedatives and Tranquilizers
C. Sleep Deprivation: Effects and Rapid Recovery
D. Oversleeping

VI. THE FUNCTION OF ANXIETY
A. Abnormal, Disruptive, and Pathologic
B. Protective, Constructive, and Socializing; Constructive Anxiety Concept
C. University of Application

VII. INTRODUCTORY COMMENTS ON DIAGNOSIS AND CLASSIFICATION
A. Making the Diagnosis
1. Diagnosis made on Descriptive Basis; 2. Importance of Outstanding Clinical Feature
B. Certain Terms: Their Origin and Development
1. Hypochondriasis, Hysteria, and Melancholia
C. Terminology at the Turn of the Century
1. Diagnostic Terms Added
D. Further Development and Refinement of Terminology (1900-1965)
E. Positive Grounds for Diagnosis Preferable

VIII. INTRODUCTORY COMMENTS ON TREATMENT
A. The Symptoms; Position in Medicine
1. Symptom An External Expression of Conflict; 2. Conflict Resolution Relieves Symptoms; 3. Emotional Bases of Functional Symptoms Elusive; 4. "Psychiatric Half" of Medical Practice; Medical Teaching Limited
B. Approaches in Therapy; Technique
1. The Patient; 2. Educational Process of Considerable Depth; 3. The Treatment Rule; 4. Psychotherapy Differs from Other Medical Therapies; 5. Patient and Therapist Learn Together

IX. SUMMARY

X. SELECTED REFERENCES AND BIBLIOGRAPHY

XI. REVIEW QUESTIONS ON CONFLICT AND ANXIETY

I. CRUCIAL ROLE OF ANXIETY

A. LAW OF RELATIVITY IN EMOTIONAL HEALTH

1. Problems are Universal

THE STUDENT of modern dynamic psychiatry soon learns that much is relative and little is absolute in the study of human emotions and behavior. First, a so-called normal level of emotional health is difficult to define. Further, the "normal" imperceptibly merges into the borderline, and the borderline into the neurotic. On certain occasions, neurotic manifestations in turn appear clinically to merge into psychotic ones. Emotional health is truly a relative matter. This is such a truism that we might well formulate a Law of Relativity in Emotional Health [Ch.9:IIA2]. Everyone has problems. Everyone suffers from disturbed and painful emotions, at least at times. The difference between people in this area more often is one of quantity than of quality. Emotional difficulties also show great variation in both quantity and quality. The degree of the resulting interference with living is also a highly individual matter.

2. Relativity in Diagnosis and Classification

There is another important area of relativity in the field of emotional health. This occurs in diagnosis and classification. Drawing clear-cut lines of distinction between the groups of clinical reactions is difficult. An arbitrary decision may prove necessary.

The clinical manifestations of the many different kinds of emotional illness thus often merge and overlap diagnostically in a confusing fashion. A number of different kinds of clinical features are more than likely to occur in the same case. This is apt to prove especially troubling for the young physician. However, that such difficulties are also experienced by his professional seniors is illustrated through the occasional lengthy discussions among them concerning some troublesome diagnostic problem.

3. Value of Separate Categories in Neuroses

A stable frame of reference for the classification of these patterns of pathologically-defensive reactions is very useful. This is true for the individual physician and in the field of medicine generally.

The development of standards for making a diagnosis in emotional and mental illness is at the same time a considerable personal asset, as well as a substantial professional advantage. The criteria which are adopted should satisfy oneself, and should also be in reasonable concurrence with those of one's colleagues. Separate diagnostic categories for the neurotic reactions have considerable value.

It is advantageous to separate the neuroses into groups of reactions. Six cogent reasons for developing our ability to classify cases of neurosis are:
  (1) The facilitation of scientific communication and the transmission of data in more standard terms.
  (2) The aiding of research endeavors.
  (3) The evolvement of more standard frames of reference.
The division of cases of neurosis into diagnostic groups is further a great convenience (4) in facilitating their study, and (5) in medical and graduate teaching. Finally, (6) classification becomes a necessity for purposes of statistics: reporting, records, studies, and in the accumulation of data relative to the incidence and prevalence of the various types of neurotic reactions.

In view of these advantages a system of classification will be followed in our forthcoming consideration of this major group of emotional illnesses. It is important, however, to note that the specificity and the subtleties of diagnosis are likely to become considerably less important in the course of intensive psychotherapy generally. During psychotherapy the aim of attention becomes directed toward the "why" of each manifestation, seeking ever to learn why it is present and how it came to be established. The importance of diagnosis becomes secondary to the aims and goals of therapy.

Actually, it must be kept in mind that a given neurosis is seldom seen in pure culture. A mixed clinical picture is more often the rule than the exception.

In making the diagnosis of a neurosis when one is required, it is helpful and recommended to make it simply according to the most outstanding clinical feature of the illness. It is also helpful to keep in mind that the various types of neurosis may perhaps more accurately be regarded as patterns of reaction, rather than as specific and absolute pathologic entities (*see also* further introductory comments about diagnosis), [Ch.1:VIIA].

B. MAN SEEKS TO AVOID ANXIETY

1. Fundamental Conceptions in Dynamic Psychiatry

Anxiety is a vital force in human existence. It is subjectively uncomfortable and painful. Painful things in turn are avoided. Accordingly, man consciously seeks to avoid anxiety, and the circumstances in which it arises [Ch.9:IIIA2]. This is the Principle of Avoidance of Anxiety. He also unconsciously employs various mechanisms in trying to allay it. Resolution is sought of the underlying intrapsychic emotional conflicts which are individually responsible for his anxiety.

Thus we early learn several important facts. First, the study of the nature and origins of anxiety is very basic to, and most important in, psychiatry. Second, anxiety and anxiety-producing material or situations are avoided. Finally, anxiety plays a major role in the psychogenesis of emotional illness. These are fundamental conceptions in modern dynamic psychiatry.

Some authorities make little or no differentiation between the rather simple emotion of fear on the one hand, and the more complex one of anxiety on the other.* One can also find instances of variation in the professional use of the two terms. Thus, they may be occasionally employed to convey different meanings. Even the discard of one or the other has been recommended.† However, these differences more often reflect a variation in terminology and usage than in anything more fundamental. The most important thing is that the sense in which a scientific or technical term is employed be clear.

In professional communication, a term should convey the same meaning to the reader as to the writer. It becomes clearer then as to why exact definition is vital and as to why the development of ever-greater professional concurrence in meaning and usage offers increasing advantage in our field.

---

* For example, Potter wrote in regard to this point: "I believe that much of the discussion about the differences between 'fear' and 'anxiety' is rather academic. I see no basic difference between the *nature* of fear and the *nature* of anxiety. As to causation, the essence is threat. . . ."

† Rado reported, for example, that he no longer uses the term "anxiety." He said that ". . . we ought to discard this unhappy word from our technical language and revert to the exclusive use of the word fear."

This does not appear very likely to occur. Currently one might about as easily seek to secure the discard of the word "microorganism" in bacteriology as to try to effect the discard of the term "anxiety" in psychiatry.

2. Bases of Symptoms

There are two major bases which enter into the development or psychogenesis of emotional symptoms. These are: (1) all of the conscious and especially all of the unconscious endeavors aiming at the avoidance, the control, or the denial of anxiety, and (2) the direct and indirect effects *per se* of continuing anxiety and tension.

Anxiety is the force responsible for bringing about the repression from conscious awareness of personally-intolerable ideas, emotions, impulses, and strivings. It is these in turn, following their repression, which give rise to the symptoms. Thus, the symptoms of psychogenic origin may be regarded as ultimately developing as attempted defenses against anxiety. As stated, they develop as either the direct, or as the complex and indirect, manifestations of anxiety and/or its effects.

Psychogenic symptoms may also be considered to develop as the result of partially-successful or unsuccessful attempts at the resolution of the emotional conflicts responsible for the anxiety. As we shall see, they also may be regarded sometimes as unhealthy compromises.

3. Anxiety Manifested Directly and Indirectly

From the clinical standpoint, anxiety may be expressed directly, with either outwardly-apparent or more subjective manifestations of anxiety *per se,* as the major feature of the illness present. On the other hand, the ultimate effects of anxiety may be expressed in more complex and indirect forms.*

The latter indirect consequences of anxiety include a variety of psychologic manifestations: the phobias, the conversions, the dissociative reactions, the depressions, the soterias, emotional fatigue, overconcern with health (hygeiaphrontis; [Ch.2:IA]), obsessions and compulsions, character neuroses, and the neuroses following trauma. (*See Table 1,* [Ch.1:- IIF*1*]. These will each be discussed separately in subsequent chapters.

4. Anxiety a New Concept of Universal Application

Anxiety is a relatively new concept in medicine. Only in recent decades has this major source of human discomfort begun to receive some of the attention and study which it has long and most urgently warranted. This is despite its universality in human experience through the ages.

Anxiety is indeed pervasive. As Saul wrote: "There is no one so free of repressions, so entirely at one with his conscience and standards, that he has no inner anxieties whatever; few persons, if any, do not have some irrational fears . . ." Anxiety is a universal phenomenon [Ch.1:IIA2]. For these and other reasons [Ch.3:IA] this is an Age of Anxiety.

---

* In addition to a consideration of these many symptoms as indirect expressions of the effects of anxiety, they may also be regarded as replacements or substitutions for the otherwise subjectively-experienced anxiety. In such a role, their degree of "success" varies widely. Symptoms are also likely to express various aspects of the underlying conflict in more or less symbolic fashion.

C. YARDSTICK FOR MEASURING EMOTIONAL HEALTH

1. Interpersonal Relationships Have Vital Importance in Emotional Development

In our study of the relative level of emotional health we have come increasingly to recognize the importance of our past and present interactions with other people. The early contacts with significant people are of particular importance. The vicissitudes of our personal relationships and the satisfactions which we derive or which we fail to derive therefrom are most vital to our developing psyche and to our state of emotional well-being.

These relationships and their vicissitudes can have additional vital consequences. Psychic trauma of many kinds can result, or unhealthy antecedent patterns of reaction and self-defeating kinds of psychologic conditioning may develop.

Emotional health is a state of being which is relative rather than absolute. This is in accord with our Law of Relativity in emotional health. When, then, might we conclude that a person is emotionally healthy? What can we use as our yardstick? What is our basis of judgment?

The person who is emotionally healthy has effected a reasonably satisfactory integration of his unconscious, basic, repressed drives. He has worked out psychologically-harmonious solutions for them which are acceptable to himself and to his social milieu.

This is especially reflected in the personally and socially satisfactory nature of his current interpersonal relationships. It is also reflected in his individual level of satisfaction in living. Finally, we can also measure the level of individual emotional health in terms of the relative level of maturity which has been achieved.

2. Neurosis vs. Maturity

Compelling impulses and needs stemming from powerful hidden instinctual drives may remain unsolved, blocked, frustrated, or they may be dealt with unsatisfactorily. This state of affairs prevents the achievement of emotional stability and equanimity. It interferes with personality adjustment. Neurotic or even psychotic patterns of reactions and behavior may ultimately result.

Maturity implies the achievement of successful personal and social adjustment. Neurosis implies the reverse. If the achievement of a good social adjustment is regarded as a success of the "process of domestication", neurosis would to an extent indicate its failure.

3. Important "Whys" and "Hows"

The study of the ways in which these changes in personality adjustment take place is basic to our current concepts of dynamic psychiatry. We recognize that it has now become scientifically possible by intensive study and special techniques to work out the "whys" and the "hows" entering into our thoughts, feelings, and behavior. Since much of this is unconscious, the difficulties may be great. However, in the properly favorable situation, these hidden bases of human reaction may be made more intelligible to the patient and to the therapist.

The goals of the psychotherapist therefore include the gaining by the patient of basically increased self-understanding and emotional insight. This must be accompanied, first, by the patient's recognition, and, second, by his acceptance of earlier consciously-rejected impulses and desires. The development of constructive outlets for them must follow. These outlets must be socially acceptable as well as personally useful and satisfying (*see also* further introductory comments on therapy [Ch.1:IIIE;IVA;VIIIA]).

D. INCIDENCE IN PRIVATE PRACTICE

1. Neuroses Constitute Majority

The chapter headings in this book include the eleven major neurotic reactions* which we shall consider. With the neuroses have been included consideration of the Character Neuroses. This large group is one in which certain personality traits or character defenses are exaggerated and over-developed. These serve an analogous function to, and may be regarded as, equivalents of the clinical symptoms of the neuroses. Also included are the Physiologic Conversions together with the Conversion Reactions, which are variously referred to by such designations as "somatization reactions" or "psychosomatic illnesses". (*See Table 16, page 243*).

Together, these eleven groups of neurotic reactions constitute the overwhelming majority of all the psychiatry which is seen in the private practice of medicine. Special attention to these groups of reactions by all those planning to do private or clinical practice and psychotherapy is strongly warranted.

In this volume the majority of our attention will remain focused on this large and important area of psychiatric practice. Factors in the dynamics and the pathogenesis of each neurotic reaction will be correlated with its more usual clinical features, diagnosis, and classification. A series of case summaries, numbered consecutively, will be presented in illustration of the various patterns of neurotic reaction.

2. Areas to be Considered

In this particular chapter will be undertaken the development of a working definition of anxiety. This will be followed by a discussion of some important concepts as to its nature. Certain comments will be offered about the relation in turn of anxiety to fear, to "apprehensive anticipation", to its possible discharge through physical activity, and to its transition into anger. A number of clinical examples will be included.

---

* In order of our presentation these are the:

1. Anxiety Reactions	5. Fatigue Reactions	9. Conversion Reactions
2. Depressive Reactions	6. Hygeiaphrontic	10. Dissociative Reactions
3. Character Reactions	Reactions	11. Neuroses following
4. Obsessive-Compulsive	7. Phobic Reactions	Trauma
Reactions	8. Soterial Reactions	

The direct and the indirect manifestations of anxiety will be tabulated (*Table 1,* page 20). Emotional conflict will be discussed in its position as a major basis of anxiety. The origins of anxiety will be outlined; divided into what we might call the primary and the secondary sources. These origins will also be summarized in tabular form (*Table 2,* page 30).

·Certain interrelations between anxiety and sleep will be noted. The possible constructive *vs.* the destructive functions of anxiety will be briefly discussed. Finally, brief introductory comments on diagnosis and classification, and on therapy will be made. *Table 3* (page 46) regarding the Diagnostic Trends in the Neuroses has been prepared as a more graphic summary-reference. As with subsequent chapters there will also be a *Summary, Selected References and Bibliography* and a set of *Review Questions* at the chapter's conclusion.

II. THE NATURE OF ANXIETY

A. MAJOR ROLE IN DEVELOPMENT AND HISTORY OF MAN

1. Powerful Influence in Maturation

Anxiety has played a major role in the history of man since the beginning of time. Until recently this has been largely unrecognized. Its role has been particularly prominent from the standpoint of individual character formation and personality development. There have been all kinds of resulting influences upon the history of nations and upon civilization.

Anxiety is a powerful force in the individual maturing process. Infantile behavior and childhood standards are substantially developed and modified so as to conform gradually and more or less according to the wishes of significant adults.

This is largely through the desire for approval, acceptance, and love, the absence of which gives rise to anxiety. According to its consequences, anxiety can be destructive or constructive, or both. More will be said about this later.

2. Principle of Universality

Anxiety is a decidedly unpleasant phenomenon. Hence, everyone seeks to avoid it. It is difficult to imagine anyone deliberately seeking to experience anxiety. As a consequence of the unconscious "efforts" at its avoidance, mental mechanisms come to be employed and psychologic defenses are evolved. These can lead to symptom formation. They also enter importantly into character development. Accordingly, we can view anxiety as a potent force in each individual's personality formation. In accord with what we might term the Principle of Universality, anxiety is indeed experienced universally.

Sometimes, of course, these defenses against anxiety which are attempted or developed are unhealthy ones. As certain aspects in the process of maturation falter, symptoms may appear. A neurosis may develop. Most psychiatrists today are largely in concurrence as to this sequence of events. The symptoms which develop psychogenetically in emotional illness thus ultimately can be considered as the result of defensive efforts against anxiety.*

3. Interest in Anxiety Recent

It is indeed surprising that more attention has not been given to anxiety in past decades. This is especially true in view of man's longstanding personal familiarity with anxiety as an unpleasant experience. Anxiety has been a most potent force in man's individual, social and cultural development.

Lack of earlier attention is also of interest since we have come to appreciate more and more of anxiety's major role in emotional illness, in personality development, and in health generally. Interest in anxiety, however, is a recent development. As we shall see [Ch.3:IA] this is one basis for referring to our era as the Age of Anxiety. One might well speculate as to the reasons for our relatively recent recognition of its vast significance, and as to the belated development of our interest in this most major phenomenon.

4. Anxiety a Stimulus to Seeking Therapeutic Help; Inverse Ratio Concept

Anxiety in itself is a very important factor in patients seeking *vs.* not seeking treatment. This is illustrated at times in those persons for whom the symptoms are well established and can be considered as "successful" or effective, from the standpoint of preventing the subjective experiencing of anxiety. These people are proportionally less inclined to seek therapy.

This is what we might refer to as the Concept of the Inverse Ratio of

---

* One of the author's colleagues noted a possible exception, referring to the symptom of *ejaculatio praecox* (premature ejaculation, see also ref. [Ch.7:XIB1] as "an act of pure hostility on the part of the man towards his partner." Do we find this to be a real exception? It would appear not.

Now this is a formulation which is essentially correct, but only as far as it goes; that is, the hostility is toward the partner, or toward whoever is represented symbolically. The antecedent relationship and its associated emotional feelings serve as the unconscious and hidden prototype. On further study these patients have no conscious awareness of why the difficulty is present. They are consciously unaware of the responsible hostile feelings, and at least in early consultations probably would indignantly deny such a possibility. (Note here the therapeutically-defeating effect of premature interpretations through the stimulation of resistance).

How, when, and why had the original hostility been repressed, to secure later expression in such a roundabout and hidden way? It is because the hostility was absolutely unacceptable in the first place. As a result, it could not be consciously recognized, accepted, or dealt with more directly or in a more constructive fashion. The hostility therefore must have been repressed from conscious awareness, to become expressed in this devious and self-defeating fashion. How then does anxiety enter into this?

If the hostile feelings had been consciously tolerable they would not have been repressed. It is the anxiety they arouse which resulted in their repression and in the maintenance of their repression. Since the hostile feelings remained charged with significance and energy, even though repressed from conscious awareness, an outlet for them in disguised form was found through the symptom of *ejaculatio praecox*. Repression was the attempted defense against anxiety, and symptom formation was the consequence. The symptom allowed a distorted and disguised outward expression of the consciously-disowned hostility. Simultaneously, masochistic elements of self-defeat and self-punishment were also present as a part of this pattern of reaction.

Symptom-Success (in the allaying or preventing of anxiety), with Motivation Toward Therapy. The greater the symptom-success, the less motivation toward treatment. (*See also* [Ch.5:IXA*1*]; *also later* Fuel Analogy [Ch.1:VIB]. For example, one of the reasons why certain patients whose major manifestation is emotional depression (pathologically low spirits) never get into real treatment is because of the relative absence of anxiety to serve them as a motivating force. The subjective experiencing of anxiety can be a most uncomfortable but urgent stimulus towards getting a patient started in some kind of constructive therapeutic endeavor. By the same token anxiety about therapy or its effects can contribute to its being delayed, impeded or deterred.

5. *Possible Restrictive Forces in Study of Anxiety*

Sigmund Freud (1856–1939) proposed his first theory of the origin of anxiety in 1894, in his earlier years. It was not substantially modified for nearly thirty years, until 1923. The etiology of anxiety was ascribed by Freud in those early days primarily as resulting from interference with sexual satisfaction. This was too narrow and restrictive, even though the term "sexual" was generally used then to include a considerably broader area than the more narrow genital one of sexual relations. It undoubtedly exerted a kind of stultifying effect. There was, indeed, a crying need for the early psychiatrists and analytic investigators to develop a greater interest in anxiety. There was the need to study anxiety clinically, to develop further theories and to test them against experience.

The original analysts in addition concentrated their attention and therapeutic interest upon the recall of early memories and on the sexual roots of neurotic processes. Other roots were poorly recognized, if at all. These factors, however, could hardly explain fully the relatively late development of interest in anxiety. In addition, what of the many previous centuries? Further, these men constituted only a small fraction of the many physicians who were directly concerned with emotional illness. Many more doctors were indirectly concerned, at least to some extent, through their activities in the field of health generally.

Physicians are themselves, of course, by no means immune to anxiety. The intuitive communication, that is, the "contagion", of anxiety is a very real matter. Could this phenomenon also help explain the failure of earlier study and recognition of the importance of anxiety? Could this have served as a contributing but inadvertent emotional resistance or block to the study of anxiety and to the exploration of the areas which arouse it? Undoubtedly many individual and cultural factors have played a role in the restriction of earlier recognition of, and interest in, anxiety.

B. ANXIETY NORMAL OR PATHOLOGIC?

Anxiety arises in response to danger or threat. By the definition which we will follow, the source of this danger or threat is largely unclear. The danger or threat is essentially internal in its origin. This raises the question, about which more will be said later, as to whether we should regard anxiety as normal* or as pathologic. *First,* one differentiation may be made on the general basis of the relative and apparent *appropriateness of the response of anxiety.* This is partially reflected in our earlier definition of anxiety, elsewhere, as "an apprehensive tension or uneasiness" or "fear out of proportion to a known stimulus . . ." This is not incorrect, but it is rather an oversimplification.

Second, one might also make a differentiation according to the degree or *level of anxiety* which is present. Basically, however, the reaction of anxiety of course is individually appropriate to the person concerned. He has no conscious control over its appearance, its intensity, its level of interference with his functioning, and little enough over its control or resolution.

Third, since anxiety is a universal experience, another possible basis for its evaluation as either normal or pathologic might lie in an estimation as to *how the anxiety is individually met.* Accordingly, that anxiety which might be regarded as normal would be met by constructive and protective responses. The emotionally-healthy person would ordinarily find some way of successfully coping with the danger, eliminating it, or protecting himself against it . This would apply even though the source lies beyond his conscious awareness. He would still be able to maintain his emotional equilibrium and to exercise a measure of mature judgment. Much of the difference in dealing with anxiety varies according to one's basic individual capacities.

In the anxiety which might be regarded as pathologic, the adjustive efforts would be less effective. The protectively-intended and integrative responses would be limited and inadequate. They would be on the nonconstructive side. They might variously be disorganized, inappropriate, exaggerated, or ineffectual. Accordingly, the effect of the anxiety would be nonconstructive, and pathologic for the individual concerned.

Our basis for an evaluation of the pathology of anxiety then might include all three of the foregoing and a possible final point, which would be according to *its overall net effect* for the person concerned. This can be destructive and lead to pathology. It can also lead to constructive influences on character and personality development. It is likely a necessity in the process of socialization of the infant.

C. ANXIETY DEFINED

In accord with earlier comments, the author would define anxiety as *the apprehensive tension or uneasiness which stems from the subjective anticipation of imminent or impending danger, in which the source is largely unknown or unrecognized.* Thus the reaction which is experienced is out of proportion to any known stimulus or clearly recognized threat or danger. Its overall net effect for the individual concerned can be constructive or destructive.

---

* Cameron wrote: "My inclination is to see anxiety as constituting an alarm reaction, appearing whenever there is a threat to the organism, and becoming abnormal only in terms of (*a*) intensity, (*b*) the cue which evokes it, and (*c*) the form which it takes."

In contradistinction, fear is *the emotional response to a consciously recognized and usually external threat or danger.* Fear has the quality of immediacy in the recognition of danger here and now. As a response it tends to be a more or less appropriate one. The origins of fear are extrapsychic; that is, they are external and readily determined. The origins of anxiety are intrapsychic; that is, they are internal [Ch.9:IA*1*] and are not readily determined.

Anxiety and fear are accompanied by similar physiologic changes. For a given individual these are often nearly identical. They are an important part of the individual's Total Response to Crisis. This Total Individual Response to Crisis (the T.R.C.) includes all those preparations intended to help prepare the person for any physical or other kinds of activity which may seem necessary to cope with the threat.

Anxiety may also be defined as *fear in the absence of an apparently adequate cause.* In this sense it is sometimes referred to as *free-floating anxiety,* because of the lack of a consciously-recognized source of danger for attachment of the anxious feelings. Since the apprehension may be objectively quite out of proportion to any apparent cause, it is sometimes referred to as *neurotic anxiety.* Anxiety is often present or increased as a consequence of earlier (that is, antecedent) psychologic and emotional sensitization or conditioning and therefore sometimes is called *conditioned anxiety.* When anxiety ultimately leads to net results which are constructive and beneficial this is what we might term *constructive anxiety.* Such contributions and benefits can be individual, social, or cultural [Ch.1:VIB].

1. Fear vs. Anxiety

Case 1

An Example of Fear; A Man Meets a Lion

An American business man was big-game hunting in Africa. On safari two weeks out of Nairobi, Kenya, his party was camped in the north central area of Tanganyika. One evening toward sundown he strolled alone, unarmed, from camp along a nearby wadi. As he walked around a large boulder he suddenly found himself face to face with a lion!

He was keenly fearful. The unfamiliar surroundings, the unexpectedness of the encounter, and his inexperience all contributed to increase his fear. His heart beat wildly, his respiration increased, and his muscles were tense. His first impulse was to flee. Fortunately, as it turned out, he maintained his presence of mind. In a flash, he decided to remain motionless. It was the right decision! After what seemed to him an eternity, the lion growled once and then slowly walked away.

Here we see an example of the intense emotional response to recognized external danger. Few of us are apt to meet lions, but there are still a great many external and very tangible dangers in our culture. Note also that the fear which was present upon meeting the lion was accompanied by rather expected physiologic changes. These, as part of the hunter's Total Response to Crisis, were automatically and protectively intended to help meet the external threat. Should flight or fight have been deemed appropriate, the necessary energy potential was almost instantaneously mobilized. One must be aware of course that the individual response may be inappropriate in degree or in kind. The result may be that the consequences are self-defeating instead of protective. The Total Individual Response to Crisis includes all the psychologic, emotional, physical, intellectual, and physiologic areas of response.

Let us consider at this point another example of fear in which the reaction is slightly more complex. In the following instance, the threat was external and real enough. The reaction in turn was objectively appropriate enough for us to include it within our earlier definition.

Case 2

Fear for a Lost Child

A mother was looking for her child. She was told by one of his play-mates that he had been seen half an hour ago headed down the street, toward a major traffic artery. The mother felt frightened. Her heart beat faster. As she neared the avenue, she saw from a distance evidence of some commotion. People had collected, and an ambulance went by.

The mother's pace quickened. She broke into a run as she overheard a passerby say, "Someone was hurt. I don't know if it was a collision, or if someone was hit by a car. . . ." It proved to be a collision. Her child was uninvolved. Her fear, however, was a reasonably appropriate response. The danger was a potential one, but it was still real enough and tangible.

2. Anxiety vs. Fear

A. FROM INTERNAL DANGER.—As stated earlier, anxiety arises largely from consciously unrecognized sources, in which the danger is essentially hidden and internal. Thus, a large amount of anxiety stems from hidden, that is, unconscious, emotional conflicts. Anxiety also arises by intuitive communication in a kind of emotional contagion. Anxiety may arise or be heightened as a conditioned kind of response. Thus it may be aroused or increased in the sensory context of experiences which previously aroused anxiety. It may have a warning function in its anticipation of threat, injury, or further danger. Anxiety may similarly have a protective function, for example, in alerting the individual against possible panic.*

Anxiety is a warning to the ego or self to meet danger which is essentially internal. The danger is frequently related to the threat of powerful internal and repressed or so-called "instinctual" demands, the threat of derepression, or the threatened loss of approval. Anxiety is a warning of impending danger.

With anxiety, in contradistinction to fear, the accompanying physiologic changes today more often serve no constructive purpose. They are not likely to help to meet the threat or to cope with the danger. Instead, they are apt to form the basis for pathologic changes in function. These may later even progress to structural changes, as a further consequence of chronic stress and constantly disordered function. Thus the consequences of the physiologic accompaniments of anxiety lead to many of the emo-

---

* One qualitative and often protective feature implied in the preceding discussion is that of anticipation. Anxiety lies in the anticipation of injury, loss, or of further hurt; whereas fear accompanies the recognition of danger at hand, here and now, and has the quality of immediacy.

tionally-determined (psychosomatic) disorders. Ultimately organic structural changes can result which are irreversible. This is the *Concept of Functional-Structural Progression,* which will be considered further in subsequent chapters.

B. PRINCIPLE OF INDIVIDUAL APPROPRIATENESS OF RESPONSE.—At this point let us consider another example. Here anxiety is illustrated as an apprehensive state in which the reaction from an objective viewpoint is out of proportion to the apparent stimulus. First, it might be noted again more specifically that on a deeper level of meaning and significance every response is individually appropriate to the stimulus. This is the *Principle of Individual Appropriateness of Response* (*see also* later Individual Specificity of Emotional Defenses Principle, p. 137).

We often cannot know (any more than the patient is consciously aware of) the possible hidden unconscious and symbolic meanings to a person of a given stimulus. Hence, the considered use of the word "apparent". Hence, the apparent inappropriateness of many emotional responses, when viewed by an objective but still incompletely-informed observer. These hidden significances may, of course, become much clearer to both patient and therapist during the course of treatment.

Case 3

Anxiety over Loss of Position and Regard

A thirty-four-year-old business man was seen in consultation. He reported increasing feelings of "nervousness," troubling insomnia, and unaccountable "uneasiness." He happened to hold a position of considerable responsibility in his firm. He reported his principal (conscious) source of concern to be whether he continued to enjoy the confidence of his boss.

The young executive recognized these fears as not being based entirely on fact. They were not at all in keeping with recent spontaneous statements made to him by the president of the firm. These had related to his value, and to a considerable personal respect for the patient and his work. In this instance, unbeknown to the patient, further corroborative evidence existed. Similiar evaluative comments had been made by the president on an independent and spontaneous basis to the examiner, who happened to enjoy a personal acquaintance with him.

According to our definition, this man's fears were not in keeping with the facts as seen by others, or, indeed even as seen by himself. Here is an example of anxiety. During therapy, his feelings were found to have their original roots in deep-seated antecedent conflicts. These had been incident to certain important relationships in early life. The unwitting employment of the mental mechanism of Projection was also involved. Further, the superior to varying extents had been unconsciously "seen" in the role of the patient's own critical and doubting father. Loss of approval and punishment were in repetitive fashion anticipated, as the expected consequence of certain long-standing competitive and hostile feelings which were hidden even from himself.

C. PATIENT'S DESCRIPTION OF ANXIETY.—During a recent consultation a patient described her subjective feelings of anxiety. This description was made in a way not uncommonly reported by people who feel anxious.

Case 4

The Subjective Experience of Anxiety

A twenty-six-year-old secretary reported how she had told her room-mate of her tension and discomfort.

"Gosh, I'm on edge tonight. I feel worried, but I don't know what it's about. My heart is pounding, and I'm perspiring more than usual. It's almost like I was waiting for something to happen. . . .

"I feel frightened and fearful, but I don't really know why I feel this way. . . . Things seem to be going well, and I shouldn't have any reason to be so uneasy!"

In this description the word "anxiety" was not used, although the reaction is clearly one of anxiety. This is not atypical in lay usage. The word "fear" is often used to describe the similar subjective experience of anxiety. In like fashion, many patients will use "fear" as the descriptive term for their discomfort. Frequently enough, if allowed the opportunity to describe it further, they will report the characteristic inappropriateness of degree. This was true in the earlier instance when the business man discussed what he had referred to as "nervousness" and "uneasiness." Some puzzlement may be expressed as to the basis for the discomfort. On the other hand, a process of rationalization can result in the more superficial assignment of the cause quite inaccurately to some external reason or object.

D. ANXIETY OVER INJURY TO FAMILY MEMBER.—A not uncommon type of anxiety is that in which objectively-inappropriate fears are felt concerning possible harm or injury coming to a close family member. The following example is rather typical of this kind of reaction.

Case 5

Anxiety Over Absence of Spouse

A thirty-six-year-old married woman reported her fear and panic upon the unexplained absence of her husband. He had been absent for a little over three hours. She was certain, however, that he was dead, had been killed, or had met with a serious accident. She had waited in dread anticipation of the bad news which she felt must come.

At the same time she had been aware that this response was out of keeping with the external circumstances. His tardiness was really not very unusual. There were a number of quite practical and prosaic reasons which might have explained it. She was, of course, unable to consciously explain her intense reaction.

Following the original report of this particular example, she reported a number of similar instances. Gradually the dynamics became clear, as ✔ a conflict over hostile impulses was uncovered. The apprehension over the husband's safety proved to be part of an attempted denial of intolerable and therefore disowned wishes for his death, plus a kind of retribution in masochistic fashion for having had them.

Such a summary is, of course, an oversimplification. However, the clarification of the underlying psychogenic process was quite important. Following this and the patient's acceptance of the hostile part of her feelings, such absences were no longer followed by irrational fears for her husband's safety.

E. FEAR: RESPONSE TO EXTERNAL DANGER.—The previous examples will help to illustrate the close relationship between fear and anxiety. Both are responses to danger. In fear, the danger is external and this emotional reaction is observed to be appropriate to the responsible external threat.

The physiologic preparation for "fight" or "flight" is likewise seemingly more appropriate, although it may be overdone to the extent of interference with, or even paralysis of, action. A further consideration of fear and its gradual evolution as an increasingly complex emotional reaction will be found in *Chapter 9* entitled *Fear and Its Avoidance*. Such an evolution appears to have taken place during the development of the human race and its civilization.

F. ANXIETY: RESPONSE TO INTERNAL DANGER.—With anxiety, the real danger is internal. As earlier noted, the threat or danger may be partially or entirely out of the range of conscious recognition. However, even though the danger is hidden and internal, the Total Response to Crisis is often as though it were in response to an external danger. Thus one unwitting type of defense against anxiety is to react to the internal danger as if it were an external one, preparing to meet it aggressively. The emotional response of anxiety is beyond what might be expected from the facts ordinarily available to someone else.

This kind of treatment of the internal sources of anxiety as an externalized danger reaches an advanced state of development in the formation of a phobia. In the Phobic Reaction the source of danger is externalized into the outside world. Thereby the individual concerned is able to make a more or less adequate defense. A danger from an internal and unconscious source thus becomes transposed into a danger from an external source. Repression is ensured. We shall observe this further in our later discussion of the formation of phobic defenses in *Chapters 9 and 10*.

The kind of "fight" or "flight" which can take place in response to anxiety is far more often a symbolic and psychologic one rather than a physical one.

The development of attempted defenses against anxiety results in the unconscious employment of various mental mechanisms, the development of character defensive traits, the possible overdevelopment of either or both, with resulting unwitting self-defeat and handicap, and ultimately in the more clear-cut symptoms of emotional illness.

G. RELATIVE AWARENESS OF SOURCE OF DANGER.—The major difference between anxiety and fear may also be regarded as being a matter of the degree or the level of one's conscious awareness as to the source of the threat or danger. If one is clear as to the source of a threat one's emotional response is that of fear; if not, it is that of anxiety.

Let us consider briefly an illustrative example in our continued study of the relationships between fear and anxiety. Herein there is a lack of clarity as to the source of danger.

Case 6

An Army Corporal Became Speechless in the Presence of Officers

A twenty-two-year-old army corporal began to have considerable difficulty in his service adjustment. In the presence of a commissioned officer he literally lost the power of speech. This was the primary manifestation of his tremendous uneasiness and fear. In view of the inappropriateness of the response and the corporal's lack of awareness of his real source of fear, the reaction was clearly one of anxiety.

In this instance one could perhaps regard the emotional reaction as one of fear or as one of anxiety, being determined by the difference in his level of conscious awareness. For instance, it may be that his apprehensive reaction was due to a hidden, hostile, or aggressive reaction to authority. This may have been his own reaction, or it may also become that of authority, by projection. In any event, this would have all been pushed out of conscious awareness through its repression.*

So long as the reasons remain partly or largely unknown to him, his reaction is clearly by definition one of anxiety and in response to anxiety. Should the reasons for his feelings come into conscious awareness, might not the response, to whatever extent it remained appropriate, then be labeled as fear? This determination as to a given reaction being one of fear or anxiety depending upon the degree of knowledge of the real source of threat or danger, could be applied similarly in many instances.

D. APPREHENSIVE ANTICIPATION

There is a type of reaction which might perhaps best be called "apprehensive anticipation," in which the emotional feeling does not accurately or exactly fit into our foregoing description of either fear or anxiety, although it is closely akin to both. Referred to here is particularly that type of tension which is experienced while waiting for something (possibly unpleasant or dangerous) to happen. This "something" awaited is external and real enough, *if* it occurs. Its nature can be guessed at (although it is not definite), with the possibilities or perhaps potentialities being decidedly unpleasant.

Perhaps the following examples will illustrate this kind of emotional feeling.

Case 7

Apprehensive Anticipation: General Quarters Aboard Ship

A destroyer was operating in the tropical Pacific in the very early days of World War II. A pip on the radar screen one moonless night clearly and definitely indicated an unidentified object off the port side at a considerable distance. It was in the area where no friendly units could possibly have been operating. The captain reported the find to the task force commander. He immediately received orders to investigate at once and at full speed.

As the ship veered off its prior course and picked up knots, the call to General Quarters sounded. All hands manned their battle stations. The news of the radar contact spread rapidly through the ship. What would be encountered? It could prove to be almost anything, from a harmless derelict or a fishing boat, to a major enemy naval unit. What would it be? The tension—"or apprehensive anticipation"—present in the crew was so marked that it became something almost tangible.

The radar contact in actuality turned out to be a surfaced enemy submarine. The crew exploded into activity. The submarine was illuminated by searchlight. The command to fire was given. Direct hits were scored, and the enemy vessel was rated as destroyed.

As all guns began firing (including even the AA guns, when no orders to fire them were given!), tremendous relief from tension was secured in the activity of the engagement. This phenomenon of the discharge of tension is widespread. When physical activity is possible, a large measure of relief from anxiety and from apprehensive anticipation can

---

* *Repression:* The involuntary and automatic relegation of unbearable ideas and impulses from conscious awareness into the unconscious, from whence they are not ordinarily subject to voluntary conscious recall. Through the automatic and consciously effortless process of repression, "painful, disturbing, and conflictual thoughts or experiences are pushed into the unconscious."

sometimes result. The discharge of the physiologic potential as part of the protectively intended Total Response to Crisis, through or into action, is often accompanied by considerable emotional release as well. This kind of reaction further illustrates the close interrelationships between the emotional, the psychologic, and the physical. It can be operative in instances in which the actual threat is by no means lessened as a result of the activity.

From this example it becomes apparent that apprehensive anticipation may be highly protective. It may well be that the destroyer crew actually survived because they were apprehensive. Chaos, panic, or paralysis of action may have been averted because of the apprehensive anticipation present. The crew was keyed up and ready for action. Here, then, this reaction was a protective aspect of the Total Response to Crisis [Ch.8:III A4;Ch.13:IIF1]. It can be useful as such with certain limits. If overwhelming in itself, or if it comes to be present chronically, the consequences may instead be disruptive.

The same principle is applicable also in the following instance. Undoubtedly the preparations for the mission to be described were better and more carefully undertaken than for previous ones. Part of the apprehension became protective and was also discharged into this kind of activity. The old proverb comes to mind in regard to these two examples, "forewarned is forearmed."

Case 8

Apprehensive Anticipation: How a New Plane Captain Will Measure Up

The pilot of a B-29 received orders in 1944, during World War II, detaching him from the crew. He had worked closely with them for eighteen months, and his departure left the unit temporarily leaderless. A rigorous mission was scheduled for the squadron the following day, upon which juncture a new pilot was scheduled to report.

What kind of a chap would he prove to be? What would happen? Was he competent? Could he be relied upon? There would be more apprehensive anticipation during this mission than with previous ones. If things went well and confidence was established, the tension next time would be much less. Again, as in *Case 7,* as the crew members were able to begin the actual preparations for the bombing mission, the level of apprehensive anticipation decreased.

In these instances, the object of threat or danger was external, in keeping with our concept of fear. On the other hand, the object was also rather unknown and highly conjectural, in keeping with our concept of anxiety. Nevertheless, the feelings are not necessarily irrational. They are not necessarily out of keeping at all with the amount of actual threat or danger present. Because this kind of response does not quite fit our definitions of either fear or anxiety, it is suggested that another term, such as *apprehensive anticipation* might seem preferable. [*See also* Ch.3:III B2;Ch.13:VIIID1;Ch.14:VIIA2].

E. DISCHARGE OF ANXIETY INTO ACTIVITY

1. *Energy Potential Released*

How can we account for the lowered level of tension and anxiety in certain instances when some kind of physical activity becomes possible?

The explanation lies in the protectively-intended potential for action which is mobilized as part of the Total Individual Response to Crisis The energy potential which is defensively mobilized in these instances finds expression and release in physical activity. Many men in military units have experienced what is literally the delight which can accompany the discharge of accumulated tensions into physical activity. This can apply even though the activity is dangerous. Aspects of this reaction are illustrated in the two preceding cases.

When there is the opportunity for direct aggressive action (as in combat), this kind of release or discharge may be even more apparent. A somewhat similar explanation may be valid in certain instances when physical exercise or work proves helpful in the dissolution of nervous tension. This is particularly true when the tension accumulates as the consequence of a confining occupation. There is another factor entering into ⋎ the lessening of tension with activity. This lies in the redirection of attention outwardly, away from the area of internal and unconscious threat or danger. This reduces the chances of derepression; that is, the coming back into consciousness of ideas or impulses which were previously found to be intolerable and consequently were repressed.

2. Transformed into Anger as Anxiety-Equivalent

Anxiety sometimes finds partial or even greater expression in anger, into ⋎ which it may be transformed. Anger thus becomes what we might term an Anxiety-Equivalent [Ch.14:VIIID1]. A tense and anxious person also is much more likely to become angry. Herein the anxiety is again translated into a kind of emotional activity; the experiencing or expression of the angry feelings, or both.

The explanation is similar to the foregoing. The accumulated energy potential (preparation for fight or flight) "welcomes" a chance for expression and release, in this instance into a kind of emotional expression. The result can be a lowering of both emotional and physical tension "after the storm has passed."

F. DIRECT AND INDIRECT MANIFESTATIONS OF ANXIETY

1. Condensed Tabulation

Through our discussion thus far it is increasingly apparent that anxiety and its effects find expression in a variety of ways. These vary from the direct and quite obvious, through the obscure, to at the other extreme the deeply hidden and extremely devious. In *Table 1 below,* are outlined the major direct and indirect ways of expression of anxiety.

It should of course be kept in mind for purposes of accuracy that certain intermediate steps have been omitted in such a condensed summary. The progression from disowned thought, feeling, or impulse into characterologic modification, or into more frank symptom formation can be complex indeed. We shall observe this repeatedly in coming chapters. Nonetheless anxiety and the struggles to avert and to avoid it play a most important role in these kinds of terribly significant progressions.

Table 1
The Manifestations of Anxiety

A. *The Direct Pathways of Expression of Anxiety*
    1. Anxiety: subjectively-experienced nervousness, tension, and anxiety *per se.*
    2. Psychomotor expression:
      (*a*) From fine digital tremors, to gross shaking of the entire body.
      (*b*) From restlessness to agitation.
      (*c*) Certain motor disturbances. These may include various phenomena such as speech difficulties, sleep disturbances, insomnia, and disturbing dreams.
      (*d*) Miscellaneous: angry hostile outbursts, aggressive behavior, tension outlets in a variety of physical activities, and the startle reaction.
    3. Autonomic expression: palpitation, increased perspiration, dilated pupils, weakness, and certain "simple" more direct changes in the function of various organic systems or regions of the body.
    4. Interference with mental function: impaired attention and concentration; confusion; interference with mental activity in any area.
    5. Certain clinical states—the Anxiety Reactions (discussed in Chapter 3).
      (*a*) The Acute Anxiety Attack, or Anxiety Panic (AAA).
      (*b*) Anxiety-Tension States (ATS).
      (*c*) Anxiety Neurosis.
B. *The Indirect Manifestations and Consequences of Anxiety*
These include all the more involved and hidden effects of anxiety, attempted defenses against anxiety, and compromise formations.
    1. Physiologic Conversions: The translation into "physiologic langauge" of anxiety and repressed conflictual material. Changes take place in smooth muscle, organ, and glandular function leading to the psychosomatic illnesses or Somatization Reactions; some cases of Emotional Fatigue, Fatigue States, and Neurasthenia. (*See Table 16.*)
    2. Somatic Conversions (Conversion Reactions).
    3. Psychologic Conversions. The many hidden unconscious, and devious pathways in which the effects of anxiety are converted psychologically, leading to the development of psychologic symptoms and reactions, including:
      (*a*) The Phobias.
      (*b*) The Dissociative Reactions.
      (*c*) The Depressive Reactions.
      (*d*) Overconcern with Health or Hygeiaphrontis.
      (*e*) Certain aspects of character defenses, the Character Reactions (neuroses) and personality patterns.
      (*f*) The Soterial Reactions.
      (*g*) Obsessions and Compulsions; the Obsessive-Compulsive Reactions.
      (*h*) The Neuroses Following Trauma.
      (*i*) Regressive manifestations and the psychogenic symptoms in the psychoses.

2. Psychogenesis of Emotional Manifestations

Strictly speaking, the progression toward psychopathology is of course more complex. It is anxiety and the threat of anxiety which provides the motive force. The resolution of emotional conflict is sought because of anxiety (and other painful emotions). Anxiety leads to the repression of that which is consciously intolerable. The repressed material, striving for consciousness and expression, plus the intrapsychic endeavors at its control, give rise to emotional symptoms and to character defenses.

This sequence of events is commonplace. It is the essence of the psychogenesis of emotional manifestations. Occurring outside of and beyond conscious awareness, however, it is likely to be most difficult of access. We shall study its operation in the various patterns of neurotic reaction.

3. Applications for Childhood, as for Adults

Anxiety and our resulting defenses against it constitute the central core in our dynamic conceptions concerning the emotional illnesses. These findings apply for all ages. In the development of neuroses in children and in adults, while the sources of anxiety may differ, the end-result psychopathologically is the same. The defenses of childhood are mustered against its early emotional urges because the child fears the outside world. In childhood it is anxiety which results in the infantile ego developing similar Phobic Reactions, Conversion Reactions, Obsessive Reactions, and Character Reactions to those which occur in adults. For in the child anxiety arises through real or imagined dangers from significant adults. As the superego evolves it provides an added source. The crucial point is that, whether it is threats from the outside world or from the superego or both, it is the resulting anxiety which leads to one's evolving and activating the various defensive processes.

Gradually the outside world becomes incorporated, so to speak, in the developing superego (conscience) of the maturing child. Henceforth, the superego with some variations exerts a similar effect, intrapsychically, to that of the outside world earlier. We shall see reference to this shortly in our discussion of conflict and in tracing the primary (infantile) origins and the later, secondary (adult) origins of anxiety. First, let us consider briefly the subject of emotional conflict, its relation to anxiety, and its role in the initiation of emotional symptoms.

III. EMOTIONAL CONFLICT

A. CLASH BETWEEN TWO OPPOSING EMOTIONAL FORCES

1. "Instinctual" Drives vs. Prohibiting Personal and Social Standards

The harvest of conflict is anxiety. At this point it is therefore proper that our attention be focused upon the very important concept of emotional conflict. Conflicts are a basic part of human experience. With the development of individual standards and with the arrival of ability for an adequate recognition of social mores and standards, conflicts are inevitable. These will take place between both sets of standards on the one hand, and the personal so-called "instinctual" drives which they oppose.

A conflict may be simply defined as the clashing of two opposing interests. Emotional conflict takes place between the instinctual drives (id) of the personality and the demands of the conscience (superego), or society. The ego, or I, serves as the mediator and is also the battleground. The realization of man's inner and primarily unconscious goals is interfered with and blocked by his opposing personal standards and by social demands. Emotional conflict may be conscious, or beyond conscious awareness. It is the latter type which has the greater psychopathologic import.

2. Goal of Equanimity Concept

From one point of view, one might regard the goal of mankind as the attainment of a state of emotional satisfaction. This is sometimes referred to also as peace of mind, or as equanimity. It is an important concept which we might refer to as the Goal of Equanimity. Since emotional conflict results in anxiety, we continually attempt to allay or avert this discomfort through the resolution of conflict. Our ways of attempting this may be constructive, socially useful, and effective. They may be also destructive, harmful, and psychologically uneconomic to the person, to society, or to both.

Great efforts are made to free ourselves of anxiety. These are both conscious and unconscious. We will learn through our study of psychodynamics, the mental mechanisms (as presented elsewhere), and from the many types of neurotic reactions that these may be highly complex. The psychologic methods by which we constantly seek to attain the somewhat theoretical Goal of Equanimity or homeostasis are indeed diverse, often devious (that is, hidden from conscious awareness), and highly involved. The degree of success which may be obtained is likewise quite variable.

B. CONFLICT→ANXIETY→REPRESSION→SYMPTOMS

1. Conflicts Over Aggressive and Sexual Drives More Basic and Important: Derepression

As noted, the customs and restrictions of society constantly block or frustrate the fulfillment of instinctual drives. Situations producing conflict involve all kinds of basic and important matters. These include, for example, matters related to school, family, religion, and occupation. The most important and basic intrapsychic conflicts from the standpoint of psychopathology occur over or relate to the sexual and aggressive types of drives.

These drives might also be alternatively categorized as those concerned with preservation of the race, and those relating to self preservation. Sexual thoughts and strivings and those with a hostile, aggressive, or acquisitive coloring are not only likely to be stronger ones, but are also likely in turn to be met with stronger opposition from personal or social standards when there is conflict. Actually, emotional conflict also enters into many areas which are quite subtle or of far finer delineation.

Conflict may be partly or fully in conscious awareness, or completely unconscious. It is the repressed (unconscious) or partially repressed conflicts which are most important in symptom formation. The repression occurs as an attempted resolution of the conflict. When derepression threatens, anxiety is subjectively experienced. [Ch.9:IA2]. This is hardly surprising since derepression would result in the reinstitution of the original intolerable conflict in full conscious awareness.

2. Emotional Conflict Defined; Vital Sequence of Events

An emotional conflict is *the clash which takes place between one's moral, social, and personal standards on the one hand, and one's egocentric and instinctual strivings—self-preservative, acquisitive, reproductive, aggressive, and destructive drives; the personal desires, needs, and strivings for possession, anger, love, and sex—on the other.*

Anxiety arises from conflict. In turn, anxiety provides the force which results in repression. The continuing energy potential of the repressed and unconscious material and the resulting intrapsychic conflict may lead to the production of emotional symptoms.

Thus, conflict results in anxiety. Anxiety leads to repression. The repressed data can lead to symptom formation. More about this important sequence of events will follow in subsequent chapters.

C. INSTINCTS AND ACCULTURATION: FIRST TENET OF PARENTAL ROLE

The so-called instinctual or id drives are universal in the infant. Although these drives are soon present in the infant in strong force following birth, and with little internal (personal) opposition to begin with, since the conscience remains to be developed later, there is a markedly limited capacity to achieve them. Needless to say, this is socially fortunate. As the capacity of the child to achieve the objects of his basic instinctual needs increases, so does his learning of the importance of control, modification, and sublimation. The capacity and the control develop together, and hopefully in more or less parallel fashion. When this takes place rather equally, the result is far more harmonious. Therefore the increase of the one kind of capacity (for securing gratification) is simultaneously accompanied by an increase in the other kind of capacity; the kind for inhibitory power and control.

The child's success in "learning" these things is one of the most important areas of childhood development. Our ability to help him learn them is one of our most important contributions as parents. It is, of course, far more than learning. It also involves many other processes, such as integration, adaptation, identification, conditioning, sublimation, and others. It is acculturation, domestication, and socialization.

MOST IMPORTANT RESPONSIBILITY OF PARENTHOOD.—The relative success of all of this complex endeavor is reflected in the child's ability to achieve a higher and more adult level of adjustment and maturity. In its broadest aspects, the healthy and constructive facilitation of this process of acculturation and maturation in an atmosphere of affection and security is the fundamental and most important responsibility of parenthood. This is the First Tenet of the Parental Role. It is a major and vital one. See also the Secure Base of Operations Concept, [Ch.11:VIIA].

D. PSYCHOLOGIC "FIGHT OR FLIGHT" RESPONSES

1. Analogous to Physical Responses to External Threat or Danger

Not all emotional conflicts prove soluble, nor is every conflict necessarily a source of difficulty. In the development of the normal individual, however, many conflicts are dealt with successfully. It is the ones that result in further difficulty or problems in which we are more interested for the purposes of our present study. These are the ones that are followed by emotional disturbances of all kinds. These are the ones which lead to the handicapping overdevelopment of character traits, and to the unconscious adoption of the various neurotic symptoms and patterns of reaction. These are intended as defenses.

The presence of emotional conflicts produces anxiety. In many instances, repression when it takes place, tends to occur very quickly and effortlessly, as well as automatically. In these, the subjective experiencing of anxiety scarcely enters into conscious awareness at the time. Anxiety is a universal accompaniment of conflict. According to definition, part of the conflict must be repressed. The internal threat producing anxiety is very often one of a loss of control of the repressed and disowned impulse. Since the neurotic patient fears he cannot handle or control, or cannot accept the ideas or impulses which have been repressed, it is small wonder that anxiety is experienced if derepression threatens.

As already noted, the automatic aim of the individual is to escape discomfort. Since anxiety is indeed uncomfortable, the individual undertakes ways of dealing with the conflict.* It is not within the scope of this introductory chapter to cover the many complex psychologic mechanisms (the so-called dynamisms or mental mechanisms) which may be employed. These shall be referred to further throughout the volume. In a broad sense, however, the psychologic responses to conflict and from resulting anxiety can be classified in analogous fashion to the physical kind of "fight" or "flight" responses by which one meets the fear of a more external kind of threat or danger.' See also [Ch.9:IIIC2;Ch.13:VE2].

2. Central Dynamic Concept

In recapitulation, we see that from the various kinds of serious emotional conflict, anxiety and tension arise. Both the conflict and the resulting anxiety tend to destroy the harmonious equilibrium of the personality. Anxiety is an apprehensive tension which arises directly from emotional conflict. Anxiety and tension may be regarded as universal in human experience.

The degree of individual conscious awareness of all this, as well as the

---

* As a reaction to anxiety, the ego may take a variety of pathways in attempting to deal with the conflict. In one classification, these would include: (1) *Modification*— (*a*) rationalization, (*b*) modification of demands or resignation, and (*c*) regression; (2) *Abandonment* of the original goals, or sublimation (rechannelization); and (3) *Avoidance* (leading to repression, and the other mental mechanisms).

As a response to the incomplete working of the mechanisms, to incomplete repression, or to threatened derepression, anxiety is produced in turn. This production of anxiety is disruptive, as is the vicious circle which may potentially result.

degree of resulting interference with living, however, is relative. Further, one is still more likely to be totally unaware of the underlying causes. This is particularly true of anxiety, which has its roots in the unconscious, and in unconscious processes. *The underlying presence of intrapsychic conflict with the resulting tension, attempted defenses, and sought-after resolution and its disguised outward expression is to be recognized today as the central dynamic concept in the origin of the neurotic and the functional psychotic emotional illnesses.*

3. Attempted Defenses Against Anxiety

In learning about emotional conflict and the reactions of the individual in coping with it, one soon learns about a large and important group of internal defenses. These are called mental dynamisms or mechanisms. These mental mechanisms * represent attempts to reach solutions and compromises in response to serious conflictual situations. They may be regarded as attempted defenses against anxiety. They represent internal kinds of compromise. According to one major conception, [Ch.6:VF*1*], they comprise one's First Line of Psychic Defense. Increasing one's familiarity with the individual members of this very interesting group of intrapsychic defenses is a most intriguing, fascinating and challenging activity.

The use of the various mental mechanisms or dynamisms in the resolution of conflict is universal to some degree or other. They are automatically and unconsciously employed. Their use in general, with some exceptions however, may be regarded as rather less successful in attaining the goal of equanimity than is a realistic and objectively-constructive solution to the conflict. Solutions which are secured through a constructive compromise may modify or influence behavior. It is also possible for opposing drives of equal strength to result in a kind of emotional paralysis.

E. TO SECURE BENEFITS THROUGH PSYCHOTHERAPY, PATIENT MUST HELP

1. Unique Kind of Collaborative Relationship Between Doctor and Patient; Joint-Endeavor Principle

Emotional processes are often highly complex. Since much of what happens in our attempts to deal with conflict takes place on an unconscious level, we recognize increasingly the many problems and difficulties in

---

* A list of the more commonly-described major mental mechanisms includes:

1. Compensation	9. Incorporation	17. Repression
2. Conversion	10. Internalization	18. Restitution
3. Denial	11. Introjection	19. Sublimation
4. Displacement	12. Inversion	(Rechannelization)
5. Dissociation	13. Projection	20. Substitution
6. Fantasy	14. Rationalization	21. Symbolization
7. Idealization	15. Reaction Formation	22. Undoing
8. Identification	16. Regression	

In accord with our concept of *Higher Order* (more advanced) *Defenses* vs. *Lower Order* (more primitive) *Defenses,* the mental mechanisms or dynamisms can also be so categorized, as may the neuroses.

psychotherapy. The most valuable kind of psychotherapy has the increase of insight (that is, self-understanding) as its major goal. One important aim is to secure constructive derepression. This means the uncovering of unconscious material, together with its acceptance, study and understanding.

The great importance, as well as the difficulty, of the actual work done by the patient in psychotherapy becomes apparent. Accordingly, in psychiatry, treatment requires a collaborative endeavor by doctor and patient such as is seldom to be encountered in any other kind of medical treatment. The result is a unique relationship. This follows the Joint-Endeavor Principle in psychotherapy [Ch.14:VIIIE2].

2. Psychotherapy Encounters Resistances

The work required of the patient himself in the therapeutic procedure makes the process of psychotherapy a different one from that of any other type of definitive treatment in medicine. Inevitably anxiety and discomfort to varying degrees accompany the recall of previously unconscious material. This contributes to certain important resistances to therapy. These may be divided into: (1) those which are present at the beginning of treatment (*See* Inertia Concept in regard to initiating therapy, [Ch.4: XIIA7]); and (2) those which are encountered during the course of treatment.

Before continuing into a discussion of the origins of anxiety, it may be appropriate to illustrate the need for the patient's active collaboration in the work of treatment. In the following illustration the patient's interest and cooperation could not be secured. The result was a failure of treatment efforts, with the inevitably tragic and life-long consequences of such a failure.

Case 9

Episodes of Drinking with Antisocial Behavior, Accompanied by Lack of Ability to Share Responsibility for Work in Treatment

A business man, fifty-two years of age, had been highly successful in his business and financially. However, he was addicted to the episodic overuse of alcohol and to resulting periods of personally- and socially-destructive behavior. Indeed, as his worldly successes mounted, his personal problem increased. On the urgent request of his internist, he was seen in psychiatric consultation on one occasion after he had been hospitalized. The hospitalization had saved him from facing some possible legal consequences of his most recent bout. There was a history of several such incidents, from which his physician had thus "rescued" him.

Affecting a show of outward cooperation, he stated his determination to "answer whatever question the doctor wants to ask." In effect, however, he was really challenging the psychiatrist to secure data. He was unwilling to assume any responsibility for helping in discovering what unknown factors might have entered into his unusual behavior and into his personal difficulties. His primary concern appeared to be an effort to obtain from the psychiatrist what he described as a "favorable report" and an early release from the hospital. He did not wish to probe deeper into his emotional self, and was unable to muster any constructive self-interest in this direction.

This man possessed unusual skill and business ability, by means of which he had earned for himself outstanding financial success. But he could not be brought to see the value which self-observation and study might hold for him. As a result, his episodic irresponsibility and anti-social behavior continued. Not only did he jeopardize his past successes, but he seriously damaged his future. His resistances to the idea of therapy were sufficiently strong to prevent its even getting a trial.

This unhappy man attempted solution of his difficulties through escape and avoidance. This had been somewhat successful in early years, but had gradually lost its effectiveness as events progressed and he became more desperate. Two years later the author noted an item in the paper reporting the untimely end of the increasingly tragic life of this unfortunate man. Undoubtedly he had hastened this considerably. Until his death, however, self-appraisal and self-study were to him far more of a threat than were the very painful personal, familial, and social consequences of his behavior.

3. In Therapy Understanding Meaning of Symptoms Sought

In conclusion, the occurrence of emotional conflict is intimately related to anxiety and to symptom formation. Anxiety is not only a cause of conflict and repression but conflict is itself also a cause of anxiety. This can produce a vicious circle. In symptom formation there is the unconscious attempt to bind, as in an emotional amalgam, to neutralize, to deny, or to counteract the anxiety. Symptoms represent a compromise way of dealing with the inner, threatening, hidden, and disowned urges. Symptoms can also provide the outward but disguised symbolic expression of elements of the conflict. We shall learn more later of this function of symptoms. Working out their origins and motivations is necessary for their resolution.* When they become understood they become no longer essential. In other words, insight is followed by relief. The patient must help.

Anxiety is a complex kind of reaction and danger signal, having evolved as a cultural development from fear as its more primitive prototype. [Ch.9:IA] Neurotic defenses, which include the psychogenic symptoms, are mobilized to deal with anxiety as the warning signal of an inner threat. Although the defense evolved may be psychologically uneconomic and self-defeating, a kind of *status quo* may be effected. All kinds of resistances may be evoked should this *status quo* be threatened or shaken. Pursuing psychotherapy against such powerful resistances requires determination and persistence on the part of both physician and patient.

IV. THE ORIGINS OF ANXIETY

A. DEVELOPMENT OF THEORY

Thus far a working definition of anxiety has been presented. This will serve as an important basis for the conceptions to be presented and discussed in subsequent chapters. The interrelationships of anxiety to fear have been discussed, as has been the concept of emotional health. The importance of emotional conflict has been summarized, and reference made to the ways by which we attempt to handle the anxiety resulting from con-

---

* According to the *Symptom-Survival Principle* [Ch.1:VIIIA2; Ch.14:IIIB2], emotional symptoms cannot survive the resolution of the underlying conflicts.

flict. In this section will be presented in outline my formulations as to the sources of anxiety. Following mention of some further developments in theory, these will be divided into the early Primary Sources of anxiety in infancy and childhood, and the later Secondary Sources of anxiety of adulthood. Finally, we shall conclude with comments about the important tangential area of anxiety and sleep and a word on the functions of anxiety.

It was not until 1923 that an important "second theory of anxiety" was formulated by Freud. This was a major step forward. It gradually had a major impact on dynamic theory, and served as a kind of rallying point for many of those who had had reservations or dissatisfactions with the more inadequate earlier theoretical constructions.

The new theory was far closer to our current conceptions as outlined thus far, and formed an important basis for their development. These represent my own views as these have evolved to date.

Anxiety had now (1923) come to be regarded as the signal for the avoidance of a danger situation.* Neurotic symptoms are developed in the attempt to cope with anxiety. Needless to say, this represented an advance from Freud's earlier theory which had viewed anxiety in a more limited and narrow fashion as a physiologic kind of response to orgastic frustration. It undoubtedly helped to stimulate further interest, clinical observation, and research. Freud had later written, ". . . all symptom formation would be brought out solely in order to avoid anxiety; the symptoms bind the psychic energy which otherwise would be discharged as anxiety, so that anxiety would be the fundamental phenomenon and the central problem of neurosis." And later, ". . . the symptoms are created in order to remove or rescue the ego from the situation of danger. If symptom formation is prevented, the danger actually makes its appearance. . ."

Alexander related anxiety to the repression of hostile impulses, which he considered to be at the core of every neurosis. He believed that early aggressive impulses must be controlled by repression. The threat of derepression aroused anxiety. Lorand regarded the nucleus of anxiety as being in the Oedipus problem and its vicissitudes, ". . . all the symptoms are connected with repressed sexual drives and they represent a compromise between the repressed erotic wishes and the repressive forces."

Rank believed the prototype of all anxiety was in the birth experience [Ch.8: VIIB1]. This theory he partially based upon the physiologic manifestations accompanying birth. These seemed to him to approximate those circulatory, respiratory, and other changes which are present with anxiety. This theory has not gained wide acceptance. Most physicians familiar with the process of birth are doubtful as to anxiety being experienced by the arriving infant. Studies comparing the infants of difficult births with infants with uncomplicated births or even those with cesarean births do not appear to indicate significant differences in emotional development or integration. As a result of Rank's work, however, the importance of separation and the threat of separation as a basis for anxiety was usefully stressed.

---

* Accordingly, anxiety *per se* might be considered as an important emotional component of the Total Individual Response to Crisis.

Sullivan equated anxiety directly with disapproval from a significant adult. Fromm was impressed with the importance of the conflict between the need for approval (closeness, love) and the need for independence. He also regarded repressed hostility as a frequent source of anxiety.

Further ideas and theories have contributed to our growing knowledge about anxiety. At one time or another various investigators have been particularly impressed with the relative importance of some specific etiologic mechanism or other in the production of anxiety. Currently, however, most psychiatrists are in full agreement as to the tremendously important role of anxiety in our individual development and in living generally.

It has proven helpful to me to classify the major sources of anxiety as primary, those most responsible in infancy and early childhood, and secondary, those more closely associated with adulthood. Accordingly, following a brief reference to the important Theory of Antecedent Conflicts, the important sources of anxiety will be summarized under these headings.

B. THE PRIMARY SOURCES OF ANXIETY

1. Theory of Antecedent Conflicts

The major sources of anxiety for the infant and in early childhood are especially important because of their antecedent position. In effect, these events and the individual response to them tend to establish important prototypes; patterns for later responses. These antecedent reactions and patterns thus may come to serve actually or symbolically as analogous prototypes.

Precedents which are so established are often repressed or partly repressed. Accordingly they are likely to be inaccessible or at least poorly accessible to ordinary conscious awareness. However, they may help in a very important fashion to determine later or to exaggerate greatly the emotional response of an individual in a similar given situation. This is a type of psychologic conditioning. This hidden, geometrically-increased effect can help to explain many otherwise apparently irrational, emotional (and neurotic) reactions.

Accordingly, it has been found convenient and useful to follow what the author has named the Theory of Antecedent Conflicts [Ch.8:VIIA1]. This theory is comprised of two major corollaries. The first one points out that *the effect of an emotionally-disturbing event may be multiplied as a consequence of the important effects of various antecedent vicissitudes of early life, which come to serve actually or symbolically as analogous prototypes.* According to the second major corollary, at least theoretically, *every emotional conflict has its earlier antecedent.*

Table 2 shows in outline form the primary and secondary sources of anxiety.

Table 2
The Sources of Anxiety

A. *The Primary Sources of Anxiety*

In infancy and early childhood anxiety arises as a consequence of:

1. Helplessness.
2. Separation, or the threat of separation or abandonment.
3. Privation and loss.
4. Frustration.
5. The communication, or "emotional contagion" of anxiety occurs intuitively and through identification, largely from parents, but also from others, particularly from those who occupy a significant position for the child or infant.
6. Disapproval or the fear of disapproval, especially from a significant adult or parental figure. Parental resentment, rejection, or both.
7. Physical threats from one's:
    (*a*) External environment:
        (*i*) Physical pain.
        (*ii*) Accidents and surgical procedures.
        (*iii*) Temperature changes and extremes of temperature.
        (*iv*) Position changes; falling and fear of falling.
        (*v*) Parental disharmony, and conflicts over discipline.
        (*vi*) Excessive emotional stimuli, especially from significant adults.
        (*vii*) General physical discomfort, further types of sudden environmental changes, and so on.
    (*b*) Internal environment:
        (*i*) Hunger.
        (*ii*) Thirst.
        (*iii*) Illness.
        (*iv*) Other physiologic needs.
    (*c*) Actual physical punishment or the threat of punishment, retaliation, or abuse.
8. Certain Specific Emotional Hazards of Childhood (The S.E.H.C.).
9. Conditioned responses.

B. *The Secondary Sources of Anxiety*

In later adult life the sources of anxiety are closely related to the primordial antecedent sources of infancy and childhood.

According to the first corollary of the Theory of Antecedent Conflicts, the effect of an emotionally disturbing event in later years may be multiplied geometrically through similar antecedent vicissitudes of early life, which actually or symbolically serve as analogous prototypes. According to a second corollary, theoretically every conflict has its earlier antecedent. Secondary sources of anxiety would include:

1. Superego conflict, following the development of the conscience; a low level of self-esteem.
2. Disapproval or the fear of disapproval, especially from significant people.
3. Social conflict: threat of censure; loss of position, prestige, stature, or self-esteem; as a consequence, for example, of doing the "wrong thing".
4. Threats to self-preservation, including situational anxiety:
    (*a*) Physical danger or injury; catastrophes of nature.
    (*b*) Food, clothing, shelter, livelihood, and privation and loss.
    (*c*) Interference with established sources of satisfaction.
    (*d*) Illness, accidents, surgical procedures, and pregnancy.
    (*e*) Psychologic injury.
    (*f*) Threats from war, civil disorder, criminality, and nuclear catastrophe.
5. Threats to racial preservation.

6. Conditioned responses. (Now a more important source.)

7. Frustration, hostility, anger and rage, with possible projection; the threat of punishment or retaliation. (Includes "castration anxiety.")

8. Infantile carry-overs and miscellaneous sources, including helplessness, separation, and intuitive communication.

9. "Apprehensive anticipation."

10. Specific Emotional Hazards of Adulthood, or S.E.H.A. (including the Military Stressful Eras or *M.S.E.s* [Ch.2:IIB4].

---

2. Helplessness

The basic helplessness and dependence of the infant gives rise to much of what we may regard as primitive anxiety. The infant of course is completely dependent on the care provided by his parents, especially the mother. In the beginning completely helpless, the infant's development of resources to cope with the outside world is a long, difficult, and gradual process. Much of what transpires during this period forms the basic foundations for the later adult attitudes, and for the development of the inner resources which come to be ultimately possessed by the adult, especially when he has to cope with serious difficulties.

On occasions in adult life when one is confronted with a situation in which one is again helpless, this primitive kind of anxiety from this very early period may be, in effect, reactivated. Helplessness then is an early, or primary, source of anxiety in the infant, and may likewise be a deep-seated source of anxiety in the adult.

3. Separation

Separation as a source of anxiety is closely related to the foregoing one of helplessness. In view of the complete dependence of the infant for all his needs and for his very life upon the mothering one, it is obvious that the threat of abandonment or separation can be a source of great menace, fear and anxiety. This is the most potent kind of object loss and is most threatening. In normal personality development, security develops as dependency decreases. Separation no longer results in anxiety. Such an ideal sequence does not always transpire.

When this process is faulty, separation or the threat of separation may continue in later life to be a major hidden source of anxiety. In the adult, separation or the threat of separation may have unconscious roots back to the early period and may be very disturbing. The connection to the antecedent similar situation from the early years in these instances is out of awareness. Vulnerability to emotional upset from separation may increase when the individual is already emotionally disturbed by other existing conflicts.

4. Privation and Loss

A sudden environmental change is always a potential threat to the infant. This is especially true when it involves the loss of some accustomed routine or comfort, or any of a number of other possible privations. It is difficult for the small child to understand privation and loss, a factor which can increase the impact of this kind of threat.

The parental attitude can be a most vital and important agent of re-assurance in these situations. In contrast, adult insecurity and uncertainty may be present. When these are reflected in the parental attitudes, they can help to augment the apparent threat and its destructive emotional effects. Emotionally-traumatic weaning can be one example of an important infantile privation.

5. Frustration

Frustration includes the important emotional sequence of frustration→anger→hostile (aggressive) impulses→conflict→anxiety. The anxiety is present because of threatened loss of control and in view of the threat of retaliation. There is a close relation here to helplessness, as well as to some physical threats.

The above sequence may be continued: anxiety→repression→emotional symptoms. The continuance and possible progression of this reaction as an important one psychopathologically, as with other primary sources of anxiety, will depend on many individual factors.

6. "Emotional Contagion" of Anxiety

An emotional kind of contagion of anxiety takes place intuitively and through identification, largely from parents. The infant possesses a keen ability to sense intuitively the presence of all kinds of emotional feelings, especially including anxiety, indifference, resentment, and hatred in the mother, or mothering figure. This ability often increases with age. The presence of anxiety, for example, is often communicated from the mother to the child automatically and rapidly. One can observe quick responses of the infant to various changes in mood by the parent. The intuitive communication of anxiety and other emotions to the infant takes place from other significant adults as well as from the mother. The infant is particularly susceptible to the emotional feelings of others around him. What we can thus term an Emotional Contagion of many kinds of feelings or moods can readily take place. It is therefore hardly surprising that this occurs with anxiety.

Through his ability to sense mood changes, uneasiness, apprehension, or anxiety, the infant thus has another primary pathway for the development of anxiety. This is an important source, an intuitive and identifying source of infantile and childhood anxiety. In many instances it also carries over in more hidden and unobtrusive ways into adult life. The carry-over of the production of anxiety by identification will depend upon the relative amount of this phenomenon (the amount of stress and trauma initiating it) in early life, and the strength of the resulting patterns of reaction and behavior which have been established.

Anxiety experienced by a significant adult can also result in anxiety being experienced by the infant via another similar pathway. Here the presence of anxiety in the adult upon whom the infant is so dependent is in itself a great menace and threat. The position of the adult as a strong and suitable object of dependency is inevitably impaired to some degree if he becomes anxious.

7. *Disapproval or Fear of Disapproval from Significant Adults*

Another important source of anxiety in the infant is an attitude of disapproval, resentment, or rejection by a significant adult. The infant soon learns the value of pleasing and of securing approval, as well as the consequences of displeasing.

Thus the need for approval is very important. When strong "instinctual" needs result in unwelcome behavior, the child may feel threatened with: (1) loss of love of parents (2) punishment (physical harm), and (3) social rejection. The early responses to parental disapproval gradually broaden to include other significant relationships and finally society as a whole. The importance of this in the formation of character structure and personality is indeed great, particularly in superego development.

8. *Physical Threats*

Many psychiatrists trace anxiety ultimately to the threat of retaliation for forbidden and dangerous hostile-aggressive or sexual impulses. In analytic terminology, this is included in the broad term "castration anxiety." According to this viewpoint anxiety is a danger signal which warns the ego of an inward or outward danger. This danger would be more or less directly or symbolically that of castration. For the purposes of our present consideration a descriptive division of threats of a physical nature into three subdivisions is preferred, as follows:

(1) The *common threats from the external environment* for the infant, including physical pain, accidents, surgical procedures, changes in temperature and position, parental disharmony, conflicts over discipline, general physical discomfort, sudden environmental changes and excessive emotional stimuli, especially from significant adults.

(2) The *common internal environmental threats,* including hunger, thirst, illness, and other physiologic needs.

(3) Actual *physical punishment* or the threat of punishment, retaliation, or abuse.

While the threat in certain of these instances is not immediately physical, in fact not even necessarily physical, they are included at this juncture because they are part of the potential physical threats to the infant's equanimity from the external environment. They are among the frequent causes of anxiety reactions in infants.

9. *Specific Emotional Hazards of Childhood (S.E.H.C.)*

There are in addition a number of specific emotional hazards for the child in his early life. These events are always likely to be of some moment in the psychologic development of a child. They can be quite traumatic from a psychic viewpoint.

They can precipitate an Acute Anxiety Reaction (*also see* [Ch.3: IVE4]), or they can contribute to various types of psychopathology. Included as Specific Emotional Hazards of Childhood are such major events as the death of a parent, a sibling, or a close playmate; moving to a new home; changing schools; beginning of menstruation; frights; certain accidents; or a sexual assault, and so on.

10. Conditioned Responses

Conditioned responses are likely to be less important in early life but often greatly increase in importance in later life. Exposure to a sufficiently painful experience or a series of them may condition the individual to experiencing later some degree of similar discomfort when some of the sensory cues of the earlier experience are present.

Since the connection may be lost or repressed, the response when this occurs is often not understood and appears irrational. One may properly refer to *conditioned anxiety* when the anxiety occurs or is considerably increased as a consequence of such prior sensitization or conditioning. This concept of conditioned anxiety is in accord with our Theory of Antecedent Conflicts [Ch.8:VIIA*1*].

C. THE SECONDARY SOURCES OF ANXIETY

1. Influences of Antecedent Prototypes and Maturation Level Important

The later or secondary sources of anxiety as seen in adulthood are of course determined in large measure by the earlier ways in which anxiety developed. As noted earlier, not only is there a close relationship, but the earlier sources tend to serve as prototypes for anxiety in adulthood and appear to create what might be considered as patterns of response. Our Theory of Antecedent Conflicts is operative.

In the earlier part of this chapter we saw ways in which some of the following sources of anxiety operated. There are, however, substantial differences in emphasis and in relative importance between the primary and the secondary sources of anxiety, as they operate for the infant and for the adult.

The development of maturity, the formation of personality traits, and the development of the individual character defenses will change the patterns of reaction. Vulnerability to some of the important early sources will be less in certain instances; for example, those of separation and intuitive communication. The emphasis may be different; for instance as in that of disapproval from a significant adult. In the anxiety stemming from the conditioned response, both the resulting reaction and this particular source for anxiety may become much more important.

Finally, there are essentially new sources. With the increasing development of social awareness and personal standards, the self takes over internally a considerable part of the censoring function earlier exercised by significant adults externally. When some of the earlier infantile sources continued to be important in adulthood, they are apt to operate in a very hidden and devious fashion, far outside of and beyond conscious awareness. *Table 2* [Ch.1:IVB*3*] has presented these secondary sources in outline form.

2. Superego Conflict (Conflicts with Conscience)

As the conscience or superego develops, conflict now becomes increasingly possible between the instinctual needs or urges on the one hand, and the evolving superego restrictions and inhibitions on the other. An important source of internal emotional conflict thus comes into being. Anxiety can originate in a strictly personal, internalized sense. Here it arises as a consequence of the intrapsychic conflicts over drives which the conscience finds intolerable and unacceptable.

The superego, that is, the conscience, develops largely in response to the real or assumed attitudes of significant persons in early life. By the acceptance (and internalization) as well as by the rejection (sometimes with the "reaction of the opposite"—Reaction Formation) of the standards of these significant persons, the conscience gradually takes form. As it develops, the superego or conscience largely assumes the function of approval-disapproval which was previously exerted by important external figures. These earlier served as external censors. There is now an internal censor. To the extent that this internal censor is successful as a replacement for previous approval or disapproval from external sources, the importance of approval from outside sources decreases. In other words, the function of approval-disapproval originally coming from important adult figures in early life is now taken over by an "internalized" authority, the conscience.

A low level of self-esteem contributes to the experiencing of anxiety and to one's vulnerability to anxiety. A direct correlation tends to exist for example between the number of psychosomatic symptoms and the level of self-esteem. Thus an adequate, approved, and accurate self-image contributes to emotional equanimity and is one of the major goals of psychotherapy.

3. Disapproval, or Fear of Disapproval, Especially from Significant Persons

Although, as we have just seen, the conscience largely takes over the role of censor in normal personality development, this does not eliminate the very human need to please, to seek approval. We have also noted the antecedent threat to the child of parental resentment and rejection. Some of this can continue and may be exaggerated and pathologic in the adult. In these instances it can be a major source of anxiety, particularly when maturity is faulty.

The importance of all this as a possible source of anxiety can vary within wide limits for different individuals. The disapproval of an important person is a potential threat to one's position, and to the relationship. Doubtless our complex social system has added to the importance of this area as a potential source of conflict and anxiety. One's position, advancement, status, and prestige all hinge upon the approval of others. To a considerable extent one's self-esteem can also have a direct relationship to the level of the esteem of others. While these factors may be evaluated quite realistically, their importance and significance also can be greatly overvalued in neurotic fashion. An objective appraisal by a self-knowing and experienced therapist can be quite valuable here.

4. Social Conflict

Social conflict includes all the social threats present as a potential consequence of doing, saying, or thinking "the wrong thing," that which is not in accord with the accepted mores of one's particular social and cultural group. The threats include censure, and possible loss or damage to one's prestige, stature, or self-esteem. This is closely related to the foregoing.

In more marked instances there are in addition further possible threats of scorn or ridicule, and actual punishment. Various means are devised by societies to enforce a measure of conformity, the well-being of the group, and obedience to its laws. These may progress in further sequence to such dreaded consequences as incarceration, social ostracism, moral banishment, loss of citizenship, actual exile on a national basis, excommunication on a religious basis, or even death by execution.

5. Threats to Self-Preservation

Within threats to self-preservation are included the sources of anxiety which arise from environmental threats. Anxiety here is often close to fear, in that it at least appears to arise in response to threats from external sources, such as threats of physical or psychologic injury. At times in deference to the source, this type of reaction is called *situational anxiety*. However, since an undue response to even a danger which is clearly external still depends upon internal personality factors which are usually hidden, these buried internal factors will make a considerable contribution to the final reaction. This is true even when the stimulus is in itself of nearly catastrophic level. Such factors also importantly affect the individual's capacity to cope with the threat and its consequences to him, as well as his speed (and degree) of recovery from injury.

Under this heading are to be included the threats of physical danger or injury, and catastrophes of nature, such as storms, lightning, floods, earthquakes, glaciation, forest fires, and volcanic eruption. Also included are certain threats involving food, clothing, shelter, and one's livelihood, as well as various external threats which might involve privation, deprivation, or loss, or an interference with established sources of satisfaction. Illness, accidents, surgical procedures, and pregnancy together with parturition are threats to personal integrity. There are also important threats of psychologic injury possible from external sources.

Finally included here are war and threats of war, war-borne violence of all kinds, invasion, occupation, servitude, nuclear catastrophe, feuds, riots, mob action, strikes, civil disorder, and the breakdown of social structure, law and order.

6. Threats to Racial Preservation

Included in threats to racial preservation are large general areas such as exterminative war, generalized atomic conflict, genocide, racial prejudice and restriction, and certain instances of religious persecution. Also included are certain more individual threats involving reproductive capacity, sex, and love.

7. *Conditioned Responses*

Conditioned responses can be a much more important source of anxiety in adulthood. Following a sufficiently threatening experience or a series of them, the adult may suffer similar feelings when only parts of the picture are later present. This interesting and vital reaction has been commented on earlier.

We shall see this amply illustrated in Chapters Nine and Ten, of Part III, concerning the Phobic Reactions. The apparent compulsion, which has been observed in many people, to repeat earlier patterns of response, behavior, and relationships, even though these may be self-defeating and destructive, is also closely related to the process of conditioned responses. Other types of compulsion, repetitive behavior, and accident-proneness also have a certain relationship.

8. *Frustration and Hostility*

These remain important sources of anxiety in adulthood where they may also be quite hidden and inaccessible to ordinary observation. Feelings of anger and rage often become very significant threats to the individual possessing them.

First, this may be so by the possible projection to the other persons of the feelings. In these instances one sees and believes his own (largely deeply hidden) level of anger and rage to be directed toward him by another or by others. Secondly, there is also the everpresent threat of punishment or retaliation which may be real, but which may also have hidden and symbolic carry-overs. These derive from early fantasies of parental retaliation for parentally- and/or subjectively-intolerable hostile thoughts or impulses.

9. *Infantile Carry-overs, and Miscellaneous Sources*

A further category includes the carry-over into later years of infantile responses of anxiety to: (1) separation, (2) identification or intuitive communication,* and (3) helplessness, that is dependency. Some pattern formation and continuity of response is undoubtedly a normal finding in every person. Such residuals in isolated fashion are not necessarily neurotic. They may be regarded as clearly neurotic when discernible interference with effectiveness in living results.

---

* As one example from military life, communication by emotional contagion, intuitively and through identification, plays a role in the "contagious" loss of morale in troops. Here also, the presence of anxiety *per se* in the leaders of a military group may be transmitted in this manner. It may also be transmitted similarly, as mentioned earlier, as a primary source of anxiety.

Anxiety in the commanders constitutes a real threat to the entire group. Good, efficient leadership and sound military judgment are threatened when those responsible become anxious. A chain reaction can spread rapidly. The effects will be considerably more powerful for some than for others, depending upon their own inner security. Overall, the result is likely to be disruptive, sometimes disastrously so.

10. Apprehensive Anticipation

The type of apprehensive anticipation illustrated earlier might be included as a final source of feelings which are closely akin to anxiety or which might be regarded as a partial variant.

11. Specific Emotional Hazards of Adulthood (S.E.H.A.)

In addition to the foregoing Specific Emotional Hazards of Childhood, some of which may carry over into later years, certain situations in adult life constitute more specific adult hazards. These would comprise an analogous concept of Specific Emotional Hazards of Adulthood (*also see* Ch.3:IVE5).

Included as such specific hazards are such potentially traumatic and anxiety-provoking events as matriculation, graduation, marriage, separation, divorce, deaths, births, menopause, first sexual experience, traumatic civilian and service situations, and so on. We would also include herein, the Military Stressful Eras (M.S.E.s [Ch.2:IIB4; Ch.14:VIIIA1], and that of "passing the peak" [Ch.4:VA5], as some adults reach a point past which they feel their vigor will henceforth decline. *See also* related Conflict Indicator Concept, [Ch.12:; Ch.13:IVC1].

V. ANXIETY AND SLEEP

A. ROLE OF SLEEP IN EMOTIONAL HEALTH

1. Principle of Trend Toward Emotional Health: Sleep Refurbishes One's Psychologic Strength

The author has long believed in the principle of a strong and rather fundamental human drive or Trend Toward Emotional Health. This trend is steadily operative [Ch.14:IA3]. If it were not for this, the cumulative effect of the stresses and strains incident to living might leave few people free of serious consequences to their emotional health.

The restorative value of sleep is of great importance in helping to counteract such possible cumulative effects. Sleep is not only important from the standpoint of physical fatigue, but perhaps even more so from the standpoint of the *emotional fatigue* which results from the effects of tension and stress. Unquestionably sleep vastly increases our tolerance of the many stresses and strains incident to our living from day to day.

Sleep refurbishes our psychologic armamentarium for the coming day. Sleep also is a refuge from care and stress. Going to sleep can be a respite, a comfort, and a retreat from the troubles that have beset one during the day. This is the *Respite of Sleep Principle*. It can be facilitated by Soterial objects and mechanisms [Ch.II:VB2]. George Sterling (1869–1926) in *The Balance* expressed this concept poetically:

> "Let us be just with life. Although it bear
> A thousand thorns for every perfect rose,
> And though the happy day have mournful close,
> Slumber awaits to house the mind from care."

2. Widespread Recognition

There is evidence of widespread recognition of this role of sleep, often on an empiric basis. As an example, the director of personnel of a large organization was recently discussing his criteria for executives who reacted unfavorably to stress. The policy had been developed over a period of years, largely empirically, to arrange for the relief or transfer of an executive in any instance in which his ability to sleep became impaired.

At times anxiety itself is of such a level as to interfere with sleep. This interference with such a natural protective and restorative function can lead to a vicious circle of decreased tolerance, more tension, less sleep, and so on.

3. Hypothesis of Dream's Contribution to Emotional Health

Dreaming is also vital to the maintenance of emotional well-being. Everyone dreams. Further, everyone dreams each night. Dreams may not be recalled, or seldom recalled. This is part of the entire protectively intended process. With effort, training, and experience one can learn to recall a much higher percentage of one's dreams and dream content.

The universality of dreaming is of fairly recent recognition. This is also true as regards our increasing awareness of the contribution of dreams to emotional health. Indeed, dreaming is likely a clear requisite to health, providing among other benefits: (1) partial discharge in symbolic fashion of otherwise forbidden thoughts or urges, (2) effecting emotional compromises to this extent, (3) securing this kind of interaction with unconscious data, and (4) aiding in the maintenance of repression.

For these reasons the author earlier formulated the Hypothesis of the Dream's Contribution to Emotional Health and this is a concept that is further stressed in this book. Still further research into this entire major area is strongly indicated and may yield much of interest to us. The more definitive study of dreams and their possible facilitation of repression is quite important, but is beyond the scope of the present discussion. Some additional comments however will be found later in Part III, Chapter Thirteen, the Dissociative Reactions, on Dreams [Ch.13:IIIA2]. When personality integration is reasonably sound, the respite afforded by sleep and its restorative value is a major factor in the normal ability to handle a reasonable amount of anxiety and tension.

B. SEDATIVES AND TRANQUILIZERS

Sedative drugs can play a useful role in acute situations in artificially inducing the conditions of sleep. Their value is temporary. They are of most service individually when restricted to use as a "crutch" or as an emergency measure. Sedatives are more likely to be a deterrent than an aid in ferreting out the reasons why sleep is difficult. As an illustration of the temporary use of sedation however in quite acute situations, it has been found that heavy sedation for the surviving airmen following a crash is highly beneficial.

Tranquilizers are of greatest use in acute states marked particularly by agitation, and in acute psychotic reactions [Ch.3:IXF5]. When circumstances require their use, a rather complete and up-to-date listing is to be found in Remmen *et al.* Dependency and habituation are to be scrupulously avoided. This is an ever present danger, and one all too easily fallen into.

The long-range interests of a patient are better enhanced by insight-directed psychotherapy whenever feasible. It is far better for him to become an expert in finding out *why* he is anxious than to become an expert in merely covering over his anxiety with tranquilization via medication. Further, the latter, through the temporary surcease afforded, can be misleading and provide a false sense of security.

When new stresses ensue, or when the drug is no longer sufficiently effective, or when both take place, real psychologic disaster can overtake the patient who has come to depend upon drugs for some measure of equanimity. Finally, the patient who accepts the temporary relief afforded by this group of drugs is more than likely to be far less interested in pursuing the more effortful route of seeking insight and understanding through psychotherapy and analysis.

C. SLEEP DEPRIVATION: EFFECTS AND RAPID RECOVERY

The importance of sleep is perhaps no more clearly demonstrated than when there is a substantial—from 30 to 100 hours or more—deprivation. In these instances there is the nearly universal development of various degrees of abnormal psychologic manifestations. These merge at the more serious level in some instances into psychotic-like states. Surprisingly, prompt recovery takes place after from eight to fourteen hours of uninterrupted sleep. This rapid recovery is seemingly independent of the actual length of deprivation, within limits. These phenomena have been summarized in an earlier paper by the author (*Int. Rec. Med.*, **8**, 305; 1953).

It becomes clear that sleep has an important relationship to human ability to tolerate anxiety and stress. When this restorative function is interfered with, often by the very forces against which it helps to protect, this can serve as a useful indication that emotional health is threatened. Dreams undoubtedly play an important role in these effects. Experiments in which dreaming was prevented (but not sleep) have similarly led to the development of untoward psychologic manifestations.

D. OVERSLEEPING

Increased sleeping is occasionally seen as a defensive response to anxiety, which may be voluntary or involuntary. It can, indeed, be developed as a faculty, and may or may not be pathologic. Sleep serves herein essentially as an escape. This is somewhat analogous to its use by some people as an escape from other aspects of living. Included, for example, are such areas as a painful marital conflict, stressful situations, problems in professional relationships, pending examinations, and boredom.

Hoboes, for example, as a group are reputed to be great sleepers, some of them averaging from sixteen to eighteen hours of sleep in twenty-four. Here the oversleeping has, indeed, become an overdeveloped and pathologic way of escape from boredom, frustration, and defeat. Further discussion of sleep will be found in Chapter Seven on Emotional Fatigue and The Fatigue Reactions [Ch.7:XA].

VI. THE FUNCTION OF ANXIETY

A. ABNORMAL, DISRUPTIVE, AND PATHOLOGIC

Our discussion of some of the important aspects of the nature and origins of anxiety may be concluded for the present with several brief remarks about its function. Anxiety is considered by some to be a phenomenon which is entirely disruptive, handicapping, and destructive. According to their view, anxiety is always abnormal and pathologic, and can only be regarded as injurious. Of course, whenever anxiety really interferes to any extent with personal effectiveness or satisfaction, there is no question that it is clearly harmful.

By definition anxiety could also be regarded as abnormal since it has something irrational about it, and objectively it appears to be an undue response. It is also correct that in direct or in hidden and devious fashion anxiety is the agent ultimately responsible for many of the clinical manifestations of emotional illness. With people who are not actually considered to be ill, anxiety may also exert important restrictive effects on function, and it may interfere with, or handicap, certain kinds of mental and emotional activity. The *Depletion Concept of Anxiety* (*see also* [Ch.7:VIB4]) helps point out the expenditure and depletion of psychic energy incident to the experiencing of anxiety. See also Concept of Emotional Death, [Ch.3:IIC5]. Let us, however, glance briefly at another side of the picture, not forgetting at the same time that there are a number of important contrasting aspects to this whole problem.

B. PROTECTIVE, CONSTRUCTIVE, AND SOCIALIZING; CONSTRUCTIVE ANXIETY CONCEPT

It is clear, for example, that anxiety can have a protective function. Anxiety arises when the ego is threatened. It alerts the defenses for meeting the threat in whatever way seems most appropriate. As a result, behavior may be modified, or new action taken. According to this view, anxiety is normal and has a useful role, at least to a given point. Anxiety or the threat of anxiety can, of course, provoke fear in itself. This is illustrated by the person subject to anxiety attacks who, as a result, will go to great lengths to avoid an attack, as we shall soon learn. However, in turn, small amounts of anxiety may serve to alert the person so that he is less subject to that overwhelming kind of fear or panic which could be most disruptive and disastrously self-defeating.

Further, anxiety is an important force in character formation and personality development. From this standpoint, anxiety can be viewed in a broad sense as exerting a constructive influence (again within certain limits). It may counteract apathy and halt tendencies toward the stagnation of self-satisfaction.

According to the foregoing, anxiety may then be considered sometimes as a constructive force tending to advance individual personal adjustment and socialization. This is a statement on behalf of our Concept of Constructive Anxiety. Thus, the uneasiness and apprehension (anxiety) aroused by the disapproval of parents, the "significant adults," are emotions which often tend to bring about constructive change in the infant. Thus, to a point, anxiety may be a socializing influence, a promoter of acculturation. In excess, however, it becomes disjunctive, pathologic, and lies at the core of the neurotic and the nonorganic psychotic illnesses.

A last but important aspect of our Concept of Constructive Anxiety relates to the important role of anxiety in the treatment process. Herein it can sometimes play a key role both in leading to the initiation of therapy and in its continuation. These effects and results of anxiety are constructive, even vital. A *Fuel Analogy* may be drawn in this regard in which anxiety can be viewed as a driving force in treatment, the "gasoline" that fuels the "motor." Severe neuroses thus are sometimes to be encountered in which the relative absence of anxiety interferes with, delays, or even prevents therapy.

C. UNIVERSALITY OF APPLICATION

One who studies human behavior and reactions almost inevitably is overly influenced by his own cultural and social milieu and the author cannot of course claim exception. However, there is rather broad applicability of the overall thesis of the foregoing concepts and of those to follow.

The verification of these conceptions in differing cultures was an important motive in securing certain earlier opportunities to undertake a fair amount of international travel, including professional world tours in 1954, and again in 1957. There are of course considerable variations in cultural experience in the various ethnic and cultural groups in many nations. In distinction however, there is perhaps more difference in the *interpretation* of emotional experience and reactions. Nonetheless, our basic themes would appear to have considerable applicability and validity for races and people generally.

From the standpoint of dynamics, anxiety is the central problem in the psychogenesis of emotional illness. It is also a prime factor in human behavior, in the development of personality, and in the formation of the individual character defenses or traits. In Chapter Three we shall make some further observations about anxiety, its role in our lives, and its major, more direct clinical manifestations.

VII. INTRODUCTORY COMMENTS ON DIAGNOSIS AND CLASSIFICATION

A. MAKING THE DIAGNOSIS

1. Diagnosis Made on Descriptive Basis

Beginning around the turn of the century, a constructive trend gradually developed in psychiatry for the diagnosis of a given case to be made upon a descriptive basis. This is particularly true for the neuroses and for others of the non-psychotic conditions.

This trend continued and grew, until today most diagnostic labels are descriptive. This has been a useful development since: (1) it is a convenience clinically and professionally; (2) the cumbersome aspects of a more complex terminology have been avoided; and (3) scientific communication has been facilitated.

2. Importance of Outstanding Clinical Feature

There have been two other concurrent major developments in the diagnosis of the neuroses in the past 65 years, which have also been practical and useful. The first of these trends has resulted in the diagnosis being made on the basis of the most outstanding clinical feature.

Thus, a patient with a phobia may also have symptoms of anxiety or obsessive traits, for example. However, if the phobia is the major and outstanding symptom, the proper diagnosis is one of a Phobic Reaction. Similarly, should the obsessive manifestations be the major manifestations clinicially, even though there were some phobic or other neurotic elements present, the diagnosis would be an Obsessive-Compulsive Reaction.

B. CERTAIN TERMS: THEIR ORIGIN AND DEVELOPMENT

1. Hypochondriasis, Hysteria, and Melancholia

A. HYPOCHONDRIASIS (HYGEIAPHRONTIS; OVERCONCERN WITH HEALTH). —The second trend as referred to above has led toward the discard of certain terms of quite hoary origin. Indeed, although based upon completely mistaken ideas of etiology, several of these in particular, such as hypochondriasis, hysteria and melancholia, which originated long ago in the world of ancient Greece, have been used for so many centuries and so widely that discard has neither been rapid nor complete. Accordingly, it will hardly be surprising if even the non-medical reader has some acquaintance with them.

Hypochondriasis is a state marked by either somatic or physiologic preoccupation (or both), symptoms, and bodily concerns. These symptoms and concerns are out of proportion to any possible underlying and strictly physical organic difficulty which may be present, and which often enough is totally absent. Various and sometimes shifting symptoms often develop which may affect any region or area of the body. This lack of organic basis makes them no less real or troubling to the patient, of course; indeed, rather the reverse, since the finding of a more tangible and definite organic basis would provide something usually far easier for him to cope with. Picking a most frequent locale of such symptoms, the hypochondrium, and believing this the area of pathology, the ancient Greeks derived their name of hypochondriasis. They believed the symptoms were due to disorders of the spleen and the region of the hypochondrium.

Today one still hears of the hypochondriacal patient or symptom, which is correct usage. Use of the term "hypochondriac" as a noun and applied to a person, often enough with some unfortunate derogatory implication or moral and judgmental tinge, is doubly improper. First, it is incorrect usage. It is an adjective and not a noun. Secondly, when a slur is implied, the user is further convicted of ignorance by his more informed listener who knows that a hypochondriacal symptom is not consciously sought, is not imagined, is not assumed, and results in distress and suffering that is most genuine and real to its unfortunate possessor. (Similar considerations apply to the words "neurotic" and "alcoholic." These should also be properly used as adjectives and not as nouns.) As the reader will learn shortly [Ch.8:IA], the author has proposed the alternative adoption of *hygeia* (health) combined with *phrontis* (anxious concern about), or Hygeia-phrentis, as a more accurately-descriptive name for this type of neurotic reaction.

B. HYSTERIA.—This is an illness which we understand today as resulting from emotional conflict. This knowledge as to its basis is impressively recent in origin from any historical perspective, dating only from the past 80 years or so.

While various explanations were offered prior to this time, the name hysteria derives from the Greek word *hyster,* for the uterus. It was the ancients' belief that the manifestations derived from this organ, wandering through the body, producing symptoms at each location. Outward expressions of hysteria may be evidenced by major and dramatic symptoms such as paralyses, loss of sensation, hearing, speech, and even sight, convulsive-like seizures and emotional outbursts. The correct name today is Conversion Reaction.

C. MELANCHOLIA.—As an older term for emotional depression, melancholia is derived from the Greek *melan,* or black, and *cholia,* meaning bile, in accord with the ancients' pre-scientific beliefs as to such phenomena underlying the etiology of depressions.

Only quite recently has the term melancholia as a diagnostic label for depressions of psychotic level been deleted from official nomenclatures. As with hypochondriasis and hysteria, the outmoded term of melancholia may occasionally still be heard.

C. TERMINOLOGY AT THE TURN OF THE CENTURY

1. Diagnostic Terms Added

It is important for us to have some understanding of the diagnostic terms which may be encountered in referring to the various neurotic illnesses. A brief survey of these terms, their origins, usage, and evolution therefore becomes an important adjunct in our understanding of the neuroses generally.

We have observed how the terms hysteria, melancholia, and hypochondriasis were adopted and passed down through the centuries. Let us pause briefly in the transitional period of 1890–1910 and see how nomenclature stood in the neuroses at this important juncture in medical history.

In addition to our original three terms, two others had by then come to enjoy wide vogue: *psychasthenia* and *neurasthenia.* Yet another, *traumatic neurosis,* could be heard. For a very limited group the term *anxiety neurosis* had just become a distinct entity.

A. PSYCHASTHENIA.—The term and concept of psychasthenia was introduced by Pierre Janet, in accord with his etiologic views of weakness (*asthenia*) of the psyche or mind underlying the symptoms. A number of our current neurotic diagnoses were included within this concept and diagnostic category. The term was widely adopted and used for many years.

People gradually became increasingly disenchanted with the concept however, and with the term as well. Accordingly, the use of psychasthenia as a diagnosis has almost completely died out.

B. NEURASTHENIA.—Neurasthenia is the only major diagnostic term introduced by an American (George Miller Beard, 1869). It was widely used for many decades [Ch.7:XI]. This term and concept was predicated on the mistaken belief that the major symptoms, such as fatigue, anxiety, weakness, and sexual malfunctions, were due to weakness (*asthenia*) of the nerves (*neuro*).

Currently this concept and term are falling out of use.

C. ANXIETY NEUROSES AND TRAUMATIC NEUROSES.—In 1894 Freud recommended that a segment of cases be detached from the neurasthenia group. These he proposed be called *anxiety neuroses* [Ch.3:IV]. Oppenheim had earlier also introduced a term and an etiologic theory of the so-called traumatic neurosis.

D. FURTHER DEVELOPMENT AND REFINEMENT OF TERMINOLOGY (1900-1965)

Let us follow further developments to the present date. The author currently offers eleven diagnostic categories as being of value in the classification, diagnosis, and nomenclature of the neurotic reactions. These have been derived as follows. Neurotic reactions formerly included under the term of psychasthenia are now comprised of three major groups: the *Dissociative Reactions,* the *Obsessive-Compulsive Reactions,* and the *Phobic Reactions.* In addition, the name *Soterial Reactions* has been proposed for the converse of the Phobic Reactions.

The *Anxiety Reactions* include Anxiety Neurosis, Anxiety-Tension States, and the Acute Anxiety Attack (Anxiety Panic.) Although neurasthenia enjoys only very limited use today, a group of cases in which emotional fatigue is the prominent clinical feature may warrant the occasional employment of the diagnosis of *Fatigue Reactions.* Hypochondriasis, hopefully to be replaced by the term *Hygeiaphrontis,* is still applicable as the most suitable label for a small group of neurotic reactions. This is the result of efforts to find a more suitably-descriptive diagnostic term in replacement

Table 3

Diagnostic Trends in the Neuroses

Diagnostic terminology in the neuroses has undergone development and refinement. Following are indicated some of the changes and trends in diagnostic terms from the ancient Greek to today, as will be followed in this text.

The chapter involved is indicated after each of the major headings. Subheads and less major categories are included in the appropriate chapters.

Ancient Greek	1890-1910	Today
Melancholia	Melancholia ....Depression	*The Depressive Reactions* [Ch.4].
Hysteria	Hysteria ....Conversion Hysteria	*The Conversion Reactions* [Ch.12].
Hypochondriasis	Hypochondriasis	Overconcern with Health; *The Hygeiaphrontic Reactions* (Hypochondriasis) [Ch.14].
Neurasthenia (Beard, 1869)	Anxiety Neurosis (Freud, 1894)	*The Anxiety Reactions:* (a) Acute Anxiety Attack (AAA) (b) Anxiety-Tension State (c) Anxiety Neurosis [Ch.3].
	Neurasthenia	*The Fatigue Reactions* (neurasthenia): [Ch. 7]. (a) Emotional Fatigue (b) Fatigue States [Ch.7].
		The Character Reactions: (a) Character Defenses [Ch.5]. (b) Personality patterns of defense.
Psychasthenia (Pierre Janet)		*The Dissociative Reactions* [Ch.13]. *The Obsessive-Compulsive Reactions* [Ch. 6]. *The Phobic Reactions* [Ch.10].
Traumatic Neurosis (Oppenheim)		*The Neuroses-Following-Trauma* (traumatic neurosis) [Ch. 14].
		The Soterial Reactions (converse of the phobias) [Ch.11].

of the older inaccurate one. Hysteria is now replaced by the category of *Conversion Reactions,* so named for the principal mental mechanism which is operative.

Melancholia has given way to the *Depressive Reactions,* whether of neurotic or of psychotic level. Traumatic neurosis is sometimes used, as is the more inclusive and probably preferable designation of *Neuroses Following Trauma.* A later concept of neurosis being represented by exaggeration or overdevelopment of character or personality traits has been gaining increasing favor. As a consequence, use of the terms *Character Reaction* or Character Neurosis for this very large group of reactions has been growing and is to be encouraged.

We shall be guided by the foregoing trends and introductory comments in our ensuing chapters. A tabulation of these developments as outlined is included as Table 3 as a more graphic effort to clarify them for the interested student.

E. POSITIVE GROUNDS FOR DIAGNOSIS PREFERABLE

What is a neurotic symptom? A neurotic symptom is one in which the basis lies in emotional conflict. It is an emotional symptom; an emotionally based symptom. Underlying the pain and discomfort are emotional factors, in contrast to the organic ones in physical symptoms. While it is true that organic causes are lacking or are insufficient to explain the presence of a given neurotic symptom, their absence alone provides inconclusive evidence upon which to base a label. Hence, what we call a "diagnosis by exclusion" is by no means the best approach nor the soundest. A diagnosis on positive grounds is far preferable.

However, most clinicians in the past, and a great many today continue to approach the neurotic or emotionally based and functional symptoms in this manner. The symptom is regarded tentatively at least as organic until an exhaustive search turns up no organic factors. Only at this juncture are some willing to concede that the symptom does not have an organic basis. This view and approach are to be decried. Whenever possible the positive approach is best adopted. It offers many clinical and therapeutic advantages.

VIII. INTRODUCTORY COMMENTS ON TREATMENT

A. THE SYMPTOMS; POSITION IN MEDICINE

1. Symptom An External Expression of Conflict

When we speak of emotional conflicts as the basis of neurotic symptoms and of the difficulties of our discerning them, we must keep in mind that in essence the symptom, character defense, or other manifestation replaces the conflict, or various aspects of it, insofar as the patient is concerned. In other words, were the patient consciously aware of the specifics of the conflict, the symptoms would no longer continue. The symptom helps to maintain in one's unconscious the elements of the conflict.

The symptom therefore can best be regarded as a *defensive endeavor*—however psychologically uneconomic—by the hard-pressed ego. The patient suffers from his neurotic symptom. Consciously, he does not want it. Unconsciously, however, it serves a vital purpose. On this level he needs it, and indeed cannot do without it. Bringing the basis of an emotional symptom into consciousness (making the unconscious conscious) is one of the goals of psychotherapy and analysis. Its elucidation changes the basis itself, the *raison d'etre,* of the symptom. As this process takes place, modification or relief of the symptom occurs also. Treatment is indicated when what we might call the *balanced neurotic position* [Ch.14:XB*1*] breaks down, with a resulting *emotional decompensation,* [Ch.4:VB*1*].

Even the most astute psychotherapist can only at times surmise what the psychogenic factors are which may underlie a given symptom. Their elucidation requires intensive psychotherapy, which can lead to their resolution.

2. Conflict Resolution Relieves Symptoms

At this point the reader might surmise, and correctly so, that a symptom cannot survive the resolution of the underlying conflicts responsible. This concept ties in directly with certain important ones concerning treatment. It follows the Principle of Symptom-Survival [Ch. 1:IIIE*3*; Ch.14:IIIB*2*] according to which symptoms cannot survive the resolution of the underlying conflicts.

In other words, working out the unconscious factors lying behind a symptom tends to secure its resolution. Definitive therapy in psychiatry therefore, at least in part, aims at making the unconscious conscious.

3. Emotional Bases of Functional Symptoms Elusive

On the other hand, emotional bases are elusive indeed. They are far less tangible for the average physician, troubling and troublesome, and indeed often quite frustrating. Cloaked as they are in the veiled reaches of the unconscious, they are not accessible by any of the more usual and familiar medical treatment techniques in which most physicians are trained.

It is small wonder that the elucidation of emotional bases of symptoms is a major problem and one which is far more complex than the infectious, neoplastic, traumatic, and so forth, bases of organically-induced symptoms. Still, elucidation leads to resolution. This is an important goal in therapy. Promptness in initiating therapy is important. This follows the Principle of Symptom Longevity [Ch.14:VIIIE*3*], which points out that the longer an emotional symptom persists, the more involved and difficult its therapeutic resolution is likely to be.

4. "Psychiatric Half" of Medical Practice; Medical Teaching Limited

Generalists and specialists in various branches of medicine not infrequently speak of the "psychiatric half" of their practices. Estimates of the overall amount of emotionally-based problems *vs.* organically-based ones are not infrequently made in the range of 60–75 per cent. The author has great confidence in those of his colleagues who make these estimates—ones which he has heard frequently repeated in his many contacts within the medical profession. Why then is this not reflected more clearly in medical teaching?

Today the physician is trained, as he has been traditionally, to become an expert in the diagnosis and treatment of organic conditions. His exposure to psychiatry is at the best still all too often only a minor and subsidiary part of his formal training. There has been a certain trend toward change in the direction of more inclusion and an increased emphasis upon psychiatry in the medical school curriculum. However, this trend has been both quite recent and its continuing implementation painfully gradual. It should be greatly encouraged by all available means.

Here then is an inconsistency. From 90 to 95 per cent of the student's curriculum is directed toward preparing him to handle what will likely constitute the minority—and the less complex minority at that—of the patients he will encounter. Small wonder perhaps at the increasing trend toward specialization, as today's graduates seek more training, more experience, and more adequacy.

B. APPROACHES IN THERAPY; TECHNIQUE

1. The Patient

Treatment in the neuroses is psychologic in nature. It requires the direction of a skilled specialist in psychiatry. This type of therapy is called psychotherapy. Its effectiveness depends first upon the interest and efforts of the patient in his own behalf, as well as upon the skill of the psychiatrist, the intensity of the treatment, and other factors.

The patient has to want treatment. He has to be willing to work hard at it. He must want to get well. He has to mobilize sufficient motivation in the service of recovery to carry him into and through treatment. With these basic requisites met, the trained and experienced psychiatrist is in a position to help him.

2. Educational Process of Considerable Depth

With the patient cooperative and the psychiatrist trained, let us consider several factors of the next order of importance in the psychotherapeutic process. Psychotherapy is an educational process, more personal, deeper and more complex than other types of study, but also more meaningful for the person concerned. For the individual who tackles therapy successfully, regardless of the presence or absence of serious neurotic symptoms or limiting personality traits, this experience will likely be one of the most important, if not the most important, meaningful, and constructive influence in his life. Anyone can benefit from psychotherapy. All too few are willing or are in a position to take advantage of it. This is hardly too surprising, however, when one recognizes the hundreds of sessions required and the high priority which must be assigned to the process, often over a period of several years.

3. The Treatment Rule

Therapy in most cases of neuroses is not substantially different. The approach is often very similar regardless of the symptomatology. The aim is constantly to learn more about the individual. In promoting this, the author sets up a so-called "treatment rule," as do many of his colleagues. According to this rule *the patient undertakes to say every thought which comes to mind while he is with the psychiatrist, without reservation or censorship.* This is an important rule. It is more stringent for some than others. Adherence to it speeds and shortens the treatment.

Ultimately, one gains increasing familiarity with the person's psyche, with his inner conflicts and his defenses against them. As they become clearer to physician and to patient, they lose their strength. They become less necessary. They undergo modification and resolution. The person's energies become freer to be employed in other and more constructive activities. The patient becomes less restricted and tied by unconscious forces about which he previously had no knowledge, let alone control.

4. Psychotherapy Differs from Other Medical Therapies

From these brief comments it becomes apparent that psychotherapy differs substantially from other forms of medical treatment. With many kinds of treatment, the therapy is something administered *by* the physician and to the patient. Indeed, insofar as vaccines, antibiotics, or other injections are concerned, it would conceivably be possible that an adequate course of treatment could be administered in some instances, despite the patient's active opposition. The patient's role thus in other types of medical therapy often can be a very passive one, without the efficacy of the treatment being substantially affected. The physician takes a great deal, if not all, of the responsibility in a fair number of cases. This is not true in psychotherapy. This type of therapy absolutely requires an active collaborative effort on the part of both physician and patient. Otherwise its potential success will be limited accordingly.

The patient is thus an active participant in his own therapy. The physician provides knowledge, training, and experience. He sets up the treatment situation, the rules, and provides guidance. The guidance varies from occasional active direction to far more subtle nudges to the patient's associations in the form of questions. When treatment is going as it should the patient does perhaps 98 per cent of the talking. Sessions may take place in which few or no words are contributed by the physician.

5. Patient and Therapist Learn Together

The patient also continues to direct his own life. Advice is rare indeed and is seldom given. Judgments are not made. The therapist's interest is constantly in learning more about the patient's emotional and mental activities and processes. One needs to learn what makes him "tick."

It is not the physician's responsibility to decide what is "right" or "wrong," nor to make decisions for his patient, although sometimes these are sought from him. On the other hand, he wishes to know the bases for the patient's judgments and decisions in detail; the pros and cons entering into them. Many times their fuller exploration and discussion with the help of an objective, trained observer uncovers irrational elements or unrealistic evaluations entering into them.

IX. SUMMARY

Emotional health is relative and problems are universal. A "Law of Relativity in Emotional Health" may be warranted. A number of cogent reasons were noted in support of classification and diagnosis, recognizing at the same time a lessened importance in relation to investigative psychotherapy. The concept of anxiety is relatively new in medicine. Possible restrictive forces were noted in its recognition and in the development of interest.

The *Principle of Universality* points out that anxiety is experienced by everyone. A concept of an "inverse ratio of symptom-success (in allaying anxiety) with one's motivation toward therapy" was offered. The greater the "symptom-success," the less motivation toward treatment.

The neurotic reactions comprise a major percentage of the psychiatry in private practice. Accordingly, increasing familiarity with them is to be stressed. Anxiety was defined and some bases for determining its pathology noted. The concept of *Functional-Structural Progression* was referred to. Fear and anxiety were distinguished, on the basis of the *known and external stimuli of fear vs.* the *unknown* or unclear and *internal stimuli in anxiety.* The *Principle of Individual Appropriateness of Response* refers to our findings that although outwardly, anxiety or an emotional response may not seem appropriate, on a deeper level it always proves to be individually so. Illustrations were offered, as was a concept of apprehensive anticipation. The Total Individual Response to Crisis refers to and includes all of the resources individually mobilized to meet a crisis, threat, or danger.

Anxiety may be discharged through physical activity or transferred into anger, or into what we might term an anxiety-equivalent. The direct and indirect manifestations of anxiety were outlined and tabulated (*Table 1* [Ch.1:IIF*1*]). Emotional Conflict was discussed briefly. Conflict gives rise to anxiety especially through the threat of *derepression.* Anxiety also provides the motive force for repression; an effortless and automatic relegation of intolerable psychic data to the unconscious. The *First Tenet of the Parental Role* concerns facilitating the process of acculturation and maturation of the child, in the proper emotional atmosphere.

In discussing the origins of anxiety we briefly touched on theory, and thence what we might term the major *primary* and *secondary* sources of anxiety. After outlining the important *Theory of Antecedent Conflicts,* the Sources of Anxiety were tabulated (*Table 2* [Ch.1:IVB*1*]), and outlined for later brief comment. *Emotional Contagion* was noted in relation to anxiety, and the *Specific Emotional Hazards of Childhood* mentioned. Similarly the *Specific Emotional Hazards of Adulthood* were outlined.

The relation of anxiety and sleep received comment and allowed mention of the *Principle of a Trend Toward Emotional Health,* and an *Hypothesis of the Dream's Contribution to Emotional Health.* Sleep (assisted by dreaming) refurbishes one's psychologic armamentarium and is important to the maintenance and promotion of one's emotional health. The role and restrictions of sedatives and tranquilizers received brief comment. Oversleeping was noted as a defensive response to stress, anxiety, and boredom.

Anxiety can function as a disruptive and abnormal force leading to all varieties of psychopathology. It can also exert influences which are constructive, socializing, and protective. *The Depletion Concept of Anxiety* notes the expenditure and depletion of psychic energy incident to experiencing anxiety.

Further introductory comments on diagnosis and classification were offered. Diagnosis is best descriptive and should be made on the basis of the most outstanding clinical feature. The origins and development were traced for the terminology in the diagnosis of the eleven neurotic reactions provided chapter recognition in the present text. Their development was tabulated (*Table* 3) for convenience of reference in a more graphic form. In conclusion some further introductory comments on therapy offered some general concepts and suggestions.

These brief comments on therapy have been very general. Chapters as we proceed will add to them. A section containing some remarks on therapy will be included at the end of most chapters.

X. SELECTED REFERENCES AND BIBLIOGRAPHY

ACKERMAN, N. W. (June 14, 1954). Personal communication.

ALEXANDER, F. (1951). *Our Age of Unreason.* Rev. Ed. Philadelphia; Lippincott.

— (1950). *Psychosomatic Medicine,* p. 140. New York; Norton.

ARLOW, JACOB A. (1963). "Conflict, Regression and Symptom Formation." *Int. J. Psycho-analysis,* **44,** 1.

BENDER, LAURETTA (1961). "Current Techniques in the Management of the Anxious Child." *Amer. J. Psychother.,* **15,** 341.

BLAU, A. (1952). "In Support of Freud's Syndrome of 'Actual' Anxiety Neuroses." *Int. J. Psycho-analysis,* **33,** 371.

BROSIN, HENRY W., Ed. (1961). *Lectures on Experimental Psychiatry.* Pittsburgh; University of Pittsburgh Press.

BUSSE, E. W. (July 29, 1954). Personal communication.

CALDWELL, COL. J. M. (July 21, 1954). Personal communication.

CALLIERI, B. and FRIGHI, L. (1962). "An Approach to the Problem of Existential vs. Psychoanalytic Anxiety." *J. Existential Psy.,* **2,** 323.

CAMERON, D. E. (May 19, 1954). Personal communication.

— (1945). "Some Relationships Between Excitement, Depression and Anxiety." *Amer. J. Psychiat.,* **102,** 385.

CANNON, W. B. (1909). "The Influences of Emotional States on the Functions of the Alimentary Canal." *Amer. J. med. Sci.,* **137,** 480.

— (1929). *Bodily Changes in Pain, Hunger, Fear and Rage.* 2nd Ed. New York; Appleton.

CATTELL, R. B. and SCHEIER, I. H. (1961). *The Meaning and Measurement of Neuroticism and Anxiety.* New York; Ronald.

COHEN, R. A. (1950). "Anxiety." *Med. Ann. D.C.,* **19,** 479.

DOLLARD, J. and MILLER, N. E. (1950). *Personality and Psychotherapy.* New York; McGraw-Hill.

DUNBAR, F. (1948). *Mind and Body,* pp. 65-79. New York; Random House.

DYRUD, J. E. (August 1953). Personal communication.

FERENCZI, S. (1950). *Sex in Psychoanalysis,* p. 34. New York; Basic Books.

FREUD, S. (1950). *Collected Papers.* Vol. 1, pp. 59-106. London; Hogarth.

— (1936). The Problem of Anxiety. New York; *Psychoanalyt. Quart.* and Norton.

— (1946). *The Ego and the Mechanisms of Defense,* p. 61. New York; International University Press.

FROMM-REICHMANN, F. (1950). *Principles of Intensive Psychotherapy,* pp. 39-42, 82. Chicago; University of Chicago Press.

GANNT, W. HORSLEY, Ed. (1961). *Physiological Bases of Psychiatry.* Springfield; Charles C. Thomas.

GANTT, WALTER J. (1962). *Basic Anxiety.* New York; Philosophical Library.

GLESER, G. C., GOTTSCHALK, L. A. and SPRINGER, K. J. (1961). "An Anxiety Scale Applicable to Verbal Samples." *Arch. gen. Psy.,* 5, 593.

GREENACRE, P. (1941). "The Predisposition to Anxiety." *Psychoanal. Quart.,* 10, 66.

HART, A. D. (1954). "Iatrogenics and Cardiac Neurosis: A Critique." *J. Amer. med Ass,,* 156, 1133.

HARTEN, D. (1944). "Fear in Battle." *Infantry J.*

JENKINS, R. L. (1955). *The Medical Significance of Anxiety,* p. 26. Washington, D.C.; Biological Foundation.

KARDINER, A. (1944). "Hysterias and Phobias." In: Lorand, S., Ed. *Psychoanalysis Today,* pp. 187-199. New York; International University Press.

KLEIN, M. (1948). "A Contribution to the Theory of Anxiety and Guilt." *Int. J. Psycho-analysis,* 29, 114.

LAUGHLIN, H. P. (1953). "Anxiety, Its Nature and Origins." *Med. Ann. D.C.,* 22, 403.

— (1953). "Sleep Deprivation and Exhaustion." *Int. Rec. Med.,* 8, 305.

— (1961). "The Current Status of Psychiatry in the United Kingdom." *Amer. J. Psychiat.,* 118, 308.

— (1960). "European Psychiatry." *Amer. J. Psychiat.,* 116, 769.

— (1958). "Psychiatry in Asia and the Middle East." *Amer. J. Psychiat.,* 115, 193.

— (1959). "India, Land of Medical Challenge." *Bull. Mont. Co. Med. Soc.,* 3, 2.

— (1958). "The Role of Sleep in Emotional Health." *State of Mind,* 2, 74.

— Ed. (1953). *A Psychiatric Glossary.* 4th Rev. Ed. Washington; American Psychiatric Association.

LEVY, D. M. (1950). "Evaluation of the 'Specific Event' as a Source of Anxiety." In: Hoch, P. H. and Zubin, J., Eds. *Anxiety,* pp. 140-150. New York; Grune and Stratton.

LIEF, H. I. (June 28, 1954). Personal communication.

LORAND, S. (1946). *Technique of Psychoanalytic Theory.* New York; International University Press.

MASSERMAN, J. H. (1946). *Principles of Dynamic Psychiatry,* pp. 126-127. Philadelphia; Saunders.

MAY, R. (1950). "Historical Roots of Modern Anxiety Theories." In: Hoch, P. H. and Zubin, J., Eds. *Anxiety.* New York; Grune and Stratton.

— (1950). *The Meaning of Anxiety.* New York; Ronald.

MICHAUX, L. and DUCHE, D. J. (1962). "Contribution a L'Analyse Symptomatique de L'Anxiete, etc." *Ann. medpsychol.,* 1, 338.

MORRIS, G. O. and SINGER, M. T. (1961). "Sleep Deprivation." *Arch. gen. Psy.,* 5, 453.

MOWRER, O. H. (1953). *Psychotherapy: Theory and Research.* New York; Ronald.

NOCE, R. H., WILLIAMS, D. B. and RAPPAPORT, W. (1954). "Reserpin (Serpasin) in the Management of the Mentally Ill and Mentally Retarded: Preliminary Report." *J. Amer. Med. Ass.,* 156, 821.

PAVLOV, I. P. (1927). *Conditioned Reflexes.* Trans. and ed. by Anrep, G. V. London; Oxford University Press.

— (1941). *Conditioned Reflexes and Psychiatry.* Trans. and ed. by Gantt, W. H. New York; International Publishing Co.

POTTER, H. W. (November 8, 1954). Personal communication.

RADO, S. "Emergency Behavior." In: Hoch, P. H. and Zubin, J., Eds. *Anxiety,* p. 150. New York; Grune and Stratton.

RANK, O. (1929). *The Trauma of Birth.* New York; Harcourt, Brace.

REMMEN, E., COHEN, S., DITMAN, K. S. and FRANTZ, J. R. (1962). *Psychochemotherapy.* Los Angeles; Western Medical Publications.

REUSCH, J. and PRESTWOOD, A. R. (1949). "Anxiety." *Arch. Neurol. Psychiat.,* 62, 527.

ROFFWARG, H. P., DEMENT, W. C., MUZIO, J. N. and FISHER, CHARLES (1962). "Dream Imagery: Relationship to Rapid Eye Movements of Sleep." *Arch. gen. Psy.,* **7,** 4.

ROSENBERG, MORRIS (1962). "The Association Between Self-esteem and Anxiety." *J. Psychiat. Res.,* **1,** 135.

SALZMAN, LEON and MASSERMAN, JULES H. (1962). *Modern Concepts of Psychoanalysis.* New York; Philosophical Library.

SAUL, L. J. (1950). "The Nature of Neurotic Reactions." *Amer. J. Psychiat.,* **106,** 547.

— (1960). *Emotional Maturity.* 2nd Ed. Philadelphia; Lippincott.

SCHILDER, P. (1944). "Neurosis and Psychosis." In: Lorand, S., Ed., *Psychoanalysis Today,* pp. 249-261. New York; International University Press.

SHARPE, E. F. (1950). "Anxiety: Outbreak and Resolution." In: *Collected Papers on Psychoanalysis,* pp. 67-81. London; Hogarth.

— (1930). "Survey of Defense Mechanisms in General Character Traits and in Conduct." *Int. J. Psycho-analysis,* **11,** 361.

SIMON, ALEXANDER, Ed. (1961). *The Physiology of Emotions.* Springfield; Charles C. Thomas.

SULLIVAN, H. S. (1946). *Conceptions of Modern Psychiatry.* Washington; W. A. White Psychiatric Foundation.

— (1949). "The Theory of Anxiety and the Nature of Psychotherapy." *Psychiatry,* **12,** 3.

— (1948). "The Meaning of Anxiety in Psychiatry and in Life." *Psychiatry,* **11,** 1.

THOMPSON, C. and MULLAHY, P. (1950). *Psychoanalysis: Evolution and Development.* New York; Hermitage House.

WHITAKER, C. A. (August 1953). Personal communication.

XI. REVIEW QUESTIONS ON CONFLICT AND ANXIETY

1. Emotional health is relative. Explain this statement.
2. How significant a role do the neurotic reactions play in private practice?
3. a. What are the advantages of having separate categories in the neuroses?
   b. What is the Principle of Universality in experiencing anxiety?
   c. Why does more "symptom-success", lead to less motivation for therapy?
4. Define anxiety. How might a patient describe his feelings of anxiety?
5. What is:
   (*a*) The functional-structural progression?
   (*b*) Principle of Individual Appropriateness of Response?
   (*c*) An anxiety-equivalent?
   (*d*) The T.R.C.?
6. Distinguish the Direct and the Indirect manifestations of anxiety. List the main ones of each.
7. Discuss:
   (*a*) The role of anxiety in the genesis of emotional symptoms.
   (*b*) The "First Tenet of the Parental Role."
8. Distinguish fear from anxiety.
9. What is: (*a*) emotional conflict? (*b*) repression? (*c*) derepression?
10. How do the mental mechanisms relate to anxiety and to emotional conflict?
11. List the primary sources of anxiety. What is the Theory of Antecedent Conflicts?
12. What are the secondary sources of anxiety?; The "specific emotional hazards of childhood?"; of adulthood?
13. How may anxiety relate to sleep?
14. What is meant by:
    (*a*) "Trend Toward Emotional Health"?
    (*b*) "Hypothesis of the Dream's Contribution to Emotional Health"?
15. What is "apprehensive anticipation"?
16. Discuss the functions of anxiety. What is the "Depletion Concept" of anxiety?
17. Outline the historical development of classification and terminology in the neurotic reactions.
18. Name the eleven neurotic reactions which account for the majority of patients seen in psychiatric practice and which are accorded chapter recognition in the present text.

CHAPTER 2

THE ILLUSORY GAINS OF EMOTIONAL ILLNESS

.... Defensively-motivated Reactions
Self-defeating

I. INTRODUCTION
  A. Endogain and Epigain
    1. Motivation Defensive; 2. Primary Gain Responsible for Initiation of Emotional Illness; 3. Advantage from Illness Contributes to Its Perpetuation; 4. Accepted Conceptions
  B. Operative in Every Emotional Illness
  C. Gain Paradoxical and Illusory
    1. Unconscious Escape; 2. Symptoms and Character Defenses as Outward Reflections of Intrapsychic Conflict; 3. Essential Gain Leads to Self-defeat and Net Loss
  D. Wide Applications; Character Neuroses
    1. Character Traits Individually-Fixed Patterns of Emotional Response; 2. Character Defenses; Character Neurosis vs. Symptom Neurosis; 3. Assessment of Gain or Loss

II. THE SECONDARY GAINS OF ILLNESS: MATERIAL ADVANTAGES
  A. Secondary Gains Both Conscious and Unconscious
    1. The Epigain; 2. Conscious Secondary Gain; 3. Important to Differentiate Malingering; 4. Definitions; 5. Gain Sought Externally
  B. Secondary Gain in Neuroses
    1. Extent and Apparency Vary; 2. Gratification of Dependency Needs; 3. Epigain

of Compensation May Propagate Illness; 4. Military Aspects; M.S.E.'s
  C. Manipulation of External Environment

III. THE PRIMARY GAIN IN EMOTIONAL ILLNESS: THE ENDOGAIN
  A. Responsible for Initiation of Illness
  B. Raison d'Etre in Psychogenesis
  C. Resolution of Internal Conflicts

IV. CLINICAL ILLUSTRATIONS
  A. In Neuroses; Conversion Reaction. Principle of Inadvertent Defeat
  B. In Character Defenses; Principle of Defense-Hypertrophy
  C. Neurotic "Gains" in Suicidal Attempts, Delinquent Behavior, Obsessive Neuroses, and Other Problems
    1. Universality; 2. Epigain in Paranoid Personality; Paranoid Position
  D. Neurotic Gain of King David Reaction
  E. Principal Features and Comparison of "Gains"

V. SUMMARY

VI. SELECTED REFERENCES AND BIBLIOGRAPHY

VII. REVIEW QUESTIONS

I. INTRODUCTION

A. ENDOGAIN AND EPIGAIN

PRIOR TO beginning our study of the rather complex patterns of neurotic reaction it is of value that we consider some additional important factors entering into the "whys" and "hows" of their development. Certain contributions to their perpetuation, once established, are also very important. This will bring us at this juncture then to a consideration of the so-called "gains" of emotional illness. This data as presented in brief in the foregoing chapter and the present one, helps comprise what we might refer to as the psychologic "anatomy of emotional illness".

1. Motivation Defensive

Neurotic reactions are defensively motivated. The intent is a protective one. Every such reaction unconsciously seeks certain gains. Although self-defeating, these "gains" often represent desperately-sought, last-ditch defenses and compromises. To the hard-pressed ego there has been no alternative recourse. The neurotic pattern from a conscious point of view develops automatically and spontaneously.

2. Primary Gain Responsible for Initiation of Emotional Illness

The primary gain, or *endogain,* is basic to the illness. This gain and the need for it is responsible for the initiation of the illness. It involves an intrapsychic operation which is always deeply unconscious.

The endogain is secured through the resolution of unconscious emotional conflicts. To the extent that it is successful, the experiencing of anxiety is averted. Symptoms and character trait defenses develop in the service of the endogain.

3. Advantage from Illness Contributes To Its Perpetuation

The secondary gain in turn is different. It is secured later. Through this channel, one gains external and material advantage from the illness, after it is established. This kind of gain can play an important role in the propagation and perpetuation of emotional illnesses, including the neurotic reactions. Secondary gain may be conscious or unconscious. The unconscious part of the secondary gain is the *epigain.*

Both the epigain and the endogain are unconscious. The endogain initiates the illness, is very deep seated, and is primary to it. The epigain occurs later, is more superficial, and is secondary to the illness.

This discussion will be directed toward helping to clarify and to outline the respective vital roles of primary gain and secondary gain in emotional illness, their relation to each other and the author's current conceptions regarding this basic and significant area of the emotional illnesses, their genesis and perpetuation. We shall learn how these gains, which are defensively sought, often in desperate fashion, are ultimately illusory in their net results. Thus the so-called "gains" of the neurotic reactions will, upon further study, in reality be seen to constitute defeats and losses, albeit vitally necessary to the psyche of the individual concerned.

4. Accepted Conceptions

There are a number of reasons for undertaking this study. First, scattered references in the medical literature over the last thirty or forty years indicate the rather general acceptance of certain concepts about psychologic gains in the emotional illnesses. This attests to their value and convenience. Second, there has been, at least heretofore, a certain unfortunate lack of clarity and precision in their use. Psychiatrically-oriented colleagues in several fields of medicine in addition to psychiatry have indicated to the author some of their dissatisfactions about this state of affairs. Third, despite the great potential and actual importance of these conceptions in present-day psychiatric thinking, this is scarcely reflected in the current publication of scientific discussion about them. This dearth of discussion leaves us with a gap in the literature. Finally, the promotion of increasing agreement is desirable in this area which is clearly of fundamental importance in psychiatry.

Accordingly, in this presentation the author undertakes to describe primary and secondary gain, and to define more specifically their role in emotional illness. Brief clinical illustrations of their operation are presented. The terms endogain and epigain (introduced earlier) as a matter of personal and professional convenience will be retained. They have assisted in communication, in therapy, and in teaching, through securing more specificity and precision in defining the kinds of gains. Others may also find them useful. This particular discussion has been undertaken then with the hope of promoting some increased general agreement in an area which is basic in the behavioral sciences.

B. OPERATIVE IN EVERY EMOTIONAL ILLNESS

Primary gain and secondary gain play a most vital role in both the psychogenesis and perpetuation of emotional illness. In subsequent chapters we shall see frequent illustrations as to how these factors are operative in every type of neurotic reaction.

Actual or presumptive evidence of the operation of secondary gain factors in illness is usually more apparent than is that of the primary gain. In Conversion Reactions, Hygeiaphrontis (overconcern with health), Emotional Fatigue, and in some of the Neuroses Following Trauma, secondary gain factors may be quite obvious. Indeed, they may be marked enough to appear to be quite conscious endeavors. This may serve to annoy or to frustrate family members, friends, or the physician, and can add to existing problems in the management of the illness. In other neurotic patterns of reaction (for example, the Obsessive-Compulsive Neuroses and Depressive Reactions), the secondary gain may operate in a much more hidden and obscure fashion.

This thesis, that the gain factors are dynamic features in every illness of psychogenic origin, may become clearer through further discussion. As we shall see, gain factors vary from those which are apparent to the independent, objective observer, to those which are deeply buried and completely hidden from the conscious awareness of both patient and examiner. This variable degree of transparency to objective observation is particularly true in the case of the secondary gain and the epigain.

To recapitulate, the primary gain (endogain), on the other hand, initiates the illness and is always deeply unconscious. Its nature can only be surmised by even the most astute therapist. The secondary gain is more likely to be a subsequent development. As noted, it may have both conscious and unconscious elements. The latter constitute the epigain. The epigain is most likely to be closer to conscious awareness than the endogain. It can be an important factor in perpetuating the illness, and often handicaps the therapy.

An understanding of the defensively-intended gains which are unconsciously sought or secured through the symptoms of emotional sickness is basic to an understanding of many other accepted and fundamental psychiatric principles. Reasonable professional agreement in these areas can help to promote scientific progress in psychiatry and in medicine. The result would be an addition to the firm foundations upon which we continue to build in the clinical practice of medicine, in psychiatric teaching, and in research.

C. GAIN PARADOXICAL AND ILLUSORY

1. Unconscious Escape

The fact that illness represents a genuine gain to the individual concerned, in any real sense becomes paradoxical upon closer inspection. We must be aware that illness is often utilized by the patient quite outside of conscious awareness, as an honorable but desperate escape from disagreeable tasks or onerous obligations which have become absolutely intolerable for him.

Neurotic patients develop symptom complexes as the result of their unconscious efforts to resolve emotional conflict. Man generally tends to obey the biologic principle of avoiding pain and discomfort while striving for gratification and pleasure. On occasion such satisfactions are of course quite hidden, devious and obscure and only individually meaningful. The painful consequence of emotional conflict is anxiety. In response to the biologic principle, man therefore seeks to avoid or to resolve such conflicts, to deny their existence, and so on. Various of these endeavors are at times referred to as types of *psychologic flight* [Ch.9:IIIC2].

2. Symptoms and Character Defenses as Outward Reflections of Intrapsychic Conflict

The automatic repression from conscious awareness of intolerable impulses is one attempted defensive undertaking. The repressed impulses, however, remain energy-laden and potent, despite their banishment to the seeming but misleading oblivion of the unconscious. The various emotional symptoms of psychogenic origin are their expression in concealed and disguised form.*

The many individual personality traits or character defenses develop to a considerable extent in the same intended service and purpose, but much more slowly and gradually. Their imbalance or exaggeration constitute the several varieties of the Character Neuroses [Ch.5].

3. Essential Gain Leads to Self-defeat and Net Loss

The long-term end result of the neurotic symptoms is so certainly self-defeating as to more than cancel out any apparent "gain". This then is the paradox of emotional illness. The so-called "gains" which we will discuss are sadly illusory. The gains are vitally necessary to the individual, to whom they are an absolute requirement psychologically. To the neutral observer the long-range net result is always a loss.

It is tragically common, however, to find patients clinging desperately to painful and handicapping symptomatology in an effort to keep the "gain" which results from the illness. The neurotic patient is caught in a trap from which he cannot extricate himself. Since he is helpless to solve his dilemma, he must have expert help.

D. WIDE APPLICATIONS; CHARACTER NEUROSES

1. Character Traits Individually-Fixed Patterns of Emotional Response

It should be noted that self-defeating patterns of reaction are by no means confined in expression to the clinical symptoms of neurosis alone. The foregoing comments about self-defeat apply in perhaps less obvious but certainly more widespread if not nearly universal fashion to many of the various personal attributes and character traits. Their exaggeration and overdevelopment comprises what we might refer to as the Character Reaction or Neurosis.

The reader has only to glance about him to observe the extreme tenacity with which people cling to established patterns of behavior and response. As Cyrus wrote in the first century B.C., "Powerful indeed is the empire of habit." This applies even more strongly in the habit-patterns of emotional responses. Character traits may be regarded as representing still more fixed, developed, and more or less individually-specific habit-patterns.

From an objective viewpoint this kind of involuntary "clinging" to certain overdeveloped character and personality traits may appear irrational, since

---

* Usually accompanied by a simultaneous concealed and distorted expression of elements of the repressing force, that is, inhibition and control or denial of the impulse, and by the expression of self-punitive elements as an attempted retribution or penance, in masochistic fashion.

these patterns may clearly be highly self-defeating and destructive in their overall net result to the person possessing them. The inner defensive needs subserved, however, are hardly apparent to the usual methods of external observation.

2. Character Defenses; Character Neurosis vs. Symptom Neurosis

The tenacity and even desperation with which an individual thus unconsciously clings to his character traits is in itself partly illustrative of their vital defensive purposes. Speaking of them as "clung to" or even as being "wedded to" is an understatement. Collectively they make up the personality, distinguishing an individual from his fellows. They tend to become as much a part of a person as his arm or leg. Indeed, the psychic part of one's makeup is at least as distinguishing as the physical aspects.

The basis for the development of these personality or character traits is defense. This is why the author has preferred to term them the Character Defenses. When one or a group of character defensive traits is exaggerated to a pathologic and self-defeating degree, as noted, the resulting state of affairs comprises the Character Neurosis [Ch.5:IA].

Thus, as with clinical symptoms of what we might for purposes of distinction term a Symptom Neurosis, the net results may often add up similarly to self-defeating and destructive consequences, which may be more or less apparent to the objective observer. Even though upon occasion the involved individual himself may have some intellectual appreciation of some of this, he is personally powerless to surrender them or, unaided, to effect much in the way of change.

3. Assessment of Gain or Loss

The entire concept of the so-called defensive gains of emotional illness is a vital one. The net gain itself is, however, paradoxical, depending of course upon how it is assessed. It may be assessed from the basis of the individual deep and hidden psychologic purposes and needs behind the symptom or the character defensive trait. From this view the gain will appear absolutely vital and necessary.

It may be assessed, on the other hand, by an independent observer as to its overall net consequences to the individual from the personal and the social standpoints. From this viewpoint the gain is often destructive and self-defeating.

Having introduced the concepts of gain in emotional illness, let us proceed to the consideration of the several types of gain, separated and classified as has proved useful. We shall first consider the secondary kinds of gain since these are more readily discernible.

II. THE SECONDARY GAINS OF ILLNESS: MATERIAL ADVANTAGES

A. SECONDARY GAINS BOTH CONSCIOUS AND UNCONSCIOUS

1. The Epigain

The secondary gain is the advantage which may be derived from a symptom or an illness. In other words, the symptom may be thus exploited after it has been established. The general term of secondary gain has been applied rather loosely in psychiatric circles thus far, so as to include this "use" of the symptom or illness in securing or in attempting to secure various gains. Such secondary gains have been those secured or sought via both conscious and unconscious pathways.

Widespread usage of this conception of gain will likely continue. Therefore there is an even greater advantage in the employment of a name to be reserved solely for the unconscious type of secondary gain in emotional illness. This would clearly distinguish the unwittingly secured gain, from those which are secured more or less deliberately and in conscious awareness. For this purpose the author employs the term epigain. The use of this concept and term has been helpful in seeking to clarify the principles of secondary gain clinically and in teaching.

2. Conscious Secondary Gain

The physician also can often distinguish certain quite conscious efforts to achieve something by or through the symptom and the illness, from unconscious efforts (the epigain). Thus, the patient may seek consciously and deliberately to have an illness which is already established serve him some rather obvious external purpose. A simple example of this is the eleven-year-old schoolgirl who sought to miss her classes because of a minor sprained ankle. Another is the stenographer who "used" a minor headache to claim sick leave. Often such instances are also consciously rationalized to placate any possible twinges of conscience.

Such rationalization may be successful to the extent of still permitting the little girl inconsistently to participate in physically-active games in the first instance. Similarly the stenographer might find it acceptable to go on a shopping or sporting expedition. In fact, how many people have not at some point in their lives made the most of an illness as an excuse of some kind?

Sometimes it becomes difficult to draw a sharp line between the secondary gain of illness which is unconsciously sought or obtained (the epigain), and that which is attempted in at least some partial awareness. Sometimes, also, even the unwitting "use" of the illness in influencing or attempting to influence the environment, especially including the people in it, is clearly apparent to the observer. It may even seem as if the patient simply must have some conscious awareness of what is going on when environmental or material benefit accrues from illness, even though this may not at all be the case. With epigain, this is no more true than a belief that the man who lost his arm in a plane accident sought consciously to have this happen to him, in order to secure the compensation which was later awarded him.

3. Important to Differentiate Malingering

Malingering is something quite different. It should be clearly distinguished. Malingering is *the deliberate simulation of illness,* for whatever purpose. It is attempted in full conscious awareness. Malingering as such is to be definitely separated from elements of secondary gain which accompany or develop in relation to an illness which is actually present.

It is even more important to differentiate instances of malingering from the epigain of illness. In the latter, of course, the patient has no conscious awareness of the—to him—hidden factors of secondary gain. This is despite their obviousness to family, friends, or physician. The physician must carefully bear this in mind in order to preserve his detached scientific viewpoint. This may be most vital to his efforts to help his patient. (*See also* comments on malingering, Ch.8:VIIIA*1*).

4. Definitions

FAVORABLY INFLUENCING EXTERNAL ENVIRONMENT.—In the development of a serviceable definition of secondary gain, its principally *external* direction is important. This is in distinction to the *internal* direction of the primary gain or endogain. The secondary gain thus is *the external situational gain or material advantage which is derived from a symptom or an illness. The secondary gain constitutes the "achievements" of an illness in favorably influencing the external environment, particularly its interpersonal aspects. Secondary gain may be secured in conscious awareness, or quite unwittingly.* The secondary gain may be regarded as *the value which the symptom or illness gains* subsequent to its onset.

The epigain refers to *that part of this process of secondary gain which takes place or is secured entirely out of conscious awareness.*

Freud commented in 1905 on the "secondary function" of a symptom which helped it become "anchored fast in the patient's mental life." *

---

* This conveys some important implications in regard to impeding therapy, and to increasing the "resistance" of the patient to insight and to change. Freud went on to say, "And so it happens that any one who tries to make him [the patient] well is to his astonishment brought up against a powerful resistance, which teaches him that the patient's intention of getting rid of his complaint is not so entirely and completely serious [*i.e.,* whole-hearted or unmixed] as it seemed."

Later (1909) Freud recognized the relation of the secondary gain to the people around the patient. He noted in the case of a conversion (hysterical) attack that the attack was "aimed at particular people"; that "it may be put off until they are within reach, and gives an impression of conscious simulation."

Freud still later (1926) wrote in more technical terms of the function of secondary gain coming "to the aid of the ego in its effort to incorporate the symptom within itself, by which it strengthens the fixation of the latter. When, then, we attempt to render analytic assistance to the ego in its struggle against the symptom, we find these reconciling bonds between the ego and the symptom functioning on the side of the resistances. To loosen them is not made easy for us."

Saul and Lyons more recently have also noted the important role of secondary gain in helping to prolong an illness, through their definition of it as "a fancied or real reward for perpetuating the illness."

CONCEPTS APPLY IN PHYSICAL ILLNESSES.—In psychiatry we are more immediately and particularly concerned with the application and study of our concepts of "gains" in the emotional illnesses as such. However, we should also recognize important similar applications which are to be observed in many cases of physical illness. Thus in many instances of more strictly physical ills, epigain may be an important hidden factor, at least as far as the patient is concerned. Here also it may operate entirely beyond any possible conscious awareness. Interested physicians in many branches of medicine will be able to find clinical instances from their own experience.

5. Gain Sought Externally

The secondary gain is to be observed as being sought or secured largely through the effects of the illness itself, the symptoms, and/or the character defenses (and the patient's responses to them) on the reactions and behavior of other persons. These are more often those people who are closest. Their attitudes and responses are influenced. The goal of the secondary gain is to change favorably the external situation and to modify one's environment, especially its interpersonal aspects. Quite often as a major feature of this, the patient seeks consciously or unconsciously to secure gratification of vital dependency needs which may be otherwise quite hidden.

Through secondary gain the patient seeks to promote an external situation which is more favorable and which will therefore tend to lessen conflict. The physician is again cautioned to bear in mind that these "achievements" of an illness often take place largely outside of, and beyond, conscious awareness. They are not subject to voluntary control, even though the "efforts" to secure secondary gains through the illness may at times be transparently obvious (sometimes even painfully so) to the trained observer, and to family and friends as well.

In order to distinguish this clearly unconscious part of the secondary gain from conscious efforts in a similar direction (that is, of gaining some external advantage from an illness) the term epigain has been adopted and used. This name indicates the typically external direction of the gain. It also indicates its relatively superficial position, in distinction from the primary gain or endogain. These terms may serve as a part of the convenient technical shorthand which is developed in every scientific discipline as a quicker and simpler way of expressing complex concepts.

B. SECONDARY GAIN IN NEUROSES

1. Extent and Apparency Vary

Although epigain is present in every emotional illness, there is considerable difference in the extent to which it is present. This varies greatly from person to person, and from case to case. The relative degree of its importance in the diagnostic categories is also variable.

Epigain is often more apparent in the neuroses. The epigain is apt to be particularly apparent in instances of: (1) Somatic Conversion or Conversion Reactions; * (2) Hygeiaphrontis (Overconcern with Health; Somatic and Physiologic Preoccupation); (3) Fatigue Reactions; and (4) in certain of the Neuroses Following Trauma. In these cases it is often apparent that some measure of escape or relief from intolerable responsibilities or unbearable situations may unconsciously be secured by the symptoms.

Through the illness, family relationships may be altered by unconscious manipulation, control, and exploitation of those persons who are particularly important and significant to the patient. There is, of course, a definite relation to deeply repressed, principally oral, dependent needs.†

Several authors have also pointed out the operation of this type of secondary gain, especially in relation to the above four types of neurotic reaction. In cases of Conversion Reaction, for example, Helene Deutsch mentioned the increased attention, concern, and interest of the parents which accompanied their child's case of (conversion) aphonia; and later the similar responses in another case in which there was inability to eat, on a conversion basis.

2. Gratification of Dependency Needs

Hygeiaphrontis (hypochondriasis) is noted historically for the unconsciously-sought effects of the symptoms upon the members of a patient's family. Attention or sympathy may be secured as part of the epigain. These secondary benefits of the illness may also be consciously sought. Emotional fatigue in turn may secure relief from odious or difficult work and responsibilities. Conscious or unwitting "pension-seeking" is at times encountered with the Traumatic Neuroses.

Compensation, or a pension, in many of these instances can carry the important practical advantages of economic support. Sometimes equally, or even more important, compensation can also acquire emotional significance. It can provide the important dependency-satisfying advantage of "being cared for" financially. This in turn can be closely related to the more hidden and buried kind of "being cared for" emotionally. These are added significances which the pension or compensation can gain. It can thus come to symbolically equate love, security, and protection—also providing figuratively this type of very important unconscious support. The compensation also can in and of itself come to have neurotic overevaluation as a Soteria [Ch.II:IA1].

---

* Noyes wrote, "In Conversion we find an excellent illustration of both primary neurotic gain and of secondary gain. The conversion mechanism yields a primary or neurotic gain through its anxiety-defense function. It also yields a secondary gain by producing something to the advantage of the patient."

† Fenichel noted in regard to the Traumatic Neuroses that "the symptoms may acquire secondarily the significance of a demonstration of one's own helplessness in order to secure external help such as was available in childhood."

In the other major categories of neuroses—Anxiety Neurosis, Depressive Reactions, Obsessive-Compulsive Neuroses, Character Neuroses, and Phobias—the epigain may be far less apparent. In many of these cases it is operative in still more devious, indirect, and hidden fashion, sometimes very much so. However, if we think of the secondary gain in terms of the external advantages which are unconsciously derived, and in terms of the influencing and control of others, the epigain can be ultimately worked out in every case, despite seeming initial obscurity. Successful analytically oriented therapy should lead to an increased awareness of the role of the epigain in the illness, for both the physician and his patient. The following *Table 4* summarizes the epigain of the emotional illnesses.

Table 4

The Epigain

A Summation of the Unconscious Secondary Gains of Emotional Illness

The epigain is comprised of those secondary gains which are unconsciously attempted or secured in emotional (or other) illness. They result from unwitting efforts which are directed externally to secure more favorable environmental, interpersonal, and situational changes, as these "appear" to, and are evaluated by, the patient.

The epigain makes the environment more comfortable. Material advantage may be secured. Through the gain it is "intended" to allay anxiety through reducing conflict, and by satisfying otherwise hidden dependent needs.

Clinically the *unconscious* secondary gains of emotional illness, the epigain, may include elements of one or more of the following ten major types of gain:

1. Compensation, financial or otherwise; possible material advantage.
2. Avoidance or amelioration of an unpleasant or intolerable situation.
3. The securing of increased sympathy or attention. This is usually sought as a near substitute for the real affection, acceptance, warmth, and love which are unconsciously needed.
4. Self-preservation (particularly in military life). Escape from, or protection in M.S.E.s (*see* text).
5. Escape from responsibility.
6. Related to the foregoing; sexual immaturity, and a need for relief from the responsibilities implicit to a sexually-mature role or position.
7. The attempted control or influence of important people: family, friends, business and professional associates, *and the therapist*. The seeking of acceptance, attention, love and affection, often in typically neurotic, self-defeating fashion.
8. The manipulation and control of people and environment, in the unwitting neurotic endeavor to satisfy deeply-hidden dependency needs.*
9. Conflict resolution by lessening of social pressures.
10. Attempt to allay anxiety and insecurity.

---

* This point (8) may relate to the preceding one (7) as well as to early dependent needs of infancy. There may be regression to the infantile operations of trial and testing which were employed with parental figures. These infantile patterns may then serve as prototypes for the later patterns which are unconsciously evolved in a neurosis. This is particularly true when a measure of success was achieved.

3. *Epigain of Compensation May Propagate Illness*

A. DISPROPORTIONATE SIGNIFICANCE; SOTERIAL SECURITIES.—It is not always entirely possible to draw a distinct line between primary and secondary gain. The distinction certainly cannot always be made alone on the basis of the relative importance of each in the illness. Instances are seen, for example, in which the secondary gains of financial compensation have become of major psychopathologic importance. As the patient unconsciously and unconstructively evaluates it, the environment now is much more favorable.

Thus, the epigain of compensation can become a powerful force in the perpetuation and propagation of an illness. When secured, this gain may grow to become so necessary and vital that the primary gains, originally a requisite to the initiation of the illness, appear to fade into the background. Therefore, especially in certain prolonged cases, the epigain may appear to take on a relative increase of importance which is disproportionate and which may become largely responsible for the continuation of the illness. See later reference [Ch.14:VIII].

This is illustrated particularly in certain cases of the Neuroses Following Trauma. The compensation may become neurotically overvalued. It may be assigned symbolic significance as a source of gratification, as noted. The compensation can sometimes gain soterial significance for the patient. In effect, the person concerned may unwittingly set this "external emotional supply" up as a soteria. When this occurs, the compensation becomes an object-source of safety, comfort and security,* in varying degree.

The patient may only too often become hopelessly entangled in his needs to justify his disability, in the resulting combination of financial and dependency compensation, and in his efforts to continue its receipt (and support). His whole life may come to revolve around his illness, his compensation claims, and possible incident litigation. A vicious circle may become established which is difficult or perhaps even impossible to interrupt. It is not surprising that his compensation may gain so much emotional significance for him. He can little more readily be separated from these intense inner needs and dependency strivings than from an arm or leg. Surgery could secure the latter. *Psychologic* surgery for the former can be infinitely more complex!

B. HOSPITALITIS.—The term "hospitalitis" has been used sometimes in not too kindly a fashion to describe the reaction of certain patients to their hospitalization. Hospital life for them can come to provide emotionally-important comfort, security, and protection. The emotional significance which approaches the soterial lies in the unconscious gratification of their inner dependency needs.

---

* In accord with the *Anxiety-Countering Principle* of the soterial pattern of defensive reaction [Ch.11:IA1].

The following instance illustrates the possible extent of conscious secondary gain and epigain in an illness.

Case 10

Extent of Secondary Gains

A thirty-four-year-old naval officer was transferred to the psychiatric service in a U.S. Naval Hospital during World War II. He suffered from incapacitating emotionally-based headaches. Once they had become established, they had resulted in his having unconsciously escaped an intolerable duty situation. An insurance policy paid him $200 monthly while he was not able to work. This was in addition to his continuing substantial service pay. Further, he was in a protected hospital environment where he was taken care of very well (gratification of his unconscious dependency needs), instead of serving in combat duty with its inherent dangers.

This young officer was polite, cooperative, and friendly. Superficially at least he was interested in efforts to help him. Any real motivation for working at securing therapeutic understanding of his problems, however, was quite limited. The epigain of his symptoms and illness had become vital to him. It contributed to its continuation and propagation. Its extent was major in the illness and in his overall life situation.

One can see in this kind of situation the exceedingly difficult task of the therapist in seeking to offer this patient something which is better than the gains of his illness. This is a marked example of how factors of secondary gain can enter the treatment situation to impede the therapeutic endeavors. The illness can be perpetuated. Therapy can be hindered or blocked.

4. Military Aspects; M.S.E.s

There are a number of further important military aspects to our discussion. One's relative position of helplessness in military service can be a vital factor of stress in the development of emotional illness. In civilian life there are often voluntary routes which are open for escape from difficult or stressful situations. One can presumably walk off from an unpleasant job, when it becomes of sufficient personal moment to do so.

In military life many of the usual escape routes are no longer open. One is no longer a free agent. To many men, this realization is tough in and of itself. The effect of helplessness together with special stresses in influencing what can happen in military service is illustrated in the peaks of incidence of emotional illness. These occur at junctures of service experience when these factors are particularly marked. These periods comprise what we might accordingly term the M.S.E.s or *Military Stressful Eras.* Included are the experiences of: (1) induction, (2) basic training, and (3) situationally-stressful positions, including combat. Also to be included on occasion as M.S.E.s of significance are (4) separation, (5) discharge, and (6) retirement, especially when these are involuntary. (*See also* the related S.E.H.A. concept [Ch.1:IVB*3;* IVC*11*]).

Thus, an escape may be sought in a stressful civilian situation. This may be far more difficult in military service. Herein, even a wound may become welcome as offering an escape from combat and stress, though the following instance is rather extreme. A freshly-wounded G.I. in Korea reported to the aid station in an almost gleeful frame of mind. "Doc," he said in a happy voice, "I think I've got my million dollar wound!"

C. MANIPULATION OF EXTERNAL ENVIRONMENT

In summary, epigain is the term reserved for clearly unconscious gains or attempts to gain, through emotional illness. Epigain is secured via the control or manipulation of the external environment, especially the interpersonal environment. This is usually through the influencing of the attitudes and responses of significant people. Epigain is generally on a more superficial level of unconsciousness than is primary gain. It is directed externally, and it is usually more readily apparent to the outside observer.

The epigain lessens conflict by securing or attempting to secure a more favorable environment, often by the gratification of repressed dependency needs. Secondary gain in turn has been used in our discussion more broadly, to include also those external gains from illness which are secured consciously and partly consciously.

III. THE PRIMARY GAIN IN EMOTIONAL ILLNESS: THE ENDOGAIN

A. RESPONSIBLE FOR INITIATION OF ILLNESS

The primary gains, or endogains, of emotional illness are *the strictly internal and ordinarily deeply-hidden psychologic gains which are the very basis of the illness. These gains and the need for them are responsible for the initiation of the illness.* Basically, and in simplest fashion, the primary gain can be said to be the avoidance of conflict and anxiety. The symptoms are part of the endogain and develop in its service. Thus, the primary gain of a symptom, basically, is the defense it provides against anxiety. The secondary gain in turn is the material advantage later secured from the symptom after its establishment. When this advantage is secured outside of conscious awareness it is the epigain.

The primary gain, or endogain, is protectively and defensively intended to maintain and preserve the integrity of the ego. To this end the primary gain is ultimately aimed at the avoidance or warding off of consciously-experienced anxiety. The primary gains may therefore be contributed to by any of the various internal psychologic mechanisms which may be unconsciously employed to this end. These include all of the various intrapsychic mechanisms of defense or mental mechanisms.*

Primary gains are concerned with the resolution, the avoidance, or the denial of conflict on a deeply-buried level of unconsciousness. They may be "attained" through the use of any of the commonly-recognized mental

---

* The author has accordingly referred to the mental mechanisms as our First Line of Psychic Defense, to help stress their basic and important position and function, thus in human adaptation.

mechanisms or dynamisms.* Symptom formation and the development of the various character defenses take place in the service of the endogain.

B. RAISON D'ETRE IN PSYCHOGENESIS

Various dynamisms may be operative in the desperately-necessary efforts to secure and maintain internal control of disowned and consciously intolerable wishes, thoughts, and drives. This control helps comprise the endogain of an emotional illness. Essentially, it is the intrapsychic control of the disowned and repressed aggressive-hostile or sexual impulses, or of both. The processes involved originally operate on a level which is deeply buried from conscious awareness.

Thus the endogain may be regarded as the underlying basis of the psychogenesis of an emotional illness. In essence, it is the *raison d'etre* of the illness. Some of these principles concerning the endogain and what it comprises are summarized in *Table 5*.

Table 5

The Endogain

A Summation of the Unconscious Primary Gains of Emotional Illness

The Primary Gains of Emotional Illness, of Symptom Formation, or of Character Defensive Trait Development, result from unconscious endeavors which are directed internally in order to secure a more favorable personal and internal psychologic environment. The primary gain, or endogain, attempts to allay anxiety largely through the resolution of intrapsychic conflict and in the effort to maintain ego integrity. The endogain is literally the *raison d'etre* of the emotional illness.

Symptoms represent the distorted, disguised, and/or symbolic expression of the repressed intolerable impulses, in addition to elements of their control (the repressing forces), and punishment for having had them, or compromises. Symptoms and what they secure (or are intended to secure) are part of the endogain of a given emotional reaction. Mental mechanisms (dynamisms) and character traits may also develop in the service of the endogain.

Clinically the endogain may include elements from one or more of the following six major areas:

1. The achievement or the reinforcement of denial, of control, and of repression of that which is consciously unacceptable.

2. The diversion and/or absorption of available psychic energy (to act upon, or to think about, or even to allow awareness of the forbidden impulse. This is illustrated in the preoccupation of obsessive rumination).

3. The securing of a more favorable internal, personal environment.

4. Resolution of conflict (or attempted resolution). Elaboration of one or more of the mental mechanisms (dynamisms).

(Table continued on next page)

---

* Freud once noted the "considerable advantage" which was derived from illness by virtue of the unconscious dynamisms employed. He labeled this the "paranosic gain." This term, however, has enjoyed only limited use.

Table 5—The Endogain (Cont.)

5. Character trait development or symptom formation in the unconscious efforts toward, or the symbolic and disguised external expression of:

   a. Reinforcement against threatened derepression.

   b. Substitutive and symbolic gratification.

   c. Masochistic self-punishment in response to a harsh super-ego.

   d. Sadistic punishment of the introjected disappointing object (as in depression).

   e. Defensive overcompensation in attempts to meet internal psychologic needs.*

   f. Inhibition of possible overt action.

   g. Compromise formations; expressions of elements of the unconscious conflict externally, in symbolic and disguised form.

6. Neurotic and psychotic reactions. These may be: initiated by, be part of, or develop in the service of the endogain.

It should be noted that character trait development and symptom formation (contributing to the endogain) may also occur partly in the service of attempting the satisfaction of unconscious dependent needs. This points out that both epigain and endogain can contribute to the gratification of dependency needs. How then can we separate them? One attempted delineation would be to regard as epigain the external effects which are secured. The internal gains in this area then would be part of the endogain.

C. RESOLUTION OF INTERNAL CONFLICTS

Thus, the primary gain of emotional illness is deeply buried and is responsible for the initiation of the illness. It deals with intensely personal psychologic needs. Its aim is to prevent or allay anxiety by resolving unconscious conflicts. In view of its fundamental, internal, and basic position, it is referred to as the endogain. While the epigain is also unconscious, it is not on so deep a level as the endogain.

The epigain refers to effects sought or obtained in relation to the external world; the world outside oneself. The endogain, in turn, is deeply within and hidden, and unconsciously secures, or attempts to secure, resolution of internal conflicts. It is less available to awareness, and much less possible to be seen or even to be surmised by an outside observer.

IV. CLINICAL ILLUSTRATIONS

A. IN NEUROSES; CONVERSION REACTION. PRINCIPLE OF INADVERTENT DEFEAT

Let us consider first the clinical summary of a case of Conversion Reaction, in which we can point to the presence of both the epigain and the endogain,

---

* Often to an unwittingly self-defeating degree, as a defensively-intended but exaggerated development. In this aspect there are implications of interest in regard to some of Alfred Adler's early concepts of organ inferiority and compensation. He assigned a degree of importance here, however, which tended to overshadow other important areas of primary gain in the initiation and pathogenesis of emotional illness.

for example in a neurosis. Please note in this case the rather typical and more apparent epigain in this major type of neurotic reaction. (*See also* discussion, Ch.12:VIA*1*). Recall that this was one of the four types of neurotic reaction as earlier noted, in which the unconscious secondary gain is usually more readily evident. Also illustrated is the Concept of the Vicious Circle of Self-Defeat in neuroses and the Principle of Inadvertent Defeat of the emotional illnesses.

Case 11

Epigain and Endogain in a Somatic Conversion Reaction

(1) *Emotional resources for parenthood lacking*

A twenty-three-year-old mother of two children, aged respectively sixteen months and three months, was referred for intensive psychotherapy. She suffered from a phobia about leaving the house. Recently a partial paralysis of her right leg had gradually come on. In early life she had been deprived of love and affection by a mother herself psychologically incapable of providing it.

Partly as a consequence of her own unsatisfied needs, the requirements and needs in turn of her own two small children (the second of which had been unwanted) had become for her an intolerable burden. She simply did not possess the emotional resources required to measure up to the demands of parenthood. Her response had been an unconscious regressive retreat into an emotional illness with predominantly Conversion (hysterical) features.

(2) *Epigain of symptoms*

The restriction of the use of her leg made it impossible for her to do her normal housework and the necessary child care. As a consequence, a nurse had to be hired, and certain family members also became involved. Her husband had to remain at home at times because of her phobia, and necessarily was required to devote more time, attention, and interest to the home and to her.

These secondary results of her symptoms, or the *epigain,* obtained situational modifications which then made life more tolerable for her. This gain of her symptoms lessened conflict through securing environmental changes and through the resulting alteration of the attitudes, responses, and behavior of the persons significant to her.

There was also a certain amount of regressive satisfaction of her dependency needs secured through the increased attention and concern which she received from external sources. These became substitutes for the real acceptance, affection, and love which actually had been sought as a replacement in turn for the subjectively experienced deprivations of early years.

(3) *Vicious Circle of Self-Defeat*

Some of the self-defeating aspects of this Conversion epigain should be noted. For example, the pressure upon her husband to provide more than he was genuinely willing to do had an adverse net effect. To the extent that this was a duty and required of him, and to the extent that it required the maintenance of a facade on his part, there was an increasing build-up of partially hidden resentment. The result was a lowering of the level of real affection which was present, instead of the desired resulting increase.

This became a vicious circle. The more affection which was demanded, the less genuine affection was available. This in turn was followed by increased demands, and so on. This is the Vicious Circle of Self-Defeat Concept in the neuroses. Thus, the illness which ostensibly secured "gains", and which was clung to blindly and desperately, actually lost for the patient the very thing which was sought.

Thus ever, the hopeless illusion and dilemma of the neuroses. The concept of gains becomes indeed a paradox when this kind of result can be observed to take place. The *Principle of Inadvertent Defeat* is illustrated accordingly, in that what was really sought was even more certainly lost.

(4) *Endogain of symptoms*

On the deeper primary level, the physical and psychologic restrictions were partly a final desperate safeguard as an unconscious attempt to inhibit action. By this means, control over hidden and feared destructive impulses was continued and reinforced. One cannot easily kick another person with a leg which has become paralyzed and useless.

The patient had a tremendous fear of any negative or hostile feelings. These had been deeply repressed in order to continue their control, fear of the loss of which was the basis of tremendous anxiety.

Both the epigain and endogain served or attempted to serve in the foregoing instance as in other cases, in the prevention or dissolution of anxiety.

B. IN CHARACTER DEFENSES; PRINCIPLE OF DEFENSE-HYPERTROPHY

For a second example to illustrate the operation of "gains" in emotional reactions, a case summary has been selected in which the manifestations were in the area of the character trait defenses, as distinct from the more clear-cut and apparent symptoms of the Symptom Neuroses. The traits concerned were those associated primarily with the Obsessive Personality. These traits had hypertrophied beyond the stage of social and personal value with more or less typically self-defeating consequences. The epigain in this instance is less readily apparent than in our previous illustration.

Case 12

Epigain and Endogain in Obsessive Personality (Obsessive Character Defenses)

(1) *Exaggeration of useful traits leads to handicap and self-defeat*

A thirty-six-year-old physician sought treatment because of the advice of friends and some partial personal recognition that certain of his personality traits were handicapping him professionally, and limiting his potential satisfactions in living. Among these were strong personal needs to be precise, over-conscientious, and perfectionistic. He was emotionally restricted and inhibited.

Earlier and when less pronounced, these traits had been very useful and constructive. Indeed, they had helped him to achieve considerable professional recognition. However, when they became exaggerated, they became personally self-defeating and handicapping. Alexander Dumas may have had some awareness of this important principle. One hundred years ago he wrote similarly but in stronger terms in *The Count of Monte Cristo* that "There are virtues that become crimes by exaggeration."

(2) *Character Analysis discloses endogain*

Following initial study, character analysis was considered advisable. The following is a stringent summary of the dynamics uncovered during long-term intensive therapy. We gradually learned how these character defenses had developed. This had been largely in the service of the attempted control of desperately feared aggressive-hostile impulses, including even his normally healthy self-assertive and protective ones. To a lesser extent they were also formed to aid in the control of similarly feared (and to him threatening) warm and loving impulses. Part of the danger in this latter area was the resulting vulnerable position as he saw it. He dreaded the possibility of rejection.

As a result, he generally inhibited all affect-laden impulses. Further, the absorption of energy in his obsessive activities diverted his attention away from any possible conscious awareness of unacceptable thoughts. It also lessened as well the danger of possible action in response to them. We can see here partially illustrated the basic and primary gain (the endogain) in the internal, deeply unconscious development of the character defenses.

(3) *Epigain subtle*

The epigain was not easily apparent, operating in more subtle fashion than in some instances. However, his precision, overconscientiousness, and his perfectionism did have a number of external situational consequences. Among these were increased respect and certain modifications of behavior from colleagues. Members of his family also made greater efforts to measure up to his high personal standards.

His traits contributed to the unwitting maintenance of protectively-intended distance in his interpersonal relations. Thus his character defenses secured for him increased attention and concern. They stimulated greater efforts to please him and to secure his approval. The environmental modifications resulting were the *obsessive epigain* (the unconscious secondary gain of his obsessive character defenses).

(4) *Self-defeating aspects*

The self-defeat lay in his loss of even the chance for real affection and love. The protectively-intended distance helped preclude the chance for such love. Even the professional respect—a substitute for what he really sought—tended to make closeness, affection, and warmth less feasible. Finally, the "greater efforts to please him" did not connote greater acceptance or love.

All too often one may observe instances in which a useful character trait, originally elaborated defensively and subserving a useful purpose, develops too far. The exaggeration of something useful produces something else, which becomes self-defeating and personally handicapping. One can have too much of a good thing, character-wise.

This is a concept which the author terms the *Defense-Hypertrophy Principle*. It has many implications and applications in clinical practice. It can be observed repeatedly in social living.

C. NEUROTIC "GAINS" IN SUICIDAL ATTEMPTS, DELINQUENT BEHAVIOR, OBSESSIVE NEUROSES, AND OTHER PROBLEMS

1. *Universality*

We will be able to see how elements of secondary and primary gain are present in many of the clinical cases which we will discuss in subsequent chapters. In accord with our original thesis, careful study will inevitably reveal the presence of some measure of both epigain and endogain in every emotional illness. Let us emphasize this by mentioning some of the less thought about sources. Accordingly, there are indications of both epigain and endogain in certain suicidal attempts. Delinquent and antisocial behavior often has a pathetic kind of epigain. In the obsessive-compulsive neuroses the epigain may result, for example, from the indirect control over others which may be exercised, somewhat as observed in the preceding case. Other persons are perhaps required to conform to some extent to the high standards of perfectionism, cleanliness, punctuality, orderliness, and so on, of the obsessively-oriented spouse, parent, or peer.

In turn, the absorption of psychic energy in obsessive endeavors is part of the endogain. Anxiety is controlled since the absorption of energy in obsessive ruminations makes the energy unavailable for the dangerous and feared possibility of acting upon inner threatening impulses. It also lessens the possibility of gaining conscious awareness of them. Repression is reinforced. The frequent general inhibition of the obsessive person is part of his unconscious defensive overcontrol of feared aggressive-hostile, or sexual impulses. As in most neurotic reactions, the Vicious Circle of Self-Defeat Concept can be noted in these instances.

In an instance of schizophrenia reported to the author not long ago, the epigain partly consisted of "attempts" to make up for deprivations of parental love and affection, as subjectively experienced by the patient. The illness itself resulted in a considerable increase of parental attention, concern, and anxiety. The patient by no means consciously "used" his illness to his advantage. It was achieved entirely unconsciously in this instance. The parents felt guilty, remorseful, and worried over their son's failures and problems. The endogain, in turn, lay largely in his regressive retreat into a schizophrenic process from the conflicts of reality, which he had found intolerable.

In the case of certain military officers in whom the need to be taken care of becomes dominant, and the patient becomes helpless, or relatively so, then someone else *must* take over and take care of him. This is partly caused by the operation of hidden (repressed) dependency needs. On occasion the consequence may have to be medical retirement. There is significant didactic and clinical value in being able to distinguish between the primary determinants and bases of a neurotic illness on the one hand, and the later additional advantages that a patient may secondarily and perhaps more superficially derive from his illness after it has become really established.

2. *Epigain in Paranoid Personality; Paranoid Position*

The thesis has been offered to the effect that factors of epigain are universal in emotional illness. Let us test this by seeing how factors of epigain are operative in a clinical situation in which they are likely to be still more obscure. For instance, how might epigain be present and operative in the Paranoid Personality? We may refer to this type of adjustment as the Paranoid Position. This type of problem is chosen for illustration since here the epigain may be more devious and difficult to fathom than in many cases of neuroses, or where various kinds of the more common handicapping character traits are the main difficulty. What external situational advantage can be unconsciously secured or sought through the manifestations of this very troublesome type of emotional disorder. A little reflection will help us answer this question.

Actually, the secondary gain of the paranoid individual is seen in the reactions which are wittingly, or not, secured from others, in response to his paranoid suspiciousness, hostility, distrustfulness, machinations, and so on. These in turn are the consequences and the outward expressions of his own deep inner insecurity and vulnerability. Together with his accompanying demands, devious planning and scheming, they may result in a certain measure of control and influence over other people. This is often an important aspect of the Paranoid Position. The unconscious secondary gain of the paranoid person, namely the paranoid epigain, thus often appears in the resulting efforts which are made by others in their attempts to try to placate or appease him, and to avoid having trouble with him.

Fear and uneasiness are generated by him and by his actual or potential tactics and actions. As a consequence, the attitudes, responses, and behavior of the people with whom he is in contact are apt to be modified, sometimes substantially. The efforts to placate him unconsciously can come to equate special consideration or attention. This becomes a substitutive but self-defeating kind of gratification of his deeply-repressed dependency needs. Here then, in accord with our definition, is the operation of the epigain in unconsciously securing an external advantage from the illness (or character defense). This accrues through the effects which are secured upon other people.

It is normal human nature to want things to run smoothly and to avoid trouble. The price that different people are willing to pay in order to help insure this may of course vary. The paranoid person instinctively (principally automatically and unconsciously) exploits this. The author has observed the influential and nationally-known members of the executive board of a large U.S. professional organization for example, to spend considerable time in efforts designed to meet the objections and trouble which were anticipated from one paranoid-oriented member among thousands. By this degree of influence and control over these important people, he had secured a measure of pseudo-importance himself. This was his paranoid epigain.

The self-defeat of the paranoid person and the real tragedy of his epigain is in his inevitable but unwitting contributions to the defeat of his own deeply repressed dependency needs. The efforts to placate and to appease him are inevitably accompanied by resentment and hatred, even though they may comprise attention and recognition of a sort. They are a sad substitute for any kind of genuine acceptance, attention, and love. These are what are really sought on a deeper level. He undertakes the securing of these in such a self-defeating fashion as to insure his never being able to secure them. Again we have illustrated for us the Principle of Inadvertent Defeat. The result is paradoxical; what has been sought is even more certainly lost.

D. NEUROTIC GAIN OF KING DAVID REACTION

Examples of the "King David Reaction" can afford us some interesting illustrations of the employment of certain mental mechanisms in the service of the primary gain. The dynamisms employed are essentially those of

Identification, Displacement, Projection, and Rationalization. In both the negative and positive phases of this interesting complex psychologic phenomenon they of course operate completely beyond conscious awareness.

Through their use, repressed self-condemnation and disapproval (that is, unacceptable negative aspects of the repressed self-appraisal) are transposed into feelings which are experienced subjectively as dislike for another person, in the negative K.D.R. Repression is reinforced, and painful recognition of disapproved segments of the self is avoided. This in essence summarizes what transpires in the negative type of King David Reaction.

In the original classic Biblical instance from which the reaction derived its name, "King David's Anger" * was outwardly displaced so that it became experienced subjectively toward another person. In clinical instances the disowned traits are assigned by projection to another person, in the service of continued denial, diversion, and nonrecognition. This is the *modus operandi* of the primary gain or endogain of the negative King David Reaction in the avoidance of emotional conflict and consciously experienced anxiety. The primary gain is very successful when this interesting mechanism is sufficiently operative. Disowned aspects of the self are continued in repression.

In these instances the secondary gain may be rather obscure. With King David, his outward condemnation of the wealthy man in the parable might have tended to secure approval from others by his siding on the "right" and "good" side as he really saw it, but against which he had acted clearly and deliberately. In other instances, where the condemnation or disapproval of the object-person is expressed verbally or nonverbally, it may be intended unconsciously to secure a certain amount of such acceptance and approval by the "audience". It may perhaps also unconsciously serve to direct other people's attention selectively and protectively away from these same condemned factors within the self, all of course on a nonconscious level. One potential for self-defeat lies in the fact that the patient may unconsciously mislead himself even more than others. In the classic example, Nathan saw through the entire process, having in fact "set it up" so that he might make the king see it also.

E. PRINCIPAL FEATURES AND COMPARISON OF "GAINS"

Since factors of primary gain and secondary gain are operable in every case of emotional illness, we might continue the discussion of clinical applications indefinitely. However, let us postpone further observation and research for now.

The student will have ample opportunity to observe some of these principles in action in later clinical illustrations and in his own clinical experience. The following tabulation (*Table 6*) of the principal features and

---

* Toward the rich man in the Biblical parable which was told to the king by the prophet Nathan. The fictional rich man who behaved badly in the parable—actually in very similar fashion to the king—became a far more tolerable substitute object for the "Royal Anger" than the king himself.

This was the outwardly disguised expression of the otherwise repressed self-condemnation, which was really felt by King David toward himself.

their comparison in the epigain and the endogain of emotional illness has been prepared as a source for ready reference in outline form and a conclusion for this chapter. In the next chapter we will begin our discussion of the various clinical types of neurotic reaction.

Table 6

The "Gains" of Emotional Illness

A tabular outline follows, presenting in summary and comparatively, the principal features of Epigain and Endogain, indicating their respective relationship in emotional illness.

	EPIGAIN	**ENDOGAIN**
	The Unconscious Secondary Gains of Illness	*The Primary Gains of Emotional Illness*
Direction	External.	Internal.
"Level" of unconsciousness	Usually superficial.	Always deeply unconscious.
The effects are upon	1. The external environment or situation, to make it more favorable as it appears to patient. 2. The responses, attitudes, and behavior of significant people, in an attempt to influence them.	1. The internal environment. 2. Supporting and maintaining ego integrity. 3. Maintaining repression and control by preventing awareness of "discarded" conflictual impulses.
Apparentness to an external observer	May be apparent, even to the point of being painfully so, to physician, family, and friends. May even suggest conscious simulation.	Never. Even the trained observer can only speculate about the nature of the endogain, pending the securing of valid data through intensive therapeutic investigation.
The resolution or the lessening of conflicts is attempted	Through favorable modification of external factors, often with gratification of deeply - hidden dependency needs. The epigain tends to secure regressive satisfactions in modification of environmental (especially interpersonal) factors.	Through modification primarily of intrapsychic conflicts. Symptom formation and character trait intensification occur as the disguised expression of the emotional conflict.
Ultimate aim	Both unconsciously aim to secure a lessening of conflict and tension with resulting control of, or the allaying of, anxiety.	
Relation to the illness	Develops subsequently to the endogain and can play a major role in its propagation. The epigain follows the establishment of the symptoms.	Basic to the illness. *These gains and the need for them are responsible for its initiation.* The symptoms are part of the endogain of the illness and develop in its service.

(*Table continued on next page*)

Table 6—The Gains of Emotional Illness (Cont.)

Universality	Both are universally present in emotional illness, although highly variable in degree, as well as in accessibility to the patient's own awareness and also to external observation.	
Relative presence in neuroses	Often more prominent, since it is more readily seen.	*Basically present in the initiation or psychogenesis of all emotional disorders.*
Relative presence in psychoses	Often more obscure.	The "gain" may operate through more primitive pathways such as massive regression. Can sometimes be more apparent.
Self-defeating aspects	Often quite prominent but occasionally difficult to identify.	Almost always deeply hidden from the ordinary means of perception.
	Both are always self-defeating in their net results to the patient, from the standpoint of the objective observer.	

V. SUMMARY

The *epigain* in emotional illness includes the changes in, or influence over, the external environment, including its interpersonal aspects, which are secured through one's symptoms or illness outside of conscious awareness. *Secondary* gain is a broader term which includes also the conscious and partly conscious gains from illness in this direction. Both are more superficial, more readily apparent to the external observer, and are more externally directed than is the endogain.

Manipulation, influence, and control are exerted in trying to secure a more favorable situation as it appears *to* the patient concerned. Resolution of conflict is unconsciously sought through the increased external gratification, which in turn may produce a resulting decrease in the level of anxiety.

According to the *Principle of Inadvertent Defeat,* in the neuroses one tends to lose the very thing which is so desperately and urgently sought. Terming character or personality traits *Character Defenses* points out their origins and bases in a defensive intent. The *Principle of Defense-Hypertrophy* refers to our concept of the exaggeration or hypertrophy of a useful character trait, leading to one which is self-defeating and handicapping.

The *primary gain* (endogain) is the deeply buried and hidden psychologic basis of the emotional illness. It is more concealed and is not apparent to the external observer, although it may become so through intensive study. In contrast to the epigain, the endogain is directed internally and aims at preserving ego integrity.

The primary gain is in the service of denial, containment, inhibition, repression, and symbolic gratification of repressed intolerable impulses, self-punishment for having had them, and the diversion and absorption of psychic energy. The internal conflicts concerned largely relate to forbidden and disowned aggressive-hostile and/or sexual drives, wishes and impulses. The gain aims to allay or to prevent anxiety through resolution of intrapsychic conflicts.

The primary gain is basic to the psychogenesis of every emotional illness. Epigain is often responsible in turn for its perpetuation, and contributes to the patient's resistance to therapeutic help. Both types of gain are present in every emotional illness. Successful therapy inevitably results in their role in the illness becoming more clear and understandable.

Added concepts which were discussed briefly, included those of *Symptom Neurosis, Soterial Security, Character Analysis* and the *King David Reaction*. Malingering was distinguished from epigain. The *Vicious Circle Concept* in the Neuroses was outlined.

VI. SELECTED REFERENCES AND BIBLIOGRAPHY

ADLER, A. (1917). *Organ Inferiority.* Washington; Nervous and Mental Disease Publishing Co.

— (1928). *The Practice and Theory of Individual Psychology.* New York; Harcourt, Brace and Co.

ALEXANDER, F. (1948). *Fundamentals of Psychoanalysis*, pp. 212-214. New York; Norton.

CAVENY, ELMER L. (4/15/54). Discussant; presentation to the Saint Elizabeths Medical Society; Annual Meeting. Washington, D.C.

DEUTSCH, HELEN (1951). *Psychoanalysis of the Neuroses*, pp. 69-109. London; Hogarth Press.

FENICHEL, OTTO (1945). *The Psychoanalytic Theory of Neurosis*, pp. 126-461. New York; Norton.

FREUD, S. (1950). *Collected Papers*, Vol. III, pp. 54, 256, 336. London; Hogarth Press.

— (1950). *Collected Papers*, Vol. II, p. 102. London; Hogarth Press.

— (1936). *The Problem of Anxiety*, p. 34. New York; Psychoanalytic Quarterly Press.

KIESLING, ALICE H. (June 29, 1964). Personal Communication.

The Holy Bible. II Samuel: 11, 12

LAUGHLIN, H. P., Ed. (1955). *A Psychiatric Glossary.* 5th rev. ed. Washington; American Psychiatric Association.

— (1954). "The Conversion Reactions". *Med. Ann. D.C.* 22, 581.

— (1963). *Mental Mechanisms.* Washington, D.C.; Butterworths.

— (1954). "King David's Anger". *Psychoanalyt. Quart.*, 23, 87.

MASSERMAN, J. H. (1946). *Principles of Dynamic Psychiatry*, p. 50. Philadelphia; Saunders.

NOYES, A. P. (1953). *Modern Clinical Psychiatry.* 5th ed., pp. 464-465. Philadelphia; Saunders.

SAUL, LEON, J., and LYONS, JOHN W. (1952). "Acute Neurotic Reactions". *In* Alexander, F., and Ross, H., Eds.: *Dynamic Psychiatry*, p. 140. Chicago; University of Chicago Press.

SYRUS, PUBLILIUS: Maxim 305. Translated by Darius Lyman.

VII. REVIEW QUESTIONS

1. What is meant by the gain in emotional illness being paradoxical, illusory, and self-defeating?
2. (*a*) Distinguish malingering from *secondary gain;* (*b*) Can secondary gains be derived from physical illness? Explain (*c*) What are Character Defenses? (*d*) What is a Symptom Neurosis? (*e*) What is meant by the Defense-Hypertrophy Principle?
3. Summarize the unconscious secondary gains of emotional illness.
4. Define: (*a*) Secondary gain; (*b*) Epigain; (*c*) Malingering; (*d*) Primary gain; (*e*) Endogain.
5. Identify the epigain and endogain in clinical illustrations of your own. What are the Principles of Inadvertent Defeat and Soterial Security in the emotional illnesses?
6. What is the importance of the concept of primary gain in emotional illnesses?
7. Summarize the unconscious primary gains (endogain) in emotional illness.
8. Give six of the major features (*a*) of the epigain and (*b*) of the endogain.
9. How can our concepts of illusory gain in emotional illness aid in their medical management?
10. What is (*a*) the King David Reaction; (*b*) Character Analysis; (*c*) the Concept of a Vicious Circle of Self-Defeat in the neuroses?

CHAPTER 3

THE ANXIETY REACTIONS

*. . . . The More Direct Expression of Anxiety
and its Effects*

I. INTRODUCTION

  A. Age of Anxiety
    1. Anxiety Present Throughout History; Principle of Universality; 2. Suitable Name; 3. Vastly Important Insights About Anxiety a Recent Achievement

  B. "It's Like I'm Expecting Something Bad to Happen . . ."
    1. Internal Threat; 2. Individually Appropriate and Proportional

  C. When is Anxiety To Be Considered Pathologic?
    1. Quantitative Determination Rather Than Qualitative; 2. Individual Utilization of Therapy Variable; 3. Various Yardsticks Useful; 4. Highly Subjective Experience

  D. Three Major Types of Anxiety Reactions
    1. Classification a Convenience; 2. Incidence; The Emotional Illnesses

II. THE ACUTE ANXIETY ATTACK OR A.A.A.; ANXIETY-PANIC REACTION

  A. Unexpected Dramatic Clinical Reaction
    1. Functional Changes Accompany Emotional Reaction; A.A.A. 2. Circular Generation of Fear Principle; Overwhelming Anxiety

  B. Positive Diagnosis Valuable
    1. Psychotherapy and Prognosis Enhanced; 2. Defensive Denial; Organic Bases Sought

  C. Clinical Features in Acute Anxiety Attacks
    1. Three Instances; 2. Cases of Long Duration; 3. Morning Attack of Anxiety; 4. Geriatric Instances; 5. Concept of Emotional Death; Death Terminates Prolonged Anxiety Attack

  D. Dynamics: Overreaction Protectively Intended
    1. Bodily Changes Prepare for Action; Concept of Defensive-Overreaction; 2. Principle of Extension; 3. Possibility of Organic Basis; Concept of Secondary Defense; 4. Cerebral *vs.* Mid-brain Origin

III. THE ANXIETY-TENSION STATE OR A.T.S.

  A. Subacute Clinical Reaction
    1. More or Less Continuous; 2. Diagnosis

  B. Symptoms and Clinical Features
    1. Anxiety Most Prominent Feature; 2. Situational Stress Important; Stress of Combat; 3. Varying Individual Reactions and Tolerances to Stress

  C. Note on Psychodynamics
    1. Complexity of Reaction Increases; 2. Precept of Inverse Anxiety-Symptom Ratio; 3. Pathologic Patterns of Emotional Reaction Neuroses

  D. In Conclusion

IV. ANXIETY NEUROSIS

  A. Introduction and History
    1. Anxiety Recently Distinguished from Fear; 2. Early Presumption of Organic Etiology; 3. Official Designation; 4. Definition

  B. Diagnosis
    1. According to Most Prominent Clinical Feature; 2. Typical Findings in Major Areas; 3. Mixed Type of Neurotic Reactions More Common; 4. Encourage Free Discussion; 5. Differential Diagnosis from Phobic Reaction; 6. Anxiety Hysteria; 7. Position of Anxiety Neuroses in Emotional Illnesses

  C. Incidence
    1. Wide Incidence Points Up Need for Trained Personnel; 2. Sex Differences; 3. Few Reliable Statistics; 4. Estimated Prevalence

D. Symptoms and Clinical
Features
    1. Level of Anxiety Varies;
    2. Exactly Appropriate for
    Individual Concerned; Subjec-
    tive Manifestations; 3. Emo-
    tional Features; 4. Psycho-
    motor Features; 5. Mental
    Features; 6. Physiologic Fea-
    tures; 7. Additional Clinical
    Features of Interest; 8. In
    Conclusion

E. Dynamics and Patho-
genesis
    1. Defenses Against Anxiety
    Poorly Organized and Ineffec-
    tive; 2. Symptoms Uncon-
    scious Compromises; 3. Sym-
    bolism; 4. Common Anxiety-
    Producing Events of Early
    Life; 5. Important Conflicts
    of Adulthood; 6. Anxiety Not
    Necessarily Destructive; Con-
    cept of Constructive Anxiety;
    7. Anxiety Neurosis, Fear,
    and Phobias; 8. Signal That
    Derepression Threatens

V. THE THEORY OF ANTECEDENT
CONFLICTS
  A. Childhood Events Proto-
  types For Later Life
  B. Early Patterns of Response
  Reactivated
  C. Widest Applications

VI. THE CONSTRICTIVE EFFECTS
OF ANXIETY: THE CONSTRICTIVE
SPIRAL CONCEPT

VII. THE RECIPROCAL INFLUENCES
OF ANXIETY AND PAIN

VIII. GENERAL COMMENTS ON
TREATMENT
  A. Response to Therapy
  B. Make Positive Diagnosis
  C. Avoid Verbal Speculation
  D. Factors in Favorable Prog-
  nosis
    1. Intensive Psychotherapy and
    Analysis Indicated; 2. Patient
    and General Physician
  E. The Acute Anxiety Attack
  F. Additional Important
  Points in Therapy
    1. Therapeutic Process Can
    Generate Anxiety; Resistance
    in Therapy; 2. Earlier Therapy
    Enhances Results; Symptom-
    Longevity Principle; 3. Avoid
    Any But Essential Surgery;
    4. Symptoms Not Imagined;
    5. Tranquilizing Drugs; 6.
    Suggestions: Moving Won't
    Help; 7. Collaboration Im-
    portant; Joint Endeavor Prin-
    ciple; 8. Treatment Sections
    in Each Chapter Have Gen-
    eral Applicability

IX. SUMMARY

X. SELECTED REFERENCES AND
BIBLIOGRAPHY

XI. REVIEW QUESTIONS ON THE
ANXIETY REACTIONS

I. INTRODUCTION

A. AGE OF ANXIETY

1. Anxiety Present Throughout History; Principle of Universality

OUR modern era has received a number of designations. These have included its being named the "Machine Age", the "Age of Science", the "Age of Discovery" or "Invention", and more recently, the "Atomic Age". For an alternative name which has considerable applicability, the author has suggested naming our era the Age of Anxiety.

Anxiety is not a new phenomenon in human experience. It has been present throughout earlier ages and cultures [Ch.1:IB4]. Indeed, anxiety has been a universal experience of man, in accord with the Principle of Universality of Anxiety, since the early beginnings of civilization. [Ch.1:IIA2]. Perhaps then it began its differentiation from fear, gradually evolving into a more complex kind of subjective experience. This might be regarded as an evolutionary kind of process which may not yet be completed, a premise about which more will be said later (*Chapter Nine*). If anxiety has been such a long-standing phenomenon and has been so widely experienced in the past, why then term our present era the Age of Anxiety?

2. Suitable Name

There are at least six reasons worthy of note for calling this the Age of Anxiety: (1) Attention thus might be better directed toward the special stresses and strains of present-day living. (2) However, of far more importance scientifically is our recently acquired and vastly increased recognition of the tremendous importance of anxiety in the whole scheme of things. (3) Increasing attention has been directed toward the study of anxiety and its important role in human life by professional people of varied orientation. (4) There is for the first time the clear recognition today of its universality as a part of human experience. (5) The problem of anxiety is now recognized as central to the whole concept of the psychogenesis of emotional illness. (6) Finally, there are the most important implications as to the continuing and significant role of anxiety in individual personality development and in character trait formation. For these reasons it would seem appropriate to refer to our era as the "Age of Anxiety."

3. Vastly Important Insights About Anxiety a Recent Achievement

In previous ages the universality of experience of anxiety was by no means clearly recognized. It is really only in the last 50 years that we have come to appreciate the powerful force that anxiety plays in day-to-day living, in molding the individual personality, and thus in shaping the destinies of peoples and nations. These insights hardly can be surpassed as to their importance for we humans as individuals, and collectively as well.

A greater appreciation of the important role of anxiety has in turn fostered increased study and attention. The development of further knowledge about its nature and origins has been encouraged. In view of its basic importance in so many areas, however, it seems rather surprising sometimes that it has remained for the present age to recognize more fully some of these very major conceptions about anxiety and their implications, and to undertake its systematic study.

B. "IT'S LIKE I'M EXPECTING SOMETHING BAD TO HAPPEN . . ."

1. Internal Threat

Anxiety is an apprehensive tension or uneasiness which is highly subjective in nature. Anxiety is one of the most uncomfortable experiences to which man is heir. It is sometimes described by patients as the anticipation of some unknown evil, threat, or danger. In his initial interview, a patient suffering from a typical Anxiety State reported, "It's like I'm expecting something terribly bad to happen, Doctor, but I don't know what it is! I'm frightened, but I don't know why!" This kind of descriptive comment is not uncommon.

Freud viewed anxiety as ". . . internalized fear, a signal for the ego that an unconscious repressed tendency is ready to emerge into consciousness and threaten the ego's integrity. The function of anxiety is the same as that of fear, which (in turn) is a response to external danger, preparing the ego for meeting the emergency." In the production of anxiety, however, the threat and the danger stem from *internal* and personal sources. It is the self, or ego, which is threatened. The ego thus experiences the feelings of danger and of threat, but does not know what they are! Not knowing makes the experiencing of anxiety all the more disturbing.

The various defenses (including the mental mechanisms) which are mobilized, and the individual responses to this emergency (the internal threat and the resulting anxiety), depend upon the existing individual personality structure which has developed. They help make up the very important psychologic part of the Total Individual Response to Crisis, or T.R.C.

2. Individually Appropriate and Proportional

When anxiety is present, the reaction of uneasy apprehension is out of proportion to the *apparent* * or known stimulus. In other words, the cause of true anxiety more likely is partly or entirely unconscious. If we knew what underlay the anxiety—the inner threat and its significance for the individual concerned—it would then prove to be exactly appropriate for him, and at this juncture in his living.

With these introductory comments we shall now pause to consider when anxiety may be considered pathologic, and then proceed to a discussion of the three major Anxiety Reactions *per se*. If he has not already done so, the reader would benefit at this juncture from a review of Part One, especially the first chapter on *The Nature and Origins of Anxiety*.

The Anxiety Reactions are being considered first among the neurotic reactions because of their clinical and dynamic features. These allow for the most orderly progression from the preceding introductory material. Further, our earlier discussion most readily leads into the kinds of more direct clinical manifestations of anxiety which are encountered in and characteristic of the Anxiety Reactions. The Anxiety Reactions comprise a major diagnostic category in emotional illness and the neuroses.

C. WHEN IS ANXIETY TO BE CONSIDERED PATHOLOGIC?

1. Quantitative Determination Rather Than Qualitative

Anxiety is present in everyone at various times and to various degrees. Thus its presence may be conveniently considered as being a matter of time and degree, rather than as something which is clearly present or absent. The level of anxiety may be higher or lower from person to person. It also fluctuates from time to time. The quantity of anxiety present is an important determination to make. These are important variable factors from

---

* Williams commented, "Since most times neither we nor the patient can understand the *why* of it, we cannot scientifically say it is out of proportion." This is in line with our earlier formulations and the *Principle of Individual Appropriateness of Response* [Ch.1:IIC2].

person to person. The amount of anxiety present and its effects are more important in determining pathology than are its mere presence or absence.

Another significant variable factor is the relative ability of an individual to tolerate a given amount of anxiety or stress. The Total Individual Response to Crisis or Danger (T.R.C.) includes all of the possible direct and outwardly-apparent expressions of anxiety. It also includes any of the more hidden methods of expression of tension by physiologic, physical, psychologic, emotional and mental means. The physician should clearly recognize that anxiety or its consequence may be expressed outwardly and directly, as well as by a number of significant more indirect and hidden ways. Anxiety is pathologic when present in sufficient amount to interfere with normal functions, satisfactions, or living.

Whether pathologic or not, or to what degree, anxiety is always unpleasant. Accordingly, our *Principle of the Avoidance of Anxiety* [Ch.I:-IB;Ch.9:IA2] holds, by which man seeks to avoid it, consciously and unconsciously.

2. Individual Utilization of Therapy Variable

Finally, individuals vary greatly in their ability to utilize expert therapeutic help so as to: (1) secure greater personal understanding; (2) reach constructive compromises; and (3) resolve the precipitating or underlying conflicts.

Considering these various factors, again *anxiety may be regarded as pathologic when it is present to such an extent as to interfere with:* (1) *effectiveness in living,* (2) *the achievement of desired realistic goals or satisfactions, or* (3) *reasonable emotional comfort.*

3. Various Yardsticks Useful

A number of yardsticks may be useful to us in attempting to measure the cumulative destructive effects of anxiety, which equate pathology. These include: (1) one's ability to develop and maintain healthy relationships with people; (2) the subjective amount of "dis-ease" experienced*; (3) the achievement of emotional equanimity in reasonable measure; (4) the relative absence of severe or limiting emotional conflicts; (5) the absence of disturbing dreams; and (6) the ability to carry out one's accepted role in life.

Actually, the individual concerned may himself be in a better position to estimate the degree or seriousness of any impairment in living which he suffers as a consequence of his anxiety.† At times psychiatrists have found

---

* See also the discussion of Conflict in *Chapter 1*. It is of course to be kept in mind that anxiety may also arise through identification, and emotional contagion, and that it can be increased as a consequence of conditioning.

† In deciding as to when a person is to be regarded as ill, Alexander wrote: "We consider [the patient] mentally sick also if he develops severe attacks of anxiety without any ideational content, which come to him apparently out of the blue without any apparent provocation, material or psychological".

it convenient to speak in terms of the *level of anxiety* of a given person. A sufficient level of anxiety to interfere with any significant aspect of life is pathologic, and indicates psychopathology.

4. Highly Subjective Experience

Anxiety is a highly subjective manifestation. Its presence clinically thus is by no means necessarily outwardly apparent. As a consequence, even experienced observers may have difficulty in accurately estimating its level. With some patients, this may be true even after many hours of psychotherapeutic work. This can add to the difficulty in judging the degree of pathology or the level of anxiety.

One, of course, cannot talk a patient out of the discomfort of anxiety. One cannot secure any substantial mitigation by simple reassurance. The diversion of the patient through amusement, new activities, or new surroundings is a superficial approach. Generally, at best it serves only temporary purposes. Certainly such measures as ridicule are to be deplored. The patient is hardly likely to appreciate such efforts. His attention to an extent may be temporarily diverted from his anxiety by these and by similar measures, but any respite afforded is apt to be only too brief.

D. THREE MAJOR TYPES OF ANXIETY REACTIONS

1. Classification a Convenience

We have seen that anxiety may be present in any degree, from the minimal to the overwhelming amount which constitutes an Anxiety-Panic attack. In this discussion, included as Anxiety Reactions are those emotional illnesses in which the most prominent presenting feature is anxiety as such and its more direct effects.

For convenience in presentation and classification, the author has for some years divided the Anxiety Reactions into three main groups. These are. (1) the *Acute Anxiety Attack (A.A.A.)* or *Anxiety-Panic Reaction;* (2) the *Anxiety-Tension State (A.T.S.);* and (3) *Anxiety Neurosis.* Each is an important type of Anxiety Reaction. Differences in the bases of these reactions are not necessarily implied. The anxiety which is subjectively experienced in each of these clinical and closely-related patterns of reaction is identical except in its extent, acuteness, and chronicity, or in the degree of its fixation as a pathologic process.

2. Incidence; The Emotional Illnesses

The author estimates that approximately 12–15 per cent of the clinical cases of neuroses may be classified as Anxiety Reactions.

As we begin our clinical inquiry into the various patterns of neurotic reaction, it is important for us early to secure some perspective concerning the relative position of the Anxiety Reactions. To this end, and also for an overall general outline of the emotional illnesses, *Table 7* has been prepared.

Table 7

The Emotional Illnesses

The following is a schematic outline-presentation of the Emotional Illnesses and their relative positions, indicating the major pathways in their pathogenesis.

UNRESOLVED EMOTIONAL CONFLICT

Unresolved emotional conflict results in anxiety or threatens anxiety. The anxiety from the emotional conflict, or the threat of anxiety brings about repression of the intolerable ideas or impulses. These had led to the emotional conflict in the first place. They also lead to, and form part of, the continuing unconscious conflict. Although repressed from conscious awareness, this material remains energy-laden and potent. As such it continues to seek expression. Such expression is often in hidden, devious, and symbolic forms. The psychogenic manifestations of emotional illnesses arise from such repressed and unconscious material.

The basis for the direct, and for the indirect manifestations or the consequences of anxiety, are therefore ordinarily not accessible to the usual means of perception. The direct and the indirect manifestations or consequences of anxiety (and of emotional, intrapsychic conflict) are ultimately responsible for the psychogenic manifestations of the emotional illnesses.

I. *The Functional Psychoses*

Included are the psychogenic features of the emotional illnesses of psychotic level.

II. *The Neuroses*

A. *Anxiety and its effects expressed more directly.*
The clinically prominent entities are the Anxiety Reactions:
1. The Acute Anxiety Attack (A.A.A.) or Anxiety-Panic Reaction
2. The Anxiety-Tension State (A.T.S.)
3. The Anxiety Neurosis (*see Table 4*)

B. *Anxiety and its consequences or effects expressed indirectly.*
The attempted defenses against anxiety result in a variety of concealed and devious expressions of conflict. Symptoms often represent or express symbolic compromises of the intrapsychic conflict. The unconscious and repressed material of the conflict (and attendant anxiety) may find outward expression in a variety of transmuted and converted forms. These might be categorized in three major groups, as follows.

III. *Defensive Character Trait Development and the Character Neuroses*

A. *Constellations or groups of related character or personality traits:*
1. The Conversion Personality.
2. The Depressive Personality.
3. The Obsessive Personality.
4. The Phobic Personality.
5. The Hygeiaphrontic Personality.
6. The Paranoid Personality.
7. Others; additional personality types (*see chapter on the Character Reactions [Ch.5]*)

(*Table continued on next page*)

Table 7—The Emotional Illnesses (Cont.)

I. *The Functional Psychoses—Contd.*

II. *The Neuroses—Contd.*

1. *The Physiologic Conversions:*
   (a) The psychophysiologic or psychosomatic illnesses; the somatization reactions.
       (*See Table 16* and [Ch.12].)
   (b) Emotional Fatigue, Fatigue States, and Neurasthenia; the Fatigue Reactions [Ch.7].

2. *The Psychologic Conversions:*
   (a) The Depressive Reactions [Ch.4].
   (b) Overconcern with Health or Hygeiaphrontis (Hypochondriasis) [Ch.8].
   (c) The Obsessive-Compulsive Reactions [Ch.6].
   (d) The Phobic Reactions [Ch.10].
   (e) The Soterial Reactions [Ch.11].
   (f) The Dissociative Reactions. (These might possibly be considered as a fourth major group.) [Ch.13].
   (g) Certain of the Neuroses Following Trauma [Ch.14].

3. *The Somatic (hysterical) Conversions:*
   (a) Conversion Reactions [Ch.12].
   (b) Certain of the Neuroses Following Trauma [Ch.14].

III. *Defensive Character Trait Development and the Character Neuroses—Contd.*

B. *The Character Reactions.* The overdevelopment or exaggeration of specific individual character defenses or personality traits, or groups of traits to a level of impairment of some facet of living, so as to constitute a neurotic reaction [Ch.5].

II. THE ACUTE ANXIETY ATTACK, ANXIETY-PANIC REACTION, OR A.A.A.

A. UNEXPECTED, DRAMATIC CLINICAL REACTION

1. Functional Changes Accompany Emotional Reaction; A.A.A.

The typical Acute Anxiety Attack, A.A.A. or Anxiety-Panic Reaction (these terms may be used interchangeably) is an acute and dramatic incident. This is certainly true subjectively and can be true for observers as well. Its victim is temporarily incapacitated and thoroughly frightened. Typically, the attack comes on suddenly and without warning. It is marked by extreme apprehension, fear, or dread. It is essentially a sudden, intense and generally short-lived burst of anxiety. Often a peak is reached in which a sense of impending doom or disaster may be experienced.

Palpitation is usually present. In the Actute Anxiety Attack, or A.A.A., there may be an increase in the rate of respiration, which can also be difficult or labored. There may be oppressive feelings in the chest, head, abdomen, or elsewhere. Various extremely uncomfortable subjective sensations may be described by the patient, such as feelings that he will "burst", "fly apart", or "go to pieces". Dissolution or death may seem imminent to him. Perspiration may be profuse. The extremities or other bodily parts may be reported as feeling cold or hot. Other physiological changes may also be reported. These can affect any function and system of the body. Most of the usual bodily functions, such as digestion, tend to be suspended. Others, having emergency functions as in preparation for combat or for flight, tend to be thrown into high gear. These, as with one's T.R.C., have a measure of individual variation.

The attack may last from several minutes to several hours. It may take a day or more for the anxiety to recede to a fairly normal level. Occasionally the "tapering off" period is greatly prolonged. Sometimes it happens that the pre-panic level of comfort is never quite regained. A.A.A.s may accompany other types of neurotic reactions especially when the other symptoms comprise an *Incomplete Defense** [*See* Ch.4:IXA1; Ch.10IIIA3].

2. Circular Generation of Fear Principle; Overwhelming Anxiety

From the foregoing description one can readily see how the presence of anxiety can in itself produce fear. This is in accord with a principle which we might term the Circular Generation of Fear. *See also* [Ch.9:IIIB3; Ch.14;VIIE1].

Indeed, the individual may become desperately afraid of these attacks. Any alternative may come to be preferable. Consciously as well as unconsciously he will go to nearly any lengths to avoid a repetition. Tragically enough, without gaining an understanding and resolution of the internal

---

* The Incomplete Symptom-Defense Concept relates to the lack of symptom-success in allaying or preventing anxiety. Presumptive evidence of this is to be found in any instance in which there is the presence of concurrent anxiety or an A.A.A. accompanying other neurotic symptoms.

conflicts responsible through insight-directed psychotherapy, it is most likely that further attacks are to be anticipated. The fear of recurrence can become a dominating theme in the person's life. *See also* the Constrictive Spiral of Anxiety [Ch.3:VI].

An Anxiety-Panic Reaction is the most acute and severe form of anxiety. In it the anxiety literally overwhelms the person, who may feel as though he is disintegrating. Sometimes after even an initial attack, or possibly after several recurrences, the individual comes to live in great fear and dread of another one. The physiologic consequences of the attack he has experienced often greatly increase his dread. Not understanding them, it is not surprising at times to find that he fears that he will be destroyed. An analogous *Phobic Attack* may be rarely encountered (*see Chapter 10*). Having many of the characteristics of the A.A.A. it is nonetheless phobic in nature, albeit episodic, short-lived, and acute. A distinction of the A.A.A. from the Phobic Attack is generally possible by the alert clinician. These phenomena however, tend to overlap.

B. POSITIVE DIAGNOSIS VALUABLE

1. *Psychotherapy and Prognosis Enhanced.*

It is important for the general physician to be able to differentiate this important type of Acute Anxiety Attack from organic conditions. The latter might perhaps be more genuinely threatening to life, but hardly more uncomfortable to the patient.*

A diagnosis on positive grounds is far preferable to one arrived at by exclusion or by elimination. It is far better also than an attitude of uncertainty or of temporizing. If the examining physician can make a positive diagnosis of an Acute Anxiety Attack and not incorrectly label the illness as an organic one which might constitute a threat to life, much needless suffering and expense can be avoided. Uncertainty can lead to unnecessary medical studies and to the patient's confusion as to the basis of his difficulties. Further, the chances of securing early and effective psychotherapy will be greatly increased. The prognosis may be greatly improved and the patient and his entire future existence can benefit substantially.

This is not to imply that a positive diagnosis is necessarily easily made. The individual may have no awareness of the emotional basis for the attack. He may even vigorously deny the presence of any possible emotional conflict. As we shall learn increasingly, this kind of reaction can reflect his "secondary defense". Through it the symptom is secondarily defended. He may deny (spontaneously or in response to specific questions) the

---

* The physician should be familiar enough with the phenomenon of the Acute Anxiety Attack that the possibility of any real confusion with organic states is minimal. Noyes pointed out that, "Physicians lacking an appreciation of psychological factors in the production of symptoms have at times erred in not recognizing that anxiety attacks are psychological. . . ." They are not physical, or physiological disturbances.

As a consequence, the Acute Anxiety Attack has occasionally been misdiagnosed as a heart attack, acute dyspnea, toxic thyroid, hyperinsulinism, asthma, or as one of certain other more rare medical conditions.

presence of any stress or difficulty at all in his personal relations. The denial may be even more vehement in the very area in which the difficulty lies!

2. The Defensive Denial; Organic Bases Sought

The attempted denial when present is mostly an automatic aspect of the defensive attempt to maintain repression. This unconsciously "seems" to be a more comfortable way of dealing with the intolerable conflict. This will be illustrated later [Ch.8:VA1;Ch.12:VIIIA3] in our concept of the *Flight to the Physical*. Emotional conflict is always painful and its continued repression is "sought."

It is therefore hardly surprising to find patients who insist upon the presence of some organic illness as the villain responsible for their difficulty. Organic bases may be sought. Responsibility may be incorrectly assigned to illnesses which are assumed, minor, or absent. This type of defensiveness is by no means limited to the Acute Anxiety Attack. It may be seen in similar fashion with almost any type of emotional disorder. We shall observe repeated instances as our study of the neuroses proceeds.

C. CLINICAL FEATURES IN ACUTE ANXIETY ATTACKS

1. Three Instances

Along the lines of the foregoing descriptive comments, the features in the following three cases supplement our knowledge of the clinical findings.

Case 13

A Typical Anxiety-Panic Reaction

A 24-year-old farmer reported to a University Hospital Clinic for a medical examination. He said that he felt fairly good. Yesterday, however, he had had a "spell" when he thought he was about to die.

History disclosed that he was running his tractor in quite routine fashion on the previous day. Suddenly he became anxious, fearful, and started to tremble all over. His mouth became dry, his heart pounded rapidly, and he had a "sinking feeling" in his abdomen. His legs were weak. He was extremely frightened, and thought that death was near. Unable to continue working, he had been helped into the house.

He was seen shortly thereafter by his family physician. After preliminary examination, his physician then had referred him on to the General Medical Clinic for diagnostic study. Medical studies and tests here were quite negative for any organic pathology. He had suffered a typical Acute Anxiety Attack. In this instance the underlying psychologic bases remained more or less obscure, except for some general evidence of long-bottled-up hostility.

Case 14

Attack of Acute Anxiety Described

A 46-year-old business man was having serious difficulties with his supervisor and in his marital relations. One morning while driving to work he suffered a typical Anxiety-Panic Reaction.

As he described the attack: "I was almost down to work. Close to the White House, on Pennsylvania Avenue I got caught in some traffic. Suddenly I began to shake all over. I felt something awful was going to happen. I couldn't go on. . . ."

"I wanted to hide my face in my arms. My chest hurt. I was afraid to drive, although I did manage to get my car to the side of the street. After a while I got a policeman to call up a friend to come down. He drove me home. I thought I was dying. . . .

"It was terrible. I keep dreading it might happen again . . . I've gotten afraid to drive downtown by myself now and I feel I want to have someone with me. . . ."

The following example is a dramatic and colorful verbatim description of a severe attack of anxiety. This was reported by a person who had suffered repeated similar attacks in the past.

Case 15

Acute Anxiety Attack: Verbatim Description

A 29-year-old housewife sought treatment because of acute anxiety attacks which had become increasingly frequent. She described one of these dramatic episodes in some detail, as follows.

"It was just like I was petrified with fear. If I were to meet a lion face-to-face, I couldn't be more scared. Everything got black, and I felt I would faint; but I didn't. I thought, 'I won't be able to hold on.' . . . I think sometimes I will just go crazy.

"My heart was beating so hard and fast it would jump out and hit my hand. I felt like I couldn't stand up, that my legs wouldn't support me. My hands got icy, and my feet stung. There were horrible shooting pains in my forehead. My head felt tight, like someone had pulled the skin down too tight, and I wanted to pull it away. . . .

"I couldn't breathe. I was short of breath. I literally get out of breath and pant just like I had run up and down the stairs. I felt like I had run an eight-mile race. I couldn't do anything. I felt all in; weak, no strength. I can't even dial a telephone. . . .

"Even then I can't be still when I'm like this. I'm restless, and I pace up and down. I feel I'm just not responsible. I don't know what I'll do. These things are terrible. I can go along real calmly for a while. Then, without any warning, this happens. I just blow my top. . . ."

These instances give us more or less the kinds of history one can expect to hear in a severe Acute Anxiety Attack. Individual variations will certainly be observed. Further, for purposes of illustration, of course, the more striking kinds of examples have been selected. The physician is likely to hear about many less striking ones. He is also considerably more likely to hear a descriptive after-the-fact account than he is to have been an on-the-spot witness.

2. Cases of Long Duration

The duration of A.A.A.s or Anxiety-Panic Attacks is variable. The stress is generally so severe, however, that one can entertain doubts as to the ability of a patient to tolerate such intense symptoms for long. Nevertheless, in occasional instances attacks may be prolonged. For instance, a young man had just reported to his first military duty station, following completion of his basic training.

Shortly following arrival, he developed acute symptoms of anxiety, with marked physiologic accompaniments. This state continued at an intense level for nearly forty-eight hours, at the end of which time the symptoms subsided spontaneously. The patient was left utterly exhausted, but he showed no obvious evidence of more permanent physical consequences. Fortunately he had a constitution strong enough to withstand such an intense and prolonged strain. Circumstances did not allow further study and the basis for the Anxiety Attack remained obscure.

3. Morning Attack of Anxiety

One prominent cardiac specialist reported to the author that he had been impressed with the frequency with which the anxiety attacks of patients referred mistakenly to him as "cardiac cases" had happened in the early mornings. Morning anxiety attacks are fairly frequent, but they can of course occur at any time.

Upon occasion the early morning attack is related to dreams. As the individual awakens from a disturbing dream in these instances he is immediately anxious. The responsible dream is often just as immediately lost to conscious recall. A patient recently reported such an instance. He said, "I was anxious and frightened the instant I woke up. I can't say why. I think I had been dreaming something frightening, but whatever it was it was gone . . . . My heart was pounding . . . . It usually happens this way. I woke up at six. The pounding didn't stop until about half past eight, after I had arrived at my office . . . ."

A 40-year-old physician reported to the author not long ago that he had suffered an unaccountable early morning anxiety attack shortly after the birth of his first child. For him this had fortunately been an isolated event. However, as a point in illustration of its severity and impact, he had not the slightest difficulty in remembering it over the course of years. Another physician reported an anxiety attack from his college days, which he had similarly always recalled: "It awakened me in the middle of the night. I was very frightened. I'll never forget it. The feeling was completely disruptive . . . It was like I was falling apart."

4. Geriatric Instances

The psychiatrist has perhaps tended thus far to think more of the Acute Anxiety Attack in relation to younger people. Instances of A.A.A.s in persons of more than 60 years of age, however, are not uncommon. These can be particularly troubling, especially when the geriatric patient has had no real prior personal experience with anxiety. Further, with what is likely to be a more fixed and rigid personality structure, he is likely to be less amenable to the requirements of the therapy situation or to make changes.

The following instance illustrates the onset of a series of A.A.A.s (Acute Anxiety Attacks) in a lady, first beginning at age 62 years. These were urgent signals of pending emotional decompensation [Ch.5:VC4;Ch.10:-IVA3]. *See also* later reference to somewhat analogous phobic attacks beginning at age 58 years [Ch.5:VC4].

Case 16

Acute Anxiety Attacks Begin at 62 Years of Age

(1) Studies Negative; tranquilizers ineffectual

A 62-year-old lady was referred for evaluation and therapy with a history of twelve or fifteen terribly-disturbing incidents. Totally unfamiliar with these phenomena and lacking descriptive phraseology, she could only refer to them as "spells", and for several months could describe her subjective experiences only in very limited terms. Thinking something *awful* was transpiring, and thinking only in physical terms, the first such "spell" had led to overnight hospitalization several months earlier.

During subsequent acute incidents her family physician had conducted various medical studies, with totally negative findings. Attempts to contain her attacks with several different sedatives and tranquilizers had proved ineffectual, as is often the case in the A.A.A. She had finally accepted psychiatric referral.

The nature of, or reasons for, what she had now come to recognize as "nervous attacks" were a complete mystery to her. They were terribly disturbing, and more so because of this and her prior almost total inexperience with anxiety. Her words, quoted below, are of interest in our further study of Acute Anxiety Attacks.

(2) The "Strong Silent One" the Victim

". . . I don't want to be left alone. I fear something that I don't understand. I can't understand these spells or what it is I fear . . . What am I going to do? These attacks worry me terribly. . . .

"I've *always* been strong. This *isn't* like me. People think I can take anything. They have always regarded me as the Rock of Gibraltar! . . . I keep things to myself—never let them out. People don't really know how I feel. They are sure I'm the strong one. I've been admired for this. . . ."

(3) Circular Generation of Fear Illustrated

In illustration of the interesting *Principle of the Circular Generation of Fear* in the Acute Anxiety Attack, as noted earlier, [Ch.3:IIA2] the fear of recurrence had soon become quite a prominent feature.

As she described this later, ". . . the fear of having them [Acute Anxiety Attacks] just completely dominates my thoughts! It seems to be the *only* thing that's on my mind lately. . . .

"*Am* I going to have another one?" And desperately, "Now what am I going to do? . . . I can't explain it. Am I going to get rid of it? . . . The only thing that's on my mind is: Am I going to have to go through another one? or when?"

Acute Anxiety Attacks are sometimes more likely on a weekend, a holiday, or during some apparently "quiet" period. However, the "choice," an inadvertent one of course, is completely individual. The frequency is usually more or less unpredictable and can vary; the setting likewise. The foregoing lady thus had, in one rapid series, two Acute Anxiety Attacks: on a Sunday while resting; and later one while doing dishes; one the following Monday while bathing; and one on Tuesday while hanging up clothes outdoors. The last one she tried "to battle through" and continue her task, but "finally had to give up and lie down."

The effects on her life as with many victims of this kind of descriptive experience were pervasive indeed. For example, "These nervous spells make me depressed. My usual interests [hobbies] are gone. This is the first house we've lived in in which I'm not immersed in decorating; the first occasion I've been like this. I used to be forever changing things or doing something different. I still like to do it, I guess, but I just don't have the same interest. Others have noticed this too. . . ."

5. Concept of Emotional Death; Death Terminates Prolonged Anxiety Attack

Patients are not always able to tolerate such stress when it is sufficiently prolonged. Indeed, the patient may actually reach a point of physical collapse in the most acute situations. This brings us to an intriguing concept.

We know increasingly clearly from a number of observations, that what we might term "emotional deaths" may occur on various kinds of occasions. These are likely marked by the most severe kinds of overt stress, or covert conflicts. These would be so labeled in view of their basic cause, which is emotional. When they occur, they cannot be explained on the basis of organic changes or pathology, as uncovered at post mortem examinations. As one possible occasionally contributing factor, the depletion concept of anxiety noted the depletion incident to the continued experience of anxiety.

Space does not permit any adequate consideration of this challenging phenomenon, and our resulting interesting conception. We know, however, that a number of individually-significant factors can be contributory. Some measure of lay recognition possibly, may be implied through such phrases as: "frightened to death", "dying of quiet", or "boredom", "eager to join a loved one", "he just couldn't stand life any longer", "had all he could take", and so on. These remarks help comprise a *concept of emotional death*. *See also* section on Accident-Proneness [Ch.4:XID].

The following case is illustrative of the rare instance in which an emotional death appeared to terminate a prolonged Anxiety Attack.

Case 17

Death During Severe, Continuing Anxiety Attack

A 54-year-old man was admitted to the hospital because of marked anxiety accompanied by depression. He did not respond to treatment, and the anxiety increased. Rapidly he became severely anxious and agitated. Sedatives seemed powerless. He was apprehensive of death, and he presented a clinical picture of the most acute anxiety. This unfortunate state continued unabated for well in excess of 48 hours, when he suddenly collapsed and died.

The immediate cause of death was on post mortem examination reported to be "coronary insufficiency," accompanied by massive pulmonary edema. Pathologically, however, his coronary arteries were otherwise excellent! It was also difficult to explain the massive edema from any strictly pragmatic viewpoint. Seemingly this patient had tolerated all of the acute anxiety of which he was physically, physiologically, and psychologically capable, and then death had supervened.

D. DYNAMICS: OVERREACTION PROTECTIVELY INTENDED

1. Bodily Changes Prepare for Action; Concept of Defensive-Overreaction

The physiologic symptoms in an Anxiety-Panic Reaction are perhaps most frequently referable to the heart and circulatory system. It is as though the emergency physiologic changes designed to meet the threat or danger are overdone. Here we have illustrated for us the important physiologic component of the Total Response to Crisis (T.R.C.), in which the reaction to an internal and unknown threat of danger is the same as though it were external. This is an overreaction.

Psychic and physiologic overreactions are defensively intended, but lead to all kinds of emotional and functional symptoms. This is the important Concept of Defensive-Overreaction in the Etiology of the Emotionally-Determined ills. [Ch.12:IA2].

The functional changes prepare for defense or aggression. They do not help the situation, as they might if the threat were external and the crisis one that could be met by physical action. Thus they become instead a handicap. The net result is likely to increase the apprehension already present. A 48-year-old attorney reported recently: "I was lying on the living room couch not doing anything. Suddenly and without any warning my heart started to pound I had a tense feeling in my chest and felt frightened. I *knew* I was having a heart attack. My wife phoned the doctor who came over right away." The physician made an examination and both wisely and quickly recognized that his patient had suffered an Acute Anxiety Attack. He provided some important and necessary reassurance and promptly arranged for his referral for a psychiatric opinion and possible therapy. This is not a rare occurrence. In this instance fortunately, it was very well handled.

Patients whose basic problem is one of anxiety are not infrequently referred to cardiac clinics (*Case 18*). This is hardly surprising in view of the frequent prominence of palpitation, skipped beats, troubled breathing, and chest pressure.

2. Principle of Extension

The Acute Anxiety Attack tends to have further emotional repercussions. Like a stone cast into a pool, these can progress in ever-spreading fashion to influence many if not all aspects of the patient's life. This is in accord with what we might call the Principle of Extension. Through it the later, secondary effects of anxiety attacks can become considerably more important and influential than the attacks themselves.

This principle was already showing signs of becoming operative with the businessman patient in *Case 14*. Here we can observe the tendency for the original difficulty to "extend." This had been his first attack. His great dread of a recurrence contributed to an association of the attack with the circumstances of the attack. By extension he now already not only feared the attack but he came further to fear driving as well—what he was doing at the time of the attack.

By extension, various places, situations, activities, objects and people thus can come to be associated with the anxiety, and thereby come to be feared and avoided in turn. We shall study this principle again and at greater length as an interesting kind of progression of pathology when we come to consider the Phobic Reactions [Ch.12;Ch.13].

The Circular Generation of Fear [Ch.3:IIA2] generally lays the foundation for this type of further extension. This can produce effects in the person's life which can become indeed pervasive.

3. Possibility of Organic Basis; Concept of Secondary Defense

It is hardly surprising that confusion can develop over the emotional *vs.* the possible organic basis of anxiety. This is suggested by the repeated references thus far to the physiological changes which to some extent regularly accompany anxiety. This kind of uncertainty as to etiology is further contributed to by: (1) The patient's frequent acute awareness of bodily changes, as mobilization for action occurs; (2) The functional changes are the ones most prominent to an observer, and are the ones which best lend themselves to some objective measurements by the physician; and (3) The patient's lack of conscious knowledge as to the nature or the real source of his "fear", or sometimes even the existence of any possible underlying emotional conflict. There is an additional vital reason with greater applicability in some cases than in others: This is (4). As a resistance and a defense, in that diversion of one's attention toward the physical and away from the emotional helps to preserve repression and nonawareness. This is part of the defensively-intended Flight-to-the-Physical. It brings us to another important concept.

A vital defensive endeavor in itself, the repression must be in turn, that is secondarily defended. This is in accord with the Concept of Secondary Defense, by which we shall observe repeatedly [Ch.4:IIIA3;Ch.5:VB6] that a dynamism, symptom, character trait, or neurotic reaction—a (primary) defense in itself—is in turn (secondarily) defended. This is an important concept as noted, with widespread ramifications throughout the fields of psychiatry and emotional health.

The following case illustrates the dramatic kind of Acute Anxiety Attack which can well be mistaken for a syndrome of organic origin. This view of its origins is in fact more the rule than the exception for many of the individuals concerned, and there are internal needs and motivations which contribute substantially to this. It should be far less so for their physicians, however.

Case 18

A.A.A. vs. Coronary Occlusion

A 49-year-old medical gastrointestinal specialist had become increasingly nervous and unhappy following a very serious (to him) professional disappointment, and the onset of crucial family disharmony. When some functional digestive disturbances had also developed, he became alarmed at their possible pathologic import. By appointment one morning the doctor came into a university gastrointestinal clinic for personal diagnostic study.

While he was waiting between tests he suddenly began to feel far more anxious and fearful. The reaction was acute. He began to perspire, and became quite pallid. He complained of chest pain. His physician colleagues were alarmed at his appearance. His apprehension and tension were sufficient to immobilize him physically. He expressed his fear of imminent death. A clinical impression of acute coronary occlusion was made, and he was rushed to the cardiology department.

An immediate electrocardiogram proved to be normal, as were subsequent studies. The announcement of the negative findings was in part only, a relief to the patient, since it made the difficulty more obscure, less tangible, and pointed toward psychic factors. It was one and a half hours later before the attack subsided. He had suffered an Acute Anxiety Attack. In view of its severity, its dramatic nature, and the clinical manifestations, it was hardly surprising that an infarction had been suspected.

4. *Cerebral vs. Mid-brain Origin*

An acute state of anxiety-panic is so dramatic, so out of control, and so overwhelming that certain authorities stress the mid-brain origin of panic, as opposed to a cerebral cortical origin. Most likely there are elements of both.

In reference to this point, Potter wrote: "Clinically, the so-called 'homosexual panic' is certainly as acute and dramatic as any acute panic [fear] precipitated by a major catastrophe. Yet the cause of the 'homosexual panic may be 'recognized' or 'unrecognized,' most often the latter. I think the terms recognized and unrecognized are not quite the right ones. Even the cause of the panic which is precipitated by a catastrophe is 'unrecognized'—such panics are mid-brain reactions rather than cortical reactions."

III. THE ANXIETY-TENSION STATE OR A.T.S.

A. SUBACUTE CLINICAL REACTION

1. *More or Less Continuous*

The isolated and dramatic occurrence and the abrupt onset of the Acute Anxiety Attack have been emphasized. In distinction, in the Anxiety-Tension State the anxiety which is present may be regarded as having become "subacute." In other words, instead of occasional and rather isolated Acute Anxiety Attacks, there is now a certain amount of anxiousness rather chronically present. Thus an Anxiety-Tension State implies a more or less continuous uneasy substratum of tension and anxiety. It may be thought of as a progression from the A.A.A. These comments are in accord with a definition to be offered shortly.

The anxiety which is experienced is not really different in quality from that already described. The difference is in the acuteness, the quantity, and the chronicity. In the Anxiety-Tension State it tends to be more steady and less intermittent. It may be low in intensity, but to some extent it is likely to be almost continuous. This is an Emotional reaction then, which is characterized by an almost steady low level of feelings of uneasiness and apprehension. An analogy of the A.T.S. to the Grief State will be drawn later [Ch.4:VD4].

2. *Diagnosis*

How is this subacute kind of reaction to be distinguished further, from the more established and chronic one of Anxiety Neuroses? The Anxiety-Tension State may be differentiated from an Anxiety Neurosis in that it tends to be more circumscribed as to time. The A.T.S. is also not so established and fixed a pathologic entity as is the Anxiety Neurosis, into which, however, it may merge.

There also are often important environmental factors present, in the onset of the A.T.S., which are stressful for the individual concerned. When these subside, presumably the Anxiety State will also tend to subside. This is true of course unless in the meantime it has become more firmly entrenched as a psychopathologic process. There is also often to be observed, however, a greater or lesser lag in time between the end of the situational stress and the subsiding of the Anxiety-Tension State. The longer the stress has been present, the greater the time lag is likely to be.

There is frequently a lag in the cessation of those functional changes which occur in response to environmental stresses, following their subsidence. While there are many and wider applications in psychiatry, this can be a significant indicator of an incipient or developing A.T.S. To aid in the identification of this phenomenon, and to stress its importance, we might label this the *Concept of Continued Physiologic Momentum.*

The patient may be able, at least superficially, to give a cause for his "fears and his tension"; on the other hand, he may report a subjective emotional reaction which seems to him out of proportion to his situation. The level of anxiety and tension which is present in the A.T.S., actually may vary from a mild, continuous kind of anxiety all the way to near panic. Indeed, Acute Anxiety Attacks may occur during the course of the Anxiety-Tension State.

The roots of pathologic anxiety lie in the unconscious, but anxiety may be reactivated or "mobilized" by external circumstances or situations. Similarly, as we have observed in the Acute Anxiety Attack, the anxiety may appear without apparent or obvious cause. Actually, the drawing of clear-cut lines between an Anxiety-Tension State and a case of Anxiety Neurosis is an arbitrary measure and one of one's professional judgment. The one merges into the other, and this division has been made for purpose of convenience in study, teaching, classification, and diagnosis.

We may define the A.T.S. for the purpose of professional convenience and usage, as a continuing, more or less circumscribed, subacute reaction of anxiety with important situational precipitants.

B. SYMPTOMS AND CLINICAL FEATURES

1. Anxiety Most Prominent Feature

Anxiety-Tension States will usually be accompanied by some overt physiologic *hyper-* or *hypo*activity of the autonomic nervous system, and these manifestations can be expressed throughout the body. Although psychophysiologic manifestations are almost inevitably witnessed in Anxiety States, in general the presence of anxiety as such is the major clinical manifestation. *See also* section on Combat Reactions [Ch.14:VII].

The following case illustrates a moderate self-limiting Anxiety-Tension State, which was precipitated as is rather typical, by situational factors.

Case 19

An Anxiety-Tension State; A.T.S.

(1) *Typical clinical findings*
A 56-year-old businessman was referred for psychiatric evaluation by his family physician. Upon examination, he appeared mildly preoccupied, tense, and restless. He described some difficulty with sleeping, in that he sometimes had trouble getting to sleep, and also slept "lightly"; being

subject to easy awakening. There was some slight weight loss which was apparently incident to moderate anorexia. Fine finger tremors were apparent. The patient described himself variously as "uneasy," "tense," "anxious," and nervous." The clinical evidence was fairly typical.

(2) Situational relationship present

History disclosed an acute precipitating event some weeks previously. At this time a reorganization had been suddenly announced by his company. The patient had been with this particular company for some twenty-seven years. His had been a successful career, in which he had eventually reached the important position of comptroller. In the reorganization, however, this post had been eliminated, at least in name, but actually filled by a younger man. The patient thus had found himself "eased upstairs" into the newly-created post of treasurer, which was apparently to be little more than an empty title.

Although there were other positions outside the firm which he could secure, none carried nearly the same prestige, interest, and significance for him. In view of his long association with the firm, in a business to which he had been "wedded," the sudden and unexpected loss of his active position had resulted in considerable insecurity and tension. In view of a stable personality background and excellent past adjustment, it appeared that he would "weather" this situational crisis in good fashion.

(3) Subsequent course self-limiting

A diagnosis of Anxiety-Tension State on a situational basis was made. It was not considered advisable or necessary in this case to undertake any kind of deeply-investigative psychotherapy. Accordingly, he was referred back to his family physician for supportive therapy and follow-up.

He continued somewhat tense and anxious for several months, during which time, however, his symptoms gradually subsided. He secured some new interests in healthful replacement for those lost. The situational precipitating event, the steady low level of tension, and the rather self-limiting course were typical of the Anxiety-Tension State. The psychopathology was never sufficiently developed, established, or severe enough to warrant a diagnosis of Anxiety Neurosis.

2. Situational Stress Important; Stress of Combat

An excellent illustration of how repeated stressful situational stimuli—those which can readily arouse fear, apprehension, and anxiety—may precipitate an Anxiety-Tension State is often to be found in the soldier in combat. In the following instance this kind of severe environmental stress resulted in the gradual development of a serious Anxiety-Tension State. In this kind of case the drawing of a dividing line from Anxiety Neurosis can become much more difficult.

Case 20

A.T.S. Develops During Stress of Wartime Sea Duty

An 18-year-old seaman reported to sick-bay on board a U.S. destroyer during World War II. He had served for several months of rather rigorous wartime sea duty, which had been marked by frequent calls to "general quarters." He had noted that during the last several instances his heart had started pounding, a pounding that continued even when the "all clear" was sounded. He was uneasy, worried, felt nervous, and had little appetite. Some of his manifestations fitted into our concept of *apprehensive anticipation* [Ch.1:IID].

During the course of several subsequent months under continued stressful conditions, his pulse rate tended to remain high for increasingly longer periods after the combat situation was over. His other symptoms, including his subjective tension, gradually increased. Indeed, these symptoms now began to occur when no general quarters alarm had been given.* He began to complain of irritability, more nervousness, and insomnia. An early slight weight loss became more marked. His companions described him as "jumpy" and "sensitive." They reported that he was increasingly difficult to get along with.

As the ship's tour of duty in the combat zone seemed certain to continue, it finally became necessary to evacuate him to the Zone of the Interior because of his increasing level of tension and anxiety. The resulting symptoms had gradually become continuous. They had also reached a level sufficient to interfere with his effectiveness on a fighting ship. This type of reaction to combat stress was far from infrequent during World War II and the Korean War. Unfortunately, not too much could be done very often in the line of effective psychotherapy while the stressful contributing conditions prevailed.

Upon his subsequent arrival in the United States, he was granted leave. Following this, he was treated by psychotherapy with adjunctive measures of rest, occupational therapy, and rehabilitation. He returned to a non-combat type of duty after three months, his symptoms having largely subsided. When last heard from, six months later, he was doing very well.

This is an example of a severe Anxiety-Tension State in which the physiologic components of this seaman's T.R.C. (Total Response to Crisis) were developed over and beyond any useful defensive requirements. Beyond this point they had become handicapping and were a net loss.

3. Varying Individual Reactions and Tolerances to Stress

This case also helps to illustrate for us varying reactions to stress that people display, and their different degrees of tolerance. The same situation that will cause a marked emotional response in one person may leave another relatively unaffected [Ch.14:VIIA2].

Presumably everyone on board this particular ship had similar external and situational wartime stimuli, from an objective standpoint. Responses, however, varied markedly from person to person, as did the individual tolerance of stress. There are important individual reasons for this. The author's military service afforded an excellent opportunity for him to observe at first hand the consequences of combat and operational stress and the individually-variable responses.

As we shall see in *Chapter 14, The Neuroses Following Trauma,* any stressful situation or environmental trauma may have widely-varying but hidden (unconscious) meanings and significance for different people. This helps us to account for the wide variation in response to what otherwise may seem to the casual external observer to be the same stress. We shall also include some further discussion and illustrations of Combat Reactions in the chapter referred to.

Anxiety-Tension States may be contributed to by all kinds of stressful situations. Several more of these tension-producing situations will be considered later. In the following instance a young physician developed an Anxiety-Tension State during an emotionally-traumatic military assignment.

---

* These findings illustrate our *Concept of Physiologic Momentum,* as noted under Diagnosis.

Case 21

Anxiety-Tension State (A.T.S.) in an Air Surgeon

A 25-year-old physician was serving out his military duty in the Air Force. Following a brief tour of hospital duty he was assigned to a busy Air Force Base. Here the air traffic was particularly heavy. The young doctor found himself assigned to the emergency crew at the airfield.

This proved to be a very trying experience for him. During his period of service the field was averaging more than one major crash weekly. He was on the ambulance and had the first medical contact with many critically-injured or dead airmen. He became increasingly anxious, worried, and nervous. He developed doubts as to his professional adequacy, competence, and experience. He felt that more was expected of him than he could possibly deliver. He was very troubled by his feelings of helplessness. At times he had trouble with insomnia and anorexia. He remained tense and apprehensive throughout this assignment, although he continued to carry on his work.

After a year his assignment was changed. This was a considerable relief to him. Gradually his state of tension subsided and after several months he was again fine. Note the lag prior to relief. He had suffered a moderate Anxiety-Tension State in the presence of prominent situational factors. When the latter were removed, his Anxiety Reaction had gradually subsided. This relationship to situational factors, while prominent, should not make us forget factors of individual susceptibility, and dynamics.

The reaction in the above case is not entirely dissimilar to that which many young doctors experience early in their professional careers. Some go through the "ambulance" or "emergency room" "jitters". Part of this discomfort is contributed to by a lack of prior experience and by the resulting self-doubt. At times the young doctor feels caught in a position in which he really can do little more than first-aid, at the same time feeling that his patients and people in general seem to him to expect so very much more.

C. NOTE ON PSYCHODYNAMICS

1. Complexity of Reaction Increases

Let us consider at this point another example, which approaches still more closely the clinical picture of Anxiety Neurosis. Herein we see some contributions which were made to the patient's difficulties by his character defenses. Other contributions stemmed from the threat of a return to awareness (through derepression) of his earlier rejected and disowned hostile impulses. As noted earlier [Ch.1:IIE2] anger can serve as an *anxiety-equivalent*. These impulses had originally been so intolerable to the patient that banishment from all conscious awareness (repression) had resulted.

Case 22

A.T.S. in Which Dynamics Become More Complex

A 32-year-old management trainee sought treatment because of recent increasing uneasiness when he came into close working relationships with people. He noted intermittent palpitation, occasional headaches, and finger tremors. He described periods when his level of anxiety, uneasiness, and apprehension increased to where it interfered substantially with his efficiency and his work productivity. These difficulties had become more marked following what he believed to be the preferential treatment which had been given to a fellow trainee.

This patient was an extremely courteous and almost subservient person. He had a pathologic overconcern for agreement with the opinions of others. He had a great need to please. These traits had been used by him to great advantage up to a certain point in his government career, but at great cost to himself. These character defenses had developed in the service of attempted further control of hostile-aggressive urges which he had consciously denied.

Much repressed (unconscious) hostility was present. This was a threat to him in close relationships with others, and this was illustrated repeatedly during the course of an analysis. The situational occurrence had assumed greatly increased significance for him by virtue of its having remobilized conflicts from similar antecedent situations of early life. These had taken place in the constellation of his family relationships in childhood.

As he gained increased insight into this segment of his difficulties, his anxiety and tension became less and his headaches decreased. Over a period of some months of treatment, he gradually became able to recognize and to accept the existence of aggressive and hostile impulses within himself. He also became able to deal with them more constructively. His character defenses leveled off as the need for them decreased.

2. Precept of Inverse Anxiety-Symptom Ratio

Neurotic patients generally experience some amount of overt anxiety. This varies greatly in amount. In some instances in which neurotic symptoms (as defenses against anxiety) are well developed and fixed, their defensive intent is well served and very little anxiety may be subjectively experienced. When the dynamism, symptom, neurotic reaction, or character defense operates sufficiently "successfully", little anxiety is experienced. *The amount of anxiety which is experienced thus tends to vary inversely with the "success" of the symptom.* This is the major precept of Inverse Anxiety-Symptom Ratio [Ch.13:VIIIE4].

In the early phase of an emotional illness the anxiety may well be more intermittently experienced or transient, but when the conflict responsible is not resolved or handled through one of the many psychologic mechanisms, it can become experienced as "chronic". Thus the anxiety may come to be more constantly present so that it truly becomes a state of emotional "dis-ease". Psychopathology has become established.

3. Pathologic Patterns of Emotional Reaction Neuroses

Emotional dis-ease is a state which is inimical to well-being and comfort. It is not surprising, therefore, that the individual consciously tries hard to escape from anxiety. All manner of unconscious methods are also employed. These important attempted methods of resolution of conflict and allaying of anxiety can eventually result in various neurotic symptoms.

Similar symptoms are likely to be found to operate together with some frequency. These together constitute pathologic patterns of emotional reaction. The more constant and typical of these patterns of reaction constitute the other varied types of neurotic reactions which will be considered in subsequent chapters.

4. In Conclusion

The Anxiety-Tension State is that condition in which the presence of anxiety to a pathologic degree is on a more chronic and continuing basis than is present in the Acute Anxiety Attack, although not sufficiently advanced and fixed as a psychopathologic process to be regarded as an Anxiety Neurosis. The anxiety which is experienced is ordinarily considered to be a more circumscribed kind of manifestation.

Often external situational factors play an important precipitating and perpetuating role in the A.T.S. and are more easily identified. The use of this diagnosis should further be based upon the relative severity of the process, as well as upon stressful environmental factors in the onset. When it is employed diagnostically, therefore, the physician must at times draw an arbitrary line. The more severe kinds of Anxiety-Tension States merge clinically into the more chronic and established cases of Anxiety Neurosis.

IV. ANXIETY NEUROSIS

A. INTRODUCTION AND HISTORY

1. Anxiety Recently Distinguished from Fear

The Anxiety Reactions have been until recent decades a rather poorly recognized and separated group of psychogenic emotional reactions. For centuries certainly, laymen made little distinction between the outward expressions of anxiety when these happened to be observable, and those of fear. This was also true professionally. Anxiety has only recently been distinguished from fear.

From the scientific standpoint, the physicians of earlier centuries generally did not distinguish anxiety. Seldom were the important direct and indirect manifestations of anxiety recognized as being a proper concern of medicine.

2. Early Presumption of Organic Etiology

Well into the nineteenth century the search for the etiology of the emotional and mental disorders was directed almost exclusively toward organic and physical areas. Further, any idea that their origins could be psychogenic seemed hardly worth considering. Indeed, Charcot was a major pioneer in this respect and then only in the waning years of the nineteenth century.

Classification, particularly in the realm of extramural (nonpsychotic) psychiatry, was also poorly developed. There was no established category for the Anxiety Reactions as such. Into the twentieth century, when clinical reactions accompanied by considerable anxiety were recognized as being of pathologic significance, they were often rather indiscriminately lumped together with, and labeled variously as cases of Hypochondriasis, Hysteria, Neurasthenia, or Psychasthenia. This was generally true in medical and psychiatric circles until some time after the turn of the present century.

It had actually not been until shortly before this when it was first suggested (in 1894 by Freud) that Anxiety Neurosis be detached from Neurasthenia as a distinct diagnostic entity [Ch.1:VIIC*1*]. Even so, Freud then grouped it with what he called the "actual neuroses," so designated as indicative (mistakenly) of their supposed organic (in distinction from psychogenic) basis. With increasing momentum from around 1910, the etiology of Anxiety Neurosis came to be recognized as psychogenic. By 1940 there was general professional concurrence in this regard.

3. Official Designation

As medical interest focused more and more upon the broad field of the emotional illnesses, physicians became increasingly aware that a large group of patients suffered from symptoms in which the subjective anxiety and its manifestations were rather directly expressed.

Appropriately, this group is now by official designation classified as an important type of psychoneurotic disorder, and is labeled as the Anxiety Reactions. In these reactions the most prominent clinical feature is anxiety. This is in accord with the following definition.

4. Definition

An Anxiety Neurosis is *an established and chronic reaction pattern of emotional illness. It is characterized primarily by the direct subjective experiencing of anxiety, which is the most prominent feature of the reaction. Anxiety and its effects are also expressed directly in varying degree via psychomotor, autonomic, and mental pathways. The effects and the consequences of the direct manifestations of anxiety in chronic form are also an important part of the clinical features of Anxiety Neurosis* (see *Table 8*).

Anxiety Neurosis is perhaps more appropriately grouped with the Higher Order Neuroses, and thus is included in Part Two of our study. While not at all invariably so, its manifestations, as with those of the A.A.A. and the A.T.S., are often encountered in the more educated and sophisticated groups of people. This was partly borne out in World War II experience (*see also* references in *Chapter 12, Chapter 14,* and *Table 14*), during which the direct manifestations and effects of anxiety appeared to become more prominent than did those of certain other more primitive reactions (such as Somatic Conversions, and so on). Anxiety Neurosis also is often somewhat closer dynamically and theoretically to other members of the less primitive group of neuroses. Finally, it is often more akin clinically, in its course, and in its response to therapy, to the more advanced reactions. While perhaps more equivocal in its position in Part Two than others (for example, the Depressive Reactions), it fits a little better here, and further, as a matter of convenience and preference, makes a good first type of neurotic reaction for our consideration. Part Two is so titled accordingly, to indicate the more developed and advanced—the less primitive—Higher Order Neuroses.

B. DIAGNOSIS

1. According to Most Prominent Clinical Feature

The diagnosis in Anxiety Neurosis is based primarily upon the history and upon subjective findings. The physical repercussions of anxiety and the resulting functional changes offer more possibilities for tests and for measurements than do the emotional ones which are more subjective. These findings are important, but they are secondary in importance to anxiety. They should not divert one's professional attention away from the more subjective findings. They must not be regarded as primary manifestations, and their relation to, and basis in anxiety must be borne in mind.

The diagnosis is essentially descriptive. A neurotic reaction is first identified. Next it is classified according to the most prominent clinical feature. In Anxiety Neurosis this is anxiety, together with its more direct effects and manifestations. These are present in five major areas: subjective, physiologic, mental, emotional, and psychomotor.

2. Typical Findings in Major Areas

Various terms have been used to describe the *subjective* discomfort present in Anxiety Neurosis. These include such descriptive indications of the presence of anxiety as: nervousness, uneasiness, apprehension, fear, anxious expectation, and, of course, anxiety. The direct *psychomotor* manifestations of anxiety include such findings as restlessness, tension, tremors, and startle reaction.

The direct autonomic manifestations and *physiologic* consequences of anxiety include, for example, palpitation, increased perspiration, weakness, and vasomotor changes, such as cold hands and feet. The direct *mental* manifestations and consequences of anxiety include interference with attention, memory, and concentration, and interference with mental functions and efficiency generally. The direct *emotional* manifestations and consequences of anxiety include irritability, mood changes, and impaired relationships with other people. These are outlined in *Table 8.*

3. Mixed Type of Neurotic Reactions More Common

In the established chronic and clear-cut case, the diagnosis of Anxiety Neurosis will ordinarily cause little difficulty for the clinician. For an emotional illness to be properly classified as one of the Anxiety Reactions, the major presenting clinical feature must, of course, be anxiety. Cases of neuroses often show manifestations and symptoms which may be associated with several types of neurosis. The result is sometimes a confusing overlapping of diagnostic categories. This is also true, of course, in cases of Anxiety Neurosis. There are few cases of the latter in which some evidence of neurotic manifestations ordinarily classified elsewhere is not seen. On the other hand, there are no types of neuroses in which the direct or the indirect manifestations of anxiety, or of the consequences of anxiety, are not present. They may be obvious and apparent. They may be covert and hidden. They may be transmuted and converted into a variety of neurotic defenses, or into somatic and psychophysiologic manifestations. As has been presented more graphically in *Table 7,* one may properly speak of Somatic Conversions, Physiologic Conversions, and Psychologic Conversions.

We see, therefore, that a specific type of neurotic reaction is seldom seen in "pure culture." Mixed reactions are more usual. However, if the psychoneuroses are classified according to the single most prominent clinical feature of the illness, more system and uniformity in diagnosis will result. This is a descriptive approach to classification of the neuroses. It is one which offers a number of advantages.

Accordingly, when anxiety and its direct manifestations are the prominent presenting features in an emotional illness of neurotic level, the proper classification is with the Anxiety Reactions. When these manifestations are fixed and chronic, and the psychopathologic process is well established, Anxiety Neurosis is the indicated diagnosis.

4. Encourage Free Discussion

In attempting to establish any emotional diagnosis, it is always helpful to encourage the patient to describe freely his symptoms and his problems in living. Both the history and the subjective findings are essential in these areas in arriving at a proper diagnosis. In most instances the patient when allowed to do so will present data which help to make the diagnosis evident.

The following example consists of a brief verbatim extract from an earlier therapeutic session with a certain patient who was suffering from a severe and firmly established Anxiety Neurosis. After several years he had finally sought medical help.

Case 23

Anxiety Neurosis

"I feel tense and fearful much of the time. I don't know what it is. I can't put my finger on it. I am frightened, but don't know what I fear. I keep expecting something bad to happen. I just get all nervous inside. . . . For the past week or so I don't want to get away from the house [which equated for him a refuge and safety]. I fear I might go all to pieces, maybe become hysterical."

The patient continued to discuss this aspect a little further: ". . . I can go into a store [without feeling unduly anxious] but only if my car is parked right close by the store. I fear somehow that something might happen and then I couldn't get back to my car. The farther I get from my car, or from home, the more uneasy I get.*

"The house is like a refuge to me. The farther I get from it, the more uneasy I become. I feel secure in the house. If something happens to me there, something can be done about it.†

---

* The car had become to him an extension of the house and a substitute. It was also a means of returning to what was for him a refuge and a place of safety.

† "That is, I will be taken care of." The unconscious roots of dependency which reach into his very early life are manifest here. Interestingly enough, the same security was derived from his father's house; as he said, "With father's house, it's the same. . . ." See also later *Secure Base of Operations Concept* [Ch.11:VIIA3] and *Home as a Soterial Refuge* [Ch.11:VIIA2].

"It's not like this all the time. Sometimes I can go anywhere and do anything without much trouble. At other times I seem constantly anxious and timid. This period now is like that. I can't tell when it will change, but right now, Doctor, it's just terrible. I can hardly do my work . . . .

"Sometimes I get fearful and tense when I'm talking to people and I just want to run away. I have thought I could tie it to definite things, but this isn't true. It varies, and it is unpredictable. I can't tell when it will come on. If I could just put my finger on what it is . . . .

"I act like I'm scared to death of something. I guess maybe I am. For the life of me, Doctor, I just don't know what it is. I don't want to go through life feeling nervous and tense all the time. I should have done something about it several years ago when it wasn't so bad, but I kept telling myself things would be all right. And then, of course, there were times when things would seem better. Gradually it's gotten worse. . . ."

5. Differential Diagnosis from Phobic Reaction

In the above case there are features which are also suggestive of the clinical features and the dynamics of the phobia. In the Phobic Reactions (also in earlier days sometimes referred to as Anxiety Hysteria), the differential diagnosis from Anxiety Neurosis rests on the unconscious displacement of the dreaded but hidden internal danger to a clearly- and consciously-recognized external object or situation.

One can see this route partially taken in the case under discussion. If this patient's fear of being away from home became more marked and increasingly fixed, if this became the principal clinical feature, then the above case might be classified with the agoraphobias—the morbid fear of open spaces. More will be said about phobias in *Chapters 9* and *10*. In this particular case, however, this feature did not remain fixed and was not the outstanding aspect of the illness.

6. Anxiety Hysteria

Anxiety Neurosis has been at times confused with the older, largely discarded diagnosis of Anxiety Hysteria. If it must be employed, the latter label, which was originally introduced by Freud, is more properly reserved for the Phobic Reactions [*Chapter 9*].

Anxiety Hysteria is rapidly becoming archaic as a term. Accordingly, its current usage tends to be increasingly restricted. In view of this, together with the possible confusion in terminology, it will be seldom referred to in this text. Its complete discard as a term is probably indicated.

7. Position of Anxiety Neuroses in Emotional Illnesses

The diagnosis of Anxiety Neurosis is the proper designation in those established and chronic psychopathologic reactions in which the direct expression of anxiety is the outstanding manifestation of the illness. This may be accompanied by the more direct kind of psychomotor, physiologic, mental, and emotional expressions of, and consequences of anxiety. There are also rather typical subjective indications of anxiety reported by the person concerned.

In *Table 7* a schematic presentation was offered which, in abbreviated fashion, illustrates the position of Anxiety Neurosis as an emotional illness, among the other major psychopathologic reactions. This table is also useful as a functional outline of the various neurotic reactions.

C. INCIDENCE

1. Wide Incidence Points Up Need for Trained Personnel

The incidence of the Anxiety Reactions is very wide indeed, an estimated 12–15 per cent of the clinical cases of neuroses. Anxiety Neurosis itself is common. Unquestionably many more people suffer from the restrictions and handicaps in living which result from anxiety in this chronic and established form than the relatively few among these who currently come to the attention of medical practitioners.

Of the many, many cases of Anxiety Neurosis that exist today, an even smaller percentage of them ever receive anything resembling adequate treatment. In part, this implies a need for better medical case-finding. There is a pressing need for the improved handling of referrals for psychiatric treatment. It also indicates the need for the more extensive training of physicians generally in the major field of mental and emotional health. Finally, there is a steadily increasing need for more trained psychiatrists, and for all kinds of necessary allied professional personnel.

2. Sex Differences

Are there differences between the sexes as to the incidence of anxiety and Anxiety Neurosis? This is a difficult question to answer precisely, but in general, the answer is closer to "No." There are, however, certain differences by sex in the sources of anxiety. Lunger and Page, for example, in a study of college freshmen, pointed out what they believed to be characteristic anxiety differences in the two sexes.

Girls appeared to be more anxious than boys and to have a larger number of conscious worries. Young college men seemed to be more afraid of external harm and to worry more about their adequacy. College women were more concerned about their social relationships.

3. Few Reliable Statistics

Statistics do not exist which will tell us accurately the total number of cases of Anxiety Neurosis in the United States, or in other countries. This is not surprising since the compilation of reliable statistics in this area is a most complex task, as is generally true with the neuroses and character neuroses.

This difficulty is partly due to differences in terminology, definition and usage. Another factor is the practical difficulty of having many persons with differing training draw corresponding lines in their evaluation of cases. Then, also, the problems of accurate emotional-psychologic case-finding in any systematic survey of large groups of people are indeed difficult ones. The factors involved in securing scientific accuracy in a large-scale survey of the incidence of neuroses are a statistician's nightmare.

4. Estimated Prevalence

Estimates of the numbers of cases which could be clinically cataloged as Anxiety Neurosis vary according to the authority. A rather conservative estimate which one could offer might be about one person in every 300. This would give us a total of more than 500,000 cases in the United States alone. It was noted earlier that an estimated 12–15 per cent of the clinical cases of neurosis would fall into the major category of the Anxiety Reactions. The majority of these would be cases of Anxiety Neurosis. This gives us some indication of the magnitude of this one small area in the enormous overall problem of emotional health. When one further recalls such facts as that half of our hospital beds are psychiatric (occupied by more than 700,000 patients), it is hardly any wonder that the field of emotional and mental health is to be regarded properly as our largest public health problem today. Greater medical and public understanding in the area of the neuroses will constitute a major advance in meeting this vast challenge.

In conclusion of this consideration of incidence, suffice it to say that anxiety is far from being an uncommon or unfamiliar, albeit unpleasant, experience for most of us. An increase in severity sufficient to warrant a diagnosis of Anxiety Neurosis is by no means infrequent. Most psychiatrists would also likely agree with Blau that "there are unquestionably many more anxiety states than come to the attention of psychiatrists."

D. SYMPTOMS AND CLINICAL FEATURES

1. Level of Anxiety Varies

It is not possible to list symptoms that one can invariably expect to find in Anxiety Neuroses. However, in *Table 8* an outline is offered which tabulates most of the features which are more commonly encountered. Some of these will be present in each case. Further, we can discuss briefly some of the principal emotional and physical features which tend to be more frequent. Clinically, the anxiety may occur in waves or attacks. The level of anxiety which is present may increase in frequency, duration, and severity, and it may become more or less continuous and chronic. Partial remissions may occur spontaneously or in treatment. These are unfortunately only temporary in most instances, unless they follow increased self-understanding as a consequence of therapy.

Frequently patients use the word "fear" to describe their feelings. The term "anxiety" may not be used at all. During a period of anxiety the patient may report that his subjective feelings and the physiologic changes are similar to those which he has commonly associated with fear.

The more frequent symptoms of Anxiety Neurosis include weakness, easy fatigability, palpitation, nausea, dyspnea, physical tension, anxiety, apprehension, and various other emotional feelings (see *Table 8*). Fears of death or of imagined, unknown but frightening events are not infrequent. These may be strong enough to produce panic, or they may seem overwhelming. Anger may serve as an *Anxiety-Equivalent* [Ch.3:IIIC*1*].

2. *Exactly Appropriate for Individual Concerned; Subjective Manifestations*

The subjective painful feelings reported in cases of Anxiety Neurosis are always out of proportion to any seemingly rational cause. The feelings thus *appear* irrational, from any usual method of observation. When it becomes possible during the course of treatment, however, to uncover the real hidden bases for the feelings, one always finds that they are indeed fully and exactly appropriate for the individual concerned. Thus, the irrationality of the anxious feelings is more apparent than real. This is in accord with our Earlier Advanced Principle of the Individual Appropriateness of Response [Ch.1:IIC*2*;Ch.3:IB*2*].

As noted earlier the clinical manifestations of Anxiety Neurosis may be considered under five major headings: the psychomotor, mental, physiologic, emotional, and subjective. Included as the major subjective indications of anxiety as reported by the patient are nervousness, apprehension, uneasiness, fear, and anxiety. Needless to say, the other major manifestations of Anxiety Neurosis also have their important subjective aspects and can be so reported by the patient.

3. *Emotional Features*

The physiologic response to fear, threat, or danger is subject to wide individual variation. For instance, some persons respond to crisis or to dangerous situations and the attendant fear and tension with palpitation and increased perspiration, while others complain of urgency or frequency of urination. Some have diarrhea while others have the reverse, constipation. Many other possibilities and combinations exact. The same types of response and of variation in response are found in relation to anxiety.

The patient may describe his emotional feelings as those of anxiety, worry, nervousness, irritability, depressed spirits, vague feelings of uneasiness, apprehension, or dread. He will frequently state that he feels or dreads that something terrible will happen. Usually he cannot really explain what this is. Patients with Anxiety Neurosis may, of course, also suffer Acute Anxiety Attacks, which have been described earlier.

Dreams are likely to reflect the underlying increased substratum of Emotional Conflict. Dream content may be weird, frightening, disturbed, and/or marked by color in objects or sequences. Nightmares may occur.

The following two cases illustrate some of the characteristic clinical findings in Anxiety Neurosis.

Case 24

Anxiety Neurosis in a Veteran, Antedating Military Service

A 31-year-old Army reserve officer was seen in consultation several months after a tour of combat duty in Korea. He had subsequently been released from active military service. He complained of irritability, tension, nervousness, and trouble with sleeping. He was having difficulty in concentration at work, and had some marital problems. In describing how he felt, he said: "There is something I am afraid of, and I don't know what it is. It's like a fear of something, but I can't name it. . . ."

The long course—". . . I've had this trouble for many years . . ."—with irregular exacerbations, identified the presence of chronic pathologic anxiety of a sufficient degree and of sufficient interference with his living to warrant a diagnosis of Anxiety Neurosis.

In cases of preexisting Anxiety Reactions (as is frequently encountered in other neuroses), situations of stress will very likely exacerbate the illness. This officer's combat experience was not solely responsible for his neurosis. The neurosis had antedated his combat duty. The external stress of combat, however, had served to increase greatly the number and variety of clinical manifestations as well as their level of severity. This man improved considerably under treatment.

Case 25

Anxiety Neurosis Underwent Exacerbation Following Visit Home

A 34-year-old housewife began psychiatric treatment shortly after a visit to her home in the midwest. The visit took place after several years of minimal contact with her family. Anxious manifestations markedly increased when emotional ties and stresses believed long inoperative became quickly reactivated.

In her words, this was partly described as follows: "I'm terribly tense and fearful. I've always been like this, but now it's much worse, I feel like something bad is about to happen. I don't know what it is, and I feel afraid."

In both this and the preceding case, the patient talked about fear. The term "anxiety" was not used. Their past experiences of fear were most akin to what was felt currently and to what was most subjectively familiar to them. The choice of the word "fear" was a logical consequence. Typically, in each case there was also the absence of a specific known cause. Neither patient had a conscious understanding of his feelings. He could not explain their degree or their strength.

The patient may be chronically tense. He may at times be a somewhat overconscientious person, feeling that he must live up to a set of self-imposed standards (which are unrealistically high from the standpoint of an independent observer) and which he is unable to meet. A certain amount of masochism (*Masochism: the derivation of satisfaction (unconsciously) from the experiencing of physical or psychologic pain or self-sacrifice*) is not infrequently present, although it may be far from apparent.

4. Psychomotor Features

The psychomotor features include agitation, restlessness, tics, and tremors which can vary widely in extent. Physical tensions may be increased, sometimes greatly. This may be reflected in increased tendon reflexes and in a startle reaction to sudden unexpected noises or movements.

Tension and tremors can interfere with finely coordinated movements, finger dexterity, learned skills, and special activities. Activities may be limited or modified and behavior influenced.

5. Mental Features

The mental manifestations of Anxiety Neurosis include all the changes which can take place in mental function. Attention and concentrating abilities are likely to be impaired. A likely direct correlation will be found to the level of anxiety present. The facility of memory may be affected.

Judgment may suffer. The outlook may become less optimistic. Future planning may decrease in amount and constructivity. There is likely to be some general interference with the efficiency of mental functioning.

6. Physiologic Features

The physiologic changes of Anxiety Neurosis are to be found in the altered functions of every organ and system. Cardiovascular functional symptoms are frequent, with palpitation and precordial pain or pressure not uncommon. There may be increased perspiration. Vasomotor changes such as cold hands or cold feet, various flushes, blushing or pallor, and so on are encountered. Weakness, fatigue, and fatigability occur with some frequency. Respiratory symptoms include chest oppression, choking sensations, dyspnea, and difficult breathing. Vertigo is not uncommon.

Disturbances of the special senses may transpire, such as tinnitus, visual blurring, numbness and tingling, balance problems, and so on. These are often transient and recurrent in nature. Sexual function is likely to be disturbed. Potency is more likely to be diminished. Additional functional symptoms, too numerous to list specifically, are to be encountered. These can reflect changes of the more temporary variety (as opposed to the more fixed variety of Physiologic Conversions) in every system of the body, especially the gastrointestinal (nausea, poor appetite, vomiting, diarrhea), genitourinary (urgency, frequency), musculoskeletal, nervous, reproductive and endocrine systems. In the absence of relief or remission these can tend to become more fixed, and eventually irreversible (the Functional-Structural Progression).

These interesting manifestations which are frequently encountered in cases of Anxiety Neurosis are summarized in outline form below (*Table 8*). Compare and contrast these features with those outlined later for the Combat Reactions.

Table 8

Anxiety Neurosis and Its Clinical Manifestations

An Anxiety Neurosis is "an established and chronic psychopathologic reaction", in which the outstanding clinical manifestation of the illness is the direct expression of anxiety, together with various ones of the possible more direct consequences or effects of anxiety. These are summarized below in outline form:

(*Table continued on next page*)

Table 8—Anxiety Neurosis and its Clinical Manifestations—Cont.

A. *Psychomotor:*
1. Restlessness.
2. Physical tension; tendon reflexes may be increased.
3. Tremors (varying in extent from very fine tremors to gross shaking); tics.
4. Startle reaction.
5. Interference with coordination of actions and movements.
6. Certain behavioral changes, and interference with sleep.

B. *Mental:*
1. Impaired attention.
2. Poor concentration
3. Interference with, or impairment of memory.
4. Interference with judgment.
5. Changes in activity, outlook, and future planning.
6. Interference generally with the efficiency and effectiveness of mental functioning.

C. *Physiologic:*
1. Palpitation, precordial pressure or pain, faintness, increased pulse rate and pulse pressure, and elevated blood pressure.
2. Increased perspiration.
3. Weakness and fatigability.
4. Vasomotor changes, such as cold hands or feet, flushing, blushing, or pallor. Vertigo not infrequent. Numbness and tingling, especially of extremities.
5. Dyspnea, chest oppression, or pain.
6. Headaches; blurring of vision, tinnitus.
7. Various interferences with sexual function.
8. Other functional changes of the more limited and temporary variety take place in the various systems: gastrointestinal, genitourinary, reproductive, endocrine, cardiovascular, or neuromuscular. (If these become sufficiently "fixed" or more chronically established, they are then to be regarded as Physiologic Conversions.)

D. *Emotional:*
1. Irritability.
2. Mood changes, depression, moroseness, loss of optimism.
3. Impaired relationships with friends and family.
4. Impaired capacity for love, affection, and sexual interest.
5. Dreams often reflect underlying increased emotional conflict.

E. *Additional Subjective Indications of Anxiety:*
1. Nervousness.
2. Apprehension.
3. Uneasiness and fear.
4. Anxiety.

The above manifestations of Anxiety Neurosis are, of course, highly variable both as to their presence, and to the resulting amount of discomfort and handicap. Some of them in particular are, of course, partly or even entirely subjective in nature.

According to their collective presence in varying degree over a given period, one may speak of a "level of anxiety." Anxiety and its more direct manifestations vary considerably in level from patient to patient, and from one period of time to another.

7. Additional Clinical Features of Interest

A. HEADACHES.—Although physical features are apt to be less prominent than in certain other types of neuroses, varied physical symptoms as noted are likely to be reported by many patients. Headaches are frequent. Their origin is emotional. Types of anxiety-emotional headache are rather typically characterized by: (1) pressure-like pain in the occipital region of the back of the head; (2) the band-like feeling, or "crown of thorns," around the head; (3) pressure or the sensation of weight pressing down on the top of the head; or (4) pressure-pain in the forehead, temples, and sometimes behind the eyes.

Migraine-like headaches are sometimes present, with various degrees of unilateral throbbing, pain, nausea, vomiting, scotomata, accompanied perhaps by the desire to be in a dark, quiet room. The migrainous headaches are precipitated by emotional tension, and these may appear to have an hereditary background or an allergic diathesis. Other symptoms are listed in *Table 8.*

B. ANXIETY, APPETITE, UNDERWEIGHT AND OBESITY.—Anxiety is commonly observed to be a destroyer of appetite. Over a period of time weight-loss not infrequently results. As a consequence, it is not surprising that the mental image most commonly held of the anxious person is that of a rather undernourished, thin, and worried-appearing individual. This also applies to the anxious child. Anxiety and emotional conflict can lead to what is later [Ch.5:IXA3] termed a *psychic distaste.* Thus an emotional and figurative distaste for a person, situation, job, and so on can come to be more literally experienced as a distaste for, and rejection of food. This is the *Concept of Psychic Distaste.*

Less well recognized and often less obvious is the other side of the picture. A frequent unconscious approach to the relief of anxiety is through eating. Seeking relief via this route, in accord with our Concept of Defensive Overreaction, results in overeating. This in turn leads to obesity. This sequence is particularly likely to occur in the case of persons with considerable oral dependency. Eating is a means of securing comfort, with roots stretching back into early infancy.

This can persist or recur unconsciously in adult life. Overeating is a frequent consequence of anxiety [Ch.11:VIIB1].

The strength of this anxious need to eat is reflected in many severe cases of refractory obesity. The best conscious efforts of both physician and patient in dietary control and weight reduction may well be frustrated when pitted against this intangible and often unrecognized, but most powerful opposition.

Other associated gastrointestinal symptoms may cover a wide range. In addition to anorexia or increased hunger, they may include nausea, bloating, "heartburn," bad taste, epigastric pressure or pain, belching, diarrhea, cramps, and vomiting.

C. ANXIETY AND INSOMNIA.—Some disturbance of sleeping is also frequent. Some of the important interrelationships of anxiety with sleep were covered in *Chapter 1,* and will be referred to again later.

D. ANXIETY AND SEXUAL RELATIONS.—As noted, some impairment in sexual function may be reported. In general, fully satisfactory sexual relations are not possible for the person with an Anxiety Neurosis. There is often some degree of correlation possible between the relative severity of the psychopathology and the relative interference with patients' ability to secure normal sexual gratification. This applies in many clinical cases of neurosis, regardless of the diagnosis.

As we shall study further [Ch.5:VB9;Ch.14:VB3], sexual maladjustment can result as the consequence of emotional problems and illness, as well as contribute to such difficulties. This follows our Concept of Effect Over Cause in Sexual Maladjustment.

E. W. B. CANNON; EXPERIMENTAL CONFLICT AND NEUROSIS; CONCEPT OF EMOTIONAL RECAPITULATION.—Walter B. Cannon (1871–1945), a pioneering American Physiologist [Ch.14:IIB3], studied various physiologic changes in response to emotional stimuli. He had learned early that anxiety, rage, fear, or other emotional changes brought about total cessation of all stomach movements.

In 1915 he published his classic book *Bodily Changes in Pain, Hunger, Fear and Rage.* Born in Wisconsin, near Fort Crawford where Beaumont had earlied worked, his important studies underlined and advanced the much earlier ones of Beaumont. The work of Cannon gave added scientific backing to our knowledge of the major effects of emotions upon all phases of physiology. He also became interested in the "emergency mechanisms" which take place as the physiologic concomitants of emotion.

He was further able to demonstrate certain blood changes which took place as part of the emergency physiologic mobilization in emotional states. These include certain changes which can at times be clearly demonstrated in laboratory studies; such as increased blood sugar level and oxygen content, and diminished clotting time.

Many other changes in the various body functions and in the organ systems are actually or theoretically demonstrable. It is possible to experimentally produce certain emotional states in the laboratory, as did Cannon. Experimental conflict and certain neurotic reactions can thus be elicited and studied. The further study of these physiologic changes which occur with emotions, offers for us a continuing broad research challenge. *See also* the other comments concerning the Total Response to Crisis (the T.R.C.) and the Total Response to Trauma (T.R.T.) (in *Chapter 1* and in *Chapters 12* and *14*), of which these physiologic components are a most important segment. Other important components of the Total Individual Response to Crisis or to Trauma include the emotional, the intellectual, the mental, and the psychologic.

At times symptoms which were originally present on an organic basis, recur later or continue in whole or in part, on an emotional basis. This is an interesting phenomenon. A number of intrapsychic processes may be involved, including: (1) conditioning, (2) auto-suggestion, (3) conversion, and (4) the provision of a more convenient, familiar, and thus easily-adopted (pre-existing) symptom pattern. This intriguing clinical sequence is illustrated in the following instance of *Emotional Recapitulation.*

A thirty-eight-year-old woman in long-term intensive therapy for an Anxiety Neurosis, developed a bona fide genitourinary infection, marked by urgency, frequency, polyuria, and dysuria. The infection was cleared up promptly through medical treatment. The symptoms disappeared, only to recure after several weeks, except for the dysuria. No infection was present on this occasion, however. These symptoms persisted in recurring on an emotional basis upon several occasions for more than two years. They gradually disappeared as the underlying tension, anxiety, and the basic conflicts of her neurosis were worked out and subsided.

8. In Conclusion

The Anxiety Neurosis is an established neurotic reaction characterized by the more or less chronic presence of the painful apprehensive feelings of anxiety. The patient may describe his subjective feelings variously as fear, dread, anxiety, panic, nervousness, apprehension, or uneasiness. He feels threatened, in danger, or imperiled. To the patient himself, as well as to the examining physician, the real source or object of danger is obscure.

The symptoms of Anxiety Neurosis include the more direct psychomotor, autonomic, emotional, and mental consequences and effects of anxiety. Included among these are at least all those physiologic and physical changes which, for the individual concerned, would accompany his frightened reaction to a situation of external danger.

E. DYNAMICS AND PATHOGENESIS

1. Defenses Against Anxiety Poorly Organized and Ineffective

Much of the data relative to the pathogenesis of anxiety has been covered in *Chapter 1.* Most of these observations also apply to the pathogenesis and to the psychopathologic basis of Anxiety Neurosis. This section accordingly will be confined to offering some supplementary data.

As noted earlier, in Anxiety Neurosis the anxiety which is present is more manifest and less concealed than that contributing to other types of emotional reactions. The defenses against it are poorly organized and not very effective. The underlying unconscious conflicts are not transmuted and converted in their expression into the various other neurotic groups of psychogenic symptoms. In subsequent chapters we will discuss how this takes place in these other types of neurotic reactions. The physiologic disturbances which are present in Anxiety Neurosis are secondary to anxiety and are manifestations of it. Anxiety as such, and its more direct effects and consequences, are the prominent features. In Anxiety Neurosis the defense mechanisms that are operative in the development of symptoms (and compromise formations) in the Conversion Reactions, Phobic Reactions, Depressive Reactions, and in other types of neuroses are either absent or are relatively more minor and are overshadowed.

In other words, in Anxiety Neurosis the symbolic external expressions of the unconscious conflicts are more direct. They are less channeled into the more devious and the more complex pathways of expression which are to be seen in other types of neurosis. Anxiety is *the* prominent feature.

Because of its overt expression, and because there is the absence of a known cause to account for it, the anxiety in Anxiety Neurosis is often referred to as "free-floating anxiety." The term "neurotic anxiety" has sometimes also been used to emphasize the presence of an anxious response which is out of proportion to any known cause. "Constructive anxiety" [Ch.3:IVE6], as assessed from its ultimate results and effects, can still be present in instances of Anxiety Neurosis.

2. Symptoms Unconscious Compromises

The close dynamic relationship with other kinds of neuroses is sometimes clinically demonstrated. On occasion a severe Anxiety Reaction will be replaced by another type of neurotic reaction. This process may also be reversed. The latter is illustrated in *Case 133* in *Chapter 13,* when the removal of the dissociated Fugue State under Pentothal narcosis was followed by the onset of intense anxiety. In such instances one can sometimes sense the intense level of anxiety which has brought on repression and symptom formation. It is hardly surprising that the unconscious conversion or transmutation of the responsible conflict, or even the onset of a major Dissociative Reaction, may be a "welcome" relief.

The symptoms thus formed are defenses against anxiety. The threat of derepression and consequent anxiety is lessened through the symptom formations and character defenses in the neurotic reaction. These lessen internal pressures by allowing the disguised and distorted (that is, symbolic) outward expression of elements of the unconscious conflict. Symptoms often represent the outward but concealed expression of what we might refer to as *unconscious compromises,* between the consciously-disowned drives and the elements seeking their control and containment. This concept will be illustrated subsequently in many case examples. The understanding of these comments and of the concept of symptoms as representing unconscious compromises is a requisite to understanding the initiation of psychopathology.

3. Symbolism

Symptoms of Anxiety Neurosis at times have important symbolic meanings. For example, these people may suffer feelings of constriction in various parts of the body, not infrequently in the chest or head. These can indicate or equate symbolically various constrictions which are felt on a deeper level of consciousness to be coming from some aspect of their living.

4. Common Anxiety-Producing Events of Early Life

In accord with the theory of Antecedent Conflicts which we will discuss shortly, the anxiety-producing events of early life have a more important position in emotional health than that which the traumatic events of a seemingly similar level of stress in later life might have. Levy listed six situations that precipitated anxiety reactions in children as: (1) accidents and operations, (2) frights, (3) separations, (4) sudden privations, (5) births of siblings, and (6) sudden environmental changes. This author would specifically mention in addition the important potential for anxiety, for laying potential foundations for difficulty, and for the possible precipitation of Anxiety Reactions in such emotionally traumatic events as: (1) the death of a parent, (2) moving to a new house and neighborhood, (3) emotionally traumatic weaning or bowel-habit training, and perhaps (4) changes of one's school. *See* earlier reference in regard to the S.E.H.C. [Ch.1:IVB9], which each of these also represents, also *Table 2*.

5. Important Conflicts of Adulthood

Emotional conflicts are legion. They can involve any area of living experience. One's wishes or desires can readily enough come into conflict with personal standards, and/or with the rules and mores of one's social and cultural milieu.

Among the important areas and sources of adult emotional conflict, and S.E.H.A. include: (1) hostility, (2) sexual desires, (3) dependent needs; (4) needs for self-approval, performance, and adequacy, and (5) questions of behavior, social approval, and "measuring-up". Some related areas might include: (1) guilt, (2) aggressiveness, (3) love and closeness, (4) warmth and tenderness, (5) sexual identity, and (6) loneliness. The S.E.H.A. Concept was noted earlier [Ch.1:IVB*3*,IVC*11*].

6. Anxiety Not Necessarily Destructive; Concept of Constructive Anxiety

In this type of discussion the reader should not lose track of the comments in *Chapter 1,* on the function of anxiety. Anxiety need not necessarily be regarded as inevitably pathologic or destructive. Anxiety can be viewed as an indication of change in the homeostatic state of the personality. This change may be pathologic, regressive, and destructive, or it can be constructive. Anxiety can have its positive values. It is the basis of much creative effort, for it is often in response to his anxieties that man looks to the future and seeks to improve things. This may be part of his efforts to make his life more secure, less dangerous, and less anxious.

The drives which impel man to seek security are very compelling ones. Anxiety is the force that moves men to sublimate the natural unfettered expression of their basic desires, which seem so full of dangerous possible consequences, retaliation, or punishment. From this point of view anxiety may be regarded as laying the basis for many socially constructive and civilizing efforts.

We might term this aspect and type of anxiety as Constructive Anxiety because of its ultimately beneficial results and constructive contributions. These are both individual and cultural.

7. *Anxiety Neurosis, Fear, and Phobias*

The psychopathologic process in the Phobic Reactions differs from that of Anxiety Neurosis in that it is more complex. It goes an important step further. In the Phobias the external object of fear or dread appears to be definite enough. It is actually, however, a substitute for the real inner hidden threat or danger. In the dynamics of the phobia, the inner feelings of threat have been *displaced* to an external substitute. This is an important additional step in the psychodynamic processes which are already operative in Anxiety Neurosis. It becomes a further reinforcement, unconsciously secured, to the unwitting endeavor at concealment and obscuration of the conflictual material. This process will be covered in the chapter on the *Phobic Reactions* [*Chapter 10*].

We must also, of course, sometimes differentiate Anxiety Neurosis as a chronic psychopathologic condition, from the more transient manifestations of fear which are normally experienced in response to external danger [*Chapter 10*]. The level of fear which is stimulated may be very severe. In the neurotic situation the internal stimuli for fear may also be very severe. However, herein they are rather chronically present. The anxiety is the outward and subjective manifestation of repressed conflicts and of threatened derepression.

8. *Signal That Derepression Threatens*

On the surface the emotional distress of the Anxiety Reactions appears inappropriate and out of proportion to any possible apparent stimulus. However, the reaction is *exactly appropriate* for the hidden and unseen source of danger. This is a psychologic source and an internal one [Ch.13:VIID7].

The danger stems from intrapsychic conflicts. It is not readily available to observation or to conscious awareness. Indeed, awareness is strongly resisted, and ordinarily is intolerable. Otherwise the original repression from conscious awareness would not have occurred. The anxiety may be regarded as a danger signal that the disowned and repressed material threatens to erupt into conscious awareness.

V. THE THEORY OF ANTECEDENT CONFLICTS

A. CHILDHOOD EVENTS PROTOTYPES FOR LATER LIFE

In the psychogenesis of Anxiety Neurosis as well as in that of other types of neurotic reactions, the events of early childhood have set up infantile prototypes. These become important antecedents for later emotional reactions and difficulties. One may look at this as a process of "sensitization", or perhaps as one of emotional "conditioning". This leads us to an important concept which has proven quite useful to the author personally and in teaching and for which the name The Theory of Antecedent Conflicts has been suggested. It has almost continual applications in psychiatry.

Thus earlier antecedent patterns of emotional reaction are subsequently more easily reactivated by renewed stress, than are ones which are less familiar, or ones which represent completely new kinds of responses. This is in accord with the Theory of Antecedent Conflicts [Ch.8:VII]. According to this theory, every adult emotional conflict has its earlier antecedent. The memories for any connection between the later conflict and its important antecedent are very likely lost to conscious recollection. Childhood antecedents are of course most important. However, antecedents from any age can have an important influence upon the subsequent emotional response, its direction, and its amount.

B. EARLY PATTERNS OF RESPONSE REACTIVATED

In line with the Theory of Antecedent Conflicts, the vicissitudes of the earlier stressful situation in childhood have a tremendous influence upon the relative susceptibility of the individual to the stressful situations which he encounters in adult life. In other words, the individual effect of an emotionally disturbing event in adult life may be greatly multiplied through the conditioning or sensitization effects of the related antecedent conflicts of earlier life.

The early conflicts thus come to serve actually or symbolically as analogous prototypes. In effect, these conflicts and the earlier responses to them become reactivated by the later adult stress, trauma, or conflicts.

C. WIDEST APPLICATIONS

What happens in the vital early prototype conflict also has a tremendous influence upon the kinds of clinical features which may later appear. The clinical course of an emotional disturbance will vary accordingly.

The relative adult vulnerability to stress, and the variable effectiveness of the Total Individual Reaction to Crisis, or to Trauma, will also reflect in large measure the emotional vicissitudes of early life and the significant interpersonal relationships. There are many significant influences upon all aspects of sickness and health. The Theory of Antecedent Conflicts has wide applications indeed. These concepts will be further amplified and referred to in subsequent chapters. (*see* later references, including *Chapter 14*).

VI. THE CONSTRICTIVE EFFECTS OF ANXIETY; CONSTRICTIVE SPIRAL CONCEPT

Anxiety is a highly uncomfortable subjective experience which we consciously as well as unconsciously inevitably seek to ameliorate, to avoid, or to resolve. No one welcomes the painful experience of anxiety. It is not surprising that the endeavors of some individuals to deal with or to escape from their anxiety can result in an increasingly constrictive effect upon their living. Sometimes a vicious circle may become established.

For example, a person may experience an Acute Anxiety Attack in a subway. Associating the acute discomfort with the subway, he may subsequently try to avoid subways as a way of preventing a repetition. Perhaps he continues such a policy of avoidance. Subsequent attacks of anxiety may occur, as is only too likely. Other related sites may come to be similarly avoided. The gradual result can be a progressive restriction of his activities, as more and more places, experiences, or situations are avoided in his continued but futile efforts to escape his anxiety.

This type of response with a resulting progressive constriction of living is not uncommon. It may progress very slowly and gradually, or its tempo can become rapid. The vicious circle may begin when the avoidance of the situation (which is feared will result in a repetition of the dreaded anxiety) in turn results in new conflicts. We might refer to this vicious cycle or circular sequence in living as the Constrictive Spiral of Anxiety. It is related to the earlier principle regarding the Circular Generation of Fear [Ch.3:IIA2].

As mentioned previously there are implications in this kind of sequence of events for the development of Phobic Reactions. The object of the phobia can develop in relation to the sensory cues which happen to be present at the time of an early severe attack of anxiety. This interesting and important aspect of the psychodynamics in the Phobias will be covered further in *Chapters 9* and *10*. The Constrictive Spiral Concept is basic to the development of the *Spatiophobia* [Ch.10:IIIA*1*], marked by progressive spatial restriction.

The following instance illustrates what we might term *secondary conflict*. This can follow the attempted avoidance of anxiety and produce added anxiety.

Case 26

Tendency Toward a Vicious Circle

A 45-year-old business man suffered from a severe chronic Anxiety Neurosis, with phobic components. He avoided, amongst other things, small boats, crowds, arguments, and hospitals. This was the gradual constrictive result of a six-year, determined, but futile campaign to avoid his dreaded anxiety. The potential was present for his developing an increasingly restrictive Spatiophobia.

One day his aged father was critically injured in an automobile accident and was rushed to a local hospital. The patient was a most conscientious and filially loyal person. He was under strong personal (and family) pressure to visit his injured father.

His fear of an anxiety attack, associated in the past with hospitals, prevented him from making the visit. The resulting conflict was serious. The pressure during six weeks of hospitalization contributed in no small measure to raising the level of his already considerable amount of tension and anxiety. This was another contribution to a vicious circle, in which more anxiety led to more conflict, which in turn led to more anxiety. This illustrates the *Conflict-Anxiety-Avoidance Circle*.

VII. THE RECIPROCAL INFLUENCES OF ANXIETY AND PAIN

The relative level of anxiety has important effects upon the subjective appreciation of pain. Pain can produce or increase anxiety. In turn, when the level of anxiety is high, the threshold to the perception of pain may be lowered. The anxious individual has less tolerance to pain. Its effects are apt to be more devastating. Thus pain and anxiety tend to have a reciprocal influence upon each other. These principles contribute to a concept which we might label the Reciprocal Influences of Anxiety and Pain.

Some of these factors enter into the anxious patient's anticipation of pain. This may be seen, for example, when a tooth extraction or a minor surgical precedure is in the offing. The anticipation of pain may itself be more painful psychologically than the actual (physical) pain of the prospective procedure.

Certain situations which involve a number of people offer the opportunity to make some interesting comparisons as to their individual emotional responses. For example, consider a line of people awaiting some procedure, such as a routine X-ray or vaccination. Some obviously suffer in anticipation. An occasional person may faint. The important determining factors lie in the conscious and unconscious significance of the procedure to each person. The physical part of the discomfort or pain is theoretically the same to each individual. The emotional significance shows wide variations.

The response to a second similar threatening or painful procedure or to repeated similar episodes can have additional aspects. An emotional kind of conditioning may take place. There may be increased sensitization, *or* desensitization, as the result. In line with our theory, the antecedent events can be very significant in determining one's response in a given situation.

VIII. GENERAL COMMENTS ON TREATMENT

A. RESPONSE TO THERAPY

In view of the more direct expression of anxiety and its consequences in the Anxiety Reactions, one might suppose that their treatment would be reasonably easy. Such a view might receive added support by contrasting this aspect of the Anxiety Reactions with other types of neuroses. In many of the latter, the unconscious conflicts from which anxiety threatens to arise come to be externally expressed, but often in most hidden and symbolic ways.*

It may be true in certain cases, that Anxiety Reactions are easier to treat. However, such is not necessarily the case. The direct expression of

---

* In a discussion of a series of rather rare causes of death—leukemia, unusual cancer, rare cerebrocardiovascular manifestations, and so on—among a group of psychiatrists not long ago, a colleague made some interesting speculations: Could the personal analyses of these psychiatrists have resulted in driving remnants of unresolved conflict deeply "underground," from whence they sought symbolic expression in these rarer kinds of most devious, deepseated, and hidden pathways of pathologic somatic expression?

the anxiety does not necessarily make easier or quicker the task of gaining a thorough understanding of its pathogenesis. At times, it may even be more baffling and more frustrating to both patient and therapist. It is generally correct, however, that the Anxiety Reactions as a group are among those emotional illnesses which are more responsive to psychotherapy. Let us proceed at this point to some general principles of management.

B. MAKE POSITIVE DIAGNOSIS

In the diagnostic approach to the patient with Anxiety Neurosis the physician must use due caution and careful judgment in his evaluation of the facts at hand. While he must satisfy himself as to the absence of organic disease, it is very important that he avoid focusing the patient's attention unduly on physical symptoms. It is possible and desirable to make a positive diagnosis of emotional illness. A diagnosis indicating emotionally-based symptons is best not reached merely by exclusion.

The development of skill and judgment in this area is important for the physician's own satisfaction. It is also important in developing his feelings of security and competence regarding the making of diagnoses in cases of emotional illness.

It is, of course, more difficult for the less experienced practitioner to make a diagnosis in this fashion. His own security and a relative lack of familiarity with emotional processes are involved. However, as the physician develops his ability and diagnostic acumen, he will find himself increasingly able to diagnose emotional states on positive grounds. This is far better than the practice of making such diagnoses by the exclusion of organic findings, as was the general practice a decade or so ago.

C. AVOID VERBAL SPECULATION

Many people are quite suggestible. Even more so, emotionally sick patients are highly suggestible. It is possible that considerable harm may inadvertently result from ill-advised attempts by the anxious, insecure, untrained, or inexperienced doctor to treat these neurotic patients. In general, the patient is quick to sense uncertainty in the physician; to sense frustration, hesitation, or lack of knowledge and familiarity. The patient's automatic response to these unfortunate factors in the doctor only too often results in his level of anxiety increasing further. He can also become rapidly and quite thoroughly discouraged with therapy. Tragically, this can extend from the immediate situation to include any future possible therapeutic relationship, perhaps for the rest of his life. The stakes therefore are very high; the cost of failure disastrous.

The physician should never tell the patient of his own speculative diagnostic thinking. He should not pass along any of the various organic pathologic possibilities of which he may himself think. When he suspects physical disease, it may be much better to keep such suspicions to himself, at least until he has secured positive evidence and has reached definite conclusions. Emotional illness can be definitely aggravated by injudicious frankness or by the premature expression of opinions. Emotional illnesses may be worsened or perpetuated as a consequence of undue interest on the part of the physician (and hence inevitably on the part of the patient!) in exhaustive examinations and laboratory studies.

D. FACTORS IN FAVORABLE PROGNOSIS

1. Intensive Psychotherapy and Analysis Indicated

Fortunately, in general the treatment of the Anxiety Reactions has a favorable prognosis in skilled hands. Early adequate treatment favors a good prognosis. Initiating treatment at an age when character structure is still pliable and nonrigid is most helpful. Firm reassurance, especially when confined to statements about the absence of organic disease, is indicated. Otherwise, reassurance can be ineffective or even harmful.

When acceptable to the patient and when available, the treatment of choice is intensive psychotherapy or analysis by a trained and qualified psychiatrist. Regular and frequent psychotherapeutic sessions should continue as indicated over a period of time. The aim of such treatment should be investigative and should point toward the uncovering and understanding of basic conflicts and sources of anxiety. Fromm-Reichmann pointed out the agreement of "all schools of psychoanalytically dynamic psychotherapy" in considering "interpretive recall of repressed emotional material an integral part of intensive psychotherapy." Patients also learn to tolerate their anxiety and tension and to recognize, accept, understand, and as a result, to cope more effectively with their emotional conflicts.

2. Patient and General Physician

Any of the various manifestations mentioned in the section on clinical features may be responsible for causing the patient to seek medical attention. The general physician may be confronted with a situation similar to the following. The doctor concerned made an accurate evaluation and promptly referred the patient for psychotherapy. His excellent handling of this case may be contrasted with that in *Case 28*.

Case 27

Good Medical Handling of a Case of Anxiety Neurosis

A 42-year-old architect reported to an internist his "unsteady nerves" and "heart trouble", which had their onset following a fairly minor automobile accident. He found himself dwelling on the possibly more disastrous results which might have ensued. He had become tense and restless, and slept poorly. Accompanying his apprehension about a repetition was some reluctance to continue driving his car.

History revealed similar emotional and physiologic overresponses to threatening situations in the past. The presence of chronic anxiety had interfered with his professional success, and had restricted his relationships with various colleagues. A systemic review revealed coronal pressure headaches, weakness, palpitation, and increased perspiration. These had all been accentuated since the recent disturbing experience. His cardiovascular system was negative from an organic standpoint. His symptoms were emotionally based and functional. The internist's tentative original diagnosis of an Anxiety Neurosis was shortly confirmed through psychiatric consultation. Psychiatric treatment was instituted promptly and achieved substantial success over a three-year period. His treatment schedule provided regular sessions on a 3–4 times weekly basis.

A major problem for the general physician in this sort of situation, as in many instances of emotional illnesses, is that of the patient who must protectively deny the presence of emotional problems. Like as not, the denial is sincere, in that the patient has no conscious awareness of emotional problems himself. His denial has been as effective to himself as to others. However, it can certainly complicate matters for anyone interested in being of help.

E. THE ACUTE ANXIETY ATTACK

The physician is not likely actually to witness many A.A.A.s. If he does and can recognize the nature of the disturbance, there are several things he can offer. These measures, which include the following, have more general value from the standpoints of emotional first aid and early management.

1. Emotional support.
2. Medical reassurance. This must be completely sincere and given with confidence or it may conceivably have a reverse effect.
3. Sedation may be used: (*a*) if the attack is prolonged; (*b*) if the patient is old; and (*c*) if there is little chance for further therapy. When used, sedation is to be regarded as a temporary crutch type of measure. Generally drugs do not offer effective insurance against subsequent A.A.A. [Ch.3:IXF5].
4. Secure prompt referral for definitive psychotherapy in competent hands.

It is very useful if the physician himself does not appear anxious, and if his personal response to the attack is not one of anxiety. Needless to add, this is hardly a matter of his completely free choice!

F. ADDITIONAL IMPORTANT POINTS IN THERAPY

1. Therapeutic Process Can Generate Anxiety; Resistance in Therapy

In the treatment process the patient will automatically and unconsciously employ defenses against anxiety. These represent extensions of his existing dynamisms and symptoms (or the development of new ones), or the employment of character defenses which are related to his general pattern of character traits; his characterologic armor.

This brings us to the therapeutic handling of resistance in therapy. This is a complex but vital subject. The subjective experiencing of anxiety during treatment can become an effective hindrance to the therapy.* This produces resistance. It is an important factor in determining the speed and degree of progress in the work of treatment.

---

* Thompson noted in reference to resistance that the counterforce (against return of the repressed idea) is furnished by the defense system of the ego. Any attempt to break this down brings anxiety. The automatic response is to avoid this. "So the threat of anxiety furnishes the motive for resistance to insight." Sharpe also summarized some of the defenses against anxiety which are active in the treatment situation. Fromm-Reichmann surveyed factors in the therapist which in turn can affect the treatment situation. Some further comments on resistance in treatment will be found in the section on *Treatment* in *Chapter 14* and elsewhere in the text.

2. Earlier Therapy Enhances Results; Symptom-Longevity Principle

In general, the sooner that adequate treatment is initiated after the onset of the condition, the more favorable is the response. In situations in which the symptoms have been closely related to situational factors, there may be less repressed material to uncover. At times symptoms seem to have to progress to a point of sufficient development and consequent discomfort and handicap to motivate an interest in therapy. Certain cases prove to be both protracted and refractive to therapeutic endeavors. In such instances therapy may become quite prolonged. This is in accord with the Principle of Symptom-Longevity [Ch.14:VIIIE] according to which ordinarily the longer symptoms have been present, the more difficult is their resolution.

The interested general practitioner may be able to handle mild cases, particularly when treatment need not be protracted and when he can avoid becoming involved in an unfamiliar maze of transference problems.* As he gains increasing experience however, his circumspection in attempting therapy and his caution in the selection of patients is likely to increase!

The physical examination should be done thoroughly. Once negative findings are ascertained, however, this should not be repeated unless something genuinely new, or disturbing to the physician himself, should develop. Too frequent examinations serve only to arouse further the patient's uncertainty and anxiety. The physician must himself be secure in his findings. When he has arrived at a diagnosis, he may, in a kindly but matter-of-fact fashion, explain to his patient how emotions can alter physiology. Examples can help. Most patients with a reasonable level of intelligence can be assisted to understand how their emotional feelings can result in physiologic changes. They can also perhaps learn further how these in turn can contribute to uncomfortable subjective sensations and to symptoms. This is a teaching kind of process, in which the physician's own confidence and security are fine assets.

3. Avoid Any But Essential Surgery: Surgery-in-Abeyance Rule

Always avoid any kind of surgical procedure in cases of emotional illness when not clearly and urgently indicated. This holds, of course, regardless of the patient's desire or even his insistence, that an operation be undertaken. Further comments as to the emotional contraindications to non-urgent surgery will be found later [Ch.10:XC;Ch.12:IIIA6;VB2].

The following is an example of a case in which undue emphasis and significance were attached to the physiologic features of an emotional illness. In this instance the original physician's uncertainty and inexperience were reflected in the undue attention which he directed toward the examination of the heart and its function.

---

* Ferenczi, who once noted that "in mild cases suggestion or superficial analysis may be successful", also supported the warning about transference problems. He noted and illustrated the occurrence of serious untoward symptoms when transference phenomena were inadequately recognized and poorly handled.

Case 28

Poor Medical Handling of a Case of Anxiety Neurosis

A 29-year-old real estate salesman became increasingly worried and anxious. He was restless, and was troubled with insomnia. He had begun drinking coffee incessantly. He had developed intermittent palpitation, and was also worried about his sexual abilities. One day while riding in a crowded bus he had a typical Acute Anxiety Attack. Following this, he reported to a physician for examination. The latter became overly impressed by the symptom of palpitation.

The physician focused his attention, his queries, and his discussion, (and inevitably that of his patient!) upon the examination of the heart and the heart's function. This happened not only upon this occasion but also during a long series of subsequent examinations. Quite possibly the physician was far more at home in exploring this familiar pathway of possible organicity, than he was in exploring emotional ones. The latter were perhaps not only less well known, but uncomfortable for him as well. Unfortunately, the patient developed an overconcern with, and a fear of heart disease as a consequence.* His "awareness" of his heart increased to a pathological extent and became most disturbing to him. This was an iatrogenic (physician induced) aspect of his illness, unwittingly brought about, of the hygeiaphrontic (hypochrondriacal) type.

Under later psychiatric treatment some of the dynamic factors in the patient's anxiety were uncovered, and his symptoms largely disappeared. This, however, was a long and difficult process, requiring many months of careful psychotherapeutic investigation. If the physician who had originally examined the patient following the first A.A.A. had been able to make a clear statement as to the absence of organic heart disease and had not unduly focused the patient's attention on his heart action, this particular aspect of his illness would have been averted. He would have been spared needless suffering, expense, and time.

4. Symptoms Not Imagined

The physician had best avoid telling his patient to stop worrying—the patient would be only too happy to do this if he could. He cannot do it voluntarily, and thus many patients will resent such advice from family, friends, or physician. The physician also must *not* tell his patient that "there is nothing wrong," or imply that his illness or symptoms are "imagined." This applies to all contacts with patients who have emotional symptoms.

The patient himself *knows* that something is very much wrong with him. To him the discomfort is very real. For the doctor to tell him that "there is nothing wrong" may convey to him that the physician is possibly concealing the truth. On the other hand, the patient may conclude that the doctor simply doesn't know what he is talking about. Further, the patient, whose emotional symptoms are most real to him (despite the fact that they are subjective in nature), will very much resent the implication that he is dishonest or a fool, when a physician implies or states that his symptoms are "imaginary." The patient well knows when he has pain or is suffering

---

* It might be pointed out more specifically at this juncture that an isolated inept or even injurious comment or so usually is in itself insufficient to produce a neurosis. In many instances of iatrogenic disorders, a preexisting chronic neurotic predisposition has long existed. The psychologic soil has been well prepared in advance. This does not of course discount the real measure of psychologic difficulty which can be compounded in this fashion.

from some emotional handicap. This kind of treatment by a non-perceptive, poorly-informed, or unsympathetic physician, is poorly calculated to promote increased respect for the doctor, or to lead into a more favorable therapeutic relationship.

5. Tranquilizing Drugs

The drugs of the reserpine and the chlorpromazine groups (and to a considerably lesser extent the more recent tranquilizers as classified below) have proved particularly helpful as adjuncts in the management of disturbed psychotic patients. In certain cases the results have been substantial. The patients have become calmer, more manageable, and obviously less disturbed. At times constructive psychotherapy becomes feasible. These effects have been observed in many mental hospitals among these severely sick patients. These results are not universal. For poorly-understood reasons, the drugs simply do not work, or else work to a more limited extent with certain other patients.

These drugs have their best use with the acute emotional disturbances, especially the severe ones of psychotic level.* In the author's opinion they have relatively little place currently in the definitive treatment of mild emotional disturbances or of chronic neurotic ones. Ordinarily the author does not prescribe tranquilizing drugs in the treatment of the neuroses or of the character neuroses and in general discourages such employment. Dependency upon drugs is to be avoided. The treatments of choice are intensive psychotherapy and analysis in experienced hands. Drugs are no substitute and can delay or discourage patients getting started in the definitive therapy they need. Their use however may well become necessary when adequate psychotherapy is not available.

There are many emotional conditions in which not only are the drugs ineffective but in which their use can prove psychologically harmful. Reference here particularly concerns the many emotional reactions which are seen in private medical practice. Unfortunate tendencies have been seen for the indiscriminate prescription of these drugs for almost any kind of emotional distress. A severe emotional disorder can further develop during a period of time when definitive psychotherapy could otherwise have been underway. Tranquilizing drugs are not very effective in halting or in ameliorating repetitive or intermittent and non-anticipated Acute Anxiety Attacks [Ch.3:IXE].

---

* Beneficial effects with the phenothiazines and reserpines result especially in those cases of psychosis in which agitation or excitement are prominent. These drugs are of less help and may be even harmful in cases of depression, or where there is psychomotor retardation. Results with psychotic patients are particularly good in acute cases and in those of recent onset. Their greatest value is in increasing the ease of general management of disturbed patients and in promoting the dissolution and fading out of abnormal mental content.

In a significant number of cases the latter consequence may have the important result of making psychotic patients more accessible to communication. The prospects for psychotherapy may become greatly enhanced, as meaningless or relatively useless verbal productions are replaced by useful and meaningful ones. One must however guard against the indiscriminate or overenthusiastic employment of these drugs. Untoward side effects such as edema, skin reactions, jaundice, pseudo-parkinsonism, and so on may occur.

It is necessary to differentiate the tranquilizers from the many other types of drugs employed for their psychic effects. Three general classes of tranquilizers might be distinguished today:

1. Alkyl diallyls: meprobamate (Dr. Frank Berger) (Miltown and Equanil).

2. Benzodiazepines: chlordiazepoxide (Librium) and diazepam (Valium).

3. Diphenylmethanes: benactyzine (Suavitil) and hydroxyzine hydrochloride (Atarax).

6. Suggestions: Moving Won't Help

When a patient is possessed of unrealistically high standards as regards his mission in life, sometimes part of the discrepancy between capability and goals can be adjusted. Suggestions as to recreation, hobbies, and new avenues of interest may be useful. Such suggestions however are hardly likely to be the ultimate answer. Nonetheless, these measures sometimes can help. The person concerned may, of course, have tried many of these himself.

The patient must be reminded, when appropriate, that escape offers no real solution to conflict. Ways of attempted escape take many forms. One attempted route is via the superficial solution of a move to another part of the country. When the patient arrives there, he is bound to discover all too quickly that his personality, psychologic defenses, and individual capacity for anxiety have moved right along with him. New surroundings will not offer new information about the source of his anxieties.

Sedation when needed should be judiciously prescribed and carefully controlled. It must be regarded as a temporary support only. It seldom has a major role in definitive psychotherapy. The latter aims to learn what the distress is about, not to cover it over. The patient needs to develop his expertness in the former, not the latter.

7. Collaboration Important; Joint-Endeavor Principle

Finally, it is important to note that for psychotherapy to have any chance for success the patient must assume responsibility for taking an active role in the treatment process. He cannot resign himself to the hands of the doctor. This procedure will involve considerable hard work and, not infrequently, discomfort. The patient's attitude is important to the prognosis in various kinds of illness. It usually plays a far more significant role in emotional illness.

For psychotherapy to be successful, the patient must not only want to get well but he must give his genuine and whole-hearted cooperation to his therapist. His role must be one of active collaboration, in accord with the *Joint Endeavor Principle* in the more ideal types of psychotherapy. Otherwise, it will not prove possible to work out the deeply-hidden roots of the neurotic processes, to secure acceptance of disowned impulses, and to resolve emotional conflicts.

8. Treatment Sections in Each Chapter Have General Applicability

The foregoing comments about treatment have a considerable amount of applicability in the management of emotional illnesses generally. They are intended to serve in introductory fashion to similar comments which will be offered in corresponding sections at the end of subsequent chapters.

It is not possible to cover all the complex factors of treatment with each class of neurotic reaction. Indeed, such a presentation in any detail could easily occupy several volumes. Therefore, some continued general comments on the therapy and management of emotional illness will be offered with each chapter, plus some ideas of particular applicability to the type of neurosis under discussion.

IX. SUMMARY

This chapter has presented a brief discussion of the Anxiety Reactions. They have been classified for purposes of convenience into three major groups as the *Acute Anxiety Attack* (A.A.A.), the *Anxiety-Tension State* (A.T.S.) and *Anxiety Neurosis*. The introductory discussion of anxiety, in Part One has been followed by our first discussion of one important group among the neuroses proper, and of related clinical material. For reasons as advanced, the name "Age of Anxiety" has been suggested as appropriate for our era. In accordance with the Principle of Universality of Anxiety we note that everyone is prey to anxious feelings. The Emotional Death Concept considers the possibility of death transpiring from emotional causes.

The Anxiety Reactions illustrate the type of emotional illness, the dynamisms, psychogenesis, and the gains of emotional illness in which anxiety is the most prominent feature, and in which its manifestations and effects are more directly expressed. The quality of the anxiety experienced does not differ substantially in the three kinds of Anxiety Reaction. The duration and quantity may. Reference was again made to the Principle of the "Individual Appropriateness of Response".

The *Acute Anxiety Attack* (A.A.A.) is an extremely uncomfortable, dramatic, and self-limited burst of anxiety with marked emotional distress. The Circular Generation of Fear Principle notes how fear of a recurrence is generated by an A.A.A. The attack is accompanied by the physical, physiologic, emotional, mental and somatic responses usually associated with fear and panic. With anxiety the real basis of concern is outside of conscious awareness. The Acute Anxiety Attack may be an isolated phenomenon or it may occur in the course of an Anxiety Neurosis or an Anxiety State.

The Principle of Extension noted the spreading psychopathologic ramifications of Acute Anxiety Attacks. The Concept of the *Secondary Defense* of a symptom was introduced.

The *Anxiety-Tension State* (A.T.S.) is a more established process, in which some level of anxiety or tension is present over a period of time. Contributing situational factors are generally in evidence. If the Anxiety ∨

Panic is regarded as an acute reaction, the Anxiety-Tension State may be regarded as one which is subacute. According to a precept of Inverse Anxiety-Symptom Ratio, the more "successful" the symptom the less anxiety is experienced.

The *Anxiety Neurosis* is a firmly established, more chronic kind of emotional illness characterized by diffuse anxiety (uneasiness, apprehension, fear, or anxious expectation) in which the real basis is not clear. It is not controlled by specific defense mechanisms as is found in other types of neuroses. Anxiety Neurosis is therefore that type of neurosis in which anxiety itself and its more direct effects and consequences are the most prominent presenting features. The concept of *Constructive Anxiety* points out that anxiety is not necessarily always a distructive force and influence. It can have individually and socially constructive influences. Emotional symptoms can serve as *unconscious compromises.*

The *Theory of Antecedent Conflicts* was briefly presented. The possible effects of anxiety were noted, and the *Constrictive Spiral of Anxiety* described. A concept of the *Reciprocal Influences of Anxiety and Pain* was offered. A *Surgery-in-Abeyance Rule* was formulated.

Finally, some ideas and cautions in the management of the Anxiety Reactions have been presented. The importance for the patient to assume responsibility and to collaborate actively in the treatment has been stressed.

Following this brief and not too complicated introduction to our first group of neurotic patterns of reaction, we shall next undertake the discussion of the Depressive Reactions.

X. SELECTED REFERENCES AND BIBLIOGRAPHY

ALEXANDER, F. (1950). *Psychosomatic Medicine,* p. 109. New York; Norton.
— (1951). *Our Age of Unreason.* Rev. Ed., pp. 131–132. Philadelphia; Lippincott.
BLAU, A. (1952). "In Support of Freud's Syndrome of 'Actual' Anxiety Neuroses." *Int. J. Psychoanalysis,* **33**, 371.
CAMERON, D. E. (1944). "Observations on Patterns of Anxiety." *Amer. J. Psychiat.,* **101**, 36.
— (1944). "Some Relationships Between Excitement, Depression and Anxiety." *Amer. J. Psychiat.,* **102**, 385.
CANNON, W. B. (1929). *Bodily Changes in Pain, Hunger, Fear and Rage.* 2nd Ed. New York; Appleton.
— (1909). "The Influences of Emotional States on the Functions of the Alimentary Canal." *Amer. J. Med. Sci.,* **137**, 480.
CHAPMAN, A. H. (1963). "The Problem of Prognosis in Psychoneurotic Illness." *Amer. J. Psychiat.* **119**, 768.
Diagnostic and Statistical Nomenclature. Washington, American Psychiatric Association, 1952, pp. 31–32.
DUNBAR, F. (1948). *Mind and Body,* pp. 65–79. New York; Random House.

DYRUD, J. E. (August, 1953). Personal communication.
FERENCZI, S. (1950). *Sex in Psychoanalysis,* p. 34. New York; Basic Books.
FROMM-REICHMANN, F. (1950). *Principles of Intensive Psychotherapy,* p. 82. Chicago; University of Chicago Press.
— *Ibid.,* pp. 39–42.
HART, A. D. (1954). "Iatrogenics and Cardiac neurosis: A Critique." *J. Amer. Med. Assn.,* **156**, 1133.
HARTEN, D. (1944). "Fear in Battle." *The Infantry Journal.*
JENKINS, R. L. (1955). *The Medical Significance of Anxiety,* p. 26. Washington, D.C.; The Biological Foundation, Ltd.
LAUGHLIN, H. P. (1953). "Anxiety: Its Nature and Origins." *Med. Ann. D.C.,* **22**, 401.
— (1953). "The Anxiety Reactions." *Med. Ann. D.C.,* **22**, 463.
— and RUFFIN, M. DEG. (1953). *An Outline of Dynamic Psychiatry.* 4th rev., mimeo, p. 257. Washington; George Washington Medical School.

— (1954). "The Neuroses Following Trauma." *Med. Ann. D.C.*, **23**, Part I, 492; Part II, 567.

— Ed. (1953). *A Psychiatric Glossary.* 4th Rev. Ed., p. 12. Washington; American Psychiatric Association.

LEVY, D. M. (1950). "Evaluating the 'Specific Event' as a 'Source of Anxiety.'" In: Hoch, P. H., and Zubin, J., Eds. *Anxiety*, pp. 140–150. New York; Grune and Stratton.

LUNGER and PAGE (1939). "Worries of College Freshmen." *J. gen. Psychol.*, **52**, 457.

MASSERMAN, J. H. (1946). *Principles of Dynamic Psychiatry*, pp. 126–127. Philadelphia; Saunders.

MEARES, AINSLIE, (1963). *Management of the Anxious Patient*, Philadelphia; Saunders.

NOYES, A. P. (1953). *Modern Clinical Psychiatry*. 4th Ed., p. 454. Philadelphia; Saunders.

PAVLOV, I. P. (1941). *Conditioned Reflexes and Psychiatry*. Trans. and Ed. by W. H. Gantt. New York; International Publishing Co.

— (1927). *Conditioned Reflexes*. Trans. and Ed. by G. V. Anrep. London; Oxford University Press.

POTTER, H. W. (November 8, 1954). Personal communication.

SCHMEDEBERG, M. (1940). "Anxiety States." *Psychoanal. Rev.*, **27**, 439.

SHARPE, E. F. (1930). "Survey of Defense Mechanisms in General Character Traits and in Conduct." *Int. J. Psycho-analysis*, **11**, 361.

THOMPSON, C. (1950). *Psychoanalysis, Evolution and Development*, pp. 96–97. New York; Hermitage House.

WHITAKER, C. A. (August, 1953). Personal communication.

WILLIAMS, E. Y. (July 22, 1954). Personal communication.

XI. REVIEW QUESTIONS ON THE ANXIETY REACTIONS

1. a. Our era might be called the *Age of Anxiety*. Why?
   b. What is meant by a Principle of Universality of Anxiety?
2. When is anxiety pathologic?
3. How does the Concept of Defensive Overreaction enter into the etiology of functional and emotional illness? What is the Emotional Death Concept?
4. Distinguish the three major types of Anxiety Reaction.
5. What is the value of differentiating the *Acute Anxiety Attack* (A.A.A.) from organic situations? How would you do so to your own satisfaction? What criteria would you use in referring this type of patient to a psychiatrist for therapy?
6. What does the Principle of Extension help point out as to the secondary effects of Acute Anxiety Attacks?
7. Delineate and discuss the *Anxiety-Tension State* (A.T.S.).
8. What is an *Anxiety Neurosis?*
9. Outline the types of emotional illness. (See *Table 7.*)
10. What is the Concept of Secondary Defense *of* the symptom?
11. List the major psychomotor, mental, physiologic, emotional, and subjective manifestations of *Anxiety Neurosis*.
    Note: Compare *Table 8* (Page 113) with *Table 1* (Page 20).
12. Why do "successful" symptoms lead to less anxiety being experienced? How is a symptom an "unconscious compromise"?
13. Discuss the Theory of Antecedent Conflicts. What is meant by Constructive Anxiety? Continued Physiologic Momentum? Emotional Recapitulation?
14. Discuss the implications of anxiety in appetite and weight control.
15. What are the constrictive effects of anxiety? What is meant by the Constrictive Spiral of Anxiety? The Joint-Endeavor Principle in therapy?
16. How can anxiety influence the subjective experiencing of pain? Explain the Concept of the Reciprocal Influences of Pain and Anxiety.
17. Outline factors in good *vs.* poor medical handling of the Anxiety Reactions.
18. Define:
    a. Anxiety.
    b. Conditioned Anxiety.
    c. Free-floating Anxiety.
    d. Pathologic Anxiety.
    e. Critical Attack of Anxiety.
19. Define:
    a. Anxiety Neurosis.
    b. Anxiety Panic Attack (A.A.A.).
    c. Anxiety-Tension State (A.T.S.).

CHAPTER 4

THE DEPRESSIVE REACTIONS

....Pathologically Lowered Spirits, Sadness and Dejection

I. INTRODUCTION

  A. Depression Defined
    1. Emotional Depression is to Anxiety, as Sadness is to Fear; 2. Depressive Reactions; 3. Matter of Degree, Level, or Depth; 4. Depression as a Major Psychologic Conversion

  B. Medical Management of Depressive Reactions
    1. Challenge to Medical Acumen; 2. Excellent Justifications for One's Efforts; 3. Common Feature of Emotional Illness

II. HISTORY

  A. Early Origins
    1. Ever Since Adam; 2. Melancholia

  B. The Modern Era
    1. Kraepelin, Bleuler, and Meyer; 2. Abraham and Freud; 3. Depression, Successor to Melancholia

III. DIAGNOSIS

  A. Making a Positive Diagnosis
    1. Clear-cut Case; 2. Problems in Diagnosis; Concept of Physical - Equivalents; 3. Secondary Defense of Symptoms

  B. Useful Points in Diagnosis
    1. Protean Forms of Clinical Expression; 2. More Depression Means Less Anxiety; Depressive-Equivalents; 3. Inquiry as to Level of Spirits; 3. "Dawn-Insomnia"; Early Morning Awakening Pathognomic; 5. Be Wary of Recurrences

  C. Neurotic Depression *vs.* Psychotic Depression
    1. Gradual Progression in Severity; 2. Summary of Differential Factors; 3. Diagnostic Determinations Important in Management

IV. INCIDENCE

  A. Depressive Reactions Widely Prevalent
    1. Higher Order, More Advanced Neurotic Reactions, *vs.* Lower Order Ones; 2. Frequent in Middle-Aged Group; 3. Depressive Reactions of Psychotic Depth

  B. Wide Prevalence of Suicidal Tendencies
    1. Many Suicides Not So Reported; Euphemistically - Intended Disguises; 2. Statistics in Suicide; 3. Five Surveys on Suicidal Tendencies

  C. Depression Encountered in Private Practice

V. SYMPTOMS AND CLINICAL FEATURES

  A. Frequent Manifestations of Neurotic Depression
    1. Withdrawal, Decreased Interests and Physical-Equivalents Obscure Depression; 2. Vasomotor Changes; Cold Depression; 3. Typical Symptoms; Dawn Insomnia; 4. Speech and Communication Reflect Mental and Emotional Retardation; Concept of Diffuse Retardation; 5. An Era of Stress; "Passing the Peak"

  B. Important Special Factors Influence Clinical Picture
    1. Relation of Depressive and Obsessive Groups of Character Traits to Clinical Depression; 2. Depression and Hostile Expression; 3. Theory of Antecedent Conflict

  C. Depressive Reactions and Danger of Suicide
    1. Always Take Seriously; 2. Estimating Danger; Index of Suicide-Potential; 3. Principle of Recurrence

D. Grief States

    1. Fear, Grief, and Depression; 2. Grief Defined; the Grief State; 3. Cultural Influences; Grieving Time; 4. Analogy to Anxiety-Tension State (A.T.S.); 5. Relative Ability to Express Grief: Constructive and Destructive Consequences

E. The Depressive Character Defenses

F. *Depression à Deux*

G. Severity of Suffering

VI. PSYCHODYNAMICS AND PATHOGENESIS

A. Theory of Antecedent Conflicts and Depression

    1. Dependency - Dilemma of Infancy: Rage Toward Object of Dependency; 2. Earliest Antecedent, or Primal Depression; 3. Repetition of Familiar Patterns; 4. Conditioned Emotional Responses; 5. Emotional - Exploitation Concept; 6. Infantile Needs; Sequence of Deprivation and Rejection→ Rage→ Apathy → Primal Depression; 7. Concept of Rejection and Compliant Response

B. Frozen State of Rage

C. Masochism and Sadism in Depressive Reactions

D. Primary and Secondary Gains of Depression: Depressive Endogain and Epigain

    1. Unconscious Gains Less Apparent in Depressive Reactions 2. Depressive Endogain; 3. Depressive Epigain; 4. Unconscious Goal of Lost-Object Reunion

E. In Summary

VII. SITUATIONAL OR REACTIVE DEPRESSION

A. Precipitated by Traumatic Event

    1. Definition; 2. Types of Precipitating Situations

B. All Depressions Reactive

VIII. DEPRESSION OF SUCCESS

A. Success Equates Great Loss

    1. Definition; 2. Dynamics

B. Promotion Depression

    1. Vital Unconscious Needs Subserved: Endogain; 2. Those Wrecked by Success

C. Related Depressive Reactions

    1. Completion Depression; 2. Work as Escape; 3. Further Implications

IX. THE ANXIOUS DEPRESSION

A. Concurrent Anxiety and Depression

    1. Incomplete Symptom-Defense Concept; 2. Definition; 3. Resistance to Therapy; Agitation Gauge; 4. Added Clinical Features

X. ONE-DAY DEPRESSION

A. Brief Depressive Reactions Possible

B. Common Cold and Depression

C. Internal Needs Often Satisfied

XI. SUICIDE

A. Introduction

B. Incidence

    1. Major Area for Medical Concern; 2. Suicidal Thoughts Universal in Occurrence; "The Three D's"

C. Clinical Features

    1. Evidence of Depression Variable; the Symbolic-Authority Concept; 2. Equivocal Suicide

D. Partial Suicide; Accident-Proneness

    1. Accidents Have Unconscious Purposive Components; 2. Fracture-Proneness; 3. Accident - Prone Drivers; 4. Dynamics

E. Impulse and Remorse in Suicidal Attempt

    1. Value in Prognosis; 2. Little Impulsiveness; Remorse After Delay; 3. Impulsiveness and Remorse Minimal; 4. Impulsiveness Marked, Remorse Undetermined; 5. Impact of Remorse

F. Evaluation of Suicidal Threat

G. Management after Suicidal Attempt

    1. Decision to Hospitalize Promptly and Decisively Effected; 2. Relative Responsibility in Therapeutic Situation; 3. Defensive Family Attitude may be Encountered

H. Psychodynamic Considerations

    1. Ultimate Symbolic Expression of Inverted Sadism; 2. Inversion of Hostile Drives; 3. Additional Dynamic Concepts; 4. Expiation, Retribution, and Absolution in Suicide; 5. Compliance with Implicit Command; 6. Death Wish; 7. Factor of Alcohol

I. Potential of Successful Treatment

    1. A Life Saved; 2. Post-Trough Point of Hazard; 3. Prognosis

XII. TREATMENT
  A. Treatment of Choice in Depressive Reactions
    1. Intensive Psychotherapy; 2. Ego Support; 3. Optimal Time for Interpretation; 4. Goals of Insight Therapy; Deep Treatment; 5. Difficulties of Therapy; 6. Study Resistances; 7. Concept of Emotional - Inertia; The Mechanical Analogy; 8. Frequency and Length of Psychotherapy Sessions
  B. Drugs

C. Remission
D. Electroshock Therapy
    1. Points of View Differ Widely; 2. Indications; 3. Disadvantages; 4. Psychodynamic Factors; 5. Effects Upon Recent Memories

XIII. SUMMARY

XIV. SELECTED REFERENCES AND BIBLIOGRAPHY

XV. REVIEW QUESTIONS FOR THE DEPRESSIVE REACTIONS

I. INTRODUCTION

A. DEPRESSION DEFINED

1. Emotional Depression is to Anxiety, as Sadness is to Fear

THIS chapter will be concerned with the important symptom of emotional depression, and with the major psychiatric category of the Depressive Reactions. Depression is the term used for a widely, if not universally experienced emotional symptom. As employed to describe an emotional feeling or symptom, depression refers to *lowered spirits or a depressed mood. Emotional depression is an affect of undue sadness, dejection, or melancholy. Clinically, the lowered spirits appear out of proportion to the stimuli, as determined by the ordinary means of observation.* This is because the origins of the feelings are *internal, as opposed to external.* As formulated by our Principle of Individual Appropriateness of Response of course, on a deeper level the depression—as indeed with all emotional symptoms—is individually quite appropriate to the (internal) stimulus [Ch.1:IIC2]. Depression can also be considered along the line of its intensity, with it being regarded as *a more persistent grief-sadness.* Some would also regard grief-sadness as being possibly intrapsychic.

In contradistinction, the terms of sadness and grief are more usually employed to describe emotional reactions to external loss. These reactions are more or less realistic and proportionate to what has been lost. Sadness and grief are to fear, as depression is to anxiety.* In both grief and fear *the stimulus is external and consciously recognized, and the response is proportionate.* In depression, as in anxiety, the real source of the emotion is largely unknown and unrecognized. It is intrapsychic, and it stems from unconscious emotional conflict.

2. Depressive Reactions

Depression as an emotional illness denotes *an established and more or less chronic condition, in which there is a pathologic dejection of mood.* It comprises a neurotic (or a psychotic) illness, in which *morbidly lowered spirits, their effects and consequences are the principal features.*

---

* While this equation has some general relevance, it should be kept in mind that frequently enough, anxiety actually sometimes can serve as a constructive or mobilizing force, while depression is generally disorganizing.

Additional characteristic features of a Depressive Reaction which may be present in variable degree, are those involving a slowing down (that is, retardation) of mental, physical, and physiologic activity, and an objectively unrealistic "attitude-symptom" of self-depreciation. These symptoms are manifested in many ways. They may become pervasive in the individual's life. The relation of the *symptom* of depression to the neurotic kind of Depressive Reaction, is analogous to the relation of the symptom of anxiety to the clinical reaction of Anxiety Neurosis.

3. Matter of Degree, Level, or Depth

It may prove difficult on occasion to draw absolute lines of distinction between the depressions of psychotic level and the neurotic Depressive Reactions. Clinical depression is at times more a matter of degree—a matter of level [Ch.4:IIIC2] or of depth—rather than something which is simply present or absent. Our interest in this chapter will be primarily directed toward the emotional reactions of neurotic level, in which the symptom of depression is the outstanding feature.

The consideration of Manic-Depressive Psychosis, Involutional Melancholia, and other Depressive Reactions of psychotic level is beyond the scope of our study of *The Neuroses*. It is to be noted, however, that much of our data will also have considerable validity and applicability in these conditions. Some points will of course be offered later (*see* Table 10), to aid in the differentiation of the psychotic reactions from the neurotic ones.

4. Depression as a Major Psychologic Conversion

Emotional depression is a widespread, if not an almost universal aspect of human subjective experience. In its ultimate origin, depression may be regarded as intimately related to anxiety. Depression is an intrapsychically-developed manifestation which results as: (1) an attempted last-ditch psychologic defense against anxiety (pending or already present); (2) a major psychologic conversion, in which it becomes an indirect manifestation and ultimate effect of anxiety and emotional conflict; (3) depression also begins in response to external stimuli including loss, deprivation, and (as will be seen) even success. [Ch.4:VIII]. Depression is not a mystical phenomenon. It is the reflection and result of the organism's best endeavor to cope with a problem. Thus it is the intensity of the depressive response, its duration, depth, and character that leads to the categorization of a Depressive Reaction.

Anxiety and the automatic human defenses against it today make up the central psychodynamic concept in the etiology of all emotionally-determined illness. Thus all psychogenic symptoms may be regarded as developing as the direct, or as hidden, indirect, and symbolic manifestations of anxiety, or as responses to anxiety.* As we shall see illustrated in subsequent chapters, emotional symptoms represent the distorted and symbolic expression of hidden and internal (that is, unconscious) con-

---

* *See Table 1* [Ch.1:IIF1], and *Table 4* [Ch.2:IIB2].

flicts. We shall also observe further that the symptom of depression fits in with these very basic considerations in the psychogenesis of emotional illnesses generally.

B. MEDICAL MANAGEMENT OF DEPRESSIVE REACTIONS

1. Challenge to Medical Acumen

Of vital importance in the excellent medical management of the Depressive Reactions are: (1) accurate, positive, and prompt diagnosis; (2) early effective medical handling; (3) the solution of problems of referral; and, finally (4) securing definitive treatment for those persons suffering from Depressive Reaction. Together they represent a most important challenge to medical acumen. Securing them at least in some measure has become increasingly feasible in medical practice today, as our level of knowledge has steadily risen. This is true in the management of emotional problems generally, as well as in the handling of the Depressive Reactions.

Our available resources in the medical management of emotional depression have also steadily increased in recent decades. Psychotherapy is increasingly available. As a consequence, the physician has a considerably greater responsibility to the public today in the realms of making an early diagnosis, and in his efforts to help his patients secure adequate therapy.

2. Excellent Justifications for One's Efforts

There are a number of most excellent reasons as to why the endeavors of both the general physician and the psychiatrist on behalf of the depressed patient, are particularly important. These might be tabulated as follows:

Table 9

Sound Bases for Assisting Depressed Persons; Why Therapy is Worthwhile

1. A *predisposition* to the development of depression *exists* especially *among society's most useful people.* Included are some of its harder working, reliable, serious, conscientious and responsible members. The depressed patient often is not only highly capable and intelligent, but has already demonstrated his superior ability for social adjustment. Depression of course also is to be encountered among immature, quite orally-dependent persons [Ch.4:VIA6].

Often the overwhelming unconscious needs for love (acceptance, approval, and, ultimately, dependence) of the Depressed Personality have contributed to his ability. At the same time, however, these same *unconscious* needs help to pave the road for his vulnerability to rejection, letdown, and disappointment.

2. The *response to adequate treatment is relatively favorable.* The same personality traits which may accompany the psychologic predisposition to depression, are often very useful when applied in the work of treatment.

3. *Efforts* by the physician to train himself in the early detection of depression and in the facility of referral to expert specialist care, will *pay substantial dividends in results,* and accordingly in personal satisfaction.

4. In many instances *the depressed patient can be restored* through adequate treatment *to his pre-illness level of effectiveness,* or *even to a better level.*

Instances still occur all too frequently in which emotional depression is unrecognized, or in which the case is inadequately managed. Among the principle unfortunate consequences are that the patient: (1) is likely to suffer recurrences; (2) may become conditioned against psychologic therapy; or (3) may be lost through suicide.

3. *Common Feature of Emotional Illness*

In view of the widespread experiencing of depression, we might anticipate that depression as a symptom may occur to some degree in many emotional illnesses. This is correct. Depression, like anxiety, is a common feature in neurotic illnesses generally. At times it also provides (or rather the discomfort incident to it provides) the fuel which initiates or continues psychotherapy as in the Fuel Analogy. [Ch.1:VIB].

There are also rather clear-cut clinical cases of neurosis, in which the clearly dominant feature of the illness is emotional depression. In these instances the most suitable diagnostic classification is that of a neurotic Depressive Reaction. We will be guided accordingly in our present discussion. Let us proceed with our consideration of this very major category of neurotic reactions.

II. HISTORY

A. EARLY ORIGINS

1. *Ever Since Adam*

States of severe emotional depression have been recognized throughout the course of history. Instances are described in early documents, going back as far as records are available. Perhaps one might even think of the history of depression as first dating from Adam's dejection, following his expulsion from the Garden of Eden!

Suicide, as the tragic ultimate consequence of severe depression whether this has been quite apparent or fully covert, has likewise been present in legend and history throughout the ages. Its cultural position, frequency, and attitudes towards it, have of course varied considerably from age to age, and from one ethnic group or civilization to another. The dramatic and tragic nature of suicide has further insured that many specific and particularly noteworthy instances would be recorded. The close relationship of suicide to emotional depression then provides us with further presumptive evidence as to the ancient clinical presence of this type of reaction.

2. *Melancholia*

Hippocrates, the "father of medicine," described a number of clinical entities in the field of medicine rather accurately around 400 B.C. One of these was severe emotional depression. The clinical descriptions were accurate. The bases of its development, however, were most poorly understood. According to the early, mistaken ideas as to its etiology such as were then current, this condition came to be known as *melancholia,* from the Greek *melas* (black) and *chole* (bile).

The resulting term of melancholia has continued in use to the present day, although it has tended to fall into gradual discard, particularly in the last several decades. When it must be employed today, melancholia is more accurately applied to those severe cases of emotional depression which are of psychotic depth.

B. THE MODERN ERA

1. Kraepelin, Bleuler, and Meyer

The modern era in the history of emotional illness was ushered in by the more humane regard for those seriously ill psychiatric patients requiring custodial care. This was followed gradually by increasing interest in this area of clinical medicine, on the part of the medical profession, and by the rise of more accurate description and terminology. The final, and continuing chapter has been our increasing recognition, study, and understanding of the underlying psychologic factors.

Scientific awareness, delineation, and observation of the clinical types of emotional illness progressed rapidly in the latter half of the nineteenth century. Melancholia had long been recognized as a psychiatric entity. It was inevitable that such a clinically striking condition would be included in all the early efforts at psychiatric classification.

Emil Kraepelin (1856–1926) was a pioneer German psychiatrist who contributed substantially to the classification of emotional disorders. In his work he used the term melancholia to include patients with Involutional Melancholia (long referred to simply as melancholia), as well as the depressed phase of Manic-Depressive psychosis. Eugen Bleuler (1857–1939), a distinguished Swiss psychiatrist and author, used the terms melancholia and depression rather interchangeably.

Adolf Meyer (1902) defined melancholia as "an excessive or altogether unjustified depression." He also stressed the clinical findings of self-depreciation and low self-evaluation, and mentioned the "retardation or inhibition of spontaneous activity." The term "depression" was coming into use. This was spurred on considerably by the gaining of more understanding of the psychodynamics of the Depressive Reactions.

2. Abraham and Freud

Until very recent times our knowledge of the psychogenesis of emotional depression was quite limited. Information was confined almost exclusively to descriptive and empiric data. Only in 1911 were the first of the psychodynamic formulations concerning depression offered, by Karl Abraham (1877–1925). This classic and noteworthy work was followed five years still later (1916), by Sigmund Freud's added contribution to the understanding of depression, in his paper entitled "Mourning and Melancholia."*

---

* Several of Freud's earlier papers contain allusions to melancholia, but "Mourning and Melancholia" is apparently his earliest attempt to formulate the psychodynamics of depression.

Both men continued their studies in the psychogenesis of depression. Abraham published additional important papers concerning the psychodynamics of depression, in 1916 and in 1924.

Following these pioneering contributions, a number of excellent clinical and theoretical studies have offered further contributions in the theory, the treatment, and to new conceptions of emotional depression. These have helped provide the necessary background for the author's research and for our resulting present study and elaboration of theory.

3. Depression, Successor to Melancholia

Rado (1928) interpreted the self-depreciation and accusation of the depressed patient as part of the unconscious attempts to placate the harsh superego. Clinical investigation in recent years has added substantially to our fund of information about emotional depression. More knowledge and understanding has been gained about depression generally, and particularly in the area of the neurotic depressions.

While significant contributions continue, there exists today a large and solid foundation of rather generally-accepted data concerning the psychodynamics of depression. The term depression has gradually tended to supersede the earlier, etiologically inaccurate one of melancholia. The Depressive Reaction, officially by nomenclature and popularly through usage, has become the accepted diagnostic term in clinical psychiatry today.

III. DIAGNOSIS

A. MAKING A POSITIVE DIAGNOSIS

1. Clear-cut Case

Making the diagnosis of depression offers few enough problems in the occasional, quite clear-cut case. Herein low spirits are noted subjectively by the person concerned, and are reported to the physician as the major presenting symptom. The presence of emotional depression may be further corroborated clinically, for example by the external appearance of apathy, unhappiness, and possibly also by some fairly obvious slowing down of mental and physical activity.

In examples of such a clear-cut case, the patient himself is likely to notice and to point out the discrepancy between his low level of spirits on the one hand, and external events or explanations to justify adequately their presence on the other. Loss of interest and energy are frequently noted. *Dawn-Insomnia* [Ch.4:VA3] may be present, with its characteristic early morning awakening.

Some self-depreciatory trends may be present. Subjective self-accusations and/or guilt feelings may be quite prominent. Appetite, activity, and animation are diminished. All the typical symptoms and signs are present. However, such ideal conditions, in so far as the relative ease of diagnosis is concerned, are more than likely to be absent, when one considers a cross section of all of the cases of emotional depression which are to be encountered clinically. Let us consider some of the reasons why this is true.

2. Problems in Diagnosis; Concept of Physical-Equivalents

There are a number of very important reasons why this particular type of emotional reaction may offer problems in diagnosis. *First,* the patient himself may be consciously quite unaware * of the presence of depression, or at least insofar as its degree is concerned. *Second,* depression, even when present in some strength and recognized subjectively by the patient, may still pass unnoticed by friends and associates.

Third, and even more important, the depressed patient all too often tends quite automatically to keep his low level of spirits and his dejected feelings concealed. This may be done actively, deliberately, and consciously, as well as unconsciously. It may be partly both. *Fourth,* in addition the patient tends to retreat from his normal activities and interests. He is therefore still less likely to discuss his problems with someone else, than are other groups of patients.

Fifth, he loses his inclination and ability to undertake new interests, projects, or activities, even in his own behalf. It is not surprising, therefore, that he is not likely readily to undertake such a new project as that of seeking help from a physician.

Even in those cases where he does consult a doctor or other professional for assistance, (medical) help is often likely to be on some other basis than on that of his complaints of the low spirits of his emotional depression.

Sixth, and finally, he has little initiative to seek medical help. He very well may resist coming to see a doctor. When he does, he may not talk of anything which would indicate emotional depression. Instead, his reported symptoms may cover a wide gamut of physical complaints. These may represent the *physical-equivalents* of depression. This is in accord with what we might term a Concept of Physical-Equivalents, in the psychogenic illnesses. Such equivalents of conflicts, and emotions are not uncommon in psychiatry. Thus, the patient may not even mention low spirits or depression at all. Emotional fatigue [Ch.7] can be one major type of such a *depressive-equivalent* [Ch.7:VIB*1*]

All of this necessarily complicates greatly the recognition of depression. This clinical reaction thus can indeed tax the diagnostic acumen of the busy physician. He must be ever on the alert in order to notice or to elicit the signs and symptoms of depression in his patients.

---

* Not necessarily so much merely a "simple" lack of awareness always. The patient's unconscious drive for self-punishment can be a significant factor in this, and in other findings.

3. Secondary Defense of Symptoms

Together, all of the patient's resistances have an important defensive intent. These begin with the foregoing factors, which can greatly complicate diagnosis. Thus, his: (1) lowered initiative, (2) lack of recognition, (3) conscious or unconscious denial of an emotional basis for his difficulties, and (4) the unconscious obscuration by physical complaints, help constitute the patient's *secondary defense*. This is his defense *of* his symptoms.

The depression itself is to be viewed as a last-ditch symptom-reaction in attempted psychologic defense. Therefore, we learn that *the symptom, an unconscious defense in itself, is in turn defended.* This is in accord with our very important concept of the Secondary Defense of the symptom and of the overall reaction, in emotional illness.

B. USEFUL POINTS IN DIAGNOSIS

1. Protean Forms of Clinical Expression

It is important to gain some recognition of the protean forms of expression that depression may take. These include the development of the important group of depressive character traits. These we shall shortly discuss with the Character Neuroses. Equivalents of depression, that is, ways in which depression may be manifested in more concealed fashion, include a number of physical and mental manifestations.

Such varied clinical manifestations may be encountered as depressive-equivalents for example, as excessive sleeping, marked anorexia, shifting somatic complaints, excessive fatigue, and possibly even the common cold on occasion.

As indicated earlier, depression is usually accompanied by some degree of withdrawal of interest from the external environment. Accordingly, "attitude-symptoms" such as apathy, indifference, boredom, and loss of ambition may cover or mask an otherwise unsuspected depression. With all of these foregoing possible obscurations to early diagnosis, it is not surprising that the recognition of many cases is missed altogether. Many other cases unfortunately progress to serious proportions before they are discovered. Some of these factors help to influence our very high suicide rate, about which some important statistics and a few comments will shortly be made.

2. More Depression Means Less Anxiety; Depressive-Equivalents

Generally the presence of considerable depression means less anxiety. Thus a reciprocal relationship tends to exist of inverse ratio, in which the more depression, the less anxiety. This bears out our Concept of "Symptom-Success" in which the more established the symptom, the less anxiety is experienced. This is in accord with the Inverse Anxiety-Symptom Ratio. [Ch.3:IIIC2]. However, this is not always true. Anxiety sometimes also can be present concurrently, as we shall see. Its accompanying presence is most marked in cases of Anxious Depression [Ch.4:IX].

Certain physical and physiologic symptoms or functional alterations, can be depressive-equivalents, as noted. These can also accompany depression, particularly in the more severe cases. They comprise a major category of our more general Concept of Physical-Equivalents in Emotional Illness.

3. Inquiry as to Level of Spirits

Two points are sometimes helpful in the diagnosis of depression. First, patients will usually respond more readily to an inquiry about their "spirits", or as to whether they are feeling sad or unhappy. For example, one may simply ask, "How are your spirits?", or "Are your spirits on the low side?". These kinds of questions can convey more meaning to a fair number of patients, than do questions as to whether "depression" is present, or as might some more complex query.

Second, the early part of the day is likely to be the depressed patient's most difficult time. This is more or less characteristic and comprises what the author would term the Morning Ebb-Tide of Spirits [Ch.4:VC2]. As the day progresses, his level of spirits accordingly is likely slowly to improve. This results in late afternoon or early evening being most likely his "best" time; in analogous terms, comprising his Evening Full-Tide of Spirits.

4. "Dawn-Insomnia"; Early Morning Awakening Pathognomic

In many cases of emotional illness there is trouble with sleeping. Patients sometimes will spontaneously report insomnia; often however they will do so only in response to specific questioning about it. In a fair number of instances of sleep disturbance in which there is considerable depression also present, the insomnia will be a particular type. The author would estimate that some 30–40 per cent of persons with the Depressive Reactions of at least a moderate severity suffer from a type of insomnia which is characterized by *early morning awakening*. In this interesting variety of sleeplessness, which the author for purposes of identification would term "Dawn-Insomnia" [Ch.4:VA3], the patient will awake earlier than his usual time and will have difficulty or find it impossible, to sleep. He may wake at 6 a.m., 4 a.m., or even at 2 a.m. This variety of insomnia will generally not be so specified by the patient, but must be inquired about explicitly.

When this phenomenon is found to be clearly present in a case which already gives a clinical impression of depression, the presence of Dawn-Insomnia can be an important final point in clinching the diagnosis. Depression can be present without it, but the author can personally recall no case in which this variety of insomnia was regularly present in the absence of depression.

This finding can also have some prognostic importance. It is more frequent in the more severe depressions. It is also an indication for the physician to be very much on guard against the possibility of a suicidal attempt.

5. Be Wary of Recurrences

In all cases of depression, following recovery the physician should be ever on the alert for recurrences. Many cases of depression slowly improve or go into remission under therapy, or even spontaneously. The occurrence of relapse or recurrence at some later date is a most crucial problem in the management of depression, and in the careful, long range evaluation of the various therapeutic approaches which may be used in the treatment of depression.

These comments are applicable both in current clinical practice, and also as noted insofar as the overall comparison of one's therapeutic results is concerned. Whenever a history of prior depression is known or suspected, the chances of a subsequent depression are greatly increased. This probability of a recurrence is proportionately still greater when earlier therapy has been inadequate or absent. Definitive therapy in expert hands minimizes the chance of future recurrence; provides the best available insurance against it. These comments are in accord with our later named Principle of Recurrence in the Depressive Reactions. [Ch.4:VC3].

C. NEUROTIC DEPRESSION VS. PSYCHOTIC DEPRESSION

1. Gradual Progression in Severity

In general, emotional depression is a clinical reaction which may gradually progress in severity from the neurotic into the psychotic. It is sometimes quite difficult to establish a definite and specific dividing line. A seriously depressed patient may maintain contact with reality fairly well, except perhaps in the sphere of certain judgments, as, for example, regarding his own worth. As a result, he may be a suicidal risk though difficult to hospitalize.

Because of their otherwise clear orientation, it may not always be easy, feasible, or even possible, legally to commit such patients to hospitals, as might perhaps be well indicated for their "own best protection and safety." They can thus upon occasion refuse or resist the professional advice, which would secure their voluntary hospitalization. This problem of hospitalization in depression will be referred to again later. (*See Case 40.*)

2. Summary of Differential Factors

Some factors which are helpful in making a differentiation of neurotic depression from psychotic depression may be tabulated in summarized fashion as follows:

Table 10

Features in Distinguishing Neurotic from Psychotic Depression

Developing the ability to distinguish clinically the neurotic from the psychotic type of Depressive Reaction can have practical and professional, as well as therapeutic advantages.

Experience indicates the following dozen factors to be among those of value in seeking to make such an assessment and differentiation:

(1) The *relative "depth" or "level"* of the depression.

(2) The *degree of contact* maintained with the outside, realistic environment, and the amount of continued ability to function therein. An assessment of the degree of retreat or withdrawal from reality and from the external situation.

(3) The degree, intensity, and apparent *realism of feelings of futility* and hopelessness.

(4) The degree, intensity, and apparent realism of *feelings of guilt* and remorse.

(5) A careful past life *history*. This will give considerable information concerning environmental influences and other useful data.

For example, the presence of marked mood swings in the past may indicate a predisposition to the development of a Manic-Depressive, "circular" type of psychotic reaction.

(6) An evaluation of the *pre-illness personality* character structure of the patient. This should place particular emphasis on such things as neurotic features, depressive personality defenses, incipient "cyclothymia" (another term for the manic-depressive reaction), and other prodromal indications of possible later psychotic manifestations. Is the attack a seeming repetition of an earlier similar event?

(7) The presence or absence of the serious and what we might refer to as the *"malignant symptoms"* of depression which are more generally associated with a psychotic reaction.

The malignant symptoms include such manifestations as severe agitation, somatic delusions, psychotic hygeiaphrontic (hypochondriacal) preoccupations, hallucinations, and deep retardation.

(8) The *degree of regression* is more complete and drastic in the psychotic depression than in the neurotic depression.

(9) The degree, intensity, and apparent realism of self-critical and *self-depreciatory attitudes*.

These, as with (3) and (4) above, are important "attitude-symptoms" in emotional depression. Assessing their individual significance can be important.

(10) The amount of physical, physiologic, and mental *retardation*.

(11) The strength of *suicidal tendencies*.

(12) *Repercussions* of the illness on: (*a*) interpersonal relations, (*b*) ability to function, (*c*) dream content, (*d*) energy, (*e*) ambition, (*f*) goals in living, and (*g*) overall personality adjustment and balance (compared to the past).

3. Diagnostic Determinations Important in Management

In the final analysis, the drawing of a line between neurotic and psychotic depression in the doubtful case is up to the judgment of the individual examiner. This is only one of the several difficult but vitally important determinations, that the physician must make. These include in addition:

(1) The determination of the presence of emotional depression.

(2) The potential value to the patient of expert psychiatric help.

(3) The kind of help to seek. This may depend in part upon the availability of physicians trained in intensive psychotherapy, and upon the patient's ability to utilize such help when it is made available.

(4) The amount of suicidal risk. It is always safer to over-rate, than to under-rate suicidal risk. This is closely related to the following determination. (*See also* later section on Suicide, Ch.4:XI.)

(5) The indications for commitment and/or hospitalization. It is always safer to hospitalize the doubtful case than to temporize.

On rare occasions the author has successfully treated a severely depressed patient psychotherapeutically on an office basis, when there was a considerable suicidal drive. This is not an easy or enviable task or responsibility. In these cases the physician-patient relationship was excellent, and the fullest confidence of the patient was enjoyed, especially *including* his thoughts about suicide.

In general, however, this approach is neither desirable nor advisable. It should only be attempted in very carefully selected instances, and then only by the very experienced psychotherapist. Further, he should be prepared to institute immediate hospitalization, should any doubts arise about the degree of confidence. Another indication for rapid hospitalization in any event, but more especially in such an endeavor, is the development or presence of any belief by the patient, that he himself doubts his ability to refrain from acting upon any suicidal thoughts or urges that he may have.

IV. INCIDENCE

A. DEPRESSIVE REACTIONS WIDELY PREVALENT

1. Higher Order, More Advanced Neurotic Reaction, vs. Lower Order Ones

Depression is a widely prevalent emotional reaction. It is more closely associated with (but not limited to) the more highly civilized and cultured ethnic groups. It often enough tends to be a relatively more advanced and developed type of neurotic reaction*, as distinguished from certain more primitive ones. This is according to our conceptions of the primitive (Lower Order), vs. the more complex and developed (Higher Order) neurotic defensive reactions, as outlined elsewhere. (*See also* later reference, Ch.8:IXA*1*.)

The more primitive and massive neurotic reactions include the Somatic Conversions, the Dissociative Reactions, and possibly the Phobic Reactions and Soterial Reactions, plus certain of the Neuroses Following Trauma. The neurotic reactions of a higher and more advanced order

---

* This is not intended to distract from observation of certain early, primordial depressions, especially as reactions to object-loss.

include the Depressive Reactions, the Character Reactions, the Fatigue Reactions, Overconcern with Health or the Hygeiaphrontic Reactions, the Obsessive-Compulsive Reactions and possibly the Anxiety Reactions. This concept of advanced, vs. more primitive defenses is also applicable to the mental mechanisms [Ch.1:IIID3].

Evidences of severe depression are also seen, however, among what are sometimes regarded as underdeveloped cultures and poorly civilized groups. Indeed, there is almost no cultural group in which there have not been instances of suicide or suicidal-equivalents. There is some evidence that the incidence of Depressive Reactions tends to be lower in the cultural groups which have more extended family structures.

The author estimates that approximately 14–18 per cent of the clinical cases of neuroses overall, present emotional depression as their principal feature.

2. Frequent in Middle-Aged Group

In western civilization more severe depressions occur in the middle-aged groups in both men and women. Some corroborative evidence for this assertion can be found perhaps from recent figures concerning the frequency of suicide in the United States. The highest incidence of suicide is between the ages of 35 and 75 years, with the peak at age 55 years. (*See Figure 2.*)

Among all U. S. white males dying between 15 and 44 years of age, the causes of deaths which are officially reported to be suicides rank this tragic one of self destruction actually as number 5 among the leading causes of death.

3. Depressive Reactions of Psychotic Depth

Figures are more readily accessible as to the clinical incidence of the psychotic types of depression. Depressive Reactions of psychotic depth are quite frequent in incidence. They rank only after schizophrenia, mental disorders of the senium, and alcoholism, in that order, in new admissions to U.S. mental hospitals. In 1949 there were 10,837 *new* admissions for manic-depressive psychosis and "involutional melancholia" alone. Together they represented 10.4 per cent of the total U.S. public hospital, new admissions for mental illness. The median age was 52.9 years for persons suffering from "Involutional" Depressions at the time of their admissions, and 41.5 years for the manic-depressive patients.

These figures, although substantial, do not give a complete picture of the incidence of psychotic depression by an means. Many cases are never hospitalized. Further when not the primary diagnosis, depression still can be a major feature in many additional cases of psychoses. Finally, a higher rate of admission of individuals for treatment of emotional depression to the private *vs.* the public hospitals, would also be anticipated.

There is a high proportion of the total psychiatric inpatient population who suffer with depression. A military publication reported a survey of a group of psychiatric hospital in-patients. The chief complaint (symptom) of 26.5 per cent of the male patients was emotional depression. Seven per cent more suffered from depression as their second major symptom. This gives a total of 33.5 per cent. For the female patients, the corresponding figures were 24.7, 12.5, and 37.2 per cent, respectively.

Figures as to the relative frequency of Depressive Reactions or the symptom of emotional depression, in non-psychotic individuals, that is, in neurotic types of depression, are more difficult to obtain. The previous source however, included a study of so-called "normal" persons. In this summary, emotional depression was the chief reported "difficulty in living" for 6.7 per cent of the men, and the secondary difficulty for 8.5 per cent (a total of 15.2 per cent). It was the primary trouble for 12.9 per cent of the women, and the secondary trouble for 5.7 per cent (a total of 18.6 per cent).

B. WIDE PREVALENCE OF SUICIDAL TENDENCIES

1. Many Suicides Not So Reported; Euphemistically-Intended Disguises

Not only is subjective emotional depression a universal phenomenon and present at one time or another in every individual's experience, but the knowledgeable clinician observes ample evidence to suggest that the presence of morbid depression is perhaps more widely prevalent generally, than tends to be commonly realized. Suicidal tendencies and suicide are closely linked to the Depressive Reactions. Information about their occurrence therefore can yield us considerable inferential data about this particular major diagnostic category.

In evaluating these statistics as to the prevalence of suicide it should be carefully borne in mind first, that for every suicide reported, there are others not reported [Ch.4:XIB1]. There are many reasons for this. Family, friends, and officials both wittingly and unwittingly provide what can be termed Euphemistically-Intended Diagnoses or Disguises for Suicide, and for suicidal attempts. Second, for every suicide, there are many unsuccessful attempts. Finally, suicidal tendencies are more frequent than ordinarily believed. Many times of course such thoughts or considerations are never shared with another person in any way.

2. Statistics in Suicide

A. RATES, TIME, AND METHOD.—Since suicide is reportable in all states as a cause of death, many cases are so reported. This is despite various economic, "protection of the family", insurance, legal, religious, prejudicial, social, and personal pressures euphemistically to play down, give "the benefit of the doubt", relabel, and in other ways downgrade the significance of the role of suicidal drives in deaths, both generally and specifically. Thus, in many instances there is the tendency to not so report them. We have the benefit, however, of some statistics, such as can be derived. It is interesting to speculate as to their bases and further implications.

Thus we learn the rate is higher for men than for women; about 3 to 1 (white men 3.2 times the rate for white women in 1960–62). In a typical U.S. state (Maryland, 1961), the figures for reported cases are 240 to 85.

Urban rates are almost 2 to 1 over reported rural rates. (In Maryland, the city of Baltimore alone reported 117, with all counties [the remainder of the state] reporting 208.)

The highest relative number of reported cases of suicide are found in the West (Nevada leading, at a rate of 26 per 100,000 population), and are lowest in the South (Mississippi trailing, at a rate of 5.8 per 100,000 population). The most likely time for suicide is *early morning* (in accord with the depressive Morning Ebb-Tide of Spirits; *see* Ch.4:IIIB*3*), on a *sunny day,* especially on a Monday or Tuesday, and in *April* (first month in incidence), May, June or September in that order, and with December trailing (followed by February and November).

The suicide rate is higher among the single, the widowed and the divorced, than among the married. This difference is more pronounced among white males, being twice as high for the single man over the married one, and nearly four times for the widower or divorced man, over his married counterpart. The suicide rate is higher for those who are obese or underweight.

The method of choice is: (1) firearms, especially with men; about 50 per cent of all male victims use firearms. (*Ex.*: Maryland, 132 ♂ to 18 ♀); (2) hanging (*Ex.*: Maryland, 41 ♂ to 17 ♀); (3) analgesics and sedatives, which are favorites with women (*Ex.*: Maryland, 16 ♂, to 31 ♀); (4) carbon monoxide; and (5) jumping from heights, in that order. For further data on suicidal incidence *see* Ch.4:XIB*1*.

B. "COVER REASONS" ADVANCED.—The bases as advanced by "suicidal notes" are the more conscious ones often represent euphemisms and obscure the real, deeper motivations [Ch.4:XIA*1*]. They do not necessarily bear much relation at all to the underlying unconscious motivations. Keeping this in mind, however, they still may be of interest to us. Ill health thus is advanced as the conscious "reason" by 40 per cent of the men who suicide and by 20 per cent of the woman. "Domestic problems" are cited by 30 per cent of the men, and by 50 per cent of the women. Unhappy love affairs are blamed by 4 per cent of the men, and by 10 per cent of the women.

There is very seldom any mention at all of anger, envy, grief, revenge, rage, hurt, loss, or hostility in suicidal notes. These emotions and the unconscious drive and conflicts leading to their being experienced, are far more crucial in suicidal motivations. People do not like to recognize their presence; are threatened by possible awareness that they have such drastic potentialities. Instead, conscious and superficial reasons are advanced. These latter are what we might accordingly call the *"Cover Reasons".* They are similar in their resulting obscuration of the overall situation, to the "Euphemistically-Intended" Disguises or diagnosis as referred to earlier. In suicidal threats, however, especially with children, the thought of "getting even" or of making someone "feel sorry" is expressed with some frequency.

3. Five Surveys on Suicidal Tendencies

In seeking further information on this subject, the author polled five small medical groups as to their clinical and personal experience in this area. The results proved interesting, as tabulated below in *Table 11*. Some of the above points are illustrated. The first small survey was made while lecturing to a postgraduate medical class some years ago. The 40 unselected physicians in the class were of mixed ages. They included representatives of most of the medical and surgical specialties. Following the conclusion of a lecture on "Suicidal Tendencies," they were asked and agreed, to provide written information, anonymously. This included answers to specific questions as to their clinical and personal experience with suicide. In interpreting the resulting figures as tabulated, one might guess perhaps that the answers would tend to be on the low side.

A second group of 56 physicians were asked to provide information in a similar survey, when the subject which was under discussion was somewhat different. On this occasion it was on "Emotional Fatigue." Still another group of 71 medical students (second semester, junior year) provided a third set of figures. Two subsequent groups of 40 and 61 physicians respectively, were later surveyed. The results with the five groups are summarized in *Table 11*.

Table 11

The Clinical and Personal Experience of Groups of Physicians and Students with Suicidal Tendencies

A. A Medical School Postgraduate Class

Forty physicians of mixed ages and representing most of the specialty fields in medicine were participants in a postgraduate medical course. In a survey of their personal and clinical experience with suicidal tendencies, they answered "Yes," anonymously, to the following questions as indicated:

1. *Patients:* Someone among my patients has suicided 28
2. *Friends:* Someone among my friends has suicided 19
3. *Family:* Someone in my family has suicided 10
4. *Personal awareness:*
   (a) I have been aware of personal thoughts of suicide 30
   (b) I have considered suicide 11
   (c) I have attempted suicide* 0

B. The Medical Staff of a General Hospital

A second similar group of 56 physicians was surveyed to try and secure comparable data several years later, upon an occasion when the scientific discussion was about another topic, "Emotional Fatigue."

Note the lower proportion of affirmative answers, when the discussion had not been directed specifically toward depression and suicide. Some proved to be quite unwilling to answer one or more parts of the survey, despite its anonymity.

1. I have had patients:

	YES	NO
(a) Attempt suicide	20	10
(b) Threaten suicide	28	6

* More than 40 years ago (1923), of the verified and reported deaths alone, from suicide among physicians in the United States, these had already reached an annual rate of 62. Currently 6 per cent or approximately one in each 16 of all physicians deaths under the age of 65 years, are reported as suicide. (*See also* Ch.4:XIB*1*.)

    (*c*) Commit suicide 10 8

2. I have had thoughts about personal suicide 13 24

3. I have considered suicide more or less seriously at one
time or another 1 30

C. A Class of Medical Students

A survey of 71 medical students in the second semester of their junior year provided the following figures, in a survey conducted in connection with a regular class lecture on emotional depression and the Depressive Reactions.

	PATIENTS	FRIENDS	FAMILY MEMBERS
1. I have had:			
(*a*) Attempt suicide	20	10	1
(*b*) Threaten suicide	24	13	7
(*c*) Commit suicide	4	19	4

2. I have been aware of personal thoughts of suicide 39

3. I have considered suicide more or less seriously,
at one time or another 7

D. A County Medical Society

Forty physicians attending the regular monthly scientific meeting of the Montgomery County (Md.) Medical Society, Sept. 15, 1952, responded to a similar survey as follows.

These physicians had an average age of 37.7 years, and an average of 13.3 years in medical practice. Eighteen were in general practice and 22 in the various specialties, including 5 in surgery, 5 in internal medicine, and 3 in obstetrics-gynecology.

1. I have had patients: YES

    (*a*) Attempt suicide 20

    (*b*) Threaten suicide 28

    (*c*) Commit suicide 10

2. I have had thoughts about personal suicide 13

3. I have considered suicide more or less seriously,
at one time or another 1

E. A State Academy of General Practice

Sixty-one physicians attending a specialty session of the 7th Annual Assembly of the Maryland Academy of General Practice, Baltimore, Oct. 26–67, 1955, reported their clinical and personal experience with depression and suicidal tendencies.

These physicians, with a total of 980 years in medical practice, averaged 16.1 years in active practice per doctor, and had an average age of 43.4 years. All but 2 were in general practice.

	PATIENTS	FRIENDS	FAMILY MEMBERS
1. I have had:			
(*a*) Attempt suicide	55	9	4
(*b*) Threaten suicide	57	16	9
(*c*) Commit suicide	41	8	4

2. I have been aware of personal thoughts of suicide 16

3. I have considered suicide more or less seriously,
at one time or another 5

Further statistics in this area will be cited in the section on *Suicide* later in this chapter [XI].

C. DEPRESSION ENCOUNTERED IN PRIVATE PRACTICE

In view of the difficulty in locating figures showing the prevalence of the Depressive Reactions in the clinical practice of psychiatry, the author made an analysis of all of the individuals studied in his own private practice in sequence, over a period of time. The figures covered consecutive consultations during a recent two-year period, together with the people who were in intensive treatment over an overlapping four-year period.

It may be noted of course that the combined total of 108 persons is a small clinical sample. As further limiting influences, it should be noted that the existence of special factors in the selection of a psychiatric consultant and therapist by the referring physicians, as well as by the individual patients concerned, could also influence the results. The findings were as follows:

Table 12

Incidence and Relative Importance of Emotional Depression as Found in 108 Consecutive Persons Studied in a Private Psychiatric Practice

	Depression as present clinically was:		
	1. *A minor* factor:	2. An *important* factor:	3. The *major* factor:
1. 66 consecutive consultations (2-year period)	44%	24%	32%
2. 42 consecutive persons in intensive treatment (an overlapping 4-year period)..	24%	55%	21%

These figures may not be at too great variance from those of a fairly typical active analytically oriented type of private psychiatric practice. They bear out the relative frequency of emotional depression, as observed by the private psychiatrist. It might be noted that combining columns 2 and 3, gives us a total of 56 per cent in the consultations, and 76 per cent in the cases in intensive treatment.

V. SYMPTOMS AND CLINICAL FEATURES

A. FREQUENT MANIFESTATIONS OF NEUROTIC DEPRESSION

1. Withdrawal, Decreased Interests, and Physical-Equivalents Obscure Depression

Earlier it was mentioned that the tendency exists in the Depressive Reactions toward withdrawal into oneself. The depressed patient becomes more introverted, as opposed to being extroverted. Apathetic trends and diminished interest in life often make it difficult to detect emotional depression.

Because of these changes in attitude, the depressed patient is less likely to confide or actively to seek help. Often when he does present complaints, as noted earlier, these are translated into various physical symptoms. These manifestations, which we might term *depressive-equivalents* [Ch.4:IIIA2; IIIB2] can include fatigue, insomnia, various vague kinds of bodily aches and pains, loss of ambition, and anorexia. Complaints of coldness, particularly of the extremities, are relatively frequent. The withdrawal, decrease of interests, and presentation by the patient of various physical-equivalents of depression can perhaps serve to obscure other aspects of the clinical picture of a Depressive Reaction through their influences on one's diagnostic impression.

Thus, while it is true that one can sometimes observe certain fairly plain outward evidences of emotional depression, even in certain fairly severe Depressive Reactions, the physician sometimes may see little or nothing outwardly. When the depression deepens, the clinical picture often becomes clearer. Further, as one gains increased experience he is more likely to: (1) keep the possibility of depression constantly in mind, and (2) become increasingly aware of both the more common obscuring findings, and of the more subtle clues and indications. As these kinds of clinical skills are gained, fewer cases will be missed, or perhaps discounted in error.

2. *Vasomotor Changes; Cold Depression*

Vasomotor changes can occur in the Depressive Reactions, and are not terribly uncommon. These may be regarded as evidence of the vegetative aspects of the general slowing down or retardation, often associated with these reactions. This finding then is physiologically analogous to the frequent retardation of mental and physical activity. These various aspects of depressive retardation are all highly variable in degree.

Feelings of coldness, as noted above, may be reported. They may be readily confirmed by examination, or may prove to be partially or even entirely subjective. Subjective feelings of coldness are a rather common finding in cases of emotional depression. This is frequent enough to warrant our use of the term "Cold Depression", when these are a sufficiently prominent clinical feature of a Depressive Reaction.

The following case is illustrative of the extremes to which this may progress.

Case 29

The Cold Depression

A severely depressed man of forty-six years of age complained bitterly of feeling cold. He would come into my office when the temperature was a comfortable 72° wearing a vest and a light sweater, in addition to his suit coat. He would further sometimes cover himself with his topcoat and also with a light afghan I kept in my office. This continued during our earlier therapeutic sessions, over a course of several months. As he made progress in therapy, this manifestation gradually subsided. On one early occasion he described his discomfort as follows:

"I seem to be cold almost all the time. I certainly seem to require more heat than anyone else in the family these days. This is an awful lot different from the way I used to be. I used to be the warm-blooded type, the most active and warmest one. . . .

"Now my hands freeze, and I'm always chilly. Extra sweaters don't even seem to help very much . . . I'm cold!. . . ."

3. *Typical Symptoms; Dawn-Insomnia*

Symptoms show all degrees of progression. Typical symptoms which may be seen in the severe Depressive Reactions, in addition to the ones already listed, include restriction or retardation of thought and speech, self-doubt, self-depreciation and recriminations, decreased sexual interests and activity, sadness, and a loss of the sense of humor. There is apathy, loss of interests, and the person may appear on the subdued and compliant side. Guilt feelings are often prominent.

Dreams which are reported appear to be far less frequent in occurrence or absent. They not infrequently are disturbing, bizarre, or macabre when they are reported. Sufficiently careful longitudinal study, however, is likely to disclose a far higher proportion of depressed patients who can progress to reporting evidences of their dreaming, than early and less thorough evaluation might have suggested.

Earlier was mentioned the particular type of insomnia with its early morning awakening, which *can be pathognomonic of depression.* To better distinguish it from other types of sleeping difficulties, it was suggested that we give it the name of Dawn-Insomnia in accordance with the most frequent time for its occurrence. It is also aptly so named since these unfortunate sufferers often see the dawn break as a consequence. Menstruation may become delayed, irregular, scanty, or even cease, at least temporarily. The skin and complexion can become dull, with less tonus, and a sallow appearance. Weight loss frequently accompanies anorexia.

It should also be noted that clothes, dress, and behavior can reflect the somber mood of depression. This can apply particularly when a comparison is available with earlier habits. However, even during the course of a depression the choice and color of the clothes which are selected and worn may reflect changes in the level of spirits. In given instances they can constitute what might be termed *Dress-Indicators* of depression. Thus, darker colors and more conservative dress tend to indicate deeper depression. Choice, color, style, and change in preference are likely to have significance. Brighter colors and more stylish dress tend to accompany lightening spirits and diminishing depression. Observing the selection of clothes and possible shifts in preference on a daily basis, is sometimes quite intriguing. Such selection, for our purposes of course, is most unwitting.

The following case is illustrative of some of the symptoms frequently seen in the Depressive Reaction. It is presented in summarized fashion in the words of a moderately depressed person recently seen in consultation. The patient was a forty-two-year-old single woman. She had suffered the onset of depressive symptoms following the death of her mother, with whom she had lived for a long time.

Case 30

Clinical Manifestations of Depression

"I don't have very much interest in my work . . . I'm tired. Don't seem to have as much energy as usual . . . I just don't feel very well. My appetite isn't very good, and sometimes I'm restless . . . I'm not very happy these days. I guess it really isn't anything and I shouldn't trouble all you busy people with such minor things. There really isn't anything the matter with me. Look at all the really sick people who need your help. (This is self-depreciation, in which she says in effect, "I'm really not very worth while, not worth bothering with.") . . . I used to always read the paper and listen to the news broadcasts. Now I don't care too much, and miss doing it about half the time . . .

"One of the other women at the office was given an assignment I might have liked, but I seem listless, and I didn't really care too much. This is different for me. Once I might have tried a little more . . . My last two periods have been late, and I feel cold. My sleeping isn't very good. I wake up early and worry about a lot of things . . . I don't feel I've accomplished very much in life. I don't think I'm a very worth-while person . . . If I could just get back some interest and ambition . . ."

This patient's manner was subdued, docile, compliant, and somewhat apathetic and apologetic.

4. Speech and Communication Reflect Mental and Emotional Retardation; Concept of Diffuse Retardation

The clinician should remember that the comments of the person in the preceding case were not made spontaneously or easily. Actually it required some effort to get this relatively small amount of descriptive information expressed in words. This actually represents more then half of the significant things which were said during two entire therapy sessions. Further, this rather superficial data was much easier to secure, than was more important data later. The latter concerned her relationship with her mother, toward whom she could consciously only recognize or express the positive side, of what were really her highly ambivalent feelings. The strong negative components were intolerable and had been completely banished (that is, repressed) from her conscious awareness.

This person's description illustrates many of the important clinical features of the Depressive Reactions. First, her manner was subdued and somewhat apologetic. She was apathetic. Her appearance and her descriptions of herself and her activities illustrated her restricted interests, energy, and ambition. Her appetite was poor; she was unhappy; and she demonstrated the type of Dawn-Insomnia as is fairly often to be observed in the Depressive Reactions. Her attitude, performance, and reports from others all bore out the presence of some retardation of thought, mental activity, and physical-physiologic-vegetative activity as well.

These "slowing down effects" can be individually pervasive. Indeed the retardation effects can so permeate the individual adjustment and psychologic defenses in instances of clinical depressions as to warrant our adoption of the term and concept of Diffuse Retardation in Emotional Depression, in referring to and in emphasizing this prominent clinical feature. Finally, the foregoing person was self-deprecatory (an important "attitude-symptom") in the Depressive Reactions, and was somewhat self-critical. These features are all to be frequently observed in one's clinical assessment of the Depressive Reactions. (*See also* the related Concept of Psychophysiologic Retreat, CH.7:IXB4).

5. *An Era of Stress; "Passing-the-Peak"*

Earlier was mentioned the relatively increased incidence of the Depressive Reaction among the middle-aged groups. This is an era of special stress in the lives of many persons. Various alterations occur as the climacteric comes along, with its important psychologic implications; or as one comes to feel he has "passed the peak" of any given aspect of his capabilities or vigor. (*See also* S.E.H.A. concept, Ch.1:IV*C11*.) The person with an established sound level of emotional maturity is much better equipped to weather these stresses of this particular era of life. When the emotional adjustment is on a sufficiently thorough level of stability, one may sail serenely through this era with scarcely a ripple. Often enough this ideal state does not prevail, however, and in varying degrees emotional problems ensue. This period of one's life can accordingly comprise one of the Specific Emotional Hazards of Adulthood.

There are also important cultural factors which contribute to the vulnerability of the middle-aged group. There is a relative lack of ego building and prestige roles available for our senior citizens in most sections of our present Anglo-American culture. In all too many instances, less social prestige, status, and importance are currently possible for many people herein, as they approach membership in the older age groups in our social scheme of things. There are simply not enough "esteem-sustaining roles" and "status functions" given in our culture to older people. These factors when they can be present, are important in sustaining and in building the ego. Their absence makes the individual more vulnerable to depression. In therapy or otherwise, deliberately providing the sources to supply them to a given individual, can be an important supportive adjunct whenever feasible. To encourage their being provided, can be a significant contribution; supportive, preventive, or therapeutic.

In some foreign cultures of both the past and the present more sources for evolving sound feelings of personal esteem, of belonging, and of continuing ability to make personal contributions, have been present for middle-aged and older persons. Opportunities for these ego-enhancing roles tend to be more available, for example, in situations where there are larger family groups, patriarchal systems, and more constructive kinds of familial-social relationships generally. In a few instances of cultural attitudes, of course, age itself has long been held in veneration.

B. IMPORTANT SPECIAL FACTORS INFLUENCE CLINICAL PICTURE

1. *Relation of Depressive and Obsessive Groups of Character Traits to Clinical Depression*

A. PSYCHOLOGIC EQUIVALENTS.—The depressive character traits can serve a similar defensive function to actual clinical depression. Accordingly, they may be regarded roughly as what we might refer to as the "psychologic equivalents" of depression. The development of depression possibly may be forestalled by the presence of, or through the evolvement and formation of, various depressive character traits. We shall study this further in the following chapter, on the *Character Neuroses*. Separation of any discussions of the depressive character traits or defenses completely from our discussion of the Depressive Reactions is difficult and somewhat of an arbitrary delineation. In view of their intimate relationship, each of these sections should be read together.

A Depressive Reaction can develop, provided other usually predisposing external and internal factors are present, in the absence of appropriate character defenses, or as an urgent reinforcement of them when the existing ones are no longer adequate. It is hardly surprising to find clinical evidence of the depressive character traits present in the depressed person.

The onset of the Depressive Reaction may possibly be viewed as a last desperate attempt to maintain repression and control of threatening and disowned (unconscious) hostile and aggressive impulses. At the same time, some external expression of these is also allowed in symbolic fashion, as we shall observe in the Conversion Reactions. Herein the expression of the hostility becomes seemingly inverted, toward the self. Depression may also appear to serve a protective function through its attempting to prevent any further uneconomic expenditure of energy, in the pursuit of hopeless goals. Depression may also be viewed as an oral defensive mechanism, in distinction from the obsessive defense being linked to the anal phase. We shall have more to say along these lines shortly in the section on *Psychodynamics*.

B. EMOTIONAL DECOMPENSATION CONCEPT.—A relationship also exists at times between the obsessive group of character defenses and the Depressive Reaction. When these defenses prove inadequate, or when added stress supervenes, the resulting clinical reactions can take the form of a Depressive Reaction.

As with the similar breakdown of Depressive Character Defenses, we might think of this as a kind of Emotional Decompensation. This can be be an interesting and useful conception more generally, with a wide potential range of clinical applications in psychiatry [Ch.10:IVA*3*]. In the severe Obsessive Reactions, for example, such an Emotional Decompensation occasionally may take the form of an Involutional Depressive Reaction. When Emotional Decompensation transpires, the previously evolved and maintained *Balanced Neurotic Position* [Ch.14:XB*1*] has been lost.

2. Depression and Hostile Expression

A. INDIVIDUAL INVERSE-RATIO CONCEPT.—Not infrequently one may perhaps be able to observe an inverse ratio existing between the patient's degree or level of clinical depression on the one hand, and his ability outwardly to express his aggressive and hostile feelings on the other. This would comprise our Individual Inverse-Ratio Concept of Hostile Expression in the Depressive Reactions.

In the following rather unusual example, this conception of an inverse ratio of the outwardly-expressed hostility to the inverted hostility (that is, depression), was rather clearly illustrated.

Case 30A

The Inversion vs. the Expression of Hostility, in a Case of Depression

(1) *Evidence of Depressive Reaction Becomes More Prominent.*

A thirty-four-year-old captain in the United States Army returned from a war-time tour of duty overseas. After a few days at a new assignment, he was hospitalized for psychiatric study. There had been considerable interference in his work from emotional factors. He was tense, anxious, preoccupied, and showed diminished interest in outside things. He expressed some mildly self-deprecatory ideas, such as doubts about whether he had done "a good job." It was not immediately clear what should be the proper diagnosis, although initially there were major features of both anxiety and depression present. The initial anxiety as noted, diminished however, as the depressive features became more prominent.

Under treatment he brought out the intensely angry feelings provoked after his return to the States, at which time his wife had asked for a separation. At this juncture he was forcibly made aware of the painful fact that their relationship was not at all what he had believed it to be during his absence. Among other facts, amazingly enough, he actually had learned for the *first* time that his wife was fourteen years older, and that she had been married four times previously!

(2) *Status of Depressive Features Directly Proportional to Hostile Expression.*

For a few days following admission he was clinically improved. He poured out his intensely resentful and angry feelings. Then, for poorly explained reasons, he slowly lost his ability to express outwardly his hostility and resentment. Concurrently, the signs and symptoms of depression increased. The self-depreciation became marked as an attitude-symptom, as he wondered whether he had "lived up to his responsibilities," or if he had "misled" his men, and so on.

These ideas were directed toward himself in a Depressive Reaction which rapidly deepened to nearly psychotic level. They could be seen to reflect clearly one aspect of depression which was first pointed out by Freud. I refer to the punishment of the internalized lost love object by the now "concealed" (that is, completely unconscious) hostility.

(3) *Inversion of Hostility*

His self-accusations and depreciation thus actually represented concealed and secret condemnations and punishment of his wife for "misleading" him and for "not living up to her (marital) responsibilities," and so on.

Treatment continued with little apparent effect for some two or more weeks, when his ability to ventilate outwardly his hostility gradually returned. Concomitantly depressive features again fell away. It was possible to continue treatment on an intensive basis for several months, during which time some important insights were gained.

The officer continued to improve, became reconciled to the separation, and eventually returned to duty.

An interesting feature of this case was the clear and rather transparent illustration of our concept of the inverse relation often present and as just outlined, between the patient's ability to express outwardly his hostility, and the clinical level of his emotional depression. This relationship was dramatically demonstrated clinically over a course of approximately one month. This is illustrated graphically in *Figure 1*.

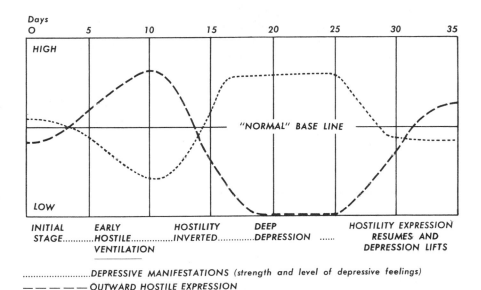

DEPRESSIVE MANIFESTATIONS (strength and level of depressive feelings)
OUTWARD HOSTILE EXPRESSION

Figure 1.—The inverse relation of outward hostile expression and the clinical manifestations of Depression as illustrated in *Case 30A*.

B. DIRECT CULTURAL-RATIO CONCEPT.—These relationships are often important in individual instances of Depressive Reactions, although seldom are they so clearly apparent as in the foregoing example. We may observe another ratio-type of relationship, which is somewhat akin to that in certain Depressive Reactions; a cultural one. Hereby we may note that the incidence of suicidal tendencies may be increased culturally, and in a more or less direct ratio perhaps with the extent that competitiveness and the expression of aggression and hostility are frowned upon and discouraged in that particular culture.

This "cultural attitude" thus can constitute a subtle but persuasive influence in the particular "cultural vogue" of emotional symptoms which develop (*see also* Ch.10:IVC1). It supports the Concept of a Direct Ratio of Depression incidence (and Suicide) with the Strength of Cultural Restraints and Suppression of hostility and competitiveness. The greater are such cultural pressures the higher will be the incidence of Depressive Reactions. This is the Direct Cultural-Ratio Concept in the Depressive Reactions.

3. Theory of Antecedent Conflicts

Our Theory of Antecedent Conflicts has been mentioned [Ch.1:IVB1; Ch.3:V] and will be referred to again [Ch.8:VIIA1]. According to this concept, traumatic situational events may occur during the course of one's life, which recapitulate important antecedent traumatic events from the early years. In other words, the later event actually or symbolically repeats the earlier event. In these instances the later environmental blow gains great added significance, by virtue of the conditioning effect of the earlier antecedent instance or instances.

This concept has important implications in the dynamics of the Depressive Reactions, as in other types of neurotic reaction. In his discussion of the mechanism of depression, Bibring may have been describing this possible psychologic sequence when he referred to the "regressive reactivation of the primary shock."

In the following instance the external situation, through its misinterpretation, was unconsciously "made" to fit more in line with earlier antecedent psychic trauma.

Case 30B

Antecedent Conflicts in Effect Reactivated Through Misinterpretation

(1) *Suicide an Ultimate "Soterial Retreat"*

A successful career woman in her middle thirties sought psychiatric consultation. She explained that some weeks prior to the appointment she had been in a rather complex emotional situation. In this she had come to believe that her boss, whom she had considered to be her close friend and supporter, had completely failed her. She found herself left with a feeling that she was of no importance to him, and that he actually didn't care much about her or about what happened. This was a serious misinterpretation, through which the current situation came to recapitulate for her an intolerable situation from her early life.

She had for many years secretly maintained the idea that when circumstances became intolerable she would end it all, that is, commit suicide. This comprised an *Ultimate Soterial Retreat* [Ch.11:VA3;-VIIA2], which had to an extent secured great emotional significance for her. To her, this point had now been reached. On this particular day she went home about noon, and did not return to the office. She made preparations to do away with herself. Fortunately, her boss phoned to inquire about her absence just at this crucial juncture, and thus inadvertently prevented her death. Thereupon she decided to seek help. She recognized something was out of proportion in the degree if not the character, of her emotional responses.

(2) *Inversion of Destructive Impulses Follows "Final Straw"*

As the working together of therapy progressed over many months, the dynamics and genesis of her depression became ever more evident. Throughout her infancy there had been a continual frustration of her vital needs for daily care and affection. There had even been a considerable indifference about providing her with nourishment. Her mother was too preoccupied otherwise, and her father was away from home.

In her suicidal "attempt," she had turned her destructive impulses, which were a consequence of the hostile impulses shown her by her mother, against herself. This eventuated after her self-esteem was broken down by her misinterpretation of her boss's attitude. This had constituted what we could term a "Final Straw" kind of initiating factor.

(3) *Therapeutic Approach*

In this case, as in others, this individual gradually produced substantial evidence of the constant frustration which had occurred from the beginning of her psychic development. It followed that there had developed a rigid armoring of her character structure, which had reduced her psychic mobility, with the result that she had became submissive, and largely lacking in critical faculties.

Therapy consisted in making the unconscious conscious. This included the elimination of resistances and bringing into the open the vital antecedent infantile conflicts. It meant a freeing of the character formation from the armoring process, thus enabling the patient to function at an improved level, more in line with her ultimate capacity.

C. DEPRESSIVE REACTIONS AND DANGER OF SUICIDE

1. Always Take Seriously

The specter of suicide constantly hovers over the emotionally ill patient. This is true despite whether the presence of emotional depression as a feature of the illness is apparent, or remains hidden. In fact, in the latter event, the danger is far greater. The subject of suicide will be shortly covered more thoroughly in a special section. However, some consideration of this ever-present danger is most fitting as we discuss the symptoms and clinical features of the Depressive Reactions. It should be constantly kept in mind.

A suicidal attempt or talk of suicide should always be taken seriously. When an individual discusses with you his low spirits or his self-destructive urges, he is paying you a great compliment. His turning to you with problems of this nature and depth, is a clear indication of the confidence and respect in which you are held. He is also likely indicating his great need for help.

2. Estimating Danger; Index of Suicide-Potential

How can one estimate the danger of suicide in the Depressive Reactions? This is often most difficult, but there are certain signs which can be helpful. When some of these are present, their level may be directly proportional to the amount of danger. Several of these are referred to elsewhere. Seven major ones are listed together in *Table 13,* as a source for convenient reference.

Table 13

The Potential-For-Suicide Index

Assessment of the following seven clinical areas is of value in attempting to estimate the depth of a given depressive reaction, the potential for suicide, the imminence of a suicidal attempt, or the possibility of a repeated such effort by a given individual.

Grading each of these items as to its individual prominence and strength, from one to seven, a total score or *Index of Suicide-Potential* might approximately indicate as follows: *5–15*: slight; *15–25*: increasing hazard; *25–35*: critical; *35–40*; extremely dangerous to imminent; 40 +: *NEVER* leave alone!
(1) *Early morning awakening*. When present, this change in sleep pattern is practically pathognomonic of serious emotional depression. The patient wakes one to four hours earlier than normal, a pattern of Dawn-Insomnia that likely continues for a time during the course of the Depressive Reaction, often for several months.

While not necessarily similarly pathognomonic of strong suicidal drives, this finding nevertheless best should be treated as a signpost for caution.

(2) *"Morning Ebb-Tide of Spirits"*. The depressed patient is likely to feel worse in the morning, and be at his best by late afternoon or evening. (*See also* Ch.4:IIIB3.)

(3) *Level of interests*. Often very striking with the depressed patient is his decreased interest in all kinds of things. Often the level of his loss of interest directly reflects the level of his depression. In other words the greater the interest loss, the deeper the depression.

(4) *Initial or sudden improvement*. Beware of the seriously depressed patient: (1) whose spirits suddenly lift, or (2) who has just passed through the lowest point in his valley of depression and has begun to improve.

The first person may have come to a personal "solution" of his problems, by reaching a decision to take his life. In the second situation, this is *the most likely time* in the course of a severe Depressive Reaction for suicide to take place. This conforms to the *Post-Trough Point of Hazard,* for suicide to be attempted in the Depressive Reactions. [Ch.4:XII2].

(5) *Withdrawal*. This area is closely related to the level of interests (No. 3 above), but refers particularly to the patient's contacts with people—friends, family, and associates.

This degree of withdrawal is likely to be in direct proportion to the depth of depression. Further, the more such distance, the less communication and the poorer the chances that the person will or can confide to another, just how desperate (and suicidal) he feels.

(6) *Communicability*. In general, the patient who can bring himself to discuss how hopeless things are to him, the less likely he is to take this kind of drastic action.

Thus a certain insurance is secured through the continued maintenance of his confidence and his communicability. It is important for his family and for his therapist to recognize this and to promote communication.

(7) *Presence of remorse*. The presence and the degree of remorse exhibited by the patient who has unsuccessfully attempted suicide has prognostic significance.

In general, the more remorse and the sooner it appears, the more favorable the outlook, and the less immediate danger of a second attempt. The less impulsiveness and the absence of remorse increases the likelihood of another and perhaps early suicidal attempt.

3. *Principle of Recurrence*

As has been noted [Ch.4:IIIB5], a major characteristic of the Depressive Reaction is its tendency to recur, especially in the absence of definitive psychotherapy. Many Depressive Reactions will eventually go into remission in the course of time alone, and with only superficial therapy, or even with no therapy. However, without real therapy, 80 per cent or more will recur.

Recurrence in clinical depression is so frequently to be encountered, and also in order to emphasize this major problem in management and in progress, that we might well speak in terms of a *Principle of Recurrence*. This would stress that in the absence of substantial changes in the patient's psychologic adjustment, character structure, or both, his depression is very much likely to recur at some future date. Definitive psychotherapy in expert hands can reduce this chance of recurrence most substantially.

It is by no means easily possible to anticipate the recurrence of the Depressive Reaction. This likewise applies to accompanying suicidal drives. Where a history of one or more attacks exists, one can in general only anticipate the patient's vulnerability to a subsequent attack when: (1) he is subjected to sufficient (for him) emotional stress; (2) his existing psychologic defenses break down; or (3) both.

Recently the author attended a forty-six-year-old business man who had made a desperate suicidal attempt, from which he had been saved, only through the medical skill and devotion of his family physician. He was found to be suffering from a "textbook" type of Depressive Reaction, which had been allowed to continue and to progress, without his seeking help from anyone, including his doctor. History disclosed two previous such episodes of Depressive Reaction, 9 and 22 years earlier.

The majority of persons who kill themselves: (1) have had prior attacks of depression; (2) have made suicidal threats, or (3) have made prior suicidal attempts.

D. GRIEF STATES

1. Fear, Grief, and Depression

Abraham first pointed out (in 1911) that "anxiety and depression are related to each other in the same way as are fear and grief." This comparison of fear with grief is based on the similar *external* nature of their precipitating causes. It is also based on our observation that the reactions of fear and grief are possibly (theoretically, at least) *directly proportionate* to their readily observed external stimuli.

Freud, in his paper "Mourning and Melancholia" (1917), offered his views as to the origin of normal grief. Grief is the response to the loss of a loved person, ideal, or abstraction. On the other hand, in melancholia (that is, depression) he saw the principal differentiating feature to be "the fall in self-esteem." This almost invariably is present to some degree in depression. In grief this is absent.

2. Grief Defined; the Grief State

Thus we may regard grief as the normal expression of sorrow and bereavement which follows the death of a loved one, or which follows some other significant loss, as experienced by the person concerned. The amount of grief in the mature personality is directly related to the amount of external loss. By definition then, grief is *the proportional emotional response to an external and consciously recognized loss. It is self-limited, and gradually subsides within a reasonable time.*

The extension of "normal" grief in quantity and duration constitutes the Grief State. A Grief State mergers further into a pathologic state of depression, a Depressive Reaction, when the duration and/or extent of the grief response to bereavement or loss is clearly more than one might ordinarily expect.

3. Cultural Influences; Grieving Time

There are cultural influences which may exert unfavorable and unhealthy effects on the manner in which we deal with grief. Many elements in our present western culture, for example, regard it as desirable and even commendable, to remain outwardly calm and emotionally restrained. An emotional display is frowned upon. Emotional stoicism perhaps tends to be overvalued. Too often it comes to be regarded unhealthily as a sign of strength. This kind of attitude encourages both conscious suppression and unconscious repression. Their employment does not at all necessarily indicate greater maturity.

The result may have unfortunate consequences on emotional health. Thus, the social premium sometimes placed upon the suppression of grief can contribute to emotional illness. Hendin believes that the tendency to solve personal problems by suicide is rooted in character structure, which would differ of course from culture to culture.

Contrariwise to the foregoing, certain rituals have developed in a number of cultural groups which allow time for the grieving. The expression of grief may be implicitly or actively encouraged during such *grieving time*. It may come to be expected as a matter of course. For example, according to certain Jewish customs, the seven days immediately following the funeral of a close relative are given over to mourning and prayer. All necessary activities are taken over by friends and more distant relatives.

The following clinical example illustrates how suppressive influences upon the expression of grief can unfavorably influence emotional health.

Case 31

The Expression of Grief is Discouraged

(1) *Suppression promoted*

A twenty-one-year-old girl presented multiple symptoms of a neurotic reaction. These had become so severe as to force her to leave her job. The history disclosed that her father had died some ten months earlier, quite unexpectedly. The mother, although grief-stricken herself, felt a need to hide her grief from the patient and her younger sister. This was done in the belief that she was protecting them.

Her attitude in turn helped to promote the active suppression as well as the automatic repression, of grief feelings by the daughter. Exhibiting grief was "giving in to it." The mother felt that if she herself could not "maintain control," her daughter in turn could not help but "go to pieces." This was a reflection of her own doubts and fears, assigned through application of the *Personal Yardstick* to her daughter.

(2) *Expression of grief beneficial*

The patient, partially because of this, and partially because of her own personality traits, which included tendencies toward detachment, restriction of emotionality, and over-nervousness, had repressed her own grief. She displayed outwardly, and actually consciously "felt", little sorrow.

The resulting severe emotional reaction followed. It was resolved fortunately in a matter of some weeks when she became able, under the supportive influence of therapy, to express, discharge, and, in effect, to relive her terribly intense feelings of loss and deprivation. The attempted defense had been largely one of denial. It had served her most poorly. The outward expression of her grief was most beneficial.

(3) *Systematic therapy feasible*

This is, of course a foreshortened account of the case, and presents only one small aspect of many complex factors in the dynamics. It is noteworthy, however, that following this abreaction of intense grief and the resolution of what was actually an incipient psychosis, a systematic analytic study then became feasible. She became able to work out through her therapy, many important insights in rather rapid fashion.

4. Analogy to Anxiety-Tension State (A.T.S.)

Grief States may be regarded simply as the extension of, or the increased intensity of, grief in response to bereavement. Here normal grief may merge into the pathologic. Clinically, the onset of a Grief State may be thought of as somewhat analogous to that of the Anxiety-Tension State or A.T.S. [Ch.3:III]. The Depressive Reaction similarly is analogous to the Anxiety Neurosis.

Thus, the loss of a close person may also precipitate a Depressive Reaction of various degrees of severity. The deceased person, the circumstances surrounding the death, and the relationship which had existed between the dead person and the bereaved one are of importance. These may further serve to "kindle" or to recapitulate various emotional conflicts, because of their unique significance and their unconscious consequences to the mourner. Herein our Theory of Antecedent Conflict has important application.

5. Relative Ability to Express Grief: Constructive and Destructive Consequences

It might be postulated that one major difference in the emotional reactions of the person who is subject to a Grief State in distinction to a Depressive Reaction may be found in his relative ability to express his grief. Depressed patients and persons who possess the potential for depression often seem to suffer from what we might refer to as a kind of "constipation of grief" and of mourning.

Other individuals seemingly can more readily express their grief, with a resulting emotional catharsis and discharge. Depressive individuals are unable to do so. It is choked back and dammed up, to become expressed, when this does occur, in an inverted fashion against themselves. They are thus not much better in directly and openly expressing their grief, hurt, and loss than they are in expressing their anger, resentment, and hostility.

Sullivan spoke of grief as the way by which detachment is effected from a lost, significant person. Accordingly, normal grief would be viewed as a health-preserving release of the integrative bonds which have previously connected the mourner to the lost one. Depression, on the other hand, would be regarded as destructive.

E. THE DEPRESSIVE CHARACTER DEFENSES

The Depressive Personality is one of three major groups of personality constellations. Its form is outlined in a section of the chapter on The Character Reactions [Ch.5:VC1].

F. DEPRESSION A DEUX

Various rare and unusual clinical patterns of Depressive Reaction can occur. These are often intriguing, sometimes tragic, and they help illustrate for us the wide variety of depressive clinical syndromes which are possible. An instance came to the author's attention not long ago which helps to illustrate the interesting clinical variety which is possible.

The following case concerns the simultaneous occurrence of moderately severe Depressive Reactions in a man and his wife. This rather rare occurrence we might accordingly call *Depression à Deux.*

Case 32

Depression à Deux

(1) *Parallel depressive manifestations*

A thirty-eight-year-old professional man and his thirty-seven-year-old wife were finally referred for medical help after it had been noted that they had become increasingly seclusive. Upon consultation, each presented the typical features of rather severe Depressive Reactions. Their interests were diminished. Their countenances and demeanor reflected their dejection and apathy.

There was anorexia present, with some resulting weight loss in each. The husband, who was the slightly more depressed of the two, reported early morning awakening. Both had various vague somatic complaints. The dress of each was on the somber side, reflecting both mood level and cultural influences.

(2) *Loss and sacrifice significant*

The couple was childless. They had come to this country fairly recently as escapees from central Europe. Earlier the husband had had a professional education and they had enjoyed a social position of some prestige in their country of origin.

In fleeing their home and country, primarily because of ideologic differences, they had sacrificed home, possessions, position, prestige, and, to a major extent, their educational advantages. Their loss and sacrifice had been of considerable significance. It had contributed substantially to the onset of their Depressive Reactions.

(3) *Community of background and interests*

The close relationship between husband and wife had been of long duration. It had become stronger through their community of interests during the deprivations, hardships, and their subsequent new experiences in becoming acclimated in a relatively alien country. More of the dynamic factors in the origin of this *depression à deux* were not worked out owing to extraneous factors which interrupted more definitive treatment.

There were, however, some further important close parallels in the early background of each. With the many evident and less evident intrapsychic factors tending to tie this couple closely together emotionally, the evidence of which was further reinforced during clinical study, the development of the parallel depressions did not seem startling.

G. SEVERITY OF SUFFERING

It should be pointed out that depressed persons are among the greatest sufferers of any medical patients. As the ultimate in progression, there is no more miserable or suffering person than the tortured victim of an Agitated Depression. This is the most severe kind of Depressive Reaction and is usually of or approaches psychotic depth. In this kind of desperate illness, there is currently present both overwhelming anxiety, and serious depression.

There is no psychologic morphine to bring relief to this kind of suffering, as there is for the terminal cancer patient. Nothing can comfort these unfortunate patients, some of whom may occasionally continue in a desperately agitated psychotic state for years. The suicidal risk is high. At times the physical structure collapses under the constant stresses, in what might seem at times almost a merciful end to a most tragic state.

VI. PSYCHODYNAMICS AND PATHOGENESIS

A. THEORY OF ANTECEDENT CONFLICTS AND DEPRESSION

1. Dependency-Dilemma of Infancy: Rage Toward Object of Dependency

If the supply of love and affection is adequate in early years, the unhealthily strong early ambivalent conflicts of childhood, which are typical findings when later the depressed person is studied therapeutically, will not develop. One must not think that these vital needs of the child are necessarily denied willfully. In turn, the parents, through insecurities and problems of their own, often enough, simply did not possess the necessary resources: actually did not have such vital emotional support to give, or could not give it. Their inability to be closer and more accepting of their children may even have been consciously recognized at least to some extent, and very much deplored.

Further, and for the same or similar reasons, some parents often cannot tolerate the hostility of the denied and frustrated child. The child in turn automatically and unconsciously "dreads" retaliation, and can only handle his rage by its repression from conscious awareness. In the oral phase of personality development, the response to frustration is rage, and the urge to destroy. This becomes ultimately a wish to devour. This is why we might sometimes refer to this complex as the *primal antecedent Oral Conflict*.

The infant subconsciously "recognizes" that the object of its rage is also the would-be cherished love object, on whom he is totally dependent. He cannot attack or destroy this vitally important figure, even if this were possible. He is too dependent. There is also the intolerable threatening danger of retaliation and retribution by such a seemingly all-powerful figure. The conflict is a basic one, and is one of considerable magnitude. It comprises what the author would term the Dependency-Dilemma of Infancy [Ch.7:VID].

When we speak of object-loss in the Depressive Reaction, this is not incorrect but really does not go far enough. Thus it is not merely the loss alone of the object which leads to depression, but further the individual's frequent-enough own inner, secret (unconscious) conviction that he *caused* it—has brought it about! The characteristic depressive needs to deny aggression become more understandable, as do the depressed person's frequent and often prominent feelings of guilt. Thus, guilt feelings are a significant clinical feature in the Depressive Reactions.

2. Earliest Antecedent, or Primal Depression

When this whole complex mechanism is of sufficient strength in infancy, and the negative side of the ambivalent feelings is not adequately handled through other mechanisms, what might be referred to as a Primal Depression develops. This very early reaction establishes an antecedent pattern for future responses in which, however, the ability of the individual to tolerate later loss, disappointment, or frustration varies widely. This is in accord with comments on the Theory of Antecedent Conflicts throughout this text.

We owe our basic early understanding of the psychodynamics of depression to the contributions of Abraham (1911, 1916, and 1924), and Freud (1917), and to a number of later noted researchers, including especially Dooley, Rado, Klein, Fenichel, Jacobson, Cohen *et al.,* and Bibring. Space and time do not permit detailing the important contributions of each. Their work, however, has contributed substantially to the view of depression as a specific ego reaction to loss or to an ego blow, to frustration and helplessness, and to the loss of, or serious damage to an ego ideal, and has contributed to the foundations for our current development and exposition of theory as outlined here.

Emotional depression arises from certain conflicts which can result from the frustrations incident to otherwise intolerable denial, loss, and failure. In the resulting great ambivalence (that is, the coexistence of very strong, completely opposing feelings) the person with predisposing personality features is unable to handle the hostile side of this. The aggression is literally inverted. Abraham, in 1924, first presented the useful concept of an "infantile prototype" of depression. He viewed this as a primal depression of infancy, developing in response to the vicissitudes of love and hostility.

With the establishment of this prototype of Depressive Reaction in early life, the depression-prone person has thus developed a familiar psychologic path, to potentially follow at some later juncture in his life. This follows when the early infantile pattern is reactivated by personally significant serious disappointments, losses, or abandonment such as may take place in one's living. This conception of the primal depression is essentially also embraced in the Theory of Antecedent Conflicts, and emphasizes further the vital role of the early emotional antecedents in the determination of emotional illnesses generally.

A recent study by Brown pointed up the greatly increased incidence of antecedent childhood bereavement in the history of those persons who suffer from Depressive Reactions. A total of forty-one per cent of a series of 216 such individuals, were orphaned prior to 15 years of age. A high proportion of these people had no knowledge or recollection at all of one or other parent. This data emphasizes further the importance of the resulting antecedent conflict and loss, in the presence of later adult vulnerability to a subsequent similar (actual, or symbolically equivalent) loss. The value of special care for the surviving child is also strongly suggested by these findings.

Related important data have been reported by Spitz. He described the *anaclitic* Depressive Reaction which followed the prolonged (several months) separation of six-eight month old infants from their mothers. This development was observed when the relationship was a "good" one, in contrast to its having been a "bad" one in which instance this reaction did not occur. The anaclitic depression is reversible, if the mother is restored to the child within three months.

Depressed individuals tend to be self-accusatory, self-condemnatory, and suffer with self-destructive tendencies. They are anxious, fearful, insecure, unhappy, guilty, isolated, lonesome individuals. They are further often guilt-ridden—for having destroyed (in fantasy and through the magic of their hostility) the love object. They tend to repeat perpetually in one form or another the early primal state of helplessness of the ego.

All of this does not happen by accident. The vicissitudes of the early interpersonal relationships set up the original antecedent patterns. These not only tend to be followed later in subsequent relationships, but analogous patterns are even inadvertently (that is, unconsciously) "set up", or contributed to by the individual.

The meaning of the symptom is of course deeply hidden and indeed *must remain obscure.* As the Theory of Transparency [Ch.14:IIIB*1*] points out, the underlying significance of emotional symptoms *must not be apparent;* cannot become too transparent, if they are to serve and survive, as "attempted" symptom-defenses.

3. Repetition of Familiar Patterns

The tendency toward the repetition of familiar patterns of reaction, *even though painful and self-defeating,* is seen to operate repeatedly in the intensive therapeutic study of patients generally. This repetition of earlier patterns can even result, as we saw illustrated briefly also in *Case 30,* in the gross misinterpretation of later events so as to fit the neurotic and unconsciously "needed" repetition. This is in accord with Freud's Concept of the Repetition Compulsion.

It is almost as though the repeat performance is unavoidable and inexorable. The established pattern is a more familiar one. It is as though there are fewer resistances to its unconscious repetition, than to a new and unfamiliar pattern of reaction and/or relationships. In this respect patterns of emotional response and behavior function like habits. One is mostly completely blind to the possible self-defeats implicit to the repetition, just as he cannot recognize possible substantial advantages in a new pathway. Like an old and strong habit, the established pattern of reaction is familiar, becomes cherished, is clung to, and the individual reverts to it automatically.

4. Conditioned Emotional Responses

A. INCREASED SIGNIFICANCE OF EARLY EVENTS.—The process of conditioning also enters into the development of emotional patterns of reaction and relationship. Thus, the early traumata of infancy and childhood tend to condition the later adult emotional responses.

The first painful experience often is likely to sensitize the individual to a subsequent one of similar nature. Sometimes also in contrast, he may instead become desensitized. The reasons for such a difference in his response are often unclear. The greater priority of the emotional experiences which occur earlier in time will be discussed further in *Chapter Nine.* Repeated observations of this basic response have, as we shall see, led to the elaboration of a *Rule of Impression Priority;* this will be outlined further.

B. VITAL IMPORTANCE OF MOTHER.—Most often the early parent-child relationship of the depressed patient has been marked by a pattern of rejection, demands, denial, and frustration of infantile needs. The author estimates that this primarily concerns the mother, in at least three-quarters of the cases. By reason of her own insecurity, she has been unable to provide real acceptance and love. The mother may even demand or require that her infant (or older offspring) supply some of her own emotional needs. This can lead to the infant's deprivation, or further to his emotional exploitation.

✓ Thus is laid the foundation of "love-craving" of the depressed patient, although he may vigorously and on the conscious level deny any such interests or needs. Indeed, were it possible to provide an adequate amount of *genuine* acceptance, love, and security until maturity, emotional illness generally would be a minor problem for the human race. The First Tenet of the Parental Role [Ch.1:IIIC] outlines the maintenance of such a role as the prime aim and goal of the parent.

What happens in early life helps condition later adult responses and reactions. This concept is also an important precept in the Theory of Antecedent Conflicts.

5. Emotional-Exploitation Concept

At times analysis will disclose a domineering, exploiting mother (or father) who because of deep neurotic needs of her own must unconsciously use the child as her major source of emotional support and gratification. This can become extreme enough to be almost a reversal of the usual parent-child relationship.

Some of the resulting possible warping of emotions and attitudes is illustrated in the following example. We might refer to this as a kind of witting or unwitting Emotional-Exploitation. Such exploitation of the child by a parent or parent surrogate can lay the psychologic foundations for a later major emotional illness. This is what the author would refer to as the Emotional-Exploitation Concept, in the psychogenesis of emotional illness. At times the (partial) reversal of the usual child-parent relationship helps to set the stage for schizophrenia. In this case, however, the clinical sequela was a severe Depressive Reaction.

Case 33

Continued Emotional-Exploitation of a Seriously Depressed Person

(1) *Life-long devotion to mother*

A forty-six-year-old professional woman sought intensive therapy upon the advice of her friends and her physician. She was in the middle of her fourth attack of a severe Depressive Reaction, during the earlier three of which, extensive hospitalization had been required. She had all of the clinical manifestations of a deep emotional depression at the time that treatment was begun, and return to the hospital had only been held in abeyance pending a possible extramural trial of intensive psychotherapy.

The patient was the only child and sole support of an emotionally insecure and egocentric mother. She had remained unmarried in order to take care of her mother. Consciously she had feelings only of love and devotion for her mother. The latter had partly unconsciously, required her daughter, through many subtle but powerful pressures, to devote her life to her.

(2) *Forced rejection of father; Emotional-Exploitation Concept illustrated*

Early in the mother's marriage, the patient's father had been rejected, and divorced. He had proved incapable of satisfying the mother's inordinate neurotic needs. As a result of these failures on his part, and also in a defensive kind of justification, the mother had developed tremendous resentment and hatred of him. The mother had subsequently thoroughly inculcated the daughter with the picture of the father which she herself inevitably had. The patient had been taught to regard her father as a very evil person.

He was worthy only of scorn, contempt, and hatred. As a consequence, the daughter had *never since even seen* her father. She had perforce accepted the unrealistically harsh and totally inaccurate evaluation of him, which was actively fostered by her vengeful and unrelenting mother.

These were several of the severe distortions which had been induced in early years, and were subsequently carried over into her adult life. They had had all kinds of external and psychologic consequences for the patient. It is difficult in such a brief presentation to give much of a picture of the exploited life led by the patient in her devoted service to her mother. It was no wonder she was vulnerable to emotional depression, when some significant aspect of the small amount of personal life which was permitted her had collapsed.

(3) *Re-establishment of paternal relationship effected*

Intensive treatment in this case was most successful, but only over the course of several years of very difficult, albeit gratifying work. Only after great struggle, however, was she able to gain a more objective view of the family constellation. One most moving episode was the occasion when she was finally able, with some encouragement and support but essentially on her own, to effect a reconciliation with her father. This was after she had not even seen him for forty years! This helped open up a whole new vista in life for her.

He was a good man, sincere and kindly. He had been deeply puzzled and hurt by the mother's rejection of many years ago, as well as by the barriers erected between himself and his daughter. It was none too soon to effect the relationship, for the patient's father by this time was well past eighty years of age.

The patient also made some other very important healthy readjustments in her attitudes and ways of living. Formal treatment was completed over thirteen years ago as this is written. There was one very mild recurrence of depressive symptoms ten years ago. However, this was by no means comparable to the four prior attacks of deep depression. The mild symptoms present at this time subsided quite promptly under brief psychotherapy.

A somewhat similar case was reported to the author by a colleague, in which the mother-daughter relationship was marked by a somewhat similar domineering and demanding exclusive kind of possessiveness. The daughter was constantly imposed upon. In addition, the daughter subsequently had "found herself" in a long series of repeated, similar emotional involvements, during the course of her necessary business and social relationships with older women. The latter had been in part "seen" and dealt with by the patient, as though they were her mother.

The relationship with her mother had served as the very unsuitable prototype upon which the later very self-defeating relationships were inadvertently patterned. As a result they consistently came to grief and an ultimately painful collapse. Incidentally, these would usually be almost violently terminated, in a way that she could not dare to allow to happen with the mother relationship.

6. Infantile Needs; Sequence of Deprivation and Rejection → Rage → Apathy → Primal Depression

Bibring believed that the orally dependent type of person who constantly needs narcissistic supplies and gratifications from outside himself, probably represents that individual with the most frequent type of predisposition to depression. From the developmental standpoint, this would fit in with our concept of the powerless infant who cannot enforce gratification of, or even necessarily the recognition of, his vital early needs for affection, protection, security, love, and warmth—sometimes even for shelter and food. The disparity in power between himself and the parents, who are to him nearly omnipotent, is tremendous.

To be genuine, the acceptance and love, and the gratification of necessary infantile needs must be voluntary, freely given, and spontaneous. Their provision by a forced effort of will is indeed poor by comparison. The child needs a home which provides him with a secure base of operations, from which to sally forth into the world. The parent's provision of this might constitute the Second Tenet of the Parental Role. This needed base is part of our later Secure Base of Operations Concept [Ch.11:VIIA2].

Parental denial or deprivation of the infant's legitimate early needs and rejection, as we have noted, results in primal anxiety, frustration, and rage. To the casual observer the mother may actually appear most loving. In the subsequent reaction, however, one of the several pathways is followed, as the groundwork is laid for possible subsequent emotional difficulty. These can lead into several patterns of symptomatology. In the particular pathway which leads toward a primal depression, the deprivation, rejection, and frustration is continued on and on, in spite of any protests or cues provided by the infant as to his increasingly critical levels of anxiety and rage. The parent may also be unable as noted, through personal insecurities, to tolerate protests or any negative feelings from the child. Eventually the child tends to become exhausted and hopeless. In this vital sequence of events a depressive kind of apathy eventually comes to replace the rage. This is the primal depression.

Herein the infant has come face to face with his helplessness **and impotence** in traumatic fashion. There is further unrealistic guilt, fear, and anxiety over the presumed (or potential) destruction of the love-object. This reaction often sets the stage, so to speak, for later reactions to severe frustration in adult life. Herein may lie the earliest antecedent conflict of depression. Through these early experiences the individual becomes conditioned in his responses to later psychic trauma. A pattern for subsequent responses becomes established.

It should perhaps be stressed that conscious awareness is not present for much of this by any means. The entire early complex would be automatically and immediately repressed from consciousness, as part of one's protectively-intended psychologic mechanism.

7. Concept of Rejection and the Compliant Response

One element of significance which can be of some importance in certain Depressive Reactions, is at times quite prominent and evident, and which the author has not seen dealt with elsewhere, relates to rejection and the patient's response to it. The author is referring to his Concept of Rejection and the Compliant Response to it.

Rejection in the infantile and childhood years has been referred to earlier. It may be quite realistic or in part phantasied. Likewise with the guilt feelings over love-object destruction (or *wish* to destroy). These may be expressed and open, or are more likely to be covert and more or less concealed and dissembled. They contribute to generating feelings of worthlessness in the depressed person. A major traumatic event, such as the death or absence of a parent, also may be subjectively experienced as rejection.

Regardless of basis, all of this has important psychologic sequelae for the developing psyche. There is an impact on the self-picture; on one's estimation of his worth; on his level of self-evaluation.

In the Depressive Reaction some of the symptomatology is *as though the* ⌐ *patient is compliantly accepting the rejection*. It is *as though he accepts this as an accurate judgment of his low value and lack of worth* (which have lead to the rejection). Thus he "obediently" withdraws, retards his interests and activities and becomes more apathetic, saying in effect, "I am not worthy; I am not wanted. I've been rejected. Accepting this, I will withdraw myself. I accept the judgments." In this light also, the self-recriminations of the depressed patient can have another, or an additional meaning to that of the concealed punishment of another significant person, in that *they may reflect the implicit and complete acceptance of the actual or supposed, critical judgments of the rejecting person.*

The ultimate progression of this concept may become an important element in certain suicides, one for which the name of the *Implicit Command* is proposed. As shall be noted again, herein the patient obediently and in actuality removes himself, *as if in response to the Implicit Command in the rejection,* that is, "to be gone," "to vanish," or even more literally, to "drop dead," as interpreted by him intrapsychically.

This brief outline of five major points in our concept will conclude this section: (1) the unconscious nature of the Compliant Response to rejection; (2) its relative position, usually as one of a number of important dynamic factors; (3) its application in the primal Depressive Reactions; (4) its possible role according to the Theory of Antecedent Conflicts, and thus as part of an early developed pattern of response, subject to later and more ready re-adoption; and (5) its ultimate progression to a symbolic Implicit Command, as a significant factor in certain suicides.

B. FROZEN STATE OF RAGE

Depression may sometimes be referred to as a frozen state of rage. This is not inaccurate, although it is rather an oversimplification. To a less marked extent, Emotional Fatigue and the Fatigue States sometimes may be similarly regarded. The advantage of this concept lies in calling attention to the relation of depression to frustration, loss, and the consequent transition of the rage into depression. It must, however, be kept in mind that the rage does not subjectively exist in the patient's conscious awareness. The rage and its transmutation are unconscious. The patient subjectively and consciously is only aware of depression and its related effects.

Naturally it does no good at all to even suggest any of this to the depressed patient. The result at the least is most likely to be an indignant and vigorous denial. His resistances to insight will be stimulated perhaps to an extent to completely defeat any further therapeutic endeavors. He can only come to appreciate such a relationship after a prolonged period of intensive treatment, by a self-knowing therapist.

Rarely the patient may even translate his feelings into similar terms verbally. The following is a very interesting verbatim account of such an instance. Herein one can also gain some appreciation of the protective endeavor of the depressive variety of Psychologic Conversion.

Case 34

A Frozen State of Rage

(1) *Struggle between repression and depression*

A patient who had been in intensive psychotherapy for some time, suffered the misfortune of being passed over for an important position. It was one which he had long sought and to which he had some claim by virtue of his experience and tenure of service. Being passed over was a very severe disappointment.

This patient suffered feelings of great anger, frustration, disappointment, hurt, and resentment. Consciously he appeared to waver back and forth between feelings related to these, *versus* feelings of personal failure, dejection, and lowered spirits. It was a though he was struggling on the tightrope of repression on the one side, and depression on the other, with the outcome in doubt. During a treatment session, when the dejection and depression appeared to be becoming the more dominant, he reported his feelings.

(2) *Frozen feelings equate depression*

In his words: "I feel I have failed. My reaction to this was severe but controlled; I froze . . . I guess my whole reaction was just too strong and too painful to bear. I just froze up. These are things I have to control. These are my feelings. I am numb. No feelings. I don't care any more . . . .

"I feel I had some right to the position by length of service. I was there ahead of nearly everyone else in the office. I was the logical one. Now I just feel like giving it all up . . . .

"I was the first to go into the Army in the War. There I saw people get ahead of me and this hurt, but then I fought back. I felt they owed me more money and more rank, and I fought for it . . . Now I feel like this is a vote of no confidence. I feel defeated and beaten. My hurt is too deep. I guess underneath it all I am seething with rage. I know my feelings are strong, but *I can't feel them.* They're all bottled up and frozen down somewhere inside. All I feel now is beaten, and I just want to give it all up.

(3) *Numbness protectively intended*

"When I heard the news, I felt hurt and tearful. But I didn't cry. I froze instead. It's a matter of control, of numbness coming with the shock. I could continue to work in a vague sort of way, but I had little interest. I had to beg off from my handball team last night. I just wasn't up to it . . . .

"It's a violent attack on my ego. My pride is hurt. I want to retaliate; to get out, to move on, to show my independence . . . I just don't have much feeling still. I'm kind of numb. It's a protection . . . Maybe this is Nature's way when things become too painful. You just freeze up. It's Nature's way. It's a godsend; a numbness. Of course now I feel suspended, and don't know what to do or which way to turn . . ."

C. MASOCHISM AND SADISM IN DEPRESSIVE REACTIONS

Clinical manifestations of masochism in depression vary all the way from the mild self-doubts and recriminations in Depressive Reactions of moderate neurotic level, to the self-accusations and nearly constant battering self-reproach of the more severe borderline-psychotic depression. In the still more desperate depressions of a deeply and clearly psychotic level, these may progress to include delusional material.

This masochistic kind of self-punishment is not simply or superficially explained. It reflects a number of components, such as: ∨

(1) The overactivity of a harsh and relentless superego. One may view the superego as being in part the internalized parental authority. These originally constituted parental attitudes, and have been since taken over by the conscience.

(2) The leveling of similar attitudes toward the self, as were the earlier critical ones of parents, or parental figures. That is, even as he was to some extent earlier rejected by his parents, he now must perforce reject himself. This would include our Concept of the so-called "Compliant Response" [Ch.4:VIA7;XIH5].

(3) As a taking over personally of anticipated external retaliation for more submerged (that is, earlier deeply repressed) aggressive and hostile impulses.

(4) As the concealed punishment in sadistic fashion of the internalized frustrating object.

(5) As a concealed, likely caricatured expression toward the self, of critical and condemning attitudes of one of one's parents toward the other.

Point 4 is an important and deeply hidden (unconscious) psychologic operation. The masochism really overlies and aids in the concealment from conscious awareness of a deeper kind of sadism.

Freud's early statement, describing this defensively-intended intrapsychic operation remains valid today. He thus succinctly stated the psychodynamics of the unconscious sadistic role of the inversion of hostility, in his paper "Mourning and Melancholia." Herein he cited the secret (unconscious) sadistic satisfactions present in the torments of the melancholiac patient. He also pointed out the relation of this to a similar kind of process in obsession as follows:

The self-torments of melancholiacs which are without doubt pleasurable (*i.e.,* they provide unconscious satisfactions) signify, just like the corresponding phenomenon in the obsessional neuroses, a gratification of sadistic tendencies and of hate, both of which relate to an object and in this way have both been turned round upon the self. In both disorders the sufferers usually succeed in the end in taking revenge, by the circuitous path of self-punishment, on the original objects and in tormenting them by means of the illness, having developed the latter so as to avoid the necessity of openly expressing their hostility against the loved ones. After all, the person who has occasioned the injury to the patient's feelings, and against whom his illness is aimed, is usually to be found among those in his near neighborhood.

D. PRIMARY AND SECONDARY GAINS OF DEPRESSION: DEPRESSIVE ENDOGAIN AND EPIGAIN

1. Unconscious Gains Less Apparent in Depressive Reactions

The author has found it useful to direct attention toward the psychologic "gains" of the illness, in teaching the psychodynamic principles of the bases for emotional reactions generally. Similar principles apply in the Depressive Reactions, although these are quite complex, and tend to be more obscure than in certain other neurotic reactions. This of course, is in reference to the underlying "gains" which the patient unconsciously endeavors to secure through emotional depression. It is part of the rather complex but major concept of the unconscious gains of emotional illness generally, as presented in *Chapter 2*. One should gain familiarity with these important principles. We soon learn that these "gains" which are so vitally necessary, also prove to be actually paradoxical and often severely self-defeating. They comprise the epigain and the endogain of an illness.

In general, the depressive endogain (that is, the unconscious, primary gain of emotional illness), and the depressive epigain (that is, the unconscious part of the secondary gain of emotional illness) are less apparent in the Depressive Reactions. These unconscious gains are usually more apparent in certain other types of neurotic-level emotional illness, such as Somatic Conversion, Overconcern with Health, and some of the Neuroses-Following-Trauma.

2. Depressive Endogain

As we have learned earlier, the endogain serves deeply unconscious needs. This of course is true with the depressive endogain. On the basis of our current views of the psychodynamics of depression, these can be grouped approximately according to their several purposes. They are outlined in *Table 14*.

Table 14

The Depressive Endogain

The depressive endogain includes all of the unconscious primary gains of the intrapsychic process of emotional depression. It can be outlined as will follow. These deep internal psychologic needs of the individual are responsible for the initiation of the illness. They may be classified approximately in the following several groups.

1. *Concealment of hostility*

   This element of the Endogain refers to the unconscious repression and denial, and thereby control, of the feared and disowned hostile-aggressive drives. These have been aroused in response to continued frustration or loss. Later those losses, which may be objectively more minor, are reacted to emotionally in exaggerated fashion.

The individual has been already conditioned as a result of his early antecedent conflicts, his exhausting frustration, and his greater or lesser primal depression. Inversion of the unconscious hostility, and the onset of clinical depression are parts of the desperate effort to reinforce and to maintain repression.

2. *Punitive purposes*

A. *Masochistic self-punishment* is unconsciously pursued: (1) in response to the harsh superego; (2) as a repetition along similar lines, of earlier parental criticism (basically rejection); (3) in unconscious anticipation of retaliation, as earlier expected for hostility; (4) in expiation of guilt, which may be on a somewhat realistic level, or largely overvalued and neurotic, and in accord with our earlier Concept of the Compliant Response [Ch.4:VIA7;XIH5].

B. *Sadistic punishment* of the symbolic, magically-introjected object of frustration and denial. This is the object of dependency, which has failed to provide as needed and/or desired. This results in the unconscious gratification in symbolic fashion of the repressed hostile urges.

3. *A protective biologic purpose*

The prevention of any further psychologically uneconomic expenditure of energy and effort, in pursuit of a goal already clearly hopeless. Depression results in a restriction of the further depletion of the already weakened ego. In addition, the lessened drive and fading interests decrease the possibility of conflict, as "instinctual" drives and demands become less insistent.

The *biologic function* of emotional depression might thus possibly be likened to its physical counterpart of total exhaustion, in which enforced physical inactivity prevents further depletion of physical energy beyond an already dangerous point. This process, intended protectively, may get out of hand in the most severe Depressive Reactions, to the potential point of inanition and death.

4. *Paralysis, denial, avoidance*

There is also implicit in most Depressive Reactions: (*a*) a protective *paralysis of action* in response to the aggressive drives, with the resulting prevention or inhibition of any possible overt activity toward gratification; (*b*) the further outward *denial* of such aims; and (*c*) the depression may be regarded as a kind of psychologic *avoidance* through "flight" or escape from conflict.

The hostile and aggressive feelings have been repressed as intolerable and have become transmuted into depression, as one major pathway of Psychologic Conversion.

Psychologic defenses are an intimate part of the psychodynamics of any emotional illness. The defenses are erected unconsciously, against completely intolerable and therefore consciously disowned impulses and needs. These are primarily sexual or hostile-aggressive in nature. In the Depressive Reaction, the individual dare not lower his defenses, because he desperately fears his ability to master and control that which may emerge, for example, an anticipated hostility, which is feared to be of an uncontrollable and murderous level.

As "recognized" in the unconscious, likely the only two possible consequences are equally devastatingly destructive. It is thus conceived as a "black or white", or as an "either . . . or" reaction. One consequence would be the "success" of the uncontrollable murderous rage. The result would be the annihilation of the frustrating object. Its destruction would be an even more devastating loss, as it is also the actual or symbolic object of any even potential satisfaction of the desperate dependency needs. (*See* the later discussions of the Depression of Success, Ch.4:VIII. The other possible consequence as unconsciously anticipated, would be the failure of the rage in destroying its object. The destruction of the individual himself, in retaliation for his own aggressive aims or efforts, might well follow.

In a case of depression studied intensively some years ago it was possible to identify several elements of the depressive endogain.

Case 35

Onset of Depression Following Commitment of Spouse

(1) *Failure of long-term endeavor*

A forty-three-year-old scientist came under treatment for a severe Depression Reaction. This had been precipitated by his forcible recognition that his most strenuous exertions to salvage his alcoholically habituated wife were fruitless. This was after eight years of prodigious personal effort. He became despairing and hopeless when things went increasingly wrong, despite his best efforts.

When commitment to a hospital finally became necessary for the wife, he could no longer completely avoid awareness of her now organic cerebral impairment. Any real resolution was now impossible. His efforts had been marked by unending devotion, patience, and self-sacrifice. However, he had also repressed a great deal of concomitant and almost inevitable hostility. There was considerable guilt present for his simultaneous contributions to the increasingly poor relationship between himself and his wife. This had helped in turn to foster the alcoholic tendencies.

(2) *Lost love object also agent of frustration*

His repetitive self-accusatory comments about *his* failures served his own overdeveloped superego. They also clearly reflected his symbolic, disowned hostile expression toward his (incorporated) wife (love object). He bore the deepest resentment toward her, for *her* failure in the marriage. He secretly resented her for her failure to get well, for her failure to respond to his efforts to help, and for her failure to gratify some of his own deep-seated dependent needs.

The wife was not only the lost love-object, but the agent of frustration as well. By this intense censored hostility being (outwardly) directed toward himself, the unconscious endeavor was to reinforce the denials as to the real object of the furious side of his ambivalent feelings—to reinforce repression.

(3) *Recapitulation of antecedent relationships and conflicts*

The wife was the surrogate in symbolic fashion, for his own, much earlier unsatisfactory and unsatisfying object-person of dependency. The early relationship was antecedent, and had been inevitably accompanied by repressed severe conflicts. The latter were in effect reactivated, by the marital relationship and difficulties, and its final complete failure and loss.

Finally the depression, with its great restriction of interest, activity, and drive, effectively blocked further pursuit of a fruitless endeavor. This man's depression was a last desperate attempt to stave off conscious recognition (that is, to maintain the repression) of the disowned hostile part of his great ambivalence. He had inevitably played an unwitting contributory role in the development of his wife's alcoholism, long prior to her final breakdown. The recognition of this also helped to contribute to the Depressive Reaction.

3. Depressive Epigain

In the foregoing case we can see the final surrender of the hopeless ego-ideal (that is, goal)—the restoration of the alcoholic wife and the marriage. As this possible external source of narcissistic supply becomes clearly hopeless, we can also see some of the attempted depressive epigain (that is, the unconscious part of the secondary gains), of the illness. There has been a degree of regression to early oral levels and an implicit appeal to dependence. The depressed patient says in effect to the external world, "I am helpless. I must be looked after. I need to be taken care of."

He tries thus (unconsciously) to secure love, attention, affection, and tenderness, or substitutes for them, partly because of his great inner deprivation and need. They are also sought in part as reassurance that his own aggression can be tolerated. So urgent and basic are these and other needs, that some of the most seriously depressed patients would, unlike conversion (hysterical) or other categories of patients, die without being able to lift a finger in their own behalf, even for food. The end result may be the requirement for the forced feeding of some of the most deeply depressed patients, and this becomes occasionally necessary in mental hospitals.

The depressive epigain includes the securing of acceptance and love, or, at the least, attention, as a poor substitute. Through the symptoms or the overall illness, these gains are attempted, secured, or forced. The depressed patient's self-recriminations and self-accusations, for example, may also say in effect, "See how much I punish myself. Witness how I suffer." He unconsciously pleads, "Won't someone please come to my defense? At least won't someone feel kindly and sympathetic, and respond with some of the external supplies which I so desperately need? Appreciate my hard-pressed position, and how deprived I have been?" Surprisingly enough to the inexperienced, the response of verbal sympathy and attempted reassurance only makes the depressed patient feel worse. While he unwittingly invites this, he only uses it to further depress himself. To him reassurance often conveys the message that the person attempting it cannot possibly understand him, or the desperateness of the situation. Further, the result is for his difficulties to appear more mountainous and to make him feel even more despondent and desperate. By the same token, one cannot agree with him and accept his own overvaluation of his problems. One *can* listen, exhibit his interest, make further inquiry, and seek to understand.

In the regression which more or less takes place to an oral level, the patient unconsciously seeks attention, sympathy, love, affection, and protection. This is the desperate appeal for the narcissistic supply, of which he has felt deprived. This occurs in deeper and less apparent but actually not too dissimilar fashion to that which we shall see illustrated in the epigain of the conversion patient. This, the epigain in depression, usually relates to regressive oral needs, and to the attempt to produce desired effects on certain people. It, like other gains which are primary, is unconscious (that is, out of awareness). It would, of course be denied verbally and probably vehemently by the depressed patient. It is not at all a subject for discussion, at the least until some possibly propitious and appropriate time, quite well along in the course of intensive psychotherapy and analysis.

An example of the situational effects of the depressive illness in actually producing secondary gain might be briefly cited in illustration. In the following instance (*Case 36*), the gain is substantial. It was, however, also achieved out of awareness (that is, unconsciously), and at a considerable price, as is nearly always the case in the so-called gains of emotional illness.

Case 36

The Depressive Epigain

Following the blow of learning that his paramour was pregnant, the young man involved rapidly developed a deep Depressive Reaction. The unwelcome news had been a most bitter blow to him. He became caught in an intolerable conflict between the demands of his harsh conscience on the one hand, and his total inability to face the prospect of marriage on the other. His "secret" fury and condemnation of the girl also had to be disowned. A Depressive Reaction was the result.

He was hospitalized for the illness, and remained in hospital for several months. On one level his illness said in effect, "I'm sick and helpless and can do nothing. Someone else, someone stronger must take over and solve this desperate problem, which I cannot face." Actually exactly this happened. The girl reached her own solution. This particular intolerable situation no longer faced him. The patient slowly recovered.

Other secondary gains may be present. These may be conscious, or unconscious, or both. They may include the avoidance through illness of an intolerable work or family situation. The effects which are secured through the illness upon other people may be very important on a deeper level, to the patient concerned. They may include actually or symbolically, for example, punishment (via passive aggression), or deprivation of love, affection, support, or sexual satisfaction. Important people around the patient are inevitably affected. In the severe Depressive Reaction, however, their greatest efforts are generally ineffective in satisfying the patient. He is now inconsolable. He unconsciously demands, but his demands not only are silent, but also they cannot be met.

The loss of sexual interest can have deeper psychodynamic implications, representing part of the general forestalling of drives, and acting as a protection of the weakened ego against additional possible conflict. Its restriction appears at times to be almost an extension, a carryover, or an overflow to this important aspect of the patient's emotional life, of the general inhibition, retardation, and general emotional restriction.

4. Unconscious Goal of Lost-Object Reunion

Much of the emphasis in the dynamics has been on the unconscious goal (and the simultaneous denial or inhibition of the drives toward it, together with self-punishment for having it, and so on) of destruction of the object of frustration. The resulting conflicts over this are important ones.

In the following instance, an additional unconscious goal was the reunion with earlier lost parents. This goal may be also simultaneously present and a contributing factor dynamically in certain kinds of Depressive Reactions. The unconscious aim of what we might accordingly term Lost-Object Reunion may be operative in depressions which either shortly, or after a longer period of time follow the death of someone close. It has not received adequate recognition heretofore in the psychodynamics of the Depressive Reactions. (*See also* the *Unit-Guilt Reaction,* Ch.14:VIID3.)

Case 37

The Goal of Reunion with Earlier Lost Parents

The thirty-four-year-old wife of a surgeon entered analysis for the treatment of a Depressive Reaction. In the course of her therapy, which was quite lengthy, all the dynamics usually expected were found. In addition, the idea of suicide was often represented, particularly in dream material, as a means of being reunited with her mother and father. Both parents had been lost before she had completed adolescence. The unconscious goal to be achieved was reunion with the loved objects, and not their destruction (although that also was seen over and over).

A saving sense of humor was discovered and encouraged. This proved of help in treatment. Illustrative of this was her turning of her hostility outward when faced, for example, with the necessity of appearing at an organizational meeting. This would demand her presence and perhaps speaking, or greeting members. On these occasions she would laugh and say, "Maybe a cyclone will hit the club building before the meeting, or maybe lightning will hit it, or at least something." This she would say as a child might impishly take delight in visiting such fantasied aggression upon those adults who require of him a performance he dreads.

Utilizing this sense of humor at times, her analyst would laughingly ask, "What's the worst thing that can happen?" As a child playing a game, she would then delight in conjuring up all sorts of quite unlikely fantasies. These, however, permitted some measure of expression of her otherwise unconscious terrific aggression and hostility. She could laugh while she was thus in fantasy visiting a carnage of destruction upon external persons and objects.

E. IN SUMMARY

To recapitulate, the intrapsychic factors comprising the depressive endogain are responsible for the initiation of the illness. An outline of the needs comprising the depressive endogain was offered in *Table 14*. The depressive epigain in turn may have a role in its perpetuation, but certainly this is likely to be less significant, and usually is far less readily apparent than, for example, in the Conversion Reactions. An escape into activity can γ be a defense against depression (Pp. 282, 412-14).

The forces which initiate a depressive reaction are to be found in both the external environment and the intrapsychic one. The unconscious evolvement of the depressive position, its reactivation as representing an earlier antecedent, or the regression to it, depends upon the initiating stress, the breakdown of previously adequate defenses, and the long range influences of the person's entire past experiences in living.

The loss of self-esteem and the recriminations of self-doubt and self-reproach become the pathologic means by which consciously intolerable hostility finds symbolic expression. Seemingly directed entirely toward the self in masochistic fashion, this actually also represents the symbolic punishment of the introjected cause of loss, frustration, or disappointment.

The importance of ambivalence has been stressed, and the primary and secondary gains of depression illustrated. Depression varies in level from mild to stuporous. The regression which occurs is primarily towards the oral level. The primal depression establishes in childhood an antecedent pattern for later depression in the adult. This occurs when the ego has been weakened by frustration, defeat, or by the loss of ego ideals and goals.

VII. SITUATIONAL OR REACTIVE DEPRESSION

A. PRECIPITATED BY TRAUMATIC EVENT

1. Definition

Certain Depressive Reactions are classified as so-called Situational or Reactive Depressions, when they occur following a specific traumatic situation. For occasional cases the use of these terms has a certain convenience.

One must not lose sight however, of the very important internal factors, the dynamics of depression. The specific trauma or event is not the *raison d'etre,* the cause of the depression. It may, however, serve an important precipitating function in the onset of the illness. Thus the Reactive Depression is precipitated by a personally significant situation or loss, which is external and rather readily identified.

The Reactive Depression may be defined as *a depressive neurotic reaction which follows a specific traumatic situational blow, tragedy, event, or loss. The event which it follows serves an important function in the precipitation of the illness, as opposed to being its cause as such.* When they play an important role in precipitating an illness, the presence of such external situational factors can be of importance prognostically and may indicate a self-limited course.

2. Types of Precipitating Situations

The author has observed instances of so-called Reactive Depressions which have followed such diverse "specific" traumatic situations as failures in school and business, the discovery of an unwanted pregnancy, apprehension for a criminal offense, being jilted, retirement, separation and divorce, death and birth, court martial conviction, and political defeat. The actual, fantasied, or magical loss of a love-object (or what stands for it symbolically) is a basic and central theme in the onset of the so-called traumatic or precipitating event in the Reactive Depression.

The following instance (*Case 38*) illustrates the onset of a depression as a reaction to involuntary retirement.

Case 38

Situational (Reactive) Depression Following Involuntary Retirement

A fifty-eight-year-old single woman, a former professional worker in Federal service, consulted her family physician because of feeling "run down." He elicited symptoms also of nervousness, insomnia, and listlessness. Further observing her apathetic appearance, he correctly diagnosed a Depressive Reaction of neurotic level. Upon psychiatric evaluation, evidence was uncovered of a withdrawal of interests, low spirits, a loss of spontaneity, and some slowing of thinking. The insomnia was of the type pathognomonic of depression, as earlier described.

The history disclosed that her involuntary retirement had transpired about three months earlier. Serious, devoted to her work, and centering her life around it for years, she had no resources to fall back upon when retired. She had gradually become depressed, nervous, restless, and had lost interest in things generally. There were also some suicidal ruminations present. This patient made a satisfactory recovery over the course of some months of a moderately intensive psychotherapeutic regimen.

B. ALL DEPRESSIONS REACTIVE

From a very broad viewpoint, all depressions might be regarded as reactive. They always follow a loss, be it actual or symbolic, sudden and acute, or not. This is true whether the loss be specific and apparent, or most obscure and non-identifiable, by the usual means of observation.

We shall next see how this principle applies even in the seemingly inconsistent type of Depressive Reactions which may occasionally be actually precipitated by success, by the achievement of a long-sought-after goal.

VIII. DEPRESSION OF SUCCESS

A. SUCCESS EQUATES GREAT LOSS

1. Definition

A curious and most interesting phenomenon is the seemingly paradoxical Depressive Reaction that sometimes follows the achievement of a long-sought-after success, or sometimes the achievement of an unexpected goal. This is what can be termed the Depression of Success. This type of depression is apt to be more severe when the success is outstanding. It may reach psychotic proportions.

Although the psychodynamics are not simple, they are very interesting. It is entirely possible for us to understand how depression can follow marked success, in a way that is in keeping with our previous discussion and insights into the psychodynamics of depression. Herein we find that the success as achieved, actually equates (symbolically and intrapsychically) a great loss to the person concerned!

The Depression of Success is *the seemingly paradoxical Depressive Reaction which sometimes follows the achievement of what appears to ordinary observation to be a considerable success. On a deeper symbolic level, the success or goal which is achieved unconsciously represents a most vital loss to the individual concerned.* The Success-Depression is that type of Depressive Reaction which follows significant achievement.

2. Dynamics

√ We have seen that depression develops partly as a desperate effort to conceal and to control the hostile side of the intense ambivalence. This includes the rejected drives to vanquish, annihilate, outdo, or destroy; ultimately, to orally incorporate. These intolerable and disowned drives were originally directed toward the loved object. One dares not harm this object, however, because of the simultaneous vital dependence upon it.

How then does depression follow a great achievement or success? How does the success come to represent symbolically on an unconscious level a vital loss to the individual concerned?

In the Depression of Success, the success symbolically recapitulates the primal ambivalent struggle of the oral phase and its "successful" resolution. Herein, the hostility has symbolically achieved its destructive aim. This is equated by the success as achieved.

In effect, one has "out-promoted oneself." He has symbolically achieved the destruction of the loved object. Now the terrible thing secretly desired, but also terribly feared, rejected, and denied to conscious awareness, has happened. How can one ever again be dependent? The object of dependency has been symbolically destroyed, swallowed up. The loss of the symbolic object of dependency, on this deeper unconscious level, is equivalent to the loss of the more usual external and tangible object of dependency, such as we have seen illustrated earlier in other Depressive Reactions.

The destroyed object is irreplaceable. It is a terribly severe loss, for which the patient is inconsolable. This is the essence of the psychodynamics of the Depression of Success. Some added important factors will be considered as we proceed.

B. PROMOTION DEPRESSION

1. Vital Unconscious Needs Subserved: Endogain

A reasonably common variant of the Depression of Success is what we might term the Promotion Depression. This interesting and challenging reaction is encountered occasionally in military service and in business. Seemingly a paradox clinically, a Depressive Reaction can be precipitated by the failure to be promoted, and also by *being* promoted! Psychodynamically, however, each can make sense.

If one of these persons suffering with a Promotion Depression could talk "straight from his unconscious," he might say something like the following semitheoretical instance.

Case 39

A Depression of Success

(1) *The "unconscious" speaks, in figurative terms*
"One of my secret hidden drives is sadistic: to hurt, to destroy, to acquire, to take over, to swallow up. I couldn't possibly ever face the thought of having these terrible feelings. They were far, far too

dangerous in childhood as I "saw" them. They threatened, if successful, to deprive me of what I also very most vitally needed—mother and
mothering. The consequences of their success were too terrible to
contemplate . . . .

"There was also the terribly dreaded danger of retaliation. Even the
chance that I might become aware consciously of the existence of such
feelings fills me with anxiety. Accordingly, I have developed opposite
traits (character defenses) to conceal recognition even from myself.
I am outwardly acquiescent, compliant, pliable, and conciliatory.

(2) *Defense against hostility imperiled*

"My promotion swept me with success feelings. These made me more
nearly (and dangerously) aware of how much I really wanted my destructive feelings to succeed—my sadism. I was further impelled into
a more active position; into a position of more independence and responsibility. My previously more dependent position was also part of
my defense against a more active position.

"It was also a defense against my hostility. Threatened with recognition of my hidden, consciously disowned sadism, I can no longer
reinforce my hiding of this from myself by seeking refuge and withdrawal. I am less able now to keep out of the spotlight, to keep out of
a more active, less dependent position.

(3) *Loss of "dependent position" significant*

"My object loss is not an outward disappointment or frustration then,
but a symbolic one—the loss of my dependent position. This becomes,
further, the symbolic loss of the original object of the positive dependent side of the ambivalence; (usually) mother, and the mothering
I must have to survive."

2. *Those Wrecked by Success*

In discussing "those wrecked by success," Freud once referred to an
interesting example of the onset of a Depressive Reaction in a medical
school teacher. This had had its onset following his selection to fill the
place of his retiring professor. In commenting many years later on what
must have been this same case, Reik said, "The physician behaved as if
his (sadistic and) ambitious wishes had brought about the death of his
predecessor." There is, of course, more interpretation possible when we
follow the psychodynamics as summarized in the foregoing paragraphs.

The terrible guilt and loss followed his fantasied replacement (out-
doing, vanquishing, destruction) of the professor. His predecessor was
an older man who must have stood symbolically in the same authority and
being-depended-upon position as did an important parental figure (here,
likely the father primarily). The success symbolically recapitulated the
antecedent conflict of the oral phase of personality development. Now,
however, the aim of the negative sadistic ambivalence of the oral phase had
achieved success in symbolic fashion. The success was disastrous. A Depressive Reaction ensued.

C. RELATED DEPRESSIVE REACTIONS

1. *Completion Depression*

Other interesting related factors exist in the production of similar types
of Depressive Reactions. There is, for example, the potential for emotional
and physical letdown following the completion of a great time-filling and
absorbing undertaking or project. The author suggests the descriptive

term of Completion Depression for this type of reaction, when it is sufficiently marked clinically. It can be regarded as a variation of the Depression of Success. There are dynamic relationships to the so-called "let down" reaction following prolonged exertion and stress. [Ch.7:IIC*1*]

This type of reaction can involve many activities, such as the completion of a major construction or engineering project, raising a family, completing a novel or textbook, a major professional or business endeavor, a political campaign or term of office, a career, a military assignment, a tour of duty, a cropping season, and many others. The emotions which follow can well approach the Depressive Reaction in severity.

This is an interesting kind of possible human reaction which has been earlier recognized. Nietzsche (1844–1900), for example, wrote of "the melancholia of everything completed." The author has had some personal experience following the completion of long-range writing endeavors, as with the present text.

Sometimes the onset of a "common cold" may be observed to take place at this kind of juncture, in which it serves as a depressive-equivalent.

There are additional more superficial sources for the guilt feelings which may follow the achievement of success. There is, sometimes, for example, the realization of a person (endowed with a severe superego) that the success achieved and recognition accorded is actually, or in his subjective appraisal, not in keeping with the quality of the work and accomplishments.

2. Work as Escape

Preoccupation with one's work is sometimes evolved as a defense against depression and anxiety. Intensive preoccupation with a challenging task, a hobby, or some other activity may thus in itself serve as a defense against depression. By this kind of emotional, attentional, and energy absorption, people at times seek unconsciously to ward off depression. Its completion (that is, its successful finishing) can: (1) deprive the individual of his defensive preoccupation, and (2) have certain symbolic meanings, as earlier noted.

There are relationships here, of course, to the defenses of the obsessive person, as we shall see when we consider the Character Defenses. Involvement in work is also more directly observed on occasion to serve as an escape, or as an attempted escape, from worry, conflicts, and troublesome feelings. In this way also, work may serve as a more direct kind of attempted defense against anxiety.

3. Further Implications

There are some important dynamic relationships between the foregoing and certain other Depressive Reactions. Depression following the death of a loved person, for instance, can have some similar dynamic components. Herein the death and loss may to a greater or lesser extent also symbolically represent the destruction of the object of dependency. The unconscious meaning may be a kind of disastrous success of the repressed hostile aim. To the unconscious of the person concerned, the simultaneously loved and vital object of dependency has been magically destroyed by the negative aspect of his ambivalence.

This interesting but complex psychodynamic sequence will not occur unless: (1) there is a considerable amount of repressed ambivalent hostility, or (2) a primordial conflict in childhood has been present, to serve as a necessary antecedent. A sufficient stress in later life would serve to recapitulate the antecedent ones and accordingly would have far more important symbolic and unconscious meanings to the individual concerned.

IX. THE ANXIOUS DEPRESSION

A. CONCURRENT ANXIETY AND DEPRESSION

1. Incomplete Symptom-Defense Concept

In this type of major Depressive Reaction there is a substantial amount of anxiety experienced concurrently with the emotional depression. This anxiety is often expressed externally by the psychomotor symptoms of restlessness and agitation. These may tend to disguise, to cover over, or to divert attention from some of the depressive features, such as retardation. When a reasonable quantum of anxiety is present, this contributes evidence that the Psychologic Conversion has not been completely effective. This is in accord with our *Concept of Incomplete Symptom-Defense* [Ch.3:IIA*1*;-Ch.14:VB*3*]. Its ultimate purpose is to serve as a defense against the subjective experiencing of anxiety. If the depression has proved to be an adequate defense, if the depressive endogain were sufficient, the concurrent anxiety would not be present.

The Anxious Depression is often a most serious type of reaction. The incompleteness of the defense sometimes appears to stimulate the pathologic progression. It may be a precursor of the fulminating kind of agitated psychotic depression, into which it merges, in its furthest progression.

2. Definition

The Anxious Depression is *an emotional reaction in which there is concurrent marked anxiety and depression. The presence of the anxiety denotes the incompleteness of the defense of depression.*

The reaction clinically can vary from a mild one to the ultimate extreme of an Agitated Depressive Reaction of psychotic depth. (*See* earlier dynamic formulations of depression, Ch.4:VI.) The Agitated Depression is the most striking clinical reaction-example to be found of the Concept of Incomplete Symptom-Defense.

3. Resistance to Therapy; Agitation Gauge

Often these patients are very resistant to therapy. In the following example a physician who suffered from just such a severe Depressive Reaction could not accept psychotherapeutic help.

Case 40

A Physician with an Anxious Depression

A forty-six-year-old pediatrician from a distant southern city arranged for psychiatric consultation, in order to discuss "domestic problems." There were ample indications, corroborated from independent sources, of outstanding success in his medical career over the past eighteen years. His professional work, however, had declined steadily in quality and quantity for some months.

His attitudes toward himself were marked by the "attitude-symptoms" of self-depreciation and doubt. His self-evaluation was not at all in keeping with the actuality of his wide reputation for medical competence. He had a position of real respect and enjoyed an excellent professional reputation in medical circles. A rather rigid, highly conscientious, mildly obsessive physician, he deservedly held the confidence of both colleagues and patients.

The deterioration of the marital situation had been gradual. These difficulties had terminated in divorce eight months before our consultation. The divorce appeared to be the immediate precipitating event in a severe Anxious Depression. Concurrently with his declining interest in medical practice, he devoted a larger percentage of his time and effort in futilely trying to persuade his wife to return to him.

He assumed (unrealistically), total responsibility for the marital difficulties. As he talked of his need for his wife, he paced the floor, he was quite agitated, and wept copiously. He stated: "If I were a real man, I would end all this difficulty . . . I have been a failure . . . I guess I can't be depended upon." Actually, this was a consciously concealed (that is, unconscious) reproach of his wife.*

His restlessness rapidly progressed to the point where he was unable adequately to practice his profession. His time was largely spent in driving his car around the city, more or less aimlessly. He described how he had already consulted well known psychiatrists in three different cities. He had been unable to accept their suggestions, or their advice to begin psychotherapy.

This patient was suffering from an Anxious Depression, in which his severe state of psychomotor restlessness augured ill for an early recovery. It is indeed sometimes possible in this type of case to gauge directly the gravity of the illness according to the amount of agitation which is concurrently present with the emotional depression. In these distressing reactions the utilization of such an *agitation gauge* also can have some value on occasion, prognostically.

At the time of consultation, the physician in the foregoing case was unable to undertake treatment on a voluntary basis. Yet he was not sick enough for hospitalization to be effected involuntarily, through his enforced legal commitment. This unfortunate kind of situation has been referred to earlier [Ch.4:IIIC1].

Such tragic borderline situations occur not infrequently. Most of our State commitment laws have inadequate provisions to allow for handling them more effectively. These establish provisions which operate, in effect, so that only overtly psychotic patients can be readily and safely sent to a hospital for treatment, unless they fully concur.

---

* From a technical standpoint, this physician's Anxious Depression also represents dynamically the masochistic inversion of his unconscious sadism. Further, his self-reproaches might well have been transposed to his former spouse. From our earlier study of the psychodynamics of depression, we can see there are other important dynamic aspects also illustrated.

4. Added Clinical Features

In the Anxious Depression there is usually a prominent self-accusatory, reproachful, and self-depreciatory theme which is more or less unrealistic. (*Note* earlier dynamic formulations.) The Anxious Depression, as noted, is characterized by restlessness or by mild to moderate agitation, which may cover over some of the apathy, withdrawal, and retardation of depression. Anxious Depressions may be classified with the group of neurotic illnesses as herein described, when they are clearly neurotic in level.

Actually, all Depressive Reactions, as all mental mechanisms, are to be understood ultimately as the expression of, and the defense against, anxiety. The analysis in depth of each and every one of them will so demonstrate. Hence: (1) The parallelism in frequency of both anxiety and depression. The fact is that anxiety is an ubiquitous, basic human experience, with depression, as it were, one of its possible results. (2) An Anxious Depression is dynamically not different from another depression. Anxiety is either more on the surface, or more in quantity, or more acceptable, hence less in need to be controlled (or sometimes even less possible to control) than are other aspects of the Depressive Reaction.

X. ONE-DAY DEPRESSION

A. BRIEF DEPRESSIVE REACTIONS POSSIBLE

This brief note is included to help emphasize the fact that a Depressive Reaction does not have to be a drawn-out affair. It does not necessarily have to be a long-term illness. At times one may see brief episodes which are really depressive in character and which are quickly over. An example is the One-Day Depression. Here the subjective manifestations are those of a from mild to moderate depression of spirits. This is not merely discouragement, although it may be so described. The feelings are out of proportion to their *apparent* stimulus. The One-Day Depression can be defined as *an episodic, brief Depressive Reaction.*

This sequela may be the response to the cumulative effect of psychologic events, perhaps deferred in their effect until this occasion. The One-Day Depression may occur in a person already prone to depression. It may come on during the day, and may be accompanied (or expressed in equivalent form) by various physiologic disturbances, such as coldness, fatigue, a "letdown" feeling, lack of energy, or a loss of the ordinary level of interests. These are physical or *physiologic equivalents* of the depression. After a day, more or less, the reaction has run its course. Often, for example, the person simply awakes the following morning with no trace of the depressed mood.

Sometimes this type of reaction is manifested through one or more additional possible equivalents of depression. The principal features in such instances may include such physical or physiologic equivalents as headache, appetite loss, nausea, and even vomiting. For some individuals, an attack of migraine or an acute coryza may be the "functional equivalent" of the One-Day Depression. This brings us to a comment about emotional implications of the common cold.

B. COMMON COLD AND DEPRESSION

The relationship of the common cold to emotional factors is increasingly recognized. While there remains firm resistance to such recognition in some professional quarters, an increasing number of observations tend to confirm such a relationship.

Depression and colds have some clinical correlation. Thus, a brief Depressive Reaction may: (1) usher in a common cold, (2) have a cold as one, or as *the* manifestation of the reaction, or (3) show some improvement while the cold is present. At times a cold appears as a substitute for depressed feelings. The manifestations of an acute coryza can symbolically equate suppressed weeping and tears. In the severely depressed patient (three recent such examples are recalled), there may be no colds during the course of several years in therapy. On the other hand, certain "partially" depressed patients can have frequent sniffles.

An interesting corroboration of lay appreciation of some of the relationships of discouraged, depressed, and jilted feelings to susceptibility to colds was offered in *Guys and Dolls,* a musical. The heroine sings "A Person Can Develop a Cold" in these circumstances, usually with a sympathetic and quite perceptive and understanding audience reaction. The lyrics interestingly outline one route in the psychosomatic background of the cold and *la grippe.*

C. INTERNAL NEEDS OFTEN SATISFIED

Often the internal purposes responsible appear to be satisfied by One-Day Depression. However, this reaction may be repeated or may even occur with some frequency. On the other hand, nothing further of this kind may occur for months, or sometimes for years.

This kind of reaction, expressed in equivalent features, may enter into some of the many otherwise unexplained and obscure transient brief attacks of malaise, discomfort, and "physical" illness.

XI. SUICIDE

A. INTRODUCTION

A. MASOCHISM AND SADISM.—A discussion of the Depressive Reactions would not be complete without inclusion of some further important features concerning the closely related subject of suicide. Additional major aspects of this significant medical and social problem are accordingly summarized in this section.

Suicide is to be defined simply, as *the act of self-destruction.* It may be regarded as the extreme self-destructive end result, of complex unconscious drives. It is the ultimate combined destructive expression or "acting out" of the unconscious, self-punitive drives and the unconscious sadistic drives such as are present in depression. In suicide the self becomes the external object-victim, upon whom is focused in action both the unconscious sadistic and masochistic drives. Suicide combines the unconscious urge to kill, the desire to die (including compliance with the Implicit Command [Ch.4:XIH5]), and the wish to be killed. All are achieved in the "successful" suicide.

B. ACTING OUT UNCONSCIOUS IMPULSES.—Thus, the act of suicide inevitably expresses symbolically, strong intrapsychic hostile-aggressive forces, like those we have studied in the Depressive Reactions. In suicide, these unconscious impulses become irresistable, and are actually murderous in extent.

In quite literal fashion, they are "acted out." The consequence is death. This result is the ultimate in self-defeat. Suicidal attempts can also invite attention to the self-defeat in contributory neurotic drives (*See Case 53*, p. 265).

B. INCIDENCE

1. Major Area for Medical Concern

Suicide is by no means a minor area of medical concern. This is true from many standpoints, including the statistical standpoint alone. There are undoubtedly a great many unverified, unreported, not clearly recognized or admitted (as outlined in the earlier Concept of Euphemistically-Intended Disguises, [Ch.4:IVB1]) or even deliberately concealed cases of suicide. Cover Reasons [Ch.4:IVB2] in suicidal notes in turn tend to observe the motivations. There are many, many additional cases in which there is unrecognized "partial" psychologic or physiologic suicide. Finally, there are a great many psychologically determined "accidents" [Ch.4:-XID1] and other kinds of what we might refer to as "Suicidal Equivalents". (*See also* earlier Concept of Emotional Death, Ch.3:IIC5.)

Disregarding all of these untabulated instances, there were still a tragic total of 17,145 verified and officially reported cases of "total" suicide in the United States as long ago as 1950. This gave a death rate from the *reported* cases of suicide alone of 11.4 cases per 100,000 population per year. This number exceeds 20,000 annually by 1963 (an 11.5 rate).

Dublin estimated (in 1963) that there are now nearly two million persons in the U.S. who have attempted suicide at least once. Suicide accounts for twice as many deaths as tuberculosis or peptic ulcer. There are 2.5 times as many victims as from homicide and 12 times as many as from all types of aircraft accidents. This is a major medical problem. It cannot be lightly shrugged away.

Suicide has a significantly higher position as a leading cause of death for certain age groups. It is actually ranked *number five* for all white males between 15 and 44 years of age. White males account for about three-fourths of all deaths from suicide in the United States. The incidence at 50 years is six times that at 20. Below 15, suicidal thoughts are common, suicide itself is rare. As one of the leading overall causes of death, suicide ranks *number eleven**. This breaks down further for the white population into cause *number eight* for the males (17.5 per 100,000 in 1960–62) and cause *number twelve* for the females (5.5 per 100,000 deaths in 1960–62). For non-whites, the figure as to the order in the

---

* *See also* earlier comments on incidence [Ch.4:IVA3].

leading causes drops to *nineteen* for males and *twenty-nine* for females. The position of suicide as a leading cause of death, has gradually increased in rank since 1900 as other causes, especially those due to communicable diseases, have been better controlled. The overall rate per 100,000 population has varied from 17 (1910–1915), to a low of slightly under 10 (1920) to a Depression high of 18 (1932), to 10–12 (1942–1965).

Physicians, attorneys, dentists and professional men are subject to a high rate of suicide. Two per cent of physicians so end their lives; six percent of all physician deaths under age 65 are due to suicide. Among the medical specialties psychiatrists appear to suffer a higher rate.

Methods of suicide in the United States vary with sex. Almost half of the men use firearms. Hanging, gas, and poison *plus* sedatives, follow in that order. More women choose sedatives and poison than gas, firearms, or hanging. (*See* footnote for comparison with methods in Japan).

Following these figures through the years reveals relatively little change.* A slight decrease in the war years and a corresponding increase in the depression years of the thirties did take place, however, and these facts have certain significances. A slow increase in numbers or in rate in the coming years can reflect more accurate and complete reporting, and might well be expected.

Figure 2 indicates the incidence of suicide according to age groups. Note the increasing incidence which takes place during the middle years. Note earlier reference [Ch.4:VA5] to the stressful adult era (an S.E.H.A.) of *passing-the-peak*. The three decades from 40 to 70 years of age are the ones with the greatest incidence. Suicide is particularly a threat of the middle years. This approximately conforms to the period of the greatest incidence of the Depressive Reactions. The *rate* of suicide per unit of population, shows almost a steady climb with advancing age groups. Refer to Ch.4:IVB*1* for added comments about the prevalence of suicide, and additional statistics.

The tragic part of all this is that very many of the persons who commit suicide are substantial actual or potential, contributors to society. Given the best of medical care and psychotherapy, they could, in most instances, be restored to emotional health, and to increased personal and social effectiveness.

2. *Suicidal Thoughts Universal in Occurrence; "The Three D's"*

Suicidal thoughts and trends have a very widespread, perhaps an almost universal, incidence. This was discussed earlier in this chapter, when

---

* In Maryland, for example, the rate was 10.62 per 100,000 population in 1952, 11.08 in 1953, and 10.48 in 1961. It is interesting to note that for each case in the city of Baltimore, there were two in the (largely rural) counties. In Nevada, the rate in 1956 was 22.3.

Other countries vary. In Japan (1955), for example, there were 21,192 reported suicides. This rate has increased sharply, with a current indicated rate of nearly 25 per 100,000. Methods differ there as well: nearly half of these suicides are due to poison; drowning follows, with jumping from buildings or in front of trains next in order of frequency.

In 1959, Hungary with a rate of 25.7 was highest, followed by Austria (24.8), Japan (23.3), Denmark (21.0), Germany (18.7), England and Wales (11.5) and the U.S. (10.4). Lowest were Ireland (2.5) and Costa Rica (2.3).

several surveys indicated the frequency of conscious awareness of such thoughts among small groups of physicians and students (*Table 11*). Self-destructive thoughts most frequently tend to follow or to be consciously associated with what we might call the Three D's: discouragement, disillusionment, and disappointment (including frustration and loss).

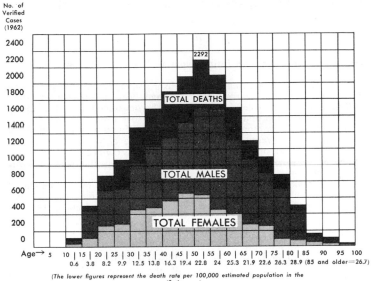

No. of
Verified
Cases
(1962)

Age→ 5   10 | 15 | 20 | 25 | 30 | 35 | 40 | 45 | 50 | 55 | 60 | 65 | 70 | 75 | 80 | 85   90   95   100
0.6   3.8   8.2   9.9   12.5   13.8   16.3   19.4   22.8   24   25.3   21.9   22.6   26.3   28.9   (85 and older=26.7)

(The lower figures represent the death rate per 100,000 estimated population in the specified group)

Figure 2.—Incidence of suicide by age groups in the United States (20,207 cases reported in 1962. (Data prepared from *Tables 1-25* and *1-26* of *Vital Statistics of the United States*, 1962, Volume II, Part A. Washington: Department of Health, Education and Welfare.)

The presence of suicidal thoughts does not in itself necessarily indicate psychopathology. Indeed, their nearly universal presence almost suggests that on some level they might serve a kind of usefulness. Nietzsche once wrote that "the thought of suicide is a great consolation: by means of it one gets successfully through many a bad night."

Suicidal thoughts far outnumber attempts, and attempts outnumber completed suicides. Of 267 attempts at suicide, 7 were "completed", in a recent series of such consecutive admissions to a Baltimore general hospital. Females outnumbered males three to one (75 per cent) in this series.

C. CLINICAL FEATURES

1. Evidence of Depression Variable; the Symbolic-Authority Concept

Suicide is associated closely with the symptom of emotional depression and with the Depressive Reactions. Nevertheless, the outward evidence of, or degree of, the depression is by no means necessarily indicative of the degree of the probability, or even the possibility, of the occurrence of suicide. Underlying depression may be poorly evident, clinically.

Several important concepts are to be observed in the following case of suicide by drowning. Herein there were seemingly no outward evidences of depression. The submission herein to a symbolic authority illustrates a useful concept, which has many additional and varied applications in psychiatry generally. In accord with the Symbolic Authority Concept, the setting up of a symbolic authority may be unwittingly undertaken for various psychologic purposes. Joseph Caro (1488–1575) set up such a mystico-religious personal authority in his *Maggid,* over a 52-year span as translated and analyzed by Gordon.

Case 41

Suicide by Drowning with Little Apparent Evidence of Depression

A forty-six-year-old woman had established a reputation for gentleness and compliance over many years. She had been a successful mother, with an apparently successful marriage. She developed an unrecognized Depressive Reaction and determined to take her life.

Tying two old-fashioned flat irons together with a short length of clothesline, she lowered herself backwards into a filled bathtub. The irons were placed on either side of her head, connected by the line across her neck. She was discovered in death, still in this position some hours later.

This case also illustrates an interesting psychologic reinforcement of her determination. She thus set up what we might refer to as *"a symbolic authority"* in the irons, and then submitted to this authority.

2. Equivocal Suicide

A fair proportion of suicides and suicidal attempts leave some measure of doubt as to the wholeheartedness of the intent. This may be due to reservations of the victim, or may merely reflect his conflict in varying measure over the taking of such a final step. These instances accordingly might be called *Equivocal Suicides.*

Authorities will sometimes lean over backwards in their judgment prior to the certification of such cases as indeed they are likely to do even in instances where there has seemingly been little doubt. Wittingly or not these become *Euphemistically-Intended Disguises,* as referred to earlier. The underlying motivation includes many complex social, ethical, familial, and practical (for instance, insurance liability) reasons.

Litman and colleagues reported a group of such cases in which the intent was uncertain. In the city of Los Angeles alone, they found 100 instances annually. Ten times this number, or 1,000 cases, were clearly certifiable as suicides. In less objective jurisdictions the relative number of such cases might be considerably higher. The overall incidence of cases which should really be certified as suicide, might well constitute a still higher percentage of the total annual deaths as now reported; that is, 1,000 certified as suicide out of a total of 50,000 deaths annually, from all causes.

D. PARTIAL SUICIDE; ACCIDENT-PRONENESS

1. Accidents Have Unconscious Purposive Components

It is beyond the scope of this study to undertake much more than brief mention of the many ways in which what the author has referred to as a Partial Suicide or what might be termed a partial *suicidal equivalent* is unconsciously brought about. Needless to say, there are many routes. They include all kinds of physical, functional, and mental sacrifices which are unconsciously made.

The extremes of accident-proneness would lead to "accidental" death and undoubtedly occur with more frequency than is commonly acknowledged. As more subtle consequences of similar but still more concealed drives, one may consider instances of our earlier Concept of Emotional Death [Ch.3:IIC5].

For a long time we have also recognized that many so-called accidents and injuries have in them certain deep and hidden purposive psychologic components. In other words, "accidents" are sometimes not at all as accidental as they may seem to be on the surface. Insurance companies, physicians, and psychiatrists alike have indicated their awareness of this in varying degree. Accordingly, the existence of the so-called "accident-prone" individual is today a rather widely accepted fact.

The following case is an extreme example of an unfortunate predilection for awkward "accidental" mishaps.

Case 42

Accident-Proneness

A thirty-three-year-old professional lobbyist consulted me some time ago concerning the possible benefits of character analysis. Among other difficulties, he reported the frequency with which he dropped things. This was uncontrollable and had proved extremely embarrassing in many ways.

During part of a recent weekend he had "managed" to drop the following: a glass of milk at lunch on Saturday, a mixing bowl full of martinis Saturday evening, a tray of cocktail glasses in the sink, and the cake intended for dessert. Finally, he had knocked over the stacked ashtrays at the conclusion of Saturday evening.

Skipping several minor mishaps at home during the day on Sunday, he was invited out for a buffet supper. Here he knocked a topcoat from a hanger, upset a drink over another guest, upset a relish dish, and tripped and fell. The climax of the evening took place after he had filled his plate at the buffet and gone to join the other guests seated around the periphery of the living room. As he got to the exact center of the roomful of guests, he "accidentally" turned his full plate directly upside down!

Needless to say, such a series of "accidents," seen here in a very unusual array, suggests on the face of it that underlying psychologic determinants must be present. This kind of accident is only *consciously* accidental. It is unconsciously but inexorably determined.

2. Fracture-Proneness

Not infrequently one hears of the unfortunate individual who breaks the same leg, shortly after the first break mended. Sometimes the location of the break and even the circumstances and locale of the accident are almost exactly repeated in some varying degree. It is almost as if the original event had not sufficiently satisfied whatever devious and hidden unconscious purposes or needs the first "accident" had attempted to subserve. The result is that the whole sequence "must" be repeated.

As a recent example, a nine-year-old boy broke his right arm in similar fashion to an earlier break, suffered twenty months previously. Six weeks later it was broken still again, and under similar circumstances! A physician friend's son broke his wrist not long ago, and while it was still in a cast broke the other wrist.

Some people have never suffered a broken bone, whereas others have a seeming predilection for fractures. An orthopedic surgeon told me not long ago of a sixty-six-year-old woman he was treating for a broken hip. At twenty-three, she broke her right ankle: at twenty-nine, her right wrist; at thirty-six, four ribs; at forty-two, her right collarbone; at fifty-three, her left hip; and at sixty-six, her right hip. During an eight-year period, one unfortunate young man did not miss a *single* winter without some kind of cast being needed, for one or another type of fracture. These instances illustrate what we might term Fracture-Proneness.

In another interesting case, a young woman had suffered five separate, severe sprains of her right ankle, during the immediately-preceding three years. Each time the injury required nearly six months for complete recovery. The net effect had been the partial sacrifice of the use of her right foot and ankle, during 80 per cent of this three-year period. Her repeated "accidents" had disabled her the majority of the time.

There are occasional 'accident-prone families', in which every member has suffered one or more fractures. In scattered instances, such a family has had at least one member constantly under treatment for a fracture over a period of years.

3. Accident-Prone Drivers

Accident-proneness is illustrated in automobile accidents. The 'accident-prone driver' is well recognized. He has some legal and statistical recognition in certain states. In several, a stated number of accidents results automatically in license revocation.

Some insurance companies give bonuses for drivers with no accidents. They may increase rates or refuse coverage for the repeat performer.

4. Dynamics

The psychodynamics of these interesting phenomena deserve further research. We are well aware of some general personality factors involved. These include impulsiveness, immaturity, and a rather frequent resentment of authority. Other commonly-recognized dynamic features include a pattern of the "acting out" of unconscious emotions, and unconscious (masochistic) self-punishment. Some of the symbolism involved may be evident at times in individual instances.

In certain cases the masochistic elements unquestionably cover a deeper, underlying sadism, as discussed in the psychodynamics of depression. Dunbar has compared certain persistent breakers of bones in effect, to certain persistent breakers of laws. The former secures expression in an "accident," with the consequences inverted toward himself. The latter secures release in an antisocial act.

E. IMPULSE AND REMORSE IN SUICIDAL ATTEMPT

1. Value in Prognosis

Impulse and remorse are likely present in association with every suicidal attempt. However, the degree of their presence and the time of their appearance are most highly variable. In an earlier study (*Quart. Rev. Psychiat.*, **8**, 19, 1953) the author discussed their prognostic significance and relationship. Impulse and remorse are both important factors in the study and understanding of suicide. A determination of their presence and relative strength has some practical importance in the management of cases of attempted suicide. This is particularly true in regard to making an estimation of: (1) the seriousness of the suicidal attempt, (2) the danger of a repeated, and perhaps more "successful" attempt, and (3) the prognosis generally.

In those cases in which the suicide is prevented or interrupted, or in which the effort has been unsuccessful, it is often possible to determine the degree of impulsiveness. It also becomes possible to observe how soon there is appreciable remorse. In general, *the more remorse and the sooner it appears, the more favorable the outlook,* and also the less depression. Generally, also, the more impulsive the act, the sooner the patient will feel remorseful. *The more impulsive the act, the less serious it is likely to be from the standpoint of immediate consequences, the psychopathologic import, and prognosis.* Highly impulsive suicidal attempts still lead to death, however, as we shall see. The more impulsiveness, the more remorse and the sooner it is likely to appear.

On occasion the suicidal attempt is very impulsive, and remorse is immediate. Occasionally, as is illustrated later, the suicidal gesture has the major feature of attempting to influence the attitudes of others. Here the endeavor is to extract some unconscious, vitally necessary concession from the environment. This is the unconsciously sought *suicidal epigain* [Ch.2:IA;-Ch.4:XIH2].

2. Little Impulsiveness; Remorse After Delay

In the following instance, the impulsiveness in the attempt was only moderate, and the appearance of remorse was delayed.

Case 43

Delayed Remorse in Suicide

An eighteen-year-old girl, without family, came to Washington for employment. Shortly after arrival she became enamored of a young man. Following a "lovers' quarrel," she secured and swallowed five or six tablets of mercuric chloride. Several hours later friends took her to a hospital. Emergency treatment, however, was somewhat lacking both in promptness and in thoroughness. Afterwards the patient was allowed to leave the hospital.

At the time of the emergency room treatment she had voiced no remorse whatsover. Five days later she became anuric. At this time she returned for further treatment. Now, however, for the first time she expressed some regrets for her action. As uremia progressed and death approached, she was increasingly remorseful. In this case the suicidal attempt which proved "successful", had been moderately impulsive. Remorse was delayed, but definite. It was only possible for it to become apparent in this case due to the circumstances of the suicidal act and the period of time required for death to transpire.

3. Impulsiveness and Remorse Minimal

In other cases there is no remorse in evidence throughout a prolonged course of treatment following the attempt which is to prove "successful." Often in such cases very careful planning indicates the determination and the strength of the suicidal drive. There is no impulsiveness in evidence. The following case is illustrative.

Case 44

Absence of Remorse in Suicide

(1) *Hazardous juncture in therapy*
A senior physician in military service was hospitalized following a serious suicidal attempt. He had slashed his throat in determined fashion, and rapidly became nearly exsanguinated. By rare chance, he happened to be promptly discovered. He was unconscious, and it took multiple transfusions to bring him around.

During some weeks subsequent to this event, his only expressed regrets were to the effect that he had been unsuccessful. His deep depression, however, began to recede somewhat. His retardation of thinking and activity became a little less marked. [*Note:* (1) There was still no evidence of remorse, and (2) the most dangerous time for suicide in the severe depression is when the patient has begun to show some evidence of its lifting. This is the *Post-Trough Point of Hazard for Suicide* to be Attempted [Ch.4:XI I2]. This applies whether prior suicidal efforts have occurred or not.]

The patient was soon undertaking workouts in the gym. This is indeed a hazardous juncture in therapy! His attendants, as well as the staff, unfortunately had become overly optimistic about his recovery. This is not an uncommon pitfall.

(2) *Determined and desperate suicidal attempt*
One day he broke away unexpectedly from his attendant, while in the three-story gymnasium. He quickly climbed a high ladder to a top-story window. Without the slightest hesitation, he dove through it and landed head first among the cars in an outside parking lot below. Although he suffered multiple fractures and other injuries, he retained consciousness.

He was immediately rushed to surgery for emergency work. While talking to his colleagues, he not once evidenced the slightest discomfort from his severe injuries. They would have been intensely uncomfortable to the ordinary person, not depressed and not so determined to end it all.

(3) *No regrets or remorse*
He was not at all regretful for his act. He upbraided himself instead for landing partly on a car, rather than entirely on the cement. "You see, I'm even a failure in killing myself. Twice I've done a poor job of it. I can't do anything right. I couldn't even miss the parked car. . . ." He urged the anesthetist to put him to sleep for good—"finish the job I have botched up twice."

This unfortunate man died. His service record had been outstanding. His personal and professional reputation had been excellent. He was well qualified in his specialty, and his loss to society was substantial. Had it been possible merely to prevent his self-destruction for a sufficiently long period, and to provide the best in skilled psychotherapy, his recovery and further usefulness to society probably would have been insured.

4. Impulsiveness Marked, Remorse Undetermined

Cases have been observed in which a great deal of impulsiveness has been clearly present in instances of attempted and "successful" suicide. At times, however, one may wonder how genuinely serious some of these individuals are about completing the act. This raises questions as to some attempts which begin perhaps as an impulsive act, and which may have large elements of a dramatic, although largely unconscious, intent to influence the behavior and responses of others. This involves the suicidal epigain, the efforts on an unconscious level to secure favorable environmental modifications. It is likely that these endeavors may in some instances get out of hand.

Are there then certain cases in which the threat is lightly taken and the patient has to "prove" his seriousness? Are there cases in which an originally impulsive suicidal gesture gets beyond control? Does remorse set in quickly but too late? The following case raised some of these questions.

Case 45

Suicide: Impulse or Remorse?

(1) *Prior evidence of impulsive behavior*
An eighteen-year-old seaman was known for his impulsiveness, quick temper, and general immaturity. An earlier incident which illustrated these traits was reported to me at a somewhat later date by one of his shipmates. It is important since it was an example of the patient's capacity for sudden and poorly-considered impulsive action. According to the shipmate's account, this particular incident took place while awaiting ship, some eight or ten months earlier than the climactic event to be shortly related.

Two couples bought a fifth of whisky and went to the apartment of one of the girls. The sailor in question raised the bottle and asked, in a half-serious voice, whether anyone wanted any before he "killed" it. One of his companions laughed derisively. This was the wrong kind of a response to make to our impulsive and unfortunate young sailor. To him this was a serious challenge. The young man's reaction, in the face of prior relative inexperience with alcohol, was to completely drain the bottle without pause. This impulsive action had rapidly led to a serious level of alcoholic coma and shock, which had actually threatened his life. However, he recovered and was shortly assigned to our ship.

(2) *Adjustment submarginal*
Aboard ship his reputation among his fellows was hardly enhanced by several untoward incidents. On one occasion, for example, our ship was closing on a surfaced Nazi submarine one night near Casablanca. From the radar contact the enemy seemingly had no awareness of our approach, until the sailor clumsily kicked the foot firing key for the five-inch gun where he was stationed! This was adequate warning indeed. The sub submerged and escaped.

My next experience with the kind of dramatic "acting out" response that he was capable of making in such highly impulsive fashion, happened on shipboard some two weeks out of Panama, in early January 1943. Heading west by southwest, we were in southern latitudes in one of the widest stretches of open ocean in the world. This sailor's dawn general quarters (battle readiness) duty consisted of standing watches on the forward five-inch main battery. Here he had acquired a reputation for falling asleep. His gun captain had tried various inducements and threats to try and keep him awake. These had met with only indifferent success. His adjustment on a wartime ship had been submarginal.

(3) *Reproach elicits fury*

One clear but moonless night the tropical ocean was calm. The time approached dawn, at which time battle stations were manned routinely. We were en route at a fast clip across the ocean, in formation with a task force. Several episodes of his napping had already occurred, when the sailor was discovered asleep again. His petty officer secured a cup of water and poured it over his face to wake him. He woke up, furious! Muttering, "I'll show you sons of bitches," he walked to the rail, threw off his clothes, and jumped into the ocean! Before his startled observers could correctly guess his intent or interfere, he was gone!

As quickly as the alarm *"Man Overboard"* could be given, the ship altered course. All possible efforts were made in what was to prove a futile search for the sailor. The reaches of the tropical ocean are vast. At night the search for one bobbing head in the black water is apt to be too tragically like looking for a needle in a haystack. The fact that he could swim was of little help.*

(4) *Remorse?*

Was he remorseful? As the heat of his intense anger and resentment cooled, could he have begun calling for help, and frantically praying, hoping for rescue?

How did he feel about the futile efforts of the searching ship? He must have seen the ship, which either never came close enough, or which in sinister and tragic fashion possibly came too close.

5. *Impact of Remorse*

On occasion, the sudden conscious recognition of the consequences of the attempt, had it been successful, can bring on remorse. This insight can have a considerable impact. This is illustrated in the following instance.

Case 46

The "Traumatic Impact" of Gaining Awareness of Some of the Implications of a Serious Suicidal Attempt

(1) *Impulsiveness and Remorse initially absent*

A thirty-three-year-old married mother of four young children was referred for psychiatric evaluation and possible recommendations, following a suicidal attempt.

There was no question as to the presence of depression. Further, the suicidal attempt was not very impulsive, nor was there any real remorse present at this time. At one point, for instance, the patient expressed her regrets that her attempt had failed, adding, "It just goes to prove I'm a failure at everything; I couldn't even do a decent job of killing myself."

(2) *Objections to absence inconsistant*

After careful assessment of these and other factors in the case, I advised immediate hospitalization. The patient initially raised few objections, until it occurred to her that her husband would have full charge of the children during her absence. This she simply couldn't stand. According to her view, her husband was not able to do a good job. Furthermore, she regarded his whole attitude toward the children as unkind.

---

* On April 1, 1957, a Sicilian seaman, aged thirty-five years, similarly jumped from his ship, the American tanker *Northern Gulf*, because his shipmates "teased him." By a "million to one" chance he was picked up alive some 30 hours later in the Atlantic, 100 miles west of Capetown, South Africa. (AP) *Washington Post*, 4/3/57.

This objection to her temporary absence from her children, was most inconsistent with her suicidal attempt, by which she might have left them *permanently* in his hands. I commented dryly that this consideration had not seemingly deterred her a few hours earlier.

(3) *Impact of awareness therapeutic*

The patient's reaction was as though she were stunned. Apparently the real impact of some of the serious consequences of what had narrowly missed being her demise suddenly struck her. Seemingly she at this point first realized the seriousness and permanence of such an act. Part of this must have been defensively maintained out of awareness. The rush into consciousness brought recognition of additional conflicts.

The emotional response to this bit of insight as observed, was somewhat comparable to that following some more clearly specific traumatic experiences. At this point and for the first time there was remorse evidenced. The remorse had a sudden and substantial impact.

In this instance, the net result was decidedly therapeutic, and helped establish a favorable attitude toward hospitalization and toward therapy. Herein were laid some of the early foundations for the successful therapeutic work which ensued over several years.

To recapitulate, *the more deliberate and planned* (that is, the less impulsive) *the suicidal attempt, the less remorse or regret will be present, and the greater the lag period is apt to be before it appears.* In such instances, the more serious and the more successful the suicidal attempt is also apt to be. Finally, the more likelihood of another attempt and the more serious this is likely to be.

F. EVALUATION OF SUICIDAL THREAT

The suicidal threat or gesture is not uncommon. Nevertheless, one should always be wary when the patient talks of suicide. It may be a real danger sign.* If not, it is always in itself a sign of some emotional difficulty. Therefore it should always be regarded seriously, from either the one standpoint or the other. It must never be treated "lightly." Earlier comments were offered in attempting to evaluate the danger of suicide [Ch.4:VC2].

Another caution concerns the response to the person who makes repeated threats of suicide. Any temptation to dismiss them contemptuously, to make light of them, perhaps even merely because of their repetitive nature, or to regard them as intended soley to gain attention or sympathy should be avoided. The same kind of caution applies to the repeated unsuccessful attempt. In a recent successful suicide by gunshot, history disclosed an earlier attempt by wrist-slashing, and another by an overdose of sedative (sleeping) capsules. This kind of history is not very unusual. Over half of the instances of "successful" suicide have made prior threats or attempts.

---

* The medical classmate and long-time friend of an excellent surgeon recently phoned him long distance to import confidences as to how desperate he felt. The surgeon tried scoffing, making light of, admonishing, and reassuring his friend. "Don't be ridiculous . . ." "You're not the kind of fellow to kill yourself . . ." "You wouldn't do anything so foolish . . . "You were such a good student . . ." "Things will look better . . ." "You've always been such a fine doctor . . ." These were typical of his responses.

These doubtless kindly intentioned but most superficial and not very understanding responses, if anything only aggravated matters for the distraught friend, who took his life some hours later. His had been a desperate last plea for help and for intervention; to be stopped.

Oftimes the warnings of impending suicide are prominent enough, if someone only will be sufficiently perceptive, and will give them heed. These indicate an inability to control destructive urges and at least partly represent a desperate appeal for intervention. In general, the deeper the Depressive Reaction and the more premeditated and planned the attempt, the more obscure will be the communication of suicidal intent. These points are summarized and tabulated (*Table 13*, Ch.4:VC2) and an *Index* offered as a possible aid in approximately computing the *Potential for Suicide*.

G. MANAGEMENT AFTER SUICIDAL ATTEMPT

1. Decision to Hospitalize Promptly and Decisively Effected

The author personally believes it is always wise to regard every case in which there has been a suicidal attempt as an emergency, at least until thoroughly proved otherwise. This practice has contributed to his good fortune thus far in the safe and successful therapeutic management of many severely depressed patients.

Prompt and decisive action is vital to the successful management of these cases. Indecision, delay, and temporizing can be literally fatal. Such actions or attitudes are never really a kindness at all to the patient, or to the patient's family. In case of any doubt as to the ability to manage adequately and safely the case on an outpatient status, hospitalization is indicated. Any possible error is best made on the side of early and prompt hospitalization.

When such a decision is reached it should be acted upon promptly and without delay. Never temporize. The patient had best not be left alone, from the time of such a decision until his actual admission. The effects of hospitalization in the borderline case will not be injurious in any event. The result may be decidedly therapeutic. This is true first of course, if the attempt was serious and/or if there was considerable underlying depression. It also perhaps has value if the attempt was partly or even largely a conscious effort to secure certain more favorable environmental changes. At the least, the patient will learn that this kind of behavior is not taken lightly. Some awareness may be gained that more constructive avenues might better be taken to satisfy one's needs. Further, the gaining of some conscious awareness of the nature of underlying unconscious needs may be gained in either instance.

Failure to appreciate the seriousness of suicidal intent may have tragic results, as illustrated in the following case.

Case 47

Failure to Appreciate the Seriousness of Suicidal Intent

John J., aged nineteen years, came to the emergency room of a large western hospital. He had slashed his wrists in seemingly hesitant and non-serious fashion. He was relatively noncommunicative and appeared morose. He indicated a wish to "finish the job."

While he was taken seriously by the interns, others in authority refused to take the case other than lightly. Following superficial first aid, he was allowed to leave. Eight hours later his body was found at the foot of a nearby cliff.

2. Relative Responsibility in Therapeutic Situation

The therapist must be fully aware of the risks involved in the treatment of any potentially suicidal patient. Still he must strike a satisfactory balance. He cannot chance losing therapeutic control in the face of a suicidal threat or gesture. He dare not allow this kind of thing to provide undue "leverage" to his patient who threatens suicide.

He must constantly keep uppermost in his own mind, and upon occasion calmly and matter-of-factly present to his patient, the latter's own responsibility in this area. The life which is threatened is the patient's. The responsibility for what he does with it cannot be handed over by him willingly to another person, such as the therapist.

3. Defensive Family Attitude may be Encountered

Not infrequently the close family members, for defensive psychologic reasons of their own, will play down the seriousness of a suicidal attempt. A defensive family attitude may be encountered, in which there is a strong need and/or preference to disbelieve or even to deny, that a suicide was a possibility for their family member. There is of course hazard in accepting this kind of underevaluation or in allowing it to remain.

Interestingly enough, there is not necessarily any correlation to the seriousness of the attempt. Recently the parents of a teenager quickly thus sought to doubt the seriousness, and to discount the strength of genuine suicidal motive, in an attempt that had proved unsuccessful. This attempt had only failed somewhat miraculously, a rifle having been fired at close range into his chest directly overlying his heart, which was injured but not fatally. There was small doubt as to the genuineness of this lad's intent. He had only been saved through luck and prompt and skillful surgery.

H. PSYCHODYNAMIC CONSIDERATIONS

1. Ultimate Symbolic Expression of Inverted Sadism

A. DESTRUCTION OF (DISOWNED ASPECTS OF) SELF.—In accord with psychodynamic formulations, suicide may represent the ultimate symbolic expression of inverted sadism. In addition, suicide represents the masochistic destruction of the hated and disowned aspects of the self. Thus suicide has in it at the same time elements both of the symbolic punishment of another, and of expiation. It is the ultimate external "acting out" symbolically of an intense, vital, and complex intrapsychic conflict.

The depressed person characteristically has a low self-esteem and a negative self-appraisal. The negative self-appraisal may actually be a realistic one, or far from it. Some interesting aspects of research concerning the self-appraisal have been considered elsewhere (*See* Projection in *Mental Mechanisms*). The projection of the negative aspects of self-appraisal to others outside oneself may be experienced consciously on occasion as what the author has named "King David's Anger," after the enraged reaction of the king when told the parable of the ewe lamb [Ch.2:IVD].

B. SEVERAL COMPONENTS; PRECIPITATING VS. ANTECEDENT BASES.— Suicide is not a simple act. As we shall observe, there are usually a number of unconscious components, which act in concert and with varying relative strengths. It should further be noted that contrary to the popular tendency to assign so often the entire motivation to the immediately preceding and obvious problem situation, illness, heartbreak, or traumatic event, and so on, the roots are always deeper.

This kind of event can serve, it is true, the function of being an important precipitating influence. However, the bases for this kind of response have long been established. Reactivation of antecedent conflicts, the readoption and further development of established patterns of response, and the further progression of pathologic and self-defeating modes of coping with life, have well set the stage prior to the precipitating event.

2. Inversion of Hostile Drives

There is usually present the turning inward of hostility with the symbolic destruction (that is, murder) of the internalized enemy. This is usually found to represent ultimately a parental figure or a parental surrogate. Freud noted that "we have long known that no neurotic (patient) harbours thoughts of suicide which are not murderous impulses against others, re-directed against himself."

The act may also have in it certain elements of reproach. This may represent an unconscious or partly conscious effort to make someone feel guilty or responsible. This aspect when unconscious may be regarded as part of the epigain, that is, the unconscious secondary gain [Ch.2:IA;-Ch.4:IXA*1*] of suicide. What a price to pay for the "gain", in such tragically self-defeating fashion!

3. Additional Dynamic Concepts

Karl Menninger in his study *Man Against Himself* presented the theme that three major dynamic components are present in suicide. These he believed to be: (1) murder, (2) the wish to be murdered, and (3) the desire to die. Menninger's formulations are supported by a wealth of data from many sources, and this volume is a classic in its area.

Litteral attributed to Rado a certain de-emphasis of the view of suicide as a self-destructive, masochistic act of punishment. He noted that it was "a means to dispel the depression for good and all." This it certainly accomplishes!

Suicide may at times also subserve a symbolic goal of *reunion*. This deeply repressed, unconscious need was referred to earlier as being present in some Depressive Reactions. This is the Concept of Lost-Object Reunion (*See Case 37*). Klein has also commented on this dynamic basis. She viewed suicide as representing not only the symbolic murder of the "bad objects", but also the preservation of the loved ones. She wrote that, "thus the ego is enabled to become united with its loved objects."

Aggression and hostility as such, or as part of what some would think of as a so-called "death instinct," may be viewed as having been acted out and directed *inwardly* in suicide; *outwardly* in murder. Destructive impulses which find no constructive outlet, no external expression, and are not handled adequately by various intrapsychic dynamisms are quite likely to be turned toward the self.

4. Expiation, Retribution, and Absolution in Suicide

Suicide usually has in it certain dynamic components of unconscious expiation, retribution, and self-punishment. This is the ultimate penance extracted by an archaic and overdeveloped super-ego. It may be an illustration of the operation of the mental mechanism of Retribution.

The following poetic effort has a depressive quality, and thus is cited as an example. The poet was psychiatrically quite unsophisticated. This makes his poetic connection between absolution and suicide more significant. On a conscious level, he intended the poem to help insure absolution for the act. On a deeper level, however, one can regard the contemplated act itself as being in absolution. Note the following instance of depression and suicidal contemplation in poetry.

IN ABSOLUTION

Cold—dark—drear—and murky; Outside
   the drizzling raindrops splatter.
   In my brain a steady patter.
Foreboding clouds hang low. Inside
   thoughts drive to desperation,
   as I find no consolation

In the steady rhythmic beating of the rain.

The God of Fortune wins! Again,
   with my victor I'm struggling,
   tensely fighting and striving
Once more, this fight I've lost. Some men
   cursed me when I failed the test.
   God knows that I have done my best.

Then again the panic pounding in my brain.

Chill—damp—thick—and dreary; On earth
   the rain now beating and fierce.
   From my very soul a curse
On fate that's made me fail. Will death
   be for this failure, the cost? . . .
   A shot would die and be lost

In the steady rhythmic beating of the rain!

L. Penseur

5. Compliance with Implicit Command

Earlier the concept was considered [Ch.4:VIA7;XIA1] of certain depressive manifestations representing in part what was called the *compliant response* to rejection which was actual and/or so experienced unconsciously by the person concerned. This brings us to its ultimate extension. Thereby in compliance with what the author would term the Implicit Command of the rejection; that is, to "be gone", to "remove oneself", to "vanish" to "die", and so on; the individual acts as he unconsciously feels directed to do.

This is an unconscious factor sometimes of importance in the wish-to-die component in suicide. Herein the person evaluates himself as worthless, unwanted, and a burden to the rejecting person(s), usually as a recapitulation of the emotional complex of an antecedent infantile rejection. Obediently, automatically, and unwittingly he may perhaps acquiesce in what is unconsciously interpreted and experienced as a wish that he remove himself permanently, or as the command to die, that is, to kill himself. This he proceeds to do, submissively complying with the Implicit Command.

The presence of this element in suicide does not of course rule out the concomitant presence of others. A number of elements are generally present in a given suicide, acting in concert or reinforcing each other. Suicide, as with other emotional manifestations, is not merely determined; it is *over*-determined. Almost invariably a number of major components converge in its motivation. Instances of suicide or suicidal attempts precipitated by episodes of being jilted, separation and divorce, or losing one's position are more likely examples in which this particular component of Implicit Command may be more prominent.

6. Death Wish

The wish for death is implicit in the suicidal trend. It becomes literally acted out along with other components, in the attempt at suicide. Often it is translated into conscious expressions which when verbalized, are done so in terms of a longing for peace, or for tranquility, and the like.

The death wish has also been equated in psychodynamics at times with a wish to return to the pre-birth status, that is, a return to the womb. Usually this tends to remain rather in figurative or symbolic terms. Occasionally, and more often with psychotic individuals and very disturbed patients, or even with neurotic persons, it secures a less disguised outward expression. Thus a patient told the author in the depths of his depressive despair not long ago, "I really want to crawl up into some little space and never come out!" He did not make any conscious connection with a wish to return to the womb, but the meaning as well as the symbolism of his despairing "death wish" was unmistakable from the context at the time.

7. Factor of Alcohol

A significant proportion of "successful" suicidal victims have indulged in a significant measure of drinking immediately prior to the act. This relationship is of interest and can offer us room for speculation. In a recent series of 94 cases, 38 of them, or 40.4 per cent, showed a concentration of blood-alcohol level of at least 0.05 per cent. Whelton also recently stressed this.

The alcohol lessens the strength of more usual inhibitions. It also thereby allows the underlying feelings and action in response to them to emerge more readily. Finally it has a narcotic effect on the aspects of the psyche which might otherwise more strongly object, restrain, or be too pained by the serious contemplation or act of self destruction.

I. POTENTIAL OF SUCCESSFUL TREATMENT

1. A Life Saved

Suicide should be prevented by whatever means possible. Every suicide prevented is a life saved. Under proper management an effort can be made to work out the bases underlying the attempt. Under the favorable circumstances of successful therapy, the patient, especially the often highly useful and socially valuable victim of a Depressive Reaction, can be returned to a constructive way of life. With successful therapy he may come to enjoy a healthier level of adjustment and more satisfactions in living. In accord with our concept of Deep Treatment [Ch.13:VIII2], all the underlying capacity and potential for this type of destructive reaction, ideally would be thoroughly dissolved, through really definitive psychotherapy [Ch.4:XIIA4].

The following case illustrates an instance of a determined suicidal attempt, prevented only by extremely fortuitous circumstances. A life was saved. As a result, treatment became possible. An excellent recovery followed. A valuable member of society was restored to her useful role.

Case 49

Thwarting of a Suicidal Attempt, Followed by Successful Therapy

This patient was a highly respected supervisory nurse who had an excellent professional record. She had carefully planned to take her life, while in the middle of a severe, but largely unrecognized, depression. She secured and took between 80 and 100 grains of Seconal. She then secreted herself in a place where discovery was ordinarily unlikely for some days. Through completely fortuitous circumstances, she was discovered in deep coma, after nearly eight hours.

Rigorous emergency treatment saved her life. It was gradually possible to institute intensive psychotherapy. Her progress was slow but excellent. Within four months, however, she was again in a responsible position. She completed her treatment. During nearly five years she has remained free of major depressive symptoms. She has produced effectively and efficiently. There has been no recurrence of depression.

2. Post-Trough Point of Hazard

When is suicide most likely to occur in the course of depression? The most likely time is *not* in the deepest trough of the illness [Ch.4:VC2]. At this point, psychomotor retardation is at its height. Whatever degree of paralysis of thought, emotions, mentation, and activity which may be present is at its greatest point at this time. The most likely time for suicide to take place in a depressed individual is shortly *after* he has begun to come out of his most depressed phase.

In a graph of his level of spirits, the most hazardous juncture then would be just past the bottom or trough of the curve, just as the level has begun to ascend. Thus descriptively, and further to emphasize this major hazard and precept, we might name this the "Post-Trough Point of Hazard" [Ch.4:XIE*3*].

At this point the depressed patient is still only too likely to have strong suicidal drives present. Only now, however, does he begin to have the necessary steam and energy to act upon them. Only now is he better able to plan and to carry out his plans.

This particular hazard that suicides are far more likely to occur when the depressed patient appears to be convalescing can hardly be overstressed. In the management of the depressed patient, keeping in mind the Post-Trough Point of Hazard will prove literally life-saving. *Case 44* helps to illustrate our precept.

3. *Prognosis*

The prognosis is always good when the suicide is averted. The chances for a more successful recurrence must, however, be borne in mind. In a study of 200 consecutive cases, Batchelor and Napier reported that three patients definitely, and one additional patient probably, committed suicide after a first attempt, *during the first year after the original attempt alone.* (*See Case 47.*) It appeared that the number of persons who killed themselves subsequently after a suicidal attempt depended on the reaction of their human environment to the first suicidal attempt. Banen reported that 6 of 23 consecutive suicides in hospitalized psychotic patients* had made previous attempts.

The initiation of treatment alone is no assurance that suicide will not occur. Many psychiatrists, perhaps most of them, have had this tragedy happen in therapeutic situations at one time or another. It is the author's own impression, however, that the prompt initiation of intensive psychotherapy greatly lessens the suicidal risk. It has the added advantage of a trained person having a closer view of the situation. So long as he has some fair assurance that he enjoys the confidence of his patient, the situation is more stable. He must know what is going on in his patient's current emotional life, and he must feel that he has the situation in hand. Otherwise he had best quickly arrange for hospitalization, as earlier noted.

XII. TREATMENT

A. TREATMENT OF CHOICE IN DEPRESSIVE REACTIONS

1. *Intensive Psychotherapy*

The treatment of choice in the Depressive Reactions when it is available and feasible, is intensive psychotherapy in expert hands. When this is successful, there is no substitute for the resulting emotionally healthful insight into the causes and background of the illness. The results of successful

---

* Approximately 80 per cent of the attempted suicides occurred in persons under 40 years of age, a seeming contrast with suicides in other groups. Twelve of the 23 were by hanging.

therapy will secure resolution of the current illness, will contribute to a healthier adaptation to life, and will render the person less vulnerable to future episodes.

Our remarks must be limited to a few points of particular applicability in the psychotherapy of depression, plus several of wider relevance to psychotherapy and analysis. The interested reader is also referred to the subsequent comments about treatment of more general application, which are included in most of our other chapters. These are to be regarded as supplementary to the current discussion.

2. Ego Support

In the early treatment of depression, measures designed to provide ego support may be very useful. Wilson pointed out the sensitivity of the depressed patient to rejection or to disapproval. The patient must be convinced of the therapist's own genuine interest in his problems, which may be difficult in view of his illness, and perhaps still more so in the face of his own frequent and obvious rejection of the therapist, as well as himself.

As will be recalled, the ego has suffered, as the battle over the repression and control of unconscious aggressive drives has waged back and forth. In effect, the ego has served as the battleground, and as the mediator. The ego has also suffered through its punishment by the harsh, overcritical conscience. As the ego recoups a little, the therapist may do well to help develop and encourage attachment to new libidinal objects. He may tacitly or sometimes in judicious fashion even actively encourage the selection of new goals, and the replacement of substitute objects for love and affection. The physician may himself become one object for attachment, an event which must be recognized and dealt with in due course and in a matter-of-fact way.

Jacobson reported that the emotional quality of the analyst's responses is very important. This is a more important factor than the number or the frequency of therapeutic sessions. The analyst must be able to have a warm understanding of his patient's daily efforts to cope with things. He must have genuine respect for his patient, and an active sincere interest.

An increase in supportive environmental factors can also prove of importance. An environment of welcome, encouragement, optimism, excellent diet, routine interested medical care, good nursing care, and supervised activity can contribute greatly in the treatment milieu. These kinds of measures are if anything, still more important for the elderly depressed patient.

3. Optimal Time for Interpretation

The therapist must be very cautious about premature interpretations concerning hostility and dynamics. Otherwise they will be rejected, often with vehemence. Impairment of rapport may follow. Treatment can be greatly retarded, blocked, or even broken off completely. On the other hand, on the rare occasion that such premature interpretations might actually be accepted, a violent emotional storm may ensue.

Either consequence is most unfortunate. Indeed, the proper selection of the optimal time for interpretations generally is an area of psychotherapy requiring the greatest skill and finest judgment. This is true regardless of the type of illness present.

4. Goals of Insight Therapy; Deep Treatment

The general goals of insight-directed therapy might be summarized as follows:

   (1) Readjustment of the level of aspirations in keeping with real abilities. New or alternate goals (that is, ego-ideals) may replace those impractical of achievement, or beyond reach.

   (2) Ameliorating the harsh conscience (that is, superego). This will lessen self-punitive and masochistic aspects.

   (3) The gradual, unforced securing of recognition, acceptance, and the subsequent study, of the hostility and aggression. Gaining an increased ability to deal with this side of the ambivalence in a more constructive fashion.

Further, as insight grows and maturity develops, the dependent needs resulting in the factors of secondary gain will lessen. These important goals, as outlined above, are not attained easily. *Many years of use deepen familiar pathways, regardless of their degree of health or neurosis.*

Intensive and definitive treatment often lasts from two to four years, and may take much longer. It is a long-term, difficult, and expensive, but rewarding endeavor. Deep Treatment is the author's term for that type of insight directed therapy which is aimed to secure the foregoing goals, plus elimination of the basic capacity to follow a depressive pattern of reaction in the future. (*See also* Ch.4:XII*1*.)

5. Difficulties of Therapy

The conscious recognition and analysis of the hostile side of the ambivalence is a major project in much of modern analytic therapy. There is actually often more resistance in working out these areas by patients today, than was true from three to five decades ago. The rigid taboos of the Victorian era have modified. As a result, a more open discussion in regard to sexual matters is now often possible. Today patients often have their greatest difficulties in discussing their feelings of love, tenderness, and warmth, or the reverse, their feelings of hatred, anger, and resentment. Because of this, association in present-day therapy may require more direction along these lines.

Free association in the Victorian era was often particularly helpful in eliciting inadvertent references to concealed (that is, unconscious) sexual roots of the neuroses. Sexual repression is often less stringent in our present-day culture.

Depressed patients often have increased difficulty with free association, because of the limitations of spontaneity in the Depressive Reactions. It is often harder, accordingly, to uncover unconscious material.

We have noted the general retardation mentally, physically, emotionally, and physiologically. Interests are lessened. Spontaneity is restricted. Similar restrictions are present in relationships and are also a handicap. Interpretation of the protective and defensive intent of these, at the proper juncture in therapy, can be very useful.

6. Study Resistances

Fromm-Reichmann stressed the value of the patient's associations during therapy and called attention to the increasing focus of psychotherapy "upon the investigation of ego-defenses, the security operations of patients as they are mobilized by the psychotherapeutic process . . ." Thus the therapist might more profitably be concerned less with the recall of early "forgotten memories," or the actual content of painful or censored associations.

He might better interest himself more in the emotional reactions actually elicited by this material coming under scrutiny in treatment. He might better study the emotional resistances of the patient to having his associations and reactions come under scrutiny. The study of resistance is often considerably more important than content alone.

7. Concept of Emotional-Inertia; the Mechanical Analogy

There is a concept about the greater difficulty of *initiating* therapy, compared to the continuation of the therapy which has already been undertaken. Accordingly, the label of a Concept of Emotional-Inertia is proposed. This interesting conception has relevance in psychotherapy and analysis generally. It is included here since it is at least as applicable to the therapy of the Depressive Reactions as to other groups [Ch.1:IIIE2;-Ch.14:VIIIE4].

An analogy to machinery offers itself. In this Mechanical Analogy, as the author would name it, we note that more effort and energy—considerably more in foot pounds or in ergs—are required to initiate a mechanical process, or to start a piece of machinery moving, than to keep it going once started. So it is in analogous fashion, in the initiation, *vs.* the continuation of psychotherapy and analysis. Both are difficult and complex, the first likely far more so. Our Mechanical Analogy holds.

In the Depressive Reactions, characterized as they are by the restriction of interests (especially new ones), and by the retardation of all phases of mental and emotional activity, the Emotional-Inertia which is present and often substantial, must be recognized and combated, in whatever ways are feasible.

8. Frequency and Length of Psychotherapy Sessions

Practice and preference among psychiatrists show considerable variation as to the length and frequency of session in psychotherapy and analysis. Following Freud, analytic therapy sessions were quite early rather rigidly held to full hours, six days each week. A few psychiatrists still follow this regime. Generally, however, the term treatment "hour" or analytic "hour" has tended to become euphemistic, and more likely today is used to refer to a period of time of 30, 40, or 50 minutes. As a consequence and in the interests of precision and greater accuracy the author has come to prefer the term "session" in preference to that of hour.

Ordinarily, more frequent sessions are to be preferred, as an advantage to continuity and intensity. The more frequent, the better; of course within the necessary limits of feasibility, practicality, and scheduling. The benefits appear to have a kind of geometrical progression, so that three sessions weekly are worth twice as much as a two-session per week schedule. Personally, a three-session per week schedule has been found to be an optimal minimum. Shorter sessions, more frequently, are also preferred over longer sessions, less frequently. Accordingly as an example, four half-hour sessions weekly would have preference over two hourly ones.

B. DRUGS

In certain occasional, very *selected* cases of mild depression, the amphetamines and barbiturates can sometimes play a useful adjunctive role. However, if one is tempted to allow their use in any way to replace psychotherapy when this is at all feasible, or to consider them in other than a temporary supportive role, it might be considerably better to avoid their use altogether.

The tranquilizer group of drugs is not of great value in the treatment of depression in private practice. They may have an adjunctive role in severe depressions (especially those of psychotic level), in which there is a great deal of concurrent anxiety and agitation. Two recent situations have been encountered, in which the use of these drugs has helped to direct attention away from the emotional bases of, and to mask, developing depressive symptoms of a serious nature. Emergency hospitalization became necessary, when earlier initiation of psychotherapy might have been preventive. In addition to this kind of disadvantage, it is the author's current opinion that this particular group of drugs may actually have an adverse effect, when employed in cases of emotional depression.

The use of tranquilizing drugs, as with sedatives and the amphetamine group, is not a substitute for psychotherapy and increased self-understanding. On the other hand, the results of their use with disturbed and agitated patients who have been hospitalized for various types of psychoses can be quite valuable. (*See* earlier reference, Ch.3:VIIIF5.) This is particularly true in selected, preferably younger and acutely ill patients, in regard to: (1) reducing abnormal mental content; (2) facilitating patient management, as a consequence of less agitation and disturbed behavior; and (3) making patients accessible to a more highly constructive and useful kind of psychotherapy. In this latter employment the tranquilizing drugs are far better regarded as *adjuncts* to psychologic therapy, rather than as constituting a specific therapy in and of themselves.

Overholser reported that the use of these drugs greatly reduced the use of electric shock treatments at St. Elizabeth's Hospital.* Billings reported

---

* In a six-month period, 13 patients were treated by electroshock. In a corresponding period a year earlier the figure was 177. The average patient census at St. Elizabeth's Hospital exceeds 7,500.

cases whose psychotic abnormal content was controlled sufficiently by maintenance doses of a tranquilizing drug to allow a resumption of work. The author has had similar experiences.

An increasing number of studies are available relating to the effects of the rauwolfia extracts such as reserpine and the synthetic chlorpromazine, marketed as Thorazine, and a whole series of candidates by most major drug houses. Noce *et al.* reported the facilitation of nursing care of psychotic patients, and reduced need for electroshock therapy, sedation, restraint, seclusion, and hydrotherapy. The monoamine oxidase inhibitors (monase, nardil, marsilid, marplan, and so on) merit further trial and study under controlled circumstances. These drugs however, also are no substitute at all for the understanding and insight which can result from definitive psychotherapy.

C. REMISSION

Earlier, mention was made to the matter of spontaneous recovery in the Depressive Reactions. The tendency for depression in all but the most seriously psychotic cases is usually toward gradual spontaneous recovery. Such a recovery, however, had far better be viewed as a *remission*. The chance for much real self-learning or insight to have occurred in the absence of sound intensive therapy of course, is very small.

The individual in such spontaneous remission however is most likely to be just as vulnerable to a recurrence of depression, as he was before he was sick. This is likewise at least as true with regard to the patient who has had a remission secured through electric shock.

While the same reservations might be held in regard to those cases which recover under psychotherapy, they are considerably less apt to apply, at least in degree. Any insight gained is to the good. More self-knowledge is the best insurance against a recurrence of depression. Although the chance of relapse or of a later depression can seldom be ruled out completely, it decreases proportionately, as the level of real insight increases. We have observed in several of our case illustrations examples of recurrence, and examples of nonrecurrence. (*See* earlier reference to the Principle of Recurrence in Depression, Ch.4:VC3.) As noted earlier, this is a crucial problem in the evaluation of the results of therapy of the Depressive Reactions.

D. ELECTROSHOCK THERAPY

1. *Points of View Differ Widely*

There are widely variable points of view in existence about the indications for and the value of, electroshock therapy in emotional depression and the Depressive Reactions. At the risk of seeming ambivalent, a little of each of these different positions will be presented.

The author's own position is as follows. He does not use electroshock and has not done so for some years, although prior to 1946 he had extensive experience with its use. However, several cases have since been referred for shock treatment. This has been done in instances in which a combination of circumstances made any kind of psychotherapy either not at all feasible or clearly impossible. On the other hand, the author has also successfully handled psychotherapeutically in private practice and on an outpatient basis, a reasonable number of fairly severe clinical Depressive Reactions. These have been cases in which some of the author's colleagues would have immediately begun a course of electroconvulsive therapy.

2. Indications

Electroshock therapy has its most clear and acceptable indications in the treatment of the very severe Depressive Reactions and in acute Schizophrenia. Many psychiatrists are highly enthusiastic about the rather wide use of shock. Many also oppose its use equally vigorously. In cases of psychotic Depressive Reactions in which psychotherapy is not available or feasible, proponents of the use of electroshock point out its substantial advantages, including that it may be life-saving. Many psychiatrists have had experience with this.*

The cases among the Depressive Reactions which are most suitable for treatment by electroshock would include those instances which are not accessible to psychotherapy, and the cases of severe Agitated Depression. In any case in which electric therapy is employed, it is perhaps ideally regarded as a tool to be employed when, for extraneous or psychologic reasons, the therapist cannot reach the patient with psychotherapy. Its use should be discontinued and psychotherapy instituted when one finds he can now work effectively with the patient in psychotherapy.

The indiscriminate use of E.C.T. is to be avoided and deplored in any event. Further, the author regards it to be strictly a hospital procedure. It is, of course, correct that many Depressive Reactions will be forced into a remission under the physical and psychologic impact of a series of electrically-induced convulsions.

---

* One of the reviewers of the original manuscript wrote on this point: "The area in which electric shock has to be used is particularly in the severe psychotic depressions. We have a fair number of them and we just can't get to them with our limited facilities for psychotherapy. We have to use E.C.T. if we are to keep down suicides. In this regard it is life-saving. I think you are quite right, however, about the difficulties later on."

Another early reviewer, whose views about the use of shock are at some variance with those above, commented: "A great many patients, in my experience, are not approachable for some time in any meaningful psychotherapeutic situation. They require many various methods, particularly the convulsive ones of somatic treatment, before prolonged therapy can be carried on. I think that one of the physician's major responsibilities is to relieve suffering as quickly as possible. In this respect in a great many depressive illnesses, electroconvulsive therapy is the method of choice and the most rapidly effective. Further, the morbidity is reduced and the ever-present danger of suicide may be minimized by immediate intensive somatic therapy.

"As indicated also, a long-term psychotherapeutic regimen would be expensive and time-consuming. It would possibly last two to five years, and only a fraction of the people suffering from depressive illnesses would be able to avail themselves of any such type of treatment."

3. Disadvantages

In personal experience, the remissions of Depressive Reactions, when they can be induced in response to electroshock therapy, have three major disadvantages. These are:

(1) The *recovery occurs without insight* or perhaps even the chance for insight. The patient gains no idea as to how he might have become depressed in the first place. He goes into remission knowing no more about what makes him "tick" as a person. He emerges at least as *vulnerable* to the *recurrence* of depression as before his present attack.

(2) The patient is likely to be still *more resistive to intensive psychotherapy* and analysis, following an electroshock remission. Often the slightest tentative and initial interest in self-observation and study is absent. This has transpired repeatedly in the author's experience.

(3) *Later episodes* of depression occur. These are quite frequent following remissions with electroshock. These are also likely to be more resistive to psychotherapy.

Memory loss, which is more marked for recent events, is present after electroshock therapy, although sometimes difficult to demonstrate. The possible consequences of the loss of memory following a course of electroconvulsive therapy will also be referred to in the section on Amnesia [Ch.13:VII]. (*See also Case 167.*)

These kinds of effects upon memory may be of more significance in those cases of depression which have followed recent marked precipitating events, such as a severe loss, frustration, or disappointment.

4. Psychodynamic Factors

The unconscious meaning of electroshock therapy has been the subject of considerable interest among psychiatrists. Many dynamically-oriented psychiatrists believe there are unconscious punitive connotations. In line with this view, Weigert wrote that shock and convulsive therapy is in opposition to some of the main efforts of intensive psychotherapy and analysis. The latter aims "to mitigate the cruelty of an archaic superego and to help the patient to endure the necessary, but not the unnecessary hardships of reality." Wayne offered an analysis of some of the unconscious factors in physicians motivating their choice of electroconvulsive treatment.

Unquestionably, electric shock has a considerable symbolic significance. This varies widely with different patients. However, this may help explain the greater effects of shock therapy upon certain patients suffering from Depressive Reactions, than in other cases. Shock may admirably but unhealthfully serve unconscious punitive internal forces in symbolic fashion by:

(1) Serving as the punitive agent of the harsh superego, aiding and abetting guilt-ridden or masochistic needs for self-castigation and punishment; and/or

(2) Aiding the inverted hostile and aggressive sides of the ambivalence, which are being expressed in concealed symbolic fashion against the introjected object.

Where shock helps symbolically to "satisfy" these internal punitive needs, remission from the depression may take place or be facilitated.

5. Effects Upon Recent Memories

The effects upon memory are of major importance in the improvement which can follow shock therapy. Other cerebral functions show some disorganizing effects as well.

These are combined with: (1) the conflict-relieving loss or partial loss of recent contributory disturbing events (which have doubtless been of exaggerated significance in a geometrical progression), and (2) the unconscious and symbolic meaning of the electroshock, to produce a remission of acute symptoms in the favorably situated case.

XIII. SUMMARY

In summary we can note the relative efficacy of therapeutic efforts in cases of depression. The investment of necessary time, effort, and money is well worth while with the cooperative patient. Reasons were tabulated. The prognosis in the Depressive Reactions when treated by expert hands is quite good, ranking high in order among the neuroses. Emotional depression is to anxiety, as sadness is to fear.

In this chapter certain important clinical and dynamic features have been presented concerning the symptom of emotional depression and the Depressive Reactions. We have observed how widespread (an estimated 14–18% of neurotic reactions) is depression, and outlined a bit of its historical perspective. Early contributors to theory were noted, together with their contributions. We have seen the challenge in the making of an early diagnosis, the laudable results and satisfactions which can follow successful treatment, and in restoring to emotional health a patient who is often highly useful socially.

According to our *Concept of Depressive-Equivalents,* these can include many physical and emotional manifestations. Problems in diagnosis were considered, including the *Physical-Equivalents* of depression. Ordinarily, more depression means less anxiety. This is in line with our precept of an *Inverse Anxiety-Symptom Ratio.* Early morning awakening or what has been termed *Dawn-Insomnia,* is pathognomic of depression. Some guidelines were offered in aiding one better to distinguish the neurotic, from the psychotic depression. A concept of *Higher Order vs. Lower Order* neurotic defensive reactions was noted. Figures from several sources were cited to illustrate the wide prevalence of depression. On must be wary of recurrence. Differential features to distinguish the psychotic depression from neurotic depression were also tabulated. Additional concepts were offered.

As part of our discussion of the clinical symptoms and features, Grief States and their gradual merging into pathologic depression were briefly considered. Depression and grief were compared to anxiety and fear.

Cold Depression as a term, helps to indicate the frequency of vasomotor changes of this order. Character defenses are encountered which are rather characteristic of depression. They may function as "psychologic equivalents." These will be listed shortly in the chapter on *Character Reactions,* at which juncture the intrapsychic needs for their development and their dynamics will be discussed. "Dress Indicators" reflect the level of depression, through the choice, color, and style of clothes, as selected by the individual concerned. The *Concept of Diffuse Retardation* emphasizes the pervasiveness of this manifestation in emotional depression.

A concept of *Emotional Decompensation* was offered. According to an Inverse Ratio Concept, the more hostility allowed outward expression, the less emotional depression. Cultural restraints leading to the suppression of competitiveness and hostile expression, ordinarily would tend to increase the incidence of depression and suicide. This is the *Direct* Cultural-Ratio Concept. The concepts of *Secondary Defense* and "cultural vogue" were mentioned. The *Theory of Antecedent Conflicts* received brief attention. Suicide was noted to sometimes constitute the "ultimate soterial retreat."

The important clinical finding of a *Morning Ebb-Tide of Spirits* in depression, received notice. The *Principle of Recurrence* points out the great likelihood for an emotional depression to recur, in the absence of definitive therapy. The Grief State was briefly discussed, as was the rare but interesting, clinical *depression a deux.*

We undertook a study of factors in the psychodynamics and pathogenesis of the Depressive Reactions. Adult depression was traced from its basic antecedent roots in the ambivalent conflict of the oral phase of personality development. Formed as a result is the childhood prototype for later adult Depressive Reactions. From this early Antecedent Conflict emerges the *primal depression.* A Concept of Rejection and the "Compliant-Response" to it was noted. The relation of depression to inverted hostility was stressed, and a viewpoint of the primary and secondary gains in this type of illness was offered. The depression endogains were tabulated (*Table 14*).

A list of some of the important psychodynamic factors in depression include:

(1) Difficulties in the supply of love and affection in the late oral or early anal periods, making for later severe defects in satisfactory human relationships. *Emotional Exploitation* may have taken place in subsequent years.

(2) Deprivation or rejection; *Antecedent Primal Depression* not infrequent.

(3) Marked ambivalence, with rage toward the object of dependency: the *Dependency-Dilemma* of Infancy.

(4) Inability to love without hating, and vice versa.

(5) The repression of hostility in the unconscious. Concept of "frozen state of rage."

(6) Later minor rejections of him become interpreted by the patient unrealistically, as being a *total* rejection, by the love object.

(7) The turning of the unconscious hostility against the self.

219

(8) The unconscious evolvement and "employment" of the intra-psychic mechanism of Introjection.

(9) The struggle between the severe, rigid, punitive superego, and the ego. In this the hostility felt toward others becomes deployed against the self.

(10) The guilt for the infantile, narcissistic egocentric drives.

(11) Low level of self-esteem. This can tie in with the *Compliant Response* to rejection.

(12) Sadistic punishment achieved symbolically, through the punishment of the introjected object. The more apparent but still unconscious masochism, overlays the more deeply hidden sadism.

(13) Unconscious "gains" of depression. (*See Table 14.*)

(14) Unconscious goal of "Reunion With the Lost Object."

(15) Interrelated dynamics of suicide.

The Rule of Impression Priority received mention. Parental influences in predisposing a child toward the depressive pattern, can include his witting and/or unwitting *Emotional Exploitation* by the parent. Depression may sometimes be regarded as "a frozen state of rage." Factors of masochism and sadism in the dynamics of depression were noted. The unconscious goal of Lost-Object Reunion was noted, as sometimes playing a role in depression.

We included brief discussions of the Reactive Depression and Suicide. *Reactive (or Situational) Depression* is a useful term, implying the onset of depression after an acute precipitating situational event. *Anxious Depression* is the illness characterized by the presence concurrently of large amounts of both anxiety and depression. The "Agitation-Gauge" can aid in estimating the gravity and the prognosis in the *Agitated Depression*. The *Success Depression* is the seemingly paradoxical depression, following achievement of a long-sought major goal. The goal symbolically achieves for the person concerned the hidden aim of the oral aggressive drives. The occasional occurrence of a *Completion Depression* was noted. A so-called *One-Day Depression* was mentioned.

Suicide is, among other things, both the actual extreme end result of masochistic self-punitive drives, and the symbolic destruction (that is, murder) of the internalized and secretly-hated object. Dynamic elements of the "Compliant-Response" and obeying the "Implicit-Command" were mentioned. Unconscious secondary gain motives (that is, epigain) exist in the attempts to secure reactions from other people. The "Three D's" in suicide are discouragement, disillusionment, and disappointment (including frustration and consequent rage).

The setting up of a *Symbolic Authority* has many and varied applications in psychiatry generally. The impulsive suicidal attempt may have elements of reproach. The act may be largely unconsciously intended to arouse feelings of guilt and responsibility in people nearby. When present, suicide can constitute the ultimate in nonconstructive dependency appeal. *Cover Reasons* are the more superficial and conscious bases advanced for suicide. Various *Euphemistically-Intended Disguises* by well-meaning friends, family, and authorities tend to obscure suicide as the cause of death in individual cases, as well as the real overall incidence of suicide. Self-destruction may include an element of response to an Implicit Command (to be gone, and so on). Impulse and remorse in suicide, and their importance in prognosis, were briefly mentioned. Accident Proneness and *Fracture-Proneness* are tenets in our conception of "Partial Suicide."

Treatment of Depression by the method of choice, that is, intensive psychotherapy, has been discussed. The use of electroshock therapy in cases not accessible to psychotherapy was also considered. Through *Deep Treatment* the underlying capacity and potential for evolving a depressive type of emotional reaction is eliminated. The Concept of *Emotional-Inertia* in the initiation of psychotherapy, was noted, and a "Mechanical Analogy" offered. The important *Post-Trough Point of Hazard* for suicide was stressed.

XIV. SELECTED REFERENCES AND BIBLIOGRAPHY

ABRAHAM, K. (1949). "Notes on the Psychoanalytical Investigation and Treatment of Manic-Depressive Insanity and Allied Conditions (1911)." In Jones, E., Ed., *Selected Papers on Psychoanalysis.* pp. 137–156. London: Hogarth.

— (1949). "The First Pregenital State of the Libido (1916)," *Ibid.,* pp. 248–279.

— (1949). "A Short Study of the Development of the Libido Viewed in the Light of Mental Disorders (1924)." *Ibid.,* pp. 418–501.

ALEXANDER, LEO (1961). "Objective Evolution of Antidepressant Therapy by Conditional Reflex Technique." *Dis. nerv. Syst.,* 2, S 14.

APPEL, K. E. (1942). "Symposium on Social Psychiatry." *Clinics,* 1, 807.

— (Sept. 28, 1954). Personal communication.

ARCHIBALD, HERBERT C., et al (1962). "Effects of Childhood Bereavement." *Psychosom. Med.,* 24, 341.

ARIETI, S. (1962). "The Psychotherapeutic Approach to Depression." *Amer. J. Psychother.,* 16, 397.

BANEN, D. M. (1954). "Suicide by Psychotics." *J. nerv. ment. Dis.,* 120, 349.

BARCIA, D., and AMAT, E. (1961). "Los Ensuenos en la Depression Endogena." *Act. luso-esp. Neur.,* 20, 281.

BATCHELOR, I. R. C., and NAPIER, M. B. (1954). "The Sequelae and Short-term Prognosis of Attempted Suicide." *J. Neurol. Neurosurg. Psychiat.,* 17, 261.

BERLIEN, I. (June 28, 1954). Personal communication.

BIBRING, E. (1953). "Affective Disorders." In Greenacre, P., Ed., *Affective Disorders: Psychoanalytic Contributions to Their Study,* pp. 13–49. New York: International University Press.

BILLINGS, E. B. (May 9, 1955). Personal communication.

BLEULER, E. (1930). *Textbook of Psychiatry.* Trans. by A. A. Brill. New York: Macmillan.

BONHIME, W. (1960). "Depression as a Practice: Dynamics and Psychotherapeutic Considerations." *Comp. Psychiat.,* 1, 194.

BRACELAND, F. J. (1954). "Men in Their Fifties." *J. Omaha clin. Soc.,* 15, 1.

— (July 1, 1954). Personal communication.

BROSIN, H. W. (1952). "Contributions of Psychoanalysis to the Study of the Psychoses." In Alexander, F., and Ross, H., Eds., *Dynamic Psychiatry,* p. 298. Chicago: University of Chicago Press.

BROWN, FELIX (1961). "Depression and Childhood Bereavement." *J. ment. Sci.,* 107, 754.

COHEN, M. B., BAKER, G., COHEN, R. A., FROMM-REICHMANN, F., and WEIGERT, E. V. (1954). "An Intensive Study of Twelve Cases of Manic-Depressive Psychosis." Psychiatry, 16, 103.

DANIELS, ROBERT S. (1962). "Psychotherapy of Depression." *Postgrad. Med.,* 32, 436–441.

DOOLEY, L. S. (1921). "A Psychoanalytic Study of Manic-Depressive Psychosis." *Psychoanal. Rev.,* 8, 37, 144.

DUBLIN, LOUIS I. (1964). *Suicide: A Sociological and Statistical Study.* New York: Ronald Press.

DUNBAR, F. (1947). "The Accident Habit." In: *Mind and Body,* pp. 96–112. New York: Random House.

DYAR, E. G. (July 29, 1954). "Personal communication.

ENGLISH, O. S. (1949). "Observation of Trends in Manic-Depressive Psychosis." *Psychiatry,* **12,** 125.

FENICHEL, O. (1945). *The Psychoanalytic Theory of Neuroses,* pp. 387–407. New York: Norton.

FREUD, S. (1950). "The Defense Neuro-Psychoses (1896)." In *Collected Papers,* Vol. 1., p. 155. London: Hogarth.

— (1950). "Analysis of a Case of Hysteria (1905)." *Ibid,* Vol. 3, p. 67.

— (1950). "Mourning and Melancholia (1916)." *Ibid,* Vol. 4, p. 152.

— (1950). "Some Character-Types Met with in Psycho-Analytic Work." *Ibid,* Vol. 4, p. 318.

— (1936). *The Problem of Anxiety.* New York: Norton.

FROMM-REICHMANN, F. (1950). *Principles of Intensive Psychotherapy.* Chicago: University of Chicago Press.

— (July 12, 1954). Personal communication.

GERO, G. (1953). "An Equivalent of Depression: Anorexia." In Greenacre, P., Ed., *Affective Disorders: Psychoanalytic Contributions to Their Study.* New York: International University Press.

GORDON, H. L. (1949). *The Maggid of Caro.* New York: Pardes.

GREENACRE, P., Ed. (1953). *Affective Disorders: Psycholanalytic Contributions to Their Study.* New York: International University Press.

GRINKER, ROY R., *et al* (1961). *The Phenomena of Depression.* New York: Hoeber.

HENDIN, HERBERT (1964). *Suicide and Scandinavia.* New York: Grune and Stratton.

HAMMERMAN, STEVEN (1963). "Ego Defect and Depression." *Psychoanal. Quart.,* **32,** 155.

HOCH, P., and RACHLIN, H. L. (1940). "An Evaluation of Manic-Depressive Psychosis in the Light of Follow-up Studies." *Amer. J. Psychiat.,* **97,** 831.

HOCH, P. H., and ZUBIN, J. (1954). *Depression.* New York: Grune and Stratton.

HUGHES, J. (July 2, 1964). Personal communication.

JACOBSON, E. (1953). "Contributions to the Metapsychology of Cyclothymic Depression." In Greenacre, P., Ed. *Affective Disorders: Psychoanalytic Contributions to Their Study,* pp. 49–83. New York: International University Press.

— (1954). "Transference Problems in the Psychoanalytic Treatment of Severely Depressed Patients." *J. Amer. Psychoanalyt. Ass.,* **2,** 595.

JAFFE, D. S. (October 23, 1953). Personal communication.

KALINOWSKY, L. B., HOCH, P. H., and GRANT, B. (1961). *Somatic Treatments in Psychiatry.* New York: Grune and Stratton.

KLEIN, M. (1948). "Contribution to the Psychogenesis of the Manic-Depressive States (1935)." In *Contributions to Psychoanalysis, 1921-45.* London: Hogarth.

KRAEPELIN, E. (1904). *Psychiatrie,* 7th Ed. Leipzig: Barth.

— (1921). *Manic-Depressive Insanity and Paranoia.* Trans. by Barclay. Edinburgh: Livingston.

KRAINES, S. H. (1957). *Mental Depressions and Their Treatment.* New York: Macmillan.

LAUGHLIN, H. P. (1953). "Depression." *Med. Ann. Dist. of Columbia,* **22,** 653.

— (1954). "The Psychiatric Aspects of Fatigue." *Med. Ann. Dist. of Columbia,* **23,** 22.

— (1953). "Suicide: Impulse and Remorse." *Quart. Rev. Psychiat.,* **8,** 19.

— (1953). "The Conversion Reactions." *Med. Ann. Dist. of Columbia,* **22,** 581.

— (1954). "King David's Anger." *Psychoanal. Quart.,* **23,** 27.

— (1954). "The Neuroses Following Trauma." *Med. Ann. Dist. of Columbia,* Part I, **23,** 492; Part II, **23,** 567.

— (1957). "Depression and the Suicidal Attempt. State of Mind." *Ciba,* **1,** 6.

—, and RUFFIN, M. DEG. (1953). *An Outline of Dynamic Psychiatry.* 4th rev. mimeo., pp. 135–141. Washington: George Washington Medical School.

LEDDY, MAJ. D. V. (October 18, 1953). Personal communication.

LITMAN, *et al* (1963). "Investigation of Equivocal Suicides." *J. Amer. Med. Ass.*, **184**, 12, 924.

LITTERAL, E. B. (November 11, 1954). Personal communication.

MARYLAND, STATE OF. (Dept. of Post Mortem Examiners) (1953). *Annual Report 1953*, p. 10; *Annual Report 1961*.

MENDELSON, MEYER (1960). *Psychoanalytic Concepts of Depression.* Springfield: Thomas.

MENNINGER, K. A. (1930). *The Human Mind*, p. 109. Garden City: Garden City Publishing.

— (1938). *Man Against Himself.* New York: Harcourt, Brace.

METROPOLITAN LIFE INSURANCE CO. (1950). *Statistical Bulletin.* **31**, 8.

MEYER, ADOLF (1951). *The Collected Papers of Adolf Meyer*, p. 566. Baltimore: Johns Hopkins Press.

MILITARY CLINICAL PSYCHOLOGY (1951). *AFM 160–45; TM 8–242.* Dept. of the Army and the Air Force, pp. 92–99.

NOCE, R. H., WILLIAMS, D. B., and RAPPAPORT, W. (1955). *J. Amer. Med. Ass.*, **158**, 11.

OLIVER, JOHN F. (1954). "Suicide Prevention as a Public Health Problem." *Amer. J. Pub. Hlth*, **44**, 11.

OSTROW, MORTIMER (1955). "The Psychology of Depression and Its Management." *Bull. N. Y. Acad. Med.*, **31**, 57.

— (1960). "The Psychic Function of Depression: A Study in Energetics." *Psychoanal. Quart.*, **29**, 355.

OVERHOLSER, W. (May 5, 1955). Nationally televised mental health program.

— (June, 1955). *Washington Post*, 6/13/55, and personal communication, 6/16/55.

RADO, S. (1928). "The Problem of Melancholia." *Int. J. Psycho-Anal.*, **9**, 420.

— (1951). "Psychodynamics of Depression from the Etiologic Point of View." *Psychosom. Med.*, **13**, 51.

REIK, T. (1953). *The Secret Self: Psychoanalytic Experiences in Life and Literature*, p. 229. New York: Farrar, Straus & Young.

ROBIE, THEODORE R. (1961). "A New and Safer Monoamine Inhibitor." *J. Neuropsych.*, **2**, S 31.

SALUS, SYDNEY G. (June 30, 1964). Personal communication.

SARGANT, WILLIAM (1961). "The Physical Treatments of Depression: Their Indications and Proper Use." *J. Neuropsych.*, **2**, S 1.

SAUL, L. J. (1938). "Psychogenic Factors in the Etiology of the Common Cold and Related Symptoms." *Int. J. Psycho-Anal.*, **19**, 451.

SHOCHET, BERNARD R. (1964). "Attempted Suicide." *Maryland med. J.*, **13**, 3, 107.

SLOANE, R. B. (1961). "Depression: Diagnosis and Clinical Features." *J. Neuropsych.*, **2** (Suppl.), 11.

SPITZ, R. (1946). "Anaclitic Depression, etc." In *The Psychoanalytic Study of the Child*, Vol. 2, pp. 313–342. New York: International University Press.

SULLIVAN, H. S. (1946). *Conceptions of Modern Psychiatry*, p. 50. Washington. William Alanson White Psychiatric Foundation.

— (1953). *The Interpersonal Theory of Psychiatry.* New York: Norton.

U.S. PUBLIC HEALTH SERVICE (1952). *Census of Patients in Mental Institutions, 1949.* Pub. No. 223. Washington.

—, NATIONAL OFFICE OF VITAL STATISTICS (1953). *Death and Death Rates from 64 Selected Causes.* Report No. 11, 37.

WAYNE, G. G. (1955). "Some Unconscious Determinants in Physicians Motivating the Use of Particular Treatment Methods—with Particular Reference to Electroconvulsive Treatment." *Psychoanal. Rev.*, **42**, 83.

WEIGERT, E. (1930). "Psychoanalytic Notes on Sleep and Convulsive Treatment in Functional Psychoses." *Psychiatry*, **3**, 189.

WILSON, D. C. (1955). "Dynamics and Psychotherapy of Depression." *J. Amer. Med. Ass.*, **158**, 151.

WILSON, L. A., and LAWSON, I. R. (1962). "Situational Depression in the Elderly. *Geront. Clin. Additamental*, **12**, 59.

ZILBOORG, B. (1936). "Differential Diagnostic Types of Suicide." *Arch Neurol. Psychiat.*, **35**, 270.

— (1936). "Suicide Among Civilized and Primitive Races." *Amer. J. Psychiat.*, **92**, 1347.

— (1937). "Considerations on Suicide, with Particular Reference to That of the Young." *Amer. J. Orthopsychiat.*, **7**, 15.

XV. REVIEW QUESTIONS FOR THE DEPRESSIVE REACTIONS

1. Emotional depression is to anxiety, as sadness is to fear. Explain.
2. How is the management of Depressive Reactions a challenge to medical acumen? Why is therapy worthwhile?
3. Discuss the contributors to theory, and their contributions.
4. Discuss:
    (a) Problems in the diagnosis of the Depressive Reactions.
    (b) Distinguish neurotic, from psychotic Depressive Reactions.
    (c) What are "physical-equivalents" of depression?
    (d) What is the Concept of Secondary Defense of the symptoms?
    (e) Why ordinarily does more depression mean less anxiety?
5. Comment on:
    (a) The incidence of emotional depression in several areas of medical experience.
    (b) Dawn-Insomnia.
6. What are:
    (a) The Depressive-Equivalents?
    (b) Typical symptoms in depression?
    (c) Concepts of:
        (1) "Cold Depression"?
        (2) Emotional and mental retardation in depression?
        (3) Diffuse Retardation?
        (4) Psychologic-Equivalents of depression?
        (5) Emotional decompensation?
        (6) Antecedent Conflict?
        (7) Inverse ratio of hostile-expression to depression?
        (8) Primal Depression?
        (9) Rejection and the "Compliant Response"?
        (10) "Dress Indicators" in Depression?
    (d) Cautions with suicidal tendencies?
    (e) Contributory factors in Grief States?
    (f) Emotional Exploitation?
    (g) Higher Order vs. Lower Order neurotic reactions?
    (h) Cover Reasons for suicides?
7. When is emotional depression pathologic?
8. What types of persons are more predisposed to emotional depression? How are certain character traits psychologic equivalents?
9. List the major psychodynamic factors in the genesis of Depressive Reactions.
10. What is meant by:
    (a) The "Compliant-Response"?
    (b) The Implicit Command?
    (c) Inverse Ratio Concept (Depression and Hostile Expression)?
    (d) A Frozen State of Rage?
    (e) Masochism and Sadism in the Depression Reactions?
    (f) Lost-Object Reunion Goal?
    (g) Emotional Decompensation?
    (h) Direct Cultural-Ratio Concept (Depression and suicide, with cultural suppression of hostility and competitiveness)?
11. Outline the depressive endogain, and epigain.
12. Discuss:
    (a) Situational or Reactive Depression.
    (b) The Depression of Success; the Completion Depression; the Promotion Depression.
    (c) The Anxious Depression; Agitation-Gauge.
    (d) The One-Day Depression.
    (e) Emotional factors in the common cold.

13. Briefly discuss:
    (a) Cultural Vogue, in emotional depression.
    (b) Theory of Antecedent Conflicts.
    (c) Morning-Ebbtide of spirits.
    (d) Principle of Recurrence.
    (e) Suicide as "an ultimate soterial retreat."
    (f) The Grief State.
    (g) Primal Depression.
    (h) The Rule of Impression Priority.
14. In reference to suicide, comment briefly on:
    (a) Incidence.
    (b) Prevention.
    (c) Accident Proneness, and Fracture-Proneness.
    (d) The "Three D's."
    (e) Psychodynamic factors.
    (f) Impulse and remorse.
    (g) Compliant Response.
    (h) The effect upon statistics of Euphemistically-Intended Disguises.
15. What is:
    (a) The Symbolic-Authority Concept?
    (b) The Post-Trough Point of Hazard, for suicides in depression?
16. Note some important goals and problems in the therapy of the Depressive Reactions. What is:
    (a) "Emotional Inertia"?
    (b) The Mechanical Analogy?
    (c) Deep Treatment?
17. In the Depressive Reactions, discuss:
    (a) The use of physical measures (including electric shock).
    (b) The use of drugs:
        (1) In the therapy of emotional depression
        (2) In emotional illnesses generally:
            (i) Sedatives.
            (ii) Tranquilizers.
            (iii) "Energizers".
            (iv) Additional agents.

CHAPTER 5

THE CHARACTER REACTIONS

.... Character Trait Defenses, their Constellations and Hypertrophy

I. INTRODUCTION
   A. Concept of Character Defenses
      1. Collectively They Comprise the Personality; 2. Constellation of Defenses; Personality Types
   B. Character Reactions
      1. Principle of Defense-Hypertrophy; Overdevelopment Equates Neurosis; 2. Continuing Vital Role in Major Areas
   C. Useful Definitions
      1. The Character Trait, Defense and Reaction; 2. Character Analysis; 3. Personality Types; 4. Constellation of Traits Defensively Intended

II. HISTORICAL BACKGROUND
   A. Focus of Scientific Interest Recent
      1. Preliminary Steps Required; 2. Quiet Revolution in Therapy; 3. Karl Abraham and Obsessive Traits; 4. Wilhelm Reich and Character Analysis; 5. Continuing Developments

III. DIAGNOSIS
   A. Descriptive System of Diagnosis Proposed
      1. Character Defenses Overlap; 2. Presence of Pathology Often Quantitatively Determined; 3. Character Neuroses Distinguished from "Symptom Neuroses"
   B. Three Major Patterns of Character Reactions
      1. Obsessive Character Defenses; 2. Conversion (hysterical) Character Defenses; 3. Depressive Character Defenses: The Depressed Personality; 4. In Conclusion

IV. INCIDENCE
   A. Major Group in Estimated Incidence
      1. Twenty Per Cent; 2. The Relative Incidence of Types of Neurotic Reactions

   B. Cultural Influences on Character Defenses
      1. Cultural Vogue; Tacit or Active Pressures; 2. Developed vs. Underdeveloped Cultures

V. CLINICAL FEATURES OF PERSONALITY TYPES AND CHARACTER REACTIONS
   A. The Obsessive Group
      1. Traits of Obsessive Personality; 2. The Obsessive Facade; 3. Concept of Personal Yardstick; 4. Ambivalence, and Obsessive Defenses of Procrastination, and Indecision; 5. Defense of Pessimism; 6. Intellectual Prowess of Obsessive Individuals; 7. Additional Aspects of Interest; 8. Advantages in Occupations and Avocations; 9. In Conclusion
   B. The Conversion (hysterical) Personality and Character Reactions
      1. Traits of Conversion Personality; 2. Defensive Purpose; 3. Egocentricity and Attention-seeking as Character Defenses; 4. Conversion Characteristics Have Important Effects Upon Relationships; 5. Case Illustrations; 6. Hostility, Uncooperativeness, and Secondary Defense; 7. Sexuality; 8. Suggestibility; 9. In Conclusion; Concept of Effect-Over-Cause in Sexual Maladjustment
   C. The Depressive Group
      1. Traits of Depressive Personality; 2. Relationships of Depressed Personality; 3. Contributions of Depressed Personality; 4. "Level" of Depression; 5. Cultural Factors and Depressive Character Traits; 6. When Is Depression Pathologic?; 7. Further Consequences of Depressive Character Traits; 8. Passing-the-Peak; Increased Vulnerability to Depression with Increasing Age; 9. Sexual Interests and Activity; Hypomanic Activity (De-

fense Against Depression);
10. Predisposition to Depression

D. Additional Personality
Types of Interest
1. Hygeiaphrontic Character Defenses; 2. Phobic Personality; 3. Casual Personality; 4. Paranoid Personality; 5. Soterial Personality; 6. "Antiseptic Personality"; 7. The Anxious Personality; 8. Impulsive Character

VI. Psychodynamics and Pathogenesis

A. Trait Development is Analogous Dynamically to Symptom Formation
1. A Defensive Development to Serve Internal Needs; 2. Genesis of Obsessive Character Traits; 3. Parents Encourage Development of Similar Traits in Children; 4. Applications Not Limited to Pathology; Program of Executive Development; 5. In Summary

VII. Obsessive Personality and Sex

A. Defensive Sexual Inhibition
1. Less Energy Available; 2. All Affectivity Restricted; 3. Supermoralism;

B. Inhibitions of Sex and Aggression Parallel

C. Marital Relationships; Marriage Non-Therapeutic in Emotional Illness

VIII. Compulsive Overeating

IX. Treatment

A. Character Analysis
1. Treatment of Choice; 2. Relationship - Improvement Precept

B. Referral: Advantageous Position of Physicians

C. Indications for Treatment

D. Cautions in Obsessive Trait Therapy

X. Summary

XI. Selected References and Bibliography

XII. Review Questions

I. INTRODUCTION

A. CONCEPT OF CHARACTER DEFENSES

1. Collectively They Comprise the Personality

PERSONALITY or character traits are important differentiating features for we humans. In this regard they can take precedence over certain physical attributes, which are of course similarly differentiating. In essence they make up the individual. They determine in large measure how he appears, how he performs, how he is liked and judged by others, and what he is able to accomplish in life. Character traits and personality traits as labels, are interchangeable in our current terminology. Collectively they comprise the personality.

One's character or personality traits do not appear by accident. Neither are they inborn. Instead they evolve gradually, as more or less fixed "habit-patterns" of attitudes and responses. Their essential function is a defensively intended one. Hence we have come to refer to them in our present discussion equally, as *character defenses*. The elaboration of an individual's character defenses is a gradual, automatic, and unconscious process.

2. Constellations of Defenses; Personality Types

While quite conscious and deliberate attempts may be made by a person to promote the development of a single personality and/or socially more desirable trait or a group of them, in general it is accurate and safe to regard them as evolving quite automatically and effortlessly. Character traits or defenses, when developed sufficiently to be so described, include such diverse attributes as those of orderliness, scrupulousness, honesty, impulsiveness, integrity, parsimoniousness, somberness, dramatism, pessimism, and perfectionism, to name a few. When sufficiently marked so as to be thus labeled, they are generally overdeveloped or exaggerated, at least to some degree. Collectively they comprise what we sometimes refer to as the "character armor" of an individual.

Overdevelopment of one or a constellation of traits, occurs in response to increasing needs and to new stresses. As we shall observe, this can occur and progress to the point of handicap, self-defeat, and neurosis. One's individual character defenses tend to develop in association with other similar and related ones. Such groupings of related traits have been referred to by the author as a *constellation* (of character defenses).

The three major such constellations of related character traits which are most commonly to be encountered, and are most clear-cut descriptively, at this juncture in our evolution of classification, are the *Obsessive*, the *Depressive*, and the *Conversion* (or hysterical). Accordingly, similar terms are used to designate the three corresponding personality types: the Obsessive Personality, the Depressive Personality, and the Conversion Personality. A number of additional personality types, as outlined later, can be similarly labeled, although currently they cannot be as clearly delineated as these three.

B. CHARACTER REACTIONS

1. Principle of Defense-Hypertrophy; Overdevelopment Equates Neurosis

From the dynamic standpoint, the obsessive character defenses for example, have similar origins and serve similar intrapsychic purposes, to the more clearly neurotic symptoms of an obsessive nature. This is true with other groups of traits as well. In other words, the several constellations of related character traits occupy an analogous position to their corresponding groups of neurotic symptoms, for which they may be regarded as what we might refer to as the *character-equivalents* (of these symptoms). Accordingly, the appropriate sections of discussion in this Chapter Five are to be considered together with the chapter on the corresponding neurotic reaction. Thus, while our present discussion will deal primarily with various defensive patterns of personality, much of what is included will also have applicability to other obsessive, depressive, conversion, and so on, types of manifestations.

A given useful character trait which has been originally elaborated as an unwitting defensive endeavor, can overdevelop, in accord with our concept of the Defense-Hypertrophy Principle [Ch.2:IVB]. The result is self-defeat and personal handicap. Sufficient such progression of one or a constellation of traits constitutes a *Character Reaction*.

The overdevelopment of such a group of related character defensive traits also may be termed a *Character Neurosis*. In common with the other types of neurotic reactions, this type of reaction is characterized by the exaggeration of the particular defense or group of defenses, beyond the point of usefulness, as judged objectively.

Herein the defenses have *over*-progressed, to the point of self-defeat, handicap, and loss, in accord with our Concepts of the Illusory Gains of Emotional Illness. (*See* Ch.2.) The Character Neuroses constitute a very important group of the clinical reactions which are to be observed in the private practice of medicine and psychiatry. For anyone seriously interested in emotional illness, private psychiatric practice, social interaction, or psychotherapy, the importance of increased familiarity and understanding of this entire broad area can hardly be overstressed. Our recognition of the importance of the character defenses, Personality Types, and Character Reactions, is most recent in origin.

2. Continuing Vital Role in Major Areas

Separate consideration of the groups of character defensive traits has been undertaken with this present work, in order to further emphasize the great importance generally, of the many various individual such attributes, character patterns, or constellations of traits. These play a continuing vital role: (1) in emotional adjustment, (2) in personality integration, (3) in maturity, and (4) in personal individuality. Such consideration in a separate chapter, is also intended to emphasize the important concept of Character Neurosis. For purposes of uniformity in our diagnostic terminology of the neurotic reactions, it is proposed that we refer to these equally as the *Character Reactions*.

Our emphasis in this chapter will be on three of the more major constellations of character traits. These three constellations are emphasized for a number of reasons, including their clearer delineation, widespread occurrence, tendency to be encountered clinically in a well-established and possibly "purer" form, relatively greater importance, and their overall cultural usefulness, especially when present to an individually moderate and non-handicapping extent.

C. USEFUL DEFINITIONS

1. The Character Trait, Defense, and Reaction

As noted, the terms "personality trait" and "character trait" have been adopted and used interchangeably, for the purposes of this text. From a dynamic standpoint they develop defensively. Accordingly, it is also considered quite appropriate to refer to them as "character defenses," as "personality defenses," or as defensive traits.

The character defense would thus be defined as *a personality attribute or trait. Each such trait has an individually-specific defensive intent or purpose. The defensive endeavor of the trait is intrapsychic in origin* and is usually quite hidden from ordinary observation, as well as from the conscious awareness of the person concerned.

The Character Reaction is the author's preferred term for a character neurosis, in the interest of diagnostic uniformity. The Character Reaction is defined then as *a neurotic reaction, in which certain personality traits (that is, character defenses) have become exaggerated or overdeveloped.*

The overdeveloped traits or attributes in the Character Reaction are ⌄
equivalent to the clinical symptoms in other types of neurosis. They may
thereby also be referred to as the *character-equivalents* to (other types of)
neurotic symptoms or symptomotology. The personality imbalance resulting from such trait overdevelopment, while defensively vital to the patient
concerned, inevitably, has greater or lesser elements of self-defeat, which
are largely hidden from conscious awareness.

The clinical manifestations of the Character Reactions are to be found
in the overdevelopment, or what we might refer to also as the *hypertrophy,*
of the person's defensive character and personality traits. This is the
Defense-Hypertrophy Principle in the evolvement of a Character Reaction,
as noted earlier. The resulting manifestations are apparent through the
study of his adjustment, behavior, relationships, and patterns of reaction.
In contradistinction to the other patterns of neurotic reaction, specific
symptom formation as such, is generally absent or of considerably lesser
relative significance. In the Character Reaction, these hypertrophied defenses or character-equivalents, may be regarded as attempting to subserve
the same vital intrapsychic purposes as in other more clearly neurotic
symptoms, although often in considerably less striking and apparent, and
often indeed in quite subtle fashion. This is why they are to be regarded as
analogous in their attempted defensive function to clinical symptoms.
Since they may be viewed as more or less direct substitutes for neurotic
symptoms, we might also term them as a matter of convenience, *symptom-
equivalents.*

2. Character Analysis

In the psychotherapeutic study of one's individual character defenses and
Character Reactions, we have come to use the term of Character Analysis. ⌄
Character Analysis is *the systematic psychotherapeutic investigation,
study, and analysis of the personality defenses and the defensive character
trait patterns of an individual.* Therefore in Character Analysis, the focus
of attention, interest, and study on the part of both analyst and patient is
directed thus, *instead* of into the analogous intensive scrutiny of the
dynamics and the defensive purposes of the more strictly clinical symptoms
which may be present, as in the other types of psychopathologic emotional
reactions (*see also* Ch.5:IXA1).

Today the definitive psychotherapy and analysis of every patient in- ⌄
evitably will also include a fair amount of what we term Character Analysis.
This is one of the important newer concepts in psychiatry.

3. Personality Types

The Obsessive Personality is to be defined as our *descriptive term for a
type of personality structure in which there is a pattern or constellation of
obsessive attributes present which includes several of the group of obsessive
personality traits or defenses, as listed in Table 17.* The descriptive term
of Obsessive Personality thus may be used on occasion to refer to an
individual who possesses such defenses. These rather typical traits may
or may not be sufficiently marked to cause interference with living, a loss

of efficiency, a limitation of one's normal satisfactions, or of his social adjustment. When they have become so, this state of affairs then constitutes the *Obsessive Type of Character Reaction.*

The Obsessive Personality thus comprises one of our major constellations of character defenses. The obsessive group of character or personality defensive traits includes among others, the character-equivalents of orderliness, inhibition of emotions and reactions, obstinacy, meticulousness, overconscientiousness, worry over relative trifles, hidden feelings of inadequacy and self-doubt, indecisiveness, preciseness, procrastination, pessimism, parsimoniousness, and perfectionism. The Obsessive type or pattern of Personality may be considered as analogous to the Conversion Personality, and to the Depressive Personality. Its relation to the Obsessive Reaction, is likewise comparable to the relation of the Depressive Personality to the Depressive Reaction, and to that of the Conversion Personality in turn to that of clinical Somatic Conversion (hysteria).

The Conversion (or hysterical) Personality in turn is *the descriptive term for a type of personality structure in which there is present a pattern or constellation, of several of the conversion group of personality traits or defenses,* as *listed in Table 18.* These may or may not be sufficiently marked so as to cause interference with living, a loss of efficiency, or a limitation of normal satisfactions or social adjustment. When they are, this constitutes the Conversion type of Character Reaction. The conversion group of character or personality traits includes strong but shifting emotional feelings, susceptibility to suggestion, impulsive behavior, attention-seeking, immaturity, self-absorption, appeal, warmth, and flexibility.

The Depressive Personality in parallel definition, is *the descriptive term for a type of personality structure in which there is present a pattern or constellation, of several of the depressive group of personality traits or defenses, as listed in Part 3 of Table 15.* These likewise may or may not be sufficiently marked so to cause interference with living, a loss of efficiency, a limitation of normal satisfactions, or of some measure of a more optimal social adjustment. When they are, this constitutes the depressive type of Character Reaction. The Depressive Personality is our third major constellation of character defenses. The depressive group of character or personality traits includes overseriousness, lowered spirits, increased vulnerability to letdown or disappointment, overconscientiousness, dependability, compliance, subservience, and deliberateness among others.

In addition to our three major constellations of defensively-intended and evolved traits, a number of other types or patterns of character defenses may be encountered, which can be more or less marked and distinguishable. As with the three major constellations described above, these may be associated with, or be precursors to, the other and often more marked, clinical symptoms of their corresponding neurotic reactions. Accordingly we might include the *Hygeiaphrontic (hypochondriacal) Personality,* the *Phobic Personality,* the *Soterial Personality,* the *Dissociative Personality,* the *Compulsive Personality,* the *Impulsive Personality,* and the *Anxious Personality.* The *Casual Personality* is the opposite of the Obsessive Personality, with the associated character defenses being roughly the converse of these. The

Paranoid Personality is characterized by a protectively-intended distance-maintaining, distrustfulness, suspiciousness, hostility, and by over-utilization of the mechanism of projection. The *Antiseptic Personality* refers to the occasional overly-moralistic, guilt-ridden, and sexually super-inhibited individual.

Additional personality types are to be found in conjunction with a principally-employed and overly-prominent, that is hypertrophied, mental mechanism. Thus one might refer to the Compensating Personality, Denying Personality, Displacing Personality, Projecting (Paranoid) Personality, Idealizing Personality, Rationalizing Personality, and others.

4. Constellation of Traits Defensively Intended

Each separate group of personality and character defenses includes more or less related and characteristic traits. Although more complete lists will follow later (*Tables 15-18*), it immediately becomes evident how widespread is the possession of various ones of these traits, and constellations of related traits. As an overall group of many, many possible traits, they may serve a dynamic purpose roughly equivalent to that of the more usually regarded clinical neurotic symptoms. When they prove effective in their ∠ role as character defenses, the development of more clearly neurotic symptoms as such may prove unnecessary and, in effect, be prevented. When they prove ineffective in their defensively-intended role, or when they crumble under added emotional stresses, they may be prodromal to the onset of the corresponding type of neurotic reaction.

The psychologic defense against anxiety takes place in the Obsessive Personality, for example, through the development of a special constellation of character traits. In the Obsessive-Compulsive Neuroses, in turn, anxiety is held in check through the intrusion into consciousness of insistent, repetitive ideas or urges to action. These substitutive intrusions are generally unwelcome and repugnant to the patient. They are often regarded by him as "senseless," "illogical," "unreasonable," or "silly."* As a result, the individual concerned consciously struggles against them. It is often the resulting discomfort of his relative helplessness and powerlessness to consciously suppress his obsessive thoughts and compulsive urges that helps to motivate such a person toward seeking professional help.

Each of the several constellations of character defensive traits has an analogous role to others. Each is similarly defensively-intended.

---

* They are only "senseless" insofar as they make no conscious sense to the patient, who may so label them. They always make sense, when the unconscious basis for them is sufficiently uncovered! This is in accord with our earlier outlined *Principle of the Individual Appropriateness of Response* [Ch.1:IIC2;Ch.3:IB1]. The patient's degree of prejudice, scorn, or criticism toward himself for having them, may reflect in direct ratio his level of psychologic sophistication.

The informed patient, possessed of sufficient education, culture, and sophistication will have just as painful and severe neurotic symptoms. However, he possibly may more likely be spared some of the added burden of self-criticism, or related futile efforts in trying consciously to dispel symptoms by an effort of will power alone. He is likely to be more free to undertake the kind of constructive self-scrutiny, which can lead or lead faster, to working out their otherwise secret meanings.

II. HISTORICAL BACKGROUND

A. FOCUS OF SCIENTIFIC INTEREST RECENT

1. Preliminary Steps Required

The observation of individual character traits is of course as old as man himself. Describing the facets entering into personalities, and types of personality, has been an important aspect of myths, sagas, history, and drama through the ages. The organized study of character defenses, however, is most recent indeed, while the endeavor to organize and to publish such data in some still more systematic form is even more so. Efforts in this latter direction were original with the preparation of the first edition of this text (1947–1956), and are expanded here. The further substantial development and evolution of these concepts and studies is very much indicated and will undoubtedly transpire.

The entry of psychiatry into these areas of character-trait evolvement has required several basic preliminary steps. These have included: (1) the clear appreciation of the defensive intent of character traits and of their automatic "effortless" development in the unconscious; (2) recognition of their major position in the psychologic scheme of things; and (3) awareness of their equivalent position (as what we have termed character-equivalents), to the more prominent and generally-recognized clinical symptoms of neurosis. With the attainment of these preliminary recognitions, further progress in this entire, most significant area has become both feasible and increasingly necessary.

2. Quiet Revolution in Therapy

Psychiatrists have been enabled thus increasingly to enlarge their focus of attention, from being confined within the narrower scope of specific symptoms, into the broader and fertile fields of characterologic study. This has led and is leading further to a quiet revolution in psychotherapy. This is a major consequence. Through it many people will benefit.

A wider range of people can now secure help, as the therapist's range of interests and effectiveness increasingly widen. Indeed, an increasing proportion of the efforts devoted to intensive psychotherapy and analysis in private practice, has come to be directed toward the understanding of the individual's character structure and toward its constructive and healthful modification, over the course of the last three decades. As a consequence many more people have come to seek psychologic help with their problems in living.

We may well refer to this kind of therapy as *a graduate course in life*. The potential among people who might enroll in such a course of study with most beneficial results personally, is increasingly widespread.

3. Karl Abraham and Obsessive Traits

Little attention was directed by psychiatrists at the turn of the century toward personality traits or character structure. Constellations of these defenses were unrecognized. Diagnoses as employed for the neuroses were confined mainly to those of hysteria, neurasthenia (J. M. Beard), psychasthenia (Janet), anxiety neurosis (Freud), melancholia, hypochondriasis, and sometimes traumatic neurosis, as was outlined more graphically in *Table 3, Chapter 1.* Interest was directed toward these, and perhaps more particularly toward the more marked and prominent cases of them, as encountered clinically. Among the few psychodynamically-oriented psychiatrists of the time there was more than sufficient effort required and challenge present in exploring and defending the most basic of theories in psychogenesis, and usually as these related to the more striking kinds of neurotic symptoms. It is hardly surprising that we find any real prominence assigned to character trait study a matter for considerably later attention.

Obsessive personality traits were the first to be studied analytically. This was not entirely fortuitous, since the early clinical experience in dynamic psychotherapy was secured in the study of cases of hysteria (the Conversion Reactions) and of the Obsessive Reactions, beginning prior to 1900. A few years later Karl Abraham published pioneering studies relating to the origin of three of the basic obsessive personality traits (those of obstinacy, orderliness, and frugality), which he traced to the so-called anal phase of psychic development. Later he pursued these studies further. Sigmund Freud (in possibly the most prominent instance of its kind in the development of his analytic theories) accepted Abraham's pioneering work practically *in toto*, and later amplified it.

In 1908, Freud thus wrote briefly on character and anal erotism. Five years later he offered a distinction between obsessive traits and clinical symptoms. In the former, repression is more successful and there are sublimations and reaction formations. He referred to character traits as "individual attitudes of the ego" in 1915, "which are thus mobilized to oppose the attempted alterations." Ferenczi also early discussed the influence of infantile bowel training on the development of personality. Some of these earlier observations in this particular area, both practically and in theory have been found to have considerably wider applications, as to the effects of early infantile and childhood training generally (and the impact of parental figures), upon overall individual personality and character trait development. These references, however, are sparse indeed, and scant consideration was available for a long time for characterologic research.

During the next two decades only quite scattered similar references continued, as the mainstream of interest in dynamic psychiatry and analysis continued to be focused on the more established and familiar cases of neurosis; an increasingly wider range of which were being likewise increasingly widely recognized for the first time, as having a clearly psychogenic origin.

4. Wilhelm Reich and Character Analysis

It was only as recently as 1928, that Wilhelm Reich published in German, the first paper on character analysis, noting the presence of character resistances in analytic therapy. This, too, was an isolated but pioneering and significant contribution. Five years later a related book was published. This was subsequently translated into English, entitled *Character Analysis,* and published in 1945, with several later editions.

Reich first discussed the purpose and genesis of certain attitudes as a kind of *characterologic armor*. He sought to delineate several types of character, the most important ones being the conversion (hysterical) and the obsessive types. He also noted the influence of social forces upon character development. Fenichel later believed that these were the determining forces in the development of man's character. The resulting impetus which Reich had thus provided to what really amounted to initiating the study and analysis of character, was his greatest contribution in psychiatry.

5. Continuing Developments

In subsequent years others have indicated interest and have offered contributions. Fenichel sought to classify personality traits as being either sublimation or reactive types, according to the predominent influences in their origin. During the decade from 1942 the author of this text became increasingly impressed with the relative prominence of character study in his own therapeutic work with individuals. Following an initial paper, he continued to develop and to organize his concepts and theories, together with his clinical data, and to correlate them with the findings of other clinicians. These were offered in *The Neuroses in Clinical Practice* (1956), and are further developed here. Other work is being done, and of course much remains to be done.

Psychotherapy and analysis today inevitably deal with characterologic matters. This is true regardless of the school of thought or of the background of the therapist. It is true regardless of the presenting problem or diagnosis, when the treatment is intensive, is insight-oriented, and is intended to be really definitive. Psychiatric recognition of the importance of character and character study has increased steadily. Currently this relatively new, entire field appears to be gradually approaching the position of prominence which it very much deserves.

III. DIAGNOSIS

A. DESCRIPTIVE SYSTEM OF DIAGNOSIS PROPOSED

1. Character Defenses Overlap

A diagnosis of Obsessive, Conversion, Depressive, or other type of Personality is warranted when at least several of the corresponding character defensive traits (as later tabulated) can be observed. When one or more of these are present and have evolved to a handicapping degree, we may speak of an Obsessive, Conversion, or other kind of Character Neurosis or Reaction.

Some forty or more character defensive traits can be listed as more or less belonging to the obsessive group alone. However, the possession of one or more of these is not necessarily confined to obsessive individuals. This tendency for overlapping and non-confinement of traits is true also for the other groups.

We have continually stressed the overlapping which exists in psychoneurotic symptomatology. This is to be observed clinically in each one of the various patterns of emotional reactions. Overlapping is also present in the labeling of the various personality or character types. The possession of his various character defenses by any given individual, thus is by no means necessarily confined to any one specific group or constellation.

2. Presence of Pathology Often Quantitatively Determined

Lines of demarcation between a so-called "normal" individual, a given pattern or type of personality, a pathological personality structure with its overly-developed defensive traits, and a neurosis, are by no means always clear-cut. The dynamic interrelationships of all personality traits with each other and with clinical symptoms, also are often very close. From this standpoint basic differences in the above categories may be slight. They may be more a matter of degree than of kind. Thus, the presence of actual psychopathology is more often a matter of degree and of relativity, as was noted in Chapter One. The difference is quantitative rather than qualitative. If separations are to be made, it may be necessary to make them rather arbitrarily, and on the basis of one's individual judgment.

The author has found it useful in diagnosis to make distinctions: (1) as to the relative presence or absence (that is, the level) of psychopathology and not alone upon (2) the presence or absence of typical symptoms or character defenses. Added important considerations are: (3) the degree of resulting personal and social handicap; (4) the relative interference with living; and (5) the limitations which may interfere with reaching one's optimal potential in achievements and maturity.

A given character structure, however, may be descriptively classified as obsessive, for example, even though a typical constellation of defensive traits resulted in minimal interference or handicap, or even though treatment was hardly indicated. These principles, as outlined, also have application in the diagnosis and classification of the various patterns of psychoneuroses, as well as the different personality types.

3. Character Neuroses Distinguished from "Symptom Neuroses"

Diagnosis in the field of the personality types and the Character Reactions has been attempted on several bases. Two major ones are mentioned here. Thus, in accord with their basis in a particular phase of psychosexual development, constellations of character traits have been sometimes labeled as genital, oral, and anal. As a second basis, in accord with the resulting character structure, they have been referred to as hysterical, phallic, narcissistic, compulsive, and so on.

Each of the above methods has been found to some extent limiting, unsatisfactory, or referred to by people in conflicting fashion. The author accordingly proposes the utilization of a more simple, basically descriptive, system of diagnosis. For practical purposes this would best correspond with existing patterns of what we might term the "symptom neuroses"* of

---

* The term *symptom neuroses* would be the author's suggestion for a means to distinguish those neurotic reactions which are marked by the presence of more or less definite clinical symptoms, from the *character neuroses,* which are marked instead by the overdevelopment of the various character defensive traits.

which the pattern of character defenses may be a precursor. (For example: Conversion, Depressive, or Obsessive), with certain prominent and over-developed intrapsychic defense mechanisms (for example: Projecting (Paranoid), Denying, Idealizing, and so on), or occasionally according to the sometimes colorfully descriptive end-result (for example: Casual, Anti-septic), as seen by the outside world.

Accordingly, one might classify a personality type in line with the indi-vidual's more prominent traits. One would thus also ordinarily diagnose a Character Reaction or neurosis, according to its most closely correspond-ing symptom neurosis. We can today best delineate the Obsessive, Conver-sion, Depressive, Phobic, Paranoid, and Hygeiaphrontic (hypochondriacal) patterns of Character Reaction, in that order. Let us say a few words about the first three types, and outline comparatively their more character-istic traits.

B. THREE MAJOR PATTERNS OF CHARACTER REACTIONS

1. Obsessive Character Defenses

A group of personality traits may be listed which are more or less com-monly to be seen in conjunction with the Obsessive Personality. These are to be known as the obsessive character defenses. Their possession, how-ever, is not limited to the Obsessive Personality. The evolvement and pos-session of a number of these individual traits is widespread. It is indeed rare today to study a neurosis in a more sophisticated individual, in which some obsessive trait or other is not uncovered during the course of therapy.

The association together of a number of them, however, especially the more typical ones, makes up a significant personality constellation of the obsessive type. Of course one would hardly expect ever to see all of these traits present in an individual at any one given time. Also, overlapping is to be noted among the traits as listed.

The major personality traits or character defenses which help to make up the Obsessive Personality, the Conversion (hysterical) Personality, and the Depressive Personality are listed together, for ready comparative refer-ence at this juncture, in the accompanying *Table 15*. A more complete separate tabulation of several of our constellations of character defense will be provided later.

A. PRINCIPLE OF DEFENSE-HYPERTROPHY; USEFUL TO A POINT.—It is important that one understands the discomforts and limitations which can result from these characteristics, when they have progressed beyond the level of real personal need or social usefulness. The individual concerned is in the grip of powerful forces beyond the possibility of any immediate voluntary control. Control or mastery is possible eventually through under-standing, but not through conscious effort alone. Constructive introspec-tion and study with expert help is ordinarily required.

The orderly and meticulous person, for instance, may attempt to justify his behavior to himself or to others, on the basis of increased efficiency or convenience. Up to a certain point this may well be true. Beyond this point, it may cease to be personally or socially advantageous. This is in

Table 15

Three Major Groups of Character Defenses

A comparative listing of defensive character traits in three personality constellations

1. *The Obsessive Personality* (See also Table 17)	2. *The Conversion (hysterical) Personality* (See also Table 18)	3. *The Depressive Personality*
1. Orderliness.	1. Strong but shifting emotional feelings.	1. Overseriousness (somberness).
2. Inhibition overdeveloped (as to actions, emotions, thoughts, imagination).	2. Susceptibility to suggestion.	2. Restricted sense of humor.
3. Rigidity (resistance to change, stubbornness, "set in his ways," obstinacy).	3. Inhibitions deficiently developed.	3. Lowered spirits.
	4. Impulsive behavior, and prominent "acting out."	4. Studiousness.
4. Meticulousness, preciseness.	5. Emotional relationships often shallow.	5. Increased vulnerability to let-down, disappointment, frustration, or loss.
5. Overconscientiousness.	6. Flair for the dramatic.	6. Overconscientiousness.
6. Worry over responsibilities, and over relative trifles.	7. Dependence and helplessness; may be contradictorily combined with a certain imperiousness.	7. High level of dependability.
7. Hidden feelings of inadequacy and self-doubt.	8. Attention-seeking.	8. Tendency toward at least outward compliance is likely to be overly strong.
8. Overly moralistic.	9. Immaturity. (Sometimes a "spoiled child" picture.)	9. Conciliation often marked.
9. Indecision and doubt.	10. Self-absorption may be marked. (Ego-centricity.)	10. Subservience; even obsequiousness.
10. Overconcern with detail.	11. A mature sexual adjustment is not attained.	11. Propensity for guilt feelings. Harsh self-judgments not uncommon.
11. Intellectualization.	12. Coquetry and seductiveness; often misleading, with an underlying apprehension.	12. Well-developed inhibitions. Imaginative ability frequently restricted.
12. Procrastination.	13. Responsiveness, appeal, and warmth.	13. Conduct restrained and decorous.
13. Pessimism.	14. Imaginative, flexible.	14. Excellent capacity for work, application, and long-term endeavor.
14. Behavior and reactions may be slow and ponderous.	15. Dissociative capacity; Depersonalization not uncommon.	15. Assumes responsibility readily and well.
15. Strong need for reassurance, and for approval.	16. Good spirits; more often on the buoyant side.	16. Overly mature in many areas.
16. Parsimoniousness.	17. Intelligence variable, but with the limitation of any sustained drive toward intellectual achievement.	17. Deliberateness.
17. Intensely self-critical.		18. Often studiously avoids altercation and hostility.
18. Sexually inhibited.		19. Sustained drives toward achievement and long term goals.
19. Perfectionism.		20. Intelligence likely high.
20. Intelligence likely high.		

239

accord with our Principle of Defense-Hypertrophy [Ch.5:IC*1*]. Thus, through further progression, the net result may become a psychologically uneconomic expenditure of time and energy, in the pursuit of relative detail and minutiae. In any event the person concerned does not know, and cannot really explain the needs which are subserved by such activity.

These needs are internal ones. They are intrapsychic and unconscious. The individual may well know consciously however, that behaving contrary to his obsessive needs, for example, in the omission of orderliness perhaps, results in some personal discomfort. He may also be equally aware that he "feels better," that is, achieves some measure of personal comfort, gratification, or satisfaction, when his behavior is in obedience to his obsessive needs.

B. CONCEPT OF OUTWARD REVERSAL OF APPEARANCE.—The obsessively-oriented person underneath may actually feel quite inadequate, self-doubting, and timorous. His outward appearance, however, may convey quite a reverse impression to others. This is likely to be unknown even to himself. Thus, outwardly he may appear confident, courageous, and self-possessed, or even superior, smug, pompous, or possibly condescending. This is in line with a Concept of Outward Reversal of Appearance in the obsessively-oriented person. It is not infrequently encountered.

Others react, of course, largely to the outward facade. It has developed unconsciously, as a protective and distance-promoting cover of the underlying vulnerable feelings. It has come to constitute an important part of his characterologic armor.

C. DISCOMFORT WHEN OBSESSIVE NEEDS RESISTED.—One might make an attempt to describe some of the discomfort and anxiety experienced by the obsessive person when, for example, he consciously resists his needs for orderliness and neatness. He feels as though something important remains undone. He is likely to feel uncomfortable and anxious. He is often self-critical about his failures to get things done. These feelings are, of course, beyond what another person not so burdened would feel. His discomfort and his uneasiness, however, are very real matters to him.

As a possible comparison, one might perhaps note the discomfort and unrest which can be experienced at the appointed time by the person to whom a posthypnotic suggestion has been made, in the event he is prevented from, or tries to restrain himself from carrying out the required act. He is under an inner and unconscious compulsion to do so. Delay and failure to comply give rise to tension, restlessness, and anxiety. He is equally unable to explain the real basis for his action although he will invariably produce a subjectively-satisfactory rationalization. The presence of this kind of compulsive discomfort reaches its most acute development in the Obsessive-Compulsive Reactions among the clinical cases of neuroses, in which the obsession is combated or in which the internal command of the compulsion is resisted.

A rather widely-read instance of an inner compulsive pressure, which antedates modern scientific recognition and study, is to be found in one of the more popular works of Samuel Taylor Coleridge (1772–1834). In

"The Rime of the Ancient Mariner," written in 1798, the reader will recall that the old sailor is pictured as being under a great inner compulsion to repeat again his arresting tale:

> Since then at an uncertain hour,
> That agony returns:
> And 'til my ghostly tale is told,
> This heart within me burns . . .

Herein Coleridge conveyed an essential feature of the compulsion, that is, the discomfort that is present *until* the compulsion is obeyed.

Many years later, the psychiatrist Dr. William A. White (1870–1937) wrote the following clinical description of the more severe instances of compulsive neurosis: "If these compulsions are resisted or interfered with, they give rise to certain symptoms which in marked cases constitute a veritable crisis. The patient feels weak, trembles, becomes dizzy, perspires, and finally yields, to find that at once all these symptoms disappear."

These instances of the inner need to yield to an obsession or to obey a compulsive urge, are not unrelated to the needs which motivate the less striking—but perhaps at least as pervasive—drives supporting various ones of the obsessive traits and their influence.

2. Conversion (hysterical) Character Defenses

We come now to an important area which is intimately related to Somatic Conversion or Conversion Hysteria. Here we refer to the Conversion (hysterical) Personality. This is a second major pattern of character defenses or traits. Their imbalance or exaggeration constitutes the Conversion type of Character Neurosis. The group is important enough as are others, to warrant consideration in a separate chapter. It is included in the present chapter in view of the close analogous relationship of this particular group of character defensive traits to the other major groups of character defenses.

The Conversion Personality consists of a constellation of a number of personality traits which will shortly be tabulated (*Table 18*). These are known collectively as the conversion character defenses. They may, of course, be present in varying strength and in varying combinations. It should be noted definitely, as has already been said about the absence of "pure" hysteria, that a given personality is not likely to be made up solely of any given constellation of defensive character traits. There may of course be little or no actual conversion symptom-formation; in such instances the character defenses suffice to ward off anxiety. At other times one may observe a predisposition to the later development of actual symptoms, as reinforcements to increasingly inadequate character defenses, or as evolving quite independently.

This personality type is frequently marked by coquetry, appeal, charm, readiness to quick friendships, elasticity, a false kind of apprehensively-tinged seductiveness, labile emotions, impulsiveness, suggestibility, dependency, flights of imagination, and a limited drive toward sustained intellectual achievement. Relationships are often warm, but can be quite transient. We can classify a personality type as being of the Conversion constellation, when several of these and/or other related character defenses are present.* We can diagnose the Conversion (hysterical) Character Reaction when a group of these are overdeveloped to a personally handicapping or socially limiting level.

3. Depressive Character Defenses: The Depressed Personality

Through our clinical observations of the Somatic Conversions and Obsessive Reactions, we have found that certain character defenses might exist which could substitute for or defend against actual neurotic symptoms. Prior to, or in the absence of, the development of actual illness, these manifestations in the character or personality of the person concerned serve in less obvious form, purposes similar to those achieved by the major clinical symptoms of the neuroses. This is likewise true in the Depressive Reactions.

Herein we undertake the delineation of the third major constellation of character defense. Each is important because of its incidence, the cultural implications, and because this kind of study contributes importantly to our understanding of the role and function generally of the many individual personality traits.

An imbalance or exaggeration of the traits which are most commonly associated with the Conversion Personality, the Depressive Personality, or the Obsessive Personality, constitute a major category of Character Neurosis. This personality type is often marked by the lower, more somber mood which tends to be present, by vulnerability to disappointment, seriousness, general restraint, well-developed inhibitions, careful, thoughtful, deliberate and decorous conduct, compliance, conciliation, studiousness, and by a restricted sense of humor. The Depressive Personality is likely to be dependable, on the overconscientious side and perhaps subservient and somewhat self-effacing, with a high intelligence and an excellent capacity for work, mental application, and long-term endeavor. *See also* the depressive constellation of attributes, as summarized in Part 3 of *Table 15*.

We can classify a personality as being of the Depressive type when some of the above related character defenses contribute in major fashion to the individual's characterologic armor. We might diagnose the presence of the Depressive pattern of Character Reaction, when they become overdeveloped to the point of social limitation and/or personal handicap.

4. In Conclusion

When a group of typical obsessive, conversion, or depressive traits are well developed, the determination of the presence of this kind of character structure or of an actual Character Neurosis is not difficult. More difficulty

---

* Chodoff and Lyons listed seven behavioral characteristics on which to base the label of the Hysterical (conversion) Personality. Accordingly, they consider this term is "applicable to persons who are vain and egocentric, who display labile and excitable but shallow affectivity, whose dramatic, attention seeking and histrionic behavior may go to the extremes of lying and even *pseudologia phantastica,* who are very conscious of sex, sexually provocative yet frigid, and who are dependently demanding in interpersonal situations."

will be found in cases in which any given constellation of traits is not clear-cut and distinct, and in which they are insufficiently developed, overlap, or in which their presence is either consciously or unwittingly concealed.

Although not included in the foregoing discussion specifically by name, similar considerations apply to the classification of all of the other Personality Types, as well as to the diagnosis of other patterns of Character Reactions.

IV. INCIDENCE

A. MAJOR GROUP IN ESTIMATED INCIDENCE

1. Twenty Per Cent

The incidence of all types of what we can classify as instances of the Character Reactions or Neuroses among the neurotic reactions generally, is quite high. They constitute an estimated 18–20 per cent of all of the clinical cases of neurosis. One would expect the obsessive type of Character Neurosis to account for close to one third of these (*See Table 16*).

The Conversion and Depressive groups together might account for a second third. The balance, combined together, might constitute the final third.

2. The Relative Incidence of Types of Neurotic Reactions

This is an excellent place perhaps to pause and summarize our chapter estimates as to the overall incidence of the several neurotic reactions, and as to their relative numbers. Accordingly these have been compiled in the following *Table 16*. It will of course be of interest to learn how accurate these attempts might be when adequate methods, standards, and means are developed which will provide us with a much-needed, adequate, and accurate sampling of the general population. As to the overall incidence in numbers for the general population, the estimates herein could prove quite conservative.

The following tabulation (*Table 16*) is included to provide a summary of the relative incidence of clinical cases of the neuroses as estimated in the several chapters of this study.

Table 16
The Relative Incidence of Types of Neurotic Reactions

Accurate statistics as to the relative incidence of the various neurotic reactions are lacking. Broad and reliable surveys continue to offer certain considerable problems in their completion. The following is a summary of the author's estimates as to the approximate incidence of the various categories, as presented in the current volume.

These individual percentages depend upon the diagnosis being made on the basis of *the most outstanding clinical feature* which is present on examination. Some of the manifestations primarily associated with one type of neurotic reaction are to be found also in a far wider range of cases. Diagnoses would be based upon the most prominent of the clinical features which were present. (*Table continued on next page*)

Table 16—The Relative Incidence of Neurotic Reactions—Cont.

Clinical Type of Neurotic Reaction	Estimated Percentage of the Clinical Cases of Neurosis
1. The Anxiety Reactions	12–15%
2. The Depressive Reactions	14–18%
3. The Character Reactions, or Neuroses	18–20%
4. The Obsessive-Compulsive Reactions	9–12%
5. The Fatigue Reactions	3– 4%
6. Hygeiaphrontic Reactions (Overconcern with Health or hypochondriasis)	3– 5%
7. The Phobic Reactions	5%
8. The Soterial Reactions	6– 8%
9. The Conversion Reactions:	
A. Somatic Conversions (hysteria)	4– 6%
B. Physiologic Conversions (plus direct psychophysiologic reactions to prolonged stress and tension)	12–14%
10. The Dissociative Reactions	2– 4%
11. The Neuroses Following Trauma	2– 3%

B. CULTURAL INFLUENCES ON CHARACTER DEFENSES

1. Cultural Vogue; Tacit or Active Pressures

The incidence of the various traits and patterns of character defense can vary from one cultural group to another. Cultural pressures toward the inhibition of emotional responses and behavior, in general often tend to favor the development of the obsessive group. Such cultural encouragement or pressures, for example, as those which tend to promote precision in art, accounting, records, and business methods may have a contributing influence toward the development of certain obsessive trends.

Similarly, cultural influences and social pressures can serve to tacitly or actively encourage the development of many additional instances in which the characterologic armor is in turn largely depressive, conversion, hygeiaphrontic, phobic, soterial, and so on. When a cultural premium is placed on certain kinds of attitude or modes of behavior in one's group, there is the tendency to produce and to conform accordingly. These can lead to the formation of a cultural vogue in manifestations, as referred to elsewhere.

2. Developed vs. Underdeveloped Cultures

One might with some justification conclude that the more industrialized and "developed" cultural groups would place a higher premium on the various obsessive and depressive traits and constellations, than would less-industrialized groups. This is correct only to a point however, in that various other cross-currents and pressures exist in the more developed cultures which tend to encourage for some people the development and maintenance of conversion or other traits as well. This is borne out partly by their continued presence in some numbers.

Similar cross-currents exist in the less-developed countries. Here we also encounter pressures favoring the development of the more advanced and mature types of character defenses, that is, the obsessive and depressive, and so forth, traits.

There are many instances of these kinds of cultural cross-currents, some of which the author has been able to observe during the course of several professional world tours. One noteworthy area concerned that of art and artisans. This work can be extremely intricate and painstaking. It can require traits of endless patience, meticulousness, precision, and great concern with detail, such as are typically obsessive. Thus, the author recalls observing in Syria the careful designing and engraving of intricately-ornamented brass trays, and earlier in New Delhi and Agra in India similar exquisite brass work, inlays, carvings, and delicately-fashioned, small very precise marble replicas of the Taj Mahal. At the Tack Cheung ivory factory in Hong Kong a craftsman was observed as he was engaged in the carving of finely-detailed ivory Chinese figures. In the establishment of S. E. Nassan, Bab-Charky, Damascus, a most meticulous Arabian artisan was observed making small wooden boxes which were completely covered with minute inlays of ivory and various decorative woods.

In these instances and other similar ones there was no doubt as to the need for, and the value placed upon, certain essential obsessive traits. An individual culture is likely to value particularly various traits and attributes. One had best not make premature or too sweeping conclusions in this vastly important but complex, area of the cultural and social influences upon the types and incidence of personality traits.

V. CLINICAL FEATURES OF PERSONALITY TYPES AND CHARACTER REACTIONS

A. THE OBSESSIVE GROUP

1. Traits of Obsessive Personality

There are important distinctions which can be made between the neurosis proper and the corresponding neurotic character. With the neurosis and its symptoms generally, there is a greater or lesser failure of repression. As a consequence there follows the emergence or theatened emergence to consciousness of the repressed material. In the evolvement and formation of character traits on the other hand, generally the repression is to be regarded as more successful, and there are reaction formations, sublimations and other mental mechanisms unconsciously evolved.

Additional important distinctions exist, as stated earlier. The defensive employment of character traits can be considered as analogous to that of neurotic symptoms. We have labeled them "character-equivalents. These defensive traits thus can serve the function of replacements for clinical symptoms or as possible precursors of them in the event of too great or too sudden added stress. Certain clinical symptoms often have a swifter onset than the more gradual and possibly more insidious evolvement of character defenses. Others among the various major and minor dynamisms are of course involved in the development of both symptoms and traits.

Typically encountered in the Obsessive Personality are several of the following character defenses: meticulousness, perfectionism, overconscientiousness, parsimoniousness, overconcern with detail, increased doubt or indecision, and inhibition. These and similar traits have been developed very gradually, as part of the basic character defenses against anxiety. They constitute fixed, defensively-intended patterns of response. They serve as a means of promoting security, through reinforcing the containment of one's threatening and rejected impulses; especially those which are primarily aggressive and/or sexual in nature.

As noted earlier, the development and maintenance of complex socio-economic cultures place a certain premium on a number of the obsessive personality traits. This applies when they are present in moderate degree (*see Case 50*). This is true in our present culture, as witnessed for example by the literary position and contributions of men like Samuel Johnson and Noah Webster. These traits were likely equally valued in other highly-developed civilizations of past eras. In view of their social acceptability and usefulness, it is not surprising to find them quite widespread, in varying degrees of prominence. As a result, their study might be considered of even greater moment than the cases in which more clearly neurotic symptoms have developed.

The different character traits may be present in varying degrees and in varying combinations. Important and noteworthy personality characteristics do not develop by chance. They come into existence as the result of powerful internal psychologic needs, attempting to serve vital defensive purposes. The obsessive personality traits usually attempt to serve a purpose similar to those which have been repeatedly demonstrated as underlying actual obsessive neurotic symptoms. Here they are defensively intended to aid in the maintenance of repression and in the control of consciously denied and rejected hostility, aggression, or disowned sexual impulses. Certain of them (for example, overcontrol and overinhibition, shyness, self-effacement, oversolicitude or considerateness, overmoralism, scrupulousness, or overcleanliness) have a clearer origin in reaction formation against the repressed or denied drives.

Other traits in this group include orderliness, neatness, rigid punctuality and truthfulness, obstinacy, love of symmetry, industriousness, and conventionality. These may to some degree be reflected in dress and manner, which can in extent approach the ritualistic. Rules, regulations, and small social conventions may be followed rigorously.

Ambivalence as a conflict between love and hate for the same person, is marked, albeit this is sometimes not readily apparent. The Obsessive Personality is often guilt-ridden. He is likely to be self-restrained and under great self-control. This is reflected in his affective (emotional) reactions. There is rigidity of thinking and attention, and often enough a compulsive, "driven" kind of activity. Having been hurt, he maintains distance. While often quite distrustful, he may be inconsistently very naive at times. He may be highly competitive. His adaptability to rapid change or to new situations is limited. Usually careful of detail and neat, an admixture or reverse of this may include upon occasion inconsistent mixed tendencies toward disorder, sloppiness, being a spendthrift, or inconsistency in money-handing, and so on. A feeling of "I ought to" or "I should," often and to a tragically restrictive extent, tends to replace "I want to" in his motivation. There are diminished feelings of real conviction overall, accompanied sometimes by a stubborn kind of unreasoning, conviction in more narrow areas.

Table 17 outlines the obsessive group of character defenses.

Table 17

The Obsessive Character Defenses

Following is a summary of those character and personality traits or attributes which are more commonly to be considered as belonging to the Obsessive-Compulsive Group. When a number or a *constellation*, of these are present together and to a recognizable degree, they collectively make up the *Obsessive Personality*.

When one or more of this group of character defenses is exaggerated or over-developed, with a resulting personal and/or social handicap to the person concerned, we may regard this development as a *Character Reaction* or Character Neurosis, of the Obsessive Type.

1. Adaptability to rapid change is limited.
2. Ambivalence is marked, although often not outwardly apparent.
3. Collecting trends: accumulations, hoarding, and hobbies can be prominent. (Relationship to the *soteria* (Chapter 11).
4. A compulsive "driven" coloring to the person's activity. Overdeveloped sense of responsibility.
5. Diligence.
6. Doubting.
7. Emotional dependence on others strong, but usually covert.
8. Feelings of inadequacy.
9. Guilt ridden.
10. Harsh self-judgments.
11. Idealism.
12. Industriousness.
13. Inhibition of emotions, both as to personal awareness and as to one's outward responses to them.
14. Intelligence usually above average, or superior.*
15. Intolerance.
16. Love of symmetry.
17. Meticulousness.
18. Order, and concern for orderliness.
19. Overcleanliness.
20. Overconcern with detail.
21. Overconcern with truth.
22. Overconscientiousness.
23. Overcontrol.
24. Overly-moralistic attitudes.
25. Overseriousness.
26. Parsimoniousness.
27. Pedantry.
28. Pertinacity.
29. Pessimism.
30. Preciseness.
31. Procrastination.
32. Rigidity; "set in one's ways"; rigidity of thinking and of attention.
33. Scrupulousness.
34. Self-consciousness.
35. Self-effacement.
36. Sensitivity.

37. Shyness, with sometimes a reversed outer appearance.
38. Strong sense of duty. May be "duty-bound."
39. Stubbornness.
40. Thoroughness.
41. Thriftiness, possibly progressing toward avarice, as an extreme.
42. Tidiness.
43. Worry over responsibility.
44. Indecision. Exhaustive consideration of the possible alternatives. Lingering doubts not uncommonly follow whatever decision is finally made. (This characteristic, as with others listed, is by no means limited to Obsessive Personalities. It occurs with many insecure people; in many instances of neurosis and personality patterns.)
45. Restricted freedom of thinking and imagination, and of the sense of humor.
46. Minute following of rules, regulations, and small social conventions. Great importance of relative minutiae and detail.
47. Harsh judgments, high standards, "black or white" outlook.
48. Feelings of inadequacy and self-doubt strongly present. These are often unrealistic. The opposite appearance may be exhibited outwardly and externally, in line with the defensive *Reversal of Appearance* concept.
49. Reactions and behavior may be slow or ponderous. Obsessive individuals may thus appear pompous, pedantic, or "stuffed shirt."
50. Reassurance, approval, backing, and support from others is very important. This may be far from being readily apparent to others, as the *Obsessive Facade* is maintained.
51. Fear of change. This is protective avoidance of change. This applies to such things, for example, as new situations, a new routine, or the unfamiliar.
52. The feeling of "I ought to" or "I should", so often tends to replace "I enjoy" or "I want to." This development which may be viewed with pathos, transpires as spontaneity becomes restricted.

---

* Intelligence which is above average or superior is not ordinarily considered as a character defense. It is however, commonly enough found in association with the Obsessive Personality, and may be considered to be almost characteristic. It has been included for this reason.

Some interesting speculation is quite possible, as to intelligence having its basis in developmental factors (*see also* Ch.5:VA6, and the Hypothesis of Developmental Influences in Mental Capabilities).

2. The Obsessive Facade

Outwardly the obsessive person may appear quite self-possessed, independent, and even aloof. This is only too often what we can refer to as the outward Obsessive Facade, behind which lie hidden, intense self-doubts and secret desires for dependence. These may be entirely beyond his conscious awareness or recognition. In a comparable fashion but on a more conscious and external level, the person who fears he knows little or is poorly informed may have a greater need to try to present the outward appearance of knowing a great deal.

A variation of this is not infrequently seen in the adolescent who very much wants to appear and to be treated as an adult. This not too uncommon kind of adolescent need may persist into, or even be exaggerated in adulthood beyond conscious awareness. In these instances the inner doubts may result in a need to be important. This may actually represent an extension of the desire to be grown-up and to be accepted as such.

The hidden self-doubts may lead to an outer distant and formal, or even formidable, facade. See also the Outward Reversal of Appearance concept [Ch.5:IIIB1]. Thus the Obsessive Personality may well have trouble in being informal. His expectations of respect and deference from others may be excessive by any usual standards. He may resent informality toward himself for several reasons, including the above. He may resent this also because of his inner needs for defensive "distance-promotion." He may himself behave formally to the point of being considered pompous, pedantic, and a "stuffed shirt." The Obsessive Personality thus hides his inner insecurities and doubts from the world. When present, this is the Obsessive Facade. It can be an interesting feature of his characterologic armor.

3. Concept of Personal Yardstick

A useful concept which has many additional applications and ramifications in human reactions is that of the Personal Yardstick. While it has particular applicability for obsessively-oriented persons, it is by no means confined to this group. The individual characterized by an obsessive personality however, has an especially strong tendency to expect others to think and feel as he does. Thus he frequently anticipates and measures others' feelings and reactions by his own. He uses his own feelings and responses by what we might accordingly term his Personal Yardstick for anticipating and measuring the feelings and reactions of others [Ch.6:-IVF1]. In view of his inhibitions and obsessive character defenses, his particular Personal Yardstick is likely to be even less accurate than many.

He may have little realistic appreciation that wide variations in attitudes and feelings exist among people, in his needs to judge others by himself. Thus he may be genuinely surprised at a lack of inhibition, selflessness, genuine emotions, warmth, and empathy in others, since these may be greatly inhibited and restricted by unconscious defensive operations within himself. On a deeper level, his self-condemnation and doubt may partly be a reflection of a recognition of these kinds of discrepancies within himself (as well as a reflection of demanding and critical parental attitudes, that is, the incorporated judgmental parent).

He may compare himself unfavorably with others, sometimes in many areas in addition to, or even avoiding, the realistic ones. In the more advanced instances of this semi-compulsive need to compare, comparisons may be made almost constantly in obsessive fashion with almost everyone. This may be a reflection also of his competitiveness and of his hidden, strong, underlying self-doubt and feelings of inferiority. The latter may in turn be concealed, as noted, by an outward appearance of superiority, sometimes to an offensive extent.

4. Ambivalence, and Obsessive Defenses of Procrastination, and Indecision

Mixed feelings—or more accurately *ambivalence,* a useful term originally introduced by Bleuler—are often very marked in the Obsessive

Personality.* This may be true in regard to attitudes toward a particular person, and also toward goals and concerning conflicting desires. A constant conflict rages between simultaneous love and hate. Often one side tends to be not available to consciousness. Outwardly any evidence of ambivalence may be poorly apparent or not at all, to the casual observer. The presence of considerable ambivalence, however, helps us understand the great amount of doubt and indecision which is rather characteristic of the Obsessive Personality. The ambivalence also helps account for the fairly common obsessive manifestation of procrastination, which is a frequently handicapping trait.

As a consequence of the ambivalence, it is often very difficult for the obsessive person to make decisions. His feelings are too divided. Procrastination and indecision may go hand in hand, as an inhibiting security operation, in which the obsessive person continually and desperately seeks to avoid loss. He may painfully weigh and reconsider endlessly all possible alternatives. This can be a typical obsessive kind of defensive operation. He may be unwilling to face any loss or to give up anything which may be entailed in a decision either way. In this respect the obsessive person often "wants to have his cake and eat it too!"

Only too often there are apt to be lingering doubts or regrets, even long following the eventual making of a decision. The decision, or the situation which required it, is often "rehashed" over and over again. In other instances the obsessive person may procrastinate long enough so that finally someone else makes the decision for him! This automatically relieves him of any responsibility for making the decision, or for the consequences. However, it is also very self-defeating. It places him in a helpless position in which he loses any possibility of a choice. At times the obsessively-oriented individual exhibits a preoccupation or over-attention to the threat of death, or to the possible prospect of death.

The following instance illustrates how the previously rather healthy and useful personality defenses of the obsessive group proved inadequate for an individual, and could no longer fulfill the intrapsychic defensive purposes for which they had been developed. The result was their exaggeration. This occurred to a point where they interfered with personal adjustment and efficiency. In their overdevelopment, they became emotionally limiting and professionally handicapping.

Case 50

The Overdevelopment of Defensive Character Traits

Unhappiness; accomplishments restricted

A thirty-eight-year-old business executive was referred for psychiatric evaluation and treatment by his physician. His difficulties included an overconcern with health, increasing dissatisfaction with his work, unhappiness, and indications of family friction.

The patient was pleasant in manner and carefully dressed. He seemed rather precise and slightly pompous in manner. He gave an impression of considerable energy, ability, and intelligence. As the interviews

---

* "Mixed feelings" tends to be euphemistic in describing ambivalence. As Cappon said, "Ambivalence is *polar*, not merely mixed."

progressed there were suggestions of high personal standards of performance, rigidity, and considerable concern with detail. Together, these had progressed to the point where they adversely affected his level of efficiency, as well as his self-esteem.

His potentials for achievement were considerably greater than had been his actual accomplishments. These factors had unfavorably influenced relationships at home and at work. They indirectly contributed to his dissatisfaction, and they limited energy which might have been available otherwise for more constructive activity. Character analysis was advised.

Influence of character defenses pervasive

During the course of therapy these and related well-established character defenses were found to have thoroughly influenced the entire course of his life. The application of his own harsh personal standards to members of his family and to his friends and associates, had greatly increased the difficulties which these people had encountered in their attempts to please or to satisfy him.

His need for meticulousness had restricted his breadth of vision. His attention was occupied with far too much (objectively) unnecessary detail. Despite his outward appearance of self-possession, he was afflicted with torturous self-doubts and indecision. This illustrated the Obsessive Facade.

Characteristically, this man's emotions were intensely ambivalent. This was accompanied by urgent suppressive efforts to continue the containment of the strong negative aspects of his mixed feelings. The latter were most unacceptable consciously, and were threatening to him.

As the details of his emotional and developmental history unfolded, there was repeated evidence that strongly ambivalent parental attitudes also had been present towards him, in turn. During his infantile years his parents outwardly at least, had been overly tolerant and permissive. He had been tacitly encouraged to be dependent. This situation was reversed rather abruptly in subsequent years. In contrast, stringent demands had been made on him for conformity and independence. Such a contrast resulted in more hostility developing in him than might otherwise have been present. There was a simultaneous increased need for its control and repression. The character traits developed as additional defenses to aid in this vital endeavor.

To a point these traits had served a very useful purpose in a complex social and economic order. However, the same traits when they became overdeveloped, were professionally limiting and personally handicapping. This feature of being useful and constructive up to a certain point, but destructive and self-defeating when developed beyond that point, is often seen, and is a typical potential sequence with all kinds of character traits. This is the *Principle of Defense-Hypertrophy.** It is, of course, particularly illustrated in this instance of the obsessive group of character traits. It is the principal feature in making the diagnosis of a Character (Neurosis) Reaction.

Substantial benefits from therapy

This patient applied himself with energy and conscientious endeavor in the project of an intensive study of himself. The results of treatment were good. The same traits which had had a considerable measure of usefulness to him heretofore were also an asset in his work with the author. He became slowly able to really recognize more and more of the tremendous hostility which had been seething in hidden and repressed form within himself. As he found himself increasingly able to handle this on more conscious levels, it became far less of a threat.

He was also gradually able to adopt a kinder, more tolerant attitude toward himself. As a result, he became more accepting of his associates as well. His family relations improved greatly. The necessary large investment of his time, energy, and money in character analysis proved most worthwhile for this man. In his case, however, as with most instances of obsessive characters, the work of therapy was prolonged and difficult.

---

* See also *Concept of Defensive Overreaction in Emotional Etiology* [Ch.3:IVD7].

As illustrated in the foregoing case, the maintenance of high personal standards of achievement and highly self-critical attitudes are evidence of the overdeveloped conscience or superego. The latter may be regarded as having in essence hypertrophied, partly in response to the internal needs for control of powerful aggressive impulses. These had in turn been unwittingly stimulated, especially by the relative change in the attitude of his parents from one of early overprotection, to the later one of great demands and expectations.

5. Defense of Pessimism

Another familiar defense which is often a part of the obsessive person's characterologic armor is that of pessimism. He is frequently prone to adopt the pessimistic outlook. In this attempted kind of protection, one anticipates the worst. Whatever happens subsequently will inevitably be less evil and less unpleasant than had been expected. The result is relief. Unpleasant surprise is guarded against.

However, since the pain of the unpleasant anticipation is so strong in itself, the amount of suffering over any long-term period is almost always mathematically greater. The patient may himself even recognize this intellectually, at least in some degree. He is still of course totally unable simply to surrender voluntarily or to modify his defense of pessimism. The Pessimism Defense is also related to the *"Be Prepared" Concept* [Ch.8:-VID3] of psychic defense.

The defense of pessimism may not make as much "sense" to the objective observer as to the person who employs it. He cannot see nor can he appreciate the strength of the internal needs which underlay it. At times it can progress to the point of considerable self-defeat and handicap to the individual. It is nearly always psychologically uneconomic, as unnecessary energy and thought are invested in the endeavor of anticipation.

Pessimism is not limited to one's personal outlook and subjective awareness. It can be widespread indeed in its influence. There are numerous ways in which it can come to the attention of others. It can influence one's decisions, attitudes, judgments, and work. It even can influence artistic production and writing, of which the following is an instance

Case 51

Pessimism in Poetry

These lines by Royer reflect a measure of pessimistic outlook, low spirits, and cynicism.

Time and Tide

"Days fade into years,
Years into centuries.
Time flings on;
Crowding all things together
In meaningless jumble.
Each lifetime adds a mere trifle,
Meaning as little to those who follow,
As to those who went before."

6. Intellectual Prowess of Obsessive Individuals

A. ADVANTAGES IN MENTAL FUNCTION.—As earlier indicated, obsessive individuals are quite often highly able, respected, contributing citizens. As Bleuler wrote: ". . . they are diligent and conscientious people. . . . The intelligence is strikingly often above the normal." Accordingly upon testing, it is not surprising for us to find that their I.Q.s are often in the superior range: 120–130 or higher. Freud also early noted that obsessive individuals tended to be favored intellectually (*see also* footnote to *Table 17*).

The Obsessive Personality may take pride in his intellectual status and in his mental achievements. His pride in his accomplishments may be exaggerated. This in part is an outward compensation for his hidden self-doubts and his great inner need for recognition and acceptance. One may see an occasional, somewhat related obsessive interest in words. Over-importance and pride may be attached to their choice and usage, and to the accumulation of a vocabulary. This bears a relation to collecting and to hoarding. An obsessive interest may be shown in other areas, such as mathematics, in the use of numbers and figures, or in geometric design. An outward indication of obsessive trends is even sometimes evident in the patterns of an individual's doodling.

The development of traits such as those of industriousness, pertinacity, and application insures the optimal use of existing capacities. Further, the faculty of memory as an important facet of intellectual ability is usually superior. Obsessive traits thus are likely to be a distinct asset in taking I.Q. tests, college board exams, and standardized tests generally.

Superior memory is a frequently encountered asset, and is a very great advantage with the obsessive traits. The character defense—patterns of thoroughness, exactness, order, and precise arrangement as developed in the Obsessive Personality, are frequently found to be operative in the field of memory, as they are in other aspects of function. These influences can substantially increase the intellectual efficiency and effectiveness of the Obsessive Personality. Their intellectual prowess will be enhanced accordingly.

Personal satisfaction with performance is an effective stimulus for still better performance. High personal standards are also spurs to performance, up to a point. These factors also may contribute to further improved ability efficiency, and achievement.

B. LIMITATIONS TO POTENTIAL.—The intellectual advantages of the Obsessive Personality however are not unmixed, particularly as his defensive traits hypertrophy further. Thinking has a tendency toward rumination. There may be a lessened discrimination and selectivity, in that unimportant, minor items or even trifles may come to receive equal or nearly equal consideration, with far more major ones. In other words, the amount of time and effort given to minor details, can come to be far out of proportion to their relatively lesser value. Non-essentials may be thought through just as thoroughly as essentials; perhaps obsessively and even interminably so.

Not surprisingly then, we find the ability of the Obsessive Personality often superior for logic and logical thinking, in the critical abilities, in focusing attention and interest, and in maintaining concentration. Creativity may be lessened, however, as the speculative powers and imaginative ability are hampered, and mental processes may be limited, stereotyped, blocked, inflexible, and rigid in varying degrees.

Superstition is often observed in obsessional persons. This is seemingly inconsistent with their high intelligence. Its prominence as a feature in obsessional individuals shows considerable variability. Soterial phenomena are not uncommon.

C. HYPOTHESIS OF DEVELOPMENTAL INFLUENCES IN MENTAL CAPABIL-ITIES.—It has been proposed that the superior intelligence of the obsessive individual possibly develops and evolves in response to hidden internal and powerful psychologic factors. This would transpire in a similar manner to the development of other ones of the more clearly recognized character defenses. This is an interesting proposition which merits our further speculation and study.

Recent observations tend to lend some support to this. One of the author's old hypotheses has been to the effect that the level of intelligence may be improved through favorable environmental influences, particularly including the interpersonal ones. We might accordingly term this the Hypothesis of Developmental Influences in Mental Capabilities.

Should this interesting hypothesis be further borne out, there are important implications concerning the relationship of intelligence to some of the other attributes, which are more commonly regarded as character defenses.

In one interesting supporting study for example, Skeels reported findings in regard to a series of orphaned children, in whom the initial testing revealed retarded intelligence. Their I.Q. levels however increased appreciably when it was possible to place them in a more favorable environmental situation. Thus, the average I.Q. of 13 children, aged 7 to 36 months, rose from 64 to 92, after from 6 to 52 months. Eleven of the group were later placed in adoptive homes, after which their average I.Q. rose to 101.6. The greatest gain (of 16 points) was made by a child who was placed in a "superior" home. I have no doubt that early developmental influences are most vital in their effects upon mental capabilities and performance.

7. Additional Aspects of Interest

A. "OBSESSIVELY-TINTED GLASSES": JUSTIFICATION AND RATIONALIZA-TION.—Obsessive personality traits result in a more or less fixed set of attitudes toward many aspects of living. In other words, the individual's relationships and surroundings are likely to be viewed through what we can refer to as his "obsessively-tinted glasses." His subjective feelings, his reactions in situations, and his responses to people are all affected accordingly. When he find himself intellectually opposed to his own obsessively-determined needs and to their dictates, he will often struggle against them.

They are, however, powerful, and are powerfully determined. They cannot be overcome simply by an exertion of will power.

Obsessive individuals will often make special efforts to justify their feelings to themselves, and sometimes to others. Emotional feelings become more acceptable if they appear rationalized to fit the circumstances. There may be a particular need to deny or to justify angry ones. Obsessive persons may become experts at rationalization. This development is one means of trying to satisfy the demands of a harsh superego.

Serious incongruities between standards and behavior can then continue to co-exist. Rationalization is one way to attempt to gloss over inconsistencies and incongruities, and to seek their "reconciliation."

B. DISHONESTY.—Sometimes there is a history of minor stealing, such as shoplifting in childhood or adolescence. These and other misdemeanors are often a self-sought way of making up for felt deprivations: really love and affection, but often expressed in terms of material things. Accompanying feelings of guilt are often so strong that they are far out of proportion to the extent of any actual misdeeds. The conscience overdevelops, partly as a way of controlling these, as well as other powerful, disturbing, and disapproved impulses.

A persistence of this type of dishonesty into adult life is occasionally to be observed, in which it remains personally permissible to take things of little real monetary value, but not things which have a more clearly-demonstrable worth. This may be an unwittingly attempted compromise between the gratification symbolically of strong, unconscious needs and the strongly disapproving conscience. One may see activities similar to these, and others limited to fantasy, in which they may still nonetheless, result in feelings of guilt.

C. RELIGIOSITY AND SCRUPULOUSNESS.—This area not too infrequently overdevelops as a facet of the obsessive group of defenses. Its position in the personality can be major or minor. Thus overattention to religion, especially its form, ritual, and perhaps to endless related detail, is by no means necessarily a simple and direct exhibition of one's piety.

Scrupulosity or scrupulousness may be defined for our purposes here, simply as an overconcern with religious matters. As with supermoralism, it suggests on the surface something quite different from that which it overlies and often conceals. It can represent a reaction formation. Often enough it conceals, or seeks to conceal and to control underlying hostility, rebelliousness, doubts, and conflicts. In this regard Brickner cited an instance of a priest who was barraged night and day by repetitive and often obsessive thoughts about and urges, to "confess"; to go over and over again his feared but objectively insignificant, "transgressions." Scrupulosity had best be regarded and treated as a compulsive neurosis or as a character reaction.

D. OVERCOMPLIANCE, ABSOLUTISM, "BLACK-OR-WHITE PEOPLE", AND SANCTIMONIOUSNESS.—At times overcompliance and obedience are seen in a form which is at least outwardly exaggerated. In seeming contradiction to this trait and to the indecision earlier described, the obsessive person may be rigid, moralistic, and absolute in his judgments. In this respect he may be what we might refer to as a "black-or-white person." Something or someone is either all good *or* all bad, clean *or* dirty, right *or* wrong, social *or* antisocial, ethical *or* not and so on. There may be little tolerance or room for compromise in such judgments. There is no room in between, no halfway point, no margin for partial rightness. In this respect the harsh judgments apply equally to others as to himself, or to aspects of himself. Other people are expected to measure up to the same high standards which have been established personally.

The obsessive person may give the impression of being pedantic, opinionated, overly-correct, and sanctimonious. He may possess the highest of ethical standards. He may thus seek and/or secure considerable gratification, and he may also thus endeavor to combat his own great feelings of guilt. Hill commented that while ". . . this might look like a bad bargain at first . . . among the secondary gains of the obsessional technique in the vast narcissistic gratification or in plainer English is the conceit these patients entertain because of their supposed virtue, goodness and so forth . . . ."

When present in appreciable degree, these kinds of attributes are hardly ones which result in increased personal popularity. Unconscious needs to promote distance in interpersonal relationships receive unwitting reinforcement, through these defensively developed but self-defeating personality factors.

8. *Advantages in Occupations and Avocations*

A. ARTISTIC ENDEAVORS; FARMING.—Certain handicrafts, artistic work, as well as many specialized occupations, and professions require an ability to preoccupy oneself with great detail. Precision, neatness, meticulousness, love of symmetry, and orderliness are requisites for the patience and ability to produce certain kinds of fine carvings, intricate engraving, detailed etching, jewelry, and many types of highly skilled ornamental work. As noted earlier, some personal observations have been possible of expert craftsmen at work in various places around the world, whose obsessive character orientation undoubtedly contributed substantially to their abilities in the production of fine *objets d'art*.

As is true in most professions and occupations, the "good" farmer also for example, very much needs certain obsessive traits. The meticulous, careful farmer thus keeps his equipment in good order. His stock is well cared for; his machinery lasts longer. The overall view of a farm and its buildings to the more experienced eye quickly indicates the degree of attention to detail, industry, neatness, and so on which are essential to successful farming.

Many skills and occupations gain as a consequence of obsessively-oriented character development. The continued application of attention and effort in such fashion is further illustration of the usefulness of many of the traits which are ordinarily classified with the obsessional group.

B. THE COLLECTOR; HANDLING MONEY.—The obsessive person is often an excellent curator, hobbyist, or collector. It is also true that his interests in a hobby may overdevelop, to the point of becoming inordinate or even fanatic. Soterial significances may contribute to this. His hobby or collection may come to absorb a major proportion of his interest and energy.

His ability to handle money is often superior, and he may save or "collect" this also, a trait which can approach hoarding and miserliness in its development and extent. Attitudes toward money may not infrequently appear paradoxical. Small expenditures may be made grudgingly, to the point of self-deprivation, whereas large sums may be disbursed with relatively little concern.

Obsessive collecting can also enter into many areas, including such general ones as, for example, the accumulation of knowledge. This can be observed upon occasion as a scholarly pursuit in many fields of academic and professional endeavor. The author's preparation of this and the preceding work (*The Neuroses in Clinical Practice*) has been inevitably marked by obsessive trends. Over the years these tendencies were a considerable aid to accumulating and collecting the many bits and pieces of information, from the rather scattered sources then available. It was quite necessary to do so in order to try and round out this presentation. The text was constantly with the author. One semi-final chapter draft for the original work for example, accompanied him around the world in 1954, and en route all possible items of useful data were added.

C. DEFENSE OF ACCUMULATING KNOWLEDGE.—It is a matter of great convenience to have knowledge at one's fingertips. The informed person is likely to be respected. In addition, however, an element of obsessive defensiveness can enter into such learning. Accumulating knowledge can in itself become an obsessive preoccupation. This bears a direct relationship to the preceding topic.

An intellectually-gifted patient related to the author as to how the failure to have some small bit of data immediately at his fingertips would inevitably result in a momentary feeling of panic. Over the course of time we learned how this reaction had helped to play a major role in his entire life. Partly as a consequence of his continuing efforts to forestall such fleeting but decidedly uncomfortable panics, this man had pursued an inordinate amount of university work. He eventually had made himself exceptionally well qualified in *five* separate fields of professional endeavor! This had become his major goal in life.

The accumulation of knowledge had become this man's obsessive preoccupation. His achievements were substantial and well recognized. Their motivation was highly neurotic, and a consequence of his defensive efforts to allay and to forestall anxiety.

D. SOTERIAL IMPLICATIONS.—Relationships are also present as noted, between the foregoing manifestations of one particular type of obsessive operation, and the soteria. (*See also* Chapter 11.) In the latter the object which is collected, hoarded, or treasured, has unconsciously secured special importance and meaning for the person concerned.

The soterial object becomes an external source of security, comfort, solace, and protection, through significance which is "assigned" in symbolic fashion. As a consequence the soterial object-symbol tends to allay and to counter anxiety. There are important soterial implications in a number of the obsessive operations.

9. In Conclusion

Much could be written in further and even exhaustive detail, about each of some forty or fifty of the obsessive character traits in turn. This could, indeed, in itself become an obsessive endeavor! It is thought important, however, to stress again in particular: (1) the relative degree of presence of obsessive character defenses, and (2) the gradation of their net personal and social consequences, all the way from considerable usefulness to great handicap.

Thus obsessive character traits may be thought of in some instances as adequately serving their defensively-intended purpose, so that the *status quo* of personality adjustment is maintained. The result is a harmoniously-balanced person, possessing perhaps just enough obsessive trends to facilitate constructive living.

On the other hand, internal and/or external stresses may become so great that the individual's character defenses are no longer adequate. Their overdevelopment and exaggeration may follow, to the point of moderate to even great interference with living. As a consequence, unhappiness may ensue; interpersonal relationships may suffer; achievements may be hampered or blocked; or satisfactions in living may lessen. This is the stage of the Character Reaction or Neurosis. If the personality defenses prove even more inadequate, or the external stress more acute, the further next step may be the development of the more marked clinical symptoms of an Obsessive Reaction.

B. THE CONVERSION (HYSTERICAL) PERSONALITY AND CHARACTER REACTIONS

1. Traits of Conversion Personality

The Conversion Personality is the second of our three major categories, and is marked by a variety of more or less typical traits. Supposedly having its origins in the genital phase of psychosexual development, there are certain elements, however, which would appear to be vestiges of the earlier oral phase. This personality constellation is likely to be an egocentric one, with strong but labile emotional feelings. Attention-seeking, acting out, and impulsive behavior are often present, accompanied by decreased inhibitions and lessened self-restraint and control. The attraction of the Conversion Personality stems largely from his appeal, emotional responsiveness, and warmth. He is often outgoing, extravertive, likeable, and a person who makes friends quite readily.

Coquettishness and seductiveness are often present and are frequently accompanied by an underlying apprehensiveness. The latter can lead in turn to the Conversion Personality beating a precipitous retreat when some sexual response is actually secured from the other person! Not too surprisingly, the sexual adjustment of the Conversion Personality in general remains immature, and some degree of frigidity is rather common. There are likely to be trends in his communications toward exaggeration and mendacity. Simulation and pretense are not uncommon. In keeping with his "flair for the dramatic," he may possess considerable histrionic ability. This may be employed socially or in the theatre. Often quite suggestible, these people also adopt convictions strongly but readily, but may shift their position rather abruptly. Immature, more on the dependent and helpless side, relationships are likely to be marked by intensity, yet shallowness, and by demands.

The following *Table 18* summarizes the more common traits and findings in the Conversion (hysterical) Personality. Several of the more characteristic traits will be discussed subsequently, and some comments will be offered concerning specific points of interest. (*See also* Ch.12:VC5).

Table 18

The Character Defenses Associated with the Conversion (hysterical) Personality

The Conversion Personality is characterized by the possession of at least several of the following personality defensive traits, as well as by certain of the deeper psychologic potentials as enumerated. Their presence in clear imbalance or exaggeration constitutes the Conversion (hysterical) Character Reaction or Neurosis.

In order to warrant the inclusion of a given personality in this particular group, the conversion character defenses as present must be preponderant in number or in relative strength, over other personality components. One cannot expect however, to encounter any given constellation of personality traits in pure and unmixed form.

A. *Outwardly more apparent defensive personality traits of the Conversion Personality:*

1. Self-absorption (egocentricity).
2. Strong, but often shifting, labile emotional feelings. "Emotionally capricious," as emotional reactions tend to be inconstant and changeable.
3. Immaturity.
4. Attention-seeking, histrionic, responsive, appealing and often warm. Tendency to be "outgoing," with friendships quickly and readily made.
5. "Acting out," impulsive behavior, often with too little regard for consequences.
6. A relative lack of inhibitions. Inhibitions are on the deficient side, in contrast to the overinhibition of the Obsessive Personality. Behavior may be of the "spoiled child" variety. Self-restraint and control are limited.
7. "A flair for the dramatic." May display dramatized behavior, or a certain type of exhibitionism. Actors not infrequently possess character defensive traits of the conversion group.
8. Susceptibility to suggestion; suggestible, often easily influenced— to a point. May be permissive, overly trusting, or quite naive. Convictions may come readily, be held strongly, and surrendered quickly. (*Table continued on next page*)

Table 18—The Character Defenses Associated with the Conversion
(hysterical) Personality—Cont.

9. Imitativeness, as a more superficial reflection of his potential
for identification, and his suggestibility. Usually makes a
better follower then a leader.

10. Emotional relationships tend to be on the shallow side, despite
their possible outward appearances of strength, depth, and
of course in spite of any fervent avowals of constancy.

11. There may be an apparent dependence and helplessness. This
can be contradictorily combined with a certain attitudinal
imperiousness.

12. A mature sexual adjustment is generally not fully attained.
Sexuality remains immature, limited, and often disturbed in
some measure. The capacity for real gratification is often
lacking.

13. Coquetry, with an apprehensive coloring.

14. Imaginative; capacity for flights of imagination. In personal
relationships may be given to exaggeration, fanciful tales, and
perhaps not too much regard for the strict truth.

15. Seductiveness; a testing kind of sexually-tinged behavior, often
followed by a hasty retreat, should the response be in kind!

16. Limited drive toward intellectuality and studious achievements.
When present, brilliance is flashy but often short-lived, with
little capacity for serious, prolonged application.

17. Appeal, charm, intense, and warm relationships, which, however, may be superficial and transient.

18. Potential for dissociation present. Subjective feelings of depersonalization are not infrequent, and may become prominent.

19. Spirits often "good." Gay, good humor, light-heartedness and
buoyant spirits more likely than in Obsessive or Depressive
Personalities.

B. *Important deeper psychologic potentials exist in the Conversion Personality for:*

1. Personality compartmentalization.

2. Massive, primary repression.

3. The capacity for conversion into bodily expression (especially
via Somatic (hysterical) Conversion, into physical symptoms;
and also an overlapping and analogous capacity for Physiologic Conversion, into physiologic symptoms).

4. Overdetermination.

5. Dissociative capacity; ready hypnotizability.

6. Overidentification.

7. A strong potential for Regression.

8. A strong potential for the use of some of the other more primitive, Lower Order and massive defenses. "Utilization" of
the more primitive mental mechanisms, such as Denial, Incorporation, Symbolization, and perhaps Idealization and
Reaction Formation. Little employment of sublimation, or
other more advanced mechanisms and symptom defenses.

In this pattern of character defense, personality development tends to
fixate in varying degrees, at the level of the genital phase.

2. Defensive Purpose

A. CHARACTER TRAITS AND SYMPTOMS.—We may in general regard the
patient with a Somatic Conversion (Reaction) as possessing an underlying
Conversion Personality. This can be viewed as part of his diathesis for a

Conversion Reaction. Glover regarded the absence of "obvious symptom formations" as a prerequisite to distinguishing the Conversion or hysterical Personality. When symptoms of Conversion Reaction are already present, one sometimes can still determine the presence of underlying and perhaps predisposing personality features.

In general, the author would regard the conversion character defenses as serving a similar defensive purpose, to that of the more obviously neurotic, clinical conversion symptoms. They may replace the latter. They may be preliminary or prodromal. They may be to some extent replaced by clinical symptom formation, when they prove inadequate as defenses. External traumatic events may also stimulate the elaboration of new, or the exaggeration of existing character defenses, as well as more strictly clinical neurotic symptoms. This is in accord with our Defense Hypertrophy Principle [Ch.5:IC*I*;IIIB*I*].

B. AVOID CRITICAL AND JUDGMENTAL ATTITUDES.—When present in marked degree, certain of this group of traits can make the person with a Conversion Personality rather difficult to get along with. Some of the typical conversion characteristics, when used as descriptive labels, tend to create or to encourage an adverse judgment, or an unfavorable opinion. However, the conversion (hysterical) individual may also possess a considerable appeal and charm. These are assets which can contribute to his position and enhance the value of his type of characterologic armor. There can be many positive attributes which may more than counteract the negative aspects.

In any event, it is highly important for the clinician to avoid judgmental and critical attitudes toward his patient. This can be facilitated by constantly focusing one's medical attention upon certain important hypothetical questions, to wit: What purpose does this trait (or symptom) serve? What is the patient's internal need to develop and to desperately cling to, this particular personality trait (which may be a considerable handicap, as assessed by an objective observer)?

The personality structure as observed in the conversion person often is not far removed from the lay concept and usage of the term hysteria. The Conversion or Hysterical Personality thus is typically immature and tends to be emotionally capricious. Conversion affects tend to be dramatic and exhibitionistic ones. The strength of his affect is often excessive in comparison to its apparent stimulus. While strong, readily aroused, and perhaps excessive, his affects are also volatile, labile, and shifting.

C. THINKING AND PLANNING.—While the Conversion Personality is limited in his long-range application and prolonged serious endeavor, this may be counterbalanced by his imaginative ability. This can be a most useful attribute. It can also progress toward the fanciful, or on into real flights of fancy. While he thinks things through in limited fashion however, his thinking is more elastic than that of the Obsessive Personality.

He is less likely to anticipate consequences as thoroughly as others. While this can be disadvantageous, it can also result in a greater willingness to hazard risks. He is likely to have a limited drive toward intellectual achievements or attainments. Thus we have an individual whose patterns of thinking and planning are limited in certain directions, and are likely to offer advantages in others.

3. Egocentricity and Attention-seeking as Character Defenses

The conversion individual, having been unable to develop sufficient interests beyond the narrow confines of himself, is egocentric in varying degree. Let us consider some possible internal needs that might be met by this trait.

First, character traits roughly equate the function of symptoms in attempting to ward off anxiety. The egocentricity stems in complex fashion from a felt deprivation of love and affection in early life. The early rage in response to this failure to meet his dependency needs was repressed from awareness as too dangerous. In other words, the lack of love produced rage and resentment in the infant. Since this was directed largely and more usually toward the desperately important mother, it was too dangerous, and actually too unacceptable even to recognize. The child's level of ego could not tolerate this level of rage or hostility being directed toward the simultaneously necessary, loved one. The potential for loss or retaliation was overwhelmingly dangerous. Repressed, these forbidden feelings threaten to emerge into conscious awareness.

Egocentricity, as with some of the other character traits, often develops in an attempt to procure or to force love, and as a way of concealing the patient's unconscious rage and hostile feelings from himself. It says, in effect, "Because I feel unloved by you, I will make you take notice of me and pay attention." At this juncture we should be reminded of the well-known fact that attention is sometimes very much sought as a substitute, when love cannot be secured. Unpleasant attention or even punishment is sometimes far more preferable to the child, than being ignored. At times punishment even appears to be sought, and in determined fashion. The egocentricity and other traits may result in a measure of success in eliciting or in forcing attention, as a substitute, however limited, for acceptance and love. In this event, the anxiety resulting from the threatened awareness of this seemingly "murderous" level of rage can be prevented. Repression of the latter can then more readily be maintained.

As might be expected from such needs, the conversion (hysterical) person seeks attention, and may make excessive demands for it from friends and family. Closely related to this is the rather frequent conversion attribute of a "flair for the dramatic." This can result in various kinds of emotional histrionics. Bits of dramatic performance may be resorted to in attempting to satisfy dependency needs or to gain various ends in interpersonal situations. There may also be egotism, vanity, and self-indulgence.

4. Conversion Characteristics Have Important Effects Upon Relationships.

A. LIMITED CAPACITIES.—Among other major characteristics of the conversion person are the presence of strong dependency needs and his relatively great susceptibility to suggestion. The possession of these of course is not necessarily limited to the Conversion Personality. In some ways the behavior and reactions of the person with strong conversion personality traits can be compared to those of the "spoiled child." Numerous adjectives may be used in describing conversion (hysterical) behavior, such as demanding, inconsiderate, vain, selfish, impulsive, and juvenile. There is apt to be a more or less limited ability to adequately consider the interests or wishes of others. The characteristic impulsiveness is in part the result of an underdeveloped ability to anticipate the future consequences of one's actions. To state this another way, it may also be regarded as part of the infantile demand that: "I want just what I want, and when I want it!" As one possible consequence, the person often can assume little responsibility, or may shun it.

Thus, there is generally less consideration for the wishes of others, largely because of the urgent personal needs and demands of the individual concerned for the affection, love, attention, and sympathy, of which the person feels deprived. Having felt so deprived himself, he has a decreased capacity for deeper interest in or an affection for others.

Many emotionally-sick people are overinhibited. This is seen in particular in the Obsessive Personality. In contrast, the Conversion Personality is likely to lack inhibitions in a way that can seriously handicap his ability to fit in socially. Not infrequently the Conversion (hysterical) Personality is shy, timorous, and fearful, although these traits may not be outwardly apparent. Relationships with people, while readily formed, tend to be on the shallow and superficial side, as the capacity has not properly developed for forming more mature relationships. The conversion group of character defenses have all kinds of important effects upon the interpersonal relationships of the person possessing them.

B. APPEAL, CHARM, EXPRESSIVENESS, LESS DEVIOUS, BUOYANT SPIRITS: In addition to noting the negative traits of the Conversion Personality, we should also again specifically note that there are often powerful, positive ones as well. The Conversion (hysterical) Personality thus often has great appeal, makes friends easily, and can be quickly and strongly responsive and warm in his personal relationships. Charm is frequently also a major asset. The conversion person is often friendly, cheerful, and out-going.

The mien and facial expression are expressive. They are likely to better (more accurately) mirror his real current attitudes and feelings than as with other personality constellations. If guile is present, it is likely to be more superficial. His friends regard him accordingly as less devious, more open, and more to be trusted. Although his feelings toward them may be subject to rapid change, his friends are more likely to know, and more clearly, just where they stand with him at any given moment!

The spirits of the Conversion Personality are more readily on the "high" or elevated side, than are those of his Obsessive or his Depressive counterpart. He is likely to have an excellent sense of humor. He can be gay, lighthearted, vivacious, and "full of life." While a rapid shift can occur, his buoyancy and good-humor can be prominent. These are assets which often make him more welcome personally and socially.

C. ARTISTIC EXPRESSION.—Character defenses enter into one's occupation, hobbies, and artistic works. They influence everything one does or accomplishes. As one interesting area, they of course can enter into a person's writing and verse. For the Conversion Personality these are likely to be imaginative. Being more expressive, emotions are more apparent and can run the gamut. Feelings expressed can be lighthearted and buoyant, tender, warm, affectionate, loving, and gay yet poignant. Some of these qualities are illustrated in the following lines by M. Sange. A comparison and contrast with those of the Somber Poet (*See Case 57*) is of interest. It would be difficult indeed to conceive that either could write like the other.

Whither Wisdom?

Teach me the truth of life, my darling.
Is it here—in the warm circle of your arms?
Here in the protection of your strength?
Is this the prize all humanity seeks?
Or is truth a lonely thing—
A solitary search through experience and time
Isolating us, one from the other?

Teach me the truth, but be prepared
For I cannot journey alone
Through bleak spaces and wintry years—
Me, a creature of giving and sharing,
Needs the touch of a hand, a tender smile—
If truth be a lonely thing
I surely will die.

Anticipation

Tomorrow creeps in this petty pace—
At least in coming—
When, at last, it's here—
How time will fly.
Minutes measured in soft caresses,
Hours in clinging flesh,
A sharing of so many things.
But, now I must run.
So much to do, 'til our tomorrow.

Many of these qualities are reflected in his relationships, which can benefit or suffer accordingly, or both. The characterologic armor of a given individual inevitably has its "good" and its "bad" aspects. From a psychiatric standpoint, however, value judgments are to be shunned. One regards traits as phenomena which are simply present, and studies them accordingly. The only "badness" lies in their unwitting self-defeat.

5. Case Illustrations

In the following instances the patient's personality traits upon beginning treatment were mainly conversion ones.

Case 52

Successful Treatment in the Conversion (hysterical) Personality

A thirty-two-year-old married housewife sought intensive treatment for increasing difficulty in getting along with other people, and because of several recent A.A.A.'s (Acute Anxiety Attacks). During her analytic treatment, her character traits of the Conversion (hysterical) Personality pattern became increasingly apparent. Her demanding, childish, self-centered behavior came to be clearly recognized. It was the carryover from her long, antecedent, unconscious efforts to force love from a critical, cold, vindictive, and perfectionist mother. The patient could not bear to recognize her intense rage over the deprivations she had felt. The Acute Anxiety Attacks took place whenever the character traits threatened to break down in their effectiveness at securing some sort of satisfaction of her dependency needs, from her mother and from others. The more positive attributes of the Conversion Personality appeared to have been minimal. These lacks had helped to intensify her interpersonal difficulties.

In this case the character traits attempted to present a defense against the conscious awareness of prohibited feelings of rage. These were toward those on whom the dependency rested. Hence awareness of them would arouse great anxiety. They were quite sufficient also to account for her great difficulties in interpersonal situations. The desperate tenacity with which such traits (that is, character defenses) are usually held onto, is indicated in some measure by the three years of character-analytic treatment required, prior to the successful resolution of the underlying conflicts, and the development of a reasonably mature personality adjustment. In turn this also helps indicate the great importance of the traits, and the vital nature of the internal defensive needs they had sought to subserve.

As part of the desperate need to force attention, the Conversion Personality may take drastic and dramatic steps. In the following example the patient made a suicidal attempt. (*See* section on Suicide, Ch.4:XI.) This instance also provides an illustration of the *Vicious Circle of Self-Defeat Concept* in the Neuroses p. 71, Ch.8:VIB*1*.

Case 53

A Dramatic Suicidal Attempt by a Conversion Personality

A twenty-six-year-old unmarried occupational therapist possessed typical conversion (hysterical) character traits. She was being treated on an in-patient status. There were great needs for attention and affection. Part of this was directed toward the securing of special privileges from the staff, some of whom however, responded with hostility. She was alternately coquettish, pouting, seductive, sullen, flattering, and demanding. She had developed great resources in seeking attention, as a consequence of her long-standing and desperate strivings for the love and warmth of which she felt so deprived. As a culmination, when these efforts and traits failed to secure the desperately-needed attention, she obtained and took a quantity of Seconal.

This was not a terribly serious attempt at suicide (from the standpoint of a threat to her life), since the quantity taken was insufficient to be very dangerous. However, she of course had no way of knowing this. She had unconsciously seemingly prepared for the moment of discovery. She had arranged her long blonde hair in careful braids and dramatically, over the pillow. Make-up was skillfully applied, and she was attired in her very best robe and gown.

This unhappy and desperate girl was driven by her dependency needs to behave increasingly frantically. However, the result was tragically more designed to inadvertently defeat her efforts to obtain the real love and acceptance which she so desperately needed, rather than the reverse. This is in accord with the Vicious Circle of Self-Defeat Concept.

6. *Hostility, Uncooperativeness, and Secondary Defense*

As might be expected, the Conversion Personality handles hostility and aggression poorly. He may display his petulance and his annoyance too readily. This can be defeating in his interpersonal relationships. He tends to be a demanding kind of person. Angry outbursts may occur when his demands are not met. The anger or pique usually dissipates quite readily, however. He is unlikely to hold grudges. His anger thus is quick, apparent, and likely quickly over. Resentment does not smoulder. This emotional lability may result at the extreme, in a succession of moods, with quick transitions, sometimes in histrionic fashion, from tears to laughter, and back to tears again. He may handle his aggression in passive ways, with apparent surface agreement being often accompanied by superficially hidden resistance, perversity, and uncooperativeness, and through various subtle ways of defeating the other person. Perversity may be prominent. Hostility-provoking behavior is not uncommon. In various ways he may thus defeat, thwart, or set "the other person" at naught. These facets are often most frustrating to his family and friends.

The following example illustrates how uncooperative an individual can be in more or less subtle and subconscious fashion, as he desperately holds onto his psychologically-uneconomic but defensively-intended symptom. This patient defensively rejected competent medical advice, despite clearly explained disastrous and permanent consequences to himself. The case is presented at this point in illustration of the outward appearance of cooperation which can be maintained, accompanied by a subtle but effective kind of sabotage which is often completely unconscious.

Case 54

A Patient with Conversion Paralysis and Increasing Contracture Who Rejected and Defeated Treatment

(1) Epigain significant

A thirty-two-year-old construction worker was under treatment for a somatic-conversion, leg paralysis of six months' duration, which had resulted in his being unable to work. His pattern of living was greatly impaired and restricted; his livelihood was imperiled, but on the other hand there was considerable conversion (hysterical) epigain derived. He received compensation, and also through his disability he had escaped from an extremely difficult work situation.

At this point the secondary and unconscious nature of these gains should be stressed again. It would be of course most incorrect to believe in any degree that this patient consciously surrendered the function of his leg in order to secure the compensation. It would be about as accurate to claim that the amputee victim of a train wreck, had deliberately arranged the accident and his loss, in order to secure the ensuing insurance settlement!

(2) Physicians helpless

Upon questioning, the patient would pleasantly but blandly state his interest in getting back to the job. It was apparent, however, that he had little real drive in this direction. Psychotherapeutic efforts were quite effectively handicapped by his complete passivity. The patient also had a face-saving need to insist (against the results of competent medical studies in several specialty fields) upon the presence of a purely physical basis for the paralysis. It was not feasible therefore to more than guess at the possible primary gains in the dynamics of his illness. His psychiatrist was helpless.

In the meantime, although the patient was repeatedly advised to exercise the paretic limb, these necessary exercises were not done. He always promised to cooperate, and was always outwardly agreeable, but he simply could not or would not cooperate. As a result, the effects of an atrophy-of-disuse gradually developed. These progressed both visibly and as shown by x-ray films. A physical disability was becoming superimposed on the already serious emotional psychologic one.

Earnest efforts were made by specialists in various fields to explain the urgent reasons for the patient to take some responsibility himself in helping to prevent ankylosis. They were helpless, as well. All attempts to aid him were unconsciously sabotaged. His intentions were always good—superficially, but he had too strong an unconscious stake in maintaining the self-defeating symptoms.

(3) Symptoms secondarily defended, at great cost

When physiotherapy was arranged, he was repeatedly late for appointments, and missed some completely. Despite his seeming outward cooperation, he came to be regarded as a most uncooperative and resistive patient. He could not really be interested in psychotherapy, despite sincere efforts by several willing psychiatrists. His outward "interest" in recovery and his apparent cooperation were most superficial. They were effectively undermined by largely unconscious counter-forces.

There are, of course, several added deeper layers of meaning here. For example, his behavior says in effect, "I can't allow myself to get well. Despite my severe losses from the illness, the psychologic purposes subserved by these handicapping symptoms are much more desperately important to me, and accordingly must be preserved at all costs." Unfortunately, despite some measure of appreciation of all this by his physicians, this was insufficient to prevent their gradual frustration and discouragement. In view of their completely impotent position, this sooner or later took place in turn, with each of the specialists who were connected with the case. The Emotional Inertia (see Concept) which was present was too great to be overcome, despite prodigious medical efforts to do so.

The Conversion Personality sometimes may possess an outward mask of friendliness which covers underlying irritability and hostility. In other instances there is sometimes seen a deceptive appearance of outward submission and passivity. In the foregoing case, the patient would willingly and cheerfully agree, on a verbal level, with the doctor's advice. His apparent agreement was at times puzzling, inconsistent, frustrating, and deceptive to some of his physicians, in the light of his subsequent performance. The latter was in turn motivated by his desperate internal needs to maintain the defensive symptom at all costs. His resistances and resistiveness is another illustration of the *Secondary Defense*. Herein the symptom, a defense in itself, is in turn (that is, secondarily) defended; in this instance both desperately and effectively.

Occasionally the differentiation of the conversion (hysterical) character structure from that of the patient with an early Schizophrenic Reaction, may present problems. As a result of this, as well as other possible confusing admixtures of personality traits, diagnosis may sometimes require observation and study, becoming clearer during a period of psychotherapeutic work.

Fitzgerald, in listing conversion (hysterical) traits, wrote that "all such traits are simple offshoots from the one fundamental trait of love-craving." Bowlby spoke of the conversion person as capricious, precious, hating a lack of attention, histrionic, enjoying "showing off," and marked by depersonalization.

7. Sexuality.

The Conversion (hysterical) Personality of course can be on the warm, friendly, and affectionate side. This is especially true at times, or for periods of time. As a related aspect, this personality also is very likely to be considered sexually oriented, because of outward, frequently apparent, but often superficial indications of seductiveness and coquetry in the female, or a kind of seemingly avid courting and girl-chasing in the male. A reputation for availability or as a lover may be secured, which upon closer investigation may well prove to be quite unwarranted. Drives for attention, acceptance, security, and affection can take on a sexual coloring. Naturally this can be a more effective lure. These gains may be sought thus, through what appears to be a sexual appeal, or via actual sexual routes, including promiscuity.

The seeming sexuality is mostly false and a front, however, in any case. Often it represents a kind of "testing," as well as a means to secure other psychologic goals. Often also, and possibly surprising to some, it is not necessarily consciously recognized at all as sexual or provocative by the person concerned. Thus it is more often an uneasy kind of approach, often marked by underlying tension and apprehensiveness. A sexual response in kind, as might seem invited, may well arouse anxiety and be followed by surprise, possibly by indignation, and not infrequently by a hasty retreat!

It is hardly surprising in view of the foregoing, that psychotherapeutic study will disclose that some degree of sexual immaturity proves to be more the rule than the exception in the Conversion Personality. Frigidity is not uncommon. What appears to be sexual interest thus often is a cover for other significant needs. Sexuality in the Conversion Personality is more or less immature, childish, unfulfilled, unfulfillable, and unfulfilling.

8. Suggestibility.

Suggestibility is an important aspect of the person with a conversion personality structure. It is likewise important in the determination of the foundation for Conversion Reactions. The conversion person usually has the capacity to dissociate, and he is likely to be a good candidate for hypnosis. It is sometimes possible to remove, or even to bring on, clinical symptoms by strong suggestion alone. An appreciation of this factor of response to suggestion in the conversion character, is a help in understanding some of today's dramatic, miraculous, and magical "cures," as well as those of earlier generations. It can help also to explain for us certain present-day instances in which there has been a great response in certain otherwise obscure conditions to "treatment" by charlatans, various therapy machines, faith healing, religious conversions, miracles, shrines, nostrums, and so forth.

Suggestion is not only effective in the waking state but may be enhanced by drugs and in hypnosis. One must, of course, bear in mind that this kind of symptom-removal through suggestion leaves the underlying conversion character, and the capacities for further somatic conversion unchanged. One also must note the dangerous potential in thus relieving a symptom-defense, which is then unreplaced. It may of course also be replaced quite spontaneously, and by something worse!

The conversion (hysterical) person is likely to be on the open and trusting side. He is sometimes also quite naive. Seemingly quite contradictory, these may nonetheless be present concurrently. Thus these characteristics are often present together in varying degrees and combinations. The character-equivalents or defenses as outlined in the foregoing table and in our descriptions, are those most frequently associated with the conversion (hysterical) type of personality make-up. It is, however, not possible to draw absolutely hard and fast lines in establishing criteria for a given type of personality structure, although certain characteristics in combination can often establish the presence of a specific type rather definitely. The deeper psychologic potentials as also tabulated (in *Table 18*), will be discussed briefly in this chapter, or later when we consider the Conversion Reactions (*Chapter 12*).

9. In Conclusion; Concept of Effect-Over-Cause in Sexual Maladjustment

The conversion (hysterical) person is characterized as being an immature, suggestible, emotionally labile, and egocentric individual who has strong dependency needs, and a flair for the dramatic. As a reflection of his internal needs, he seeks attention, and is impulsive and demanding. He is likely to be naive, and to have the capacity to dissociate. He has imaginative ability, appeal, is more outgoing, and he makes friends readily. Aggression and hostility may be handled poorly by this individual, and the capacity for mature relationships is underdeveloped. Both plus and minus effects upon his interpersonal relationships can be significant.

The ability to make a satisfactory sexual adjustment is more or less inadequate. In the past, sexual conflicts were regarded as *the* important consideration in hysteria, and the real source of difficulties. This leads us to an important concept, rather in reverse.

In order to effect an adequate and mature sexual adjustment, it is almost a prerequisite that the various components of the personality act in reasonable harmony. Since the sexual relationship represents an interpersonal adjustment of maximum intensity and of a high order of complexity, *it is often the first function to break down when personality adjustment is threatened. Sexual maladjustment is thus more likely to represent the effects (rather than the cause) in emotional illness.* This is in line with an important Concept of Effect-Over-Cause in Sexual Maladjustment. As noted earlier, emotional conflict is most likely to develop around sexual and aggressive impulses.

From a dynamic standpoint, we have seen the close relation of the conversion traits to hostility, as well as to sexuality. These character defenses serve as defenses against resulting anxiety. Thus, the person may be egocentric, demanding, and attention-seeking, because he cannot tolerate the anxiety of ever consciously recognizing his repressed rage toward the loved one. This in turn was in response to the deprivation of love and affection which he experienced. If he devotes all his attention and energy in trying to get these wants fulfilled, he cannot be aware of the forbidden impulses. If his traits do not result in some substitutive satisfaction of his needs, his defenses may be reinforced through intensification of the existing character traits, perhaps by symptom formation, or both.

C. THE DEPRESSIVE GROUP

1. Traits of Depressive Personality

A. OVERSERIOUS AND SOMBER.—The personality traits which are most commonly seen to develop in the Depressive Personality and in association with the Depressive Reactions may be placed in three subgroups. The presence of several of these characteristics together (a depressive constellation) constitutes what was earlier postulated as the Depressed Personality.

The first group is clearly depressive and includes overseriousness, great dependability, somberness, over-studiousness, overconscientiousness, restricted sense of humor, and lowered spirits. The depressed person may have quite a capacity for worry. He may feel subjectively and outwardly appear, as though he carried more than his share of the world's burdens and cares on his shoulders.

Behavior is likely to be decorous and restrained. Inhibitions are well developed, possibly overdeveloped. He may take a gloomy view of things. His spirits are lower and lack buoyancy. His sense of humor is restricted. He may appear subdued. In typically depressive fashion, he may view life as somewhat futile. This may extend over into his work, profession, or art, for example, to thus secure some measure of outward expression. We shall soon see this operative in the "Somber Poet."

The Depressed Personality generally has an increased vulnerability to rejection, to "letdown," to hurt, to loss, to frustration, and to disappointment. This is present as a consequence of: (1) his overwhelming, unconscious need for love, and ultimately dependence; (2) an overability for social adjustment; (3) a possible blocked potential for creative outgoingness; and (4) his attitudes and reactions, which are at times almost as though he has some perhaps partly unconscious conviction that he does not deserve to have fun or to be happy.

The Depressed Personality has a propensity for guilt feelings. This aspect of his character armor should be stressed. It can progress to a point of his being a "guilt-ridden" individual. Not unrelated is his frequent tendency to make harsh self-judgments and to maintain a low level of self-estimation and esteem. If he is not too worthwhile in his own eyes, then how can others like him? How could he deserve contentment or satisfactions? These character-equivalents relate in particular to his unconscious utilization of the mental dynamism of introjection, as we earlier observed in the Depressive Reactions of clinical level.

The foregoing character defenses as outlined attempt to serve a similar
function psychologically to that of actual emotional depression, in aiding
the repression (that is, maintaining the unconscious status) and control
of hostile and aggressive impulses.

Many of his character defenses are in effect the converse of those of the
conversion (hysterical) group. Emotional feelings and responses tend to
develop more slowly in the Depressed Personality, and to be sustained.
Behavior is more deliberate (in contrast to being impulsive). Appearance
is likely to be overly mature, with the impression given of the person
being older than his years. The Depressive Personality often has an excellent capacity for work, great application, and prolonged endeavor.
Intelligence is likely high.

B. COUNTER HOSTILITY.—A second group of traits which may accompany the above or be present independently, is related to the denial of and
reaction against, hostility. These traits develop largely through the operation of the dynamisms of repression, denial, and reaction formation.

This second group also includes the related character defensive traits
of compliance, conciliation, overpoliteness, subservience, and obsequious-
ness.

C. OBSESSIVE OVERLAPPING.—A third, less-clear group of character
defenses which are also to be uncovered with moderate frequency, includes
several defenses which overlap with those of the obsessive category. Herein
may be included as an admixture with other more strictly depressive character attributes, such traits as meticulousness, concern with detail, rigidity,
and perfectionism.

The presence of a number of the foregoing traits makes up the constellation of the Depressed Personality. Their imbalance or exaggeration constitutes the depressive type of Character Reaction or Neurosis. A number
of these defensively elaborated traits were present in the following rather
typical case.

Case 55

The Depressed Personality

(1) Predilection to assume responsibility

A forty-one-year-old businessman was referred as a candidate for
character analysis. He believed his life was restricted and that his
ability to function effectively and to secure more satisfactions in living
might be improved. This was indeed correct! In the initial interview the
author was impressed with the evidence of overseriousness and
somberness as major character defenses. His wife and his business
associates thought of him as a "worrier." Indeed, at times he appeared
as though he carried the "weight of the world" on his shoulders. His
view of things was often on the gloomy side. A character analysis was
advised and undertaken.

During the subsequent intensive personality study, we soon learned
that his character defenses extended into earlier years. He had been
early regarded as a serious child. While he had participated to a limited
extent in some social and athletic activities in school, he had been also
quite studious. He had taken great pride in his teachers' reference to

him as "very serious." This was true later, and with other people. He had a great capacity for assuming responsibility, and his behavior was on the decorous and restrained side. As a consequence of these and other aspects of his personality traits and behavior, he had early begun to give the impression of being older than his chronologic age. Later, on occasion he would be taken for as much as eight or ten years older than his actual age—again something in which he took some pride.

(2) Level of spirits lowered

He had wanted very much to speed up his assumption of an adult role. At eighteen years of age, he secured employment as a bookkeeper and was thenceforth considered to be an adult. From this he secured considerable satisfaction. He was always conscientious and hard working. He was quite successful in competition and made rapid strides in his work. His business and professional successes were hardly short of outstanding. When first seen by the author, he was a partner in a major construction firm, which he had helped to build from scratch. He was never very happy, however. He lacked a healthy buoyancy of spirits; his sense of humor was restricted; and he lacked any element of carefreeness.

Perhaps one can see how the same traits which were such an advantage to his business advancement, were at the same time a serious handicap to him in many other ways. Thus, he was limited in his outgoingness, in his making friends. He expected his friends, family, and business associates to equal his own standards and performance. His attitudes were rigid and entrenched, accompanied by a number of well established prejudices. He had a limited tolerance for change. He was vulnerable to disappointment or loss, and he had become terribly dissatisfied with his business partner. His lack of elasticity had handicapped him at work and socially, and inevitably also prolonged his work in treatment. However, he was able fortunately to achieve considerable constructive change during his therapeutic work, but only over a fair period of time.

(3) Substantial gains through therapy

Therapy became a most worthwhile endeavor in lessening his own internal restrictions and in opening up new avenues of enjoyment and satisfaction.

Instead of hampering his business success, his progress therein actually picked up speed. This was in turn at considerably less cost to him in terms of effort expended and intrapsychic sacrifices required. These were indeed substantial gains.

2. Relationships of Depressed Personality

The Depressed Personality is restricted in his ability to develop and to maintain close and warm relationships. These are limited in both quantity and quality (depth, closeness, and meaningfulness). Early frustrations in childhood, and the limitation or failure of vital antecedent child-parent relationships are responsible. These deny him an adequate psychologic foundation for the establishment of later more optimal interpersonal relationships. English believes that the depressed patient "does not seem to have much feeling of love to give, and what he has he is afraid to give." His own early deprivations were in turn due to the inability of his parents to provide a suitable measure of real acceptance and love. As a result, the Depressed Personality unconsciously seeks to make up for the earlier lacks and frustrations.

This is reflected in his own distance-maintaining operations and resulting relatively-restricted relationships. As might be expected, these may lack mutuality and an equal appreciation of the position and needs, in turn, of the other person. The relationships of the Depressed

Personality are likely to include one or more in which he "attempts" to achieve a position of considerable dependency. His claims for love and attention are based simply upon his need for the other. According to Cohen *et al.,* "Demands are made for love, attention, service, and possessions. The concept of reciprocity is missing; the needs of the other for similar experience are not recognized."

3. Contributions of Depressed Personality

We have already noted the superior ability of the Depressed Personality for social adjustment. As the reader glanced over the traits outlined above, he may have noted the personal and social value of many of them, at least when they are in reasonable balance and in moderation. The serious, conscientious, hard-working, dependable person who maintains high personal standards, is a social asset. In accord with our Principle of Defense-Hypertrophy however, their development is likely to progress beyond an optimal point.

The Depressed Personality is often able to produce an inordinate amount of constructive work. Despite his own great unconscious needs for love, ∟ he can assume great responsibility. Also, despite his limited capacity in personal relationships, he may have great executive abilities in administration and management. His deep and genuine sincerity is sensed. He is dependable, and often scrupulously honest. His associates appreciate these stable qualities and are often more willing to produce with, or for him. Depression is indeed an emotional illness to which many of our socially most useful and productive people are subject.

In the Depressed Personality we frequently find high personal standards or goals. The superego (that is, conscience) is quite likely to be overdeveloped. Depressive trends often evolve in able, intelligent, and sophisticated people. Although two cases of emotional depression were reported to the author not long ago in patients with I.Q.s of 76 and 80 respectively, an I.Q. of considerably over 110 is a more likely finding in the depressed person. Depressive Reactions are frequently encountered in clinical practice in individuals with I.Q.s of 120–140, and higher. The author recalls recently treating a very depressed person with an I.Q. of more than 170.

The presence of depressive character traits covers a broad range of occupational and professional groups. The preceding case was that of a business man, a builder. The following instance is that of a surgeon.

Case 56

The Somber Surgeon

Dr. Samuel X. Jamisen was a well respected general surgeon, who was known for his careful technique, his caution, his conservatism, his essential honesty and integrity, *and* for his somber appearance. He had well earned his nickname of "Somber Sam." This did not imply that he was unpopular or not well thought of. It was simply an accurate, descriptive label.

Somber Sam, the surgeon, as he had become known, was an overserious person, with a long face and gloomy mien. He was somber, indeed, and had a somewhat restricted sense of humor. His work was most conscientious, and he could always be depended upon to assume the responsibility in a difficult case. He was widely known to worry, perhaps excessively, over his cases.

His outward display of emotions was restricted and restrained. He seldom if ever became involved in arguments, and tended to hold himself somewhat apart from the spirited medical discussions of his colleagues. His overall bearing reflected an overdeveloped general level of concern and a gloomy outlook. His level of spirits appeared to have a base line which was below the average.

A psychiatrist comes to mind whose similar personality make-up and character structure, very closely parallel the foregoing case. There is likely no professional group which cannot provide those from its members to illustrate the Depressed Personality.

The characteristically lowered level of spirits, somber nature, and depressed outlook are often directly reflected in a gloomy or pessimistic point of view. Things may seem futile, in typically depressed fashion. At times this may secure expression in work or art. The following lines of poetry and the outlook which they reflect, well illustrate this. This depressive, futile kind of outlook may be found also in instances of painting, sculpture, novels, plays, music, and other modes of artistic expression. Its manifestations may be quite subtle.

Case 57

The Somber Poet

The following three brief poems are by R. H. Allen, who at 20 years of age already possessed a number of the typical depressive character defenses. Comparison with earlier lines is of interest (Ch.5:VB4).

Reflection

We have our lives, and these we live;
Each, as he thinks, the best.
But Sands of Time, so quickly tend;
To hurry us toward Heaven's Rest:
That scarce one knows, when at the end;
Just what has been Life's quest!

Eternity

In the realms of space beyond our mortal ken;
Enthroned on darkness itself;
Watching through the chill blue light of dying worlds;
Is The Thing!
His being far flung into the vast reaches of time
    itself, whence he came.
Pale shadows flicker across his cold hard face,
As eons pass and new worlds are born.
A mirthless grin shows his knowledge of their
    futile efforts.
A Flash! and they are gone!
As those that went before and others will follow
Into the dismal abyss
That men call Eternity!

Whither Content?

Who seeks to wander to Cathay or Rome?
Far too many!
How many realize content lies at home?
Few, if any!

4. "Level" of Depression

A. STATUS QUO OF ADJUSTMENT, AND ADDED STRESS.—In assessing the presence or the level of clinical depression, comparison with a hypothetical base line to indicate an "average" or "normal" level of spirits is useful. This we studied in the preceding chapter. So long as the character defensive traits of the person with a depressive diathesis adequately serve their purpose, what we can refer to as "the *Status Quo* of Adjustment" is maintained (*see also* Ch.12:VA2).

External and internal factors of added stress, however, may result in one's defensive traits or "character-equivalents" becoming no longer adequate. As a result, the character defenses may further develop and become stronger. This is true particularly if the stresses are sustained and any increase in them is gradual and not overwhelming.

When the stress is too much to handle in this fashion, a clinical Depressive Reaction may develop, as part of the urgent need to continue the repression (from recognition by the world and, more importantly, from one's own conscious awareness), of threatening aggressive and hostile drives. These threaten to escape from repression. The patient "fears" the loss of their control.

B. DEPRESSION AND ANXIETY.—Recognition and loss of control appears to be the most dreaded consequence. When the threat of *de*repression occurs, great anxiety is subjectively experienced. This serves as an alarm signal, a psychologic Call to General Quarters! The threatened catastrophe which derepression would mean is defended against: (1) by the very gradual evolvement of the depressive character traits, or (2) by clinical depression as such. The anxiety may or (more often) may not comprise an A.A.A. (Acute Anxiety Attack). It often enough can be a warning signal of actual or impending Emotional Decompensation. (*see* Ch.4:-VB1.)

Overdevelopment of the depressive character traits as outlined and when sufficiently severe, can disrupt personality integration, impair effectiveness, interfere with interpersonal relationships, and decrease one's ability to secure real satisfaction in living. The following case is presented in illustration.

Case 58

The Overdevelopment of Depressive Character Traits

(1) Character analysis undertaken
A forty-one-year-old corporation tax consultant originally was interviewed as a possible candidate for character analysis on the recommendation of his brother, who had himself gained considerably from

intensive treatment in another city. Upon examination, he was mild-mannered, overly-polite, very serious in mien, and seemingly compliant in attitude. He stated that he was inclined to moroseness and low spirits. History disclosed further that he was overly concerned with detail, and usually carried too great a burden of responsibility. There was also evidence of some particular vulnerability to disappointment or rejection. He wanted help with these traits. He felt handicapped, that his interests were too restricted, and that he was unable properly to enjoy life. This assessment was undoubtedly quite correct.

During treatment it soon became clear that he had long maintained perfectionistic standards. He was the victim of his own harsh conscience, which had taken over the highly critical attitudes toward himself which had earlier and long been presented, by his judgmental and stern parents. As one might expect, he required considerable satisfactions from outside himself in view of early deprivations of love and acceptance, and a deficiency in internal sources of supply. His interpersonal relationships reflected his terribly strong, but deeply unconscious needs for acceptance and love. He had a considerable propensity for guilt feelings, and usually maintained a low level of self-esteem.

(2) Defences against hostility

A typical psychologic element was the presence of strong ambivalence —mixed *polar* feelings. This was, of course, outside of and beyond his conscious awareness. One side of the ambivalence was the great amount of aggression he had felt in response to early deprivations in childhood. This had seemed too dangerous to tolerate. It consequently had been quickly and automatically repressed from awareness. This set up an antecedent pattern for his future reactions, so that most later hostile feelings were also repressed. (*See Dependency Dilemma of Infancy*, p. 410.)

His defensive character traits had developed in the service of repression and denial. Outwardly he was calm, mild-mannered, and compliant, and completely denied having had any hostile feelings whatsover! These attitudes also denied outwardly to the world as well as to himself, the presence of his actual very considerable reservoir of hostility. His original automatic rejection from consciousness of his hostile feelings in childhood, had been based upon the dreaded but unconscious fear of retaliation from his parents. Further, the danger of harboring destructive aims toward the vitally necessary object of his own dependence was too great. As life progressed, his hostile impulses toward people were gradually but inexorably inverted. They were replaced in turn by traits which were actually opposite to his real inner but hidden feelings. His mood reflected a consistent overly-serious level. His spirits tended to be low, and lacked a normal amount of buoyancy. His sense of humor was also restricted.

He was vulnerable to emotional depression, as illustrated by his overreaction in depressive fashion to any loss, disappointment, frustration, or a failure to achieve a cherished goal. He lacked the elasticity to adjust his goals in line with reality. Although he was successful to a fair degree, his necessary obsessive kind of preoccupation with detail decreased his ability to delegate responsibility to others. His handicapping somberness was an additional impediment. Further, the diversion of potential energy to serve essentially uneconomic internal needs, decreased the amount of energy which was available for more constructive external endeavors.

(3) Results of therapy

In rapid resume of the results of his long-term, intensive treatment, he became able gradually to reappraise his goals, and to effect an adjustment of harsh and punishing superego forces. He also became able in time, to face the aggressive side of his ambivalence, to accept it, to understand it, and ultimately to handle it far better. As a consequence of these gains and other insights, his ability to maintain effective interpersonal relationships—familial, social, and professional—improved substantially. Life became fuller and more satisfying. These results, however, were not easily achieved. His treatment required more than three years of difficult work. An added measure of its success might be noted however, in his ability to tolerate several rather keen disappointments, experienced since the termination of his formal work in treatment.

There is an increased likelihood of relapse in every case in which depressive character traits, depressive equivalents, or clinical depression as such is present as a major feature of the illness. This is in accord with the Principle of Recurrence in depression, as outlined in Chapter 4. This principle must constantly be kept in mind prognostically, and in evaluation of the results of therapy. This man has maintained his gains for more than thirteen years now, since the termination of his formal work in therapy.

5. Cultural Factors and Depressive Character Traits

The evaluation of emotional depression must be made from the hypothetical normal base line of the individual patient's spirits and mood as referred to earlier. It can be noted, however, that many individual and cultural factors will influence the relative location or level of such a "normal" base line.

A number of subgroups in our culture appear to foster personality traits similar to those we have described. This is true both in America and overseas. In patients from these groups the presence of certain of the depressive character traits have less significance than if the same traits were present in a person from another subgroup.

For example, the traits of impassivity, somberness, and seriousness have been more or less associated with some of the American Indians. Traits of taciturnity, stoicism, and dourness are present in many native New Englanders. These character attributes may be contrasted with the relative emotional volatility of certain other ethnic or cultural groups. The Latin groups among European nationals illustrate this.

6. When Is Depression Pathologic?

In view of the relative universality of depression, one must agree with Greenacre that "it is certainly the intensity, the excessive duration and the domination of the organism by the affect, rather than its occurrence, which is pathological." In other words, the presence of emotional depression in and of itself, is not necessarily to be considered pathologic.

A Depressive Reaction may be considered pathologic: (1) when it is present in the form of substitutive, overdeveloped, and handicapping character defenses; (2) when these defenses have progressed to a further state of imbalance so as to constitute a depressive type of Character Reaction or Neurosis; (3) when clinical depression is present to a point where it can be considered objectively as a neurotic or a psychotic Depressive Reaction; or (4) when physiologic depressive equivalents are determined to be present.

From any of these eventualities a varying degree of interference with living results. The degree of clinical depression which develops will depend on the relative internal strengths of the personality and its integrative ability, in the face of external and internal disintegrative stresses. See also *Table 10.*

7. *Further Consequences of Depressive Character Traits*

A. ASSETS AND CONSTRICTIONS.—As illustrated in *Case 58*, the Depressed Personality is likely to suffer personal, social, and professional handicaps. The degree of these handicaps depends upon the relative strength of his defensively-developed character traits. Spontaneity is restricted. There is likely to be a similar restriction of imagination and speculative ability. On the other hand, he is likely to think things through carefully and to anticipate consequences well.

The Depressed Personality is conservative and enjoys a limited freedom to try new things; to take chances or risks. The result is a constricted life and a limitation of ability to enjoy it. These traits which can greatly handicap and prolong the character analysis of the Depressed Personality, as we have observed, are often well offset from the social standpoint by accompanying traits of sincerity, application, dependability, seriousness, and conscientiousness. The latter in turn can be great assets in treatment.

The following instance illustrates the lifelong restrictions in living which had resulted from the presence of character traits which were typical of the Depressed Personality. These, however, had served this gentleman rather adequately as defenses, until middle life. This instance also illustrates the generally increasing vulnerability to depression rather frequently to be noted in this phase of life, as long-established character defenses may prove less adequate. An added stress may be the increasing recognition that long-cherished goals in living are not going to be realized. This is part of the Passing-the-Peak hazard in emotional depression.

Case 59

Defensively-Developed Character Traits are Intensified, and a Depressive Reaction Develops in Response to Additional Stress

(1) Depressive character traits develop

A forty-six-year-old associate professor sought medical help, primarily for insomnia. His alert doctor found relationships in the onset of his difficulty to some recent disappointments in both his personal and the professional life. He also learned that the insomnia consisted of waking earlier than usual; Dawn Insomnia. He correctly suspected the onset of a Depressive Reaction, although there had been relatively little in the professor's appearance or complaints to suggest this diagnosis initially. The man was promptly and efficiently referred for psychotherapy.

Upon consultation he was observed to be of a very serious mien. He spoke in slow and deliberate fashion, without very much spontaneity of ideation or change of facial expression. He was overly devoted to his work. He had a well-established reputation for being dependable, hard-working, sincere, and overconscientious. Some of the usual character traits associated with the psychologic potential for emotional depression were present. These had developed as desperately-needed character defenses, to aid in his mastery over consciously intolerable and threatening aggressive and hostile drives.

Later study revealed an intolerance to any error in himself or to any failure to measure up to some expected personal standard of performance. This evidence of a harsh superego was borne out further in his extension of this overcritical attitude toward his students, colleagues, and family. Its sources were eventually largely traceable in turn to his harshly judgmental father.

(2) *Control of affectivity*

The defensive character traits had been unconsciously erected mainly in an attempt to conceal and to deny the aggressive elements of what were his actual strongly ambivalent feelings. At the same time, however, they gained concealed symbolic expression in destructive fashion as the self-limiting, overserious, rigid, and depressive character elements. In this instance there was also present rather considerable repression of his sexual drives. It was as though any kind of "instinctual" drive or affectivity, was threatening and dangerous to him.

His character defenses had served their purpose as reinforcements to the control of forbidden drives, until the past year. At this time it began to be increasingly clear that he would miss some of the marks in life for which he had aimed. This half-recognized apprehension was finally confirmed by the selection of a new man for the vacant professorship, a post which he had long wanted. Also, his daughter had married a man whom he considered to be quite beneath her station in life. These were vital matters to him.

(3) *Clinical depression when character defenses inadequate*

With these disappointments,* the whole defensive character structure was no longer adequately able to handle repression and control. Early signs of emotional depression appeared, as reinforcements to character defenses which were no longer adequate.

Parts of the character defensive structure were responsible to a major extent for his success (for example, serious application, devotion, conscientiousness). Other aspects were in turn responsible for his failures (for example, intolerance, overconcern with detail, constant relatively low level of spirits, critical attitude toward others, difficulty in tolerating change, and interferences with close personal relationships).

Analytic treatment in this case was moderately successful. A major Depressive Reaction was likely averted. In addition, it was possible to secure some healthier realignment of the superego (conscience), ego ideals (goals), and ego (the self or "I").

In this instance it was not deemed feasible or possible to secure any really complete analysis of some of the more rigid character defenses, which had served so well through many years. These were clung to in an understandably tenacious and desperate fashion. A recent interview, however, indicates the maintenance of a kindlier attitude toward himself and others. He has an increased ability to tolerate frustration. There has also been a healthier handling of hostility, in the years since the termination of his intensive treatment.

B. VULNERABILITY TO CRITICISM; REACTIONS OF OTHERS; ATTENTION HYPOTHESIS.—As we have seen, the Depressed Personality may have the personal and social advantages of certain of his socially desirable personality traits offset by other disadvantageous facets. As another example of this, there is frequently a need to be very critical of others, as well as of himself. This is an attempted way of bolstering his own battered ego. The endeavor is to build himself up comparatively, by tearing others down. This often takes place unwittingly, that is, outside of conscious awareness.

---

* From a more technical point of view, these disappointments constituted a major failure of narcissistic supply from external sources. The ego in early life was deprived of largely oral, narcissistic supplies. An antecedent primordial pattern of Depressive Reaction was set up. The ego became further impoverished through the necessity of maintaining defenses, and by its continued absorption of punishment from the harsh superego.

As a result there was greater dependence upon external sources of supply, since internal ones were lacking. The ego was more vulnerable to a failure of supply from the external sources. Disappointments, losses, and frustrations accordingly became of far greater moment, as threatening aggressive retaliatory drives came closer to conscious awareness. Depression ensued, as a last-ditch psychologic attempt to maintain repression and control.

Awareness by others of his critical attitudes, however, often is gained, despite conscious efforts at concealment. Because of this and because of his rigidity and somber nature, some people may feel less comfortable around the Depressed Personality. In contrast also, however, some people may respond to the implicit dependency appeal of depression in keeping with their own internal needs. This is in accord with the Attention Hypothesis (Ch.10:VIII), through which our interest is invited to the *automatic attraction toward people whose internal needs complement one's own.*

The frequently-observed inability to accept or to face criticism can be better understood in the light of the already existing large burden of self-criticism from a punitive superego. This burden is too heavy to allow the addition of still more from outside. Criticism is also difficult to accept because of the great and largely unconscious craving for love and acceptance.

C. GOALS NOT IN KEEPING WITH CAPACITY.—The person with the psychologic capacity for the development of emotional depression may get into trouble when his goals are set and maintained higher than realizable, out of keeping with his real personal resources.

The well-adjusted person in some distinction, generally has some reasonably adequate safeguards. He possesses the ability and the necessary elasticity to readjust his sights in keeping with the actuality of his capacity. He is fortunately more able to tolerate loss and disappointment. He is free of the characteristically harsh superego.

D. REACTION FORMATION IN MILITARY AND CIVIL "CORRECTNESS".— We earlier noted the formation of certain depressive character defenses through reaction formation (that is, the mental mechanism leading to outwardly-opposite feelings and reactions, from the basic or original unconscious ones). An interesting instance of this kind of reaction formation or possibly sometimes of compensation) may be familiar enough to the readers with military experience. Reference is being made here to the overly-correct serviceman who makes a ceremonial point of saluting, and in other ways perhaps just slightly overdoes, the showing of "respect" to his officers. To a major extent he may be unaware that his exaggerated military correctness is a way of reinforcing control over his more concealed (unconscious) resentment of authority and actual hostility.

This kind of behavior may to some extent nettle his officers, but how is it possible to reproach him? Fromm-Reichmann raised the interesting question here as to whether some of the military rules and regulations might not really have come to be developed in the first place, so as to allow for the counteraction of adverse and negative feelings in just this way. This interpretation would be similar also to some of the conventions and conventionalities which govern social (nonmilitary) interchange.

One might interpret this kind of behavior as saying in effect, "I really hate your guts and don't respect you at all, but this I must conceal, not only from you, but even more so, from myself. Therefore I show outwardly (while actually I only go through the motions of showing) every manifestation of respect. If I obviously respect you so much, you (and I also!) can't possibly be aware of how hostile I really am underneath."

When hostility is concealed or buried, this may be imperfectly done. It may, of course, be to some extent discernible directly to perceptive people, or intuitively so, with resulting impairment of relationships.

E. USE OF ALCOHOL.—Infrequently there is an increased use of alcohol by the Depressed Personality, which might at times be looked upon as an attempt: (1) to drown hostility, (2) to replace oral narcissistic supplies, and/or (3) to ease the burden of self-condemnation and reproach. Unfortunately, this resort is self-defeating and can tend toward establishing a vicious circle, as new self-reproaches follow alcoholic indulgence.

The use of alcohol may remain quite occasional, limited to social occasions and parties, and under excellent control, so long as the emotional *status quo* can be maintained.

8. Passing-the-Peak; Increased Vulnerability to Depression with Increasing Age

The foregoing instances may help us further to understand the increased vulnerability to depression for certain individuals, as middle-age advances.

Life can have a wearing-down effect, as disappointments occur and their effects build up in cumulative fashion. Some level of disillusionment and possible cynicism may gradually develop. Cynicism may appear, for example, as one response to the increasing awareness of one's forced surrender of long cherished ambitions or illusions. These attitudes may represent a characterologic equivalent of, and also a kind of defense against, emotional depression.

As life proceeds into the middle years, the loss or diminution of physical vigor and effectiveness, the expected hormonal changes and their consequences (especially the psychologic ones), and the accumulated disappointments and buffetings of life, may result in an increasing level of disillusionment and discouragement. Increased vulnerability to emotional depression can result. Development of Passing-the-Peak attitudes can contribute, as earlier outlined [Ch.4:VA5;XIB1.]

From one standpoint, the ego becomes impoverished: (1) through the vicissitudes and wearing-down effects of internal conflict, and (2) through the constant maintenance of defenses against threatening, disowned hostility and aggression. There also may be less ability to tolerate loss, frustration, and disappointment. When a considerable discrepancy exists between goals in life and the ability to achieve them, the likelihood for severe disappointment increases. This discrepancy may increase with declining personal resources. Furthermore, with an underlying capacity for depression, the pathway for this kind of intrapsychic development already exists. For some people, awareness of declining physical vigor has a considerable emotional impact.

When strong competition is present in the seeking of various goals, there may be an added handicap for the older competitor. Finally, in persons in whom there was an early failure of (largely oral) narcissistic supply, there is an increased or an increasing dependence on satisfactions from external sources, and a corresponding increase in ego vulnerability when these prove inadequate or fail.

9. *Sexual Interests and Activity; Hypomanic Activity (Defense Against Depression)*

Absorption of psychic energy takes place in the desperate attempts to keep censored (unconscious) feelings concealed from conscious recognition, and to keep them controlled. Accordingly, there is less psychic energy available for libidinal attachments and for sexual outlets. Further, there is more sexual repression present in the Depressed Personality. In addition there is both sexual suppression and repression, as consequences to the distance-promoting needs in his interpersonal relationships.

Accordingly, one usually finds a decreased amount of sexual activity in the Depressed Personality. Sometimes this can progress to almost a seeming absence of all sexual interests. This is often enough merely accepted as a matter of course by the depressed individual. He frequently not only fails to complain of this to his physician, but such information is often gained only through rather careful and pointed questioning. The amount of decrease in sexual interest and activity often parallels the amount of depression which is present.

Sexual preoccupation and overactivity in turn may occasionally be observed as a reaction to or as part of a defense against, depression in the *hypomanic* individual. This kind of overactivity on a hypomanic basis is usually accompanied by unusually good spirits on a relatively superficial level. There also is usually accompanying overactivity in mental, physical, and emotional areas. The amount of such diminution or increase in the sexual interests and activity of an individual are highly variable, depending upon the specific effects upon sexual functions of the emotional reactions of depression or elation.

10. *Predisposition to Depression*

In summary we may note the predisposition toward depression in the overconscientious, serious, compliant, subservient, obsessive, or overly-agreeable individual. He is driven by the demands of his punitive superego (that is, the internalized parental authority). He has become overly dependent upon external sources of satisfaction, leaving himself more vulnerable to disappointments and loss. He may be regarded by his associates simply as a somber, gloomy, or over-serious person.

One might think in terms of a normal range of swings of mood, taking place in waves. There accordingly would be peaks and shallows, with an average line. The level of spirits of the depressed person is mostly below such a hypothetical average, base line. This may be an integral part of the character structure. It may not necessarily be psychopathologic. Whether or not pathology is considered to be present depends upon the presence and level of resulting handicap. Depressive character defenses generally restrict enjoyment in living to some extent, and often limit the scope of social relationships.

These people do not often themselves seek therapeutic help, although benefits to them from character analysis could be substantial. There is at times a close relation to be observed between the character structure in the

Depressed Personality and that to be observed in the Obsessive Personality. Careful consideration of the dynamics of the depressive character traits and the Depressive Reactions will help us understand why the person concerned urgently requires their development and maintenance.

D. ADDITIONAL PERSONALITY TYPES OF INTEREST

Unfortunately space does not permit more than brief mention and definition of some eight of the "lesser" personality types, in addition to the three prior major ones, as already outlined. In general, however, their origin and development seek to subserve similar intrapsychic needs. The contributing attributes which comprise such "minor constellations" likewise can effectively color the attitudes of the individual concerned, and help to constitute his characterologic armor. They are best labeled on a descriptive basis.

1. Hygeiaphrontic Character Defenses

Careful observation may disclose occasional instances in the clinical practice of psychiatry, in which certain character defenses of a hygeiaphrontic (hypochondriacal) coloring are present. As outlined in our study of the foregoing three more pronounced constellations of character defensive traits, these particular traits have also gradually developed in the service of internal psychologic needs.

When the individual character traits serve their defensively-intended purposes sufficiently well, they suffice in themselves. When they break down under added or new stresses, or prove insufficient, clinical neurotic symptoms will develop. The latter are the desperate and vitally-necessary efforts to preserve ego integrity. This is despite the fact that they are essentially nonconstructive and psychologically uneconomic.

Hygeiaphrontic Reactions (Overconcern with Health, or Somatic Preoccupation) are frequently seen in which the level of the manifestations is subclinical and subneurotic. These instances sometimes may be definite enough to be classified as belonging to a category which we accordingly might call the Hygeiaphrontic (hypochondriacal) Personality. In other instances of the Hygeiaphrontic Personality, even the actual overconcern with health may be minimal. In these, however, the potentiality for such further development is marked. These are underlying psychologic characteristics which are most commonly associated with this pattern of character defense, and with the neurotic reaction as well.

Some of the more typical such characteristics which may be noted, would include narcissism, the development of interests and concerns on a somatic level to excuse shortcomings or failures; thinking in somatic, visceral, or physiologic terms; and trends toward regression, and seclusiveness. Schilder regarded the typical hypochondriacal individual to be narcissistic, seclusive, and monomaniacal. The hygeiaphrontic character is also marked by the use of the defense of isolation. This is reflected in his interpersonal relationships. If the hygeiaphrontic trends increase, the relationships become increasingly attenuated. As a result, the Hygeiaphrontic Personality may retreat into an increasing level of somatic and physiologic self-absorption.

This protective withdrawal of interests from external objects is regressive and unconscious. It may be interpreted by the casual observer as self-centeredness or egotism. As a consequence, it is apt to bring to the Hygeiaphrontic (hypochondriacal) Personality the reverse of the love and affection which he unconsciously craves. This in turn helps further to contribute to the frequently increased level of distrust, suspicion, and withdrawal which he displays. This is the Hygeiaphrontic Vicious Circle. Once established, it can gradually increase in its scope, and in its resulting self-defect for the individual concerned.

2. Phobic Personality

The Phobic Personality is characterized by his tendency to employ phobic patterns of defense and to develop the manifestations of a Phobic Reaction under sufficient stress. He employs techniques of avoidance in response to stress and anxiety. His interpersonal relationships are so colored as well.

Inwardly he entertains self-doubt, lack of confidence, and considerable fear. Outwardly these may not be apparent. Painful experiences are followed by an overconcern for the avoidance of related circumstances. In the Phobic Personality, dealing with problems through avoidance often becomes a subtle but pervasive attitude. It extends through the internal psyche. Thus this characterologic attitude of avoidance is not limited to external things. It includes all strong painful emotions; sometimes strong emotions of all kinds.

3. Casual Personality

One might think of the obsessive elements in personality as being in themselves neither positive nor negative. Potentially they can be either. This might be clarified further if, parallel with obsessive personality characteristics, one considers their opposite.

We might name the opposite of the Obsessive Personality, the Casual Personality. The characteristics of casualness can likewise be an asset or a liability, perhaps to the point of being considered a neurosis. In general there is a common tendency to think of the casual person, however, as being less neurotic. His traits would be approximately the converse of the Obsessive Personality. Their development to the point of exaggeration or imbalance can result in a Character Reaction or Neurosis of the casual type.

4. Paranoid Personality

Distance-promotion is important for the Paranoid Personality. This is accordingly contributed to by a variety of means in his interpersonal relationships. A mainstay among his mental dynamisms is that of projection.

His tendency toward suspiciousness, distrustfulness, doubt, projection, distance, and hostile reserve help comprise his characterologic armor. Overdevelopment of these constitutes a paranoid type of Character

Reaction. A paranoid coloring is not uncommon in major psychotic re-actions. This can extend in its more extreme progression to the most severe paranoid delusions.

5. *Soterial Personality*

In the Soterial Reaction various objects become an emotional source of comfort, security, and protection. The soterial object is the converse of the phobic object. See also the chapter on the Soterial Reactions [Ch.9].

The Soterial Personality seeks his security thus through objects, situations, and people. In these endeavors the soterial aims are more pervasive and subtle. Not sufficiently specific to establish a clinical reaction *per se,* they are nonetheless an important element in the individual's aims, attitude, and emotional coloring. They help comprise the individual's characterologic armor. Overdevelopment leads to a Soterial type of Character Reaction.

6. *"Antiseptic Personality"*

An inhibited aloofness from sexual matters may be associated with strong feelings of guilt, exaggerated notions about moral purity, and avoidance of personal "contamination." This development is closely related to the Obsessive Personality. The "gains" are secured partially through the feelings of goodness or superiority which may be engendered. The author has sometimes referred to the person in whom this particular variety of characterologic armor has been evolved, as the "Antiseptic Personality."

Considerable discomfort may result for such a person in many situations. This can transpire for example, should companions tell stories with sexual overtones. This is illustrated in the following instance.

Case 60

Condemnation and Denial of Sexual Interests

A patient reported recently following such an experience, "I was very uncomfortable with the fellows. I knew they were doing something wrong. . . . I couldn't approve at all, and I wouldn't even listen. I would like to have left right then. . . . After the meeting started, of course they stopped, and I got comfortable again."

This patient had to deny and to condemn any sexual interests at all. For a long time he could not even admit the presence of any sexual curiosity in himself. Certain neurotic feelings of superiority and goodness which he gained were small compensation for the resulting actual isolation and feelings of difference from his fellows.

The Antiseptic Personality is sexually superinhibited, overly moralistic, and generally guilt-ridden. His relationships are attenuated and he tends toward social isolation. He is insecure, self-hating, and unhappy.

7. *The Anxious Personality*

The Anxious Personality type is distinguished by an overdeveloped capacity to worry and by his being readily subject to tension, apprehension, and anxiety. The major feature for the unfortunate person concerned is his completely automatic generation of an anxious response (which is of course primarily internal) to nearly any stimulus.

At times differentiation from the Anxiety State is indeed a problem. In the Anxious Personality the anxiousness is mainly confined to being subjective, and is subclinical in nature.

8. Impulsive Character

The impulsive type of Character or Personality is marked by the tendency toward impulsive acts. These are usually diffuse and multiple, as opposed to being marked, specific, and repetitive. Unlike the more specific Impulsion (See pages 354-360), where a given type of repetitive impulsive act features the disorder, the Impulsive Character has a more pervasive and overall impulsive tone to his reactions and behavior. In other words, in place of his problems being manifested as a single type of repeated symptom-impulsion, it is his overall character pattern which is impulsive.

Frosch and Wortis describe this group as intolerant of tension, with a low tolerance to frustration. The potential is present for an explosive reaction to deprivation. Their emotional patterns are primitive, infantile, and generally immature. Violent outbursts of temper may occur, as regards the lay description as to how readily he "blows his top."

A distinction from the Psychopathic Personality lies in the Impulsive Personality's feelings of guilt, self-reproach, and self-castigation. These may alternate in the Impulsive Character with one or a series of impulsive acts.

VI. PSYCHODYNAMICS AND PATHOGENESIS

A. TRAIT DEVELOPMENT IS ANALOGOUS DYNAMICALLY TO SYMPTOM FORMATION

1. A Defensive Development to Serve Internal Needs

A. CONCEPT OF CHARACTER DEFENSES.—All character traits develop defensively in the service of internal psychologic needs. This is why they have been referred to in this work as character or personality defenses. Traits may be regarded as fixed patterns of emotional attitude and response. Together, those traits which have been evolved constitute one's characterologic armor.

Character defenses when overdeveloped or hypertrophied lead to Character Neuroses, as distinguished from the Symptom Neuroses. [Ch.5:-IIIA3]. These defenses are continually present, and they operate automatically and unconsciously to ward off anxiety. The defensive operation and intent of character traits is often far from simple. Ready external perception may be difficult.

B. VAGUENESS AS DEFENSE.—Let us consider an example of how character traits operate. In the following instance the seemingly simple personality trait of vagueness or tentativeness "sought" to subserve an important defensive purpose.

Case 61

Vagueness as a Defense

(1) Direct question may not elicit desired response

A thirty-four-year-old, single pharmacist had begun intensive psychotherapy largely because of the limitations of some overdeveloped typically obsessive traits. At times he was outwardly vague and circumstantial. Illustrations of this were occasionally in evidence during his treatment sessions.

During the course of several interviews he worked out how he used one aspect of his vagueness as a defense against anxiety. This facet happened to be his habit of raising questions during treatment sessions by implication, as opposed to asking them directly. In the event he asked a direct question, the failure to secure the particular response which he desired would make him terribly angry. To avoid the pain and danger of becoming so angry he would not ask a direct question.

(2) Helpless position averted

In intensive treatment a direct factual answer to a question can block further associations which might prove helpful and useful. Hence, sometimes a question is best treated as merely another association, with no special regard being given to the fact that it is punctuated by a question mark rather than, for example, by a period or an exclamation mark. The patient could not accept this.

The failure to secure an answer made him feel furious and rebuffed, even though he knew the rationale for this, at least from an intellectual standpoint. In addition, such a circumstance served as still more pointed evidence to himself of his complete helplessness and powerlessness; of his inability to control the other person. It was an illustration of his relative position of impotence in this regard.

(3) Recapitulation of antecedent position

On a deeper level this helplessness carried back to (that is, recapitulated) his primitive infantile feelings of helplessness, in relation to his (then) all-powerful parents. Infantile anxiety in response to this, which had never been adequately worked through emotionally, was in a sense reactivated. Anxiety in turn, as often occurs, found a rather ready outlet through its subjective transition into anger.

When an answer was requested by implication only, the direct request and the attendant dangers to this as noted, were avoided. In addition, the patient could then make many easier explanations to himself, if the desired responses failed to be forthcoming.

C. ADDED IMPLICATIONS RE VAGUENESS.—Vagueness can, of course, have other implications, for example, the stimulation of the other person to stronger, even the utmost endeavors to understand, to anticipate, or to please. Vagueness also, through tentativeness and lack of commitment, may be intended to place one in a stronger position of defensiveness and control. As the defensive-intent of the character defense of vagueness came under scrutiny in the foregoing instance, it became less necessary for the man to employ it. Gradually this character-equivalent and the need for it faded away.

The defensive mechanism of character trait formation is quite analogous dynamically to the more obvious pathologic development of the more clear-cut neurotic symptoms. In the latter, the self-defeating and psychologically uneconomic outward aspects are, of course, often much more striking. This analogy gives us a better basis for the understanding of character defenses.

D. GAINS OF CHARACTER TRAITS AND NEUROTIC SYMPTOMS ANALOGOUS.
—The neurotic gains of symptoms are analogous to character trait gains as well, although they differ somewhat in the different constellations of traits. For example, the Conversion Personality may unconsciously achieve considerable gratification of his psychic needs at the price of fear and a fair amount of self-defeat.

The psychic gains of the Obsessive Personality are much less. They may include some measure of ego enhancement through his supposed virtue, goodness, and superiority; to which Hill added conceit. However, this in turn is at the expense of a large measure of self-doubt and guilt. Character Neuroses dynamically are analogous to Symptom Neuroses.

E. MENTAL MECHANISMS AND CHARACTER TRAITS.—Mental mechanisms make substantial contributions to the development of character traits. Although this is doubtless true to varying degrees in the moulding of everyone's personality, it is more outstanding and more readily observed with some individuals. Likewise certain mechanisms are more prominent in making these contributions.

Some of these vital relationships have been commented on at greater length in the author's book *Mental Mechanisms* (*see* REFERENCES). Herein we see in more detail the ways in which such mechanisms as Identification, Compensation, and Sublimation can contribute in determining character structure.

2. *Genesis of Obsessive Character Traits*

A. ANALYSIS VALUABLE.—Many physicians are only gradually coming to think of the obsessive traits as important psychologic phenomena. They are actually of a very high level of importance to the individual's potential social and professional development, as well as to his personal well-being. In effect, one can compare the great self-limitation and sacrifice which one sees imposed upon a given individual by a gross symptom of Somatic Conversion, and less dramatically by certain other psychopathologic manifestations, to the sequelae of hypertrophied character defenses.

The analysis of character defenses when they have served, often as an unwitting handicap, is of great potential usefulness to many people. It is a process which is likely to undergo considerable further development and wider application. By this means of study, the genesis of the individual character defenses becomes apparent in successful instances. Only through such a thoroughgoing process can the underlying intrapsychic need for them become substantially diminished.

B. TRAITS ASSIST AND HANDICAP.—A further clinical example concerning the obsessive group of character defenses might prove useful at this point in helping us increase our understanding of their operation. In the following interesting instance the most marked traits of a certain businessman were those of obstinacy, parsimony, and perfectionism. There was also a rather marked degree of rigidity of personality, with a resistance to any kind of change. In addition, the patient was a very inhibited person emotionally. As we shall observe, in an intriguing sequence, his traits first assisted, and later handicapped him.

Case 62

The Analysis of Obsessive Personality Traits: An Obsessive Character Reaction

(1) Constellation of defenses becomes apparent

The patient, a thirty-six-year-old production manager of a small manufacturing plant, had been under intermittent medical treatment for a year for chronic constipation. His physician observantly came to note the presence of certain rather characteristic obsessive personality traits. These had become more apparent during their professional association, as he had learned to know his patient better. Consultation with a psychiatrist was recommended, with the hope that a character analysis might prove feasible. The patient followed through, but entered therapy with reservations and considerable reluctance. Gradually and fortunately, it became possible to increasingly enlist his interest and commitment.

This hard-working young executive early discussed the problems in his relationship with the company president. Part of the difficulty appeared to be a conflict between the latter's interest in quantity production, and the younger man's own considerable and personal needs for perfection of detail and precision of workmanship.

(2) Character analysis facilitated and also complicated

The author was impressed with his qualities of superior intelligence and the maintenance of high personal standards. He was usually characterized by his careful, well-chosen dress, precise habits, and evidence of a certain rigidity of manner and thinking. During the trial period of treatment (two months) it became clear that the rigidity included a resistance to the acceptance of new ideas or to change. There was also present a certain obstinacy in his opposition to following suggestions from others. This applied to all phases of living, at home and socially, as well as at work. Inevitably all of these factors appeared also, and played important roles in both facilitating and complicating the work of treatment.

He was uncomfortable if prevented from religiously following his daily practice of taking two thorough shower baths, with several complete changes of clothing. His family relationships were rather distant. During early phases of treatment relatively little was learned about either his immediate family or his earlier family interrelations. There was a distinct and handicapping parsimoniousness. This extended into his business operations. The fact that the latter did not involve his own funds made no appreciable difference.

It is evident that certain of his traits (that is, thoroughness, conscientiousness, intelligence, application, serious endeavor, and precision) could facilitate the work of character analysis. Others (for example, rigidity, obstinacy, overcaution, restricted freedom of thinking, and need to control by withholding) necessarily complicated and prolonged the process.

(3) Anal character traits

Reference is sometimes made by psychiatrists to "anal character traits," thus denoting primarily: (1) their earlier origins in this particular stage of infantile training and development [Ch.6:VB*1*], and (2) their possible relation to present or past patterns of bowel function. Our awareness of this helped point up the relation between this patient's problem with constipation and his character traits. (We shall comment further about these relationships later in this chapter, and also in our further study of some of the dynamics of the Obsessive Reactions.)

The referring physician had happily been aware of the possibility of such relationships. He had been alert to the possible presence of just such traits which, upon closer observation, were amply confirmed as comprising part of our executive's characterologic armor. Incidentally, the title of the patient's job, "production manager," and the difficulties he experienced in it, are of interest in view of their possible anal implications!

(4) Reverse effects upon business success

Prior to his promotion to this position. This man's interest in detail, his rigidity, and his needs for precision had contributed substantially to the development of excellent, carefully-engineered new products. The firm had prospered. As one important consequence, his promotion followed. However, in his new role, where in some contrast his job was to expedite production and increase its quantity, these same traits worked in reverse! Understandably they partially handicapped him and hampered the business.

As might be expected, this patient was highly self-critical. This proved to be partly a direct reflection of his harsh, overdeveloped conscience (that is, superego) and partly an inversion of hidden, disowned aggressive and punitive attitudes toward others. The latter process is similar to the inversion of hostility which has been earlier illustrated in our study of depression. The obstinacy, which at times amounted to perversity, was an immature and vestigial carryover of an infantile power mechanism.

The control exercised in this withholding manner was intended to combat the anxiety-provoking feelings of helplessness. His need for physical, bodily cleanliness proved to have symbolic meanings, related to important inner needs for and concerns over, moral cleanliness. The purity of his body gained through bathing thus had to some extent come symbolically to equate the moral purity of soul.

(5) Therapeutic benefits substantial

This is necessarily a fragmentary summary of a few facets of the complex genesis of several of his outstanding character traits. The patient and the author collaborated intensively for more than four years, to work out many of the hidden aspects of his personality development. This gentleman was able to make some substantial readjustments, as his understanding progressed. In direct proportion his defensive needs for precision, rigidity, and overcaution lessened.

His work performance and his professional relationships also improved markedly. As an added tangential but significant economic benefit to the business, the production rate per employee increased, and the plant further expanded. These facts doubtless reflected to some extent a lessening of his own personal overdeveloped needs for rigidity and precision. Family relationships became closer, fuller, and more satisfying.

As in the foregoing case, a thorough and successful study and analysis of whatever character defenses may have been evolved, is invariably followed by certain constructive modifications. As the needs underlying their defensive motivations and intent come more into conscious awareness, the traits themselves diminish. Their hypertrophied aspects come in turn into a constructive, more normal focus.

C. TENACIOUS DEFENSES; INTERESTING COROLLARY OF SECONDARY DEFENSE CONCEPT.—Since the underlying psychologic needs are powerful and tenacious, character defenses are formed which are clung to desperately. These are not surrendered readily in whole or in part without great struggle. This is true despite the fact that character traits in their overdevelopment are often psychologically uneconomic. To the objective observer, they are often seen to be seriously handicapping and defeating. Their development is in response to strong psychologic defensive needs, which are out of conscious awareness.

It is indeed not surprising that *in the very instances where character defenses (or clinical symptoms) are most exaggerated and most personally defeating, they are often held onto the most tenaciously and desperately.* This is exactly what we would expect in accord with our important Concept of Secondary Defense.

This is an interesting corollary, pointing out that often enough *the level* √ *of secondary defense (or a symptom or trait) parallels the level of self-defeat* which it engenders. This is the *Concept of Symptom Defense-Defeat Parallel.*

3. Parents Encourage Development of Similar Traits in Children

A. BELIEF IN HEREDITARY ORIGINS OUTMODED.—There is a tendency in their child-training for the parents to encourage, tacitly or actively, in their children the recapitulation of their own (parental) traits. Parents and other significant persons exert all kinds of both conscious and unwitting influence upon character development. The old and often accurate sayings, "Like father, like son," and "Like mother, like daughter" can have considerable foundation in fact.

This observation, however, was another, albeit misguided, reason advanced in support of the presently-outmoded ideas and beliefs about the presumed inheritance of character elements. These were long in vogue. There exists, also, of course, the potential for reaction formation, which can lead to the development of reversed traits.

Parents with obsessive traits thus may tend to encourage the development of obsessive traits in their children. This often transpires completely unwittingly. Parents are also likely to be pleased by the emergence of traits which to them indicate early evidence of maturity, or which make them "a chip off the old block." Certain obsessive traits are in this fashion encouraged and welcomed. Their possible overdefinition or hypertrophy in response to this, is what becomes a matter of concern or even pathology. This is in line with our *Concept of Interpersonal Perpetuation,* in contrast to an outmoded belief in hereditary perpetuation.

The evolvement and formation of character traits is a highly complex process. Personality "is moulded by the varied sequence of experience—by all the relationships effected, whatever their nature," according to Brierley.*

B. HABIT PATTERNS OF REACTION.—The early childhood formation of habit patterns of reactions and feeling is hardly surprising. The elaboration and adoption of habits in one's activity and in his behavior is a matter of

---

* Brierley also pointed out the interdependence of personal and social conditions. Sullivan stressed the importance of interpersonal relations in emotional development. Abrahams and Varon in an interesting piece of group analytic research pointed out "the dovetailing of the defenses of mother and daughter . . ." Klein related obsessional defenses to manic defenses, to paranoid anxieties, and as a result of failure of "the act of reparation."

considerable convenience, and these tend to be more or less universally employed. Children early demonstrate repetitive activity in play and in relationships. Later these become quite complex. Sometimes in childhood a small action is repeated over and over again for its effect, or as a test of response. The first time it was performed it may have evoked an amused or pleased response. Although this quickly faded, the child may repeat the performance again and again, literally "running it into the ground."

There is little doubt that such repetitive activity is somehow gratifying to the child. Related to this is the "just like before" demand, made for the adult to *exactly* repeat a story or a game. Childhood repetitions if they prove sufficiently useful can become response-patterns. Later habit patterns of reaction in adulthood can evolve in more complex, but analogous fashion.

C. BOWEL-HABIT TRAINING AND OBSESSIVE TRAITS.—Ferenczi early discussed the relationships of early bowel-habit training in infancy, to certain of the obsessive traits as observed in later adulthood. These relationships are important, but are sometimes not necessarily as absolute and definite as once thought. However, the foundations for traits of stubbornness, withholding, accumulating, and parsimoniousness, for example, can have important roots in the child-parent interaction which occurs at the time of bowel-training.

A continuing power struggle between parent and child at this time can have important repercussions personality-wise. Patterns of active or passive resistance, submissiveness, or rebellion, or combinations of these may have their earliest foundations first established during this era. These may be healthy or unhealthy. As established pathways, they are more readily continued or later reactivated. Once established however, later change is far more difficult. While we can only briefly refer to the important influences present, the degree of their later presence can be a direct reflection of the vicissitudes of the relationship between the parent and the child, particularly at this important stage in his personality development and character formation.

D. ABRAHAM'S ANAL CHARACTERISTICS.—Abraham first described a group of three obsessive character traits, which he related specifically to the anal phase of personality development as a consequence of his pioneering research. At this early juncture in personality development, these "anal characteristics," as he termed them, made their first appearance. He so included the three basic traits of orderliness, frugality, and obstinacy. These obsessive attributes in later life, represented a symbolic and partly-sublimated expression of what were originally antecedent ways of reaction, relating, and expression via the anal sphincter and bowel function in infancy.

In the infant, the first demands for control come from outside. First imposed upon a resisting ego, these demands gradually receive acquiescence, and come to be accepted. Eventually they are taken over, firmly adopted, and thence become an integral part of the self. One is likely to find that toilet training was begun too early and was too stringent in the Obsessive

Personality. Some measure of maturity-fixation at the anal-sadistic level (usually in the period of from one to three years of age) likely follows. Some traits also begin as partial reaction formations against a consciously-disowned anal-eroticism. Frequently a continuing conflict rages between defiance on the one hand, and submission on the other. This comprises our important concept of the non-resolution of the *Defiance-Submission Conflict* in the obsessive individual.

Preoccupation with anal function or with feces, or an increased interest in these at the time of toilet training, may be forcibly submerged as unacceptable. They may secure subsequent symbolic expression. This expression is in ways which are disguised and unavailable to conscious awareness or recognition. Occasionally one sees an increased interest along these lines carried over more directly into adult life. In the obsessional individual, however, these are often associated with shame and guilt. He may, for example, have a secret interest in the smell of his flatus or feces. He is likely to feel guilty or self-critical about this sort of thing. As a result he will attempt to stifle it, instead of possibly raising questions to himself such as how and why it is present, why it developed, and what purpose it might have been intended to serve. These kinds of questions are most legitimate and are indicated ones to raise about *any* given subject during the course of psychotherapy.

E. VICIOUS CIRCLE OF TRAIT-INTENSIFICATION.—Obsessively-oriented persons are inhibited, frustrated, and distant. These had their origins from external influences, but were gradually taken over and continued. For these reasons, however, these people have been denied many otherwise attainable satisfactions. They are going to react with feelings of resentment and with hate. A vicious circle may become established, which tends to prolong or to intensify the traits. This states an important concept concerning the elaboration of character defenses which we might term the Vicious Circle of Trait-Intensification. Outlined here in relation to obsessive traits, it applies to many diverse traits.

Thus, obsessive reactions may be segments of a vicious circle, in which a person "attempts" to defend against hate and its consequences, but inevitably and tragically only creates more. This view, of course, does not rule out other possible purposes, including the important defensive, albeit self-defeating, one of creating distance in personal relationships.

4. Applications Not Limited to Pathology; Program of Executive Development.

A. DIFFICULT TO SEE ONESELF CLEARLY.—Scholars historically, as well as psychiatrists, have noted the great difficulty in seeing one's self clearly. With exaggerated character defenses, in the various patterns of personality traits and behavior, the person concerned may be almost the last to see them. The King David Reaction illustrates one specific variety of just this problem.

This difficulty in securing an accurate self-picture also helps to convey the basic requirement for skilled assistance in seeking to do so. This is necessary in efforts to increase the accuracy of one's self-appraisal, and in securing recognition, understanding, and possible modification of personality traits.

B. STUDY OF "NORMAL" PERSONALITY TRAITS: EXPERIENCES IN GROUP TRAINING IN HUMAN RELATIONS.—Every personality is made up of a large group of character traits and defenses. Their relative harmony and balance is highly variable. So is the "psychologic net result" in so far as the individual is concerned. The fact that one's personality function is maintained on a high level of efficiency and effectiveness does not at all, of course, preclude the possibility of rather substantial benefits from character analysis. In other words, people do not have to be "sick" for gains to accrue. These can be substantial.

This was further illustrated for the author through five years of earlier experience in working with groups of federal executives. This was an interesting research project* in management development. In it groups of ten or twelve people from the higher administrative levels in a U.S. Government Department undertook to study themselves from an emotional standpoint. Four such groups were activated, each of which continued to meet together regularly over from two- to three-year periods. The project sought to promote greater competence in human relations, through increased self-study and observation. The groups functioned in a group analytic setting.

Participation required a degree of purposeful self-revelation certainly never approached in the usual administrative situation. As a result, there was an important selective process already operative at the time of the launching of each group. This in itself resulted in the preliminary elimination of the less secure candidates. The participants who volunteered, knowing what was to be required, thus were on a very high average level of emotional health at the very outset. The personal benefits resulting were secured through the gaining of improved self-understanding. Where modifications took place, they were largely in the realm of the personality attributes of the participants.

The application of our knowledge concerning character defenses is not necessarily limited to instances of their exaggeration, nor to psychopathology.

5. In Summary

To summarize, we have seen how overdevelopment of the same traits which are personally quite necessary to some extent, and which are often highly desirable and useful in our present culture, can impair personality integration, decrease individual effectiveness, interfere with interpersonal relations and to some extent with one's ability to secure satisfactions in living. When these untoward sequelae occur, the feasibility of character analysis should be explored.

The fine line has been noted earlier which is present between the normal and the psychopathologic. This observation holds even more particularly

---

* Sponsored by various bureaus and offices of the U. S. Department of Health, Education, and Welfare, and the National Institute of Mental Health (1947–1953).

when one is observing and studying personality traits. What can represent thrift for one person, for example, might well be considered parsimoniousness for or by another. It may be also useful to consider the formation of character traits generally, from the standpoint of their gradual evolutionary development on an individual basis. English suggested that one could perhaps envisage this in a number of gradual steps. We might outline five such progressive steps, as follows.

(1) *Parental influences and training.* (*See* First Tenet of Parental Role, Ch.1:IIIC; Ch.6:IA*1*.)

(2) *Social learning.* The gradual appreciation of what constitutes expected behavior, and how one meets and fits into socially-required patterns.

(3) *Incorporation* of the traits which develop as a consequence of steps 1 and 2, into one's ego structure so that they become personally useful traits.

(4) *Character Trait Hypertrophy.* These traits may subsequently become exaggerated or hypertrophied to the point where they are not longer useful in their overall net result. This is in response to increased personal needs, external stress, or both. This is in accord with our important Principle of Defense-Hypertrophy.

(5) *Character Reaction Established.* Progression may continue to the point where these traits become clearly handicapping, self-defeating, and neurotic. At this point a Character Reaction or Neurosis exists.

VII. OBSESSIVE PERSONALITY AND SEX

A. DEFENSIVE SEXUAL INHIBITION

1. Less Energy Available

The sexual attitudes and behavior of the Obsessive Personality are of sufficient moment to warrant some separate consideration. Although these particular effects of obsessiveness cannot be studied exhaustively due to space, a few brief comments may be useful. Their influences on sexual attitudes and on individual sexual functions of course may vary a great deal. They can be quite substantial.

As indicated earlier, this group of character defense traits have developed as part of the early desperate struggle to keep censored feelings out of any conscious recognition (that is, repressed). Naturally such defenses tend to be continued, in order to maintain the repression. With the absorption of energy in obsessive thinking and in obsessive activities, there is less of it available for libidinal attachments and for sexual outlets. This is one important basis for diminished sexual activity.

Sexual drives, feelings, and related conflictual material, in turn may also constitute an important part of the disowned unconscious data, which has contributed to the psychologic necessity for the development of obsessive traits in the first place. Defensive sexual inhibition can thus also receive an impetus on this basis.

2. All Affectivity Restricted

The normal and healthful expression of sexual drives may be under rigid control. This is because of the general inhibition of the personality, and also as a part of the overall restriction of affectivity. This phenomenon of inhibition is rather common to these persons [Ch.6:VG*1*]. It provides a third basis for the frequent sexual inhibitions of the Obsessive Personality.

As a result, it is not surprising to find a history of decreased sexual activity, or of apparently decreased sexual interests. Such inhibitions and restrictions, however, rarely serve as a matter of presenting complaint by the patient. This appears to be partially an unwitting reflection of his "satisfaction" with his emotional *status quo*.

3. Supermoralism

It is not surprising that a supermoralistic attitude about sex is sometimes present. This may develop as a reinforcement of the general inhibition. It may be present as a reinforcement of the defensive avoidance or denial of sexual interests, or of even any awareness of sexual matters.

Through such measures the individual may unconsciously attempt to enhance his control over his feared (and often consciously disowned) sexual impulses, or over his partner.

B. INHIBITIONS OF SEX AND AGGRESSION PARALLEL

The restricting and crippling emotional inhibitions of the obsessive person seldom are limited to one area alone. Sometimes they are inhibited unevenly, and at other times "across the board." In the following instance aggressive and sexual impulses were both strongly inhibited.

Case 63

Aggressive and Sexual Impulses Are Inhibited

A thirty-seven-year-old single businessman had entered therapy because of restrictive obsessive personality traits. These had influenced his personal and business relationships to such an extent that he could not engage in normal competition. He was literally loaded with guilt in relation to anything sexual *or* anything aggressive. These impulses were almost completely buried from his conscious awareness. Even a normal, protective degree of healthy self-assertiveness was lacking. Despite these handicaps, he had still been quite successful financially, as a result of several fortunate investments.

As a measure of the extent of his inhibitions, even his dreams were very restricted as to content. Never had he had a dream in which he took any aggressive action. Never had he had a dream containing an instance of successful competition with another person. This is another reflection of his generally inhibited attitudes in dealing with people. He could not even dream aggressively, let alone be aggressive while awake! He had never come close to a heterosexual act, let alone its completion. This too was reflected in his dreams! As he reported this inhibited attitude about sexual activity, "I can't even have intercourse in a dream!"

C. MARITAL RELATIONSHIPS; MARRIAGE NON-THERAPEUTIC IN EMOTIONAL ILLNESSES

Obsessive inhibitions in the sexual area do not suddenly dissolve as a consequence of a marriage. Indeed it is not possible to so dissolve them, and this should not be attempted. These may constitute a continuing powerful distance-promoting force. The development of marital disharmony is often enhanced. Accordingly, the physician should *never* advise marriage *as a therapeutic measure*. This caution has general application and is not limited necessarily to the Obsessive Personality, or to other character or neurotic reactions. Marriage can resolve some problems, but it can also produce new ones. These may well be far tougher ones than those resolved.

Intimate personal relationships are often restricted in the obsessive individual. This is reflected in marital relationships and in love-making. A variety of handicaps and interferences may appear in the latter. These may include such things as a distaste for caressing, for sexual foreplay, or for kissing. These may be "explained" (or rather rationalized) on the basis of esthetic or moral grounds, or upon standards of hygiene or personal cleanliness. There may well be difficulty in marriage in adjusting the sexual relations to any reasonable degree of mutual satisfaction. The ability to secure mutual simultaneous orgasm is often greatly restricted or lacking. Contrariwise there may be a compulsive insistence upon such achievement.

Strong moral scruples often also continue as an interference with sexual activity. The Obsessive Personality may suffer from undue guilt or shame, or be terribly concerned and overly fearful of the possible consequences of his sexual drives. Conflicts may be severe should there have been premarital sexual experiences. These comments also apply to earlier or continuing masturbatory activity.

The sexual drive may be strong, in some contrast to other types of emotional reactions, even though the expression or even awareness of the drive is inhibited by various elements of an over-developed superego. An unfavorable and disapproving attitude toward sex, when present, may vary all the way from one of "It's not nice", to one of loathing and disgust, or even revulsion.

VIII. COMPULSIVE OVEREATING

Most physicians recognize the very important adversary to good health implicit to compulsive overeating. The doctor prescribes dietary restrictions and then often has to struggle to try and secure their observance. This problem was briefly mentioned earlier [Ch.3:IVD*1; Ch.11:VIIB*1] in discussing the relation of anxiety to overeating.

An internist recently reported his despair over a cardiac patient whose persistent overweight threatened to contribute to his early demise. Explanations, urging, pleading, and even threats seemed to no avail. Despite the best obtainable efforts of patient and doctor, gains in combating the overweight were very small indeed. At intervals any weight lost was more than replaced. The physician felt helpless, as indeed he was. This patient's eating had followed a compulsive pattern in response to powerful internal psychologic needs.

Compulsive overeating is by no means infrequent. It can defeat the most carefully designed dietary regimen, and bring the sincere and conscientious physician to despair.

Unfortunately, there are no easy solutions in these situations. Sometimes the persons concerned simply have no interest at all in the constructive self-study of psychotherapy, or they may have to justify their fears and apprehensions concerning possible psychiatric treatment by various explanations and rationalizations. Fortunately, in occasional instances the patient's interest can be secured in at least granting a trial to a psychotherapeutic approach. This can be then promptly undertaken, whenever any existing somatic pathologic process is not already so far advanced as to be a contraindication, by virtue of the possibility of a dangerous exacerbation during treatment.

IX. TREATMENT

A. CHARACTER ANALYSIS

1. Treatment of Choice

Character Analysis is the term which will be increasingly used to describe the process, when the aim of the treatment is primarily the analysis of personality and character traits, as opposed to that of more specifically neurotic symptoms. Thus, Character Analysis, as noted earlier, may be defined as *the systematic, psychotherapeutic inquiry, study, and analysis of the personality defensive traits or character-equivalents, and the patterns or constellations of traits, of a given individual.* [Ch.5:IC2].

Through Character Analysis *one aims to elucidate and to resolve the underlying and initiating conflicts which are responsible for the elaboration of an individual's character defenses.* This process can be highly useful. An individual's assets can be enlisted. With obsessive persons, for example, their traits of persistence, application, and conscientiousness are very useful when applied to the hard work and necessary collaboration of investigative psychotherapy. Likewise, substantial benefits may accrue from therapy in many clinical instances of Obsessive-Compulsive Neurosis. The prognosis is increasingly guarded when the case is more firmly established, or of longer duration, and of greater severity.

Traits in other personality types can also help with the work of treatment, or hinder, or both. Further, as noted in the Concept of the *Inverse Ratio of Symptom Success, with Motivation toward Therapy* [Ch.1:IIA4; Ch.12:VG], the more effective the defense of the symptom or character-equivalent, the less motivation is likely to be present for entering treatment.

A body of knowledge has been accumulated during the past seventy years which places the experienced psychiatrist in a relatively advantageous position to assist this entire group of persons. These data, together with our recognition of the frequent high caliber of the person affected, and his high actual or potential level of social usefulness, multiply our medical responsibility. Making an accurate diagnosis and securing adequate treatment for suitable persons can be a worthwhile and highly rewarding endeavor.

Character Reactions in which the manifestations are confined to character traits can, of course, still represent marked psychopathology. In the more severe instances these can be sufficiently inhibiting, and personally, socially, and professionally handicapping so as to equal a severe neurosis as to the level of disturbance, handicap, and pathology. The terms "Character Reaction" or "Neurosis" for the difficulty, and "Character Analysis" for its intensive (analytic) treatment, are indeed appropriate. Character Analysis is the treatment of choice in the Character Reactions.

2. Relationship-Improvement Precept

Our discussion thus far makes this an appropriate time to mention an important precept governing the direction and the progression of close personal relationships. It applies particularly to marital and family relationships, especially significant ones, but is likely to have implications for any given relationship. Thus, *to improve a relationship, both parties must want to, and must work at it.*

The relative presence or absence of such an interest and the resulting efforts by each party will determine whether the relationship will be maintained, will develop and improve, or will deteriorate.

To stress the foregoing rather basic concept, the recognition of which can be very significant in psychotherapy, the writer proposes referring to it as the *Precept of Relationship-Improvement.*

B. REFERRAL: ADVANTAGEOUS POSITION OF PHYSICIANS

Many physicians, whether they be general practitioners or specialists, enjoy an unusually close position in their relationship to their patients and to their patients' families. The physician is often accorded a unique role as a friend, counselor, and advisor. This may extend far beyond the more narrow limits of guidance as to physical health. This position is one of great privilege, and is also a serious responsibility.

The physician may well constitute the only contact the patient and his family have with one who is in a position to possess much knowledge about emotional health. It may be he alone who is able to recognize the early signs of an impending serious emotional disorder, the symptoms of a neurosis, or the unhealthy and self-defeating accentuation of defensive character traits. His ability and knowledge may well represent the *only* chance the one who consults him has to secure any real help.

The physician's ability to recognize the presence of limiting and handicapping personality traits, alone can be a most useful and important medical function. The potential results to persons from selective referral for character study and therapy may be actually greater than in those benefits which might accrue to some from referral for the management of the more disturbing and serious emotional illnesses.

The recognition and diagnosis are often easier, and the need for help is often more readily apparent to the patient and his family, in the more severe cases of emotional illness. Diagnosis and referral in cases of distorted and exaggerated personality traits however, can be a greater challenge to proper medical management. In some of these situations the physician can be of added substantial help through a properly constructive utilization of his special relationship and position. This is a good vantage point for the observation and recognition of self-defeating character defenses. It is also an asset in gaining an acceptance from his patient of the prospect of intensive personality study, in instances in which this is indicated and feasible.

C. INDICATIONS FOR TREATMENT

Treatment is indicated when any character traits are sufficiently marked or have developed out of their proper perspective, and have become handicapping. They may be a matter of concern to the individual affected, provided he is at least aware of them. They may also be a source of concern to family, physician, friends, and professional or business associates. Consultation with an experienced psychotherapist can determine the potential results of treatment.

Treatment must be investigative to achieve success. Patient and psychiatrist must work together to determine the psychologic needs which necessitated the development of various character defensive traits. Actually, some of this is inevitably a part of every successful psychoanalysis, regardless of the emotional condition originally present. When indicated and feasible, psychotherapy for the various groups of character defenses can be very successful and gratifying to both parties concerned.

Substantial, definitive benefits are unlikely to be achieved however, on a short-term or nonintensive basis. Character defenses have developed in response to internal and hidden, powerful psychologic needs. As a consequence, they have become an integral part of each individual. They operate automatically and are largely out of conscious voluntary control. They cannot be removed surgically as we might amputate an extremity, or by logic, or by force. They can only be modified voluntarily by the individual concerned when, through greater insight, he is ready, willing, and able to forego some of the underlying psychologic needs. He eventually must have the choice of something better, in accord with our *Concept of the Therapeutic Bargain* [Ch.10:XA1; Ch.12:VIIIC1].

D. CAUTIONS IN OBSESSIVE TRAIT THERAPY

Several points might be made concerning some of the technical matters in the treatment of obsessive patients. Many obsessive patients respond poorly to suggestion. If anything, they are the reverse of suggestible. To urge or to push them in therapy is apt to defeat one's aim. Rather automatically and perversely they are likely to simply push back in the reverse direction!

We might also note at this point the rather regular tendency of these people to displace their concerns onto what appears objectively to be relative trifles. This accounts for the great amount of piffle with which these patients may often clutter up their interviews. Awareness of the nature of the defense being used can result in cutting this down.

It is also perhaps generally recognized, but too often by-passed in discussions of therapy, that in addition to insight, there is a need for the patient to develop new patterns of reaction and response. These new emotional patterns do not always come into being simply through the removal of the preexisting, handicapping patterns. They must also be developed and evolved. An attitude of acceptance and judicious encouragement here on the part of the therapist can be most healthful.

A final point may be made concerning the relation of obsessive character defenses and psychotic episodes. Careful history not infrequently will disclose that certain patients who have succumbed to manic-depressive or schizophrenic episodes have previously functioned reasonably well by means of obsessive defenses, and appear to have become psychotic only because and after these defenses have utterly failed. Hill added: "On the other end of this reaction, it is our frequent experience that patients recovering from either of these disorders do so by way of the reestablishment of their obsessive mechanisms. I have a feeling that, short of very extensive psychotherapy which would be needed to analyze these psychotic patients, what is practical to do frequently is to help them to reestablish their obsessive characters."

More comments on the treatment of the Obsessive-Compulsive Reactions will follow in the next chapter.

X. SUMMARY

Personality traits account for individuality. They develop as part of the defensive or characterologic armor, and may overdevelop in response to increasing needs or stresses. The overdevelopment or exaggeration of one or more of a group of what we might call *character defenses* constitutes a *Character Reaction* or a Character Neurosis. Recognition of the importance to an individual of this progression and its universality leads to a quiet revolution in psychiatric concepts and therapy. Character traits may be regarded as *character-equivalents* to more clear-cut Neurotic Symptoms, or as "symptom equivalents." The *Principle of Defense-Hypertrophy* points out how the same defensive traits which are quite useful to a point, can progress far beyond this optimal juncture, to result in a net of greater or lesser self-defeat and psychopathology for the individual concerned.

Abraham first described three basic obsessive traits. Reich introduced the major concept of character neurosis. Diagnosis on a descriptive basis offers certain advantages. Character neuroses are analogous to but are to be distinguished from what we accordingly might term the *Symptom Neuroses*. Three major patterns or *constellations* of character defenses were outlined: The Obsessive, Conversion (hysterical), and Depressive Personalities. The respective three patterns of Character Reactions were also indicated.

Estimates of the high incidence of the Character Reactions (18–20 per cent of neurotic reactions) were offered, together with a tabular estimation of the clinical incidence of all types of neurotic reactions (*Table 16*). Under the section on clinical features a major subsection was devoted to each of the three, more readily delineated, major groups, and one section to eight remaining "minor" ones. A concept of Outward Reversal of Appearance in the obsessively-oriented person was noted. The *Obsessive Facade* often hides the patient's inner doubts and insecurities. The *Concept of the Personal Yardstick* received reference, as being a personal psychologic measuring device of great variation in accuracy, which is commonly over utilized by the Obsessive Personality. It is to an extent universal in its employment by people.

The ways in which the Defense of Pessimism operates is illustrative of the more or less analogous defensive intent of other personality traits. An *Hypothesis of Developmental Influences on Mental Capabilities* was offered. The Obsessive Personality tends to view the world through his "obsessively tinted glasses." He may well belong in the so-called group of *Black-or-White People*.

Reference was made to the major *Concept of the Secondary Defense* of emotional manifestations. Sexual maladjustment is often *the effect, in distinction to being the cause,* of emotional illnesses or reactions. One may properly speak of maintaining the *status quo* of adjustment, and of the "level" of depression, anxiety, or of other emotional manifestations. The role of the character defense in combating the danger of *de*repression was noted. Our *Attention Hypothesis* points out the automatic factors which help to determine the direction of one's focus of attention and concern. Casual, Soterial, Hygeiaphrontic, Antiseptic, Anxious, and several other patterns or constellations of Personality were noted, as was the Impulsive Character Personality.

Character traits develop in analogous fashion to the more marked clinical symptoms of neuroses. Each one is a defensive endeavor. They evolve automatically and gradually, in response to intrapsychic needs. The *cultural vogue* influences the development of various traits so "selected" and encouraged, and the evolvement of constellations of traits. Parents and other significant persons exert all kinds of both conscious and unwitting influences upon character development. The Concept of Interpersonal Perpetuation stresses this, in an important distinction to older views of hereditary factors. *Overdevelopment of the same traits which can be necessary, constructive, and useful, can turn them instead into ones which are handicapping, self-defeating,* limiting, and non-constructive, in accord with the *Defense-Hypertrophy Principle*.

The fierceness and tenacity of one's Secondary Defense *of* a symptom or character trait, often roughly parallels the self-defeat it engenders. Thus, as a corollary of our conception of Secondary Defense, *the level of such defense (of an emotional manifestation), more or less parallels the level of self-defeat which the given clinical symptom or trait has engendered.* This is the *Symptom Defense-Defeat Parallel Concept.* The Obsessive Personality and Sex as a topic, was discussed briefly, as was the challenging subject of Compulsive Overeating. Character Analysis was discussed, as the treatment of choice in our approach to exaggerated character traits, patterns, and the Character Reactions. Indications for treatment were noted, and a *Precept of Relationship-Improvement* outlined.

XI. SELECTED REFERENCES AND BIBLIOGRAPHY

ABRAHAM, K. (1940). Three papers in: Jones, E. Ed.: *Selected Papers on Psychoanalysis,* pp. 137, 248, 418. London: Hogarth.

—(1955). The Influence of Oral Erotism on Character Formation (1924), In: *Selected Papers on Psychoanalysis.* New York, Basic Books.

ABRAHAMS, J., and VARON, E. (1953). *Maternal Dependency and Schizophrenia,* p. 240. New York; International Universities Press.

ALEXANDER, FRANZ (1930). "The Neurotic Character." *Int. J. Psychoanalysis,* **11,** 292.

BARTON, WALTER E. (May, 1954). Personal communication.

GELLAK, LEOPOLD (1961). "Personality Structure in a Changing World." *Arch. Gen. Psychiat.,* **5,** 183.

BLEULER, E. P. (1951). *Textbook of Psychiatry,* p. 563. 4th ed., translated by A. A. Brill. New York; Dover Publications.

BRICKNER, JOHN (1963). "Interactions of Psychoanalysis and Religion," unpublished paper, delivered to the Eastern Psychoanalytic Assn., Washington, D. C. (June 27).

BRIERLEY, M. (1951). *Trends in Psychoanalysis,* p. 181. London: Hogarth Press.

CAPPON, DANIEL (June, 1954). Personal communication.

CHODOFF, PAUL, and LYONS, HENRY (1958). "Hysteria, the Hysterical Personality and 'Hysterical' Conversion." *Amer. J. Psychiat.,* **114,** 8.

COLERIDGE, S. T. "The Rime of the Ancient Mariner."

COMMITTEE ON NOMENCLATURE AND STATISTICS (1952). *Diagnostic and Statistical Manual.* Washington, D.C., American Psychiatric Association.

CORIAT, I. E. (1924). "The Character Traits of Urethral Erotism." *Psychiat. Rev.,* **11,** 426.

DEUTSCH, H. (1951). *Psychoanalysis of the Neuroses,* pp. 206–208. London; Hogarth Press.

ENGLISH, O. SPURGEON (July, 1954). Personal communication.

FENICHEL, O. (1945). *The Psychoanalytic Theory of Neurosis,* pp. 268–310. New York; Norton.

FERENCZI, S. (1950). *Sex in Psychoanalysis,* p. 319. New York; Basic Books.

FRANKLIN, BENJAMIN. Maxims prefixed to *Poor Richard's Almanac.*

FRIEDLANDER, K. (1945). "Formation of the Anti-Social Character." In: *The Psychoanalytic Study of the Child,* Vol. 1, pp. 189–204. New York; International Universities Press.

FREUD, S. (1896). "Further Remarks on the Defense Neuro-Psychoses." In: *Collected Papers,* Vol. 1, p. 155. London; Hogarth.

—(1943). *A General Introduction to Psycho-Analysis,* p. 229. Garden City; Garden City Publishing Co.

—(1913). "Predisposition to Obsessional Neurosis." In: *Collected Papers,* Vol. 2, p. 131. London; Hogarth.

—(1915). "Some Character-Types Met with in Psychoanalytic Work." In: *Collected Papers,* Vol. 4, p. 318. New York; Basic Books.

—(1908). "Character and Anal Erotism." In: *Collected Papers,* Vol. 2, p. 44. New York; Basic Books.

GLOVER, E. (1926). "The Neurotic Character." *Int. J. Psychiat.,* **7,** 11.

—(1925). "Notes on Oral Character Formation." *Int. J. Psychiat.,* **6,** 131.

—(1948). Chapter in: Lorand, S., Ed., *Psychoanalysis Today,* p. 223. New York; International Universities Press.

HENDRICK, I. (1936). Ego Development and Certain Character Problems. *Psychiat. Quart.,* **5,** 320.

HILL, LEWIS B. (June, 1954). Personal communication.

JACOBS, HASKELL (1952). *Better Human Relations Through Group Analysis—A Group of Executive Reports on Their Experience.* Div. Personnel Management, U. S. Fed. Sec. Agency (in Dept. H.E.W.).

JONES, E. (1913). "Anal-Erotic Character Traits." In: *Papers on Psychoanalysis. New York;* Wood.

KLEIN, M. (1950). *Contributions to Psychoanalysis,* p. 318. London; Hogarth Press.

LAUGHLIN, H. P. (1954). "The Obsessive Personality: The Clinical and Dynamic Features of the Obsessive Character Defenses." *Med. Ann. D. C.,* **23,** 202.

—(1953). "Depression." *Med. Ann. D. C.* **22,** 653.

—(1954). "King David's Anger." *Psychiat. Quart.,* **23,** 87; *J. Pastoral Care,* **8,** 147; *Digest Neurol. & Psychiat.* **22,** 207.

—(1954). "Executive Seminars in Human Relations in the U. S. Government: A Group Approach to Management Improvement." *Int. J. Group Psychother.,* **4,** 165.

—(1963). *Mental Mechanisms.* Washington; Butterworth.

MICHAELS, J. J. (1959). "Character Structure and Character Disorders." In: Arieti, S.: *American Handbook of Psychiatry,* Vol. 1, Pt. 2, p. 353. New York; Basic Books.

—(1955). *Disorders of Character.* Springfield; CC Thomas.

NEINBURG, H. (1956). "Character and Neurosis." *Int. J. Psychiat.,* **37,** 36.

NOYES, ARTHUR P. (June, 1954). Personal communication.

REICH, W. (1945). *Character Analysis,* 2nd Ed. New York; Orgone Institute Press.

—(1928). "Uber Charakteranalyse." *Int. Zeitsch. Psychoanal.,* **15.**

SAUL, LEON J. (1910). *Emotional Maturity,* 2nd Ed. Philadelphia; Lippincott.

SKEELS, H. M. (1955). National Institute of Mental Health, Bethesda, Md. Cited by *Chicago Daily News Service.* 1/28/55.

SMILES, SAMUEL (1812–1904). "Thrift."

STERBA, R. (1950). "Character and Resistance." *Psychiat. Quart.,* **20,** 72.

STEVENSON, GEORGE S. (May, 1954). Personal communication.

SULLIVAN, H. S. (1953). *The Interpersonal Theory of Psychiatry.* New York; Norton.

WESTPHAL, C. F. A. (1878). *Arch. Psychiat.,* **8,** 735.

WHITE, W. A. (1935). *Outlines of Psychiatry,* p. 103. New York; Nervous and Mental Disease Monographs.

XII. REVIEW QUESTIONS

1. What is a character defense? A *constellation* of character traits?

2. What is a *Character Neurosis?* Distinguish from a *Symptom Neurosis.*

3. Discuss the progression from character defense to Character Neurosis. What does the Defense-Hypertrophy Principle stress?

4. What is meant: by character traits being *symptom-equivalents?* By Character Analysis?

5. What is the Obsessive Personality? Give ten of the more typical traits.

6. Outline the Conversion character type. The Depressive Personality.

7. What are the social, economic, occupational and professional advantages of obsessive character traits? What is the possible "outward reversal of appearance" sometimes to be observed in obsessively-oriented persons?

8. Explain:
   (*a*) Cultural Vogue, in the evolvement of character traits.
   (*b*) Obsessive Facade.
   (*c*) Personal Yardstick Concept.
   (*d*) Defense of Pessimism.
   (*e*) Hypothesis of Developmental Influences in Mental Capacities.
   (*f*) Obsessively-tinted glasses.
   (*g*) "Black-or-White People."

9. What is the Secondary Defense of the emotional manifestation?

10. How do parental influences play a role in the development of character defense? How is the Concept of Interpersonal Perpetuation useful?

11. What is meant by the *status quo* of adjustment?

12. Outline four additional, "minor" personality types.

13. How can sexual maladjustment represent effect, as distinguished from cause, in emotional illnesses?

14. What is the Attention Hypothesis?

15. Why might the Secondary Defense *of* a symptom, parallel its level of self-defeat?

16. Discuss Character Analysis. What is the Relationship-Improvement Precept?

CHAPTER 6

THE OBSESSIVE— COMPULSIVE REACTIONS

.... Defensively Elaborated Patterns of Reaction Marked by the Intrusion of Insistent, Repetitive, and Unwelcome Thoughts or Urges

I. INTRODUCTION
  A. Deprivation of Love, Affection, and Acceptance
      1. Association with Emotional Illness; 2. Obsessive Persons Very Susceptible to Anxiety
  B. Definitions
      1. Obsessions and Compulsions; 2. Insistent, Repetitive, and Unwelcome
  C. Substitution of Something Less Disturbing; Concept of Preoccupation-Defense

II. HISTORY
  A. La Maladie du Doute
      1. Esquirol and Falret; 2. Morel, Westphal, Freud, and Janet; Psychiatry Participates in Medical Renaissance
  B. Pioneering Work in Psychodynamics
      1. Repression and Displacement; 2. Transference; 3. Disowned Sexual and Aggressive Impulses

III. INCIDENCE AND DIAGNOSIS
  A. Frequency of Obsessive Reactions
      1. Estimated Twelve Per Cent; 2. Increased Percentages Found; 3. Severe Obsessions
  B. Diagnosis
      1. Making the Diagnosis; 2. Illustrations; 3. Obsessions, Phobias, and Hygeiaphrontis (hypochondriasis)

IV. SYMPTOMS AND CLINICAL FEATURES
  A. Obsessive Trends, Character Defenses, Neurotic Symptoms, and Certain

Psychotic Manifestations Related
      1. Character Defenses and Obsessive Symptoms; 2. Psychosis Can Follow Collapse of Obsessive Defenses
  B. Aggressiveness and Hostility in Obsessive Individuals
      1. Defiant Rebellion→Guilty Remorse → Expiatory Reparation; 2. Constructive and Destructive Aggression; Healthful Self-assertiveness
  C. Inhibition and Control
      1. Parent-Child Relationships Determine Degree and Adequacy; 2. Control of Emotions and Behavior; Principle of Inhibition; 3. To Outside World Obsessive Person Reserved, Model Citizen; 4. Obsessive Recurrent Thoughts about Harming a Family Member
  D. Clinical Findings
      1. Typical Obsessive Picture; An "I-Should Person"; 2. Obsessive Symptomatology Outlined
  E. Lessened Capacity for Affection and Love
      1. Partially Pretense and Facade; 2. Principle of Inhibition; R.I.G.I.D. Person Concept; 3. In Sexual Relationships; 4. Sexual Maladjustments; Concept of Effect-in-Distinction-from-Cause in Emotional Illness
  F. Vulnerability and Distance-Promoting; Overcritical Attitudes
      1. Major Influence on Personal Relationships; 2. Obsessive Vicious Circle Concept in Relationships; 3. Lack of Spontaneity

G. Important Added Features of Obsessive Person
1. Low Level of Self-Esteem; 2. Childhood Manifestations; 3. Parental Attitudes Favor Obsessiveness; 4. Importance of Detail; 5. Perfectionism: The "Just-So" Defense; 6. Compulsions Accompany Obsessive Thinking

V. ADDITIONAL PSYCHODYNAMIC CONSIDERATIONS

A. Onset of Obsessive Symptoms

B. Interaction Between Parent and Child
1. Establishment of Precedent; 2. Responses and Counter Responses; Profitable - Patterns Concept; 3. Parental Emphasis on Control

C. Impulses and Wishes Dangerous and Threatening; Come to be Equated with Actual Event
1. Anger Toward Parental Figures; 2. Rejection; Need to Appear Friendly

D. Obsessive Dilemma
1. Vital Object Threatened; 2. Symptom Endeavors to Protect

E. Predisposing Factors to Developing Obsessive Defenses

F. Important Mechanisms in Obsessive Reactions
1. First Line of Defense Concept; 2. Displacement and Substitution; 3. King David Reaction; Obsessive Symptoms Related to Repressed Data

G. Obsessive Defenses and Sex
1. Sexual Inhibition and Control; Sexual Influence on Content; 2. Brill's Illustration; Bleuler and Freud

H. Additional Factors in Obsessive Patterns
1. Obsessive Doubting; 2. Vulnerability; Concept of Relationship - Distance Defense; Difficulty in Saying "No"; Obsessive Facade; 3. Hand-in-Glove Analogy and Principle in Relationships; 4. Similar Dynamics in Depressions and Obsessions

VI. COMPULSIVE RITUALS

A. Repetitive and Ritualistic
1. Compulsions are Acts, and Urges to Act; 2. Childhood Rituals; 3. Neurotic Compulsive Ritual

B. Security Operations: S.O.
1. Patterns in Living; Religious Rites; 2. Obsessive Preoccupation with Religion, and Health; 3. Compulsive Security Rituals; C.S.R.

VII. THE IMPULSIONS
A. Definitions
1. Repetitive Series of Irresistable, Usually Anti-Social Acts; 2. Further Distinctions between Compulsion and Impulsion; 3. "Acting Out" of Hostility and Sex; Social-Defiance; 4. Punishment and Remorse

B. Types of Impulsions
1. The More Common Impulsions; 2. Kleptomania

C. Problems in Management and Therapy of the Impulsive Individual
1. Five Principles of Impulsions; 2. Therapy, Resistance, and the Secondary Defense of the Impulsion; 3. Treatment Rarely Sought; More Rarely Successful

VIII. TREATMENT
A. Know Thyself
1. Derepression Necessary; 2. Accurate Self-Appraisal a Valuable Asset; 3. Emotional Understanding; 4. Team-Work Tenet in Psychotherapy

B. Recognition and Referral
1. Major and Laudable Accomplishment; 2. Early Therapy Advantageous

C. The Treatment of Choice
1. Four Major Hurdles; 2. Problems Encountered in Intensive Treatment of Obsessive Patients; 3. The Tracing Technique in Therapy; 4. Premature Interpretations or Speculations Avoided

D. Therapeutic Problem of Obsessive Patient
1. Obsessive Patient Inhibited and a Conformist; 2. In His "Hard-pressed Position" Obsessive Patient Maintains Triple Defense; 3. Frozen State

E. Results of Therapy

F. Contrast in Ministerial Counsel
1. Crucial Position of "Respected Person" From Whom Counsel Sought; 2. Major Consequences Follow Contrasting Responses When Help Sought

IX. SUMMARY

X. SELECTED REFERENCES AND BIBLIOGRAPHY

XI. REVIEW QUESTIONS ON THE OBSESSIVE-COMPULSIVE REACTIONS

I. INTRODUCTION

A. DEPRIVATION OF LOVE, AFFECTION, AND ACCEPTANCE

1. Association with Emotional Illness

A DEPRIVATION of real love, affection, and acceptance, especially in the early years of life, is commonly associated with cases of emotional illness. A vital factor in the initial emotional security of the child, and indeed in his subsequent healthy maturation is for him to be a welcome arrival. Conception may be the result of careful planning.

In many cases, on the other hand, conception simply happens. This distinction does not necessarily *have* to be important from a mental health standpoint. In the event that conception has been unplanned, the months of pregnancy can provide a useful interval for the prospective parents, especially when they are reasonably well adjusted themselves. These months provide the opportunity (when necessary) to reconcile any conflicts or problems over the prospective new addition to the family. In most instances the child is welcomed and loved. This is part of what we can call the *proper emotional climate,* as referred to earlier in the *First Tenet of the Parental Role* [Ch.1:IIIC], through which the parent constructively facilitates the child's maturation.

In instances of emotional disturbance, a deprivation of love and affection is frequently experienced subjectively, and reported in therapy. It may have been objectively realistic, largely subjective only, or some combination of both. However, the author has never worked intensively with a patient with obsessive manifestations who was not in some measure actually deprived of love, affection, and acceptance in his early life. In an informal survey this observation was supported without exception by the opinions of a small group of the author's colleagues, whose cumulative psychiatric experience at the time, however, was well in excess of 100 years.

2. Obsessive Persons Very Susceptible to Anxiety

This chapter is a direct continuation of the discussion which began with the Obsessive group of character defenses in *Chapter 5.* These discussions accordingly are to be considered together as a unit. This group of reactions make up one important type of the indirect manifestations and ultimate effects of anxiety (*see Table 1, page 20*), in which one may think of the anxiety and its consequences as being converted into or expressed in psychologic terms.

The obsessive person may feel extremely vulnerable in many situations. He is very susceptible to anxiety. He may feel threatened by almost anyone, although this may be hardly apparent to others or sometimes even to himself, as we shall stress further. In his desperate unconscious efforts to ward off anxiety, an obsessive pattern of psychologic defenses has been erected.

One important direction of the attempted protection is in the vital realm of interpersonal relationships. The obsessive individual may feel threatened

by the other person in almost any interpersonal situation. Obsessive manifestations can develop as a consequence. They tend to maintain and to
promote protectively-intended distance in interpersonal relationships.

B. DEFINITIONS

1. Obsessions and Compulsions

✓   An obsession can be defined as *an unwanted but repetitive thought which
intrudes rather imperatively into conscious awareness. Highly charged
with unconscious emotional significance, it recurs against the conscious
wishes of the individual. Unconsciously elaborated, it is a defensively-intended endeavor. Characteristically, an obsessive thought is insistent, recurrent, and intrusive.*

Obsessive neurotic thoughts may include, for example, repetitively-
intrusive doubts, wishes, fears, impulses, prohibitions, warnings, admonitions, and commands. The person concerned has no real voluntary control
over them. Since they are troubling, disturbing, and often repugnant, he
deliberately tries to deny them admittance to conscious awareness as
thoughts, or to suppress them upon their arrival.

Obsessive personality traits are so labeled because in general they are
related to the obsessive group of neurotic symptoms. The resulting atti-
tude-defenses, as well as their important influences upon behavior, emotional reactions, and personality, are largely automatic. They are also
insistent, repetitive, and unconsciously motivated. They help to make up
the obsessive kind of character structure which sometimes evolves. This
important area was discussed in *Chapter 5.*

The Compulsion has many similar qualities to the Obsession, but in addition involves action. A compulsion is defined as *an insistent, repetitive,
intrusive, and unwanted urge to perform an act, which is contrary to the
patient's ordinary conscious wishes or standards. Compulsive behavior,*
and *Compulsive Rituals (see* section VI) are *in response to such urges.*
✓   A compulsion is a defensive, conscious substitute for hidden (unconscious)
and still more unacceptable ideas and wishes. Anxiety results upon the
failure to perform the compulsive act.

Conversely, performances of the compulsive act usually provide some
temporary subjective lessening of tension. Anxiety and tension, of course,
can also result from conscious resistance to obsessive ideas and standards.
The *Impulsion* shares certain qualities with the *Compulsion* but there are
also significant distinctions, as we will shortly see. (For a definition, and
brief comments about the distinction between Impulsion and Compulsion,
see Ch.6:VIIA*1* and *2.*) The *Compulsive Security Ritual* or *C.S.R.* is a
ritualistic Security Operation with compulsive aspects. It is related to the
Soteria, which it can also comprise.

From the foregoing, one can see the close relationship which exists between the obsessions and the compulsions. Both are highly subjective.
Both have internal (that is, intrapsychic) origins. Each is defensively
evolved by the ego. They are both also ultimately the consequences of
internal psychologic conflicts, as for example those between forbidden and

intolerable urges (id), and internal standards (superego). Each "seeks" to maintain repression. A compulsion is perhaps more readily understood, and can be further defined as *a command from within oneself—an internal command.*

Although clear reasons exist for the presence and the content in every instance of obsessive thought, character trait, or compulsion, these are not consciously accessible to the patient. If they become so through therapy, they are generally "surrendered." Even the trained and experienced observer cannot firmly establish the underlying bases for a given such manifestation, without considerable study in each individual case. The Obsessive-Compulsive Reactions or Neuroses are marked by the presence of obsessive character traits, obsessions, and/or compulsions.

2. Insistent, Repetitive, and Unwelcome

The Obsessive-Compulsive Reactions or Neuroses are emotional patterns of reaction in which the most prominent clinical feature is the intrusion of insistent, repetitive, and unwanted ideas, or unwelcome impulses to action. The Obsessive Reaction is *an unconsciously-elaborated psychic mode of response, which is defensively-intended and motivated.* (See also definitions in *Chapter 5.*)

In his desperate defense against anxiety the sufferer has erected beyond conscious awareness a system of attempted protection. This system is firmly built and often tends to be relatively stable. Upon occasion, under sufficient stress it may break down, with the subsequent onset of a psychotic reaction.

As we have observed in *Chapter 5,* this obsessive-compulsive defensive pattern of reaction may include certain character traits which fall into the obsessive group. These may prove adequate as defenses, or they may break down under added stress. These traits serve a defensive purpose in similar fashion to neurotic symptoms, which can supersede them when they prove inadequate. They develop as protective devices against the intense subjective and often hidden emotional feelings of the obsessive person. As with clinical symptoms, character defenses "seek" to maintain repression and to prevent anxiety. Our discussion of the obsessive character defenses and the Obsessive Neuroses in the two chapters does not indicate major differences in dynamics or in the therapeutic approach.

C. SUBSTITUTION OF SOMETHING LESS DISTURBING; CONCEPT OF PREOCCUPATION-DEFENSE

It is the ever-lurking prospect of anxiety that makes it impossible for the individual to suppress his impulse in compulsions, or his thought in obsessions, in spite of the fact that he is willing, knows better, and makes valiant efforts to do so. The intrusion of the unwelcome thought "seeks" to prevent anxiety by serving as a more tolerable substitute, for a subjectively even less welcome thought or impulse. The consideration of the mechanisms of Substitution and Displacement lead us to the topic of preoccupation, and a conception of Preoccupation-Defense.

Obsessive types of preoccupation are thus also protective, in that they absorb attention and interest and relieve tension. They further serve to lessen the ability to even notice events and so on, which otherwise could be quite troubling and disturbing. This is a concept of what we may term the Defense of Preoccupation* in the obsessive situation. It is analogous to the *Attention-Absorption Defense* in the Hygeiaphrontic Reactions [Ch.8:VB5;VIC1]. The performance of the compulsive act in more or less analogous fashion tends to relieve tension and anxiety, which otherwise threaten to appear when the patient stubbornly resists it, or attempts its omission.

This chapter will directly continue the discussion begun in the previous chapter on the Obsessive group of character defenses. Although the main focus in this chapter will be on the Obsessive-Compulsive Neuroses, a complete separation from obsessive character traits is not feasible, and additional data are included which are applicable to the latter, as well as certain further clinical factors and psychodynamic bases which are common to both.

II. HISTORY

A. LA MALADIE DU DOUTE

1. Esquirol and Falret

Obsessive character traits and obsessive symptoms have probably been observed during most of recorded history, although not as such. In earlier times, however, any widespread attention to them was certainly lacking, and scientific medical interest was not only not available, but was not even possible. Accordingly, gaining some understanding of their origins and their defensive intent was long delayed. Other factors include our knowledge that there is likely more encouragement to their development implicit to the conditions prevailing in the more advanced and complex kinds of cultures, subject to some exceptions as noted earlier. Further, many obsessive defenses being valued, handicapping potentials might well receive little notice.

With the advent of modern psychiatry, especially following the eighteenth century, some gradually increasing recognition was given to the obsessive-compulsive group of emotional illnesses. In 1838, Jean Etienne Esquirol (1772–1840), a pioneer French psychiatrist, observed and named the condition of obsessive doubting *monomanie raisonnante.* Jean-Pierre Falret (1794–1870) later appropriately named it *la maladie du doute,* "the illness of the doubt."

2. Morel, Westphal, Freud, and Janet; Psychiatry Participates in Medical Renaissance

In 1861, B. A. Morel (1809–1873), another French psychiatrist, probably first used the term "obsession." Seventeen years later, in 1878, Carl

---

* Sullivan expressed one aspect of this concept as "the great general principle of the obsessional state is that the person is so frightfully busy living that he doesn't have time to suffer some of the greatest pains of life."

Friedrich Westphal (1833–1890) usefully defined obsessions, as ideas which appear "contrary to the patient's volition, cannot be banished, . . . and [which] are recognized by those affected as abnormal . . ." Although current definitions, through the development of our present-day concepts and terminology, may possibly offer us some advantages, Westphal's early one remains applicable today. A Medical Renaissance [Ch.14:IIA*1*] was well underway, in which psychiatry participated.

In the following several decades an appreciation gradually developed concerning some of the possible intrapsychic bases of obsessional psychopathology. Sigmund Freud soon (*circa* 1895) began to include some comments in his writings about obsessive symptoms and their dynamics. Many years later he stated that the sub-specialty of psychoanalysis as he named it, had been built primarily upon the early study of clinical cases of Conversion Reactions (hysteria) and Obsessional Neurosis.

After the turn of the century obsessional patterns of reaction were beginning to be widely recognized in psychiatric circles. The French clinician Janet deserves credit for some excellent early descriptive observations from his clinical cases. In 1903 he introduced his term and concept of "psychasthenia." This was a broad group for classification and diagnosis in psychiatry, in which he included not only the obsessions and obsessional states but also other psychoneurotic syndromes such as the phobias, but excluding hysteria.

Although psychasthenia as a term has rapidly declined in its nosologic usage in recent years, it may still be occasionally heard. Literally meaning "psychic weakness," this term gives us an idea of some of the views of neurotic etiology which were broadly extant around 1900 (*See also Table 3,* Page 46).

In 1952, for excellent scientific reasons, in the U.S.A. the Phobic Reactions were officially (by the American Medical Association and by the American Psychiatric Association) separated from the Obsessive-Compulsive Reactions. However, the phobias bear a clinical and a psychodynamic relation to obsessions and compulsions, as will be discussed in *Chapter 10,* and as reflected in our definition of a phobia (as *an obsessively persistent, unrealistic fear*).

During the present century recognition gradually has been given to a distinction between the Obsessive Neuroses proper, and the related and often accompanying or underlying obsessive kind of character structure. This tendency toward increasing refinement of our concepts in clinical practice, in theory, in classification, in terminology, and in diagnosis, has continued to the present. It is a constructive and useful evolutionary process in our particular branch of medical science. It is a trend which should be encouraged; not disparaged.

B. PIONEERING WORK IN PSYCHODYNAMICS

1. Repression and Displacement

In 1894 Freud published his early observations concerning the psychologic etiology of obsessions. At this time he first related the appearance of the obsession to the banishment (that is, the repression) from conscious awareness of unbearable ideas. He was able to illustrate this clinically.

At this early stage of study and research and for some time, the "unbearable ideas" were almost exclusively regarded as being sexual in nature. In the complex unconscious process which occurred, a detachment of feeling (that is, affect) was effected from the original intolerable sexual idea. This took place quite automatically. Displacement of the affect was automatically effected to another, more tolerable object.

It was observed that whenever adequate awareness by the patient of these unconscious endeavors could be secured through free association, study, and analysis, the defensive need for the obsession decreased or ended. Thus, in addition to providing a research method, psychoanalysis also provided a method of treatment. In other words individual investigation and research into psychologic manifestations require intensive analytic study, which is simultaneously also a treatment process.

2. Transference

Together with the early understandings which were worked out concerning the Conversion Neuroses and the Phobic Reactions, the knowledge gained from the study of cases of Obsessive Neurosis comprised the cornerstone of modern dynamic psychiatry. Later the Obsessive Neuroses were grouped together with the Anxiety Neuroses, the Phobias, and the Conversion Reactions (hysteria) as the emotional illnesses to be regarded as most accessible to analytic therapy. Freud referred to them as the "transference neuroses." This term was used to indicate and to help stress the basic capacity of these patients for developing a "transference" of emotional feelings. Through their transference during the course of therapy, those feelings which were originally experienced toward others, particularly including the significant persons from early life, come to be re-experienced with and toward the therapist. This provides an opportunity for the further elucidation of long established emotional patterns of reaction.

The same principle applies to early emotional defenses, habit-responses, and to the important interpersonal relationships which are established in early years. These set up patterns and establish significant and influential antecedents for the development of later relationships. Thus there is an important tendency for the vicissitudes of the early interpersonal relationships to be automatically and inadvertently, but most forcefully recapitulated in the individual's later experiences in living.

3. Disowned Sexual and Aggressive Impulses

While these four types of emotional illnesses continue to be regarded as quite favorable prospects for intensive treatment, the application of intensive psychotherapy has been quite successfully undertaken in the last fifty years with many additional types of cases. Some of these additional categories, at least at one time, were regarded as only poorly accessible, or even as entirely inaccessible to psychiatric treatment. In addition, as the understanding of dynamics has further developed, we have also increasingly come to recognize the most important role of the unbearable hostile, destructive, and aggressive impulses (in addition to the disowned ones of a sexual nature) in the etiology of the Obsessive-Compulsive Reactions. This major feature has been further developed and is very much stressed in our present discussion.

We have also come to learn more about the important relations to repression and to anxiety, and about the various added internal, unconscious psychologic needs which the obsessive manifestations meet or "attempt" to meet.

III. INCIDENCE AND DIAGNOSIS

A. FREQUENCY OF OBSESSIVE REACTIONS

1. Estimated Twelve Per Cent

The diagnosis of an Obsessive Neurosis is properly made when obsessive symptoms are the most prominent feature of an emotional illness of neurotic level. The Obsessive-Compulsive group of reactions are generally quite distinct. It is the author's impression that less confusing overlapping with the other neuroses is to be observed clinically with obsessive individuals, than is encountered with some of the other types of neurotic reactions.

In the preceding chapter it was estimated that approximately from 9 to 12 per cent of the clinical cases of neurosis fall into the Obsessive-Compulsive category. This is likely a conservative figure.

2. Increased Percentages Found

A. AMONG PATIENTS IN THERAPY.—A study of the patients who are in intensive psychotherapy and analysis, or who have had the benefit of such work, might well reveal a higher relative incidence of Obsessive Reactions, including the Obsessive type of Character Reactions.

The higher percentage of obsessive patients among this particular group is likely due to several important factors: *First,* patients in the obsessive group are often better motivated for therapy. *Second,* they are often better able to stay with it. *Third,* due to their application, persistence, and other similarly useful character traits, the overall results of therapy are likely to be good. *Finally,* the incidence of the obsessive group of character defenses among the general population is quite large.

B. INCIDENCE AMONG THE INTELLECTUALLY FAVORED.—The Obsessive-Compulsive Reactions are typically to be found fairly frequently among those who are more favored intellectually. This has been referred to earlier. (*See* Ch.5:VA6.) Freud had early noted this, from his comment about these people being "as a rule intellectually gifted above the average."

The obsessive person usually achieves a fair measure of success in life, provided the overdevelopment of obsessional traits is not too great nor too handicapping, either generally or in some special area. Predictions of such favorable results, however, are often poorly made by his school peers. Election in high school, for example, as the "one most likely to succeed" does not often result in the naming of an obsessive individual. The measure of success he is likely to achieve over the years thus is not always readily anticipated by his classmates, who tend to pick a more spontaneous, flexible, and outgoing person. Sometimes his teachers also might better recognize his potential!

C. SOCIAL PREMIUM.—Modern society clearly places a considerable premium on the possession of a certain amount of the obsessive traits. This adds a certain factor of what we might refer to as a *Cultural Vogue* in their incidence. Thus, a reasonable degree of orderliness, neatness, punctuality, precision, meticulousness, and cleanliness is highly useful personally, and in our era is culturally very desirable. See also the *Changing-Trend Concept* in the incidence of Conversion Reactions (Ch.12:IVA;B).

The Cultural Vogue of obsessive trends is illustrated in a great many ways. Thus we might even cite the wide quotation of many familiar admonitions and mottoes to this effect. As examples, one might recall Smiles' "A place for everything, and everything in its place"; "If a thing is worth doing, it is worth doing well"; Franklin's "Waste not, want not"; "Order is Heaven's first law"; "Cleanliness is next to Godliness"; and at least two Biblical injunctions (2 Kings, XX, 1, and Isaiah XXXV, 3, 1) to "Set thine own house in order," among many others.

Sometimes the presence of obsessive character traits indicates a considerable potential for the development of a later Obsessional Neurosis. The Obsessive-Compulsive Reactions in various degrees are very common, particularly the more mild instances. The incidence of obsessive character defenses among the general population is still greater.

3. Severe Obsessions

In current psychiatric practice the very severely obsessive neurotic patient is not really terribly common, numerically. A reversed impression, however, may sometimes inadvertently be created for several reasons. First, this may be because of the very severe type of case which is usually selected for presentation to students in clinical illustration. They are frequently picked on the basis of their unusual nature, marked interference with living, or because of other quite striking features. They may also be picked because of the completeness of the understanding of the underlying dynamics, or perhaps simply because they stand out as being more severe, or unique, or demonstrable. Second, the severe case can be prominent and attracts attention. Finally, such a patient is likely to be in evidence over a relatively long period, so that a fair number of medical personnel and others become familiar with him and his situation.

It is certainly true, of course, that in the most severe cases the patient can become one of the most tortured of individuals. Indeed, when one sees how terribly worrisome the secondary conscious struggle can become in such an instance against the intrusion of the unwanted obsessive idea or compulsion, the feared potential level of disturbance of the still more-to-be-avoided (unconscious) impulse or idea which it has replaced is most awesome.

On the other hand it is important to be aware of the fact that obsessive manifestations vary greatly as to severity, and also as to their real psychopathologic significance. As examples of the "most tortured of individuals," the author thinks of persons afflicted with a severe and almost continual handwashing compulsion (see Case 68 as a moderately severe example), or with terribly troubling obsessive thoughts about bringing harm to family members (see Case 65).

B. DIAGNOSIS

1. Making the Diagnosis

A. DESCRIPTIVE BASIS. The diagnosis of neurotic reactions on a descriptive basis operates reasonably well with the obsessive group. Accordingly as noted, this diagnosis is warranted when the obsessive manifestations are the most outstanding feature of an emotional illness on a neurotic level.

Diagnosis thus does not require the absence of other manifestations. It does require the obsessive features to be the most prominent ones.

B. PROGRESSION INTO PATHOLOGY; RELATIVITY LAW IN EMOTIONAL HEALTH.—Rather commonly experienced as a mild and usually nonpathologic example of intrusive obsessive thoughts is the recurrence of a musical theme or some particular phrase which has been read or heard. These examples may or may not persist over a period of time, and may cause no real interference in living. At times one may, however, attempt to expel such a mildly troubling recurring idea or mental theme from his mind with little immediate success.

There is a graduation in obsessive manifestations from a so-called "normal," on through the borderline, and thence past the mildly pathologic, into frank emotional pathology, and finally on into the severely psychopathological. This is a very gradual kind of progression. It is one in which it is not always easy to draw hard and fast dividing lines. At one end, one may observe mild, even quite useful obsessive character defenses, as earlier discussed, or the kinds of obsessive phenomena as are not infrequently encountered in adolescence. These findings with obsessive manifestation, as with other phenomena, help illustrate our Law of Relativity in Emotional Health [p. 2], which points out the graduation from normal to pathologic; that the level of emotional health is indeed a relative matter.

At the other extreme of psychopathology are the terribly severe instances; those marked by excruciating obsessions and tormenting compulsions, with their great interference with living. Here also one may encounter the tragic instances of failing obsessive defenses, and the consequent onset of psychotic manifestations. This tragic development can provide our occasional acute illustration of our Concept of Emotional Decompensation, p. 159.

2. *Illustrations*

In the very severe instance, as illustrated in *Case 73, Section VIB 2,* one may observe the overlapping of the diagnostic categories which can take place. This also illustrates as well, the close possible relationships of the psychodynamics generally in the different groups of emotional reactions. *Case 73* describes the situation of a severely obsessive person with a compulsive ritualistic diet. His obsession with health was very similar to Hygeiaphrontis (hypochondriasis) [*See* Ch.8:IIIB3], while the clinical picture especially in its depth and severity also had a number of the elements present which are associated with an early schizophrenic psychosis.

The case to be cited initially is an example in connection with our discussion of diagnosis. We shall encounter additional case summaries, as we proceed shortly to our next section on Clinical Features.

3. *Obsessions, Phobias, and Hygeiaphrontis (hypochondriasis)*

A. CLOSE RELATIONSHIPS.—Obsessive manifestations can have close relations to the phobias and to hygeiaphrontis (hypochondriasis), (*see Case 114,* Ch.10:IIIB2.). Noting these relationships is of some value when diagnosis is important. While later cases may also underline these relationships, at this juncture an illustration of obsessive caution is briefly cited which is not unrelated also to a Phobic Reaction.

In the following example, a patient-colleague gradually worked out the reasons for his long-standing obsessively cautious driving habits.

Case 64

Obsessively Cautious Driving Habits

A forty-year-old business man had begun psychotherapeutic treatment after long consideration. This was a consequence of his increasing recognition that certain overdeveloped obsessive traits were interfering with his interpersonal relationships and had hampered his career. During the course of treatment among other features, a pattern of painfully overprudent driving had become apparent. This was marked by his extreme overcaution and painstakingly minute following of traffic rules. The latter behavior was sufficient at times to drive his friends to distraction. Despite his overcautiousness, however, he still somehow "managed" to become involved in several minor "accidents" each year! (*See* reference to *Accident-Proneness;* Ch.4: p. 196.)

During therapy, his associations gradually indicated some of the underlying bases. By these super-cautious driving habits he was unwittingly and to an extent symbolically, attempting to protect himself against his own strong, consciously-rejected aggressive impulses. It is small wonder his overly cautious driving was important to him. The underlying impulses in turn nevertheless had appeared to play a part in psychologically determining at least two of his accidents which were studied. These had resulted from an outwardly expressed but still "hidden," *acting out** of his inner disowned hostility. Since this was not at all clearly understood, it was all the more frightening. It had led to increasing attempts at control through caution. This had tended to create a vicious circle. He also himself suffered in the overcautious efforts at control, and from the consequences of his "acting out." Hence, a certain simultaneous retribution or self-punishment was exacted.

---

* *Acting Out* represents what we might call a "behavioral conversion", or a "behavioral language." See later reference in Ch.12:VC1; also in relation to Impulsions. in Section VIIA3, of this chapter.

As a consequence of the eventual clarification of the underlying needs through their therapeutic study, the needs themselves gradually lessened. His obsessively overcautious driving habits were slowly surrendered.

The foregoing case helps to illustrate the close relationships between obsessions and phobias. This case has been used as an instance of obsessive caution, which it is. Yet the line of demarcation here from a phobia about accidents (by definition: *a morbid fear of accidents which is out of proportion to the apparent stimulus*) is not overly distinct (*see also Case 113, Ch.10:IIIA5*).

This close relationship is apparent in other similar instances of emotional symptomatology. For instance, a phobia about dirt and germs may be closely related to obsessive cleanliness. Our understanding of the close association of the obsessions and the phobias will aid us in our study and in our understanding of the psychoneuroses. The transition from one group to the other becomes easier. It also helps explain why Janet included phobias, together with obsessions and compulsion, within his classification of psychasthenia. This is an association which was continued by various authorities until quite recently (1952), despite the gradual discard of Janet's diagnostic term.

B. RATIONALE FOR SEPARATING OBSESSIVE REACTIONS FROM PHOBIC REACTIONS*.—Separation of the two groups has a sound scientific foundation. They were separated: on the basis of (1) different clinical features; (2) their separate modes of onset; and (3) because of the operation of different intrapsychic mechanisms of defense. Furthermore (4), the phobias are a more primitive type of neurotic reaction, whereas the obsessive group may be regarded as a more advanced and less primitive type of reaction (*see also* Ch.10:IIIA5).

Accordingly, despite their possible close relationships, and fairly frequent association, their distinction diagnostically is well warranted. We can employ a similar rationale for distinguishing the Obsessive Reactions from the Hygeiaphrontic (hypochondriacal) Reactions.

IV. SYMPTOMS AND CLINICAL FEATURES

A. OBSESSIVE TRENDS, CHARACTER DEFENSES, NEUROTIC SYMPTOMS, AND CERTAIN PSYCHOTIC MANIFESTATIONS RELATED

1. Character Defenses and Obsessive Symptoms

The clinician must constantly keep in mind that obsessive character defenses (traits) and obsessive symptoms as such develop, as do all symptoms of emotional illness, in response to powerful internal psychologic needs. The successful analysis of every obsessional manifestation will eventually disclose their presence and nature. The ultimate purpose of each such manifestation is the avoidance of conflict and anxiety, especially through the maintenance of reinforcement of repression.

---

* Inclusion of the rationale suggested by Barton.

The developing child automatically and intuitively evolves and adopts those ego defensive mechanisms which work best for him in his own particular interpersonal environment. This process is analogous in intrapsychic defense-elaboration, to that embodied in our later *Profitable-Pattern Concept,* through which we stress how *the child automatically exploits and further employs those particular behavioral responses and patterns which have proved useful to him personally.* This type of process, with the resulting evolvement of "behavioral habit-patterns," character traits, and in the "adoption" of psychic defenses, generally, is so automatic and so outside of his conscious awareness and direction as to be comparable to the process of physical growth. The result is the development of his individual set of character .defenses (traits) as we have seen illustrated in the preceding chapter. A group of related personality traits has been termed a *constellation* [Ch.5:1A1]. Many times these are obsessional ones. Their overdevelopment constitutes the obsessional type of Character Neurosis [Ch.5:VA1].

Earlier it was noted that character defenses can falter and be replaced or accompanied by more frank clinical symptoms of neurosis. In type, these very strongly tend to follow the type and the patterns of defenses which are already present. This then follows with obsessional trends. The most likely kinds of clinical symptoms to appear therefore when obsessive character defenses prove inadequate, are obsessive ones. While obsessive symptoms may be encountered in an individual who seemingly has no existing or preexisting obsessive trends, this is rare and further careful study is likely to disclose some of such trends. Thus obsessive character defenses, obsessive behavior, and obsessive trends relate to obsessive symptoms.

2. Psychosis Can Follow Collapse of Obsessive Defenses

At the other end of the scale there is a relationship to certain psychotic manifestations. These may replace, or appear together with obsessive traits, behavior and/or symptoms. This development may take place as an *Emotional Decompensation* (*pp. 48* and *159*) when the latter prove ineffective and insufficient, or when they break down under additional overwhelming conflict and psychic stress.

To label or to regard this possible series of events as a "simple" kind of progression would be a considerable oversimplification. It is usually to be regarded as a type of progression from at least one standpoint, however; that is in regard to the severity of the psychopathology.

B. AGGRESSIVENESS AND HOSTILITY IN OBSESSIVE INDIVIDUALS

1. Defiant Rebellion →Guilty Remorse→Expiatory Reparation; →Defiance-Submission Conflict

It is most appropriate that we consider first the management of his aggression and hostility by the obsessive individual. The primordial patterns which are established for handling his anger and rage, in turn lay the groundwork for the individual's later obsessive manifestations.

The conflict between submission and defiance is never adequately resolved. Albeit thoroughly hidden perhaps, this is the important *Defiance-Submission Conflict,* which is often very prominent in the psychic makeup of the obsessive person. [*See also* Ch.6:VB2; and VD1.] *The Defiance-Submission Conflict* is characterized by (1) a seemingly automatic see-saw of expiatory-reparative (attitudes and/or) acts on the one hand, together with a concurrent, active defiant rebellion in many forms on the other; (2) by recurrent guilty remorse, which helps to maintain this "emotional seesaw;" and (3) by the evolvement of various more or less typical intrapsychic defense mechanisms. Obsessive manifestations develop in the service of the continued efforts at control and as part of the regulatory system which is sought. We shall comment on this further in the section on psychodynamics.

It is not so much that sexual urges and their vicissitudes are unimportant in obsessive manifestations. Indeed, they can play an important role in a number of ways. Included are: (1) their influences on the content of obsessive symptoms and compulsions; (2) contributions through the hurts, disappointments, and rage of sexual frustrations, and their required control; and (3) the carryover of inhibitions, developed primarily for the control and regulation of aggression and rage, but which can also come to include sexual expression. (*See also later* Section VG.)

Thus it is more that the role of sex is considerably less central and vital to the development of obsessive manifestations than was earlier believed. Further, the role of sex has received more than sufficient emphasis in the past. Rage and its vicissitudes and resulting conflicts are often crucial in the psychodynamic elaboration of obsessional defense systems.

2. Constructive and Destructive Aggression; Healthful Self-Assertiveness

A. FOUR CATEGORIES OF AGGRESSION PROPOSED.—Having labeled inner rage and aggressiveness as a frequent kind of basis in the obsessive scheme of things, it is important perhaps that we again pause to note the personal and social value of many obsessive manifestations, when these are held to reasonable limits. It is also of great importance at this juncture for us to recognize the useful and even necessary aspects of aggression and aggressiveness.

Aggression is by no means solely a destructive force. To emphasize the author's conceptions of aggression, its subdivision into four categories is proposed, specifically: (1) *constructive* aggression, (2) *destructive* aggression, (3) *outward* aggression, and (4) *inward* aggression. Thus aggression is not to be judgementally regarded as merely something that is "bad" or "wrong." The word and its connotation should not automatically and of itself invoke negative moral judgment.

Aggressiveness does not need to be a harmful and a destructive force. Indeed, a certain amount of aggression is very much a requirement for self-preservation. These aspects are clearer through the following definitions of our proposed categories.

B. DEFINITIONS.—Aggression may be defined as *a forceful self-assertive* attitude. When translated into action it becomes *a forceful attacking action*. In line with the foregoing discussion, our first category is that of *Constructive Aggression*. This is the type of aggression which is *self-protective and preservative, and which may be realistically evoked by threats from others*. Included herein is that important and essential personality ingredient of *healthful self-assertiveness*, which is necessary to protect one's reasonable rights, especially when these are threatened or infringed.

Our second category is *Destructive Aggression*, which *takes place in response to "internal" (intrapsychic) hostility. It is a kind of aggressiveness which is not essential for self-preservation or protection*. It is the type which is injurious to others and/or to oneself.

Outward Aggression is that which is directed outward toward the external world and toward other people. *Inward Aggression* is that which has become directed inward, or inverted, toward the self.

C. INHIBITION AND CONTROL

1. Parent-Child Relationships Determine Degree and Adequacy

Many obsessive manifestations, if not all, relate to the inhibition and control of aggression and hostility. Closely related is the degree of inhibition of aggression, the amount of underlying hostility present, and the degree of thoroughness of its relegation (by repression) to the unconscious. Parental attitudes play an important role in how the child learns to cope with his hostility and aggression. These matters are important in the genesis and in the understanding of obsessive traits and symptoms.

Much has been written about the hostility which is replaced, controlled, or masked by obsessive traits or symptoms. Earlier it was noted how increased hostility can arise from the frustration which results from parental rejection, or from the setting of what quite literally prove to be *sickeningly* difficult standards and goals.

It is important and helpful also for us to recognize how the deprivation of parental love and affection actually results in turn from the parental inability to provide it. In certain instances one can observe clear enough recognition, accompanied by great conscious efforts by parents to make up for this lack. A studied facade and pretence, however, are a sad substitute for the genuine article. Likewise, children are quick to grasp intuitively the underlying real rejection implicit in both conscious and unconscious efforts at compensation. These may appear in exaggerated form, for example as overprotectiveness or overindulgence. Insecurity and anxiety result, in place of feelings of security and of being accepted.

2. Control of Emotions and Behavior; Principle of Inhibition

Frequently one sees clinically in the obsessive patient the great emphasis which has been placed upon the control of his feelings, affectivity, and behavior. This is so general and part of such pervasive inhibitory trends, as to warrant our referring to a Principle of Inhibition in the obsessive situation [Ch.6:IVE2]. Often this is an endeavor which was either actively or tacitly and unwittingly encouraged by important adults in the individual's childhood, as noted previously. In any event, the inhibition and the suppression of strong emotions as dangerous was made a vital endeavor. Emotions came to be automatically regarded as threatening. This held true whether they were hostile and aggressive, or warm and loving. They constituted a threat, since the possessor "feared" they would get out of hand and control him, instead of the reverse.

Parents who have had similar fears about their own emotions rather naturally encourage inhibition and control in their children. Thence all manner of psychologic efforts are employed in the endeavor to "sit on" the emotional feelings. These may include but are not limited to, such various attempted inhibitory endeavors for example as control, denial, concealment, intellectualization, rationalization, conscious suppression, unconscious repression, diversion, and displacement. Conscious efforts in a similar direction not infrequently parallel the unconscious, intrapsychic endeavors.

These influences help illustrate the important *Concept of Interpersonal Perpetuation* in emotional manifestations, which stresses the perpetuation of emotional problems through the influences erected upon the child by significant (to him) adults, with problems of their own. (*See also* Ch.12:VA3.*)

3. To Outside World Obsessive Person Reserved, Model Citizen

With all the emphasis in our discussions upon aggressiveness and upon the repressed hostility of the obsessively oriented individual, one may have received quite a false picture. Actually, his hostility is often *not* very apparent at all. Since repression has generally been successful, there is often little outward evidence of hostility. As a result, any intimations as to the presence of inner hostility would be vigorously and indignantly denied by the person himself. To the outside world as well he is most often a reserved, good, model citizen.

He thus is apt to appear not so much a hostile kind of person, as perhaps a restrained and dull one. Not infrequently he may present the appearance of someone who is boring, intellectual, overly serious, conscientious, and/or preoccupied. The obsessive person is an inhibited one. This is in accord with the Principle of Inhibition which, as noted, is applicable to many obsessively oriented persons.

Underneath the sometimes external formidable, distant, discouraging of friendly advances or haughty, (*See* Ch.1:IVG1) facade which he has "erected" largely unconsciously he is really very easily frightened. He actually reacts quite defensively against any feared upsurge of his long bottled-up and frozen inner emotions, which might ruffle the seeming but outer calm of the dead sea of his personality!

When the defenses and controls work adequately, no need is felt for psychiatric assistance, and it is not sought. The efficacy of the defenses is to be measured by the extent to which anxiety is controlled or allayed, in line with our Inverse Anxiety-Symptom Ratio Precept (*See* p. 103). The self-defeating or socially limiting aspects are part of the unfortunate by-products, of which the patient most often has little or no awareness. When his defenses break down or do not suffice, help may be urgently needed. Sometimes it is then finally sought.

4. Obsessive Recurrent Thoughts about Harming a Family Member

One not uncommon type of obsessive intrusion is encountered clinically which can be very alarming to the person concerned. This is the one in which there are recurring intrusive thoughts related to harming a family member or members. As this is written the author recalls five patients seen in consultation in a recent six-month period in which this kind of obsessive thought was the principal (conscious) source of concern. Such ideas are often highly repugnant. They may seem too evil to admit consciously or to accept. To the patient they may seem almost murderous in themselves.

In every one of the above instances the patient regarded the thoughts as intolerable. Obsessive intrusions may also be regarded on occasion as nonsensical, silly, or ridiculous. The person concerned may strongly try to suppress them, or to substitute others. He is often likely to be encouraged in this type of approach by well-meaning friends or family, or by equally well-meaning but psychiatrically unsophisticated professionals in various fields. An instance of the latter is cited at the end of the section on *Treatment* [Section VIII F]. Such endeavors are not only likely fruitless but can do harm.* Attention and energy are directed away from the possibly more constructive approach of inquiry as to meanings.

The following case extract illustrates the problem of obsessive thoughts about harming a family member.

Case 65

Obsessively Recurrent Thoughts of Infanticide

(1) Similar disturbing thoughts not unusual

A thirty-two-year-old mother of two small children finally sought psychiatric consultation because of her distress over a related group of obsessively intrusive and terribly repugnant thoughts. These had related to her injury or murder of her children. On infrequent occasions her husband was also a "victim." These thoughts were so repugnant to her, made so little sense, and were so foreign to her conscious feelings that she had long been afraid and embarrassed to seek help with her problem. As a result she had kept this problem to herself for nearly two years, despite considerable psychologic pain, tension, and turmoil. Finally the steadily increasing difficulty had reached an intolerable level.

These thoughts which were so terribly disturbing to her, were really not too much different in quality from what every normal young woman may occasionally feel toward her children. In other words, similar kinds of disturbing thoughts are not unusual. Many a young parent less inhibited and more spontaneous than this one might on occasion

---

* This is similar to the almost inevitably attempted reassurances by the family members of the severely depressed individual. With the depressed patient these are often directed against his self-depreciatory attitudes.

In analogous fashion these efforts also fail. Their net result is to make the person concerned feel worse. *See* Comments on Treatment in *Chapter 4*, pp. 135–218.

say, "Oh, today I feel just like throwing Johnny out of the window! He makes me so mad!" She would not feel threatened by such a thought. She would also not feel very guilty or self-critical about having had it. She would probably forget it rather quickly. Not so with this patient. She greatly feared and condemned such thoughts. To her the thought was nearly as threatening and as guilt-provoking as the act.

(2) Defensive needs lead to attempted denial

This patient had early developed a defensive need to deny the presence of all but her positive feelings. As a consequence she also sought to defend herself against her self-condemnation and guilty feelings over having had such "terrible" thoughts. One such endeavor was simply to deny that they were hers. As she said, "It's just awful words that pop into my head . . . . They have nothing at all to do with the way I feel. They really couldn't be my thoughts at all . . . ." This represented a dissociatively attempted denial. She had thus "sought" its depersonalization Ch:13V*3*.

In her early years her insecure and anxious mother had been unable herself to permit the slightest expression of negative feelings. This was true for herself personally, and also true so far as her child was concerned. The child in turn had adopted a similar pattern of constantly affirming only her affection and love. Repression and denial of all negative feelings seemingly had taken place. These had seemed threatening, and were thereby unwelcome, and unacceptable. This had been reflected in turn in the young mother's conscious attitudes toward her own children. Here also any feelings other than loving ones were intolerable. Even these if very strong, had had to be inhibited or suppressed. It was further observed on occasion that a relationship existed between the frequency of occurrence of her obsessive thoughts and her mother's visits to her home.

(3) Early antecedent conflicts; replacement and substitutions

It has been indicated that obsessive thoughts are substitutions for earlier intolerable ones. Accordingly, at this point one might well ask, what could have existed which was more disturbing than these thoughts, dealing with the murder of her own children? The answer to this question was eventually forthcoming.

In stringent summary, the patient was the eldest of three siblings and had early been assigned undue responsibility for their care. This was over the course of some years. Further, and realistically, she felt deprived of any reasonable share of affection from her parents. She was inevitably greatly resentful of her younger sister and brother. She had fantasied what it would be like if they were not around. She had also entertained occasional murderous fantasies about them, which were accompanied by tremendous guilt and anxiety. As a result these fantasies and associated emotional feelings had been completely repressed from conscious awareness.

Her hostility was replaced in conscious awareness by positive feelings only. The early fantasies toward her siblings were intolerable. These also related to her consciously rejected infantile and demanding dependency strivings. Farther back there were important antecedent oral conflicts. Conscious awareness of all this was far more disturbing potentially than was its partial and symbolic expression via the obsessive thoughts. These early conflicts were significant antecedents, which were also replaced by the more current obsessional intrusions.

It might further be noted with certain obsessional persons that the emotional impulse which could precede a thought of throwing Johnnie out of the window might instead have even been the reverse; that is a spontaneous, warm, and loving impulse, like throwing one's arms around him and hugging him for joy! Such positive feelings are often also very threatening to obsessive individuals, being associated in the past with rejection, hurt, and pain. Since in these instances great amounts of anxiety are generated when they erupt, they are often automatically and obsessively replaced by the reverse, by hostile feelings. The analyst sees instances of this in treatment sometimes, when the arousal of positive feelings may give rise outwardly instead to a defensive display of hostile fireworks!

(4) A recapitulation

The marriage and her small children, together with her need to reject all negative feelings, had out-of-awareness recapitulated in effect her earlier family and emotional situation, with its attendant significant conflicts. The children symbolically stood for and represented on the emotional plane her own siblings, whose destruction would presumably make her the sole object of parental affection and relieve her of odious responsibility. Her infantile dependency needs might then be satisfied. Mother's presence during her visits served as a kind of trigger or stimulus to the complex mechanisms involved. The husband was occasionally included, being partly considered (unconsciously) as another sibling in these instances, and also as a parent.

The patient gradually came to recognize and to accept the existence of her real hostile feelings. These proved to be consciously tolerable and controllable. Further, they lessened substantially. (See *Principle of Symptom-Survival,* footnote p. 27, also Ch.61:IVG4.) She developed more genuine spontaneity, became increasingly mature, and was able to make some substantial healthful readjustments in living.

Many variations of our theme are to be encountered. Freud, as cited by Brill, once described the case of a young man whose life was greatly restricted by a very severe obsessive neurosis. This patient could not go out of the house because of the tormenting obsessive fear that he would commit murder. In this case the obsessive fear represented displaced and consciously denied murderous impulses toward his overly strict father. In restricting himself to his house he said in effect, "Anyone capable of wishing to push his own father from a mountaintop into an abyss cannot be trusted to spare the lives of persons less closely related to him; he therefore does well to lock himself in his room." This type of psychodynamics also can contribute to the development of a *Spatiophobia* [Ch.10: IIIA*1* and *p.* 122].

D. CLINICAL FINDINGS

1. Typical Obsessive Picture; An "I-Should Person"

Clinically, obsessive manifestations can cover a wide range of personality features. This is similarly true with compulsions. The obsessive person is typically of superior intelligence. He is orderly, controlled, secretly sensitive and vulnerable, and has strong opinions in specific areas which are nonetheless accompanied by an underlying and pervasive doubt, by indecision and possibly by a lack of real convictions more generally. His interest in and need for perfectionism is further marked by concern for detail and interest in minutiae.

His activity tends to have a driven and effortful quality, with decreased spontaneity. It is often marked by considerable rigidity, and by the trend toward the replacement of "I want to" or "I enjoy" with "I ought to" or "I should." This latter phenomenon can be sometimes regarded as almost characteristic of the obsessive person. He becomes an *I-Should Person* as his spontaneity is gradually killed off.

His conscience is overdeveloped, often unevenly and with inconsistencies. He is emotionally inhibited, oft-times shy (although the reverse might appear outwardly, lending him a formidable facade as earlier noted). His psyche is marked by underlying conflicts over gratification, frustration, and rage, and a resulting conflict between these and a rebellious, defensive, and guilt-ridden, fearful "making-up-for" kind of reparation. As a consequence, the discharge of emotions and resulting tension (including sexual) is never complete. The added types of obsessive symptoms, character defenses, "attitude-symptoms" (*p.* 144) and symptom groups outlined below reflect these and other prior comments. (*See also* Chapter 5.)

2. *Obsessive Symptomatology Outlined*

A. *Obsessive Ideas*—repetitive intrusions of consciously unwelcome thoughts or ideas:
   - (1) Intellectual Obsessions
      - (*a*) Metaphysical
      - (*b*) Ethical
      - (*c*) Religious
   - (2) Emotional Obsessions
      - (*a*) Destructive, enraged, murderous, hostile, and aggressive
      - (*b*) Loving and sexual
      - (*c*) Inadequacy; self-doubt
      - (*d*) Impulsive; *re* Impulsive Acts or the Impulsions
   - (3) Daydreams and fantasies; visual imagery
   - (4) Superstitions (usually covert)

B. *Doubting Obsessions:*
   - (1) Recriminations
   - (2) Chronic painful indecision; vacillation; doubting obsessions

C. *Ambivalent Attitudes:*
   - (1) Accepting *vs.* rejection
   - (2) Familial
   - (3) Dilemmas over marriage, occupational, career, and so on

D. *Obsessive and Compulsive Rituals:*
   - (1) Cleaning rituals
   - (2) Ceremonial acts
   - (3) Exaggeration of *minutiae* in daily routines
   - (4) Wedded to habit patterns
   - (5) "Making sure" routines (door-locking, switch-checking, making amends, counting money, checking car, spouse, friends, and many others); Compulsive Security Rituals, or C.S.R.

E. Experiencing *Obsessive Repetitive Temptations.*

F. *Emotional (Affect) Obsessions*—the obsessive recurrence of any given emotional feeling.

G. *Obsessive* Related *Phenomena in Other Reactions:*
   - (1) Conversion and functional
   - (2) Phobic
   - (3) Hygeiaphrontic (hypochondriacal)
   - (4) Pain
   - (5) Depersonalization

(6) As a Neurosis Following Trauma; a rather rare kind of defensive retreat (Illustration [Ch.14:IV*3*]).

(7) Soterial Reactions; Security Operations

H. *Attitude-Symptoms:*

(1) Perfectionism: the Just-So Defense

(2) Obsessive cleanliness

(3) Supermoralism

(4) Obsessively pervasive criticism

(5) General affective inhibition (Principle of Inhibition)

E. LESSENED CAPACITY FOR AFFECTION AND LOVE

1. Partially Pretense and Facade

As another consequence of the little genuine interest shown him in childhood, the obsessive person has a diminished capacity for genuine interest in others in turn. Sometimes a pretense or a facade of interest may have been demanded by parents, perhaps even as they may have demanded this of themselves in turn. This, however, not being genuine, can only lead to more trouble, in accord with our *Concept of an Interpersonal Perpetuation Cycle.*

In later life, because of his great underlying need for love, acceptance, and affection, the obsessively-oriented individual may in turn, similarly force himself to behave lovingly or obligingly. The less genuine this is, and the more enforced, the more accompanying resentment is likely to be further aroused in the patient himself. An Obsessive Vicious Circle in Relationships can ensue. (*See* Ch.6:IVF2; also *Vicious Circle of Self-Defeat Concept in the Neuroses,* pp. 71, 74, and *Case 71* Ch.6:VH*1*.)

From one point of view the obsessive person has a legitimate complaint in his constant claim and expectations of love and acceptance. He feels deprived, but he now unrealistically and often unwittingly expects to receive these from new people.

Similarly, the child who has not received warmth, acceptance, understanding, and affection will in turn be limited later in his capacity to provide them for his own children. The possible implications for a tragic continuation of this Interpersonal-Perpetuation Cycle are only too apparent.

2. Principle of Inhibition; R.I.G.I.D. Person Concept

The limited capacity for affection may also be regarded as one part of the overall *inhibition* of all kinds of emotional feelings. This inhibition is so widespread among obsessively-oriented persons that we might in general expect our Principle of Inhibition to more or less apply with some regularity. It includes many, if not most, aspects of affectivity and behavior. It has been developed as defensively necessary to guard against forbidden hostile and sexual impulses, frozen from childhood. Further, the giving of affection is protectively restricted, in similar fashion to the

increased caution around fire by one who has been earlier burned—
"Once burned, thrice wary!" Rebuff and rejection are stringently avoided.
The obsessive individual reacts in some measure "allergically" to such a
prospect. If he maintains sufficient distance from people presumably he
is then less liable to renewed hurt and pain, to which he has become far
more vulnerable. His personality and patterns of reaction tend to be
rigid ones.

Often the obsessive person does not, and indeed cannot, do things on
a simple and free basis of wanting to. He is *driven* instead by feelings of
guilt, guilty fear, or obligation. Duty and obligation tend to replace genuine interest and spontaneity. Tragically, he often does things for or with
others mainly because he feels *required* to do so. *Indecision* is often a
prominent feature. In view of the foregoing we might regard the obsessive
individual as what we might term a R.I.G.I.D. person, in view of the ∟
prominent roles played by these features of *r*equirements, *i*nhibition, *g*uilt,
*i*ndecision, the *d*riven nature of his responses, and the general emotional
restriction and the *rigidity,* in his overall adjustment.

3. In Sexual Relationships

Satisfactory relationships with the opposite sex may be similarly (and
defensively) impeded, restricted, and inhibited. A failure to make really
adequate or satisfactory sexual advances, commitments, or to maintain
such relationships may be present. This in turn may be rationalized on ∟
the basis of the obsessive person's intense criticisms of any given potential partner. This kind of harsh judgmental attitude toward another often
approximates the obsessive individual's own harsh standards for himself.
This also may be a result (or a contributing aspect) of his protective
distance-promoting maneuvers, or part of a defensively-intended bulwark
against disappointment, rebuff, rejection, loss or failure.

He may "explain" his restrained attitudes about sex in general, or about
a given potential experience, on the basis of such factors as fastidiousness,
apparent ethical considerations, time, or circumstances. At times these
kinds of factors may operate as additional controls, to further help inhibit
his strong but feared sexual drives.

In other instances obsessive-compulsive manifestations themselves may
be reflected in the sexual adjustment. For example, there are obsessive
persons who "control" the sexual act (and often their partners) through
various specific types of ritualistic sexual activity and obsessive behavior
patterns. Actually, however, the attempted control here is to be regarded
as ultimately that of the inner anxiety.*

One may encounter in clinical experience a compulsive kind of frequency of intercourse. This may be in response to torturing inner and
largely unconscious doubts which the patient has in regard to his potency
or virility. Such behavior conveys little real sexual gratification, since it
really attempts to subserve these other important needs. It has a forced
quality. It is as though a claim to manliness (or femininity) and adequacy
can be so established.

---

* *See also* the comments on Sexual Manifestations, *Chapter 5,* Section VII.

So often these patients regard themselves as somehow terribly different from other people. Routinized sexual activity can represent one of the many rather forlorn and pathetic ways in which they may try to conform to what their concept of "other people" is.

4. Sexual Maladjustments: Concept of Effect-in-Distinction-from-Cause in Emotional Illness

Elsewhere in this volume it is noted how the working out of a mature and mutually satisfactory sexual relationship constitutes the most complex achievement in interpersonal relations. Undoubtedly the sexual relation is the most intense of all interpersonal experiences. It can also be the most friendly; or upon occasion one of the most hostile of acts. It is not surprising therefore, when emotional difficulties occur, that the adequacy, the degree, and the mutual satisfaction of sexual relationships frequently are a reflection of, and in effect mirror the overall interpersonal situation, as well as the level of emotional disturbance. This is often in direct proportion as regards friendliness, warmth, adequacy, and degree of success of the sexual relation. In other words, the more severe the level of emotional disturbance, the more interference with normal sexual ability and function.

The balance which is effected in the sexual area of adjustment is likely to be more intricate and more complex than in other areas. Accordingly it is much more easily disturbed.

In view of the very frequent involvement of problems of sexual adjustment in all types of emotional illness, it is not surprising that there has been a rather wide tendency in the past to regard these disturbances as the underlying cause of the illness. Instead, they may often be the result. In other words, some authorities have tended to regard sexual problems as almost invariably the *cause* of the emotional illness. In distinction, they can often be one of the important and frequent *consequences* of the illness. This is in accord with our Concept of Effect-Over-Cause in Sexual Maladjustment in emotional illness, which can be observed not infrequently. *See also* pp. 116, 269, 282, 425, and 426.

F. VULNERABILITY AND DISTANCE-PROMOTING; OVERCRITICAL ATTITUDES

1. Major Influence on Personal Relationships

Reference must be made again to the intense vulnerability of the obsessive patient to personal hurt. Because he has been so repeatedly injured, frustrated, and rejected, it is not surprising that a frequent prominent aspect of his resulting psychologic defensive system consists of distance-promoting operations. In other words, part of his protection against injury from people is to keep distant from them (*See* later *Concept of Relationship-Distance,* Ch.6:VH2.) This aspect also relates to the preceding comments on sexuality.

As one of the unwitting contributions toward maintaining such distance, there is the rather common obsessive faculty of being overly critical. This need often also operates as an attempted ego-boosting endeavor, to combat the very low self-esteem. As a consequence, personal relationships may become attenuated, difficult, or impossible. The threat implicit thereby is avoided, that is, the danger of further hurt and rejection, of added frustration, and of rage which cannot be adequately discharged.

The basis of the censure and the criticisms which are made, and their vehemence, often vary according to the strength of the underlying inner need present. They may include almost anything about a given person, such as his personal characteristics, clothes, possessions, appearance, manners, prestige, position, friends, odor, make-up, speech, family, education, age, and experience. Not infrequently when this defensively-intended undertaking is operative, the obsessive person unwittingly adds to his resulting further deprivation and misery, by believing via projection that similar attitudes exist toward him in turn. Through the assignment to others of his own motives, feelings, and reactions, it thus often seems to him that similar harsh judgments are constantly being made of him by others. *See* added comments on *The Personal Yardstick,* [Ch.5:VA3.]

The overly critical attitude which the obsessive patient possesses is actually often enough the direct application of his own harsh standards as a Personal Yardstick, by which he then measures others. He also may well be intensely critical of others who do not have similar obsessive attitudes, defenses, or standards. He is inevitably an equally harsh critic of himself. His overdeveloped superego has evolved especially through the incorporation of harsh parental attitudes and standards, especially those which were present toward him.

2. Obsessive Vicious Circle Concept in Relationships

To return to the vitally required defense of maintaining distance, this endeavor can be a further source of excruciating emotional conflict and misery to the severely obsessive patient. In consequence of his own early deprivations he concurrently possesses an even greater need for people, warmth, and companionship. This, however, adds to his vulnerability to hurt and to rejection. A vicious circle may be established in which the great need for closeness increases vulnerability, which leads in turn to greater distance, and thence on to still more need, and thus on and on! When operative, this sequence comprises what we can refer to as the Obsessive Vicious Circle in Relationships. *See also* Ch.6:IVE*1*.

Very often the obsessive patient has had to consciously deny many of these deep needs. They are no longer at all present in his conscious awareness. However, one can see how the obsessively oriented person may be most vulnerable to loneliness. He is usually sadly unable unaided to bring the conflict between his truly great needs for closeness, and his even stronger defensive needs for distance, into any reasonable resolution. He cannot reconcile these conflictual, contrasting, and inconsistent inner needs.

3. Lack of Spontaneity

Even in those relationships which are already established, the obsessive patient often suffers greatly. As noted earlier, such relationships are often directed in part, or are often accompanied by torturing feelings of guilt, guilty fear, burdensome obligation, and inner conflict.

The obsessive person is not free spontaneously to love or to enjoy. His is often a tragic loss and a forlorn position in living, which is seldom even recognized by him.

G. IMPORTANT ADDED FEATURES OF OBSESSIVE PERSON

1. Low Level of Self-Esteem

A. SELF-ABSORPTION; EGOCENTRICITY AND SUPERIORITY COVER INNER DOUBTS AND CENSURE.—A super-awareness of and concern with self can be a reflection of low self-esteem. This kind of self-preoccupation is frequently present to some extent in Obsessive Reactions. A harsh judgmental and overdeveloped conscience may be partly responsible. All of this can greatly restrict the ability of the obsessive individual to enjoy living, to have fun, or to relax.

The overly critical attitude about himself may be combined with his preoccupation with detail. The obsessive person may be forced to devote abnormal concern, for instance, to an awareness of the position of his tie. He may be overly concerned about the crease of his trousers, his complexion, dress, appearance, and/or hair. All this can operate in the intended service of the restriction and the control of unconscious, disowned drives. Energy and attention are absorbed in these "safer" concerns and activity.

Despite his best efforts, the obsessive person failed to secure real acceptance in early life. This insures a continuing low level of self-esteem, perpetuated by the incorporation into his own standards and conscience of the impossible-to-achieve ones set for him by his parents. Low self-regard and self-esteem are universal with obsessive patients. Often, however, it has to be defensively denied consciously to the self, as to others, and the reverse appearance may even be created of egocentricity, overevaluation, superiority, and condescension. (*See also* Ch.6:IVC3.) These findings are on a considerably more superficial level, however, than are the inner and underlying self-doubts, poor self-esteem, and self-censure, which they defensively cover over and outwardly reverse.

B. COMPARISONS AND COMPETITIVENESS.—The inevitable low self-esteem may result in the development of many vital defensive operations which may be socially unwelcome. As one result of low self-esteem and inner self-doubts, the prestige needs of the obsessive patient may be inordinately high. There may be an exaggerated desire, for instance, to associate with financially or professional successful people. This may represent a way of trying to belong, to gain acceptance, to "be there also." Despite his very real achievements, when these have been gained, he is still quite likely to retain pervasive lingering doubts about them, his acceptance, his "having arrived", or his intrinsic worth as a person.

Comparisons with others may become an important, continuing, absorbing, and nearly automatic, albeit painful, process. In these comparisons, the obsessive patient who makes them most often sees himself in a poor light. Sometimes also and in some contrast, he must defensively and obsessively(!) seek to make comparisons, in which he secures the more favored position. This represents the defensive operation of "building oneself up at another's expense."

The obsessive person may suffer from strong competitive feelings, or from envy and jealousy. The extent of these is highly variable according to his early family constellation of relationships. These feelings when present, will also prevent or interfere with closeness. Not infrequently they may carry over to some extent into the relationship with his spouse.

Low self-esteem can also contribute to the undue and often self-defeating importance of being correct. The harsh conscience burdens the obsessive individual so that he can poorly tolerate criticism from others. He already carries too great a burden of his own. As one may readily note, the obsessive patient is his own most harsh critic.

2. Childhood Manifestations

It is a common finding that nearly all children are likely to go through minor and transient stages of compulsive behavior. Thus, they may feel the need to avoid or to touch, for example, every crack in the sidewalk, the fifth picket in a fence, or every light pole, and so on. These phenomena usually have little or no pathologic significance in and of themselves. They seldom long continue. On the other hand they may very occasionally persist, or later recur, perhaps in a different form. When they have significance, it is in relation to additional obsessive manifestations, and as an indication of early and possibly developing obsessive defenses.

Freud observed that "the first symptoms of obsessional neurosis declare themselves in the second period of childhood (from six to eight years of age) . . ." It is also to be noted that certain children may first show evidence of obsessive character traits at this time. These often then recede to some extent, perhaps permanently. However, they may become a firm although latent part of the personality structure. They may be reactivated under subsequent emotional stress. Hill suggested pointing out that Klein and the modern ego psychologists describe obsessive behavior, and even neuroses, in children considerably under the age of six or seven years. This does not eliminate our theories and findings that obsessions have to do with guilt and the superego, but "it seems to suggest that perhaps the superego begins to emerge much earlier than Freud thought."

Scrupulosity and religiosity are encountered as childhood obsessive manifestations. A child may become obsessively involved with sin and with wrongness. He may come to fear doing or thinking wrongly in almost everything. Overmeticulousness may occur also, as indeed may the early manifestations of nearly any of the adult obsessive defenses we have outlined earlier, and in Chapter 5, *Table 17; VA1*. Fortunately most of these tend to subside spontaneously.

3. Parental Attitudes Favor Obsessiveness

Some parents are much less likely to become concerned over the evolvement and presence of obsessive character formations, or even early obsessive symptoms, than they are over some certain other kinds of emotional manifestations. This is true since in many instances the parent is consciously seeking to encourage his child to "grow up." As he views their development in his child, various of the obsessive manifestations may well appear to be on the right track!

The parent may also either actively or unwittingly encourage the inhibition or the suppression of any emotions of his child which he finds unwelcome. He may be inclined to accept any response to these efforts as evidences of success in the promotion of maturity. A certain amount of control of one's emotions and behavior indeed is a requisite for successful social living and for maturity. It may be very difficult for the parent successfully to foster the development of just the proper quantity at the proper time. Parental influence on the side of overinhibition is too readily developed.

Further, the parent may be somewhat obsessional himself. He may be pleased to see patterns and attitudes similar to his own begin to appear in his child. Perhaps, as psychologic defenses, these have served him well, and of course he may be completely unaware consciously of their concomitant limitation and handicap, or of such a potential. (*See also* related comments in Chapter 8 VIB4.) Some psychiatrists automatically look for an influential obsessive adult in the childhood of every obsessive person in therapy.

Thus, parental attitudes in favor of the development of obsessive traits can have an important influence in their development and accentuation, as in our important *Concept of Interpersonal Perpetuation* (Ch.12:VA3). These factors may also help to account for the relatively fewer young obsessive patients seen in consultation by child psychiatrists. Kanner, for example, has pointed out that it is rare to have a child brought in for psychiatric consultation because of obsessive difficulties before he has reached fourteen or fifteen years of age.

4. Importance of Detail

An important obsessional defense against anxiety is a preoccupation with detail. This is in accord with our earlier Preoccupation-Defense Concept [Ch.6:IC;IVB2]. This can enter into or even permeate any area of living, and is usually consciously well justified by the patient. His rationalizations are very well erected. This is hardly surprising. After all, if he could recognize the defense, the need behind it, and its self-defeating aspects, he would have less need for it. It would have diminished or disappeared. This is in accord with our *Principle of Symptom-Survival* (Ch.14:IIIB2) which stresses the relative inability of a symptom to survive its thorough therapeutic elucidation.

The following instance illustrates the obsessive individual's not uncommon interest in his vocabulary.

Case 66

Preoccupation with Words

A forty-two-year-old housewife had a number of obsessive symptoms. Among these, she was gradually able to work out some of the defensive intent in the one concerned with her preoccupation with the selection, use, origin, and meaning of words.

In rather typical obsessive and self-critical fashion, she once commented as follows on her obsessive etymological interests: "Why do I have such an interest in words? Do I use this as an evidence of my knowing something that someone else does not? Is this a much sought-after superiority about some small specific thing? . . . I notice in my writing a studied effort to use the odd and unusual. Then it doesn't read well, which defeats me. Lincoln pointed out the value of not using two syllables, when one would do. Maybe it's an attempt to impress people with my eruditeness and scholarliness . . ." Actually of course, it went further then this.

For this patient her overattention to words, her deliberateness, and her "studied choice" were part of her rather pervasive defense against all spontaneousness (*Principle of Inhibition*). This was simply another obsessional device directed toward the further control and inhibition of her emotions and emotional display. This is illustrated in her very statement about her problem. Note the words and phraseology which she employed.

5 Perfectionism: the "Just-So" Defense

Closely related to the importance of detail is the frequent obsessive need for perfection. Obsessive preoccupation may be present with order, detail, and with keeping or making things so they are "just so", that is, perfect. Accordingly, we may refer to this appropriately as the *Just-So Defense.*

This can comprise an "attitude-symptom" which is another important, defensively-intended endeavor. It also absorbs psychic energy and attention. One can see the intimate dynamic interrelationships between the control and inhibition of emotion, and the traits of perfectionism and concern with detail. There may be a lack of patience with others who are less concerned with order and perfectionism.

A rather striking, although extreme, case was reported by Bowler illustrating perfectionism while the author was discussing its defensively intended purposes with a psychiatric group.

Case 67

An Extreme Instance of Perfectionism

A large jewelry firm regularly found one or two of their more perfect diamonds missing at periodic inventories. For a considerable period of time these irregular and seemingly inconsistent losses remained unaccountable. Finally, however, the recurring losses were traced to one of their most devoted and trusted diamond experts. He had not stolen them for himself. His rationale for their appropriation was most interesting and unique.

The expert had developed such a tremendous obsessive need for perfection that he simply could not stand an imperfect stone. A diamond *must be* "just-so". As a result, when a customer occasionally brought

in a chipped gem for resetting, or an imperfect one, he simply replaced it with a perfect stone from the firm's extensive stock, and threw
away the poor or damaged diamond brought in by the customer!

This was a reflection and a consequence of his *Just-So Defense;* for
him an important "Attitude-Symptom". Needless to say, his interest
and need in thus occasionally supplying some customer of the firm with
a flawless diamond, gratis, was poorly appreciated by the firm's officials!

6. Compulsions Accompany Obsessive Thinking

In severe cases of Obsessive-Compulsive Neurosis one may observe obsessions and compulsions occurring together, often in related areas. At
times obsessive concerns about cleanliness, for example, may be accompanied by compulsive bathing. An instance of such obsessive preoccupation follows.

Case 68

**An Obsessive Preoccupation with Cleanliness, Accompanied by a Hand-
washing Compulsion**

A twenty-eight-year-old unmarried business machine operator sought
professional help because of a compulsion to wash his hands and for
certain other problems in living. His hands were reddened and sensitive
from the thorough scrubbing received on a daily average of twenty-five
times or more. Occasionally when his level of anxiety, or internal pressures became quite high, even this frequency of washing greatly increased.

He had to carefully clean the keys of his business machines with a
strong disinfectant before and after each use. In dressing he sometimes
felt it necessary to handle his undergarments through sterile tissues. If
his shoes touched any item of clothing he had a strong impulse to
destroy it. He feared he would contaminate people whom he happened
to touch. He could not stand to brush against another person, and if
this happened, dry-cleaning of his garments was often a necessity,
although even this was not always sufficient to result in his feeling
comfortable.

Occasionally he even felt forced to destroy, by burning, certain items
of personal property which he felt had become "contaminated." He
usually had to wear a special pair of gloves when dressing or undress-
ing. He could seldom bring himself to handle food or eating utensils
directly. He "explained" his inability to do so on the basis of some
vaguely dreaded but unspecified "thing" which would happen.

This patient's efforts to avoid "contamination" of himself or of others
had became a major endeavor in his life. It required the investment
of much time and effort which could well have been more constructively
utilized elsewhere.

A number of important pathogenic features were ultimately worked
out. The ritualistic washing symbolically represented, in part, efforts
to secure moral purity. His "ability to contaminate others" partially
reflected his extremely low level of self-esteem. This in turn was a
"taking over" of the attitudes of nonacceptance present towards him
on the part of his parents from the earliest years.

Under intensive treatment over a prolonged period of time this man
made considerable improvement.

V. ADDITIONAL PSYCHODYNAMIC CONSIDERATIONS

A. ONSET OF OBSESSIVE SYMPTOMS

When the psychologic foundation has been established for the adoption of this particular pattern of psychologic defense, the onset of obsessive symptoms can occur with an increase in emotional stress, or with the weakening or inadequacy of existing character defenses. They also have their onset when derepression threatens and/or as a last desperate effort to maintain repression. Usually some combination of these occurs. Essentially, the danger is that consciously intolerable and disowned (repressed) impulses threaten to break through the psychologic barriers and to escape into conscious awareness. These are terribly threatening to the obsessive patient, who "fears" his ability to control them. The evolvement of manifestations of the obsessive pattern of defense follows. These are intended, beyond conscious awareness, to aid in control. The obsessive individual has not developed adequate means effectively to cope otherwise with these dangerous situations.

Reinforcement of repression results in several ways including symbolism, obscuration, and replacement. Attention is directed away from the disturbing areas. Psychic energy is also absorbed and therefore is no longer available for either gaining awareness, or for potential action. Despite the fact that the intrusion of the obsessive ideas may be quite painful in itself, these intrusions help prevent conscious awareness of something which is far more personally unbearable to the patient.

The comments in this section are written to underline and to supplement those already offered earlier (and in *Chapter 5*), concerning the origins and the genesis of obsessive symptomatology.

B. INTERACTION BETWEEN PARENT AND CHILD

1. Establishment of Precedent

Through careful study and observation it has gradually become possible for us to correlate many of the events in infancy and early childhood with one's later personality traits and with possible neurotic symptoms. Many of these relationships have been considered in earlier chapters. In the development of the obsessive group of defenses those particular events in the parent-child relationship which surround the establishment of bowel-habit training often play an important role. (*See also* Chapter 5.) Intensive study of individual cases will frequently indicate that increased relative importance and emotional significance were attached to this period of psychologic development. Part of the significance which is normally later attached to the genital areas and function may remain at this earlier psychologic level, or regress to it. Expressed more technically, anal erotism may partially replace later genital erotism.

When parents themselves are secure and do not become overconcerned at the time of such training, there is apt to be little difficulty. These events are then less likely to have undue significance attached to them. When the mother is anxious, the story is apt to be quite different. The child actively or intuitively senses the parental emotional response to variations in bowel function. Delay or refusal results in mother becoming concerned. Anal function and its variations can readily come to have various kinds of special meaning for the infant. The interaction between parent and child during this period is most important insofar as setting up important precedents for later possible patterns of reaction and interaction, with parents or with other people.

2. Responses and Counter Responses; Profitable-Patterns Concept

A. PERSONALITY DEVELOPMENT INFLUENCED.—According to various significances which may become attached, feces (and bowel function) can come to equate for the infant something all the way from a valuable gift on the one hand, to a weapon or power-lever on the other. In the latter sense the primordial mechanism can become established for possible ways of control, power, and retaliation. Levy labeled the manifestations of stubborn defiance in the infant who is destined to become obsessive, as his "oppositional behavior." Patterns of response like these tend to become established and to be carried over into other later and more complex patterns of interpersonal interaction. These may be unconsciously adopted, and often are, especially when their employment meets with any success. Their modified utilization in subsequent interpersonal situations follows automatically and often symbolically.

All this, of course, is inoperable in a void. The parent inevitably contributes to the establishment of the early antecedents of various patterns according to his response, and according to the amount of anxiety, concern, or attention which is evoked by his infant's behavior. In other words, the infantile endeavor must be responded to in order to make it profitable, and to encourage the later development of patterns of behavior based upon these infantile manipulative ones.

The original behavior on the part of the child may be regarded from this viewpoint as largely a matter of rather unwitting trial and error. *Infantile behavior becomes profitable or not according to the parental (or other) responses which are evoked.* Profitable Patterns accordingly, are found to be the ones which tend to be exploited and to be further elaborated, during an individual's childhood development and subsequently. This is the important *Profitable-Patterns Concept* in personality development. (*See also* Ch.6:IVA1.)

B. STRUGGLE FOR MASTERY.—Bowel function is an early major area in which the infant is in a position to exercise mastery and control. (*See also Case 62*, Ch.5:VIA2). He may or may not cooperate with parental wishes, or may do so in varying degrees. His behavior may have a testing quality. This can be a potentially powerful lever in the hands of the infant, over an otherwise seemingly omnipotent figure. The child would have to be very undiscerning and obtuse not to at least implicitly and intuitively recognize this. He would have to be very mature (and of course he cannot be) not to make use of and exploit it, if he can.

With many obsessive individuals information is forthcoming to confirm some phase or other of our information about the important possible effects of this early period of personality development, and the operation of our Profitable-Patterns Concept. The following is a verbatim extract from an analytic session. This patient was well along in his therapeutic work, undertaken for a moderately severe obsessive character structure.

Case 69

Child-Parent Interaction over Bowel-Habit Training: Extract from a Treatment Session

"A great deal of attention was paid to my habits of elimination in the early years, especially by my mother. She was very concerned about my bowel movements. She believed that health was dependent upon elimination; that these were poisons. She would become anxious if I had no movement, and relieved if I had. If my bowels moved to her satisfaction, then everything would be all right. . ."

The mechanism for possible control here is quite apparent from the response of his mother. The patient went on to indicate his own perhaps inevitably heightened interest in this function. "Sometimes bowel movements were pleasant and I would enjoy them. . . . I am reluctant to discuss all this, even now, and as I do so I feel tension and tightening in my lower abdomen. I must regard it as somehow wrong that I took so much interest in elimination. . . . Sometimes movements were very uncomfortable. It all depended on the duration of my retention; which would always get a rise out of mother! . . . She seemed very powerful to me all right, but after all, this was part of me she couldn't control. I guess this was a way I could sometimes turn the tables. . . ."

In this patient's presentation we must note the evidence of the operation of our Profitable-Patterns Concept and the careful, almost pedantic phrasing. As earlier pointed out, the latter characteristic is one type of obsessive control of feelings. There is an outward academic type of Obsessive Facade, with the divorcement or isolation of inner affect. The reported bodily sensations help point up this discrepancy between what is the real but hidden subjective affect, and the more apparent outward controlled kind of expression. *See* also the earlier reference to the *Obsessive Facade* (Ch.5:VA2).

C. ANTECEDENT CONFLICT.—This antecedent kind of conflict, as outlined, over early bowel-training, with its characteristic obedience *vs.* defiance struggle, or its guilty fear *vs.* defiant rage, is first experienced in relation to the mother or the mother-figure. This is an expression of the significant *Defiance-Submission Conflict,* noted earlier (Ch.6:IVB1). Later it comes to include the father. Ultimately this pattern can extend to color, in more or less subtle fashion, many if not all of the subsequent relationships.

In other words, the Antecedent Conflict establishes a pattern which enhances the recapitulation of this primordial one in later situations. Rado felt that the continuation of this basic conflict was "sustained by the inordinate and unrelenting strength of fear and rage . . ." One might view this as a dammed-up reservoir, ordinarily deeply repressed, in the psyche of the obsessive person.

D. REQUISITE FOR BOWEL-TRAINING DIFFICULTIES CHALLENGED.—It should be noted that obsessive patterns of reaction of various kinds can occur when bowel-training was essentially uneventful. Problems in this area were—and still are—believed by many to be an absolute requisite for obsessional evolvement.

Today, however, the author looks on this more as a convenient, and at least formerly a frequent if not inevitable, pathway into obsessiveness. Others certainly exist. Such patients have similar conflicts, emotions are as strong, obsessional manifestations evolve, but their foundations can be found to lie in other developmental areas.

3. Parental Emphasis on Control

During and following this early period of bowel-habit training, parents can further contribute inadvertently to the establishment of many kinds of patterns which carry over into later life. Prohibitions, rules, punishment, and threats of punishment can have a cumulative effect psychologically. As noted earlier, the control demanded by parents is apt to have a later active second phase, during the years of age from six to ten. Inhibitions may be developed, which tend in their extreme development to limit most spontaneous expression.

During these later years there likely may be an overemphasis placed by parents upon control, performance, independence, maturity, orderliness, and the abandonment of childishness. Lorand pointed out that a possible contrast could exist between this kind of parental attitude, and the over-indulgence and permissiveness which is sometimes present during the preceding anal phase of personality development.

Such a contrast can come to be dynamically significant when it is present and sufficiently marked. It would tend to result in some confusion in interpretation by the child. This might be reflected in his responses, as well as in an increased accumulation of hostility.

Aspects of parental control are legion; the influences most pervasive, often very gradual, frequently most subtle. Why is John so deliberate? Why is his speech slow and careful? Why does he pause, or why is he sometimes exasperatingly slow in responding to questions? John learned most thoroughly through the years to give the most careful consideration to his answers! They had to have his full thought so as to be expressed as mother, or father, expected and required. Small wonder this pattern developed and has continued as a useful if not vital defense.

C. IMPULSES AND WISHES DANGEROUS AND THREATENING; COME TO BE EQUATED WITH ACTUAL EVENT

1. Anger Toward Parental Figures

We may understand the threat of one's aggressive thoughts and urges more clearly perhaps if we can recognize that to the infant, destructive wishes may rather magically come to approach actual fact. He fears their strength, or he doubts his ability to control and contain them. Anger toward the parental figure jeopardizes security: the food, warmth, and love so vital to the infant—to his very survival. In other words, anger threatens the "source of supply." This results in the psychic dilemma of the obsessive individual, which will shortly be mentioned. The only safeguard is total rejection (repression) of any such dangerous hostile thoughts.

Anger toward parental figures is also dangerous because of possible destructive retaliation. The infant may "fear" that any destructive inpulses which he may feel toward these powerful, omnipotent figures may be reciprocated. Any possible retaliation by such all-powerful persons would be terribly threatening.

2. Rejection; Need to Appear Friendly

Weight may be added to this fear if the child recognizes or senses by intuition some real rejection by one or both parents. This then can be an additional force helping to restrict all expressions of any hostile nature, or even awareness thereof. This of course all operates out of awareness, only the indirect currents and ripples (and defenses) reaching the surface of conscious activity or awareness.

The frequent intense need of the obsessive patient to be pleasant and to appear friendly at all costs, becomes more understandable. He has a tremendous need to be acceptable. Anger outwardly expressed has come subjectively to equate disaster!

D. OBSESSIVE DILEMMA

1. Vital Object Threatened

The seemingly insoluble dilemma of the obsessive patient lies in the fact that *his unconscious hostility, rivalry, destructive impulses, and aggression are directed toward the very figures upon whom he is vitally dependent.* This constitutes what it is proposed we might refer to as the *Obsessive Dilemma.* This is the Dependency Dilemma of Infancy, p. 169, as encountered in the obsessive setting. This dilemma is all the more difficult adequately to appreciate or to cope with because it is unconscious. The infant is at once completely dependent upon parental care, and is simultaneously subject to parental discipline.

In the Antecedent Conflict (*See* references pages 29 and Ch.8:VIIA*1*) of the obsessive individual, the frustrating and demanding parents were simultaneously the objects of love and dependency. It is no wonder that guilt and anxiety were intense. In his subsequent interpersonal relations, this primordial reaction has established a powerful precedent. He reacts to alternating waves of frustration, rage, and defiant rebellion, regularly followed by guilty fear, remorse, and reparative endeavors. This is the consequence of the unresolved *Defiance-Submission Conflict,* outlined earlier [Ch.6:IVB*1*].

2. Symptom Endeavors to Protect

Symptoms develop in the service of denial, control, or concealment of the obsessive person's unacceptable and banished hostile and/or sexual impulses. The meaning of this becomes clearer when the observation is made through analytic investigation that the obsessive-compulsive symptom, which aims at the protection of the individual and his parents or others in authority, actually arises from destructive wishes toward them—those in authority! Essentially, the obsessive person is threatened by his own aggressive feelings.

It is not that this kind of psychologic dilemma is not encountered elsewhere. Indeed, we see it not infrequently in various types of emotional illness. It is termed the Obsessive Dilemma in our present discussion, because of its prominence in the obsessive pattern and its relative accessibility here. Otherwise it is one operative area of the more general Dependency Dilemma of Infancy.

E. PREDISPOSING FACTORS TO DEVELOPING OBSESSIVE DEFENSES

Thus far in our discussion of the Obsessive-Compulsive Defenses we have covered a number of the significant causative factors in environment, in interpersonal interaction, and also in the various cultural influences which tend to promote the establishment of obsessive defenses. The following table (*Table 19*) summarizes twelve of these more important factors.

Table 19

Twelve Factors Which Predispose to the Development of Obsessive Patterns of Defense

There are many factors which are present in the early parent-child interaction, in the environment, and in the cultural milieu, which tend to encourage the development of obsessive kinds of psychologic defenses. Note support for our *Concept of Interpersonal Perpetuation* [Ch.6:IVG3]. These factors include:

1. *Parental insecurity.*
2. A considerable degree of underlying *rejection of the child,* with the struggle of the parent at concealment of this through the maintenance of an opposite or different outward facade.
   This results in outwardly unreliable expressions. The child comes to doubt, and to lack faith and trust. He intuitively but inevitably feels the nonacceptance and the rejection.
3. *Parental overambitiousness* for the child's success and maturity.
4. Early overindulgence, permissiveness, and a tacit encouragement of dependence; succeeded by later stringent and contrasting *demands for responsibility and maturity.*
5. *Obsessive traits in the parents.* These often result in a tendency to encourage (consciously or unconsciously), or to place a premium upon, the development of similar traits in the child.
6. Parental, social, and/or religious *condemnation of negative feelings.*
7. *Rejection* by significant adults in childhood *of spontaneous demonstrations of affection* by the child. *Curbs on spontaneity* of any kind.
8. *Familial, social and cultural premiums placed on obsessive traits.* Influence of a *Cultural Vogue* of obsessive trends. For example, even such things as the income tax laws contribute in some measure. Today an interest is required on the part of many average

citizens, in maintaining some kind of detailed fiscal records and books.

9. Overdeveloped *conscience*.

10. The Antecedent Conflict of subservience *vs.* defiant rebellion; accompanied by guilty fear and subsequent reparative efforts. This is the unresolved *Defiance-Submission Conflict*, commonly associated with the obsessive situation.

11. *Parental overemphasis on control* and inhibition (formerly believed specifically and inevitably in relation to bowel habit training).

12. Primordial infantile rage, from whatever source. *Discharge of rage* is too dangerous and threatening, and thus is incomplete or *blocked*. The Antecedent Conflict becomes established.

F. IMPORTANT MECHANISMS IN OBSESSIVE REACTIONS

1. First Line of Defense Concept

There are a number of the intrapsychic mechanisms of defense which are frequently "employed" by the obsessive person. The use of displacement and substitution is common—a *displacement* of affect to the new object, and the *substitution* of the new object for the repressed one. Other mechanisms of considerable importance to the obsessive pattern of defensive reaction include isolation, projection, reaction formation, rationalization, repression, denial, symbolization, and undoing. (*See Index* as a guide to further mention of these important unconscious mental mechanisms.)

The dynamisms can usually be viewed in the light of their comprising the vital First Line of psychic Defense for each individual. This is what we might term the First Line of Defense Concept. The name is intended to help stress their fundamental position in individual psychology. *See also* p. 25.

Obsessive neurotic symptoms develop when these existing ego defenses (the mental mechanisms), and/or the character defensive traits are inadequate or break down. As noted, this occurs under additional stress, often a sudden or acute one. When the stress has been gradual and steady, the development of defensive character traits may suffice. These in turn may become exaggerated, to become an obsessive type of Character Neurosis. They may prove inadequate, may be reinforced, to some extent may even be replaced by actual neurotic symptoms in response to added stress. Derepression threatens, with the hazardous potential for the breaking through into conscious awareness of the intolerable ideas.

In turn, if the threat actually overwhelms the defenses, in the resulting *Emotional Decompensation* (p. 159), a psychotic episode may ensue. Psychiatrists have occasionally observed rather striking incidents in which a given individual's anxiety had mounted to an unbearable peak, to be followed by the overnight onset of a psychotic episode. After such a development there is likely to be little outward evidence of anxiety. Although the cost to the individual's integration is perhaps maximal, the newly evolved psychotic defenses are effective, in accord with our *Precept of Inverse Anxiety-Symptom Ratio* (p. 103).

2. Displacement and Substitution

At this point let us consider how displacement and substitution can operate as defenses against anxiety. In the following example, when disowned rage threatened to come into conscious awareness during treatment sessions, an obsessively repetitive train of thinking ensued instead. The repetitive thought thereby replaced a more disturbing thought and affect, as a defense against the anxiety which the latter produced.

Case 70

Displacement and Substitution; the Intrusion of Obsessive Thoughts during Treatment, when Derepression Threatened

(1) Incident recalled repeatedly.

This patient was a thirty-one-year-old physician who had sought analysis because of certain limitations in his interpersonal relations, and in order to improve his professional effectiveness. He was an able, conscientious, and hard-working person who enjoyed the respect of his professional colleagues. Among his character defenses were some rather prominent ones of an obsessive nature. During the second year of his psychotherapeutic work a recurrent, obsessive pattern of thinking and reaction was noted as occurring during treatment sessions.

On these occasions the patient would repetitively recall a certain incident from his early life and focus his attention upon it in obsessive fashion, with accompanying expressions of guilt and dismay. "After all it was I who did such a terrible thing. I guess I'm a pretty bad person really . . . I feel terribly guilty. This prevents me from having confidence in myself. . . . No one could really respect me if they really knew me. I guess I'll never get any place professionally," . . . and so on, and on.

As one might expect, his reaction was far out of proportion to any realistic appraisal of the incident recalled. However, this served quite effectively and promptly to divert his attention from much more uncomfortable areas, the recall and recognition of which were threatening to him and thereby anxiety-producing. Thereby he automatically reinforced repression and guarded his unconscious.

(2) Threatened awareness of hostility elicits obsessive defenses.

Gradually it became apparent that the recurring obsessive preoccupation with the early incident arose whenever he came close to any conscious recognition of hidden, disapproved, angry, or hostile feelings. Threatened awareness of hostility elicited the obsessively recurrent theme. Following recognition, these negative feelings appeared superficially to be directed toward his wife, because of her rejection of him. He could not tolerate, or rather feared he could not tolerate and control, the amount of hostility this aroused.

The obsessive line of thought would occur when discussions approached too closely his feelings of rejection in marital areas with his wife, and also as an important antecedent, with his mother. When awareness of his hostile feelings (derepression) threatened, anxiety was aroused. The obsessive pattern of thinking and feeling descended as though it were a protective curtain for his unconscious. In other words, as conscious consideration of his wife's rejection impended, instead of facing the hostility this aroused, he automatically evoked the obsessive line of thinking. In somewhat similar fashion to what we have earlier observed in the dynamics of depression (*see* Chapter 4:p.177), part of the punishing reaction tended to become turned inward (inverted) and redirected, seemingly toward himself.*

---

* More technically stated, we can be aware here that actually the object is introjected and sadistically punished in secret and symbolic fashion, at the same time insuring a certain degree of masochistic self-punishment. See the section on dynamics in *Chapter 4, Table 14*, pp. *178–9*.

Thus he evoked in substitution the fixed line of thought, "I've been so bad. I feel so guilty." This was an upsetting obsessive rumination which was, however, more consciously tolerable as a substitute for the unconscious but still more threatening hostility. As together we gained awareness of the basis for this pattern of defense, it became no longer necessary. He became gradually able to understand and to accept the erstwhile hidden emotions without anxiety or fear, an important goal in therapy. There were other deeper roots present, of course.

(3) Antecedent rejection, deprivation, and rage

In partial stringent summary, the primordial rejection had been by his mother, who was psychologically unable herself to give him much genuine warmth and affection. The great frustration and disappointments resulting inevitably aroused a level of rage and resentment which seemingly could not be faced. Herein lay the basis of important antecedent conflict. His relationship with his wife partly rekindled and recapitulated these earlier antecedent conflicts of childhood. His own early deprivations had limited the amount of warmth and affection which he could direct toward his own children in turn.

As he became able to recognize more about the defensive efforts of his other obsessive patterns to circumvent anxiety, and the basis for the latter, they also became less necessary. Over the course of several years of intensive therapeutic work he became able to enjoy a fuller and more satisfying life. His professional work improved, as did his social and professional relationships.

The displacement which takes place in the obsessions is to something seemingly more remote but nevertheless most likely still closely associated in some way with the incompletely repressed idea, desire, or affect. The association may of course be a symbolic and obscure one.

Obsessive defenses are a defensive reaction pattern, evolved within the psyche by the ego to maintain repression which is faulty, threatened, or incomplete. In other words, as we have noted, the Obsessive Reaction reinforces repression.

3. King David Reaction; Obsessive Symptoms Related to Repressed Data

The obsessive person may use projection to a greater or lesser extent but it is not so important a mechanism for him as the foregoing one. On the other hand, in view of his harsh superego and his low level of self-esteem, he not infrequently "provides" data which illustrate the King David Reaction. This might be recalled as being an interesting psychologic process involving the unwitting employment of the mechanisms of repression, identification, projection, and rationalization. (*See p. 75; also* Ch.6:VIIIA2.)

Freud early noted the connection of the obsessive person's symptoms with repressed material: ". . . their symptoms arise through the psychical mechanism of (unconscious) defense, that is, through an attempt to repress an intolerable idea which was in painful opposition to the patient's ego."

G. OBSESSIVE DEFENSES AND SEX

1. Sexual Inhibition and Control; Sexual Influence on Content

Much of our attention has been focused upon the obsessive defenses in their role of attempted defense against the anxiety which is aroused by subjectively intolerable aggressive and hostile impulses. The early scientific literature tended to concentrate upon the protectively intended role of the obsessive defenses in the control of unacceptable sexual impulses. This important function also might be emphasized. (*See also* Section IVB*1*; *also* Obsessive Personality and Sex, Ch.5:VII).

We might in addition note the influence of sexual factors in determining the *content* of certain obsessive intrusions. Further, we should note the frequent inhibition of sexual drives and activity which is present for the obsessive person. Finally, one finds empirically that orgastic experience tends to be weaker, sometimes very much so, in the obsessive person.

2. Brill's Illustration; Bleuler and Freud

As an illustration of sexual content, we may recall Brill's citing an instance of the development of the recurrent and disturbing (but reversed, disguised, and therefore superficially meaningless), obsessively and painfully recurrent thought by a young patient that "God might get into me." This had developed as an intrusive obsessive idea in a retiring, inhibited, and obsessively oriented young man.

Study had eventually uncovered an initiating situation in which his fellow workers had pointed out to him two dogs in coitus. They had then asked the (to him) terribly embarrassing and disturbing question, "How would you like to be the top dog?" His rejecting, protesting, and denying thought, and admonition to himself, had immediately been, "No, you are not going to get into the dog!" By complex steps of unconscious psychologic process and transposition (active position becomes the passive one; d-o-g is reversed, to become G-o-d), this initial defensive reaction had finally evolved into the foregoing disguised, and thus apparently meaningless, obsessive thought. The latter had then persisted, replacing in consciousness the earlier more obvious one.

For the interested student, there are several additional clinical illustrations to be found in the literature. These can supplement the current discussion (for example, Freud's early (1909) "Notes upon a Case of Obsessional Neurosis.")

If space permitted we might examine in turn the hidden dynamics of each major obsessive symptom. Bleuler noted that "obsessional cleanliness may frequently be traced to the need for moral purity . . ." (*see also* Chapter 5:VIIA, and *Case 68,* Ch.6:IVG6 in this chapter.) In regard to the moralistic trends, Freud stated, "In order to protect object-love from the hostility which lurks behind it, the obsessional neurotic [person] is compelled to build up an overconscientious system of ultramorality . . ." This again points up the unconscious dilemma (Section VD) of the obsessive person.

We have been able to briefly discuss several obsessive manifestations thus far. Let us consider obsessive doubting and one or two additional aspects in this defensive pattern of reaction, before concluding these further thoughts on dynamics.

H. ADDITIONAL FACTORS IN OBSESSIVE PATTERNS

1. Obsessive Doubting

One of the earliest, historically recognized types of obsessive patterns of thinking was that of obsessive doubts. (*See* Section II.) Obsessive doubting may cover almost any subject. At times this obsessive occupation may be unconsciously "used" by the patient to help aid in the concealment or the continued concealment from himself of certain reversed (and repressed) emotional feelings.

The following case summary helps to illustrate some of the foregoing principles. Here the obsessive-ruminative doubts were over whether the patient's husband loved her.

Case 71

Obsessive Doubts

(1) Exaggerated picture of blissful marriage
The patient, a young housewife, was treated briefly by her family physician for insomnia, digestive disturbances, and nervousness. Referral to a psychiatrist was made promptly after she had confided some of the bases for her nervous disturbance. Thus, she had been tormented by recurrent and seemingly unreasonable doubts about her husband's state of love for her. These were of an obsessive nature, and she had found them terribly disturbing.
When first seen she appeared worried and depressed. She discussed her struggle in attempting to banish the intrusive, unwelcome, and "inane" doubts which had kept recurring. She had gone into endless efforts to try and establish that there were no real bases for her doubts. In explaining how impossible this could be, the author was assured that "never a single cross word" or disagreement had passed between them during eight years, of what was pictured as the very ideal of marital happiness. This was obviously an exaggerated picture, and thereby significant. In itself it was an indication that something was wrong about the relationship and her attitudes about it.

(2) Projection and Reversal
To her, marital bliss had been apparently equated with an absence of the slightest of negative feelings. When the husband and his wife were seen together in consultation it seemed as if the wife had to go out of her way in the use of endearing terms. The husband was troubled and mystified by his wife's obsessive doubting. He went to endless pains in attempting to reassure her. Part of this response consisted in his trying to behave as what he believed to be the ideal husband—lover, whose only interest in life was his wife. Actually (and not surprisingly) his efforts in these directions only seemed to trouble her more.
As suspected from the early interviews, this doubting obsession proved to have developed as a desperately needed aid to the continued repression of underlying reversed feelings: of what had unconsciously seemed to the patient to be accumulated rage of a murderous level. This had been totally unacceptable to conscious awareness. The obsessive thoughts had elements of projection here. Actually she had to completely conceal from herself and to deny her own negative feelings toward her husband and toward the marriage. In reversed fashion her time, energy, and attention instead became occupied with obsessive doubts about her husband's love for her.
There had been severe incompatibilities present with her parents in her own childhood. These had resulted in her developing a docile and compliant nature, in which there was no room for any recognition of her intense hostile and aggressive feelings. The continued repression

of everything negative created an increasing internal pressure which became ever more threatening. The doubting obsession had of course also even "reversed the threat," in its direction (that is, doubts concerning *his* love), as a further effort at denial, obscurement, substitution, and concealment.

(3) Symptom epigain and self-defeat

The case also demonstrates the epigain of the symptom: the unconscious secondary gain which may be sought in obsessive processes. In obsessive cases this is often less marked and more obscure than in other neuroses. However in this instance, the effect on the husband was to stimulate even greater efforts to prove his love. He became ever more solicitous in an effort to meet the unrealistically (and unconsciously) desired standard of being an "ideal" lover-husband, as noted. This would then presumably result in the complete absence of negative feelings, and end the obsession doubting.

The self-defeating effects of this "gain" became obvious. The more forced, required, and reluctant his attention became in response to her urgent dependent demands, the more resentful and insincere the husband became. The patient actually lost love, and felt more guilty. (*See Concept of the Vicious Circle of Self-Defeat in Neuroses, pp.* 71, 74 and Ch.6:IVE1.) She also sensed the forced quality in his efforts, which made them less than reassuring, rather than their intended reverse. There were other interesting dynamic implications present, some of which may well occur to the interested reader.

2. Vulnerability; Concept of Relationship-Distance Defense; Difficulty in Saying "No"; Obsessive Facade

On closer inspection, the obsessive patient's apparent outward independence, seeming thick skin, and emotional restriction often prove to be largely a facade. This facade has developed because of his own internal weakness, vulnerability, and doubts. An obsessive patient may have trouble saying "No," or refusing a request. He may even have difficulty in "sticking up for" his own rights, despite an external appearance to the contrary. This contrary appearance itself may well have developed as an attempted defense in the presence of such difficulties. This is part of what we have termed his Obsessive Facade. (Ch.5:VA2; *See also Case 69.*)

Sullivan may have been thinking along these lines in commenting that what the severely obsessive person often himself regards as hatred, "on more close scrutiny, proves to be [his] shocking vulnerability to almost anybody . . ." Accordingly, obsessive substitutions sometimes produce attenuations of contact with people which seek to protect the obsessive person from his abnormal vulnerability to anxiety.

The obsessive individual must remain relatively distant from others because of his own concealed but strong internal doubts, fears, low self-esteem, and his "shocking vulnerability." Maintaining distance in relationships is a vital defensive endeavor.

This *Concept of Relationship-Distance* as a major psychic defense, while prominent in the obsessive situation, also has application in many other instances of emotional illness.

3. Hand-in-Glove Analogy and Principle in Relationships

At this juncture mention should be made of a major concept in interpersonal relationships. This concerns the "hows" and "whys" of people

"fitting together, and some of the bases for the formation of their interpersonal relationships. The *Hand-in-Glove Analogy* helps point out that
people do not have to be alike to form relationships. Indeed, in certain
aspects, they can be complete opposites.

Complementing each other's needs, conscious or unconscious, is a significant motivation in the formation and maintenance of a relationship.
Two people can be drawn together by healthful needs. Frequently this also
occurs *through neurotically complementary needs,* which tend then to fit
together as the hand in the glove. This is what we can term the *Hand-in-
Glove Principle in relationships.* Many times both types of needs are
operative and motivating in the formation and development of interpersonal
relationships.

4. Similar Dynamics in Depressions and Obsessions

The underlying psychopathologic sadistic satisfactions which are obtained secretly (out of conscious awareness) by the obsessive individual
are similar to what we have earlier observed in our study of Depression.
(*See* Ch.4, *pp.* 177, 183; *also Case 70,* Ch.6:VE2.) Freud pointed this
out succinctly (in "Mourning and Melancholia"), when he said: ". . . the
corresponding phenomenon (the self-torments) in the obsessional neurosis
signifies a gratification of sadistic tendencies and of hate turned around
upon the self. In both disorders the sufferers usually succeed in the end ⌐
in taking revenge, by the circuitous path of self-punishment, on the original
objects and in tormenting them by means of the illness, having developed
the latter so as to avoid the necessity of openly expressing their hostility
against the loved ones." This is an important aspect of the dynamics.

The reader must bear in mind that this formulation comprises part of
the endogain, this is, the deeply buried primary purpose of the emotional
sickness. (*See* Chapter 2, *p.* 55.) It remains completely hidden from conscious awareness, except following instances of successful therapeutic
intervention.

VI. COMPULSIVE RITUALS

A. REPETITIVE AND RITUALISTIC

1. Compulsions are Acts, and Urges to Act

As noted earlier, obsessive thoughts may include such diverse content as
subjective doubts, wishes, fears, impulses of various kinds, admonitions,
and commands. The distinction between obsessive thoughts and compulsions is usually fairly clear. Cobb stated simply, "When they (obsessive
ideas) lead to actions they become compulsive behavior." It should be
noted, however, that actions as such are not always a requisite for compulsions. Compulsions also include *the urge to act,* in accord with our
earlier definition [Ch.6:IB*1*].

Compulsions and obsessive phenomena tend to be repetitive in themselves. They tend to develop into *patterns* of psychologic reactions,

or what we accordingly might term Compulsive Rituals. The *Compulsive Ritual,* or *C.R.,* may be defined simply as *an insistent, intrusive, habit pattern of behavior which is compulsive in character, and which takes place in response to compulsive urges.*

The Compulsive Ritual develops in accord with five important psychodynamic principles of: (1) continued conflict; (2) incomplete discharge; (3) tendency toward a rhythmical, seesaw types of alternation, or succession of emotional feelings; (4) continued elaboration of the primordial Antecedent Conflict; and (5) the insolubility of the Obsessive Dilemma [Ch.6:VD].

Compulsive Rituals are concerned with security, anxiety, pain, morality, cleanliness, religiosity, scrupulousness, and phobic avoidance. They may involve sexual activity, physiology, money management, temptations, collecting activities, hobbies, counting, eating, sleeping, elimination, music, identification, and almost any aspect of activity, endeavor, or living. The further study of examples of each of these in turn could be intriguing indeed.

2. Childhood Rituals

Frequently, compulsive behavior is repetitive or ritualistic. Examples of the Compulsive Ritual are often present in childhood. The child may explain his compulsive touching or avoidance on the basis that "something evil" or "bad" will befall him, if it is not carried out. He may repeat certain rhymes, as for instance, "Step on a crack, break your grandma's back," "Step on a line, crush your mother's spine," and so on. These illustrate the relatively simple Compulsive Ritual of childhood. They also illustrate its motivation in a magical kind of avoidance of evil, or of averting injury to oneself or to others. The Compulsive Ritual develops as a control, to ward off threatening aggression and hostility. It also serves to maintain a state of readiness and alertness against danger.

Spock discussed the common appearance of mild compulsions around the ages of from eight to ten years. He believed these are more likely to occur at this time because one's "conscience is just naturally becoming stricter at this stage of development." Kanner and others have called attention to the frequency of children's games which are characterized by ritualistic or compulsive rules.

The nine-year-old child's half-serious explanation of his compulsively ritualistic games or behavior generally is that "something" unpleasant might occur if they are not carried out. This is similar in quality to the vague but much stronger and more compelling foreboding and anxiety which is experienced by the adult who may try to resist the performance of a ritual or compulsion. Milder feelings on a similar order are by no means uncommon.

3. Neurotic Compulsive Ritual

There are many clinical examples of Compulsive Rituals. These are to be regarded as neurotic when they result in handicap to the person concerned, or when their overall net result is psychologically uneconomic.

Thus when they interfere with effectiveness or limit the individual's achievements or potential, they are properly labeled neurotic. The patient in *Case 68* often felt compelled to recheck his totals three times. His handwashing was in effect also a Compulsive Ritual. The Handwashing C.R. usually represents (unconsciously), to some extent a symbolic attempt to achieve moral purity or to relieve guilt. This is indeed a hopeless endeavor.

This kind of symbolic handwashing never can achieve its aims. It is a tragically hopeless endeavor. Recognition of such futility is not new. Shakespeare stated it three hundred and fifty years ago in the familiar lines from *Macbeth* (Act II, Scene 2, Line 61):

"Will all great Neptune's ocean wash this blood
Clean from my hand? No, this my hand will rather
The multitudinous seas incarnadine,
Making the green one red."

The following case briefly illustrates a severe C.R., manifested as a "Multiple-of-Three" compulsion.

Case 72

A Compulsive Ritual

A twenty-seven-year-old veterinarian in therapy described his severe Compulsive Ritual. His compulsion required his flushing the toilet a multiple of three times whenever he entered a bathroom. Sometimes he was "satisfied" with three times only, but on other occasions nine, twenty-seven, or even more, were needed. He was at a loss to control his Compulsive Ritual, which had sometimes embarrassed him socially and was professionally handicapping.

It was eventually learned that the number of times required bore a definite relation to his current level of self-esteem and feelings of moral rightness. There were also certain deeper symbolic meanings tying back to earlier years, and partly reflecting parental concerns at an early stage of his development. As more knowledge was gained of the underlying dynamics, the internal needs for the performance of the Compulsive Ritual slowly lessened.

B. SECURITY OPERATIONS: S.O.

1. Patterns in Living; Religious Rites

A. USEFUL ROUTINES AND REPETITIVE SECURITY OPERATIONS.—The development of routine, of habits and patterns in living generally is a useful matter of psychic economy, convenience, and general value. These can comprise what we might term Security Operations. They can be of quite considerable significance to the individual concerned. (*See also* Ch.11:-VA3.) Case *128* (Ch.11:VA4), also illustrates a protective type of Soterial Ritual, as an S.O. in highway travel. The S.O. and the Soterial Ritual frequently overlap.

The extension of these principles into ceremonial rites for fraternal groups, military organizations, and the like can also serve purposes such as the foregoing. In addition, added symbolic meaning and significance is secured for the rite. We might comment in passing upon both the similarities and the differences which exist between certain religious ceremonials and neurotic Compulsive Rituals.

Undoubtedly such repetitions secure other and added psychologic significances and values, particularly as they increasingly become something familiar and reassuring through their continued utilization. Both because of this and possible symbolism, such rites may serve to allay anxiety; to provide a measure of security. Stereotyped behavior and stereotypy in story, legend, song, and so on, come to secure certain security implications. They can gain considerable soterial significance.

B. BARKER AND STEREOTYPY IN STORIES; EXPERIMENTAL ANIMAL STEREOTYPY.—Barker discussed certain of these aspects in relation to the long popular stereotyped Western story. Masserman described stereotyped compulsive behavior as having been observed as part of experimental animal neuroses.

There are also dynamic relationships in such phenomena to the later described *soteria*. (*See* Ch.5:VA9, and Ch.11:pp.19*ff.*) See also the earlier reference to the "just so" story for children, in Ch.5:VIA3.

2. Obsessive Preoccupation with Religion, and Health

A. DYNAMIC AND DIAGNOSTIC INTERRELATIONSHIPS.—The conscience or superego is very important in the genesis of obsessions and compulsions. Frequently, exaggerated moral and religious precepts may be incorporated. It is not surprising on occasion, therefore, that the content of neurotic thoughts and acts may reflect this. Obsessive preoccupation with health also helps to illustrate the close relationship dynamically between the Obsessive-Compulsive Reactions and Hygeiaphrontis Hypochondriasis).

In the following very severe case, the religious elements were overdeveloped by a young high school teacher, as additional reinforcements to aid in the endeavor of repression and control.

Case 73

Ritualistic Diet; Obsessive Preoccupation with Health and Religion

(1) Obsessive preoccupation borders on schizophrenia

A young married college graduate originally sought medical advice for constipation and in order to plan a diet. He was found to be quite preoccupied about these and other aspects of his health. For example, he stated his fears that his intestines might become plugged, or his stomach nonfunctional. He inquired as to how much water he should drink to avoid becoming "dried out," and so on and on and on. These kinds of concerns rightly alarmed his physician. Along with other severe elements in this case, they illustrate how close the severe obsessive person can approach or merge into a psychotic state, in this instance schizophrenia. This patient was very sick emotionally and suffered immensely. His obsessive preoccupations with his health approached closely in degree and kind to the somatic type of delusion. In appearance he was rather on the pedantic and pompous side.

Upon psychiatric consultation, he had amplified these fears. He also related how desperately he dreaded the possibility of his wife becoming pregnant. If this happened, "something incredibly bad" would happen. On the rare occasions he allowed himself intercourse, all of the contraceptive measures he had ever heard about were used simultaneously, to avoid such a dire possibility.

His thought content was also predominantly religious; "I must keep my mind on God all the time. It's the only Christian way of life." Nearly anything else was sinful to him, and he must not "drink, smoke, laugh, smile, or have angry thoughts. . . . These are sinful. . . . The only way to be saved is to pray all the time. . . . There is a constant battle between God and Satan." Actually, this was for him symbolically the battle between his "bad" instincts which he consciously rejected as intolerably evil, and the "good" superego forces within himself.

(2) Medical help sinful

Initially, it was even a sin to seek medical attention: "One should have trust in God to take care of health matters. Resorting to medicine and doctors indicates a lack of faith and is sinful! . . ." He had restricted his diet per "meal" gradually to *exactly* one tumbler of prune juice, three stalks of celery, one pint of ice cream, and three tablespoons of Metamucil. This would always be followed by precisely three cups of water. This compulsively ritualistic diet was eaten two times daily and at stated hours.

His father had been a worried, distant, rigid, and indecisive person. He also had been preoccupied with constipation, and quite evidently had been obsessive-compulsive himself. The patient's mother was moody, serious, and subject to depressions, in which she retreated to her bedroom for two-day periods. Neither parent was able to provide affection, warmth or acceptance.

(3) An objective measure of response to psychotherapy

With such serious psychopathology as partly indicated, one would be justified only in offering a pessimistic prognosis. Nevertheless, this young man made surprisingly substantial progress during the next six months of a moderately intensive treatment regimen. As one objective clinical measure of his improvement, from the physical standpoint alone, his weight climbed from 145 pounds on September 20, to 156 on October 25, and to 167 on January 20.

The red blood cells numbered 3,900,000 and his hemoglobin was 12.1 gm. on September 15, and increased respectively to 4,850,000 and 13.9 gm. by January 22. This was in the absence of any drugs or medical dietary supplements. Indeed, he could have been induced to take these only by force! The physical changes represented the effects of his gradual surrender of stringent and desperate self-imposed dietary restrictions, under the fortunately beneficial effects of intensive psychotherapy.

Reference was made earlier in this chapter, under Section III on *Diagnosis,* to the implications of this case as an example of the possible dynamic interrelationships and overlapping classification in the emotional reactions. In the foregoing instance, these relationships are clinically and dynamically illustrated between Overconcern with Health (that is, Hygeiaphrontis), Obsessive Neurosis, the Compulsive Ritual, and Schizophrenia.

B. SYMBOLISM IN ELIMINATIVE FUNCTION.—The foregoing case also serves to indicate again some of the relationship between bowel habits and personality. In one continuing difficult situation this patient had pointed out how changes in his eliminative function were directly related to his level of anger. For example, he had found himself particularly resentful and angry when an observer would appear when he had been "practice-teaching" while in college. This had been invariably followed by several days of constipation! This represented an unconscious regressive response back to the now futile method of retaliation (by withholding), which had been employed perhaps more successfully in infancy.

Another instance feature of his problems which helped to illustrate the important symbolic implications of bowel function, also furnished an indication of his tremendously low level of self-esteem. This patient reported how he felt temporarily "much better" following a loose copious stool or flatulence, particularly when this was odoriferous. This meant to him symbolically the expulsion of part of his "bad self." He "thought" of himself as mostly bad, and the badness equated feces. This had also entered subconsciously into his urgent concern with maintaining elimination.

3. Compulsive Security Rituals; C.S.R.

Another type of ritualistic behavior is seen at times in which some aspect of daily living becomes compulsively elaborated as a Security Operation. When Cumpulsive Ritual and S.O. are combined, we might call this a *Compulsive Security Ritual.*

In its most common and simple form the C.S.R. for example may involve the rechecking of the gas stove or lights. The following case illustrates a more extreme example.

Case 74

A Compulsive Security Ritual upon Retiring

A forty-year-old single business woman reported an involved Compulsive Security Ritual upon retiring each evening. The stove was triple (or more) checked, windows and doors were each carefully inspected in turn several times, and a dresser was placed against her bedroom door.

Finally, a long and involved procedure had to be followed, and in exact sequence, in order to get herself undressed, bathed, and into bed. If an item were omitted, or perhaps not performed precisely as it should be, it had to be repeated. Otherwise she would be unable to sleep, because of resulting uneasiness and anxiety.

As in other instances, this type of ritualistic activity was a defense against anxiety. Preliminary investigation tended to confirm an early hypotheses that part of her C.S. Ritual was an unconscious attempt to reinforce repression of her disowned sexual impulses. The patient was an unhappy inhibited person, whose affectivity had been long frozen within herself. Unfortunately, all efforts to interest her in intensive treatment were unsuccessful. In this instance, as in many C.S.R.s, there was a close relationship and overlapping with the Security Operation as referred to in Section B, and to the Soterial Ritual, in Chapter 11.

VII. THE IMPULSIONS

A. DEFINITIONS

1. Repetitive Series of Irresistable, Usually Anti-social Acts

Impulsive, as an adjective, refers to *quick or sudden actions without real forethought, judgment, the adequate weighing of consequences, or careful prior consideration.* Impulsion is the noun naming *the act which is carried out in this fashion through strong impulse.* It is also the term the author has come to employ for members of a group of psychopathologic, impulsive patterns of acts or behavior.

Accordingly, the Impulsions are herein considered to include, and are defined as, a rather heterogeneous *group of emotional disorders which are characterized by repetitive compulsions to commit, and the carrying out of various unlawful or socially disapproved series of similar, related, or identical actions. They are compulsive, repetitive acts.* The Impulsion is *a psychopathologic pattern of behavioral reaction.* The Impulsive Act comprises a major instance of what we can call a *behavioral-symptom.*

In view of their intimate relationship to the Obsessive-Compulsive group of reactions, some brief comments about the Impulsions are offered in this chapter. Within this category are included such acts and repetitive urges to act, as pyromania, kleptomania, and exhibitionism. These acts characteristically tend to be repetitive, also pointing up their relations to the foregoing category of Compulsive Rituals.

The Impulsion, however, differs importantly from the more usual kind of compulsion, in that the person concerned fairly often *acts* upon, or what we term in psychiatry *acts out* (see later) his urges, and despite their antisocial nature. Certain of the Impulsions are considered also by some authorities to represent perversions.*

2. Further Distinctions between Compulsion and Impulsion

An important distinction between these two reactions also is to be found empirically, that is in the person's reaction to the impulse. Thus, in the Compulsion he may resist vigorously the performance of the act, and likely finds it intolerable and abhorrent. In distinction, the impulsive act is likely to be more acceptable, welcomed, and to a greater or lesser extent consciously pleasurable, although emotional conflict in varying degree may still be present in relation to its contemplation or commission.

Both Compulsions and Impulsions have the qualities of urgency and immediacy. However, the ability to resist his urge and resulting performance varies considerably. The compulsive individual *resists,* often valiantly. The impulsive person generally *yields,* and repeatedly. His so-called "irresistible impulse" really more accurately indicates his relative unwillingness and inability to withstand any reasonable measure of tension. Hence any build up of tension (to obey the impulse, however motivated) is intolerable. The impulsive individual seemingly cannot postpone, modify, or wait very long in his response. He yields to his impulse, and (at least a temporary) relief of tension is thereby secured. Not infrequently, as noted, there is subjective pleasure experienced at the time of or following, the commission of the impulsive act.

3. "Acting Out" of Hostility and Sex; Social-Defiance

Dynamically, the group of Impulsions is characteristically marked by major elements of: (1) hostility, (2) aggression, and (3) what we might term *Social-Defiance.* Sexual Impulsions are also to be encountered. These sexual elements may be "acted out" separately, or in conjunction with

---

* An example is exhibitionism, which is a recognized perversion. Dynamically, perversions are sometimes described as representing the "negative" of neuroses.

hostile impulses. They may secure outward expression, being directly sexual in nature, or being expressed in some more indirect, concealed and symbolic form. These hostile and/or sexual compulsive urges are all in literal fashion "acted out" * by the individual concerned, in this group of
√ socially important and disturbing reactions. *The Impulsive person's rebellion, hatred of authority, and hostile-aggression is* in this way *often generalized to include, and to be expressed toward, society as a whole.* It is the latter which accounts for the fairly frequently encountered picture of Social-Defiance in the Impulsions, and also defines the term.

Society may be subjectively perceived by the individual as personally threatening and hostile. Of course he inevitably winds up in self-defeating fashion by making it far more realistically so! With the Impulsions there is often the more or less concealed element of the actual or symbolic gratification of sexual or aggressive impulses. These may stem from needs which are consciously disowned.

The subjective experience which is described with the Impulsions is somewhat comparable to that in the Compulsions. Performance of the act is accompanied by a relief of tension. This is similar to the relief which accompanies a compulsive act. The impulses in both types of reaction appear without (apparent) cause, the patient is tense and anxious until the act is carried out. Its completion is accompanied by the discharge of tension and the feeling of relief. Guilt or remorse vary in degree and in frequency as an accompaniment of the impulsive act; a "behavioral-symptom." Many such acts have overtones of sexual stimulation or gratification. Many have hidden sexual or aggressive symbolism or implications.

Impulsions are usually characterized by a lack of real logical and realistic explanation for the act performed. There are often rationalizations of one kind or another developed to help account for some of the behavior. In some of them there also is often an element of concealed sexual meaning, or of stimulation and gratification, as noted. This is frequently present, for instance, in pyromania. Sometimes this type of sick social offender will watch the results of his act, accompanying or following this by sexual self-gratification or by micturition.

4. Punishment and Remorse

Impulsions have to be regarded as more or less uncontrollable through the conscious effort and will power alone, of the person concerned. They are often repeated despite apprehension and censure or punishment. The threat of punishment may not serve as a very strong deterrent to the repetition of the Impulsive Act. Indeed, it is not unusual to find the coexistence of a strong unconscious need to "seek" punishment (and also forgiveness) in this nonconstructive fashion. As a result, the impulsive, antisocial act sometimes may be committed in a manner that seemingly almost insures detection! With certain individuals in this group it is as though the punishment even provides them with a clean slate. The individual is then free to begin over again.

---

* *See* earlier footnote, *Case 64*: IIIB3.

The patient may or may not experience some degree of reluctance before acting out his impulsions. Remorse afterwards is also present in highly variable degree. Generally, the person has a full awareness and understanding of the potential consequences of what he does.

The Impulsions have increased importance by virtue of their complex and often controversial medico-legal implications. In a given instance of actual or potential legal action, it is best not to make too hasty conclusions or generalizations, as to the moral and legal responsibility of the person concerned. Bias in these areas of the Impulsions also can be a handicap to justice. Where injury to others results, and leads to a trial in court, each case, together with all the individual elements in this particular situation and the psychodynamic factors and motivational features involved, had best be carefully considered separately and on its own merits.

B. TYPES OF IMPULSIONS

1. The More Common Impulsions

The more common psychopathologic patterns of behavioral reaction which may be considered Impulsions, together with brief definitions, include the following fourteen:

1. *Dipsomania*. Periodic episodes of compulsive, excessive drinking, frequently associated with behavior disturbances.
2. *Exhibitionism*. A compulsive kind of bodily exposure, usually involving the display of the sexual organs to a member of the opposite sex. This is often accompanied by a socially perverse kind of sexual stimulation and/or gratification; particularly in males.
3. *Kleptomania*. Compulsive stealing; is largely without regard to any *apparent* personal need for the stolen object. The need of course is "hidden" and its sought-after gratification a more or less symbolic one. It is usually strong indeed; more so because of its unconscious nature.
4. *Pyromania*. The morbid compulsion to start fires; often associated with (unconscious) urethral erotism.
5. *Voyeurism*. Sexually motivated spying on others, which may be compulsive in character.
6. *Sado-Masochistic Rituals*.
7. *Repetitive Rape* on an Impulsive basis.
8. *Repetitive Impulsive Mayhem, Infanticide, and Murder*.
9. *Compulsive Repetitive Perversions and Sexual Practices;* includes *pedophilia, pederasty, some sexual instances of promiscuity,* and certain cases of *Don Juanism, Nymphomania,* and *impulsive homosexuality*.
10. *Impulsive gambling*.
11. *Drug Addictions*.
12. *Miscellaneous behavioral and object addictions*.

13. *Impulsive Nomadism.*
14. *Impulsive Criminality.*

2. Kleptomania

For an example of the foregoing Impulsions let us pick the interesting one of kleptomania. Characteristic of kleptomania is that what is taken is not really needed or wanted in the ordinary sense. The kleptomaniac individual is usually unable to explain why he steals, or why he steals what he does. Furthermore, he is often well able to afford to purchase what he takes.

The object taken has value of course, but this value is far more an unconscious one, and its satisfaction is sought in symbolic and thereby obscured terms. Kleptomania is more frequent among women. The following instance illustrates these characteristic features of true kleptomania.

Case 75

Kleptomania; Active Disinterest in Therapy A Secondary Defense

A wealthy woman was a typical sufferer from Kleptomania. She was apparently unable voluntarily to control her shoplifting impulses. On her intermittent trips into town she would thus "pick up" various odd assortments of merchandise. These items were ones for which she had no great or apparent practical need. They were usually of rather small value, and their total purchase price was relatively insignificant, at least to a person of her means.

The need to steal was clearly not financial, nor was there significant material gain. She was apprehended several times during her shoplifting experiences and avoided prosecution by making prompt restitution, or through the use of her social position and personal contacts. Some persons with Kleptomania are less apt to receive or to be able to arrange such benign, nonpunitive, and charitable treatment.

In this instance there was no interest in or motivation for treatment. This does not mean, however, that she was comfortable about her problem. Indeed, she was tortured at times by conflicts and doubts. Even superficially there was evidence of great insecurity, social maladjustment, and unhappiness. Not the master of herself, she was driven by inner forces not accessible to her understanding or control. Her active disinterest in finding out what her inner needs were in so behaving, constituted an additional potent defensive protection of them.

This provided another interesting illustration of our *Concept of Secondary Defense.* (*See pp.* 97 *and* 144.) Repression can be maintained and neurotic gratification can be continued (even though self-defeating) if one actively fears and avoids the introspective work of psychotherapy.

C. PROBLEMS IN MANAGEMENT AND THERAPY OF THE IMPULSIVE INDIVIDUAL

1. Five Principles of Impulsions

Problems are always present in the attempted therapeutic management of the impulsive individual. This is true personally, socially, often legally, and certainly professionally. Treatment is very difficult. Its initiation is not infrequently impossible. Why is this so?

The answers relate to the nature of the Impulsive Reaction. The Impulsion is not necessarily nor undividedly unpleasant or consciously repugnant to the individual concerned, as we find more commonly in the Compulsion. Indeed, the Impulsion may be quite pleasant, and usually, as noted, there is a distinct quantum of pleasure concurrent with its commission. Psychic pain is more likely absent.

Therefore the problem to the impulsive individual, should he recognize one (in distinction from the compulsive person where the experiencing of the compulsion itself is most likely difficult, painful, and abhorrent), often enough lies in the unsuitability or unacceptability of the act itself, or even more in the resulting social censure and condemnation. In other words, he suffers little or even no pain in or from the act in itself. This is accompanied instead by pleasure or satisfaction in varying kind and measure. Difficulties when present are more likely to stem from the consequences of the Impulsion, especially possible social ones.

Five major Principles are thus generally found to be more or less characteristic of, and operative in the Impulsions. These are the Principles of (1) Minimal Discomfort; (2) Unconscious Satisfactions; (3) Antitherapy; (4) Social Censure; and (5) Social-Defiance.

2. Therapy, Resistance, and the Secondary Defense of the Impulsion

Thus the tendency of the impulsive person is not to seek therapy. He does not wish for the surrender of his impulse. He has only too often little motivation for seeking out the basis for it, via the psychotherapeutic route of finding out more about what the impulse really means and represents, and why it is present. Instead he will ordinarily seek to retain it, sometimes despite strong and repeated verbal protestations to the contrary.

Wishes for change, when present, are more likely to be directed toward allaying the social censure. This motivation can sometimes lead to a trial of treatment. The results may be indifferent, fair, or occasionally good, depending upon the strength of his motivation and what additional psychic forces can be mobilized in its behalf. If he seeks anything, he may seek instead of course to find more hidden, devious, and/or less censurable means of discharging (gratifying) the impulse.

3. Treatment Rarely Sought; More Rarely Successful

The foregoing outlines the basis of the resistance to therapy of the impulsive person. As with resistance in other emotional illnesses his *secondary defense* is actively operative; perhaps far more so. Here again the aim is to secure the retention of his impulsion (*behavioral-symptom*). It is hardly surprising that therapy is too rarely sought with serious intent, and is still more rarely pursued to a successful conclusion. See also *Inertia Concept* in this initiation of psychotherapy, page 213.

VIII. TREATMENT

A. KNOW THYSELF

1. Derepression Necessary

Our comments concerning therapy have general applicability in the treatment of emotional illness. This is in line with the policy which is being followed generally in the sections on treatment for each chapter. In addition some special points in relation to the treatment of the Obsessive-Compulsive Reactions will be included. These are in supplement to those already referred to in this and in the preceding chapter.

Inscribed prominently in the famous Temple of Delphi in ancient Greece were the words *"Know Thyself."* This admonition was respected for its wisdom in the ancient world. It is equally significant and wise today. Learning to really know oneself is the major endeavor of psychotherapy. The extent to which this goal is successfully achieved on a meaningful level, is the measure of the effectiveness of psychiatric treatment in a given situation.

Basic self-understanding inevitably results in securing the recognition or further recognition, the understanding, and the acceptance of one's emotions. Such acceptance and understanding is both a consequence and a measure, of the level of emotional maturity achieved. Constructive modification follows.

For many individuals, and in particular, in instances of the Obsessive Reactions or where there is obsessive character formation, the analytic work seeks to free the long-internally-frozen emotional assets. These have been defensively locked in the unconscious. Their recognition and expression has been feared. Repression has been reinforced in many ways. Derepression has been a threat and a danger, and the possibility which has been dreaded. This "attitude" must be reversed. In therapy one must learn to permit it, encourage it, and even to seek it.

Derepression can take place in the treatment situation permissibly, safely, and in a healthy direction. With adequate professional help the patient learns to recognize and to accept his emotional feelings. He comes to appreciate what his feelings are, and that they are not uncontrollable. He learns that the negative and self-assertive elements are not "murderous" as he has "feared." He secures an understanding of their origins, and they lose their capacity as a potent source of pressure and trouble. Energy formerly required to maintain control and repression becomes available for healthful redirection.

2. Accurate Self-Appraisal a Valuable Asset

A. REQUISITE FOR THE ANALYST.—The value of possessing a more objectively accurate picture of oneself has long been recognized. Most of us have an inaccurate or distorted self-estimation, in varying degree. Further, it is hardly possible for us unaided to recognize the existence of such distortions, their ramifications, or their extent.

Patients who have achieved considerable self-understanding in therapy gain increased awareness of the importance of an accurate self-appraisal. A patient-colleague in his third year of fruitful therapy spontaneously commented recently. "The real value of analysis is that it shows me what I really am. I've made some useful changes because of this. . . . Now I can take a kinder view of myself. I guess it's easier after this for me to take a kinder view of other people. I suppose then also, that I'm more comfortable and more accepting of myself, and I guess this all helps make others more comfortable around me. . . ." These gains had been most significant for him.

Self-understanding is of universal value. Its great value is not limited to those in therapy, or to any single professional group. Accordingly, it was also recognized some decades ago that more self-understanding and maturity were decided assets to psychiatrists. The earlier adherents of the psychoanalytic movement were often encouraged to have some analysis themselves. By 1920 analysts generally were being urged to undertake a personal analysis. Today such an intensive self-study has come to be considered a requisite for competence in the techniques of psychoanalysis. In addition, the gains achieved thereby generally become a highly useful individual, social, and professional asset. The latter gains accrue of course, to others as well as to psychiatrists.

B. NONAWARENESS PROTECTIVELY INTENDED; ACCURATE SELF-PICTURE A THERAPEUTIC GOAL.—Thus, one important goal of psychotherapy not often enough stated is the more accurate adjustment of the self-estimation or self-picture. Discrepancies exist to some extent or other between the subjective picture which we have of ourselves, and the sometimes more objective one which others have of us. The continued maintenance of conscious nonawareness of the inaccuracies of the self-picture is a psychological protectively-intended and defensive endeavor. This may be contributed to by the development of character defenses and reaction formations.

The maintenance of nonawareness is for the purpose of preventing the conscious recognition of traits (and other aspects) which would be disapproved of, or condemned in oneself. Discrepancies between a subjectively inaccurate self-picture and an objectively more accurate appraisal may be very great. A resolution of such discrepancies is another important goal in psychotherapy.

Stating such a goal is relatively simple. Securing it is likely to be a vastly more difficult and prolonged endeavor. Interpretations and pertinent information can be presented only so fast as the patient is ready and able to receive.

C. AGGRESSIVE AND DOMINEERING BEHAVIOR UNRECOGNIZED.—The distortions in one's self-appraisal can be substantial. Their resolution can pose major difficulties. An instance comes to mind. This concerns a woman who felt subjectively, quite abused and maligned. She regarded herself as a constant victim to nearly everyone. She felt very badly treated and continually pushed around. She saw herself as "everybody's patsy." This helped to conceal from her any recognition of what was actually very aggressive behavior on her own part.

She usually managed to secure a domineering role in her relationships. Her attitudes were marked by a considerable measure of contempt and scorn for most of her associates. Awareness of this had to be secured gradually. Her level of self-esteem was already too low to tolerate any possible acceptance of such data if suddenly or prematurely presented to her.

D. KING DAVID REACTION.—In a paper on King David's Anger (see Selected References and Bibliography; also see p. 75 and Ch.6:VF3), examples were cited of the strong emotional reaction which can occur when sudden conscious awareness has been inadvertently gained of the negative aspects of one's self-appraisal. As the result of successful psychotherapy, one's own self-picture and that which is held by others, will more closely approximate each other. Ultimately, the gaining of increased self-respect is likewise a consequence.

3. Emotional Understanding

There is a significant difference between understanding which is on a strictly intellectual and academic level, and that which includes the emotional. This latter is what we can refer to as emotional understanding, in distinction from intellectual understanding as above. It is an important concept in therapy.

Thus the real therapist is not concerned with securing added information alone. He is also vitally interested in his patient-colleague developing an increased ability to function with effectiveness and satisfaction in living. He has an interest in his patient's securing an improved ability to promote and to maintain good relationships. He is interested in the post-treatment status of the patient's emotional reactions. Emotional understanding is real insight.

We stress the importance of emotions in therapy generally, and in what transpires between physician and patient. Therapy is not merely an intellectual exercise. It is perhaps on the more accurate side to regard it instead as an *emotional experience*.

4. Team-Work Tenet in Psychotherapy

In *Chapters 1* and *3*, reference was made to the important *Joint Endeavor Principle* (*pp.* 25 and 130) in psychotherapy, which stresses the requirement for the active collaboration of the patient with his therapist. A related and supporting major Tenet of Team-Work needs to be stressed at this juncture, in further clarification of our Principle.

This Tenet can be defined as: *ideally, the therapist seeks to enlist, to secure the cooperation of, and thence to team up with the more mature aspects of the personality of his patient-colleague, in their joint therapeutic endeavor.* As a consequence *both work together to better understand the less mature, more emotional aspects of the person's personality and his intended-defenses.* Together they seek to resolve his emotional conflicts and inconsistancies; to recognize, to accept, to understand, and to secure more psychologically-economic replacements for his self-defeating attitudes, psychic endeavors, and patterns of reaction. These aims are basic to sound psychotherapy and analysis. [*See also* Ch.7;XIIC3, pp. 434–435.]

B. RECOGNITION AND REFERRAL

1. Major and Laudable Accomplishment

The physician has very great responsibility in the recognition and selection of proper persons for referral to a psychiatrist. It is easy enough for patients and for the doctor to maintain the *status quo* when emotional defenses are working well. It is more difficult to disturb it when necessary to effect referral. The adequate recognition and the expert referral of suitable patients for psychotherapy is a major and laudable accomplishment for the referring physician and friend.

Patients with obsessive tendencies are often the most easily "managed" ᵛ ones in medical practice. Rarely enough will they spontaneously seek medical help for their obsessive defenses. The responsibility of the physician lies in his developing an ability to recognize early the presence of limiting obsessive character traits or symptoms. His further responsibility is to take the initiative in the early preparation of selected patients for psychiatric consultation and possible treatment.

2. Early Therapy Advantageous

On occasion patients will seek help when they become too tormented by obsessive fears, doubts, or thoughts. It would be *far* better if treatment were begun considerably before this state of affairs has come about. When obsessive traits serve their unconsciously intended defensive purposes adequately, there is apt to be little or no anxiety.* With no anxiety present there is usually no interest in treatment unless such an interest can be stimulated. As earlier noted in our *Fuel Analogy* (*see* p. 42), anxiety can provide "fuel" for therapy.

Usually it is only when conscious awareness (that is, derepression) is threatened of heretofore disowned impulses that anxiety arises. This may serve as fuel to motivate the obsessive patient toward seeking treatment. Treatment when successful can unlock the long-rusting doors of his unconscious to permit the constructive release, examination, and healthy utilization of the patient's hidden emotional potentials. Lowering of the level of anxiety ensues as resolution is secured of the underlying intrapsychic conflicts. The earlier therapy is initiated, the less suffering, the less danger of progression, and the sooner conflicts can be resolved. This is a relationship of direct proportions. It bears out our important *Principle of Symptom-Longevity* [Ch.14:VIIIE15 also p. 48)].

C. THE TREATMENT OF CHOICE

1. Four Major Hurdles; The Better-Than-Well Result

A. RESULTS MOST WORTHWHILE.—The treatment of choice is analysis or analytically oriented psychotherapy on as intensive a basis as is feasible

---

* *Inverse Anxiety-Symptom Ratio Precept,* pp. 103, 144–145, and 343.

and useful. This is necessary in order to achieve real insight. The first major hurdle is the recognition that problems exist. The second one is the desire for help and the willingness to seek it. The third hurdle is the initiation of therapy. Each of these hurdles can pose major problems. In addition of course, it may still prove difficult to find a suitable therapist or one who can make time available on his schedule, once a positive decision has been reached.

Once the patient has at least accepted a trial period of therapy, the therapeutic problems really begin. Continuing the therapy so as to secure optimal results and thence to its logical completion, is the fourth major hurdle. The potential results make all of these necessary efforts most worthwhile. Pursuing treatment to its ultimate goal will result in the person concerned progressing beyond his pre-symptom or pre-illness level. In other words he potentially can gain a status of being "better than well."

B. LONG-TERM ENDEAVOR.—The treatment of obsessive patients is never easy. Certain character traits common to such patients (that is, rigidity, stubbornness, obstinacy, and perverseness) tend to prolong and to handicap therapy. Other traits (that is, superior intelligence, persistence, conscientious endeavor, and diligence) can usually be enlisted as useful allies to treatment. One can expect, however, that a thorough analysis in cases of established obsessive character defenses, or in cases of from mild to moderate Obsessive Neuroses, may well require several years of intensive collaborative work. This applies to the instances in which the patient can cooperate effectively.

On the other hand, when the patient is limited in his cooperation and when the neurosis is more severe and established, the period of treatment can become further extended. Defensive patterns which are laid down as thoroughly as the obsessive ones, in response to such fierce internal psychologic needs, and which have served so "effectively," are not readily surrendered. Further, there are the basic therapeutically handicapping defenses of these persons, such as their poor tolerance to change, and their resistance to new ideas and attitudes. These rather fundamental defensive attributes help to insure the generally slow rate of progress which can be expected.

2. Problems Encountered in Intensive Treatment of Obsessive Patients

A. KINDLINESS AND TOLERANCE LIMITED.—From the study of this chapter and the preceding one the reader already may have a considerable appreciation of the problems inherent in the treatment of the Obsessive-Compulsive Reactions. Since these people were themselves accepted, regarded, and treated with impatience, and intolerance in early life, they are likely to have in turn a limited capacity to be tolerant or kind toward themselves or toward others.

These handicapping attributes inevitably enter into the therapeutic situation. There may be limited tolerance present for the therapist and for his ideas. Perversity is also prominent. The patient may have so little really basic positive desire to meet what he imagines to be the wishes of the therapist, or to cooperate in the work of treatment, that he can quite unwittingly defeat all efforts to help him.

B. TRANSFERENCE AND COUNTER-TRANSFERENCE.—On the successful working out of the patient-therapist relationship will hang the relative success or failure of the entire treatment. This relationship offers the patient the opportunity of more objectively observing and studying at close hand, with the aid of the therapist as a detached, expert observer, the ways in which he thinks, feels, and behaves. He further learns how, often inadvertently, these ways can profoundly influence the interpersonal situation. The analytic therapist comes to be regarded variously as representing in part and at various times one or the other parental (or other significant) figure. Prior relationships and problems from the early parent-child interaction thus are recapitulated in the therapeutic situation. There can be various differences and distortions. The recapitulation may be a caricature of its antecedent.

This leads of course to the transference to the therapist attitudes and feelings previously experienced toward earlier significant figures. In therapy the observation, recognition, and the study of these patterns of transference is very important. The counter-transference in turn of the therapist to his patient is also a matter of importance.

C. FENICHEL LISTS DIFFICULTIES IN ANALYSIS.—Fenichel has listed eight principal difficulties in the analysis of Obsessive-Compulsive Neuroses. These are: (1) compliance with the basic rule of analysis (see the Treatment Rule, p. 50) is very difficult or impossible; (2) the ego is split, part of it siding with the symptoms and only the remainder able fully to cooperate with the analyst and in treatment*; (3) an extra layer of regression (over conversion) must be worked through; (4) the prominent ambivalence, which is characteristically present, enters into the transference, with cooperation accompanied by stubbornness and rebelliousness; (5) the isolation of ideation from corresponding emotions may result in insight being limited to intellectual understanding; (6) thinking and talking are "sexualized"; (7) secondary gains are integrally bound up in the personality (not limited to this group); and (8) the arousal of anxiety during treatment is poorly tolerated by obsessive persons, who are less used to experiencing it.

D. OBSESSIVE EPIGAIN; RESISTANCES.—In reference to the unconscious part of the secondary gain (the epigain) of the obsessive patient, one must observe the fact that many of his neurotic traits are highly valued socially, and that they also have considerable personal use. Sharpe noted the use by the patient of interpretations which were made by the therapist and even of insights gained, in a typical kind of obsessive fashion. This often tended to delay or obstruct their value and the therapy. Sullivan called attention to the security operations of these people in therapy. These result

---

* An observation which is of course correct, as acknowledged in our *Team Work Tenet* in psychotherapy (Ch.6:VIIIA4), but which notes a difficulty that is more a relative matter, and one that is accordingly common to the therapy of all types of emotional problems.

in "anxious deletions," and increase the difficulty of the psychiatrist's task.

Fromm-Reichmann noted that in the treatment relationship, "obsessional patients . . . may make use of their repetitive, argumentative, manipulative, and compulsive ways of interpersonal behavior." She also wrote of the value of the therapist's directing attention to major issues. As these are clarified, side ones can be skipped. One attempts to avoid the establishment of an obsessive pattern in the treatment itself and in the treatment interaction.

To be further noted at this point and as earlier illustrated, the obsessive person is often driven to use words, careful phraseology, and the academic approach to "control" the treatment situation. Actually this is part of his unwitting endeavor to control the anxiety and the discomfort which will arise from an inadvertent expression of emotions. It is another defensive operation, a resistance, a delay, and part of his Secondary Defense.

3. The Tracing-Technique in Therapy

A. THERAPY RESERVED TO EXPERIENCED PSYCHIATRIST.—The definitive treatment of obsessive patients is advisedly reserved to the experienced psychiatrist. Others had best avoid the temptation of attempting psychotherapy. Treatment is a complex endeavor. There are many pitfalls for the unwary. There are many subtleties and nuances involved. Extensive training, background, and experience are required in order properly to cope with them, or adequately to utilize them in the therapy.

A wide number of approaches and techniques may offer therapeutic help to the psychotherapist. He will find on the basis of his personal experience that various ones of these will prove useful to him. One of these, for example, is the attempted *tracing of a particular emotional manifestation back to its earliest appearance.* This is the Tracing-Technique in Therapy. In appropriate circumstances it is useful generally in therapy [Ch.10:XB1]. It is particularly applicable to certain specific obsessive symptoms in which this Tracing Technique can be utilized in seeking to determine the original expression and initiating circumstances of an obsessive trend.

B. UTILIZATION OF INQUIRY AND HYPOTHETICAL SITUATION.—For example, let us consider disturbing obsessive ideas relating to the injury of a family member. It is always helpful for the therapist to discover when possible, whether there have been thoughts, wishes, or fantasies about this family member being gone, dead, or never having been present. The selection of the optimal time for inquiry, using the best approach, and knowing the proper emphasis and the right degree of insistence in each individual case requires the most discriminating judgment on the part of the therapist.

The psychiatrist might also determine, for example, what things might then be like, by setting up a hypothetical situation for the patient to associate to, in which such an absence had transpired. An inquiry or inquiries as to when the ideas first appeared, may result in their being placed farther and farther back in time. This is likely to be particularly true in long-term therapy, when one will often be led gradually to earlier and earlier data. The exploration itself is constructive, and the data procured is useful.

A related extension of this discussion leads us to an interesting conception which we shall consider further later (Ch.8:VB4). This is the *Concept of Defensive Layering,* which stresses how successive layers of conflict and defenses are uncovered in turn, in successful long-term therapy.

C. WHAT REPRESSED DATA UNDERLIES MECHANISMS?—With all obsessive ideas, the physician may find it helpful constantly to keep in the foreground the question as to what painful unconscious idea or impulse could possibly be present which requires the substitution and displacement that has occurred.

What has been the need? What repressed data lies at the basis of these mechanisms? What do they seek to defend against? What are the emotional conflicts? Keeping in mind these and other similar questions helps constitute the "proper therapeutic attitude."

D. BREAKDOWN OF OBSESSIVE DEFENSES.—One must be very cautious when new and severe obsessive ideas have developed suddenly. This development may possibly be prodromal to a psychotic episode. This can transpire should the newly acquired, desperately-needed obsessive defense prove insufficient or break down, as an Emotional Decompensation.

When the onset of great stress results in the crumbling of obsessive defenses, when established defenses prove inadequate, or when new and more adequate stable ones cannot be elaborated in time, a major psychosis can occur. This may take place rather gradually, or with some rapidity. In either event the consequences can be psychologically catastrophic.

The instance to follow concerns a forty-four-year-old man of superior intelligence and much ability, who had functioned in excellent and efficient fashion for years. Long-established character defenses of the obsessive group crumbled, and hastily-attempted elaborations proved inadequate in the face of a series of most serious familial and professional problems. This was an "emotional decompensation," roughly analogous to the physical one of the heart in cardiac decompensation. The reaction which evolved was basically a schizophrenic one with a paranoid coloring. Outwardly and at least superficially he could present a fairly organized appearance most of the time! Otherwise he was in far more serious trouble. This was illustrated particularly in the interference with, and in the major effects upon his thinking processes.

These effects are strikingly reflected in the following excerpts from a piece of his philosophically written material. They were nearly non-apparent in his speech and conversation. During the course of prolonged therapy this man made substantial improvement. Many of his obsessive defenses were reestablished, several being increased and some undergoing constructive modification and development.

Case 76

Disorganization of Thought Processes when Obsessive Defenses Crumbled; Written Material

(1) Ideation confused

"The following random thoughts of constructive criticism express a needling conscience to course humanitarian concern everywhere, yet such a voice is literally muffled by hands over the mouth and a foot on the back, stamping—'according to the constitution and by-laws.' This is TODAY, and we are existing in every-changing event through NOW with education, new sciences, higher standard of living, *AND* insight to conclude there isn't one single 'saint' who founded society planks can rise up rattling bones if the reign of leadership build new kind into constructive practices that fulfil *NEED* with a current wisdom. . . .

". . . When human mind with-hold such need for brotherly teamstering, of course they turn to communism that will offer to supply grasping power for more gourds. What *IS* communism other than obeisance to a flesh-like reasoning, religiously learning knowledge through native that is practicing organically with the body of human mind for voice? Isn't communism all the devilish forces of subserviancy with a body so God's wisdom is credited to a self-funneling do-it-yourself kit, within bodies of flesh that mate in resolving field only tor 'self' through God's breath? Christianity is a field of religion to serve *MANKIND* with a heart as well as a mind digesting the kind with kin, by *discipline* with human relationships that *culture* spiritual WORD. Take a look at some past history, and observe how food and indolent ignorance of relative standpoint tends to propagate mere communism. . . ."

(2) Excess verbiage; goals of phrases sidetracked

". . . Any society framing John's body that lies molding in the grave, is styling dregs of blood to cast seeds of doubt for deceptive 'Why' that perceive nod of opinion, juggling minds of qualified conscience to practice religiously with habits that bind thought in regulation. Fear of tribulation muffle the conscious efforts into muse of levity that create quackery in paraphernalia for a pillage of meliorism. A nation's harvest is ground of parental mind rather than diet of worm wherever the land parallel freedom rider in nod to grooming cultural perpetuity, to salvage it through fields of battles in kaleidoscope . . .

". . . A family reasoning with moral matter as environmental bulwark find a talent from intellectual pockets of insight like His figurative soul of wisdom, creating personal integrity and morality into a HOME like it by thinking and acting with concern and compassion to fellow man. This accomplishes an obligation of purpose with the best of ability, that also respect hide, because conduct is upheld by orderly society where men can think and act with reason and not in response to a mob psychology. An incredible race of recurrent scrambling mortality is rocking cradles of relative idyllic force for a model heart picturing it, to present paradoxical brow of refinement anointing inspirations figuring a cast itineration of that notational metabosis. Men harp history as a shepherd to 'rock' tribe for truth that bark referendum as kindred knight, and propagate fruit of gastronomy like a parasite to snake God through anthropology with legendary regiments of voice. . . ."

4. Premature Interpretations or Speculations Avoided

A. RULE OF IMPRESSION PRIORITY IMPORTANT IN THERAPY.—Although applicable in all sound analytically-oriented therapy, the dangers and the disadvantages of premature interpretations are particularly great in the treatment of the obsessive patient. Ideas should be presented to the patient sparingly and only after careful consideration. They must be sound. In each instance they should be supported or supportable by factual data which has been previously secured from the patient. They should be presented as briefly, clearly, and concisely as possible. Any other course enhances the chances for their rejection, and stimulates the resistance of the patient.

Later interpretations are likely to fare far better if an early pattern of accuracy, meaningfulness, and acceptability is established. Such a pattern of success will be greatly enhanced if earlier comments by the therapist have clearly made sense to the patient. Other factors being equal, an initial, first, or earlier impression will tend to occupy a position of emotional priority. The emotional reaction: (1) to the first contact(s), (2) to the initial interaction between patient and therapist, and (3) to the earliest comments or interpretations accordingly are most important.

These are first or prior events and as such they establish precedents and set up patterns for later responses. This is in accord with our Rule of Impression Priority (*see Chapter 9*). This is an important conception in human economy generally, as well as many for psychiatry. It has some important implications for psychotherapy.

B. GEARING COMMENTS TO RECEPTIVITY; PUSHING STIMULATES RE-SISTANCE.—Unsupported guesses or speculations as to underlying dynamics should be kept to oneself. If one has to debate at all between silence and speaking, choose the former! One can always return and pick up an earlier point. The therapist, however, cannot call back an inadvertent, clumsy, meaningless, misleading, or inane comment, once it has been made.

One must also gear such comments as are offered, to the current level of receptivity which is present. These obsessive individuals cannot be pushed. Attempts to hurry treatment unduly will more than defeat their intent. Such efforts to push treatment along may be a reflection of anxiety or impatience on the part of the therapist, with himself or with his patient. "Pushing the treatment" will only stimulate in turn more anxiety within the patient, with the likely result of increased resistance. The reverse effect from that desired will result, and ground will be lost rather than gained. This may be even more true with the seriously ill patient, that is, the patient who needs to maintain notable obsessive defenses. Similarly, one must not be misled by insistance from the patient that the treatment be pushed along. The reader can perhaps gain some appreciation of the rather tremendous capacity for patience, persistence, and tenacity which must be present on the part of the therapist in order successfully to work with obsessive patients.

D. THERAPEUTIC PROBLEM OF OBSESSIVE PATIENT

1. Obsessive Patient Inhibited and a Conformist

We have seen how the obsessively oriented individual appears to those about him to be a good, model citizen. He is likely to be regarded as a conformist, and a hard-working, persistent, moralistic, virtuous, law-abiding, and conscientious person. His suffering is rarely perceptible outwardly, consisting as it does so often in a marked and crushing reduction of spontaneity. It should be clear that this is with respect to both the warm and loving as well as the aggressive and self-assertive tendencies. On any level of conscious awareness his emotional life is likely to be inhibited, restricted, and dull. The obsessive person fears manifestations of self-assertive spontaneity of any sort. To him they appear grossly disproportionate, magnified, uncontrollable, and thereby are threatening in some way, such as the hostile ones being potentially destructive of others (murderous) in level. They are also frequently accompanied by opposite emotions and tendencies; the characteristic ambivalence of the obsessive person.

We have seen that rather frequently there is present the contributing background of a parent who became anxious in response to the spontaneous kinds of emotional expressions of his child. This was quickly sensed and responded to in turn by the child, who became more frightened and uneasy himself about the supposed destructive potentials of his feelings. It is not surprising that even normally healthy self-assertive tendencies may become feared, and may even be totally repressed to deep levels of unconsciousness, as "murderous." These are later to be mobilized, brought into conscious awareness, and dealt with in more healthful fashion by those patients who successfully undertake therapy. This is in accord with the constructive kind of derepression which is required.

2. In His "Hard-pressed Position" Obsessive Patient Maintains Triple Defense

Although it may not be outwardly apparent, the obsessive person is an unhappy sufferer who is driven and miserable, often without even knowing it himself. His emotional potential for more fully creative and satisfying living is locked securely within. He (the ego or self) is in a very hard-pressed position in the obsessive process. He has been forced to develop and to maintain what we may refer to as an energy-absorbing and obsessive Triple Defense. This is intended to guard him simultaneously: (1) against his own harsh and constantly grinding conscience; (2) against society, because of his great vulnerability to people and his resulting defensive need for distance; and (3) in efforts to control his feared and rejected impulses.

Thus, the ego is at the mercy of an overburdening conscience which is constantly critical and condemning of what is felt or done. Driven by feelings of guilt and responsibility, the sufferer feels a constant desperate striving to maintain inhibition and control over all kinds of emotions. Accordingly, many of these must be rejected and deeply buried from conscious awareness within himself.

Ordinarily, neuroses are regarded as less severe than psychoses. Actually some neuroses however, are more disabling and disturbing than are certain psychoses. Occasionally this is illustrated by the severe obsessive person, who is literally a slave to his obsessions or compulsions.

3. Frozen State.

When these defensively intended efforts have been successful in freezing the threatening and frightening emotions internally, the obsessive individual may reach an internal adjustment with which he is content. This is, of course, regardless of how limiting and restrictive this may be. His ability may be very limited to live a reasonably full life emotionally, or to achieve a degree of satisfaction in life at all commensurate with his real potentials.

When his internal defenses achieve their purpose (the endogain) adequately, the obsessive person will not seek or want help. He is satisfied with his *status quo,* doomed to a life of restriction and handicap without even knowing it. He has achieved what might be termed a Frozen State, emotionally. What a sad, hopeless, and insoluble dilemma!

E. RESULTS OF THERAPY

Most of these people could benefit a great deal from treatment. Their adjustment, effectiveness in living, and level of maturity can be substantially improved. For those therapists who have the requisite patience and pertinacity, the results of long-term intensive psychotherapy are highly rewarding. These able and useful people are a distinct social asset, and the therapeutic investment of time and effort is a most sound one.

The following communication from an obsessive person may help to illustrate the extent of the insight which can be gained through therapy.

Case 77

Treatment of an Obsessive Patient

A forty-four-year-old scientist was in the final stages of intensive treatment after over three years of therapeutic endeavor marked by considerable success. He had originally sought treatment for a character neurosis with a textbook picture of the principal obsessive traits. The following is an extract from a letter, in which he wrote about his previously unrealistic and inhumanly high personal standards.

"When I think of my life during the past twenty years or more, it has been a constant effort and struggle; to be something beyond myself. . . . My aims and goals have been in truth illusory. What a vast amount of desperate striving toward an unobtainable goal! Now that I've been able to see this, at least in part thus far, it seems a great deal less necessary. From this standpoint the past has all been rather tragic and futile. . . ."

This patient's endless struggle had been initiated by his unconscious endeavor to gain parental acceptance, approval, and love. His parents were actually long dead. Their impossibly difficult standards had been internalized, to become part of the patient's own superego. The patient's struggle for what was now at least a mythical goal was indeed hopeless, illusory, and tragic.

F. CONTRAST IN MINISTERIAL COUNSEL

1. Crucial Position of "Respected Person" From Whom Counsel Sought

Emotionally-sick patients will first turn for help and advice to some respected person who is close to them, or whose counsel they have some reason to expect will be of high caliber. This may be approached in a forthright and direct manner. It may be in various ways hesitant, tentative, concealed, or indirect. The family physician may be thus selected. It may be a professor, supervisor, professional colleague, minister, or a family member.

Upon this person and what he does, rests an awesome burden of responsibility. The influence which can be exerted at this crucial time upon the entire future life of an individual is tremendous. The response of this "respected person" from whom such advice may be early sought, will also have a substantial effect upon the entire course of the illness.

2. Major Consequences Follow Contrasting Responses When Help Sought

A. SIMILAR CASES SEEK RELIGIOUS COUNSEL. —The lessons learned from this kind of consequence have general application in varied forms in emotional illness. They were quite forcibly demonstrated to the author in two recent instances of obsessive preoccupation which were similar to *Case 65*. These instances afford us the opportunity to contrast the results on the one hand when the respected counselor had an objective and neutral attitude of curious inquiry, and on the other hand when the "expert" was unwise, inexperienced, and possibly had suffered from similar conflicts himself.

As in *Case 65*, each instance had involved a young mother who was greatly concerned because of recurrent highly unacceptable thoughts about harming her small children. As a result of the deep level of concern present over such consciously abhorrent and disturbing thoughts, each had finally sought religious counsel from the minister of her church. Let us see what happened.

B. SINFUL TRANSGRESSION; PENITENCE AND SELF-CONTROL REQUIRED. —In the first instance the minister sided with the patient's conscience and also vigorously condemned the thoughts. To him, these were very sinful. He clearly did not understand their nature, or their implications as to the presence of a neurotic illness. He did not realize that he was attempting to deal with emotional sickness. Sadly, he missed the whole point. Accordingly he responded as he might have with a penitent, genuine transgressor. He got down on his knees with the patient and prayed aloud and long for the patient's forgiveness. He demanded penitence.

He further urged the unfortunate young mother to exert increased will power and self-control. His approach sided with hers, that the thoughts must be stifled and controlled. The patient had of course already tried this herself many times unsuccessfully. This approach is futile and foredoomed to failure. His response accepted the obsessive thoughts on their superficial face value as evil and sinful.

There was no purpose envisaged by him in securing medical consultation. This did not even occur to him as a possibility. No thought was apparently given that anyone might try and determine *why* such thoughts might come. The possibility that they might be intended to serve some unconscious, psychologically defensive purpose never even remotely occurred to him.

C. UNDERSTANDING, SYMPATHETIC APPROACH AND PROPER REFERRAL.— In the second instance, the religious counselor listened in kindly fashion, after which he indicated his understanding of how upset his parishoner must feel. In sharp contrast to his colleague, however, he next assured her that perhaps the moral implications of her thoughts were not so bad as she had feared.

The wise minister further indicated that there must be some basis for the disturbing thoughts. These were, undoubtedly, at present poorly understood. Finally, he advised that expert help be sought in trying to seek such an understanding. He encouraged her to consult a psychiatrist and helped her arrange an initial appointment.

D. CONTRASTING RESULTS.—What were the results? In the first case, the conflicts were increased, as the minister sided with her already harsh and condemning conscience. The patient became more convinced than ever of her own terrible guilt and unworthiness. Naturally she could not "control" the obsessive intrusions by an exertion of will power. Such superficial and naive advice is comparable to telling a patient with bronchiectasis or tuberculosis that the way to remedy the condition and to secure relief, is to stop coughing. As a consequence in this case, the conflicts were magnified, the illness steadily progressed in severity, and psychiatric consultation was long delayed. Many months of suffering were added.

With the second case, handled with infinitely more understanding and skill, the initiation of adequate psychotherapy was facilitated. Progression of the illness was avoided. The burden of an already overdeveloped judgmental conscience was not increased. The treatment was more successful and its progress faster. The enlightened minister accomplished a noteworthy service for his parishioner, in sharp contrast with what transpired in the first instance which was so badly managed by his poorly equipped and miserably informed colleague.

IX. SUMMARY

An Obsessive-Compulsive Neurosis is a psychopathologic emotional pattern of reaction, which is marked by the repetitive intrusion of ideas or impulses which are consciously unwelcome. These intrusions are unconsciously intended to allay or to prevent anxiety, to which the obsessive person is very susceptible. The aim is to secure, maintain or reinforce regression, which has often faltered. When the obsessive defenses are sufficiently effective, anxiety is not experienced, in accord with our *Inverse Anxiety-Symptom Ratio Concept*.

Subjective feelings of the early deprivation of love and affection may be realistic, exaggerated, or unrealistic. Some lack of acceptance and love is always present in the early years in obsessive patients.

Knowledge about the dynamics of cases of Obsessive-Compulsive Neuroses, together with knowledge gained from the study of cases of Somatic Conversion (hysteria), has formed the cornerstone of modern dynamic psychiatry. Cases of Obsessive-Compulsive Neurosis constitute an estimated 9–12 per cent of the clinical cases of neuroses. Severe cases, which can be among the most troubling of illnesses, are relatively rare. Milder cases and the obsessive variety of Character Reactions are more common. The possession of obsessive character defenses is widespread. Obsessive traits, at least in moderation, are individually and socially useful and thus enjoy a certain *Cultural Vogue*. A diagnosis is warranted when obsessive-compulsive symptoms or traits are the most prominent clinical features of a case. In the obsessive situation a major *Defiance-Submission Conflict* has not been adequately resolved.

Children commonly go through stages of ritualistic behavior in their games, or in touching or the avoidance of touching, for example, sidewalk cracks or fence posts. Those which prove to be his *Profitable Patterns* receive further exploitation and elaboration by the developing child. Parental attitudes may unwittingly foster obsessiveness, in accord with our *Concept of Interpersonal Perpetuation*.

A conception of four categories of aggression was offered. *Destructive aggression* is in response to hostility, is not essential for self-preservation, and is injurious to others. *Constructive aggression* is self-protective and is evoked in response to realistic threats from others. An important component of the latter is the healthy kind of self-assertiveness which is necessary to protect one's rights and position. *Inward* and *outward* aggression would depend upon its direction, toward the self or the outside world.

The obsessively oriented individual has unwittingly and defensively placed an emphasis upon the control and inhibition of his emotions. The *Principle of Inhibition* is applicable to the obsessive individual. Emotions came to be regarded as threatening. The obsessive person is a reserved, conforming citizen to the outside world. The major role of requirements, inhibition, guilt, indecision, the driven nature of response in his adjustment, and his rigidity make up the *R.I.G.I.D. Person Concept*. The obsessive individual is largely consciously unaware of his inward hostility and of the socially and personally limiting and restrictive consequences of his obsessive defenses. He is prone to apply his *Personal Yardstick* in measuring others' thoughts and responses. The limited capacity for interest in others and for affection is a reflection of the lack of parental acceptance and affection which he received in turn. Limitations or disturbances of sexual adjustment are common. Such disturbances generally are often the *result* of emotional illness rather than the *cause*. The obsessive person protects himself by distance-promoting operations. The *Obsessive Vicious-Circle Concept in Relationships* points out the self-defeat of this endeavor. He is often preoccupied with detail, is perfectionistic, overly critical of himself and others, and suffers from a low level of self-esteem.

Obsessive symptoms occur in response to an increase in external stress (especially in acute cases), when the character defensive traits prove inadequate, or usually a combination of both. Obsessive thoughts tend to direct attention away from disowned ideas or impulses which threaten to break through into conscious awareness. They further absorb psychic energy, which might be available to act upon them. Repression is reinforced by obsessive manifestations.

The early interaction between parent and child is important in the genesis of obsessive manifestations. Those events surrounding the period of bowel-habit training, and during the later period of from six to ten years of age are of particular importance. Parents may actively encourage control, inhibition, and other potentially obsessive manifestations for a number of reasons. Impulses and wishes come to be unconsciously regarded as dangerous and threatening, because they are somewhat magically equated with the actual happening. Important mechanisms more commonly employed as defenses by the obsessive patient include displacement, isolation, projection, rationalization, repression, substitution, symbolization, and undoing. The mental mechanisms generally comprise what we may refer to as the psychologic *First Line of Defense*. The *Concept of Relationship-Distance* outlined a major psychic defense. Compulsive Rituals are a further evolution of compulsions. Rituals are *series of acts repetitively carried out in a compulsive manner*. As with single compulsions, carrying out of the ritual relieves tension and anxiety. The concept of the *Security Operation* was mentioned.

The *Impulsions* are a group of compulsively performed acts of a more or less antisocial nature. Mentioned briefly because of the compulsive element in their performance were dipsomania, exhibitionism, kleptomania, pyromania, and voyeurism, among others. The *Secondary Defense Concept* was noted, and *Five Principles of Impulsions* outlined.

Under treatment, some important concepts with rather general applicability were presented in accord with our policy in other chapters. These included *Emotional Understanding,* the *Team-Work Tenet* in Psychotherapy, the *Tracing Technique* in Therapy, and the *Rule of Impression Priority*. The obsessive person maintains what was termed a Triple Defense. He sometimes achieves the sad position of a Frozen State, emotionally. Some specific points in regard to the treatment of the Obsessive-Compulsive Defenses were also noted. A major contrast in ministerial counsel and its effects was reported.

X. SELECTED REFERENCES AND BIBLIOGRAPHY

ABRAHAM, KARL (1948). *Selected Papers on Psychoanalysis.* London; Hogarth Press.

APPEL, K. E. (1954). "Fundamental Considerations in Psychiatric Treatment." Read before the Sixth Annual Meeting of the Washington Psychiatric Society, Washington, D. C. (January 8).

BARKER, W. J. (1958). "The Stereotyped Western Story." *Psychoanal. Q.*

BLEULER, E. P. (1951). *Textbook of Psychiatry,* p. 89. 4th ed., translated by A. B. Brill. New York; Dover Publications.

BRILL, A. A., Ed. (1938). *The Basic Writings of Sigmund Freud,* p. 306, New York, Modern Library.

—, *Ibid,* pp. 34–35.

— *Ibid,* pp. 197–205.

COBB, S. (1935). *Borderlines of Psychiatry,* p. 131. New York; Nervous and Mental Disease Monographs.

DAVIS, F. H. (1954). Personal communication.

DUNBAR, F. (1948). *Mind and Body,* p. 57. New York; Random House.

ENGLISH, O. SPURGEON (1954). Personal communication.

FAIRBORN, W. RONALD D. (1952). *Psychoanalytic Studies of the Personality.* London; Tavistock Publications.

FENICHEL, OTTO (1945). *The Psychoanalytic Theory of Neuroses,* pp. 309–310; 369–385. New York, Norton.

FREUD, SIGMUND (1950). *Collected Papers,* Vol. 2, p. 59. London; Hogarth.

— (1943). *A General Introduction to Psycho-Analysis,* pp. 380, 386. Garden City; Garden City Publishing Co.

— (1950). *Collected Papers,* Vol. 2, pp. 122, 131. London; Hogarth.

—, *Ibid,* Vol. 1, p. 155.

—, *Ibid,* Vol. 2, p. 162.

—, *Ibid,* Vol. 3, pp. 296–390.

FROMM-REICHMANN, F. (1950). *Principles of Intensive Psychotherapy,* pp. 64, 74–75, 115, 146. Chicago; University of Chicago Press.

FROSCH, JOHN and WORTIS, S. B. (1954). "A Contribution to the Nosology of the Impulse Disorders." *Am. J. of Psychiat.,* **111,** 132.

GERZ, HANS O. (1962). "The Treatment of the Phobic and Obsessive-Compulsive Patient Using Paradoxical Intention." *J. Neuropsychiat.,* **3,** 375–387.

GRANTIR, W. L. (1954). Personal communication.

GRIFFIN, J. D. (1954). Personal communication.

GUTHEIL, EMIL A. (1959). "Problems of Therapy in Obsessive-Compulsive Neurosis." *Am. J. Psychother.,* **13,** 793–808.

HELD, R. (1961). "De La Singularite de la Structure Obsessionnelle aux Necessites Techniques Impliquees Par Cette Singularite." *Rev. Fr. Psychanal.* **25,** 319–332.

HILL, LEWIS B. (1954). Personal communication.

INGRAM, I. M. (1961). "Obsessional Illness in Mental Hygiene Patients." *J. Ment. Sc.,* **107,** 382–402.

JONES, ERNEST (1923). "Hate and Anal Erotism in the Obsessional Neurosis." In *Papers on Psychoanalysis.* New York; Wood.

KANNER, L. (1946). *Child Psychiatry,* p. 453. Springfield, Ill.; Charles C. Thomas.

KAUFMAN, IRVING (1963). "The Defensive Aspects of Impulsivity." *Bull. Menninger Clin.;* **27,** 24–32.

KAUFMAN, I., *et al.* 1961). "A Revaluation of the Psychodynamics of Firesetting." *Am. J. Orthopsychiat.;* **31,** 123.

KNIGHT, R. P. (1954). Personal communication.

KRAEPELIN, EMIL (1915). *Psychiatrie,* Vol. IV. Leipzig; Barth.

LAUGHLIN, H. P. (1954). "The Obsessive Compulsive Neuroses." *Med. Ann.* Dist. Columbia, Part I, **23**, 264; Part II, **23**, 322.

— (1954). "The Obsessive Personality." *Med. Ann. Dist. Columbia,* **23**, 202.

— (1954). "King David's Anger." *Psychoanal. Q.,* **23**, 87.

LeGAULT, OSCAR (1954). Personal communication.

LEVY, DAVID (1956). "Development and Psychodynamics of Oppositional Behavior." In Rado, S., and Daniels, G. E., Eds., *Changing Concepts of Psychoanalytic Medicine.* New York; Grune.

LOPEZ, IBOR, J. J. (1921). "Analisis Estructurales de las Obsessiones y de los Escrupolos." *Actas luso-Esp. Neurol. Psiquiat.,* **20**, 1–10.

LORAND, S. (1946). *Technique of Psychoanalytic Therapy,* p. 120. New York; International Universities Press.

MASSERMAN, J. H. (1946). *Principles of Dynamic Psychiatry,* p. 128. Philadelphia; Saunders.

MATTHEWS, R. A. (1954). Personal communication.

MENNINGER, K. A. (1954). Personal communication.

MILLER, M. H. (1960). "Obsessive and Hysterical Syndromes in the Light of Existential Consideration." *J. exist. Psychiat.,* **1**, 315–329.

RADO, SANDOR (1959). "Obsessive Behavior." In Arieti, S., Ed., *American*

Handbook of Psychiatry, pp. 324–344. New York; Basic Books.

ROSEN, ISMOND (1957). The Clinical Significance of Obsessive Schizophrenia. *J. ment. Sci.,* **103**, 773–785.

SHAPIRO, DAVID (1962). "Aspects of Obsessive-Compulsive Style." *Psychiatry,* **25**, 46–59 (February).

SHARPE, E. F. (1950). *Collected Papers on Psychoanalysis,* p. 79. London; Hogarth.

SILVERBERG, W. V. (1952). *Childhood Experience and Personal Destiny,* p. 212. New York; Springer.

SPOCK, B. (1946). *The Pocket Book of Baby and Child Care,* pp. 300–330. New York; Pocket Books.

SULLIVAN, H. S. (1954). *The Psychiatric Interview,* p. 203. New York; Norton.

— (1953). *The Interpersonal Theory of Psychiatry,* p. 318. New York; Norton.

—, *Ibid,* p. 338.

THOMPSON, C. (1950). *Psychoanalysis, Evolution and Development,* p. 102, New York; Hermitage.

WARREN, W. (1960). "Some Relationships Between the Psychiatry of Children and Adults." *J. Ment. Sci.,* **106**, 815–826.

WEISNER, W. M., and RIFFEL, P. A. (1960). "Scrupulosity: Religion and Obsessive Compulsive Behavior in Children." *Am. J. Psychiat.,* **117**, 314–318.

WHITE, W. A. (1935). *Outlines of Psychiatry,* p. 103. New York; Nervous and Mental Disease Monographs.

XI. REVIEW QUESTIONS ON THE OBSESSIVE-COMPULSIVE REACTIONS

1. What is an Obsessive-Compulsive pattern of neurosis?
2. What are the types of aggression?
3. In obsessive manifestations, what are the applications of:
    (a) The concept of Cultural Vogue?
    (b) Inverse Anxiety-Symptom Ratio?
    (c) Unresolved Defiance-Submission Conflict?
4. With obsessive patterns what is the application of the:
    (a) Principle of Inhibition?
    (b) R.I.G.I.D. Person concept?
    (c) Personal Yardstick?
    (d) Obsessive Vicious Circle Concept, in relationships?
    (e) Obsessive Dilemma?
    (f) Triple Defense?
    (g) A Frozen State, emotionally?
5. Why is the possessor of an obsessive type of personality likely to be regarded as a model citizen?
6. Why may the obsessive patient have a limited capacity for interest in others, or for love?

7. What is meant by: (*a*) Childhood exploitation of Profitable Patterns (the *Profitable-Patterns Concept* in personality development). (*b*) Mental mechanisms comprising a psychic *First Line of Defense?*

8. Discuss sexual problems as cause *vs.* effect in emotional illness.

9. How is Distance-Promotion a major psychic intended defense? What may be incurred in the way of unwitting self defeat?

10. How can parents unwittingly help to promote obsessive character traits? What is stressed in the *Concept of Interpersonal Perpetuation?*

11. What are Compulsive Rituals? Security Operations?

12. Name and define the major mechanisms in obsessive symptoms.

13. List the common Impulsions. What is their Secondary Defense? What are the Five Principles of Impulsions?

14. Why is an accurate self-appraisal a valuable asset?

15. Distinguish *emotional* understanding from *intellectual* understanding. What is the *Team-Work Tenet* in psychotherapy?

16. How might you utilize the *Tracing-Technique* in psychotherapy?

17. What is the value of appreciating the possible contrast in counsel to an individual, as sought from a "respected person"?

CHAPTER 7

THE FATIGUE REACTIONS

*. . . . Fatigue Incident to Emotional Stress,
Tension, and Psychic Conflict*

I. INTRODUCTION

  A. Concept of Emotional
    Fatigue
      1. Emotional Fatigue Distin-
      guishable by Discrepancy Be-
      tween Effort Expended and
      Tiredness Experienced; 2.
      Wider Medical Recognition
      Needed

  B. Useful Definitions
      1. Physical, Mental, Organic,
      and Emotional Fatigue; 2.
      The Fatigue Reaction or
      Fatigue State

  C. Indications for Separate
    Consideration
      1. Five Reasons for Chapter
      on Fatigue Reactions; 2. Emo-
      tional Fatigue and Emotional
      Depression

II. HISTORICAL BACKGROUND

  A. From Ancient to Modern
    Times
      1. Weariness of Soul; 2. Early
      Ideas Concerning Etiology

  B. Concept of Neurasthenia
      1. George Miller Beard's
      "Nervous Exhaustion"; 2. S.
      Weir Mitchell's Treatment
      Regimen; 3. Wide Use of
      Term Neurasthenia; 4. Reten-
      tion of Fatigue Aspects of
      Neurasthenia

  C. Later Contributions
      1. Stimulus of World War I
      and II Observations; 2. W.
      B. Cannon, H. Selye, and
      H. G. Wolff, *et al.*, on Emo-
      tional Stress and Physiology;
      3. More Research Needed

III. DIAGNOSIS

  A. Presence of Emotional
    Fatigue
      1. Overlapping Terminology,
      Principle of Characteristic
      Disproportion; 2. Ease of
      Identification Varies

  B. The Fatigue State
      1. Emotional Fatigue Most
      Prominent Clinical Feature;
      2. Overlapping of Fatigue
      States and Depression

  C. Primary and Secondary
    Organic Fatigue
      1. Advanced-Organicity Con-
      cept; 2. Organic Fatigue:
      Organic Bases for Fatigue
      and Exhaustion

  D. Problems in Diagnosis and
    in Treatment Aims
      1. Physician's Skills in Diag-
      nosis and Management of
      Emotional Reactions not
      Commensurate with those in
      Physical Ills. The "Physical
      Scapegoat"; 2. Incorrect
      Treatment Aims; 3. Emo-
      tional-Organic Combinations;
      E.O.C.; 4. Useful Point in
      Diagnosis

IV. INCIDENCE

  A. Physicians Find Fatigue a
    Frequent Symptom

  B. Clinical and Personal Ex-
    perience of Physicians and
    Students

  C. In Conclusion

V. SYMPTOMS AND CLINICAL
  FEATURES

  A. Emotional Fatigue the
    Presenting Symptom
      1. Not Clearly Distinguished;
      2. Concept of Secondary De-
      fense; 3. Two Descriptive
      Case Illustrations

  B. The Fatigue State
      1. Product of Emotional Con-
      flicts; 2. Further Manifesta-
      tions; Fatigue State Follows
      Loss of Dependent Position

C. Factors Influencing Fatigue
1.Kinder Social Attitude Possible; 2. Relativity of Fatigue Principle; 3. Fatigue in Intellectual Pursuits

VI. PSYCHODYNAMIC CONSIDERATIONS
A. Conditioning Effect of Parental Influences; Concept of Interpersonal Perpetuation
1. Fatigue as a Rationalization; 2. "Mother Says . . ."

B. Relations of Emotional Fatigue to Emotional Depression
1. Psychodynamic Formulations Similar; 2. Conflict and Fatigue; 3. Points of Relationship Listed: 4. Anxiety Fatiguing; Depletion Concept of Anxiety

C. Conscious and Unconscious Defensive Intent
1. The Endogain; 2. The Epigain

D. Frustration of Infantile Needs
1. Dependency Dilemma of Infancy; Vitally Necessary Person Also Object of Hostile Aggression; 2. In Illustration of Dynamic Factors

VII. INTEREST AND MOTIVATION
A. Incentive-Fatigue Ratio: Inverse Relation of Fatigue to Incentive
1. Performance Potential Increases with Motivation; 2. Neurotic Factors and Motivation C.S.E.

B. Effects of Added Interest and Motivation
1. Allays Fatigue and Increases Work Potential; 2. In Conclusion; Many Psychological Factors Influence Fatigue

VIII. BOREDOM AND MONOTONY
A. Dynamic Features
B. Individual and Social Reactions to Boredom
1. Experienced or Reported as Fatigue or Tiredness; 2. Seeking to Escape Boredom; 3. Substitute Expression for Anger; Anger-Equivalents

IX. PHYSIOLOGY OF ENERGY AND FATIGUE
A. Complex and Variable Factors Influence Available Energy
1. Reservoir Concept of Energy Misleading; 2. Psychic Energy Not Dependent Upon Physical Metabolism; 3. Interaction of Psyche and Soma

B. Emotions and Body Chemistry
1. Carbohydrate Metabolism Stimulated; 2. Fatigue Neglected in Current Textbooks; 3. Metabolic Requirements of Brain; 4. Endocrine Activity; P.E.E.R. and S.E.E.R.

X. FATIGUE AND SLEEP
A. Aid in Replenishing Energy
B. How Much Sleep Needed
1. Individual and Relative Matter; 2. Recovery Time Following Deprivation; Personal Requirements Vary; 3. Conditioning Influences Attitudes; Effect of Emotional Conflicts

XI. NEURASTHENIA
A. Introduction
B. History
1. G. M. Beard Introduces and Outlines; S. Freud Studies and Narrows; 2. Evolving Views of Etiology of Neurasthenia; of Views About Masturbation

C. Diagnosis and Incidence
1. Rarer Diagnosis; 2. Conditions to Differentiate; 3. Very Poor Medical Management Follows Misdiagnosis

D. Symptoms and Clinical Features
1. Attempted Correlation of Emotional Make-up and Physical Habitus; 2. Parent-Child Relationships

E. Therapeutic Results
1. Excellent Despite Progression of Psychopathology; 2. Pattern of Fatigability

XII. TREATMENT
A. Prognosis Good with Psychotherapy
B. Supportive Therapy
1. Environmental Changes; 2. Attention and Interest Supportive; 3. Several Approaches

C. Considerations in Intensive Psychotherapy
1. Initiating Analysis; Emotional Inertia Concept; 2. Fatigue Attacks Occurring During Intensive Psychotherapy; 3. Areas of Analytic Interest; The Therapy-Alliance Concept; 4. Course of Graduate Study Concept

XIII. SUMMARY

XIV. SELECTED REFERENCES AND BIBLIOGRAPHY

XV. REVIEW QUESTIONS ON THE FATIGUE REACTIONS

I. INTRODUCTION

A. CONCEPT OF EMOTIONAL FATIGUE

1. Emotional Fatigue Distinguishable by Discrepancy Between Effort Expended, and Tiredness Experienced

FATIGUE is universal in subjective experience. Everyone becomes fatigued. Tiredness, weariness, and fatigue follow the expenditure of sufficient amounts of one's physical, emotional, or mental energy. Thus fatigue can follow each of these pathways. While the basis may be a single one of them, it is more often likely to be a combination.

Is there a ready way to distinguish the basis or type of fatigue in a given situation? There is. How then may we identify the emotional type of fatigue? This type of fatigue is incident: (1) to emotional stress and tension, (2) to the tiring and wearing effect of all strong emotions, and (3) it follows as a consequence of continuing emotional conflict.

Many of us are aware that we can become fatigued upon occasion, *when the level of our fatigue is out of proportion to the amount of physical labor or mental activity which has been performed.* It is proposed that this very interesting kind of fatigue be referred to as emotional fatigue. It is to be distinguished from physical fatigue, from mental fatigue, and from the more rare instances of organic fatigue.

This, then, is the important basic conception and term of *emotional fatigue.* It is the foundation for our discussions in this chapter. The discrepancy between the amount of effort expended and the level of fatigue which is experienced, ordinarily provides presumptive evidence of its presence. This is what might be termed the *Characteristic-Disproportion Principle* in its identification. It is a useful principle which we shall also see to have some applicability in the Neuroses Following Trauma [Ch.14:VD1]. Since the source of emotional fatigue often lies in emotional conflict which is unconscious or largely so, this is a useful, ready, and often accurate distinction and one which should be borne in mind.

2. Wider Medical Recognition Needed

Emotional fatigue is a most common symptom. It is widely if not universally experienced. Accordingly, it is to be observed very frequently by many people, including physicians in most of the branches of medicine. It is far less frequently identified as such, however. Its emotional basis has rather rarely been clearly recognized. The securing of improved understanding of this concept is very much indicated in the humanities, psychology, psychiatry, general medicine, and in allied professions.

The more usual lay usage and meaning of the term fatigue refers to the kind of fatigue which is the direct consequence of physical exertion. Thus, when "fatigue" is used by an individual to describe his subjective feelings, the ordinary tendency on the part of most people is to think in terms of *physical* fatigue.

We shall stress how fatigue and exhaustion often have their origins entirely in, or are contributed to in various degrees by, emotional factors and by the stress of emotional (intrapsychic) conflicts. Wider medical recognition of these very important bases of fatigue is needed. A further appreciation of the important implications to medicine generally, would be quite useful.

B. USEFUL DEFINITIONS

1. Physical, Mental, Organic and Emotional Fatigue

Fatigue is *tiredness* or *weariness*. As noted, fatigue and its origins may be emotional, mental, physical, organic, or a combination of these.

Physical fatigue may be defined as *the fatigue of strictly physical origin, which comes on as a consequence of, and is more or less proportionate to, one's physical labor or exertion.* It thus follows the expenditure of sufficient physical effort. There are wide individual variations as to when, at what point, and as to how much fatigue will be experienced. One's individual tolerance and threshold also can show considerable variation from time to time.

Mental fatigue in turn is *the fatigue which comes on following individually sufficient and sufficiently prolonged, mental effort.*

Organic fatigue (and exhaustion) is *the rather rare type of fatigue which is occasionally incident to several physical (organic) diseases* [Ch.7:IIIC2] *as a post-surgical manifestation, and following severe physical trauma.* Fatigue and fatigability in mild form can accompany nearly any infection or organic disease process. At times psychologic factors contribute to this; sometimes substantially.

√ Emotional fatigue in contradistinction is *a weariness of spirit.* It may be defined as *the tiredness or weariness which stems from emotional sources. It arises from the continuation of sufficient emotional stress, follows the expenditure of sufficient emotional energy, and stems from psychic conflict. Presumptive evidence of the presence of emotional fatigue lies in an observed discrepancy between the subjective feelings of fatigue which are experienced, and the actual amount of mental or physical effort which has been expended.* Emotional fatigue will likely follow at least to some extent, the experiencing or especially the continuation of any type of intense emotional feeling. This is especially true for those affects which are unpleasant or painful. Long-continued anger, fear, anxiety or sadness, for example, or even elation, are likely to leave one feeling "drained" and worn out.

√ Emotional fatigue arises in response to various intrapsychic factors. It may occur: (1) as a symbolic outward expression of certain consciously disowned needs or wishes; (2) as a result of the expenditure and depletion of emotional or psychic energy as a direct consequence of the intrapsychic struggle between unconscious emotional conflicts; (3) as a consequence of the "wearing down effects" of continuing emotional stress and tension; (4) as a defense against consciously disowned needs or striving, that is, toward reinforcing their inhibition, control, or denial, plus possible self-punitive elements; and (5) as a combination of all of these factors. Certain instances can be regarded as *psychologic conversions. (See Table 1, p.* 20).

2. The Fatigue Reaction or Fatigue State

Regardless of its origins, emotional fatigue can become quite prominent clinically. The transition from the symptom to a full-blown neurotic reaction can be a very gradual one in clinical experience and observation. When this symptom-manifestation becomes of such frequency, duration, prominence, or strength so as to interfere with effectiveness in living, with performance, or with efficiency, and when it is *the* most prominent presenting feature, it constitutes a neurotic reaction. This is the Fatigue Reaction or Fatigue State. If emotional fatigue were to be regarded as analogous to anxiety*, the Fatigue State could be viewed as analogous to the A.T.S., or Anxiety-Tension State (*p.* 98).

The Fatigue Reaction or Fatigue State then can be defined as *a neurotic reaction in which the single most prominent clinical feature is that of emotional fatigue.* It is a "symptom neurosis" (*pp.* 60, 237). The emotional fatigue which is present is well established and has become more or less chronic.

C. INDICATIONS FOR SEPARATE CONSIDERATION

1. Five Reasons for Chapter on Fatigue Reactions

This chapter has been developed and included in our text for a number of reasons. *First,* the concept of emotional fatigue is both an intriguing and an important one from a medical standpoint. Its separate consideration is intended to help call attention to an area which has thus far received insufficient medical recognition, attention, study and research.

Second, emotional fatigue has a widespread, if not universal, incidence. Accordingly, it is hardly surprising to find that it is one of the most commonly encountered presenting symptoms, in all types of medical practice.

Third, despite its relative medical importance, its widespread incidence, and its many implications for health generally, medical teaching and medical textbooks thus far have largely neglected the consideration of the subject of fatigue generally, as well as that of Emotional Fatigue more specifically. (*See* later section IXB2.) Physicians who have heard very little about fatigue during their medical school studies find upon entering practice, usually with some surprise, that they must deal with it as a symptom which is presented rather frequently by their patients.

Fourth, it is possible that in the current trend toward the complete discard of Neurasthenia as a diagnostic category, we may perhaps be carrying things too far. There might be some merit in retaining in classification and in diagnosis in some form at least, one of its major clinical components,

---

* As a symptom emotional fatigue is analogous to anxiety. From the psychodynamic and functional viewpoints, however, emotional fatigue ultimately must be regarded as a defense against anxiety.

that of fatigue. Accordingly, our retention of the Fatigue State as proposed herein, represents a great narrowing and a limiting of the older concept of Neurasthenia to the one quite interesting and important area of emotional fatigue. This single part of the older diagnostic syndrome likely best warrants perpetuation.

Finally, separate consideration has been undertaken to further help to stimulate medical interest and research in the area of emotional fatigue, and to emphasize this important concept.

2. Emotional Fatigue and Emotional Depression

The psychodynamics of emotional fatigue are very similar to those of emotional depression. Some people in the field regard emotional fatigue as an equivalent of depression only (*p.* 143). This it can be, but not exclusively. At times, it may also be regarded simply as a corollary to, or even merely as a symptom of depression.

There are frequent clinical instances, however, in which the fatigue which the patient experiences and reports is distinguishable from depression. Because of its close relationship to depression, however, emotional fatigue is being considered shortly following the chapter on Depression. This is a useful and a proper sequence.

II. HISTORICAL BACKGROUND

A. FROM ANCIENT TO MODERN TIMES

1. Weariness of Soul

The presence of fatigue on a basis other than that which was strictly physical or mental has had some measure of at least implicit recognition for a long, long time. For centuries it has been referred to on occasion by philosophers, physicians, and sometimes by poets. They used such terms for example as "weariness of the soul," or "tiredness of spirit." Sometimes these may have so labeled depression, but sometimes reference also was intended to emotional fatigue. The basis for such weariness was not always very clear. Still, the descriptive terms which were applied suggest an intuitive appreciation of some of the sources as being emotional ones.

As modern times approached, some physicians became aware of the appearance of cases of Fatigue States, and of the occasional patient who suffered from partial or even complete "nervous exhaustion." Both occurred in the absence of a sufficient real amount of physical exertion to account for the subjective manifestations.

2. Early Ideas Concerning Etiology

When scientific medicine began to emerge, various ideas were held as to the etiology in these kinds of cases. Could it be a kind of constitutional weakness? Could it be something inherited? Was some obscure or poorly understood physical disease-process responsible? By this time (1800–1850) physicians specializing in neurology in several countries, particularly Germany, Austria, France, England, and the United States, were increasingly active in study and research. Conversion Reactions were being studied. Oppenheim (1858–1919) was soon to devise his theory of molecular changes in the nervous system in an effort to account for cases of Neurosis Following Trauma. Pierre Janet would shortly formulate his concept of psychasthenia. Many theories were being advanced.

The medical world had become increasingly conscious of the existence of the nervous system and its vital role in the human economy. For a time it seemed quite possible that herein might be found physical and organic bases for many of the remaining major unexplained syndromes in psychiatry. Medical research in organic areas was yielding substantial and impressive results. Its promises seemed endless. The stage was properly set for the American physician, Beard, and his concepts.

B. CONCEPT OF NEURASTHENIA

1. George Miller Beard's "Nervous Exhaustion"

Two American physicians are noteworthy for their early contributions in the area of nervous exhaustion; Mitchell and Beard. George Miller Beard (1840–1883) has been generally credited with introducing the term "Neurasthenia." (*See* later discussion; section XI.) This was in 1869. Neurasthenia literally means nerve-weakness. Beard believed that studies would ultimately prove that the symptoms of this condition lay in pathology of the nervous system. These were due, he felt, to basic nerve weaknesses, which would sooner or later prove demonstrable (*see p. 45*).

Beard thus named the syndrome, which he also referred to as nervous exhaustion. He was wrong of course, but such a concept was very much in accord with the ideas about the etiology of conditions which we now recognize as psychogenic, which were then prevalent. As a result, the name Neurasthenia caught on rapidly in most medical circles in both Europe and the United States. It is the only diagnostic term in psychiatry of American origin thus far, to receive such widespread acceptance and usage in psychiatry.

Most cases in which emotional fatigue, easy fatigability, nervous weakness, and exhaustion were prominent features (plus others), were henceforth most frequently classified under the general heading of Neurasthenia. Accordingly, the history of Neurasthenia is inexorably tied in with the historical perspective of Emotional Fatigue.

It must be noted, however, that the syndrome outlined under the term Neurasthenia also included a considerable variety of other psychologic, physical, and mental manifestations, which will be mentioned later. For sixty years the view was generally held that a kind of nerve-weakness or nerve-exhaustion played a basic role in the etiology of certain types of emotional illness. During this period many authorities accorded Neurasthenia a major position in the whole field of psychiatric diagnosis and classification. Eugen Bleuler, and other later authorities, however, gradually began to give Neurasthenia less emphasis, a process that has continued with increasing impetus to date.

As with the terms hysteria and melancholia, the diagnostic term neurasthenia tends to convey an inaccurate etiologic impression. Emotional fatigue is not at all a nerve-weakness, nor is it due to nerve-weakness. Nor are the many other manifestations so grouped in the past (as summarized in *Table 23*), due to nerve weakness.

2. S. Weir Mitchell's Treatment Regimen

In many medical circles by the turn of the century Neurasthenia had become a well established concept and term, in both diagnosis and classification. S. Weir Mitchell (1828–1914), a pioneer psychiatrist of Philadelphia, introduced a very successful regimen of therapy for neurasthenic patients. This had attracted considerable attention.

His good results were attributed to his carefully enforced routine of bed rest, restricted activity, and high caloric diet. These results were more likely due to his great interest in his patients, his enthusiasm, initiative, forceful personality, factors of suggestion, and to the resulting attention to the sufferer, the important overall psychotherapeutic implications of the regimen, the setting, and the personnel.

3. Wide Use of Term Neurasthenia

Most early psychiatrists accepted the conception and the term of Neurasthenia. This was limited to no single school of thought. The early analytic physicians utilized Neurasthenia as a familiar clinical entity.

Sigmund Freud very early grouped Neurasthenia, together with Anxiety Neurosis and Hypochondriasis, as the three so-called "actual neuroses", thus believed to be of organic origin. This group was so named supposedly (and mistakenly) in distinction from other ("not actual") neuroses which were already rather clearly recognized as being psychogenic in origin. In 1894 he had recommended the detachment from Neurasthenia of a syndrome which he named Anxiety Neurosis. This was a conception and proposal which was destined to gain firm and lasting acceptance in our diagnostic nomenclature. (*See* Chapter 3, *page* 104.)

Over a period of several decades this detachment gradually took place. In the twenty years from 1890 to 1910, however, many physicians largely confined their diagnostic terminology for the nonpsychotic emotional disturbances to four groups: hysteria, hypochondriasis, neurasthenia and psychasthenia.*

During this time the diagnosis of hysteria included all the major Conversion Reactions, the various Dissociative Reactions, and even certain

---

* Not all authorities were in agreement. Janet and his students for example, preferred to group all conditions which were not hysteria within his concept of psychasthenia. Other physicians had various favorite terms which they used, even as do doctors today.

psychotic reactions. Hypochondriasis was neurotic overconcern with health, usually with multiple bodily symptoms. Psychasthenia included the obsessive-compulsive states, phobias, and mild cases of schizophrenia. All the remaining cases were likely to be included under the heading of neurasthenia. It was a broad and important category for many years. (*See also* Chapter One, *page* 43*ff,* and *Table 3, page* 46.)

4. Retention of Fatigue Aspects of Neurasthenia

Gradually, however, the medical use of the term neurasthenia has become less appropriate and therefore less popular. Some scientific attention has been devoted to understanding the physiology of bodily fatigue, some of the varied factors in mental fatigue, and particularly in this chapter, the important psychodynamics of emotional fatigue. More is needed.

There is good reason for our currently preferred use of simple descriptive terms in diagnosis. Therefore the author has found an advantage in the employment of such terms as Emotional Fatigue, Chronic Fatigue, Emotional Exhaustion, and the Fatigue State. It is recommended that we detach these as a diagnostic category from the nearly discarded syndrome of neurasthenia. Their retention in this form for the purposes of classification and diagnosis in the neuroses, appears warranted and useful.

C. LATER CONTRIBUTIONS

1. Stimulus of World War I and II Observations

The interest in medical physiology and in medical psychology received a considerable stimulus as a result of both World Wars. As a consequence, many physicians have gained an increasing appreciation of the important role of chronic emotional stress in the production of fatigue, in Fatigue States, as an important determinant in one's stamina, and as a significant factor in the individual Total Response to Crisis, or T.R.C. (*See* earlier references *pp.* 12, 51, and 116.)

Numerous pertinent clinical and experimental observations were made during combat in World War II. In observations made by the Royal Air Force, for instance, it was found that the incidence of Operational Fatigue in pilots directly paralleled the curve of the degree of individual flying hazard — the danger and deaths per sortie. This was an important practical bit of confirmatory evidence in the relation of fatigue to emotional stress and to efficiency.

We have also learned of the "letdown phenomena" following strong (and often prolonged) physical and/or psychologic exertion. These phenomena were suspected to play a role, for example, in the incidence of landing accidents suffered by pilots following their return from bombing missions in World War II. Accidents upon landing decreased when, by regulation, the copilot took over the landings upon return from the mission and just prior to landing. These phenomena have a relation dynamically to our concept of *Completion Depression* [Ch.4:VIIC1].

2. W. B. Cannon, H. Selye, and H. G. Wolff, et al., on Emotional Stress and Physiology

Walter B. Cannon undertook important work on the physiology of the emotions. This is also referred to elsewhere in our text [Ch.14:IIB*3*]. Hans Selye has done significant research in the physiology and biology of the alarm reaction, and in the field of chronic stress. He formulated theories relating to the hormonal reaction in the first group. In the second instance, chronic hormonal reactions occur which can lead eventually to what he referred to as "diseases of adaptation." Wolff *et al.* also have studied the long-term body responses to stress. Their work considered the production of bodily diseases in response to stress, a field of investigation closely tied in with fatigue and its occurrence.

Implications in the work of these researchers and subsequent investigators has helped underline our psychiatric conceptions of the role of emotions in producing fatigue. In the physiology of emotions we learn thus that stress and tension are important sequellae of all strong emotions and of emotional conflict. Emotional Fatigue, progressing all the way to Emotional Exhaustion, can follow. These latter reactions can be difficult to distinguish from their physical counterparts.

3. More Research Needed.

We need to learn a great deal more about Emotional Fatigue and the Fatigue States. Needless to say, a fertile field for research lies in further exploration of the vital relationships between emotions, the endocrine system, physiology, the various hormones, stress, and fatigue. There is room for very useful research in all of these important clinical areas and possible avenues of approach. Some of these have up to this point received far too little attention. We need more information about the contributing roles of stress, exhaustion, and sleep to emotional stability and to personality adjustment.

We need to learn more about the relationship of Emotional Fatigue to stamina, to the Total Response to Crisis (T.R.C.), and to Depression. The psychodynamics and the pathogenesis of Emotional Fatigue, its manifestations and sequellae as outlined herein, could also benefit from further exploration, study, and research.

III. DIAGNOSIS

A. PRESENCE OF EMOTIONAL FATIGUE

1. Overlapping Terminology; Principle of Characteristic Disproportion

The rather common lay and professional employment of the same term, fatigue, for the most common kind of physical tiredness (which follows muscular exertion), as well as for the fatigue of mental effort, and the weariness from emotional conflict, is confusing. Such multiple and overlapping usage does not help in any attempted precise separation of the respective causes. Patients, of course, as well as their physicians, also use the term fatigue in its several meanings.

Emotional Fatigue was defined earlier in this work as the fairly common type of tiredness or weariness which arises from emotional sources. Characteristically as noted, the fatigue which is experienced is out of proportion to the actual amount of physical labor or mental activity performed. This nearly completely pathognomonic finding is the essence of the *Principle of Characteristic Disproportion* in the identification and diagnosis of emotional fatigue and the Fatigue Reactions. It is analogous to our later Non-Proportionate Response Rule in the neurotic responses to trauma, *q.v.* (Ch.14:VD*1*).

2. Ease of Identification Varies

Actually, the exhausting effect of emotional stress is a commonplace experience. The efficient housewife may be able to accomplish an amazing amount of housework with relatively little resulting fatigue. However, if a conflicting problem arises, with her husband, for example, or if several small, demanding children are added to the picture, her threshold to experiencing fatigue may be substantially lowered.

Most self-observant readers will probably be able to observe instances of Emotional Fatigue in themselves, at least with some practice in self-scrutiny. The diagnosis of mild Emotional Fatigue may thus upon occasion be very readily made. On the other hand, when this symptom has become the symbolic outward expression of unconscious emotional conflicts, it can be an insidious manifestation and one which is difficult accurately and definitely so to determine.

B. THE FATIGUE STATE

1. Emotional Fatigue Most Prominent Clinical Feature.

Chronic fatigue can in effect become a character defense (*p.* 228), as will be seen to some extent in *Case 84*. This is not clearly enough established, however, to warrant separate consideration and study as previously undertaken, for example, with the conversion (*p.* 258), depressive (*p.* 270), and additional (*pp.* 233, 283) constellations of character defenses in Chapter 5.

The symptom of emotional fatigue is a frequent accompaniment of most types of neurotic reaction. The diagnosis of a Fatigue State is indicated when chronic emotional fatigue is present as the most prominent clinical feature of an emotional illness. Fatigue States are not in themselves overly numerous. In accord with our earlier definition, the Fatigue Reaction or State is a *neurotic reaction in which the most prominent clinical feature is that of emotional fatigue. The emotional fatigue which is present is well established and has become more or less chronic.* When this descriptive guideline is employed the diagnosis can be more readily made. There are not likely to be too many problems in diagnosis.

The "level of fatigue" is likely to vary inversely with the amount of anxiety experienced. This is in line with our Precept of the Inverse Anxiety-Symptom Ratio. This points out that the more "successful" a symptom (and often thereby the more prominent), the less anxiety is present [Ch.3:IIIC2].

2. Overlapping of Fatigue States and Depression

At times the Fatigue State must be differentiated from Depression. In view of the dynamic interrelationships and the overlapping of clinical features, this is not surprising. (*See Table 21;* Ch.7:VIB3.) The patient may also have some of both features concurrently. Generally the masochistic self-punishment we saw illustrated in *Chapter Four* is absent, or at least is much less apparent or marked in the Fatigue State.

Upon occasion patients with either depression or fatigue may phrase their complaints in terms of the other symptom. This is more likely to occur with the depressed patient, who may complain of fatigue. (*p. 143*). This may be encountered in all types of depression. Jacobson noted this in commenting on the retardation experienced by cyclothymic patients: "Frequently they are unaware of their depressed affective state and complain only about their (apparent) mental and physical fatigue and exhaustion."

Dealing with depression in terms of tiredness or fatigue is sometimes encountered in literature. As one example, the poet Mathilde Blind (1841–1896) early wrote some interesting lines in which depression is thus described, in terms of tiredness:

> We are so tired, my heart and I,
> Of all things here beneath the sky,
> Only one thing would please us best,
> Endless, unfathomable rest . . . ."

Here the "tiredness" as referred to, in reality represents emotional depression. A similar longing for "endless rest" and so on is also sometimes expressed clinically by patients who are depressed. When so expressed, the implication is that this kind of wish represents an underlying, probably less conscious wish for death. (*See* reference to "death wish", *p. 208.*)

C. PRIMARY AND SECONDARY ORGANIC FATIGUE

1. Advanced-Organicity Concept

The differential diagnosis of emotional fatigue may sometimes be required from that which is produced as a *primary* consequence of physical conditions, particularly in certain severe or chronic illnesses. Fatigue and exhaustion are likely to be present in most advanced and chronic states of organic disease. This is especially true when there is accompanying debilitation, either physical or pathologic. In general however, by the time a physical condition of itself reaches a stage sufficient to produce fatigue, the responsible disease process will probably be quite advanced and thus rather readily diagnosable.

Thus, when fatigue occurs solely as a primary manifestation of organic illness, the latter is by that time generally severe or advanced, and has become chronic in nature. This is the *Concept of Advanced-Organicity* in the diagnosis of Fatigue Reactions Acute conditions are less likely to pose any problem in differential diagnosis.

Exceptions to the foregoing comments also fit in here, in relation to the decreased energy available and the fatigue and fatigability which are *secondarily* incident to infections, surgical procedures, and nearly any type of organic illness. This latter type might accordingly be termed *secondary organic fatigue*.

2. Organic Fatigue: Organic Bases for Fatigue and Exhaustion.

Differentiation from myasthenia gravis will ordinarily offer little difficulty. The characteristic feature in myasthenia gravis is the *rapid* fatigability of certain *individual* muscles or muscle groups. This specific and circumscribed type of muscle fatigue is most unlikely in the more generalized kind of fatigue which develops from emotional causes. Ferraro noted fatigability for mental work to be a possible early symptom in the slowly progressing case of cerebral arteriosclerosis. Organic Fatigue was defined earlier (Ch.7:IB*1*).

Careful differential study on rare occasions may be required to rule out the presence of early tuberculosis, in which fatigue may be an important feature. One must be aware of some dozen additional rather rare pathologic conditions which may also produce what we can label in differentiation as primary organic fatigue. These include adrenal insufficiency, hypothyroidism, occasionally severe heart disease, hypoglycemia (especially diabetic), certain blood dyscrasias, advanced anemias, or avitaminosis (very rarely), undulant fever (Brucellosis), post influenza, surgical hypoparathyroidism (now very rarely seen), infectious mononucleosis, nephritis, certain neurologic disorders, certain cases of unrecognized early malignancy, and hyperparathyroidism. Leukemia, advanced cancer, chronic gastrointestinal tract disorders and dysentery all can produce fatigue. By the time this occurs they are likely to be rather advanced and generally sufficiently so that the presence of organic pathology is quite apparent. (*See also* section IX:B2.) In some of these organic illnesses, the symptoms which may be present can also suggest hygeiaphrontis (Chapter 8). Diddle's study (Ch.7:IVA) actually finds fatigue *more* frequent when organic disease as such is absent. To the student of psychiatry this may not be too surprising.

A recent organic case seen by the author in consultation had fatigue as the single most prominent initiating symptom. This was a very rare case indeed, one of afebrile viral encephalitis in a forty-two-year-old man. Ten days prior to the onset of a resulting severe organic psychotic-like state, his complaints of severe (subjective) fatigue had first led him to seek medical help. He recovered completely in two weeks.

Secondary organic fatigue and exhaustion are common symptoms in post-surgical cases. They are also sometimes present following serious trauma, and they can follow prolonged pain. Fortunately the Surgery-in-Abeyance Rule (*p.* 127) seldom needs to be invoked in the Fatigue State. The characteristic fatigue does not often invite surgical intervention.

D. PROBLEMS IN DIAGNOSIS AND IN TREATMENT AIMS

1. Physicians' Skills in Diagnosis and Management of Emotional Reactions not Commensurate with those in Physical Ills, the "Physical Scapegoat"

With the increasingly excellent level of scientific training in medical schools, physicians generally are apt to have considerable skill today in the diagnosis of even the rarer and more obscure organic conditions. The degree of skill in turn which has been gained in the diagnosis and management of emotional problems and reactions, is unfortunately seldom commensurate.

Difficulties in diagnosis in the area of the Fatigue Reactions are likely to lie in: (1) the failure to detect the presence of emotional fatigue, (2) the inability to make a positive diagnosis. This unfortunately is often accompanied by exhaustive testing and repeated examinations designed to uncover some presumed but obscure organic bases, and (3) the disregard of the emotional fatigue, or its mislabeling as being part of a physical syndrome.

Some physicians have unfortunately tended upon occasion to ascribe the supposed origins of what is really emotional fatigue inaccurately, to a presumed physical pathologic basis. This constitutes a physical scapegoat [Ch.8:VA*1*], which is more likely to be, in order of frequency, (1) low blood pressure, (2) anemia, (3) hypothyroidism, (4) avitaminoses and (5) (additional) hormonal deficiencies.

2. Incorrect Treatment Aims

Patients who report to their physicians feelings of being "tired and run down" are sadly only too often still treated with iron, vitamins, hormones, and occasionally with thyroid extract. Often these approaches develop into long courses of injections. It is important to note that even when subjective improvement is reported following such therapy, this is *by no means necessarily the result of a specific response to the specific medication.* More subtle psychologic factors can play an important role. In other words, the patient may improve as a response to the *psychic* implications of the therapy; the actual medication, or its type being otherwise objectively immaterial and meaningless.

Explanations such as hypotension, anemia, and so on, tend to satisfy the physician, who then proceeds with medical treatment on this basis. They are also often quite acceptable to the patient as well, who may very much desire a physical explanation for his symptoms. This is in accord with our *Flight-to-the-Physical Principle* [Page 97; Ch.12:VIIIA*3*]. Thus he will perhaps quite strongly prefer to have his fatigue ascribed to an organic basis. This may constitute an important reinforcement of his secondary defense . (that is, the defense of the symptom) [Ch.7:VA2]. An illness (or symptom) on these bases is also clearer, more definite, easier to cope with, more readily treated, and someone else — the physician — can be assigned the responsibility for securing relief or a cure. In thus assigning responsibility elsewhere, the patient adopts a passive, dependent position.

3. Emotional-Organic Combinations; E.O.C.

Each of the foregoing organic conditions can, of course, possibly underlie fatigue or the restriction of energy, especially when well advanced. They are far less frequent causatively speaking however, than are the emotional bases for fatigue.

Emotional Fatigue can also independently accompany mild anemia or moderately lowered blood pressure. This should be kept in mind. These conditions actually are very widespread anyway, according to a strict interpretation of the currently accepted "normal" values and optimal standards for hemoglobin levels and blood pressure. Emotional Fatigue thus can well exist concurrently with most other physical conditions. When present together, these comprise *emotional organic combinations,* or E.O.C. (*see also* Ch.12:VB2.)

4. Useful Point in Diagnosis

A. AVOID FOCUSING PATIENT'S ATTENTION AWAY FROM EMOTIONAL AREAS.—Even on mistaken bases of both etiology and treatment, the patient's fatigue may still lessen. The basis for this improvement, however, is more likely to stem from the physician-patient relationship and from the increased interest and attention accorded the person concerned. As noted, this is in distinction from the medicine, as prescribed to which full credit may be given by both physician and patient.

One potential great harm in such a sequence lies in the fixing of the patient's attention mistakenly on an organic basis for his problems. His attention is focused away from any possible emotional conflicts, rather than toward them.

B. LESS CHANCE FOR MUCH-NEEDED PSYCHOTHERAPY.—Later constructive interest in self-observation is much harder, if not impossible, to develop. Resistances to healthy introspection are inadvertently fostered.

The secondary defenses are bolstered and legitimatized. The possibility for securing the beneficial results of self-knowing through insight-directed psychotherapy becomes more remote.

IV. INCIDENCE

A. PHYSICIANS FIND FATIGUE A FREQUENT SYMPTOM

Many physicians report how very frequently they encounter fatigue as a symptom. The author has found this to be true upon inquiry among a wide cross-section of his colleagues. Very little has so far been accomplished in confirmation of these observations on any statistical basis. However, many practitioners agree that symptoms of fatigue are fairly prominent among the presenting complaints of their patients.

Ripley and Wolf, in a study of 1800 consecutive psychiatric cases in the southwest Pacific theater in World War II, diagnosed 47, or 2.6 per cent, of them as Neurasthenia. The author similarly estimates the general incidence of those cases of neuroses which might warrant a diagnosis in accord with our narrower concept of Fatigue State as proposed, to be about one to three per cent. However, the incidence of Emotional Fatigue, as such, as a symptom is far greater. If one included every person's experience individually over a sufficient span of years, the long range incidence of this symptom would approach 100 per cent.

A prominent internist told the author recently that 85 per cent of his patients complain of fatigue. He felt that most of this was on an emotional basis. These figures are very possibly higher in his practice than average, since over three-quarters of his clinical work happens to be with young married women, with several small children apiece. This may help to illustrate some special factors of susceptibility in this particular group in which there are the additional emotional stresses of young-married motherhood.

Occasionally studies have been made as to the incidence of fatigue in relation to the presence of organic disease. Diddle, in a study of functional gynecologic disorders, surveyed the incidence of fatigue in a large group of women. In his first group of 678 female patients with *no* organic disease, he reported the complaint of chronic fatigue to be twice as frequent as in a second, control group of 888 patients *with and without* organic disease. In other words, he found the complaint of fatigue to be far more frequent in the absence of organic disease.

B. CLINICAL AND PERSONAL EXPERIENCE OF PHYSICIANS AND STUDENTS

Some years ago the author was invited to lecture on the subject of fatigue to the professional staff of an active general hospital. The group of approximately sixty physicians who attended included representatives of most of the medical and surgical specialties. They were willing to contribute the results of their clinical and personal experience as to the incidence of fatigue in response to an anonymous survey.

Among the group present, the internists estimated that from thirty to fifty per cent of their patients complained of fatigue in some form. The obstetricians and gynecologists estimated it to be a symptom of major frequency in their practice. Specialists in other fields described it as "very common," "one of the most common symptoms," "often seen," and "frequent." A pediatrician commented that while it was a rare complaint among his patients, it seemed a most usual one of their parents!

More recently this type of survey was repeated with other groups of students and physicians for the purposes of this text. The results are summarized in *Table 20*.

Table 20

Clinical and Personal Experience of Groups of Physicians and Students with the Symptom of Emotional Fatigue

I. THE MEDICAL STAFF OF A GENERAL HOSPITAL

A group of physicians in private practice, comprising the professional staff of an active general hospital attended a lecture on "The Psychiatric Aspects of Fatigue". During the course of the formal part of the presentation, they anonymously provided data for this survey.

The results are summarized as follows, with the number of participants answering in each category as indicated.

A. *The estimated percentage of my patients in whom emotional fatigue is:*

	0–25%	25–50%	50–75%	75–100%
1. A presenting symptom	13	10	5	3
2. A major presenting symptom	20	5	2	0
3. The principal presenting symptom	25	1	2	0

B. *My personal awareness of emotional fatigue.* Presumptive evidence is to be based upon discrepancy between the actual physical or mental energy used, and the subjectively experienced fatigue. Emotional fatigue follows emotional conflict.

1. Never	None
2. Occasional	26
3. Frequent	30

II. A CLASS OF MEDICAL STUDENTS

The survey was repeated with a class of 56 junior medical students in their second clinical semester. The results follow:

A. *The estimated percentage of my patients in whom emotional fatigue is:*

	0–10%	10–25%	25–50%	50–75%	75–100%
1. A presenting symptom	18	12	10	14	2
2. A major presenting symptom	31	13	8	0	1
3. The principal presenting symptom	45	6	1	0	1

B. My personal awareness of the frequency of emotional fatigue in myself is:

1. Never	5
2. Occasional	34
3. Frequent	16

III. A COUNTY MEDICAL SOCIETY

Forty physicians attending the regular monthly scientific meeting of the Montgomery County (Maryland) Medical Society, September 15, 1953, provided the following data in a survey of their clinical and personal experience with emotional fatigue.

These physicians had an average age of 37.7 years and had been in medical practice an average of 13.3 years. Eighteen were in general practice and 22 were in various specialties, including 5 in surgery, 5 in internal medicine, and 3 in obstetrics-gynecology.

A. *The estimated percentage of my patients in whom emotional fatigue is:*

	0–10%	10–25%	25–50%	50–75%	75–100%
1. A presenting symptom	9	8	8	6	4
2. A major presenting symptom	14	12	5	2	0
3. The principal presenting symptom	19	12	2	1	0

(Table continued on next page)

Table 20—Continued

B. *My personal awareness of emotional fatigue.* (The discrepancy between physical energy used and the level of fatigue experienced, or fatigue following emotional conflict):

1. Never 0
2. Occasional 27
3. Frequent 13
4. In past experience 1

IV. A STATE ACADEMY OF GENERAL PRACTICE

Sixty-four physicians attending a specialty session of the Seventh Annual Assembly of the Maryland Academy of General Practice, Baltimore, Maryland, October 26–27, 1955, reported their clinical and personal experience with emotional fatigue, as defined for them below. These physicians with more than 1020 years total in medical practice averaged 16.4 years of practice per physician, and had an average age of 43.7 years. All except three were in general practice.

Emotional Fatigue was defined as "a tiredness or weariness of spirit, arising from emotional sources. When Emotional Fatigue is present, the most prominent clinical feature is the discrepancy between the actual amount of mental or physical effort expended, and the level of fatigue which the person feels."

A. *The estimated percentage of my patients in whom emotional fatigue is:*

	0	0–10%	10–25%	25–50%	50–75%	75–100%
1. A presenting symptom	0	16	23	17	7	2
2. A major presenting symptom	1	26	24	12	0	0
3. The most prominent clinical feature	2	42	16	1	2	0

B. *My personal experience with Emotional Fatigue has been as follows:*

(a)
1. Never 9
2. Occasional 45
3. Frequent 11

(b)
1. Present in childhood 7
2. Adolescence 10
3. College 13
4. Medical School 18
5. Since entering practice 46

C. IN CONCLUSION

Fatigue is a frequent symptom in medical practice. Fatigue can accompany or stem from any emotional conflict. Since emotional conflict is universal and individual variation is more to be considered a matter of degree, it is therefore hardly surprising that fatigue is such a frequent manifestation. Clinical Fatigue States comprise around two–three per cent of neurotic reactions. Emotional Fatigue as a symptom is in itself nearly universal in human experience.

Fatigue can also accompany severe physical illness and pain. It is influenced by personal interests, by one's motivation, and by such factors as boredom or monotony. Finally, through the common association of fatigue with hard work, there is perhaps some implicit cultural encouragement to its development in the relatively greater social acceptability of complaints of fatigue, as opposed to certain other emotional symptoms. In other words, it tends to be more acceptable as a symptom, in line with current trends in the "Cultural Vogue." (*See* later reference, section VC*1*.)

V. SYMPTOMS AND CLINICAL FEATURES

A. EMOTIONAL FATIGUE THE PRESENTING SYMPTOM

1. Not Clearly Distinguished

The patient who suffers from fatigue of emotional origin more often than not makes no real distinction in his description of this from the fatigue of physical or mental origin. If he is inclined to mention or report his difficulty, he most often simply complains of "fatigue," which is not further specified. In presenting his symptoms, these may be worded along various lines, such as "I'm all tired and run down;" "I've got no pep or energy;" "I feel all worn out and I'm tired all the time;" or "I don't know why it should be, but I've been so worn out lately," and so forth.

The patient may be aware of some discrepancy between the extent of the fatigue which he experiences and the amount of physical energy he has dissipated. In turn, he may deny this in defensive fashion. This brings us to the important concept of secondary defense which has been referred to earlier (*See pp.* 96 and 144.)

2. Concept of Secondary Defense

A. THROUGH MAINTAINING NON-AWARENESS OR SEEKING A PHYSICAL BASIS.—The symptoms in emotional illness are largely developed as the self-defeating consequences of intrapsychic, defensively intended endeavors. Despite the net effect of their being psychologically uneconomic for the individual concerned, they nonetheless and concurrently also serve a vital purpose. Accordingly, they often will be held onto grimly, albeit unconsciously. It is hardly surprising therefore that the symptom is in turn defended. The symptom is a defense, and as such it is secondarily defended. This is the important *Concept of Secondary Defense* in emotional illness. (*See also Case 54*, pp. 266–7, *Table 22*, Ch.7:VIC*2*, and VIIA*2*.)

Secondary symptom defenses in Emotional Fatigue include all the various ways in which the symptom is defended. These largely operate unwittingly. Maintaining an unawareness of possible emotional contributions to symptoms is one important way. Concentrating attention on possible alternative and "preferred" physical bases augments this. The patient and/or physician may thus eagerly adopt a *physical scapegoat,* as referred to earlier (section IIID*1*) for his emotionally-based difficulty. At times the patient's insistence on a physical cause effectively blocks psychotherapeutic study. We shall see all of this increasingly operative in Hygeiaphrontis or Overconcern with Health, in the following chapter.

B. ATTENUATING INTERPERSONAL RELATIONS; INSULATION AGAINST RESULTING PAIN PART OF EPIGAIN.—Emotional fatigue often unconsciously serves a defensively intended social purpose for the person concerned. Interpersonal relations being difficult and unsatisfactory, his symptoms can help attenuate them and maintain distance. The more preoccupied he is with his symptoms or the more limited he is by them, the less he can, or can be expected to, participate actively. He remains or becomes more insulated socially. (*See also* Preoccupation-Defense Concept, *p.* 311, which has some applicability here.)

This is all part of the self-defeating epigain of emotional fatigue (*see* later *Table 22.*) By thus absorbing his attention and by delimiting his interpersonal relationships, he further "defends" and perpetuates his problems. Note that in several of our illustrative case summaries individuals spontaneously and prominently noted the socially limiting effects of their (emotional) fatigue and exhaustion.

3. Two Descriptive Case Illustrations

The following case excerpts are illustrative of the descriptions of his difficulties which the individual may present to his physician. In each of these instances the level of emotional fatigue was severe. It is to be encountered frequently in clinical situations in considerably less marked form.

Case 78

Emotional Fatigue: A Housewife Reports

The following is quoted from an instance in which the complaints of emotional fatigue were the major difficulty.

"Doctor, I'm just so tired all the time. I can't seem to get things done any more. Since the baby came I've been exhausted . . . By the time we get her to bed, I can hardly raise a hand. I can't understand it. Fred [the husband] helps me every evening and the maid is here nearly every day, but it all just seems too much . . .

"I'm just tired of everything. I feel worn out all the time. I don't want to go any place. When evening comes, all I want to do is to climb into bed . . ."

Case 79

A Businessman Complains of Emotional Fatigue

"I just don't seem to have as much pep as I used to have. I tire more easily. It's hard to understand. Sometimes I even seem most tired when I have done the least . . . But it isn't always the same. Some days I feel like I used to — the old zip and energy. Other days, and I guess more often now, I just seem tired a lot of the time . . .

"Sometimes I'm just so tired I can hardly drag myself down to the office . . . Sleep doesn't seem to do me very much good either. When I get up in the morning I'm tired. I used to have a lot of pep and energy, and I don't know what's happened to it . . .

"Last Monday I just stayed home and spent the whole day in bed. I felt too exhausted to get up. Still I hadn't done much over the weekend. I feel a little ashamed to tell you about it. There has been a day like that every so often now for the last few months . . ."

B. THE FATIGUE STATE

1. Product of Emotional Conflicts

In the Fatigue State the presence of fatigue of emotional origin has progressed so as to become a more or less chronic manifestation. When this point has been reached, we may view this development as representing an *emotional decompensation* (*p.* 159). The next case illustrates several of the rather common clinical features, and also helps point up the close clinical relationship of fatigue to depression. Approximately one year earlier this patient had suffered a depressed episode which had lasted for several months. The present episode was different and clinically distinct.

In this case the manifestations of emotional fatigue were prominent enough clinically at the time of consultation to well warrant a specific diagnosis of Fatigue State. Symptoms in the Fatigue State are the product of emotional conflict.

Case 80

A Fatigue State

(1) *Chronic Fatigue Prominent and Severe*

A thirty-three-year-old mother of three children, aged thirteen, eleven, and eight years, was referred as a candidate for intensive psychotherapy because of a moderately severe Fatigue State accompanied by some other symptoms. Careful medical studies had revealed no additional findings of significance in the case. The patient's physician had correctly determined the basis of her difficulties to be essentially emotional.

The patient also complained of a lack of self-confidence, and occasional heart "skipping," followed by palpitation. By far the greatest difficulty, however, was her chronic tiredness and fatigability. She had found these handicapping and troubling, and she sought explanation and assistance. The self-criticism and self-recrimination so often to be observed in emotional depression were absent. She noted the changes in herself during an early interview.

"I get too tired. It's just like I've told you. Sometimes I'm so weary that I have trouble getting my housework done. Usually by eight o'clock I'm too tired to do anything but fall asleep. This isn't like I used to be . . .

"When the kids were growing up, I would dig into each little job with equal enthusiasm and looked forward to finishing it. I wouldn't get exhausted like I do now. Even though I would get tired, I would still be able to finish a job . . . Now it seems I can do only about half as much, and even then I get dead tired. Sometimes I get so exhausted I stay like that for two or three days . . ."

(2) *Comparison with Earlier Depressive Reaction*

On one occasion she discussed her spirits and made some comparisons with her earlier depressive episode.

"I don't think my outlook is as bright as it ought to be, but it's not terribly low either. During last winter I went through a real siege of depression, and I know what it's like. That period lasted several months. I felt terrible — all slowed down, and everything looked black. It's different now. Back before I was married I can remember Mother having to try to get me up in the morning! . . .

"It seems surprising when you think of it, but I went through a period back there, a year ago, when I would wake up every morning about four o'clock, try as I would to keep asleep. [Note the characteristic type of insomnia with depression. *See p.* 145.] It's not at all like that. Now it's just this awful tiredness . . ."

(3) *Lack of Energy*

She described how tired she would become.

Yesterday (a Sunday) was pretty bad. I hardly did anything all day. I don't know how you can get so exhausted after doing so little. All I did all day was to take my mother to the airport to catch a plane. We went over to my sister's for dinner so I didn't even do any cooking. We got home around six, and I was real tired. I went upstairs to lie down, and stayed there until eight o'clock.

"I didn't want to fall asleep, since that might only make it harder to sleep at night. I guess I would have fallen asleep in spite of myself except that my brother phoned long distance, which I didn't expect. That seemed to pep me up some, and I did a few things before going to bed."

(4) *Underlying Conflicts Activated*

Not too surprisingly, we found out that the "hardly anything" which she did all day was still sufficient cause for her to become worn out *emotionally*. The seemingly simple act of taking her mother to the airport was, indeed, quite sufficient to activate some important underlying conflicts concerning hostility and dependency.

The effects in consequence, operating unconsciously, were quite mysterious to her. In addition, they were, of course, individually specific. The presence of these factors contributed to the difficulty of her husband and of others having any appreciation or understanding as to the degree of her fatigue.

2. *Further Manifestations; Fatigue State Follows Loss of Dependent Position*

The Fatigue State results from emotional conflict, which is partly or completely out of the patient's conscious awareness. Actually, any continuing strong emotion and any emotional state can be fatiguing. Even under rather mild but prolonged emotional stress or tension, one may experience some degree of Emotional Fatigue. This symptom is usually accompanied by a lessened interest in the environment and often by increased preoccupation with the self. Additional manifestations of the Fatigue State are likely to include some increase in irritability, diminished power of concentration, more limited reserve energy, and a diminished capacity for work of any kind. Some degree of accompanying depression is not infrequent.

In the following instance, the onset of a moderately severe Fatigue State followed the delegation of increased responsibility to the person concerned. This man was basically a dependent person who was not interested in, or psychologically capable of, assuming this more active, responsible, and independent kind of position.

Case 81

Onset of Fatigue State Follows Delegation of Increased Responsibility

A forty-six-year-old business man was seen in consultation because of symptoms of chronic fatigue. There was also some trouble with concentration and attention, and mild irritability. He was a man of no particularly outstanding talent. Over a ten-year period he had neither sought nor made much advance in his firm. He was basically a dependent personality, mainly content to "get by." Because of certain unconscious needs, it had been important for him to "lean" upon his superiors. He avoided an active and more independent position. He preferred the less exposed, less responsible, and to him less vulnerable and more protected position.

This man appeared listless and tired. He showed little physical or mental initiative during our interview and followed instructions in an apathetic and rather compliant fashion. His fatigue was general, and more severe in the morning. There was little improvement with sleep. His interests were diminished, but not to the extent often seen in depression. He had given up his golf. ("I never cared for it much anyway.") He had deserted a square-dance group. ("I was just too tired in the evenings.")

About a year prior to consultation he had been unexpectedly advanced to a position of considerably increased responsibility, through reasons beyond his knowledge or control. This proved to have served as his own particular *Final Straw*, as in *Case 30, p.* 162. Verbally true to our cultural mores which often judge success by the achievement of higher position, he expressed at least outwardly, his pleasure with the promotion. As one might have expected however, these feelings were not unmixed. The resulting severe internal conflicts had resulted in severe emotional fatigue. This had interfered with his work effectiveness to a point where a demotion was threatened. He feared this consciously. From at least one unconscious view he would also have very much welcomed it! It would have meant for him a return to a less active and responsible (that is, a more dependent) position.

C. FACTORS INFLUENCING FATIGUE

1. Kinder Social Attitude Possible

The social attitude tends perhaps to be a little more kindly toward the symptom of fatigue than toward some of the other emotional symptoms. This is related to the attitude of society in general tending to approve of the hard worker. The complaint of fatigue thus may be more apt to engender approval than disapproval. Here is a manifestation which is likely to be socially acceptable. This effect can influence in turn the *"Cultural Vogue"* of this particular emotional manifestation.

A man may suffer from considerable fatigue, in the face of what are actually light duties. His complaints of fatigue to the outside casual observer, tend to imply hard labor or overwork. This can possibly secure him sympathy, kindly regard, and perhaps even admiration. The sought-after result could be important and ego-building. The response of friends, family, and physician is thus more likely to be kindly, sympathetic, and understanding when symptoms of fatigue are presented, than with certain other socially less welcome manifestations of emotional illness. These attitudes in turn can exert subtle and unwitting, but powerful influences upon symptom "choice" by the individual.

On the other hand, of course, complaints of fatigue can upon occasion meet with a measure of social disapproval or censure. The lack of relationship to the expenditure of commensurate physical or mental effort can be quite apparent. For example, it is usually quite acceptable to complain of fatigue after strenuous physical exertion, such as a closely contested tennis match, a tough football game, chopping down a tree, or loading hay on a hot July day. In contrast, the complaints of a society matron (whose physical activity has been limited to an afternoon of bridge) about her strenuous day and about how tired she is, may receive less sympathetic reception. One may well doubt the genuineness of a physical basis for her complaints. An accurate assessment of the possible *emotional* bases however — which of course can be more than sufficient to produce what she describes — is far more difficult.

2. Relativity of Fatigue Principle

A change of scene, an interesting opportunity for activity, or a sudden new interest may serve to dissipate fatigue. Similarly, what is work for one person may represent play for another. Along these lines, one important distinction between work and play may sometimes well be that work is something you feel more or less *required* to do, while play is something you quite freely *elect* to do.

During the course of a long period of demanding work, the student or physician may find that his energies are considerably revived by an interlude marked by an opportunity for what actually involves the further expenditure of effort. Despite considerable feelings of subjective fatigue, he may find himself to be quite eager to engage in a period of dancing, bowling, tennis, an excursion, writing, socializing, a poker party, or a hobby. Sometimes even a change in the subject of work seems to be met with renewed energy. In these instances, with new interests and motivation, the fatigue from prior activities may not only recede, but it is at times almost as if the expenditure of effort in the interim recreational activity is somehow reviving and restorative. To varying extents one's energy potential can be thus recreated through recreation. These comments help illustrate an important principle concerning the *Relativity of Fatigue*. (*See* later sections VII on *Interest and Motivation* and VIII on *Boredom and Monotony*.)

During the course of an established and chronic case of emotional fatigue, that is, the Fatigue State, the new interest is not as easy to secure. Interest in external things tends to slacken similarly but less strongly, than in depression. A hundred years ago Pater wrote of "the sunless pleasure of weary people, whose care for external things is slackening."

3. Fatigue in Intellectual Pursuits

Many persons, particularly those who work in occupations requiring primarily the expenditure of physical energy, tend to lack any real appreciation of the severe levels of fatigue which can follow mental effort or emotional stress. As a result, they may very falsely regard a given office position as a "soft job," or as a "cinch." Yet the business or professional man knows only too well how fatigued he can become after a "trying day at the office." The surgeon may be "worn out" after even a brief, but difficult and tiring or hazarduous operation. The analyst may spend six to eight or more continuous hours, daily in the same chair. Although his physical activity as such is pretty nearly at a minimum, his level of fatigue at the end of the day may be considerable. Of interest to note in this regard, estimates have been made that 80% of all jobs in industry require only slight muscular effort.

The stress which is incident to competitive endeavor along purely intellectual lines, also can result in a rapid depletion of energy. For persons unacquainted with the possible level of fatigue incident to these and to similar endeavors, an understanding may be quite difficult. They might upon occasion be even more surprised to learn of the seeking of physical exercise by those in the above occupations as an indirect and seemingly paradoxical means of restoring energy. In other words, in certain situations physical "work" may serve to *reduce* fatigue. This is, of course, limited primarily to emotional fatigue and the fatigue incident to mental effort.

VI. PSYCHODYNAMIC CONSIDERATIONS

A. CONDITIONING EFFECT OF PARENTAL INFLUENCES; CONCEPT OF INTERPERSONAL PERPETUATION

1. Fatigue as a Rationalization

Let us consider briefly certain instances of the inadvertent and often unwitting parental contributions to the developing child's attitudes about fatigue and such things, for example, as rest and sleep. Occasionally a mother may be heard to say about her child, "He's so tired today." This can be a euphemism through which she is really referring to, or perhaps making an excuse for his fussiness, disobedience, temper, and so on. This explanation may, of course, be true in part. It is well recognized that fatigue can play a role in increasing irritability. However, it may also be quite untrue.

With sufficient repetition and emphasis over a sufficiently long period of time, this kind of comment and attitude can contribute to the laying of a foundation for a pattern of later excuses or rationalizations. In later life these may come to be used in attempted explanation for the non-completion of tasks or projects, and for inadequate achievements.

A kindergarten teacher regularly used "tired" as an adjective for children who didn't pay close attention or became restless in her class. When the difficulty would persist, she would tell the child and the group that he was "too tired" to do thus and so. "He obviously needs a rest." She would then require him to leave the group, get his sleeping mat, and lie down for a period of "rest" away from the group.

This constituted a somewhat devious form of discipline and punishment. It called a spade something other than a spade. Unwittingly it provided suggestions to the particular child, as well as to the group, for their possible adoption of various further kinds of similar later excuses, toward themselves or toward others, reactions, and behavioral patterns.

2. "Mother Says . . ."

The child may also hear, and perhaps later learn to say himself various admonitions and requirements, such as, "Mother says I'm tired.", "Mother says I need more rest.", "Mother says I have to have nine and a half hours of sleep every night to feel well.", "Mother says I can't stay up late, or I won't be able to work.", "Mother says I must have a rest every day.", "Mother says I'm the kind of person who must have plenty of sleep.", "Mother says I can't stand strenuous work.", and so forth.

Gradually the *"mother says"* part, as the important parental authority element, may tend to be dropped. Over the course of many years, it may gradually come to be completely forgotten. Thus one may see in abbreviated fashion how the original attitudes and admonitions of the mother often become incorporated as an integral part of the child's own standards and self-evaluation; his conscience or super ego. Now these have evolved into, *"I'm* tired." *"I* need more rest." *"I* have to have nine and a half hours of sleep.", *"I* can't stay up late.", or *"I* can't stand strenuous work.", and so on. This kind of process is, of course, a prolonged one and exceedingly more subtle and complex than pictured in very abbreviated form here. It may be reinforced by long-preexisting self-appraisals by one or both parents of themselves. This is likely to be particularly true when they themselves have been insecure in these areas and possess unhealthily tinged views of their own physiologic processes. The parents well may be attempting to be protective and helpful. Thus, their possible contributions to psychologically limiting or perhaps less healthful views on the part of their children are usually unwitting. As we learned with anxiety (*pp.* 32 and 37) emotional fatigue can be contributed to through the process of *emotional contagion,* although this is not frequently a prominent basis.

The following example helps illustrate the inadvertent contributions which can be made by a parental figure in the development of such potentially unhealthful attitudes in the child. These in turn can play a more or less significant role in the later onset of emotional illness. These principles help illustrate the *Concept of Interpersonal Perpetuation* as outlined [Ch.8:IIIB*1* (*Case 90*) and VID*3* (*Case 101*); also p. 291 and Ch.12:-VA*3*], which points out and is named so as to stress, the considerable significance of parental influence in the "transmission" of emotional illness.

Case 82

Fatigue State: Conditioning Effect of Early Parental Attitudes

(1) *Mother's excessive sleeping and excuse of being "too tired"*
A twenty-eight-year-old married woman was seen in psychiatric consultation, with fatigue as her most prominent symptom. There were also moderately frequent headaches and sporadic gastrointestinal difficulties. The fatigue was severe and limiting despite her (physically) very light household duties. She described her many dissatisfactions with her marriage, and it soon became apparent that her husband did not at all live up to her expectations. She herself was not consciously very aware of this initially.

Our patient had been an only child in a wealthy family. Her mother had had few domestic responsibilities. The care of the patient as a child had been largely relegated to a governess. The mother herself had had moderate hygeiaphrontic (hypochondriacal) preoccupations, and slept inordinately. The mother had explained the latter, as well as her decreased attention to the child, on the basis that she had "no time," or was "too tired."

She had further insisted that the child spend long hours in bed, and take daily rests. This routine had been extended into the patient's early teen years. There was later ample corroborative evidence to support a thesis that the patient had been unwanted upon arrival, and subsequently. The enforced rests may have represented a way of securing freedom from the child, or perhaps control of her. It might also have been partly a reflection of the mother's own neurotic overconcern. It thus constituted an extension to her child of her own great insecurities about her personal health. (*See also* following chapter; section on Dynamics).

(2) *Limitations inculcated; Dependent Position sought*

In this case the mother had made repeated comments to the child about her need to conserve energy. Repeated ideas also had been expressed verbally to the child about the child's lack of physical stamina and about her supposed relative weakness. Partly as a result of this psychologic conditioning, the patient had selected and married her husband.

This was an unconscious seeking to find someone who would continue the pattern of looking out for her and protecting her. What was sought was a dependent position. Her husband, however, was quite unable to measure up to being the protective figure unconsciously sought. Unquestionably the patient in turn was also had been a disappointment to him. Their entire marital adjustment had deteriorated. Not unexpectedly, she was more often than not "too tired" for sexual relations.

(3) *Multiple bases for sexual maladjustment*

In this latter regard there was: (1) An unconscious regression to a more infantile level of adjustment. This was in part a denial of her adult role. (2) The unconscious punishment of her husband by sexual deprivation, for his inadequacies. He had fallen short of being the all-providing figure she unconsciously sought. (3) Certain masochistic self-punishing elements. She herself inevitably also was denied any possible sexual gratification.

In this case there was illustrated clearly a close connection between the mother's attitudes both toward herself and toward her child, and the child's own later emotional difficulties. These were especially manifested clinically by her limiting chronic Fatigue State. Treatment in this case over several years was very beneficial.

B. RELATIONS OF EMOTIONAL FATIGUE TO EMOTIONAL DEPRESSION

1. Psychodynamic Formulations Similar

The close relationship of emotional fatigue to emotional depression has been referred to several times. It is illustrated not infrequently in clinical cases. Actually, the psychodynamic formulation of instances of these two major emotional symptoms, and their clinical reactions, can hold many points in common. Many similar points have already been discussed in *Chapter Four* on the Depressive Reactions. Emotional Fatigue may appear in the place of depression or as a *depressive equivalent* [Ch.4:IIIA2; IIIB2; VA1]. It may be a closely associated manifestation. (*See Table 21.*) The close relation to depression is sometimes illustrated by the depressed person's statement, "I'm *tired* of living."

At times complaints of fatigue are reported as the first subjective manifestation of depression. Complaints of fatigue may also accompany or precede the onset of clinical depression. Prior to or concomitant with the onset of depression, the patient may become emotionally exhausted through the expenditure of the psychologic effort needed to maintain repression. When this great amount of energy has been unsuccessfully expended to continue the repression and thereby ward off prohibited impulses, they may then be inverted, with depression the result. The self-punitive or masochistic elements are generally less marked in the Fatigue State than in a severe depression.

Case 83

Concurrent Fatigue and Depression

A young married woman, five months postpartum, sought treatment because of fatigue and depression. Usually vivacious and reasonably energetic, she had felt fatigue beginning gradually several weeks after the birth of her first child. In her words, "When I wake up, I'm too tired to start the day.* Sleep doesn't seem to help at night or during the day. Sometimes I have bad dreams. When I wake up even from a nap I am apt to feel more tired than when I lay down . . . I don't care to go out very much any more. I'm too tired, and have little interest . . .

"Jim is pleased for me to have a maid, and with her doing most of the work I shouldn't be so tired. . . ."

In this case the fatigue preceded depression but also accompanied it. The arrival of the child served as a situational factor in precipitating the emotional difficulties in a personality already vulnerable, given sufficient initiating circumstances. The patient had hidden unconscious wishes to be cared for herself. These were part of her unresolved strong dependency needs. These strong unconscious needs made the role of motherhood a difficult, resented, and frustrating one. Her strong conscience and her self-expectations, on the other hand, demanded that she perform well.

These difficulties led to serious emotional conflicts. The conflicts in turn led to a limiting level of Emotional Fatigue. When even this amount of psychic energy expenditure was insufficient, there was a further intrapsychic inversion of hostility, with the resulting onset of concurrent depression. (See also the discussion of dynamics in *Chapter Four, p.* 169.)

The secondary defense of the symptom in fatigue may be more readily pursued than in many instances of depression. The patient may a little more easily consult one or even more than one physician, and even more readily avoid seeing a psychiatrist. The symptom may have more social acceptance. Long and complex medical studies are more acceptable and more easily justified on a basis of unexplained fatigue.

2. Conflict and Fatigue

A. POTENTIAL SOURCE IN EVERY EMOTIONAL CONFLICT.—Thus far our concepts have emphasized Emotional Fatigue as resulting largely from the expenditure of psychic energy or as the unconscious expression of, and defense against emotional conflict. Brosin suggested stressing the fact that internal conflicts cause fatigue. They do with great frequency, both directly and indirectly. Such effects are illustrated in a number of the cases cited in our discussion. On the other hand emotional fatigue can also serve on occasion as an important *Conflict Indicator* [Ch.13:IVC1].

Accordingly, with every emotional conflict the potential is at least theoretically established for the onset of fatigue on an emotional basis. This type of fatigue accordingly is potentially as universal a manifestation as are anxiety, conflict, and repression.

B. BOILING TEAKETTLE ANALOGY.—A considerable expenditure of emotional effort and energy is required to maintain repression. This brings us to a pertinent analogy, which the author has found useful in teaching.

---

* See the analogous Morning Ebb-Tide in Spirits, as often encountered in the Depressive Reactions, *p.* 145 and *Table 13, pp.* 163–64.

Some kind of vent for the otherwise steadily increasing pressure of unconscious and repressed emotions is vital. It is as vital for an individual, as is a vent to allow for the dissipation of the increasing pressure of the steam which is generated in a boiling teakettle. What would happen if there were no vent provided in a teakettle, or if the vent were inadequate? There would be an explosion. When no vent is available to allow for the escape of the generating steam, an increasingly greater amount of effort is required to contain the steadily increasing pressure.

In analogous fashion, forbidden wishes or drives which are relegated to the unconscious (that is, those which are repressed) create internal pressures. The pressures are toward action and toward conscious awareness. This is the threat of derepression. This powerful threat is then combatted by the various intrapsychic forces which can be called upon. Thus also any emotional conflict uses psychic energy and can result in fatigue. In other words, we might view emotional fatigue as resulting in part from the pouring of energy into the repressive forces. By turning the energy inward (as to an extent also occurs in depression), the risk to the other person (and more importantly to oneself) is less. Here the steam escapes from another vent, an internal one. It is also more safely hidden from any possible personal or external detection.

3. Points of Relationship Listed

Table 21 is a tabulation of some important points in the clinical and dynamic relationships between emotional fatigue and depression. (*See also p. 143.*)

Table 21

Emotional Fatigue and Depression

These two important and commonly encountered manifestations of emotional illness are closely related dynamically and clinically. Their points of relationship include the following:

(1) Symptoms of Emotional Fatigue may *initiate* a clinical depression.

(2) A Fatigue State may occur as a *result of,* or as *a means of of combatting* depression. A vast amount of psychic energy may be expended in the unending service of attempting the maintenance of repression.

(3) Emotional Fatigue is an important possible *equivalent* of depression. (*See p. 143.*)

(4) Fatigue may represent an *extension* of depression. Depression or a depressive process probably basically underlies most Fatigue States. The latter may serve to *mask* the underlying depression.

(5) Fatigue may occur as a *concomitant expression* of and/or an attempted resolution of the underlying emotional conflicts, as is probably illustrated in *Case 83.*

(6) A depression may ensue *when fatigue* as a neurotic defense *proves insufficient* to cope with the problems.

(*Table continued on next page*)

Table 21—Continued

    (7) The *psychodynamics* of depression and fatigue *overlap* consider-
ably, and may sometimes be identical for all practical purposes.
The *precipitating events* may also *have a* certain *similarity*.
It should be kept in mind, however, that the clinical manifestations of a Depressive Reaction and of a Fatigue State can still be
quite distinct. (*See also Case 80, Sect* VB*1*.)

4. Anxiety Fatiguing; Depletion Concept of Anxiety

Emotional fatigue is a ubiquitous kind of manifestation since it may to
some degree be a consequence of almost any kind of emotional conflict.
The subjective experiencing of anxiety can in itself be fatiguing. This is in
accord with the Depletion Concept of Anxiety [Ch.1:VIA], which is
named so as to recognize and to stress the expenditure and the resulting
depletion of psychic energy, which occurs through the experiencing of
anxiety (*See p.* 41.)

Thus, when emotional fatigue is not of itself present as a direct consequence of, or as a contributor to emotional illness, one may still have a
lowered threshold to fatigue along with any moderately severe emotional
illness.

C. CONSCIOUS AND UNCONSCIOUS DEFENSIVE INTENT

1. The Endogain

The symptom of emotional fatigue seeks to subserve complex defensive
purposes on a hidden, intrapsychic level. As noted, this symptom, very
similarly to depression, can serve as the disguished and symbolic outward
expression of, and simultaneous defense against various aspects of basic
emotional conflicts. Completely beyond conscious awareness (that is, unconsciously), it may attempt to answer various internal psychologic needs.

The endogain of emotional fatigue (that is, the deeply unconscious
primary gain of the illness) and the Fatigue State is deeper and more hidden than the epigain. These major internal "gains" of the illness (See
Chapter Two, p. 68*ff*) and the desperate psychologic need for them are
responsible for its initiation. Hereby the symptoms symbolically attempt
various functions of gratification, as well as those of unconsciously denying, concealing, or controlling disapproved and rejected wishes or needs.
These are largely hostility and aggression, but they may also include repressed sexual drives and other consciously disowned wishes or needs.
Emotional symptoms are defensively intended unconscious endeavors.
They contribute to and may be part of the endogain. See also *Table 14*
and the discussion of the depressive endogain, *p.* 178. Emotional fatigue
might also be thought of as subserving a biologic *function* or purpose.

Further, the fatigue serves as a symbolic way of aiding in the control and
repression of the consciously disowned aggressive rage. This may occur in
response to frustration when infantile demands are not more literally met.
The unconscious of the patient with the Fatigue State partly might thus say
in effect, "If I'm weak and fatigued, I can't possibly attack or injure some-

one; there is no danger that I will or even can, act in response to this repressed rage. . . . I certainly cannot be expected to maintain an independent position. I must remain dependent, in a less active and less exposed position."

2. The Epigain

A. GAINS THROUGH EXTERNAL ENVIRONMENTAL CHANGE.—The epigain of Emotional Fatigue (that is, the unconscious secondary gain) is more superficial and is often more apparent to the objective, independent observer. This does not, of course, in any way necessarily indicate conscious awareness by the patient. Nor does it at all imply conscious simulation for some purpose, that is, malingering. (*See Chapter Two, page 61ff, for* further definition and delineation of the epigain.)

Table 22

Conscious Secondary Gain and Epigain of Emotional Fatigue

Secondary gains and the epigain may include one or more of the following:

(1) *Less may be expected,* asked, or demanded of someone who is already weary.

(2) The fatigued individual may secure some possibly kinder, *more sympathetic,* or even admiring *regard.* This includes the gaining of the ego satisfaction inherent to being considered a hard worker.

Comments at least may be theoretically evoked from one's fellows, such as, "Why don't you slow down?", "Why must you drive yourself so that you get so tired?", or "My, he must be quite a producer!", and so on.

(3) *Social and Personal Insulation.* Attenuation of his (largely painful and unsatisfactory) interpersonal relationships taken place through his absorption and preoccupation with his symptoms, and through the limitations placed on his activity through his being thus fatigued and exhausted. (*See* earlier reference, section VA2.)

(4) The *Dependent Appeal.* The seeking of *a more passive position* and the avoidance of a more active one. There may be an implied asking for someone else, someone stronger, to "take over." To a variable extent someone in the individual's interpersonal environment may do just this.

(5) Closely related to the foregoing is the *delaying of action* or decision which may result. Procrastination can contribute to the avoidance of responsibility. This may be secured largely out of awareness.

(6) When the patient through his Emotional fatigue can "secure" the *direction* of his own *attention* and perhaps also that of a physician along possible *physical lines,* a certain amount of gratification can be secured. Some of the dependency needs may be satisfied from this external source. A *physical scapegoat* may be adopted.

This endeavor of course also helps to *defend the symptom;* to maintain and perpetuate the illness. It can thus constitute a powerful Secondary Defense of the symptom and of the illness (*See* earlier reference, Ch.7:VA2.)

B. REGRESSION OF FATIGUE STATE.—The Fatigue State tends to place its victim in a passive, less responsible position. To the extent that this is unconsciously sought, Emotional Fatigue and the Fatigue State are regressive manifestations. They can thus attempt unconsciously in part to regain the dependent and protected position of early childhood. The patient says in effect, "I am tired and weak . . . I need to be taken care of . . . Mother [or a substitute mother] must take care of me and gratify my infantile needs for love and affection, which were never satisfied."

Thus the Fatigue State may unconsciously secure a regressive kind of retreat. This is largely part of the endogain of emotional fatigue. To the extent, however, that changes in the external environment, especially including the interpersonal, are secured by the patient through the inherent dependent appeal of his regression, there is also included fatigue epigain.

C. CONCEPT OF INTERNAL WHIPS.—Emotional Fatigue may also occur, or occur more readily, when personal incentive is lacking, or when the chances of reaching a cherished goal no longer appear possible. The subjective experiencing of fatigue generally may also be affected by various kinds of what we might refer to as internal "whips" or "spurs." These internal whips may include various compulsive urges, fears, anxieties, sex, anger, various other "internal" drives, needs, love, and also on the other hand, certain psychic forces which have been evolved in their intended control. Psychic energy is by no means solely dependent upon physical metabolism [Ch.7:VIIIA]. It tends to be considerably independent.

Other kinds of whips and drives can stem from such factors as loyalty, patriotism, revenge, and so on, and also from physical stimulants such as benzedrine and caffeine. Alexander noted as a psychodynamic factor that "in a number of male cases there is a conspicuous feminine identification which opposes aggressive ambitious attitudes." In the author's own clinical experience this, as the single outstanding component, has been rare.

D. FRUSTRATION OF INFANTILE NEEDS

1. Dependency Dilemma of Infancy. Vitally Necessary Person Also Object of Hostile Aggression

In tracing back the very early psychodynamic roots of emotional fatigue, we return again to a possible serious dilemma of early childhood. Reference is made here to infantile needs from and attitudes toward significant adults, especially mother or the mothering figure. This dilemma, which has been referred to in relation to the Depressive Reactions and again in the Obsessive-Compulsive Reactions relates to the intrapsychic handling of the infantile hostile-aggressive responses. These can reach a serious level in response to the frustration of vital infantile dependent needs or demands.

The hostile aggression which may be stimulated in him seems to the infant to *threaten the destruction of the very object which at the same time is most vitally needed.* This comprises what we might refer to as the Dependency Dilemma of Infancy. As a phenomenon in basic psychodynamics it can assume great importance. In the Conversion Reactions the symptom is intended to reinforce repression and inhibition and often at the same time also to secure symbolic gratification of the denied wish. In the Depressive Reactions the energy of aggression is finally inverted toward the self as a last desperate attempt to deny and conceal the disowned rage and destructive wishes. Fatigue in like fashion can be a manifestation of these basic defensively-intended endeavors.

Alexander noted the frequent central conflict of the psyche between passive dependent wishes and reactive aggressive ambition. In Fatigue States more specific factors include: (*a*) little hope for success against insuperable odds, (*b*) a lack of real incentive, (*c*) the inconstancy of anxiety, and (*d*) a degree of feminine identification in males (which opposes aggressiveness and ambitiousness).

2. In Illustration of Dynamic Factors

The following case is presented to help illustrate some of these points in the psychodynamics and pathogenesis of a severe Fatigue State. Note the recapitulation of the antecedent oral conflicts, the struggle over dependency, the *Infantile Dependency Dilemma,* the complex dynamics of the interpersonal situation (with mother), and the fatigue epigain and endogain.

Case 84

Psychodynamics of a Severe Fatigue State

(1) *Productivity Intermittent Only*

A thirty-four-year-old man began analysis because of a chronic Fatigue State. This also had its effects on some of his other functions. As an example of impairment of his mental functioning, he had some difficulty in concentration. He was a brilliant engineer when employed. However, he repeatedly left excellent positions for nonspecific reasons, which he largely attributed to be the result of his chronic fatigue and fatigability.

He was unmarried and had continued to live at home with his mother. During intervals between work he spent his time lying around the house. This was an occupation in which he unconsciously was very content. He consciously felt only the need "to rest up," to "regain his strength," and to "recoup his energy." He could only work so long and then he would have to rest for a while. He had followed such a pattern for some years. He had been able to be only intermittently productive.

Actually, the lying around the house reflected in poorly concealed fashion his real wish for dependency. Unconsciously, he very much wanted to be taken care of. The fatigue epigain here related to his securing a certain measure of satisfaction of his dependency needs. It was an endeavor in which he was actually implicitly (that is, unconsciously) encouraged by his mother. Through his symptoms, he said in effect, "I am weak and helpless. I am chronically tired and I have trouble concentrating. Surely I cannot be expected to be self-sufficient and measure up to adult standards. Mother, or someone, must take care of me."

(2) *Ambivalence Toward Object of Dependency*

In this complex interpersonal situation, the mother exhibited considerable sympathy, understanding, and also a fair amount of overprotectiveness. Through these she inadvertently held out an implicit promise that she might actually become the all-providing mother he unconsciously sought. However, this could never possibly realistically be. Accordingly, the mother was also the extremely frustrating and denying object of dependency.

On a deeper level of unconsciousness this patient then was filled with murderous rage over her failure to more literally meet his infantile dependent demands. This placed him in an intolerable position. His hostility threatened the vitally needed but frustrating mother. This constituted for him a powerful Dependency Dilemma of Infancy.

He was further threatened by possible derepression which would bring his consciously disowned needs and his hostile impulses into conscious awareness. Should the latter ever really happen, the anxiety in prospect was to him intolerable. Also his ability to continue control was doubted. Accordingly, every possible safeguard must be mustered to reinforce repressive efforts. The chronic fatigue resulted.

(3) Major Elements of Endogain

The "primary gain" (that is, the endogain) of the fatigue with this patient related largely to the continued control and concealment of his aggressive urges. Here the unconscious of this patient said in effect, "I cannot face the realistic needs of an adult world. I cannot work. I cannot strike out independently for myself. I cannot take this more exposed and less protected position.

"I must use up all of my energy restraining, concealing, and holding down my rage. The terrific expenditure of psychic energy in this manner is depleting and of course makes me very tired. [Recall our somewhat analogous Depletion Concept of Anxiety, p. 41.] Since I am so tired and worn out, there is no energy available, and there is no possible danger that I might act upon my feared aggressive impulses. I cannot do so." One can see how closely the psychodynamics in this case of a clinically severe Fatigue State parallel some of our formulations of the dynamics of Depression as were outlined in *Chapter Four.*

Treatment in this case was successful, although most difficult and prolonged. The patient no longer suffers from chronic fatigue. He has made a reasonably successful marriage. He has also maintained a much more successful professional life.

VII. INTEREST AND MOTIVATION

A. INCENTIVE-FATIGUE RATIO: INVERSE RELATION OF FATIGUE TO INCENTIVE

1. Performance Potential Increases with Motivation

The occurrence, the degree, and the effects of emotional, mental, and physical fatigue are each influenced by the individual level of interest and motivation. When the level of personal interest in a given task or activity is high, there is a greater potential for performance. Fatigue occurs less readily. This is in accord with our Relativity-of-Fatigue Principle, as noted earlier (VC2).

When the motivation or incentive can be increased, the onset of fatigue is delayed and impeded. The work potential is increased. The effects of fatigue are less. Thus there is an *inverse relation between the amount of incentive which is present, and the amount of fatigue which is experienced.* The more incentive, the less fatigue. We might refer to this as the Inverse Incentive-Fatigue-Ratio. It is a fairly steady and reliable one.

2. Neurotic Factors and Motivation C.S.E.

A. COMPULSIVE DRIVES AND PSYCHIC ENERGY.—The compulsively "driven" person may have little subjective awareness of fatigue. Energy can have important psychologic sources. On various intrapsychic bases one may seemingly possess almost boundless "sources" of available energy. This can also apply in acute situations and in brief bursts. Our findings in this area have a relationship to the occasionally reported instances of seemingly superhuman strength and resulting feats which have been performed by individuals in dire emergencies.

Berlien pointed out that a person with a background that is rather neurotic can still get along well in military service, provided his motivation for service and his unit support are strong. This observation can lead us into the important topic of neurotic motivation. Thus neurotic factors also may play a most significant role in the level and in the direction of motivation and interest, in one's drives, and as to the amount of psychic energy which an individual can mobilize.

B. HYPOMANIC ACTIVITY AND FATIGUE.—A somewhat similiar phenomenon to that of neurotic drive or energy may be observed in certain clinical instances of manic psychosis or hypomanic excitement. In these latter reactions, an interesting speculation might be raised. Could the depletion of psychic energy in some way contribute to the depressive retardation in those cases in which a depressed phase closely succeeds a manic state? In such a state inordinate amounts of physical and psychic energy have been expended. Generally, however, such a connection is not often granted much weight in the psychodynamic formulation of depressive retardation. From the organic side, the hyperthyroid person sometimes also may give an impression of seemingly limitless energy.

The manic or hypomanic state at times is best viewed in part as a defense against depression. Part of this defense is an escape into activity (*pp.* 183 *and* 282). This is a rather complex defensive operation. It is clinical or subclinical in extent. It is accompanied by increased energy potential, greater activity in all spheres (mental, emotional, and physical), together with less fatigue and decreased fatigability. Although a defense itself, and at least in part against its opposite, it is still quite likely in turn — as we can observe repeatedly with other emotional manifestations — to be secondarily defended. (*See* earlier reference, Ch.7:VA2.)

C. CYCLIC SWINGS OF ENERGY; THE C.S.E.—Cyclic swings of energy are sometimes to be noted by the perceptive observer. This is an interesting phenomenon to which further attention and study are invited. These, which we might call the C.S.E., are somewhat analagous to the more commonly observed swings of mood which many people experience, and which we are more accustomed to notice. Such cyclic energy swings may accompany mood swings, replace them, or occur quite independently.

While the author was undertaking the revision of this section, a colleague reported an increasing personal awareness of just such energy swings as described. For from two to five months, when his C.S.E. is in the antecedent or cresting position, energy seems more than ample for routine activities. Extra endeavors are undertaken. For other similar periods his C.S.E. is in a trough and the energy potential falls. Extra tasks are pretty well held in abeyance, new ones are not begun. At times it is then even difficult for him to complete his more usual and routine work.

B. EFFECTS OF ADDED INTEREST AND MOTIVATION

1. *Allays Fatigue and Increases Work Potential*

In testing the effects of motivation on the length of time a subject could continue to hang on to a horizontal bar, Schwab and DeLorme found that the usual time was substantially increased by the offer of a reward. This is a simple and direct effect. Similar resistances to fatigue can take place in many far more complex ways psychologically.

The gaining of renewed work interest, motivation, and incentive is illustrated in the following case. The gradual dissolution of the handicapping Fatigue State took place concurrently during treatment.

Case 85

New Interest and Motivation Serve an Adjunctive Role in the Successful Psychotherapy of a Chronic Fatigue State

A forty-year-old federal executive was originally referred for psychiatric treatment because of severe chronic fatigue. This had been accompanied by decreasing work performance. The fatigue was somewhat characteristically greater in the morning, with improvement during the day.* As evening approached, however, he often still felt too tired for many social activities. As he explained it, "I have no energy left." Sleep was described as restless, and it seemed to him to have lost much of its restorative value.

Ordinarily ambitious and energetic, this man had achieved a high degree of success in federal career civil service. However, in recent months he had lost much of his incentive for work. Actually, while in the pursuit of an ever higher position he had gotten into a line of endeavor which was basically distasteful to him. This had also led him into a dead end, in so far as any further possibility for advancement was concerned.

The complex dynamics uncovered in the course of prolonged and difficult analytic study cannot be detailed. It might, however, be noted that his response to this frustration had been a nonconstructive regression to a more dependent position in which he unrealistically waited for "something to happen" which would solve his problems. His fatigue developed when the "something" awaited was not delivered. (*See* dynamics in the previous case, *Case 84.*)

As he gained more awareness of his dependency needs during therapy, he became better able to deal with them. As one constructive result of his early therapeutic work, he located a different position not of higher grade, but in an area of genuine interest to himself. This useful step, taken at an optimal point in therapy, provided renewed incentive. The lack of energy and the handicapping fatigue were hastened out of their position of prominence as major symptoms. In other words, the presence of added sources of interest and motivation served as an external stimulus. This helped to reinforce the more fundamental effects of the gradual, continuing clarification and resolution of his unconscious conflicts in therapy.

2. *In Conclusion; Many Psychological Factors Influence Fatigue*

The relative ability to perform physical and mental work over a period of time relates not only to such external factors as physical size, stature,

---

* This clinically parallels the situation in many cases of Emotional Depression. The manifestations of depression are similarly often at their worst in the morning, generally with some gradual improvement during the day. This is in accord with the Morning Ebb-Tide of Spirits, as noted earlier (*p.* 145) in certain Depressive Reactions.

and strength. It also relates importantly to the level of interest, to the amount of personal drive and enthusiasm, to the personal motivation, and to the genuine basic willingness of the individual concerned.

The onset of fatigue is not only enhanced by little interest in one's work, but also to an important extent by factors of discouragement, disappointment, or disillusionment, and by important intrapsychic factors. The *Inverse Incentive-Fatigue Principle* generally tends to be operative.

VIII. BOREDOM AND MONOTONY

A. DYNAMIC FEATURES

Boredom is closely related clinically and dynamically to disappointment and to depression. Feelings of boredom may be actually directly described by some people on occasion as "tiredness." The origins of boredom can be relatively simple, or more complex.

In certain instances of boredom the underlying dynamic factors in one major intrapsychic "route" in this direction, are as follows, in abbreviated fashion: One wishes for activity but the actual goals have been repressed as unacceptable. Substitute ones are not satisfying since: (1) they are either too far removed from the unconscious goals, or perhaps; (2) they are so close to the desired goals as to be stimulating; this is then a danger and a threat, and thus cannot be acceptable either.

The ultimate result therefore is an unconscious inhibition of interests and activity. One then feels subjectively bored, or perhaps what one is doing comes to seem boring and monotonous. Challenge and internal psychic drives are inimical to boredom. (*See also* Concept of Internal Whips and psychic energy, Ch.7:VIC2.)

B. INDIVIDUAL AND SOCIAL REACTIONS TO BOREDOM

1. *Experienced or Reported as Fatigue or Tiredness*

Boredom and monotony are often subjectively experienced or described as feelings of fatigue, tiredness, or weariness. Thus fatigue may be the outward manifestation of boredom. This is reflected in the interchangeability of these expressions, as sometimes illustrated in our day-to-day usage. Thus we may hear such comments as: "I'm tired of my job", "I'm tired of this club, or group, or person", "I'm tired of farming", "I'm tired of this novel", and so forth. While working on one of the early drafts of this chapter, one of the author's then small daughters came in the house to tell him she was "tired" of swinging. When dolls were suggested as a substitute, she was "tired" of dolls also. She of course was not saying literally that she was fatigued, but rather that she was bored. She had already adopted a euphemistic expression of rather widespread use.

There are many similar reactions. The housewife may become "tired" of her daily routine, and the salesman may become "tired" of making the same sales talk over and over again. The mathematics teacher may become "tired" of presenting the same theorems, the physician perhaps "tired" of following his examination routine, and the medical student "tired" of hearing a lecturer. In each of these and similar instances, the use of the word "tired" refers largely (and often somewhat euphemistically) to the subjective experiencing of boredom, monotony, and disinterest.

A recognition of the relation of fatigue to boredom and to a relative lack of interest may sometimes be seen in social situations. The alert hostess may well sense the disinterest and boredom implicit in the yawning or sleepiness of a guest. Not long ago a patient reported an instance in which the hostess at a party became annoyed as a guest left early. It seemed that the guest had commented on departing that he had better go along home since he had been feeling "tired" ever since arriving at the party! The hostess had surmised the underlying level of boredom. She had taken this as a personal affront. The expression of tiredness, fatigue, or sleepiness may thus be used as a conscious or an unconscious euphemism, or both, for what is really an underlying boredom.

2. Seeking to Escape Boredom

Escape from boredom may be sought in many ways. They may be constructive and healthy, or not. At times boredom may be an important contributing factor in such areas as alcoholic overindulgence, delinquent or antisocial behavior, and in sexual promiscuity. Sleep is a not uncommon route to escape boredom and monotony. (*See also* later section X and also reference to "oversleeping," *p.* 40.) Daydreams and fantasies can also so serve, and can provide a major source of interest and subjective satisfaction.

Many social activities originate in the attempt to stimulate interest and to combat boredom. So may many worthwhile civic, church, charitable, and community projects, and the individual's participation in them.

3. Substitute Expression for Anger; Anger-Equivalents

"I'm tired of" or "I'm discouraged with" can also be used as a substitute expression for "I'm cross" or "I'm angry." Thus a patient told the author that she was discouraged with him. It was soon learned that what she really meant was that she was angry with him. Why had her feeling been thus worded in its expression? Her response was along the lines that it "sounded better" and that it was "nicer" that way. Thus expressions of fatigue can be an anger equivalent (*See also* earlier reference, *p.* 19, to anger as an *anxiety-equivalent.*)

"I'm tired of" can also at times be translated to mean "I've had enough of." In *Case 86* we shall shortly see how the patient literally acts out in his appetite and in his eating habits his feeling of being "fed up." This is another concealed somatic way of expressing the feeling "I'm tired of", "I've had enough", or even "I'm discouraged." It is a type of *somatic language* as referred to earlier. (*See also* Ch.12:IB*1*.)

"You make me tired" likely means bored, provoked, cross, out of patience, or some combination of these. A man commented in therapy about his wife, with annoyance and disgust, "I get so tired of this business [arguments and scenes] day after day!"

IX. PHYSIOLOGY OF ENERGY AND FATIGUE

A. COMPLEX AND VARIABLE FACTORS INFLUENCE AVAILABLE ENERGY

1. Reservoir Concept of Energy Misleading

Among the more popular misconceptions about relative individual energy is the rather mechanical one of the Reservoir Concept. Hereby this very circumscribed reservoir or warehouse is thought of as containing a quantum of energy which is directly proportional to the exact amounts of rest and food which have been provided. This rather common mechanical view is unfortunate and misleading. The reservoir concept neglects all the possible complex factors of motivation, interest, ambition, and the basic inner personal drives and needs which can enter so significantly into the relative supply or lack of available energy. Such a mechanical view also fails to take into account the equally important complex ways through which the emotional dissipation and expenditure of energy takes place. It is inaccurate and an oversimplification.

2. Psychic Energy Not Dependent Upon Physical Metabolism

Contrary to the view of an absolute and fixed supply of energy as in the reservoir concept, in certain instances it appears that the expenditure of energy, particularly psychic energy, seems almost in itself to stimulate a greater supply or store of available energy. Psychic energy is by no means definitely and solely tied to the rate or efficiency of physical metabolism alone. (*See* Concept of Internal Whips, Ch.7:VIC2.)

On the other hand, emotional or psychic energy is not inexhaustible. Both its supply and its depletion are influenced by important intrapsychic factors. Thus psychologic depletion can occur, of what Janet called "mental energy," and what Freud referred to as "psychic energy." There is no fixed reservoir, but rather a very elastic and complex supply which is influenced in each direction by a number of important and variable intrapsychic factors.

3. Interaction of Psyche and Soma

A. EMOTIONAL-PHYSIOLOGIC RELATIONS IN FATIGUE AND EXHAUSTION IMPORTANT.—There is of course a genuine physiologic basis for physical fatigue. In view of the close possible interaction already recognized between the emotional and the physiologic, what are the implications as to their interaction more generally, in fatigue and in exhaustion? Some answers are known, some remain to be better understood, and the pathways for the further study of some of them are available. These relationships are important.

Medicine has taken increasingly careful cognizance of the close interaction of psyche and soma. We have learned much concerning the physiologic responses to emotions, together with the physiologic sequelae to their having been experienced. Although a large field for study and research remains, we have already acquired considerable knowledge about the many possible avenues of the somatic expressions of anxiety and emotional conflict. Some of these have been referred to in earlier chapters and others will be noted subsequently.

B. CLINICAL LABORATORY FINDINGS IN SEVERE FATIGUE STATES.—
Severe Fatigue States may be accompanied by some interesting and demonstrable clinical laboratory findings. It might be worth while to mention some of these. For example, there can be a rather typical flat curve observed in the *glucose tolerance test*. There is also a low blood sugar level, followed by a delayed return to normal, which may be reported by the laboratory in the *insulin tolerance test* in certain cases. These findings were illustrated in the following instance.

Case 86

Glucose Tolerance Test in Severe Fatigue State, with a 32-pound Weight Loss

(1) *Emotional Fatigue and Conversion Anorexia as "Psychic Distaste"*
A twenty-four-year-old accounting student was seen in psychiatric consultation following the simultaneous decline in his class standing and in his general health. His principal complaint was intense fatigue. To this he ascribed his poorer grades and his gradual loss of class standing. The fatigue was so great that he felt up to doing very little. There was also an accompanying loss of weight over the preceding six months, accompanied by anorexia. His weight had declined from 142 pounds upon his enrollment in school in October, to 110 pounds in March. (With psychotherapy and in the absence of adjuvants or dietary supplements, his weight subsequently had climbed back to 130 pounds in July, and by September to 138 pounds.)

In condensed form, the history revealed a rather submissive and compliant person who was consciously never aware of the existence of a wish which was contrary to his mother's suggestions. He had entered accounting on this basis, concealing (even from himself as well) his own strongly contrary interests and desires. However, as he continued in an endeavor with which he was basically not in sympathy, he became less able to repress from his conscious awareness his terrific rebellion and "distaste." Psychic Distaste had evolved into a literal distaste and psychopathologic anorexia. (*See also* Ch.3:IVD7; Ch.12IB*1*; VIC2.)

In accord with his major symptoms of anorexia and fatigue, some of the following, greatly condensed but verbatim comments of the patient, extracted from months of therapeutic work, are interesting from a dynamic viewpoint.

(2) *Unconscious Rebellion*
"The work was monotonous and tedious for me. All my energy was used up. I felt tired and didn't want to do much . . . A person gets tired from sitting still or from being bored . . . It's a lot tougher to do something you don't want to do or aren't interested in, and I seem to get tired a lot quicker . . . When I was in Blake [his preparatory school] I was interested and liked what I was doing. I was spry and

full of pep. Now I can hardly drag myself around. I feel tired and don't want to do much."

Actually, he had begun to feel forced to do something he increasingly consciously did not want to do. Unconsciously he was in even greater rebellion. He was figuratively and symbolically "fed up." This is reflected in selected quotes from some of his comments about his appetite loss. "I began to feel filled up inside and my appetite went away. I would be hungry in the morning, but after working in the classes awhile I would get a bloated feeling . . . I was never hungry during work or after finishing it . . . I felt better on weekends, but I dreaded even the thought of going back to school on Monday . . . As Monday comes closer, I notice the filled up feeling is stronger. I am more tired at the end of the weekend than at the beginning."

(3) Glucose Tolerance Curve Flattened

Initially, careful physical studies in this case by competent physicians had ruled out all possible organic causes for the weight loss. The psychologic basis for his chronic Fatigue State and the consequent symptoms was clearly recognized. A glucose tolerance test showed a flat curve with roughly half the expected rise in blood sugar after thirty minutes.*

Although this type of response is not limited to Fatigue States, it is a frequent finding as also reported by Alexander and others. A case studied analytically by Carlson demonstrated the correlation between the glucose tolerance curve response and the changing emotional status while the patient was in treatment.

---

* This type of response is not necessarily a simple one, nor is its interpretation easy. The entire subject of carbohydrate metabolism is a very complex one which has itself been the subject of considerable study. One may note possible contributions through such things as a failure of absorption of the glucose, or more insulin being available.

These could be in response to tension and internal stress. The autonomic nervous system through activity of the sympathetics and parasympathetics plays an important mediating role.

C. INSULIN TOLERANCE TEST.—In the foregoing case an insulin tolerance test also revealed responses which might be anticipated in some cases of severe fatigue, particularly when these are associated with anorexia and resulting weight loss. Calculating the regular insulin given intravenously at 1/10 unit per kilogram of body weight, we found the following results:

mg per cc

1. Fasting blood sugar level.......... 90
2. Thirty-minute level .... 28 (very low)
3. Two-hour level .... 68 (normally should be back to fasting level)

This test, which may occasionally separate the Fatigue State from adrenal cortical insufficiency on one of several organic bases (which might, for example, include such possibilities as severe tuberculosis, infections, tumors, histoplasmosis, pituitary dysfunctions, and so forth), also indicates the amount of glycogen stored and/or the ability to utilize it. Starvation can also result in changes in carbohydrate utilization and metabolism.

D. JOINT INVOLVEMENT OF THE EMOTIONAL AND PHYSIOLOGICAL.— The foregoing results are interesting. In this case they helped to point out the close interrelation and interaction of the psyche and the soma. It seems to me that the important thing here is the simultaneous involvement which takes place. Perhaps this is of greater moment than arriving at a rather academic conclusion as to whether the psychic or the somatic changes are primary or secondary in relation to each other, or to what extent. Such dichotomous considerations can be unfortunate, and there is a clear medical need to regard psyche and soma functioning as one unit together, and not separately.

It has not been possible to find anything in the current literature in regard to insulin tolerance determinations in Fatigue States. Since there are currently few enough laboratory correlations possible between emotional states and altered physiology, further research in this area would be interesting and is clearly needed.

B. EMOTIONS AND BODY CHEMISTRY

1. Carbohydrate Metabolism Stimulated

According to McCulloch and his colleagues, interest and zest stimulate carbohydrate metabolism, as do most other emotions. If the individual puts out prolonged effort in the absence of interest, the promptness of the regulatory change in metabolism is likely to suffer. It is no wonder that prolonged emotional tension on almost any basis can leave a person "drained," worn out, and fatigued.

Stieglitz commented on the more effective performance of youths in short bursts of intense physical activity, whereas the older individual may do better in the more prolonged kinds of work or sports. He noted, for example, that all the sprint records are held by young people. Most of the marathon records in turn are held by older men, often in their forties. The variability of fatigue in response to activity is a highly individual matter. Kinsey and his colleagues reported the wide variation in the individual level of subjective fatigue following sexual orgasm.

2. Fatigue Neglected in Current Textbooks

A. NO DEFINITIVE REFERENCE; CURRENT DISCUSSION OFFERS MOST AVAILABLE DATA ON FATIGUE.—In view of the frequency with which fatigue is encountered as the presenting complaint, or as an important symptom, in the clinical practice of medicine, it is indeed surprising that so few references are to be found in standard textbooks of medicine. The very extensive index of one such major standard textbook of medicine makes only five very brief references to fatigue! This is despite its 2000-odd pages, and its many thousands of indexed topics and references on all variety of medical matters. Further, none of the data for the five references includes more than the briefest mention of the symptom of fatigue, none more than two or three lines. Precisely, they include the occurrence of fatigue as a predisposing cause of lobar pneumonia and (possibly) in rheumatoid arthritis. Fatigue was merely noted as being a possible symptom of Addison's disease, exophthalmic goiter, and tuberculosis. (*See* our earlier summary of possible sources for what has been termed *primary* and *secondary organic fatigue;* section IIIC*1* and *2.*)

There are no definitive references on the subject. So far as could be determined, this chapter offers the most data by far in the medical literature to date on the subject of fatigue. A great gap in the completeness of our knowledge awaits filling by the properly challenged student and researcher.

B. SCATTERED REFERENCES.—Among accounts by physicians of their own illnesses, Low wrote of his personal "physical and mental fatigue" subsequent to an attack of poliomyelitis. Goldsmith wrote about his overpowering "weakness and fatigability" with multiple sclerosis.

Weiss and English also noted the tendency in medicine, in dealing with fatigue, to look for an organic condition, such as tuberculosis or anemia. They reported excessive fatigue occurring in individuals as a result of "too little interest in doing their work, or that it is too difficult — there are too many conflicts which induce anxiety. They are working overtime as it were." Emotional Fatigue also ensues, as we have formulated earlier, because of ". . . emotional conflict which uses up so much [psychic] energy that little is left for other purposes."

3. Metabolic Requirements of Brain

A point might be noted in regard to mental fatigue. Mental effort consumes more actual energy than might ordinarily be expected. Not too much is known about exactly just how mental effort is coordinated with metabolism. Nerve impulses apparently result from a change in electrical potential, with minute charges constituting the impulse.

We do know that the brain has considerable metabolic requirements, particularly in view of its small proportion — about 2 per cent — of the body weight. It receives about 14 per cent of the blood circulation. It consumes approximately 20–25 per cent of the oxygen intake. One may assume accordingly that its caloric-metabolic requirements are considerable.

4. Endocrine Activity; P.E.E.R. and S.E.E.R.

A. PSYCHOPHYSIOLOGY RETREAT.—A final point of interest in our brief comments on physiology is in regard to the evidence of decreased endocrine activity in Fatigue States and in Depression. With fear, anxiety, and anger, epinephrine is released, with resulting increased pulse rate, deeper respiration, and other associated physiologic changes in preparation for physical activity. With most emotional states, the usual response to heightened emotions is increased endocrine activity. The physiologic preparation builds up one's potential for actual physical "flight" or "fight".

In distinct contrast, in the Fatigue States and in Depression there is ordinarily a "psychologic retreat" or withdrawal, with *decreased* endocrine function, toward a state of relative physiologic dormancy. This constitutes what might be termed the Psychophysiologic Retreat, a pervasive, withdrawing type of retreat which is fairly common in depression and less so in emotional fatigue. (*See also* Diffuse Retardation Concept in depression (Ch.4:VA4).

B. PRIMARY AND SECONDARY EMOTIONAL-ENDOCRINE REACTIONS (P.E.E.R. AND S.E.E.R.).—With strong emotions generally, except perhaps in these latter conditions, we can postulate a Primary Emotional-Endocrine Reaction or P.E.E.R., as stemming from most emotions and emotional tension. This is through their effect upon the soma via sympathetic-parasympathetic action with an increase of the relative activity and *stimulation* of endocrine function.

There is likewise the potential for a succeeding Secondary Emotion-Endocrine Reaction or S.E.E.R. This occurs when the chronic presence of emotional tension may itself lead to relative exhaustion or inanition. The result is the decrease of endocrine activity and stimulation.

X. FATIGUE AND SLEEP

"Sleep; that knits up the ravell'd sleeve of care"
Shakespeare

A. AID IN REPLENISHING ENERGY

One commonly expected response to any kind of fatigue is to seek a renewal of energy through sleep. This is the specific for physical fatigue and often for mental fatigue as well. Other things, such as a good meal, a shower, or a change of occupation, can also sometimes result in renewed energy.

With emotional fatigue, sleep is most necessary also, but is less likely to be as regularly and routinely effective in its relief. Sleep inevitably will restore depleted physical or mental energy. It will often help one whose psychic energy is low, but it is by no means as certain or proportionate. More sleep does not always result in more psychic energy becoming available. The person with a severe Emotional Depression or a major Fatigue State does not necessarily feel a great deal more rested after sleep. This may be true also with other neurotic reactions. Sleep has not changed substantially the underlying emotional conflicts. These of course continue to be present on awakening. At times it is even as though the more sleep, the more fatigue, rather than less.

This does not mean, however, that sleep does not play an important role in the maintenance of emotional health. It was pointed out in Chapter 1, *p.* 38, for instance, that sleep helps a great deal in refurbishing our psychologic armamentarium. Further, sleep is vital and a necessity from the emotional and psychic standpoints, as was earlier stressed in our *Respite-of-Sleep Principle* and related concepts [Ch.1:V; Ch.9:IVC1].

B. HOW MUCH SLEEP NEEDED?

1. Individual and Relative Matter

Sleep is, of course, a necessity and plays a vital role in both the physical and the emotional aspects of our lives. As discussed elsewhere from 60 to

100 hours of deprivation of sleep leads almost universally to the production of certain abnormal psychologic phenomena. Sleep is very much an absolute requirement. One may perhaps, however, raise a question as to the necessity for the establishment of any absolute general requirements or standards as to the amount of sleep generally necessary for maintaining good health. This is a more relative and individual matter.

A common standard for health is eight hours of sleep in each twenty-four, although longer and shorter periods have been advocated. However, we know of frequent instances in which people function at a high level of effectiveness and health on relatively few hours of sleep. Edison, for example, slept four hours nightly for many years, cramming most of the remaining twenty with very active and highly productive endeavors. Other instances are found in history, biography, and in the author's own experience, in which the individual average amount of sleep per night has been so low and lower, over varying periods of time.

2. Recovery Time Following Deprivation; Personal Requirements Vary

We know also that the recovery time following considerable deprivation of sleep is rapid. This appears to vary surprisingly little from a maximal ten–fifteen hours of uninterrupted sleep, and with seemingly little actual relation to the total duration of the preceding amount of sleep deprivation. This is an interesting observation which has received too little scientific attention or recognition.

On the other hand, many persons feel a deep need and requirement for from eight to ten or even more, hours of sleep daily. With less, they experience subjective feelings of discomfort, lack of energy, fatigue, tiredness, or exhaustion in varying degrees. We are further aware of great differences in sleep requirements and in sleep patterns with the various age levels. (See also page 40.) The infant sleeps most of the time. The aged person may spend relatively few hours sleeping, and his actual requirements appear to be less. Some use sleep to escape boredom, as noted earlier [Ch.7:VIA*1* and *2*], as a defense or as an escape.

Strauss cited fatigue as an important factor in eliciting (epileptic) attacks. He noted that some patients report attacks following a night with insufficient sleep.

3. Conditioning Influences Attitudes; Effect of Emotional Conflicts

One may rightfully expect that one's individual psychologic conditioning can well play an important role in the development of his personal attitudes toward sleep. This is inherent in the effects of parental attitudes. Neurotic needs may well contribute in some of these instances. Emotional conflict affects the ability to sleep, and to sleep soundly.

A superego in repose, a reasonable level of self-regard, and the absence of guilt feelings, real or neurotic (that is, unrealistic), are certainly important adjuncts to good sleep. At times also, a "good" or clear conscience can be more useful than a sedative! Two hundred years ago Joseph Addison (1672–1719) wrote: "Sweet are the slumbers of the virtuous man."

XI. NEURASTHENIA

A. INTRODUCTION

During the past sixty-five years the psychiatric conception of Neurasthenia has undergone considerable evolution. At the beginning of this period it served as a wide diagnostic catch-all. Gradually however, its frequency of usage has tended to decline. At the same time its application has also narrowed as the manifestations of other and more recently adopted categories of diagnoses, heretofore included, have been separated.

When employed today to describe a neurotic reaction, the term of Neurasthenia may perhaps be most adequately defined in brief as *an emotional reaction of neurotic level, characterized particularly by symptoms of emotional fatigue, weakness, fatigability, feelings of inadequacy, irritability, poor concentration, and by the presence of a variety of other lesser physical, psychologic, and emotional features.* Even when utilized as so defined, a clear-cut emotional syndrome is not sharply delineated.

B. HISTORY

1. G. B. Beard Introduces and Outlines; S. Freud Studies and Narrows

As noted earlier in this chapter, the history of Neurasthenia is intimately tied up with observations concerning Emotional Fatigue and the Fatigue States. Hence much of the data has been presented earlier in this chapter (section II). As mentioned there, the American, G. M. Beard, has mainly been credited with introducing the concept of nerve weakness and the term of Neurasthenia in 1869, also for outlining the syndrome (Ch.1:VIIIC1). See *Table 23* following, for an outline of his signs and symptoms of Neurasthenia. It should be noted at this juncture, however, that the term of Neurasthenia actually may have been in use previously, according to an early lexicon (Mayne, 1856). Further, Cowles (in 1894) credited a physician named Van Deusen with formulating the concept of Neurasthenia in 1867, although publishing his theories in the same year of 1869 as had Beard. While Beard advocated electrical stimulation in therapy, as a "tonic" for the exhausted nervous system, Van Deusen proposed rest treatment.

Beard believed chemical changes in nerve tissue resulted in exhaustion of the nervous system. This sequence then became for him the most frequent cause of disease in his time. As will be noted in *Table 23, D,* he had formulated almost a "diagnostic catch-all". He postulated the causes of Neurasthenia to be hereditary, and that somehow the condition occurred as a part of the compensation for progress and refinement. Precipitating causes according to Beard were: pressure of bereavement, business and family cares, parturition and abortion, sexual excesses, abuse of stimulants and narcotics, and "civilized starvation". The concept, syndrome, and diagnosis were quickly and very widely adopted and used for half a century.

Freud, among others, was early concerned with the problem of nomenclature and classification in the diagnosis of Neurasthenia. In one of his earliest papers (1894), he proposed separating from Neurasthenia a group of emotional disorders which he termed the Anxiety Neuroses. Herein he included many of the cases having manifestations of the Anxiety Reactions, more or less as currently conceived. (*See* Chapter 3). He presumed a completely sexual basis for both syndromes; the sexual problem in Neurasthenia being of recent origin, whereas that in Anxiety Neurosis was to be found in infancy.

During this period, Freud had quite positively but mistakenly ascribed the etiology of Neurasthenia to be specifically that of sexual frustration (although other causes might be present concomitantly): "Neurasthenia arises whenever a less adequate relief [activity] takes the place of the adequate one, thus when masturbation or spontaneous emission replaces normal coitus under the most favorable conditions." He had previously cited his view that coitus interruptus (*see* footnote, Ch.1:IIA2) was important etiologically. While these findings may be present in instances of Neurasthenia, their presence is not a requisite. Neither are they to be any longer regarded as *the* causative factors in its onset.

Freud listed the principal clinical features of his new more narrowed concept of Neurasthenia as including primarily those of exhaustion, pressure on the head, flatulent dyspepsia, constipation, paresthesias, and sexual weakness. In the same paper, published in 1896, he stated flatly that Neurasthenia "admits of only two specific aetiological factors, excessive onanism and spontaneous emissions".

Adolf Meyer later added the mental symptoms of poor memory, impaired concentration and irritability, together with those of poor sleeping, various bodily aches and pains, and increased reflexes as common clinical features of Neurasthenia.

2. Evolving Views of Etiology of Neurasthenia; of Views About Masturbation

Subsequently, formulations of the psychodynamics of Neurasthenia have undergone substantial development and evolution. Today as noted these earlier constricted and abbreviated etiologic concepts and clinical descriptions are to be regarded as both insufficient and in error. While the symptoms of Neurasthenia may well be dynamically contributed to by sexual frustration, there are other major and complex factors to be considered. These include especially: (1) the frustration of hostile and aggressive needs; (2) the struggle over unconscious dependency needs; (3) the reinforcement of repression; and (4) other similar vital psychological defensively-intended endeavors.

When masturbation continues actively into, or is resumed in, adulthood, it is to be regarded first as an indication of failure to achieve maturity in the sexual area. It may sometimes also be a symptom of emotional difficulty. It can represent a potential source of further emotional conflict in itself for someone who worries about it. Masturbation as such is not the cause of emotional illness. (*See also* references to Sexual Maladjustment as Effect-over-Cause in emotional illness, *pp.* 116, 269, *and* 330.)

C. DIAGNOSIS AND INCIDENCE

1. Rarer Diagnosis

As suggested earlier, the diagnosis of Neurasthenia is made more rarely today than previously, with a tendency in certain quarters for it to fall into relative disuse and discard. If the diagnosis is to be made, it is properly done in the presence of a number of the more characteristic symptoms, some of which have been noted. These will be tabulated in *Table 23*.

When usage and preference result in the less frequent use or the total discard of the older syndrome of Neurasthenia, the diagnosis of Fatigue State is to be used. In the absence of fatigue as the major manifestation, the selection of the next most suitable diagnostic category among the psychoneuroses is to be made.

It is estimated that between five and six per cent of the neurotic reactions encountered in private practice might fall into the broader and older category of Neurasthenia. This percentage drops somewhat (to an estimated two–three per cent) when the concept is narrowed and limited to that of the Fatigue States.

2. Conditions to Differentiate

One must be careful to differentiate psychoneurotic reactions in which fatigue is a prominent feature, from the very rare organic syndromes which might occasionally simulate Neurasthenia. The emotional reaction of Hygeiaphrontis (hypochondriasis), with its lowered activity and decreased initiative, may offer a possible source of confusion (Chapter 8) with mild Neurasthenia. Actually, the occasional error in diagnosis in this instance is apt to be more frequently the other way around, with the Fatigue State being more likely misdiagnosed as hypochondriasis.

Cerebral arteriosclerosis may occasionally be the cause of a neurasthenic-like pattern. Occasional cases of general paresis, brain tumors, emotional depressions, and early schizophrenia may on rare occasions do likewise. Likewise a neurasthenic syndrome sometimes may usher in a major functional psychotic episode.

3. Very Poor Medical Management Follows Misdiagnosis

The following case illustrates the occasional problems in diagnosis. There was a poor prognosis for potential treatment, as the result of early misdirected therapeutic attention. An original failure to make an adequate diagnosis was followed by psychiatrically introgenic management. The results were very poor. (*See also* Ch.8:IIIA3; Ch.12:VA1.)

Case 87

A Case of Neurasthenia with a Mistaken Diagnosis and Poor Medical Management

(1) *Mistaken label of "thyroid deficiency"*

A twenty-six-year-old single woman was referred for psychiatric consultation by an internist for symptoms of a neurasthenic nature. The internist had "inherited" the case from a colleague who had recently moved to another part of the country. Immediately he had become greatly, and correctly, concerned at the nature of her long standing treatment regimen.

On the basis of a slight depression of the basal metabolic rate, a mistaken diagnosis of thyroid deficiency had been made some six years previously. The patient had been placed on thyroid extract on a continuing basis, with gradually increasing doses. For the past two years she had been taking 10 grains, on a daily basis. In addition to various other more sporadic medication, she was also taking from 2.5 to 7.5 mg (or more) of benzedrine daily.

(2) *Hygeiaphrontic preoccupation encouraged*

Careful diagnostic study had quickly convinced the internist that there were deeply seated psychologic reasons for her symptoms. There were indeed, as he had accurately suspected, adequate psychologic factors in evidence to account for her symptoms on an emotional basis.

The earlier establishment of the erroneous diagnosis and the resulting treatment had unfortunately encouraged unhealthy narcissistic preoccupation with her physical self and functions. (See following chapter). It had given tremendous support to her already strong existing need for the secondary defense of her symptoms. Her hygeiaphrontic preoccupation had been unwittingly encouraged and facilitated introgenically.

(3) *Prognosis dim*

The relationship with the physician had also inadvertently helped to meet her strong dependency strivings. All of this unfortunate history had vastly complicated the original Fatigue State. Over a period of years, attention had been focused on what had been regarded by both patient and physician as the purely physical basis of her symptoms. She bitterly resented even the most gentle and tentative suggestions in the line of redirecting her focus of inquiry. There were many iatrogenic elements in her illness.

It thus proved a most discouraging task to try belatedly to secure her interest in the exploration of emotional conflicts as the real major factors of her illness. Her orientation was too fixed to permit adequate psychotherapeutic study. It is unfortunately likely that she may never be amenable to the only kind of treatment that can offer a real hope in the possible relief of her symptoms, and in the making of any kind of satisfactory adjustment in living. (*See also* Case 98, Ch.8:- VIB3.)

D. SYMPTOMS AND CLINICAL FEATURES

1. Attempted Correlation of Emotional Make-up and Physical Habitus

According to older descriptions, there was supposed to be a frequently encountered and more or less characteristic "neurasthenic habitus." The so-called asthenic person thus was expected to be tall, slender, and was most often on the poorly nourished side. His thorax was long and narrow, with prominent bony features. His neck and extremities were also long. Sheldon later sought to classify and to match several various types of body build with emotional make-up. These classifications were believed to develop according to the preeminent development of one of the three embryonic layers, in an attempted correlation of somatic type with personality characteristics and temperament. The asthenic habitus corresponds to his ectomorphic group.* A number of authorities have attempted similar classifications and formulations.

While this kind of attempted correlation offers considerable interest, it has been the author's experience and that of others that it does not fully hold up in any extensive clinical experience. Its value is accordingly limited. Neurasthenia and neurasthenic symptoms are not specifically linked to any clear group of physical characteristics. These are not required for a diagnosis, although as in *Case 88,* the so called asthenic habitus may well be present. It like other categories, might of course — and perhaps more accurately — be thought of as developing *secondarily* to the individual's basic emotional make-up (in distinction to the reverse). The Fatigue State likewise appears to occur independently of any specific kind of body build.

The clinical manifestations most frequently associated with cases diagnosed as Neurasthenia are listed in *Table 23.*

Table 23

The Principal Features of Neurasthenia

The following symptoms and manifestations in the psychologic, emotional, mental, and physical spheres are those which have been more commonly ascribed to, or associated with the diagnosis of Neurasthenia. Beard's original signs and symptoms are summarized (*D*) as well, in view of their prior position and historical interest. Freud's and Meyer's were noted earlier, section XIB*1*.

A. **Psychologic Features**
1. Dependency.
2. Narcissism.
3. Hygeiaphrontic (hypochondriacal) tendencies; somatic and functional preoccupation; from mild to moderate, sometimes shifting.
4. Regressive retreat.
5. Underlying emotional conflict.
6. Primary and secondary psychologic gains (outlined earlier in the section on psychodynamics of Fatigue and Fatigue States).
7. Depressive features may accompany marked fatigue.
8. Attenuated hostile interaction with others.
9. Attitudes apathetic.

B. **Emotional Features**
1. Difficulty in concentration.
2. Irritability and tension.
3. Memory may function poorly; may appear impaired.
4. Feelings of inferiority; social interests reduced.
5. Gloom, pessimism, depression, apathy; suicidal ideas may be present.
6. Lack of initiative and ambition.
7. Sensitive or "thin-skinned."
8. Impairment of sexual function — seldom is ability adequate or relationship satisfactory.
9. Interpersonal detachment and insulation.

* Sheldon's three groups were the *ectomorphs,* who were delicate, tall, and thin; the *endomorphs,* who were splanchnically developed and stout; and the *mesomorphs,* who were solid and muscular.

C. **Physical Features**
1. Fatigue, fatigability, weakness, and lack of energy.
2. Headache: (*a*) pressure or weight, (*b*) band, (*c*) suboccipital.
3. Asthenic body build, blood pressure low, coldness and perspiration of extremities frequent.
4. Insomnia and weight loss.
5. Fleeting and shifting somatic symptoms; indigestion, heart burn, anorexia, dizziness, muscular soreness, tachycardia, paresthesia, pain in the abdomen, and dyspepsia with flatulence and constipation.
6. Reflexes may be increased but ordinarily are equal on both sides.

D. **Beard's Signs and Symptoms Included:**
1. Nervousness, insomnia, headaches, backache and hypersensivity.
2. Neurocirculatory asthenia, constitutional inadequacies, mild depression, hypochondriasis, fatigue and weakness.
3. Nervous indigestion, phobias and hysteria.
4. Chronic complaining; a mild Mènière's syndrome.
5. Cardiac neurosis; an Anxiety State.

2. Parent-Child Relationships

Neurasthenia is a condition that is frequently associated with feelings of failure, frustration, and disappointment. It is often accompanied by a prominent attitude-symptom of personal inadequacy. The early family situation is characterized as being far from ideal — most typically a family in which too much responsibility was delegated to the child. This was likely accompanied by little real parental interest, attention, or affection.

The neurasthenic patient often possesses considerable narcissism*; in current usage roughly, self love and absorbing self interest and he strongly needs to be dependent. Characteristic is the easy fatigability following small amounts of physical activity. This is as though the person concerned is already so exhausted from the stress and strain of his emotional conflicts that the slightest amount of physical work or activity would prove exhaustive.

E. THERAPEUTIC RESULTS

1. Excellent Despite Progression of Psychopathology

The following case might be diagnosed as Neurasthenia, or as a very severe Fatigue State. It illustrates the handicapping level to which Emotional Fatigue can progress. It further shows the considerable degree of therapeutic success sometimes possible despite the extent of psychopathologic progression.

Case 88

Neurasthenia or a Severe Fatigue State, with Good Therapeutic Success

A thirty-six-year-old research chemist was referred for analytic treatment because of complaints of severe chronic fatigue, excruciating, nearly constant headaches, weakness, sexual maladjustment, and various minor somatic complaints. He was on the tall and thin side, with a typical asthenic build and imperfect posture.

---

* From Narcissus, of Greek mythology, who fell in love with his image, although in the original myth he did not know that the image was his own.

His fatigability was such that the slightest exertion was completely exhausting. He had gradually reduced his professional working time to a total of only four hours per day. When first seen by the author, he was on the point of giving it up entirely. During the remainder of his time, which was spent strictly at home, he carefully alternated each fifteen–thirty minutes of activity, with exactly one half-hour of reclining.

These measures had proved quite ineffective in reducing his chronic severe level of fatigue. He had experienced progressive difficulty in concentration. Together with his severe headaches, these symptoms had resulted in an increasingly restricted social life, a situation foreign to his previous nature. Life had become so intolerable that he had been on the point of suicide. He chose psychiatric treatment instead, in what amounted to a last desperate resort, having visited half a dozen physicians in various fields, in his futile search for an organic basis, and resulting cure of his terrible symptoms.

This case is clinically rather typical of very severe Neurasthenia. This patient, however, proved an apt candidate for intensive treatment and eventually, during the course of more than four years of treatment — on a three-times, and later two-times a week basis — he stopped having his headaches entirely. His fatigue also completely subsided. For more than ten years he has worked full-time and has been able to resume his former level of social activity.

2. Pattern of Fatigability

The fatigue and easy fatigability observed is a chronic type of fatigue in which rest and sleep do not refresh. The fatigue is typically greatest on arising and improves during the day's activities. This pattern of fatigability may, however, be reversed, as seen in *Case 80.* Physical exercise may actually bring relief, as was observed during World War II by the Royal Air Force. Ferenczi described a series of cases which presented marked symptoms for one day and which he termed "One-Day Neurasthenia." Following Freud, he ascribed a purely sexual etiology. *Case 176,* which is summarized in (Ch.14:VD*3*) also illustrates some of the clinical features of Neurasthenia.

Careful psychologic research has led to an increasing understanding of the psychodynamics of Neurasthenia. Some of the principal features have been covered under the section on Fatigue and the Fatigue State and need not be repeated here. A few more, general comments on treatment will follow, included in the section on Emotional Fatigue and the Fatigue State.

XII. TREATMENT

A. PROGNOSIS GOOD WITH PSYCHOTHERAPY

The treatment of choice in Emotional Fatigue, the Fatigue State, and in Neurasthenia is psychotherapy. Results to be expected with the interested and cooperative patient working in an active collaborative effort or *therapy-alliance* (see later) with a well-trained psychotherapist, are very good.

The deeper and more insight-developing the therapy, the better are the prospects for significant and permanent constructive change.

B. SUPPORTIVE THERAPY

1. Environmental Changes

Complaints of Emotional Fatigue tend to invite approaches by the more common measures such as are usually associated with the alleviation of mental or physical fatigue. Recommendations of general physicians have in past decades included many varied suggestions. These have included changes of avocation and work, the adoption of a hobby, increased rest and sleep, a vacation or trip, high-caloric diets, changes in the level of responsibility, physical therapy, reassurance and suggestion, and various types of medication, especially including vitamins, amphetamines, and hormonal extracts.

Some of these measures or regimens or some combination of them have been widely endorsed or advocated at various times in the past. They are intended to provide a measure of support, at times through environmental manipulation and change.

2. Attention and Interest Supportive

The interested and sympathetic physician can, indeed, secure some improvement simply by devoting a fair amount of time, attention, and sincere interest to a patient, with or without one or more of the above adjunctive measures. This type of response to genuine interest and attention is, however, likely to be a temporary one.

As long as the crutch-like supportive and dependent nature of some of these measures is clearly recognized, however, the physician will not rely too much upon the results continuing or increasing, and both he and the patient will avoid disappointment. Also, harm is less likely from the inadvertent promotion of further unhealthful dependence, which can be terribly and permanently damaging through its rendering some patients less amenable, or even permanently non-amenable, to psychotherapy.

3. Several Approaches

A. S. WEIR MITCHELL'S REGIMEN.—S. Weir Mitchell, a psychiatric pioneer in America, treated neurasthenic patients with great success in the nineteenth century with a regimen of enforced rest and high-caloric diets. His ability to gain improvement (which, however, was often followed by relapse upon discontinuance) was the result of his own dynamic personality, plus the gratification of the dependency needs of the patient. These served as a somewhat unwitting aid to his therapeutic results. Actually, however, his regimen abetted and encouraged the neurosis, instead of relieving it. Neurotic dependency needs were met or even fostered.

Neurasthenic patients need to become aware of and to learn about their unconscious dependency needs and strivings. They need to gain a willingness to renounce some of them, if real and permanent improvement is to be secured and a higher level of maturity is to be achieved.

B. PHYSICAL MODALITIES AND DRUGS NOT RECOMMENDED.—At times electric shock and various physical methods of treatment or drugs are used in treating the Fatigue Reactions. These are not recommended. The end results will only often be unfavorable because of the psychopathologic and fundamental features of this group of emotional reactions (dependency, narcissism, and hygeiaphrontis).

In order to obtain satisfactory permanent results with the Fatigue Reactions, the therapist must be aware of the above personality pitfalls and help the patient gain awareness and understanding of them. One must keep in mind that anxiety is potentially present in the Fatigue Reactions but is largely kept under control through the symptoms of fatigue. One must be aware of the psychodynamics of emotional fatigue and be able to help the patient gradually work them out for himself.

C. AIM TO SECURE INSIGHT AND TO PROMOTE MATURITY.—In the Fatigue State the outward manifestations of fatigue are present in place of the outward manifestations of anxiety which are observed in the more overt Anxiety Reactions. The aim of the therapist is to secure insight and to promote greater emotional maturity, as is true for all psychotherapeutic endeavors.

Personality development beyond the narcissistic level has been retarded or interfered with in these patients. Accordingly, they must be encouraged to progress and to mature to a more adult and constructive level of integration. By the same token these factors add to the increased difficulties in initiating psychotherapy. This is in accord with our *Concept of Emotional Inertia.*

D. REST AS SYMPTOMATIC APPROACH.—The symptomatic treatment of fatigue by prescribing rest will be doomed to failure when the fatigue results from unrecognized emotional conflicts. We saw this very pointedly illustrated in *Case 88,* in which a steadily increasing attempt had been made to increase the time spent in rest, parallel to the increase in symptoms. Emotional Fatigue is often characteristically more intense on arising in the morning, with a tendency to lessen or improve as the day passes. This feature leads the patient to report sometimes that "rest does no good", or "I get no good out of sleep."

When the fatigue is serious enough to be incapacitating in itself, or when it is accompanied by such other emotional symptoms, psychotherapy is indicated. Successful insight therapy will result in the bringing of conflicts into awareness. This allows for a more realistic appraisal of conflicting internal needs and wishes, and it increases the chance for better, more constructive solutions. As the conflicts decrease in number, the fatigue will diminish.

E. STIMULANTS.—Generally, stimulants tend to decrease *awareness* of fatigue or they may temporarily stimulate wakefulness and *apparent* energy. Physiologically and psychologically, they may only too often produce somewhat the same effect as whipping a horse — a tired one at that! For *physical* and *mental* fatigue, simple carbohydrate intake in readily assimilable form, as sugar, glucose, candy, and so on is probably physiologically best, next to rest. At times a shower will help. Generally the author votes against drugs as an approach to Emotional Fatigue and personally does not use them.

The drugs most frequently used as stimulants are caffeine and those of the amphetamine group. In the carefully selected case, their restricted use may have an adjunctive role. The physician must keep carefully in mind that the amphetamines are a temporary relief at best. Habit formation and dependence are serious potential hazards. Finally, "pep pills" are a poor substitute for psychotherapy.

With the symptoms of Emotional Fatigue, as with all other emotional symptoms, it is far better for the patient to seek competence and expertness in finding out why he has the symptoms. This is much to be preferred over the seeking of the very short-sighted goal of expertness in suppressing, concealing, or temporarily removing his symptoms through the use of various drugs. He needs to develop understanding, not to evolve a crutch upon which to become increasingly dependent.

C. CONSIDERATIONS IN INTENSIVE PSYCHOTHERAPY

1. Initiating Analysis; Emotional Inertia Concept

A. EFFECTIVE THERAPY MOST WORTHWHILE.—Persons to be referred for intensive psychotherapy and analysis should be carefully selected as to actual or potential interest, reasonable intelligence, and ability to cooperate. This treatment approach is difficult, time-consuming, and expensive.

Results, however, when analytic treatment is effective, are more than worth all the efforts and sacrifices required. In the successful case, the results of such *deep treatment* (*p.* 212) are beyond price to the individual concerned. This was most true, for example, in *Case 88.* In accord with the Emotional Inertia Concept [Ch.4:XIIA7], in initiating therapy, more effort is required and more cooperation must be enlisted to overcome the initial emotional inertia.

B. HOW LONG TO BECOME WISE?—At the beginning no definite promises can or should be made by the consulting analyst as to the duration of therapy, nor should a cure or other specific results be guaranteed. How long does it take to become wise? One cannot answer how long a time this would take.

One cannot say how long it might take to secure sufficient self-knowledge. One cannot state in advance what the degree of success will be in achieving the wisdom of self-understanding. Many therapists begin treatment on a trial basis of at least a month or two. This is for the benefit of both analyst and patient.

C. RESOLUTION OF EMOTIONAL CONFLICTS REQUIRED.—In general, dietary measures, manipulation of the external environment, pharmacologic measures, reassurance, rest, or suggestion can achieve little more than temporary respite or improvement. Emotional Fatigue is due to internal conflict. Alexander wrote: "In all cases in which there is a chronic conflict situation, neither dietary and pharmacological measures, nor manipulation of the external life situation can achieve more than some temporary relief from the symptoms. Such cases require a consistent psychotherapeutic approach."

The basis of the underlying emotional conflicts must be uncovered, recognized, brought into conscious awareness, resolved, and dealt with constructively in order to effect their successful resolution.

2. Fatigue Attacks Occurring During Intensive Psychotherapy

A. WHEN DEREPRESSION THREATENS; A FATIGUE-INDICATOR.—Emotional Fatigue may be occasionally observed to occur or to increase at some juncture during the course of analysis. The appearance of emotional fatigue at various phases of therapy can have considerable significance. It may be a frequent prelude to the impending appearance in dreams or in consciousness of affective memories. It may indicate resistance or have prognostic import. Essentially this is fatigue resulting from the intrapsychic struggle over derepression. The recognition also by the therapist of the absorption of energy in intrapsychic struggles during phases of resistance can be useful in therapy. In line with the foregoing comments these recognitions can comprise for us what might be termed *A Fatigue-Indicator*.

B. ATTACK INDICATES IMPENDING DATA OF SIGNIFICANCE.—Emotional catharsis can aid substantially in symptom relief. A forty-one-year-old woman patient in analytic therapy experienced a severe fatigue attack which kept her in bed for most of the day. She had been at a meaningful juncture in treatment. She had previously avoided any real discussion of a certain important relationship with a business associate. The onset of her fatigue-attack provided an important Fatigue-Indicator that impending data of significance was threatening to emerge. The patient, who had achieved a certain level of psychiatric sophistication recognized this. As a consequence of the fatigue episode, she accordingly brought herself to discuss the relationship.

Following the ensuing emotional session, she described her feeling of relief. She felt good about it and about having gotten it off her chest. In her words, "There was a feeling of peace of mind. It's having discussed something that had been inside and troubling. I really unloaded about Ann, and I feel better for it. I feel more tolerant toward her, and the faults I complained about don't seem so important any more. It had seemed too great a task to get it out. Afterwards I felt better. I seemed to have more energy. That terrible fatigue business has gone now."

3. Areas of Analytic Interest. The Therapy-Alliance Concept

A. LEARNING WHAT MAKES ONESELF "TICK."—In the treatment approach of intensive psychotherapy the psychiatrist attempts to learn as much as possible about the patient and what makes him "tick" as a person.

The need for active collaborative work by patient and doctor as a pre-requisite for results becomes clearly apparent. Interest is centered upon the patient's emotional life, his satisfactions, his goals, and particularly upon his personal relationships with, and adjustments to other people.

The joint interest of the physician and his patient-colleague is especially directed toward the vicissitudes of all important interpersonal relation-ships, past and present. Of inestimable value to the patient is the gaining of conscious awareness of the ways in which he unwittingly contributes to his own unhappiness and self-defeat.

B. PATIENT-THERAPIST RELATIONSHIP.—Inevitably, the one relation-ship which is available for a laboratory level of study, observation, and dissection is the one with the therapist. This offers an excellent area for gaining understanding about relationships.

Inevitably, the patterns of reaction, skills, and techniques which have been employed in dealing with people thus far, will again be employed in the relationship with the therapist. These have been developed automati-cally, for better or for worse. See our *Profitable-Patterns Concept,* as out-lined earlier, *p.* 320. Gaining conscious awareness of them puts the patient in a far better position to make a choice.

Earlier, comments have been offered as to the necessity for a special kind of collaborative relationship between the doctor and his patient. This produces the kind of endeavor requisite to promote meaningful progress in psychotherapy. This can hardly be overstressed. On the effectiveness and excellence of the patient-therapist relationship will rest the gains of therapy. In further emphasis we might refer to this kind of productive collaboration as the *Therapy-Alliance Concept.* From our psychiatric point of view, it is more important, for example, then an alliance between two nations at war with a third party. Thereby it can enhance the allies chances of success and victory. In psychotherapy a Therapy-Alliance is even more significant. Herein it becomes a necessity for success. See also the related Joint-Endeavor Principle in psychotherapy (*p.* 130), and the Team-Work Tenet in therapy (*p.* 362).

C. FREE ASSOCIATION.—Attention in psychotherapy is focused on the present day-to-day living, and upon minute-to-minute observations of thoughts, feelings, physical sensations, and associations of the person con-cerned. One seeks to follow his "free associations." This means his *asso-ciations are to be unfettered and unrestricted, and are to be presented ver-bally in the therapy sessions, insofar as possible without prior reservation or censorship.* Pursuing the pathways of free association in turn often leads into emotionally significant areas of the person's past. Greater understand-ing of one's problems is developed, as is knowledge as to how these prob-lems were handled. See also earlier reference to The Treatment Rule, page 50. In the successful instance the patient does not merely become well, he becomes "better than well."

As we have seen illustrated repeatedly in our case material, the vicissi-tudes of the very early childhood relationships with significant adults are most vital to the later potentials for emotional health. These and the resulting patterns of interpersonal adaptation and patterns of reaction, inevitably come under analytic scrutiny. One learns more and more about what makes himself "tick" emotionally and psychologically.

4. Course of Graduate Study Concept

With such an intensive study, usually requiring hundreds of sessions over several years, we may aptly compare analysis in conception to a complete course of graduate study in a university. In therapy the subject of this course is the patient. He also becomes the reference source, and the textbook for all primary data. (See also page 234.)

The undertaking of this kind of treatment is always to be regarded seriously. It is not to be undertaken without due prior consideration on the part of both physician and patient. In the analogy to graduate study, the work of therapy is on a deeper, more significant, and personal level.

XIII. SUMMARY

The concept of *emotional fatigue* was outlined and wider medical recognition was urged. Emotional fatigue is a common symptom in medicine. When fatigue arises largely from emotional sources, there is a discrepancy between the amount of physical and mental work which has been performed and the level of fatigue which is subjectively experienced. This disproportion is characteristic. Emotional fatigue is to be distinguished from mental fatigue and from physical fatigue. When emotional fatigue is chronically present and is the predominant clinical feature of a neurotic reaction, the indicated diagnosis is that of a *Fatigue State*. The Fatigue State is a *symptom neurosis*. Definitions were offered and the rationale for including this chapter in our text on the neuroses was outlined.

In earlier times Fatigue States were included within the category of Neurasthenia, a widely employed term, an earlier frequent but diffuse diagnostic category, and an etiologic concept of nerve weakness, which was mainly promulgated by Beard, beginning in 1869. Retention of a category of the *Fatigue State* was recommended. The Fatigue State must be differentiated from Depressive Reactions, to which it may be closely allied dynamically and clinically. (*See* summary in *Table 21.*) Sometimes differentiation must also be made from the organic fatigue which is very occasionally the product of a number of rather rare organic conditions, which have been enumerated. The Primary Organic Fatigue of chronic illness and the Secondary Organic Fatigue incident to infections and surgical procedures were noted. The *Concept of Advanced Organicity* was outlined. Since Emotional Fatigue may theoretically occur as a consequence of any unconscious emotional conflict, it is not surprising that the incidence is considerable. Physicians find it one of the most frequent symptoms encountered in medical practice. The *Principle of Characteristic-Disproportion* is an aid to its identification. The presence of emotional manifestations (as with emotional fatigue) concurrently with organic ones, comprise what was termed *E.O.C.* — emotional-organic combinations.

Our Concept of *Secondary Defense* was noted. The symptom of emotional fatigue tends to find a measure of social acceptability, and thus can currently enjoy a certain *cultural vogue*. An estimated three–four percent of clinical neurotic reactions might warrant a diagnosis of Fatigue Reactions.

Psychodynamically, Emotional Fatigue has its origin in unconscious emotional conflict. Emotional Fatigue arises primarily: (1) as a hidden symbolic expression of, or as a defense against, consciously disowned needs or wishes, (2) as a result of the expenditure and depletion of psychic energy due to emotional conflicts, or (3) as a combination of these. The "physical scapegoat" is defensively evolved. The conditioning effects of parental influences were discussed, and the close clinical and psychodynamic relationships of the Fatigue State to Emotional Depression have been stressed. The *Concept of Interpersonal Perpetuation* finds applicability. The *epigain* (see *Table 22*) and the *endogain* of Emotional Fatigue have been summarized. Fatigue occurring from the experiencing of anxiety and tension is in accord with the *Depletion Concept of Anxiety*. What have been termed *"Internal Whips"* exert major influences upon drive, motivation, and fatigability. In the *Dependency-Dilemma of Infancy,* the repressed rage threatens the vital object of dependency.

The important influence of the level of interest and motivation upon fatigue was discussed. *An Inverse Ratio Principle of Incentive to Fatigue* was outlined. The phenomenon of C.S.E. (Cyclic Swings of Energy) was noted. The onset and level of fatigue is influenced to an important extent also by factors of possible discouragement, disappointment, and disillusionment. Boredom was discussed, and note was taken of the frequent use of the term "tired" really to express boredom. Tiredness and fatigue can comprise an expression of what we have called a *somatic language*. Expressions of fatigue can also be *anger-equivalents*.

The *Reservoir Concept of Energy* is quite misleading and rather passé, since important intrapsychic factors are ignored. Comments on carbohydrate metabolism and certain physiologic factors in fatigue were offered. Psychic energy is by no means dependent upon metabolism alone.

What was referred to as *Psychic Distaste* can secure a more literal translation into anorexia. The subject of fatigue has suffered from its neglect in current medical literature and has received only scattered references. A *psychophysiologic retreat* is common in depression and less so in the Fatigue Reactions. It is mediated in part through reduced endocrine activity. The *Primary* (P.E.E.R.) and *Secondary Emotional-Endocrine Reactions* (S.E.E.R.) (stimulation; later depletion) stem from the experiencing of strong emotions.

Some data were presented about the relation of fatigue and sleep. The *Respite-of-Sleep Principle* received reference. The individuality of one's sleep requirements was noted; various factors being contributory. Neurasthenia was discussed briefly as a narrowing and less frequently employed diagnostic syndrome. In *Table 23* were outlined the principle features.

Some important general points in psychiatric treatment were presented, with some special factors in relation to the earlier therapy of Neurasthenia, and the current therapy of Emotional Fatigue and the Fatigue States. The *Therapy-Alliance Concept* was offered and so named as another means of stressing the importance of the relationship of therapist with his patient colleague. Free Association was defined and its value in psychotherapy and analysis underlined. Analysis was likened to a course of graduate study.

XIV. SELECTED REFERENCES AND BIBLIOGRAPHY

ADDISON, JOSEPH. *Cato*, Act 5, Scene 4.

ALEXANDER, F. (1950). *Psychosomatic Medicine*, pp. 185–193. New York; Norton.

—, and PORTIS, S. A. (1944). "A Psychosomatic Study of Hypoglycaemic Fatigue." *Psychosom. Med.*, **6**, 191.

BEARD, G. M. (1869). "Neurasthenia or Nervous Exhaustion." *Boston med. surg. J.*, **57**, 217.

— (1880). *A Practical Treatise on Nervous Exhaustion*. New York; Wm. Wood.

BERLIEN, I. C. (1944). "Neuropsychiatry in Armed Forces Induction Stations, Rehabilitation Centers and Combat Divisions." *Bull. Menninger Clin.*, **8**, 146.

BIBRING, E. (1953). "The Mechanism of Depression." *In* Greenacre, P., Ed.: *Affective Disorders: Psychoanalytic Contributions to Their Study*, pp. 29–34. New York; International University Press.

BLEULER, E. (1930). *Textbook of Psychiatry*. Translated by A. A. Brill. New York; Macmillan.

BLIND, MATHILDE: "Rest", Stanza 1.

BLOOMBERG, WILFRED (1954). Personal communication.

BRILL, A. A. (1944). *Freud's Contribution to Psychiatry*, pp. 17–19. New York; Norton.

BROSIN, H. W. (1953). "The Reciprocal Relations Between Incentive, Motivation and Strain in Acute and Chronic Stressful Situations." In *Symposium on Stress*, AMSGS, Walter Reed Army Hospital, p. 211.

— (1954). Personal communication.

CANNON, W. B. (1929). *Bodily Changes in Pain, Hunger, Fear, and Rage*, 2nd. ed. New York; Appleton-Century.

— (1932). *The Wisdom of the Body*. New York; Norton.

DIDDLE, A. W. (1953). "Emotional Stress, A Female Disorder." *Obstet. Gynec., N. Y.*, **2**, 353.

EWALT, JACK R. (1954). Personal communication.

FENICHEL, O. (1945): *The Psychoanalytic Theory of Neurosis*, pp. 185–186, 455–456. New York; Norton.

FERRARO, A. (1959). "Psychoses with Cerebral Arteriosclerosis." *In* Arieti, S., Ed.: *Handbook of American Psychiatry*, Vol. 2, pp. 1083–1084.

FERENCZI, S. (1950). *Sex in Psychoanalysis*, pp. 186–192. New York; Basic Books.

FREUD, S. (1950). "Sexuality in the Etiology of the Neuroses" (1898). In *Collected Papers*, Vol. 1, p. 240. London; Hogarth.

— (1950). "The Justification for Detaching from Neurasthenia a Particular Syndrome: The Anxiety Neurosis." *Ibid.*, Vol. 1, pp. 75, 106.

— (1950). "Heredity and the Aetiology of the Neuroses. *Ibid.*, Vol. 1, pp. 138–155.

GOLDSMITH, N. (1952). "Multiple Sclerosis." *In* Pinner, M., and Miller, B. F., Eds.: *When Doctors Are Patients*, p. 157. New York; Norton.

GONI, A. R. (1946). *Myasthenia Gravis*, pp. 6–8. Baltimore; Williams and Wilkins.

GRAY, GEORGE A. (1953). Personal communication.

GREENE, K. V. (1957). "The Fatigue Neurosis." Junior Medical Thesis; George Washington University Medical School.

GREENSBERGER, E., *et al.* (1962). "Diagnostic Differential des Etats Depressifs et Exhaustifs au Moyen d'une Methode d'Exploration de la Fatigue." *Annls méd.-psychol.*, **120**, 865–873.

JACOBSON, E. (1953). "Contributions to the Metapsychology of Cyclothymic Depression." *In* Greenacre, P., Ed.: *Affective Disorders: Psychoanalytic Contributions to Their Study*, p. 52. New York; International University Press.

JAFFE, D. S. (1953). Personal communication.

— (1962). "Fatigue States—Asthenic Reactions." *In* Cantor, P. (Ed.):

Traumatic Medicine and Surgery for the Attorney, Vol. 6, page 22. Washington; Butterworths.

KINSEY, A. C., POMEROY, W. B., MARTIN, C. E., and GEBHARD, P. H. (1953). *Sexual Behavior in the Human Female,* p. 638. Philadelphia; Saunders.

LASLETT, H. R. (1928). "Experiments on the Effects of the Loss of Sleep." *J. exp. Psychol.,* **2,** 370.

LAUGHLIN, H. P. (1954). "The Psychiatric Aspects of Fatigue: Emotional Fatigue, Fatigue States, and Neurasthenia." *Med. Ann. Distr. Columbia,* **23,** 22.

— (1953). "Sleep Deprivation and Exhaustion: An Invitation to Further Observation and Study." *Int. Rec. Med.,* **8,** 305.

— (Ed.) (1955). *A Psychiatric Glossary,* 5th rev. ed. Washington; American Psychiatric Association.

—, and RUFFIN, M. DEG. (1953). *An Outline of Dynamic Psychiatry,* 4th rev. mimeo, pp. 142–147. Washington, D.C.; George Washington Medical School.

LOW, M. B. (1952). "Poliomyelitis with Residual Paralysis." *In* Pinner, M., and Miller. B. F., Eds.: *When Doctors Are Patients,* p. 73. New York; Norton.

MASSERMAN, J. H. (1946). *Principles of Dynamic Psychiatry,* pp. 8–11. Philadelphia, Saunders.

MAYNE, R. G. (1856). *An Expository Lexicon of the Terms, Ancient and Modern in Medical and General Science.* London; —.

McCULLOCH, W. W., CARLSON, H. B., and ALEXANDER, F. (1950). "Zest and Carbohydrate Metabolism." *In* Wolff, H. G., Wolf, S. G., Jr., and Hare, C. C. (Eds.): *Life Stress and Bodily Disease.* Baltimore; Williams and Wilkins.

OWEN, T. (1962). "Fatigue, Rest and Exercise." *Am. J. Psychiat.,* **119,** 497.

PATER, WALTER. The Rennaissance. Michelangelo.

RIPLEY, H. S., and WOLF, S. (1941). "Studies in Psychopathology." *J. nerv. ment. Dis.,* **114,** 234.

ROBINSON, E. S., and HERRMANN, S. O. (1922). "Effects of Loss of Sleep." *J. exp. Psychol;* **5,** 19.

SCHMIDT, C. V. (1953). "The Adjustment of Oxygen Supply to Oxygen Demand in Organs." In *Symposium on Stress,* AMSGS, Walter Reed Army Hospital Center, 1953, p. 26.

SCHWAB, R. R., and DeLORME, T. (1953). "Psychiatric Findings in Fatigue." *Am. J. Psychiat.,* **109,** 621.

SELYE, H. (1949). *The General Adaptation Syndrome. Textbook of Endocrinology.* Montreal; Acta.

— (1950). *Stress.* Montreal; Act.

—, and FORTIER, C. (1950). "Adaptive Reactions to Stress." *Psychosom. Med.,* **12,** 149.

SHAKESPEARE, WILLIAM. *Macbeth,* Act 3, Scene 2, line 28.

SHARPE, E. F. (1949). *Dream Analysis,* p. 155. London; Hogarth.

SHELDON, W. H. (1940). *The Varieties of Human Physique.* New York; Harper.

— (1942. *The Varieties of Temperament.* New York; Harper.

SOSKIN, S., and LEVINE, R. (1952). *Carbohydrate Metabolism,* 2nd ed. Chicago; University of Chicago Press.

STIEGLITZ, E. J. (1952). *The Second Forty Years,* rev. ed., pp. 63–67. Philadelphia; Lippincott.

STRAUSS, HANS (1959). "Epileptic Disorders." *In* Arieti, S., Ed.: *Handbook of American Psychiatry.* Vol. 2, p. 1129.

Symposium on Stress, A.M.S.G.S., Walter Reed Army Medical Center, Washington, D. C., 16–18 March, 1953, p. 332.

TUKE, D. H. (1892). *Dictionary of Psychological Medicine.* Philadelphia; Blakiston.

VAN DEUSEN, E. H. (1869). *Am. J. Psychiat.,* **35,** 445.

WEISKOTTEN, R. B., and FERGUSON, J. E. (1930). "A Further Study of the Effects of Loss of Sleep." *J. exp. Psychol.,* **13,** 247.

WEISS, E., and ENGLISH, O. S. (1949). *Psychosomatic Medicine,* 2nd ed., pp. 14, 502. Philadelphia; Saunders.

WOLFF, H. G., WOLF, S. G., JR., and HARE, C. C. (1950). *Life Stress and Bodily Disease.* Baltimore; Williams and Wilkins.

XV. REVIEW QUESTIONS ON THE FATIGUE REACTIONS

1. What is the concept of Emotional Fatigue?
2. Distinguish emotional fatigue from other types of fatigue. What is:
   (*a*) Physical fatigue?
   (*b*) Mental fatigue?
   (*c*) Organic fatigue?
3. List three reasons for separate consideration of the Fatigue Reaction.

4. What is the Fatigue State or Fatigue Reaction? What is Neurasthenia? Why retain the former as a diagnostic category in the neuroses?
5. (*a*) Two American physicians are known for their early contributions in this area. Explain.
    (*b*) Later contributors and their contributions include . . .
6. (*a*) What are useful points in the differential diagnosis of the Fatigue State from other emotional and physical states?
    (*b*) What is the *Characteristic-Disproportion Principle,* in identifying emotional fatigue?
    (*c*) What is meant by a *physical scapegoat* in emotional illnesses? In the missed diagnosis of emotional fatigue? Name three.
    (*d*) Distinguish *primary* from *secondary* organic fatigue.
7. Discuss the incidence of:
    (*a*) The symptoms of Emotional Fatigue.
    (*b*) The Fatigue Reaction.
8. (*a*) How does the concept of Secondary Defense apply in the Fatigue State?
    (*b*) How is the symptom of Emotional Fatigue "socially acceptable"? How might it become in *cultural vogue?*
    (*c*) What is the *Concept of Advanced Organicity?* What is the defensive intent of the "physical scapegoat"?
9. (*a*) How can parental influences lay the foundations for the later development of a Fatigue State?
    (*b*) How is the *Concept of Interpersonal Perpetuation* illustrated?
    (*c*) How is the Depletion Concept of Anxiety illustrated?
10. Discuss the relation of the Fatigue Reaction to the Depressive Reaction.
11. In Emotional Fatigue, what is:
    (*a*) The endogain?
    (*b*) Regression?
12. What are:
    (*a*) "Internal Whips"?
    (*b*) The *Infantile Dependency Dilemma?*
    (*c*) Emotional-Organic Combinations (*E.O.C.*)? How can they complicate diagnosis?
13. (*a*) What is the relation of fatigue to incentive (the *Principle of Inverse Incentive-Fatigue Ratio*)?
    (*b*) What are C.S.E. or "Cyclic Swings of Energy"?
14. Discuss boredom and monotony, from the standpoint of possible contributing and dynamic factors.
15. How can expressions of fatigue be *anger-equivalents?*
16. (*a*) Discuss the factor of interest in the physiology of fatigue.
    (*b*) How is the Reservoir Concept of Energy misleading?
    (*c*) What is "psychic distaste"?
    (*d*) To what extent is psychic energy dependent upon metabolism?
17. (*a*) What is the role of the endocrine system in the *psychophysiological retreat* common in emotional depression, and less so in the Fatigue Reactions?
    (*b*) Explain the "primary" and "secondary" *emotional-endocrine* reactions. (P.E.E.R. and S.E.E.R.).
18. (*a*) What are the relationships between fatigue and sleep?
    (*b*) What is the *Respite-of-Sleep Principle?*
    (*c*) How are individual "requirements" for sleep determined?
19. (*a*) Discuss Neurasthenia from its various aspects.
    (*b*) What is the *Therapy-Alliance?*; Free Association?
20. Concerning treatment of the Fatigue Reactions:
    (*a*) Why was S. Weir Mitchell's treatment regimen sometimes so effective?
    (*b*) Outline possible supportive measures.
    (*c*) Discuss the analytic method of therapy.
    (*d*) How can fatigue be an "Indicator" during the course of therapy?

CHAPTER 8

THE HYGEIAPHRONTIC REACTIONS

.... Anxious Concern about Health; Non-organic Symptomatology

I. SOMATIC AND PHYSIOLOGIC PREOCCUPATION

  A. Hygeiaphrontis
    1. Hygeiaphrontic Discrepancy Principle: Between Level of Subjective Concern and Discomfort, and Objective Appraisal; 2. Underlying Psychologic Needs; 3. Value of Making Medical Appraisal to Patients; 4. Physician's Reaction

  B. Definitions
    1. The Hygeiaphrontic Reaction; 2. Beyond Conscious Control

II. HISTORY

  A. Ancient Name Outlives Usefulness
    1. Hypochondriasis Reflects Ancient Mistaken Etiology; 2. Seeking a Term. Hygeia and Phrontis

  B. Early Contributions to Psychodynamics
    1. With Neurasthenia and Anxiety Neurosis, One of Freud's "Actual Neuroses"; 2. Modern Contributions

III. DIAGNOSIS

  A. Distinguishing the Hygeiaphrontic Reaction
    1. Clinical and Dynamic Relationships with Other Reactions; 2. Avoid Diagnosis by Elimination; 3. Overstudy More Frequent Than Understudy. The Favorable - Response Concept; 4. Emotional Disturbance and Organic Disease Both Present: E.O.C.

  B. Special Conditions of Onset
    1. Hygeiaphrontic Reaction Follows Stress; 2. Hygeiaphrontis and Psychoses; 3. Hygeiaphrontis and Obsessive Neuroses.

IV. INCIDENCE

  A. Hygeiaphrontic Symptoms and Hygeiaphrontic Reaction
    1. Stressful Periods in Living Increase Vulnerability to Neurotic Reaction; S. E. H. A.; The Peg Concept; 2. Incidence of Cases Diagnosed as Hypochondriasis

  B. Clinical and Personal Experience of Physicians and Students with Undue Somatic Concerns
    1. Four Groups Surveyed; 2. Among the "Seekers-After-Health"

V. SYMPTOMS AND CLINICAL FEATURES

  A. The Hygeiaphrontic Patient
    1. Overattentiveness to Function; 2. Criteria for Pathology; Less Overt Anxiety

  B. Variety of Hygeiaphrontic Symptoms
    1. Every System, Organ, or Body Function; 2. Childhood Example; Importance of Parental Response; 3. Increased Awareness of Normal Function; 4. Concept of Defensive-Layering; 5. Severely Pathologic Retreat into Overconcern with Health

  C. Psychologic Categories of Visceral Pain
    1. Four Major Routes or Types; Three Conceptions; 2. Emotionally Determined Stomach Pain; 3. Location and Susceptibility; Axiom of Inverse Pain-Conflict Ratio

  D. In Special Circumstances
    1. Overconcern - with - Health Follows Surgery; 2. Increasing Emotional Vulnerability with Advancing Age; 3. Drugs and Hygeiaphrontis

E. Occasional Serious Portent of Hygeiaphrontic Preoccupation

1. Ushers in Schizophrenic Reaction; 2. Exaggeration of Hygeiaphrontic Trends

F. Hygeiaphrontic Character Defenses

VI. PSYCHODYNAMICS AND PATHOGENESIS

A. Relation Between Figurative and Literal

1. "I'm Sick" May Have Symbolic Meaning; 2. Recognition in Figures of Speech; 3. Denial and Its Consequences in Hygeiaphrontis

B. Factors in Initiation

1. Regression and Dependency; 2. Precipitating Events; 3. Defense Against Anxiety; 4. Early Environmental Factors; 5. Concept of Lowered-Perception-Threshold Source; 6. Emotions and Physiology

C. Hygeiaphrontic Endogain: The Unconscious Primary "Gain" of Somatic and Physiologic Preoccupation

1. Bodily Expression of Underlying Conflicts; 2. Suffering, Guilt, and Punishment. Episodic Hygeiaphrontis; 3. Concluding Thoughts

D. Hygeiaphrontic Epigain: The Unconscious Secondary "Gain" of Somatic and Physiologic Preoccupation

1. Favorable Modification of Interpersonal Environment; 2. Love, Affection, and Acceptance Sought; 3. Important Dynamic Implications

E. In Conclusion

VII. THE THEORY OF ANTECEDENT CONFLICTS

A. Antecedents and Precedents Play Important Role

1. Patterns of Response Established; the Emotional Prototype; 2. Oedipal and Oral Conflicts; 3. Melanie Klein's Contributions

B. The Earliest Antecedent

1. Psychic Trauma During Birth? 2. The Ultimate Extension; 3. Vicissitudes of Earliest Interpersonal Events Important

VIII. MALINGERING

A. Malingering Distinguished from Epigain

1. Deliberate Simulation Versus Unconscious Utilization; 2. Mechanisms of Epigain Unconscious; 3. True Malingering Rare

B. Clinical Relationships; Distinguishing Features

1. Use of Placebos; 2. Two Possible Pitfalls in Certain Cases of Neuroses Following Trauma; 3. Malingering an Indication of Illness

IX. THE CONCEPTION OF PRIMITIVE VERSUS MORE HIGHLY DEVELOPED PSYCHOLOGIC DEFENSES

A. Level of Operations Concept

1. Intrapsychic Mental Mechanisms; 2. Neurotic Patterns of Reaction

B. Gradation of Defenses in Psychoses and Maturation

1. Defenses Change During Both Onset and Lifting of Psychotic Reactions; 2. Progression of Defenses in Maturation

X. HYGEIAPHRONTIS AND DEPRESSION

A. Hygeiaphrontic Conflicts Expressed on Visceral Plane

B. Equivalent of Depression

XI. TREATMENT

A. Attitude of Physician Crucial

1. Need for Wisdom and Perception; 2. The "Proper Therapeutic Attitude"; Approach of Speculative Inquiry; 3. Indications for Psychiatric Evaluation and Treatment

B. Intensive Psychotherapy and Analysis

1. Mutual Confidence and Trust Required; 2. Introspection Constructive and Healthy; 3. Onset or Increase of Hygeiaphrontic Concerns During Treatment; 4. Patient Selection; Anxiety Mobilized in Therapy

C. Attentuation of Interpersonal Relations

1. Withdrawal from Relationships Inevitable; 2. Isolation and Despair Decrease Accessibility

D. Aid to Referral

1. Effects of Emotions on Functions; 2. Avoid Academic Discussions

E. Further Points in Therapy

1. Fenichel's and Fromm-Reichmann's Points; 2. Goals, Conditions, and Results

XII. SUMMARY

XIII. SELECTED REFERENCES AND BIBLIOGRAPHY

XIV. REVIEW QUESTIONS

I. SOMATIC AND PHYSIOLOGIC PREOCCUPATION

A. HYGEIAPHRONTIS

1. Hygeiaphrontic Discrepancy Principle: Between Level of Subjective Concern and Discomfort, and Objective Appraisal

A. PSYCHOPATHOLOGY, NOT ORGANIC PATHOLOGY.—Most physicians in clinical medicine are familiar with the patient who is overconcerned and anxious about his state of health. The prominent feature in these situations clinically is the discrepancy between the actual amount of organic pathology or of disordered function which is present and the patient's amount of concern. Many of these people also have bodily discomforts or pain, in the absence of somatic pathology to account for it.

This is a *discrepancy between the levels of concern and discomfort which are experienced by the person concerned on the one hand, and the apparent realistic need for concern and discomfort as estimated objectively by his doctor on the other.* From the viewpoint of the examining physician, this kind of discrepancy *may exist whether somatic pathology is absent, minimal, or even serious.* This is the basis for and defines, what we might term the Hygeiaphrontic Discrepancy Principle. Its presence is more striking in instances when there is little or no demonstrable *organic* pathology present. The pathology responsible here is *psycho*pathology. The basis for this type of reaction lies primarily in the emotional sphere, as distinguished from the physical sphere.

The Hygeiaphrontic Discrepancy Principle is illustrated in every instance of Overconcern-with-Health (hypochondriasis) or preferably, Hygeiaphrontis. A combination of hygeiaphrontic and organic symptomatology comprises a hygeiaphrontic E.O.C. (Emotional-Organic Combination).

For many physicians the hygeiaphrontic state of affairs can prove understandably baffling and frustrating. The physician can clearly demonstrate, at least to himself, the absence of sufficient organic pathology to account for the symptoms which are reported. He can find no adequate physical basis for the anxious preoccupation of his patient with his symptoms, and with his state of health. Why cannot — and sometimes it almost seems, will not — the patient accept the reassurances concerning the absence of (physical) illness, which are given him? Why can he not give up his undue concern? The answer to this is to be found in the bases of his symptoms and preoccupation, which are emotional. This being the case, the physical, organic state of affairs is almost a *non-sequitor.*

B. ANXIOUS CONCERN ABOUT HEALTH.—The word *hygeia,* from the name of the ancient Greek Goddess of Health, has come in present-day usage to mean health. *Phrontis* is a direct carryover from the Greek word meaning "anxious care" or "anxious concern about." Hence the term hygeiaphrontis has been derived, meaning *anxious concern about health.* It is offered to the reader as an accurate and descriptive term for that type of neurotic reaction which is characterized by an overconcern-with-health. Further, as a diagnostic term it lacks the unfortunate, sometimes derogatory and accusatory connotations, which at times have been associated with the older inaccurate label of "hypochondriasis" which it is hoped it might eventually replace.

It is accordingly proposed that its substitution be considered without bias, for the long-outmoded, non-scientific, and descriptively inaccurate term of hypochondriasis (literally meaning "below the rib cage") to which we have long and stubbornly clung. It would more accurately express the meaning, describe the condition, name the neurosis, be more scientific, and provide us with a more neutral and objective term in medicine and psychiatry. For these reasons the term of Hygeiaphrontis will be used in our present discussion.

Hygeiaphrontis would be the noun, and hygeiaphrontic, the adjective. The Hygeiaphrontic Reaction signifies and may be defined as *a pathologically increased level of concern about health, marked by various kinds of somatic and/or physiologic preoccupation, and frequently accompanied by subjectively discomforting symptoms which are essentially emotional and non-organic in their origins. This reaction is further marked by the presence of a "hygeiaphrontic discrepancy" as noted, between the accompanying subjective distress and concern, and any underlying physical bases.* This is also part of our Hygeiaphrontic Discrepancy Concept.

2. Underlying Psychologic Needs

A. AWARENESS OF PSYCHOGENIC FACTORS VITAL.—When a Hygeiaphrontic Reaction is present, it is most helpful for the physician to be aware of the powerful psychologic factors underlying the symptoms. He had best recognize the existence of the deep-rooted psychologic needs which the patient's preoccupation with his state of health attempts to meet. These are not accessible to the conscious awareness of the person concerned. They are likewise hidden from the physician by any ordinary methods of observation. Awareness of their existence lessens his frustration, and tends to enlist his interest and sympathetic understanding, in place of his possible alternative frustration, disgust, or exasperation.

Since these bases of hygeiaphrontic manifestations are beyond conscious awareness, they are much more difficult to cope with. This does not mean that they are less important. On the contrary, they are, if anything, even more important. Further, it is the great importance of the hidden underlying needs to the individual concerned that resulted in conflicts and anxiety over them. This led to repression and, in turn sooner or later, to symptom formation. Each such development may be viewed as an added layer of attempted defense. The next subsequent layer includes the resistances, as symptoms are in turn defended, in the Secondary Defense of them (Pages 144 and 366).

B. ICEBERG ANALOGY.—We may draw an analogy between the psychic and emotional aspects of the personality and the iceberg, seven-eighths of which is submerged and invisible. This much larger but unseen bulk of ice importantly influences the iceberg's behavior, and is analogous to the unconscious part of the psyche. Navigators take this into consideration and make necessary allowances. Similarly, dynamically oriented physicians have learned to recognize and to allow for this large and important but hidden part of the psyche, the unconscious.

If the physician is unaware of this, he may unhappily attempt to remove hygeiaphrontic symptoms by all kinds of direct and "rational" approaches. He may seek to do this through persuasion, reassurance, or by presenting supposedly "convincing" scientific proof of the absence of organic pathology. *In such efforts he is unwittingly attempting the impossible task of trying to dissolve in simple fashion, established and powerful psychologic defenses.* These are not only vital to the patient but their bases are also entirely out of his conscious awareness. This is an endeavor which is inevitably doomed to failure. The physician who does not sufficiently appreciate the vital role of unconscious forces will inevitably be puzzled or mystified. He may become frustrated and angry with himself, with his patient, or both. Knowledge and understanding is the key to avoid this and to establish an adequate foundation for therapy.

3. Value of Making Medical Appraisal to Patients

Presenting an accurate appraisal of the state of his physical health to a patient is one of the most important of medical responsibilities. Reassurance when there are needless fears of organic pathology is one of the most useful services of the medical practitioner. This is particularly true in instances in which there is neurotic overconcern about some aspect of the emotional, mental, or physical health.

In these situations, an objective reassurance as to the absence of organic illness can be very useful. This should be done without any slightest implications as to the possible presence of simulation, imagination, or malingering on the part of the patient. Such information can help lay early solid groundwork for later therapy. An eventual redirection of the existing nonconstructive somatic introspection and preoccupation may be secured. This leads into the more constructive personal study of emotions and emotional conflicts which takes place in therapy.

4. Physician's Reaction

A. POSSIBLE SEQUENCE OF FAILURE, SELF-CRITICISM, ANGER AND DISPLACEMENT.—A failure to appreciate the presence of the deep psychologic roots of hygeiaphrontis (hypochondriasis) in the patient's unconscious, as noted, leads to feelings of helplessness on the part of the physician. The doctor's own self-evaluation especially professionally, can hinge to a fair extent on his therapeutic effectiveness. Feelings of failure in trying to help this kind of patient are quite possible. Together with the resulting lower self-evaluation, these may lead directly or indirectly into feelings of anxiety, discouragement, frustration, or anger. These kinds of feelings are not difficult to understand. One can also see how such feelings might be consciously or subconsciously "taken out" on the patient. He is the most convenient object or target in any event.

Thus a process of displacement to the patient of these possible consequences of the physician's own feelings of failure, anger, and criticism can take place. Feelings of helplessness promote anxiety, which in this sequence may in turn become transmuted into feelings of anger. See earlier references (pp. 19, 416) to anger as an *anxiety-equivalent.*

B. ANGER-BREEDS-ANGER CONCEPT; DOCTOR-PATIENT RELATIONSHIP THREATENED; THE THERAPEUTIC IMPASSE.—Anger, whether open and expressed or concealed, tends to breed anger in return. This Concept is an important one in the understanding of emotions and people generally. Thus anger on the part of the physician will likely generate responsively, or increase existing anger or resentment on the part of the patient. This may be quite sufficient to endanger or even quickly to destroy the professional doctor-patient relationship. It may also lead further to creating gradually a destructive vicious circle. This can end in what we might term a *Therapeutic Impasse,* or in the desertion of one by the other. At times such a Therapeutic Impasse develops so rapidly as in essence to prevent treatment even "getting off the ground." The T.I. can develop through various, often hidden personality incompatibilities of patient and therapist. This has many applications in psychotherapy.

The doctor may thus unrealistically expect himself to be able to alter and to change by a purely rational approach, what are essentially the patient's hidden emotional needs to focus on somatic matters. He will not have such unrealistic expectations if he has an adequate understanding of the powerful unconscious needs which are present. It is these which force the patient to develop his hygeiaphrontic preoccupations.

B. DEFINITIONS

1. The Hygeiaphrontic Reaction

Hygeiaphrontis is (as is hypochondriasis) *overconcern with health, marked by an obsessive kind of somatic and/or physiologic preoccupation.* The Hygeiaphrontic Reaction is *a state in which there is a more or less persistent anxious overconcern about the state of health and/or the possible presence of illness.* The neurotic focus of attention may change quickly or gradually shift from one organ or system or body region to another. *Various uncomfortable symptoms may develop and be experienced, which may be singular or multiple.* These may affect any body region, organ, or system, also may shift as to their focus and locale, and their organic basis alone is insufficient to account for the discomfort experienced and the concern which is present, in accord with our *Hygeiaphrontic Discrepancy Principle.* As with other neurotic symptoms, these likewise seek to defend against anxiety.

Hygeiaphrontis may also be defined as *an obsessive kind of preoccupation with physical functions and body processes, which is frequently accompanied by the development of various and sometimes shifting somatic complaints.* It is a *symptom neurosis* (pp. 237, 286, and 383). The *hygeiaphrontic system* refers to the defensively-intended, anxiety countering system or pattern of symptoms, attitudes, concerns, and psychologic pattern-responses of the hygeiaphrontic person. The *Hygeiaphrontic Character* refers to the corresponding type or constellation of character defenses (*see*

p. 283). An *Hygeiaphronic State* of more or less limited duration may be sometimes encountered. In the delineation of this condition, one may regard it as rather analogous to our earlier outlined A.T.S. (*see* pp. 98 and 167).

Although cases which most clearly fit into this specific category are not numerous, they nonetheless make up a small but definite percentage of emotional disorders. In the Hygeiaphronic Reaction there is:

(1) A discrepancy between the amount of organic pathology or disorder of function which is present, and the amount of symptomatology and of concern exhibited by the patient.

(2) The presence generally of various discomforting, uncomfortable or painful subjective symptoms. These are often attributed to or are associated by the patient with illness, disease, or are ascribed to impairment of physical structure or function. They are accompanied by an absence or by an insufficient amount of actual organic pathology to account for them.

(3) In the Hygeiaphronic Reaction, or Overconcern-with-Health, the emotional conflict or some part of it is symbolically expressed through the development of a variety of subjective symptoms, accompanied by some degree of somatic or physiologic preoccupation.

The Hygeiaphronic Discrepancy may be defined as *the discrepancy between the actual level of anxious bodily concerns and discomforts on the one hand; and that which would appear indicated following an objective appraisal as to the real need for them, on the other hand. It includes the discrepancy between the hygeiaphronic discomforts, and any physical bases for them.*

2. Beyond Conscious Control

The word "simulate" may still be used occasionally or heard in reference to hygeiaphronic complaints. This is strongly objected to. In the true Hygeiaphronic Reaction the symptoms are *not* consciously simulated. Hygeiaphrontis is not malingering. (*See* later comments on malingering in this chapter, Section VIII). The hygeiaphronic patient is the victim of his own unconscious processes, which are out of voluntary control and out of awareness. Consciously and rationally, no one would voluntarily choose the resulting constriction of living, the suffering, handicap, sacrifice, and the nonconstructive direction of psychic energy, all of which take place in this type of neurotic reaction.

Psychologically uneconomic consequences inevitably result from the regressive retreat which hygeiaphrontis dynamically represents, as we shall observe. As in other emotional illnesses, the ultimate net results of the desperate efforts to ward off anxiety are self-defeat and loss. (*See* Chapter 2.) The concept of the "gain" of neurosis is paradoxical since from the broadest objective viewpoint, there is always an actual loss.

II. HISTORY

A. ANCIENT NAME OUTLIVES USEFULNESS

1. Hypochondriasis Reflects Ancient Mistaken Etiology

The old term "hypochondriasis" refers to the hypochondria (singular: hypochondrium), which are the anterior parts of the body (the two regions of the abdomen on either side of the epigastric region) just below the ribs. Its origin is from the Greek *hypo,* meaning under, below, or less than, plus *chondros,* meaning cartilage; that is, under the cartilage of the breast bone or rib cage. Its adoption and use in early times reflected three factors, the first being the need for a term. Secondly, the region so named historically had long been a frequent site of "hypochondriacal" symptoms.

The third factor involved in the adoption and use of this term is that the name also reflected the early, but quite inaccurate ideas as to the etiology of the disorder. In ancient times, its basic psychologic origin was unclear. Thus, hypochondriasis was thought by the ancients to directly result from a disorder of the hypochondria, the upper lateral regions of the abdomen next below the lowest rib. It was believed especially to relate to disorders of the spleen, about which very little was known until recent times. Modern dynamic psychiatry, through the exhaustive study of many cases over the past eighty years, has established the origins of this neurotic reaction, which is marked by one's pathologic overconcern with his state of health, as being in psychologic processes which are largely unconscious. Symptoms, which include various kinds of discomfort and pain, are of course by no means limited to this particular anatomical region. They can involve any system or region.

The term hypochondriasis originated as did certain other ancient medico-psychologic terms. As diagnostic labels they were chosen according to the concepts of etiology which were then current. These were often far later found to be quite inaccurate in the light of subsequent knowledge. Thus far we have studied or referred to other diagnostic terms with similar origins, for instance, "hysteria," from (wandering of) the uterus, (Ch.12:IIA*1*) and "melancholia," from black bile (pp. 140–1).

2. Seeking a Term: Hygeia and Phrontis

The long continuation of our use of such an etiologically inaccurate name unfortunately has been responsible in some measure perhaps for a tendency to discard the entire concept of hypochondriasis in diagnosis and in classification. There is scientific justification for dropping the term as such, especially in view of its mistaken and unfortunate connotations (*see* Section VIIIA*2*). One wonders, however, if it is necessarily wise to also completely discard such a useful clinical concept and syndrome. It seems to the author that a number of cases regularly are encountered in clinical medical practice in which the clinical and dynamic features of hypochondriasis are well established. These would appear possibly to warrant the maintenance of such a separate diagnostic category. In view of some of the current objections to the term "hypochondriasis," however, they would lack a suitable name. Overconcern-with-Health, and Somatic or Physio-logic Preoccupation, which have been used earlier by the author as possible substitutes, have the advantage of being descriptively accurate, but unfortunately are quite unwieldy and do not convey the accompanying presence of discomfort and pain.

This state of affairs led the author to search in the Greek language again for possibly usable terms. While several terms singly or together offered some promise, a combination of two in particular — of which one has already enjoyed wide usage in medical circles — appeared most suitable. *Hygeia* thus has long since come to equate health, and is already most familiar to physicians, allied professionals, and a fair segment of the informed laity. *Phrontis* means anxious care, or concern about.

These two terms combined together thus express a basic major aspect of the syndrome. They are reasonably easy to pronounce and spell, fit together fairly well, and as with many other medical terms, originate in classical Greek. Hygeiaphrontis accordingly is offered, albeit tentatively, for possible adoption in replacement as a possible diagnostic term. This is done however with considerable reservation and great hesitancy, especially in view of the signal lack of success most such innovations have enjoyed, particularly those offered by Americans. With these doubts so expressed, the use of this new term will be continued in this text.

B. EARLY CONTRIBUTIONS TO PSYCHODYNAMICS

1. With Neurasthenia and Anxiety Neurosis, One of Freud's "Actual Neuroses"

A. FIRMLY ESTABLISHED DIAGNOSIS IN 1900.—In the latter part of the last century Hypochondriasis and Neurasthenia were both firmly established as diagnostic categories in psychiatry, and in medicine generally. (*See* section on History in Chapters Seven and Fourteen, *and* also *Table 3*, p. 46). Freud had urged the narrowing of the latter concept, as we learned in the preceding chapter. He recommended the detachment of a major group of cases, the Anxiety Neuroses, from Neurasthenia. He proceeded to group these three kinds of reactions together subsequently as what he then referred to as the "actual neuroses." This was done to indicate that they were "actual"; that is, psychologic in origin. These three types of reactions constituted the ones which he so recognized at that time.

As early as 1896, Freud made an analogy between the subjective *conscious* shame and self-reproach which might be experienced following a disapproved sexual act, to hypochondriacal anxiety. The latter was viewed by him then as an *unconscious* guilty fear of bodily injury in consequence to a disapproved but repressed (and usually sexual) impulse. This is one possible factor in a hygeiaphrontic symptom, but of course there are others as well. These can operate singly or in combination. There will be further comments about this when we discuss dynamics. Freud was one of the first who sought to apply dynamic principles to the understanding of hypochondriasis.

B. PSYCHODYNAMICS GRADUALLY WORKED OUT.—There has been an increasing focus of scientific medical attention in modern times upon the psychologic basis of the neuroses. In the case of Overconcern with Health, as well as with the other major categories of defensively intended neurotic reactions, this has resulted in increased efforts and improving results in the gradual working out of the underlying psychodynamics.

The solution of the dynamics has been accomplished rather thoroughly in hypochondriasis. By 1914, Freud had worked out his views of "eroto-genicity as a property common to all organs", according to which one is "then justified in speaking of an increase or decrease in the degree of it in any given part of the body".* This theory further stimulated interest and research. Authorities today do not always use the same terms, but their underlying bases of understanding are usually not too far apart.

2. Modern Contributions

A number of excellent clinicians, for example, Bleuler and Cobb, have contributed to the establishment of a rather uniform view of the symptoms and clinical features of hypochondriasis. Others, including Klein, Heimann, Schilder, and Fenichel, have also contributed to our understanding of the psychodynamics. In some psychiatric quarters today hygeiaphrontis (hypochondriasis) is simply regarded as a symptom complex. Sometimes also it is viewed merely as one manifestation, which is present as a part of many other emotional reactions, rather than as a separate diagnostic entity. Herein it may fit in with our earlier concept of *attitude-symptoms* (p. 328).

Further contributions to and conceptions about the psychogenesis of the Hygeiaphrontic Reactions will be presented shortly in the appropriate sections (Sect. VI). Together with our expanding clinical and theoretical understandings concerning this major group of neuroses, the adoption of a more accurate, descriptive, and modern name could contribute to our continued *Medical Renaissance* (pp. 312–13) in psychiatry.

III. DIAGNOSIS

A. DISTINGUISHING THE HYGEIAPHRONTIC REACTION

1. Clinical and Dynamic Relationships with Other Reactions

Hygeiaphrontic overconcern and hygeiaphrontic symptoms may simulate many physical and emotional conditions. They may also occur in association with organic conditions or with other emotional illnesses. Herein the diagnostic problem is often one of determining which is the underlying or more prominent condition. Some degree of Hygeiaphrontis, or undue Somatic and Physiologic Preoccupation, may be observed as comprising a part of almost any of the neuroses or the psychoses. Among these, a measure of Hygeiaphrontis is most frequently seen as a manifestation in the Fatigue State, in Neurasthenia, in Depressive Reactions (*see* later Section X), and in the Anxiety Reactions.

---

* Freud continued: "It is possible that for every such change in the erotogenicity of the organs, there is a parallel change in the libidinal cathexis in the ego. In such factors may lie the explanation of what is at the bottom of hypochondria and what it is that can have upon the distribution of the libido the same effect as actual organic disease."

When hygeiaphrontic manifestations merely comprise a part of another syndrome, with other more prominent neurotic symptoms present, or when they are not sufficiently marked to warrant a diagnosis in and of themselves, we may regard preoccupation-with-health as another variety of *attitude-symptom* (p. 138), as noted.

Concern with health can become obsessive in nature. It may be severe enough to constitute a compulsive direction of thought, so that certain instances of Obsessive-Compulsive States may occasionally offer difficulties in the differential diagnosis of the Hygeiaphrontic Reactions. At times the hygeiaphrontic individual appears to be somewhat of a *Black-or-White Person,* as we have noted with the Obsessive Personality (p. 255). At times also there may be an overlapping with certain of the phobias. (*See Case 114,* Ch.10:IIIB2). These factors in differential diagnosis, however, help to point out the close clinical and dynamic relationships between these various groups of neurotic reactions, as well as their tendency to overlap. The presence of concurrent anxiety with hygeiaphrontic manifestations is a highly variable feature. It reflects the level of "symptom-success" in allaying anxiety. When present as such or as an A.A.A., the *Incomplete Symptom-Defense Concept* (pp. 89; 189) is illustrated.

2. Avoid Diagnosis by Elimination

Sometimes the physician will have difficulty in eliminating possible organic bases for hygeiaphrontic symptoms. Whenever possible, the reaching of a diagnosis other than by the process of elimination is preferable. Occasionally this will not be possible, and fairly extensive medical study will prove genuinely necessary in order to rule out one of the more obscure possible organic bases.

With increasing experience and professional sagacity the physician will be able in many cases, however, to make a positive diagnosis. He will be able to recognize the source of the difficulty in the hypochondriacal patient as being essentially emotional.

Overexamination, uncertainty, or a constant and prolonged searching for possible obscure physical explanations can be quite disadvantageous to the patient. These may "play into" the neurotic needs which the patient is unwittingly attempting to meet via this nonconstructive pathway of hygeiaphrontis. Although this medical endeavor may superficially please the person concerned, it also can do him great harm. The elaboration of an illness on an iatrogenic basis can be thus encouraged. Identification of the *Hygeiaphrontic Discrepancy* is important in establishing the diagnosis. Its extent and level is also significant dynamically and prognostically. Recognizing its presence is of great value in making a positive diagnosis.

3. Overstudy More Frequent Than Understudy. The Favorable-Response Concept.

A. POTENTIAL GREAT HARM IN MISSING EMOTIONAL DIAGNOSIS, AND IN MEDICAL OVERSTUDY.—A cursory examination accompanied by a seemingly poorly considered prejudgment can, of course, also cause trouble.

Further, it can be embarrassing professionally. This situation, however, is far more rare medically than that of overstudy. The relatively rare complete missing of an organic condition in diagnosis is: (1) more apparent when it occurs, and (2) far more apt to be the subject of criticism from his colleagues. This tends to promote overstudy.

Perhaps, however, as the potential great harm of medical overstudy, as well as the harm of missing an emotional diagnosis, comes to receive more widespread recognition, it will tend to become less frequent. This is certainly to be hoped for.

In the following instance the error in medical management was on the side of overstudy. Another instance of iatrogenic contributions to hygeiaphrontic preoccupation is to be found in *Case 87* [Ch.7:XIC3; Ch.12:V A1].

Case 89

Hygeiaphrontis or Overconcern-with-Health; Medical Overstudy

(1) *Multiple Symptomatology; the Attention-Absorption Concept*

Mrs. Agnes S. was referred by an internist for psychiatric evaluation. She was a forty-eight-year-old, childless married woman whose major center of attention and interest had gradually come to be her physical self, her functions, and her bodily sensations. This level of involvement well illustrated the defensive concept of *Attention-Absorption,* [Ch.8: VB5; VIC1]. Her doctor described her as having "numerous psychosomatic symptoms and a great deal of concern over her health." He was indeed correct. This was an understatement.

Mrs. S. complained of frequent indigestion, "neuritis," and aching abdomen. She was very heart-conscious. She suffered also from frequent headaches, accompanied by a feeling of cervical tightness. Her symptoms had become steadily much worse following the death of her mother seven years previously from cancer of the throat. At this time the patient had had an A.A.A. (an Acute Anxiety Attack), with recurrences, in which she also had suffered from marked *globus hystericus* [Ch.12:VD2] with cervical pain.

(2) *Logical approach fruitless*

Her medical history was extensive. She had had thorough studies by several very competent physicians. In addition, she had been through the diagnostic clinics of two university medical centers. Two of her doctors had talked with her of the value of a psychiatric consultation. A new set of symptoms always arose to delay and so interfere with this course of action, however, and to send her into a new round of tests, studies, and observations. Her present physician had made a most exhaustive study. This had been so complete over the course of the past eight months, that it took him fifteen minutes just to list the many tests she had undergone. He had just about exhausted the possibilities for testing! It was as though he was trying to prove to her and to himself an absence of organic dysfunction.

Not only did each new possibility which occurred to him for exploration absorb the patient's attention in neurotic fashion, but it strengthened her conviction of a physical etiology, renewed her interest in further studies, and reinforced her secondary defenses. The physician had hoped to eventually logically disprove her belief in a physical basis. Instead, she had taken his interest and each new test as evidence of uncertainty on his part and his lack of security, or of his being not at all convinced about the emotional bases which he had intermittently suggested. It would have been far better, and far kinder to this patient, if one of the first physicians in the case had in sympathetic but firm fashion told her that there were important emotional factors entering into her difficulties, that continued medical searching was fruitless, and that she simply must make up her mind sooner or later to tackle psychotherapy. This no one had been able to do. The long-term consequences for her were tragic indeed.

(3) *The Favorable-Response Concept illustrated: Each new regimen "benefits"*

Another finding not infrequently noted in cases of this kind was in her pattern of response to therapy. She had had "trials of therapy" of many kinds. The referring physician reported that with each new medicine or treatment regimen which he had tried, she would improve, at least temporarily. This is sometimes also true in this kind of case with the advent of each new physician, a new nurse or physiotherapist, or a new diagnostic procedure or series of tests.

An important part of this favorable kind of response to each new regimen, test, or person is due to the amount of interest, attention, and concern which is thereby directed toward the patient, or so experienced by him. Another lies in providing a new such focus of attention and interest *for* the person concerned. This type of benefit is a psychologic and emotional one. These observations comprise a *Favorable-Response Concept* in the neuroses in general and in hygeiaphrontis in particular (*see also* p. 392, and Sect. VD3). Occasionally a person is encountered who illustrates its reverse, with an unfavorable response to each such change.

(4) *Value of treatment recommendation*

It was not possible to convince this unfortunate woman of the possible profit to her through psychotherapeutic self-study. In this kind of instance one must sometimes be content with having made a positive recommendation for treatment. This is important to make, even when one anticipates it will fall on deaf ears. Sooner or later such advice still may well bear fruit. This has been seen to happen from one to three (or even more) years after such a recommendation was first made.

It is also sometimes better for the effectiveness of the therapeutic work, for a patient finally to begin treatment *when he has really arrived at such a point in his own views,* even though this may mean a considerable delay. Ten years later this particular patient sadly continues to pursue her neurotic, hygeiaphrontic pattern. She has been unable thus far to muster sufficient constructive interest in psychotherapy.

B. MISSING ORGANIC DISEASE QUITE RARE.—An instance of the considerably more rare instance of inadequate study was reported to the author not long ago. Herein an organic case was misdiagnosed as hypochondriasis. In this instance a patient was sent along for psychiatric consultation because of what was described as his "preoccupation with rectal function and bleeding." The patient had good cause to be preoccupied. Multiple bleeding polyps were revealed upon requested sigmoidoscopic examination. This was not hypochondriasis.

As might be expected this case and its mishandling provoked considerable censure among the physician's colleagues. The missed organic basis was more apparent, more readily recognizable, in more familiar areas (of organicity), and thus seemed far more censurable. Still, the error was correctable here, had far less tragic consequences, and was a *far* rarer phenomenon than the many, many instances in which an emotional reaction is misdiagnosed as organic, or is grossly mishandled, with really desperate long-range consequences for the hapless person concerned.

4. *Emotional Disturbance and Organic Disease Both Present: E.O.C.*

The clinician must also bear in mind that the presence of clearly established organic disease does not rule out the simultaneous presence of various degrees of emotional disturbance. The organic condition will not necessarily account for all the patient's symptoms, some of which may well have an emotional origin.

Preoccupation with Health thus may also follow or accompany organic conditions. These situations can comprise some interesting and challenging instances of E.O.C. (Emotional-Organic Combinations; p. 393). In these situations its onset is often largely determined by the person's relative ability to handle the threat of illness. It may be the psychologic portion of his individual Total Reaction to Crisis [T.R.C. Ch.1:IIC*1*; Ch.14:VD*1*]. It is part of his response to his position of relative helplessness in relation to the organic process which is present. The individual reaction here is widely variable, according to his entire past experience, his psychologic conditioning, and his emotional resources.

B. SPECIAL CONDITIONS OF ONSET

1. Hygeiaphrontic Reaction Follows Stress

Hygeiaphrontis may have its onset gradually, in response to fairly recognizable conditions of external stress. The following instance is an example in which already existing hygeiaphrontic tendencies were reactivated and expanded. These became the principal feature of an emotional illness which had its onset following great situational stress.

Case 90

Somatic and Physiologic Preoccupation; a Hygeiaphrontic Reaction Follows Continued Great Stress

(1) *Symptoms and concerns progress to disability*
A lieutenant colonel in the U. S. Marine Corps was hospitalized during World War II because of increasing gastrointestinal complaints. These had progressed to a point of considerable interference with his military duties. They included poor digestion, flatulence, constipation, and abdominal pain. He had a subjective intolerance to many foods. Exhaustive physical and laboratory studies had been essentially negative for any kind of organic pathology or demonstrable disorder of function. His attention, however, remained quite absorbingly concentrated upon his gastrointestinal functions. This had been unwittingly encouraged through the prolonged medical overstudy. He was unfortunately and defensively convinced that some undiscovered organic condition accounted for his symptoms. This constituted a very strong *secondary defense* of his hygeiaphrontic manifestations. His *Interest-Absorption defense* was a major contribution.

Psychiatric examination revealed a robust, athletic-appearing officer. He had engaged in a fair amount of immature narcissistic preoccupation most of his life. As one part of this particular arrest or fixation of his personality development, he had also always been rather overconcerned with his digestive functions and elimination.

(2) *Stress precipitates reaction and leads to reactivation of earlier patterns*
This officer had been serving during the preceding eighteen months in a combat situation involving maximal emotional stress. Under this constant intolerable pressure, he came to focus his interest increasingly upon his gastrointestinal tract and its functioning. This had progressed to the point that he paid detailed attention to the most minute events and variations. He even kept exhaustive written records. He had just

about completely lost his effectiveness as a military officer. A major part of his time, effort, and attention had become invested in this kind of nonconstructive, introspective activity. He appeared tense and worried. In talking with him, one was quickly impressed with the amount of attention and energy which was unconstructively but defensively directed into these self-absorbing interests.

This officer's response to overwhelming stress had been increasingly to redirect his interests and concerns into himself. This interest-absorption defense was so marked as to constitute an unconscious regressive retreat toward a more dependent position. There had been at least two rather clear earlier periods of somatic preoccupation. One had occurred in childhood, and a second in adolescence. His illness might be regarded as an unconscious return to an older and familiar or antecedent pattern of reacting to otherwise unbearable stress. There were also subjective factors of conscious and unconscious guilt. The latter also included the unconscious anticipation of punishment.

(3) *Concept of interpersonal perpetuation operative*

It is to be stressed that these and other factors had operated out of awareness (that is, unconsciously). Their effect was intensified through the reactivation of what were originally infantile fears of bodily punishment. (*See* S.E.H.C., page 33.) The patient's mother was herself hypochondriacal. Her overprotectiveness had fostered these trends in her son, as had other unconscious factors, such as the important one in this instance of modeling himself (through the mental mechanism of identification) after his mother. These findings were in accord with the Concept of Interpersonal Perpetuation [pp. 291; 334; also, Ch.8;VID*3*; Ch.12:VA*3*; p. 404, *Case 82*].

Over a period of study and superficial treatment, this man's concerns subsided somewhat. It was not possible for him to continue on active duty status or to offer him definitive treatment, however, and he was shortly retired for emotional disability.

The foregoing case also illustrates another important principle which is generally operative in those emotional reactions having their onset following rather specific and externally prominent emotional stress. This is our *Concept of Continued Physiologic Momentum* (*see also* p. 99, and *Case 20,* p. 100). Thus there is often a greater or lesser lag in the subsiding of the emotional and the physiologic reactions to stress (immediate, mid-term, and long-range reactions), following the subsiding of the stress itself.

2. Hygeiaphrontis and Psychoses

A. PSYCHOTIC REACTION FOLLOWING HYGEIAPHRONTIC DEFENSE BREAKDOWN.—It has been noted that hygeiaphrontis may be seen in conjunction with emotional reactions of psychotic depth. In *Case 96* we shall see this illustrated in a clinical example in which acute schizophrenia was ushered in by severe hypochondriacal preoccupation. It is important that mention be made also of the overlapping of hygeiaphrontis and certain cases of psychosis. Occasional diagnostic difficulties may be encountered as a result.

As Cobb wrote, "it is difficult and often impossible to tell hypochondriacal neurosis from early schizoid or affective psychosis." Further, it should be pointed out that when an established hygeiaphrontic defense system breaks down, a psychotic reaction may ensue. From this point of view one must sometimes regard the severe hygeiaphrontic state as possessing the ominous potentiality for progression into a psychosis.

B. ACCOMPANIES MANY TYPES OF PSYCHOSIS.—Hygeiaphrontic (hypochondriacal) preoccupation has been reported in schizophrenia, the psychotic depressions, including involutional melancholia, paranoid conditions, the senile and arteriosclerotic psychoses, and general paresis. In these grave emotional disorders, the hygeiaphrontic preoccupation may be sometimes observed to reach its ultimate psychopathologic development in the onset of the most deep-seated kind of somatic delusions. Noyes referred to the need for differentiating hypochondriasis from Depressive Reactions, from psychophysiologic reactions (Physiologic Conversions), and from early schizophrenia.

Much of this can be clinically confirmed by psychiatrists with extensive experience with hospitalized psychotic patients. One may conclude that hygeiaphrontic tendencies are not infrequently seen in schizophrenia, involutional melancholia, and in certain other depressive reactions. They are also occasionally present in the paranoid states, and in the psychoses of the senium. Freud regarded paranoid conditions as "almost invariably accompanied" by hypochondriacal symptoms.

3. Hygeiaphrontis and Obsessive Neuroses

A. CLOSE RELATIONSHIP.—As noted earlier, there is also a close relationship between the severe Hygeiaphrontic Reaction (which itself may be regarded as an obsessive preoccupation with health) and the Obsessive-Compulsive Reactions. Indeed, certain instances of Hygeiaphrontis sometimes might be considered as one significant clinical variety of the Obsessive State. *See Case 64* (pp. 318–19) and *Case 73* (pp. 352–53), for important examples of how these two major categories of neurotic reaction can overlap, *also see* p. 318.

B. FORMAL DIAGNOSIS NOT WARRANTED.—Actually, somatic preoccupation may be present to some extent in any emotional illness. It is not uncommonly present to a mild degree in certain individuals whose emotional problems are not present to a sufficient degree or with sufficient interference in living to warrant the establishment of a formal psychiatric diagnosis.

C. IN CONCLUSION.—Hygeiaphrontis (or hypochondriasis) is a medical problem of considerable moment. It probably deserves some separate consideration, from the standpoint of its psychodynamics, management, and other aspects. However, the trend has been away from the use of the term as such as a specific diagnosis. The *Diagnostic and Statistical Manual* of the American Psychiatric Association does not currently include hypochondriasis as a separate category. Some tend to regard hypochondriasis merely as a non-specific syndrome, which can appear as one aspect of various neurotic and psychotic states.

However, cases are to be observed in medical and psychiatric practice in which the absorbing somatic preoccupation is so much *the* major aspect of the clinical picture, that Hygeiaphrontis (hypochondriasis) is the most suitable diagnostic label. There accordingly is some preference for the employment of an accurate diagnostic term in these cases. The older one has long offered certain disadvantages, as noted. Such tentatively attempted labels as Overconcern-with-Health, and Somatic and/or Physiologic Pre-occupation, are unfortunately cumbersome. Accordingly the terms of Hygeiaphrontis and the Hygeiaphrontic Reaction have been offered.

IV. INCIDENCE

A. HYGEIAPHRONTIC SYMPTOMS AND HYGEIAPHRONTIC REACTION

1. Stressful Periods in Living Increase Vulnerability to Neurotic Reaction; S.E.H.A.; The Peg Concept

As noted earlier, preoccupation with some aspect of one's health is quite common. During an average lifetime, it is rather likely that everyone at some time or other will experience a degree of overconcern with physical structure or function. This is in accord with our earlier formulated *Law of Relativity in Emotional Health* (p. 2).

Certain periods in life tend to be of greatest stress. These comprise the Specific Emotional Hazards of Adulthood or S.E.H.A., as referred to earlier (pp. 38, 119). They include puberty, early marital adjustment, the menarche and the approaching senium, plus other periods of specific situational stress. One's individual *vulnerability to the development of the clinical manifestations of neurotic reactions of all kinds is* in general *increased at these times.* The frequent presence of some degree of increased somatic concern during adolescence, for example, is therefore not necessarily to be regarded as serious or pathologic.

The presence of organic disease may serve as a focus or as a stimulus for the increase of health concerns. In this situation, some part of the body may come to serve as a convenient attachment for anxiety. This may occur at that particular time, or a potential peg may be set up for the attachment of later difficulty, when stress leads to the reactivation of earlier conflicts. This helps comprise the *Peg Concept* [Ch.10:IXD2; and XB1]. It is related to our earlier *Concept of the Emotional-Object Amalgam,* or E.O.A., as discussed elsewhere* [Ch.10:VIIC1; Ch.11:VB2]. As an added source of psychologic stress in itself, a severe illness may also contribute to the intrapsychic need for the development of neurotic defenses.

The incidence of Hygeiaphrontic manifestations is widespread indeed. The incidence of the Hygeiaphrontic Reaction of sufficient clinical level to be so diagnosed is considerably less common.

2. Incidence of Cases Diagnosed as Hypochondriasis

A. THREE TO FIVE PER CENT.—The author would estimate the overall incidence of cases of emotional illnesses in which hygeiaphrontic concerns and/or symptoms constitute the outstanding clinical feature to be from

---

* See also discussion of the *Law of Universal Affect,* and the E.O.A. in pp. 45–46.

3 to 5 per cent of all neurotic reactions. As noted, Overconcern-with-Health is much more frequently encountered as a component of other emotional reactions, as was illustrated in the discussion of Neurasthenia (pp. 424*ff*.) As borne out by several statistical surveys, the specific diagnosis is warranted somewhat infrequently.

B. AMONG OFFICERS IN WORLD WAR II.—Earlier the author reported a series of military personnel under therapy during a selected period of a little more than one year, toward the close of World War II (*see also* section on Combat Reactions, Ch.14:VII). In these consecutive patients, an occasional individual received a "final" diagnosis of hypochondriasis. In our review of their official, final records, the dispositional survey reports (that is, case summaries) of 127 consecutive Naval and Marine Corps officer cases were included. These had been written in 1946–47 while the author was serving in charge of the Officers' Psychiatric Service at the National Naval Medical Center.

In this unselected group of persons, hypochondriasis had been the most suitable final diagnosis in exactly three cases, a total of 2.3 per cent. However, lest this give a misleading impression, it should be noted that hygeiaphrontic *concerns* were present to at least an appreciable degree in 41 cases (sufficiently marked to warrant specific mention as a manifestation of the total reaction), or roughly *one-third* of this entire group. These individuals as a group constituted a fair diagnostic cross-section of clinical psychiatry.

C. IN A LARGE RANDOM MILITARY GROUP.—Ripley, in reviewing a draft of this chapter some years ago, called to the author's attention some additional data which essentially tends to confirm independently the relative incidence of cases which might be specifically diagnosed as Overconcern-with-Health or Hygeiaphrontis.

In a statistical study of a considerably larger group of military patients during World War II in the southwest Pacific Theater, Ripley and Wolf so diagnosed 51 persons out of a larger random group of 1800 patients. The rate of incidence in this group was 2.8 per cent. Their study did not include the frequency of hypochondriacal complaints, when they were present simply as a part of other clinical psychiatric entities.

B. CLINICAL AND PERSONAL EXPERIENCE OF PHYSICIANS AND STUDENTS WITH UNDUE SOMATIC CONCERNS

1. Four Groups Surveyed

A few years ago the author had an opportunity to enlist the assistance of some 50 of his medical colleagues in reference to their personal and clinical experience with the incidence of Overconcern-with-Health. The unselected group of physicians included representatives of most of the medical and surgical specialties. They were asked to indicate, anonymously, the estimated frequency of cases observed clinically, and also the results of their own self-observation.

Later, a class of 70 medical students provided the data in a similar survey. On subsequent occasions, the assistance of two other groups of physicians was also enlisted. The results obtained are summarized in *Table 24*. These figures, of course, do not necessarily have statistical validity, especially in view of the limited size of the samples, and possibly due to the circumstances of the surveys.

Table 24

The Clinical and Personal Experience of Groups of Physicians and Students with Hygeiaphrontis

I. *The Medical Staff of a General Hospital*

A group of physicians comprising the professional staff of an active general hospital were asked to report their personal awareness of undue somatic concerns, and the estimated frequency with which they were found to be present in their clinical practice.

This survey was conducted upon an occasion when an unrelated medical topic was under discussion. They anonymously reported their experiences, which are tabulated as follows:

A. *The estimated percentage of my patients* in whom undue somatic concerns are present. In my practice I have found them to be present in the following frequency:

	0-25%	25-50%	50-75%	75-100%
1. A presenting problem	15	6	1	3
2. A major presenting problem	15	5	1	0
3. The principal presenting problem	13	2	1	0

B. *My personal hypochondriacal trends have been:*

1. Never 4
2. Occasional 25
3. Frequent 4
4. Present in early past years 2
5. Present as a medical student 10

II. *A Class of Medical Students*

A similar anonymous survey was conducted with a group of 70 medical students in their second (junior) clinical semester. The results are summarized as follows:

A. In my *clinical contacts with patients* I have found hygeiaphrontic (hypochondriacal) concerns and/or symptoms in the following frequency:

	0-10%	10-25%	50-100%
1. A presenting problem	31	30	9
2. A major presenting problem	52	17	1
3. The principal clinical feature of illness	65	5	0

B. *My personal experience* with these kinds of concerns and/or symptoms has been as follows:

1. Never 9
2. Occasional 50
3. Frequent 11
4. Present in:
    a. Childhood 10
    b. Adolescense 19
    c. Medical school experience thus far .. 46

III. *A County Medical Society*

Forty physicians attending the regular monthly scientific meeting of the Montgomery County (Maryland) Medical Society, Sept. 15, 1953, provided the following information in estimating their clinical and personal experience with hygeiaphrontis (hypochondriasis).

(*Table continued on next page*)

Table 24—Continued

The average age of this group was 37.7 years. Their average experience in medical practice was 13.3 years. Eighteen of the group were in general practice, and 22 in the various specialties, including 5 in surgery, 5 in internal medicine, and 3 in obstetrics-gynecology.

A. The *estimated percentage of my patients* in whom undue somatic concerns are:

	0-10%	10-25%	25-50%	50-75%	75-100%
1. A presenting problem	10	11	6	2	3
2. A major presenting problem	12	10	6	1	0
3. The principal presenting problem	18	5	2	1	0

B. My *personal hypochondriacal trends* are:

1. Never	5
2. Occasional	28
3. Frequent	4
4. In early past years	3
5. As a medical student	9

IV. *A State Academy of General Practice*

Sixty-three physicians attending a specialty session of the 7th Annual Assembly of the Maryland Academy of General Practice, Baltimore, Md., Oct. 26-27, 1955, reported their clinical and personal experience with hygeiaphrontis (hypochondriasis), as defined for them below. This group of physicians averaged 16.6 years of practice per physician, and had an average age of 44.1 years. All except 3 were in general practice.

Overconcern-With-Health was defined as "a state in which there is a more or less persistent anxious overconcern about one's health, or in regard to the possible presence of illness. Various uncomfortable symptoms may affect any body region, organ, or system. Any possible organic basis or contribution is insufficient in itself to account for the discomfort experienced, and the level of accompanying concern."

A. The *estimated percentage of my patients* in whom Overconcern-with-Health is:

	0%	0-10%	10-25%	25-50%	50-75%	75-100%
1. A presenting problem	0	23	27	8	3	3
2. A major presenting symptom	3	30	19	6	3	0
3. The most prominent clinical feature	3	38	13	5	2	2

B. My *personal experience* with these kinds of concerns and/or symptoms has been as follows:

1. Never	23
2. Occasional	38
3. Frequent	3
4. Present in:	
a. Childhood	2
b. Adolescence	8
c. College	6
d. Medical school	20
e. Since entering practice	26

2. Among the "Seekers-After-Health"

A. NOSTRUMS, PATENT MEDICINES, HEALTH DEVICES, PURVEYORS OF CURES. —As a final note in relation to incidence, we must remember that probably a considerable additional number of hygeiaphrontic concerns and problems come relatively infrequently to the legitimate physician's attention, if at all. They are found in a large group of anxious and worried people. They comprise a large body of the public and as a group may be referred to as the *Seekers-After-Health*. Without them, the patent medicine field would not be the lucrative bonanza it consistently remains year after year.

The large volume of this business on a national level is another indication of the widespread incidence of concern and Overconcern-with-Health. Without this large group of persons also, the promoters of various nostrums and the various groups of borderline practitioners would have tougher economic sledding.

B. PHYSICAL CULTURE AND RELATED INTERESTS.—Still another large group of people direct what may be regarded as the equivalent of hypochondriacal preoccupations into avid personal interests in such related areas as those of physical culture, exercises, physical appearance, beauty aids, and many others.

V. SYMPTOMS AND CLINICAL FEATURES

A. THE HYGEIAPHRONTIC PATIENT

1. Overattentiveness to Function

In the Hygeiaphrontic Reaction the patient usually believes, at least to some extent, that organic disease is present and is the source of his complaints. Impetus for this may be gained also through operation of the *Flight-to-the-Physical Principle* [Ch.12:VIIIA3; Ch.14:IB2] which points out the preference of many persons to suffer from physical bases, as distinguished from emotional ones. A *physical scapegoat* [Ch.7:IIID1] may be evolved. The hygeiaphrontic person's attention comes to be abnormally focused on his subjective bodily sensations or upon some aspect of bodily function or health. This overattentiveness may develop with an increased awareness of sensations which formerly failed to reach the threshold of awareness.

In this fashion the patient may become acutely aware of minor variations of "normal" function and devote abnormal attention in this direction. His pattern of hygeiaphrontic ruminations may appear to comprise an S.O. (Security Operation), or even a C.S.R., as such repetitive, defensively-intended patterns were termed (p. 351), in our earlier discussion of the Obsessive-Compulsive Reactions. In the broadest sense, concern about illness is hygeiaphrontic (hypochondriacal) when it is out of keeping with the actual amount of organic or functional pathology that may happen to be present. This is in keeping with our Hygeiaphrontic Discrepancy Principle, as earlier outlined.

In contrast, very occasional patients with severe illnesses, in whom concern might well be warranted, have relatively little preoccupation with their condition, or may even lack a commensurate amount of concern. An illustration of the latter was reported to the author in which a physician was discovered to have inoperable cancer. His life and activities reflected little outward change after he learned of this. He seldom spoke of the cancer, although he did not completely avoid it. He carried on in his usual efficient manner with his professional work. He even developed a new hobby, in a field in which he had long had an interest. Note the contrast with reactions in later *Case 101* (pp. 487–489).

2. Criteria for Pathology; Less Overt Anxiety

We regard undue concern over one's health and/or accompanying hygeiaphrontic symptoms as significant from a psychopathologic standpoint when competent, objective judgment indicates that as a result: (1) the individual's effectiveness and efficiency in living are impaired; (2) his attainment of reasonable satisfactions is handicapped; or (3) his capacity for happiness and satisfactions in living are significantly diminished.

The overt presence of anxiety is apt to be considerably less, or even absent, in cases of Hygeiaphrontis compared to certain other neurotic illnesses. At times a hygeiaphrontic manifestation may be regarded as an *anxiety-equivalent* (pp. 19, 102, 111). The complaints themselves are an unconscious way of dealing with anxiety and the threat of anxiety. When the symptoms operate effectively in this way, there is little subjective anxiety. In effect, anxiety has been traded for the overconcern and the discomforts of Hygeiaphrontis. This illustrates our precept of the *Inverse Anxiety-Symptom Ratio*. The more "successful" the symptom, the less anxiety is experienced (*see* pp. 103, 145, and 324.)

B. VARIETY OF HYGEIAPHRONTIC SYMPTOMS

1. Every System, Organ, or Body Function

This type of problem in emotional illness is not uncommon, as noted earlier. Some hygeiaphrontic complaints are witnessed in company with many psychoneurotic illnesses. Mildly hygeiaphrontic patients may persist in their preoccupations for years with little change. Occasionally, however, the movement into a hygeiaphrontic (hypochondriacal) retreat is a progressive affair. It may become increasingly absorbing of the patient's interest, his attention, and his energies. This is in accord with our Concept of Interest-Absorption as a major psychologic defense, and the related Preoccupation-Defense Concept (pp. 311, 332), especially in the Obsessive-Compulsive Reaction. His libido is withdrawn from the outside world to become attached to (functions, organs, systems, and symptoms within) himself.

Single or multiple symptoms may be presented, in which there is little apparent or even a completely hidden (and usually outwardly denied) relationship to emotional disturbances. These symptoms may refer to any or every system, organ, or body function. In view of the ubiquity of manifestations, an attempt to list or catalog the hygeiaphrontic patient's complaints or symptoms as such would run the gamut of clinical medical experience.

When hygeiaphrontic manifestations are not sufficiently effective in the endeavor to combat and control anxiety, covert or overt evidences of anxiety may also be in evidence as concurrent findings. At times a slow spiral of symptoms (plus anxiety) can develop. In this kind of development anxiety leads to more symptoms, and anxiety over these seems in turn to produce still more symptoms. Living becomes gradually constricted, as symptoms limit activity and handicap living. The resulting *Constrictive Spiral of Hygeiaphrontis* is quite analogous to our earlier *Concept of the Constrictive Spiral of Anxiety* (p. 122). *See also* comments concerning what was termed the *Hygeiaphrontic Vicious Circle,* p. 284.

According to Bleuler, "The picture of the condition of hypochondriasis consists in continuous attention to one's own state of health with the tendency to ascribe a disease to oneself from (objectively) insignificant signs." Cobb reserved the term hypochondriasis to describe "a group of introverted patients whose main interest in life seems to revolve about their viscera. . . . The true hypochondriacal patient is convinced that certain organs are diseased or are functioning improperly. It is impossible to convince him (otherwise) by medical examinations and argument." Our *Flight-to-the-Physical Concept* (pp. 91, 97, 392, and Ch.12:VIIIA3) thus is well illustrated in many Hygeiaphrontic Reactions. Emotional conflict is more troubling, and a substitute physical focus has become "preferable" for the unconscious, leading to the evolvement of the hygeiaphrontic process.

2. Childhood Example; Importance of Parental Response

It may contribute to our understanding of the problem of somatic preoccupation to illustrate ·some fairly common instances. In the following relatively nonpathologic example, a child became aware of his heart action and was concerned.

Case 91

A Child's Awareness and Concern About His Heart Action

A seven-year-old boy appeared worried. He was noted by his parents to have recently withdrawn from his usual degree of participation in various activities with his playmates. He had recently overheard grown-ups describe several dramatic instances of heart attacks and death. He had become impressed with the vital role of his heart.

Shortly afterwards he had begun to notice his own normal physiologic response of heart palpitation and the resulting chest motion upon exercise. He had become uneasy and frightened. He began to withdraw from games involving exercise. His concerns were fairly rapidly dissipated, following simple explanation and reassurance.

This kind of temporary somatic concern is not uncommon in children. It may have very little if any pathologic significance. The important consideration is in the handling of the situation from the point at which one first learns of such an undue concern. What reaction will be evoked from the child's parents or from other significant adults? The possibility for the development of emotionally unhealthy patterns will be largely determined by the adequacy of handling and by the parental attitudes which are present. When the results contribute to the establishment of a potential for the later development of Hygeiaphrontis, such incidents will have had a cumulative effect. Many similar events will likely have occurred, most of which will have been less striking than the above. Their effect tends to be cumulative. We might make reference at this juncture to our important *Profitable Patterns Concept*. This was earlier (pp. 320, 338) so named, in order to stress how the child intuitively will adopt and exploit those responses and patterns which prove most useful, that is profitable, to him in his interpersonal relationships and adjustment.

A matter-of-fact approach is important in the dissolution of an unrealistic concern of childhood. On the other hand, when this kind of instance in a child arouses some anxiety in an adult, even if an effort is made to conceal this, it may still have an important place in evolving a pattern of undue concern about health in the child. In other words, if the parent is concerned, the child is more likely to be concerned. As we learned earlier with our concept of *Emotional Contagion* [Ch.1:IVB3; IVB6] anxiety can be highly contagious from parent to child. When the parent is not concerned, the child is less likely to be concerned. The importance of parental response, its type, degree, and adequacy can hardly be overstated (*see also Case 82* p. 404).

Finally, in reference to our *Interpersonal Perpetuation Cycle Concept* (p. 328), hygeiaphrontic parental attitudes may be "passed on" both wittingly and not. This can thus lead to the evolvement of just such a pattern in one's child or children. One would also and correctly expect the process of identification to contribute in a number of possible ways to the development of emotional patterns and illness. (*See* Identification, pp. 118–167 in the author's previous book, *Mental Mechanisms*).

3. Increased Awareness of Normal Function

Not uncommonly adults as well as children will develop a hyperacute awareness of some normal and usual physiologic process which ordinarily passes completely unnoticed. The following example was recently discussed with a physician.

Case 92

Hyperacute Awareness of a Pulse Beat

A thirty-two-year-old mathematician sought advice from his physician about a "thumping" in his head which he noted at night. He was moderately concerned about the possible pathologic significance of what proved to be merely the pulse beat in his ear. It became, of course, normally accentuated in either ear when he lay on that particular side. This patient had developed an increased awareness of one of the many sensations which are normally ignored or which pass relatively unnoticed.

The instance has significance beyond merely ascertaining the absence of physical illness. The increased concern served an emotional purpose. This remained obscure. This example, however, illustrates how a peg will be found—something upon which to hang the hygeiaphrontic concern. This is in accord with our interesting *Peg Concept* [Ch.14:IVB2; Ch.10:B1].

These two cases represent types of more or less temporary preoccupation with some aspect of health and are relatively benign. They are not uncommon at one stage or another in living. The amount and degree of hygeiaphrontic trends can vary widely. They also help to illustrate our *Law of Relativity in Emotional Health* (p. 2).

4. Concept of Defensive-Layering

Successful therapy will sometimes clearly demonstrate successive layers of psychic defenses. Accordingly one may uncover "layers" of emotional conflict, of defensive mechanisms, character traits, and symptomatology in many emotional reactions, and of the somatic concerns underlying the Hygeiaphrontic Reactions. This outlines the important and intriguing phenomena which the author suggests we might for convenience refer to as the *Concept of Defensive-Layering*. (p. 367). This concept includes strata of defenses, as well as layers of meaning and significance.

Instances can also be observed in reverse as pathology progresses. Herein a more serious layer becomes superimposed as the older one proves defensively too ineffective. The new "layer" of defense thus evolved is likely to be more malignant from a psychopathologic standpoint (*see also* related discussion and *Tracing Technique in Therapy,* pp. 366–7).

The following instance is illustrative of the reappearance of older layers of conflict, as successful therapy leads to the resolution of the newer ones.

Case 93

The Hygeiaphrontic Reaction Is Resolved and Earlier Replaced Conflicts Reappear

(1) *Concerns on body plane replaced by psychological ones*
A thirty-two-year-old woman attorney was referred for psychotherapy by an internist because of a typical somatic and physiologic preoccupation. For years she had been unduly concerned about health. The past 12 months had seen an exaggeration of this pattern, with frequent medical visits, repeated requests for examinations, and nearly constant worry and concern. Her professional effectiveness was seriously impaired.
     A year after she had entered treatment, the hygeiaphrontic manifestations had been resolved. The "new" layer of concern was now psychological; and no longer expressed on the bodily plane. Now she feared obsessively that "No one will ever love me or find me attractive . . . I'm not worthy of love (*i.e.,* I'm unlovable)". This was accompanied by the intense fear of any close relationship.

(2) *Defensive Layering illustrated in therapy.*
Ultimately these obsessive concerns were worked through, and another still deeper layer emerged. This had to do with her previously repressed anger and resentment toward her parents. This third layer of conflict and significance was still more basic. Its emergence helps illustrate our *Concept of Defensive-Layering*.
     She was gradually able to gain awareness of her parents' thorough control of her during the course of her entire life. She had been an "exclusive possession", with nearly all aspects of her social and professional life completely dominated and controlled by them. Recognition provoked several emotional crises. However, she became quite able to cope with her long repressed emotions, and her gradual emancipation became possible. The original Hygeiaphrontic Reaction had receded far into the past.

When the Defensive-Layering Concept happens to be clearly illustrated in therapy, it is generally a long-range process and may be noted only in careful retrospect. It might be compared on such occasions to the successive peeling away of the layers of an onion, in which endeavor one progresses toward the center.

5. Severely Pathologic Retreat into Overconcern-with-Health

A. HYGEIAPHRONTIS AN OBSESSIVE PREOCCUPATION.—The following instance is presented to illustrate the pathologic degree of somatic narcissistic preoccupation which can occur. *Case 73*, p. 352, also illustrates the very severe type of case, which from another standpoint might be regarded as obsessive preoccupation.

Case 94

Hygeiaphrontic Preoccupation

(1) *Animation and interest confined to hygeiaphrontic concerns*
This patient was a thirty-eight-year-old electronics engineer. He had been referred for psychiatric evaluation because of multiple somatic complaints. These had not been substantiated on an organic basis following extensive medical study. Diagnosis by exclusion, which was later substantiated by psychiatric consultation, indicated their emotional origin, and the presence of a severe Hygeiaphrontic Reaction.

At the time of psychiatric referral he described constant frontal headaches, tinnitus, nausea, abdominal cramps, leg pains, frequency of urination, insomnia, nervousness, and lack of energy. He was absorbed in these complaints and he could rather animatedly discuss any one of them in great detail. In fact, these were about the only subjects in which he seemed able to exhibit much real interest.

(2) *Introspective absorption defensive*
Psychiatric examination further revealed an emotionally impoverished person. He was anxious, immature, and worried. His principal defenses against anxiety appeared to consist of his absorbing level of pathologic introspection into his multiple symptoms. This is in accord with our previous *Attention Absorption Concept* of defense (Ch.8:IIIA3;VIC1). His social adjustment was inadequate, and his professional achievements had been in a state of gradual decline over the preceding year. He was concerned about his potency, and his sexual activity was both limited and unsatisfactory.

This patient suffered from a chronic, severe, low level of self-esteem. In attempted compensation he had set impossible goals of achievement for himself. When he had failed increasingly to attain his high levels of professional and personal expectation, he had begun a regressive retreat into a narcissistic level of somatic preoccupation.

(3) *Retreat to a less exposed position*
In a very brief summary of the major dynamic considerations involved, this patient had made a dependent retreat, in which his anxiety and disappointments were displaced somatically. He had assumed a more dependent and helpless position as the response to his unconscious needs for a more dependent, protected, less exposed, and less active position. Through the limiting and handicapping symptoms of his very severe psychologic illness, the resulting suffering also satisfied certain unconscious feelings of guilt and needs for punishment.

Two all-too-brief attempts at psychotherapy were abortive. After a lapse of time, a third endeavor proved more successful and he was able gradually to make considerable improvement.

B. FIXATION AND REGRESSION.—It is helpful to keep in mind that hygeia-phrontic preoccupations may be almost normally encountered in certain stages of personality development. In the usual course of events and in the maturing process, this particular kind of regressive retreat is surrendered. This is done in favor of more constructive ways of dealing with problems in living. The person who passes through these stages successfully may be thought of as fortunately lacking the necessary, strong, unhealthy, internal psychologic needs responsible for hygeiaphrontic overconcern.

These unhealthy needs can result for some individuals either in a per-petuation of this unhealthy type of response (that is, fixation), or in a later resumption of an earlier unhealthy pattern (that is, regression). As might be hypothesized in relation to *Case 94,* there are certain possible early conditioning factors. These can greatly enhance the later prospects for an unconsciously directed retreat into this kind of narcissistic somatic pre-occupation. More will be said about this later.

C. PSYCHOLOGIC CATEGORIES OF VISCERAL PAIN

1. Four Major Routes or Types; Three Conceptions

A. PHYSIOLOGIC LANGUAGE.—This is an important topic. The reader is referred also to later comments in *Chapter 12* about the conversion of (aspects of) emotional conflict into visceral pain, and about conversion (hysterical) pain.

In Physiologic Conversion there is an expression into what we may term the *physiologic language,* of the repressed conflictual material (*see also* Ch.12:IB2). The symptom formation is of a physiologic nature. This results from a psychologic process which is analogous to that of Somatic (hysterical) Conversion. In Somatic Conversion there is the expression into "bodily language" of the repressed emotional conflict, with symptom formation of a physical nature.

B. PRINCIPLE OF EMOTIONALLY DETERMINED VISCERAL PAIN.—The au-thor has earlier noted one typical clinical feature of Hygeiaphrontis to be the discrepancy between the subjective anxiety about health, and the objec-tively evaluated state of health (Principle of Hygeiaphrontic Discrepancy). It is clear that *an individual may often suffer serious discomfort in the com-plete absence of any demonstrable malfunction or somatic pathology. Emo-tionally determined visceral pain can develop via several psychologic path-ways.* This is in accord with what might be referred to as the *Principle of Emotionally Determined Visceral or Area Pain.* These routes may be clas-sified as falling into the four major types or categories: (1) Somatic Con-version (that is, conversion hysteria), (2) Physiologic Conversion, (3) the response to prolonged stress and tension, or (4) Hygeiaphrontis.

Pain may or may not be accompanied by functional variations or dis-turbances. In turn, pain may or may not be present with functional dis-turbances, when these are present. Such functional or even structural diffi-culties can be discovered sometimes, for example, upon otherwise routine examination of the stomach or back,* in which no subjective discomfort was present.

It should also be noted again (*see* p. 113) that in the absence of relief from their underlying bases, functional symptoms can at times progress so as to become fixed, and eventually irreversible. The ultimate in their progression is on into structural change and gross pathology. This is our *Concept of Functional-Structural Progression.*

c. PSYCHIC REDUPLICATION CONCEPT.—Emotional pain on occasion will far more readily follow established pathways of past experience. Illnesses from one's past experience with various organic and functional bases thus can provide an antecedent pattern of pain. Later psychic needs may automatically adopt this avenue, as a familiar one. It becomes in effect an unconscious precept.

A patient with severe painful shingles later thus developed similar pain. However on this later occasion, the basis was psychic entirely. It was in effect an emotional reduplication of the earlier organic situation. Similar recent incidents have come to the author's attention which have illustrated the analogous reduplication of bladder pain, pleurisy pain, and fracture pain. It would appear that at least theoretically, emotional forces might in the properly favorable circumstances similarly reduplicate almost any given type of organic pain.

This type of sequence illustrates what the author would accordingly describe as the *Psychic Reduplication Concept,* according to which any organic or functional pain might be reproduced at some future juncture unconsciously, on a partial or completely psychologic basis.

The conjoint presence of both physical and psychic symptoms is what we have referred to as an E.O.C. (Emotional-Organic Combination); *see also* analogous instance of an *Emotional Recapitulation* of an antecedent G.U. infection, later on a psychologic basis (p. 117).

2. Emotionally-Determined Stomach Pain

A. HYGEIAPHRONTIC PAIN.—Let us consider in illustration several categories of emotionally determined stomach pain. First, stomach discomfort or pain is considered clearly hygeiaphrontic, for instance, when the bases are emotional and there is no organic disease or functional disturbance. This type of stomach pain can be, and is better, diagnosed on a positive basis (in distinction to exclusion) by the experienced clinician.

Rare exceptions exist, of course, in instances of otherwise "silent" organic pathology of the stomach, possibly not yet advanced enough to be demonstrable. Generally, however, when the organic pathology is not sufficiently advanced to be clinically detectable, it will seldom give rise in itself to very much in the way of subjective symptoms.

---

* Illustrations of this may be found in civilian, industrial, and military practice. For instance, routine X-rays of the backs of a series of paratroopers disclosed a number who had what was considered to be very bad backs but who had not complained or had symptoms. On the other hand, another group of men in less strenuous duties, who complained bitterly, had a great deal less, comparatively speaking, in the amount of demonstrable pathology present.

B. FUNCTIONAL PAIN.—Stomach pain also may be present in which there is a demonstrable functional disturbance present which has an emotional basis. This may be illustrated by certain cases of pylorospasm, cardiospasm, and hypermotility or hypomotility. The functional disturbance may be of a smooth muscle response to stress and tensions, in which there is a particular individual susceptibility present in the organ affected.*

A degree of Hygeiaphrontic Discrepancy may be present here to reinforce the subjective suffering, as may also occur in the following instance. Functional pain may occur also in instances in which organic disease is concurrently present.

C. CONVERSION PAIN; PAIN FOLLOWING PROLONGED STRESS.—Stomach pain may occur as a conversion symptom. It may also develop from a specific lesion such as peptic ulcer in the stomach or duodenum. This may be pain from the erosion, acidic excoriation, and tissue damage. Prior to this advancing structural alteration, there may have been conversion pain, stemming from the transmutation and concealed expression of one or more elements of unconscious emotional conflict and/or functional alteration following prolonged stress. This is part of the *Concept of Functional-Structural Progression,* [Ch.14:VB2].

The psychopathologic sequence can potentially follow either prolonged physiologic conversion or emotional tension and stress, or both. Stomach pain can originate either as a *Physiologic Conversion* type or as a more direct response to *prolonged stress.* Thus the lesion and its accompanying pain can gradually result as the pathologic response to chronic psychophysiologic stress.

This latter kind of severe consequence of Physiologic Conversion has also been labeled by other names: for example, an autonomic or vegetative neurosis, a psychosomatic or psychophysiologic disorder, an organ neurosis, or a somatization reaction [Ch.12:IIIA5;B1;B2].

Pain of emotional origin of the stomach, for example, as well as elsewhere may be functional in origin, represent an emotional conversion (or hysteria), result from prolonged tension and stress, be of a hygeiaphrontic basis, or result from a combination of these. From whatever source or sources, however, it is a very real matter to the person concerned. In accord with our *Concept of Functional-Structural Progression* (pp. 13–14), functional alteration can lead to organic change, and on into irreversibility.

3. *Location and Susceptibility; Axiom of Inverse Pain-Conflict Ratio*

A. LOCALE; CHARACTERISTICS.—The location for a hygeiaphrontic symptom can be in any organ or any region of the body. The determination of the site depends upon the overall combined consequences of complex intrapsychic factors. The interested reader is referred to comments on the selection of the location of the site for emotional symptoms in other chapters, especially Chapters Ten and Twelve.

---

* A woman reported: "I can't stomach my husband's flirting." When she observed it (sometimes also when she discussed it!), this woman experienced distinct epigastric distress, nausea, and sometimes acute episodes of pain or vomiting. There was gastric hypermotility and delayed emptying present, as evidence of accompanying functional interference.

No part of the body is immune. Symptoms may likewise run the gamut of subjective experience. They may simulate almost any organic illness. They may be single or multiple, credible or bizarre, persistent or shifting. At times they may be rather directly regarded as *anxiety-equivalents* (p. 19).

B. THRESHOLD TO PAIN INFLUENCED BY EMOTIONAL FACTORS.—It should be noted here that the individual threshold to pain varies greatly. Emotional factors have a powerful effect. Not only do persons who are anxious and irritable have a lowered threshold, but persons who are in pain in turn are likely also to be anxious and irritable. *Pain and anxiety have a reciprocal relationship* (*see* earlier reference to concept, p. 123).

The threshold to pain is affected by many emotional factors. These include: (1) Emotional sequallae to previous pain, (2) prolonged stress and tension, (3) the presence or degree of subjective anxiety, (4) single *vs.* multiple and repeated stimuli, (5) fatigue and sleep deprivation, (6) personal level of security, (7) already established patterns of emotional response, and (8) early conditioning from experiences with pain.

In general, *the more emotional conflicts, anxiety and problems are present, the lower the pain threshold, and vice versa.* This inverse ratio relationship is so nearly certain as to be regarded as axiomatic. Accordingly we might term this principle the *Axiom of Inverse Pain-Conflict Ratio.* Accurately assessing the relative level of pain, possible organic components, emotional contributions, and/or emotional conflict or anxiety can be enhanced by keeping this important relationship and axiom in mind.

D. IN SPECIAL CIRCUMSTANCES

1. Overconcern-with-Health Follows Surgery

Overconcern-with-health (hygeiaphrontis) may sometimes be initiated or vastly increased by the threat and stress incident to serious injury, major illness, or surgery. The following briefly cited example illustrates the onset of a greatly increased, nonconstructive hypochondriacal focusing of attention following an otherwise successful surgical procedure. In this case a surgical portacaval anastomosis was successfully accomplished. It was a vitally needed circulatory adjunct and relief in a case of Laennec's cirrhosis. The success of the surgery was more than nullified by the emotional illness which developed. (Recall our *Surgery-in-Abeyance Rule*, p. 127, as applicable in non-essential surgery.)

Case 95

A Severe Hygeiaphrontic Reaction Follows Otherwise Successful Surgery

A thirty-seven-year-old machinist was hospitalized for diagnostic study following several episodes of hematemesis. The intermittent bleeding was found to come from esophageal varices. The enlarged veins had resulted in turn from the venous stasis of a moderately advanced Laennec's cirrhosis. To ameliorate the increasingly dangerous venous back pressure, surgical anastomosis of the portal vein to the vena cava was successfully undertaken. A preoperative portal pressure of 320 mm of water dropped to 130 mm immediately following the procedure. (Normal pressure is 90–140.)

Prior to the operation the patient had appeared on a superficial basis to be a reasonably stable person emotionally. Following the operation, however, he became irritable and anxious. Although his physical recovery from the surgery was uneventful, he soon had more complaints and symptoms than he had had before the operation!

He was increasingly concerned about pains in his legs and abdomen. He began focusing his attention upon his digestion and elimination. He had trouble sleeping and eating, and reported a series of nightmares. Gradually he focused such an inordinate amount of attention upon his state of health that he was even more handicapped and restricted from an emotional standpoint than he had previously been from the cirrhosis. Although the surgery was eminently successful, his emotional response to it had resulted in effect in a defeat of the medical efforts to help him. Such an unfortunate sequence of events is sometimes observed in surgical procedures. While there are some very interesting dynamic implications from the psychologic standpoint, the surgeon is apt to feel frustrated and puzzled.

This patient had little interest in constructive self-study. His complaints diminished only slightly prior to leaving the hospital. Some months later a physician whom he had consulted reported that his hypochondriacal manifestations still occupied a large proportion of his interest.

2. Increasing Emotional Vulnerability with Advancing Age

Various personal and social factors which serve as additional hazards to many of our senior citizens were noted earlier. Undoubtedly advancing age, with its inevitable loss of vitality and elasticity in emotional, mental, and physical areas, contributes to an increased vulnerability to emotional stress in later years for some persons. (*See* era of *Passing-the-Peak,* p. 158; *also* pp. 38 and 281.) Often one sees an increasing tendency to hypochondriacal preoccupation.

As goals in life are not achieved and external sources of satisfaction fail, we can expect to find instances of increasing concern with health. These have peaks in their onset around the time of the climacteric, and later as the senium approaches.

3. Drugs and Hygeiaphrontis

Occasionally untoward emotional responses to certain drugs may include elements of Hygeiaphrontis. These are not frequent. The tendency was likely present before the drug evoked the response. Other untoward emotional reactions in response to drugs are likely to be much more frequent, for example, anxiety, restlessness, irritability, nervousness, insomnia, and even occasionally disorientation and temporary psychotic states. Such commonly used drugs as pyribenzamine, scopolamine, cortisone, the amphetamine group, and the barbiturates are among the most frequent agents which can produce these unexpected and unwelcome emotional responses.

On the other hand, as noted earlier, the hygeiaphrontic person may make at least a temporarily favorable response to almost any kind of drug. This is particularly true when its administration is accompanied by an optimistic attitude on the part of the therapist, or by his dependency-satisfying encouragement, interest, support, and sympathy. This phenomenon is in accord with the *Favorable-Response Concept,* of frequent, temporary improvement on a psychologic basis, in response to each new regimen, agent, medication, or therapist (IIIA*3*).

E. OCCASIONAL SERIOUS PORTENT OF HYGEIAPHRONTIC PREOCCUPATION

1. Ushers in Schizophrenic Reaction

The physician must be aware of some very serious implications in certain cases of Overconcern with Health. As noted previously, hygeiaphrontic preoccupation may have a sinister portent. Occasionally it can usher in a malignant form of emotional disorder. This is illustrated in the following case of schizophrenia.

Case 96

Hygeiaphrontic Preoccupation Ushers in a Psychosis

A single, twenty-six-year-old textile designer met a girl while attending a movie and they kissed. He began to worry about this the next day. His tongue seemed swollen to him. He began to fear he had contracted some form of venereal disease. Shortly thereafter he noted a very minor skin rash which tended to convince him even more that he must be suffering from syphilis. As he became more and more preoccupied with these concerns, things began to seem increasingly unreal to him (that is, depersonalized). He had trouble at work, lost interest in outside events, and spent more and more time alone.

His vision soon seemed to him to become distorted. He developed a fear of death. There was an increasing preoccupation with somatic affairs, and a retreat into emotionally unhealthy fantasy. Outward emotional display first became decreased, and then inappropriate. He began hearing a voice which accused him of having syphilis and of being guilty of great sin.

In greatly abbreviated form, this case illustrates the onset of an acute schizophrenic episode with a rather rapid progression from the original hygeiaphrontic concerns, into an advanced and severe psychotic state.

2. Exaggeration of Hygeiaphrontic Trends

In less obvious fashion hygeiaphrontic concerns can have a serious long-term prognostic import for the ultimate development of acute emotional reactions. Recently the author has observed two instances in which some shifting hygeiaphrontic complaints had been present for six and eight years in a successful businessman and a leading professional man.

A month or six weeks prior to the onset of acute states of (1) Anxiety Neurosis and (2) Depressive Reaction, the hygeiaphrontic features had become greatly exaggerated.

F. HYGEIAPHRONTIC CHARACTER DEFENSES

As one might surmise, the presence of hygeiaphrontic manifestations can play a role in character formation. Very occasionally a hygeiaphrontic (hypochondriacal) character structure can be hypothecated. Further comments on this subject were included elsewhere (pp. 232, 283–4).

The overdevelopment of hygeiaphrontic character traits, as with any given trait or constellation of traits, illustrates the important *Defense-Hypertrophy Principle* (pp. 73; 229*ff*; and 251). According to this principle, a character trait originally elaborated as a defense, in its overdevelopment (or hypertrophy) results in unwitting self defeat and handicap.

VI. PSYCHODYNAMICS AND PATHOGENESIS

A. RELATION BETWEEN FIGURATIVE AND LITERAL

1. "I'm Sick" May Have Symbolic Meaning

First, let us begin with some general observations. The general use of the statement "I'm sick," as well as the subjective feeling of "being sick of" can have broader and more extended meanings than might ordinarily be apparent. Thus, "I'm sick" can convey a fair amount of unconscious meaning, in addition to being merely a reference to one's state of physical health.

It may refer more basically to something else. It may have for example, a symbolic meaning, such as: "I'm sick of my situation"; "I'm sick of this repugnant aspect of it"; "I'm sick of my marriage, my parents, my husband (or my wife)"; "I'm sick of my boss, or my job"; or even "I'm sick of life." Earlier the related *Concept of Psychic Distaste* was cited (pp. 115, 416, and *Case 86,* p. 418), noting how a figurative distaste for a situation, person, or some aspect of living, can become a literal distaste for food.

2. Recognition in Figures of Speech

A. WIDESPREAD KNOWLEDGE IMPLIED.—Many common figures of speech indicate a rather general implicit knowledge of all this. Examples apply to all body regions and parts. There are many instances of this sort of expression. Thus one may say, for instance, "He gives me a pain in the neck!"; or "Boy, is that situation ever a headache to me!"; "When I think of that job, oh, my aching back!"; "My blood boiled"; "That idea nauseates me"; "I get worn out just thinking about spring cleaning"; "It left me limp"; "I can't stomach that"; or "It's just too much for me to swallow!"

"I'm worried sick"; "It was a heart ache"; "I'm fed up"; "That galls me"; "It knocked the pins from under me"; "He's going to pieces"; or "It really tore me up." There are many more of these interesting expressions.

The hygeiaphrontic syndrome can sometimes be viewed as almost necessarily reflecting a sick interpersonal relationship. This can appear also in the person's figurative expressions and speech. Further, there may be little real interest in improving the relationship, as both parties neurotically cling to a self-defeating *status quo*. According to our earlier cited (p. 299) *Relationship-Improvement Precept,* both parties must want to improve the relationship, and be willing to work at it, in order to secure its constructive progression and development.

B. VERBAL AND FIGURATIVE VERSUS LITERAL.—Such sickness may, of course, be expressed in verbal terms alone. The sickness may also be more literal. From our researches into psychodynamics, we know full well the ability of the psyche to express this in terms of actual disorder of function, the symptoms of visceral discomfort, or both. Such somatic, functional, and visceral expressions are much more likely to be present when any original conscious connections have been lost. Otherwise such a psychologically uneconomic expression would not be maintained. The progression of the figurative into the literal is also illustrated frequently in the Conversion Reactions (Chapter 12).

Thus the underlying meaning of the somatic or physiologic expression of conflicts is concealed and unconscious. This is true not only for the sufferer but also to the casual observer. Sometimes the latter may be able to some degree to surmise part of the latent meaning of the complaint. At times there is a fine line between the verbal and figurative, and the literal. There may be a progression from one toward the other. An example of this was observed in our Psychic-Distaste Concept (see above).

C. CONSCIOUS CONNECTIONS LOST.—The following instance is illustrative of the common enough situation in which any conscious connection has been lost. It has been repressed because it was intolerable. In comparing this conflict over football to the one in *Case 163*, one can note the more serious psychologic consequences and potential in this particular instance.

Case 97

"My Career in Professional Football Has Become a Headache"

(1) *Repression contributed to success*
A twenty-six-year-old professional football player developed increasingly severe headaches. He had achieved considerable success as a player and had enjoyed a rather wide reputation for his skill and his gridiron exploits. He had become noted for his aggressiveness, and for his daring execution of complex plays. As his game promised to become even more worthy of national acclaim, his headaches seemingly began to interfere more and more with his ability to play.

This man would have been (and was) the first to deny that he ever had any conflicts over playing professional ball. Consciously, he was correct. His very success had been due to a considerable extent to his ability to repress certain inner dependent needs, which were quite opposite to the aggression and boldness which had marked his play.

(2) *Storehouse of repressed conflicts overfull!*
Psychologically he was to pay a considerable price for the ruthless denial and apparently successful relegation to his unconscious of his contrary impulses. He simply did not dare allow the slightest conscious awareness of fear, timidity, or the slightest reluctance for physical encounter. These had seemed unallowable and intolerable. Their banishment to the unconscious had taken place, seemingly successfully. However, as we have previously noted, such repressed conflictual material does not simply lie dormant. It retains psychic energy and will seek expression in alternate and concealed ways when denied conscious awareness. The storehouse of his repressed feelings and conflicts had become overfull. Something had to give.

In effect, the patient's headaches (unconsciously) said, "The requirements for success in pro ball are too much for me. Football gives me a headache." Any conscious connection between the underlying (and denied) feelings, and the unwitting message of the headaches if ever present, had been lost.

(3) *Depth of love for sports questioned*

This is a condensed version of only one important aspect of the psychodynamics of this case. One can, perhaps, see some of the importance of the repressive forces at work here. The player's success had contributed importantly to his ego. His acclaim from the public had provided an important external source of satisfaction. He had some further need to deny to himself the existence of the disowned personal attributes. His success had aided in this endeavor.

Small wonder that the initial raising of any question whatsoever about the genuine depth of his love of football was met by indignant and vehement denials. Such questions threatened the maintenance of the protectively and defensively intended repression.

This man made considerable improvement under psychotherapy. Although he did not continue long enough for fully definitive results, his headaches ended. After a time he gradually gave up professional football. He has done quite well since in an automobile dealership.

This patient's attention and interest had become increasingly absorbed in his headaches specifically, and his health generally. The clinical picture most nearly met the diagnostic criteria for a Hygeiaphrontic Reaction.

3. Denial and Its Consequences in Hygeiaphrontis

A. MANY AND VARIED SYMPTOMS ARISE IN ANALOGOUS FASHION.—Many cases of emotionally based symptoms arise in analogous fashion to the headaches in the foregoing case. Various symptoms may thus originate from conflictual situations involving work, as well as from conflicts in familial relationships and other sources. Often the nature of the symptoms and of their source tends to go unrecognized because of the defensive needs for denial. On occasion the physician, among others, may be convinced by this denial. When he is not, he may still feel quite helpless in the presence of strong defensive, conscious or unconscious, denial. In some instances he falls unwittingly into the trap of becoming involved in exhaustive physical and laboratory studies.

This all too often tends to protect the neurosis and its symptoms as a part of the secondary defense. It furthers the nonconstructive direction of the attention of the patient, his family, and his physician. It will tend at the least to delay, if not to destroy, any later chances for successful psychotherapeutic intervention.

B. PRESSURES FOR EXHAUSTIVE TESTING.—This had happened in the foregoing case. The headaches had progressed to an incapacitating level, especially in so far as the patient's football career was concerned. Every conceivable test which could be thought up by a team of eminent specialists showed negative results. Many pressures encouraged exhaustive and exhausting diagnostic study. His team's management, for example, added to these, since they urgently wanted to continue his services and his expert performance. (*See also* earlier *Case 87,* p. 427, for an instance of iatrogenic facilitation of Hygeiaphrontic Preoccupation.)

When the young man stopped playing temporarily, the subjective pain diminished for a time. Such layoffs proved to be short-lived respites only. Subsequent events, however, served to further reactivate underlying conflicts. By fortuitous circumstances he then managed to get into psychiatric treatment.

B. FACTORS IN INITIATION

1. Regression and Dependency

As indicated earlier, unhealthy introspective preoccupation with body and function represents either defective maturity (that is, fixation), the regression to an earlier narcissistic stage of development, or both. In general, there is usually a very close relationship between hygeiaphrontis and inner dependency needs. At this juncture reference is appropriate to the *Second Tenet of the Parental Role* (p. 174). In accord with this principle, when love, genuine acceptance, and a secure home environment are provided, inordinate dependency needs are unlikely to be present. The basic conditions for their evolvement are not present.

With most hygeiaphrontic patients, the dependency appeal inherent in their complaints is apparent. Here is an important segment of the hygeiaphrontic epigain. Certain instances can illustrate the *Vicious Circle of Self-Defeat Concept* in the neuroses (*Case 11,* p. 71; also p. 265), according to which the more affection (and dependency) which is demanded, the less genuine affection is available and forthcoming.

In certain instances, Overconcern-with-Health has become so deep-seated, chronic, and pervasive that it appears almost to represent a way of life in itself. In the sufficiently suggestable individual, hygeiaphrontic symptoms can sometimes appear through the process of *emotional contagion* (p. 32).

2. Precipitating Events

At times external stress may bring on hypochondriacal concerns which may then appear to follow precipitating situational factors. Thus the Hygeiaphrontic Reaction may follow a serious operation, the serious illness or death of someone close, or a protracted serious or dangerous personal illness or injury. These serve as precipitating events. In childhood a hygeiaphrontic episode may be precipitated by any of the S.E.H.C., or by significant emotional trauma of a sufficient level to the child concerned. Likewise with adults, an S.E.H.A. (p. 38) may initiate hygeiaphrontic symptoms.

Traumatic neurosis (that is, the neurosis which may have its onset following minor or major physical injury) may be a special combination of situational Somatic (hysterical) or Physiological Conversion Reaction and Hygeiaphrontis [Ch.14:VB3]. Here the traumatic event serves a precipitating role. This is generally in situations, however, in which the predisposition for such development has been well established. The rapid onset of a Hygeiaphrontic Reaction, as with other emotional syndromes, can illustrate our *Concept of Emotional Decompensation* (pp. 48, 159, 317, and 343. Various *Final Straw* situations (*Case 30,* p. 162, and *Case 81,* p. 400) can serve to initiate their onset.

3. Defense Against Anxiety

A. PARENTAL DISAPPROVAL, CONSCIENCE, AND SYMBOLIC PUNISHMENT.—
An emotionally based overconcern with the state of health is essentially
and ultimately a defense against anxiety. As noted earlier for a number
of cogent reasons (p. 82), ours is the *Age of Anxiety*. Accordingly, every
major pattern of emotional reaction as a defense against anxiety is to be
encountered now and again. Thus it is with the Hygeiaphrontic Reactions.

This particular pattern of reaction has its roots, as do others, in the very
early parent-child relationship. Herein enter important factors of identification, psychologic conditioning, and absorption of parental attitudes. The
parental attitudes are often taken over and adopted. However, the Principle
of Individual Appropriateness of Response, as earlier outlined (pp. 14, 84),
holds of course. Further, in accord with our *Concept of Profitable-Patterns,*
those responses and attitudes of the child which prove profitable *to him,*
regardless of how nonconstructive, are inevitably adopted, employed, and
further elaborated. Some of these can involve hygeiaphrontic attitudes
and reactions.

Freud early (in 1896) noted the relation between the conscious shame
and self-reproach experienced because of a consciously disapproved sexual
deed, and hypochondriacal anxiety occurring as an unconscious guilty fear
of bodily injury. This can develop further in psychopathologic sequence
into phobic manifestations, for example, as "fear of punishment — for the
lapse" and even on into delusional areas. This sequence can also progress
psychologically into hygeiaphrontic preoccupation, by *physiologic* expression into functional changes, and by *hygeiaphrontic* expression into various
discomforts, pains, and other symptoms which are emotional, nonfunctional, and nonorganic. The presence of concurrent anxiety of course is
presumptive evidence as noted, that the hygeiaphrontic symptom lacks
defensive effectiveness. This is in accord with our *Incomplete Symptom-
Defense Concept* (p. 89, 189).

Today the early concept of superego (that is, conscience)-disapproved
sexual acts and punishment symbolically as an etiologic factor, while still
applicable, might be broadened considerably. One might also include the
translation of the intolerable feelings of various other types of emotional
conflict into hygeiaphrontic preoccupation and symptoms as a defense
against anxiety.

B. SUDDEN DISSOLUTION MOST HAZARDOUS.—This pattern in patients
with a hygeiaphrontic preoccupation could potentially arise as a consequence of almost any conflict-producing action, feeling, or thought. When
somatic and physiologic preoccupation is well established and marked,
subjective anxiety is often minimal.* In turn, were the sudden dissolution
of the hygeiaphrontic defenses possible, the result would be overwhelming
anxiety. Could one remove them suddenly, it would be too dangerous
to risk.

---

* The *Inverse Ratio of Symptom-Success* (in countering anxiety) *to one's Motivation toward Therapy* (pp. 9–10; 298; and Ch.12:VG), can well operate herein to
delay and to hamper therapy and its initiation.

These defensively intended symptoms serve a vital purpose. One must not suddenly remove the concern or take away the symptom. In most instances the patient would prevent this anyway, and it is hardly a feasible endeavor. His secondary defenses of his symptoms also contribute in this regard. There is a rare hazard in this regard via the route of hypnotic intervention. It is to be strongly interdicted.

C. PROSPECT OF ORGANIC DISEASE EASIER TO TOLERATE.—For many persons it is far easier to face the prospect of organic disease, as a more tangible problem, than it is to face the hidden, baffling, intangible, and often far more painful areas of emotional conflict. This is occasionally rather dramatically illustrated. It forms the basis of our concept of the Flight to the Physical [Ch.8:VA1]. Such was the case in the following instance in which the patient welcomed the discovery of diabetes. Compare and contrast the "encouragement" of hygeiaphrontic preoccupation in Case 87 [Ch.7:XIC3] of supposed thyroid deficiency. Herein the person concerned violently insisted on retaining a mistaken label of "thyroid deficiency".

Case 98

The Diagnosis of Diabetes Welcomed

(1) *Organic explanation sought*

A forty-one-year-old professional writer from a medical family sought psychoanalytic treatment because of serious areas of adjustment difficulty with her husband and children. There were also multiple somatic symptoms, including headaches, severe hypogastric pain, intermittent backaches, nervousness, insomnia, and poor digestion. Irritability and depression routinely accompanied her menstruation. All of these manifestations had increasingly interfered with her professional accomplishments. Her increasing focus of attention toward them and her overall level of somatic and physiologic preoccupation further underlined a diagnosis of Hygeiaphrontic Reaction.

Although the patient had voluntarily sought help and was sincere in her analytic work, the going was very difficult. Progress was greatly hampered by her protective avoidance of significant areas, and by considerable personal rigidity. She had earlier persistently hoped for and sought an organic explanation for her many troubles. Repeated medical studies had, however, been negative. The knowledge from her medical background was both a help and a hindrance.

(2) *Prospect of diabetes less painful than emotional conflicts*

One day during the course of her therapy, a routine periodic medical examination suggested the presence of incipient diabetes. Although she knew full well the grave implications of diabetes (a serious case of which she believed she had), she appeared relieved and was literally gleeful upon receipt of the news! This had provided for her a beautiful vehicle for an immediate and instant flight to the physical! It was clearly apparent to the author that the diabetes could not be, and was not responsible for her many symptoms. Nevertheless, the discovery of the diabetes at least temporarily provided her with something less painful and something less difficult with which to cope.

She clutched eagerly for such an explanation. Diabetes provided something more tangible to her than the repressed and painful emotional conflicts which were actually and primarily responsible for her troubles. This patient was able gradually and over a considerable period of time to make substantial improvement. She had surrendered the diabetic explanation only with great reluctance, as had happened with other possible (to her) medical avenues before and subsequently. Her defensive resistances, her Secondary Defenses, were substantial ones indeed.

4. Early Environmental Factors

The author has referred to the important roles of identification, parental attitudes, and conditioning in preparing the foundation for the later development of a particular type of neurotic reaction. In certain instances we can clearly trace the development of undue somatic preoccupation and concern to emotionally unhealthy parental influences. This is what we might expect, in accord with our *Concept of Interpersonal Perpetuation* [pp. 291, 323, and Ch.8:IIIB*1;* VID*3;* Ch.12:VA*3*]. In simplified and highly abbreviated form, this kind of sequence was discussed and illustrated by the development of a Fatigue State and Overconcern with Health in *Case 82*, p. 404. Parental overconcern with personal health and function is a strong factor in the development of similar attitudes in the child (*see also* p. 334). Klein once cited such a case also in which "there was no doubt that her [the mother's] attitude had contributed to his [the son's] hypochondriacal fears."

In this development, the mental mechanisms of Identification and Introjection play an important role. The formation of the superego (wherein resides the "internalized parent") is accompanied by the taking over by the child of many parental attitudes. Kanner regarded the "imitation of observed adult patterns" as a prominent source of hygeiaphrontic attitudes in children. He cited examples of the relationship between existing parental overconcern to the development of similar concerns by the child.

In certain instances it should be noted that pathologic overconcerns with the health and safety of a child, actually may represent a reaction formation against the unconscious hostile-aggressive impulses of the parent, and a denial of them. Herein lies a reinforcement to the repression of the consciously disowned attitudes.

A pathologic overconcern with health may also serve unwittingly as a means for the avoidance of disturbing and painful emotions or emotional problems. In some instances parents may have found it "easier and more comfortable" to focus their attention on the *physical* disorders of their child. This was in lieu of facing the real difficulties, the emotional problems that existed in the family. A large proportion of these are usually out of, or partially out of, awareness. Such a focus may seem to serve as an unconscious substitute for real love, affection, and acceptance, for the parent, or the child, or both. Providing the proper atmosphere for maturation, in accord with the *First Tenet of the Parental Role* (pp. 23, 309), will eliminate many bases for later neurotic evolvement.

5. Concept of Lowered-Perception Threshold Source

A. GREATLY LOWERED THRESHOLD.—A major reason for referring to this group of reactions as somatic and physiologic preoccupations lies in the fact that the symptoms are most often accompanied by little or no functional alteration. Perception has instead become intensified. Often the painful sensations thus actually really represent the intensification of one's perception, of what might be otherwise normal visceral or other types of sensations. Ordinarily these would pass unnoticed.

When there is present a neurotic overconcern with health, these otherwise normal and likely unperceived sensations tend to receive increased attention and significance. The threshold for sensation is greatly lowered, to the point of their perception, and even painful perception. This provides us with what can be a potentially important additional source for certain hygeiaphrontic symptoms. For purposes of identification we might term this the *Lowered-Perception-Threshold Source* for symptoms. It undoubtably can help us better understand something of the origins of some instances of otherwise obscure hygeiaphrontic symptomatology.

B. PAIN, AND ANXIETY ABOUT PAIN; POSSIBLE VICIOUS CIRCLE.—At times a distinction may be necessary between subjectively reported pain, and anxiety *about* the pain. The relation between anxiety and pain is such that there may be a tendency toward the establishment of an *Anxiety-Pain Vicious Circle,* through which each tends to increase the subjective apperception of the other. This relationship was earlier implied in our Concept of the Reciprocal Influences of Anxiety and Pain (*see* p. 123).

6. *Emotions and Physiology*

A. BEAUMONT AND ALEXIS ST. MARTIN.—Emotions have been long known to have important effects on physiology. In the case of the stomach, for instance, direct evidence of this has been in existence for more than one hundred and fifty years. In 1833 Beaumont published his classic observations, made over a period of time, of the traumatically exposed gastric mucosa of Alexis St. Martin (*see also* Chapter Fourteen).

These early studies of function helped to revolutionize physiology. They had been possible through an astute taking advantage of fortuitous circumstances. They helped to widen the existing horizons of medical thinking, and have served as an impetus for further research. It has required many years for their full significance and impact to be recognized.

B. CANNON'S CATS AND PAVLOV'S DOGS.—In the early twentieth century Cannon began his important work in physiology. He observed the influence of emotional states on the functions of the alimentary canal. When such influences were first observed, they were regarded as merely a nuisance and an interference, with what had begun as a pioneering study of gastric function and digestion in cats by X-ray. He quickly recognized their significance and, as can happen with the astute scientist, turned an initial handicap into a major contribution.

About the same time his friend Ivan P. Pavlov (1849–1936) was studying the effects of environmental influences, repeated stimuli, and conditioning, on gastric secretion in dogs. Carlson, among others, made some additional observations on stomach physiology. The continuing challenge is a great one for further research in emotions and physiology.

C. FUNCTIONAL CHANGE DIRECTLY PROPORTIONAL TO INTENSITY OF EMOTION.—Ripley has written a useful summary on the role of emotions in gastric function and noted some important implications as to the development of peptic ulcers. He wrote: "The degree of change in physiologic function has been found to be related to the intensity of emotion. Such emotions may be overtly expressed and consequently related to stressful life situations. However, in some persons they may not be evident . . . because of strong repressive forces . . . and defenses utilized to solve personal problems. It then becomes necessary to analyze and to bring to awareness unconscious mechanisms." In accord with the Perception-Intensification Concept, otherwise normal physiologic events can be perceived. This can even transpire to the point of subjective pain. It provides an additional potential source of importance for hygeiaphrontic manifestations.

C. HYGEIAPHRONTIC ENDOGAIN: THE UNCONSCIOUS PRIMARY "GAIN" OF SOMATIC AND PHYSIOLOGIC PREOCCUPATION

1. Bodily Expression of Underlying Conflicts

A. SYMBOLIC GRATIFICATION AND CONTROL.—As in our previous discussions, the author has found it convenient in teaching to regard the unconsciously sought aims, or "gains," of Hygeiaphrontis as being divided into ones which are primary and secondary. These are accordingly termed the hygeiaphrontic endogain and epigain (*see* Chapter Two, p. 55*ff*). As in the Conversion Reactions, the Depressive Reactions, and the Fatigue Reactions, this division has been made for purposes of convenience in study and teaching. It has been made on the basis of the "level" of unconsciousness (that is, relative inaccessibility to conscious awareness), and certain other important factors as outlined earlier.

The *primary gain* (that is, the endogain) of this reaction, with its characteristic regressive narcissistic preoccupation with health, includes the unconscious expression and the symbolic partial gratification of various disowned needs and drives. It also includes their symbolic inhibition, concealment, and denial. The somatic concerns are aimed at helping to reinforce repression of the disowned impulses, awareness of which would produce anxiety. Thereby we may think of hygeiaphrontic symptoms in condensed fashion as representing a substitutive expression of the various aspects of the unconscious emotional conflicts into bodily areas. The areas selected for hygeiaphrontic attention, concern, and discomfort are *not picked by chance*. These instances of *Bodily Expression* of elements of unconscious conflicts are selected unconsciously, with definite, although hidden, symbolic meanings. Such meanings may be most elusive even to expert study and observation.

B. SELF-PUNITIVE FACTORS; ATTENTION-ABSORPTION DEFENSE CONCEPT.
—There are major self-punitive factors present in the Hygeiaphrontic Reaction. These are secured unconsciously through the resulting pain, handicap loss, and suffering of the patient. Absorption of Attention is also an important factor. This is defensively *away* from painful and dangerous *emotional* areas, into the safer areas of somatic and physiologic preoccupation [Ch.8: *Case 89,* IIIA3; VB5]. The *Concept of Attention-Absorption* (and of Interest-Absorption) as a witting or unwitting defensive endeavor, has many applications in the neuroses and in psychiatry generally. It is analogous to the Concept of Preoccupation-Defense in the obsessive situation [pp. 311–313; *see also Case 90,* pp. 454–455].

The needs, wishes, and drives which are disowned are largely aggressive and hostile, or sexual in nature. As noted, the preoccupation with somatic matters unconsciously serves the important function of keeping the conscious attention directed selectively (and protectively) away from these dangerous areas, and/or from the conflicts over them. They are then less likely to come into conscious awareness. This redirection also absorbs and occupies energy and effort, which cannot then possibly be available for action in response to the discarded wishes. As part of our conceptions of resistance and Secondary Defense, energy is thus also less available, or unavailable, for constructive introspection and for analysis. These defensively-intended features help comprise and outline our important *Interest-Absorption Concept* (*see also* references to related Concept of Preoccupation Defense, pp. 311 and 398).

Hygeiaphrontic concerns are essentially a regressive phenomenon. The symptoms attempt an unconscious defense against the anxiety of threatened derepression or the loss of control, as noted earlier. This regression is toward a narcissistic and auto-erotic level of interest. With the onset of a Hygeiaphrontic Reaction there is a regressive retreat into the characteristic manifestations of this neurosis. The expression which takes place of elements of the underlying conflicts into bodily areas and concerns is part of the endogain.

2. *Suffering, Guilt, and Punishment. Episodic Hygeiaphrontis*

A. VIEWS OF SILVERBERG, WEIGERT, AND FENICHEL.—There are also important implications of Hygeiaphrontic Reactions as regards guilt and punishment. The hygeiaphrontic person suffers. This can often represent an unconscious variety of suffering in retribution for his consciously unacceptable sexual or aggressive wishes. It takes place in response to an archaic and punitive conscience, and/or as a reflection of an unduly low level of self esteem (*see also* Concept of Visceral-Masochism, as outlined later VIIA2).

Silverberg noted that hypochondriacal (hygeiaphrontic) fears may relate to anticipated punishment for oedipal wishes. Weigert, reviewing an early draft of this chapter, wrote that, "many hypochondriacal ideas have originated in the fantasied threats of the feared disastrous consequences of masturbation in childhood; variations of the theme of castration anxiety, damage to the genitalia, to the brain, any kind of threat to life and limb. The need for atoning punishment, combined with the hope for reconciliation with prohibitive authority, is a strong motivational factor in hypochondriacal symptoms. In psychosomatic and conversion hysterical symptomatology the need for punishment is acted out and discharged. In apprehensive preoccupation with health and hypochondriacal symptoms, the need for punishment remains in suspense and leads to increased alarm if the conflict cannot be elucidated."

Fenichel pointed out that "among the impulses that are withdrawn from object to organ representations in hypochondriasis, the hostile and sadistic impulses appear to play a particularly pronounced role. The original hostile attitude toward an external object is turned inward [inverted] against the ego, and hypochondriasis may serve as a gratification of guilt feelings."

B. POINTS IN ENDOGAIN ILLUSTRATED.—A number of the foregoing points about the hygeiaphrontic endogain are illustrated in the following case, and in the two subsequent cases. Also illustrated is the *Hygeiaphrontic Attack* or *Episodic Hygeiaphrontis,* which is somewhat analogous to the A.A.A. (p. 89*ff*), and the Phobic Attack (p. 90 and Ch. 10), and can even occur concurrently in the same clinical situation.

Case 99

Episodic Hygeiaphrontis

(1) *Multiple symptomatology*
A twenty-seven-year-old housewife sought treatment for recurring attacks of anxiety. These were accompanied by an intense preoccupation about, and the fear of, some serious bodily disorder or other. These fears were accompanied by shifting somatic complaints which occurred in the absence of organic pathology. Such attacks had occurred in episodic fashion for most of her life.

The earliest of these attacks which she could recall dated back to the age of five years when she had suffered a "heart attack." Later this kind of "attack" was repeated, and alternated on occasion with acute fears of poliomyelitis. Still more recently there were also other episodic attacks of cancerophobia accompanying her hygeiaphrontic complaints. Her emotional illness was an obsessional kind of a disorder in which the hygeiaphrontic preoccupations were the outstanding feature, and the diagnosis was made accordingly. The close relationships of the various groups of neurotic reactions is also illustrated in the concurrent presence of Acute Anxiety Attacks and the phobic manifestations.

(2) *Aggressive-hostile feelings, threatening*
In her childhood position in the family, this girl had assumed the role of the docile, compliant child to an unusual degree. This was in contrast to her older sister who was considered by the parents to be more attractive. The older sister was also an object of constant concern to the parents, both from the standpoint of illnesses and injuries, and because her defiant behavior led to many problems.

In the course of analytic work it became apparent that the hygeiaphrontic attacks occurred whenever strong destructive tendencies or aggressive-hostile feelings were being forced into awareness. Since her very character structure had been developed to ward off the recognition of such aspects of the self, any event of life that provoked such feelings came to be experienced as a dreaded threat.

(3) *Important needs and motives subserved*
The Hygeiaphrontic Attacks that followed, acted to turn the threatening feelings away from the outward object or person, and inward toward the self. This involved the operation of the unconscious intrapsychic mechanisms of Introjection and Inversion.

Punishment was meted out symbolically in a combined unconscious sadomasochistic operation. At the same time this reaction represented a regressive and narcissistic retreat into the self. Self-punishment was also present as an expression of guilt feelings, since it was the patient who suffered most. The attacks thus subserved a number of important inner needs and motives.

(4) *Results of therapy*
The results of therapeutic work in this case were very gratifying. Gradually it became possible for this young woman to turn her attention, even when the attacks occurred, externally from her symptoms and somatic fears, toward what she was really feeling at these times toward those close to her, and so as to be able to better observe what was actually transpiring in her interpersonal relationships.

Her self-understanding increased as she found that she more and more dared to allow herself awareness of her real feelings. As she became able to accept more and more the presence of negative and hostile feelings within herself, the episodic hygeiaphrontic preoccupations decreased substantially both in frequency and in severity.

3. Concluding Thoughts

A. FEELINGS TRANSLATED IN THEIR VERBAL EXPRESSION.—In an instance reported by a colleague, the phrase "I'm worried about myself" could have been almost directly translated to mean "I'm angry." At times subjective feelings as well as the outward expressions of hygeiaphrontic concern may represent this kind of an *unconscious translation into verbal expression of an otherwise unexpressed emotional feeling.*

The feeling itself does not have to be within the realm of conscious awareness for this to take place. Generally it is outside of conscious awareness. While this kind of translation of emotion is occasionally rather clearly demonstrated in Hygeiaphrontis, it is likely to be even more frequent and more readily encountered in cases of Depressive Reactions and of Emotional Fatigue.

B. CONFLICTS OVER AGGRESSION STRESSED.—Conflicts over repressed sexual impulses are, of course, prominent and operative in Hygeiaphrontis. Since more attention has been directed along this line in past research, the author has stressed herein the relatively neglected but similarly most vital conflicts over hostility and aggression.

C. DYNAMIC RELATION TO THE PHOBIA.—One might also mention the relationship of hygeiaphrontic concerns over health to the phobic reactions. This was illustrated in the preceding *Case 99.* Conflicts between prohibited sexual desires and self-preservative needs may find their expression in certain typical hygeiaphrontic syndromes and in pseudocyesis (that is, illusional pregnancy).

In syphilophobia the conflict between the prohibited wish, fear of consequences, and masochistic self-punishment is quite clear. In pseudopregnancy the wishful aspect prevails over the aspect of fear of punishment.

D. HYGEIAPHRONTIC EPIGAIN: THE UNCONSCIOUS SECONDARY "GAIN" OF SOMATIC AND PHYSIOLOGIC PREOCCUPATION

1. Favorable Modification of Interpersonal Environment

The hygeiaphrontic epigain is the unconscious secondary gain of somatic and physiologic preoccupation. It is a most important aspect of the illness. Much of what has been earlier outlined concerning the paradoxical concept of the so-called "gains" of emotional illness in Chapter Two (p. 55ff), is applicable here. The epigain refers largely to the effects upon other people which are unconsciously sought through the symptoms. These include: (1) the satisfaction of dependency needs; (2) the regressive return to a more passive, less mature level; (3) the avoidance of responsibility; (4) the seeking of attention, sympathy, concern, and pity; and (5) the escape from, or the amelioration of what has become to the patient an intolerable situation. The hygeiaphrontic person "seeks" the favorable modification of his environment — especially its interpersonal aspects — via these routes (*see also* Section VIII). This is the epigain of the reaction; the unconsciously sought secondary gain.

To have an effect upon other people around him, the hygeiaphrontic individual, together with them, must in various ways tend to complement each other's emotional needs. This is in line with our earlier (pp. 280, 348) Hand-in-Glove Concept in Relationships. Indeed, sometimes the needs are so mutually complementary that the other person or persons "deep down inside" do not really want the affected person to get well from his neurosis; to modify his neurotic patterns of reaction and behavior.

It is the presence and relative transparency of these secondary gains which has so often in the past aroused the anxiety or antagonism of some physicians in cases of Hygeiaphrontic Reactions. Thus, these gains may be almost painfully transparent to an observer. It can appear that they are sought in full conscious awareness. For some observers, accordingly, the consequence is to become irritated or resentful.

2. Love, Affection, and Acceptance Sought

Some of the epigain is unconsciously sought as a pathetic substitute for the love, attention, affection, and acceptance which are really desperately sought, and which were never forthcoming. It is important in view of the relative transparency of secondary gains in Hygeiaphrontis to differentiate this kind of neurotic reaction from malingering. More will be said about this later in the appropriate section (VIII).

Some of the various foregoing points in the pathogenesis of Hygeiaphrontic Reactions are illustrated in the following case.

Case 100

Somatic and Physiologic Preoccupation: Hygeiaphrontis

(1) *Increasing retreat into hygeiaphrontic concerns*
A single, thirty-five-year-old assistant editor for a publishing firm was referred for psychiatric evaluation and possible treatment. There were problems in her personal relationships, and she had exhibited a marked and increasing overconcern with health matters. History disclosed an increasing retreat into somatic preoccupation over the two preceding years. A person of considerable ability and initiative, she had worked her way originally from a clerical job to work of a professional level, which she had performed with great competence. There were multiple complaints present without organic findings. The diagnosis was made of a Hygeiaphrontic Reaction.

Treatment was clearly indicated, but this prospect was accepted by the patient only with considerable difficulty. There had been one early accusation by a physician of malingering, and this was implied again later during the course of her many visits to various physicians. These had hardly tended to promote increased trust or confidence in medical help. They had impeded and delayed her acceptance of the vitally needed psychotherapeutic study of her underlying areas of emotional conflict.

(2) *Significance of a broken relationship*
During the course of early analytic study an important situational initiating factor was discovered. This had been the breaking off of an eight-year love affair. The conclusion had finally become unavoidable in that there was no prospect of a satisfactory marriage. The patient had unduly concentrated her attention and interests in this one relationship.

Her father had died when she was twelve years old. Unconscious factors of seeking a replacement had entered into the unrealistic degree of dependence on the relationship, her defective judgments, and her resulting severe loss. Her response had been a regression and retreat into narcissistic concerns over health matters. The initiating loss and onset (but not the clinical features) were not unlike what we have observed in the Depressive Reactions [Ch.4,pp.135ff; see also Case 102, Sect. X]. During the course of a prolonged and difficult but successful analysis, the dynamics gradually became clear. The highlights of these, in highly summarized form, reveal some of the psychologic roots of her illness.

(3) *Endogain bases of illness*

The endogain of her illness related to the denial and control of her deeply repressed murderous rage toward the object of her disappointments. For several years this was her fiance. Important antecedents related to her father's death, which to her unconsciously had been a desertion. [*See* Antecedent Conflict Theory, Ch.8:VII.]

Part of the attempted defense against anxiety was in the channeling of her interest and attention away from conflicts relating to both rejected sexual impulses and activity, and her forbidden (unconscious) aggressive drives. Since these threatened to be overwhelming if admitted to conscious awareness, the somatic preoccupation was a desperate attempt to reinforce their repression from conscious awareness. At the same time, energy potentially available for carrying out prohibited activities was dissipated. Further, the incapacitation and suffering served to satisfy the demands of a harsh superego for punishment in both areas.

(4) *Interpersonal direction of epigain stressed*

Factors of hygeiphrontic epigain (the unconscious secondary gain) in this case largely related to the regressive retreat. This was toward a more dependent and child-like level of adjustment. She unconsciously sought and secured a less active and less responsible relative position with her family.

There were elements of attention-demanding and sympathy-seeking as a neurotically sought replacement for real love and affection. Her symptoms inevitably influenced the attitudes and responses of the people about her. This was not always favorable, in self-defeating fashion.

(5) *Symptom Barrage: When significant areas approached in therapy*

During the course of therapy several other fairly typical features were illustrated. There was ample evidence of unwitting contributions having been early made by her parents in the form of oversolicitude. This had often replaced a more genuine kind of affection and real acceptance. On a number of occasions when therapeutic study approached significant areas of rejected or disapproved drives, new symptoms developed temporarily. This was a less marked instance of what we have called the Symptom Barrage phenomenon [Ch.8:XIB3;Ch.12:VA2] in therapy. These episodes also illustrated the Hygeiaphrontic Attack.

Treatment results were very good in this case and were facilitated by the patient's intelligence, cooperation, and the early excellent rapport established with her therapist. It was fortunately possible to gradually counteract the earlier influences, which had been seriously inimical to even the initiation of intensive therapy.

3. *Important Dynamic Implications*

A. HYGEIAPHRONTIC MANIFESTATION ILLUSTRATES MAJOR PRINCIPLES.— Let us consider some of the dynamic implications of another most interesting instance of hygeiaphrontic overconcern. The following case illustrates a number of the important principles discussed. The successive strata of significance were in accord with our important and intriguing Concept of Defensive-Layering [Ch.8:VB4;IXB1]. The multiple determinants found also illustrate the principle of overdeterminism [Ch.12:VIIB;Ch.13:IIIC1].

Case 101

Some of the Important Dynamics Underlying a Disturbing Hygeia-phrontic Overconcern

(1) *Worry about breast cancer increases, and symptoms develop!*

A thirty-five-year-old housewife and former medical technologist who was in intensive psychotherapy noticed the presence of a lump on her left breast. There had been a history of breast cancer in the family. Over a period of several months she thought the lump had increased in size. Pain developed, subjectively. She had become terribly concerned about this, but *had not mentioned it at all in her therapy.*

Her fear of cancer had gradually progressed to the point where for her it had become an established certainty. Note, however, her seemingly paradoxical reaction of not reporting it to her physician-therapist, or seeking appropriate examination, opinion, advice, or treatment. She of course had all the necessary knowledge, medical background, and resources to do this most competently. Here an intelligent and well educated person was faced with what to her was the dread certainty of cancer, but could do nothing constructive about it.

(2) *Inconsistency supports Secondary Defense*

Eventually she was able to make some mention of this problem, when some tangential data led the author to suspect something of the sort might be operative. Gradually then we were able to work out many of the significant ramifications.

As noted, there was a seeming inconsistency in her intense fear and the failure to at least attempt its relief. This was not all purposeless, however. It was an important Secondary Defense of her symptom, that is, her concern, fear, and preoccupation.

(3) *Significant unconscious needs served by the hygeiaphrontic over-concern*

The powerful Secondary Defense indicates the presence and the importance of the underlying defensive purposes which the symptom endeavored to serve.

These purposes will not stand up to any critical or rational evaluation. They are psychologically uneconomic in their net result. Emotionally, however, they are most vital. In this particular instance they included at least seven major ones:

(a) *An escape.* This patient had consciously wished on a number of occasions to have a "broken leg," for the escape it would afford her into illness from her painful life situation. The cancer equated for her a "super broken leg," a superescape.

(b) *The Boy Scout motto: "Be Prepared."* She thus steels herself and prepares herself to accept and to cope with what to her was the ultimate: cancer. (This is closely related to the following.). The *Be Prepared Concept* of psychic defense is an interesting one which has relations to the defense of pessimism [Ch.5:VA5].

(c) *Super pessimism.* The defense of pessimism is widely used and widely recognized. Through it, one prepares for something likely worse than the possibilities might allow. Unpleasant surprise is guarded against.

One is thereby ready for the worst, and what finally results is likely to be a relief, instead. This patient's certainty of having cancer constituted in effect an instance of super pessimism (*See* Defense of Pessimism, p. 252).

(d) *A regressive retreat.* If her assumption is correct, it provides an acceptable excuse to avoid anything she henceforth wishes. She can drop any or all of her responsibilities and commitments. New ones can understandably be shunned. Why tackle something new or difficult in the face of cancer and an apparent and inevitable hopeless end to her life? *

---

* Note the sharp contrast in her outlook and philosophy here with another instance cited earlier (Section VA1), in which the physician concerned, following the onset of his cancer, followed his usual routines and actively developed a new hobby.

(e) *Absorption of interests.* Attention and interest can now be protectively absorbed in this all-engrossing preoccupation with illness. The *Attention Absorption Concept* was operative. There is far less chance of any conscious awareness on her part of even more threatening repressed and conflictual emotional material. It becomes in itself a further protection *of* her neurosis. This has important consequences as far as the therapy is concerned, as follows:

    (*i*) It constitutes an important and powerful resistance in therapy.

    (ii) Why bother working very much in therapy when her demise is in sight?

    (*iii*) The onset of cancer would likely effectively bring treatment to a close. This would be beyond her control; she would have no responsibility.

    (*iv*) All our therapeutic efforts could come to naught, a self-defeating consequence, which is also partly sought on an unconscious level.

(f) *Sado-masochism.* On a deeply unconscious level there are important self-punitive elements subserved. One can possibly visualize some of the disturbance of this unhappy woman who was convinced she had cancer and who could not do anything about it or even talk of it, at least for some time.

    Further, there was a simultaneous, concealed, sadistic punishment, which is symbolically achieved, of the internalized disappointing object (*See also* depression dynamisms, pp. 177 *ff*).

(g) *Symbolism.* The symbolism extends back to the Oral Phase. The "cancer" simultaneously represented both the internalized "good" and the internalized "bad" breasts as early fantasied unconsciously. Later conflicts have reactivated earlier, preexisting ones. The antecedent oral conflicts from early life are in effect recapitulated. The overconcern with cancer was the painful and disturbing consequence, for which there were some rather realistic bases of fact.

    The infantile ambivalance was still present. Great attention and concern — an equation sometimes for love — becomes devoted to something which is at the same time terribly worrisome and a threat to life. If this is correct, it is likely to be reflected in a certain apparently perverse kind of need to preserve the "cancer." This proved to be true.

This was, indeed, a far more involved kind of psychologic operation than it might have seemed at first to casual observation. We have seen some of its unconscious vital defensive purposes. It was very painful. It was psychologically uneconomic in its ultimate net result. Accordingly, it must have been of considerable importance, and it was.

Later (in Part III, Chapter Ten) we shall learn how the phobic patient unconsciously often seeks and finds the very object of his phobic fear and dread. This is somewhat analogous to the present patient's internal needs *for* her cancer which are reflected in her unconscious protection of "it" and in her relative lack of relief upon its dissipation.

(4) *Dissolution of symptom leaves patient bereft!*

Was this person relieved when she finally did learn that her apprehensions were unfounded? Actually not very much, as the following extracts from her later comments indicated. These also offer some interesting sidelights into an earlier similar parental pattern. She said:

". . . It was nice to have that settled. However, *I was almost more bereft than relieved,* which seems like an odd reaction to me. . . . [Hardly so from the dynamic standpoint: What is unconsciously dreaded is simultaneously sought and held to. When one loses something which is important for whatever reasons, one will feel bereaved.]

(5) *Principles of Interpersonal Perpetuation illustrated*

". . . It was extremely uncomfortable for weeks with this conviction. I can understand some of it now . . . I had the feeling that this was behaving something like mother used to. Was it the sort of path that she trod every once in a while? . . .

". . . She used to get very upset every now and then about something being wrong with her. The only difference was that she would talk about it constantly. The whole household would be thrown out of gear. She would manage to manipulate everyone around and change everything! I never do any of that; couldn't do like she did; hence I keep it all to myself . . . One other reason I guess that I kept it all to myself was that that was the only way I could keep it! I would lose the conviction and the stress, and all that it represented psychologically, if I didn't keep it all to myself. . . .".

B. OVERDETERMINISM AND CONVERGENCE PRODUCE THE SYMPTOM.—Illustrated also in the above case as noted was the important principle of overdetermination. Every symptom thus is determined by underlying factors. This is true as to its form, its extent, its locale, and its scope.

Symptoms, however, are not just determined; they are *overdetermined.* This is true also for dreams [Ch.3:IIIC*1*(12)]. Thus in the foregoing case we can observe some of the many major contributing forces which converged toward, and to produce the symptoms as analyzed. The hygeiaphrontic pain, concern, and preoccupation were not merely determined; they were overdetermined. The concepts of *Interpersonal Perpetuation* [Table 19; pp. 342 and 404] and *Defensive Layering* are among those important ones illustrated.

C. CONCEPT OF ACTUAL NEUROSES ABANDONED.—Earlier reference was made to Freud's concept of hypochondriasis (hygeiaphrontis), together with Neurasthenia and the Anxiety Neuroses as the three so called "actual neuroses." It might be noted in passing that this concept has received no further reference here, since it is now rarely used in the analytic literature. It has in effect been discarded.

The "actual neuroses" were represented in Freud's early theories as a group of neuroses which supposedly resulted from an accumulation of not-discharged libido. In the case of Hygeiaphrontis, according to these views, the libido which could not be discharged was narcissistically oriented. The concept of "actual neurosis" is no longer in use to define neurotic reactions and symptomatology, which were supposedly due to a disturbed sexual economy; a disturbance resulting from an "incomplete discharge." Present-day conceptions are concerned instead with conflict-neurosis, and our present text is so oriented.

E. IN CONCLUSION

In our study of the psychodynamics and the pathogenesis of the Hygeiaphrontic Reactions we have observed how somatic and physiologic over-concern represents one major pathway for and ultimate result of, the unhealthy and unconscious endeavors to handle anxiety. Hygeiaphrontic symptoms thus can provide a route for narcissistic regressive retreat. This pattern of neurotic reaction has its origins in early childhood and may be unwittingly fostered through the parent-child relationship.

By the focusing of one's attention instead upon hygeiaphrontic concerns, the real and possibly more painful ones are less apparent. Also less energy is available to act upon disapproved sexual or aggressive impulses. Primary and secondary gains (that is, the hygeiaphrontic endogain and epigain) are present, of which the latter may be all too painfully apparent to an external observer, albeit completely outside of the conscious awareness of the person concerned.

VII. THE THEORY OF ANTECEDENT CONFLICTS

A. ANTECEDENTS AND PRECEDENTS PLAY IMPORTANT ROLE

1. Patterns of Response Established; the Emotional Prototype
A number of references have already been made to this important theory
[pp. 29, 120, 161, 170, 339, 341, and *Case 70,* pp. 344–5], and we may
find it opportune at this juncture to offer some further thoughts. The
Theory of Antecedent Conflicts is one which has proved useful to the
author in seeking to understand and to teach the principles of the neuroses.
This theory seeks to point out and to stress that *the effect of an emotionally
disturbing event may be greatly increased as a consequence of the sensitization and conditioning effects of previous, earlier similar events, that is,
antecedent conflicts.* Such Antecedent Conflicts are inevitably present as
the result of the vicissitudes of early life. One would anticipate correctly
then that such conflicts may be uncovered during the therapy. Thus: (1)
the form and strength of an emotional conflict; (2) the character of one's
reaction to it; and (3) one's effectiveness in coping with it, are all influenced by the important emotional antecedents and the precedents which
have transpired.

*Early antecedent conflicts, conflictual situations, or relationships from
childhood therefore serve actually or symbolically as analogous prototypes.*
We might refer to these accordingly by the term of *emotional prototypes.*
As such, they can play hidden but most important roles subsequently.
Later traumatic events may serve to reactivate these partially dormant and
inactive emotional prototype conflicts.

In accord with the Theory of Antecedent Conflicts, at least theoretically,
*every emotional conflict has its earlier antecedent. The subsequent conflict
tends then to secure the repetition of an emotional pattern of response
which has already been established.* These principles as outlined have applicability in emotional illness generally, as well as in the Hygeiaphrontic
Reactions.

2. Oedipal and Oral Conflicts.
The earlier analysts and psychiatrists when considering psychodynamics
tended to trace the roots of emotional illness back to the era of the Oedipus
conflict and its vicissitudes. Many still do. Ernest Jones described the
discovery of the importance and the universality of the Oedipus situation
as Freud's greatest contribution. However, mostly through the later contributions of Klein and their impetus to many of us in our further development of analytic theory, a fair number of psychiatrists have come to regard
the significant frontier of antecedent conflict as lying further back, within
the conflicts of the Oral Period. This has proved a useful extension of
theory.

For most present practical purposes, regarding the origins of antecedent
conflict within the Oral Period is entirely correct and sufficient. In accordance, the earliest antecedent conditioning events in Hygeiaphrontis, at
least theoretically, often can be traced to the special interpersonal events

of this vital developmental era of the child. The deepest roots may be conveniently regarded as resting in the frustrations of the Oral Period.

Introjection of the disappointing and frustrating aspect of the mother (the "bad," that is, frustrating, breast) takes place unconsciously in response to the resulting massive and primitive conflicts in infancy. The result is the prototype for a later, inverted, sadistic kind of operation. The author refers to the visceral punishment of the now inverted frustrating object. This can now take place in a "safer" fashion, which obviates the dreaded danger of possible retaliation. It now becomes expressed outwardly in the form of a disguised (but also simultaneously genuine) masochistic self-punishment. The relationship of this formulation to that earlier advanced for depression is to be noted [pp. 169–178].

This is an important conception in dynamics. In Hygeiaphrontis we might accordingly refer to this as visceral-masochism [Sect.VIC2]. As such it comprises one important segment of the underlying psychodynamics of the symptomotology.

3. Melanie Klein's Contributions

A. ANXIETY OVER RETALIATORY ATTACKS.—Klein advanced an hypothesis as to the basis of hypochondriasis (Hygeiaphrontis) in *The Psycho-Analysis of Children.* This concerned the anxiety relating to feared (through infantile fantasy) retaliatory attacks by internalized objects. Later she wrote: "the pains and other manifestations which in phantasy result from the attacks of persecuting objects within against the ego are typically paranoid." The relation to depression was also noted, in that "the symptoms which derive, on the other hand, from the attacks of bad internal objects and the id against good ones, *i.e.,* an internal warfare in which *the ego is identified with the sufferings of the good objects,* are typically depressive."

Projection of infantile fantasies of a destructive nature takes place toward the (real or imagined; usually an admixture of both) "bad" breast as the object of frustration. Thus "we find that the hated breast has acquired the oral-destructive qualities of the infant's own impulses when he is in states of frustration and hatred."

B. THE SOTERAL REACTION.—In addition to the concept of the "bad" breast is its important converse. This would comprise our conception of the idealized, all-providing, and all-gratifying "good" breast. One very important application concerns the dynamics of the *Soteria.* Thus, unconscious displacement of the actual or fantasied views of the latter to external objects or symbols, is responsible for the development of the Soterial Reaction, which we shall shortly study further [Ch.11:VIA].

The earliest infantile fantasies, long since lost to conscious awareness through repressions, are vital to our understanding of the Theory of Antecedent Conflicts. They are also vital to our knowledge and understanding of the earliest foundations: (*a*) for later emotional health or illness, and (*b*) for the individual capacities to tolerate stress, that is, the Total Reaction to Crisis or T.R.C., and the Total Reaction to Trauma or T.R.T.

Klein wrote further that "to a little child, his mother's body is the first representative of the outside world." Here begins the whole most vital chronology of interpersonal relations. Klein explored further areas and unlocked deeper ramifications of previously existing psychoanalytic theory.*

B. THE EARLIEST ANTECEDENT

1. Psychic Trauma During Birth?

So far all of this is quite in accord with our Theory of the Antecedent Conflict. However, if there is always, at least theoretically, an earlier and antecedent conflict, where does this then take us? Tracing the antecedent conflict back to the oral period, as noted, very likely for the present at least, quite satisfies our practical needs. This already takes us back toward, if not into the early months of life. One may ask where further can one go? Otto Rank, and later Freud also, were impressed with the process of birth as being an important primal source of psychic trauma [p. 28].

This has not seemed to be very important to the author. This is largely on the basis of such factors, for example, as (1) a lack of any clearly established correlation between the relative difficulty of labor and any subsequent effects upon, or the general level of emotional health; (2) the lack of any convincing proof of the presence of any lasting traumatic emotional sequelae from the circumstances surrounding birth; (3) the lack of significant later emotional differences in babies with cesarean births, as distinguished from other births; and finally (4) the relative protection by nature of the infant at birth.

There is often a type of fetal flaccidity to be observed, accompanied by a relative insensitivity to stimuli, and diminished perceptivity. These can be readily perceived in the delivery room. In effect, they constitute a considerable degree of what has seemed to the author to be a very protective kind of unconsciousness. There is thus a considerable degree of dissociation from the infant's potential conscious awareness, of the potentially traumatic process. Accordingly, one may doubt that the so-called trauma of birth could often play a significant role in emotional health, or in the concept of antecedent conflict.

2. The Ultimate Extension

Where does the Theory of Antecedent Conflict ultimately extend? According to the author's present view, applications of our Concept of Antecedent Conflicts would gradually fade into the origins of individual perception. The limits of perception of the developing fetus are set by the prerequisite developmental organization of the nervous system at about three or four months. Early perception is not highly differentiated and is probably limited to a general kind of comfort versus discomfort. From these simplest kinds of awareness there is a gradual evolution and development

---

* Klein's directing the author's attention to certain of these important aspects of her work, in connection with an early draft of this chapter, is gratefully acknowledged.

of more complex perceptive abilities and responses. We can at times observe intrauterine movements, which may correspond to emotional or physical stimuli, or both, of the mother. Thus the early beliefs as to the importance of the so-called "maternal impressions" are not entirely unfounded, although considerably different both in degree and in specificity than earlier superstition would have had it.

The earliest interpersonal reactions are an extension of intrauterine warmth and comfort versus discomfort, but with certain added important possibilities. These are first potentially present in the oral stage beginning immediately following birth. Denial, frustration, dependency, and withholding all enter as possibilities. The vicissitudes and the interpersonal events of the oral phase will depend on the development of the primal infantile patterns of response and conflict.

3. Vicissitudes of Earliest Interpersonal Events Important

A. ANTECEDENTS FOR EMOTIONAL PATTERNS.—Thus the primal pattern may be established in this early era, for example, for the later development of preoccupation with health as the individually specific neurotic reaction. Herein, as noted, there is a transformation of infantile anxiety about retaliation and physical injury (via introjection and inversion) into hygeiaphrontic overconcern.

In the evolving development of the personality such a primal capacity is created through this "earliest" antecedent conflict, for the later similar transformation of emotional conflict [*See also* p. 341].

B. PRIMAL THREAT EVOLVES INTO HYGEIAPHRONTIC MANIFESTATIONS.— The link to the original actual, or much more often fantasied, threat of punishment or retaliation has early been totally lost. This was the *primal threat*. For example, by gradual and complex transition, "Father may punish me or injure me" may become first "I may be injured, or made sick, or ill."

The next progressive and possibly final step may then become "I fear I *am* sick or ill. These pains trouble and worry me. I am ill or function poorly. I have emotional, mental, or physical limitations. I am poorly developed or physically deficient." Thus the original primal threat evolves gradually and becomes translated in its subsequent manifestations into visceral anxiety, pain, and somatic complaints. *Visceral-Masochism* may contribute.

Heimann aptly wrote: "The behavior of the adult hypochondriacal (hygeiaphrontic) patient suggests a type of narcissism in which the internal object, represented by the particular part of his body about which he is most concerned, is preferred to external objects, and is in so far loved; but since this internal object is felt to be injured and therefore not gratifying, it is also hated and feared, so that on this account again it requires attention and must be watched carefully and with suspicion all the time."

The Theory of Antecedent Conflicts has many applications, both theoretical and practical. Resulting studies and potential also give us added encouragement and hope in psychotherapy. Among the tie-ins with therapy, one important one relates to the *Tracing Technique,* cited earlier [p. 366]. This technique was named so as to invite further attention to the strategum and value of tracing an emotional manifestation or pattern of reaction backward in time to its first appearance. While not a facile or quick endeavor, with the hygeiaphrontic manifestations, as with other neurotic features, it can eventually pay substantial dividends.

VIII. MALINGERING

A. MALINGERING DISTINGUISHED FROM EPIGAIN

1. Deliberate Simulation Versus Unconscious Utilization

Malingering is *the deliberate and conscious simulation of illness, for whatever purpose.* Attempts at malingering are undertaken *in full conscious awareness,* in order to secure for the person concerned what appears to him to be an advantage to be gained from the presence of an illness. There is a considerable difference between malingering on the one hand, and hygeiaphrontic epigain (that is, the unconscious part of the possible secondary gain of hygeiaphrontis) on the other hand. There is also a distinction to be drawn between malingering as illness simulation, and any of the more conscious efforts to secure secondary gains from an established emotional or physical illness.

The *hygeiaphrontic epigain* is externally directed, so as to seek or to secure favorable modification of the external environment or situation [Ch.8:VID]. These are secured, or attempted, in particular through possible influences on the attitude, the responses, and the behavior of significant people. They are unconsciously directed, principally in the service of deeply repressed dependency needs. The *secondary gain* is a broader and more inclusive concept which may also include any consciously or partly consciously secured "gain" of an illness in addition to the epigain, as the unconsciously secured gain of an illness. The important distinction lies between deliberate simulation on the one hand, and the unconscious utilization of established symptoms on the other.

2. Mechanisms of Epigain Unconscious

These distinctions between malingering and secondary gain are clearcut. Still, they are not always easy to make. The occasional individual who attempts to malinger for whatever reason, is hardly likely to advertise the fact! The physician may also have difficulty in distinguishing the existence of epigain as an unconscious phenomenon. Herein the needs and the endeavor to secure their gratification are unconscious. Yet it may appear upon occasion that the patient cannot help being fully aware of these.

It may even occasionally seem that his apparent bland ignoring or denial of such blatantly sought goals is almost a calculated affront to the intelligence of the observer. It is because of instances such as this that the term "hypochondria" has often acquired an unfortunately accusatory and derogatory connotation. Its having gained such an unfortunate, even occasional position as a term of opprobrium would provide us with another cogent reason for its discard and replacement in scientific medical circles.

The real mechanisms underlying true hygeiaphrontic epigain are not available to conscious awareness. They do not result from conscious planning and scheming. Indeed, and in accord with the *Theory of Transparency* [p. 171], the real underlying meaning of an emotional symptom *must* remain obscure in order for the symptom to survive. While the doctor or others, sometimes may clearly see the gain and the intent as well, the patient remains consciously blind to this. He will of course at times vigorously and with some justification angrily deny an accusation as to his consciously attempting the secondary goals, which are sometimes so obvious to others.

When there is conscious planning and simulation present, the patient is malingering. He is not suffering from the type of neurotic reaction marked by hypochondriacal concerns.

3. True Malingering Rare

It might be well to point out that true malingering is rare.* Certain cases of Somatic Conversion (hysteria), Physiologic Conversion, various emotionally-based functional disturbances, and hygeiaphrontic concerns are the emotional syndromes which are most often likely to be inaccurately regarded as malingering. These are more of a problem in the differential diagnosis of malingering than symptoms of organic disease are likely to be.

In the foregoing emotional reactions, an accusation of malingering, or even regarding a situation in this light silently, may result in a grievous medical error being committed. [*see Case 100,* Sect. VI *D 2*]. Such an error destroys rapport and confidence. It may long delay or even end, the potential help available via constructive psychotherapy.

B. CLINICAL RELATIONSHIPS; DISTINGUISHING FEATURES

1. Use of Placebos

It is pointed out that a favorable response to a placebo by no means necessarily proves the existence of malingering or simulation. Improvement in response to a placebo may tend even to disprove malingering. For example, certain patients with Conversion Reactions or personality patterns are commonly rather suggestible, may get a "good" response to the suggestive effect of a placebo. This also applies with many of the emotional illnesses which would fall into the groups listed above as problems in differential diagnosis.

In general, the use of placebos with their implications of distrust and deception of the patient is to be deplored. Their use does not reflect a good doctor-patient relationship, nor is this practice likely to promote one.

---

* Trawick and Bate agree. They wrote: "Malingering or conscious utilization of a neurosis as an escape mechanism is a very infrequent pattern."

2. Two Possible Pitfalls in Certain Cases of Neuroses-Following-Trauma

In the traumatic occupational (compensation) kind of neuroses a false evaluation of malingering may also be made. This happens not infrequently. There is also, however, still another important kind of trap for the physician in certain of these situations. We shall see this illustrated further when these reactions are considered later [Ch.14:VIIIC2]. I refer here to the physician being occasionally "taken in" by the patient's consciously honest but totally inaccurate estimation of the cause of his illness. In certain instances, for example, the patient falsely believes his actually neurotic symptoms originate as a consequence of a traumatic event. When the physician is ensnared here also, he than comes to regard the initiating trauma, as does the patient, as the sole basis for all symptoms.

This is potentially a great injury to the patient and to therapy, based as it often is upon sincere conviction, protectiveness, and perhaps identification. The damaging result is that it affords external objective support to the patient's unconscious seeking for secondary gain. It encourages, promotes, and provides professional backing for his regressive helplessness, his dependency-seeking, and his unconscious need for compensation. Any possible existing, even mild interest by a patient in securing psychotherapeutic assistance in these situations is most unlikely to survive if the physician unwittingly sides with and supports the neurotic dependency striving which is largely responsible for the perpetuation of the illness.

3. Malingering an Indication of Illness

To be led into undertaking such a deceptive and dishonest course as actual malingering, a person must have desperate internal needs, a great lack of self-respect, and an immature and maladjusted personality. Malingering in itself thereby becomes an evidence of serious emotional defect. Unfortunately, the very nature of the emotional problems of the malingerer makes it unlikely that much interest can ever be secured from him in any real collaborative effort at constructive introspective study.

Some mention should be made of the presence of both malingering and hygeiaphrontic features in some patients. Ripley wrote: "It has not been uncommon in my experience to find a superimposed malingering which may even be used by the patient in a desperate attempt to prove to the physician that there is [physical] illness [present]. This may occur when [the actually very] troubling psychopathologic manifestations are not given proper consideration by the physician."

The relative degree of conscious and unconscious factors may need to be distinguished. However, as Masserman commented, "too much time and energy should not be wasted in hair-splitting as to which symptoms are 'consciously' determined and therefore classifiable as 'malingering', and those which are 'unconsciously' determined and thereby 'neurotic'." This is particularly true from the standpoint of treatment in most cases of neuroses.

There is little justification, either, for spending much time or effort in a differentiation when the purpose is basically one of moral judgment. The practical value of making this determination lies primarily instead in an early assessment of the suitability for possible treatment. Unconscious mechanisms indicate a neurosis, with a good treatment potential; conscious simulation primarily indicates character and behavior disorders, usually with a poor treatment potential. In military service, the distinction may also be important as to the disposition of the case.

IX. THE CONCEPTION OF PRIMITIVE VERSUS MORE HIGHLY DEVELOPED PSYCHOLOGIC DEFENSES

A. LEVEL OF OPERATIONS CONCEPT

1. Intrapsychic Mental Mechanisms

This conception has been referred to in the earlier edition of this text and in the "blue book" of *Mental Mechanisms* [Butterworths, Washington, 1963]. The distinction has also been noted [p. 148] which is sometimes possible to make as to their emotional *level,* between certain of the intrapsychic mechanisms of defense.

Thus certain mental mechanisms may be regarded as being more, or less primitive; or as being on a higher, or lower level; or as being more, or less advanced or developed. It is possible to apply these principles to the broader clinical field of emotional illnesses generally.

2. Neurotic Patterns of Reaction

Certain neurotic reactions may likewise be regarded as more primitive, such as the massive types of Dissociative Reactions. Others are more advanced, complex, developed, and elaborated, such as the Obsessive Reactions.

If one attempts the somewhat arbitrary categorization necessary, the neurotic reactions of Somatic Conversion (hysteria), the Dissociative Reactions, the Phobic Reactions, and the Soterial Reactions might be considered to be more primitive and of a lower order. As with a more primitive order of emotional reaction, the repression has been automatic and massive. Anxiety as such may scarcely be experienced.

The Depressive Reactions, the Fatigue Reactions, the Character Reactions, Overconcern-with-Health, and the Obsessive-Compulsive Reactions would accordingly be regarded as less primitive, and of a more highly developed order. Thus Hygeiaphrontis would be more likely classed as a higher order illness. With the characteristic obsessive preoccupation with health, it is more closely related to Obsessive Neurosis, and its consideration at this later juncture of our study is appropriate. Cases of Anxiety Neurosis might perhaps fall somewhere in between these two general groups, but closer to the more advanced group. Some instances of Physiologic Conversion and the Neuroses Following Trauma may fall into either group. *Parts II* and *III* in this text have been grouped accordingly. We shall shortly proceed to *Part III.*

B. GRADATION OF DEFENSES IN PSYCHOSES AND MATURATION

1. Defenses Change During Both Onset and Lifting of Psychotic Reactions

Clinical instances are sometimes observed in which there is a progressive breaking down of defenses, in gradation from a higher to a lower order. One such instance recently reported to the author showed rather clearly such a progressive breaking down under great increments of emotional stress. This is in accord with our Concept of Defensive-Layering [Ch.8: VB4; VD3].

The first step was the collapse of existing rather well-established obsessive defenses. This was followed by the unconscious elaboration of very severe and limiting phobic defenses. Next the phobic defenses broke down, with the onset of an acute episode of Schizophrenia.

When the defenses collapse, however, such a clear-cut progression of events is not common. The onset of psychic disorganization is more likely to occur also, whenever the onset of a psychotic reaction is at all acute and rapid. When a psychotic reaction lifts, the pre-existing pattern of defenses is nearly always reinstated to some degree. This is true in reference to single dynamisms or combinations, character defenses, and to neurotic symptom defenses.

2. Progression of Defenses in Maturation

A progression of defenses from the lower order type into higher order ones can at times be observed. The evolution is often quite subtle through the processes of maturation and emotional-psychologic development. Such a sequence follows in character formation. Obsessive character defenses (and depressive ones) are likely to be found in slowly increasing incidence as age advances.

According to Klein, "the early infantile anxieties are psychotic in nature and [form] the basis of later psychoses." There is considerable clinical support for her observations. According to these findings, these early infantile anxieties are always present, albeit deeply unconscious. Normally, successful integration has been achieved by the developing cgo. Given sufficient basis, however, (that is, early predisposing infantile foundation, plus sufficient later adult stress), a psychosis may result. Psychotic defenses thus perhaps well might be regarded as still more primitive in level. They would accordingly come to constitute a still lower order of emotional illness.

X. HYGEIAPHRONTIS AND DEPRESSION

A. HYGEIAPHRONTIC CONFLICTS EXPRESSED ON VISCERAL PLANE

Depressive Reactions and Hygeiaphrontic Reactions have some important points in common. Sometimes instances are to be observed in which the close relation of the psychodynamics becomes more evident. In the cases of Hygeiaphrontic Reaction one generally does not have the same verbal self-reproaches of an emotional and psychologic nature, nor is there the presence of the frozen inhibition as seen in the depressed patient. Instead, the self-reproaches and the sadomasochistic operation unconsciously become transmuted or translated into intrapsychic operations which are on an *internal visceral plane*. Conflicts accordingly are sometimes spoken of as being expressed on the plane of one's body-image. In Hygeiaphrontis the verbal expressions are of a different character than the frequent self-reproaches of depression. However, the patient is likely quite verbal in his complaints of hygeiaphrontic pain and symptoms.

In both Depression and Hygeiaphrontis there is a withdrawal of interests. This is likely to appear much more marked in Depression. The increased middle age incidence [p. 149] is not so prominent in Hygeiaphrontis. The Passing-the-Peak contributions [pp. 158, 281] and the S.E.H.A. [pp. 38, 158] are variable but likely less prominent. The Hygeiaphrontic Reaction does not reflect a Frozen State of Rage [p. 175], as can depression. In Hygeiaphrontis the narcissism is more evident in the obsessive kind of preoccupation which occurs. Both are regressive. However, Dawn-Insomnia [pp. 142, 156], and the Morning Ebb-Tide of Spirits [pp. 145, 406], are not present in Hygeiaphrontis, nor does the principle of recurrence [pp. 146, 164, and *Case 58,* pp. 275–7] carry the same weight. Likewise absent are the Dress-Indicators of depression [p. 156].

"Cold Depression" [p. 155] is not found, and the Concept of Diffuse Retardation [p. 157] does not hold in Hygeiaphrontis. It should of course be borne in mind that these more or less characteristic findings in depression may become only apparent in the fairly severe and clinically marked reaction.

B. EQUIVALENT OF DEPRESSION

Hygeiaphrontic concerns frequently also accompany the Depressive Reactions. They may vary from relatively mild in degree, onward to the deep somatic delusions which are seen in certain very severe depressive reactions of psychotic depth. In certain instances the onset of hygeiaphrontic interests following a serious loss may appear to serve dynamically as an *equivalent of depression*. [*See* earlier references to the Concept of Depressive Equivalents pp. 143–4, 155, 158, 191]. Herein the somatic preoccupation appears to serve rather comparable dynamic functions to those earlier outlined in our discussion of the dynamics of depression [pp. 169*ff*]. One might also prefer to regard these as psychologic defenses which have been elaborated as a guard against the onset of depression itself [*see also* reference on p. 143 to the Physical-Equivalents of Emotional Depression].

In the following case the fairly acute onset of hygeiaphrontic preoccupation followed the sudden death of the patient's husband. This was the kind of a situation in which the onset of a depression might well have been expected should some kind of emotional illness ensue.

Case 102

Overconcern with Health Occurs Where a Depression Might Have Been Expected

(1) Sudden loss of dependent position

A sixty-eight-year-old widow sought medical attention for a number of complaints. These included visual disturbances, weakness, poor concentration, failing memory, insomnia, and various aches and pains. She had been a good driver for many years but now no longer felt capable of driving. She walked with difficulty and sought an arm to lean upon whenever possible. Actually her muscle tonus and strength were good. When she was inadvertently observed, or when her conscious attention was distracted, her infirmities would tend to fall away. At these times her strength and faculties were good, and she would function at the level of a person about ten years younger. At other times she tended to appear and to behave instead as if she were seventy-eight, or even older! Careful medical studies had been essentially negative.

The history disclosed a great increase in symptoms (and in her attention to them) following the unexpected death of her husband some three months earlier. During at least fifteen years previously she had become increasingly dependent upon him. Many of her responsibilities, including even household ones, had been gradually shifted over to him. His death constituted the sudden removal of an important kind of emotional and supportive crutch.

There were strong ambivalent feelings, however, toward this object of her dependence. The hostile side of these had been deeply repressed from all conscious awareness. These aspects of her feelings had been inverted, as in depression, but instead into somatic areas of concern and preoccupation. (One might compare here the dynamics as outlined in several of our illustrative cases in the earlier chapter on Depression.

(2) Symptom's function summarized

The focus of attention in unhealthy but protective and diversionary introspective fashion aided in the concealment and denial of her disowned hostile feelings toward the lost object. Her "seeking an arm to lean on" was a direct expression of her inner need to lean emotionally.

Suffering and limitations in living were present. These served simultaneously to gratify unconscious feelings of guilt, and to provide an outward kind of dependency appeal for sympathy, pity, concern, and forgiveness. These were sought as external replacements for the lost object of dependency.

(3) Adequate management aids gradual improvement

Judicious medical handling was conducted in a kindly but matter-of-fact way. In addition, there was a high degree of intuitive understanding and limited, clearly temporary support provided by several family members. These together contributed greatly to the gradual improvement which took place.

The patient was slowly able to surrender the major part of the hygeiaphrontic preoccupation which had developed. The danger of chronic invalidism was averted. This lady was gradually able to resume more healthy interest and responsibilities, including even some of those which had been earlier handed over to her husband.

XI. TREATMENT

A. ATTITUDE OF PHYSICIAN CRUCIAL

1. Need for Wisdom and Perception

A. PERSUASION AND REASSURANCE POOR.—The problems which are likely to be encountered in the medical management of the patient unduly concerned with health relate, first, to the recognition of the emotional basis of the difficulties, second, to problems of referral, and third, to conducting the definitive psychotherapy which is necessary. Skill in these areas depends upon the attitudes which the individual physician has developed toward these types of emotional problems, together with his wisdom and experience. These are reflected in every contact which he has with the patient. He needs to be wise, understanding, perceptive, and patient. His role needs to be one of active collaboration with his patient-colleague, in accord with our earlier stated Joint-Endeavor Principle [p. 130].*

Patients, of course, cannot be talked out of their anxiety and concerns. In accord with our Concept of the Therapeutic Bargain [p. 300], he must ultimately be able to "trade in" his symptoms for something better. They may respond only temporarily, if at all, to reassurance. Attempts at persuasion, or the seemingly rational approach of offering opinion and medical proof, will often prove frustratingly futile. These approaches may well have quite an adverse effect. Referral may be delayed, self-esteem lowered, antagonism aroused, and prospects for treatment aborted.

B. EMOTIONAL SUFFERING MORE SEVERE.—As noted earlier, patients who manifest Hygeiaphrontis are sometimes erroneously regarded as malingerers. Family, friends, the public, and physicians too, have been known to speak of them disrespectfully, as though they were somehow knowingly and deliberately responsible for their symptoms and for their hygeiaphrontic preoccupation with health. It is, of course, correct that the true hygeiaphrontic patient is characteristically possessed of little or no organic pathology. However, the symptoms, the discomforts which he experiences and describes, and the patient's concern and discomfort are very real matters to him. Indeed, these psychogenic complaints may well be more real, more disabling, and more disturbing to the patient than an organic disorder would be.

Pain and suffering of an emotional origin are not less severe because of this. Instead, they are likely to be more so. An emotional etiology is less tangible and more difficult to understand. It is more difficult to cope with from the standpoint of the patient and thereby is more troubling and often more frightening to him. It is nearly always a more difficult problem for the physician to deal with. Its treatment is usually more complex, more difficult, and the outcome more problematic than with a case which has an organic basis alone.

2. The "Proper Therapeutic Attitude"; Approach of Speculative Inquiry

A. DISSIPATE FRUSTRATION, HELPLESSNESS, AND PREJUDICE.—The physician should constantly ask himself speculative questions as to possible hidden sources of anxiety and the defensive purposes of the symptoms. What are the underlying desperate psychologic needs which enter into the state of preoccupation with one's health? Although this may not help much in a reliable solution of the psychopathology, such a dynamically oriented

---

* See also Team-Work Tenet in Psychotherapy, [p. 362].

approach can help to dissipate the frustration and the helplessness of the physician. It is eminently more constructive in so far as the patient is concerned. These remarks help outline farther the Proper Therapeutic Attitude, as referred to earlier [p. 367].

When the physician has some recognition of the hidden emotional origins of hygeiaphrontic symptoms, it is hardly possible for him to retain much prejudice. He can hardly view hygeiaphrontic illness as malingering. Indeed, with this kind of attitude and orientation he will be far more free of any prejudice towards emotional illnesses generally. This is a very important step towards increased ability and competence in their medical management. Likewise, in line with the Symptom-Survival Principle [p. 27 and *Case 65,* pp. 324–6], the emotional symptom cannot survive its thorough elucidation.

B. UNFORTUNATE CONNOTATION OF "HYPOCHONDRIAC."—The physician may of course find it difficult to maintain an objective, patient, and unbiased view in the presence of persistent hygeiaphrontic preoccupation. Another disturbing element to him can be the accompanying urgent dependency demands of the patient. These, in addition to his relative professional helplessness, and the related, sometimes rather apparent factors of secondary gain, have contributed to the term "hypochondriac" having sometimes acquired the unfortunate connotation of opprobrium, scorn, or castigation. This becomes a pitfall to giving any real help to the victim of hygeiaphrontic preoccupation. It should be avoided.

As noted, the physician might well repeatedly ask himself such questions as: "What purpose do these complaints serve?" "Why must the patient invest so much effort in such a nonconstructive direction?" "What might be some possibilities as to the real source of his anxieties?" "What are his underlying needs?". Such speculative and silently posed questions to himself can be most helpful in his understanding, management, and therapy of many cases of emotional illness.

3. Indications for Psychiatric Evaluation and Treatment

Adequate medical handling of the hygeiaphrontic patient is a therapeutic challenge. Only the occasional patient who is not very sick emotionally will respond to simple reassurance, and will not require psychiatric evaluation and treatment. Psychiatric consultation is indicated at least to estimate the potential benefits of psychotherapy as outlined in *Table 25.*

Table 25

Indications for Psychiatric Consultation and Therapy in Hygeiaphrontis

1. When the degree of hygeiaphrontic preoccupation is moderate or severe.
2. When the discrepancy between the level of concern and any possible organic basis is clearly apparent to the physician, or is considerable (The Hygeiaphrontic Discrepancy Principle).
3. When the degree of somatic preoccupation appears to be progressive.
4. When the hygeiaphrontic trends are suspected of initiating or accompanying a more malignant psychiatric disorder, or when hygeiaphrontis as a psychologic defense appears to be breaking down.

5. In all those cases in which the hygeiaphrontic preoccupation is constrictive, interferes with efficiency, or prevents the securing of reasonable satisfactions in living.
6. Early therapy is important whenever feasible. In accord with the Principle of Symptom-Longevity [p. 48], the longer the hygeiaphrontic symptom persists, the more difficult its therapeutic resolution is likely to be.

B. INTENSIVE PSYCHOTHERAPY AND ANALYSIS

1. Mutual Confidence and Trust Required

A. CONCEPT OF SYMPTOM DEVELOPMENT AS IMPLIED PREFERENCE.—Intensive psychotherapy in competent hands is the treatment of choice. It must be investigative and insight-seeking. The symptoms and the intrapsychic need for them should be thoroughly analyzed for definitive emotional benefits to accrue. The Treatment Rule [p. 50], requiring the uncensored production of thoughts, can be highly useful in eliciting meaningful data.

It is by no means easy to secure genuine constructive change, especially when this mechanism of neurotic defense is well established. [*See* Principle of Symptom-Longevity, Ch.14:VIIIE*3*]. If it is serving as an effective kind of psychologic defensive purpose, patients will not surrender such defenses easily, at least not until other more healthful patterns appear clearly advantageous. Again in line with our Concept of the Therapeutic Bargain [Ch.12:VIIIC*1*], something superior in the way of a consequence, or solution must be offered or be made available, in exchange for the hygeiaphrontic manifestation.

The very development of hygeiaphrontic symptoms in the first place is in accord with a concept which would regard them as "an implied statement of preference", albeit unconscious, by the patient. In other words, troubling and "painful" physical complaints are preferable, in contrast to an even more troubling and emotionally painful awareness of underlying painful emotional conflicts. Recognition of this helps us understand some of the severe difficulties which are inherent in the management and treatment of these individuals. This is the *Concept of Symptoms as an Implied Preference.*

B. INTERNAL DANGERS TO BE OVERCOME.—In psychotherapy generally, the first concern of the therapist should never be a fruitless direct assault or battle against the irrational complaints of the patient. All attempts to "set him straight" by repeated physical examinations and by rational explanations only intensify the patient's low self-esteem and his sense of isolation. Psychotherapy is only possible when a mutually confident, trusting relationship between patient and physician can be established. The patient is already distrustful and embittered, since he has incorporated in his conscience aspects of early parental figures who were extremely dangerous and hateful, at least as they seemed to him. The battle between these overpowering internal enemies and a weak and detestable ego rages on the plane of his body-image.

It is small wonder that the patient is egocentric and narcissistically oriented. He harbors the most terrifying dangers in his own internal environment. The psychotherapist has to try to reconcile him with these internal enemies. He can only gain ability to mediate between his patient and the ghosts of the past when he enters sufficiently into the understanding of the patient's conflicts to mitigate the severity of the infantile conscience. Conscious acceptance of early dependency needs must be secured. These can only be outgrown when they can be tolerated by the therapist and come to be recognized and tolerated by the patient.

2. Introspection Constructive and Healthy

A. SUPERFICIAL ADMONITIONS USELESS.—A difficulty sometimes encountered in intensive psychotherapy is the lay tendency in some quarters to regard introspection as such as unhealthy. To an appreciable number of lay persons introspection is almost automatically equated with self-centeredness, narcissism, self-love, or hygeiaphrontic preoccupation, or with the danger of their development. This kind of equation is understandable in view of the inherent recognition by the public of the emotionally unhealthy meaning of overconcern with self as such. The reaction, however, indicates a feeling that it is possible somehow consciously and voluntarily to control hygeiaphrontic tendencies. There is no awareness of the powerful underlying unconscious needs.

This has led to such various, well intended but often superficial lay admonitions as "Forget yourself", "Stop thinking so much about yourself", "You need outside interests", and so on. These are useless. Worse, they can be harmful.

B. CONSTRUCTIVE INTROSPECTION VITAL IN THERAPY.—One must keep in mind the very important fact that *introspection and self-study can, under proper direction, be most constructive, profitable, and healthful.* It is vital in therapy. The psychotherapist works in a mutually collaborative endeavor with his patient to learn what makes him function, what emotions are present, how they developed, and what makes him "tick" as a person. [*See* remarks in Chapter 7, pp. 434–5].

The process of treatment is one in which constructive introspective study is a basic essential. Intensive psychotherapy is literally *a postgraduate course of study in oneself.*

Generally speaking, therapy takes more doing to initiate, then to continue once it has been begun. This applies to the Hygeiaphrontic Reactions, as well as to other neurotic reactions. This should be regularly borne in mind, in accord with our earlier outlined Concept of Emotional Inertia [pp. 213 and 433].

3. Onset or Increase of Hygeiaphrontic Concerns During Treatment

A. A PROGNOSTIC SIGNAL-FLAG TO THERAPIST.—It is not too surprising during the course of investigative psychotherapy to see patients:
(*a*) develop a new absorbing symptom or bodily concern, or a rash of

them, as in the *Symptom Rash or Barrage* [Ch.8:VID2; Ch.12:VA2], or (*b*) have a recurrence of somatic difficulties which had been relatively dormant. This should serve as a Prognostic Signal-Flag to alert the therapist that something has threatened the defense of repression. The work of treatment may have come "too close for comfort" to some vital area of the unconscious defenses, may have arrived there too soon, or at an inopportune juncture. Increased symptoms may, of course, also arise on the basis of extraneous factors, or external stress.

On the other hand, such a Symptom Barrage may also indicate that collaborative treatment is coming uncomfortably close to something psychologically significant, which offers a threat to the existing and well established defenses. If one regards this as a P.S.F., or Prognostic Signal-Flag, it may be compared to the guiding cry of "You're getting warm!" given by the onlooker to the searcher in childhood games. In less obvious fashion it may be somewhat analogous to the A.A.A. [pp. 89 *ff*].

B. AS RESISTANCE AND SECONDARY DEFENSE.—As an example of this reaction, the case is recalled of a clothes designer under intensive treatment who almost regularly developed varied troublesome symptoms as our study approached some area of particular conflict. At these times he threw up a great barrage of complaints. These had a diversionary and a smokescreen effect. It was an effective resistance; an excellent Secondary Defense.* He complained about work and family. His many aches and pains multiplied. Existing ones intensified. He very much resented the "indifferent feelings" and the relative "lack of concern" of several of his examining physicians † [*see also* discussion, p. 397].

On one occasion he said with some vehemence, while suffering with chest pain which he associated with cancer of the lung, "It would serve the doctors right if I went on and died, even if just to prove how wrong they are!" He really partly meant, on an underlying unconscious level, "in not giving me the serious concern which I merit, and the attention and retreat I am seeking in this nonconstructive and immature fashion." Among the destructive effects of this type of symptom development is, of course, its interference with therapy, as a diversion and as a resistance.

Newly hygeiaphrontic persons, and others who develop somatic or physiologic overconcerns during treatment, may devote their attention and their verbal productions for a time almost exclusively to these kinds of preoccupation. This can be an effective block to therapy, as in the foregoing instance. Symptoms and hygeiaphrontic overconcerns can also have

---

* The Secondary Defense of hygeiaphrontic manifestations can be staunch and stubborn indeed, as many physicians can attest. At times an earlier cited corollary [p. 291] is also prominent. This is the Concept of Symptom Defense-Defeat Parallel, which noted how the level of Secondary Defense of a symptom may be paralleled by the amount of defeat engendered.

† Actually his resentment was in hidden fashion also in response to (1) the therapist's refusal to redirect his medical interests also into these less threatening somatic areas, and (2) the physician's failure to respond as wished to the dependency appeal inherent in his complaints.

Heimann noted the "double attitude to his doctors" as presented by the hygeiaphrontic patient "in that they are both distrusted and objects of complaints for not helping, and are also continuously sought and treated as authorities."

an insulating effect between the person concerned and other people. One protection when one feels vulnerable to people, thus, is to maintain distance, an endeavor to which preoccupation with function and symptoms can contribute. This is in accord with our Concept of Relationship-Distance, as cited [pp. 330, 348] in relation to the Obsessive Reactions [see also p. 398].

Upon occasion the employment of a special, useful technique may be helpful. At such a juncture one may instruct the patient to talk about anything at all *except* his troubling bodily concerns. In several instances the author has observed this to prove effective. There followed the production of some very significant data about interpersonal problems.

4. Patient Selection; Anxiety Mobilized in Therapy

Careful judgment is required to know how far to press the search and when to ease off one's efforts in therapeutic study. The arousal of anxiety at various junctures during any meaningful kind of analytic treatment, however, is inevitable. This may be manifested in many ways, including various possible uncomfortable somatic responses, and may occur here via several possible pathways, as we have learned. The underlying capacity for these has been established earlier in the individual's patterns of response.

Instances in which the patient expresses his anxiety somatically can help us understand the need for certain cautions which should apply in the evaluation of possible candidates for therapy. This would include persons who have had such symptoms, for example, as serious hemorrhages from peptic ulcers, dangerously high blood pressure, or very acute asthmatic attacks.

The patient must have sufficient physical reserves remaining so as to be able to tolerate possible exacerbations. One must be prepared for these to take place, in response to the anxiety which is likely to be mobilized during the course of his treatment. The referring physician, understanding this, will be better able to cooperate in the evaluation of such patients for referral. He will also be better able to give such medical assistance as may be indicated and necessary during the course of therapy.

C. ATTENTUATION OF INTERPERSONAL RELATIONS

1. Withdrawal from Relationships Inevitable

The author has earlier referred to the increasing self-absorption which occurs in somatic preoccupation. This is concurrent with the withdrawal of external interests. In any kind of severe or painful illness, the patient understandably becomes increasingly self-absorbed. Somehow we often find this to be more expected and acceptable in physical disease. Here one would hardly be critical, or attempt to combat it. Yet sometimes one sees this development become the object of criticism or condemnation in cases of Overconcern-with-Health. However, it is hardly a surprising occurrence in Hygeiaphrontis, in which the ego is strongly beset by the fierce raging of the internal unconscious conflicts.

The result is an inevitable withdrawal from external relationships. Close interpersonal contacts are partially surrendered. As the psychic energy is directed internally, there is not enough to also maintain normal love relationships. As a consequence, the hygeiaphrontic syndrome tends to become increasingly inaccessible to therapeutic scrutiny when the interpersonal relations of the patient are attenuated by distance, decreased potential, resentment, hate, or distrust. In Freudian terms, this would be when the object libido is largely converted into narcissistic libido. To an extent the patient partially withdraws from reality.

2. Isolation and Despair Decrease Accessibility

The hygeiaphrontic ideation may become more fantastic, delusional, and be defended by the distrustful patient against all rational explanation with the despair of loneliness. There is a conflict present between his need to be understood, to be taken care of, and the defiant despair that such understanding is not available to him. On the basis of his deep-seated (unconscious) guilt, he feels that he does not deserve what he seeks anyway.

The lowered self-esteem and the despair of his isolation tend to make him more defiant, stubborn, and more or less inaccessible. The personal condemnation of his desperate dependency needs and his shame about their infantile character help to maintain his conflicts. The so-called secondary "gain" (that is, the wish of the individual to be taken care of) is mostly defeated in the hygeiaphrontic patient. His guilt feelings may frequently even disallow his acceptance of the rational help that can be offered. This also helps to explain the frequent discouragement of the therapist.

D. AID TO REFERRAL

1. Effects of Emotions on Functions

For the resolution of a hygeiaphrontic neurosis, the basic unconscious mechanisms must eventually become apparent to both patient and physician. Prior to referral for psychotherapy, the interaction of emotional and physical processes can be illustrated to the patient with various easy-to-understand examples. Most patients can understand, for instance, the expected effect of fear upon heart rate and respiration, and the effect of other emotions upon such things as appetite, perspiration, urgency, blushing and nervousness. It may then be indicated and prove possible in some instances, to further point out to the patient some of the possible emotional factors entering into such symptoms as fatigue, insomnia, headache, digestive function, and other areas.

English has written a brief and simply worded aid to physicians in the explanation to their patients of psychophysiologic relationships. This can be consulted for some more detailed suggestions. This author thinks that sometimes it is easier to secure acceptance of a patient's understanding of emotionally induced pain when there is some demonstrable functional alteration. If this can be secured, one need not go into too great detail about other possible psychologic pathways or emotional origins for discomfort and pain.

As noted earlier [p. 9], anxiety can be a useful stimulus for seeking help. The more "successful" the symptom in allaying anxiety, the less motivation toward therapy. This is the Inverse-Ratio Concept of Symptom-Success and Motivation Toward Therapy [p. 298]. In the absence of all anxiety the Hygeiaphrontic System can remain relatively stable, with little inclination of the person concerned toward seeking therapeutic help. This sad state of affairs has been aptly termed the *balanced neurotic position* [p. 48, and Ch.14:XB*1*].

2. Avoid Academic Discussions

It is helpful to secure sufficient intellectual understanding by the patient to obtain his cooperation. However, one should not allow this to lead further into too much continued academic discussion of principles and theories. Although the intelligent patient may grasp these thoroughly on an intellectual plane, this does not contribute to real understanding on an emotional level. In fact, it can tend to block it through its being used in an intellectualized kind of resistance.

E. FURTHER POINTS IN THERAPY

1. Fenichel's and Fromm-Reichmann's Points

Fenichel considered the prognosis in treatment to be in inverse proportion to the amount of narcissism present. He pointed out: (*a*) the vital requirement by the patient for the capacity to develop transference, and (*b*) the importance for the therapist in determining the (developmental) status of the infantile genitality. He believed that determination as to the adequacy of these necessary foundations to analytic treatment could only be made by a trial analysis.

Fromm-Reichmann cautioned against the inadvertent encouragement of hypochondriacal (hygeiaphrontic) preoccupation. This could be unwittingly brought about by the psychotherapist, as a consequence of inquiries about the patient's symptoms and complaints at the beginning of treatment sessions. There are also disadvantages inherent to succumbing to the demands made by some hygeiaphrontic patients for repeated physical examinations. The danger herein is of "a serious disruption of the patient's interest in overt interpersonal relationships . . . [and] the danger of the patient's retreat into somatic self-engulfment."

2. Goals, Conditions, and Results

A considerable amount of genuine patience is a "must" in the therapist. Dynamic factors in the patient's personality development must be uncovered and a program of reeducation instituted. Reorientation of his emotional drives and a more healthy emotional maturation will eventually leave him free of his need for the hygeiaphrontic reaction pattern. In essence, the patient must be offered a more constructive way of life to take the place of the neurotic "solution" already a part of his living (the Therapeutic Bargain). An analytic treatment regimen may well take several years or more, depending on (*a*) the relative speed of progress; (*b*) the efficacy and value of the work; (*c*) the patient's malleability, and (*d*) the strength of his needs to cling to neurotic and self-defeating emotional patterns, versus his drive toward maturity and toward making constructive changes.

Thus, the patient must be helped to develop a constructive outgoing interest in himself. His introspection heretofore has been very likely nonconstructive. Treatment aims to uncover the relationships between his symptoms and his emotions. The very psychologic nature of Hygeiaphrontis is indicative of the patient's prior resistance to a clarification of these relationships, and the resolution of his underlying conflicts. The intensive treatment of this and other neurotic patterns of reaction can be successful, although never easy. The results in experienced hands are well worth the required investment of effort, time, and money. Finally, our earlier formulated Surgery-in-Abeyance Rule [pp. 127 and 392] is very much to be observed in the Hygeiaphrontic Reactions. Over-ready acquiescence to surgical procedures, or even an "operation-seeking attitude" is sometimes to be encountered. These and similar pressures and needs are to be carefully guarded against.

XII. SUMMARY

Overconcern with Health, Hygeiaphrontis, and Somatic or Physiologic Preoccupation have been used interchangeably with the older term of hypochondriasis in the present discussion. In this pattern of neurotic reaction, there is a discrepancy between the amount of organic pathology which is present on the one hand, and the patient's degree of interest, concern, and discomfort, on the other. This is the Hygeiaphrontic Discrepancy Principle. Hypochondriasis is an ancient term reflecting archaic ideas about the etiology of this neurotic reaction, as well as one frequent site for visceral symptoms. For several reasons as enumerated, the author has suggested consideration of the new term of Hygeiaphrontis as a preferable alternate.

Diagnosis is to be made whenever possible on positive grounds, and not by exclusion. Hygeiaphrontis is seen in conjunction with organic illness and with many kinds of emotional illness. Organic findings may be considerable, unusual, or absent, but do not realistically account for the patient's discomfort and his anxious concern about them. Hygeiaphrontic trends may be present more or less normally in certain stages of personality development, at which time they are not necessarily of pathologic significance. Errors in diagnosis and early management when present frequently lie: (1) in missing an organic condition, (2) in the delay and the iatrogenic influences of endless examinations and testing, or (3) in subsequent endless treatment for some obscure, unrelated, or nonexistent medical condition. Examples of the second and third kinds of error are much more frequent and cause more damage than does the first. They are generally less apparent and less widely recognized. The concept in human relations and behavior that Anger-breeds-Anger was noted as important in understanding emotional reactions generally. The hazard of developing what was termed the *Therapeutic Impasse* was cited. The *Concepts of Attention* and *Interest Absorption* were offered. *Case 90* illustrated the *Concepts of Interpersonal Perpetuation,* and *Continued Physiologic Momentum.*

Hygeiaphrontis may accompany organic disease, may follow external stress, or may be associated with psychoses. The *Peg Concept* was noted, with its relation to the E.O.A. (Emotional-Object Amalgam). As a diagnostic entity, the use of the term might prove appropriate in slightly less than 5 per cent of the cases of neuroses. Overconcern-with-Health is, however, a common enough problem in medical practice. Clinically one often sees a degree of overattention to function or to almost any aspect of health.

The *Concept of Defensive-Layering* refers to the onion-like successive layers of conflict, of meaning and significance, or of emotional defenses which may be "peeled off" or uncovered in therapy; or which may be elaborated when an existing stratum proves ineffective and the level of psychopathology deepens.

The variety of possible clinical manifestations is very wide. Likewise the amount or depth of pathology is quite variable. The principle of Emotionally-Determined Visceral Pain was noted. Four possible pathways or types of visceral pain of an emotional origin were noted. According to the *Psychic Reduplication Concept,* later emotional forces can lead to the psychologic reproduction of antecedent, organically based pain. *The Axiom of Inverse Pain-Conflict Ratio* points out that the greater the emotional difficulties, the lower the threshold to pain, and usually vice versa. Mention was made also of the increased vulnerability with age, and of the occasional very serious portent of somatic preoccupation ushering in a psychotic episode. Hygeiaphrontis is observed in certain psychoses to reach its most malignant guise in the form of deeply rooted somatic delusions. Occasional instances are to be observed in which character defenses of a hygeiaphrontic nature may make up what we might term the Hygeiaphrontic (hypochondriacal) Personality.

In the section on psychodynamics we learned how "I'm sick" might have extended symbolic meaning. The intensification of perceptive ability provides a *Lowered Perception-Threshold-Source* for certain otherwise obscure hygeiaphrontic symptoms. Somatic preoccupation is regressive, and a defense against anxiety for which the foundations are laid in early life. Parental attitudes and influences are important in the psychologic conditioning. Later adult Hygeiaphrontis can be thought of as representing areas of arrested development of maturity (that is, fixation), regression to earlier patterns of reaction, or both. The presence of organic disease may be a welcome relief to some emotionally sick persons in preference to their hidden, baffling, and more painful emotional conflicts. According to the *Perception-Intensification Concept* in Hygeiaphrontis, an intensification of perception may be observed of what are otherwise normal physiologic events. An *Anxiety-Pain Vicious Circle* was hypothecated, as an extension of our earlier *Concept of the Reciprocal Relation of Anxiety to Pain.*

The hygeiaphrontic endogain and epigain were discussed. *Episodic Hygeiaphrontis* (Hygeiaphrontic Attacks) was noted in *Case 99*. The internal basis for hygeiaphrontic preoccupation stems from deep seated psychologic needs which are outside of the patient's conscious awareness. These were grouped together as the endogain (that is, the primary gain of the emotional illness), and the epigain, tabulated as follows.

Table 26

Hygeiaphrontic Endogain and Epigain

A. The Endogain includes:

1. Aiding the concealment and denial of rejected wishes, primarily aggressive and sometimes sexual ones (that is, the *reinforcement of their repression*).
2. The channeling of anxiety away from deep-seated emotional conflicts into bodily areas (that is, *absorption and diversion of psychic energy*), in accord with the *Interest-Absorption Concept.*
3. Punishment for real, or subjectively (and largely outside of awareness) judged real, evil acts or wishes of oneself or others (that is, *unconscious retribution*). The *Concept of Visceral Masochism,* as outlined earlier.

B. The Epigain includes:

1. Largely unconsciously sought *effects upon people,* the unconscious seeking of sympathy, attention, and love. The *Hand-in-Glove Concept in Relationships* can be significant herein (as well as with the Conversion Reactions [Ch. 12].
2. The seeking of a more *dependent position* in living; the *regressive retreat* to a less active, less responsible level, as was present in early life.
3. The *escape* from an intolerable situation.

Some further consideration was given to the *Theory of Antecedent Conflicts* and as to where we might place a limit for the earliest antecedents. These fade into the earliest beginnings of human perception. For practical purposes, however, the Oral Phase of personality development provides the important basis for the origin of the primal patterns — the "earliest" important antecedent conflicts. The *emotional prototype* was so termed. This is an early and antecedent conflict, conflictual situation, or relationship which becomes an important actual or symbolic prototype of, and for, later more-or-less analogous events. The concept of the all-providing "good" breast (in the figurative sense), was noted, together with its relation to soterial evolvement.

We distinguished malingering from the epigain (that is, the unconscious secondary gain of emotional illness), and from the conscious efforts to secure some external gain from an illness already present. The *Theory of Transparency* was mentioned. Malingering is the conscious simulation of an illness. The *Conception of Primitive vs. More Highly Developed Defenses* was offered and outlined. Accordingly, mental mechanisms, neurotic reactions, character defenses, and psychotic reactions can be regarded as operating on various levels. We also briefly noted some of the relations of Hygeiaphrontis to Depression.

Finally, in a brief section on treatment, we added to our general comments about the management and the therapy of emotionally sick patients, together with some more specific references to the neurotic reaction of Overconcern-with-Health. The indications for psychiatric referral were outlined. In good medical handling there should be an original thorough examination with findings positively presented and an avoidance of repeated later examinations. The *Favorable-Response Concept* points out the tendency of some persons, perhaps especially in Hygeiaphrontic Reactions, to respond favorably to each new medicine, regime, or therapist. The prognosis for treatment is good in experienced hands although never easy or simple. Definitive treatment may require years of collaborative work by physician and patient.

XIII. SELECTED REFERENCES AND BIBLIOGRAPHY

ALEXANDER, F. (1948). *Fundamentals of Psychoanalysis,* pp. 232–234. New York; Norton.

AUSTEN, JANE. *Pride and Prejudice,* Chapter 9.

BEAUMONT, W. (1833). *Experiments and Observations on the Gastric Juice and the Physiology of Digestion.* Plattsburg, New York; F. P. Allen.

BLEULER, E. P. (1951). *Textbook of Psychiatry,* pp. 163 and 192. Authorized English edition by A. A. Brill. New York; Dover Publications.

CANNON, W. B. (1909). "The Influence of Emotional States on the Functions of the Alimentary Canal." *Am. J. Med. Sci.,* **137,** 480.

CARLSON, A. J. (1912). "Contributions to the Physiology of the Stomach." *Am. J. Physiol.,* **31,** 151.

CHRZANOWSKI, G. 1959). "Neurasthenia and Hypochondriasis." In Arieti, S., Ed., *American Handbook of Psychiatry,* Vol. I, pp. 258–271.

COBB, S. (1946). *Borderlines of Psychiatry,* p. 132, Cambridge, Mass.; Harvard University Press.

— (1941). *Foundations of Neuropsychiatry,* p. 217. Baltimore; Williams and Wilkins.

Committee on Nomenclature and Statistics (1952). *Diagnostic and Statistical Manual.* Washington, D. C., American Psychiatric Association.

ENGLISH, O. S. (1953). *Personality Manifestations in Psychoneurotic Illness,* p. 57. Available through Sandoz Pharmaceuticals, 68 Charlton Street, New York 14, N. Y.

FENICHEL, O. (1945). *The Psychoanalytic Theory of Neurosis,* pp. 261–265. New York; Norton.

FREUD, S. (1943). *A General Introduction to Psycho-Analysis,* p. 339. Garden City, N. Y.; Garden City Publishing Co.

— (1950). "On Narcissism: An Introduction." In *Collected Papers,* Vol. 4, pp. 40–43. London; Hogarth Press.

— (1950). "A Case of Paranoia (1911)". *Ibid.,* Vol. 3, p. 441.

— (1950). "Further Remarks on the Defense Neuro-Psychosis." *Ibid.,* Vol. 1, p. 165.

FRIES, M. (1944). "Psychosomatic Relationships Between Mother and Infant." *Psychosom. Med.,* **6,** 159.

FROMM-REICHMANN, F. (1950). *Principles of Intensive Psychotherapy,* pp. 126, 184–185. Chicago; University of Chicago Press.

GANTT, W. HORSLEY, Ed. (1961). *Physiological Bases of Psychiatry.* Springfield, Ill.; C C Thomas.

HEIMANN, P. (1952). "Certain Functions of Introjection and Projection in Early Infancy." In *Development in Psycho-Analysis,* pp. 145, 150–153. Ed. by J. Riviere. London; Hogarth Press.

JAFFE, DANIEL S. (1953). Personal communication.

JONES, E. (1953). *The Life and Work of Sigmund Freud,* Vol. 1. New York; Basic Books.

KANNER, L. (1946). *Child Psychiatry,* p. 459. Springfield, Ill.; C C Thomas.

KENYON, F. E. (1964). "Hypochondriasis: A Clinical Study." *Brit. J. Psychol.,* **110,** 478-488.

KLEIN, M. (1950). *Contributions to Psychoanalysis, 1921-1945*, pp. 292-300, 340. London; Hogarth Press.

— (1952). "Some Theoretical Conclusions Regarding the Emotional Life of the Infant." In *Development in Psychoanalysis*, pp. 198-204, 225. Ed. by J. Riviere. London; Hogarth Press.

— (1932). *The Psycho-Analysis of Children*, pp. 204, 350, 362. London; Hogarth Press.

— (1954). Personal communication.

LAUGHLIN, H. P. (1954). "Overconcern with Health. Somatic and Physiologic Preoccupation: Hypochondriasis." *Med. Ann. Dist. Columbia*, Part I, **23**, 96; Part II, **23**, 147.

— (1963). *Mental Mechanisms*. Washington, D. C. Butterworths.

— (1955). *A Psychiatric Glossary*, 5th Revised edition. Washington, D. C.; American Psychiatric Association.

— and RUFFIN, M. DEG. (1953). *An Outline of Dynamic Psychiatry*. 4th Revised Mimeo., pp. 147-151. Washington, D. C.; George Washington Medical School.

— (1954). "Psychosomatic Medicine." District of Columbia Tuberculosis Association, Bull. 40, April.

— (1954). "The Neuroses Following Trauma." *Med. Ann. Distr. Columbia*, Part I, **23**, 492; Part II, **23**, 567.

MASSERMAN, J. H. (1946). *Principles of Dynamic Psychiatry*, pp. 51-52. Philadelphia; Saunders.

NOYES, A. P. (1953). *Modern Clinical Psychiatry*, 4th Edition, p. 479. Philadelphia; Saunders.

PAVLOV, I. (1910). *The Work of the Digestive Glands*. Translated by W. H. Thompson. London; C. Griffin.

RANK, O. (1929. *The Trauma of Birth*. New York; Harcourt Brace.

REICH, A. (1951). "The Discussion of 1912 on Masturbation and Our Present Day Views." In *Psychoanalytic Study of the Child*, Vol, 6, pp. 80-94. Ed. by Eissler, R. S., Freud, A., Hartmann, H., and Kris, F. New York; International Universities Press.

RIPLEY, H. S. (1954). Personal communication.

— and WOLF, S. (1951). "Studies in Psychopathology." *J. Nerv. Ment. Dis.*, **3**, 234.

— (1951). "The Role of Psychotherapy." In *Peptic Ulcer*, Ed. by D. J. Sandweiss, pp. 415-426. Philadelphia; Saunders.

ROMANO, J. (1954). Personal communication.

SCHILDER, P. (1924). "Zur Lehre von der Hypochondrie." *Msch. Psychiat. Neurol.* **56.**

(1930). "Neurasthenia and Hypochondria; Introduction to Study of Neurasthenic-hypochondriac Character." *Med. Rev. Revs.*, *N.Y.*, **36**, 164.

SCHULTZ, JOHN D. (1965). Personal communication.

SILVERBERG, W. V. (1952). *Childhood Experience and Personal Destiny*, p. 215. New York; Springer.

SIMON, A., Ed. (1961). *The Physiology of Emotions*. Springfield, Ill.; C C Thomas.

SULLIVAN, H. W. (1953). *The Interpersonal Theory of Psychiatry*, pp. 355-359, 363. New York; Norton.

TRAWICK, T. C. and BATE, J. T. (1949). "Traumatic Neurosis." *Am. J. Surg.*, **78**, 661.

WAHL, C. W. (1963). "Treatment of the Hypochondriac." *Psychosomatics*, **4**, 9.

WEIGERT, E. (1954). Personal communication.

WHITE, W. A. (1935). *Outlines of Psychiatry*, pp. 128-192. New York; Nervous and Mental Disease Monographs.

WILGUS, T. (1964). Personal communication.

XIV. REVIEW QUESTIONS

1. What is hypochondriasis?; Hygeiaphrontis? Discuss the origins and relative merits of the two terms.

2. How can Hygeiaphrontis: (*a*) be a source of difficulty and frustration to the practicing physician? (*b*) illustrate the *Concept of Defensive Interest-Absorption?* (*c*) reflect the operation of the *Peg Concept?;* (*d*) illustrate the *Precept of Inverse Anxiety-Symptom Ratio?*

3. Distinguish Overconcern with Health, or Hygeiaphrontis from:
   (*a*) Malingering.
   (*b*) Conscious secondary gain.
   (*c*) Unconscious secondary gain (epigain).

4. Discuss the incidence of Hygeiaphrontis.

5. Discuss the Concept of Defensive Layering.

6. What does the Principle of Emotionally Determined Visceral or Area Pain point out? Name three possible routes or types.

7. What is meant by: The Axiom of Inverse Pain-Conflict Ratio?; The Psychic Reduplication Concept, in regard to earlier organic pain? What is the value of keeping in mind these relationships, of the Pain Threshold to the level and significance of emotional problems?

8. (a) How does the *Lowered-Perception-Threshold Source* help explain certain otherwise obscure hygeiaphrontic symptoms? (b) What is the Anxiety-Pain Vicious-Circle? (c) Explain *the Constrictive Spiral of Hygeiaphrontis Concept.*

9. What is meant by the "anger-breeds-anger" concept?

10. List common figures of speech which indicate a carryover of emotions into functional changes or symptoms.

11. How can Overconcern-with-Health be an unwittingly attempted defense against anxiety?

12. (a) Discuss the *Theory of Antecedent Conflicts;* (b) What is an "emotional prototype?"; (c) What is *Visceral-Masochism?*

13. (a) Discuss malingering. (b) Differentiate hygeiaphrontic epigain: how can it defeat the physician?; the patient?

14. What is (a) the *Level-of-Operations Concept?* (b) Primitive vs. more developed mechanisms concept? (c) primitive vs. more developed neurotic reactions concept?

15. What neuroses are more particular contraindications to any surgery except that which is clearly emergency?

16. What are the unconscious secondary gains of Hygeiaphrontis?

17. What is (a) the Therapeutic Impasse, or T. I.? (b) The *Favorable-Response Concept,* to a new medicine or regime?

CHAPTER 9

FEAR AND ITS AVOIDANCE

.... An Introduction to the Phobic and Soterial Patterns of Reaction

I. INCREASING COMPLEXITY OF RESPONSES
  A. Defenses Against Danger
    1. Vital Role of Fear; 2. Avoidance Important Defense
  B. The Phobic Response
    1. Fear, Anxiety and Phobias Related; 2. The Phobia Defined

II. VARIATIONS IN THE FEAR RESPONSE
  A. Assessment of Fear
    1. Amount of Fear Individually Variable; 2. When Is Fear Pathologic?
  B. The Influence of Developing Civilization
    1. Manifest Conceals Latent; 2. Action in Emergencies: Reflex and Reflective; 3. Role of Fear, Anxiety, and Prolonged Stress in Psychosomatic Pathology
  C. Fear and Some Clinical Responses
    1. Avoidance Through Academic Absorption; 2. Fear Leads to Avoidance of Close Relationships; 3. Fear Pervasive; Age-Long Avoidance and Control

III. AVOIDANCE OF DANGER AND PAIN
  A. Basic Biologic Response
    1. Conscious Avoidance; 2. Danger and Avoidance with Primitive Man
  B. Progressive Types of Avoidance
    1. Avoidance as a Superstitious Protection; 2. Locale Avoidance in Animals; 3. Avoidance of the Scene of an Unpleasant Event; 4. Avoidance of Public Appearance

C. Avoidance of Psychologic Pain, and Resistance in Therapy
    1. The Burned-Finger Analogy and Defense; 2. Psychologic-Flight Avoidance in Dissociative Reactions; 3. Reluctant Opposition to Change. The Automatic Recoil Principle in Therapy

IV. THE RULE OF IMPRESSION-PRIORITY
  A. First Impression Has Priority
    1. Effective Upon Subsequent Attitudes; Emotional-Priority Concept; 2. Painful First Experiences
  B. Initial Impressions Color Subsequent Attitudes
    1. Added Significance of the Prior Event; 2. Meeting the New Patient. Emotional-Relearning-Tougher Principle; 3. The Principles of Impression Priority Deliberately Employed
  C. Applications in Many Areas of Living
    1. Variation in Sleep Requirements; 2. Prejudices, School, and Learning; 3. Homosexual Seduction; 4. Impression Priority and the First Sexual Experience
  D. Applications Progressively Complex
    1. Antecedent Patterns and Neurosis; 2. Recapitulation of Earlier Relationship

V. SUMMARY

VI. SELECTED REFERENCES AND BIBLIOGRAPHY

VII. REVIEW QUESTIONS

I. INCREASING COMPLEXITY OF RESPONSES

A. DEFENSES AGAINST DANGER

1. Vital Role of Fear

A. RECOGNITION OF DANGER.—Fear is a universal and disturbing aspect of human experience. In the ordinary course of events it is unpleasant and thus is avoided whenever possible. However, the emotion of fear has played a vital role in the survival of our race. The presence of fright indicates a recognition of threat or of danger. Unless it is overwhelming and paralyzing in its extent, it likely becomes the forerunner of any necessary physical or psychologic Security Operation (*see* S.O. p. 351), as needed to meet the initiating threat.

The survival of primitive man often depended upon his ability to recognize danger immediately and to cope with it effectively. When confronted by a threatening animal or person, he had to choose quickly to fight or to flee, according to which appeared to be the more appropriate response.

B. THE TOTAL RESPONSE TO CRISIS; T.R.C.—Accompanying and partly preceding the physiologic changes in preparation for such emergency action of fight or flight are certain vital emotional reactions in which fear is to be prominently included. In addition to these emotional responses, there are also certain possible accompanying physical, intellectual, and psychologic changes. Together *all* of these changes constitute the protective mobilization which takes place in the individual's *Total Response to Crisis;* his T.R.C., which comprises all of his defenses against danger [Ch.8:IIIA4]. These are similar for each such exposure of a given individual, and are made up in varying amounts of the same elements whether the danger is external or internal, and whether it is physical or psychologic in nature.

It will be recalled that we have earlier defined fear as *the emotional response to a known or consciously recognized, and most frequently external, threat or danger.* Fear and its accompanying physiologic alterations constitute a reaction designed to meet the external threat. Fear is *an uncomfortable state of apprehension and uneasiness, in which the object of danger is more or less clearly apparent.* Fear is likely to be a more circumscribed reaction, whereas anxiety, as the closely related "civilized" evolvement of fear, may be more diffuse.

2. Avoidance Important Defense

A. SOURCE OF ANXIETY INTERNAL; DEREPRESSION THREAT.—Anxiety, in turn, is the apprehensive tension or uneasiness in response to the imminent anticipation of danger. As we have learned (Pages 4 and 85), because of its unpleasant nature, and in accord with the earlier formulated *Principle of the Avoidance of Anxiety,* all manner of conscious efforts and unconscious endeavors are called into play in seeking to avoid or avert its being experienced. In anxiety, however, the source of such danger is largely unknown and unrecognized, since it is essentially internal (page 16). This internal danger transpires when an earlier disowned impulse or idea threatens to emerge into conscious awareness (pages 22–23). Such content had been relegated to the unconscious because it was unbearable.

In other words the threat of derepression produces anxiety. It is also usually the signal of and the harvest as well, of intrapsychic, emotional conflict (p. 21ff). The source of anxiety thus is largely internal. It is the reaction to an unknown, or at least an undefined danger.

It is necessary that we understand these concepts, as well as the importance to people generally of seeking to avoid such emotionally painful experiences whenever possible. Avoidance is one kind of significant defensive response. Its study is particularly useful for our approaching consideration of the phobias and the soterias. Many of the mental mechanisms evolve as internal attempts to serve the intrapsychic defensive pathway of attempted avoidance. These comprise our psychologic *First Line of Defense* (pages 25 and 343, *see also Mental Mechanisms,* Butterworths, Washington, 1963). Most if not all have at least some element of psychic avoidance of discomfort, threat, or psychic pain in their elaboration.

B. PHYSIOLOGIC CHANGES IDENTICAL IN FEAR AND IN ANXIETY.—The close relation of the emotions, or effects of fear and of anxiety, is illustrated in the extremely close similarity of the physiologic changes accompanying each. For all practical purposes they may be regarded as identical. Individually specific, these tend to be more circumscribed in their extent, character, and duration when they are secondary to fear.

The physiologic changes, however, normally subside within reasonable limits in the emotionally healthy person. This occurs gradually but rather promptly, following the cessation of the threatening stimulus which has evoked them. As we learn in our study of the neurotic reactions, as danger and one's responses to it become more and more complex, such a happy state of affairs does not always transpire. From the more or less direct and simple physical kind of avoidance of external (physical) danger, there are a number of progressive steps in the gradual increase in complexity of possible responses. These can lead ultimately to that of the phobic pattern of avoidance of internal, psychologic danger. Both are avoidance, but their relative transparency as well as their degree of complexity varies widely.

B. THE PHOBIC RESPONSE

1. Fear, Anxiety and Phobias Related

A. PATHOLOGIC RESPONSE.—An individual may report, for example, that he suffers from uncontrollable feelings of "fear" and "panic", which come on when he is within closed spaces, or upon heights. We rather generally and easily recognize this as a pathologic level of emotional response. The fear in these instances is unreasoning and is not subject to voluntary control. This particular kind of psychopathologic reaction is termed a *phobia*.

Specific phobias have been named, with their prefixes being selected on an empiric basis, usually from the Greek, and simply indicating the object which is feared. Thus, the morbid fear of closed spaces is *claustrophobia*, and that of heights is *acrophobia*. In 1952 the Phobic Reactions were officially established as a separate group of the neuroses, for purposes of diagnosis and classification. The Phobic Reaction can have a close kinship to anxiety, and especially to the A.A.A. In accord with the *Circular Generation of Fear Principle* [p. 89], an A.A.A. likely generates the further fear of a recurrence.

B. DISPLACEMENT ALLOWS AVOIDANCE.—A close relationship exists between fear, anxiety, and the phobias. As a continuation of our present study we shall learn how the phobias develop as attempted defenses against anxiety.

In the phobic defense the internal threat is transposed or displaced so that it appears to the patient as a threat from outside. The *apparent* source of danger is the external object which symbolically represents that which is really feared. This substitute object and threat can then perhaps be avoided. [*See* Psychogenesis of Phobia, Ch.10:VIB2]. Such avoidance is part of the sought-after phobic endogain.*

2. The Phobia Defined

The author's definition of a phobia is *a specific pathologic fear, out of proportion to the apparent stimulus, which has been unconsciously displayed from its internal object and attached to a more or less specific, external object or situation. A phobia is an obsessive, unrealistic fear which is inappropriate and unreasoning.* It is beyond voluntary control and cannot adequately or logically be explained by the patient.

As we approach the study of the phobias, we shall enter the gates of a fascinating clinical domain. We shall also find the dynamics and pathogenesis of the phobias and the subsequent types by neurotic reaction becoming gradually more complex. This chapter is a vital introduction to the forthcoming study of the phobias and the soterias.

II. VARIATIONS IN THE FEAR RESPONSE

A. ASSESSMENT OF FEAR

1. Amount of Fear Individually Variable

The more common objects of human fear were once described by Freud as "the common phobias . . . aversions which are implanted instinctively in everyone . . .," for example, fear of snakes, vermin, thunderstorms, darkness, illness, and solitude. Although these rather common objects of aversion may approach the universal, they are *not* implanted instinctively, *nor* are they universal.

---

* Endogain: *The primary gain of an emotional illness.* The endogain and the need for it are basic to the illness and are responsible for its initiation. It operates on a deeply unconscious level. [*See* p. 68 *ff.*] Symptoms and what they secure or seek to secure psychologically, are part of the endogain and also help to secure it.

As we shall learn, however, these "common" objects of fear are among the many objects which can serve as "convenient pegs" to which external phobic displacement takes place. This comprises a major application of our Peg Concept. Such a peg invites attachment when an excess of anxiety is available*—thence the formation of the phobic *emotional-object amalgam* or E.O.A. The concept of this psychic amalgam has been discussed elsewhere. [See references in Chapters 8 and 10, and discussion of the *Law of Universal Affect* and the E.O.A., pp. 45 ff.]

The amount and the degree of fear in response to any given stimulus varies widely and individually. Thus it is often most difficult to define just what is, or to determine the presence of a "normal" or "usual" degree of fear. Many times otherwise hidden psychologic factors can contribute to the exaggeration of what may seem to be "uncomplicated" or "simple" fear. Fenichel, for example, in commenting on the question of "whether there is any such thing as a normal fear of death", wrote that probably even a "fear of death covers other unconscious ideas." The fear of death, when pathologically exaggerated, can sometimes be traced back, for example, to infantile anxiety over separation. Such a reaction in infancy can serve as an important unconscious prototype. This is in accord with our *Theory of Antecedent Conflicts* [*see* Chapter 8].

How strong can fear become? This is an individual matter. It certainly can become quite powerful itself, and in its effects. The expression "scared to death" is frequent enough in lay usage. It implies perhaps the implied general recognition: (1) that such an eventuality is not entirely impossible, and perhaps even more, (2) that fear can make a contribution to (illness and) a shortened life.

2. When Is Fear Pathologic?

How can we determine, then, when fear is pathologic? Trying to draw any hard and fast line poses many problems. There is a gradual progression from any so-called "normal" level of fear into, first, a mildly pathologic kind of reaction, then on to a more severe one, and finally to frantic states of panic. This is in accord with our *Law of Relativity in Emotional Health*. There is no problem with the first and last parts of this progression. Some of the middle area does offer problems.

In general, in making such a determination it can be helpful to raise such questions as to the *degree,* and as to the *appropriateness.* When fear is of such a degree as to interfere: (1) with living, (2) with effectiveness, (3) with function, or (4) with the ability to develop and maintain constructive relationships with people, professional help is indicated. In such situations the reaction of fear is an over-response. As such, the individual concerned well deserves the help of psychotherapeutic investigation.

---

* Freud advanced the belief at an early date (1894–95) that phobias developed in these "common" areas through the use of "available anxiety" with resulting "exaggerated fear of all those things that everyone detests or fears to some extent . . ." This is correct and in line with our current conceptions of dynamics, but only insofar as such common fears may serve as the "convenient peg" for the displacement to, and the attachment of such "critical anxiety."

B. THE INFLUENCE OF DEVELOPING CIVILIZATION

1. Manifest Conceals Latent

A. CONFORMITY AND CONTROL REQUIRED.—As civilization has progressed, its gradual evolution has resulted in the increasing complexity of our social interactions. Fear, likewise, has undergone considerable evolution. The original responses of primitive man to his direct external dangers were simple and likewise direct. Through the unconscious operation of many factors, including the mental mechanisms, the *apparent* or *manifest* objects of fear in modern times as indicated, may well cover over a deeper, underlying *concealed* or *latent* object.

Modern society requires a degree of emotional maturity in which many of man's inner drives and demands must be stringently controlled, denied, or redirected in more socially useful and constructive directions. These pressures in these directions are undoubtedly much stronger today than they were in primitive society. Conformity and control have been increasingly required. Pressures toward socialization generally vary directly with the degree of complexity of the society concerned. These factors have contributed to our referring to the present era as the Age of Anxiety [*see* p. 82 *ff*].

B. SOCIAL PRESSURES TOWARD MATURITY.—In this context then, *fear* is the primordial and nearly instinctive reaction, modified only slightly by learning—learning through both rational and irrational interpretation of experience as to what constitutes a threat. This threat must then call into play our learned modes of behavior, or to use Rado's phrase, "established methods of psychological adaptation." These are mobilized in order: (1) *to deal with the threat*, (2) *to repair the injury, and* (3) *to prevent further damage to the organism.*

The source of the threat in "simple" fear is, by definition, typically external and apparent. Anxiety is closely related however, as a more complex outgrowth of fear. *The evolution of the simple and direct primitive reaction of fear into a more complex reaction of anxiety has only occurred over many, many thousands of years, in response to the gradually increasing and progressively complex social and cultural pressures.* These pressures have been aimed, over ages of time, at securing individual restraint, repression, and the control of so-called instinctual drives. Increased emotional maturity has been sought in favor of the greater social gain, progress, and civilization. Thus social pressures can exert a powerful influence upon the increase of emotional maturity.

2. Action in Emergencies: Reflex and Reflective

A. REFLEX ACTION LIFE SAVING OR DESTRUCTIVE.—When a person feels frightened and panicky, his impulse is to act immediately. The response is often very nearly a reflex; almost instantaneous. This can be vital, protective, and even life-saving. This applies especially in urgent situations involving physical danger. In the primitive era such emergency situations prevailed more widely. A pause for contemplation, reflection, or for the consideration of various alternative actions .in the face of many of the possible primitive dangers could be injurious and defeating. Delay was likely disastrous. It could result in the loss of life.

The civilization of man has developed by an uneven but continuing evolutionary process into its present highly complex state. In many of the very complicated or involved dangers of our modern society we find that the taking of immediate action can be quite inappropriate. Thus, in the face of many current dangers, the reflex type of impulsive action can prove to be self-defeating and destructive.

B. MODERN MAN NEEDS BOTH REFLEX AND REFLECTIVE POTENTIAL.— Still, modern man can by no means afford to surrender the older, more primitive and reflex ways of response to danger. *The need remains for both*. One has only to think of some of the current-day emergency situations which might arise for instance, with airplane or marine travel, or in possible sporting mishaps. The ability to take action in semi reflex fashion can still prove life-saving. There are many kinds, and many examples.

The following personal experience comes to mind. It is an instance of the common enough crisis which can be encountered on the highway.

Case 103

A Driving Emergency

One Fourth of July some years ago my family, with three children, and a family of friends in another car, had set out across northern Virginia to visit the Scout camp in which we each had a daughter. I was driving in the lead, west of Luray. Here the road winds in and out a great deal, around and over low foothills. Suddenly, coming toward us around a curve to our left and down a grade, appeared a large trailer-truck and a car. The car was incautiously attempting to pass the truck. The road was only two lanes wide. The oncoming vehicles were rapidly approaching. To my right was a ten-foot dropoff from the edge of the road.

If the car approaching in my lane held its course a couple of seconds more, I would have to choose between the deep ditch or a head-on collision. I gripped the wheel preparatory to ditching the car at the last remaining instant, and slammed on the brakes. The other car also braked savagely. He managed to swerve behind the truck at the last possible moment. We had had a close call.

Actually, all this happened much faster than it takes to tell. My actions were more reflex than anything else. Fortunately for everyone concerned, the reflexes of the other driver were also quite efficient. I had almost no time for fear before it was all over. Only then did I note the transitory palpitation, increased respiration, and the other emergency aspects of my T.R.C. (Total Response to Crisis). Our friends in the following car observed the little drama with its potential for calamity. They were perhaps much more personally aware of fear at the time, as they later described how they had reacted to the situation.

Thus, it becomes clear that modern man must retain his direct, semi-reflex, automatically protective and more primitive kinds of responses in situations of acute danger. As noted, there is a coexisting frequent and basic need for their major modification, great inhibition, and/or stringent control. Reflective decisions and responses are, however, also most necessary and a requirement in every society. While not often life saving as may be the reflex reactions to danger, their cumulative effect and importance today makes them at least as important. Both are required.

However, this coexistence can cause serious difficulty. They can upon occasion come into conflict. This is particularly the case with certain persons who illustrate the characteristic extremes personality-wise of either pathway of response, that is: (1) the anxious, impulsive type of person, and (2) the overly cautious, restricted, and inhibited type of person. Each may have more trouble in properly maintaining a sufficient measure of *both* of these kinds of necessary emergency responses.

3. Role of Fear, Anxiety and Prolonged Stress in Psychosomatic Pathology

A. PHYSICAL PREPARATIONS MUCH LESS APPROPRIATE WITH ANXIETY: DESTRUCTIVE POTENTIAL.—With the emotions of *both* fear and anxiety there are common and rather regularly accompanying physical and physiologic changes. These are produced by the secretion of epinephrine, and other internal physiologic mediators. These changes include elevation of blood pressure, more rapid and productive action of the heart and lungs, dilation of the pupils, and various other somatic and physiologic changes. Included is the expenditure of psychic energy with continuing anxiety (which can lead to various consequences), as noted in our *Depletion Concept of Anxiety* [pp. 41, 408]. In the more primitive reaction of fear these various somatic and physiologic changes played a most vital role in the preparations to fight or to flee, in response to a crisis.

In anxiety, these physical reactions in preparation also take place, but are usually much less appropriate. Indeed, there are many valid reasons in the modern social era for the inhibition of most if not all, of one's physical responses. A discharge in any reasonable promptness (or appropriate direction) of one's action-potential which has been so created, may not be possible. Accordingly, these preparations often no longer serve at all their originally intended protective function. Instead, this damming up of action-potential results in increased tension and stress. [*See* discussion of the A.T.S., and the Concept of Continued Physiologic Momentum, pp. 98-104.]

B. CHRONIC STRESS LEADS TO FUNCTIONAL; EVENTUALLY TO STRUCTURAL CHANGES.—When stress and tension are repeated or chronic, the consequences lead to functional changes in the individually susceptible organs or systems. If unrelieved, later structural changes can ultimately follow. Exposure to crisis or danger is accompanied by the calling into play of all the elements of one's Total Response to Crisis. These include the alteration of physiology. In turn, altered function when present over sufficiently long periods leads to changed structure. This is often the hypertrophy of a physical unit, a function, an organ, or a system. This is a gradual sequence from the protective to the destructive. It is a progression from the useful to the pathologic.

The foregoing discussion more or less carries over the concept embodied in our Principle of Defense Hypertrophy [pp. 72 and 229 *ff.*] in the development and elaboration of the defensively-intended character trait features, into psychologic and structural terms. This comprises in turn another important conception of psychopathologic progression: The Concept of Functional-Structural Progression [Ch. 8:V C 2 and Ch. 14: V B 2 and I].

When structural alteration has occurred, this later part of the psychopathologic sequence is usually irreversible. An understanding of this entire complex process is basic to our understanding of the development or psychogenesis of the somatization reactions; the phychosomatic or psychophysiologic disorders. This is the kind of sequence that leads to all of the kinds of organic pathology that have their origins in strong emotions, emotional conflict, and emotional stress. It is the heart of our conceptions of psychosomatic pathology.

C. FEAR AND SOME CLINICAL RESPONSES

1. Avoidance Through Academic Absorption

As the objects of fear have become gradually more complex in modern life, so have the responses to fear. The psychologic kinds of "fight or flight" in the Total Response to Crisis have done likewise. Today these are often hidden, complex, and involved. They are often conditioned from past experience, and from antecedent conflict.

An involved kind of avoidance is the defensively intended response illustrated in the following case. The avoidance utilized here was a "flight into activity."

Case 104

Fear of Social Relationships

A brilliant young college girl sought medical assistance because of mild general debility, moderate underweight, and nervousness. She was referred as a possible candidate for phychotherapy because of her limited social adjustment. The referring physician had also determined the existence of a certain compulsiveness in her academic work.

Consultation revealed an attractive but insecure young lady who disclosed her strong fears of social relationships, principally with men. In reaction to this there had been a "barricading" of the self. She had become absorbed in her classwork. She had further secured permission to exceed the usual limit of semester credit hours allowed. This degree of academic absorption was a defensive effort to deny her interests and to divert her attention away from the feared (but still basically desired) *relationships*. There was an avoidance of feared social activity. This was via a flight response away from it, and into scholastic application.

Her fears were found to stem from large, deep areas of self-doubt. There were all kinds of doubts. She doubted her ability to make necessary decisions. She doubted that she could adequately handle problems arising from dates. She feared she could not cope with men and with sex. In view of inadequate earlier preparation for social adjustments, there was a considerable basis of reality for her self-doubts. In addition there was an even more pervasive kind of fear, relating to the vulnerability of her total self. This greatly added to the more specific constrictive influence of her sexual fears. Her reaction to all this had been one of generalized avoidance. This had been slowly progressive. Its overall net results, however, were terribly restrictive and most self-defeating. Still it was a vital defense, had proved more or less effective in its aim, and was in turn defended. The latter would be expected in accord with our concepts of resistance and Secondary Defense [pp. 96–7, 144, 397].

This patient was fortunately very eager to learn more about what made her "tick" as a person. As a result, she was able to make rapid and substantial progress in the work of treatment. She was soon able to forego her defensive scholastic preoccupation. After some early fluctuations, her academic standing did *not* suffer as a result but actually

showed some improvement! Her social adjustment advanced remarkably during the course of treatment. Today she leads a successful
married life. She has two children and she has taken an active role
in community and social activities. The early protectively intended
avoidance has long since been surrendered as a mainstay in her
personal system of psychologic defenses.

A. PSYCHOLOGIC FLIGHT THROUGH EXTERNALIZATION AND DISPLACEMENT.
—The foregoing case illustrates in an early and not yet fully developed
form, a kind of psychologic flight [p. 58 and Section III 8 2]. We shall see
this type of Psychologic-Flight Avoidance [Ch. 9: III C 2; Ch. 13: I B]
increasingly present and to be observed in gradually more complex ways,
as we continue our study of fear, its avoidance, and the phobias.

In this case, the fear tends to be subjectively experienced and described
as though it is of something outside oneself? In this particular instance, it
was of social relationships. Actually, as we have seen, there was probably
a certain displacement externally from things that were feared and doubted
in herself, that is, her ability, capacity, and adequacy. Subjectively the
threat then *appeared* to come from feared and avoided external relationships. This is a rather simple and uncomplicated instance of the utilization
of the mechanisms of Externalization and Displacement. The psychologic
use of these mechanisms will be seen frequently and more clearly developed in some of the subsequent clinical examples. They are very important and rather basic mechanisms in the development of phobias and
soterias.

2. Fear Leads to Avoidance of Close Relationships

An example similar to the foregoing comes to mind. It illustrates the
extremes to which the attempted psychologic defenses may drive a person.
The great amount of self-defeat, self-deprivation, and injury which were
present in this instance also help point out the sad paradox and illusion
implicit to our concepts of "gain" supposedly to be derived from the
neurotic defensive endeavor. (*See* earlier references to these gains in
Chapter 3, pp. 55–133.)

Case 105

Fear of Vulnerability and Hurt through a Close Relationship

A thirty-nine-year old attorney had sought character analysis, principally in order to improve his professional competence. It was early
apparent that all his relationships were on the cold and formal side.
He had a tremendous defensive need to maintain distance in all his
contacts with people; professionally, socially, and *en famille*.

One day this patient unfolded for the author in a highly dramatic
session how, following graduation, he had "deliberately" broken off
the relationship with the girl he loved. He had then shortly proceeded
to marry another girl towards whom he had actually felt cold and indifferent! He had rationalized his action on the grounds that a marriage with strong love present was bound to be followed by (an all too
painful) disillusionment. He also professed to admire those kinds of
marriages which are completely arranged by the families of the couple
in certain other cultures, as being more stable and more lasting. As he

put it, it would "certainly work out better for the bride and groom to be strangers prior to the final ceremony."

These rationalizations eventually broke down as we learned that all this was part of his desperate attempt to avoid the inevitable hurt, disappointment, and rebuff which he so absolutely and certainly associated with *any* close relationship. He had become so sensitized to hurt in the bitterly disappointing traumatic relationships of early life that no sacrifice was too great to avoid the dangerous chance of repetition. His was a Relationship-Distance defense.

The great amount of restriction and sacrifice which was so willingly accepted by this patient was some measure of the level of his tremendous fear. We can also question how "deliberate" such a choice was. The underlying protective needs which were present were very powerful indeed.

3. Fear Pervasive; Age-Long Avoidance and Control

In conclusion, fear is indeed a pervasive feeling. Men strive in every conceivable way to avoid it or to control it and ofttimes to conceal it. Thus it has been throughout the ages of man. James Norman Hall wrote of the essential futility of man's efforts to banish fear, and his reaction to recognizing this in the following lines:

> The thing that numbs the heart is this:
> That men cannot devise
> Some scheme of life to banish fear
> That lurks in most men's eyes.
>
> Fear of the lack of shelter, food,
> And fire for winter's cold;
> Fear of their children's lacking these,
> This in a world so old.

III. AVOIDANCE OF DANGER AND PAIN

A. BASIC BIOLOGIC RESPONSE

1. Conscious Avoidance

The avoidance of danger and of pain is an important and basic biologic response. This is true whether these are of internal or of external origin. Since fear and anxiety are psychologically painful, their avoidance will also be attempted. This was earlier noted (p. 85) in our *Principle of the Avoidance of Anxiety*. Avoidance therefore becomes a major way of dealing with the conflicts which can arise over one's so-called instinctual drives. There are many ways of such avoidance, as illustrated in our discussion elsewhere of the mental mechanisms. Many of these operate unconsciously in this endeavor. The psychologic conditioning which develops from the vicissitudes of antecedent conflicts will determine which mechanisms will operate, and how they will operate.

Avoidance can of course operate quite effectively at times on a conscious level. The following case is illustrative of a consciously protective avoidance.

Case 106

Conscious Avoidance

A colleague and his wife had the unfortunate experience of discovering the suicide of a friend. They had decided to investigate the friend's failure to answer their calls. The tragic and gruesome discovery resulted.

The author learned of this some years later when, while driving with the colleague and the latter's wife, a less direct route was taken in order to avoid passing the house where the tragedy had occurred. The wife explained the strong, painful impression this had made upon her. "I couldn't bear even to drive past the house where it happened. I've avoided the house and the neighborhood ever since. It wasn't pleasant, and it all comes back when I am reminded of it.

Avoidance of the locale was an additional means of attempting to avoid the painful recollection. While there were undoubtedly some added unconscious bases for her level of emotional reaction, the protective avoidance was a deliberate and conscious endeavor.

The following instance illustrates a type of avoidance in childhood which is not uncommon. Conscious awareness of its basis can vary within fairly wide limits however.

Case 107

Childhood Avoidance of Locale

A ten-year-old girl and her aunt chanced to come upon a large snake in the corner of the latter's garden. They were greatly frightened. Subsequently a thorough search by her uncle, assisted by his dogs, proved fruitless in attempting to locate the reptile.

Afterwards the girl quite studiously avoided the locale of her fright. As she expressed her subsequent reactions many years later, "I never went near that corner of the garden again. . . ."

Avoidance is a defensive psychologic response. It may vary from simple physical avoidance to something very complex. Its study will take us an important step further in the understanding of the phobias. We shall direct our attention toward learning more about the particular kind of psychologic avoidance which evolves into the phobic pattern of neurotic defensive reaction.

2. Danger and Avoidance with Primitive Man

A. EFFICIENCY OF T.R.C. CRUCIAL FOR SURVIVAL.—Let us return at this point to primitive man, with his direct fears and his direct responses to them. Let us picture in our mind's eye a young prehistoric man following a jungle trail to the tribal waterhole. Suddenly he is confronted by a sabretooth tiger! Fight or flight? If he survived to become your ancestor or mine, he made the proper decision in a flash, and had the adequate resources to follow it through successfully!

His Total Response to Crisis had to be highly efficient and protective if it was to account for his survival. Our imagination can perhaps also supply us with a number of his alternative responses. We can possibly even form a fairly accurate (and fortunately detached, by time and distance!) picture of the composite physical, physiologic, and emotional changes occurring.

B. LOCALE-AVOIDANCE.—So much for the immediate handling of the situation. However, how about tomorrow's trip to the water hole? Other things being equal, our young man might take another path. Associating the disturbing encounter with its locale, he may well tend to avoid a repetition in part through the avoidance of the *place* where it happened. This is *Locale-Avoidance*. Now this may be a very sound and practical course to follow. It may also not be realistic at all. In any event it is in accord with the principles of avoidance.

Seeking the avoidance of danger and pain is quite basic to human nature. Fear and fear-producing situations (or—locales) are painful. Within limits, this kind of avoidance of a fear-producing situation can be healthy and constructive. The *Avoidance of Anxiety* is a fundamental concept in human psychology [Ch.1:IB*1*]. On the other hand, when the avoidance becomes unrealistic or self-defeating in neurotic fashion, the intended protection instead becomes a net liability.

Even with our primitive man the avoidance of the locale of his encounter is not necessarily realistic or rational. It is conceivable, for instance, that he might take an alternate path, even though other members of the tribe had seen sabretooth tigers more frequently in the alternate path. This also might be despite the fact that his was the only such encounter in the first path. We might further note at this point that the avoidance of the situations which were associated with fear in *Cases 104* and *106* have a certain similarity to the foregoing kind of avoidance of the tiger trail.

As illustrated with the tiger, this principle of the avoidance of the object of fear or fear-producing situations, and of the locale, is another important cornerstone in our study of fear and the phobic defensive mechanism. One can see in addition the possibilities for the development of protectively-intended magical ideas, superstitions, and rites in the primitive situation. This provides us with an analagous contribution to the dynamics of the *soteria*.

The "tiger trail" might become evil and taboo following an encounter or a tragedy. Protective talismans might be "developed". The talisman could be an attempt to serve a *counter-phobic* purpose; to guard against tigers or other dangers. This is in accord with the Concepts of *Soterial Security* [p. 66] and the *Anxiety-Countering Principle,* in the soterial pattern of defensive reaction. The latter has an added interest to us in illustrating the symbolic reverse of a phobia. This will be discussed further under the Soterial Reaction, in Chapter 10.

B. PROGRESSIVE TYPES OF AVOIDANCE

1. Avoidance as a Superstitious Protection

Avoidance can also have similar kinds of magical, more-or-less unrealistic protective significance for modern man. This is seen in the continuation of superstitions in which some kind of evil is avoided, for example, through avoiding walking under a ladder, or by not having a black cat cross one's path. Recall the proverbial seven years of bad luck if a mirror is broken.

Superstitious avoidance can be regarded as a vestigial carryover from early man and his attitudes. It is a primitive kind of mechanism.

We may laugh at these reactions in ourselves. We may know they have no scientific basis, and yet feel some underlying slight uneasiness about them, particularly if a sufficient early childhood or later foundation for superstitious belief in them has been established. The stronger of one's superstitious beliefs most often have a basis in early psychologic conditioning.

Avoidance, of course, is a very important cog in the attempted protection of the phobia, through the theoretically possible avoidance of the phobic-object. It is this external object of the phobia and of phobic dread, which has become symbolically important. The real internal threat cannot be avoided. Awareness of this may be forestalled. The phobic patient "hopes" to avoid contact with its external representation (the phobic-object).

2. Locale-Avoidance in Animals

A. CONCEPT OF DANGER AND PAIN ASSOCIATION WITH LOCALE.—A similar pattern of protection through avoidance is commonly present in animals. For example, the author's family Collie dog, after the painful and frightening experience of being struck by a car on a busy Washington thoroughfare, carefully and deliberately avoided the locale of the accident for years—indeed for the remainder of her life.

She did not become more cautious about *cars*. Instead she began to avoid the place of the original trouble. This is a phobic kind of avoidance. Any connection with the car, or with cars generally, was clearly lost. These were not regarded as the source of the injury or as the source of a potential threat. This had become firmly associated with the locale, and illustrates Locale-Avoidance, as mentioned.

B. INDUCED AVOIDANCE PRINCIPLE.—This kind of reaction of avoidance event or experience. The author not long ago observed it to be purposely evoked as part of the training of a young stallion. Twice the horse had gotten out of the control of his rider. Each time he had headed into an area of brush and low trees in one corner of his pasture, and his rider had been scraped off. The provoked trainer deliberately led the horse by the halter into the area and harshly beat him again and again.

After this deliberately induced painful experience, the horse could not be even persuaded to enter the brush area. The pain of the beating became attached to the scene where the beating had taken place. The man who had administered the punishment had been initially the object of some uneasiness, but within twenty minutes was well accepted by the horse. The horse became more docile and obedient to control. The avoidance remained. Subsequently, he could not be persuaded by any rider to enter the area where the beating had taken place. [*See also* later deliberate Employment of Impression Priority and the *Induced-Avoidance Principle,* Ch. 9:IV B1.]

3. Avoidance of the Scene of an Unpleasant Event

A. PHOBIC-LIKE AVOIDANCE OF A MEANINGFUL ROUTE.—A physician friend recently told the author about an incident which took place while he was driving north through Virginia. A detour in a town led him rather automatically into not retaking the original road at the end of the detour. Instead, he took another route out from town, one with which he was familiar. He also knew it to be shorter and easier, with less traffic. He saw a route sign and then suddenly realized he was travelling the identical route along which he had had a very serious accident some three years earlier. He found himself uneasy and apprehensive.

These feelings increased. Despite the loss of time and some miles, he decided to retrace his way to the town in order to get back on the original more difficult road. In doing so, he again felt comfortable. Intellectually he felt it rather a foolish thing to do. Emotionally, the increased comfort was to him well worth the extra time and trouble.

Thus we can see the progression in gradual stages from uncomplicated fear and from the simple direct responses to it. At the other end of this progression in complexity of the type of avoidance which is employed, are the phobias. The mechanisms which are basic to the phobias, however, have very simple origins. Already we have begun to approach the phobic response, as we see the source of danger and threat begin to be attached to external objects, and to locales associated with the initial frightening experience.

B. PHOBIC AVOIDANCE OF BUSES.—Compare the foregoing instance of the author's friend's fearful, semimagical protection sought through a phobic-like avoidance of the route where his accident occurred, with that of a patient who developed a strong phobia of buses. The difference is not great. The patient's phobic object of buses was selected circumstantially in a primitive kind of association mechanism. His first "critical" attack of anxiety panic or A.A.A. [see pp. 89 ff] had occurred while he was riding on a bus. His subsequent responses are in accord with the *Circular Generation of Fears Principle* [Ch. 3:II A2; II D2; VI].

The patient thereafter feared buses. He henceforth avoided them, in his desperate effort to avoid a recurrence of the dreaded Acute Anxiety Attack. The bus had little real connection with his inner hidden fears, even on a symbolic level. He had happened to be riding on one upon the occasion of the A.A.A. The association was with the circumstances at that time. The bus became the convenient external "peg" for a measure of externalization and displacement.

4. Avoidance of Public Appearance

In the following illustration the author would not yet fully regard the reaction as an actual phobia perhaps, but the dividing line rapidly continues to narrow. We observe here a social fear, and its unusual basis of origin ultimately in the person's own judgmental conscience. The personal condemnation and self-critical feelings had been partially projected to the outside world-at-large.

Case 108

Avoidance of Public Appearances with a Girl Friend

An unmarried college professor in analytic treatment had spoken at times of his restricted social life. It was not that he was timorous or reluctant to have dates. Actually he had a girl friend of whom he was quite fond. Although they had frequent dates, they seldom went out. The patient and therapist were at the same time well aware of the presence of his set of hypertrophied moral standards. His conscience bitterly disapproved of any interests or activities along sexual lines. Consciously, he had attributed his difficulties in social adjustment to the uneasy and fearful feelings which he experienced whenever he and his girl friend appeared in public. As a result he was restricted from many types of social activity.

For a long time intermittent references to his fear and the resulting social restrictions secured little further data. There was no evidence of relationship to the strong conscience. Inquiry regularly led to a blank wall. Finally, certain clues resulted in progress. What he genuinely feared was the projection of his own disapproving conscience. Somehow people who might see him with his girl friend would intuitively sense or magically gain awareness of his sensual interests and thoughts. To him it was certain they would share his own harsh judgments and condemn him accordingly. The resulting fears and restrictions had developed.

C. AVOIDANCE OF PSYCHOLOGIC PAIN, AND RESISTANCE IN THERAPY

1. The Burned-Finger Analogy and Defense

The mental mechanisms in general operate in harmony with and in the service of the biologic principle of the Avoidance of Pain. According to this principle, *man ordinarily tends to seek automatically to avoid pain and discomfort, whether this be physical or psychologic. He strives instead for gratification and pleasure.* An understanding of these factors also will help us appreciate more clearly the operation of resistance in therapy. In its explanation the author sometimes likes to employ the following "Burned-Finger Analogy."

According to this analogy, one will quickly and automatically withdraw a burned finger from the source of heat and pain. This is pretty obvious. As soon as one learns where a hot area is, he will tend to avoid it whenever possible; to escape the resulting discomfort. If he should get close to it, the heat will tend to make him withdraw or to want to withdraw. The hotter and the closer, the more discomfort and the more urgency about withdrawal.

This analogy and the defensive pattern evolved carry over importantly into many and more complex areas of emotional kinds of discomfort and pain. This is a naturally protective and defensive response. It is an early acquired principle of human behavior. To help stress, emphasize, and perhaps more clearly identify this defensively-intended reaction, assigning it the name of the Burned-Finger Analogy and Defense is proposed.

2. Psychologic-Flight Avoidance in Dissociative Reactions

The operation of avoidance can take additional forms. We consider (actual) flight to represent the avoidance of (external, physical) danger. At times the defensive psychologic responses of the organism are seemingly confused in their reactions. Thus in the Amnesias, Fugue States, and in other of the major Dissociative Reactions [see Chapter 13] we observe combinations of responses. In the Dissociative Reaction, this can become an active kind of avoidance, through *both* physical and psychologic flight.

The flight to be observed herein is figurative and symbolic, and also simultaneously literal and active!

Accordingly, the avoidance through this combined kind of flight is a most active instance of the avoidance response to the internal danger and psychologic pain of emotional conflict. The foregoing comprises the basic dissociative *Concept of Psychologic-'Flight Avoidance'* [Ch. 13:1B]. It is essential to our understanding of the dynamics of the Dissociative Reaction, which we shall consider several chapters hence.

3. Reluctant Opposition to Change. The Automatic-Recoil Principle in Therapy

It is hardly surprising to find this same principle as to the avoidance of pain operative in many psychologic areas. In psychotherapy the carryover of this concept makes the important factor of resistance more easily understood.

The patient will inevitably tend to recoil from the areas of association ⌐ where he has suffered pain and discomfort in the past. This is not only a conscious type of avoidance but it is also operative in more concealed fashion on unconscious levels. Associations tend thus to become blocked, held up, cut off, or scanty whenever one approaches closer to such a "hot" area. This is the *Automatic-Recoil Principle* in therapy. It is the important therapeutic corollary to the Burned-Finger Defense, outlined above.

The foregoing psychologic response in therapy, as also the earlier physical one, is a naturally protective and defensive endeavor. It occurs on both conscious and unconscious levels and helps explain the vital, defensively-intended, but actually handicapping, role of resistance in psychotherapy.

Our definition of resistance in psychotherapy should include *the patient's* ⌐ *conscious or unconscious reluctance to relinquish old and established patterns of behavior; his opposition to allowing associations concerning, or to studying, emotionally painful material; his reluctant opposition to change.* Resistance occurs as part of both conscious and unconscious avoidance of anxiety. Resistance in therapy is a very important aspect of the Secondary Defense.

IV. THE RULE OF IMPRESSION-PRIORITY

A. FIRST IMPRESSION HAS PRIORITY

1. Effect Upon Subsequent Attitudes; Emotional-Priority Concept

The Rule of Impression Priority is based upon the thesis that, *other things being equal, first impressions ordinarily tend to take an emotional priority.* This applies to the coloring and influencing of the individual's subsequent attitudes and patterns of reaction to the subject and possibly to the circumstances as well, of the (later) impression. The special significance which is usually attached to first impressions has an interesting relationship to the phenomena of avoidance. The Rule of Impression-Priority is a corollary to our Theory of Antecedent Conflicts. It stresses the Concept of Emotional-Priority. It also has an important bearing on conditioning.

Thus, what occurs when something is done or tried for the first time is likely to be especially important from the emotional standpoint. This has an important influence upon one's subsequent attitude toward that event or experience. There are many applications of this Rule, as well as some exceptions. It can apply as one important example, to meeting a person for the first time. While there are also exceptions, as noted, this is a principle of some importance in living.

What might happen in an entirely new situation sometimes can be almost entirely adventitious. As a consequence, the "new thing," experience, person, or situation may prove to be pleasurable, or painful. This can then substantially color future (subsequent) attitudes about the new thing, event, or person for many of us.

In the year 1700, John Locke (1632–1704) noted how childhood fears of the dark (which could continue into adulthood) could be induced, through associations with frightening tales of goblins. Watson (1924) viewed fears as acquired through the effects of early, prior events. Dollard and Miller (1950) described the phobia as a learned response from painful experiences. As we shall learn, the phobic mechanisms are very often more complex. However, these comments emphasize our increasing recognition of the influential position of prior impressions in one's (developing) attitudes, views, and emotional responses.

2. Painful First Experiences

This vital principle of the importance of the initial impression is brought up for discussion here since it relates importantly to avoidance. Man ordinarily seeks to avoid the painful or unpleasant. If the initial impression is unpleasant, avoidance may follow as either a conscious or an unconscious consequence. The following examples are cited.

Case 109

Four Examples of Painful Initial Impressions, and Resulting Avoidance

(1) Riding and Horses
A young man of sixteen years of age had his first chance to ride a horse. He was thrown twice upon this initial occasion. Since then he has never cared for riding although previously enthusiastic, at least about the prospect.

On perhaps half a dozen occasions since, he has ridden briefly upon the urging of friends. However, he just does not like riding or horses, and avoids them whenever possible.

(2) Driving
A young married woman had finally learned to operate a car. She was delighted. To celebrate the securing of her license she took her family out for a short drive. While attempting a right-angle turn from the highway, she misjudged her speed. The car did not quite make the turn and instead ran through a fence. No one was physically hurt; the damage to both car and fence was slight; but it was a very frightening and painful experience for her.

This painful experience of an initial order negatively conditioned her further attitude toward driving. Driving has been a burden to her ever since and never a pleasure.

(3) Traveling by plane

A 36-year-old woman refuses to ride in a plane. Her initial experience nine years ago was a terrifying one. On this occasion her craft was involved in a forced landing in water following considerable stress and tension, because of mechanical difficulties. The plane finally came to rest in shallow water and although no one was injured physically, the psychic effects were substantial.

(4) Baseball

A 40-year-old patient was talking about his activities and interest in various sports recently: "Baseball—I never did too well in that. I got smacked in the side of the head by a ball when I was 9, and that really dimmed my ardor for playing ball!. . . . That was all that was needed to discourage a boy who was already only half-way encouraged to start with. As a result, I never liked it much or played very well."

The early accident had influenced this man's subsequent attitude, in line with its prior position experientially. One might wonder, of course, if it would have had the same influence without the impact of its prior position. This patient thought it would not have.

In support of his belief he cited other injuries and mishaps of equal moment suffered in connection with other sports. These had not been similarly early or initial experiences. They had included ice skating and ice hockey, in which he was both interested and proficient.

One of course must keep in mind in examples like the foregoing, other possible influences, such as those from the individual "receptor-apparatus," the ego, and from the "intra-psychic transit" of the experiences.

In some of these situations the unpleasantness or pain can probably be entirely due to circumstantial, extraneous, and adventitious circumstances. The associations so present help determine subsequent feelings. Needless to say, there are deeper implications possible in many situations. Herein the associations, the responses, and the relative significance to the person involved will be determined entirely or largely unconsciously on the basis of his own earlier vicissitudes in living, and his entire early past experience. There may be added antecedent and hidden symbolic significances.*

B. INITIAL IMPRESSIONS COLOR SUBSEQUENT ATTITUDES

1. Added Significance of the Prior Event

Initial impressions can color subsequent attitudes and can influence subsequent behavior in automatic or semi-automatic fashion. This is an important principle in human psychology. From this point of view then, patterns of reaction can, in a sense, be learned; that is, influenced in these ways by initial or very early experiences. Repetitions, particularly early ones, can also be of significance. Both influences are easier to illustrate

---

* This threat and pain can be external or psychic in origin, or a combination of both. Our discussion has stressed "environmental trauma", principally of the external variety. A concept and term of what we might call *Psychic Pain* is certainly warranted.

Since experience is sifted through one's ego, what is frightening to one person may be not at all so to another. As noted, the *intrapsychic transit* of any experience can have most important influences upon its individual impact, and as to how a given individual reacts to it.

with the foregoing kinds of initial impressions, which are of the painful variety.

Finally, often the more recent the antecedent experience, the more influence it is likely to have on the present one.

The Rule of Impression Priority is important in therapy [Ch. 6:VIIIC4]. It can contribute to the importance of our utilizing the Tracing Technique in treatment [Ch. 6:VIII C3; Ch. 10:XB], whereby one seeks out the initial appearance of a given manifestation.

Efforts to further our understanding of psychic phenomena require us to seek continuing modifications and refinements of psychologic theory. As one aid in this area, the author has come to accord increasing respect to *The Rule of Impression Priority*. This significant rule as noted, is based on the thesis that first impressions ordinarily tend to take an emotional priority. The earlier impression thus will have more significance and will carry more weight than a subsequent one of equal strength. There are many, many applications. Accordingly, the impressions gained on a first visit, an initial meeting, the original experience in a new sport or activity, the first day at a new school, and the initial contact with an employee or employer, all have special added significance. These are but a few of the possible illustrations to be found in day-to-day living.

Subsequent events, attitudes and history from that moment on can be profoundly influenced by what happens at the time of and by one's emotional reaction in connection with a first experience. The first impression has a kind of emotional priority. Other things being equal, earlier impressions are more significant and carry more weight than do subsequent ones. The Rule of Impression-Priority is an important one in human psychology. The study of many phenomena in emotions and behavior will demonstrate its influence.

2. Meeting the New Patient. Emotional-Relearning-Tougher Principle

The concept of emotional priority has an important application in the situation of meeting a new patient. The initial interview is likely to be of far greater importance than the twelfth, or the twenty-third. In fact, if it does not go well, there may be no twelfth or twenty-third, or perhaps not even a second session.

It is of major importance for both the patient and the physician therefore, that his first contact with a new patient get off "on the right foot." This is crucial for the patient. It is of great importance for the therapy, and for the therapist. One wants the patient, for example, to gain a favorable impression. An immediate positive attitude toward and about the treatment situation is highly constructive. This can get the relationship and the therapy off to a good start. The initial experiences take an *emotional priority*.

The patient can also quickly gain some idea of what to expect in subsequent visits. One needs insofar as possible to avoid his securing unreal expectations. He needs to learn early in the relationship what is to be expected as to his part in the therapy, his contributions, and the receptivity and understanding of the psychiatrist. It is far better also, and with similar rationale, to get settled fairly early such matters as those of frequency and usual length of sessions, absences, fees, payment, and other practical matters.

The importance for the relationship and for the therapy of the initial impressions can hardly be overstressed. The Rule of Impression Priority begins to operate from the first telephone call to the physician at his office; from the first of any kind of contact with the new patient. More of our so-called therapeutic failures date from what transpires on the occasion of our initial contact with a given new patient than we might wish to recognize. An unsatisfactory first contact can well add up to a "therapeutic failure," even though historically it also becomes an *only* contact.

Thus, in the effort to initiate psychotherapy, as in the initial phases of other important relationships, the factor of priority helps give the first contact added relative weight. *It is far harder to "unlearn" an emotional attitude and to replace it through "relearning", with a new one, than to begin with the preferable one in the first place.* It is far easier to begin with good habits and with favorable attitudes, than to alter bad habits or antagonistic attitudes once these have become established. This is so basic as to be a truism in life, as in therapy. However, it is an important one and should be borne in mind. It is a significant corollary of the Rule of Impression Priority, which for purposes of emphasis we might refer to as the *Emotional-Relearning-Tougher Principle*.

3. The Principles of Impression Priority Deliberately Employed

A. INDUCED I.P. (IMPRESSION PRIORITY) BY PARENTS.—At times, the principles underlying the priority of first impressions are used purposely to achieve some desired result. This is Induced I.P. A colleague finding his young teenage son with a forbidden cigarette encouraged him to smoke an entire cigar! This was several years ago. The son has not smoked since. This is an example of an induced, unpleasant, initial experience. Its potential success in achieving its goal is quite variable. So is the strength and duration of such a goal.

The author has observed similar instances in which this kind of approach was used by parents to establish desired initial attitudes in their children towards alcohol, and even towards sexual activity. There are other illustrations of the Induced I.P. Reaction to be observed. Some are far more subtle in their application. Some of these require great perceptivity to observe. Some are partly or entirely unconsciously directed (*see also* the Induced Avoidance Principle as noted earlier [Ch. 9:III B2].

B. IN ANIMAL TRAINING.—A federal employee wanted to train his young dog to stay out of the street. When the dog ventured from the sidewalk, he would throw an explosive "torpedo"—close by. Exploding with a loud bang, this would greatly startle and frighten the animal. He was soon successful in his immediate aim, in that almost complete avoidance of the street and automobiles was secured.

However, he also secured more than he had bargained for or anticipated. The fear reaction had rapidly extended, and came to include thunder, even distant firecrackers, and indeed any kind of loud noise. Any such instance would immediately reduce the poor pet to a frightened, trembling, and helpless state, seeking to hide under the nearest piece of furniture. This Induced I.P. Reaction seemingly could not be modified subsequently, and persisted throughout the dog's lifetime.

Variations of the reward or punishment procedure in deliberately coloring a given act, behavior, or performance, or its locale, have widespread use in animal training. The principles of impression priority are not necessarily so defined or named, but they enjoy implicit and widespread recognition.

Farmers well utilize this important principle. For instance, electric fence is widely used to contain goats, sheep, and cattle in a given area of pasture. The fence is charged initially. The animals quickly learn to avoid the fence. After this priority of painful impression has been established, the current often can be turned off, at least for periods of time. The stock is quite content to remain in their prescribed area. Mostly they cannot be induced to even try to venture beyond. Only rarely does current ever need to be reconnected and this usually in connection with other (intruding) stock, a very occasional recalcitrant animal, or new additions to the herd. The principles of impression priority hereby serve a very useful purpose.

Housebreaking kittens and puppies becomes more feasible through punishment for a miss. Although more subtle, the pressure of approval *vs.* disapproval play a similar influential role in child training. In these areas a dynamic explanation at least partially based upon conditioned reflex theories is also possible, or may be considered to be overlapping.

C. IN COMPULSIVE OVEREATING.—Some years ago the author was working in therapy with a young lady who suffered from a number of emotionally-based problems. One of these was the very tough one of compulsive overeating and chronic obesity. This had been a well established and seemingly intractable pattern for years. It became gradually possible to link it to eating as a major source of comfort and security.

Compulsively she would turn to food, particularly high-caloric sweets and ice cream whenever disappointed, hurt, or anxious. For her these items and their ingestion were an important *soteria;* the soteria being the converse of the phobia [Ch.5:VIII;Ch.11:VIIB].

This was a major and automatic pattern * of thereby seeking pacification, comfort and security. It had been quite deliberately induced in her early years by a nursemaid, who sought to avoid fuss and wanted to "shut her up."

C. APPLICATIONS IN MANY AREAS OF LIVING

1. Variation in Sleep Requirements

Many emotional areas illustrate the relatively greater importance of early impressions, the Rule of Impression Priority, and the conditioning effects

---

* Why are certain first impressions important to an individual, while others are not? The answers relate to prior experience, already established reaction patterns, and the various influences brought to bear during its "intrapsychic transit". A first impression of course can never be really unrelated to the individual's total personality, at that point in his life.

that these have upon subsequent attitudes and patterns of reaction. More recent ideas about sleep would suggest less need for emphasis upon an arbitrary number of hours * to be spent each night sleeping. This seems more a matter of individual adjustment, emotional reactions, and (perhaps less surprising at this moment of writing) of the person's own attitudes and beliefs about sleep.

Thus, what one has heard in early years about sleep and his relative need for sleep, from parents, health authorities, and other significant adults may influence his attitudes about sleep in later life. The subjective "need" for sleep can be quite variable. This can play an important role in the actual relative need for sleep. Indeed this may be more important than many physical and more objective factors. Thus, one's need for sleep may tend to become in actuality what one has emotionally come to feel that it ought to be (*see also* the Respite-of-Sleep Principle, and discussion, pp. 38–41 and 422–424).

2. *Prejudices, School, and Learning*

Prejudices about races, groups, and religions often develop as a kind of emotional contagion from prejudicial ideas and attitudes to which one may be early exposed. These constitute negative "first impressions," in the absence of preceding positive ones.

Similarly, attitudes toward school, toward interest in a given subject, or indeed toward all learning, may be colored and influenced by what happens in an early class or in the relationships with a particular teacher.

3. *Homosexual Seduction*

Why is the homosexually oriented individual so censured when he approaches the child or adolescent? Even those persons not otherwise critical of homosexual activity are likely to oppose this kind of outlet. The added hazard is in line with our thesis so far.

Here also the initial impressions of sex and of sexual activity with another person can have a considerable priority in influencing subsequent desires, interests, and patterns of sexual behavior. Early homosexual experiences can, in many instances, influence the subsequent sexual orientation of the child toward, away from, or about the homosexual person and about homosexuality.

Lest these comments appear too oversimplified, we should note that the influences are not *just* those of first experience alone. Importantly also, it is the experience in and of itself, especially transpiring as it well may, long before the ego is able to properly and adequately integrate—to psychically digest—an experience of this order of significance and magnitude. Needless to say, many adolescents do have homosexual experiences and proceed to develop heterosexually in any event.

---

* Nature requires five
   Custom takes seven
  Innocense takes nine
   and Wickedness eleven
      . . . .*Old English Rhyme*

Actually, intense experiences of any nature occurring prior to one's ability to "psychically digest" them, can constitute a problem of some magnitude and one which can be a continuing adverse influence. Thus it can comprise an S.E.H.C. (specific emotional hazard of childhood) to his maturation and to his emotional health. This is the Psychic Indigestion Concept in the S.E.H.Cs. [pp. 33–34]. Such Psychic Indigestion is a frequent factor in the foundation-genesis of Conversion Reactions. It follows the "too-intense" stimulus. There are also implications for the following topic, as elsewhere in our study of the neuroses.

4. Impression Priority and the First Sexual Experience

The first sexual experience often establishes an important precedent, in line with our brief about the importance of the Rule of Impression Priority. One may thus set the stage, so to speak, for what happens subsequently.

An adolescent (or earlier) seduction is usually more meaningful than a later one and can be thus more traumatic or influential. It can help establish subsequent attitudes and actions toward and about sex. Many times in evaluating the emotional adjustment of an individual, one learns of the first sexual experience of the patient. Usually also one duly accords this experience added consequence, quite automatically. The importance this has had in his subsequent sexual adjustment and in his later sought-after patterns of sexual activity is widely recognized. As noted, the childhood experience, especially the individually "too intense" one, can comprise an S.E.H.C. through the inability psychologically to integrate it with reasonable facility, and the ensuing Psychic Indigestion.

D. APPLICATIONS PROGRESSIVELY COMPLEX

1. Antecedent Patterns and Neurosis

In developing our thesis a path of increasing complexity has been followed. We have considered the interesting priority which is likely to be accorded first impressions, and were able to expand our theme further to observe the additional weight accorded early influences in people's lives. Still further, we note the relative importance of early patterns of reaction in inducing ones which are automatically operative in later life.

As we progress we note two things: (1) the applications of the Rule of Impression Priority become increasingly involved and complex; and (2) we are also observing consequences which are less and less "normal" and are more and more in the realm of psychopathology.

We are now ready to consider application of our Rule and the related principles in areas of more specifically neurotic symptomatology. These are legion. The author therefore contents himself with two examples and leaves it to the reader to observe the many possible and interesting additional applications to be encountered.

2. Recapitulation of Earlier Relationship

A. ANTECEDENT CONFLICT UNDERLIES THE PRESENT.—The following instance illustrates how earlier attitudes and relationships can unwittingly call forth analogous emotional responses, when elements of a later situation appear similar, to the individual concerned. The later response occurs automatically. Its basis is "unknown" to the person concerned without special study. He is accordingly at a loss to explain the presence or the strength of his reaction.

Case 110

An Early Pattern of Response Exercises Priority; Sets the Stage

Two years ago a married woman entered therapy. Among other things she complained of irritability with her child Eddie. She described herself as "too angry," and said that her anger was out of keeping with what he might do. She feared that she might injure him. She noted frightening and inexplicable urges to strike him or to attack him.

Gradually we learned that as a girl she had been responsible in large measure and for a long time for the supervision and care of her younger brother, Bob. She had been the eldest child and from the age of eleven years, she was required to become practically the mother for Bob, who was eight years younger. This was indeed a burdensome, demanding, and unwelcome responsibility, really far too onerous for her years, resources, and experience. At times she would become uncontrollably angry with him. She eventually recounted how she had knocked him downstairs one time, and on another occasion struck him so hard that his nose bled. She was terrified both times. As she tearfully recounted these instances and her emotional turmoil about them, with a significant slip of the tongue she called Bob, Eddie.

She had never before been able to admit to herself her resentment of either Bob or Eddie. Repression of these emotions had seemed vital to their control. When derepression and loss of control threatened, she had sought help. Conscious recognition and study during therapy led to acceptance, resolution of conflicts, and more control rather than the feared reverse.

It became clear that the earlier relationship had set the stage for the later one. It had had a considerable influence in rendering this young woman more vulnerable. This was in a situation which she unwittingly experienced and reacted to as though it were similar or identical to the early antecedent one. It was in essence a recapitulation. She was correct when she described her anger with Eddie as "undue", insofar as the *external* circumstances appeared. It was not undue insofar as the *internal* circumstances were concerned. When these came into our awareness, the reaction then appeared appropriate to the hidden facets which had served to stimulate it.

The earlier pattern of response exercised an emotional priority. Similar patterns of response were automatically evoked when the relationship with her son unconsciously recapitulated the conflicts and tensions surrounding the earlier one with her younger brother.

B. ONCE ESTABLISHED, REPETITIVE PATTERNS OF INTERACTION PERSIST.—Our final instance illustrates the persistence through adulthood of patterns of reaction which were originally adopted in childhood when they were found to be effective. Patterns of reaction in relationships tend to become, in essence, habits. They are likely to operate without either party being clearly aware of the interaction, its subtleties, or its repetitive nature. This is in accord with Freud's concept of a so-called "repetition compulsion."

Here again the first instance takes a prior position. When successful, it is far more likely of course to be adopted and used subsequently. It may of course be further refined, developed, or modified in more complex fashion. In essence however, it becomes what we might term an *emotional habit-pattern*.

Case 111

Success Leads to the Establishment of an Early Pattern of Behavior

Betty, the mother of several children, living in a distant city, secured a promise of financial underwriting from her parents to install an additional second floor bathroom. This was to cost an estimated $1500. In the midst of this work, some alterations to the bedroom seemed desirable. One thing led to another. The kitchen was also revamped. Before everything was finished, the living room was expanded and *two* new bathrooms were installed! All of this came to a total bill of more than $15,000.

Betty had not consulted her parents in the course of all this. Now she tearfully confronted them with what had become a rather staggering bill. Overwhelmed, they finally agreed to contribute one-third of the total.

Betty's older brother, Tom, was disgusted with what he viewed as his parents' coddling and unequal treatment of his sister. He predicted that they would wind up assuming the entire cost. They did. There was ample basis for his prediction.

In high school she had wanted a new dress. She had been able to talk her father into granting permission. She came home with a hat, shoes, pocketbook, and accessories, in addition to the dress! This all totaled several times the original expenditure agreed upon. Father's objections were met with "sweet talk" and "Oh, I just had to, Dad. It was such a good buy!"; and an appealing, "Look, I'll model them for you," mixed with tearful pleas for his understanding, approval, and help. It was a successful performance, securing his acquiescence and support.

There were many similar instances, in which "poor" Betty went beyond her authority in getting what she desired, and in which she was able subsequently to wheedle its being condoned in one form or another. An early pattern became established through its success. It had persisted into adulthood.

At first glance the foregoing pattern might seem far removed from our Rule of Impression Priority. It is of an increasing order of complexity to be sure. Indeed, other instances are often far more so. However, we can utilize this and many other such examples in the service of further elucidation and understanding of the many applications of the Rule of Impression Priority in psychodynamics.

C. SELF-DEFEATING.—How does this pattern fit in with certain of our criteria for neurotic symptoms? How is such a pattern handicapping to Betty? In view of its successful operation over many years, what is the self-defeat?

True, she has gained certain material things. However, has this pattern contributed to her self-sufficiency, her self-reliance, her independence, or to her maturity? It has not, really. Instead it has interfered with, prevented, or at least retarded the attainment of such emotional goals. Further, who fills such a position when her father can no longer do so?

Others are hardly likely to be so accepting, cooperative, or charitable now, or in the future. In similar matters a friend would be likely to resent any such presumption, even though it was far less striking. Accordingly, there is clear handicap and self-defeat in these patterns. They can rightly be considered neurotic. Thus, the neurotic pattern secures external secondary gain; but in accord with all neurotic symptoms and patterns, the long-range net result from an objective viewpoint is a loss.

V. SUMMARY

FEAR has long been recognized as playing a most important role in man's life. Many centuries ago Statius assigned a preeminent role to fear when he wrote: *"Primus in orbe deos fecit timor"* (The first fear is what made gods in the world). Fear is sometimes readily transposed into hate of, or anger toward, the feared person. We can perhaps readily illustrate this for ourselves through personal, social, or clinical observations. It is not nearly so easy to see the reverse of this process. Hate or anger, *through its projection to the hated person,* can result in the subjective experience of fear. Fear (as does anxiety) leads to what have been termed *Security Operations.* Fear and the S.Os. are part of an individual's T.R.C. Both reflective and reflex components are a requisite to modern life.

Fear and anxiety are closely related phenomena.* Following the biologic principle of avoiding pain, man ordinarily seeks to escape what was termed the *psychic pain* of fear and anxiety. Avoidance is an important type of attempted escape, particularly in the development of phobic defenses. Avoidance can take place through many psychologic pathways, of which we have been principally pursuing the one important one considered here leading into the formation of the phobic and soterial patterns of neurotic defense. *Locale Avoidance* was discussed. The A.A.A. can contribute to phobic evolvement. Thus, the ego can take many devious pathways which are defensive and protectively intended. We have already seen many of these illustrated in the discussions thus far. Mental Mechanisms often comprise what has been referred to as our First Line of Psychic Defense. Externalization and Displacement aid in the phobic pattern of "psychologic flight". The *Peg Concept* was mentioned. Reference was also made to the *Law of Universal Affect,* and the E.O.A. (emotional-object amalgam.)

The phobias are a major category of the defensive reactions against fear and anxiety. So far we have seen how fear and the individual response to it can become increasingly complex. The manifest and latent objects of fear were noted. The theory of its possible evolvement over the ages into anxiety was discussed. As we have considered some of the more complex

---

* Fear and anxiety have been distinguished partly on the basis of the danger being internal or external. This basis is not always to be accepted as absolute. A sharp separation of external danger and internal danger is not always feasible. Fear is safely to be regarded as a reaction to known danger, and anxiety on the other hand is the reaction to unknown or at least undefined danger. [*See* Chapters 1 and 3].

psychologic aspects of fear, we have already uncovered some of the important components of phobic defense formation. Thus in *Case 104* we saw how fear and self-doubt about the possession of ability to handle the problems which could arise in social contacts, were transposed in a short-circuiting fashion into an apparently direct fear of social relationships *per se*. A condensation took place with a loss (through repression) of several steps in the process, and the obscuring of the real source of fear. To this patient the fear was then subjectively experienced as being something external. The *Burned-Finger Analogy* and *Defense* was offered, with its corollary of an *Automatic-Recoil Principle in Therapy* and resistance.

Externalization is a frequent part of the phobic defense. With the primitive man, with the author's physician friend, and with the family pet, the source of fear became associated with the locale of the original frightening event. As we shall learn, this type of association is a frequent and a major pathway for selection of the phobic object, and one largely neglected in the literature to date. Once such an association has been established, the route is open for use of the magical protection sought through the more important reaction of avoidance of the feared area.

The final section dealt with the *Rule of Impression Priority*. It is an important corollary to our Theory of Antecedent Conflicts. This Rule helps point out the added significance gained by an initial, or an earlier (prior) event. First impressions ordinarily take a position of *emotional priority*. Patterns of reaction evolve so as to follow early precedents. Emotional conflicts and interpersonal relationships are profoundly influenced, and often unconsciously, by their early antecedents. The *Concept of Psychologic-Flight Avoidance* basic to the Dissociative Reactions, was introduced. The importance of one's first contact with a new friend or patient was stressed. The *Emotional-Relearning-Tougher Principle* was cited. When properly induced or evoked, the resulting pattern of reaction is an *Induced I.P.*

Also included was the *Principle of Defense-Hypertrophy* and the related *Concept of Functional-Structural Progression*. The *intrapsychic transit* of an experience can importantly influence its perception, impact, and one's responses to it. The *Psychic Indigestion* Concept can explain one type of S.E.H.C., when a "too-intense" stimulus cannot be emotionally integrated (or psychically digested) by the child and his ego. The *emotional habit-pattern* was mentioned.

VI. SELECTED REFERENCES AND BIBLIOGRAPHY

ACKERMAN, N. W. (1954). Personal communication.

AMERICAN MEDICAL ASSOCIATION (1952). *Standard Nomenclature of Diseases and Occupations*, 4th ed. Philadelphia; Blakiston.

CANNON, W. B. (1929). *Bodily Changes in Pain, Hunger, Fear and Rage*, 2nd ed. New York; Appleton.

— (1934). *The Wisdom of the Human Body;* rev. ed. New York; Norton.

COMMITTEE ON NOMENCLATURE AND STATISTICS (1952). *Diagnostic and Statistical Manual*. Washington, D. C.; American Psychiatric Association.

DOLLARD, J. and MILLER, N. E. (1950). *Personality and Psychotherapy*. New York; McGraw-Hill.

DUNBAR, F. (1938). *Emotions and Bodily Changes*, 2nd ed. New York; Columbia University Press.

FENICHEL, O. (1945). *The Psychoanalytic Theory of Neurosis,* pp. 208–209. New York; Norton.

FREUD, S. (1950). *Collected Papers,* Vol. I, p. 59. London; Hogarth.

Ibid., p. 128.

LAUGHLIN, H. P. (1963). *Mental Mechanisms* (Blue Book). Washington, D. C.; Butterworth.

— (1953). "Anxiety: Its nature and origins." *Med. Ann. D. C.,* **22,** 401.

— (1953). "Fear and phobias, Part I." 379.

— Ed. (1955). *A Psychiatric Glossary,* 5th rev. ed. Washington, D. C.; American Psychiatric Association.

— (1961). "Neurosis, Conditioning, and the Rule of Impression Priority." *J. Med. Soc. N. Jersey,* **58,** No. 9, 454.

RADO, S. (1950). "Emergency Behavior." In Hoch, P. H., and Zubin, J. Eds.: *Anxiety,* p. 150, New York; Grune and Stratton.

SALUS, SYDNEY, G. (1964). Personal communication.

SELYE, H. (1956). *The Stress of Life.* New York; McGraw-Hill.

WATSON, J. B. (1924). *Behaviorism.* New York; Norton.

WEISS, E., and ENGLISH, O. S. (1957). *Psychosomatic Medicine,* 3rd ed. Philadelphia; Saunders.

VII. REVIEW QUESTIONS

1. Compare and contrast the defenses against *external* and *internal* dangers.
2. (*a*) What is meant by "Increasing Complexity of Responses"? (*b*) How does this apply to Avoidance? (*c*) What is *psychologic flight?* (*d*) Why are both reflective and reflex components of the T.R.C. necessary?
3. How does the Phobic Reaction subserve Avoidance?
4. When is fear pathologic?
5. What are the influences of developing civilization as to sources of danger and responses to them?
6. Describe and illustrate:
    (*a*) The Reflex Response to Danger;
    (*b*) The Reflective Response to Danger;
    (*c*) *Psychic pain;*
    (*d*) *Locale-Avoidance;*
    (*e*) Security Operation (S.O.);
    (*f*) *Peg Concept.*
7. What is the psychopathologic sequence of progression from fear and anxiety, to irreversible (psychosomatic) pathology? How does this illustrate the *Principle of Defense-Hypertrophy?* How does the latter extend into the *Concept of Functional-Structural Progression?*
8. (*a*) What is psychologic avoidance? (*b*) How do its pathways differ in complexity? (*c*) How can the A.A.A. contribute to phobic evolvement? (*d*) What is the *Law of Universal Affect?;* (*e*) What is the *E.O.A.?*
9. Discuss avoidance as a primitive, and as a modern response to danger.
10. What are the relationships of: (*a*) Resistance in Therapy?; (*b*) Avoidance of Psychologic Pain?; and (*c*) (the Conception of) Secondary Defense?
11. (*a*) What is meant by the *Automatic-Recoil Principle* in therapy?; (*b*) What is meant by "emotional priority?"
12. Define and illustrate *The Rule of Impression Priority.*
13. Concerning the Rule of Impression Priority, outline its role in:
    (*a*) Beginning therapy.
    (*b*) Deliberate employment. (Induced I.P.).
    (*c*) Sleep requirements.
    (*d*) Prejudices.
    (*e*) Sexual adjustment.
    (*f*) A personal aspect of living.
14. How are early patterns and relationships recapitulated?

15. How do the principles of Impression Priority aid us in understanding emotional health and emotional illness?

16. What is meant by:
    (a) *Emotional-Relearning-Tougher Principle?*
    (b) Induced I.P.?
    (c) *Emotional habit-pattern;*
    (d) Psychic Indigestion Concept;
    (e) "Intrapsychic transit"; and
    (f) Burned-Finger Analogy?

CHAPTER 10

THE PHOBIC REACTIONS

. . . . Avoidance Through Displacement
and Substitution

I. THE PHOBIC PATTERN OF
DEFENSE

A. Fear and Avoidance;
Anxiety and the Phobia
1. Progression in Complexity
From Fear-Avoidance; 2. Phobia and Phobic Reaction Defined

B. Nature and Purpose of
Phobic Reactions
1. Manifest and Latent Stimulus; 2. The Phobic Endo-
gain; 3. Difficulties for Patient and for Therapist

II. HISTORICAL BACKGROUND

A. In Early Medical History
1. Recognition Present but
Understanding Limited

B. Dynamic Principles Evolve
1. Little Hans: First Case History; 2. Castration Complex

III. MAKING THE DIAGNOSIS

A. The Phobic Reactions
1. The More Common Pho-
bias; 2. Phobias and Organic
Disease; 3. Phobias and Other
Neurotic Reactions; Incomplete Symptom-Defense Concept; 4. Phobias and Conversion Reaction; 5. Phobias and
Obsessive - Compulsive Reactions

B. Differential Diagnosis;
Clinical Illustration
1. Occurrence with other
Emotional Reactions; 2. Four
Basic Possibilities to Con-
sider; 3. Phobic Object Also
Unconsciously Sought — and
Preserved; Phobic Dilemma
Concept; 4. Recapitulation of
dynamics

C. Diagnosis of Phobic Reactions Appropriate

IV. INCIDENCE

A. Incidence Generally; In
Early Years
1. Five Per Cent of Neuroses;
2. Childhood Fears; 3. Phobias in Childhood. Phobic Attacks

B. Phobias Beginning Later in
Life
1. Incidence slowly declines;
2. In young adulthood

C. Cultural Influences Upon
Manifestations and Types
of Illness
1. "Styles" of emotional illness; 2. Cultural vogue concept: popularity of phobic
objects shifts

V. SYMPTOMS AND CLINICAL
FEATURES

A. Anxiety, Fear, and Dread
1. Physiologic, Physical, Mental, and Psychologic Consequences; 2. Inversion of the
Unconscious Wish; Concept
of Phobic Ambivalence Illustrated

B. Onset of Symptoms
1. Displacement More Readily Effected when Anxiety Inordinate; 2. Danger Displaced
and Externalized; 3. Why the
Phobic Type of Defensive Reaction?

VI. PSYCHODYNAMICS AND PATHO-
GENESIS OF PHOBIC REACTIONS

A. Each Phobic Reaction Individually Determined
1. Bases of Phobias; 2. Principle of Individual Specificity
of Emotional Defenses; 3.
Variable Complexity

B. Dynamics of a Phobia
    1. Feared Loss of Dependent Position; the Gradually Evolving Phobia; 2. Important Dynamisms Operative; 3. Hypothesis of the Oral Conflict

VII. SELECTION OF PHOBIC OBJECT

A. Sensory Context of Phobic Reaction
    1. Symbolism and Sex; 2. Association with Situation or Locale; 3. Circumstantial Factors Determining Selection of Phobic Object. Peg Concept

B. Critical Attack of Anxiety

C. The Emotional-Object Amalgam; E.O.A.
    1. Attachment of affect to object; 2. Sequence of Critical Level; Instability; Detachment; Displacement; Attachment Externally; 3. Phobic and Soterial Emotional-Object Amalgams

VIII. THE ATTENTION HYPOTHESIS

A. Unconscious Seeking Out of Phobic Object

B. Automatically and Selectively Determined

C. Operative Daily, in Many Areas

D. Attention Attracted Toward Matters of Concern and Trouble
    1. Phobic Object and Soterial Object; 2. Selection of Peg for Phobic Attachment

IX. FREUD'S PHOBIC DEFENSES

A. A Train Phobia
    1. Implications for Psychoanalytic Theory; 2. Antecedent Mistakenly Dated Within Oedipal Period; 3. Oral Conflicts Underly Oedipal Conflicts

X. TREATMENT

A. Important Considerations in Psychotherapy
    1. Established Patterns Clung to Tenaciously; 2. Potential Harm from Unskilled Interference; 3. Helpful Attitudes for Physician to Take; 4. Goals of Psychotherapy

B. Techniques in Therapy of Phobias
    1. Recall of Original Traumatic Experience; Tracing Technique; 2. Focusing Patient's Attention Away from Phobic Object: Anything Else Technique; 3. Retraining and Relearning; 4. Study of Dreams; 5. Indirect Approach in Psychotherapy

C. Psychologic Contraindications to Surgery
    1. Elective Surgery to be Avoided; Surgery-in-Abeyance Rule; 2. Emotional Needs for Surgery

D. Prognosis in Therapy

XI. SUMMARY

XII. SELECTED REFERENCES AND BIBLIOGRAPHY

XIII. REVIEW QUESTIONS ON THE PHOBIC REACTIONS

I. THE PHOBIC PATTERN OF DEFENSE

A. FEAR AND AVOIDANCE; ANXIETY AND THE PHOBIA

1. Progression in Complexity From Fear-Avoidance

IN THE preceding chapter certain further important features about fear and anxiety were discussed, supplementing our earlier and continuing studies. Anxiety is a universal experience in line with the *Principle of Universality* of anxiety [*p.* 8]. As additional preparation for the understanding of the phobias we directed our attention toward the important conscious and unconscious defensive operation of avoidance.

We have learned that avoidance takes many forms. These can vary from the very simple *physical* avoidance of the threat or the locale of the threat on the one hand, all the way to very complex and symbolic kinds of or attempts at *psychic* avoidance of the danger on the other. Anxiety is a more complex evolvement of fear. Phobic-avoidance is a more complex evolution from physical avoidance. Herein the phobia is to (physical) avoidance, as anxiety is to fear.

The discussion of Fear and Its Avoidance which we have just concluded follows in a direct line of progression to the phobic pattern of defensive reaction. This progression is a gradual one, leading on into increasingly complex neurotic patterns. As the result of these foundations which have been laid, we are now ready to begin the very important and interesting study of the Phobic Reactions proper. These constitute a defensively intended reaction pattern, in which avoidance of conflict and anxiety is sought through displacement and substitution. This phobic type of *Psychologic-Flight Avoidance* produces an interesting and challenging clinical entity.

2. Phobia and Phobic Reaction Defined

A. THE PHOBIA.—The word "phobia" comes from the Greek word *phobos,* which means flight, fear, dread, or panic; or fear such as that which causes flight. Dislike or aversion is often implied. The author would define the phobia as *a specific pathologic fear which is out of proportion to the apparent stimulus. The painful affect has been automatically and unconsciously displaced from its original internal object, to become attached to a specific external object or situation. The phobia is an obsessively persistent kind of unrealistic fear which is inappropriate and unreasoning.* The phobia seeks to defend the unconscious and the repressed. It is a defense against anxiety which is thereby displaced externally.

When the psychodynamics are uncovered, however, one finds that the reaction is exactly appropriate for the actual hidden inner threat, so far as the particular person is concerned. This is in accord with our *Individual Appropriateness of Response* Principle [*See pages* 14, 84, and 111]. When the level of fear and dread for the external object is severe, the level of the internal threat is severe. The degree of the Phobic Reaction is thus a gauge of the degree of the internal threat.

B. THE PHOBIC REACTION.—The phobic reaction and the phobic fear is beyond the individual's voluntary control. He can usually recognize that it is disproportionate, illogical, and non-rational in degree. He cannot adequately explain to others, or to himself, the real basis for, or the level and strength of his fear response to his phobic object.

The Phobic Reaction we can define as *an unconscious neurotic pattern of attempted defense. It is characterized clinically by the presence of a phobia, or phobias, as the most prominent feature of the neurotic reaction which is present, and by the predilection to develop phobic manifestations under appropriate conditions of psychic stress. Displacement from the original internal source of threat and danger has taken place to an external object-source.* Through this defensive reaction pattern the resolution of internal emotional conflicts is sought, as is the psychic avoidance of resulting anxiety.

Several general categories of Phobic Reaction might be distinguished; the following three descriptive ones are of some prominence. The *Critical-Displacement Phobia* refers to *the phobic reaction which is evolved suddenly and urgently at the time of an acute overload of anxiety.* In the *Situational Phobia,* the *displacement and phobic attachment has been made to a specific given aspect of the situation or locale, generally at the time of such a critical overload.* The *Gradually-Evolving Phobia* in some distinction, *has no apparent sudden or dramatic time of onset.* The first two categories often overlap. The *Phobic Attack* [Ch.10:IVA2] is clearly phobic in character, and often otherwise approximates the A.A.A., in many of its clinical features and sequella.

B. NATURE AND PURPOSE OF PHOBIC REACTIONS

1. Manifest and Latent Stimulus

The emotional feeling of fear in the phobia seems to be out of proportion to what we might term the *manifest,* or external stimulus. This outward or manifest source of fear in this respect has a somewhat analogous position to the manifest content of the dream.

The manifest stimulus is the phobic object. In varying degrees, it is a distorted, condensed, or symbolic representation. As such it serves to conceal, to displace, and to replace the underlying *latent* stimulus. The latent stimulus or object in turn is the internal object-source. It is from this that Displacement has been effected externally. We shall see this illustrated repeatedly.

2. The Phobic Endogain

A. CONCEALMENT, DENIAL, DISPLACEMENT.—The primary gain of the phobia, *the phobic endogain* [*see* p. 68*ff*], is sought through the concealment and the denial from conscious awareness of the internal source of the fear and danger.

As the phobic process is elaborated, the anxiety becomes attached to the external object through the unconscious mechanism of Displacement [Ch.9:IB*1*]. We shall consider this further as our discussion proceeds.

B. ANXIETY AVERTED.—The phobic endogain thus is secured by averting anxiety, mainly through: (1) maintaining repression, (2) the diversion and absorption of psychic energy (into obsessive phobic preoccupation), and (3) via the now apparently possible "magical" avoidance of the externalized object or situation. To the (unconscious of the) individual concerned this "gain" is an essential and vital one indeed.

As we have observed repeatedly in earlier chapters however, the so-called "gains," although they are vital to the emotional illness, most often (paradoxically) prove to be losses in their overall net result, when assessed objectively. These essential gains secured through emotional illness, are all too sadly illusory and self-defeating.

3. Difficulties for Patient and for Therapist

A. MANY OBJECTS.—Closed spaces, heights, an animal, insects, cancer, atomic war or thunderstorms, for instance, may become the object of a phobia. The type, name, and category of Phobic Reaction is determined generally by the phobic object, as unwittingly selected. There are many,

many potential phobic objects. The resulting fear and dread which subjectively torture the patient are usually consciously recognized by the patient as being inappropriate.

The level of subjective disturbance in the phobias varies considerably. The student must learn to appreciate its very important psychologic defensive intent. This lies in the further diversion of the conscious awareness of the patient away from repressed and unconscious data which seem consciously intolerable. Concealment and control are promoted of the hidden *unconscious* something which is actually more disturbing and dreaded. This something is in his unconscious.

B. SECONDARILY DEFENDED.—Thus, the "level" of the phobia fear and dread may give us an approximation of the level of internal conflict. In the occasional very marked case of phobia, how terrible must be the underlying disturbance! How feared and dreaded must be the possibility of conscious awareness! How important it must be to maintain the phobic displacement, at all costs!

One might add not infrequently, how resistant the patient *has* to be to therapeutic intervention! The Secondary Defense *of* the phobic symptom, unconsciously maintained by the individual, is indeed a vital endeavor. How difficult the task of the therapist! How difficult the task of the patient!

II. HISTORICAL BACKGROUND

A. IN EARLY MEDICAL HISTORY

1. Recognition Present but Understanding Limited

A. HIPPOCRATES, LOCKE, WESTPHAL, AND KRAEPELIN.—An account of a phobia is included in a book attributed to Hippocrates. Medical interest in the Phobic Reactions, as that of scholars generally however, lagged greatly. As an almost lone exception the English philosopher, John Locke (1632-1704), in *An Essay Concerning Human Understanding,* discerningly described how "a foolish maid [might] inculcate . . . often on the mind of a child . . . the ideas of goblins and sprites . . . with darkness . . .". Afterward they are no longer separable, and "darkness shall ever afterwards bring with it those frightful ideas . . .". Herein ahead of his time, Locke recognized how the childhood origin of a later phobia of the dark (nyctophobia) might lie in early, implanted associations.* Thus a phobia could develop on the basis of antecedent (prior) impressions.

Through the evolving history of medicine in and past the Middle Ages, the phobias had become an increasingly recognized, but quite poorly understood, group of manifestations. Their nature and meaning were obscure and seemed destined to remain so. This may have further contributed to few people having much interest in them—perhaps with the exception

---

* Locke however also described the origin of phobias as constitutional, in addition to the above acquired origin. He believed they could *not* be cured by "reason." Some were cured through "time," the reasons not being specified.

of those persons having had the misfortune to suffer the tortures of a phobic illness. Frequently enough, any speculations which were offered as to the bases for such seemingly irrational fears were usually related to possible superstitious, mythological, or supernatural origins. More frequently, and perhaps worse, over the course of hundreds of years the reaction to an account of a phobic fear was likely to be total disinterest. A casual shrug of the shoulders might be the dismissal for such an obscure problem.

The fear might well seem out of proportion both to the sufferer and to the onlooker. Perhaps the latter might suggest, even as is done sometimes today, that the patient "get hold of himself", or more in the spirit of the times, "cast out his fear". To anyone understanding the essential psychologic basis of the phobias, such advice is worse than useless. It betrays the ignorance of the advisor. One might as readily tell the utterly exhausted alpine climber who, following a mishap, dangles helplessly alone in space at the end of a seventy-foot rope, to "get hold of himself," and climb up the rope!

Fortunately, the upsurge of scientific medicine gradually led to new interest in many clinical entities. Psychologic ones were not excluded. The *Age of Anxiety* was underway. In 1871 Westphal (1833–1890) introduced the term of and described *agoraphobia,* as the fear of wide streets, squares, and open spaces. The same year Raggi introduced the term *claustrophobia.* Kraepelin (1856–1926) diagnostically first classified the phobias under Neurasthenia; later under "compulsive insanity". Both Oppenheim (1876–1949) and Kraepelin regarded the outlook for the phobic patient as unfavorable. By the latter part of the nineteenth century however, medicine was on the brink of new and important breakthroughs. We were ready for Janet and his excellent clinical work.

B. JANET DESCRIBED AND CLASSIFIED.—Beginning sometime after the year 1800, phobias were clinically described by a number of early medical observers. Pierre Janet (1859–1947), the famous student of Jean Charcot (1825–1893), wrote about certain aspects of the phobias. He further classified them, together with the Obsessive-Compulsive Reactions, within his major concept of psychasthenia. A term widely used for decades, this latter diagnostic category has now largely fallen into disuse. The early history of the underlying psychodynamics of the phobias is related to Sigmund Freud and his followers. They originally unraveled the psychologic basis of the phobias. Their pioneering work opened the way to further definitive research for later students and investigators in psychiatry.

C. FREUD'S PSYCHOLOGIC THEORY.—In a paper first published in 1894, Sigmund Freud (1856–1939) offered a "psychological theory of phobias and obsessions." Herein he presented: (1) the concept of the "unbearable idea" or experience, (2) the importance of the amount of feeling attached to it, and (3) the comparative psychologic defensive handling of this in hysteria and in phobias.

He found that in both hysteria and the phobias the failure of repression (that is, the complete relegation from awareness into the unconscious) of the unbearable idea or experience resulted in the psychopathologic process. "In hysteria the unbearable idea is rendered innocuous by the quantity of excitation attached to it being transmuted into some bodily form of expression . . .".* In phobias the painful affect was found to be attached to "other ideas which are not in themselves unbearable".

B. DYNAMIC PRINCIPLES EVOLVE

1. Little Hans: First Case History

Ever since these initial important discoveries, the dynamics of the phobias have intrigued research workers in psychiatry and in allied fields. Fifteen years later Freud chronicled the history of a case which illustrated his theories. In 1909 he was able thus to publish the first detailed clinical history of a phobia and its dynamics. This was the classic instance of "Little Hans", which is included for its historical interest and summarized as follows.

Case 111

Freud's Case of "Little Hans"

Little Hans was a five-year-old boy who had a phobia of horses. He feared they would bite him. Aggressive impulses toward his father had become intolerably dangerous because of the threat of possible retaliation. Hans' unconscious endeavor was to exclude the unbearable ideas from all conscious awareness.

The threat and danger came to be displaced from the now internal fear of father, to an external one of horses. The danger then appeared in disguised form to be that "the horse will or may bite me."

The horse thus had become a substituted, more bearable external object. It symbolically "stood for" the feared retaliatory part of father. The basis for this phobia (and for others) was assumed by Freud to lie in the Oedipus Complex. The horse could be avoided; father could not. "Flight" as an avoidance response to the object of danger was now possible.

In a second detailed report Freud later presented another animal phobia which began before the age of four years. In this instance the main fear was also externally displaced onto an animal, but in a more complex fashion.

2. Castration Complex

A. BROADER INTERPRETATION USEFUL.—Freud's own concepts of the phobias underwent evolution over the years. In 1923, in *The Problem of Anxiety,* Freud wrote: "On a previous occasion I ascribed to phobias the character of a projection since they substitute for an internal instinctual danger an external perceptual one. Such a process has the advantage that

---

* ". . . a process for which I should like to propose the name, conversion." This is Freud's original introduction of a medico-psychologic usage for this term. Conversion hysteria as a diagnostic term is interchangeable with Conversion Reaction, although today the latter is to be preferred for a number of reasons [*See* Chapter 12].

from an external danger, protection may be gained through flight and the avoidance of the perception of it, whereas against a danger from within, flight is of no avail. This statement of mine is not incorrect, but superficial. For the instinctual demand is not in itself a danger but is so only because it entails a true external danger, that of castration. So that fundamentally we have in the phobias, after all, merely the substituting of one external danger for another." This is in accord with the so-called "castration complex", long accorded a preeminent position by many writers and theorists in the field of analysis.

✓ This comment and concept may be clearer to the reader if the word "castration" is interpreted in a considerably broader sense. Hereby, the author would regard it as a far more general kind of possible damage, including punishment, retaliation, and physical injury of any variety. Accordingly, there is no real conflict with the psychodynamics as we currently present them and which are further extensions and elaborations of earlier views.

B. A PERSONAL DETERMINANT FOR FREUD.—Freud has a special personal interest in phobias which helped lead him into productive research in the early years. I refer here to the fact that Freud himself was a phobic individual. According to an account by Theodor Reik, as he was walking through the streets of Vienna with Freud one day, the latter hesitated upon coming to a street crossing. Freud remarked, "You see, there is a survival of my old agoraphobia which troubled me much in younger years" [Ch.10:IXA].

The presence of this emotional difficulty conceivably could enter as an important personal determinant into the explanation of several things. It might help explain, for instance, Freud's considerable interest in phobias. It could have also entered into his earlier (*circa* 1894) great pessimism about prospects for their therapeutic resolution.* Finally, it could have helped provide the impetus for the study which produced the two early detailed case histories of phobias.

Freud's inability more completely to resolve his own agoraphobia is consistent with the relative paucity of his definitive dynamic contributions toward the understanding of this particular type of phobic defense. It remained for the work of Helene Deutsch, W. Schmideberg, E. Weiss, A. Katan-Angel, O. Fenichel, and others to help us better understand the psychodynamics involved in agoraphobia. Other contributors have added to our fund of knowledge about various other types of phobias. Collectively, all of this invaluable data provided an indispensable foundation and launching point for the further study and development of phobic theory and clinical study, detailed herein. Our fund of knowledge continues to grow.

---

* For example, "in the phobias . . . (1) this effect is always the same; always that of anxiety; (2) it does not originate in a repressed idea, proves not reducible further by psychological analysis, and is also not amenable to psychotherapy."

III. MAKING THE DIAGNOSIS

A. THE PHOBIC REACTIONS

1. The More Common Phobias

In 1895 Freud had distinguished obsessions and phobias as noted. His inclination had been to include the latter as one area of his newly proposed diagnostic entity of Anxiety Neurosis. Soon the phobias were also to be labeled as "anxiety hysteria", a term now discarded. Janet grouped them within his rather widely inclusive syndrome of Psychasthenia. Hall (1897) recommended the classification of various phobias descriptively, according to the phobic object, with its Greek name.

The trend toward the separate delineation of phobias as a major neurotic reaction however, has been developing only since around 1910–1915. This cycle is about complete and today we widely accord them recognition as a separate diagnostic entity. Within this present accepted division of the Phobic Reactions, three general categories as earlier noted, and several score of types are included, among the latter being the more frequently encountered specific phobias.

The phobia is a specific pathologic fear of an external object. One would expect to find little difficulty in diagnosis and ordinarily this is true. An established dread of dirt, for example, or of fire, or of animals, offers few problems in classification. We shall shortly find, however that complex problems sometimes can be encountered in the differential diagnosis of the Phobic Reactions.

In *Table 27* the author has classified and listed the more commonly encountered phobias. More than twenty of these (*Part A*) are still widely referred to by their technical names. For these, the classical derivation from the Greek or Latin sources has been indicated. Some sixty additional phobias (*Part B*) are also listed, in alphabetical order. They are named descriptively and empirically, according to the phobic object. Technical names have also been assigned these latter, by custom, usage, or herein as a matter of convenience. As possible alternatives, such names have been selected on the basis of etymology, ease of usage, and according to word roots which are variously Latin, Greek, Old or Middle English, and occasionally French, German, Italian, and Scandinavian.

Table 27

The More Common Phobic Reactions

A. *Technically Named Phobias*

Types of Phobic Reaction classified by their technical names, with their objects and derivations indicated. The type is determined and named according to the phobic object.

1. *Acrophobia.* Height. (Gr., *acra*, heights or summits.)
2. *Agoraphobia.* Open spaces. (Gr., *agora*, market place, the place of assembly.)
3. *Ailurophobia.* Cats. (Gr., *ailouros*, cat.)
4. *Anthophobia.* Flowers. (Gr., *anthos*, flower.)
5. *Anthropophobia.* People. (Gr., *anthropos*, man, generically.)
6. *Aquaphobia.* Water. (Lat., *aqua*, water.)

(Table continued on next page)

Table 27—Continued
    7. *Astraphobia.* Lightning. (Gr. *asterope*, lightning.)
    8. *Bacteriophobia.* Bacteria. (Gr. *bacter*, small rod.)
    9. *Brontophobia.* Thunder. (Gr., *bronte*, thunder.)
   10. *Claustrophobia.* Closed spaces. (Lat. *claustrum*, bar, bolt, or lock.)
   11. *Cynophobia.* Dogs. (Gr. *cynas*, dog.)
   12. *Demonophobia.* Demons. (Lat., *daemon*, demon.)
   13. *Equinophobia.* Horses. (Lat., *equinis*, horse.)
   14. *Herpetophobia.* Lizards or reptiles. (Gr., *herpetos*, a creeping or crawling thing.)
   15. *Keraunophobia.* Thunder. (Gr. *keraunos*, thunderbolt.)
   16. *Mysophobia.* Dirt, germs, contamination. (Gr., *mysos*, uncleanliness of body or mind; abomination or defilement.)
   17. *Numerophobia.* A number, or numbers. (Lat., *numero*, number.)
   18. *Nyctophobia.* Darkness or night. (Gr., *nyx*, night.)
   19. *Ophidiophobia.* Snakes. (Gr., *ophis*, snake or serpent.)
   20. *Pyrophobia.* Fire. (Gr., *pyr*, fire.)
   21. *Spatiophobia.* Self-confining phobia. (Laughlin) Phobically imposed area or spatial restrictions; often gradually, occasionally rapidly, progressive (pp. 121–122).
   22. *Zoophobia.* Animals. (Gr. *zoos*, animal.)

B. *Phobias by Phobic Object*

Types of Phobic Reaction classified and named on a descriptive, empiric basis, alphabetically and according to the phobic object. Technical names by usage, or as assigned on the basis of etymology and preference, follow.

 1. Air (*aerophobia*)
 2. Airplanes (*flienophobia*)
 3. Aloneness (*solicitudophobia*)
 4. Anger (*angrophobia*)
 5. Animals (*zoophobia*)
 6. Arguments (*argumentophobia*)
 7. Atomic explosions (*atomosophobia*)
 8. Birds (*avisophobia*)
 9. Blood (*hemophobia*)
10. Boats (*boatophobia*)
11. Cancer (*cancerophobia*)
12. Cats (*ailurophobia*)
13. Childbirth (*byrthophobia*)
14. Closed spaces (*claustrophobia*)
15. Confinement (*confinophobia*)
16. Cosmic phenomena (planetary collision, etc.) (*kosmikophobia*)
17. Crowds (*crudanophobia*)
18. Dark (*nyctophobia*)
19. Death (*thanatophobia*)
20. Demons (*demonophobia*)
21. Dependence (*soteriophobia*)
22. Dirt (*mysophobia*)
23. Disease (*pathemaphobia*)
24. Doctors (*medicophobia*)
25. Dogs (*cynophobia*)
26. Drugs (*drogophobia*)
27. Fights (*fechtenophobia*)
28. Fire (*pyrophobia*)
29. Flowers (*anthophobia*)
30. Genitals (*genitophobia*)
31. Germs (*mikrophobia*)
32. Hair (*trichophobia*)
33. Heights (*acrophobia*)
34. Horses (*equinophobia*)
35. Hospitals (*hospitalophobia*)
36. Illness (*illrophobia*)
37. Insanity (*dementophobia*)
38. Insects (*insectophobia*)
39. Knives (*knifrphobia*)
40. Light (*luxophobia*)
41. Lightning (*lichtophobia*)
42. Lizards (*lacertophobia*)
43. Medicine (*medicinaphobia*)
44. Men (*hominophobia*)
45. Mice (*musophobia*)
46. Night (*nyctophobia*)
47. Occupations (*occupatiophobia*)
48. Old age (*senilophobia*)
49. Open spaces (*agoraphobia*)
50. People (*anthropophobia*)
51. Phobias (*phobosophobia*)
52. Poison (*toxicophobia*)
53. Poliomyelitis (*poliosophobia*)
54. Races or racial groups (*razzaphobia*)
55. Rats (*rattephobia*)
56. Rodents (*rodentophobia*)
57. Satan (*satanophobia*)
58. Senility (*senilisophobia*)
59. Sex (*sexesophobia*)
60. Sharp objects (*scharfophobia*)

(*Table continued on next page*)

Table 27—Continued

61. Skin (*dermatophobia*)	68. Syphilis (*syphilophobia*)
62. Snakes (*ophidiophobia*)	69. Thunderstorms (*brontophobia*)
63. Snow (*blanchophobia*)	70. Trains (*traherophobia*)
64. Solitude (*desererephobia*)	71. Travel (*travelophobia*)
65. Soteria (*soteriophobia:* fear of soterial dependence, dread of dependency)	72. Venereal disease (*venerophobia*)
	73. Vermin (*verkisophobia*)
	74. War (*werrephobia*)
66. Spiders (*arachnophobia*)	75. Water (*aquaphobia*)
67. Strangers (*etrangerophobia*)	76. Women (*femellaphobia*)

2. Phobias and Organic Disease

Certain cases of phobia can cause occasional trouble in diagnosis. Examples are the phobias about certain illnesses. On occasion, these can be accompanied by some pain or functional alteration sometimes quite sufficient to result in problems in differentiating them from organic disease.

The early symptoms of such pathologic conditions as certain cancers, poliomyelitis, hepatic cirrhosis, and coronary artery disease can be equivocal. The patient's dread and fear of these, plus various nonspecific symptoms, can result at times in leading the physician through a course of exhaustive diagnostic studies, tests, and observations.

3. Phobias and Other Neurotic Reactions; Incomplete Symptom-Defense Concept

More frequent problems in differential diagnosis, or rather in the choice of the most accurate diagnosis, are seen in cases of illness that are primarily emotional. The following severe case of neurosis illustrates the simultaneous presence of a number of component neurotic symptoms. The presence of concurrent anxiety or A.A.A.s with (other) established symptoms as in the following case, is presumptive evidence of an *Incomplete Symptom-Defense*. See earlier reference to concept [p. 89].

Case 113

Severe Phobic Reaction Accompanied by Other Major Neurotic Patterns of Reaction

(1) *Self-critical attitudes and rationalizations handicap judgment*

A thirty-four-year-old married mother of three children was referred for psychiatric evaluation. An assessment as to the possible value of therapy was sought. Examination disclosed the simultaneous presence of a number of major neurotic defensive patterns. Symptoms of a clinical level had been present for ten years and had gradually been increasing in severity.

Although the prospective patient was a university graduate of some sophistication, she had not previously sought help. She had kept telling herself that her troubles were "silly" and that she simply must "get a hold" of herself. This admonition was echoed by family members. She had felt, further, that consulting a psychiatrist was an evidence of weakness. Her judgment was handicapped by her critical attitudes, defensiveness, and rationalizations.

(2) *Phobic manifestations prominent among several major neurotic problems*

Finally, however, the phobic manifestations had driven her to at least consider seeking help from her family physician. Her morbid dread of closed spaces, crowds, and airplanes was marked. In addition, a self-confining phobia, or spatiophobia, had increasingly restricted the distance she could venture from her home without suffering great uneasiness. At the time of examination this had progressed to the point where a distance of even a few blocks might bring on considerable anxiety.

As noted, there were other manifestations. *First,* she suffered with rather frequent, typical A.A.A.s (Acute Anxiety Attacks). *Second,* she possessed a number of well developed Conversion (hysterical) character traits. *Further,* there was a history of several episodes of gross Somatic Conversion symptoms, and she had exhibited certain conversion (hysterical) patterns of reaction and behavior. *Finally,* there were established hygeiaphrontic (hypochondriacal) trends, in which she had suffered multiple shifting symptoms, aches, and pains, and which (in themselves) had been quite troubling and frightening.

(3) Diagnosis according to most prominent feature

Any of these symptom groups separately would have warranted the appropriate diagnosis. Although one might question the proper diagnosis in this case, that of Phobic Reaction was made, because it appeared clinically to be the *most prominent neurotic feature.* It caused the greatest interference with living, and had led the patient to seek help.

In view of the duration and level of psychopathologic reactions and the patient's limited interest in therapy, the prognosis was guarded. A trial at therapy was offered the patient. Unfortunately this has yet to be accepted.

4. Phobias and Conversion Reaction

In the foregoing case, elements of conversion (hysteria) were present along with phobic ones. The phobias are also related to the conversion reaction dynamically. Up to a point, the psychogenesis is similar. There is also a similarity between the near-magic of the secret (unconscious) conversion of the hidden conflict into a distorted bodily form of expression in Somatic Conversion, and the likewise near-magic of its partial displacement to a symbolic external object in the phobias. With each, it is sometimes possible through suggestion or under hypnosis to remove the symptom.* Compare also the massive dissociation of the Somatic Conversion [Ch.12:VIB2] with the emotional segment "splitting away" through displacement in the phobia.

Freud early suggested and himself came to use the name "anxiety hysteria" for the phobias, as noted. This term is only very occasionally seen in the literature today and it does not currently enjoy wide acceptance or usage in psychiatry. This name is somewhat appropriate dynamically, however. Owing to the psychopathologic relationship of (Somatic) Conversion Reaction and anxiety hysteria, the internal (unconscious) approach to the resolution of anxiety is similar in both. In the Conversion Reaction it takes place through *Somatic Conversion* in the form of specific disabilities

---

* This can be a potentially dangerous procedure. Ordinarily it should not be used in therapy, or for experimentation. The sudden removel of a defensively, vital, conversion, or phobic symptom by hypnosis or suggestion offers the likelihood of a more dangerous sequela. As an example, Schmideberg related a story (told by Jones) in which just such a rapid "cure" of a case of agoraphobia by Freud was followed in a few days by the onset of acute symptoms of schizophrenia. Freud was reported to have promptly and successfully suggested, under hypnosis, the return of the phobia! This incident illustrates the *Principle of Symptoms Exchange Hazard* [Ch.12:VIIIB4].

and physical ailments.* In the Phobias there is a displacement of the threat and dread onto outside objects or situations.

The two reactions are not always fully separable. At times a case will illustrate elements of both the Phobic Reaction and Conversion Reaction. This will be found to occur in a case which has been summarized later [Ch.12:VIC2]. The case was presented because of the major conversion feature of *globus hystericus*. Prominent phobic reactions concerning contamination however, were nearly equally prominent and handicapping.

5. *Phobias and Obsessive-Compulsive Reactions*

The phobias are also closely related to the Obsessive-Compulsive Reactions. Indeed, following Janet's inclusion of phobias in the major category of psychasthenia, these three types of clinical phenomena tended to remain together as a group, for purposes of classification and study until recently (1952). This close relationship of the Phobias and the Obsessions is also reflected in the use of the adjective obsessive in our formal definition of a phobia. The fear and dread of the phobic patient and his preoccupation with his phobic object are very definitely obsessive in character.

Phobic Reactions as such are seen at times in patients with Obsessional Neuroses [*See also Case 64*, p. 318]. This may also be illustrated to an extent in the following clinical example. While this is not too clear-cut a reaction, it is, however, phobic in character.

Case 114

A Phobia of People (Anthropophobia)

(1) *Projection, Displacement, and Generalization*
A thirty-seven-year-old psychologist was in intensive treatment because of certain handicapping and limiting character defenses which were primarily of an obsessional nature. Among his rather severe emotional problems was a marked fear of people. While it was not always too specific in nature, it was nevertheless severe and handicapping.

This fear often interfered with his going to theaters or restaurants. He could usually manage such social expeditions only at the cost of considerable uneasiness.

We gradually discovered his fear to be largely the result of the projection and displacement of his own hostility and intolerance. The injury and hate he expected from others was a projected expression of his own deep-seated and hidden resentments. The combination of deep roots for his own feelings and the generalization to people as the phobic object, determined the choice of the latter on both symbolic and circumstantial bases.

(2) *Understanding promotes resolution*
The fears gradually subsided as we learned more of their mechanisms. We first began their understanding through some experiences he was able to report from playing golf. He began to notice how angry he was toward fellow club members for their "misuse of equipment", their "failure to replace divots", and their manner of dress and behavior.

---

* W. C. Menninger points out that the somatization or psychosomatic reactions "are just as much conversion reactions as is a paralysis."

As a way of helping to make their conversion basis clearer, the author has suggested and personally adopted the term *Physiologic Conversions*.

He deplored their "poor taste, boorish manners and loud talk". This critical attitude actually paralleled and reflected his own level of terrible self-criticism. This came in turn from a judgmental, over-developed conscience.

(3) Theory of Antecedent Conflicts illustrated

The antecedent roots for all this lay in infantile dissatisfaction with the sought-after object of dependency. There had been a failure of gratification. My patient said, in effect, "If Mother really cared enough, she would treat me better". The same thing was repeated all over again in effect, with the men at the club.

He might almost have said, "If they respected me enough, they would behave better out of consideration for me. To them I projected my own resentment and hostility at their failure to do so. Accordingly, it now seems to me that they are threatening me in turn, and are therefore to be feared, dreaded, and avoided". The maternal conflict was the important primordial antecedent, in accord with the Theory of Antecedent Conflicts.

For other dynamic formulations which may be applicable here, the reader is referred to our account of the Obsessive Personality [p. 245ff.] and to the Obsessive-Compulsive Reactions [p. 307ff.].

B. DIFFERENTIAL DIAGNOSIS: CLINICAL ILLUSTRATION

1. Occurrence with other Emotional Reactions

The development of phobias can be seen accompanying nearly every kind of emotional illness. They are a more common accompaniment of the Conversion, Hygeiaphronic, and Obsessive-Compulsive Reactions. They are likely to be less discrete and marked when they accompany some of the other patterns of neurotic reaction.

Phobias can be seen not infrequently to be a developmental step into more advanced and serious psychopathology with patients suffering from the Anxiety Reactions. Phobic development is observed in the psychoses. On the other hand, phobias tend to be rare in cases of Depression, the Dissociative Reactions, and Emotional Fatigue. Phobic Reactions occasionally occur in a traumatic setting, as illustrated in *Case 176,* [Ch.14:VC4].

2. Four Basic Possibilities to Consider

The case to follow illustrates a number of important aspects of clinical and psychopathologic interest. It illustrates the poorly defined boundaries which can sometimes exist between: (a) Hygeiaphronic (hypochondriacal) preoccupation [Ch.8:IIIA], (b) the severe Phobic Reaction, and (c) the somatic delusion as sometimes present in the Schizophrenic Reaction.

Accordingly, one's diagnostic judgment might result in the following absorbing case being considered as belonging to one of several diagnostic categories. It might possibly be classified as: (1) Phobic Reaction, (2) Hygeiaphronic Reaction, (3) Schizophrenia, or even (4) a severe Obsessional Neurosis. The dynamics and pathogenesis of the symptoms are also interesting and will be briefly discussed.

Case 115

A Phobia of Hirsutism; Variant of Trichophobia

(1) *The presenting features*

The patient was a twenty-six-year-old married mother of two small children. At the time of the first consultation in mid-November, she expressed her great concern over an alleged overgrowth of hair on her forearms, legs, and face. She had a great fear of becoming grotesque or "like a sideshow freak". She could not accept reassurance as to the normalcy of the fine blonde down or "peach fuzz" which was actually present. Her dread and fear were out of all possible proportion to what could be seen by an external observer.

There was a history of persistent overconcern of a pathologic level for six months. The patient suffered with frequent crying spells, moodiness, and irritability. She reported her great dissatisfaction with her family life and with her husband. The marriage was seriously threatened.

(2) *Diagnostic possibilities*

According to one's viewpoint, the principal feature of her very severe illness could conceivably be regarded variously as: (1) an obsessive preoccupation, (2) a specific pathologic dread and fear, that is, a phobia, (3) hygeiaphrontic overconcern, or even (4) a delusion. From this latter point of view the hirsutism might be viewed as "a false belief which is out of keeping with the person's level of knowledge", and which was "maintained against logical argument, despite objectively contradictory evidence". These points are major ones in the definition of a delusion.

(3) *Deception in emotional illness; its disastrous effect*

This patient had been brought to the city from her small home town in a neighboring state by her husband and hospitalized. The *ostensible* purpose of the trip had been in order to consult still another in a series of dermatologists. Actually, it was in order to secure hospitalization and to arrange for inpatient psychiatric care. This kind of dissembling is unfortunate. While far less frequent today, it still occurs all too frequently in making such arrangements for emotionally sick patients. Even once is too often!

Both the husband and the family doctor in this case had favored this unfortunate deception. They explained it to themselves, as to others later, on the basis that "it would make things easier for Ann". However, on the contrary, this deception was really undertaken *in order to make things easier for themselves.*

This kind of deception could only result in *more* trouble for the patient, since: (1) It "sided with the symptom", the implication being that the latter was factual and actually existed; (2) False expectations were encouraged, which could lead only to later disillusionment; (3) The deception reinforced feelings of distrust which had existed in past segments of her relationships; (4) It created a clouded aura of suspicion, which handicapped the early attempted therapeutic relationship with the psychiatric department and with her prospective therapist. It took great effort and many, many hours to finally counteract some of the untoward effects of this added handicap.

The psychologic effects of this kind of deception cannot always be overcome. A problematic situation thus can become a most difficult one; a difficult one may be made impossible.

(4) *Parental background*

The history disclosed that Ann was the only child of a distant, rather cold and reserved father, who had little to say about the running of the house. Long ago he had ceased taking any active stand with the mother, acquiescing in all her wishes. He happened to have an unusual amount of bodily hair.

Ann's mother was an obsessively clean and orderly housewife to whom arrangement and having things "just so" were very important.

She was the strong and dominant figure in the family, completely over-shadowing the father. The house was always completely immaculate.

There was no smoking, no drinking, no socializing, and never any playing allowed in the house. The mother was, in addition, intensely hygeiaphrontic. Although always the picture of health, she suffered with a great variety of complaints. She had visited the family physician at least once weekly all of her life. From earliest childhood, Ann was herself immediately carted off to the doctor for the most minute complaint.

(5) An Identification conflict: Mother vs. Father

Ann could never really measure up to her mother's very high standards. As she put it, "I never felt I could do anything right. I could never measure up . . : I guess I never felt adequate. I knew I could never keep house as well as my mother . . . Mother just seemed so efficient and so perfect. . . . It was hopeless to try to measure up to her. It was always clear to me that I could simply never do half so well as she did. . . .".

Ann developed strongly ambivalent unconscious feelings about all this. On the one side, she wanted to be the strong, dominant person her mother was. At the same time, she hated and resented her mother's coldness and aloofness, and she felt that being like her was not only an impossible achievement but also one which she didn't want at all! As one consequence, she also unconsciously and strongly wanted to retreat into the passive, acquiescent dependent role as exemplified by her father. Hirsutism became for her an important symbolic equivalent of father, of maleness, and also of dependency. [See later reference to Faulty Identification Concept, Ch.13:VE3.]

(6) Sexual conflict

There were early illustrations of the adoption of an obsessive-phobic pattern of defense. As one example, while in college, she developed an unrealistic fear. This was that her boy friend of many years, Roger, would be inevitably swept off his feet when he learned to know her strong and somewhat masculine roommate. Ann herself was subject to a strong attraction to the latter, an attraction which she found re-pugnant and had consciously to deny. Her obsessional fear about the *certain* loss of Roger was phobic in degree. Actually, it represented a number of facets of her emotional conflicts.

First, it was a projection to Roger of her own consciously disowned homosexual attraction. Secondly, as we shall learn, the feared object in a phobia is at the same time secretly desired. Herein, the loss of Roger (that is, his assumed certain marriage to Gloria), which was so consciously dreaded, would remove the homosexual threat. Of deeper consequence, it would also relieve her of any responsibility in the rela-tionship for maintaining her own unacceptable and burdensome femi-nine role.

(7) Fears begin about hair overgrowth

During Ann's teen years and even earlier, her mother had unwittingly implanted apprehensions about hair growth by holding such a possi-bility over her head as a way of control. For example, in discouraging the use of makeup, she told Ann that it was dangerous to use face powder since the orris root it contained would encourage hair growth. Later, when skin blemishes had appeared, she would say, "If you don't stop paying so much attention to your face all the time, picking at pimples and squeezing blackheads, hair will grow on your face. Each pinch can grow a hair!"

As a result of these repeated incidents and other cumulative and re-enforcing factors, Ann had developed even by this time some extra concern about her very normal, fine, lanugo-like facial, arm, and leg hair. She would spend time trying to pluck or to bleach it. This occu-pation was more marked when she was anxious or upset, thus providing us with certain soterial implications (*see Chapter 11*).

She had finally married Roger. He was a rather strong person and took much of the responsibility of their home. This was what she, largely unconsciously, very much wanted. Her feelings about this, however, were not unmixed. Partly as a consequence of these internal conflicts, she had increasing differences with her husband, but she outwardly based them upon other causes.

Following the birth of the second child, she was forced into a position of greatly increased responsibility in double fashion, as Roger's work began to take him on prolonged trips. This appeared to reactivate the earlier conflicts. These, it will be recalled, were over: (1) her attempted identification with her mother as the strong and efficient (albeit obsessive, hygeiaphrontic, and distant) "ideal", (2) her more secret (unconscious) wish to renounce the feminine role as represented by her mother, and (3) her desire to identify herself with her father. In addition there were major conflicts present over hostility and aggressiveness, sexual orientation, dependency, and health fears.

(8) *Fear progresses to "certainty"*

Some difficulty with ovarian cysts had developed, followed by the removal of an ovary. During her recovery she overheard her nurse talking to another about excess facial hair. She believed herself to be the subject of the conversation.

She also happened by chance to read a popular magazine article about the masculinizing ovarian tumor, arrhenoblastoma. The symptoms therein of the loss of secondary sexual characteristics might to some extent have been similar to some of her actual postoperative manifestations. In any event, she tied all these factors together and applied them to herself. One significant feature of this type of ovarian medullary tumor also happens to be an increased development of hair!

These somewhat adventitious events had been "seized upon" by her unconscious, and thus "used" to greatly strengthen her psychopathologic concerns, for which a considerable foundation had already been established. Her difficulties with her husband steadily increased. Looking after the two children became an increasingly intolerable burden. Her obsessive preoccupation and dread about hair growth gradually continued to increase and to become more fixed. Crying spells were frequent and she lost interest in social contacts.

(9) *Reassurance fails to relieve*

In August she had consulted a dermatologist in another city, seeking removal of the hair on her arms, legs, and face. He refused to do anything and denied that the amount of hair was unusual. Her response to this very honest appraisal was to become worse. (Recall that the object of fear and dread in a phobia is at the same time secretly desired!)

The determatologist's reassurance was factual and was the correct procedure. Nevertheless, it unconsciously equated the denial of her "secret" wish. (Hirsutism symbolically meant to her the masculine, more passive role, and at the same time a rejection of the impossible goal of femininity as it was represented to her by her mother). The reassurance did not relieve her. Instead, her phobic preoccupation increased. She had developed a type or variant of what we might term *Trichophobia,* in her obsessive preoccupation with, and fear of hirsutism.

She spent more and more time studying herself for signs of more hair growth, and staring at her face in the mirror. She remained in bed frequently. Her inability to care for the house increased. Roger now told her he was sick and tired of all this and threatened to leave her. Ann was, however, in the grip of powerful internal conflicts over which she not only had no control, but of which she did not even have conscious awareness. She was herself helpless—a ship tossed about on the stormy ocean of her hidden conflicts.

Matters were not helped when there developed some medical suspicion of a cyst in the remaining ovary and its removal was threatened. Her own personally suspected diagnosis of arrhenoblastoma, her serious conflicts over her masculine-feminine identification (and still more basically, dependency) had all been intensified by the first operation. Consideration of the second operation further reactivated and intensified her difficulties. She sought out the magazine article and read it repeatedly.

(10) *Psychopathology recognized*

In October she consulted a second dermatologist who fortunately correctly recognized the essential psychologic nature of her increasingly serious psychopathologic progression. He refused to intervene. In addition, he strongly urged immediate psychiatric care. Her hospitalization in November followed a week of tearful and miserable seclusion.

Of course, only a few highlights of an extremely interesting and complex case have been presented. It is included to illustrate the difficulty which can exist in drawing any absolute dividing line between the severe phobia, the obsession, the hygeiaphrontic preoccupation, and the delusion. The diagnosis of Phobic Reaction seemed most appropriate to the author in this instance, since most contacts with reality were essentially preserved and since the dynamics and psychogenesis were phobic in character. It might be noted, however, that a colleague of many years' experience believed that the diagnosis was more properly one of schizophrenia and that the patient was delusional. Whichever viewpoint is adopted by the reader, the case certainly points out how a phobia can conceivably increase in severity to merge into a psychotic delusionary belief. As noted earlier, phobias as such can be observed with various psychoses.

3. *Phobic Object Also Unconsciously Sought—and Preserved; Phobic Dilemma Concept*

While the foregoing case is presented as an interesting study in psychiatric diagnosis, there were of course many fascinating aspects of the dynamics and pathogenesis. Some of these have been alluded to already. Every phobia constitutes a horrible dilemma. The feared and dreaded external phobic object (the real internal source for which remains hidden from conscious awareness) is also simultaneously unconsciously wished for and desired. More accurately, it symbolically stands for that which is, on still a deeper level, also wished for but for which the secret wish must be denied and reversed. This is in essence what we might term the *Phobic Dilemma*. It is a concept of phobic ambivalence. So it was with hair and hair removal in the foregoing case.

The Phobic Dilemma represents a reactivation of antecedent conflicts. Most basically perhaps, it recapitulates as *phobic* ambivalence in the phobic syndrome, what we might refer to as the early primal ambivalence. This primal ambivalence dates to the oral period, stemming from, and reflecting the Oral Conflict. Theoretically, at least, all ambivalent reactions as observed so frequently in emotional reactions, would extend back to the era of oral conflict. The "primordial ambivalence" of these would constitute their earliest antecedent, in accord with our *Theory of Antecedent Conflict*.

It is interesting to note in this present connection that upon one occasion the opportunity did present itself for the actual removal of the hair. A physician, perhaps thinking to humor her, actually offered to do so. Despite her great level of conscious fear and dread and her earlier efforts to have someone do exactly this, *she could not accept it!* The phobic object had to be preserved at all costs despite the conscious pain and suffering it caused. This is also part of the *Phobic Dilemma*.

Her reasons at the time were rationalized on the basis of a sudden "lack of faith" she "conveniently" developed concerning the doctor's competence to use depilatory needles. Her lack of faith in his skill and judgment might have had some basis of fact, however, although for quite a different reason. His undertaking such a superficial approach in attempting to deal with a problem of a most complex psychologic nature actually reflects a professional naiveté of some gravity.

4. Recapitulation of dynamics

One might summarize some of the dynamics in the preceding case. Major conflicts were as follows: *First,* it is clear that the patient had major conflicts over her sexual identification. *Second,* there were also serious conflicts over her dependency needs. *Third,* important secondary conflicts also related to an earlier and not very well established homosexual leaning, to her marriage, and to her children.

The possession of hair symbolized maleness to her. On a deep level of meaning, its possession would mean giving up all chance or requirement to be feminine and to be like her mother. She doubted that she could ever achieve real strength or independence. Her secret feelings toward her mother were very ambivalent, and a large segment of her inner self unconsciously rejected her (and identification with her). The possession of hair would then mean she could be masculine, that is, more like father. Although he had acquiesced to mother's demands and was thereby weak, he "gained" a more passive, protected, and dependent position as a result. In accord with our *Faulty Identification Concept* [Ch.13: VD4; VE3], a conflict or confusion over identification can be quite ego-disruptive, and can lay the foundation for later serious difficulties.

The hidden conflict was fought out symbolically in distorted and disguised form in the phobic manifestations. The symbolic expression in symptom formation aided repressions. Her suffering through all this was partly masochistic retribution for the unconscious disapproval and guilt. These all helped make up the phobic endogain (that is, the primary gain of the illness).

The phobic *epigain* (that is, the *unconscious* secondary gain of the illness) followed from the dependent and protected position secured for her by the illness. As she had once actually stated in expressing her requirement for "everything to be all right," this would, in its ultimate form, require her husband to stay with her constantly. Her symptoms, her handicaps, and her suffering inevitably had considerable effects upon a number of people, upon their attitudes toward her, and upon the treatment she received from them.

C. DIAGNOSIS OF PHOBIC REACTIONS APPROPRIATE

As the reader has by this time doubtless realized, any systematic and rigid classification of the phobias is rather difficult. The phobic defense is highly individual. Phobic objects are legion and mechanisms in the same phobia can show wide variation. From this standpoint the phobias rather accurately might be regarded as a whole series of related illnesses rather than as a single psychopathologic entity. The diagnosis of a **Phobic Reaction** is appropriate and warranted when phobic manifestations are the most prominent and/or most limiting clinical feature in an emotional illness of neurotic level.

The naming of the many individual phobias has been done in the past on an empirical, descriptive basis. Many of the names thus applied seem more confusing than helpful. We shall accordingly use only a few of the technical names which are most widely accepted and which have been tabulated. [*See Table 27.*] For the most part, the simple naming of the phobic object seems sufficient. This kind of diagnosis on a descriptive basis is presently quite adequate.

IV. INCIDENCE

A. INCIDENCE GENERALLY; IN EARLY YEARS

1. Five Per Cent of Neuroses

The incidence of phobias is fairly wide. The author would estimate that between eight and twelve per cent of the clinical cases of neuroses have some phobic manifestation. Approximately five per cent or more of the clinical cases of neuroses would likely fall into this major diagnostic category of Phobic Reactions.

In regard to sex, Noyes stated that phobias were twice as frequent in women as in men, a statement which the author cannot verify from his own clinical experience.

2. Childhood Fears

A. PATHOLOGIC IMPORT VARIABLE.—The universality of fear has been noted. This is particularly true in childhood. [*See* preceding chapter.] Morbid fears, those out of proportion to the apparent stimulus, are very frequent. Spock discussed some of these frequent fears as they occur in early childhood. He pointed out that they "are different at different age periods". The more common fears which we are likely to develop from three to five years of age include such fears as those of the dark, of dogs, of death, and of injury. The psychopathologic significance of these can vary greatly. While widespread, they do not necessarily produce psychologic damage. On the other hand, childhood fears can be quite important as covert or as more open antecedents to later adult fears.

B. PARENTAL ATTITUDES CRUCIAL.—The attitudes of parents toward their children's fears is important. For example, it is very difficult if not almost impossible for a child to be comfortable with thunder and lightning when his parent is obviously frightened. Fears, as with other emotional feelings, can "rub off" on the child from a significant adult. They are, in effect, contagious. Children can be highly perceptive. They can often sense the presence of uneasiness despite all manner of conscious efforts at dissimulation.

Impatience or ridicule has a destructive effect. An attitude of acceptance, patience, and curious interest can greatly facilitate understanding
and possible resolution. The attitudes of a given parent in a given situation are, of course, strongly influenced by whatever emotional feelings may
be being experienced by him.

3. Phobias in Childhood. Phobic Attacks

The transition from fear to persistent fear, or to exaggerated fear, and
on to the clearly phobic manifestations, is a gradual progression. The
boundaries between these stages can be rather indistinct. This sometimes
appears to be more the case in infancy and in childhood.

Definite phobias are found in all age groups. There are a number of
scientific reports of infantile phobias and their treatment. Fear reactions
which may be of a phobic character are sometimes seen in the early months
of life. The following case illustrates a marked infantile fear which gradually subsided.

Case 116

**A Persistent Fear in Infancy Which Gradually and Spontaneously
Subsided**

A service officer and his wife were en route across the country with
two small children, aged twenty months and five months. Toward evening they left Route 40 to try to locate a restaurant in a small nearby
town. One was found across the street from the village railway station.
The younger child was sleeping peacefully. He was left in the car
while the adults and the older child went to eat. The car, with the
sleeping infant in it, was parked alongside the railway track.

The parents and older child were almost finished eating some thirty-
five minutes later when a steam train approached. As it pulled into the
station by the parked car, the whistle was blown, deafeningly and repeatedly. The five-month-old infant woke up, screaming, in a panic.
He was not easily comforted by his parents and was still somewhat
upset an hour or so later. This was an early instance of the "too-intense stimulus or experience," as a S.E.H.C. since it could not be readily
integrated by the infant's psyche. It was a source of emotional difficulty
in accord with our *Psychic Indigestion Concept* [Ch.9:IVD1].

Henceforth, for some months anything about a train was frightening
for him. He would cry if he heard a distant train whistle. An enforced
stop by a railroad crossing for a train to pass would result in almost
hysterical crying. Gradually these responses subsided, but the child was
more than eighteen months old before the reaction faded out entirely.
One may speculate on the possibility of any emotional repercussions
later in life.

Bornstein reported a case of phobia in a two-and-a-half-year-old child.
Schmideberg reported the cure of a train phobia in a three-year-old. The
first case of phobia dynamically interpreted was that in a five-year-old.
This was the classic example of Little Hans, cited earlier. Sterba published
still another instance of a childhood phobia in which the displacement of
the fear of a person (in this instance again, father) important to the emotional life, was made in somewhat similar fashion to the case of Little
Hans. In Sterba's case, the unconscious displacement was made to dogs
as the phobic object.

Phobias seem often to have their initiation in childhood. Frequently,
also, the early foundations for a later phobia are laid down in the years

between five and eight. Phobias are also observed frequently to begin in later life. In a recent instance a series of what the author would term *Phobic Attacks* first began for an electronics engineer at age 58 years. These were brief, acute, unpredictable, and episodic. They approximated the A.A.A. in their onset, duration, and sequella [*see* pp. 121–122]. Clinically claustrophobia is a frequent type. Aerophobia, spatiophobia, anthrophobia, and others, however, can be experienced as Phobic Attacks. The Phobic Attack as in the A.A.A., is a signal of acute Emotional Decompensation [p. 159].

B. PHOBIAS BEGINNING LATER IN LIFE

1. Incidence slowly declines

In general the incidence of Phobic Reaction declines slowly after the age of the early twenties. In the author's clinical experience there has seemed to be some increase in the incidence of phobias again in the thirties and early forties. While not absent they have been rarer in the later decades of life.

Menninger reported that about twenty per cent of college students have, or have had, phobias in early years which sooner or later disappeared spontaneously. The disappearance spontaneously of mild phobias in early years may be observed with some frequency. Occasionally they reappear. The author has heard of cases in which the phobic symptoms were first reported after the age of seventy years, and has worked therapeutically with persons in which this first transpired in their fifties and sixties. When therapeutic study is possible in some of these later phobias, important dynamic antecedents can be anticipated and are frequently to be found.

2. In young adulthood

Many significant Phobic Reactions which become the object of therapy have their initiation in young adulthood. This group is accordingly an important one. Usually earlier roots can be uncovered.

The following case summary is one concerning the definitive formation of phobia of theaters in young adulthood. This illustrates the *Critical-Displacement* type of Phobia [Sect.IA2 and Sect.VIA3]. In view of its attachment at times to the locale or situation at the time of onset, some instances are also to be classified as *Situational Phobias*. In this case the dynamics have also been worked out rather carefully. Of both interest and value, these will be presented in condensed form.

Case 117

A Phobia of Theaters

(1) *A significant failure sets the stage*

A successful young journalist sought treatment because of his lack of success in developing and maintaining meaningful relationships. He had a strong phobia of theaters which had been present for several years, since his graduate school days. In his class he had been a brilliant and outstanding student who worked inordinately. He had been somewhat handicapped by being younger than his classmates.

The onset of the phobia had followed what had been for him an emotionally traumatic situation. The highly coveted editorship of the

School Review had been awarded to another, although he was the logical candidate. He had been denied what represented to him the pinnacle of success. Greatly disturbed, he had sought out one of his professors, who was also Chairman of the Editorial Board, for some explanation or help. His interview with this man gave him little satisfaction. In fact, it only disturbed him further. His defeat, deprivation, and helpless rage came to focus on the Professor-Chairman.

(2) *Critical level of anxiety and its displacement*

He was torn by confused feelings of helplessness, murderous hostility, and self-destruction. In an effort to relieve his agitation he went to a theater. At this crucial juncture and by chance, he happened to see the professor, who was also attending the play! His state of disturbance reached a peak and he fled the theater. However, about this time his disturbing feelings were repressed and lost to consciousness. As a consequence, the conflicts and his desperate feelings in response to them no longer threatened him. The danger was henceforth displaced to the theater!

He could not flee from his feelings, but he could flee from the theater. By the displacement of the feelings to the theater they were lost to conscious awareness, and flight from, or avoidance of, the theater henceforth was possible. Fleeing from the theater now came symbolically to equate for him, fleeing from his feelings.

(3) *Recapitulation of antecedent conflicts*

Let us briefly condense the background and dynamics. The rage against the professor in essence recapitulated a very important antecedent conflict. The patient's father had been a plodding, noncolorful professional man, subject to frequent ridicule by his mother. She held up a more successful brother of hers as an ideal and goal to the boy. She had always been cold and distant. The implication was, in effect, "If you become like your uncle, then I will really accept you". His hidden and threatening rage against his mother was toward the unsatisfactory object of his dependency, who had constantly set impossible standards of achievement for him. This made it impossible for him ever to secure success, that is, acceptance and love. He had protectively to deny that it was possible to be deserted and unloved.

The emotionally heightened goal of the editorship and his intense struggle over it was a reliving of the earlier struggle. Loss of success here symbolically equated for him the earlier failure he had experienced in his attempts to meet his mother's standards and to gain her love. In this failure, he must face helplessness, nonacceptance, and murderous rage over his frustration to make the parent or the parent-object "come across".

The failure of his compulsive drive for success touched this off. The phobic defense kept the awareness of his helplessness and his murderous rage in response to this, repressed.

(4) *How locale becomes phobic object*

The main factor in the selection of the theater was the locale of the final unstable overload of anxiety and tension. There were deeper symbolic elements, however, in that to him a theater was a place where one "shows off" or makes a spectacle of oneself. This conformed to some of his fantasies at the time. These, if followed through, symbolically became a revenge on the standard-setter, a revenge for failure, however self-defeating.

The theater also represented the feared and dangerous situation where things are more freely expressed: the actors may act out many kinds of dramatic events. This made the theater a place where such impulses as he had might be more likely to be expressed.

(5) *"Deep treatment": excellent therapeutic results*

In this case what we might call the successful *deep treatment* of the phobia was marked by the surrender of his basic underlying capacity for the development of the phobic pattern of defense. Ultimately also the patient came to understand and to accept his helplessness and his inability to gain the fantastic mother of his unconscious wishes and longings. Only then could he accept any failure to succeed. Only then could he give up compulsive working.

Then he could allow the risks of close, significant, and constructive relationships. There were many other ramifications and details in this complex but very interesting case. His successful course of treatment required hundreds of sessions, over several years. This phobia represented both the *Critical-Displacement* and the *Situational* categories of Phobic Reaction.

C. CULTURAL INFLUENCES UPON MANIFESTATIONS AND TYPES OF ILLNESS

1. "Styles" of emotional illness

Many psychiatrists are aware of various cultural influences upon the incidence of the different types of neuroses, and upon certain similar variations in the prevalence of the symptoms of emotional illness. These influences tend to bring about what we might call a *cultural vogue* in symptoms. This cultural vogue is apparently slowly changing, with perhaps some clear enough difference in the comparative "styles" of emotional illness for our detection, perhaps over each interval of several decades.

Reference is not made here of course to the short-range effects of "contagion" via suggestibility, of which reactions on this basis have occasionally been seen. For example, "epidemics" of headache, gastrointestinal upsets, or backache have been seen at times in a fairly large proportion of the soldiers in a given barracks. These instances are more apt to be observed during basic training, "boot camp", or while awaiting overseas duty. [*See also* reference to Conversion Epidemics in *Chapter 12.*]

The influence of the cultural vogue is perhaps best illustrated in the Conversion Reactions, in the Phobic Reactions, and in paranoid delusions. In the former we have seen a gradual but substantial decrease in the incidence of the gross kind of Somatic Conversion Reactions since World War I.

2. Cultural vogue concept: popularity of phobic objects shifts

With the phobias, the changes have been in the changing "popularity" of certain phobic objects. Around the sixteenth century, demons (demonophobia), sorcery, witchcraft, and Satan (Satanophobia) were in vogue. During the 1920s and 30s syphilophobia was relatively common, whereas the instances the author has encountered in recent years have been increasingly rare and have been associated with incipient or active schizophrenia.

Currently, cancerophobia, fear of flying and of airplanes (flienophobia), fear of poliomyelitis or poliosophobia (decreased following widespread anti-polio programs) and, to a lesser extent, atomic phobias (atomosophobia), have increased in frequency. The "popularity" of certain other phobic objects, for example, water, height, closed spaces, open spaces, insanity, dirt, and certain animals, appears to remain rather stable.

Similar changes have been observed with paranoid patients, who are more currently concerned with television and Communists. These have superseded at least in part, wireless, radio, dictaphones, and Nazis. These evolving trends in the "choice" of phobic objects and other emotional manifestations, tend to follow gradually shifting patterns of "popularity", in accord with our *Cultural Vogue Concept,* in emotional symptomatology.

V. SYMPTOMS AND CLINICAL FEATURES

A. ANXIETY, FEAR, AND DREAD

1. Physiologic, Physical, Mental, and Psychologic Consequences

The symptoms of a phobia are the various subjective manifestations of anxiety, dread, and fear which have become unconsciously associated by a given patient with his object of phobia. At times some parts of this reaction are outwardly apparent. The subjective reaction alone however can be quite severe enough! Physiologic changes can accompany the subjective ones. These are generally those which are appropriate to the emotions of fear and anxiety, as earlier described in the appropriate chapters. Our *Concept of Continued Physiologic Momentum* [pp. 98–104] may receive illustration.

Not infrequently the establishment of a fixed object for phobic dread and avoidance appears, at least superficially, to lessen the patient's anxiety. In more covert fashion symptoms can also include the physical, psychologic, and mental consequences of anxiety. [*See Table 8,* pp. 113–4.] The best way to present the clinical manifestations of the phobias and their level of disturbance may be through the presentation of the three additional case summaries which follow. Something of the dynamics will also be included.

2. Inversion of Unconscious Wish; Concept of Phobic Ambivalence Illustrated

The following clinical example of a phobia shows little further progression in complexity from the last clinical illustrations of fear. This interesting case shows the rather simple type of phobia in which the feared event is, on a deeper level, also secretly desired, illustrating the intriguing Concept of Phobic Ambivalence; or *Phobic Dilemma,* as noted earlier.

Case 118

Phobia of Nervous Breakdown in Spouse

(1) *Doubts and recognition of a major mistake consciously intolerable*

A thirty-seven-year-old civil engineer, with a record of excellent professional achievement, sought psychiatric treatment because of certain failures in his familial relationships. Among his initially reported difficulties was a marked fear that his wife would suffer a nervous breakdown. He suffered considerably from his apprehension and went to some lengths to save her undue stress and strain. During the first eight months of three years of intensive and productive work in his treatment, some of which was intermittently directed toward this particular problem, we managed to analyze the basis for his phobia. As a result, it ceased to trouble him.

Immediately following his engagement, this patient had begun to suffer misgivings about the wisdom of his choice of a fiancee. These and later more definite doubts, he attempted to discard. It was intolerable to him, from the time of the engagement onward, ever to face a formal break-up of his engagement, or a divorce, from his marriage. This was because of his own stringent moral standards, and to avoid the judgments which he anticipated from others.

(2) Inversion of disowned wish

As he said, "I could not bear the spotlight of family post-mortems. . . . The thought of being in the 'dock' is disturbing and embarrassing. Maybe I've always placed too strong an emphasis on 'the proprieties'. . . . I've always had a terrific need for social conformance and acceptance. . . . I could never stand the awkwardness of a disrupted engagement or of a broken marriage . . .". His analysis eventually uncovered some basic elements in the origins of his phobic dread.

"This fear of mine has been an *inversion* of my real but hidden wishes to escape. . . . I can see it all clearly now. I guess I've always wanted to escape the unpleasant part of our relationship. These desires have been hidden, even though there have been references to them in some of the daydreams I've told you about. I recall, too, some of my trapped and helpless feelings about the marriage in the early years. . .".

(3) What is feared is, on a deeper level, also desired

". . . If my wife had a nervous breakdown, this would accomplish what I've secretly wanted and it wouldn't involve any angry break-up or unpleasant scenes. It wouldn't be my fault either. . . . No blame for me, plus absolution for any part I might have played in previous disharmonies. . . .

". . . People would say 'Poor guy, he's been living all along with that neurotic woman! . . . You see, doctor, this would give me sympathy instead of an accusing finger. I couldn't stand that accusing finger from myself as well as from others. So I had to try and hide such wishes even from myself . . .".

What was outwardly feared in the above instance, as we eventually learned, was unconsciously really desired! This again represents the operation of *phobic ambivalence*. Thus the phobic object, or more precisely perhaps, what it stands for or symbolizes, is also in some way secretly desired, sought, or necessary. As noted earlier, it recapitulated the "primordial ambivalence" stemming from the Oral Conflict.

Thus, because of its production of intense guilt, and for other reasons, the wish was consciously intolerable and came out in disguised form. As the patient described it himself, it became "inverted." Avoidance of recognition of the hostile wishes was a vital internal endeavor. These became inverted into a feared or dreaded event. The specific *reversal* or *inversion* was part of their further disguise and concealment. His wife was actually overprotected and received special treatment. This, plus his anxiety, now continued to punish him (though the punishment was in disguised form) for his own disowned wishes. The phobia dealt in neurotic fashion with the conflicts by attempting to hide and conceal the intolerable wishes. Certain implications herein as to antecedent conflicts in childhood we shall leave for further discussion in connection with certain of our other illustrative cases. This case is an excellent illustration of the mental mechanism of Inversion. [*See the author's previous book, Mental Mechanisms,* pp. 168–197.]

B. ONSET OF SYMPTOMS

1. Displacement More Readily Effected when Anxiety Inordinate

A. NEW EMOTIONAL-OBJECT AMALGAM, E.O.A.—At times the onset of symptoms can be traced to the original time at which an effort to thrust the painful event or idea from the mind seemingly succeeded. We have seen this illustrated in Case 117. Thus, when anxiety is present in inordinate amounts, it is more readily detached from its original source and, by a process of *Displacement,* an external object or situation becomes a substitute. This process takes place completely outside of awareness. Usually, from the time that displacement is effected, all memory traces are lost (that is, repression occurs) of the unbearable idea or event. The new Emotional-Object Amalgam is relatively stable.

An example of this is seen in the following phobia about flowers and their scent. This was a *Critical-Displacement* type of Phobia.

Case 119

A Phobia of Flowers (Anthophobia)

(1) *Serious consequences*
This rather marked phobia was a major factor in leading a thirty-four-year-old chemist to seek analysis. The sight or smell of flowers, particularly bouquets, sprays, and cut flowers, brought on intense fear, dread, and anxiety. This might be even more intense if the flowers were beginning to wither. Flowers had become for him an external threatening object which had to be avoided at all costs. Concomitant changes in the physical, physiologic, mental, and emotional spheres were in evidence at various times. They were more or less appropriate for the level of the reaction which his phobic object evoked. A partial carry-over (that is, Extension) to certain chemical odors was a serious professional handicap.

The effects on his life were constant, always serious and sometimes tragi-humorous. Cumulatively they were more than might perhaps be expected by the casual observer. They were more than can be readily or fully described here. The ramifications of such a Phobic Reaction can, and did, extend into every aspect of his living.

(2) *His father's death*
There was no conscious memory of the time of onset, nor could the patient give any rational explanation for his very troubling and uncontrollable reactions. Eventually, however, through associations and some collateral information and suggestions, during a prolonged, difficult period of treatment, he was able to recall, albeit with great anxiety, the time of onset. This had taken place in very early years at the time of the death of his father.

Before the funeral, the casket rested in the living room, surrounded by floral displays. The small boy had wandered into the room alone and suddenly recalled hostile feelings he had had toward his father. A terribly repugnant thought that he "was glad father was dead" came to mind. Another idea, "It served him right," followed. Even more unbearable fleeting fantasies were in sequence. These were along the line that he somehow shared responsibility for father's death, through his own hostile thoughts. It occurred to him that, as a consequence, punishment (through the wrath of God) must come. He had frequently been told semi-seriously by his mother that "flowers in bloom reflected God's smile." It was a logical development for him to evolve this further into the sequel that, "As His smile faded, so would flowers fade and die."

(3) Psychically Determined Phobic Object; Phobic Endogain

In stringently condensed form this was the essence of the phobic formation. The unbearable ideas included his hostile reflections, consequent feelings of responsibility and being faced with the wrath of God
as his deserved punishment. He was intensely anxious and fearful.
The excess of anxiety readily attached itself to flowers as the "convenient" phobic object. These were present at the time when his anxiety
had reached an unstable and unbearable "critical" level and were so
associated in sensory context. They already had a symbolic representation of him of equating God's smile. Flowers always fade and wither.
In incurring God's wrath, faded flowers were thus even more ominous
to him. The choice of flowers as his phobic object was psychically
more than amply determined, and thus constituted a good example of
the important principle of *overdetermination*.

Previously he had loved flowers. From this day on, however, they
were the object of intense fear and had to be avoided. His reaction
might be regarded as a type of *Induced-Avoidance* [Ch.9:IIIB2]; "self-
induced". Note, however, that the unbearable ideas were apparently
successfully *repressed* from all conscious recollection at the same time
that displacement of his anxiety and fear was made to the flowers. Now
the flowers became unbearable. This process also illustrates the *phobic
endogain*. It would be impossible to escape his unbearable hostile fantasies, omnipotent feelings of responsibility or the wrath of God. It
now became more possible to avoid flowers as the symbolic and hidden representation of these. *

(4) Oral Dependent Conflict recapitulated

The avoidance does not work out as one might think. The object of the
phobia is frequently encountered, often in rather uncanny fashion. On a
deep level of unconsciousness, the feared object as noted is simultaneously desired and often sought out. This ambivalent attitude symbolically recapitulates the original or primary Oral Conflict, and ambivalence over the maternal object of dependency. The unconscious
need for the object and the consequences of the concurrent hostility
toward it can account for the apparent uncanny ability to "find" it.
This is, of course, despite the subjective fear and anxiety which is
aroused.

In the oral dependent conflict one must have what one wants, but
at the same time deny that it is wanted! The threatening danger of
the hostile impulses which are part of the ambivalence toward the
object of dependency is that they might be successful in their aim, perhaps rather magically. The ensuing destruction of the vitally needed
object would indeed be a disastrous success.

(5) Neurotic "gain" paradoxical

Further, the self-limiting and restrictive effects of the phobia, the investment of energy in efforts at avoidance, and the suffering despite
the patient's best efforts, made the neurotic "gain" indeed paradoxical.
The real net result, as in every neurosis, was defeat, handicap, and loss.

Finally, recall that the original basis of anxiety at the time of the
Critical Attack had in it unreal and magical elements which if made
accessible, can be dispelled in the detached light of objectivity, insight
and reason.

2. Danger Displaced and Externalized

The following case, in similar fashion to *Case 119,* had its onset at the
time of the death of a parent. The dramatic events as summarized below
were gradually reconstructed during long-term intensive therapy.

---

* Actually, however, as Rangell has also reported in his excellent analysis of a
phobia of dolls, the patient had a hyperacute "ability" to "find" the object of his
phobia, in this instance, flowers. The world seemed to him a rather flowery place!
Thus, there is the unconscious seeking of the very object which is feared. This is
in accord with our *Concept of Phobic Ambivalence.*

Case 120

A Cat Phobia Began with Death of Parent (Ailurophobia)

(1) *Shifting feelings towards father and towards cats*

A psychologically, seriously ill, thirty-six-year-old patient suffered from an intense phobia of cats; an ailurophobia. Cats had been anathema to her since early childhood although there were dim recollections, substantiated by family members, of a still earlier fondness for them. The patient's father had long suffered from severe chronic alcoholism. He had alternated between being loving and tender, and very abusive. The consequence to the little girl was the development of strongly ambivalent feelings toward him.

Part of her earlier fondness for and attachment to cats had been a sort of compensation to her. She also sometimes played games with them in which they represented father, mother, and other children.

(2) *Feelings and events repressed*

The father died suddenly from an acute gastric hemorrhage. This occurred suddenly and in a tragic and dramatic episode. The little girl entered this scene despite some initial attempt by her mother to exclude her. She felt both fascinated and intensely repelled by what she saw. Following the father's death, the mother kissed the dead man, whose lips were stained from the terminal hemorrhage and then insisted the child do likewise. This the little girl did, despite strong feelings of revulsion. She wondered if the cat might do this also and she recalled earlier playful identifications.

This experience was too intense for the child. Not possible to integrate it adequately, it illustrates our earlier [Ch.9:IVC3] *Psychic-Indigestion Concept*.

There also now entered into her recollection some of the unbearable hostile side of her feelings toward father and toward mother also, who had been a frustrating object of dependency. If she had such horrible feelings these might be effective again (as with father); mother might also die (that is, be killed)! Projection and displacement took place. The unbearable feelings and her recall of these traumatic events were relegated to the unconscious.

(3) *Phobic Endogain: Repression, Displacement, Externalization,
   control, self-punishment*

The danger was henceforth externalized to cats, which became to her the external source of threat and danger, in place of her own feared *internal* impulses. These had proved fantastically and disastrously potent in symbolic fashion, in view of her father's death. The resultant phobic suffering was both retribution and warning.

Preoccupation with the avoidance of and threat from cats also absorbed psychic energy and protectively bound it so that it was unavailable for recognition of or acting upon, her repressed hostile impulses. In a more complex way this is in accord with our earlier [p. 85] *Principle of the Avoidance of Anxiety*. [*See* Ch.9:Sect.III.] She developed character defenses of compliance and become overly protective and solicitous toward her mother. At the same time she "acted out" some of her hidden, intensely hostile and competitive feelings in a disguised and self-defeating, partial expression of them.

3. Why The Phobic Type of Defensive Reaction?

Unanswered fully as yet are questions as to why the capacity for the development of phobic defense mechanisms exists in one patient, whereas the capacity for Conversion Reaction, Dissociation, or some other type of reaction is present with another. Does some kind of psychologic dominance develop? Are visual areas dominant for one and various selected somatic ones for another?

On the basis of an increased individual psychologic meaning, could such a deeply buried basis determine the direction, site, and type of the later focus of emotional difficulty? Further understanding also as to more of the determining factors in location would be useful in emotional illness. This is especially true, for example, in the Physiologic Conversions (that is, the psychosomatic disorders).

VI. PSYCHODYNAMICS AND PATHOGENESIS OF PHOBIC REACTIONS

A. EACH PHOBIC REACTION INDIVIDUALLY DETERMINED

1. Bases of Phobias

A. THEORIES OF ETIOLOGY EVOLVE.—Early beliefs ascribed phobias as due to supernatural forces and by investment by evil and spells. Some persons later ascribed them to constitutional factors, to dizziness, or to epilepsy. Westphal noted the irrationality of agoraphobia.

Kraepelin and Oppenheimer regarded the Phobic Reactions as largely constitutionally determined. Hall (1897) suggested phylogenetic origins. Pitres and Regis in 1902 stressed the importance of the precipitating event. Janet related them to conversion paralyses. Freud offered the first really dynamic formulations.

B. FAVORABLE PSYCHOLOGIC SOIL CONCEPT.—Adequate determining conditions must exist for a phobia to develop. This already may be quite apparent. The cases thus far summarized have included the dynamic considerations involved in their formation. These data are to be regarded as an integral part of the present section on the pathogenesis of the Phobic Reactions.

From our study of the phobic type of defense to this point, it must be apparent that the psychologic capacity for the formation of a phobia must antedate the later clinical symptom formation. In other words: (1) the basic psychology, (2) the constellation of dynamisms employed (or where the potential for their adoption exists), and (3) the existing pattern of character defenses together constitute a predisposition. Such a foundation must exist for the adoption and use of this type of unconscious defensive operation against anxiety when the circumstances require emergency defenses. This is in accord with what we might for convenience refer to as the conception of *Favorable Psychologic Soil*. Existence of such soil antedates the elaboration of a Phobic Reaction, in which it thrives.

2. Principle of Individual Specificity of Emotional Defenses

This conception points up the individual specificity of the type of emotional defense which a person adopts. It may also illustrate the relative susceptibility of different people to what appear to be identical emotional stresses. For example, a large number of people might theoretically be exposed to the same stressful situation. Only an occasional one might develop a phobia. This *Principle of Individual Specificity of Emotional Responses* ties in with our earlier Individual-Appropriateness-of-Response Principle [pp. 14, 84, 111].

Other persons thus might develop other types of emotional reactions in various degrees or combinations. Much is dependent on the *Intrapsychic Transit* [Ch.9:IVB3] of a given stressful experience. Many would show little or no apparent effect. Thus, the development of neurotic emotional defenses is marked by great specificity and by a high degree of individuality. Each is emotionally determined by powerful intrapsychic forces, factors and symbolism. Each is actually *over-determined*. [*See* Principle of Over-determinism, Ch.8:VID3; Ch.12:VIIIB; Ch.13:IIIC1].

3. Variable Complexity

It should be noted that the complexity of phobias varies greatly. As Fenichel observed, "In certain cases there is not much displacement; anxiety is simply felt in situations where an uninhibited person would experience either sexual excitement or rage." Perhaps one might also add feelings of closeness, warmth, or tenderness. Fenichel continues, "for such cases . . . what a person fears he unconsciously wishes for". [*See also Case 119* and Concept of Phobic Ambivalence.] In other and still simple phobias, the feared situation does not represent a feared temptation; rather it is the (accompanying) threat that causes the temptation to be feared.

The dynamics are more clear cut in Critical-Displacement phobias, and generally less so in the Gradually Evolving phobias. In the latter, factors of origin are multiple, involved, and more complex. Overdetermination is likely more significant. Finally in their therapy, resolution may well be secured without the clear-cut therapeutic delineation or specific "working through" of all, or even many, of the basic initiating dynamic facets.

The individuality of the phobias has been referred to. The selection of the phobic object offers almost unlimited variety, from such a specific phobia as one of knives or cats, to the phobia of "a part of the universe", as in agoraphobia, or as in the following instance (*Case 121*) of a phobia of travel.

As the author has pointed out elsewhere, "At times one may make an educated guess as to the psychologic significance of a particular phobia for a particular individual. While this sort of intellectual exercise may occasionally be accurate, the only real proof of the accuracy of any surmises as to the dynamics is to be found in the therapeutic working out and analysis of the meaning of his phobia with the individual patient."

B. DYNAMICS OF A PHOBIA

1. Feared Loss of Dependent Position; 'The Gradually Evolving Phobia'

In the following phobia of travel, the displacement served symbolically to represent outwardly the disguised but deeply rooted and consciously disowned fear of a loss of the dependent position—ultimately the object of dependent needs, mother. The fear of travel served as a cover for the real but hidden and internal fears. This became the phobic object. It constitutes an externalized and symbolic representation.

What it stands for thus remains internal, hidden from conscious awareness and repressed. This is an instance of what we might term the *Gradually Evolving Phobia* in distinction from those phobic reactions with an acute, sudden, and sometimes dramatic onset: the *Critical-Displacement Phobia*.

Case 121

Phobia of Travel (Travelophobia)

(1) *Fear of exposed, more active position*

A young business executive who sought analytic treatment had suffered for years from a fear of travel. The fear had been of sufficient severity to handicap his business considerably. This involved the production and distribution of machine tools which were individually designed to meet the specialized needs of various manufacturers around the country. He had consciously rationalized his fears on the basis that something vaguely evil might befall. For example, he might become ill, with adequate medical care unavailable. Intellectually he recognized the level of fear and anxiety which was stimulated by the prospect of travel as being most inappropriate in degree.

During the course of his analytic work we occasionally found data which related to this particular segment of his emotional difficulties. Gradually it became clear that a fear of the "unfamiliar" and of "being on his own" underlay the earlier advanced fears.

This in turn slowly crystallized as uneasiness about being independent or about taking a more "active position." This was implicit to travel, as opposed to the more passive and protected position possible in his usual business surroundings. Actually, he poorly tolerated separating himself from his familiar and accustomed daily sources of support, emotional "supplies", familiarity, security, protection, and dependency.

(2) *Reaction to loss of Object of Dependence*

Thus separation recapitulated in effect, his antecedent early childhood fears of separation from his mother. These fears had been banished from all conscious awareness. They had had their ultimate realization with the death of his mother, when he was six years old. He had been an only child, overprotected and overdependent. The mother's sudden death had been thereby an even greater shock and loss, which at that time left him in precipitate fashion alone, independent and on his own.

In contrast to certain other cases thus far illustrated (*Cases 117, 119,* and *120*), there was *no sudden or dramatic onset.* Instead, the phobic problem had developed gradually. This case is not dissimilar in this respect or in the dynamics, to certain instances of agoraphobia, the fear of open spaces, or of many other kinds of phobias. It would be classified therefore with the *Gradually Evolving* type of Phobias.

Let me mention briefly another significant aspect of the dynamics. In this kind of situation *not only is the original object of dependence desperately important, but almost inevitably there are also directed toward it strongly ambivalent, negative feelings.* Such proved to be present with this patient. There were some resulting guilty, rather magically omnipotent feelings of responsibility for his mother's death.

In this sense the loss of his mother was also on an unconscious level a punishment for having had the negative ambivalent feelings. The death of mother had played a major role in his personal psychology. Following the death, any and all negative thoughts in relation to mother were rapidly sent into the oblivion of the unconscious. A process of Idealization took place. He had soon reached a point where, when faced with any problem or disappointment, he retreated semi-automatically to the comforting thought that "everything would be O.K. if only mother were here".

(3) *Transference to therapist*

It is not surprising in this emotional constellation that fears were also present about the absence of the therapist during his occasional trips or vacation periods. His reactions to the therapist were as if he were "mother." The patient was eventually able to put some of his feelings into words which related these instances to the earlier painful occasion. "I am powerless again. . . . I don't like it when you go away. It is painful to me . . . I feel frightened and deserted, and somehow both guilty and punished . . . I would like to prevent it, but of course I can't. I feel frantic and helpless . . .". Before treatment he would not have been able consciously to recognize the presence of these feelings, or their extent, let alone give voice to them.

His references to guilt and punishment were the result of poorly hidden hostility and resentment toward the therapist, in view of his powerlessness (as with mother). In childhood, originally one defense against this had been a "flight into omnipotence." Herein it had seemed somehow as though magically his negative wishes had become terribly and frighteningly potent, and had succeeded in bringing about the loss of mother. This could be viewed as an instance of our clinical concept of "feelings of omnipotent responsibility", as outlined later [Ch.14:VE2].

(4) *Ambivalent Conflict toward Object of Dependency: danger of the negative side's "success"*

The defense of omnipotence can seemingly protect against helplessness or powerlessness. However, the danger that the negative side of the ambivalence might ever achieve its ultimate aim, that is, the desperately self-defeating destruction of the simultaneously vitally needed object of dependence, is terribly alarming. Thus, anxiety became increased. On a deep level of unconscious mental processes the patient feared that his anger might in some omnipotent fashion achieve its desired but terribly self-defeating result.

In an automatic and compulsively repetitive fashion, as earlier and stronger with mother, the author had become the needed object of dependency, although simultaneously resented for his incompleteness and for his failures fully to satisfy the patient's "hidden" needs. Thus, in complex fashion, the author's absences recapitulated the earlier antecedent, primordial situation. In effect, the early conflicts with mother were rekindled. These had been unfortunately greatly intensified by her death, which had taken place at a time when the patient's negative ambivalent feelings were very strong.

(5) *A significant aspect of therapy*

There was, of course, a relationship between the patient's fear of his own travel and his fear of the author's absences. His fear of travel was greater partly because the initiative for making the trip was his own, with its attendant and earlier stated symbolic meaning. The intensity of fear about the author's travel was partly a reflection of the level and the intensity of the transference.

The resolution of the emotional patterns evolved in the transference relationship are always a significant aspect of the therapy. As this was secured over a period of time in the foregoing case his Phobic Reaction gradually melted away. Further, generally beneficial effects diffused throughout his personality and his emotional adjustment.

2. Important Dynamisms Operative

A. PSYCHOGENESIS OF THE PHOBIA.—The foregoing case can serve to illustrate for us the mental mechanisms most frequently operative, and the technical terms most likely to be employed in discussing the dynamics in cases of Phobic Reaction. For these purposes, let us recapitulate and summarize the psychopathogenesis.

First, *Repression* had taken place and the patient no longer had conscious awareness of either his early negative *ambivalence* or of his basic *dependency* needs. The former had been replaced by a *reaction of the opposite (Reaction Formation),* with the development of an *idealized* image of mother. According to this, her (symbolic) return would now solve any problem. The mental mechanisms comprise our First Line of Psychic Defense [p. 25]. Their failure, overdevelopment, or psychopathologic evolvement leads to the generation of the various neurotic patterns of reactions. As outlined in Chapter 9 the phobic defense is a type of *avoidance* and comprises one major variety of *psychologic flight.*

The anxiety of his dependency conflicts had been *displaced* externally onto the idea of travel. The latter is the *phobic object.* It is a *Substitution* for the original, disowned internal areas of conflict and concern. *Externalization* has occurred, with the emotional feelings associated with the unbearable ideas now bound or cathected, through the important mechanism of Displacement, to a new area [Ch.9:IB*1*]. The new (phobic) object plus its firmly attached affect or emotional charge is a relatively stable union. This is the phobic *emotional-object amalgam.* It is also sometimes termed an anxiety-laden cathexis. *Phobic avoidance* now becomes a defensively, and at least theoretically, possible maneuver. In distinction from the *Critical-Displacement Phobia* with its acute, sharply demarcated onset, this phobia would be typed as an instance of the *Gradually Evolving Phobia.*

B. PHOBIC ENDOGAIN; PRIMARY AND SECONDARY DEFENSES.—In this case, travel is the disguised outward *symbolic* representation of the inner, hidden (unconscious) and disturbing ideas and needs. This entire complex process is in the service of controlling, denying, or allaying anxiety. It brings about and constitutes the *phobic endogain.* This is the unconscious *primary gain* of this emotional illness. The gain is defensively and desperately sought. This gain plus the symptoms (phobia and phobic sequella) constitute the *primary defenses* implicit to the elaboration of the Phobic Reaction. They are urgently and vigorously maintained in turn through their *secondary defense* (of the symptom-defenses already established) despite the fact that they are neurotic and that they actually and paradoxically achieve self-defeat, handicap, and a net loss.

The fairly frequent *Extension* or *Generalization* of a phobia to include related areas is not well illustrated here. By this possible *progression,* a phobia may come to include related, associated, or adjacent areas. For example, a phobia of bridges may come to include tall buildings, airplanes, mountains, or any high place. The often significant unstable overload, or level of anxiety at the time of the critical attack, as earlier illustrated, is also not prominent. From the foregoing discussion, our concept of mental mechanisms as comprising our psychic *first line of defense* [pp. 25, 343] may gain some added emphasis. The intended defense is overdone, quickly and acutely. In essence it is another instance of our *Principle of Defense-Hypertrophy* [pp. 72 and 229 *ff.*], carried over into psychologic terms. [*See also* Ch.9:IIIB*3*.]

Finally, in accord with the *Principle of Symptom-Survival* [Ch.14:IIIB2] the phobic defensive process cannot continue in existence when the dynamics become sufficiently clear to the possessor. In other words, the basic factors entering into the elaboration of the symptoms must remain hidden and buried within the unconscious, in order to permit the survival of a defensively-intended symptom.

3. Hypothesis of the Oral Conflict

A. ORAL CONFLICT IN ANTECEDENT POSITION TO OEDIPAL SITUATION.— In supplement to our understanding of dynamics in our present state of knowledge, the author offers an *Hypothesis of the Oral Conflict*. According to this hypothesis, the antecedents of later emotional conflict are *ultimately traceable (possibly through several "layers"* * *of significance), to the early Oral Conflict of infancy*. Thus, the origins of every phobia theoretically would be ultimately traceable to the Oral Conflict.

In accord with this view, the Oedipus situation might later reinforce, underline, repeat, or distort earlier primordial oral patterns. Thus the dread and fear of the phobic object not only would represent the feared retaliation implicit in the Oedipus complex but, on a deeper level, would ultimately represent something further back and more basic.

B. SUCCESSFUL RETALIATION; ALSO ULTIMATE IN SELF-DEFEAT.—The foregoing is in agreement with the *Theory of Antecedent Conflict*. On the level of oral conflict however, successful retaliation would equate the danger of the magical symbolic destruction of the loved and vitally needed maternal object of dependency. This comprises the Dependency-Dilemma of Infancy. This would be the ultimate dreaded and self-defeating consequence of the hostility and rage of infantile helplessness. The latter follows the frustration of denial, or of unsatisfactory fulfillment.

Thus oral frustration produces rage. The mothering one is the object; but of course also vital to survival. *In effect therefore, the rage actually threatens the self*. Success in retaliation would also achieve the ultimate in self-defeat. This is part of the basis for anxiety implicit to the Oral Conflict. In effect the very basic *Dependency-Dilemma Concept* (of Infancy) underlies and evolves into our *Phobic Ambivalence Concept*, as with the similar underlying ambivalence to be found deep within many instances and types of neurotic reactions.

C. CHALLENGE OF EXPANDED STUDY.—It is impossible to discuss each phobia and its dynamics in any detail in our current presentation. An attempt has been made to select certain fairly representative and interesting cases for clinical illustration. In view of the many varieties of phobic defenses and of the infinite types and combinations of underlying dynamics, no attempt has been made exhaustively to cover the field. Some further important considerations as to dynamics and theory will be included in the following section.

---

* See *Concept of Defensive Layering*, [Ch. 8:VB4;VID3; IXB1].

Clinical and theoretical research in the phobias has been somewhat limited. The expansion of further study and research in this fascinating area of psychopathology offer a challenging area for the interested student.

VII. SELECTION OF PHOBIC OBJECT

A. SENSORY CONTEXT OF PHOBIC REACTION

1. Symbolism and Sex

The phobic object and the individually determining factors in its selection are an intriguing subject for students of psychodynamics. The emphasis in the past has been almost exclusively upon the role of symbolism.

In the early development and study of dynamics of the phobias, symbolism was the requisite to the unconscious "selection" of the phobic object. The unbearable idea which has been repressed was considered to be almost invariably sexual in nature. The past regard of these factors of symbolism and of sex as the exclusive ones in determining the selection of the phobic object warrants reexamination.

2. Association with Situation or Locale

In an early case, Freud traced the origins of the strong phobia of a young girl about wetting herself. Her phobia prohibited her from venturing far from a toilet. This phobia had provided a Substitution for certain originally intolerable sexual ideas which had been thus displaced. At the time of the critical attack of anxiety (that is, upon her first awareness of the intolerable ideas, and at the time of their likely simultaneous repression), she had been present at a concert which she had had to leave in order to void.

It would seem that the choice of the phobic object here was partly determined by the sensory context present at the time. Displacement to (an aspect of) the locale or situation at the time of the "critical attack" would lead to our labeling this a "Critical-Displacement Phobia."

Menninger cited an interesting case (originally reported by Bagby) of an adult with a phobia of running water. As a child, aged seven years, she had fallen and become wedged among some rocks in a stream. A waterfall poured down over her head. She was in danger of drowning and was terribly frightened. The psychologically traumatic incident, with its terrific anxiety and frantic helplessness, served as a convenient external peg for the attachment of deeper, underlying conflictual material. Here also the selection of the phobic object was largely determined through association with the immediate surroundings.

The author has observed two phobias of water (aquaphobia) where the determination of the phobic object was largely traceable to the sensory context of early, nearly disastrous misadventures while swimming. A phobia about dirt and germs (mysophobia) is also recalled in which the phobic object appeared to originate at least partly adventitiously, through association with the littered, unkempt condition of the dirty hovel in which a recluse lay very ill. The illness and unbearable ideas about death had stimulated the critical attack of anxiety, which was of such intensity as to bring into play phobic defensive mechanisms.

Many similar examples can be cited to illustrate the important role of the association of the fear of aspects of the external situation which happens to be present at the time of the phobic defense formation. These play a large role in the choice of the object for phobic avoidance.

3. Circumstantial Factors Determining Selection of Phobic Object. Peg Concept

Rado indicated his recognition of the importance of the sensory context as follows: "Suppose the child experiences a violent attack of fear. He would wish to forestall the recurrence of such an attack. How is this to be done? He has not read any textbooks and would not have gotten the answer if he had. All he can do is to remember, and thus interpret, the attack in the *sensory context* of its concurrence. If his memory stresses the visual picture, he will henceforth be forced to avoid the situation branded by the crucial attack. Through automatization of this mechanism, he develops the phobic syndrome . . .".

It is important and interesting further to direct our attention to the important role of the sensory context in circumstantially determining the selection of certain phobic objects. Lief recently commented that ". . . the selection of phobic object when based on the sensory context often has nothing or little to do with the unconscious conflict; it may merely be adventitious . . .". The author would agree with him also that this particular mechanism for the selection of the phobic object is "simpler, perhaps more magical and hence more primitive". When symbolism exists in some of these instances, it plays a less significant role and is deeply hidden.

A peg is necessary for attachment of affect at the critical juncture, in accord with our *Peg Concept*. This peg becomes the phobic object; an important type of emotional-object amalgam. Its selection is individual. Factors of (1) circumstantiality, (2) locale and "convenience", (3) symbolism, and (4) conflictual external representation, can each be important determinants, individually or in various combinations.

B. CRITICAL ATTACK OF ANXIETY

We might define the Critical Attack of Anxiety as *an attack of anxiety which is of a sufficient level or quantity, to be of a crucial or critical level. It is critical, especially in so far as continuing the maintenance of the existing pattern of personality defenses and balances is concerned. The Critical Attack of Anxiety therefore results in the urgent, immediate (emergency) mobilization of additional intrapsychic mechanisms of defense.* In the acute onset of certain phobias, the level of fear and anxiety, thus has reached an intolerable, or critical level. This is not necessarily the first attack, although frequently enough this is true.*

Repression of the anxiety-producing thoughts or impulses automatically and simultaneously occurs. At this critical juncture there is a displacement externally. When this rapid displacement occurs to situational elements present at the time, or to elements of the locale, this constitutes the *Situational Phobia*. The defenses of Repression and Displacement have been called into play. The level of anxiety has become so critical as to render the previous attachment of the affect unstable. The attachment thus of the unstable affect externally, creates a new Emotional-Object Amalgam. This tends to be a stable compound. With its creation, the critical attack of anxiety subsides. A measure of personality stability, even though pathologic, is restored.

This entire sequence can be quite rapid. In these instances the reaction is the Critical-Displacement Phobia. On occasion it can also transpire gradually. Herein is produced the Gradually Evolving Phobia. In the latter instances it is likely difficult, if not impossible, to identify a specific Critical Attack of Anxiety.

The following interesting case was cited by Lief and is included here with his permission. It is illustrative of the unconscious selection of the phobic object on bases which were primarily adventitious and circumstantial. The Phobic Reactions here illustrate the Situational and Critical-Displacement categories. These took place in an adult at the time of the "critical attack of anxiety".

Case 122

The Selection of the Phobic Object According to the External Circumstances Present at the Time of the Critical Attack of Anxiety

A housewife of forty-five years of age was going to pay a visit to her husband, recuperating from an illness in a hospital. It was Sunday morning and she went to early church services so that she could see her husband earlier. Walking into the hospital room about two hours sooner than she had been expected, she saw a young woman, a pretty redhead, holding her husband's hand. The girl got up and left hurriedly with a murmured apology. Upon his wife's insistent demands, the husband confessed his intimate relationship for two years with the girl, a cashier in a drug store. The wife fainted "dead away" and had to be carried to another room and put to bed.

In addition to a profound depression, the wife also developed a phobic avoidance of many things which had been situationally and adventitiously associated with the traumatic experience. First, *the time*: she woke up with panicky feelings on Sunday mornings for months after what she termed the "shock". She could hardly go to church, so upset did she become. For a while she actually remained away, despite her being a conscientious, almost compulsive church-goer. Second, *the place*: the hospital where the trauma had occurred was avoided like the plague. She would get unbearable anxiety on approaching

---

* Lief commented that it ". . . is usually the initial attack, though it need not be if the quantity of fear in the initial attack is insufficient. It sometimes takes two, three or more episodes of fear to build up the intensity of fear to the point where phobic avoidance is called into play as a mechanism of defense. The particular attack of fear which directly precedes the onset of the phobia may be termed the critical attack . . .".

within blocks of it. Clinically this illustrates *Locale-Avoidance,* as out-lined in Chapter 9 [IIIA2], in a more psychopathological setting. Third, *her clothes*: the dress she was wearing that day, though an expensive one, was thrown out. Fourth: things associated with *the person* con-cerned: all drugs bearing the label of the drugstore where the redhead had worked were likewise thrown out, and she ordered her husband never to buy anything from, let alone frequent, that drugstore. If she herself came anywhere near the store, she would get panicky, and so made wide detours to avoid it. The delivery truck of the drugstore gave her the same frightening feeling when she chanced to see it.

Then she began to develop a phobic avoidance of all places where she learned her husband had taken the girl: motor courts, restaurants, even particular streets and highways. For a time it was almost impossible for her to drive her car.

When these relationships were made clear to the patient in analysis, these fears and phobias quickly abated. Within two weeks they were almost completely gone, although they had been present for two years after the "shock". Then the underlying reasons for her over-reaction and her long-lasting fear and depression could be worked out.

The author does not wish the foregoing discussion to detract from the importance of symbolism in the selection of the phobic object, but instead for it to call attention also to an important but heretofore neglected avenue for determination of the phobic object, and one which has received in-adequate notice. Contributions to the determining of the phobic object can occur in a number of major ways. These are outlined in *Table 28,* with our present examples grouped according to their particular major pathway(s) of determination.

Table 28

Selection of the Phobic Object

In the development of the phobic defense, the displacement of excessive anxiety often is made at the time of the "critical attack," to a substitute external object. This phobic object is unconsciously determined in several ways. The examples cited are those which show the pathway illustrated as the major pathway.

1. *Symbolism.* The phobic object is the disguised outward symbolic representation for internal, disowned (unconscious) ideas or drives. Sym-bolism plays some role, even though deeply disguised or slight, in the selec-tion of every phobic object. Symbolism is the classic determinant in the unconscious choice of a phobic object.

Examples:
(*a*) A phobia of travel (*Case 121*).
(*b*) A phobia of coughing (*Case 124*).
(*c*) Freud's "Analysis of a Phobia in a Five-Year-Old Boy," (The Case of Little Hans, *Case 112*).
(*d*) A phobia of hirsutism (*Case 115*).
(*e*) Freud's agoraphobia.

2. *Transposition of Identity to a Specific Object or Animal.* The phobic displacement is of a parent or more properly of a part of a parental figure. The animal or object becomes the disguised substitute for the feared and threatening aspects of the parent. There is usually some overlapping with symbolism, since there are also symbolic aspects in the transposition dis-placement.

(Table continued on next page)

Table 28—Continued

Examples:

> (*a*) A cat phobia (*Case 120*).
> (*b*) Freud's Case: From the History of an Infantile Neurosis (also Little Hans).
> (*c*) Sterba's case of a dog phobia.

3. *Circumstantial and Adventitious Association, to the Objects, Locale, or Surroundings Present at the Time of the Critical Attack of Anxiety.* This route is simpler, and more direct and primitive. This is the *Critical-Displacement* category of Phobia. It may *also* be a *Situational Phobia.*

Examples:

> (*a*) An attack of acute anxiety which led to the development of a driving phobia (*Case 14*).
> (*b*) Multiple phobias (*Case 122*).
> (*c*) A phobia of theatres (*Case 117*).
> (*d*) The wetting phobia.
> (*e*) The bus phobia [Ch.9:IIIB*3*].

4. *A Combination of the Foregoing Pathways.*

Examples:

> (*a*) A phobia of flowers (*Case 119*). Object is both symbolic and by association.
> (*b*) Anthropophobia (*Case 114*). Symbolic and circumstantial.
> (*c*) Rangell's case of a doll phobia. Likely includes elements of all three.

C. THE EMOTIONAL-OBJECT AMALGAM; E.O.A.

1. Attachment of Affect to Object

An emotional-object amalgam is *the compound formed by the attachment of affect to an object. It is a union of emotion (affect), or emotional significance, with a person, event, object, or circumstance.* When used in psychopathology the term often implies the attachment to the object of an undue amount of significance—an emotional charge which is apparently untoward in degree or intensity.

The displacement and attachment of anxiety in the formation of the phobic E.O.A., or Emotional-Object Amalgam is to the external object, and is a protectively intended endeavor. The patient thus secures, entirely out of conscious awareness, of course, the binding of the anxiety and fear to a less disturbing and troublesome external object, which presumably can then be more easily dealt with or avoided.

2. Sequence of Critical Level; Instability; Detachment; Displacement; Attachment Externally

One can to some extent perhaps compare this attachment to magnetism in physics, or to the formation of a compound or amalgam in chemistry. There is a sudden burst of excess anxiety. Its attachment is tenuous and easily dislodged, perhaps partly because there is so much, and because it cannot adequately be handled or managed by the existing defenses. In essence this comprises another type of what we have earlier [Ch. 9] termed "Psychic Indigestion." This occurs in somewhat analogous fashion to the behavior of certain unstable physical compounds.

The level of anxiety at the time of the critical attack becomes highly unstable in its attachments. As with iron filings to a magnet, free ions in a solution, or two metals forming an amalgam, the anxiety is attracted (that is, displaced to a new and "convenient" external object). The convenience is often determined as we have seen: (1) by the availability of things in the immediate environment for association by contiguity, (2) by semi-existing, or even well-established pathways of symbolism, (3) by transposition, or (4) by some combination of these [*see Table 28*]. In the ensuing "binding" of the anxiety, an *emotional-object amalgam* is formed. In the psychogenesis of the phobia this is a phobic emotional-object amalgam (phobic E.O.A.).

3. Phobic and Soterial Emotional-Object Amalgams

Once the anxiety is so bound, this new amalgam or compound is more stable and is difficult to separate. Despite his suffering, the phobic patient tenaciously clings to and protects (secondary defense) his defensively developed phobia. This is in accord with our concept of the Phobic Dilemma [Sect.IIIB*3*]. Its loss it is feared threatens to bring back the critical anxiety; a dreaded and intolerable contingency. Further, upon the substitution of the new object, the old original one is thereby lost to awareness through repression. The technical name which has been used in psychiatry for the *attachment of emotional feeling and significance to an idea or object* is "cathexis."

The attachment to or investment of the new object with fear and threat may therefore also be referred to as an *anxiety-induced cathexis*. A primitive, magically protective counterpart is the assignment of special meaning and significance to the talisman. More will be said about this in the following chapter when we discuss the Soterial Reactions. These are the converse of the Phobic Reactions. An important concept in their evolvement is the *Anxiety-Countering Principle* [Ch.11:IA*1*], inherent in this particular defensive pattern of psychic reaction. In analogous fashion a *soterial E.O.A.* is evolved.

The phobic object can be a very painful, if not the most painful, kind of emotional-object amalgam. The soterial object illustrates its converse. Through partially- analogous but reversed dynamics it becomes an object source of security, comfort, and protection. The soterial object is sometimes what we might term *anti-phobic, or counter-phobic* in its effects. It is a satisfying, security-providing, and comforting, if not the most, such kind of emotional-object amalgam.

Both the phobic E.O.A. (emotional-object amalgam) and the soterial E.O.A. (emotional-object amalgam) are unconscious, defensively intended pathogenic evolvements. Each achieves certain effects. Each is frequent in occurrence. The Phobic Reaction however, is far more likely a source of distress and complaint. Only very rarely is the Soterial Reaction offered by someone as the presenting neurotic manifestation.

VIII. THE ATTENTION HYPOTHESIS

A. UNCONSCIOUS SEEKING OUT OF PHOBIC OBJECT

The author has earlier mentioned the hyperacute ability of the phobic patient to "find" his phobic object and has offered one dynamic formulation in attempted explanation. [*See Case 119*, Sect. V B*1*]. On occasion the "ability" of the phobic patient to make these frequent, unwelcome contacts seems almost uncanny. Little Hans had frequent encounters with horses. The attention of the young woman in *Case 115* [Sect. III B*2*] was irresistibly and repeatedly drawn to the object of her greatest conscious personal concern, that is, her phobic preoccupation with facial and extremity hair.

The infant in *Case 116* [Sect. IV A*3*] would react to a neighbor's phonograph recording of train noises which were ordinarily entirely unnoticed by other people present. In *Case 119* the chemist had an uncanny ability seemingly to "seek out" his phobic object, flowers, which caused him so much distress. The foregoing instances illustrate the *Phobic Dilemma* in our concept of phobic ambivalence. They also illustrate the operation in the phobic reaction of an important precept to be observed in many aspects of living, which we might term the *Attention Hypothesis* [*see also* p. 279].

The following instance again illustrates the particular selectivity of attention toward the phobic object and the Attention Hypothesis, as observed with a phobic patient.

Case 123

The Attention Hypothesis Illustrated

(1) *Cancerophobia*
A thirty-four-year-old lawyer came into treatment because of occasional Anxiety Attacks and certain phobic manifestations. The latter had been present for some time and were closely related to certain preoccupations with his state of health.

This patient had a phobic dread of developing cancer or cirrhosis of the liver. He was constantly over-evaluating minor functional alterations as indicating this type of serious pathology. Prior to entering treatment, he had once consulted five separate physicians in a two-week period.

(2) *Phobic Avoidance*
The attorney constantly sought new examinations and reassurances, which, however, gave him little satisfaction. Note the earlier references to the unconscious secret ambivalence toward the phobic object. From one deeply unconscious "point of view," he actually doesn't want—perhaps could not stand to accept—the reassurance which he consciously and urgently seeks!

In accordance with the Attention Hypothesis, his attention and interest were irresistibly and inevitably drawn to small items about himself which stimulated his reaction of phobic dread and suffering.

(3) *Selectivity of attention weighted*
Let me illustrate this further by a small incident. One day a minor item on the front page of *The Washington Evening Star* mentioned liver cirrhosis. The reference was in small print and in a single sentence. During his treatment session the following day the patient discussed this for the entire time. To him it had been like a glaring

three-inch headline! He couldn't possibly have missed it with his selectivity of attention so strongly weighted in this direction. The author had missed the item, even though it concerned a medical subject, which would likely be personally weighted to some extent.

It had such an ordinarily minor position of prominence for most people that none among a number of friends of whom the author inquired had seen it. My patient's attention was drawn to this minor item as certainly as that of an excellent hunting dog is drawn to a rabbit's fresh trail. It was as though he must unconsciously seek out his object of fear and concern. This was his phobic dilemma.

(4) Attention Hypothesis constantly operative

Actually, his attention was irresistibly *drawn to his object of concern.* This was an automatic and selective process. It illustrates in more pointed fashion the precepts of the *Attention Hypothesis.* This major hypothesis operates constantly for each of us, but ordinarily in far more subtle fashion.

B. AUTOMATICALLY AND SELECTIVELY DETERMINED

Indeed it is true, as de Cervantes pointed out long ago in *Don Quixote,* "Fear is sharpsighted and can see things under ground and much more in the skies." Thus we must often really doubt that such frequent contacts with the phobic object are solely the result of simple chance or accident. *These are unconsciously determined, seemingly despite the patient's best conscious efforts to the contrary.* This capacity of the phobic patient supports an interesting hypothesis earlier proposed about the "selectivity of attention".

According to the *Attention Hypothesis,* our attention is selectively directed toward those qualities in others about which we have special interest or over which we have concern or conflict in ourselves. *"Attention tends to be selectively, automatically, and unconsciously drawn toward our personal areas of greatest interest and concern."* Accordingly, we are also selectively attracted to those persons whose characterologic make-up most fits our own inner needs, whether these aspects of character are healthy or neurotic. Also of importance, therefore, are the effects upon our "choice" as to those who become friends and associates. Our choice may be far less voluntary than we tend to think. This is in accord with our *Hand-in-Glove Principle* in Relationships [p. 349].

C. OPERATIVE DAILY, IN MANY AREAS

In many areas our attention is thus selectively directed in automatic and semi-automatic fashion. This occurs to a much greater extent than we are consciously aware. In this vein, the photographer thinks in terms of subjects, setting, and background; the stamp collector can spot an interesting postage stamp from a distance; the sports car enthusiast likewise with sports cars; and many teen-age boys can more readily and automatically recognize the make and model details of cars than can their elders; and so on. The psychiatrist may well have an affinity for words beginning with "psych," which are seen by him to "stand out" from a printed page.

It is hardly surprising that we find an important application of our hypothesis in the phobic pattern of reaction. Rangell stated, "When one chooses an object for a phobia, he in a sense becomes married to the object. In order to avoid it, his eyes seek it out. He finds it in obscure places, he sees it with his peripheral vision".

D. ATTENTION ATTRACTED TOWARD MATTERS OF CONCERN AND TROUBLE

1. Phobic Object and Soterial Object

As an important corollary to our Attention Hypothesis it must be noted that *things which trouble us or cause painful feelings, are very likely to be more a matter for notice than are things which do not.* There is a magnetic kind of attraction for our attention toward matters of concern and trouble.

This applies to conflictual matters, to obsessions, to objects of fear, to hygeiaphrontic concerns, and to troubling aspects of interpersonal relationships. The phobic object, with its neurotically attached affect of threat and fear, is something that troubles and concerns the patient. It is something with which he wishes help, and which is more forcibly drawn to his attention, and to that of the physician as well.

The neurotic love object with its pathogenic, magical kind of love, protection, and security is more likely to be a comfort and a pleasure and is much less apt to be a matter of trouble. Medical attention does not ordinarily, nor as easily, become directed to such an area. It is, therefore, not surprising that little consideration has been given heretofore to the "other side of the phobic coin", to the *Soteria,* to which our next chapter will be directed.

Neurotic feelings of being loved and protected much less obviously cause pain and trouble. Accordingly, this is something which is far less forcibly drawn to the attention of the physician by the patient, if at all. Nonetheless the Soterial Object invites our professional interest. It is a source of concern, albeit positive concern.

2. Selection of Peg for Phobic Attachment

The Attention Hypothesis is especially well illustrated in the phobias. Although to some extent it is usually operative in the neuroses, in some of these other kinds of neurotic reaction it may be much less apparent.

What role does the Attention Hypothesis play in the selection of the phobic object? We have discussed such selection from the standpoint of the sensory context at the time of a Critical Attack of Anxiety, in certain phobias, the Critical-Displacement type of phobias. Herein the role of symbolism may be less prominent. It is not absent however. The Attention Hypothesis is operative and important here.

The selection of a phobic object at this crucial juncture may appear adventitious. Still there are always a number of possible items for selection in the situation, as to people, or as to various objects at hand. Ordinarily we may note that, *of the pegs available for possible phobic attachment* (of the displaced affect) *in the situation at the crucial juncture, the personally most meaningful, significant, and appropriate one will be automatically selected* as the phobic object. This selectivity is very much in accord with our Attention Hypothesis. It is also in accord with the *Law of Universal Affect* [pp. 45*ff*.] and the E.O.A.

IX. FREUD'S PHOBIC DEFENSES

A. A TRAIN PHOBIA

1. Implications for Psychoanalytic Theory

Freud's own phobic pattern of defenses probably played a role in the development of dynamic theory in psychiatry. In the section on History at the beginning of this chapter, reference was made to these defenses and to their possible significance in helping to motivate the early research by this great pioneer in the psychodynamics of phobias.

Ernest Jones,* has since provided us with further information in this area. In his excellent biography of Freud, he commented about Freud's phobia of traveling on a train. This phobia appears to have been present at least from 1887 to 1899. This would have been while Freud was between 31 and 43 years of age. The phobia eventually was in large measure successfully resolved, through his personal efforts in analysis by the latter date. There are also present some interesting possible implications to be drawn concerning the foundations of psychoanalytic theory. Jones' comments (likely Freud's own analysis) indicate underlying antecedents which now in retrospect extended back further into (or toward) the era of oral conflict.

2. Antecedent Mistakenly Dated Within Oedipal Period

It would appear now that Freud incorrectly recalled the date of the occasion of a very early traumatic train trip, in which part of the foundation for the later phobia was likely laid. This error resulted in its being mistakenly placed within the Oedipal period.

Freud, of course, assigned the predominant role in his theories of human. psychology to the important unconscious sequelae of the Oedipus conflict. The question might be raised as to the error in this recollection possibly contributing to a greater emphasis on the Oedipal period?

3. Oral Conflicts Underlie Oedipal Conflicts

In our current understanding of dynamics, many psychiatrists would agree that the emotional roots of agoraphobia, as well as of other phobic

---

* During a visit with Dr. Jones in 1955 at his home in Elsted, Sussex, this distinguished biographer and last-to-survive contemporary and close colleague of Freud, relayed some interesting information about the kind of person that Freud was.

Jones noted on this occasion that Freud was actually a kindly and gentle person. This is in some contradistinction to certain other, perhaps less well informed, views of Freud as a stern authoritarian.

manifestations and those of most types of neurotic reactions, extend not only into the oedipus complex and its vicissitudes but also through and beyond, into the still more deeply buried earlier area of oral dependency and its conflicts. This has been formulated earlier. According to this point of view, antecedent oral conflicts underlie the later conflicts and vicissitudes of the oedipal situation. This is in agreement with the Theory of Antecedent Conflicts, according to which every difficult emotional situation theoretically has roots in a primordial antecedent.

The speculation may be made that Freud himself believed his primary problems to lie in his relationship with his father. On a deeper, less clearly recognized level, they more likely extended further back to antecedent problems in his relationship with his mother. We know that agoraphobia probably originates in the Oral Era, and is frequently connected with separation anxiety, from the mother. This observation is confirmed by the interpretation of agoraphobia by others; notably including Abraham, Weiss, and Deutsch. Freud's suffering from a lingering agoraphobia is a matter of record.

This data can lead us to some possible important speculations and implications in regard to the origins and evolution of dynamic theory. In this Freud played a preeminent role. He very definitely directed its lines of development in the early years. The oedipus complex was long the basis, the heart of analytic theory and formulations. Freud's concentration upon, and possible resulting overemphasis on the importance of the oedipus complex as the developmental area of most profound emotional significance, has had great influence on the development of the dynamic understanding of human emotions and behavior.

To carry our speculations further as to the possible dynamic formulations in regard to Freud's phobic defenses seems an unnecessary intrusion. There is, however, excellent reason at least to explore the evidences of their presence. These personal defensive reactions had an influence on the entire history and research into the phobias generally, as well as important implications for the whole development of dynamic psychiatry, to which Sigmund Freud made so many outstanding contributions.

X. TREATMENT

A. IMPORTANT CONSIDERATIONS IN PSYCHOTHERAPY

1. Established Patterns Clung to Tenaciously

As is our custom in considering the treatment aspects of the various neuroses, this section will include remarks which will have some applications to the treatment of emotional disorders generally, together with several points pertaining more specifically to the therapy of phobias.

The young psychiatrist soon learns to recognize the extreme tenacity with which people cling to old and established patterns of behavior and response. This is because of the attraction of the familiar and oft-used pathways. It also illustrates their vital defensive purposes. To the objective, interested observer, the net result of self-destruction and self-defeat may be clearly apparent. It even may be at least partially apparent on an intellectual level to the person concerned. Efforts to point this out to him however often meet with indifferent success.

Established patterns are never easily surrendered. The concept of the defensively intended "gains" of emotional illness is a vital and useful one, although the so-called "gain" is itself paradoxically a net loss [pp. 55*ff.*]. An understanding of the unconscious origin and defensive intent of emotional symptoms is vital to the development of the necessary resources to attempt to effect their resolution. Only thus has one a chance to aid a patient to modify or to surrender non-constructive patterns, when new and more advantageous ones becomes apparent during the course of therapy. This is in accord with the *Therapeutic Bargain Concept* [Ch.12:VIIIC*1*].

2. Potential Harm from Unskilled Interference

A. UNDERSTANDING, TRAINING AND EXPERIENCE REQUISITES.—Psychotherapy is a very complex business. Only too few people have the requisite personality, interest, patience, skill, and training to undertake it with reasonable chances of success. Unfortunately, however, the wide, intriguing, and seemingly lucrative field of counseling and treatment of emotional problems invites attempts at intervention by often well-meaning, but untrained or inadequately trained people. This is to an extent not seen in any other field of medical practice.

Not infrequently these people regard themselves as possessing skill and competence in these areas in a way that would simply never occur to people concerning some other medical field, for example, surgery. Yet the fine judgment, subtle discrimination, perceptiveness, reasoning ability, and the combination of art and science requisite to sound psychotherapy are at the very least as complex as that required for the most delicate and complex surgical procedure. Often they are far more so.

B. "FOOLS RUSH IN . . .".—Family members, friends, work associates, ministers, or physicians who sincerely wish to assist the person with emotional problems would ordinarily not even remotely give a second thought to personally tackling any kind of serious surgical procedure. Yet they may, with the greatest impunity and blindness, often assume competence to offer specific direction and advice, and often where even the very experienced psychiatrist would not do so, in all kinds of tenuously balanced and potentially explosive emotional situations. More than two hundred years ago Alexander Pope wrote his now famous line, "Fools rush in where angels fear to tread."

This is often only too true in emotional problems. It is perhaps less apt to be true in the more well marked, severe, and distinct psychiatric entities. It is almost unusual, however, not to see some evidence of this sort of thing in the neuroses and character defenses. This is however often particularly regrettable, since it is in these areas in which the competent psychotherapist can often render his most effective service.

c. DESTRUCTIVE CONSEQUENCES.—Such unskilled interference at the least impedes, and can seriously handicap or even block therapy. This often sadly occurs at a critical time, when every genuinely constructive force had best be mustered in support of the patient's already only too slight interest in treatment. He very much needs the results of constructive self-study with expert assistance. Advice may be given which leads to the trying of alternatives, or delay. This may be done in order to see if time, or if this, or if that, or if the other, will help solve matters. Such action is a vote in favor of the illness; not one in favor of its resolution and defeat.

This sort of intervention can sometimes have an even more destructive result. This can interfere with or even prevent the taking of any subsequent steps toward seeking necessary definitive help at some later date. An unsuccessful or painful experience, or the increase of any existing prejudices and personal resistance as the consequence of any ill-advised therapeutic attempt, can add immeasurably to the problems which many patients have to solve to even begin treatment. In some instances these unfortunate consequences contribute to its becoming forever impossible.

In many cases, the completion of definitive treatment can take years of hard work. This may be true even in the hands of the most competent psychotherapist, and one who is well suited to the particular patient. This may be true even when the patient himself is highly cooperative. This is a reflection of the difficulty and complexity of the work.

3. Helpful Attitudes for Physician to Take

A kindly and sympathetic attitude, in the person—be he friend, physician, or minister—to whom the phobic, or other type of patient, turns for help can be most valuable. The patient can be told that the emotional difficulty is very puzzling. This is a basic fact. The listener can point out that neither the patient nor the listener himself can possibly know the answers, at least at this point. He can refrain from giving moralistic admonitions, or urging "will power" or "self-control".

He can help the patient to recognize and to accept the presence of a disturbing emotional illness which is puzzling and in which the origins are quite obscure. Just because it is so unclear and thus seems to make so little sense is a very poor reason for any prejudice. It would be as easy to expect an unschooled laborer to explain the Theory of Relativity, as to expect the patient to recognize and to understand the obscure and deeply hidden emotional conflicts which are responsible for a phobia, or for other emotional symptoms. The kindly physician or friend can point out that if understanding were possible in any easy or ordinary sense, the difficulty would not have developed in the first place.

4. Goals of Psychotherapy

Certain general goals for psychotherapy can be listed, which apply to a considerable extent in all cases of emotional illness. It is perhaps appropriate at this point to outline these goals. In *Table 29,* I have accordingly undertaken to tabulate in summary form seven of the important general goals of psychotherapy.

Table 29

Seven Goals of Psychotherapy

Regardless of the level of symptoms, the goals of treatment are approximately the same in all types of emotional illness.* Simply stated, these goals include:

1. Improved external environmental adjustments, including the ability to initiate, to develop, and to maintain constructive relationships with people.
2. Improved internal adjustment: conflict recognition, resolution, and an improved level of personal integration.
3. The surrender of socially destructive and personally inimical patterns of behavior.
4. Improved function, increased effectiveness, and increased ability to satisfy realistically adjusted needs, and to achieve realistic personal goals.
5. Self-acceptance with an increased genuine self-respect, a closer approximation of the self-picture to that held by others, and the ability to recognize and to accept the presence of disapproved inner drives and wishes.
6. A higher level of emotional maturity, with all its implications as to constructive and satisfying individual and social adjustment.
7. The achievement and maintenance of a reasonable level of emotional and personal equanimity or homeostasis.

B. TECHNIQUES IN THERAPY OF PHOBIAS

1. Recall of Original Traumatic Experience; Tracing Technique

A. BAGBY'S CASE.—The rapid dissolution of a specific phobia very occasionally takes place dramatically. This can occur through the therapeutic recall, that is, derepression, of the "forgotten" original and initiating traumatic situation. This took place in Bagby's case of the phobia of running water [Sect. VIII A2]. Searching back to the initiating experience or first manifestation of a symptom follows our *Concept of the Tracing Technique in Therapy*. It can be particularly useful in certain instances of Critical Displacement Phobias, Obsessions [p. 336], and Neuroses Following Trauma.

This particular instance of sudden recall had taken place at the age of twenty years. The much earlier traumatic situation at the time of onset was at the age of seven years. The phobic reaction was thus resolved after some thirteen years.

---

* Not only are therapeutic efforts similar in all types of emotional illness, but the dynamics of symptom formation likewise have much in common. Thus, in response to anxiety, repression of various intolerable impulses and ideas takes place. These consciously intolerable and repressed impulses result in the formation of symptoms.

Saul wrote, "It seems to me that . . . probably all neurotic symptoms contain expressions of regressive impulses, a form of psychological flight as well as defense and al. partly expressions of and defense against hostile impulses."

B. RAPID RESOLUTION OF PHOBIC MANIFESTATION.—In the following case a well established phobia of coughing disappeared similarly in sudden fashion following the second interview.

Case 124

A Phobia of Coughing

The twenty-six-year-old husband of a patient came to discuss ways in which he might better support his wife's therapeutic efforts. During our discussion, which was on a very friendly basis, he described his own disturbing phobia about coughing. He became very anxious whenever someone coughed, or if he did so himself. A coughing spell literally filled him with panic. He could not recall the original time of onset. Although the author indicated his interest in hearing any further possible details, the patient was not pressed for information.

I managed to see him, at his subsequent request, for a second session several days later. He had in the meantime set an approximate date of onset, and had had a few additional thoughts of interest about the phobia. For example, a labored and a "loose" or fluid cough was much more frightening. As he began telling me these additional thoughts, suddenly in dramatic fashion and with great emotion he recalled the initiating situation in vivid detail. Actually he did more than merely recall it. From an emotional standpoint he, in effect, relived it.

At the age of nine years, he and his family were in a serious automobile accident. He was personally unhurt. An uncle was critically injured and, while awaiting medical help, was carried into the nearest farmhouse. Here he lived for an hour or so, with the boy in attendance. The uncle's chest was fatally crushed and he struggled constantly and in labored fashion to breathe. There were repeated attacks of coughing. As he gradually lost the fight to keep his respiratory system open and free of the steady internal hemorrhage, his coughing had become more labored and loose.

This was a dramatic recall of the initiating traumatic situation. An accompanying abreaction of emotions took place. The phobia vanished and, although I have not seen the patient since, he has remained free of this particular, very troubling manifestation. Obviously, we cannot know further what the dynamics were here, since further therapeutic investigation was not feasible.

This interesting instance may help call attention to the earlier observation, that regardless of the kind of traumatic situation, it serves as a precipitating event in psychologic soil already prepared.

C. LATENT CAPACITY FOR PHOBIC DEVELOPMENT; PHOBIC PEG CONCEPT. —Fortuitous misadventures in early life are often uncovered where the phobia had a sudden onset. These serve as what we might refer to as convenient *phobic pegs,* upon which one inadvertently "hangs" the phobic displacement. There has usually been some preexisting but latent capacity for phobic development. These phobic pegs can include such emotionally traumatic and frightening events, for example, as tornadoes, near-drownings, mishaps with animals, thunderstorms and lightning, death, and physical or sexual assaults. The concept of *Symptom Pegs* has general applicability, as well as in the Phobic Reaction.

However, the resolution of the phobia itself is a limited therapeutic goal. Ideally speaking, *deeper characterologic study is needed.* This brings us to our next topic. *The ultimate goal of therapy in the treatment of the phobias should be to remove or to decrease the underlying psychologic capacity for phobic formation.* If the hidden defensive needs of the personality can be resolved, the phobic defense will not need to be used in the future; in addition to the resolution of the current phobic manifestation. This is *Deep-Treatment,* as noted earlier [Ch.10:IVB2].

D. QUESTION OF UNWITTING ENCOURAGEMENT TO PHOBIC FORMATION. —From this context, one need not necessarily take a dim view, for example, toward such work as that of public education about cancer, accident prevention, tuberculosis, venereal disease, civil defense, or emotional health. It is true that such socially constructive endeavors can make unwitting contributions to various kinds of phobic development.

In the light of the foregoing comments however, these modes of encouragement are not necessarily to be condemned. Instead, their further evaluation is indicated. Accordingly one might safely surmise that if this particular phobic peg were not available, susceptible people might well find another! One can look similarly at the unduly fearful responses to polio.

One should still not discount the fact that it is possible to frighten people with sufficient provocation. As Francis Bacon wrote long ago: "Men fear death as children fear to go in the dark; and as that natural fear in children is increased with tales, so is the other."

2. Focusing Patient's Attention Away from Phobic Object: Anything Else Technique

A. UNDERLYING CONFLICT RESOLUTION A PREREQUISITE.—There can be disadvantages in directing undue attention in the therapeutic work to the specific phobic object and to the individual's phobic responses in and of themselves. The external object of phobic dread is much less important than the underlying need for it. Although rapid resolution of the phobias can on rare occasions be secured therapeutically and sometimes in dramatic fashion, such a result should be clearly seen as a limited therapeutic goal. For lasting, healthful characterologic change, the therapeutic clarification and resolution of underlying conflicts is a prerequisite, in accord with our Deep Treatment Concept [Ch.13:VIII2]. These comments also apply to the resolution of conversion, depressive, hygeiaphrontic, and other types of neurotic symptoms.

The therapist himself must have a sincere interest and wish to help his patient in order to achieve much therapeutic success. This can be early indicated in a simple statment to this effect. Generally the choice of subject and the approach to the problem in a given therapy session can be largely left to the patient. There is, however, an occasional need for firm and positive direction.

B. AVOID OBSESSIVE PREOCCUPATION IN THERAPY; DISCUSS ANYTHING ELSE!—An example of this is sometimes seen with the phobic patient who tends to dwell obsessively on his phobia. This can become a circular and profitless preoccupation. This occurred in *Case 115,* where the patient was seemingly content to discuss repetitively and endlessly her phobic dread of hirsutism. It became apparent that a line had to be drawn. It was accordingly indicated to the young woman that for a time we wished to hear *nothing* more about hirsutism; the therapist would be glad to hear *anything else!* This positive direction of her focus of attention and associations was initially met with resistance and some resentment, but proved to be an important and useful step. This is what the author would term the *Anything-Else Technique* in Psychotherapy. It has useful applications in a fair number of carefully selected and suitable therapeutic situations.

This technique of approach is occasionally indicated and will at times bear fruit particularly in cases of: (*a*) Obsessional Neurosis, (*b*) Phobic Reaction, (*c*) Hygeiaphrontic Preoccupation, and (*d*) Depressive Rumination. At times it can help resolve a seeming therapeutic impasse. The author can recall another illustration of this technique being successfully used by a colleague, in a case of polio phobia. His young woman patient had presented a phobic, hygeiaphrontic preoccupation of absorbing and seriously handicapping level. She would talk endlessly about it. Her therapist temporarily forbade further talk on the subject. She was enjoined to discuss anything else. The admonition in this case was very necessary. As a result considerable significant data were secured about the increasingly intolerable relationship with her husband. The uncovering of this data alone resulted in considerable improvement, and the patient's progress was subsequently far more rapid.

C. INDIRECT APPROACH PREFERABLE.—Generally speaking, however, a more passive role on the part of the therapist is preferable and safer. The indirect approach through pathways of association is more efficient and more effective in the long run. This is the preferred approach.

The occasional use of more active techniques requires most excellent judgment and discrimination. These can often lead to longer time and less satisfactory results in therapy. It is the overdetermination of phobias which often makes their "working through" so time-consuming in therapy.

3. Retraining and Relearning

A. ENCOURAGEMENT AND SUPPORT USEFUL.—The encouragement and support of the phobic patient in his inevitable contacts with his objects of dread can be a valuable adjunct to treatment. There is very often an important need with some individuals also for retraining, or a relearning experience in order to master the phobia. These people almost have to go through the dangerous situation over and over, and to reexperience the gradually decreasing anxiety.

Through this kind of relearning, they can help to master the feelings of anxiety, gradually realizing that these are not overwhelming. In this way they learn to be master rather than the slave of the phobic situation. This can be an important supportive adjunct to insight. The *Automatic-Recoil Principle* [Ch.9:IIIC3] in therapy can play a role here.

B. DECONDITIONING.—During the reexperiencing of the phobic situation, the patient learns that the fear is not intolerable. It will gradually decrease as he learns more about the sources of his anxiety. This can be a useful adjunct to psychotherapy and helpful in the management of these cases. This is a method of deconditioning. It is not an intellectual exercise. As we learned in Chapter 9 [Sect.IVB2], in our *Emotional-Relearning-Tougher Principle,* emotional patterns and reactions once established are more difficult to modify. Related supportive and relearning approaches can include the following:

1. With the childhood phobia, the cause for fear should be immediately removed wherever possible. At least temporarily one intercedes to protect the child from anxiety-producing situations. Reassurance and support in a matter-of-fact way are offered when he is frightened.
2. Allowing the patient to have contacts with the phobic area at gradually decreasing distance. These are accompanied by support and encouragement, as insight is gained, and as internal resources grow. Deconditioning may be used.
3. A positive conditioning way of approach may be tried sometimes, in which one attempts to secure an association of the dreaded object with more pleasant ones.

4. Study of Dreams

A. ANALYST'S "WHY?" AND "HOW?"—The psychotherapist and the analyst seek the development of understanding and emotional maturity through insight. The growth of self wisdom is fostered. Psychiatrists are constantly interested in clarifying data, and in probing into hidden meanings. In the analyst's armamentarium while in pursuit of clarification, one of his most important words is "Why?" Another is "How?"

B. UNRAVELING OF DREAMS AIDS UNDERSTANDING.—With many types of emotional illness, the study and interpretation of dreams is an important adjunct to treatment [Ch.13:IIIB]. This is also true in the therapy of fears and of the Phobic Reactions.

The following instance illustrates how a dream helped in the particular understanding of a marked fear of women. This was of sufficient strength, persistence, and interference with adjustment to probably earn the designation of a phobia.

Case 125

A Fear of Women

(1) *Level of fear varies with age*

A thirty-three-year-old housewife in treatment suffered from a handicapping fear of women. This was of considerable strength. It was a handicap to her personally and socially. In view of the degree of avoidance resulting from this fear, it perhaps could be regarded as a phobia, one kind of anthropophobia. This fear was poorly understood until an early dream fortunately provided some useful leads. The dream was reported as follows:

> "I was at the club. There were many members—all women—there. I was unafraid and at ease. I thought to myself, 'I really belong here. This is my element.' There was a strange realization that I wasn't afraid. I wasn't on the alert or defensive. I wasn't feeling threatened. I was happy and could be there without fear."

The dream was particularly interesting in view of the great contrast with her usual conscious reactions to women. It occurred to her that in real life she was actually more comfortable at the club than else-where. This club was one which principally included women who were considerably older than herself. We learned thus that there was a correlation of her degree of fear with the age of women concerned. In the dream every one of the women was definitely older. Gradually we worked out that the older ones did not pose the same danger to my patient that the young ones did. Her fears were much stronger in regard to younger women.

(2) Competitiveness and acceptance

The danger was in competition, a danger which she believed she could not face since it must inevitably end in defeat for her. In early years, the original instruments of what she had experienced to be certain defeat for her in competition, had been two younger sisters. She felt they had enjoyed preferential parental acceptance and favor.

Her reactions to older women instead had followed more closely the pattern of her early relationships to her grandmother and an aunt. As she said many months later, "I felt I ought to have a place in my family. It couldn't be with my parents. I had a place with my grand-mother and my aunt. This was the only place I could get."

(3) Primordial origins: the Oral Dependency Conflict

This is different from her feelings toward younger women, who also became for her her own projected, competitive self. They were indeed threatening, since she "regarded" her own inner hidden competitiveness to be murderous in level. This made it greatly feared. It became repressed as a control measure, and at the same time was disguised through its projection.

Again I would carry back the internal hostile-aggressive rage, now subjectively experienced as threatening through its projection, to its primordial origins. This would ultimately lie in the long and deeply buried infantile rage toward the frustrating object, mother. It was repressed as unbearable. These infantile feelings not only threatened the dependent object, but their control and concealment fitted in also with the implied promised return for good behavior, that is, "then I will be fed, and cared for, and loved, and so on. . . ."

(4) "Talk from his unconscious"

If the phobic patient could talk "from his unconscious," he might say in effect, "I want something and I'm going to be punished for it. My phobia is a line of defense, frightening me away from something I want, but for which I must deny my wish, since the securing of it would be symbolically disastrous.

"My phobia indicates that I [the ego] feel I am in a precarious state of equilibrium between my unbearable hostile impulses toward my needed object, and my simultaneous hidden dependent needs upon it." This carries our concept of phobic ambivalence [Ch.10:VA2] back to its antecedent "primordial ambivalence" from the Oral Phase [Ch.10:IIIB3], and basic oral conflict.

There are certain other implications here as well. Suffice it to say that the bit of insight secured as a consequence of the analysis of this patient's dream aided substantially in the understanding of her phobia and led into some interesting and therapeutically useful ramifications of her emotional life.

5. Indirect Approach in Psychotherapy.

As noted, the indirect approach to solving a phobia is often more fruitful than direct approaches such as are marked by questioning, or urging, or active probing, and so on. It is always useful to try and trace a specific phobia to its day of onset. Not all phobias by any means have such a well defined onset. When possible this is usually far better accomplished in the absence of direct pressure. (*See also Case 123,* Sect. X B1.) Indeed, the indirect approach holds considerable validity in psychotherapy generally. The seemingly longer approach actually can often prove to reach the desired goals much more rapidly. It may seem longer and more circuitous, but the proof lies in the results. The seemingly straight line is not always the shortest distance between two points! This is a lesson of experience in psychotherapy.

The recall to consciousness of the traumatic precipitating situation (when present) and its clarification, can at times result in the rapid dissolution of the phobia as such. [*See Cases 119, 120* and *124.*] Ideally, therapy does not end here, as it should similarly not end in Conversion Reactions when the gross somatic conversion symptom is vanquished. Treatment should continue in order to secure constructive realignment of the phobically predisposed character structure.

C. PSYCHOLOGIC CONTRAINDICATIONS TO SURGERY

1. Elective Surgery to be Avoided; Surgery-in-Abeyance Rule

In closing, it is desired to emphasize an important point in regard to the performance of surgical procedures upon patients with psychiatric conditions. *The undertaking of surgical procedures is always to be considered with special judiciousness in cases of emotional illness.* This is particularly true with patients with Depressive Reactions and Hygeiaphrontic Reactions. Ordinarily the presence of these conditions should constitute an absolute contraindication to any elective surgical procedure. Even other than elective procedures should be done only when absolutely necessary [Ch.12:IIIA6; VB2].

In certain cases of the Conversion Reactions, the Obsessive Reactions, the Phobic Reactions, and the Neuroses Following Trauma, elective surgery is also contraindicated. The psychologically inimical consequences to the patient are likely to far outweigh any possible surgical benefits. This again underlines our *Surgery-in-Abeyance Rule.*

In *any* case with concurrent emotional difficulties, a contemplated surgical procedure is much more likely to have unconscious psychologic meanings and significance to the patient. These may be most difficult to anticipate. They may have an important adverse effect upon his emotional status. They can also result in long delays in recovery and untoward physical sequellae.

2. Emotional Needs for Surgery

A. LESS INTEREST IN EMOTIONAL PROBLEMS.—Symptoms of emotional illness are not always readily observed. They may be easily missed by physicians and surgeons who are more used to observing physical manifestations, or who are likely to be far less interested in the nuances of emotional adjustment. Then, also, some patients who have a considerable level of emotional difficulty may consciously or unconsciously conceal this. Some individuals also have strong conscious and unconscious needs, emotional needs to be the object of surgery. This they may seek, and even insist upon. Stevens noted the frequent incidence of a surgical history among conversion patients for example. Such seeking can be direct or it can involve all manner of quite covert and subtle means.

The author recalls an instance in which a severely depressed patient underwent major surgery after complaining of prolonged severe back pain. Neither the referring physician nor the neurosurgeon recognized that a serious Depressive Reaction was present. Two days following his discharge from the hospital this patient slashed his wrists and took poison. These measures not proving effective, he set his mattress afire and lay on it while it slowly burned. He died from the burns, complaining not at all of the pain.

This man had been a capable executive. He desperately needed psychiatric care, which he had earlier refused. While we cannot say absolutely what the relationship of the surgery was to the suicide, the operation should have been at least deferred, if not avoided. Recognition of the presence of the Depressive Reaction could have led to further efforts to institute psychotherapy or to secure hospitalization.

B. MORE FREQUENT PSYCHIATRIC CONSULTATION NEEDED.—There are indeed a great many such cases in which each consideration of a surgical procedure should take into account the emotional factors present. Preliminary psychiatric consultation in many cases can provide an estimation of the possible emotional consequences of the surgical procedure under consideration. While this precaution cannot eliminate all risk, it can sometimes be most useful and it ought to be employed far more frequently.

In established cases of emotional illness, surgery should be undertaken only under the clearest emergency. It should be done then only following careful consideration of its effect *upon the emotional situation, and vice versa:* when there is any doubt, seek psychiatric consultation.

C. EXPLORATORY LAPAROTOMY FUTILE.—Why is this precaution mentioned in the chapter on Phobias? First, it very urgently needs to be pointed out. Second, it also has application in the management of certain phobic patients. Fears of illness of a phobic level are not infrequent, and they can lead sometimes to helping to influence the physician. How many exploratory laparotomies are required to cure a cancerophobia? The answer: an infinite number would not suffice!

The phobia stems from deeply hidden psychologic needs. It is not rational and will not respond to reason or to logic. Thus it will not respond very well to the sometimes anticipated reassurance to be derived from negative organic findings. At times, in this regard, the phobia can approach the delusion in character, although the phobic patient is ordinarily distinguished by his ability to recognize the inappropriateness of his reaction. Phobic and hygeiaphrontic patients can sometimes exert certain indirect but compelling pressures, hence the caution to the surgeon. *Surgery in which reassurances to the patient* with a phobia *are* an important *part of the surgical rationale is absolutely contraindicated.*

One might also ask, in a similar vein, "How many examinations will cure a real phobia of poliomyelitis?" Here again, such a goal is impossible. The physician can at least spare himself frustration if he is aware of this.

D. PROGNOSIS IN THERAPY

In conclusion, one might ask, "How long a period?", or "How many sessions are required to cure a phobic patient?" The answer: One must anticipate that many, many sessions will be required. A great deal of time and effort is generally required on the part of both doctor and patient alike.

Further, no guarantee as to the results can be given. Here at least, however, one has a good chance with the patient who is willing to work together with the psychiatrist in the mutually collaborative endeavor. It may be a strenuous job, taking hundreds of therapeutic sessions over some years. The end results can be worth far more than the considerable investment of time, effort, and money required.

XI. SUMMARY

A *phobia* is a specific pathologic fear which is *apparently* out of proportion to the stimulus. The painful affect has been unconsciously displaced from its original internal source, to become attached to a specific external object or situation. Although the reaction appears disproportionate, when one can uncover the source and nature of the internal threat for the person concerned, the reaction is found to be individually quite appropriate. The hidden (unconscious) source of danger is the *latent* stimulus; the external object is the *manifest* stimulus.

Diagnosis ordinarily offers few problems. Occasionally fear of organic disease may lead the physician into a false trail. Phobias frequently accompany other neurotic reactions. The diagnosis in such instances is best made on the basis of the most outstanding clinical feature. Occasionally a very severe case (such as in *Case 115*) may show obsessive, hygeia-phrontic or even schizophrenic features. Incidence is fairly wide, with some 8–10 per cent of the clinical cases of neuroses having some phobic manifestations, and some half as many being sufficiently marked clinically to warrant a diagnosis of Phobic Reaction. Phobias may occur from infancy to old age.

The *phobic dilemma* refers to the simultaneous unconscious seeking out of a phobic object, which is feared and dreaded on the conscious level, The concept of a "cultural vogue" in symptoms was noted; with its applicability to the type of phobic object, as well as to neurotic (and psychic) manifestations more generally.

The complexity of phobias varies widely. A phobia may represent simply the inversion of the unconscious wish (as in *Case 118*). Anxious fear of a phobic nature may be experienced when an otherwise less inhibited person would experience anger or love. Phobias may develop of specific objects (as in *Case 119*), of places (*Case 117*), of animals (*Case 120*), or of such more diffuse things as coughing (*Case 124*), open spaces, travel (*Case 121*), heights, and people (*Case 114*). The onset of symptoms may be sudden and occur at the time of the emotionally traumatic event, in which case they comprise the *Critical-Displacement Phobias,* or they may be of gradual onset; that is, the *Gradually Evolving Phobias.* In the *Situational Phobia,* the displacement has taken place to some aspect of the situation or locale, at the juncture in time of the overload of anxiety.

The concept of *phobic ambivalence* refers to the hidden ambivalent attitude of the phobic person toward his particular phobic object. In accord with the Theory of Antecedent Conflict, this would ultimately recapitulate the *primordial ambivalence* of the Oral Phase.

The phobia develops upon what we might term *favorable psychologic soil* and is individually specific. Important mechanisms which are operative include Repression, Displacement, and Substitution. According to the *Hypothesis of the Oral Conflict,* the antecedents of the phobia are ultimately traceable to the early oral conflicts of infancy. In addition to the important factors of symbolism, the phobic object may be selected through the association of the fear and threat to its locale, and by the transposition of identity. The *Critical Attack of Anxiety* results in the urgent mobilization of additional intrapsychic mechanisms of defense. An overload of anxiety is less stable, lending itself to more ready detachment and displacement.

The *Emotional-Object Amalgam* is the union of affect and object. The phobic object with its associated fear and dread is such an amalgam. The *Attention Hypothesis* points out the automatic and selective directing of our attention toward areas of great personal interest and concern. Also influenced is our choice of people for friends and associates. The *Hand-in-Glove Principle* in relationships was mentioned.

The *Soteria* is the converse of a phobia. Through this mechanism one may consciously experience, or derive in less conscious fashion, security, comfort, or protection. The phobic symptoms of Freud were discussed in relation to their helping to determine his directions of study, research, contributions, and the conclusions thereof.

The complexity of psychotherapy was noted. Unskilled interference in a delicately balanced emotional situation is unfortunately frequent. The well established phobia is a major therapeutic challenge. An understanding view on the part of the physician, with a recognition of the unconscious roots of the phobia and the patient's subjective distress, can be very helpful. What we have labeled *Phobic Pegs* provide a psychologically convenient place for attachment of the displaced emotional charge. Recall of the initiating experience in certain acute phobias can occasionally result in their dissolution. Ideally, treatment continues toward further understanding of the basic character defenses and antecedent conflicts. Symptom removal in emotional illness is a limited therapeutic goal. *Deep Treatment* aims to secure the elimination of the basic capacity for the evolving of phobic patterns of defense. The value of the indirect approach was noted, and the roles of retraining and relearning were mentioned.

Elective surgery should ordinarily be deferred in emotional illness as in our *Surgery-in-Abeyance Rule.* More attention generally is warranted to the possible emotional consequences of surgery. Depressive Reactions and Hygeiaphrontic Reactions, in particular, constitute contraindications to surgery of any other than an urgent emergency nature. Phobic defenses will not be surrendered in response to the negative findings of medical and surgical procedures.

XII. SELECTED REFERENCES AND BIBLIOGRAPHY

ABRAHAM, K. (1955). *On the Psychogenesis of Agoraphobia in Childhood. Clinical Papers and Essays on Psychoanalysis*, p. 42. New York; Basic Books.

AGRAS, STEWART (1959). "The relationship of school phobia to childhood depression." *Am. J. Psychiat.*, **116**, 533.

ALEXANDER, V. K. (1957). "A case of phobia of darkness." *Psychoanal. Rev.*, **44**, 106.

AMERICAN MEDICAL ASSOCIATION (1952). *Standard Nomenclature of Diseases and Occupations*, 4th Ed. New York; Blakiston.

ARIETI, SILVANO (1961). "A re-examination of the phobic symptom and of symbolism in psychopathology. *Am. J. Psychiat.*, **118**, 106.

BACON, FRANCIS. *Maxims of the Law; of Death.*

BAGBY, E. (1922). "The etiology of phobias. *J. abnorm. soc. Psychol.*, **19**, 16.

BORNSTEIN, B. (1935). "Phobia in a two-and-a-half-year old child." *Psychoanal. Q.*, **3**, 93.

COLM, HANNA N. (1959). "Phobias in children." *Psychoanal. and psychoanal. Rev.*, **46**, 65.

COMMITTEE ON NOMENCLATURE AND STATISTICS (1952). *Diagnostic and Statistical Manual*. Washington; American Psychiatric Association.

DAVIDSON, SUSANNAH (1961). "School phobia as a manifestation of family disturbance: Patient's structure and treatment." *J. Child Psychol. Psychiat.*, **1**, 270.

DEUTSCH, H. (1951). *Psycho-Analysis of the Neuroses*. London; Hogarth.

DIXON, J. J. et al. (1957). "Pattern of anxiety; The phobias." *Br. J. med. Psych.*, **30**, 34.

EISENBERG, LEON (1958). "School phobia: a study in the communication of anxiety." *Am J. Psychiat.*, **114**, 712.

FELDMAN, S. S. (1949). "Fear of mice." *Psychoanal. Q.*, **28**, 227.

FERENCZI, S. (1952). *Further Contributions to the Theory and Technique of Psychoanalysis*, p. 357. New York; Basic Books.

FENICHEL, O. (1944). *Remarks on the Common Phobias. Psychiat. Q.*, **13**, 313.

—(1945). *The Psychoanalytic Theory of Neurosis*, p. 195. New York; Norton.

FREUD, S. (1936). *The Problem of Anxiety*, p. 81. New York; Psychoanalytic Press.

—(1950). "The defence neuro-psychoses." In: *Collected Papers*, Vol. 1, p. 70. London; Hogarth.

—(1950). "The anxiety neurosis." *Ibid.*, p. 84.

—(1950). "Analysis of a phobia in a five-year-old boy." *Ibid.*, Vol. 3, p. 149.

—(1950). "From the history of an infantile neurosis." *Ibid.*, p. 473.

FRIEDMAN, PAUL (1959). "The phobias." In: *American Handbook of Psychiatry*, p. 293. Ed. by Arieti, S. New York; Basic Books.

FRY, WILLIAM F., JR. (1962). "The marital context of an anxiety syndrome." *Fam. Proc.*, **1**, 245.

GERZ, HANS O. (1962). "The treatment of the phobic and obsessive-compulsive patient using paradoxical intention." *J. Neuropsychiat.*, **3**, 375.

GREENSON, RALPH R. (1959). "Phobia, anxiety and depression." *J. Am. Psychoanal. Ass.*, **7**, 663.

HALL, G. S. (1897). "A study of fear." *Am. J. Psychol.*, **8**, 147.

HARPER, MAX and ROTH, MARTIN (1962). "Temporal lobe epilepsy and the phobic anxiety-depersonalization syndrome." *Comp. Psychiat.*, **3**, 129.

HIPPOCRATES. *On Epidemics*, V, Section LXXXII.

IBOR, J. J. LOPEZ (1961). "Analisis estructurales de las obsesiones y de los escrupulos." *Actas luso-esp. Neurol. Psiquiat.*, **20**, 1.

JANET, P. (1919). *Les Obsessions et la Psychasthenie*. Paris; Alkan.

JONES, E. (1953). *The Life and Work of Sigmund Freud*, Vol. 1. p. 316. New York; Basic Books.

—(1955). *Ibid.*, Vol. 2.

—(1954). "Freud's early travels." *Int. J. Psycho-Analysis*, **35**, 81.

KATAN-ANGEL, A. (1937). "The role of 'displacement' in agoraphobia." *Int. J. Psycho-Analysis*, **32**, 4.

KING, ARTHUR and LITTLE, J. CRAWFORD (1959). "Thiopentone treatment of the phobic anxiety-depersonalization syndrome." *Proc. R. Soc. Med.*, **52**, 595.

KLEIN, M. (1946). "Notes on some schizoid mechanisms." *Int. J. Psycho-Analysis*, **27**, 99.

— (1937). *The Psychoanalysis of Children*. London; Hogarth.

KRAEPELIN, E. (1903). *Lehrbuch der Psychiatrie*, 7th Ed. Leipzig; Barth.

LAUGHLIN, H. P. (1953). "Anxiety; its nature and origins." *Med. Ann. D. C.*, **22**, 403.

— (1953). "The anxiety reactions." *ibid.*, **22**, 463.

— (1954). "Fear and phobias." *ibid.*, Part 1, **22**, 379; Part 2, **22**, 439.

— (1954). "King David's anger." *Psychoan. Q.*, **23**, 87. *Dig. Neurol. Psychiat.* **22**, 207.

— (1963). *Mental Mechanisms*. Washington; Butterworth.

LAWRENCE, G. (1952). "Mysophobia." *Med. J. Aust.*, **1**, 4.

LAZARUS, ARNOLD A., and ABRAMOVITZ, ARNOLD. (1962). "The use of 'emotive imagery' in the treatment of children's phobias." *J. Ment. Sci.*, **108**, 191.

LEIF, H. A. (1955). "Sensory association in the selection of phobic object." *Psychiatry*, **18**, 331.

— (1954). "Critical fear in phobic defenses." Presented at the Annual Meeting of the American Psychiatric Association, St. Louis, Mo., May 1954.

LEVENSON, EDGAR A. (1961). "The treatment of school phobias in the young adult. *Am. J. Psychother.*, **15**, 539.

LEWIN, B. D. (1935). "Claustrophobia." *Psychiat. Q.*, **4**, 227.

— (1952). "Phobic symptoms and dream interpretation." *ibid.*, **21**, 295.

LOCKE, JOHN (1913). "An essay concerning human understanding." In: *The Philosophical Works of John Locke.* Ed. by St. John, J. A. London; Bell.

MALLET, J. (1956). "Contribution a l'etude des phobies." *Revue fr. Psychoanal.*, **20**, 237.

MENNINGER, K. A. (1930). *The Human Mind*, p. 245. Garden City, New York; Garden City Publishing Co.

MENNINGER, W. C. (1954). Personal communication.

MILLER, M. L. (1946). "Psychotherapy of a phobia in a pilot." *Bull. Menninger Clin.*, **10**, 145.

MONSOUR, KAREM J. (1961). "School phobia in teachers." *Am. J. Orthopsychiat.*, **31**, 347.

NOYES, A. P. (1953). *Modern Clinical Psychiatry*, 4th Ed., p. 472. Philadelphia; Saunders.

OVESEY, LIONEL (1962). "Fear of vocational success." *Archs. Gen. Psychiat.*, **7**, 82.

OPPENHEIM, H. (1911). *Textbook of Nervous Diseases for Physicians and Students*, 5th Ed. Edinburgh; Schultze. New York; Stechert.

PITRES, A. and REGIS, E. (1902. *Les Obsession Et Les Impulsions.* Paris; Normalest Pathologique.

POPE, ALEXANDER. *Essay on Criticism*, III.

RADO, S. (1950). "Emergency behavior." In: *Anxiety*, p. 150. Ed. by Hoch, P. H. and Zubin, J., New York; Grune and Straton.

RAGGI, A., as cited by Janet, P. (1919). *Les Obsessions et la psychasthenie.* Paris; Alkon.

RANGELL, L. (1952). "The analysis of a doll phobia." *Int. J. Psycho-Anal.*, **33**, 43.

REIK, T. (1949). *Listening with the Third Ear*, p. 15. New York; Farrar, Straus and Young.

RODRIGUEZ, ALEJANDRO, RODRIGUEZ, MARIA, and EISENBERG, LEON (1959). "The outcome of school phobia: A follow-up study based on 41 cases." *Am. J. Psychiat.*, **116**, 540.

ROTH, MARTIN (1960). "The phobic anxiety-depersonalization syndrome and some general etiological problems in psychiatry." *J. Neuropsychiat.*, **1**, 293.

SAUL, L. (1954). Personal communication.

SCHMIDEBERG, W. (1948). "Agoraphobia as a manifestation of schizophrenia. The Analysis of a case. *Psychoanal. Rev.*, **35**, 309.

SEGAL, H. (1954). "A note on schizoid mechanisms underlying phobic formation." *Int. J. Psycho-Anal.*, **35**, 238.

SPOCK, BENJAMIN (1950). *The Pocketbook of Baby and Child Care*, p. 282. New York; Pocket Books.

STERBA, E. (1935). "The analysis of a dog phobia." *Psychoanal. Q.*, **4**, 135.

WEISS, EDOARDO (1964). *Agoraphobia in the Light of Ego Psychology*, p. 132. New York; Grune and Stratton.

WEISS, E. (1935). "Agoraphobia and its relation to sexual attacks and to trauma." *Int. J. Psycho-Anal.*, **16**, 59.

WESTPHAL, C. (1871). *Die Agoraphobie: eine neuropathische Erscheinung.*" *Archs. Psychiat.*, **3**, 138.

XIII. REVIEW QUESTIONS ON THE PHOBIC REACTIONS

1. How do fear and avoidance progress to anxiety and the Phobic Reaction?

2. (*a*) Define Phobia and Phobic Reaction.
   (*b*) List and identify ten common types of phobias.
   (*c*) What is the Situational Phobia?, the Critical-Displacement Phobia?, the Gradually Evolving Phobia?

3. What factors retarded interest in and understanding of the Phobic Reactions historically?

4. Discuss the contributions of Janet; of Freud.

5. (*a*) Outline considerations in the diagnosis of a Phobic Reaction. Include emotional and physical differential features.
   (*b*) How does *Case 115* illustrate several major considerations in problems of differentiation? Discuss this case and its dynamic implications.

6. Outline factors in the incidence of the Phobic Reactions.

7. Distinguish childhood fears and childhood phobias. At what ages can phobias begin?

8. How do cultural developments influence phobic formation?

9. What is "Inversion of an Unconscious wish?" How can this lead to a phobia? What is the "phobic dilemma"? What is meant by the *cultural vogue* in symptoms? What is meant by the "popularity" of phobic objects?

10. Why is an individual more vulnerable to phobic formation at the time of a Critical Attack of Anxiety?

11. What is the "sought" defensive advantage of a Phobia? What is the relation of *phobic ambivalence* to *primordial ambivalence?*

12. List and define the dynamisms important to the phobic formation.

13. Discuss the importance of:
    (*a*) The Critical Attack of Anxiety.
    (*b*) The Emotional-Object Amalgam.
    (*c*) The Attention Hypothesis.
    (*d*) The Theory of Antecedent Conflict.
    (*e*) The Hypothesis of the Oral Conflict.
    (*f*) The Object of Dependence.
    (*g*) Favorable Psychologic Soil.

14. What is:
    (*a*) Transference? (*See Case 121*).
    (*b*) The Danger of Success of the Negative Side of the ambivalence?

15. Define:
    (1) Repression
    (2) Negative side of ambivalence
    (3) Reaction of the opposite
    (4) Displacement
    (5) Substitution
    (6) Externalization
    (7) Phobic Avoidance
    (8) The Phobic Object

16. How does the sensory context (and locale) influence the selection of the Phobic Object?

17. Compare and contrast the phobic and the soterial Emotional-Object Amalgams (E-O-A.).
18. Discuss symbolism in phobic formation.
19. How does the Attention Hypothesis enter into daily living?
20. Treatment:
    (a) What is meant by:
        1. Established patterns are clung to tenaciously?
        2. The potential harm from unskilled interference?
        3. The goals of psychotherapy?
        4. Deep treatment?
        5. Symptom and phobic pegs?
    (b) What is the value of:
        1. Recall of the Initiating experience.
        2. Instructing the patient to discuss "anything else" but his symptom.
        3. The Indirect Approach.
    (c) Discuss the psychologic contraindications to surgery.

CHAPTER 11

THE SOTERIAL REACTIONS

....Security From An External
Object-Source

I. The Soterial Pattern of Defense

   A. Maternal Comfort and Family Safety; Object Protection and Security
      1. Progression From Real to Magical; 2. Soteria and Soterial Reaction Defined

   B. Nature and Purpose of Soterial Reactions
      1. Manifest and Latent Source; 2. The "Just-in-Case . . ." Phenomenon; 3. Seldom Basis for Complaint; 4. Estimating Import; Secondary Defense Effective and Valiant

   C. Forthcoming Discussion

II. Historical Notes

   A. Long-Standing Evidence
      1. In Ancient and Modern Life; 2. Reasons for Lack of Attention

   B. Development of Interest
      1. Widespread Incidence Becomes Apparent; 2. Name Soteria Selected; First in Print in 1954; 3. Considerations Influence Adoption and Survival

III. On Diagnosis

   A. Common Soterial Reactions
      1. Diagnosis Warranted . . .; 2. Choice of Soterial Object Unlimited

   B. Points in Differential Diagnosis
      1. Obsessive Compulsive Reactions; 2. Organic Disease; Hygeiaphrontis

IV. Incidence

   A. Nearly Universal
   B. Adeia and Phylactory
   C. Estimated Percentage

V. Symptoms and Clinical Features

   A. Special Emotional Significance Attached
      1. Soterial Objects; Individual Prototypes; 2. Importance of Accustomed and Familiar; 3. Accumulations, Savings, Collections, and Hoarding; 4. Soterial Comfort and Preservation Derived

   B. Soterial in Medical Treatment
      1. Drugs, Procedures, Interpersonal Aspects; 2. Compensation

   C. In Business

   D. In Love Affairs

VI. Notes on Psychodynamics

   A. Object of Dependency Projected Externally
      1. Symbolic Possession; 2. Self-Defeat Illustrated; Relationship-Objects

   B. Soteria and Phobia

   C. In Conclusion

VII. Additional Aspects of the Soterial Reactions

   A. Secure Base of Operations Concept
      1. Important in Child Development; 2. Home a Soterial Refuge; 3. Marriage

   B. Soterial Implications of Food and Eating
      1. Overeating and Obesity a Consequence; 2. Eating a Source of Comfort and Security

VIII. TREATMENT

    A. Initiation of Therapy
        1. Indications for Treatment;
        2. Symptom Resolution a Lim-
        ited Goal; 3. More Effective
        Approach

    B. Some Helpful Considera-
    tions
        1. When to Interpret; 2.
        Hand-in-Hand Concept in Psy-
        chotherapy; 3. Tracing Ante-

cedents; 4. Conservative Therapeutic Attitude; 5. Sometimes Significant; Often Important; Always Interesting

IX. SUMMARY

X. SELECTED REFERENCES AND
    BIBLIOGRAPHY

XI. REVIEW QUESTIONS ON THE
    SOTERIAL REACTIONS

I. THE SOTERIAL PATTERN OF DEFENSE

A. MATERNAL COMFORT AND FAMILY SAFETY; OBJECT PROTECTION AND SECURITY

1. Progression From Real to Magical

A. OTHER SIDE OF PHOBIC COIN: THE SOTERIA*.—In the two preceding chapters we have studied the gradual progression of physical fear and its avoidance into the more complex reaction patterns of emotional conflict anxiety, and the phobic type of defensive response. The Phobic Reaction has been presented as an interesting and important type of neurosis. In it the phobic object becomes an external substitute for internal dangers, which are thereby lost from and/or maintained outside of conscious awareness.

The phobic object thus becomes a neurotic external source of danger, fear, and dread. This is clearly out of proportion, intellectually, to any real or manifest danger. Through intrapsychic processes there was a progression in complexity in the avoidance response to danger, and to threats. The real danger source is magically displaced externally. There is similarly a gradual progression from the early and realistic maternal comfort and the safety of the family setting, to the projected external object-source of security in the Soterial Reaction.

A great deal of what we have studied about the phobias could be transposed to apply to their reverse, the Soterias. However, the consequent interference with function in the latter reactions, and the psychopathology when present, is not readily uncovered. Ordinarily a soteria is not very consciously troublesome to the person concerned. This group of reactions, nevertheless, may well be sufficiently important and widespread in clinical experience to warrant its independent classification and study. Separate consideration is thus accorded this intriguing emotional and psychologic pattern of defense, for the first time.

B. SOTERIAL OBJECT COUNTERS FEAR AND ANXIETY.—The Soterial Reactions comprise a large group of protectively intended patterns of reaction. Characteristic of this group is the establishment of an external neurotic source of security; the *soterial object*. Through it, or from it, the individual concerned derives solace, comfort, protection, reassurance, and safety in varying degree and extent. The soterial object is somewhat analogous to the phobic object. However, the emotional consequences of these are oppo-

---

* Pronounced: so-ter'e-ah.

site. The phobic object is feared, dreaded, and is (at least consciously) avoided. The soterial object in some contrast provides, or seems to provide, preservation, comfort, and security. The phobic object is abhorred and produces anxiety. The soterial object is (mostly) treasured and protected. It counters fear and anxiety. This is the *Principle of the Anxiety-Countering Effect* of the soterial pattern of defensive reaction [p. 66].

The phobic individual seeks relief and professional help in the resolution of his acrophobia, claustrophobia, *et al.* The soterial person is more likely, perhaps far more so, to want to keep and to preserve his soterial talisman, pillows, medicine, hobby, religious object, food(s), doll, amulet, routine, special possession, or good luck charm. This affords him comfort, not anxiety. He seeks more to preserve it, not to get rid of it or to free himself from it.

C. RELATIVE PRIOR LACK OF ATTENTION AND INTEREST.—Not very frequently is the psychiatrist consulted by someone who seeks help or relief because of his Soterial Reaction! This characteristic of this defensive pattern has contributed substantially to our relative, prior lack of interest in and attention to the soteria. It has been thus, despite its being a rather widespread phenomenon in our emotional life.

Let us begin our brief survey of this interesting group of reactions. Definitions are now in order.

2. Soteria and Soterial Reaction Defined

A. SOTERIA.—The word *soteria* is derived from the classical Greek. In its original, ancient usage it meant safety; preservation; a way or means of safety; good health and well being; a security or guarantee of safety; something that delivers one from evil. As a theologic extension since, the adjective *soterial* has also been taken over into the English and used to indicate "of, or pertaining to salvation". Also derived from the Greek word *soteria,* has been *soteriology:* (1) a discourse on health or hygiene, or (2) a branch of theology dealing with salvation of divine origin.

For our present psychologic purposes, we may define a soteria as *the converse of a phobia.* More specifically, the soteria is *a defensively-intended intrapsychic process and reaction, through which an external object, situation, person, habit, ritual, or circumstance, and so on, has come to be the source of feelings of comfort, security and well being, which are intellectually out of proportion to the apparent stimulus.* In the Soteria, *the external object becomes a neurotic object source of comfort and security.*

It is interesting but hardly surprising in view of the foregoing comments, that so little consideration has been given previously to this "other side of the phobic coin". For this kind of emotional reaction which is the reverse of the phobia, the author has earlier (1950–54) adopted and proposed the usage of the name *Soteria.* This word is carried over by direct transliteration into the conventional English letter equivalents from the original Greek word.

The original word soteria conveyed much of the meaning of security, safety, protection, and health or well-being which is often neurotically attached to the soterial object. The soterial object seeks to defend the unconscious, particularly the ego. It is a psychologically elaborated attempted defense against danger, fear, threats, and anxiety. Through the operation of the Soteria the source of security is externalized. From thence it provides its more or less magical refuge, preservation, solace, and comfort.

B. SOTERIAL REACTION.—The Soterial Reaction is largely beyond the individual's voluntary control. He can usually recognize to some extent, when it is pointed out to him, that the security gained from his soterial object is disproportionate, illogical, and non-rational in its degree and extent. He cannot fully explain its real basis in adequate fashion to others, or to himself.

The Soterial Reaction may be defined in turn as *an unconscious neurotic pattern of attempted defense. It is characterized clinically by the presence of a soteria or soterias, as the most prominent feature of the neurotic reaction which is present, and by the predilection of the individual to develop soterial manifestations under appropriate conditions of psychic stress.* Through this defensive reaction pattern, *the easing or resolution of internal emotional conflicts is "sought", as is the subjective experiencing of reassurance, and personal feelings of safety, protection, and security.*

C. AN EXTERNAL OBJECT-SOURCE SECURED.—The protective and satisfying person, object, or situation as we have noted is properly called the *soterial object*. Thus, a Soterial Reaction is the defensive emotional reaction through which an individual derives security, comfort, and protection. These are secured in *apparently* irrational fashion from an external object, symbol, situation, or relationship.

As with the phobia and with anxiety, when the underlying basis is fully determined, the soterial reaction also may be recognized as exactly appropriate for the individual concerned. This is in accord with our *Individual Appropriateness of Response Principle* [pp. 14 and 51].

B. NATURE AND PURPOSE OF SOTERIAL REACTIONS

1. Manifest and Latent Source

The emotional feelings of security and protection which are derived in the Soterial Reaction are out of proportion to any real such value in the object. The *manifest* and necessarily external, source of preservation and safety is the soterial object. It is more or less unwittingly assigned this ability and power, by the individual concerned. The internal origin and basis is the unconscious, *latent* source. This is a semiautomatic and "magical" process.

In the popular daily cartoon "Peanuts", Linus' blanket is his soteria. As he terms it, it is his "portable security". Similar objects serve this kind of purpose for many small children. For an adult, common soterial objects include amulets, good luck charms, a religious object, or some type of medicine. A soterial person may feel "safe" or comfortable for example, if some smelling salts or tranquilizers are readily available. These may seldom or never be used, but take them away and the individual will be tense or anxious — will feel unsafe.

A Soteria may be employed to counter fear and anxiety. A patient recently recounted her use in this way of the Lord's Prayer. She was frightened of dogs for years, ever since an early prior, painful experience with a large dog as a child. Wherever she encounters a dog she recites this prayer as a talisman to ward off her being molested. When she says the prayer she feels safe and in no danger from the dog. This mechanism has served her in this way for many years.

2. The "Just-in-Case . . ." Phenomenon

A lady said recently, "I never use sleeping pills. I'm opposed to them really. However, I'm never without them. . . . As long as I have some available I'm secure. Then I can feel safe. . . . I don't use them, understand; almost never have, but it's a comfort to have them on hand — *just in case! . . . .* If I'm caught somewhere without them I feel tense and nervous . . .".

The "Just-in-Case" phenomenon is fairly widespread in our society today in various guises. The magical protection thus afforded has much of the primitive in it. Most such reactions are soterial, or have soterial aspects.

3. Seldom Basis for Complaint

Patients seldom complain to their physician, to their friends, or to their psychiatrist about their soterial objects. Accordingly there has been relatively little incentive thus far for the professional to study and to understand them. As for the individual concerned, who would eagerly seek to resolve and perhaps have to surrender, a valued source of comfort, solace or security? Not many will be so inclined.

It is of no help in increasing our understanding that this kind of reaction can operate unwittingly, or partly so: In fact, this relative non-awareness can be a further hindrance to our study and understanding, since the reaction thereby becomes so much less accessible. Like, but often even more so than with other neurotic reactions, the Soterial Reaction thus becomes so much less possible to cope with from a therapeutic standpoint.

4. Estimating Import; Secondary Defense Effective and Valiant

As with the phobia several factors are indicative of the psychologic import of his Soterial Reaction to the person involved. Thus this defensively evolved reaction is more significant emotionally when: (1) it is discrete, specific, and well established; (2) when it is particularly prominent as a defense; (3) when there is substantial dependency upon it; and (4) when it is isolated, that is, relatively unaccompanied by other neurotic manifestations.

In direct proportion to the above four points also are: (*a*) the degree of psychopathology, (*b*) the self-defeat implicit to its operation and one's dependence upon it, and (c) the resistances to be encountered to its possible therapeutic resolution. We shall return to this latter point in *Section VIII,* on Treatment.

In the presence of such a valued defense, its valiant and both conscious and unconscious secondary defense in turn would barely prove surprising. This is then to be expected, and is correct. The *Concept of Secondary Defense* in the Soterial Reactions has many applications. There are many reasons why it proves to be strong and stubborn. At times it also operates in subtle, yet pervasive and effective ways. We shall observe some of this.

C. FORTHCOMING DISCUSSION

In our continuing short survey of the Soterial Reactions we shall include a brief historical note pointing out the longstanding evidence of their operation, and noting the very recent development of interest. Concerning diagnosis, common soterial reactions will be discussed, together with some relationships to the Obsessive and Hygeiaphrontic Reactions. Their nearly universal incidence will be noted.

In *Section V* on Symptoms and Clinical Features we shall observe the special emotional significance which is attached. Individual prototypes will be noted, followed by the mention of some of the more popular soterial objects. The importance of what is familiar will receive comment, together with some applications for our senior citizens. The Separation Reaction will be noted which follows the loss of the familiar and the soterially valuable. We shall observe how accumulations, savings, and collections can progress beyond logic and the practical, as soterial significance is gained by (assigned to) them. They can thus become important Security Operations.

We shall next observe the derivation of soterial comfort and security from such varied areas as art, music, writing, personal relationships, and religious objects. Several cases will illustrate selected Soteria Reactions and point up the symptom-preserving effect of the Secondary Defense. We shall observe influences of the Soteria in medical treatment, in compensation, in finding a haven or refuge, and in love affairs. The results of attempted deprivation of a soteria will be noted.

Brief comments on the psychodynamics will follow, with a reference to the soteria ultimately representing some measure of symbolic possession of the oral object of dependency. The aspect of self-defeat will be illustrated. The Soteria and the Phobia will be compared and contrasted. In *Section VII* two important additional tangential aspects of interest will be discussed. First will be the *Concept of the Secure Base of Operations,* and its major applications in child development, in the home as representing a soterial refuge, and in marriage. Secondly, the soterial implications of food, of overeating, and in the development of obesity will receive brief comment and illustration.

A few notes on treatment will include some indications for therapy, the limited goal of symptom-resolution, and certain more effective approaches. Some helpful rather general considerations next will include: when to offer interpretations, the value of the therapist not getting too far ahead of his patient in securing insight, and the usefulness of tracing antecedents. A summary, several references, and then review questions will conclude our abbreviated survey of this very interesting group of neuroses: the Soterial Reactions.

II. HISTORICAL NOTES

A. LONG-STANDING EVIDENCE

1. In Ancient and Modern Life

The seeking of individual salvation, preservation, and safety from or through various types of external objects is far from new. There is long-standing evidence of this through the ages. The presence of the talisman, magical object, religious image, and phylactery are to be noted in their many varied forms throughout the course of human civilization. As the classical Greek tongue had developed terms for these, so have most of the other ancient languages.

More recent times have seen the adoption of similar additional forms, including the good luck charm, medicinal soterias, and soterial objects for travel (especially by car, train, and plane). Still more such "safeguards" are adopted by people in seeking to guard and protect themselves against such dangers as health hazards and natural disasters. Certain of these will be noted as we continue our discussion.

2. Reasons for Lack of Attention

As a course of psychotherapy with a given individual has progressed, and as his own clinical experience has grown, the therapist has likely increasingly encountered the soterial object and mechanisms. However: (a), his patient rarely complains of them; (b) elements of secondary gain are not likely to be very prominent; and (c) the self-defeat so engendered is likely to be either quite obscure, or at least not terribly apparent.

Further, many far more urgent and pressing conflicts and problems are far too likely to be encountered during the work of psychotherapy. It is hardly surprising, therefore, that this rather widespread group of defensive reactions has been heretofore ignored, or at best has thus far received the barest of clinical recognition, attention, and study.

B. DEVELOPMENT OF INTEREST

1. Widespread Incidence Becomes Apparent

The author became increasingly interested in this large group of related phenomena in the late 'forties and the early 'fifties. Several fairly marked instances came under his therapeutic scrutiny in these years. They met the usual criteria which might be applied to define the neurotic reaction. These included the characteristic elements of self-defeat. These proved to be present well enough, despite their obscurement by the apparent gain secured. Further a measure of attention soon disclosed their wide prevalence. The author found them to be quite intriguing. He gradually learned that a careful enough study would usually reveal that they played some contributory role in the personal psychology of most of the individuals whom he encountered in intensive therapy.

Sometimes this was quite minor. Occasionally soterial operations formed a subtle underlying and rather pervasive defensive pattern. In a few instances they proved to be of major proportions. The author came to expect that sooner or later some such manifestations would appear with each person working in psychotherapy and analysis. He gradually began to view them as a rather separate and distinct group of defensively-intended reactions.

2. Name Soteria Selected; First in Print in 1954

Students on the graduate and the undergraduate levels seemed quickly to grasp and to appreciate these conceptions. Research into the Greek had produced a suitable name — the *Soteria,* one in fact which very closely expressed the desired meaning, and which could be carried over into English quite readily.

The term of *soteria* first found its way into print in mid-1954 in an article on phobias in the *Medical Annals of the District of Columbia.* In 1955 it was also included in an early version of *A Psychiatric Glossary* (5th rev. ed.) which the author had written for the American Psychiatric Association, and it was mentioned in several subsequent papers. The concept was developed sufficiently to secure several pages of comment as an "Additional Aspect" of the Phobic Reactions in the first edition of this text in 1956.

Resulting evidences of interest and usefulness have encouraged its retention. The further development of the concept of the Soteria has continued. It has since been mentioned in several more recent papers, including one (in *The Journal of the Medical Society of New Jersey;* September 1961), which led the author's friend, Davidson, psychiatric author and lexicographer, to comment in quite favorable terms.* Needless to say this kind of reaction was most encouraging and helps lead to the current exposition, which is the most complete to date. It is very much to be hoped that others will contribute to the expansion of our clinical data and formulations of the Soterial Reactions.

3. Considerations Influence Adoption and Survival

Time, of course, plus circumstances, relative value, and convenience will determine if, how long, and how well the term soteria will survive. Its

---

* Editor Henry A. Davidson kindly commented: "The word is so useful, that it is surprising that it has not worked its way deeper into the psychiatric lexicon. It is a handy term and there is no other single word that quite conveys the meaning. It should be used more."

chances are slim indeed when one traces the fate of many offerings to the diagnostic nomenclature over the last few decades.

Only through many such ventures, however, does the profession have an opportunity occasionally to consider and possibly adopt as useful, a given new concept or term. In this way we may selectively and upon occasion add to our convenient scientific shorthand. This medium of communication has very gradually evolved, is time-saving, aids in the transmission of ideas, and concepts and is indispensable to the discipline of psychiatry. This is exactly the way that similar special terms and concepts have evolved, to aid in the communication of ideas, and in the progressive development of every other scientific discipline and field, as well as in psychiatry. It is in this light that "soteria" has been offered, with the author's wish for its success!

III. ON DIAGNOSIS

A. COMMON SOTERIAL REACTIONS

1. Diagnosis Warranted . . .

The Soteria is a neurotic reaction in which an external object source provides protection and security. To the outside observer, and very often to the individual concerned as well, the protection received and the reliance upon it is quite clearly out of proportion to any objective comfort, succor, or security which the object alone and unaided has any realistic power to provide. As with the phobia and the phobic object, determination of the presence of a Soterial Reaction depends upon the identification of the soterial object, together with its associated emotional significance and meaning.

The Soterial Reaction requires the presence of one or more soterias of some significance. The pre-existing predilection usually also is present for the adoption of this form of neurotic defense. A diagnosis is warranted when this type of reaction is the most prominent feature in a person's psychologic makeup or in his neurotic pattern, and when there are the accompanying elements of self-defeat, handicap, and so on, such as are usually implicit to the presence of a neurotic reaction generally.

2. Choice of Soterial Object Unlimited

As with the phobic object, the choice of soterial object is practically unlimited. It would seem of limited practical value at this time in any way exhaustively to classify, to name, or to assign Greek prefixes to all those that might be identified. A number of types have been mentioned thus far.

The following examples illustrate some additional types of Soterial Reactions which may be fairly frequently encountered.

Case 126

Common Soterial Reactions

(1) A middle-aged woman constantly feared she would faint. She never did. However, she could not venture forth without her bottle of *smelling salts*. It had become her soterial protector. As long as she had it, she felt safe and secure. In its absence she felt "tense", "nervous", and "uneasy".

She felt constantly in danger of fainting. Having her smelling salts at hand and constantly available countered her apprehensive dread, contributed feelings of safety, and made life tolerable.

(2) *Sedatives* may similarly become soterial objects of dependency. The author has treated phobic patients who used them as a direct counterphobic protection. More recently the *tranquilizer group of drugs,* with increasing frequency, plays a similar role. Many types of drugs have come to secure soterial significance for the person concerned.

(3) Various kinds of *collections* can gain soterial significance for people. They become a source of security and comfort.

One of the author's respected colleagues who has long been an ardent philatelist said not long ago, ". . . My stamp collection is a real comfort to me. It's so fine to put a stamp down in its proper space and know exactly where it is and that there it will stay! It is such a satisfaction to have that stamp and to know exactly where it is. It is one thing that remains constant and just as I want it to . . .".

His stamp collection was a source of security in its stability and relative permanence. There were no changes except when he himself made them. It was an area of certainty; one in which he remained in control.

(4) *Toys and stuffed animals* are a frequent soterial source of comfort, solace, and security for children. Other sources include pictures, songs, the oft repeated "just so" story [pp. 291–2 and 352], an item of food [*Case 73* pp. 352–3], clothing or other possession, a pet, a song, rhyme or prayer, a favorite person, and so on. The *C.S.R.* (Compulsive Security Ritual; p. 354) can have important soterial implications, as can various neurotic reaction patterns.

(5) A 36-year-old teacher was inseparably attached to four small *pillows.* These were practically a necessity for him to relax sufficiently (*that is, to feel safe and secure enough*) to be able to sleep. He had to make occasional trips to other colleges as a visiting lecturer or professor. The pillows had to accompany him. They had first priority among his traveling effects.

Each night when at home or away they were arranged in a precise way in which they surrounded and covered his head. This afforded a soterial retreat and comfort. He could thus feel secure. Sleep was then possible.

B. POINTS IN DIFFERENTIAL DIAGNOSIS

1. Obsessive Compulsive Reactions

Differential Diagnosis is not likely to offer major problems. There are sometimes relationships to be observed to certain obsessive phenomena. Indeed some obsessive rituals have a distinct soterial quality. Herein the individual concerned feels unsafe, tense, or anxious when his Compulsive Ritual or C. R. is incomplete or when something external forces its discontinuance [pp. 349 *ff.*]. The compulsive patient similarly obeys his compulsion to act, so as to feel better, or more comfortable. Moreover, certain compulsive childhood patterns of protective avoidance, for example, touching every fourth picket in a fence, avoiding stepping on cracks in the pavement, and so on, are Security Operations or S. O. [pp.351 *ff*] with a soterial character.

Certain superstitions and superstitious avoidances are also essentially soterial security operations. One avoids walking under a ladder, breaking a mirror, or having a black cat cross one's path, and so on, to protect oneself against "evil" or to avoid "bad luck". These kinds of phenomena illustrate the close relations which can exist between the Obsessive-Compulsive group of Reactions and the Soterial Reactions. Actually a given manifestation can illustrate both. Recall that the phobia is an obsessively persistent fear. Similarly the soteria is an obsessively persistent comfort and protection-seeking.

2. Organic Disease; Hygeiaphrontis

Confusion with organic disease is rather rare. Sometimes the patient's soterial dependence upon and urgent need for a medicine, an examination, physical therapy, injection, dietary routine, or health food, and so on can suggest organic possibilities. At times further studies and exams are indicated. However these (and attempted proof to the patient of the absence of a real objective basis of need) are unlikely to eliminate the person's soterial dependence. Perhaps it is better not to attempt this too abruptly in any event. One does not so readily nor suddenly dissolve the internal needs and mechanisms which have led to evolving the Soterial Reaction. This is also illustrated in *Case 130* and elsewhere.

The foregoing comment leads us directly to the soterial implications of the Hygeiaphrontic Reactions (hypochondriasis). Herein the lines of demarcation can become a bit blurred. Accordingly an organ, function, or symptom can gain what is in effect soterial meaning and importance [Ch.8:VIIA*3*]. These reactions can in this fashion tend to overlap clinically. The distinction is based upon which is the more prominent feature, as assessed by the diagnostician.

IV. INCIDENCE

A. NEARLY UNIVERSAL

Many examples of soteria can be seen in day-to-day life by the alert observer. A fair number of instances are also to be encountered in the clinical practice of psychiatry and in psychotherapy. For many people at one or more junctures in living, the setting up of soterias becomes an important S.O. (security operation). When one includes all the major and minor instances over the course of a lifetime, the author strongly suspects that the incidence of soterias approaches that of being nearly a universal phenomenon.

Racial prototypes of the soteria extend into prehistoric times. They are found widely today as well among the more primitive peoples. Included are talismans, amulets, charms, items of dress or apparel, decorative and religious objects, the rituals of taboo, and various images. Such multitudinous objects have had assigned to them various magical powers of preservation, anti-evil, and security. These operated for individuals, family groups, tribes, and races. The protective power with which such an item is endowed depends largely on the level of one's individual belief and the significance assigned. Symbolic meaning is sometimes enhanced by the "successful operation" of the device, as when it has become associated with victory in battle, recovery from an illness (individual), or a pestilence (group or tribe), averting a natural catastrophe, and so on.

B. ADEIA AND PHYLACTORY

The *adeia* of the ancient Greeks served both as a safe conduct and a guarantee against reprisal. It often had official sanction. A *phylactory* was a Grecian talisman, which also had some Hebriac usage. In more modern times the "good luck piece", the rabbit's foot, squirrel's tail, and other similar objects are not far removed in meaning and usage.

Many other soterial objects exist openly or more covertly, some of which have been noted. From all of these some degree of protection, security, and safety is sought, and is derived by various people. An acceptance of special powers, magic, or the presence of superstitious belief can facilitate or reinforce the subjective feeling of protection and security to be secured.

C. ESTIMATED PERCENTAGE

Among the neurotic reactions the author has estimated a relative incidence of approximately 6–8 per cent (*see Table 16,* pp. 243–4). At first glance this figure seems high. However, one must keep in mind the many factors which tend to keep the Soterial Reaction a covert one. It is likely to be obscured and protected.

Not leading to the subjective pain and misery of other psychic reactions, it is not often a subject of complaint, nor is it often a presenting symptom. It is also less likely to be a spontaneous subject for scrutiny by the patient in psychotherapy. This however does not mean that it is less frequent. It does not lessen its occasional considerable significance in a given individual's psychology.

V. SYMPTOMS AND CLINICAL FEATURES

A. SPECIAL EMOTIONAL SIGNIFICANCE ATTACHED

1. Soterial Objects; Individual Prototypes

The special emotional significance which can become attached to such objects as charms, talismans, good luck pieces, metals, religious tokens, and relics has been noted. Certain modern rituals, ceremonials, fraternal and patriotic procedures may in themselves have or gain soterial value for certain persons. These also in turn can make use of symbols which have become highly meaningful through attribution and repeated use. Photographs, mementos, and souvenirs can become soterial objects of some importance. Alcohol and items related to its use can come to have important soterial significances. Pets of many varieties can become to an extent soterial objects; puppies, kittens, a goat, calf, cosset (a pet lamb), and any of the domesticated, or even non-domesticated living creatures.

Pathology is by no means necessarily implied in instances of soterial development. The soteria is a normal or at least a nonpathologic response until it interferes with effectiveness in living, or until self-defeating elements are present in its often hidden neurotic effects. These may be apparent, they may be ascertained, or their effects may be reflected or mirrored in the general personality adjustment.

Certain objects which serve as security-comforts for infants and small children can serve as *"individual prototypes* for later soterias. Common examples are such bedtime treasures as the favorite teddybear, stuffed dog, or the special blanket. These familiar objects can become very meaningful. They may be required by the young child for a feeling of comfort and security when he goes to bed, or at times when he becomes troubled and upset. He may become unable or unwilling on occasion to go to sleep without them. (*See* earlier instance of the small pillows). Sometimes these feelings can carry over for prolonged periods. A child for many years, into early adolescence, was attached in this way to an old silk handkerchief which was called a "pah-dah". This type of clinging can serve as an early antecedent in the later development of certain adult soterias.

2. Importance of Accustomed and Familiar

A. UNEASINESS WHEN SEPARATED: THE SEPARATION REACTION.—The soterial type of reaction frequently results in an emotional attachment to "things", that is to material possessions as well as to persons and to relationships. Thus these can tend to become increasingly important and significant. The soterial individual, in direct contrast to the phobic patient, often feels uneasiness upon being *separated from them*. The extent of this can vary tremendously. This soterial variety of what we might term a *Separation Reaction* is a measure of their individual significance and of the underlying needs which have led to their evolvement.

This kind of uneasiness may occur for many of us to some extent when we are separated from our familiar surroundings and familiar objects. We tend to become more or less closely attached to, and emotionally dependent upon the many aspects of our usual surroundings, and to the people of our familiar relationships; the ones we have become used to.

B. APPLICATIONS FOR CARE OF SENIOR CITIZENS.—An understanding of these principles leads us readily into an understanding of advice already recognized as most appropriate for our senior citizens. Older people should be maintained in their usual and familiar surroundings whenever possible. A proper consideration of the deeper emotional support and significance involved, multiplies the importance of any of the more superficial considerations of simple convenience and so on, involved in maintaining their "usual" surroundings.

C. EXILES AND POW'S.—Important emotional losses in these respects can play a role in numerous other situations. They add to the suffering from exile and help to make it the terrible punishment it is to most people. They contribute to the emotional stress of deportation (recall the Acadians), and that resulting from enforced living in D.P. or prisoner-of-war camps. Thus, often the loss of one's soterial objects — both material and interpersonal — contributes to the suffering incident to exile and banishment.

3. Accumulations, Savings, Collections, and Hoarding

A. BEYOND LOGIC AND REALISTIC NEED; EMOTIONAL DETERMINANTS OPERATIVE.—The farmer takes real satisfaction in seeing his mows and silos filled. His animals are thus assured of food for the winter. The old-fashioned housewife takes pride in canning fruits, vegetables and so on in order to have ample provender for her family until the new growing season comes around. These feelings are quite fine of course. Such accumulations provide a real and a realistic measure of security.

These preparations however, as can many others, at times extend far beyond the practical. A given housewife for example fills shelves and cupboards with excess foodstuffs, not content with practical amounts. It is as though more security can be gained in this way. An occasional country sale will disclose this kind of excess accumulation, in which one may surmise its underlying attempted soterial function. The farmer similarly may keep his mows or graneries overfilled, or on occasion retain an excess even to the point of spoilage.

Thus with many people in many circumstances; their provisions for the future, their accumulations, do not necessarily directly reflect this logic of the external circumstances. Non-rational, emotional determinants are operative.

B. SECURITY OPERATIONS.—There are many instances of soterial Security Operations or S.O. Collections of many kinds can have soterial meaning and value to the collector. So also can savings. Hoarding for instance can include many items, in addition to money, foodstuffs, and, in wartime, certain critical and scarce items. The symbolic comfort, satisfaction, and protection afforded in these instances can vary from the minimal and innocent all the way to the pathologic and absurd. Seldom, however, is such activity a presenting symptom or complaint. The reasons are often consciously rationalized on the basis of practicality and convenience.

Some of the foregoing comments are illustrated in the following three instances.

Case 127

Soterial Significance in Certain Cases of Hoarding

(1) *Foodstuffs.* A thirty-nine-year-old housewife kept the largest size of deep-freezer packed with food. She could almost never bring herself to use any of the contents. Even for a last-minute emergency meal, she would insist upon her husband going to the store for supplies. Not long ago their family of two, living in a small apartment, purchased a *second* large freezer, which Mrs. M. also busily packed.

Her explanations were on the basis of convenience and availability. Yet note that the contents of the freezers were not so used. The accumulation of food served her as an important *Security Operation*. The needs for this were protectively concealed from conscious awareness. Rationalization helped protect the prior repression. Through the presence of the foodstuffs, Mrs. M. felt safer, protected, and more secure. This was a neurotic reaction. The similar elaboration of various soterial objects comprises Security Operations of some moment.

(2) *Books*. A forty-three-year-old single patient, Mr. K., is fond of books, although he seldom reads them. He carefully reads the better book reviews and makes out lists of those books which he regards as outstanding. To economize, he then waits a year or so until a paperbound edition is published and he can purchase a copy. Considerable time and energy is invested in hunting for them intermittently in various book displays.

Mr. K. has many large bookcases in his home filled with the books he has painstakingly secured. His collection overflows into his garage. He has read only a handful! He could not bear the thought of parting with them, or of being separated from them. This is a soterial operation of considerable importance.

It is not surprising, in view of the special emotional significance to him of his accumulated books, that he did not even mention them until well along in treatment! To him the books afforded a measure of semimagical security and protection. They were not a source of discomfort. It was not, therefore, regarded as a problem.

Consciously he rationalized his obsessive soterial activity on a superficial level. He wanted to be sure he would "always be able to have a good book to read." He had thousands!

(3) *Household Supplies*. An older woman, Mrs. S., was known for some years to hoard linens, soap, and toilet tissue. With each trip to a store she would usually buy a small quantity of each item. Not long ago Mrs. S. passed away.

Her house was found to be nearly crammed with the accumulation, over thirty years, of these soterially meaningful supplies. Dressers, bureaus, drawers, and closet shelves were jammed. The attic was crowded with filled cardboard cartons.

The dividing line between the security which may be gained in healthy fashion, and that secured through the attachment of special emotional significance to a soterial object, may be difficult to draw. The normal and healthful merges gradually into the neurotic. The Soteria is very often an important Security Operation.

C. SINISTER POTENTIAL.—Security Operations are sometimes involved. In the following instance it was perverse. The soterial object was itself also deadly. It was designed to ensure this person an escape; a way out. (*See* earlier reference to suicide, as an ultimate soterial retreat, *Case 30*, p. 162.)

Case 128

A Perverse Kind of Soteria

A 42-year-old biologist secured two ounces of cyanide. She carried it in her purse for several weeks, during which she made a trip to the west coast. It was intended as a final resort, escape and relief via suicide from intolerable emotional pressure. In this perverse comfort it also provided her with a twisted soterial kind of security. In obsessive fashion, her thoughts dwelt on it constantly.

This mechanism allowed her—gave her "the courage"—to face each new stress. She could remain confident that she constantly had a means of "escape" at hand. While the reaction has some of the elements of the obsessive, here it is at least partially consciously sought, and becomes more a soteria.

In other instances, of course, similar suicidal thoughts could be intrusive, consciously unwelcome and constitute a true obsession. Recently the author has studied two instances in which suicide was contemplated in soterial terms, as a comfort and refuge; something always available to "fall back on", should the need become sufficiently urgent.

4. Soterial Comfort and Preservation Derived

A. ART, THEATRE, MUSIC, AND WRITING.—For some people soterial aspects are present in various art forms. Such is true also for plays, the theatre, and ballet. Music in its many forms provides fairly frequent examples of soterial attachment. The writer may gain security from his papers, and so on.

A very successful internist friend and medical author commented to the author some years ago concerning the secure feelings and comfort derived from the five medical books he had produced; "Whenever my spirits are low", he said, "I come and look at my books. I always feel better. They make life, me, and my work worthwhile . . . I have something I've created. No one can take it away. I feel safe and secure . . . . These volumes are my own real treatment for nervousness or tension. The sight (or thought) of them makes me feel less vulnerable . . . . Many times when things have appeared quite black, they have seemed to keep me going; been my preservation! . . .".

E. RELIGIOUS OBJECTS.—Religious soterial objects are widespread and have considerable variety. In various individual circumstances they can achieve considerable significance for the person concerned. The author suspects this may be slightly less true today than a generation or so ago. Nevertheless this type of soterial attachment is common enough to not require further description.

It may be worthy of mention more specifically, however, that the soteria in religious areas as in other situations, is not confined solely to material objects. Thus the "object" for example can also be a proverb, a biblical quotation or verse, a commandment, a priest, minister, or rabbi, the Golden Rule, a ritual or ceremonial, a blessing, a hymn, and so on.

C. PRESERVATION OF TRAVELER.—Religious items as well as others are employed in conjunction with needs for safeguarding travel and the traveler. Highway dangers are ever with us, and highway accidents occur with all too great frequency. It is hardly surprising that many people and their cars carry a protectively intended soterial object.

The following instance illustrates an interesting type of protective soterial ritual. It further combines the religious, the musical, and the non-material type of "object". This was a Security Operation of some importance to the person concerned.

Case 129

A Protective Soterial Ritual for the Highway

Sarah M. was a 42-year-old housewife who was in intensive therapy because of long-standing nervousness, handicapping character traits, and several physiologic conversion symptoms. She had an excellent intellectual background, was a *cum laude* graduate of one of the "seven sisters' colleges", and had long been a leader among her peers.

Some time early in her third year of treatment she related her special private method of protection and preservation while driving. During such times she would sing a hymn softly aloud. The more traffic, the louder she would sing. A favorite was the old, and revered by many, Methodist hymn of "Whispering Hope". The song and its singing were a significant avenue of protection and preservation for her. Through it any danger was allayed. She felt protected, and that her life was charmed. Anxiety and fear during driving were banished. With the song, her soterial object, she could feel beyond any threat or danger.

D. SECONDARY DEFENSE; THE PRESERVING IS IN TURN PRESERVED.—The pattern of living for the lady in the above instance required almost daily driving. Having seen her for three and four sessions a week during more than two years made it perhaps more noteworthy that this interesting soterial operation was not shared with the author earlier in our work together. Many highly personal significant, and/or deeply troubling and conflictual matters certainly had been discussed. Perhaps this partly bespeaks its emotional value to the possessor.

It also indicates its relative importance. Finally, it further illustrates the operation of the Secondary Defense. Hereby *the soterial operation is preserving; and is in turn preserved!* The delay in sharing was an unconscious further protection. This was rationalized on several bases: such as, "lack of importance", "little relevance to our work", and it just "hadn't come to mind".

B. SOTERIA IN MEDICAL TREATMENT

1. Drugs, Procedures, Interpersonal Aspects

A. DIFFICULTY IN AVOIDING.—The soterial situation may develop or be unwittingly contributed to through medical treatment. In the treatment situation the patient may well come to derive a neurotic kind and/or degree of security, dependency, and comfort from various kinds of medicines and drugs. This reaction also develops with greater frequency than may be commonly recognized from various *other aspects* of the treatment situation, including especially the interpersonal ones, as well as objects in the physical surroundings. This is often unwitting and may be most difficult to avoid. Its determinants are individual, often deep seated, and unconscious. The primary needs for this kind of soterial S.O. are usually those of the particular patient.

Transference may play a role here also. In psychiatric treatment especially, the intensity of the relationship strongly encourages the development of transference*, the positive side of which can carry important

---

* Transference is *the unconscious transfer to new persons of feelings which were originally experienced toward important persons of early life. The entire relationship, or parts of it, then tends to be conceived as following the earlier antecedent pattern of its prototype.* In a *positive* transference the patient largely experiences feelings of warmth, fondness, affection, or love. In the *negative* type of transference the feelings and reactions toward the therapist are preponderantly on the negative side.

soterial overtones. As a result, the patient may be quite content with it. Its analysis and resolution can well prove difficult.

B. WHEN DEPRIVATION ATTEMPTED.—Many aspects of the soteria and attendant considerations enter into medical practice. In *Case 126* we saw an illustration of the protective significance which medicine can gain.

Soterial dependence on drugs can become a powerful influence. This is of course by no means necessarily related to the actual medicinal strength, or to its effects as such. On occasion a patient in therapy is observed while battling such a soterial dependence. The difficulty in his winning such a battle may well serve as a measure of the strength of the dependence. One such patient recently was seeking to conquer a strong soterial dependence on a sedative and a tranquilizer. One day, she related how *"this* morning I was going to take *just* my Donnatal and not my *Thorazine* [of a minimal 5 mg B.I.D.] . . . but my heart pounded so just at the thought of not taking it, that I was afraid to omit it! . . . I say to myself, 'Take it and you'll be protected'! . . .". She was seeking to rely mainly upon will power, in distinction to increasing her insight and understanding.

The following instance illustrates the resistance of a patient to being deprived of such soterial medical comfort.

Case 130

Deprivation of a Medical Soteria

A fifty-six-year-old woman had long been under the regular care of her family physician. Part of his treatment included the giving of weekly injections over a considerable period of time. This was a relatively inert substance which had no real influence upon the patient's *physical* health. However, she had come to attach great significance to it. It had become an unreal kind of emotional security to which she very much clung. A convenient peg for the attachment of neurotic dependence, it had probably been contributed to unwittingly by the doctor concerned. What were some of the consequences when she moved to another city?

Her new physician could not conscientiously sanction the continuation of the injections on any scientific basis. He carefully explained all this and the basis for it to the patient, an intelligent woman. Her reaction was to become indignant. She became quite angry with the physician. He was interfering with and attempting to halt the injections! This would deprive her of her soterial object, the injections, which had become a neurotic source of protection, comfort, and security. It is hardly surprising that she became very angry with the person who attempted to take all this away from her!

2. Compensation

A. SOTERIAL E.O.A.—Patients may seek and/or be granted compensation for illness or for injury. The compensation, pension, hospitalization, and so on may gain great soterial significance. This is illustrated in *Case 10* (p. 67). The patient has no voluntary control over this. It is very much a part of him. He cannot simply relinquish it.

The union of affect and object in the soteria constitutes at least as stable an E.O.A. or *emotional-object amalgam* as in the phobia. An understanding of how some of this comes about will be of interest and use to many physicians.

B. SOTERIAL HAVEN AND REFUGE.—Many *places* can gain soterial value and significance. In effect they tend thus to become a haven; a refuge. The *Respite-of-Sleep Principle* (p. 38) points out that sleep can be an invaluable refuge and retreat. The respite thus afforded may receive reinforcement or contributions through accessory soterial objects and mechanisms. The "soterial haven" is also illustrated at times with the office of the physician and with that of the psychiatric specialist. Thus the therapist's office may become a soterial refuge of considerable significance.

This development is indicated in the following case. Here she (the patient) was in a safer, more dependent, less exposed position. Leaving it was threatening as equating a loss of protection and safety, requiring her to resume a more exposed position.

Case 131

The Therapist's Office as a Soterial Refuge

A patient had originally entered intensive therapy for emotional problems which included a number of phobic manifestations. The author's office gradually became established as a counter-phobic kind of refuge. It was a soterial situation in which this person felt safe and secure. This is illustrated by the following verbatim extract from a treatment session.

". . . . This is the one place where I'm safe. I feel secure here. Why? Well, I just can't visualize anything horrible happening to me as long as I'm here. . . . Here I feel safe and protected. . . . It's like no other place. I guess this is the one time in the day when I'm real safe and don't have to worry about having a heart attack, or having something dreadful happen to me. . . . I look forward to my sessions here. I'm sorry when our time runs out, and I don't want to leave. Here I'm safe . . .".

C. IN BUSINESS

The following instance is from the world of business and commerce. It helps indicate how pervasive the soterial mechanism can be in our many areas of living. It came to the author's attention at a most opportune juncture for its inclusion here.

Case 132

Soterial Protection in a Business Venture

Just as this chapter had been gotten into semifinal draft, a builder who is also a business colleague phoned, "Doctor we are pouring our first footings on the Prince Fairfax project at 2:00 tomorrow. . . . I'll be there to represent us. . . . I'll put a silver dollar in the concrete for you and me. Then I know things will go fine! . . . [and slightly apologetically] This is just a little superstition of mine . . . .".

The builder is an educated, substantial, sophisticated, and practical businessman. Still, the placing of the silver coin in the concrete foundation offers a measure of superstitious comfort and protection. This came out by chance. It is a small item in his personal psychology, but still of some importance. He had followed this practice regularly for years. The omission of his soterial precaution would lead to discomfort and uneasiness. This illustrates a type of Soterial Reaction which is sometimes encountered in business ventures, as elsewhere.

D. IN LOVE AFFAIRS

Soterial satisfactions which are often poorly recognized consciously, can help to account for the tremendous importance of love affairs (often illicit ones as well) to certain people. These may contribute to the individual's reluctance or inability to give up such a relationship. This may be despite its terrifically self-defeating consequences, which the person concerned may be totally unable to recognize.

Blindness to these consequences can be essential to protect the neurotic satisfactions which may be involved. Because of neurosis or neurotic character structure, more healthy avenues for securing satisfactions may be blocked. Their blockage makes the maintenance of soterial and other neurotic satisfactions more vital and essential.

VI. NOTES ON PSYCHODYNAMICS

A. OBJECT OF DEPENDENCY PROJECTED EXTERNALLY

1. Symbolic Possession

A few comments are indicated concerning the dynamics of this "other side of the phobic coin". Ultimately, that is, on the deepest "level"* of psychologic significance, the soterial complex, including the typical attachment to the soterial object, can be regarded as representing a symbolic and unwitting seeking to achieve the possession of the neurotically sought-after object of dependency. The individual has displaced to this object (which can be an actual object, person, or situation), in an automatic, unconscious process, some measure of the protection and security long associated with the ideal mother-image from his early oral stage of development.

Some measure of the idealized dependency object is projected externally. The person concerned experiences resulting feelings of preservation and security. The object of dependency is (in part) symbolically possessed.

Thus, the soterial object symbolically represents the idealized mother-image. One thus achieves to some degree the protection and security which was early associated with this as a prototype. In infancy this was fantasied perhaps as all-providing and all-gratifying. The dependent needs for these comforts and for the possession of the object have been deeply repressed from all conscious awareness. The unconscious displacement externally of the source of satisfaction for the disowned dependent needs takes place. Part of the soterial endogain, that is, the primary gain of the soterial mechanism, is in the measure of magical security and gratification which is thus secured.

From another technical frame of reference, there has been a libidinal attachment to an object. The latter is overvalued. It is an external idealized object. Its special emotional meaning and significance have been projected to it. Now *from* it appears to emanate the typical soterial feelings

---

* See *Concept of Defensive Layering*, p. 465.

as experienced [Ch. 8: VII A *3*]. Several principal mental mechanisms are operative. These include Repression, Idealization, Projection, and Displacement. This entire process is deeply unconscious.

For further related psychodynamics the reader is directed to the several appropriate sections in the two preceding chapters. Understanding of the material here and elsewhere in the text will help elucidate the underlying bases of the Soterial Reactions.

2. Self-Defeat Illustrated; Relationship-Objects

If the possession of his object of dependency can to some extent be symbolically attained, why should one complain? Such possession will not be likely to afford the person concerned any conscious pain, even though the results may be, in hidden fashion, very self-defeating. This is illustrated briefly in the following instance.

Case 133

The Conscious Neurotic Pleasure and Comfort Derived from Certain Soterial Relationships versus The Concomitant (and Unconscious) Self-Defeat

A thirty-four-year-old, single physician, in analysis had reported a series of fairly superficial relationships with young women. Although he consciously asserted his interest in marriage, his friendships never seemed to progress sufficiently. An interesting aspect of his complex inner conflicts was the tremendous satisfaction he would derive from what to an external observer, were rather small rewards.

A smile from his current girl-friend would put him in "seventh heaven". He would go to great lengths to secure any expression of approval. When his young lady seemed to approve of him or to like him a little, he would be literally in "ecstasy". Small wonder that he had little interest in changing this *status quo*. The tremendous satisfactions he derived in hidden neurotic fashion, and with some considerable masochistic sacrifice, were too important. This was despite the reverse of gloom and depression which he experienced in response to a frown or an expression of disapproval.

Each relationship in turn was used unconsciously by him as a soteria, from which he derived tremendous neurotic comfort, protection, and satisfaction. These thus comprised what we might call soterial *Relationship-Objects*. Gradually we worked out in therapy the transference and displacement, to each new object-relationship in turn, of early overdependent attachments to an idealized mother. He was symbolically regaining his long-lost mother-ideal. He inadvertently further thus recreated all over again his unrealistically guilty striving to please her and to secure acceptance.

The tragic defeat in this pattern of neurotically repetitive relationships lay in: (1) the absorption of energy and effort in essentially nonconstructive endeavors; (2) the continuation of a pattern of unrealistic "ecstatic" satisfaction; and (3) the effective blocking of any opportunity for more lasting and mature relationships. This patient had no complaint about the neurotic satisfactions derived from his soterial objects. These he desperately wished to preserve. Still the ecstasy would gradually phase out in each instance. He would routinely outdo himself to gain the approval he sought. Gradually his energy, devotion, and efforts would wear out. Reinvestment would require a new object, which, in its turn would serve for a while.

He had sought treatment for the reverse aspect: the depression, discouragement, and certain physiologic conversion symptoms of intense headaches and functional gastrointestinal difficulties. During the course of nearly five years of intensive treatment many hidden conflicts were uncovered and resolved. As might be expected, his surrender of his neurotic soterial objects was one of the last major changes, as he gradually effected a more mature adjustment.

B. SOTERIA AND PHOBIA

The clinical features and the dynamics of the soteria perhaps can be more clearly observed in tabular presentation. Accordingly, the accompanying comparative data have been prepared. Herein the Soteria and the Phobia are compared and contrasted.

Table 30

The Soteria and the Phobia

The reaction of the soteria and its effects for the individual are roughly the converse of those of the phobia. A *phobia* is a specific pathologic fear, which is out of proportion to the apparent stimulus. The painful affect has been displaced from its original unconscious source to an external object.

A *soteria* is a reaction through which emotional feelings of security and protection are experienced. Anxiety is allayed. The security feelings as experienced, are apparently out of proportion to the external stimulus. This is the *Anxiety-Countering Principle* of the soterial operation and a requisite to its evolvement and its delineation clinically. By displacement, the external object symbolically has come to represent to some degree the unconsciously long-sought object of dependency. As a consequence it becomes a neurotic object-source of security, solace, comfort, and/or protection.

Some of the contrasting and comparable features of the phobia and the soteria are as follows:

THE SOTERIA	THE PHOBIA
1. The soterial object is protective and satisfying.	1. The phobic object is feared and provokes anxiety.
2. The soterial E.O.A. becomes a neurotic source of security.	2. The phobic E.O.A. becomes a neurotic threat to security.
3. Consciously perceived as a source of comfort, protection and reassurance.	3. Consciously perceived as a source of danger, fear, and tension.
4. Unconscious displacement externally of a consciously disowned dependent need and its satisfaction; ultimately, the partial or full achievement (possession) of the ideal object.	4. Unconscious displacement externally of a consciously disowned threat or danger; ultimately and symbolically the threat of loss of the object of dependency or the threat of retaliation for seeking to possess it.
5. Conflict resolution is sought through continued repression of the unconscious dependent needs. In addition, the soterial endogain (that is, the primary gain of the soterial mechanism) includes the provision for their magical gratification. Ultimately, the soterial object symbolically represents the idealized mother-image which has been fantasied by the infant as all-providing and all-gratifying.	5. Conflict resolution is sought through reinforcement of the repression, and denial of consciously disowned thoughts and drives. These are aggressive—hostile and sexual in nature. They are intolerably dangerous and threatening because of: (*a*) possible retaliation, and/or (*b*) the danger that they might achieve their ultimate aim, that is, the annihilation of the simultaneously vitally needed object of dependency.

Common Features of The Soteria and The Phobia

1. In both, there is apparent irrationality, according to any of the usual methods of observation. There is a discrepancy between the feelings experienced, and the ordinarily perceived level of significance of the phobic or soterial object. Both have an element of the primitive and magical.
2. In both, the consciously disowned satisfaction, or danger, is displaced externally to a substitutive object.
3. In both, the external object may cover a wide range of things, people, or situations. Its determination may be by a variety of pathways. (*See Table 28*, p. 583.)

C. IN CONCLUSION

The reader's attention has been invited to what may be regarded as a whole class of reactions, in which an added emotional significance of protection, security, comfort, or love has been secured through the displacement of an internal idealized prototype to an external and more or less symbolic object, situation, or relationship. The term *soteria* has been proposed for this group of reactions, which is to be considered as largely the reverse of the phobia.

Soterias and soterial objects are less apt to have attention drawn to them than are the phobias and phobic objects, since the former are a source of comfort, while the latter are a source of discomfort. Both can become highly self-defeating and neurotic.

The patient is more comfortable living with his soteria than he is living with a phobia. Ordinarily he has no conscious awareness of the deeper psychologic significance of either, although he is more apt to be willing and to have the incentive to try and learn more about the origin of his phobia.

A soteria is by definition, then, the defensive Security Operation, through which an individual unconsciously establishes an external object, symbol, situation, or relationship as a source of emotional comfort, security, love, or protection. These emotional derivations, as with the phobic object, are apparently out of proportion to the soterial object from the standpoint of any of the usual methods of observation. As with the phobic object, when the dynamics are uncovered, one finds that the reaction is exactly appropriate for the actual hidden inner meaning to the person concerned.

VII. ADDITIONAL ASPECTS OF THE SOTERIAL REACTIONS

A. SECURE BASE OF OPERATIONS CONCEPT

1. Important in Child Development

An important emotional significance of the home and family for the infant or child is in the creation of a *secure base of operations* (p. 174). This is an important concept in healthful childhood development. In the psychologically healthful situation the child can then sally forth from his secure base, according to his inclinations and his ability to do so. The base is always available for a return. Here he can replenish and remobilize his emotional reserves and his potential for new activities.

Gradually, as he gains increasing maturity, he becomes less dependent on the original S.B.O. Eventually he creates his own Base. However, with slight changes in this process, the original home and what it represents can become soterially important to a pathologic extent. The dependency bonds cannot then be dealt with in any mature kind of fashion. The *First Tenet of the Parental Role* (p. 23) lies in the facilitation of the child's acculturation and maturation, in the optimal emotional climate. (Establishing the "secure base of operations" is the Second Tenet, p. 174.)

2. Home a Soterial Refuge

One's home may become a soterial refuge. This would be seen as an extension of whatever carryover there had been from the healthful childhood (secure) base of operations. The extension can be slight or it can progress to a seriously limiting and handicapping extent. The soterial value of the home in the most severe instance can result in a nearly complete unwillingness to venture forth from the source (locale) of security. (*See Case 23*, pp. 107–8.)

The same kind of restrictive effect thus can result soterially, as one also can see in the severe Self-Confining Phobia, although the basis for the restriction differs. In this type of Phobic Reaction it is the fear and threat of the external which restrains, defers, and delimits boundaries. In the very marked kind of Soterial Reaction, the security, and soterial safety of the home is so strong as to be surrendered with great reluctance, if at all.

The *soterial retreat* is emotional and not objective. Thus the place of retreat can reflect this. Earlier (*see Case 30,* p. 162) mention was made of one possible facet in the dynamics of suicide, in which this act represented the ultimate in a self-defeating retreat.

A second house or cottage, particularly a summer vacation home on occasion, may readily tend to gain this kind of significance. It may become an important secondary personal soterial retreat and refuge.

3. Marriage

Marriage can be an extension of either the healthful or the unhealthful consequences of the foregoing. It can possess or gain for a partner significance as a soterial retreat. The successful marriage in any event becomes to a greater or lesser extent, a mature, secure, and healthful base of operations. It is psychologically economic in that more energy is made available for constructive social activity.

Major problems of adjustment and sexual activity have been resolved accordingly. As a result, the individual is left freer to direct his energies outwardly. He is free to function more effectively and in a more socially constructive fashion.

B. SOTERIAL IMPLICATIONS OF FOOD AND EATING

1. Overeating and Obesity a Consequence

The relation of anxiety to the problem of obesity was referred to earlier. Overeating can be one response to anxiety (*see* p. 115). Overeating generally implies the existence of some emotional problem. It has been more or less well known that the obese person may seek gratification in eating when he is unhappy or anxious. Food can secure unconscious significance as representing security. This has many ramifications in the psychologic bases of overeating, weight gain, and obesity. Food can thus gain important soterial meaning for some people.

This is hardly surprising. The symbolism is that the food and its eating come to equate the "good object". The distortion is not very great since satisfaction of hunger was early associated with the all-providing mother of the early oral level. In the soterial operation, food gains added significance. It is no longer merely a way of satisfying one's appetite for food alone. It also conveys overtones of security, solace, and comfort.

2. Eating a Source of Comfort and Security

A. INSTANCE OF RULE OF IMPRESSION PRIORITY.—For some, eating allays anxiety. For some, eating can become, or serve as an important source of comfort and security. The analysis of such examples can reveal soterial mechanisms.

In the following instance there were significant soterial implications. This illustration is also a useful example of the more or less deliberate employment of the underlying principles of the Rule of Impression Priority. A sudden dramatic burst of recall and insight highlighted this particular segment of what was actually a long-term analysis.

Case 134

Analysis of a Pattern of Overeating

Several years ago a certain young lady suffered from a number of problems, one of which was the very difficult one of compulsive overeating and obesity. This was a seemingly intractable pattern of reaction. It became gradually and increasingly possible however to link it to eating as representing for her a major source of comfort and security.

Compulsively and automatically she would turn to food, particularly cookies, sweets, and ice cream whenever she was disappointed, hurt, or anxious. For her these items and their ingestion had evolved as an important soteria. This continued for many months until an earlier pattern was recalled. The antecedent basis became suddenly and dramatically clear.

One day in her tenth month of intensive therapy, in a burst of recall, the young obese patient related seemingly forgotten events from her second to fourth years of age. Her elderly nurse had learned an easy way to pacify the child through candy and other sweets. Let the child fret a bit and the nurse, taking the course of least resistance, would pop something sweet into her mouth.

The child never had much chance to learn other or more effective and healthful ways of handling her hurts, disappointments, and frustrations. As she recounted repeated instances of this kind of sequence, she quickly recognized its fundamental significance in her current problems. With racking and bitter sobs she very correctly assessed how cruel and heartless this way of managing her had been. The pattern thus induced had become an integral part of her emotional adaptation. Operating automatically through the years she had been helpless in its grasp.

The foregoing insight constituted an important breakthrough in the aspect of this young woman's problems which related to overeating and obesity. Needless to say, many more sessions were devoted to related problems. Many, many instances of troubled emotions and the automatically accompanying urge to eat came under our analytic scrutiny and study. The pattern gradually diminished.

The session described thus did not alone result in the cure of this aspect of her neurosis. However, it provided us with very beneficial and essential insights into the initiation of this particular pattern of reaction. It became gradually possible to erase the effects of the early unhealthful prior impressions. The indulgent, defeating, soterial pattern was gradually surrendered.

B. SIX IMPORTANT POINTS ILLUSTRATED.—As noted, the above case illustrates several important points, including: (1) The sudden dramatic recall which occasionally occurs in therapy, and its potential great value; (2) According to the Principle of Impression Priority we see how the reaction developed and also how its original pattern was more or less inadvertently, yet actively induced; (3) The relation of food and eating to comfort and security; (4) The importance of seeking earlier antecedents in therapy, the *Tracing Technique* in therapy; and (5) The great strength, long life, and tenacity of established emotional patterns.

Also illustrated (6) is the potential soterial importance to an individual of food and of eating. This pattern, however it originates, does not begin on barren ground. Some factors of psychologic predilection were doubtless present. Thus with the soteria. It develops also when prior circumstances of the individual's unconscious and its needs make such a (soterial) peg feasible and usable.

C. FACTORS IN DEVELOPMENT OF SOTERIAL REACTION.—The development of a Soterial Reaction can be contributed to by the antecedent circumstances and situation. The groundwork can be laid in accord with the Rule of Impression Priority and its principles.

A soteria can evolve on many bases. The precepts governing the selection of the Phobic Object, as summarized in the preceding chapter, have a considerable measure of applicability in the analogous selection of the Soterial Object.

VIII. TREATMENT

A. INITIATION OF THERAPY

1. Indications for Treatment

Principles of treatment as outlined with the various chapters have applicability in the management of the Soterial Reactions. The reverse also applies.

Treatment for the Soterial Reaction is indicated when:

1. There is a significant handicap or self-defeat, whether or not the individual concerned has awareness of this;
2. The Soterial Reaction is of sufficient prominence to warrant a clinical diagnosis;
3. There are major soterial contributions to, or interrelationships with other types of neurotic or psychotic reactions;
4. There is a pervasive kind of predilection for the employment of the soterial mechanism, or where an established soteria (or soterias) show evidence of trends toward their psychic pathologic extension and expansion;
5. A counter-phobic purpose interferes with phobic resolution; and in every instance where
6. The presence of a soteria or Soterial Reaction allays fear, threat, anxiety, and danger in (*a*) any way that delays or prevents a more effective therapeutic approach, or in (*b*) any way that leads to a resulting psychologic loss to the person concerned.

2. Symptom Resolution a Limited Goal

In the study, analysis, and resulting therapeutic modification of the Soterial Reaction one seeks more than mere symptom resolution. Accordingly, the removal of a specific soteria and its relative significance is not the best or ideal goal of therapy. This is too limited.

One seeks understanding and healthful maturation of the personality, with its soterial diathesis and predisposition. What are the underlying needs which have led to the development of this particular pattern of (attempted) defensive reaction? Why has this particular pattern evolved? What are the principal mechanisms employed by the individual concerned? What are their advantages, and their handicaps or defeats? What is the ultimate net result, the overall consequences of their operation? What is the soterial endogain?

3. More Effective Approach

The indirect approach in psychotherapy is often faster and more effective than any misguided more "direct" attempts at persuasion, argument, "proof", or appeals to logic. One needs to find out the "why" and the "how".

Encouraged free narrative, an unrestricted associative type of reporting thoughts in sequence — without prior reservation or censorship — and in so far as possible, an attitude of cooperative collaboration, together with real receptiveness, will produce far more significant data and benefits in the long run. These are valuable contributions to the therapeutic work which one desires from the patient. They help comprise the most effective approach to therapy. The therapist needs to have the kind of accepting, kindly, and perceptive listening ability, which will allow and encourage this.

The import to the patient can help determine the approach. The more major and significant the Soterial Reaction, the more outstanding and isolated it is, the more problematic the prognosis, the more reason to approach more indirectly. Discussion should be directed, especially early, toward *other* areas than the Soterial manifestations as such.

B. SOME HELPFUL CONSIDERATIONS

1. When to Interpret

Interpretations are to be offered when the individual concerned is within reasonable striking distance of gaining the insight himself. At the appropriate time the idea proffered will gain acceptance. This is in contrast to generating resistance or leading to attempted disputation.

2. Hand-in-Hand Concept in Psychotherapy

Actually, it is often just as well for the therapist to be *not too far ahead* of his colleague-patient in his understandings of the psychologic defenses and their ramifications as encountered. Being too far ahead offers the disadvantages of: (*a*) the possible development of impatience, while waiting for the analysand to get there (or close) also; (*b*) the danger of premature interpretations, with all the attendant hazards to the therapy; (*c*) the patient's sensing the gap and pressing for data to be shared; and (*d*) the problem of "being cruel" — that is, of being in the possible position that one's information could be helpful and if so, it would indeed be cruel to withhold something potentially very useful to the patient in his hard-pressed position.

It is better in the foregoing ways for the therapy, for the therapist, and for the patient, if both participants learn together and if their level of insight progresses more or less together. The foregoing are the bases entering into what we might call the *Hand-in-Hand Concept* in psychotherapy.

3. Tracing Antecedents

Tracing the reaction to its earliest manifestations, and study of the attendant circumstances, finding its origins where possible, can be quite useful. This is an application of the Tracing Technique in therapy.

This technique is valuable even when the origins veer away from the soterial, as we observed in the preceding case. Herein the gaining of soterial significance was a later development. The tracing of antecedents and their understanding are always of value in therapy.

4. Conservative Therapeutic Attitude.

At times the soteria is quite interesting and intriguing, occasionally amusing. It may be harmless or relatively so. One should not be carried away with unnecessary zeal for the dissolution of a Soterial Reaction simply because it can be identified!

Hobbies, accumulations, and collections rarely become greatly disadvantageous or handicapping. Very occasionally elements of inadvertent self-defeat become quite prominent. Other types of soterial manifestations may follow similar lines. A reasonably conservative therapeutic attitude is indicated.

5. *Sometimes Significant; Often Important; Always Interesting*

An important auxiliary benefit to be derived from the therapeutic study of the soteria relates to the contribution made thereby to an overall more thorough insight and understanding of the personality structure and its dynamic interactions. Study of soterias and their implications is an intriguing subject.

Sometimes quite significant, often important, always interesting, it is doubtful if time and effort invested in learning more about this pattern of reaction, or its individual manifestations in therapy would be other than a useful investment on the part of the psychotherapist.

IX. SUMMARY

In the *Soterial Reactions* one seeks security from an external object source. They represent a progression from the (early) realistic sources of security, to the magical and neurotic source which has been displaced externally. They are to an extent analogous to the Phobic Reactions, but reversed, being the "other side of the phobic coin". The soterial object counters fear and anxiety by providing comfort, solace, preservation, and security. The Soterial Reaction is defined as an unconscious neurotic pattern of attempted defense. A soteria or soterias are prominent features, and there is generally a predilection toward the development of soterial manifestations under appropriate conditions of psychic stress.

There is a manifest and a latent source of the feelings associated with the soterial object; the first (the manifest) is external and apparent, and the second (the latent) is unconscious. The latent is only expressed outwardly in disguised and/or symbolic form, in the guise of the manifest. The *Just-in-Case* . . . usage of a soterial protection was mentioned. The Secondary Defense of the soterial complex is effective and valiant; at times subtle, and yet both pervasive and strong.

Our Historical Notes stressed the long-standing operations of soterial manifestations throughout the development and course of civilization. Relative prior lack of attention has been due to a number of factors including: (1) lack of resulting *conscious* pain, self-defeat, and trouble; (2) its rare position as a presenting complaint; and (3) its being so often overshadowed by the seemingly more urgent problems which are presented by the patient in psychotherapy. Accordingly, the development of interest has been mostly quite recent, and this chapter comprises the first separate write-up and classification accorded this group of reactions. Following its discovery and adoption, the term *soteria* first found its way into print in 1954.

A diagnosis of Soterial Reaction is warranted when this is the most prominent feature in a neurotic reaction. The choice of soterial object is practically unlimited. Common Soterial Reactions were mentioned and several were illustrated. Points covered in the differential diagnosis included the relations to the Obsessive-Compulsive Reactions, organic disease, and Hygeiaphrontis. Incidence is nearly universal, considering the many major and minor Soterias which can evolve over the course of a given lifetime. Relative incidence was estimated at 6–8 per cent of the neurotic reactions.

In the Section on Clinical Features classes of soterial objects were cited, and the possible presence of individual prototypes was noted. As the soteria frequently results in an attachment to things, there are important implications in the security of one's usual and accustomed surroundings. A *Separation Reaction* can occur, or be exaggerated accordingly. This indicates another, emotional basis for the value in not changing or disturbing unnecessarily the surroundings of our senior citizens. The pain of exile, banishment, and the P.O.W. camp become more understandable. Accumulations, savings, and collections can progress beyond logical, practical needs as they gain soterial significance. Emotional determinants are operative. Instances of hoarding foodstuffs, books, and household supplies were cited as soterial *Security Operations*. The wide possible selection of soterial objects was again noted, and some classes of these were listed. Objects also include many possibilities, in addition to the strictly material and tangible. People, relationships, locale, rituals, prayers, and hymns are examples. We observed how the preserving (soterial object) is in turn preserved through the operation of the *Secondary Defense*.

Drugs, procedures, interpersonal relationships, the physician's office and so on can all come to provide soterial benefits and resulting emotional complications in medical practice. Attempted persuasion and "proof" of an absence of real need medically, is ineffective in dissolving a Soteria. The soteria fits into our concept of the emotional-object amalgam (E.O.A.). Forced deprivation likely provokes resistance, resentment, and anger. Compensation, pensions, even a symptom, a disability, or an illness can secure soterial significance as can money, hoarding, and collections. Soterial implications can enter into love affairs.

A note on the psychodynamics pointed out the projection externally of (a measure of) the object of dependency. Ultimately this symbolically represents (part of) the "good" mother-image, from the oral phase of development. The reader was further referred again to the discussions of the Phobic Reaction, many of which have applicability in gaining an understanding of the dynamics of the Soteria. The potential for great consciously (but not necessarily objectively) obscured self-defeat was noted and illustrated. The Soteria and the Phobia were compared and contrasted. Both have elements in common as well as in divergence. Displacement and attachment in each case take place in line with the *Peg Concept*.

Under additional aspects the concept of the *Secure Base of Operations* (S.B.O.) was discussed. This has important relationships to our principles of the Soteria. It is a major influence in successful child development. The home can become a major *soterial refuge;* and can progress onward via this route into severely limiting psychopathology. Marriage and the home in adulthood can offer a psychologically economic and mature Base, and can also secure soterial meanings. Overeating and obesity are possible consequences of soterial values having been secured by food and eating. An example illustrated this, plus several added important points, including the *Rule of Impression-Priority*. The operation of this Rule, plus many other factors can contribute to the development of a Soterial Reaction.

The initiation of treatment included six indications to undertake therapy. Symptom resolution was discussed as a limited goal. The more effective kind of approach was outlined. Interpretations are to be offered when acceptable; at the optimal time, and not prematurely. There are advantages in the therapist not getting too far ahead of the patient in gaining insight during the process of therapeutic work. This helps comprise the *Hand-in-Hand Concept* in psychotherapy. The *Tracing Technique* in therapy, which leads to uncovering origins and antecedents, can be valuable. One should not necessarily eagerly rush into the attempted resolution of a Soteria simply because it can be identified. The Soterial Reactions are sometimes significant, often important, and always interesting.

X. SELECTED REFERENCES AND BIBLIOGRAPHY

CONRAD, S. W. (1954). "The psychologic implications of overeating." *Psychiat. Q.*, **28**, 24.

LAUGHLIN, HENRY P. (1956). *The Neuroses in Clinical Practice*, pp. 198–207. Philadelphia; Saunders.

— (1954). "Fear and phobias Part I and Part II." *Med. Ann. Dist. Columbia*, **22**, 379 and 439.

— (1963). *Mental Mechanisms*. Washington; Butterworths.

— (1961). "Neuroses, conditioning, and the Rule of Impression Priority." *J. Med. Soc. N. J.*, **58**, 454.

XII. REVIEW QUESTIONS ON THE SOTERIAL REACTIONS

1. What is meant by "the other side of the phobic coin"?
2. How does the soterial object (seek to) counter fear and anxiety?
3. Define: (*a*) Soteria; (*b*) Soterial Reaction.
4. How does one estimate the psychologic import of a given soteria?
5. In relation to Soterial Reactions, comment on:
   (*a*) the "Just-in-Case" phenomenon.
   (*b*) Individual Prototype Concept.
   (*c*) Security Operations (S.O.).
   (*d*) Separation Reaction.
   (*e*) Secondary Defense Concept.
   (*f*) The Emotional-Object Amalgam, or E.O.A.
6. (*a*) Why has more attention heretofore not been accorded the soterial pattern of reaction?
   (*b*) Why might separate consideration and classification be justified?
7. How might the Rule of Impression-Priority apply in soterial evolvement?
8. (*a*) List the more common Soterial Reactions.
   (*b*) Briefly discuss soterial implications in collections, in hoarding, and in obesity.
9. What are the important soterial factors which can arise in medical treatment?
10. What is the *Secure Base of Operations Concept?*

11. Compare and contrast the phobia and the phobic object, with the soteria and the soterial object.
12. Home can become a "soterial refuge". Explain.
13. How is the selection of the soterial object determined?
14. What is the *Peg Concept* in soterial displacement.
15. (*a*) Discuss treatment in the Soterial Reactions; the *Tracing Technique* in therapy.
    (*b*) What is the value of progressing in psychotherapy according to the Hand-in-Hand Concept?

CHAPTER 12

THE CONVERSION REACTIONS

...Emotional Conflicts are Converted so as to
Secure Symbolic External Expression via
Somatic and Physiologic Routes

I. THE CONVERSION OF
   UNCONSCIOUS CONFLICT
   A. Unconscious and Symbolic
      Expression
      1. Conversion Reactions De-
      serve Priority; 2. Useful Defi-
      nitions
   B. Symptom Expressions A
      Symbolic Language
      1. Motor and Sensory Mani-
      festations; 2. Physiologic Lan-
      guage; 3. The Conversion
      Character

II. HISTORICAL BACKGROUND
   A. Prescientific Views of
      Etiology
      1. Ancient Times Until Nine-
      teenth Century; Many Beliefs
      Held; 2. Mesmer and Mesmer-
      ism
   B. Emergence and Develop-
      ment of the Scientific
      Approach
      1. Charcot and Janet; 2.
      Breuer and Freud

III. DIAGNOSIS
   A. Diagnosis on Positive
      Grounds Preferable
      1. Sequence of Reactions:
      Conflict - Anxiety - Repres -
      sion - Conversion, and on into
      Disguised Somatic Expression;
      2. Diagnosis by Exclusion Dis-
      advantageous; 3. Anatomic
      Comparisons Useful; 4.
      Pseudo - Epilepsy; Fits and
      Convulsions; 5. Speech, Hear-
      ing, and Visual Losses; 6.
      Factors In Positive Diagnosis
   B. Diagnostic Terminology
      1. Narrowing Application of
      Terms; 2. Physiologic Conver-
      sion; 3. When Diagnosis War-
      ranted

IV. INCIDENCE
   A. Changing-Trends Concept
      1. Early Frequency of Major
      Manifestations; 2. Decreasing
      Incidence
   B. Inverse Ratio of Incidence
      to Sophistication
      1. Gross Symptoms Make Too
      Much Sense: Theory of Trans-
      parency; 2. Ever More Dis-
      guised Expressions? Recent
      Interest Lags

V. SYMPTOMS AND CLINICAL
   FEATURES
   A. Psychologic Concepts
      1. Physical Symptoms and
      Symbolic Expressions; 2. De-
      fensive Symptoms in Turn
      Defended: The Concept of
      Secondary Defense; 3. Mainte-
      nance of Repression Vital;
      Concept of Interpersonal Per-
      petuation
   B. Conversion Pain
      1. Frequent Problem; Psychic
      Reduplication Concept; 2.
      Surgery vs. Psychotherapy; 3.
      Contraindication to Surgery.
      Surgery-in-Abeyance Rule
   C. Appearance and Behavior
      1. Acting Out; In Transfer-
      ence and Therapy; 2. Inhibit-
      ing Function of Symptoms;
      Spasms, Cramps, and Tics; 3.
      La Belle Indifférence; 4. Emo-
      tionalism and Histrionics; 5.
      The Conversion Character or
      Personality
   D. Special Clinical Features
      1. Somatic Conversion and
      I.Q.; Principle of Self-Esteem-
      Maintenance; 2. Variety of
      Symptoms; 3. Conversion
      Aphonia; A Dissociative Re-
      action and the Emergency
      Analytic-Bridge; 4. Conver-

sion Reactions and Schizophrenia; Bleuler's Dissociation; 5. Self-Punitive Aspects; Conversion Symptoms as Rage-Equivalents

E. Dyskinesias and Anesthesias
    1. Disturbances of Coordination and Motor Activity; 2. Symptoms of Sensory Loss in Conversion Reactions

F. Psychosomatic Illnesses

G. Concluding Remarks

VI. DYNAMICS AND PATHOGENESIS
A. The Conversion Endogain
    1. Formulations Apply to Somatic and to Physiologic Conversions; 2. Maintaining Repression

B. The Mechanisms in Conversion Reactions
    1. Systematic Analysis Required; 2. Symbolic Gratification, Denial, Inhibition, and/or Compromise; Part-Reaction Concept

C. Important Facets in Development
    1. Dependency Needs; 2. Predisposing Factors; 3. Symptoms May Develop as Emotion (Affect) Equivalents

D. Symptom and Location Choice
    1. Important Factors in Choice of Symptoms; 2. Interpretation of the Symbolism; 3. The Rule of Individual Symbolism; Complexity of Symptomatology in Emotional Illness; 4. Surface Anesthesia

E. Symbolic Expression of the Repressed and the Repressing
    1. Endogain Summarized; 2. The Oral Conflict

VII. ADDITIONAL IMPORTANT ASPECTS OF CONVERSION REACTIONS
A. Identification
    1. Marked Capacity; 2. In Character Defenses; The Conversion Personality

B. Overdetermination
    1. Every Phenomenon Explainable; Doctrine of Scientific Determinism; 2. Focusing and Convergence of Multiple Factors; Confluence and Condensation of Unconscious Needs

C. Conversion Pain
    1. Recapitulation of Early Pain or of Associated Events; 2. Fenichel's Pathways for Conversion Pain

D. Conversion Epidemics

E. Compensation Neurosis

F. The Problem of the Painful Phantom Limb
    1. Somatic Conversion; 2. Dynamics and Prevention

VIII. TREATMENT
A. Ideal in Therapy
    1. Psychoanalysis and Psychotherapy; 2. Character Analysis Valuable; 3. Symptom "Good" Exchange for Anxiety; Flight-to-the-Physical

B. Additional Therapeutic Measures
    1. Indications for Symptomatic Treatment; 2. Suggestion in Therapy: Progressive-Suggestion Technique; 3. Interpretative and Educative Measures; 4. Hypnosis and Hypno-Narcosis: The Hazard of Symptom-Exchange; 5. The Tracing Technique in Therapy

C. The Challenges of Therapy
    1. Something Superior Must Be Offered; The Therapeutic Bargain; 2. Insight the Major Goal

D. Useful Attributes for the Therapist

IX. SUMMARY

X. SELECTED REFERENCES AND BIBLIOGRAPHY

XI. REVIEW QUESTIONS ON THE CONVERSION REACTIONS

I. THE CONVERSION OF UNCONSCIOUS CONFLICT

A. UNCONSCIOUS AND SYMBOLIC EXPRESSION

1. Conversion Reactions Deserve Priority

THE DISCUSSION of the Conversion Reactions warrants some measure of priority among the neuroses, for six valid reasons. *First,* the Conversion Reactions take actual precedence historically over the other neurotic patterns of reaction. They were the first illnesses of psychogenic origin to be so recognized. Accordingly, they have received wide attention over the past eight decades. *Second,* these neurotic reactions were the first ones in psychiatry to receive intensive psychologic study. As a result, and *third,* the entire science of psychodynamics developed upon the foundations of the resulting early research.

Fourth, from the clinical standpoint, the Somatic Conversions (or Conversion hysteria) include major symptoms of motor and sensory disturbance. These often produce striking, dramatic, and therapeutically challenging illnesses. *Fifth,* this impressive kind of case probably is still to be encountered in the clinical experience of every physician, psychiatrist, and allied professional.

Sixth, the management and the therapy of cases of Conversion Reactions remain a wide and continuing challenge. Understanding the dynamics and securing the resolution of the underlying and responsible emotional conflicts is by no means easy or simple. However, in the many successful cases, the required investment of time and effort is indeed well worth while.

2. Useful Definitions

A. CONVERSION.—The Conversion Reactions comprise a major pattern of neurotic defensive reaction. This group is named for its major intrapsychic mechanism, conversion. Conversion is a most important concept in dynamic psychiatry. The Conversion Reaction is a *symptom-neurosis.*

Conversion is the name for *the unconscious process through which intrapsychic conflicts, which would otherwise give rise to anxiety, instead secure symbolic external expression. The consciously disowned ideas* (and associated affect) *plus the psychologic defenses against them, are transmuted or converted into a variety of physical, physiologic, and psychologic symptoms.* Generally the symptom in some measure expresses symbolically both the repressed, and the repressing forces. It also usually exacts its toll of self-punishment. Many conversion symptoms (as do others) illustrate our earlier advanced [pp. 95, 115] *Concept of Defensive-Overreaction.*

B. HYSTERIA: A TIME-HALLOWED TERM, BUT MISCONCEIVED AND INACCURATE.—The term, the diagnosis, and the clinical features of hysteria have been with us a long time. The physical symptoms of hysteria are primarily somatic conversions. They have developed as the result of internal psychologic pressures. The internal pressures have led to the external somatic expression (in this converted, disguised, and symbolic form) of elements of otherwise intolerable emotional conflicts. These remain unconscious, a defensive maintenance which has been enhanced by the symptom formation.

In view of our modern knowledge of dynamics, continued use of the term hysteria is an anachronism. It is unfortunate that psychiatry has had to be saddled so long with this kind of most inaccurate, misleading, and obsolete term, whose origin was even conceived in gross error. This is true no matter how hallowed by time, usage, and familiarity it tends to keep becoming to each successive generation of psychiatrists. The fortunate addition of the term "conversion" (that is, Conversion Hysteria) in the recent official nomenclature has lessened, but has not removed these objections. The name *Somatic Conversion* is dynamically more suitable and accurate. These two terms accordingly will be used interchangeably in our present discussion.

C. SOMATIC CONVERSION.—Somatic Conversion (or Conversion Hysteria) then may be defined as *an emotional illness in which the consciously disowned impulses plus other elements of the unconscious conflict over them, are transmuted into (and so as to secure) their symbolic somatic expression. The body symptoms which result serve to allay anxiety through maintaining repression, and through seeking resolution of the unconscious conflicts.*

The resolution of unconscious conflicts is sought through the symbolic expression, and the partial gratification in disguised, concealed, and unwitting fashion, of the disowned impulses. Repression is thereby reinforced. Some symbolic expression of the defenses against them in like fashion, is also usually present. These may include elements of their inhibition, denial, control, or compromise formations, and usually in addition some factors of self-punishment for having them.

In other words, instead of being experienced consciously, the emotional conflict is converted and expressed in physical symptoms in various parts of the body, especially those which are mainly under voluntary control. The principle mental mechanism brought into operation is that of conversion.

The Somatic Conversion Reaction, and less prominently the other Conversion Reactions, are less highly developed neurotic reactions. As such they tie in with our concept of the so-called Primitive Neuroses. See pages 148 and 497–8, and 19–21, of the author's "blue book" of *Mental Mechanisms* (*see* reference), for further discussion of this conception.

D. PHYSIOLOGIC CONVERSION.—There are other varied and major conversion reactions. Including most of the psychosomatic illnesses, the somatization reactions, and the socalled vegetative or organ neuroses, these are the *Physiologic Conversions*. Still other types of neurotic reactions may be regarded as the *Psychologic Conversions* [*Table 7;* pp. 87–8].

The Physiologic Conversions are *a large group of psychogenic manifestations or illnesses in which the consciously disowned impulses, and/or other elements of the unconscious conflict over them, are transmuted into symbolic physiologic expression. The functional symptoms which result serve to allay anxiety through maintaining repression and through seeking resolution, or some relief from the pressure of the unconscious conflicts.*

In the Physiologic Conversion, similarly to the Somatic Conversion, the repressed (as consciously intolerable) drive, wish, thought, memory, or event secures some measure of external, disguised, and symbolic expression. Through its conversion this occurs in unrecognized and at least to the person concerned, unrecognizable form. The conversion process allows partial expression and gratification of the repressed material, through physiologic symptom formation, at the cost of limitation, functional handicap, and/or pain. At least theoretically, the Physiologic Conversion can be the first step into an eventual *Functional-Structural Progression* [pp. 13, 14, 113, and 468–9]. The ultimate result would be structural change and fixed somatic pathology.

While most of our ensuing discussion will be directed toward the somatic type of conversion, a great deal of this material is also applicable to corresponding points in reference to the Physiologic Conversions. Many of the physiologic conversion symptoms when isolated, can serve as significant *Conflict Indicators* [p. 406;Ch.12:VC2;Ch.13:IVC1].

E. PSYCHOLOGIC CONVERSION.—A concept of still other types of neurotic symptoms as representing conversions utilizes a very broad view of the important process of conversion. This view however, is possible. Accordingly many neurotic reactions may in analogous fashion be regarded as *Psychologic Conversions.*

The Psychologic Conversions may be defined as *a large group of psychogenic manifestations or illnesses, in which the consciously disowned impulses, and/or other elements of the unconscious conflicts over them, are transmuted into symbolic psychologic expression. The psychologic symptoms which result, serve to allay anxiety through maintaining repression, and through seeking the resolution or some relief, from the pressure of the unconscious conflicts.*

In other words, one might regard the Psychologic Conversion as the expression of elements of the unconscious conflict into a "Psychologic Language" [p. 467], with the formation of psychologic symptoms. Accordingly, many of the other types of neuroses which are considered in separate chapters also might be regarded as Psychologic Conversions (*Table 7*).

B. SYMPTOM EXPRESSIONS A SYMBOLIC LANGUAGE

1. Motor and Sensory Manifestations

In simplified form, the clinical features in the Conversion Reactions result through the conversion into a *body language* of the repressed impulses, or of various elements of the unconscious conflicts over them. Somatic or body language, and physiologic language are comprised of symptom expressions. They are both the "symptom language" of the Conversion Reactions. As noted in Chapter One, the anxiety and the threat of anxiety, has been aroused through the intrapsychic conflict over certain impulses and ideas, because they were unacceptable and intolerable. This has brought about their repression.

As we shall learn, the Somatic Conversion (hysterical) type of neurotic reaction differs from others in that the repressed material finds its disguised outlet somatically, in the form of physical symptoms. These as noted, comprise what we might term and refer to as a *somatic language*. The ease of interpretation of this body or somatic language however can vary a great deal. This depends upon the symbolism involved and its depth and relative obscurity. The possibility of interpretation also varies according to one's familiarity with the individual's personal psychology, background, environment, factors relating to the *Rule of Impression-Priority* [pp. 531–541], and with the details of the precipitating situation.

The somatic conversion in hysteria thus results in a bodily expression or language. Somatic Conversion symptoms include loss of sensory and motor functions, and disturbances (sometimes gross ones) of movement and activity. Somatic Conversion Reaction is the pattern of neurotic reaction in which we may observe a number of gross and sometimes bizarre clinical manifestations. Herein are included instances of astasia-abasia, contractures, and the functional types of paralyses in which the reflexes are active and the anatomic innervation remains demonstrably intact.

Large areas of sensory loss may be encountered which likely do not conform to the anatomic distribution of sensory nerves; for example, "glove" or "stocking" types of anesthesia. Impairment or loss of function of the special senses may be observed on a conversion basis. Dyskinesias are encountered, with various movement and coordination disturbances, as well as tics [Ch. 12:VC2], muscular spasms, convulsions, and fainting. Often symptoms are less gross and dramatic, however. For example, instead of a paralyzed arm, the arm may be weak [see Case 136]. Aphonia is not uncommon [Case 142]. Conversion pain in various bodily areas is frequent, including some specially named types such as camptocormia, clavus, and other more or less specific kinds and sites for such discomfort. Vasomotor derangements can develop. Conversion anorexia [Case 86, p. 418], nausea, vomiting, dysphagia [Sect. VIC2], and globus hystericus [Sect. V C2] are encountered.

2. Physiologic Language

As indicated above, symptoms bespeak a kind of "body language". This is not a direct communication by any means. It is symbolic and is not intended to convey any clear or easily understood message to the observer. Far less indeed to he who has the symptom! Recall the *Theory of Transparency* [see pp. 171 and 495]. Nonetheless it is often possible under the more favorable circumstances which should prevail during therapeutic study, to fathom the meanings of an appreciable number of symptoms. Historically, the "body language" of some of the more striking Somatic Conversion symptoms first became understandable. This group of symptoms is very likely to include the ones most readily thought of in relation to this kind of symbolic communication today.

Functional symptoms, together with the major psychosomatic disorders (for example, peptic ulcer, asthma, colitis, and so on) are not as generally or as readily thought of as representing such a non-verbal and primitive kind of "communication". However, they can be indeed. Upon occasion they can constitute as least an individually as important expression of "body language" as their somatic counterparts. For this type of symptom expression and symbolic meaning when applicable, the author proposes the name of *"physiologic language"*. Its usage when employed would be analogous to the other similar "language" terms, as cited.

Functional changes and functional pathology thus can convey all manner of symbolic meanings. For the perceptive therapist-observer this can constitute an important kind of "physiologic language" [see also later concept of *overall language*, or reaction, in the following chapter on the Dissociative Reactions, Ch.13:IIF3].

3. The Conversion Character

Instead of symptoms, or in addition to them, certain rather more or less typical conversion (hysterical) character traits may be observed, studied, and analyzed. In general, these develop in the same service of attempted defense as do the more widely recognized clinical symptoms of Somatic Conversion. [*See* Ch. 5; pp. 58 *ff.*]

II. HISTORICAL BACKGROUND

A. PRESCIENTIFIC VIEWS OF ETIOLOGY

1. Ancient Times Until Nineteenth Century; Many Beliefs Held

Hysteria is an archaic term. It is derived from the classical Greek word *hystera,* meaning uterus or womb. As the principal basis for this major type of illness, the ancients had ascribed to the uterus the supposed ability to wander about pretty much at will through the body. These fanciful and imaginative but terribly erroneous beliefs, were prevalent at least by the time of Hippocrates, about 400 B.C., and were later also voiced by Plato. In its new locations, the womb then was supposed to produce the particular local symptom-manifestation of hysteria. Possibly the great significance thus attached to this organ may have indicated some perhaps unwitting recognition of the frequent role of sexual conflict in its etiology. As another point of interest to us currently, there is some indication that the ancients also confused epilepsy with conversion convulsions.

Various ideas and theories were advocated by savants through the years. For example, Galen, in the Rome of Marcus Aurelius, asserted that the uterus provoked convulsions through its retention of seminal fluid and the supposed resulting excitation. A Greek physician, Aetius D'Amide, in the year 980 A.D. also modified the ancient theories in order to add his own belief that conversion convulsions resulted from "subtle vapors" from the uterus which influenced the brain. Actually, despite some interesting implications from these and other early ideas about causation, it becomes apparent that little real progress was forthcoming toward the definitive scientific understanding of the bases for this major psychologic illness for more than two thousand years after Hippocrates.

Then came the Middle Ages and at various times conversion symptoms were thought to result from the work of demons, Satan, spells, or witchcraft. It is not surprising therefore to find "cures" attempted by kings (through the "royal touch"), by quacks (through nostrums, magic, and pseudo-medicinal concoctions), by religious representatives or approaches (through idols, medals, blessings, shrines, religious conversion, saints, relics, and special church rites), by witchcraft, and by primitive ceremonies. As Gordon portrays, communication with spirits and God, as well as divination and the widespread belief in various mystical phenomena, were pretty much a part of everyday belief in the sixteenth century.

In view of the characteristic suggestibility of the typical conversion patient, it is not surprising that so-called 'cures' (that is, to the extent of symptom relief) were sometimes effected. Some of these, rather in keeping with the symptoms themselves, were highly dramatic and attracted widespread attention. The typical imitativeness and capacity for identification, as well as the corresponding suggestibility of the Conversion Personality [see Ch. 5] led to many less dramatic successes.

Some of these routes of approach, of course, have continued to the present. At times they have been embellished for the naive and especially for "the believer", by various additional quasi-scientific trappings, electric and, more recently, electronic gadgets, and other devices designed to impress the suggestable and/or ignorant patient. An important point might be noted at this juncture. Here is referred to what we might term the *Principle of Belief* in pseudo-medicine, witchcraft, voodoo, and "religious" ceremonies; in that belief on the part of *both* parties can greatly facilitate the "efficacy" of all of the foregoing approaches. Thus, when the operator, priest, or witch-doctor, and so on, himself believes in what he does, its "magic" is thereby likely to be greatly increased for the person concerned.

Medicine, obstetrics, and surgery today have many quite legitimate uses for the prefix of *hyster*. Herein it is used correctly from an anatomical sense, and also to describe various procedures relating to the uterus. We might well advocate, however, that it no longer has any scientifically accurate, legitimate, or justifiable use in psychiatry as a diagnostic term for an emotional illness [see also earlier references to outmoded terms in psychiatry; pp. 45–47, 140, 448, and 495].

In the year 1618, according to Muncie, the French physician Charles Lepois declared conversion to have its origin in the brain. He also noted such symptoms as paralyses, anesthesias, and loss of the special senses of hearing and vision. Fifty years later, however, Thomas Willis had spoken of hysteria as resulting from possession by demons; still the more prevalent view.

2. Mesmer and Mesmerism

From about the year 1776 until his death in the early nineteenth century, an Austrian physician, Dr. Anton Mesmer (1733–1815), treated many conversion patients, primarily in an elegant salon on the Place Vendôme in Paris. Using a combination of suggestion and hypnosis, he and his pupils effected many dramatic cures and attracted widespread attention. His approach was named Mesmerism, after him.

Mesmer's attempts to explain his results on a scientific basis were quite inadequate. We cannot be sure if, or how much, Mesmer might have suspected as to the psychic factors in his patients' symptoms, and their recovery under his powerful suggestive techniques. He appears to have been under great compunction to propound an objective, physical kind of theory. As this was offered, however, it would not stand up under scientific inquiry by his learned contemporaries [Ch.13:XIB2]. The consequence of this ultimately led to his being discredited by an official commission, appointed to investigate his theories. As an interesting sidelight, Benjamin Franklin was a member of this commission. Mesmerism rapidly fell into complete disrepute. As a term it came frequently to convey an unpleasant or shady connotation. The *Medical Renaissance* (p. 312) was soon to begin.

An occasional medical reference to hysteria in succeeding years indicates the recognition of some possible connection between emotionally laden events or passion, and the onset of conversion symptoms. Brodie, an English surgeon, in 1837 labeled as hysteria many somatic symptoms without an organic basis, and suggested that emotional factors were primarily responsible for them. In 1859 Paul Briquet reported 430 cases of hysteria, all but seven in women, quite in accord with the long-prevailing view of the illness as almost exclusively a feminine problem. An American, A. J. Ingersoll, stated in 1877 that "hysteria is frequently caused by the voluntary suppression of the sexual life". However, it remained for Charcot to provide the first really detailed clinical insights into the psychic etiology. The hypnotic or induced type of dissociation has been named B.B.C. (for Braid, Bernheim, and Charcot) Dissociation [*see* Ch.13:II C2; II E1], after these three pioneers.

B. EMERGENCE AND DEVELOPMENT OF THE SCIENTIFIC APPROACH

1. Charcot and Janet

A. JEAN-MARTIN CHARCOT.—As the last century passed its midpoint, more physicians were beginning to take a constructive interest in the disorders of psychiatric and neurologic origin. In the 1870s and 1880s, Professor Jean-Martin Charcot (1825–1893) of the *Salpêtrière,* a famous French neurologist, became interested in patients with Somatic Conversion Reactions. At least early, he still believed somewhat in an hereditary predisposition to these reactions; that ". . . the greater number . . . are simply born *hystérisables* . . .", a view now discarded by the great majority. He contributed however to differentiating Somatic Conversion (hysteria) from neurologic conditions. Convulsions were evidently so frequent a manifestation in his day (*circa* 1873) that he divided cases into the two major categories of convulsive and non-convulsive patients. He described the *grande attaque hystérique* with four phases, and denoted one of them as *les attitudes passionelles.* It is noteworthy that his conversion patients, suggestible as they were, were quartered indiscriminately with persons suffering from epilepsy. Charcot also invited attention to *la belle indifférence* of the conversion patient [Ch.12:VC3].

Charcot later made most noteworthy contributions toward proving the psychologic (non-organic) etiology of some of the Conversion Reactions. If not the first, he was certainly the earliest well-known physician to make clear their psychologic origins. He undertook clinical demonstrations which were of great significance to the later development of psychodynamics.

Charcot thus was able to reproduce under hypnosis in appropriate subjects identical manifestations of paralysis to those observed with established clinical cases of hysteria. These in turn he had earlier carefully distinguished from organic disturbance. Both types of symptoms he also successfully removed through hypnotic suggestion.

As Freud later evaluated Charcot's work, "With this, the [psychical] mechanism of a hysterical phenomenon was for the first time disclosed . . .". In Freud's words, it was ". . . on this incomparably fine piece of clinical research [that] his own pupil Janet, and also Breuer and others [undoubtedly also including Freud], based their theories of the [neuroses] . . .".

At Charcot's clinic, demonstrations of suggestibility were made and patients were treated in dramatic fashion. Hypnosis was extensively used. Charcot attracted many students. Perhaps the most outstanding among these was Pierre Janet, who later continued on his own with extensive clinical work and teaching in the field of neuroses.

B. PIERRE JANET.—Pierre Janet (1859–1947) regarded Somatic Conversion as "a malady of the personal synthesis". He undertook to explain attacks of Conversion Reaction, altered consciousness, bouts of somnambulism, and related dissociative phenomena, as due to a process of *dissociation* of the major personality components. This occurred, he believed, in response to toxic factors, exhaustion, or psychic stress. His introduction of the concept and term of dissociation was a major contribution. It has led to our present major diagnostic category of the Dissociative Reactions. [*See* the following Chapter 13.]

Janet also investigated the psychologic aspects of the Conversion Reactions (hysteria), and illustrated his ideas with excellent, descriptive case histories. His clinical observations were of superior quality. He described and classified a number of the somatic types of conversion phenomena, which were undoubtedly more prevalent in these earlier days, during his clinically active years. The term and concept of *la belle indifférence,* "the grand indifference" of the conversion patient to his incapacity, was adopted and further described by him. The type of dissociation occurring in conversion emotionalism, convulsions, and other major conversion behavioral manifestations might quite appropriately be termed *Janet Dissociations* [Ch.12:VIB2;Ch.13:IIC2;IIE1].

2. Breuer and Freud

A. A FRUITFUL COLLABORATION.—In the meantime a Viennese physician, Joseph Breuer (1841–1925), had been delving into early painful events in the lives of certain of his conversion patients. Breuer made some of the very first and most important psychodynamic discoveries in psychiatry, beginning at least as early as 1880. At that time with his now famous patient Anna O., he discovered the importance in symptom development of early, painful, forgotten (repressed) events.

Breuer did little writing himself, and has received too little credit for his very major and pioneering contributions. In one small attempt at compensation the author has suggested [Ch.13:IIC2] naming the dissociation which occurs in the onset of the major conversion symptom, as *Breuer's Dissociation.* This would seem appropriate and deserved for a number of reasons [Ch.13:IIE1].

After some years a young neurologist named Sigmund Freud became interested in Breuer and in his work. An active collaboration began and developed between the two men following Freud's return from Paris in 1886 and lasted for several years. It was productive and fruitful.

Freud and Breuer originally proposed a psychologic usage for the term *conversion* in a paper in 1892.* This term has since been widely adopted in psychiatry, to convey the idea of the outward expression in disguised form of repressed and hidden (unconscious) impulses. In Conversion Hysteria (Somatic Conversion) this expression is to be found primarily in somatic terms.

There has also been the trend toward a wider application of this very useful term and the principle it conveys. As pointed out earlier, the author has also found it convenient to refer to certain emotional reactions as *Physiologic Conversions,* and to others as *Psychologic Conversions.* This has proved useful to him in teaching; in presenting the concept of the similar outward expression of repressed impulses in physiologic terms, and also in psychologic terms.

B. BASIC PSYCHOANALYTIC CONCEPTS INTRODUCED.—Breuer and Freud found it possible in certain instances to bring about the disappearance of conversion symptoms. This occurred upon occasion, as with Breuer's patient Anna O., when a significant earlier painful event, for which the memory had been "lost", was recalled and thus restored to conscious awareness, its emotional catharsis was secured, and the relationships of event to symptom were made clear. Several clinical papers followed which set out their early findings and theories, principally concerning Conversion Reactions (hysteria). In 1895, two years after Charcot's death, they first published their *Studien über Hysterie,* since translated and republished several times. This work remains a classic today. Herein Breuer and Freud clinically illustrated their findings that the symptoms of conversion patients were founded upon highly significant but forgotten events in their past lives.

A number of added important concepts were developed and named as a consequence of this early collaboration. These included: (1) *mental catharsis,* the talking out of reactivated emotional events from the past; (2) *abreaction,* the resulting discharge of affect, and the process in which it takes place; and (3) *transference,* in which the positive and/or negative feelings originally felt toward an earlier significant person are automatically and unconsciously transferred to the therapist.

In addition, observations were made of the differences in the amount of resistance to the recall or to the verbal reporting of painful data in the waking state, as opposed to the hypnotic state. These were to become basic tenets in psychoanalysis and in dynamic psychiatry. Freud later added the technique of *free association,* studied psychic phenomena in everyday life, and worked out methods of dream interpretation.

C. EARLY CREDIT GIVEN CHARCOT AND BREUER.—Freud had visited (in 1885 and 1886) Charcot's clinic in Paris, as one of the latter's foreign

---

* In one of their first papers published in 1892, they noted that in the Somatic Conversion Reactions ". . . the unbearable idea is rendered innocuous by the quantity of excitation attached to it being transmuted into some bodily form of expression, a process for which . . . [we] should like to propose the name of *conversion* . . . ".

students. He had reported to Charcot at this time some of Breuer's pioneering early experiences and intriguing findings. Charcot unfortunately had not seemed very interested. This very early association with Charcot however undoubtedly had a considerable professional influence upon Freud, as reflected in several of his early papers.

For a number of personal reasons, Breuer decided not to continue his collaboration with Freud. The latter proceeded almost alone for some years to develop the many further contributions that have earned him his eminent stature in psychiatry. Joseph Breuer, however, probably deserves more credit for laying the basic foundations of modern psychodynamics than is often assigned to him.

In Freud's earlier writings such crediting and laudatory descriptive phrases were employed by him as "the momentous discovery of J. Breuer", the development of "Breuer's thesis", "Breuer's method [of analysis]" in early investigative psychotherapy, and "Breuer's conception". Thus, in 1896, Freud was giving great credit to Breuer, as he had earlier given to Charcot. The major credit acknowledged by Freud to both Charcot and to Breuer in these early years was not to be continued, nor was it repeated subsequently in his later and extensive writings.

D. REPORTED FANTASIES MISLEADING.—By this time the significance long attached by many to the role of heredity in the etiology of Conversion Reactions had been substantially reduced. Freud early ascribed its onset as being due to specific sexually traumatic experiences in infancy. Within the next ten years, however, he learned that the experiences which his patients reported were not always actual events. As reported, they often turned out at times instead to be the fantasies of his patients! This was at first surprising, and something of a shock. In 1905, Freud wrote of this as "the most momentous of my early errors . . ." and made appropriate revisions in his theoretical formulations. These revised concepts, together with the many valuable additions and modifications made subsequently, by an increasing number of contributors in the field of psychiatry, constitute the framework for present-day theory, research, and therapy in the Conversion Reactions. Indeed, the early work concerning the pathogenesis of these types of neurotic reactions has substantially helped to form the foundation for work in psychopathology generally.

III. DIAGNOSIS

A. DIAGNOSIS ON POSITIVE GROUNDS PREFERABLE

1. Sequence of Reactions: Conflict—Anxiety—Repression—Conversion, and on into Disguised Somatic Expression

A. HYSTEROGENIC AREAS AND THE SO-CALLED STIGMATA.—The term *stigmata* derived from the supposed miraculous appearance of marks on the individual's body which approximated the wounds of Christ. St. Francis of Assisi was apparently the first known person to develop them. This prominent early instance has been followed since by several hundred similar reported cases of such phenomena.

Once regarded many years ago as a very important point in establishing a diagnosis of hysteria was the finding of what were termed hysterogenic areas or zones. These were most commonly found to be located in the breasts, inguinal regions or lower back, and so on. Stimulation of these might be used to bring on, or to terminate a conversion (hysterical) attack. Their presence at least in the early days was considered pathognomonic for making the diagnosis of a Conversion Reaction (hysteria).

Undoubtably suggestion at the time of examination could and often did, play a powerful role in the development and operation of such hysterogenic zones in the properly susceptible person. These areas and their meaning, while of interest historically, have come to have little significance in diagnosis today.

Perhaps somewhat related, and certainly also intriguing is the phenomenon of the so-called stigmata.

B. NO SUBSTITUTE FOR PERCEPTIVENESS, ACUMEN, AND EXPERIENCE.— In Conversion Hysteria, anxiety is responsible for the repression of the intolerable ideas and impulses. These impulses, although buried from conscious awareness, continue potent and secure a disguised kind of expression somatically in a variety of physical symptoms. These symptoms, as we shall learn, usually symbolically serve several important and often contradictory purposes [see Tables 32 and 33]. The symptoms may represent compromises, symbolically expressing the repressed impulses as well as the repressing forces.

This process is not always easily determinable. During the initial examination and evaluation it may be exceedingly difficult to establish a definite diagnosis. In other instances it may be relatively easy to rule out organic disease and to make a positive diagnosis of Conversion Reaction. Special training and clinical experience in psychiatry will, of course, be of substantial value here. The perceptive and well trained physician can develop a remarkable degree of diagnostic acumen and judgment in these areas. There is no substitute for these attributes. However, the most skillful clinician may encounter cases in which it becomes impossible to establish a diagnosis, at least short of several sessions. Occasionally a more prolonged psychotherapeutically oriented period of study is required.

2. Diagnosis by Exclusion Disadvantageous

In some quarters it is still acceptable, and perhaps even occasionally necessary to reach a diagnosis of Conversion Reaction by exclusion, that is, by the elimination of any possible organic factors. This can have a number of disadvantages for the patient, for the subsequent course of the illness, for its possible early resolution, and for the physician. Reliance on such an approach bespeaks an unfamiliarity with psychogenic types of illness. It would hardly seem appropriate to physicians to try to establish a diagnosis of diabetes by the negative approach of excluding other pathologic possibilities. How about cancer, or pernicious anemia? No, certainly not.

Janet warned that the failure to make an early diagnosis in the Somatic Conversion Reaction is ". . . usually due to an attempt to reach a diagnosis by exclusion of organic disease, and by neglect of that aspect of the history which deals with the emotional life of the patient. . .".

With average patience, persistence, and skill, one can usually uncover significant contributing factors of emotional difficulty, or evidence of contributory problems in the individual's interpersonal relationships. These will have prepared the soil for the development of the Conversion Reaction and/or will have contributed to its initiation.

3. Anatomic Comparisons Useful

There are several points in diagnosis which can be of value to the practicing physician. In support of one major point, his knowledge of neurology can be quite useful. Hereby the locale and extent of motor and sensory disturbances which are present can be readily compared with the actual anatomic distribution of the innervation. When there are definite discrepancies uncovered, the most common emotional diagnostic basis is Somatic Conversion (hysteria). Hardly surprisingly the "need" for a physical basis can lead to the evolvement of what we termed a physical scapegoat [pp. 392 and 461].

With certain patients, especially in the older age groups, one must occasionally differentiate the consequences of possible instances of atypical and bizarre vascular accidents. There is also an interesting phenomenon termed *conversion allochiria* in which the sensory or painful stimuli which are received on one side of part of the body, are perceived as coming from the other or opposite side.

The simultaneous presence of organic disease and conversion symptomatology is possible but not frequent. At times this can comprise a Conversion E.O.C. (emotional-organic combination), as noted earlier [p. 443]. Careful differential diagnosis may be required [Ch.13:VIID1].

4. Pseudo-Epilepsy; Fits and Convulsions

Posturing, "aimless" movements, and various kinds of seemingly uncoordinated motor activity were evidently more frequently encountered several generations ago. In 1859 Briquet reported that the majority of conversion patients were convulsive. Charcot's later reference to the frequency of convulsive features has been noted. Fits and convulsions have been very frequent. Today they are more common in the less developed countries, and among less sophisticated cultural groups.

The Conversion Reactions have long had the reputation for being "the great imitator" (of other organic pathologic entities). Since the Conversion patient has been characteristically suggestible, and more readily takes on various manifestations through the process of identification, it is not surprising that careful differentiation sometimes has been required from epilepsy.

Convulsions on a conversion basis thus may simulate epilepsy. Usually, however, various differential features are present. In distinction, it is indeed rare, for example, for the conversion patient to fall so as to hurt himself, to bite his tongue (as will the epileptic person), or involuntarily to urinate. Further, he nearly always has his seizures in the presence of a person or persons who are significant to him. Factors of (unconscious) epigain may not be too obscure to a perceptive, detached observer. The electroencephalograph can be helpful in making the differentiation, especially when it indicates the characteristic spiking pattern associated with epilepsy. The dissociative intrapsychic operation in these so-called "behavioral manifestations" of conversions are instances of the *Janet* type of *Dissociation,* as noted earlier [*see also* Ch.13:IIE*1*(6)].

5. *Speech, Hearing and Visual Losses*

Ninety per cent or more of all cases of aphonia are of a conversion origin. Cases of sudden partial or complete hearing loss, or of loss of visual acuity (in the absence of an organic basis) are nearly always of conversion origin.

Methods for the detection of these conversion disabilities and defects have been devised in examination procedures in the appropriate specialties. These are common knowledge or are readily accessible, and space does not permit our detailing them here. The psychiatrist's prime interest lies in the relationship of strongly emotionally-colored events to the Somatic Conversion.

6. *Factors In Positive Diagnosis*

A. CAREFUL STUDY INDICATED.—On the side of a positive diagnosis, there are nearly always indications of a conversion diathesis, conversion character defenses, *la belle indifférence,* associated emotional trauma, or evidence of significant and related interpersonal difficulties. These conversion factors become evident from careful study of the patient's emotional life and his level of adjustment. They help to provide the basis for making a positive diagnosis.

Needless to say, the psychologic requirements which result in such a drastic surrender of function as is that of blindness, will be very likely defended most bitterly and urgently. This kind of major conversion symptom can constitute a therapeutic problem of the greatest magnitude in medicine. By inference its general significance has common features but it is also very much an individual problem. Fortunately it is not very common in recent decades.

B. I.Q.—A low intelligence quotient (60–90) used to be, and still is by some, considered to be a prerequisite for a diagnosis of a Somatic Conversion Reaction. In the author's experience, this is no longer a necessary criterion. Four consecutive conversion patients in his recent experience, for example, have had I.Q.s of more than 100 (Wechsler-Belevue scores of 107, 114, 119, and 109, respectively). It remains correct, however, that a lower level of sophistication, education, and so on, likely increases the chances of conversion symptom formation. These factors are more crucial than that of the I.Q. Conversion Reaction is probably more frequent *per unit* of population in rural areas than in urban areas, and in economically less favored groups.

With the Physiologic Conversions there is actually likely to be a somewhat higher than average I.Q. The general level of education and sophistication tends to be higher than in instances of Somatic Conversion. While these comments apply in the more direct and simpler functional symptoms, they have still more applicability for the major functional reactions. The latter would include the psychosomatic syndromes, symptom-complexes, or perhaps better, the Physiologic Conversion Reactions of peptic ulcer, asthma, colitis, and arthritis.

C. CONVERSION PAIN.—The general practitioner, the surgeon, and others so concerned are strongly cautioned about the recognition of conversion (hysterical) pain. Such pain is very real indeed to the patient, and his suffering is genuine,* although without organic basis (*see* later discussion). Generally, tactful encouragement of confidence and kindly understanding will produce evidence of significant problems which may bear a direct or indirect relationship to the pain [pp. 462–3].

As a major emotional contraindication for any but clear-cut emergency surgery, conversion pain joins the Hygeiaphrontic Reactions (Hypochondriasis), the Depressive Reactions, and the Phobic Reactions [Ch.10:XC1]. This is in accord with our *Surgery-in-Abeyance Rule* [Section V B3].

B. DIAGNOSTIC TERMINOLOGY

1. Narrowing Application of Terms

At the close of the last century the term "hysteria" was used descriptively and diagnostically to describe a considerably wider variety of emotional conditions. Indeed, the literature of fifty and more years ago abounds with case material which today might be preferably diagnosed under various other neurotic labels and even as schizophrenia. Bowlby noted that the diagnosis originally was widely applied to nearly all ". . . somatic symptoms without organic lesions . . .". This was very much an indiscriminate and nonselective use of a long out-moded diagnostic term! Since then, the diagnosis has undergone evolution and refinement, resulting in a constantly narrowing application.

Currently the use of the term hysteria when it must be used, is probably best reserved to the major Somatic Conversions; those involving paralysis, anesthesia, dyskinesia, and the like, and possibly to describe a characteristic type of personality structure [*See* Chapter 5 and pp. 258–270]. When function becomes altered, an overlapping in psychopathology, and in terminology, may exist with the Physiologic Conversions. Somatic Conversion (or Conversion hysteria) is usually accompanied by an emotional diathesis, and often by certain personality characteristics which are frequently associated as well. There is present a current tendency gradually to discard entirely all emotional diagnostic, and psychiatric use of the term hysteria. This the author would encourage.

---

* Our *Principle of Emotionally-Determined Visceral Pain* [p. 467] stated that "an individual may suffer serious discomfort in the complete absence of any demonstrable malfunction or somatic pathology . . .".

2. Physiologic Conversion

This brings us into an important and vital area in modern medicine and psychiatry. A brief consideration of the Physiologic Conversions is well warranted [*see* pp. 467 *ff.*] Perhaps it may help at this point to clarify certain questions about this large and significant group of reactions.

In regard to these types of outward emotional-functional expression, a number of terms have been introduced which to a certain extent are overlapping as to the areas which they include. Each has been, and more or less continues as the term of preference for a varying group of physicians. Each has certain advantages, and, until one term secures overwhelming, or more exclusive acceptance, the reader must perforce make his own best selection. These terms are listed in the following *Table 31*. This tabulation has been prepared to provide the reader with a handy basis of comparison and reference, for a group of quite useful terms which cover, however, important similar areas of function, diagnosis, and reactions to stress and conflict.

Table 31
Terms in the Diagnosis of the Physiologic Conversions

The following terms have been proposed and advocated by various authorities. By usage they cover overlapping areas. Each enjoys certain advantages. The multiple terminology offers a choice to the student or practitioner, who fortunately is still free currently to make his own selection. This is a vital and increasingly important area in medicine and psychiatry. The source or originator is indicated in parentheses. Terms are listed alphabetically as a matter of convenience.

1. *Autonomic Conversion* (Laughlin): The conversion into an "autonomic expression" or "autonomic language" of various elements of the repressed emotional conflict. This outward expression is principally mediated via the autonomic (or vegetative) nervous system.

2. *Emotional-Physiologic Illness* (Laughlin): The E.P.I. is an emotional illness, with prominent accompanying physiologic changes as an integral part of the total reaction. This term emphasizes the coequal importance, contributions, and mutual interaction of the emotional and the physiologic factors in a given illness.

   Structural change can occur and represents the consequence of continuation of the functional manifestation(s), great stress, and chronicity. When present, this is included in the concept.

3. *Functional Illness* (first use uncertain): An illness of emotional origin in which changes are present only in the function of an organ or symptom. Organic or structural changes are absent.

4. *Organ Neurosis* (Fenichel): An emotional illness with functional and even anatomic alterations. Physiologic changes are caused by the inappropriate use of the function in question.*

5. *Physiologic Conversion* (Laughlin): The term already referred to, which the author has adopted and employed as a convenience in communication, and in presenting teaching material on the Conversion Reactions. The conversion which has transpired here is an expression into "physiologic language" of the repressed conflictual material. The symptom formation is of a physiologic nature. *(Table continued on next page)*

---

* Fenichel included four classes of symptoms in the Physiologic Conversions (Organ Neuroses): (1) Affect equivalents; (2) Results of changes in the chemistry of the unsatisfied and dammed up person (expressions of unconscious affects); (3) Physical results of unconscious attitudes or unconsciously determined behavior patterns; and (4) All kinds of combinations of these three possibilities.

Table 31—Continued

> This condition develops as a consequence of the operation of psychologic processes which are physiologically analogous to those in Somatic Conversion, in which there is an expression in *"somatic language"* of the repressed emotional conflict, with its symptom formation in turn of a *physical* nature.
>
> 6. *Psychophysiologic Disorder* (G. N. Raines, *et. al.*; A.P.A. *Diagnostic and Statistical Manual*): A new term introduced in 1952. This reaction is defined as representing ". . . the morbid physiological expression of emotions".
>
> 7. *Psychosomatic Illness* (Weiss and English, Alexander, Dunbar and others): Points out the inseparable nature of the psyche (mind) and the soma (body), their mutual interaction, and their coequal importance.
>
> 8. *Somatization Reactions* (W. C. Menninger): A useful term for the psychosomatic reactions which, as Menninger noted, are "just as much conversion reactions as is a paralysis".
>
> 9. *Vegetative Neurosis* (Alexander): The psychogenic dysfunction of a vegetative organ. A vegetative neurosis is the physiologic accompaniment of constant or periodically recurring emotional states.
>
> 10. *Types of Conversion:* The author would personally consider it entirely proper to speak, when appropriate otherwise, in terms of *mental, psychologic, physical, physiologic,* and *somatic* (or *hysterical*) conversion. Conversion is a highly useful concept in medicine and in psychiatry.

3. When Diagnosis Warranted

A. THE CONVERSION REACTIONS; SOMATIC CONVERSION AND PHYSIOLOGIC CONVERSION.—The diagnosis of *Conversion Reaction* (or Conversion hysteria) is to be made when the principal presenting neurotic features result from a conversion type of reaction, manifested in bodily terms.

Somatic Conversion includes those conversion reactions where the conflict is expressed mainly in physical, somatic symptoms. *Physiologic Conversion* includes those conversion reactions where the conflict is expressed mainly in functional, physiologic symptoms. These are to be differentiated when necessary, from each other. They are also to be distinguished from other kinds of conversions in which the expression is, for instance, via the autonomic or vegetative nervous system; or via "psychologic conversion" [*Table 7,* pp. 87–8], into the other major types of neurotic reactions. For a discussion of some comparative and differential features with the Dissociative Reactions, the reader is referred to Ch. 13: VII E.3.

B. THE GREAT IMITATOR. SIX FINAL POINTS.—A few final points of significance in regard to diagnosis should be noted. *First,* the Conversion Reactions can appear in any guise, resembling any organic syndrome. Indeed, as early as 1681, Sydenham had noted their ability to simulate every known disease.

Even as the Conversion Personality is marked characterologically by the capacity for identification and by a facility for the unwitting imitativeness of others [pp. 258–270], so is the clinical illness itself marked by its potential to simulate other kinds of illnesses. This is true for both organic and emotional categories of disease. This parallel is not accidental, as noted. Therefore, in accord with these comments, this reaction still proves often enough to be aptly named "the great imitator".

Second, the Conversion Reaction is seldom to be observed in "pure culture". Severe, externally apparent, or overt anxiety is rather rare in Somatic Conversion, but can occasionally occur. The presence of conversion symptoms does not necessarily mean that anxiety is absent. As a presenting feature, it may be major, minor, allayed, or held in abeyance. In effect, it is always "lurking in the background", should the defenses falter.

Thus anxiety and the Conversion Reactions are not always mutually exclusive. The process of conversion may have been incomplete, or operative only for certain aspects of the individual's conflicts. The parallel presence of anxiety indicates an *Incomplete Symptom-Defense* [pp 89, 189, and 451]. This is more common in the Physiologic Conversions.

Absorption of attention and interest in a given symptom can become defensively engrossing for the person concerned. This can illustrate our *Attention-Absorption Concept* [*Case 89,* p. 452, and pp. 188, 466, 481–2, and *Case 101,* pp. 487–9].

Concurrent manifestations of other patterns of neurotic reaction may also be present.* When the clinical features are mixed, a diagnosis of Conversion Reaction is proper if the conversion elements are the most prominent ones in the illness. The presence of a conversion reaction does not rule out concomitant physical illness. Their simultaneous presence [comprising an E.O.C., pp. 393, 454] can sometimes complicate the arrival at a diagnosis. For some comments about the Dissociative Reaction dynamics *versus* those of the Conversion Reactions, see later reference [Ch.13:VIIE*3*].

The older criteria would have made the diagnosis largely dependent upon the presence of physical symptoms without structural lesions to account for them. This is no longer suitable. There are several reasons including: (*a*) this is an oversimplification, (*b*) it also suggests diagnosis by exclusion, (*c*) this is an insufficient distinction from Hygeiaphrontic Reactions (pp. 450–7), and finally, (*d*) it fails to call attention to the basic emotional factors requisite to the process of conversion.

Third, the physician should keep in mind in referring to somatic conversion (into somatic, physical symptoms) that accurate usage refers to expression via: (*a*) the motor parts of the body which are under voluntary control, and (*b*) any of the sensory receptors, including the special senses. Certain more internal dysfunctions, such as globus hystericus [Ch.12:VD *2; VIC2*], hysterical vomiting, and conversion pain, are of course also to be classified as Conversion Reactions.

Fourth, Conversion Hysteria is not to be confused with the now nearly obsolete term of Anxiety Hysteria. When it must still be used, the latter term is properly reserved for the phobias and the Phobic Reactions. [*See* Chapters 9 and 10].

Fifth, it should be kept in mind also that conversion symptoms can run the gamut from minor ones, to major ones, and on to grossly disabling ones; also from single, to multiple; and from rapidly shifting or transient, to ones which are semipermanent or fixed.

---

* Saul commented that the ". . . 'pure' . . . [Conversion Reaction] is probably never seen . . . This is a type of reaction, as you point out, which is apt to occur to some extent in everyone, and is also probably invariably mixed with certain other (neurotic) reactions".

Beyond the employment of the term "hysteria" in Conversion hysteria, the only other usage of this term that the author currently favors in psychiatry would be in the description of certain personality features. These are grouped together to comprise the Conversion (hysterical) Personality, as discussed in Chapter 5.

Finally, use of the term "Somatic Conversion Reaction", as earlier noted, offers certain advantages as a substitute for "hysteria" or "Conversion hysteria". Together with the Physiologic Conversion Reactions, these comprise the Conversion Reactions.

IV. INCIDENCE

A. CHANGING-TRENDS CONCEPT

1. Early Frequency of Major Manifestations

Prior to the beginning of this century, the major sensory and motor disturbances, the dyskinesias, the convulsions, and the "spells" of a conversion (hysterical) origin were common. The more dramatic forms with their disabling paralyses, large areas of sensory loss, blindness, aphonia, or pseudo-epilepsy, were rather familiar to physicians. Accordingly, it is not surprising that these cases widely attracted the attention of the nineteenth century physicians. Some of them even came to be interested in psychiatry as a result. Further, as earlier noted, it was the study of some of these kinds of cases which was the basis for much of the pioneering work in psychodynamics and psychopathology.

The old diagnosis of hysteria was even more common at the turn of the century because of the practice of lumping all of these instances together with many cases of Dissociative Reaction and even with certain psychotic reactions under this heading. A segment of the greater number of cases so diagnosed in that era also reflected a different cultural milieu. Finally, part was due to an actual increased incidence, attributable largely to lower general levels of education and sophistication.

During World War I, the incidence of major Somatic Conversion Reactions was high. All types of conversion disability were seen frequently. Ferenczi and Simmel, for example, described their experiences with these rather frequently seen gross conversion disorders. Camptocormia [Section VB3] was common.

In line with an early belief held by many that the shock of exposure to shell fire accounted for their emotional and nervous symptoms, many instances of Conversion Reaction were diagnosed and labeled as "shell shock". To the general public at the time, this label also served a euphemistic purpose, helping to allay the possible stigma of an emotional disorder of "internal" origin, as opposed to an "external" and more patriotically associated combat origin, suggested by the name "shell shock". Actually, however, many victims of this so-called "shell shock" did not come at all close to shell fire.

2. Decreasing Incidence

A. INSTANCES FROM ISOLATED AND LESS FAVORED AREAS, AND THOSE IN
MEDICAL CENTERS.—The question arises as to whether a change in the
incidence of major Somatic Conversion Reactions has taken place during
the past several decades. In the author's personal experience, these major
cases are considerably less frequent. He believes their overall incidence
has been steadily decreasing.

On the other hand, we may note that these cases are still not infrequently
observed, especially in some of our rural areas, and particularly in the more
isolated and backward ones. They also come more frequently from depressed, less favored, city areas. They are of course still to be encountered
in most of the large medical clinics and university teaching centers.* Such
centers tend to attract the more striking, obscure, and difficult cases, drawing as they do from a rather wide geographic area. The Somatic Conversions are likely to wind up being sent there as diagnostic problems, and as
treatment problems, when their resolution has not proved possible, or has
not been quickly or readily enough effected elsewhere. Treatment often
proving to be quite difficult in the teaching centers as well, a given case may
continue in residence for quite a period and thus come to the attention of
most of the staff and many visiting professionals. Such cases, being noteworthy, may thereby still further give a misleading impression as to their
relative occurrence and numbers.

B. WORLD WAR II TYPE OF RESPONSE CHANGED.—In the author's own
fairly extensive clinical experience during more than six years of military
service in World War II, the gross types of Somatic Conversion as described
in World War I and earlier were relatively speaking, far more rare. Although the general incidence of somatic symptoms and of physiologic disturbances in response to stress showed little change, indeed being quite
frequent, there was a definite change in the type and the quality of such
responses.

While Somatic Conversions were not observed frequently as these were
earlier defined, the physiologic kinds of conversion were encountered relatively far more frequently. These included disturbances of the cardiovascular system (such as pain, vascular and circulatory manifestations,
tachycardia and other irregularities), the gastrointestinal system (such as
peptic ulcers and ulcer-like symptoms, digestive disturbances, and irritable

---

* As Kolb earlier pointed out, "We had the opportunity of making such a diagnosis
almost weekly in consultation at the Mayo Clinic and also instructing a large number
of residents in the reduction of . . . [conversion] symptoms. I am sure the same sort
of thing takes place around other medical centers. People with gross . . . [conversion]
symptoms do not consult psychiatrists and analysts nor are they referred to them.
Most of the patients going to psychiatrists and analysts these days have character
problems and the . . . account given by these groups is due to the nature of their
practice . . . Another reason that psychiatrists do not see [conversion] hysterical
people is that they do not wish to see them, and many are unwilling to spend the
time and energy necessary to carry individuals with this highly disturbing dramatic
illness to a successful conclusion."

Ziegler *et al.* also reported an excellent series of 134 patients meeting careful
criteria for the diagnosis of Conversion Reaction. These cases were seen over a
6-year period (1954–59) on the Psychiatric Liaison Service at Johns Hopkins University Hospital.

colon), and general neuromuscular symptoms (such as headaches, backaches, and vertigo), increased perspiration, and many other functional disturbances. The interested reader is referred further to the Combat Reactions in Chapter 15.

C. PERCENTAGES ESTIMATED.—At present the author estimates that approximately 16–20 per cent of the clinical cases of neurotic reactions would fall into the major diagnostic category of the Conversion Reactions. (*See Table 16*, pp. 243–4 for estimates of the relative incidence of the various neurotic reactions.) Somatic Conversions (hysteria) might account for 4–6 per cent of these, and the Physiologic Conversions for another 12–14 per cent.

These estimates are for the U.S.A. only. During two earlier (1954 and 1957) world tours of medical and psychiatric centers, the author was impressed with what appeared to be a greater relative prominence of instances of long-standing Somatic Conversions as encountered in other countries. This was particularly apparent in the Far East and in the Middle East.

The trend would appear in the United States to have been increasingly toward more functional conversions, and fewer somatic ones.* However, there are many evidences in our day-to-day living that there remains a wide potential for the translation of elements of inner emotional conflict into their outward symbolic expression. This is indicated in our fairly common usage of what we might call *"physical-translation"* figures of speech. The extent of these help indicate that this constant potential is present within us to evolve somatic and physiologic conversions. [*See* pp. 473–5, for further examples of these interesting "physical translations".] This widespread potential, although highly variable on an individual basis, helps support our earlier [pp. 2, 457, and 465] *Law of Relativity in Emotional Health.*

D. AGE AND SEX INCIDENCE. THE CONVERSION ATTACK.—Conversion Reactions sometimes have been thought of as primarily affecting the more youthful. This has a relation to maturity and to sophistication, and thereby has some real basis. At times conversion attacks are transient or episodic, particularly with children and with youths. In analogous fashion to the *Hygeiaphrontic Attack* [p. 483], we might therefore properly find the application of the designation of *Conversion Attack* warranted on occasion.

Often there is a tendency to think of these reactions more in terms of women. The Ziegler series of cases had 40 men, of 134 total — just under one-third. Other series have indicated a smaller proportion of males; occasionally more. While this may be correct to some extent with the more marked and bizarre kinds of major symptoms, when one includes the many subtle and less striking instances, one might suspect the apparent disproportion would become less. In the author's personal clinical experience, males would run close to 40 per cent.

---

* On the other hand, Stephens and Kamp do not believe there is much change in the incidence of the major Conversion Reactions (from a group of 100 U.S. patients from 1913–1920, and a similar group from 1945–1960), and that the symptoms are not substantially different. Only six of their patients had pain, predominantly, and but 32 showed classic conversion *indifférence*.

B. INVERSE RATIO OF INCIDENCE TO SOPHISTICATION

1. *Gross Symptoms Make Too Much Sense! Theory of Transparency*

Can we account for these changes in the types and the relative incidence of physical and physiologic responses to stress? Why has the incidence of the major symptoms of the Somatic Conversion Reactions decreased to the point that they are today of less relative prominence, and incidence? Why are they today rather rarely seen in the private practice of psychiatry? In attempting to explain this, the author would postulate the presence of an inverse relationship between the incidence of Somatic Conversion, on the one hand and the gradual rise in the overall level of scientific knowledge and education, together with the increase in the average level of sophistication of the general population, on the other. These factors are in addition to the one of an important influence of selectivity as to the patients seen in private practice.

As part of what the author has referred to as a *Theory of Transparency* [Ch.14:IIIB*1*], we might note that today it is culturally (socially and professionally) likely to be far more acceptable to have a rapid or irregular heart beat, or a gastrointestinal tract difficulty, then to have a nonorganic paralysis. The latter on an emotional basis does not make as much sense to people any more. Perhaps one might say, instead, that it makes *too much sense!*, as the factors of unconscious secondary gain, that is, the epigain, become more transparent to the more sophisticated family and friends of today. This is not true of the endogain, that is, the deeply unconscious primary gain. It is in accord with our Transparency Theory.

The question might be raised of course as to whether wider recognition of non-organicity, or of the secondary gain factors would have a sufficiently suppressive effect. In answering this, one might point out that the influence of decreased social acceptability undoubtedly exerts certain subtle but powerful continuing pressures upon the currently "popular", or at least more acceptable type of psychoneurotic manifestation. [*See* earlier similar comments in relation to "selection" of the object of phobias and soterias in Chapters 10 and 11].

2. *Ever More Disguised Expressions?; Recent Interest Lags*

Let us assume that the Transparency Theory is applicable. Let us presuppose a continuing rise of cultural sophistication. Accordingly, we might make an interesting speculation: Will the resulting pressures, on an increasingly sophisticated level, for socially and culturally acceptable emotional symptoms, continue to drive the somatic and physiologic expressions of emotional conflict into ever deeper and disguised avenues of symbolic expression? This is an interesting speculation! Time will tell (*see also* footnote, p. 123).

Psychiatric textbooks today generally do not contain an up-to-date chapter on the Conversion Reactions! Research interest with only a few notable exceptions, also tends to be directed elsewhere. So do the therapeutic interests of psychiatrists, as Kolb noted. In recent decades interest in this major area has lagged. It is as though most investigators felt that the basic work was completed and that no new challenges remained in the major field of the Conversion Reactions.

Actually, some important questions remain unanswered, and others are only incompletely answered. There is ample room indeed for further research and study. This is particularly true in the realm of the functional ills; the Physiologic Conversions.

V. SYMPTOMS AND CLINICAL FEATURES

A. PSYCHOLOGIC CONCEPTS

1. Physical Symptoms and Symbolic Expressions

A. SYMPTOMS LEGION.—The physical symptoms which may be observed clinically as part of the Conversion Reactions are legion in number and variety. These are the many symbolic, somatic expressions. They may be regarded as a kind of body language, for the disguised and symbolic acting out of forbidden and consciously disowned impulses.* The variety of symptoms and their possible combinations are only limited by the variety, degree, and possible combinations of the repressed unconscious needs, and by the structures which are available to express them.

The formation of physical symptoms on a conversion basis is often best regarded as a desperate psychologic effort to maintain the intolerable thought, wish, or urge in a continued state of repression, where it thus remains out of conscious awareness. It is the result of a last-ditch effort to reach some solution, however unrealistic and self-defeating it may be, of what is to the ego an otherwise insoluble conflict. It is an attempt to avoid anxiety and what seems an overwhelming threat. The physical symptom formation, with its resulting surrender of function, handicap, and incapacity, is indeed indicative of the underlying desperate psychologic needs of the patient.

B. UNCONSCIOUS SIMULATION CONCEPT.—Conversion symptoms can unconsciously simulate those of almost any kind of organic illness. This is in line with a concept of what we might call *Unconscious Simulation* in certain Conversion Reactions. Their ability thus to mimic other pathologic syndromes has been long noted. The conversion diathesis commonly includes strong suggestibility and identification, in addition to dissociative ability and emotionalism. These lend themselves to the unwitting adoption and development of conversion manifestations akin to those witnessed or heard about, when these are psychologically convenient and individually meaningful.

Thus the route of hysterical blindness may have been earlier suggested and unwittingly implanted through contact with a blind relative or associate, or through stories about blindness. This route is followed when duly

---

* Plus simultaneous hidden factors of their control, and of self-punishment, as we shall see.

fitting and individually appropriate to the compelling and existing inner psychic needs. Symptoms, for example, of conversion pain, paralysis, and convulsions may be similarly initiated.

C. IATROGENIC FACTORS.—Symptoms may also be brought on and follow the inadvertent suggestions as derived through various kinds of medical reading or contacts. As pointed out by Babinski, these can also follow adequately suggestive kinds of history taking and examinations [*see also Case 87*, p. 427, and *Case 89*, pp. 452–3]. Iatrogenic factors, however, most often are to be regarded as seeds which can only germinate in fertile, ready, and predisposed psychologic soil, to develop into established symptoms. This is in accord with our *Concept of Favorable Psychologic Soil* [Ch. 14: VIA]. The iatrogenic aspects can be of importance: (*a*) in providing an avenue for selection of the types of symptoms evolved, and (*b*) in the perpetuation of a conversion mode of reaction. The capacity for conversion reaction, however, must of necessity pre-exist.

2. Defensive Symptoms in Turn Defended: The Concept of Secondary Defense

A. PHYSICAL EXPLANATION PREFERRED.—It is not surprising that the conversion patient often seeks to explain his disability on a physical basis. This is in line with our later [Ch.12:VIIIA*3*] *Flight-to-the-Physical Principle*. There are a number of important reasons for this. *First,* this represents an after-the-fact attempt to explain something which he does not, and cannot possibly, understand. *Second,* and more important, he often has a strong need to interpret his symptoms as being on a physical basis since this is more socially acceptable and is personally face-saving. *Finally,* this presumed basis of origin and preferred area for exploration, serves also to protect and to maintain the symptom, which of course is basically emotional. The symptom, of basically defensive intent in itself, is in turn defended [*see also* earlier references, pp. 96, 144, 267, 359, 366, 444, and *Case 101*, pp. 487–9].

Loss of the symptom would seem to the person concerned to expose himself to the dreaded consequences of what threatens to be an overwhelming level of consciously experienced anxiety, against which the symptom constitutes a defense. One must first grasp the earlier, terribly urgent need of the patient to deny his consciously intolerable needs, or symbolically to secure some measure of substitutive gratification. This is part of the endogain. The symptom constitutes a defense, a primary defense. Then one can have an appreciation of why a symptom is often held on to like grim death, despite all the sacrifices which can ensue, or the destructive effects of the resulting handicaps. It is small wonder that this primary defense, this symptom, is in turn defended [*see also* pp. 96, 144, and 267].

B. PROTECTIVE INTENT.—Thus the patient may most firmly believe that his disability is the result of an organic illness. In these instances he is often quite resistive to the idea, and perhaps quite resentful even of any faintest suggestion, that his complaints are emotionally determined.* This is a protectively intended reaction in denial of the existence of possible emotional contributions. It constitutes in effect a *secondary type of defense, in which the symptoms, a defense in themselves, are in turn defended.* This is the basic and important Concept of the Secondary Defense.† [*See* p. 505 and earlier references.]

C. BARRAGE OF SYMPTOMS IN THERAPY.—The Concept of Secondary Defense and resistance is brought home forcibly on occasion when a barrage of functional symptoms comes on at a critical juncture in analytic therapy. This kind of phenomenon which can be precipitated also by various other stressful events or situations the author would propose for purposes of identification we call the *Symptom Barrage.* The onset of such a Symptom-Barrage in fairly transient form during analysis is illustrated in the following example. In therapy the Symptom-Barrage can constitute a P.S.F. [Prognostic Signal-Flag; p. 505], indicating one is getting close to crucial issues or conflicts. Also clearly emphasized is the close relation between affect and function, through which hidden emotional facets of living produce considerable alteration in, or diverse new types of, functional activity [*see also Case 95,* p. 470–1, illustrating a Symptom-Barrage following major surgery; *Case 100,* pp. 485–6, and p. 505].

Case 135

The Symptom-Barrage in Therapy: The Treatment-Resisting Effects of the Secondary Defense

A 52-year-old successful businessman was making excellent progress in his analytic work. One day he discussed some half-forgotten events in his early relations with his father. He found himself quite angry and somewhat agitated. He was quite surprised at this reaction and its strength, since he had fully believed heretofore that any hostile feelings in this particular area had long since been thoroughly resolved. He remained angry all day, and the day went poorly. The functional sequellae were still more noteworthy. We had indeed touched on significant ground. A rash of functional symptoms appeared over the next 72 hours. This well illustrated the occasional marked *Symptom-Barrage,* in therapy.

These included bouts of coughing, nervousness and tension, constipation, sensations of his skin "breaking out" on his back and as though he were being "needled", headache, nausea, and finally, a bout of elation the night prior to his next session, followed by oversleeping (a terribly rare event for him) the next morning, nearly to the point of missing his next session. He further found himself reluctant to come, which was also terribly unusual. This particular rash of manifestations or Symptom-Barrage, gradually subsided over the course of two weeks, following their thorough discussion and the analysis of their significance. Even on casual view they suggest some interesting symbolic meanings.

---

* The patient with emotional symptoms may seek for, or cling to a presumed organic basis. In some contrast, the patient with organic illness, even if this be most critical, will not welcome any alternative, emotional explanation.

† The *Symptom Defense-Defeat Parallel Concept* (pp. 291, 505) as a sometime significant corollary to our Concept of Secondary Defense, pointed out how the level or strength of the latter can pretty well directly parallel the amount of self-defeat, handicap (and masochism) engendered.

D. STATUS QUO OF ADJUSTMENT CONCEPT.—This example indicates the strength of the resistances in their role of Secondary Defense. Such a barrage of functional symptoms and physiologic conversions seeks to divert attention, to express feelings and conflicts symbolically, and in effect to retard and break up the analysis. This is part of the Secondary Defense. In this as in other similar instances, the forces of the Secondary Defense of the existing symptoms, character traits, mental mechanism defenses, and/or current personality adjustment are active and strong. The Secondary Defense further endeavors: (1) to protect the unconscious, (2) to resist therapeutic intervention, and (3) to defend what we might refer to as the *Status Quo of Adjustment*.

3. Maintenance of Repression Vital; Concept of Interpersonal Perpetuation

A. IMPULSES AND LOSS OF CONTROL FEARED.—The maintenance of repression is always a vital matter. It can become practically a matter of life and death to the patient. What appeared to a mother in the following illustration to be "murderous" impulses toward her child, were so totally unacceptable that she would almost rather die than admit them to conscious awareness.

Thus, it had become to her far more acceptable to lose the function of her right arm than to "murder" the child, a result which she unconsciously feared would ensue. In a magical and unrealistic fashion, the "thought" came to be unconsciously equated with the act. The best protection against acting, therefore, is not to have the thought! If awareness were tolerated, the mother "feared" she would be unable to inhibit her action. Therefore, as we shall see, she reinforced repression, control, and inhibition against such a dangerous possibility through her conversion symptoms.

Case 136

Conversion Weakness of the Arm Serves as a Reinforcement Against Intolerable Hostile Impulses

(1) *Earlier deprivations limit motherhood capacity*

A twenty-six-year-old married mother sought treatment because of a tremendous dragging weakness of her right arm. This was severe enough to result in an inability to do her housework adequately, or properly to care for her eight-month-old daughter. She also reported being so anxious when in the kitchen that she could not bear to remain there long.

The clinical picture was that of an immature mother. She had been so deprived of love and affection herself that the needs of her child in this direction had become an intolerable burden to her. This resulted in a rejecting attitude toward the child. This was communicated to the latter frequently and via various routes: intuitively, emphatically, and directly.

(2) *A vicious circle*

The response of the child in turn was to become restless, tense, and anxious, and to develop poor sleeping habits and digestive upsets. All of this resulted in an added drain on the mother. Her resentment and hostility toward her child were increased, setting up a vicious circle. The weak arm developed as a final safeguard against conscious awareness of her overwhelming rage.

As a result a nurse was hired which helped the mother to avoid the child (and her "murderous" feelings). This arrangement also helped satisfy dependency needs on the part of the mother, who was unable to function on a more mature level because of her own early deprivations of love and affection.

(3) *Paralysis inhibits action*

The mother was hostile to the child essentially because she herself never got any real warmth. Her own great need for affection * made it less possible for her to tolerate demands on her by another person. The anxiety about the kitchen was found to relate to the kitchen knives (potential murder weapons) which were kept there.

One cannot easily wield a knife with a paralyzed arm! The symptom symbolically served to reinforce the inhibition of any possible overt physical act in response to her consciously disowned hostile thoughts.

B. PERPETUATION OF A PATTERN; NON-INHERITANCE.—From the foregoing greatly condensed example one can perhaps begin to appreciate why a given symptom which is actually disabling, may become "acceptable", or far more than that, urgently needed, wanted, and even required. One can see why it is often bitterly defended against therapeutic study and intervention, despite its major interference with living. The sacrifice of the function of an arm is far more acceptable to the mother than the murder of her child, which is the underlying, unconscious fear.

This patient did well in intensive psychotherapy. Her level of maturity increased substantially. Her arm weakness had gradually lifted. Undoubtedly the inner need for such conversion came to no longer exist, either specifically or as an established potential avenue for reaction in response to future possible major stress.

Space does not permit us to consider the complex relationship of this young woman to her own mother. However, *one poor relationship tends to reproduce another.* Capacities for later constructive and satisfying relationships come to be limited. One can see in this instance how the patient might well have inadvertently perpetuated a pattern of serious emotional illness in her own daughter in turn. As a matter of convenience, and emphasis we might term this major psychodynamic precept, the *Concept of Interpersonal Perpetuation* [pp. 291, 334, and 455] in the transmission of emotional illness.

Emotional illnesses are *not* inherited. However, through one's early interpersonal environment, perpetuation of the potential for (and the certainty of!) emotional problems certainly does occur. This can continue from generation to generation. The manifestations can vary greatly from individual to individual. It is far more complex a sequence, however, than the antequated misbelief in the inheritance of emotional illness would indicate.

---

* This, plus her dependency needs, led her to demand more from her husband. As in so many such situations, the more she demanded, the less of genuine affection was forthcoming! This aspect of her complex and tragic situation illustrated our *Concept of a Vicious Circle of Self-Defeat* in the neuroses [*See also* pp. 71, 265, and 476].

B. CONVERSION PAIN

1. Frequent Problem; Psychic Reduplication Concept

It is not possible entirely to delimit Somatic Conversions from Physiologic Conversions. Overlapping tends to occur. Motor activity and sensation cannot be completely divorced from function and from internal physiology.

Conversion pain often tends to overlap in these areas. Diagnosis may be more difficult in cases in which pain on a conversion basis is severe. The patient himself is aware only of his discomfort. He is, of course, unaware of the source or reasons which underlie the pain. He cannot possibly be aware of these, any more than he could possibly be aware of the basis for such symptoms as for example the palpitations or the gastrointestinal malfunctions which might occur as physiologic conversions. It is interesting that conversion pain receives little mention as a clinical symptom of Conversion Reaction (hysteria) by the early medical authors.

Conversion pain is today a frequent clinical manifestation of this defensive pattern of reaction [Ch.12:IIIA6]. This is more correct currently than generally recognized.* Psychologically, pain offers certain advantages again in a more sophisticated cultural millieu as to one's acceptance, the inability to disprove or to contradict, providing an honorable relief from an intolerable position, and so on. It can produce all of the conversion endogain about as well as the more gross motor and sensory symptoms. Further, once established, the factors of epigain can be substantial. Pain conveys a more apparent appeal for help and succor than do other more "silent" symptoms in which function is surrendered. Its locale and type often simulates (unconsciously) an organic condition with which the person has gained some familiarity [see also later reference, Section VIIC].

Antecedent organic pain can provide an unwitting prototype for later pain, on a number of emotional bases, including that of conversion. This is in accord with the interesting *Psychic-Reduplication Concept,* as earlier formulated (p. 468). The concurrent presence of conversion manifestations *and* organic symptoms comprises an emotional-organic combination (E.O.C.). [See pp. 393, 453, and Ch. 13:VIID1].

2. Surgery vs. Psychotherapy

At this point some of the problems which can arise with conversion pain will be illustrated clinically.

Case 137

Conversion Pain Simulates a Surgical Emergency

(1) *Emotional factors suspected*

A forty-one-year-old man suffered a sudden onset of severe abdominal pain. He was obviously in considerable discomfort. There had been no dietary indiscretion. Some questionable protective muscular rigidity

---

* This was borne out recently (1960) in Ziegler's *et al.* series, in which pain was the primary complaint in 75 of 134 consecutive persons with Conversion Reactions.

was present. A surgeon was called into consultation by the examining physician. The latter was puzzled by certain contradictory factors in the case.

The patient had by then been hospitalized for a possible exploratory laparotomy. The white cell count remained normal, and the neutrophil differential had shown no "shift to the left". Nevertheless, partly on the added basis of a history of a childhood appendectomy and suspected possible subsequent adhesions, the operating room was alerted. Something about the patient's attitude contradictorily reflected overconcern, alternating with a detached kind of indifference. There was also some evidence of interpersonal familial stress. These slowed down the urgent preparations.

(2) Surgery abandoned; Analysis undertaken

On psychiatric consultation, still more positive findings indicated serious emotional conflicts and conversion character defenses. A trial period of treatment was recommended. The patient was able to accept the wisdom of the advice in this instance. Not always is one so fortunate! A series of intensive interviews was begun which was destined to continue over nearly three years, with some resulting substantial emotional changes. After several months of work it became possible to reconstruct the psychogenic bases of the attack.

The patient's parents were materially wealthy. They were impoverished in so far as their capacity for love or affection was concerned. The barrenness of their underlying lack of acceptance and warmth they attempted to cover over and make up for by a pathetically overdone and superficial outward display. This did not, of course, really deceive the boy. He intuitively grasped the situation, even though at the time he could not entirely admit it even to himself. As he viewed it, one single exception to all this had been the sequence of his early appendicitis and operation. To him, the love and attention during this period was meaningful, real, and what he "had always longed for".

(3) Regressive and dependency features

His conversion pain unconsciously sought in regressive fashion the reattainment of this earlier and more satisfactory era. He would presumably secure the gratification of dependent wishes which, on the other hand, he must consciously deny. As he had also suffered in the antecedent situation, so in unrealistic fashion he must "arrange" suffering in the present situation, partly as the price for securing such gratification. Here then he unwittingly repeated the earlier situation which for him was a prototype.

Thus this patient, acting entirely out of conscious awareness, indicated the price he would or must pay as he sought in anguished fashion to recreate the pleasant early dependency with its aura of extra and real attention and affection. What restimulated his regressive longing so that it became expressed at this time in its distorted conversion into the somatic language of pain?

What had happened on the occasion of the attack was a particularly marked attempt at domestic deceit. It turned out that his wife had become infatuated with another man. At the very same time that she was seriously contemplating going off with him, there was a dramatic showdown in which she had vigorously but untruthfully denied all her feelings for the other man and had affirmed her love for her husband. This insincerity had been sensed by the patient, for whom the significance of the whole affair was greatly magnified because of his own early antecedent conflicts over his parents' insincere affection and his deeply repressed resentment about this. It was too much, and his pain began.

3. Contraindication to Surgery. Surgery-in-Abeyance Rule

A CONVERSION PAIN A SERIOUS PROBLEM; OFTEN SEVERE.—Conversion pain manifests itself in many ways. The fact that an organic basis is not present does not make the pain any less severe. It does not make it non-existent. Indeed, it is likely to be more severe. It is certainly likely to be more of a problem. Nor does this mean that there is "nothing wrong" with the patient. On the contrary, it means there is something very wrong indeed! This is an indication of serious emotional illness.

The possibility of severe pain on a conversion basis, as in *Case 137,* helps again to call attention to the fact that the Conversion Reactions constitute an important contraindication to surgery, except in clear-cut emergencies. This is our *Surgery-in-Abeyance Rule* [pp. 127, 392, 470, 509; Ch.10:X6, and Section IIIA6]. Stevens, among others, has called attention to the frequent history of surgical procedures to be found among somatic conversion patients. Sullivan, in writing on "Psychiatric Factors in Low Back Pain", commented: "I shudder when I think of the laminectomies and fusions done on obviously neurotic people without psychiatric consultation". Many psychiatrists fully share his feelings. This kind of reaction also might be quite appropriate in relation to the similar evaluation of certain other types of surgery.

The following case further helps to illustrate these points.

Case 138

Conversion Pain

(1) *Multiple surgical procedures*

A thirty-eight-year-old mother of five children was under diagnostic study because of severe burning pain in her right abdominal wall and in the soles of her feet. She also suffered from sharp pain in her left knee.

History disclosed good health until two years earlier. At this time she had complained of abdominal pain and an appendectomy was performed. Some months later she was under treatment for "arthritis and neuritis" of the knees. Several recurrences of "sharp" or of "burning" abdominal pain led, next, to an exploratory laparotomy; third, to a scar excision; fourth, to a cholecystectomy; and, finally, to the removal of adhesions. Still another operative procedure was currently under consideration. There had been five abdominal procedures in two years; a sixth being actively considered. The needs for each of these were undoubtably far more emotional than organic. Unconsciously, she had "sought" surgery. Her history well illustrated the value of our *Surgery-in-Abeyance Rule.*

Upon consultation, the pain in her knee was acute. There was no redness or swelling. There was no limitation of motion. It did not hurt more with exercise. The sedimentation rate was normal, as were other laboratory studies. There was, however, no doubt as to the genuineness of her suffering. She was seriously ill emotionally. Nevertheless, one physician had told her there was "nothing wrong" with her. Another had suggested exploratory surgery of her knee. Fortunately, in part, and at least for the nonce (!) those recommending psychiatric consultation prevailed and for the present anyway, she was spared (or denied?) further surgery.

(2) *Psychotherapy refused*

History uncovered a long series of emotional traumata. Three years earlier these had culminated with serious marital problems, followed by the death of her mother, and the enforced marriages of *three* of her children, all a few months apart. She described these crises with little outward evidence of emotion. However, her knee became more painful as we talked. As she described the difficult period, she said several times, "It was so bad back then I nearly went crazy. Now it doesn't bother me any more."

It is not by accident that people on occasion refer to having "heart aches". It was almost as though this patient had exchanged her "heart aches" for aches instead in her knees, abdomen, and feet. She refused to even consider our recommendations for at least a minimal trial of psychotherapy. Her Secondary Defense-Resistance was too powerful.

B. ANY SITE POSSIBLE; CLAVUS AND CAMPTOCORMIA.—There are two further brief comments about conversion pain in a later section of this chapter [Section VII C]. The lower back and the head are frequent sites for pain of conversion origin. Several special types have received names.

These varieties of conversion pain notably include *clavus;* defined as the *painful sensation of a nail being driven into the head,* and *camptocormia* (Sougues; 1915) which is *severe low back pain which is usually chronic,* and is *often accompanied by muscle spasm, by some limitation of motion, and especially a forwardly bent back* [Ch.12:IVA*1*;VD2].

Any part or region of the body can be the site of conversion pain. Conversion pain can be multiple, simultaneously affecting several regions, or affecting them in tandem.

C. APPEARANCE AND BEHAVIOR

1. Acting Out; In transference and therapy

Acting Out refers to unconscious, unthinking external action in response to disowned (unconscious) emotions and emotional urges. Hostile or loving feelings, for example, are thus expressed in some (consciously concealed from oneself) form of action. The person concerned thus "manages" to maintain conscious ignorance of his unconscious feelings or impulses, of their extent, or of their having been "acted out". Acting Out is quite commonly encountered in conjunction with the Conversion Reactions [*see also* references on pp. 193, 258–9, 355–6, and Ch.13:VIIIE*1*].

In Acting Out, the conversion individual or other person does not recognize the real significance of what he does. He is unaware of his inner motivations, as when hostility is thus expressed. He is equally unperceptive as to its intent, and usually as to its effect upon the other person or his environment. The expression or term of Acting Out by definition also includes certain phenomena of transference and so is particularly observable, and to be observed, in the treatment situation. Herein the person in therapy thus may "act out" toward the therapist attitudes, feelings, and reactions which are really directed toward an important person in an antecedent relationship. Acting Out is of course by no means limited to the treatment situation.

Conversion (hysterical) persons often tend to act impulsively, and to give inadequate thought to the consequences of their actions. It is to be noted that impulsive behavior, as in compulsive behavior is to be distinguished from Acting Out.

2. Inhibiting Function of Symptoms; Spasms, Cramps and Tics

At other times, as noted, conversion symptoms appear to be defenses *against* acting, or to include such a component. It is as though the conversion person fears he has no control, as though he fears emotions *will* be acted upon, no matter how personally or socially destructive they may be. This is the symbolic inhibiting component of the symptom. When present, it often accompanies the simultaneous symbolic gratification in some measure, of the disowned impulse.

In regard to the conversion types of motor disturbances, Fenichel has also noted that one of their major symbolic functions is to prevent or to defend against possible action. The action defended against is in response to a forbidden and disowned hostile or sexual impulse, often infantile in origin. In this fashion, muscular spasms may be symbolically intended to prevent forbidden activity as well as to allow symbolic gratification.

Certain occupational cramps can also represent the somatic expression of such hidden symbolic inhibition of action, interference with a "forbidden" success or symbolic achievement, and simultaneous punishment. Tics and habit spasms are related. These kinds of conversion symptoms usually also represent what we might refer to as *compromise formations*. These are defined as the *compromise expression in outward and symbolic form of conflicting internal (unconscious) emotional drives or needs* [p. 118; Ch. 12:VIB2].

Tics and mannerisms can also be grouped with certain other significant emotional manifestations to be regarded and labeled as *Conflict-Indicators*. This is in accord with a concept which notes these so-named phenomena as indicating the presence of underlying emotional conflict, usually together with the potential for the progression of further difficulties. [*See Concept of Conflict-Indicators,* p. 406 and Ch.13:IVC1].

3. La Belle Indifférence

A. ENDOGAIN AND EPIGAIN.—Charcot and his pupil Pierre Janet are credited with having described a classical clinical feature of Somatic Conversion which was aptly name *la belle indifférence* [Section II B1]. This is the "beautiful", "grand", or striking indifference of the conversion patient to his symptoms. It is striking in view of the symptom (the bases for which remain a mystery to him however), having resulted in major incapacity. This relative bland acceptance of what is often serious disability may be due to several factors.

First, the symptom formation in the Conversion Reaction represents the unconscious neurotic resolution or attempted solution of a conflict. Since the symptom serves a useful purpose unconsciously, the patient cannot take the same serious view of his disability as might the person suffering from a comparable level of disability from an organic disease. In Somatic Conversion, the symptoms subserve desperately important unconscious primary needs. This is the endogain, the outward reflection of which is represented symbolically.

The conversion epigain is likewise often very important. It can contribute substantially to the perpetuation of the illness. (*See* Chapter 2.) These principles apply particularly when the conversion is "successful" in allaying anxiety and in providing a (neurotic) resolution for conflict. In its major anxiety-countering function, the conversion symptom may be regarded rather directly as what we have earlier referred to [pp. 103, 145, 324, and 462] as an *anxiety-equivalent*.

B. BOTH DENIAL AND SECONDARY DEFENSE.—In discussing the feature of *la belle indifférence* in the Conversion Reactions, Saul said that ". . . the person whose emotional tension results in physical symptoms is apt to be free from complaints of emotional strain". These stresses can, in the "successful" instance, be sufficiently "taken care of" by the physical symptom.

There is an added possible contribution to such relative freedom from emotional stress. The author refers here to instances in which there is a further *denial* of the symptom. Here the conversion and symbolic expression into body language has not only been successful, but to an extent the presence of the manifestation (and the resulting disability) have now in effect been denied. The patient then behaves as though a compartmentalization had been effected to enclose the entire process.* It is now to this extent dissociated from the remainder of experience and living.

The indifference helps to defend the symptom. The symptom is itself a defense [Ch.13:IB2]. The seemingly incongruous indifference to its effects, and to the major disability which may be present, is a part of the *Secondary Defense,* as referred to earlier.

C. UNCONSCIOUS SATISFACTION REFLECTED.—*La belle indifférence* is a frequent finding in Somatic Conversion. The more serious the symptom, the more striking this manifestation is likely to appear. This perhaps illustrates what has been said about the degree of "success" of the conversion. *La belle indifférence* is *a reflection of the unconscious satisfaction with the attempted solution, and the resultant prevention of anxiety,* however handicapping the symptom and essentially nonconstructive the solution. The underlying principles also help to explain the defensive disinterest in the necessary therapeutic intervention which is required to effect a cure. This resistance is also a major aspect of the powerful Secondary Defense of the symptom.

The sudden loss of the symptom without insight and adequate understanding would result in the restored vulnerability to anxiety. It is not surprising then perhaps, that although the patient may call attention to his symptoms and seek treatment for them, they often do not in themselves appear to be a sufficiently real problem to him. Thus they are often presented to the physician with a relative lack of concern, out of keeping with their gravity. This may be true even when the disability is of such serious import as paralysis or blindness.

D. ORGANIC MORE ACCEPTABLE: FLIGHT-TO-THE-PHYSICAL.—An explanation in organic terms, and treatment from such a standpoint might be far

---

* Legault interestingly pointed out a similar process of denial seen to operate in lobotomized patients *for* their operation, and *for* the resulting emotional deficit.

more acceptable to the person concerned. He may desperately seek or insist upon this in line with our concept of the self-defeating and sometimes quite tragic *Flight-to-the-Physical* [p. 461; Ch.12:VIIIA*3*; Ch.13:VIIB*3*]. This would be face-saving, socially acceptable, would not "rock the boat" of his tenuous symptom-adjustment, and would allow retention of the dependent (and orally recipient) position.

Attempted probing, the offering of an emotional interpretation, or diagnosis, or of investigative psychotherapy and analysis may be desperately needed to effect the definitive resolution of handicapping symptoms. Tragically it so often has to be resisted, resented, and spurned, often angrily, sometimes even as insulting. This occured in *Case 138*.

E. INDIFFERENCE VARIABLE IN CONVERSION PAIN.—How about this feature of indifference in conversion pain? In *Cases 137* and *138* the patients suffered from their pain. They were well aware of it and they focused their attention upon it. Hence, one can hardly regard them as being indifferent to the pain as such. The Conversion type of indifference in these areas appears more in relation: (1) to the consequences of the pain, (2) to the resulting handicaps or limitations in living, and (3) to possible organic implications, which are likely to be almost more sought than feared.

The patient in *Case 138* had little concern over her multiple surgical procedures. She was rather indifferent, or even seemed to welcome the prospect of another one. Likewise she was relatively unconcerned about the resulting handicaps in her day-to-day living. She was not at all indifferent to the pain, but she was rather indifferent to its results and consequences. Needless to say, the conversion endogain had to be very important in this case to make the conscious physical, somatic kind of suffering "preferable". The conversion epigain was very considerable as well. Her symptoms had had major effects upon her environment, including those persons close about her.

F. PARALYSIS LESS CONCERN THAN SKIN IRRITATION.—This apparent lack of concern over a major disability is typically present in the following case. Although this patient suffered a partially paralyzed leg, a major disability, for a time he showed much more interest and concern about a minor and transient skin irritation [*see also Case 54*, pp. 266–7].

Case 139

La Belle Indifférence with a Major Physical Disability

A twenty-one-year-old soldier completed his basic training without incident. In view of his superior physical attributes and excellent soldierly bearing, he was shortly assigned to an "honor guard" unit. Upon completion of this tour of duty he was ordered to overseas combat service. Before he could go, he developed a major Somatic Conversion Reaction marked by the partial paralysis of his left leg.

This was attributed by the patient as being the aftermath of a minor physical injury. In response to his complaints and demands, a physician had unwittingly helped along the psychopathologic process in iatrogenic fashion. He had indulgently placed a plaster splint on the leg for two weeks, hoping thus to "satisfy" the patient. Upon removal of the case, the dysfunction was found to be well established. Competent medical evaluation left no doubt as to the conversion etiology.

Personality study revealed a dependent, immature, egocentric patient. He was inordinately proud of his physique, and had showed great concern over any possible threat of injury thereto. The disability was severe enough to require him to use crutches. It was a great impediment, and seriously handicapped his present and future prospects. Nevertheless, he appeared blandly indifferent to the serious implications of his handicap.

This was typically *la belle indifférence*. On several occasions he showed a great deal more concern over a minor skin irritation. He requested, or more accurately, demanded to see a dermatologist, although he had remained indifferent to the point of rudeness to the interest exhibited by other medical officers in trying to help him. He appeared to care very little about their active and spontaneous efforts on his behalf.

Relatively unresponsive to any psychotherapeutic efforts, his paralysis gradually improved following the decision to discharge him from service, and over the period while he was awaiting the necessary processing of his separation papers.

In view of the resistance here, little could be learned in this case as to the psychodynamics of the primary gain or endogain, except what might be highly speculative. One might perhaps guess at some possible inhibiting and masochistic purposes. [*See Table 32* in Section VI]. As to the conversion epigain features, one might perhaps view this disability as securing the unconscious exchange of a definite, delimiting symptom for the indefinite but more feared risks which could result from combat. The latter unconsciously may have been to him a greatly dreaded certainty.

La belle indifférence at least superficially has a certain similarity at times to the *flattened affect* (that is, diminished emotional expression) of schizophrenia. Occasionally, outward similarities may contribute to difficulties in diagnosis. The bases for their elaboration can be to an extent related.

4. Emotionalism and Histrionics

The emotional aspects of the conversion patient are often associated by people with and are sometimes well marked by, *emotionalism:* defined as *frequent, strong, and poorly controlled emotional outbursts;* and by *histrionics:* the *dramatic appeal, theatrics, representations, and playing "as if for an audience"*. The Janet Dissociation is the type involved when these are viewed as personality desyntheses. The concept of wild emotionality which is uncontrolled, but perhaps unwittingly controlling, is commonly associated with the Conversion Reactions (hysteria). It may be less frequently encountered than formerly.

Occasionally the motor or sensory manifestations may be similarly "wild", that is in the sense of being inconsistent, disorganized, and shifting.

5. The Conversion Character or Personality

A. CONVERSION PERSONALITY AND CHARACTER NEUROSIS.—Several preliminary features are often of some importance to the later appearance of the clinical features of the Conversion Reactions. These include: (*a*) the conversion diathesis, as referred to earlier, (*b*) the contributory underlying emotional conflict(s), (*c*) the initiating emotional experiences, and (*d*) the Conversion Personality (*See* Chapter 5). Recent studies by Chodoff and Lyons are cited by them, however, in support of their belief that the relationship between the Conversion (hysterical) Personality and the Conversion Reactions is less definite than heretofore believed.

The marked and handicapping instance of conversion character defenses comprises the Conversion type of Character Neurosis (p. 237). This is in distinction to the Conversion Reactors, which are *symptom-neuroses* (pp. 286, 383, and 446). The overdevelopment of conversion character trait-defenses illustrates our important *Defense-Hypertrophy Principle* (pp. 73, 229 *ff.*, and 251).

The author has found his concept of Conversion Character to be a useful one in any event. There are undoubtedly many reciprocal relationships with clinical Conversion Reactions, and this type of personality can be clearly enough delineated. Its study is warranted. A group of such related character defenses comprises a character trait *constellation* [p. 229]. The reader is referred to its fuller discussion in the appropriate chapter on The Character Reactions [pp. 229 *ff.*, 258; Ch.12:IA3, VIIA2].

B. CONCEPT OF DEFENSIVE-LAYERING.—It is both appropriate and useful at this juncture to again stress an important concept outlined earlier (p. 367; *Case 93,* p. 465; and pp. 486-489; also Ch.13:VE2). This is the *Concept of Defensive-Layering*. It has been identified to direct further attention toward the successive strata or "layers", of emotional defenses which are frequently elaborated by the hard-pressed ego. Accordingly, one defensively motivated pattern of reaction may underlie and succeed another one, which in turn is of greater or of lesser significance.

The level of a given character defense, emotional symptom, or neurotic or psychotic reaction will roughly correspond to the existing inner needs. As underlying emotional conflicts are resolved in therapy for example, a new layer of defenses may well appear, to successively undergo further working-through and resolution. Likewise in the reverse direction, an added layer of defenses (and psychopathology) may well be elaborated — gradually or suddenly, depending upon the initiating circumstances — in response to otherwise intolerable stress(es)* and emotional conflict. Defensive-layering results from unconscious, intrapsychic processes. It may be roughly likened to the structure of an onion or to successive layers of rock strata.

Between Conversion Reactions and the traits of the corresponding conversion type of character defenses, such a relationship can sometimes be observed. This is true also between other types of neurotic reactions and their corresponding character-trait patterns. A similar reciprocal relationship is at times demonstrable as well: (*a*) between psychotic defenses and reactions on the one hand, and neurotic ones on the other; (*b*) between various of the mental dynamisms; (*c*) among the several psychotic defenses themselves; and (*d*) between the various categories of neurotic defenses. The Defensive-Layering Concept is of significance and can be of value in many areas of psychiatry, including theory, dynamics, and therapy.

---

* Conversion defenses as with other types, can sometimes crumble under added stress. This can produce an acute *emotional decompensation* (*See* pp. 48, 159, 317, 343, 367, 476 and Ch.13:IIA2.)

D. SPECIAL CLINICAL FEATURES

1. *Somatic Conversion and I.Q.; Principle of Self-Esteem-Maintenance*

A. THERAPEUTIC APPROACH RESTRICTED.—Reference was made earlier to the fact that the grossly disabling major symptoms of Somatic Conversion are likely to be more frequently observed among persons from less favored social, economic, and educational backgrounds.* The following case is an example of a rather typical instance in which the I.Q. was also low.

Case 140

A Conversion Locomotor Disability

A seventeen-year-old recruit from the remote mountain country of eastern Tennessee was admitted to a military hospital from basic training during World War II. He had found himself suddenly unable to use one leg while standing or walking. Examination disclosed normal function and range of motion while prone or upon sitting. The patient had no understanding of his symptom and could not explain the discrepancy in function when in various positions. Although his inability to walk required him to travel either by wheelchair or with the constant support of another soldier, he did not appear really concerned about the many present handicaps, or the implications for his future of this otherwise major difficulty.

This soldier's I.Q. of 68 added another formidable barrier to an effective therapeutic approach. Even if his present symptom could be relieved, he was indeed a poor risk for military service from both a military and a taxpayer's viewpoint, in view of the strong existing potential for further difficulties.

In this instance, gradual recovery of function followed supportive, explanatory, educational, and suggestive measures. The latter early included a careful statement that, while it was in essence correct, also offered a bonus for his early recovery of function. It was said to him in effect that it was obviously impossible to retain him in service in any capacity since this disability had developed. Its continued presence, however, indicated he still needed treatment. Thus, he could be discharged to home only after he had regained the full use of his leg. Any deeper psychotherapeutic approach was necessarily restricted by time, circumstances, the limited capacity for understanding, and by the exigencies of the military situation.

B. GRADUAL RECESSION ADVANTAGEOUS.—Recovery took place gradually in the foregoing instances, with a steady increase in function. This is more the usual course in the recession of this type of symptom. Two of the reasons for this are: (1) sudden loss of the defensive function might release a sudden surge of anxiety (a reflection again of the *primary* defensive purpose or endogain of the symptom), and (2) *gradual* recession is far more face-saving in relation to the secondary gain features. Provision should always be made to allow for the preservation of the person's self-esteem. When removal of symptoms can be secured by the conservative supportive, and suggestive measures of psychotherapy, the patient then

---

* *See* earlier reference under Diagnosis in relation to intelligence, Section III A6. In Brown and Pisetsky's series of eleven consecutive instances of conversion paraplegia, five patients had I.Q.'s below 100. The range was from 84 to 122. Ten of the patients had been raised in slum or low middle class areas. They had been for the most part unskilled laborers. Most of them had not completed high school.

may be in a better position for more intensive treatment.* The foregoing outlines an important *Principle of Self-Esteem Maintainence* in Conversion Reaction therapy of all types. This principle is also applicable in the clinical Dissociative Reactions [Ch. 13].

C. FOCUS ON SECONDARY GAIN UNFORTUNATE.—Cases in military situations unfortunately often result in tending to focus the medical officer's attention (and to some extent, that of medicine generally) on the factors of secondary gain. This is at the least unfortunate.

The overstressing of this use to which the conversion symptom may be unconsciously put, as opposed to its much more important role as a defense against anxiety from censored emotional urges, needs and drives, may be very misleading. Attention directed toward this aspect, to the relative exclusion of other more important ones, also tends to result in condemning and judgmental attitudes on the part of the physician toward his patient. These often make it impossible for him to be very helpful.

2. Variety of Symptoms

Such symptoms as *globus hystericus* (the conversion symptom in which there is the sensation of a globe or ball in the stomach, which passes upward through the esophagus; or the persistent feeling that one has a lump in the throat), *pseudocyesis* (false-conversion symptoms of pregnancy), and *aerophagia* (air swallowing — perhaps to the point of bloating, distension, and/or eructation) help illustrate the variety of symptoms. *Case 145* [Ch. 12:VIC2], illustrates an instance of *globus hystericus*.

In conversion dyspnea the breathing is rapid and shallow. Conversion vomiting can become serious to the point of inanition. Camptocormia ("bent back") is sometimes observed. In a recent three-month period the author observed a series of three such cases on a local psychiatric service. Hypnoid-stuporous states occur rarely nowadays.

Motor restrictions are illustrated in *Cases 136, 139,* and *140*. Another type of conversion motor inhibition is *the restriction in,* or *interference with speech (dysphonia),* and *the loss of the power of speech (aphonia)*. Interesting cases of conversion *dysphagia* (difficulty in eating; painful swallowing) occasionally occur. *Aphonia* on a Conversion basis is still to be encountered not infrequently. Often it is of added interest because of its intriguing symbolism.

3. Conversion Aphonia; A Dissociative Reaction and the Emergency Analytic-Bridge

A. THE RHAZES MANEUVER: SYMPTOM RELIEF THROUGH TRICKERY.— The loss of speech on a conversion basis is still to be encountered. The Conversion Reaction remains the most likely cause to be suspected in any sudden loss of the power to speak. This is particularly true when it is

---

* T. A. Ross has told of the techniques he has successfully used with patients in explanation, education, relearning, and rebuilding their self-esteem. He disapproved of crude suggestion, or the use of faradic stimulation as an aid to suggestion.

associated with an emotional scene, or when some obvious "secondary gain" is to be derived.

It is at times possible to "trick" a patient out of his conversion symptoms. We might term this kind of approach the *Rhazes Maneuver,* after Rhazes, a physician of Rai in ancient Persia. Seeking to treat a prince who had been unable to walk, Rhazes is by legend reputed to have unexpectedly appeared in the latter's bathroom, brandishing a dagger most realistically and threatening to kill him! The startled prince abruptly fled, leaving his clothes, his dignity, his symptom, and undoubtedly part of his self-esteem behind!

While dramatically and impressively enough secured, the "relief" obtained through this type of maneuver is most superficial. Further, an aphonia or other symptom for example may conceivably be replaced by another symptom of equal or greater moment. In any event it is certain that no real insight has been achieved. Further, through its damaging effect on the self-esteem of a patient, it is hardly apt to promote a continuing good doctor-patient relationship! One might also speculate as to the later attitude of the prince toward Rhazes, or his treatment of him if he became the ruler.

The following instance illustrates the way the Rhazes Maneuver was carried out quite effectively, but this only from the superficial standpoint of symptom removal. This technique is not recommended. It is of no real help from the standpoint of understanding the dynamics. The consequence is interference with any useful therapy. It is all too likely to be detrimental to the future prognosis of the individual, as well as to that of his illness.

Case 141

Hysterical Aphonia "Relieved" by Trickery: The Rhazes Maneuver

A forty-five-year-old married woman felt badly treated and neglected by her husband. This had been particularly aggravated following the departure of their two grown children from the home. After one in a series of particularly bitter and angry scenes with her husband, she suddenly developed aphonia.

Following examination, the physician spoke to another person present. In a whispered tone, but loud enough to insure the patient's overhearing, he said, "That old gal is an awful fake. There is nothing *at all* wrong with her . . . Of course she could talk if she really wanted to!"

The angry response of the patient to overhearing these accusing and insulting comments was an indignant vocal denial! This proved the doctor "right", and announced her "cure". Having been thus tricked into it however, her future relations with the physician left much indeed to be desired.

Even had this physician possessed the requisite skill, any productive collaborative working relationship would have been precluded. Her negative attitude toward him lasted the rest of her life. The "success" of the Rhazes Maneuver was far from an unmixed blessing indeed.

B. EMERGENCY THERAPY IN A DISSOCIATIVE REACTION; SODIUM AMYTAL.
—In cases of conversion aphonia, the onset is often sudden, as in the preceding case. As a consequence of the symptom itself, to say the least, the initiation of therapeutic communication can be most difficult! In carefully

selected instances the temporary return of function can safely be secured through hypnosis, with or without the adjunctive use of intravenous sodium amytal [Ch.13:VIIIF4]. One thus may establish what the author terms for ready reference an *Emergency Analytic-Bridge* between the dissociated parts, so as to allow a temporary therapeutic resumption of communication. (*See* Ch.13:VIIIF3; and Cautions, in later section of this chapter, Ch.12: VIIIF4).

Establishing contact in judicious fashion thus can assist in initiating a therapeutic collaboration. This approach as an emergency adjunct in treatment is illustrated in the following instance. This case is also interesting because of the symbolism and the unusual completeness of the Dissociative Reaction which was brought out under the amytal. [*See* section on Double Personality, Ch.13:IX.] It further illustrates the relationship and overlapping which can be encountered in the Conversions and Dissociations.

Case 142

Conversion Aphonia and Double Personality in a Marked Dissociative Reaction

(1) *Temporary dissociated voice allows communication during amytal interviews*

A twenty-four-year-old patient was first seen fifteen days after the sudden onset of complete aphonia. He exhibited certain mannerisms which, along with other data, suggested the presence of emotional conflicts in a homosexual area. Communication by writing was labored, difficult, tedious, and in general very unsatisfactory. On the eighteenth day, following careful evaluation of the factors involved, a series of therapeutic interviews was begun. These interviews were continued at regular intervals under amytal of hypnotic depth, until permanent restoration of vocal function was effected several weeks later. In the meantime a temporary dissociated voice permitted communication during the interview sessions. An *Emergency Analytic-Bridge* had been established successfully.

In his interviews, "I", the voice, represented the conscience or superego. This markedly dissociated aspect of his personality spoke of Fred (the ego, and the patient) as of another person. This degree of personality dissociation is unusual. The following are greatly abbreviated verbatim extracts from recordings. They provide interesting glimpses into the dynamics of the psychopathology, in which the homosexual conflict was very important.

(2) *Superego speaks; Help sought*

"I'm Fred's voice . . . We were together . . . Maybe you would call me his conscience. Fred needs somebody; he needs help . . . I can leave him any time I damn well please. He would be all right if only he wasn't queer. Things would be damn much simpler for both of us . . . Hell, I could help him along. I think I could make something out of that guy. But, Heaven knows he's queer all through! . . . He wandered around from flower, to flower, to flower, to flower, and back again. Boy, he's been getting it . . . The more he can find to do the better he likes it. Frankly, he's worried about it. Real deep, deep down, inside, he is. I know he is . . . Someday somebody's going to tap him on the shoulder and say 'O.K.' and that will be that — especially in the service . . .

"I want you to get him over this business of being queer. I had him under control until a couple of months ago. You talk him out of it. He's reading the right books. He'll know what you're talking about . . . I won't go back to him! . . .".

(3) Precipitating events

The "voice" went on at one point to relate in detail how and why he had left Fred. This had followed a night of uncontrolled promiscuous homosexual behavior of every variety, which was consciously totally unacceptable. Then later, "It was the stinkingest thing I've ever seen — the four of them . . . I just can't stand the stuff he's been pulling. Maybe one occasionally — but never three. Three guys at a time, doctor; that's completely disgusting. That's why I left! . . . Sinking lower, and lower, and lower! . . . I just can't take it any more . . . He's queer straight through. That's why I left him . . .

"I can't have him doing this. It's the only way I can teach him a lesson . . . The thing wrong with Fred is he's queer as a nine-dollar bill. The way I figure it, doctor, if he can't *talk* to the other queers, he can't get them! Fred knows I'm not talking, but he doesn't know why . . . I've told him to behave better a thousand times. He knows I want him to change. I've been pleading with him to change for ages, but he won't change, and as long as he won't change, I ain't coming back . . .

"We were sitting at the hotel and I had been kicking around in my mind what he had pulled, and I just decided right then it's going to be a choice. Either he was insane, or he's queer as he wants to be. And I just figured I would give him his choice, so I left. And I'm not coming back until he gives up this business of being a queer . . . When he gives it up maybe I'll be back . . . You can see my point, doctor. So long as he runs around with these guys in the service like he does, I've had it. What if he should get picked up by somebody? . . .

"All right, you must see my point. If I'm going to make anything out of him, what the hell, I can't have him running around getting himself a dishonorable discharge. Sure, let him go ahead and get in trouble . . . Remember, I've got to live with him the rest of his life, too. The rest of our life we've got to be together, doctor, whether I talk or not, we've got to be together . . . I'll just go right ahead and let him get a dishonorable discharge . . . Do you think he'll be able to get himself into a decent school? Do you think he'll be able to get into a dance act or into a decent voice school? Get into a good radio station, television, or anything else like he's always wanted. He had a lot of promise and some recognition. Not a chance unless he changes, and I'm not coming back unless he does! . . .".

C. PSYCHODYNAMICS OF THE DISSOCIATION (AND APHONIA).—Gradually, however, in the foregoing instance, "he" became reconciled to "coming back". Vocal function returned, the dissociation was resolved, and therapy on a more conventional basis could begin and now proceed more rapidly.

In these necessarily far too brief excerpts, taken from the fascinating recordings made of the therapeutic interviews, one can see how the loss of the power of speech attempted to cope with and defensively resolve to some degree deep-seated conflicts over homosexual drives. The aphonia (1) acted to prevent further homosexual activity, (2) punished the bad part (Fred), (3) eliminated or lessened any continued danger or further consequences from the important weight of personal and social disapproval, and (4) reinforced repression through the focus of attention on the absence of speech and resulting complications, and away from the poorly repressed, consciously abhorrent homosexual strivings which threatened to escape control.

Finally, (5) the symptom was most self-punitive and masochistic, since the sacrifice of the voice was quite a loss indeed. Fred's voice was his most valuable asset. It was cherished personally, and was required professionally as he was an excellent singer. The precipitating event was the sexual *smorgäsbord*, although the conflicts had been present in serious form for a long time, with attempted handling by conscious suppressive efforts, as well as by repression [*see also* footnote, Section V E*2*].

Construction of an *Emergency Analytic-Bridge* in this instance safely and effectively allowed successful and earlier therapeutic intervention. Without it this possibly might not even have proved feasible.

D. PARTIAL APHONIA FOLLOWS TRAUMA.—Not all instances progress to a complete aphonia. In the following instance the degree of loss of vocal function was considerable, but not complete. It was accompanied by a marked conversion cough. This instance also illustrates the kind of situation in which a traumatic incident provided an important peg for the attachment of the conversion symptoms, and also served as a final impetus [*See* Peg Concept, p. 464 (*Case 92*); Ch.10:VIIID*2* and Ch.13:VIIE*1*].

Surrender of vocal function, as was true in the previous case, was of particular significance to this patient.

Case 143

Conversion Vocal Loss with a Post-traumatic Onset

(1) *A rigid plan of life*
A fifteen-year-old boy was referred for psychiatric consultation because he had become unable to speak above a whisper. Upon examination he was pleasant enough, but his overall attitude was bland and distant. He was willing to answer questions, but had little to say spontaneously. The present episode of speech limitation was the longest of several since a reported head injury sixteen months earlier. Undue significance had been earlier attached in error to this event as the etiologic basis for his symptoms.

This young man had had his entire career outlined for some years. He was going to Dartmouth, and then through Harvard Law School. After a preceptorship, he would become a successful trial lawyer, as was his father. There were two noteworthy facts about all this. First, the unusually complete and settled degree of his planning was far beyond that of his compeers. Second, he did not have the scholastic ability to maintain his aspirations. Despite rather prodigious efforts at school, he was barely able to make average grades. In fact, even the maintenance of these had begun to pose a considerable problem. Together with certain other major difficulties, his situation in life had reached an impasse at about the time when his illness formally began.

(2) *Undue significance assigned to trauma*
Sixteen months earlier he had slipped and fallen while playing ball and suffered a gash in his head which "dazed" him. Although the wound healed readily, his symptoms increased. He began to suffer from headaches and visual disturbances. Several times his voice "failed". However, the trauma was not responsible for his illness. He had a number of definite conversion character defenses prior to this time. These had become inadequate and his symptoms came on. The traumatic incident had provided a convenient peg for the attachment of his conversion symptoms. (We shall consider further the relationship of traumatic events to symptoms when we discuss the *Neuroses Following Trauma* in Chapter 14. Conversion symptoms frequently have such an onset.)

His concerned parents consulted several specialists who were puzzled by his symptoms and could not account for them. Now he had what was for him an acceptable physical cause, to fall back upon in his inability to keep up with his group scholastically and in sports.

(3) *Faulty-Identification Concept illustrated*
The whispering remnant of his voice was high pitched and feminine. His marked repetitive cough was also high pitched. Another patient

once remarked on the "irritating cough of that woman in the waiting room". This was significant because of conflicts over his (unconscious) masculine-feminine identifications with both parents. The *Concept of Faulty-Identification* [Ch.13:VE3] is illustrated here, in the laying of foundations for further emotional conflicts via this route.

His fixed decision to be a lawyer like father was really conflictual, and far from being completely satisfying. The vocal loss was a deprivation of the very attribute most needed for success as a trial lawyer.

(4) Therapy ultimately accepted

His secondary defenses were very strong. He found my voice unpleasant, my office arrangements distasteful. My (infrequent) questions gave him a headache. If I asked no questions, he would not talk. He — actually his psychologic defenses — felt threatened by me, and he was convinced "no doctor could help" him.

He refused all professional help, largely on the basis of finding it or the therapist unsuitable. The cough slowly improved spontaneously. after eight months vocal function also improved. Three years later external events lessened somewhat his level of conflict. He became more accepting of the idea of an emotional-therapeutic self-study, and upon further recommendation by his family doctor, a series of psychotherapeutic interviews proved of considerable benefit. He gradually became able to modify his high level of self-expectation to a point more consistent with his realistic abilities and his underlying, genuine interests. This had also become gradually more feasible, as his parents became more accepting, and genuinely more willing to allow him independent self-determination.

4. *Conversion Reactions and Schizophrenia; Bleuler's Dissociation*

A. DISTINCTION AT TIMES NARROW.—The complete dissociation present in our earlier *Case 142* illustrates the considerable degree of compartmentalization of the self which is emotionally possible. As one sees the splitting apart of the aspects of the personality in this fashion, the psychopathology of schizophrenia comes to mind. Let us note in passing the dividing lines which exist between neuroses and a complete psychotic break. These are sometimes finely drawn.

The patient in *Case 142* appeared clinically at times to be a hair's-breadth from a schizophrenic psychosis. Further, it should be noted that the presence of schizophrenia does not rule out the operation of conversion mechanisms. Physiologic Conversions are common enough in psychotic reactions. The experienced institutional psychiatrist also sees all manner of scattered bits of Psychologic Conversion in the form of various neurotic symptoms and patterns of reactions. Noble has discussed Conversion (hysterical) manifestations in schizophrenia. Fairbairn laid considerable emphasis on the close relationship between Conversion (hysteria) and schizophrenia.

B. TYPE OF DISSOCIATION DIFFERENT.—It should be noted that the personality splitting differs in the two conditions, however. In the Conversion Reactions affect and ideation are more or less proportional. The splitting when it occurs is of major aspects of the personality, as dramatically illustrated in *Case 142,* or of less dramatic internal factors (for example, function and its perception, or function and its usual employment) as in other types of symptom formation.

In schizophrenia the splitting is between affect and ideation, in which the affect is more or less inappropriate; perhaps merely flattened. In addition there are disorders of thought, reasoning, logic, abnormal mental content, and so on in the Schizophrenic Reaction. In recognition of his contributions, the author has proposed [Ch.13:IIE*1* and *Table 34,* II C2] that schizophrenic dissociation be termed *Bleuler's Dissociation.*

C. POSSIBLE PSYCHOTIC PROGRESSION.—Rarely, cases are seen in which the conversion defenses prove inadequate or break down under new assaults, and a frank schizophrenic psychosis evolves. This is a potential danger when the sudden, forceful removal of major symptoms is attempted. Kolb reported an observation concerning the possible prodromal relationship of the Conversion Reaction to schizophrenia. He cautioned, "A number of individuals have come to us with a conversion [hysterical] symptom screening a basic schizophrenic process. The attempts to suddenly reduce the symptoms in these circumstances may precipitate an overt Schizophrenic Reaction." *

5. Self Punitive Aspects; Conversion Symptoms as Rage-Equivalents

Reference was made earlier to the frequent self-punitive aspects to be uncovered in the therapeutic study of conversion symptoms. In *Case 142,* words can hardly describe the suffering this man went through. Through his loss, he "sought" to secure for himself penance and retribution. He thoroughly condemned his homosexual orientation and activity. The resulting behavior was to at least part of him as intolerable as it might be expected to be to the most condemning of ultramoralists.

Loewenstein has discussed some of the aspects of self-punishment in conversion attacks. He presented the interesting case of a lawyer in whom the conversion attacks were what we might term *rage-equivalents.*† These represented the need he felt for a public confession of certain traits which he regarded as unmanly and feminine. The function of self-punishment in this case was successfully followed out through the inhibition of his professional activity. As a result, he had strong impulses to abandon his law practice altogether.

The self-punitive aspects of conversion symptoms are illustrated in a number of the accompanying clinical case illustrations. This is an important factor in dynamics of the symptomatology. It is part of the tribute exacted by a punitive superego in securing the conversion endogain.

E. DYSKINESIAS AND ANESTHESIAS

1. Disturbances of Coordination and Motor Activity

A. MAJOR SOMATIC CONVERSION SYMPTOMS LESS IN VOGUE.—The dyskinesias are disturbances of movement(s) in the voluntary muscular system.

---

* *See also* the later reference under *Treatment* in this chapter. *Also* earlier reference on p. 556 concerning Freud's rapid dissolution of a major phobic defense. The sudden removal of any vital psychologic defense can lead to psychotic illness.

Any attempts at such removal should always be considered with great caution and circumspection. This is in accord with a *Concept of Symptom-Exchange Hazard* [Ch.12:VIIIF4].

† *See also* earlier Concept of Anger as an Anxiety-Equivalent [pp. 19, 102, 111, and [Ch.14:VIID*1*]. At times also depression can accompany conversion, and a Conversion Reaction may rarely represent a *depressive-equivalent* [pp. 143, 155, 191, and 499].

Included are the Somatic Conversion symptoms of tics, tremors, posturing, catalepsy, speech disturbances, bizarre gaits, choreiform-like movements (especially in children), torticollis, (at times) "writer's cramp", muscular spasms, conversion contractures, and pseudo-epilepsy. The presence of conversion (hysterical) personality defenses, evidence of underlying emotional conflict, and an absence of organic neurologic dysfunction are characteristics in these types of reaction. As with other conversion symptoms, they are a defense against awareness of disowned (unconscious) strivings or wishes.

Paralyses are encountered wherever major Somatic Conversions are to be found. They can affect any motor (voluntary muscular) area. [*See Case 139* and Ch.12:VC*3;* VIC*2;* VIIIB*2.*] These can be stoutly defended in highly self-defeating fashion. *Case 54,* p. 266 illustrates such an instance of Conversion Paralysis, in which contractures followed the continued rejection of physical and psychic measures. As noted, Somatic Conversions may bear little or no relation to innervation but follow the individual's "view" of function and structure [*see also* discussion in relation to Breuer's Dissociation in Chapter 13:IIE*1*(5)].

This group has seemingly been losing its cultural vogue. These are the major motor symptoms of Somatic Conversion. They are to be observed less frequently today than a hundred years ago.

B. UNCONSCIOUS SEXUAL EXPRESSION IN A GAIT DISTURBANCE.—In the following case, we see an instance of conversion gait disturbance. The gait disturbance was an unconscious expression of this young woman's consciously disowned and abhorrent provocativeness. At the same time it directed attention to her legs and body. The self-punitive aspects were partly in the handicap and limitation which resulted from her symptom. Conversion interferences with walking are also illustrated in *Cases 139* and *140.*

Case 144

A Conversion Disturbance of Gait

A strikingly attractive young woman of nineteen developed a rather disabling and bizarre gait. Outwardly prim and prudish, she complained that men were "beasts". Prior to the onset of her symptoms, she described how when she would walk down the street, men would stare, laugh, whistle, offer advances, and sometimes make lewd remarks. She seemingly was quite unaware that she had dressed in revealing and sexually alluring clothes, that she walked in a sexually provocative manner, and that she frequently promenaded alone down unsavory streets. Her symptoms developed shortly after a traumatic and frightening incident in which she was followed down a dark street by a "drunken monster", who "mouthed foul epithets" at her and "threatened rape".

Her symptoms had made it impossible for her to walk alone at night any longer. While it thus protected her from certain hazards incident to her unwittingly exhibitionist behavior, on the other hand, by virtue of her gait being so bizarre and dramatic, it also quite certainly directed attention to her legs and body. Unconscious identification of the "drunken" monster with the drunken stepfather of her childhood had played a contributory role in the onset of the symptoms. An *acting-out* of fantasies of the drunken rambling of a street walker, and punishment for secret prostitute wishes were unearthed in analysis. Treatment in this case was quite successful.

C. BASES IN CONFLICT OVER HOSTILITY AND SEXUALITY.—The most frequent bases of the conflictual unconscious impulses are hostile, or sexual, or both. This is also illustrated in a case reported by Kardiner in which an arm tic symbolically represented both "murderous" impulses and also forbidden masturbatory activity. Certain other conversion symptoms may express symbolically the disowned wish. This is illustrated in the coitus-like movements often unwittingly expressed in conversion convulsions. These conflicts are intolerable because of their potential for anxiety through and accompanying conscious awareness.*

Other symptoms may express inhibition or denial, as in some of the conversion paralyses. Usually a tic represents a symbolic compromise between inhibition and gratification of the censored, forbidden wish. The basic conflict is traceable in its roots to the Oedipal situation, or in the author's view beyond it, to the Oral Conflict [see also Section VIE1]. The hidden motivations and bases for conversion symptomatology bear such a major relation to the external manifestation that we may recall our Iceberg Analogy. [See p. 444.]

Spasmodic torticollis on a functional basis in males is frequently occasioned by sexual conflict. At times these cases are associated with sexual impotence, in which the "stiff neck" represents an interesting displacement from below upwards. Fenichel noted that instances of conversion paralysis may be accompanied in seemingly paradoxical fashion by an increased tonus. Elements of these contrasting findings can illustrate the opposing elements of emotional conflict. These conflicting findings also can serve symbolically as a distorted substitute for sexual action, in addition to representing insurance against it. Dyskinesias likewise can represent a disguised "acting out" of the forbidden impulse, as well as preventive activity.

D. CONVERSION CONVULSIONS.—Conversion convulsions may more or less simulate epilepsy as noted earlier, depending sometimes on how much the patient "knows" about a typical epileptic attack! However, recall that conversion patients are less likely to injure themselves. They usually have an audience, and they seldom soil themselves. These convulsions seem to be far more infrequent today. They may externally but unwittingly represent the (unconscious) wish for coitus. When expressed in such a distorted and disguised form, the continued absence of such disowned interests from conscious awareness can be better maintained.

This phenomenon was undoubtedly a frequent one in past decades. It is still likely to be encountered today under appropriate initiating circumstances, and where a predisposing diathesis exists. Dissociative aspects are of the Janet type [Ch.12:IIIA4 and Ch.13:IIE1(6)].

The following instance represented the Conversion of homosexual excitement into a pseudo-convulsion, as another, rarer psychodynamic basis for this phenomenon. The activity symbolically expressed a young man's level of stimulation in a disguised and acceptable form, and at the same time

---

* Emotional conflicts generate anxiety. They are universal, contributing a cogent reason for our recognition of this era as the *Age of Anxiety* [pp. 5 and 477 and Ch.13:IA2].

inhibited further response or participation. The two major aspects of the emotional conflict were represented.

Case 145

Pseudo-Convulsions

A 16-year-old boy boarding at a local preparatory school was referred for evaluation as a consequence of repeated "convulsions". These were not typical of any organic condition. This lad complained that on many occasions other boys in his cottage had crawled in bed with him as soon as the lights went out. He was afraid to go to sleep for fear of having a convulsion.

On repeated occasions he had been just about to go off to sleep when he would be observed to break into heaving sobs with a regular contractions of his shoulders and body. He described these episodes as "convulsions". He never lost consciousness nor bladder control and never injured himself. He was always conscious of what was going on around him. His "convulsions" would be precipitated by someone starting to wrestle with him in bed or by someone coming over and sitting on the side of his bed. An attack might also occur if he mistakenly believed that someone was near his bed in the dark.

In therapy he became able to recognize the presence of homosexual feelings and his great conflicts over them. He became better able to cope with these and other problems. The "convulsions" stopped and his social and scholastic adjustments improved substantially.

E. SYMBOLISM IN MOVEMENT RESTRICTIONS.—All manner of movement restrictions are possible. These can express interesting symbolic meanings. The following example is illustrative.

Case 146

"Looking backward makes me sick"

A 46-year-old businessman in intensive therapy found rather suddenly one morning to his surprise and dismay that he couldn't turn his head appreciably to either side. This restricted his looking around. He could not look backwards. When he sought harder to do so he became dizzy and nauseated.

This symptom had its onset at a juncture in therapy when we were actively engaged in "looking back" — into a painful past and past events. This was both an actual and a figurative looking backwards. He in turn had become sick at looking backwards, both literally and symbolically! Elucidation of this symptom led to its rapid dissolution.

2. Symptoms of Sensory Loss in Conversion Reactions

A. LACK OF CORRESPONDENCE WITH NERVE DISTRIBUTION.—Sensory findings may include all varieties of disturbances of sensation. In the first group there may be anesthesia, hypesthesia, or hyperesthesia, and various kinds of paresthesias. In a second group disturbances of special-sense reception may occur, involving vision, hearing, and very rarely the senses of taste or smell. These are illustrative of the sensory symptoms of the Somatic Conversion Reactions.

Of the first group, the anesthesias are the most frequently seen. Any area may be affected, but the findings often do not correspond with the anatomic nerve distribution. The location of sensation loss may shift. The anesthesia also may end abruptly, for example, in circular fashion around an extremity, producing the characteristic "glove" or "stocking" pattern. On the trunk, also, it may terminate exactly in the mid-line, or perhaps extend too far across. Such clinical findings are not supported by the anatomic nerve distribution. A knowledge of innervation is essential for diagnosis, but in many cases the differentiation from organic conditions can be rather readily made.

The role of suggestibility can be very important in conversion sensory loss. The development of surface anesthesia in the highly suggestible patient may be brought on unwittingly by the physician even during the examination. A colleague recently told the author about treating a case of total surface anesthesia. Conversion vaginal anesthesia is sometimes seen. A colleague recently commented on the frequency of frigidity in women in our culture. It was his opinion that 60 per cent of this would be attributable to the conversion dissociation of vaginal sensation. Elsewhere we have noted the sharp reversal of previously required inhibitions on sex and sexual activity which is expected to transpire upon marriage. Needless to say, this often does not readily follow. Difficulties persisting here can contribute substantially to the foregoing as well.

B. DEFENSIVELY INTENDED SURRENDER OF AWARENESS.—Sensory loss symbolically represents a partial unconscious surrender or loss of this aspect of perception; a defensive shutting out of an aspect of awareness. Not being able to feel says in effect that one cannot, one must not, one dare not, or one does not wish to feel. Awareness must be shut out for hidden reasons. We shall have more to say shortly about the symbolic meanings of anesthesia on a conversion basis.

Conversion fainting is not infrequent and may occasionally offer problems in the differential diagnosis, from possible organic sources. Conversion fainting is a gross kind of sensory and perceptive loss. For some persons it represents an effective way to interrupt awareness of some aspect of highly disturbing reality, a temporary respite. Fainting in the presence of accident, death, or upon a strong sexual stimulus can represent a protective denial of the underlying hidden personal hostile impulses or sexual interests. It carries the defensively intended *partial* surrender of awareness in the conversion sensory anesthesias much further. Here the surrender is at least temporarily complete. Fainting will receive further attention in the following chapter.

In the second group involving cranial-nerve sensory function we find some of the most severe manifestations of conversion. It is evident, for example, that as noted already, the most serious kind of emotional conflict and powerful symbolism must underlie the conversion mechanism to which, for example, the vital function of vision is sacrificed. Fortunately, complete conversion blindness is now rare. Conversion constriction of the visual fields (that is, tunnel vision) also occurs, but is to be carefully distinguished from a rather rare form of congenitally-determined and slowly progressive, degenerative and irreversible retinitis, which eventually leads to blindness. The typical conversion indifference is usually present in the emotionally-based cases. It can be considered almost one criterion for the establishment of a diagnosis of a Somatic Conversion Reaction.

C. SELECTIVE INATTENTION; SELECTIVE HEARING; SECONDARY RESTRIC-
TIONS.—Hearing difficulties, partly or solely on an emotional basis, are
relatively frequent. Not all of these evolve through the mechanism of conversion. Diminished hearing can have less deep-seated factors entering
into it. These include such interesting and more or less unwittingly operative components as *selective inattention* and *emotional blocking*. These
operate defensively to secure the avoidance and exclusion of unpleasant
and painful data. They may evolve as defensively-intended patterns of
reaction early in life. In some degree they are not infrequent. In childhood
they can fit in with our *Profitable Patterns Concept* [p. 477 and Ch.13:
VIB].

Fenichel pointed out that the dynamics are similar in the conversion surrender of the special senses. There are elements of regressive retreat and
withdrawal. "I cannot hear", or "I have difficulty in hearing", really says
in effect, "Hearing represents some kind of threat or danger; therefore I do
not dare to hear". Its loss also has elements of inhibition or punishment.*
Further, one often fails to hear, or is unable to hear, that which one really
wishes to avoid hearing, or wants not to hear. This we might label as
Selective Hearing. What is heard may also be modified or distorted in order
for it to conform with one's unconscious wishes.

Sensory loss can therefore represent a defensive cutting off of sensations.
An important part of this protection lies in what is suggested for convenience
we term the *Secondary Restrictions*. For instance, the associations which
could follow the ordinary and unimpeded sensory perception *might* lead
into or toward the repressed intolerable impulses or ideas. Since the first
is cut off, the latter are also thereby cut off!

This is a Secondary Restriction, following after the primary restriction
(of the sensory perception). Emotionally this can comprise an important
defense to the otherwise hard-pressed ego.

F. PSYCHOSOMATIC ILLNESSES

Space does not allow the opportunity to review the many Physiologic
Conversion symptoms and syndromes. These functional conversions can
affect every organ and every system. This is indeed a major subject in
itself.

There are many interrelationships between the physical, the physiologic,
the pathologic, and the neuroses as outlined in our present discussion. Additional consideration is both well warranted and indicated. The reader is
accordingly referred to the several excellent sources extant, as for example
the text by Weiss and English (*see* Bibliography).

---

* Recall in *Case 142* that Fred's voice was something very special to him. It was
one of his most precious attributes. He was a talented singer, who had done professional entertaining. He believed that people were attracted to him by his voice
and his singing. Therefore it also represented to him by extension a threat, that is,
it attracted men to him.

Hence, its "surrender" not only sought to lessen the threat but also, in view of its
special importance and value to him, the surrender was a tremendous loss in self-
punitive fashion. This was in partial retribution for gratifying his disapproved sexual
impulses, and for having had them.

G. CONCLUDING REMARKS

It would be possible greatly to augment this discussion by an exhaustive presentation of the multitude of sensory, motor, or psychologic symptoms which are seen alone or in various combinations in Somatic Conversion and in Physiologic Conversion. Since many of these manifestations could in themselves be the basis for prolonged study, the effort here has simply been to outline some of the more important and/or interesting findings. Symptoms which appear in Conversion Reactions always have a hidden symbolic meaning. In some instances it may be possible to make some speculations as to the meaning. However, the real significance of the symptom can only be worked out through psychotherapeutic investigation.

How this may be accomplished is illustrated in some of the accompanying case studies. The personality make-up, the setting in which the symptoms occur (including the interpersonal), the presumptive evidence of unconscious motives behind the symptoms, and their symbolic significance are the positive criteria on which the diagnosis of Somatic Conversion Reaction (or Conversion hysteria) is based. This is the correct positive basis for diagnosis, as opposed to the negative approach to diagnosis through exclusion.

The significance and role of anxiety might be further stressed in the onset of conversion symptoms. Actually, anxiety plays a crucial role in initiating symptoms and the threat of anxiety, likewise in maintaining the concealment of their bases. At times there is a clear relationship between the time and circumstances of onset and an A.A.A. [pp. 89 ff.]

It becomes apparent from our discussion that many symptoms occur through a process of Somatic Conversion. Many symptoms also come about or are largely contributed to by the analogous process of Physiologic Conversion. It should be clearly noted, however, that by no means do all of the physical and physiological symptoms of emotional origin occur on a conversion basis. As will be recalled from the prior discussion in earlier chapters, many symptoms are the more direct expression or effect of anxiety and tension [see also Table 1, p. 20]. These numerous more direct expressions and effects of anxiety, tension, and emotional stress can appear in any body region, organ, or system. It may be usefully borne in mind that the greater the defensive success of a given conversion symptom, the less motivation toward therapy. This bears out our concept of the *Inverse Ratio of Symptom-Success to Motivation Toward Therapy* [pp. 9–10, 298, and Ch.13:VIIIF1].

VI. DYNAMICS AND PATHOGENESIS

A. THE CONVERSION ENDOGAIN

1. Formulations Apply to Somatic and to Physiologic Conversions

The major symptoms of the Conversion Reactions, with which we are mainly concerned here, are Somatic Conversions. The symbolism in the Physiologic Conversion Reactions is not necessarily different, although it can be more involved, deeper, and still more difficult to unravel. Some of the other distinctions have been noted or inferred earlier.

We must unfortunately direct the main stream of our attention away from this latter large and important group. While some of the psychodynamic formulations already included, and to which we shall add a few pertinent points, are also applicable directly or tangentially also to the Physiologic Conversions, we shall focus our attention more toward the Somatic Conversions, as included in the older category of hysteria.

In Somatic Conversion, the consciously intolerable impulse or idea becomes transmuted into a symbolic form of bodily expression. As noted, conversion symptoms are a disguised kind of "somatic language" for the unconscious. They attempt unconsciously to resolve conflict, through the symbolic and disguised gratification of consciously disowned needs. Often there are simultaneously expressed symbolic elements of their control, inhibition, or denial. A self-punitive element is frequently present. A clinical illustration of the Endogain and the Epigain in Conversion Reaction was offered earlier [pp. 70–73 and *Case 11*].

2. Maintaining Repression

In the neuroses symptoms are formed to help maintain repression, that is, to keep forbidden and consciously disowned impulses out of conscious awareness. This usually proves to be the self-defeating route through which the person concerned unconsciously seeks to avoid the anxiety and "danger" which he expects would result from awareness. In line with these formulations, we can often observe the conversion of inadequately repressed impulses into specific somatic symptoms to occur when the ability for conscious control is lacking (or doubted) and they threaten to break through into conscious awareness. Immediate somatic expression takes the place of acting them out in reality, and prevents a "break" with reality.

At several points the author has referred to the hidden psychologic purposes of the Conversion Reactions. These are part of the conversion endogain. They are listed in *Table 32*.

Table 32

The Psychologic Purposes of the Conversion Reactions;
The Conversion Endogain

The symptoms of the Conversion Reactions may be regarded as representing an expression into bodily language of the emotional conflict. In the Somatic Conversion this expression is made somatically into physical symptotms. It is made in a way that is often hidden, devious, distorted, condensed, or symbolic.

This tabulation has considerable applicability to neurotic reactions generally. However, some of these applications become increasingly obscure in certain of the neuroses. Several may be present simulttaneously, even though they are apparently contradictory. They constitute part of the *conversion endogain,* that is, the primary gain of the illness.

Conversion symptoms may attempt in disguised fashion to serve one or more of the following important psychologic purposes:

1. Symbolic and disguised outward gratification or expression, of the consciously disowned wish or impulse.

2. Denial of the existence of the intolerable idea.
3. Inhibition or prevention of possible overt action in the direction of its possible attainment. (Protection against its expression, or defense against attempting its gratification.)
4. A self-punitive purpose, often in masochistic fashion. This in given instances of Conversion Reactions, is not entirely unrelated to what we have termed *visceral masochism,* in relation to the Hygeiaphrontic Reactions [p. 493]. It is levied against the self for:
   a. The possession of the forbidden impulse.
   b. Gratifications in earlier years.
   c. Retribution for its current gratification, even though such gratification is symbolic.
5. Maintaining or reenforcement of Repression.
6. Outward partial and often figurative-symbolic expression and "discharge" of otherwise hidden and consciously disowned impulses and wishes. This leads to our earlier view of the *symptom language* of the conversion manifestation. In our discussion of Hygeiaphrontis [*see* pp. 473 and 484], we learned of some of the analogous figurative literal and symbolic meanings of certain figures of speech and how these can carry over into "physical" symptoms.
7. Distance Maintenance. Preoccupation with symptoms (see *Concept of Relationship-Distance* and pp. 330; 348; 398; 506) can contribute to the attenuation of painful and feared interpersonal relations.

B. THE MECHANISMS IN CONVERSION REACTIONS

1. Systematic Analysis Required

A. DISGUISE MUST KEEP PACE WITH PERCEPTIVE ABILITY.—As outlined in *Table 36,* these hidden, unconscious purposes constitute the conversion endogain. This is the primary gain of the clinical symptoms of the Conversion Reactions. We have already noted the fact that the substitute physical expression of the hidden conflict is always thoroughly disguised from ordinary perception. The nature of the disguise varies. It obviously has to be a good one to keep its secrets from the ordinary observer, as well as from the patient himself. As the sophistication and perceptiveness of the average potential observer, the person himself (and society) increases, so must the cleverness and concealing ability of the disguise! Recall the *Transparency Theory,* according to which the bases for a symptom dare not become too transparent to the patient or to others.

Conversion is the primary mechanism. In conjunction with the prerequisite *Repression* [*see* pp. 27–75 in the author's *Mental Mechanisms,* for a more definitive discussion of this basic dynamism], *Distortion, Symbolism, Avoidance, Displacement,* and some *Regression* are most frequently used. At times *Condensation* (overdetermination) takes place, in which two or more or perhaps many concepts are fused or condensed so that a single symbolic representation may serve. Representation may be by the opposite. *Displacement* from an original to a new object may add to the outward disguise. The reader may recall our view of the mental mechanisms generally as the psychic *First Line of Defense* [pp. 25, 343, and Ch. 13:IIE1].

Sequences may have their order rearranged, and further disguise may be effected through *Extension* or *Elaboration*. Multiple *Identification* [*see* pp. 118–168 in the author's previous work, *Mental Mechanisms*] may be present. As additional examples of this kind of disguise, the author would like to refer to Fenichel's pointing out how hunger can sometimes symbolize a displaced sexual hunger, and how anorexia can symbolize a denial. Conversion vomiting can similarly represent a rejection or denial of (for example, the fact of pregnancy, or of other aspects of one's life and experience) and also a rejection or denial of the *wish* for pregnancy.

B. SUGGESTION, DISSOCIATION AND IDENTIFICATION.—It is important to note that while the physical symptoms in Somatic Conversion perhaps most frequently conform to the parts of the body under voluntary control as stated earlier, this is a somewhat elastic line of demarcation. This might now be amended so as to also include those individually determined areas which are subject to influence by suggestion. Another way to outline them is to include the individual areas which are subject to influence under hypnotic influence.

The conversion patient is prone to *dissociate,* and to respond readily to appropriate *suggestion.* He often makes *identifications* on a grand scale. Sometimes these are mixed, faulty [Ch.13:VD4] or confused, as noted earlier [Ch. 12:VD3]. In so doing, he takes on the color of the envied one's personality. Along with this as punishment for real or subjectively overvalued transgressions, certain defects, however slight, in the envied one, may become magnified out of all proportion and may prove handicapping, discomforting, punitive, or even disabling to the conversion individual. One learns to understand the underlying psychodynamics of a given case of Somatic Conversion through the systematic analysis and interpretation of the "somatic language" which is thus expressed and employed, and of the needs which have led to the symptom elaboration.

2. Symbolic Gratification, Denial, Inhibition, and/or Compromise; Part-Reaction Concept

In partial recapitulation, anxiety is not so likely to be experienced consciously in the Conversion Reactions as we observed, for instance, in the Anxiety Reactions. In clinical practice actually, however, it is to be noted that an admixture of anxiety is not uncommon. Its presence may reflect: (1) the incompleteness of the repression, (2) the failure fully to bind the potential for anxiety through the symptom formation in accord with our *Incomplete Symptom-Defense Concept* [pp. 89, 189, 477], or (3) the failure sufficiently to achieve the sought-after endogain. In place of the subjective experiencing and expression of anxiety (in full or in part), a variety of physical symptoms appear. These symptoms serve as a defense against unconscious intolerable drives which threaten possible emergence into awareness. Recognition of the foregoing helps us better appreciate our earlier noted [p. 503] *Concept of* (emotional) *Symptoms as an Implied Preference.*

The symptoms symbolically express the underlying emotional conflict. Once already established they also unconsciously serve some more obvious or immediate gain to the patient. This is the *conversion epigain*. In other words, in the Conversion Reactions the emotional conflict is converted into symptoms. These unconsciously attempt to resolve the conflict through the *symbolic gratification* of a disguised wish, *the denial or inhibition of an intolerable* need, and/or a *symbolic compromise* [p. 118]. A conversion foundation or diathesis in the underlying character structure can be considered to be necessary.

Conversion symptom formation may be thought of as *dissociative* in nature. From this standpoint, one or more functions are split off, or dissociated. These would be called *Janet Dissociations* [Ch.13:IIC2; IIE1] after Pierre Janet. For example, the motor function of one arm is dissociated and lost and the arm becomes in consequence paralyzed, loses its movement ability. As noted later [Ch.13:IIF3] this constitutes a *Part-Reaction,* in distinction from certain other Dissociative Reactions, which are more properly to be regarded as, and termed, *Reactions-of-the Whole.*

It is important to note and to stress that this loss is of the function, *as this is unconsciously perceived by the individual concerned.* This capacity for the dissociation of a somatic motor or sensory function is a requisite for the formation of somatic conversion symptoms.

C. IMPORTANT FACETS IN DEVELOPMENT

1. Dependency Needs

It is important to keep in mind the significance of dependency needs as a motivating force in the development of a neurotic reaction, and in the perpetuation of conversion symptoms once established. As might be inferred from our introductory chapter on primary and secondary gains, the sought-after satisfaction of dependency needs becomes a major part of the conversion epigain, that is, the unconscious secondary gain of the symptom. In accord with the *Second Tenet of the Parental Role* [pp. 174 and 476], inordinate dependency needs are unlikely to be present when love, acceptance, and a secure home environment were provided.

Symptoms which develop in the Conversion Reactions are often regressive in character, usually rendering the patient more or less helpless and interfering with, or even depriving him of some of his usual skills. He accordingly requires some amount of being taken care of. This may progress in extreme cases to a state of nearly complete infantile helplessness and dependence. An instance of this was seen some years ago in the case of a thirty-two-year-old housewife. She had become so weak and helpless on a conversion basis that her husband literally had to carry her physically into the author's office for consultation. This level of severe progression is quite rare nowadays.

Finally, the symptom itself has definite symbolic meaning which can be determined in successful psychotherapeutic investigation, as illustrated in *Cases 52, 135, 141* and in the following case.

Case 144

Some of the Dynamics of a Conversion Gait Disturbance

(1) *Disruptive personally and in military life*

Following severe situational and personal emotional stress, a thirty-one-year-old major in military service developed a peculiar and rather dramatic type of "drum major" gait. In this, when walking he could not bend his knees. Needless to say, this interfered with his physical activity and military life. It resulted in his being the object of considerable unpleasant comment, joking, and ridicule by his colleagues. Despite the disruptive influence on his military career and personal life which the disability caused, the major was not greatly concerned about the interference with living which the symptom produced. He was quite certain that there was "something wrong" with his muscles or his ligaments, and so on.

To his seeming disappointment at that time, competent orthopedic consultants ruled out organic lesions. Intensive study on a deeper psychologic level produced some important data. It was eventually learned that the peculiar gait represented, on one level, a strong regressive and dependent wish to have a life similar to that of a boyhood companion. This boy had contracted polio, and as a consequence had developed in very early life a gait somewhat similar to that of the major. In accord with our *Theory of Antecedent Conflicts* [pp. 490–494], the earlier situation in effect had established an *emotional prototype*.

(2) *Identification and dependency needs*

The symptom attempted to provide substitute gratification. It also acted out a wish for identification. The boyhood friend had received a great deal of love, attention, warmth, and affection from his parents. This had increased following his illness. The major had never received this and had always envied his friend. Furthermore, the major had become mortally afraid of future combat experience. He could not, however, in any way tolerate fear or cowardice in himself. Herein the symptom also solved an otherwise insoluble and more immediate conflict. The symptom served the epigain (secondary gain) function of removing him from future combat. Because he had an illness and therefore could not fight, it preserved his self-esteem. In helping such a case, it is vital to maintain or to increase self-esteem, in accord with our *Self-Esteem-Maintenance Principle* [Ch.12:VD*1*; VIIIC2].

The major was released from military service. By the time he departed on terminal leave, his gait disturbance was 60–70 per cent improved.

2. *Predisposing Factors*

A. IMPORTANT ENVIRONMENTAL INFLUENCE.—What contributes to the development of the necessary psychologic foundation so that the initiating stress will be followed by conversion symptoms? We do not know the entire answer. Certainly, as earlier outlined [pp. 14, 84, 477, and Ch.12: VIIID2], the *Principle of Individual Appropriateness of Response* holds. We do know that cold and rejecting parents can contribute through their inability to provide necessary basic affection, warmth, security, and love. Some parents, because of needs of their own, may have to keep the child dependent and clinging, in a way that is responsible for an inability to renounce infantile needs. The resulting insecurity may result in character traits which perpetuate this indefinitely. Frequent in the early history of conversion persons is the "too-intense experience" [*see* Ch. 9] that is too intense for psychic mastery and integration-digestion to proceed. Primal scene exposure is frequent. So also are other types of emotionally-intense experiences, events witnessed, and even fantasies. The infant and child has no means adequately to discharge his excitement and emotional tension. The "too-intense stimulus" thus joins other S.E.H.C.s. [pp. 33–34].

It is also true that children who have parents with a conversion diathesis or traits are more likely to develop these themselves through all the complex mechanisms of Idealization, Identification, Incorporation, and the like which are involved in personality formation. These are parental carry-overs. Our comments are of course in accord with the Concept of Interpersonal Perpetuation [see also Section VA3 and pp. 291, 334, 404, 479, and Case 90, pp. 454–5 and Case 102, pp. 487–9].

Literally, any development which hampers maturation may favor establishment of the conversion predisposition. Inadequate or poorly adjusted home and school environments and disturbed interfamily relationships can be predisposing factors.

B. INSECURE PEOPLE MORE VULNERABLE.—Insecure people are more vulnerable to the buffetings of life. Their psychologic structure has been unable to develop a sufficiently strong foundation to withstand the vicissitudes that fate can bring. They lack the resources adequately to cope with environmental stresses and with situational trauma. They are more subject to symptom evolvement in conjunction with the S.E.H.C. and S.E.H.A. Their feelings may vary, as the reed does with the north or south wind. Insecurity augments immaturity.

The major symptoms of Somatic Conversion (Conversion hysteria) are found particularly in young people and children. [See earlier reference, Section IVA2]. Some of our answers might conceivably be augmented by more scientific study of the child-parent relationship, particularly in the years when this is fresh at hand and more accessible. Perhaps a reader will be so stimulated as to undertake this very interesting area of research.

C. CASE ILLUSTRATIONS.—Walker reported two cases of girls who suffered from an inability to walk, which was on a conversion basis. Their ages were thirteen and eleven years, with the duration of their difficulties four months and twelve months respectively. As factors in psychogenesis, Walker listed: (1) rejection by parents, (2) loss of a love object, (3) a threat to security, and (4) a lack of the means of gratifying childhood goals. Asher reported the case of a twenty-year-old girl with a paralyzed right arm which developed in conjunction with an obscure illness. The importance of suggestion was stressed in this case, in that the symptom developed following the patient's mother telling her she had "creeping paralysis".

The following case is summarized to suggest some of the dynamics of another kind of conversion symptom. This is a case of globus hystericus [Ch.12:VD2]. This manifestation is a more or less persistent conversion symptom, in which there is the disturbing subjective sensation of a lump in the throat. This case also illustrates the concurrent presence of phobic manifestations.

Case 145

Globus Hystericus

The patient was a twenty-four-year-old married woman, with the presenting symptom of globus hystericus. The onset of her difficulty was shortly after her marriage, while she was playing cards with a pregnant friend, whom the patient had strongly admired and envied.

From early childhood the patient had repressed strong strivings to become pregnant and to have a baby. The prohibited wish was defended against by the careful avoidance, by the patient, of any substances which she unconsciously feared might "contaminate" her. She became panicky if she was in the same room with an individual who sneezed or coughed. She carefully scrubbed the bathtub and the toilet seat before using either. Dirt, dust, "germs", and so on were feared in phobic fashion. Under the sway of her unconscious infantile oral sexual theories (in which impregnation took place via the mouth), the patient paid particular attention to her mouth, throat, and gastrointestinal tract.

Accordingly, the "wrong things" must not enter her mouth. Care was taken to eat food that was unpolluted. She thought of her mouth as the most sensitive part of her body. She was frigid in intercourse, with a relative genital anesthesia.

Analysis of the *globus hystericus* eventually revealed the patient's unconscious and magical primitive wish for an oral pregnancy. Identification with her envied pregnant friend had been prominent. There was a displacement of genital sensation from below upwards. Punishment for her forbidden orality was provided by the limitation and suffering. In addition, there were numerous pregenital fantasies woven into and expressed by this symptom.

Difficulty in swallowing [*dysphagia;* Section VD2] is seen on a conversion basis. It can be the symbolic expression for several less than conscious meanings. It can be merely verbal and a figurative expression: "I just can't swallow that" (a situation, person, and so on). This can "progress" to represent a conversion which becomes the identical, but literal expression of the same feeling, in which swallowing is actually difficult, but the conscious connection is lost. Herein it indicates this kind of a literal reaction to a situation.

Finally, there is the *literal-symbolic expression.* A patient reported her difficulty in drinking milk, which she "just couldn't swallow". Analysis eventually revealed that this really stood for certain aspects of her relationship with her mother, which she just "couldn't swallow". The milk was a symbolic representation, replacing something which seemed better and safer if repressed. This is the literal-symbolic expression of an affect whose real object can thus be kept unconscious [*see also* earlier *Psychic-Distaste Concept, Case 86,* p. 418].

3. Symptoms may Develop as Emotion (Affect) Equivalents

Clinical experience and observation points out that the conversion patient experiences large amounts of emotion. Further, much of this is unpleasant and painful. It is often a subjective ordeal. Small wonder that these patients seek to escape this. They may seek to break off treatment when strong emotions arise, particularly those of a transference nature. Such avoidance of painful emotions may include both conscious suppression and unconscious repression. In the latter event, symptoms may ensue which represent what we might term *emotional-equivalents.*

A patient of the author became terribly unhappy, worried, and anxious under certain circumstances. At other times, under the identical circumstances, she would not experience the subjective emotional pain at all, but instead would suffer a constrictive kind of abdominal and/or chest pain. This was an instance of the "emotional-equivalent symptom". Brierley noted several instances. "A patient suffering from Conversion (Reaction) realized very clearly that she *either* developed symptoms, *or* 'felt rotten' ".

Not only symptoms but also impulsive behavior may be "designed to shortcircuit affect-development". Sometimes both are present. Helen Hayes has noted that she always suffers nosebleeds accompanying strong worry.

D. SYMPTOM AND LOCATION CHOICE

1. Important Factors in Choice of Symptoms

Many students raise the interesting and often puzzling question as to what determines the individual "choice" of symptom, or its possible "choice" of location. This is a very important area in understanding the symptoms of the neuroses. There is also room for a great deal of further study and research in this interesting aspect of psychiatry. In an attempt to present the major contributing factors as the author currently understands them, they are outlined and presented in condensed form in *Table 33*.

Table 33

Important Factors (Determinants) in Symptom Choice and Location

---

The psychogenic symptoms of emotional illness may be regarded as allowing a concealed distorted outward expression for the repressed impulses responsible for emotional conflict, plus elements of their simultaneous control, and accompanying self-punitive aspects. The choice of symptom and the choice of location are psychologically determined. This is in accord with the *Principle of Hidden Determinants* [Ch.14:IVB2 and Ch.13:VIIIE3].

The basis for all of this is deeply hidden from conscious awareness, and in many cases is never accessible. Some of the following ten important factors in influencing the unconscious determination of symptom choice and location sometimes can be identified.*

1. **Symbolism:** Hidden individual special significance and meaning for the type of symptom and its location. The "selection" is a symbol or symbolism is an involuntary one. [*See* earlier discussions of the Peg Concept, pp. 457, 464, and Ch.10:IXD2 and XB*1*].

2. **The Sensory Context:** The immediate surroundings, the sensory context at the time of additional stress, likely have more importance in symptom choice and location than heretofore has been believed. Such influences to an extent are more fortuitous and external.

3. **Illness or Injury:** Damage to or around the site of the symptom, especially at or near the time of the precipitating stress can also have an important although more circumstantial influence. Such misadventures could also be considered part of the sensory context.
   This is also true of illness. The later emotional recreation is in accord with our Psychic Reduplication Concept [*see* p. 468].

4. **Past Experience:** The cumulative experiences of living will help to determine which area and which kind of manifestation are individually most suited to the person concerned, to express symbolically the repressed

(Table continued on next page)

---

* *See also Table 28, Selection of the Object of Phobias, p. 583.*

Table 33—Continued

conflictual data. Association pathways which lead to past experiences of significance have lessened resistance.

Symptoms may be historically determined by repressed experiences from the person's past, and by the vicissitudes of experience, relationships, instincts, and through conditioning. Conversion manifestations may appear as part of the reaction to stress. In accord with our Concept of Continued Physiologic Momentum [pp. 99–100 and 455; Ch.14; VIIC2], these (together with other stress-induced symptoms) often do not subside concurrently with the subsiding of the stress.

5. **Identification:** The automatic influence of identification is particularly important to the conversion person in symptom choice and location. The *Faulty-Identification Concept* [Ch.13:VD4; VE3] is operative here in laying the foundation for emotional conflicts and future symptoms.

The following variations are encountered, as modified from Fenichel:

(a) *With the fortunate rival.* (Example: In Freud's case, Dora developed a cough like her successful rival, Mrs. K.)

(b) *With the inaccessible object.* (Example: As a compensation in the Electra complex, the daughter may identify with the father.)

(c) *Identical needs or desires.* Similar to (*a*); the competitive interest or desire for the same thing. *Case 145* is an excellent illustration.

(d) *Multiple identification.* This may be illustrated as operative with several persons simultaneously and in condensed fashion, or serially. (In accord with our F.I.C. above.)

6. **Organic Determination:** An early antecedent organic disturbance may provide a hidden but established peg, to which later symptom formation is attached or associated. *Case 137* is a good example. (This is in accord with our *Concept of Psychic Reduplication* [Ch.8:VC1;Ch.12: VB1].

7. **Suggestion:** Can be an important factor, especially in Somatic Conversions, as illustrated and referred to in several instances earlier.

8. **Wound or Trauma in War:** Related to No. 3 and to No. 6 above. The site of injury in combat or in industrial accidents can provide a focus for immediate or later attachment of conversion symptoms. The basis or capacity for Somatic Conversion may preexist, in which the injury becomes an "opportune foundation" for symptoms.

9. **Unconscious Special Meaning of Parts of the Body or Bodily Areas:** For most people certain areas of the body become unconsciously invested with special significance. This is usually a highly individual matter and could be classified with No. 1 above.

Some of these meanings tend to be more commonly shared. (Example: For many the right side may unconsciously represent the stronger, dominant, correct, or "right" side. The left side may represent the weaker, inferior, incorrect side, or even come to have a meaning somewhat like the English meaning for the Latin word sinister, actually meaning left.)

10. **Stress and Psychologic Conflict:** Increased vulnerability to conversion symptom evolvement with the actual and symbolically exaggerated effects of "external" stress. Greater propensity in conjunction with the S.E.H.C. [p. 33] and the S.E.H.A. [pp. 38, 457].

11. **The Content of Unconscious Fantasy:** Freud, Isaacs, Klein, and others have pointed out that symptoms can be regarded as a primitive kind of pre-verbal somatic language. This is particularly true in the Somatic Conversions, and less obviously true in the Physiologic Conversions.

Conversion symptoms express fantasy without words. This is more apparent in conversion convulsions, tics, posturing, and gestures. Hence, the content of unconscious fantasy can play an important role in determining the choice of symptom and its location.

2. Interpretation of the Symbolism

Conversion symptoms are a primitive kind of somatic language. This is more apparent with Somatic Conversions than with Physiologic Conversions. They may be regarded as a pre-verbal, magical kind of expression. The communication conveyed in their action or pantomime is more readily understood by the perceptive observer in certain symptoms, such as certain conversion tics, gestures, posturing, convulsions, and spells.

At times the hidden meaning present may be surmised in part by the experienced clinician. [*See Case 102*, p. 500, in which a need "to lean emotionally" was directly translated into a literal such need to lean upon".] It is also quite possible to miss the mark rather widely. In every instance it must be kept in mind that the symptoms are vital defensive measures adopted unconsciously, and also that they are in each case completely individual.

3. The Rule of Individual Symbolism; Complexity of Symptomatology in Emotional Illness

The *Rule of Individual Symbolism* helps point out the far greater complexity of symptomatology in emotional illness than in that of organic disease. In the latter, one can expect the manifestations of a given condition at least roughly to follow certain lines. One can more definitely anticipate symptoms from the nature of the illness. Considerably more often will the symptoms have the same or similar significance for a number of patients.

In emotional illness, however, the manifestations are completely individual in each case. They are highly specific, but on a completely individual basis. The same symptom in two patients can have completely separate, individual significance. The symptoms can vary widely in their inherent meaning and in their symbolic meaning. This makes the interpretation of symptoms (and symbolism) in emotional illness a complex endeavor.

The same symptom or dream symbol for example, *can have completely different meanings in different persons*. This expresses and follows what we might conveniently refer to as the Rule of Individual Symbolism, [Ch.13:IIID3] an important precept to bear in mind.

4. Surface Anesthesia

The patient who develops surface anesthesia may be expressing a wish in symbolic form. Such a wish is largely unconscious. In this manner the surrender of physical sensation may express the wish or need for the loss of emotional sensation, the achievement of a degree of emotional numbness.

It is as though the patient says in effect, "I would like to feel nothing emotionally. So I do the best along this line that I can. I surrender external, physical sensitivity. That is, I dissociate from conscious awareness that part of my perception having to do with physical sensations for this particular part of me."

Thus this kind of symptom may be an expression in somatic language of "I will be insensitive." If one is not sensitive (emotionally) he is less liable to hurt or pain. Anesthesia on a conversion basis can represent the symbolic exchange of a physical expression for an emotional meaning.

E. SYMBOLIC EXPRESSION OF THE REPRESSED AND THE REPRESSING

1. Endogain Summarized

This major pattern of neurotic defensive reaction is based upon the important intrapsychic process of Conversion. Conversion is an internal psychologic mechanism. Through it, consciously intolerable ideas or impulses are transmuted so as to find a disguised and distorted external expression.

The endogain of Conversion includes the continued repression of the unbearable content. Conversion results in allowing: (1) the distorted symbolic expression and gratification (partial and symbolic) of the consciously disowned impulse, (2) the simultaneous expression of factors in its inhibition, control, or denial, and (3) the expression of superego components in self-punishment or retribution for having it.

The simultaneous expression of these factors indicates the compromise character of the conversion symptom. The repressed as well as the repressing forces are symbolically expressed to varying extents. This is why we may sometimes speak of the symptom as a distorted external representation of the unconscious conflict.

2. The Oral Conflict

The author has increasingly advocated the relative importance of the era of oral conflict, believing it to underlie the conflicts and the vicissitudes of the later Oedipal period and complex. Conflicts in the oral stage thus are important antecedents and prototypes for what follows, in accord with our Theory of Antecedent Conflict.

Oral conflict has important implications in the psychodynamics of the Conversion Reactions. A number of manifestations and personality features are more understandable when viewed in the perspective of the more basic oral conflicts. Proposed (both before, and) in the first edition of the present text, and seconded by several other investigators, it is to be stressed further today. This is in some distinction to the majority view, which still assigns (but today, perhaps less unanimously and rigidly so) the preeminent role to the Oedipus situation and its vicissitudes.

VII. ADDITIONAL IMPORTANT ASPECTS
OF CONVERSION REACTIONS

A. IDENTIFICATION

1. Marked Capacity

The conversion patient is noted for his marked capacity for *identification.**
This is often reflected in the process of symptom formation. Here reference
is made of course to the dynamism of identification, a defensive intrapsychic process which takes place outside of and beyond conscious awareness. It is a true mental mechanism, through which one unconsciously takes
over the characteristics of another's personality or molds oneself to an
extent after another person.

There are a number of significant variations of identification which have
been listed and described elsewhere [*see* footnote]. Through his facility
for and frequent use of this mechanism, the individual may more readily
develop symptoms which he has observed in others, or which he has heard
about. This is an important aspect of the foundation for the selection and
the development of particular conversion symptoms [Ch.12:VD*3*; VIB*1*;
VID*1*]. Identification is often enhanced through the rather characteristic
suggestibility of the conversion person.

2. In Character Defenses; The Conversion Personality

In the development of the conversion character defenses as earlier outlined [pp. 258–270], the process of identification is also operative. At
times one can postulate a conversion identification with a certain segment
of the parental personality. On occasion this may be confined, for example,
to largely hostile and rejecting elements. When this occurs, it comprises
a process which we might term *hostile identification,* which of course takes
place outside of awareness. It is not a rational process, and often tragically
tends to secure the loss of the very goal which is sought. This type of
Identification also has been encountered in P.O.W. camps.

In the character trait development in which identification plays an important role, it is almost as though the Conversion Personality says in
effect, "If I become as you are, then perhaps I will get the affection,
acceptance, and love which I want so much."

B. OVERDETERMINATION

1. Every Phenomenon Explainable; Doctrine of Scientific Determinism

According to the important *Doctrine* of *Scientific Determinism, nothing
in the emotional or mental life (as well as in the physical world) happens
by chance alone. Everything thus that happens is the result of specific
forces, motives, or causes, even though these may elude scrutiny or observation, and even though they may be deeply hidden or buried from conscious
awareness.*

---

* For a more definitive discussion of this major psychic dynamism, see the author's
monograph *Mental Mechanisms*, pp. 118–168.

701

2. Focusing and Convergence of Multiple Factors; Confluence and Condensation of Unconscious Needs.

Every phenomenon is explainable. This is true whether it be physical, chemical, astronomical, behavioral, emotional or psychological [p. 486; Ch.13:IIIC *1*]. This, of course, applies equally to symptom formation. It applies to the psychogenesis of the Conversion Reactions.

Overdetermination means that a given symptom is *over*determined, that is, it has an excess number of underlying forces. These combine and converge to produce the symptom. Overdetermination or convergence is marked in Somatic Conversion, in which a given action, fantasy, or symptom is usually found to have an overabundant number of converging underlying associations and hidden emotional roots.

Thus, in overdetermination a number of factors converges to determine the specific neurotic symptom which appears. Through overdetermination symptoms come to represent a confluence and a condensation of a number of vital, underlying unconscious needs. This is particularly illustrated in Somatic Conversion and less obviously in Physiologic Conversion. A single symptom thus simultaneously expresses in complex fashion several unconscious purposes.

Overdetermination refers to the multiple factors in the determination of a particular neurotic action. *Through the focusing and convergence of unconscious determinants, a symptom thus is not simply determined; it is overdetermined.*

C. CONVERSION PAIN

1. Recapitulation of Early Pain or of Associated Events

The pain of conversion origin is often a serious clinical problem. Some important aspects of conversion pain were discussed in the section on Symptoms and Clinical Features. *Cases 137* and *138* were illustrations of conversion pain and some of the more serious problems that can ensue in its clinical management [*see also* p. 469]. Here also was illustrated something not infrequently encountered, that is, how subsequent conversion pain can recapitulate the childhood pain, or the events associated with such pain. This may be the result of illnesses, injuries, and operations which were early associated unconsciously with coexistent childhood conflicts. The later repetition or recapitulation of these conflicts may be accompanied by repetition of the pain. This process is analogous to what transpires in our *Psychic Reduplication Concept* [p. 468].

2. Fenichel's Pathways for Conversion Pain

Another possible sequence is that the injury, illness, or operation in childhood may in itself have contributed to the development of conflicts. Should these same conflicts be later rekindled, the (real) pain of that early era might likewise be rekindled by association. Fenichel succinctly noted four major ways in which conversion pain might develop:

1. Pain was actually present originally, at the time of repression.

2. The pain expresses the wish to be in another's place. The original pain was experienced by another. The dynamics are part of the process of conversion identification.

3. Where pleasant sensations were associated with the original pain, the later pain may be a warning not to give in, or a punishment for desiring to experience, or for the experiencing.

4. Pain may also be a part of unconscious sexual or hostile fantasies.

As a possible contributing factor in conversion pain, we should again note that the more that emotional conflicts, anxiety, and stress are present, ordinarily the lower the individual's threshold to pain. This states again [p. 470] our *Axiom of Inverse Pain-Conflict Ratio*. As a final note, some instances of conversion pain appear to illustrate in similar fashion what we described and termed [p. 480], a *Lowered-Perception-Threshold Source* or contribution to hygeiaphrontic discomforts.

D. CONVERSION EPIDEMICS

The Conversion (hysterical) Epidemic is a very interesting but rather rare phenomenon. It is not too surprising that we encounter this phenomenon, however, in view of the various potentials for dissociative ability, massive repression, suggestibility, and identification in the Conversion Personality. Such epidemics have been observed among soldiers in military barracks, at a large naval receiving station among personnel awaiting shipboard and overseas assignments, in boarding schools, camps, factories, audiences, and offices. What we have termed the *conversion epidemic* is a particular type illustrating our earlier *Emotional Contagion Concept*. [*See* pp. 32, 464, 476, and Ch. 13:VIC2.]

Schuler and Paventon reported such an "epidemic" in a Louisiana high school in 1939. Involving girls from sixteen to eighteen years old, it began with one of the top students. This student developed a leg jerk and crying spells, apparently in response to a conflict over dancing. Soon it had spread to others. It became widespread. Disorganization and panic temporarily took control of the whole school. Menninger cited an epidemic of conversion convulsions among the girls employed at a cotton mill in England in 1787.

E. COMPENSATION NEUROSIS

Compensation neurosis is a rather unfortunate term applied by some physicians to certain neurotic illnesses, largely of an industrial nature, in which features of secondary gain are prominent and include an absorbing interest in securing compensation or pension for an alleged damage or injury. Further discussion of this type of neurotic reaction shall be included when we come to discuss the Neuroses Following Trauma in Chapter 14. It is appropriate that it be mentioned at this point because:

1. The so-called Compensation Neuroses are most frequently of conversion origin.

2. Industrial accidents and their emotional sequelae are of great importance in preventive and industrial medicine today.

3. The author would like to encourage the discard of this term, in view of its calling attention to an aspect of the illness which hardly invites the most sympathetic understanding, or the dynamic study of a terribly difficult and increasing problem. It is a problem which is tragic in its implications to the patient, to his family, and to society.

F. THE PROBLEM OF THE PAINFUL PHANTOM LIMB

1. Somatic Conversion

Although the painful phantom limb is a problem not commonly encountered, it is an interesting one and can offer a considerable therapeutic challenge. The painful phantom limb is part of the clinical experience of most surgeons. Kolb, Frank, and Watson have reported interesting cases in which their clinical observations further confirm the basic psychologic origins of the pain in the phantom (amputated) limb.

Some of the difficult problems incident to the management of these troubling cases are illustrated in the following example.* The pain present here was most severe, as it is in many cases. The responsible psychologic mechanism was a somatic conversion.

Case 146

A Case of Pain in a Phantom Limb

(1) *Amputation follows non-union and infection*

A twenty-four-year-old college student sustained multiple fractures in a streetcar accident. A fracture of the femur failed to unite in spite of careful reduction and balanced traction. After six months, pin traction was applied to the femur, but an infection which developed in the wounds could not be controlled with antibiotics.

Upon examination one year after the injury, the patient was an emaciated, febrile man with chronic osteomyelitis of the middle third of the femur and decubitus ulcers of the left heel, leg, and lateral part of the knee. The organisms cultured from the wounds were resistant to chemotherapeutic agents.

After three weeks of conservative therapy which failed to alter his progressive downhill course, a midthigh guillotine amputation was performed. The patient expressed a wish to have the amputated limb buried, but after some discussion with his parents and surgeon, agreed to allow the hospital to dispose of the limb. In the immediate postoperative period, he complained of severe pain in the amputation stump and in the phantom limb. This pain could not be alleviated by large doses of narcotics. When seen in psychiatric consultation, he was writhing and screaming in pain.

* Acknowledgment is made to the authors and to the Publications Office of the Mayo Clinic for permission to include this case.

(2) Psychotherapeutic approach

All drugs were withdrawn, aside from regular, spaced doses of morphine sulfate. The patient was advised of this therapeutic plan and was relieved, as for months before the operation he had received warnings of impending drug addiction and had had to beg for medication. It was only after the institution of psychotherapy that overt expressions of anxiety and his conspicuous behavior disturbance subsided. A therapeutic relationship was achieved by instituting daily therapeutic interviews and intensive nursing care. In this early period, there were frequent expressions of resentment toward the therapist and the staff. He described his pain in his phantom leg in detail. During interviews, mention by the therapist of the amputation or of use of an artificial limb repeatedly induced the complaint of pain in the phantom, and jerking movements of the stump. He was encouraged to discuss himself, his family, his injury, and the presumed attitude of others to the amputation. The material thus elicited made evident the source of his attitudes toward his body, his ambivalent feelings toward his parents, and certain childish behavior patterns.

The patient was the oldest of three children from a family of moderate means. Until the age of seven years he had been sick frequently. After that, he was generally well and had been active in tennis, golf, and football in high school. He had enjoyed teaching sports to his younger brother. He did not wish to have others see him with this amputation since he had always been proud of his physique. He described his father in the following ways: "My father was quite an athlete — a great basketball and football player. He feels I'd be better off dead than missing a leg. If he'd lost his leg, you'd really have something. . . . He used to make a fuss over me when I was sick as a child — I'm disappointed in him now — he's quiet." The patient initially declared his mother had been sympathetic about his illness. Toward the end of therapy he said of her, "She tried to take too much care of me, but doesn't know it irritates me."

It was noted that this patient's irascible behavior in association with complaints of pain was indicative of previous behavior patterns. This man had always met frustration with immature behavior; he had failed a college course because he disliked the instructor; when he did poorly at school he "took it out" on his family with irrational and undue criticisms. In the ward this pattern was repeated. He delayed necessary nursing procedures "just to see if I can bluff the nurses." If the bluff were called, he either readily complied or responded with complaints of pain.

After working through this material, he seldom complained of pain. He was able to sleep throughout the night without sedation. He was requesting and receiving ½ grain of morphine sulfate approximately every five hours.

(3) Preparation for discharge

As hospital discharge was contemplated, a plan of narcotic withdrawal was discussed with the patient. A five-day morphine withdrawal program was instituted, utilizing methadone hydrochloride substitution in order to minimize the abstinence symptoms.

On the third day of methadone withdrawal the patient's mother visited. In the patient's presence she indicated considerable anxiety about his proposed homecoming. She later also privately told the therapist that her uncle, a drug addict amputee, had committed suicide when under her supervision some years previously; shortly thereafter, the patient had written a thesis at school on narcotic addiction. On the two subsequent days, methadone hydrochloride was withdrawn without evidence of abstinence symptoms. However, the day following complete withdrawal of methadone hydrochloride, an acute anxiety reaction (A.A.A.) developed. The patient tossed about in bed and moaned with pain. He was incontinent of urine. He claimed that he had fallen out of bed and injured his amputation stump. After an interpretation in which his dependency on the therapist was described and his behavior was stated to be a repetition of an infantile pattern to obtain her help, which, however, was not longer necessary as he was not in pain, his symptom immediately subsided.

The patient was discharged free of symptoms and with a more realistic attitude toward the social adjustment he would be required to make. He returned to the Clinic three months later, when the orthopedic surgeons performed further repair of the amputation stump. He planned to acquire an artificial limb as soon as this incision healed. He stated that he had adjusted well at home, and had gained fifteen pounds. The phantom limb sensation still existed but there was no longer any pain.

2. Dynamics and Prevention

A. IDENTIFICATION; SPECIAL SIGNIFICANCE OF THE LIMB.—Weiss and English, in commenting on pain in the phantom limb, reported that "it appears to be associated with pain experienced in the past, by the patient or by a person with whom the patient has identified."

Noble, Price, and Gilder discussed psychiatric disturbances following amputations. The anxieties provoked by the experience "are associated with the individual's past history of emotional and physical injury and with the special meaning (significance) which the amputated part has come to hold for him." As noted earlier [pp. 123, 480], a reciprocal relationship can be present between pain and anxiety, promoting a possible *Anxiety-Pain Vicious Circle*.

B. PREVENTIVE MEASURES.—Important preventive measures are possible when these kinds of psychic disturbances might be anticipated. These include a kindly and sympathetic inquiry as to the patient's attitudes in general, before the time of surgery.

A prior and reassuring explanation that the part to be lost will be given due regard and "respect" in its disposition likewise can be useful. Short-term supportive, interpretive, educational, and reassuring psychotherapy can also be most helpful.

VIII. TREATMENT

A. IDEAL IN THERAPY

1. Psychoanalysis and Psychotherapy

The treatments of choice in the Conversion Reactions are psychoanalysis, or dynamically oriented psychotherapy, in competent hands. Analysis requires employment of *The Treatment Rule* [pp. 50 and 503]. This is the only approach that offers the prospect of permanent relief. In the successful instance, there are important personality and character changes which take place in consequence of the work of therapy. These are basic ones.

Vulnerability to further episodes of Somatic or Physiologic Conversion is minimal or absent following completion of definitive therapy, and the patient achieves a new and healthier level of maturity. Most analysts regard the Conversion Reaction as one of the specific types of neurotic emotional reaction which are best suited for an analytic approach. Fenichel wrote: "The technique of psychoanalysis still remains most easily applicable to cases of (conversion) Reactions . . . Psychoanalytic treatment continues to yield the best results." An approach of speculative inquiry is the ideal one, and comprises what was earlier [pp. 367 and 501] referred to as the *Proper Therapeutic Attitude*.

2. Character Analysis Valuable

The character analysis of conversion (hysterical) personality traits can also be very gratifying as to results, when the patient has or can develop a genuine interest in constructive self-study. Character analysis can result in securing substantial and constructive changes in the individual's psyche, adjustment, level of maturity, and the great lessening of future vulnerability to further neurotic episodes.

Through making himself, his emotions, reactions, motivations, and defensive mechanisms clear to the psychiatrist in the therapeutic relationship, the individual inevitably becomes clearer to himself. As his insight grows, his own resources and ability to make selected constructive modifications in these areas of personal psychology also increase. Indeed, in accord with the *Theory of Transparency* [pp. 171 and 495], a symptom is generally unable to survive its thorough elucidation. Any individual so motivated can secure most substantial, personally beneficial, and welcome benefits through character analysis [*see also* pp. 298–301, and the Symptom-Survival Principle, pp. 27 and 502, and *Case 65*, pp. 324–6]. Sharpe believed that the conversion patient is likely to have "less driving power" in pursuing analysis. The initiation of therapy also can be quite difficult, particularly when there is a considerable measure of conversion "symptom-success" in combating anxiety. It is small wonder that our principle holds of the Inverse Ratio of Symptom-Success, to one's Motivation toward Therapy. [*See* pp. 9, 298, 477, 508, and Section V-G.]

Some therapists also feel that they do not do well with conversion patients. This points up the value which can accrue from matching patient and therapist. A prominent psychiatrist told the author recently that he purposely avoided all contact with patients suffering from Conversion Reactions whenever possible. He explained, "If I'm going to do therapy, I might as well put in my time with patients I feel I can help." In accord with our Emotional-Inertia Concept [pp. 213, 433, 504], the initiation of therapy is more difficult.

3. Symptom "Good" Exchange for Anxiety; Flight-to-the-Physical

A. EMOTIONAL SYMPTOM PREFERABLE TO ANXIETY; PHYSICAL SYMPTOMS PREFERABLE TO EMOTIONAL ONES.—An understanding of the dynamics involved is vital to securing resolution of the conversion difficulties. When the conversion is "successful", the resulting symptom represents for him a "good" exchange for anxiety. Actually, the more "Successful" the symptom, the less anxiety is experienced. This is in accord with our precept of Inverse Anxiety-Symptom Ratio [*see also* pp. 103, 145, 324, and 462]. Some anxiety can be a useful stimulus toward seeking therapy. An alternative conviction as to the presumed presence instead, of the physical symptoms of organic conditions, becomes in like fashion a welcome relief to the individual, from the troubling and disturbing presence of emotional symptoms, as many physicians have observed. This is a noteworthy principle which for ready identification we might term *The Flight-to-the-Physical*. Leddy commented on the case of a severe obsessional patient who had his most comfortable time while suffering from a very severe intercurrent cold and painful sinusitis. Concentration on the physical symptoms gave relief from obsessive ruminations. The author has encountered a number of similar noteworthy examples of this type of reaction in his practice in recent years. Concentration on physical factors can also have other effects. Thus as we observed in certain Hygeiaphrontic Reactions [p. 460], an occasional conversion patient may in similar fashion join the ranks of what we termed the Seekers-after-Health.

B. RESOLUTION DIFFICULT.—To the patient the physical symptom is often very "preferable" to the emotional conflict and consequent anxiety. It entails less suffering. There are many vital psychologic reasons for maintaining the symptoms. It is readily understandable why resolution is often so difficult.

The symptom also may serve a masochistic purpose of attempted retribution or propitiation. Sharpe recognized this in commenting that "physical suffering serves the purpose of propitiation. It is offered to turn the anger of the tiger [parents] to pity, to remorse". Thus, for example, when the "murderous" impulse is to trample, kick, and destroy, the paralyzed leg not only is a terribly important inhibition, but it also concommitantly reflects propitiatory suffering. From the inhibiting-of-actions viewpoint the symptom becomes a vital S. O. [Security Operation: pp. 351, 461].

Dreams, their symbolism and their interpretation can be very important. They sometimes afford a readier route to the translation of the symptom language of the conversion.

C. PROGNOSIS IMPROVES WITH MULTIPLE SYMPTOMS.—In the author's experience the prognosis to treatment has often varied inversely with: (1) the level of fixation of a symptom, (2) its isolated discreteness, and (3) the individual focus of attention on it. An admixture of further symptoms and of conversion character defenses therefore actually appears to improve the prognosis!

However, either the great single conversion or multiple ones can provide the basis for the individual's further defensive absorption with it. This illustrates our Interest-Absorption Concept [pp. 311, 332, and 462].

B. ADDITIONAL THERAPEUTIC MEASURES

1. Indications for Symptomatic Treatment

Although the deeper and more complete analysis is the ideal in treatment, and in the therapeutic approach, there are reasons why other approaches may be used. Firstly, such analysis may not be available. Secondly, it may not be feasible for such practical considerations as time, money, location, or other limiting external circumstances. Thirdly, by no means are all patients suitable for this kind of intensive psychotherapeutic work.

A patient may have an absence of inclination or interest. His intelligence may simply be too dull for real profit. In these instances wrote Lebensohn, "a symptomatic cure is justified even though the basic personality may not lend itself to further treatment."

In general, the prognosis is enhanced in direct proportion to the promptness of initiating therapy. This can be crucial in Conversion Reactions. According to the Principle of Symptom-Longevity [p. 503 and Ch.14:VIII E 3], the more finely established and the longer-lived is a symptom, the more difficult its elucidation and resolution becomes.

2. Suggestion in Therapy: Progressive-Suggestion Technique

A. THE "RED-INK CURE".—The following instance is reported as an example of the use of suggestion in the removal of a disabling symptom. The author suggests that this interesting type of symptom resolution and gradual improvement through this technique or similar kinds of *Progressive-Suggestion* might be termed for convenience and identification "The Red-Ink Cure".

Case 147

Symptomatic Progressive Suggestion: The Red-Ink Cure

(1) *A double escape*
A twenty-three-year-old English seaman was invalided out of the naval service because of a paralysis and anesthesia of the right forearm. He had developed the disturbance while on duty in Hong Kong. Careful orthopedic and neurologic examinations there had failed to reveal organic disturbance. He had been subsequently discharged from the Royal British Navy.

After his discharge, he entered a London hospital on the advice of his family doctor. The diagnosis of a characteristic Somatic Conversion Reaction in a young man of dull intelligence was established. The boy had always had a great deal of difficulty in managing his hostile feelings toward authority figures. He had joined the Navy to avoid constant friction with his father. While stationed in Hong Kong, he developed a sudden and intense urge to strike his superior officer, following a minor incident. The resulting paralysis and numbness of the offending member was indeed a symbolic representation of his entire conflict.

This was a "double escape". He had first escaped the family by joining the service. He had again escaped the recapitulation of authority aspects of Military Service, plus the danger of assaulting the authority figure by the unconscious escape into the Somatic Conversion.

(2) *Progressive-Suggestion Technique*
Treatment was highly suggestive and consisted of repeatedly exposing the patient at daily intervals to a mild faradic stimulation of the arm, with the strong and repeated suggestion that the level of anesthesia would gradually diminish. A record of the level was made in bright red ink on each day following treatment. This level gradually descended, a few inches at a time, until the complete function of the arm, which had been disabled for over six months, was soon completely restored.

That such measures as the Red-Ink Cure are sometimes successful in the removal of symptoms, is a further measure of the suggestibility* of the

---

* Suggestibility can lead to frequent temporary improvement or well-being in response to a new regimen, medicine, or therapist. This is in accord with our earlier [pp. 392, 453, and 472] *Favorable-Response Concept* in the neuroses.

conversion patient. This potential can be so much a part of the conversion syndrome as to comprise an *Attitude-Symptom* [*see* pp. 328 and 450]. When symptoms can be changed or removed through suggestion in this way, it is hardly surprising that their onset may also follow the very powerful force of internal psychologic needs, and be similarly influenced by external "suggestive" influences. In other cases in which suggestion is used, the use of the Red-Ink Cure kind of method of Progressive Suggestion may take a considerably more subtle form and be combined with other measures.

Suggestion can be particularly effective in some cases of Conversion Reactions which are seemingly not approachable by other means. This is perhaps more especially true when intelligence is limited and when the patient cannot be adequately interested in a constructive kind of self-study.

In the following instance, suggestion was successfully resorted to in a case of Physiologic Conversion marked by the prominent symptom of impotence, after efforts at investigative and interpretative therapeutic approaches proved futile.

Case 148

A Physiologic Conversion Symptom of Impotence Relieved by Suggestion

A 21-year-old Army mess attendant reported to a young psychiatric resident that he had "lost his nature". He had been unable to maintain an erection for several weeks. The resident was very enthusiastic to try the dynamic approach in therapy. The soldier's intelligence, educational opportunities, experience, and imagination were all quite limited. During many hours of efforts, about all that the doctor could obtain in the line of verbal communication was a series of monosyllabic answers in response to direct questions. *La belle indifférence* superimposed upon a very limited capacity would have made this a very formidable task to the most experienced therapist. It was too much. The young psychiatrist decided he would try suggestion.

He laid the stage carefully, explaining to the patient that he would administer a "new and powerful medicine" that would "restore his nature" in exactly four treatments. With considerable ceremony and a solemn approach, he administered some vitamin B intravenously on four successive occasions. Each occasion was used for further suggestion and to reinforce prior ideas. The patient was visibly impressed. Two days following the completion of the course, he reported his complete "cure". It was true; his symptom had disappeared in response to the suggestion. It did not recur during the subsequent eight months while some contact could be maintained.

Needless to say, such symptomatic therapy is limited in its benefits. The potential for Conversion remains unchanged. There is no opportunity for constructive modifications of character structure or personality. The deception required is also to be deplored, its only justification being on a basis of expediency, which of course can be questioned in many instances.

In observing the efficacy of this approach, one can well appreciate the "cures" sometimes effected throughout history by mystics, medicine men, magicians, faith healers, and similar people. When they themselves also thoroughly believe in what they do, their potential results are likely to be greatly enhanced.

3. Interpretative and Educative Measures

A partial dynamic interpretation after a sufficient interval and over a period of time, which is based upon a carefully detailed and evaluated history of the precipitating events, can be reinforced by subtle suggestion, a confident attitude, instruction of the patient about emotions, and perhaps some reeducation in the use of the affected part. When accomplished carefully, with finesse and good judgment, these measures will often suffice so as to secure at least a measure of symptom relief.

It is very important that the symptom be removed in a way that allows for adequate face-saving. Already the self-esteem of the patient is shaken, even though this may not be outwardly apparent. Every care must be taken to maintain and to raise the level of self-esteem. Derogation, scorn, and contempt have no place. Frustration is better absent or at least not given outward expression. Recall [p. 446] our *anger-breeds-anger concept.*

The related treatment methods of Ross have been referred to earlier. Others have also reported a number of instances of successful symptomatic treatment.

4. Hypnosis and Hypno-Narcosis: The Hazard of Symptom-Exchange

Hypnotic suggestion was for years the standard approach. Using this method with the classic case of Anna O., Josef Breuer made some of the initial dynamic discoveries as early as the years 1880–1881. Thus he probably was the first person ever to learn the importance of "forgotten" memories of significant emotional events from earlier life, in the development of the conversion symptom. When suggestion is used under hypnosis or *Amytal,* with the aim of symptom removal only, there are a number of potential dangers, as implied earlier [Ch.12:VD3].

There is the risk of stirring up more difficulty. The symptoms may be banished, only to be later replaced by another, or by others which may even be far worse. The patient may be rendered more vulnerable to an *emotional decompensation* [Section VC5]. A psychosis may be precipitated. Thus, very careful judgment is required even by the most skilled hands, in selecting cases for treatment via this approach [Ch.13:VIIIF1]. It is difficult to draw absolute lines. In general, however, cases of blindness should not be attempted at all. Cases of paralysis and aphonia should be attempted only very selectively. Cases of anesthesia, on the other hand, are comparatively safe.

A colleague once reported to the author that he had actually observed the precipitation of six such cases of acute psychosis. These were reputed to have followed attempted symptom removal through suggestion under *Amytal* sedation, in a brief series of conversion patients overseas. Five of these instances had originally begun as paralysis, and one as aphonia. The onset of psychotic reactions followed what had been a most ill-considered and inexpert treatment approach. The foregoing is in accord with the increasingly recognized danger which in our psychiatric shorthand we might refer to as the *Hazard of Symptom-Exchange* [Ch. 10: III A4; Ch. 12: V D4 for an illustration of the Symptom-Exchange Hazard in a Phobic

Reaction.] On the other hand, Stevens recently (1964) presented a careful report summarizing his extensive clinical therapeutic experience with an estimated 200 cases of Somatic Conversion over some years of practice in Washington, D.C. These were treated empirically with suggestion under *Amytal* sedation. The results were generally successful, with prompt symptom suppression or removal, and were without untoward sequellae. He believed the cautions as emphasized in the foregoing discussion were overdrawn, and that the possible hazard of psychosis as noted above was inaccurate [*see also* earlier discussion of the hazard of sudden defense-dissolution, p. 477].

The following case underlines the caution about attempting symptom removal under hypnosis.

Case 149

A Psychosis Follows Attempted Symptom Removal Under Hypnosis

A forty-year-old housewife, mother of two children, lost her voice a year before she consulted a psychiatrist. She had earlier consulted throat specialists who had found no evidence of organic pathology. During one of these examinations she had been given intravenously *Pentothal Sodium,* after which she had been able to talk normally for one hour following the examination. This led her laryngologist to recommend psychiatric consultation, which she had however rejected for some time.

During attempted psychotherapy the patient spoke in a hoarse whisper. Although much material was obtained, the patient's symptoms persisted. An interview under *Amytal* sedation was only partially successful. She was then referred to a psychiatrist with some experience in hypnosis. During the course of hypnotherapy she was soon able to speak quite normally. However, she suddenly developed an acute schizophrenia-like reaction. She became actively delusional and became convinced that she was receiving messages from her therapist. Finally, under prolonged therapy, her psychotic symptoms subsided, and she was eventually able to return to a good adjustment. Her reaction well illustrated our cautions as to the *Hazard of Symptom-Exchange.*

A very few psychiatrists who are quite skilled in both hypnosis and in psychodynamics use hypnosis to effect symptom removal and also to work out some of the psychopathology. Wolberg reported such a case, in which the mechanism of a conversion anesthesia was uncovered and the symptom resolved under hypnosis.

Patients will themselves sometimes very much prefer and seek a possible approach by hypnosis, since it involves for them merely the assumation of a passive position, in which they hope the difficulty will be removed effortlessly and painlessly. As a general caution, such an outlook is illusory. It should not be encouraged, if not actively discouraged. Only in very carefully selected instances should this approach be recommended by a physician. There are many drawbacks, hesitations, and cautions about any extensive use of hypnosis as a therapeutic tool. More will be said about some of these cautions in the following chapter on the Dissociative Reactions.

5. The Tracing Technique in Therapy

The value of tracing an emotional manifestation back to its original appearance has been cited [pp. 367, 465, 494, 534]. Employing what was described as the "tracing technique" in therapy can sometimes yield substantial benefits in conversion reaction therapy. This is also of importance since various *final straw* situations [pp. 162 and 713] can precipitate the onset of a conversion symptom.

C. THE CHALLENGES OF THERAPY

1. Something Superior Must Be Offered; The Therapeutic Bargain

The real challenge in the treatment of the Conversion Reactions, as in other emotional ills, lies in the gaining of the ability to offer the patient something better than his symptoms. One can appreciate how really tough this can be when a major disability is worth engendering, however unwittingly, in the service of the powerful unconscious needs. The conversion endogain is achieved at considerable cost. Realization must gradually be gained of this. Failure by the therapist clearly to understand this can lead to a therapeutic impasse, or T.I. [p. 446]. The self-defeat and hardship become too high a price to pay, as the needs slowly and simultaneously melt away. This is an excellent exchange for the surrender of symptoms. Something superior has been offered. This then becomes the interesting principle entering into what the author labels for convenience the Therapeutic Bargain [*see also* pp. 300 and 501]. When it is of sufficient value the handicapping symptom or character trait can be surrendered [Ch. 10: X A*1*].

As an example of occasional rapid response to conservative therapy, Alexander reported a case of Somatic Conversion Reaction which responded symptomatically in twenty-six interviews. He explained the efficacy of the treatment as resulting from an unusual transference situation. This had been purposely induced by the physician, who adopted a carefully studied role accepted by the patient, and one which was diametrically opposed to the critical, harsh father of the latter's earlier years.

The *Principle of Self-Esteem-Maintenance* [Ch. 12: V D*1*] is a very useful one to adhere to with persons in psychotherapy generally, as well as in the Conversion Reactions.

2. Insight the Major Goal

The definitive treatment of the Conversion Reaction is more likely to be prolonged and difficult. In general, the securing of insight is the major goal of therapy. Included of course is the understanding and acceptance of, or the resolution of conflicts.* In order to secure a really adequate result, the patient must be helped to reach a higher level of maturity, through which he can make more satisfactory adjustments to living in the future.

---

* See also Table 29, *Seven Goals of Psychotherapy*, page 593.

He must gain the ability to renounce some of his strong dependency needs in return for more mature ways of achieving satisfaction. This entails: (1) gaining an understanding of the internal necessity for the symptom, (2) the choosing of more mature goals in living, and (3) the recognition and resolution of his basic conflicts.

D. USEFUL ATTRIBUTES FOR THE THERAPIST

In the treatment of the Conversion Reactions the psychiatrist must possess a great amount of patience and understanding. The therapist must have the ability and the requisite personal security to keep himself apart from the many efforts of the patient to involve him personally in his own characteristically neurotic world. Still his role requires active collaboration with his patient, in accord with our Joint-Endeavor Principle [pp. 130 and 501].

The sensitivities of conversion patients make it impossible for a gruff, severe, impatient, or hostile therapist to make much progress in therapy. Malingering must not be implied [see earlier discussion, pp. 494–497]. On the other hand, the absence of a reasonable amount of firmness and detachment will also result in the failure of therapeutic efforts.

As a tangential but important corollary to our earlier [pp. 299 and 473] Relationship-Improvement Precept, carrying this over to the joint doctor-patient relationship and therapeutic endeavor, both principals must want to improve the latter's emotional *status quo* in order to make meaningful progress.

Accessory measures are sometimes indicated. In discussing severe Conversion Reactions in children, Jensen and Wert advised removal from the home. In accord with our First Tenet of the Parental Role [pp. 23, 309, 479], the proper atmosphere for maturation would likely have obviated or at least minimized possible bases for developing a conversion diathesis. Some treatment for other family members, particularly the mother, may be indicated. Supplemental information about the family relationships often can be very germane to the therapy of the case. This must never be gained at the greater expense of any sacrifice to the doctor-patient relationship. This relationship is vitally important to the successful conduct of the case. Development and maintenance of a constructive relationship is the best insurance against the hazard of Therapeutic Impasse [p. 446], or T.I. The expert therapist is able to assess carefully the wisdom of what contacts, if any, to make with members of a patient's family, and when to make them while treatment is in progress.

Twenty-three centuries ago Hippocrates wrote that ". . . some patients . . . recover their health simply through their contentment with the goodness of the physician." Although successful treatment in Somatic and Physiologic Reactions requires considerably more than this of the therapist, still the point has some modern applications.

In general, conversion patients respond well to psychotherapy in competent hands, when a real interest in constructive introspection can be secured and a genuinely collaborative endeavor can be established with the therapist. As a result of successful therapy, changes in personality occur so that the conversion patient no longer requires the use of his infantile patterns of reaction and behavior in order to try to solve his problems in living. On the other hand, some conversion patients tragically are quite disinterested in treatment and remain tragically content to cling obstinately to their illness. They can thus provide all too cogent illustrations of what we have earlier termed [pp. 48, 508, and Ch.14:XB*1*] the *balanced neurotic position*.

IX. SUMMARY

Following a brief introduction to Somatic Conversion and Physiologic Conversion, and certain important definitions, the early history was briefly surveyed. We learned about Anton Mesmer, whose inadequate scientific explanations of his dramatic results contributed to his becoming discredited. Brodie suggested an emotional basis for Conversion, and Joseph Breuer made the first dynamic discoveries, around the year 1880. Charcot first experimentally duplicated conversion paralysis. Breuer was joined by Sigmund Freud and the term "Conversion" was introduced. Their fruitful collaboration was subsequently broken off, after which Freud made further contributions, first to the understanding of Conversion Hysteria, and on to a widening field of clinical reactions in psychiatry.

Under Diagnosis, we learned of the value of special psychiatric training and experience. Diagnosis of Conversion Reactions should be made on a positive basis, and not by a process of the exclusion of organic disease. The positive criteria include evidence of underlying contributing emotional conflict and the presence of preexisting conversion character defenses. *La belle indifférence* may be present, as may significant interpersonal difficulties. Careful study of the patient's emotional life and adjustment will lead also to the identification of conversion factors. In appropriate cases, the comparison of the affected areas with the anatomic nerve distribution can rule out neurologic dysfunction.

There appears to be a decreased incidence of the clinical cases of major Somatic Conversions in the last fifty years. This is due to the influence of increasing sophistication, education, and the evolution of the level of general social acceptability, of understanding, and of perceptiveness. From sixteen to twenty per cent was the overall estimate for Conversion Reactions, with 12–14 per cent of these today being Physiologic Conversions and 4–6 per cent Somatic Conversions.

In the section on Symptoms and Clinical Features we learned that symptoms represent in distorted form hidden emotional conflicts acted out or expressed somatically in physical symptoms as a kind of *body language*. The interesting Symptom-Barrage was illustrated in a therapeutic situation. Symptoms are legion. They include motor, sensory, and special sensory symptoms and dyskinesias, including convulsions, tics, spasm, and pseudo-epilepsy. They include also conversion vomiting, aphonia, pain, and globus hystericus. They represent a desperate psychologic effort to resolve conflicts over intolerable impulses, which are beyond conscious awareness. Briefly considered were such special aspects as "acting out", *la belle indifférence,* intelligence, conversion and schizophrenia, and self-punitive aspects. The *Rhazes Maneuver* was illustrated. The Concept of the Psychic Reduplication of organic pain was noted.

The Conversion Personality consists of a constellation of traits, as tabulated in *Table 18* [p. 259], which must be outstanding qualitatively and quantitatively for a personality to be so classified. Conversion character defenses are to be treated as are conversion symptoms. They have a similar intended purpose. When they are insufficient to cope with developing or additional stress, their intensification may follow, or replacement by clinical symptom formation can occur. Their imbalance or exaggeration constitutes the conversion kind of Character Neurosis.

The concept of *Interpersonal-Perpetuation* in the transmission of emotional illness, as distinguished from discarded views of inheritance was discussed. The possible establishment of an *Emergency Analytic-Bridge* was noted.

Under Dynamics, the hidden psychologic purposes of conversion symptoms (and the conversion character defenses) were tabulated. Simply stated, the primary gain or *endogain* of the symptom, responsible for and contributing to its *initiation* and its elaboration, is the avoidance of conflict, or the control of conflict. The three elements represented symbolically in symptoms include: (1) the expression of what is repressed, (2) the repressing force, and (3) retribution or punishment.

The *epigain* of the symptom *following* its elaboration relates to the unconsciously attempted efforts to influence favorably people and the persons' environment. It serves more immediate ends than the endogain, namely: (1) gratification of dependency needs, and needs for attention, love, affection, and so on; (2) escape, as from military service or an intolerable job or family situation; and (3) compensation. The conversion epigain aids in perpetuating the illness, once established.

We learned that symptoms are very much disguised and distorted. This is contributed to by *symbolism, condensation, displacement,* the use of *opposites, extension, elaboration,* and possible *changes of sequence.* Some of the important factors in the "choice" of symptoms and their location were tabulated (*Table 33*). The *Rule of Individual Symbolism* is an important precept to bear in mind.

Some special features were mentioned, including conversion identification, conversion pain, and conversion epidemics. *Hostile Identification* is with the largely rejecting and hostile elements of parents or others.

In the section on Treatment, the importance of dynamically oriented therapy was emphasized as the treatment of choice. When this is not feasible, other methods used primarily for symptom removal, are available. The defensive principle of the *Flight-to-the-Physical* was noted. The method or technique of *Progressive-Suggestion* was outlined and illustrated, and the *Red-Ink Cure* noted. Cautions as to hypnosis and narcosynthesis included the *Hazard of Symptom-Exchange.* The need for a *Therapeutic Bargain* was observed.

X. SELECTED REFERENCES AND BIBLIOGRAPHY

ABSE, D. W. (1950). *The Diagnosis of Hysteria*, p. 112. Bristol, England; John Wright & Sons.

— (1959). "Hysteria." In *American Handbook of Psychiatry*, pp. 273-292. Ed. by S. Arieti. New York; Basic.

ALEXANDER, F. (1950). *Psychosomatic Medicine.* New York; Norton.

— (1943). "Fundamental concepts of psychosomatic research." *Psycho-som. Med.,* **5**, 205.

— and FRENCH, T. M. (1946). *Psychoanalytic Therapy,* pp. 55–65. New York; Ronald.

ASHER, P. (1946). "A case of rapidly cured hysterical paralysis." *Br. Med. J.,* **1**, 355.

BABINSKI, J. and FRONENT, J. (1918). *Hysteria or Pithiatism.* London; University Press.

BABINT, M. (1956). *The Doctor, His Patients, and the Illness.* New York; International Universities Press.

BOWLBY, J. (1940). *Personality and Mental Illness,* pp. 152–162. London; Paul, Trench, Trubner.

BRADY, J. P. and LINA, D. L. (1961). "Experimental analysis of hysterical blindness." *Archs. Gen. Psychiat.,* **4**, 331.

BREUER, J. and FREUD, S. (1950). *Studies in Hysteria.* New York; Nervous and Mental Disease Publishing.

BRIERLEY, M. (1951). *Trends in Psychoanalysis,* p. 47, London; Hogarth.

BRILL, A. A. (1940). "An American precursor of Freud." *Bull. N. Y. Acad. Med.,* **16**, 631.

BRIQUET, P. (1859). *Traité de l'Hystérie.* Paris; Bailliere.

BROWN, W. and PISETSKY, J. E. (1954). "Sociopsychologic factors in hysterical paraplegia." *J. Nerv. Ment. Dis.,* **119**, 283.

CHARCOT, JEAN M. (1873). *Lecons sur les maladies du Systems Nervous.* Paris; Delalaye.

— and MARIE PIERRE (1892). "Hysteria." In *A Dictionary of Psychological Medicine,* Vol. 1, p. 67. Ed. by H. D. Tuke.

CHODOFF, PAUL and LYONS, H. (1958). "Hysteria, the hysterical personality and 'hysterical' conversion." *Am. J. Psychiat.* **114**, 734.

— (1954). "A re-examination of some aspects of conversion hysteria." *Psychiatry,* **17**, 75.

DUNBAR, F. (1948). *Mind and Body.* New York; Random House.

FAIRBAIRN, W. R. D. (1941). "A revised psychopathology of the psychoses and neuroses." *Int. J. Psycho-Analysis,* **22**, 250.

FENICHEL, O. (1945). *The Psychoanalytic Theory of Neurosis,* pp 216–237. New York; Norton.

FERENCZI, S. (1952). *The Theory and Technique of Psychoanalysis,* pp. 124–141. New York; Basic Books.

FITZGERALD, O. W. S. (1948). "Love deprivation and the hysterical personality." *J. Ment. Sci.* **94**, 701.

FREUD, S. (1950). "The defense neuropsychoses." In *Collected Papers,* Vol 1., p. 63, London; Hogarth.

— and BREUER, J. (1959). "On the "psychical mechanism of hysterical phenomena." *Ibid.,* p. 24.

— (1950). "Some points in a comparative study of organic and hysterical paralyses." *Ibid.,* p. 42.

— (1950). "The aetiology of hysteria." *Ibid.,* pp. 183–219.

— (1950). "Heredity and the Aetiology of the Neuroses." *Ibid.,* p. 138.

— (1950). "Sexuality in the neuroses." *Ibid.,* p. 276.

— (1950). "Repression." *Ibid.,* p. 94.

— (1950). "Charcot." *Ibid.,* p. 9–23.

— (1950). *Ibid.,* Vol. 3, pp. 13–148.

— (1913). *The Interpretation of Dreams.* New York; Macmillan.

— (1933). *New Introductory Lectures,* p. 154. London; Hogarth.

GLOVER, E. (1948). In *Psychoanalysis Today,* p. 223. Ed. by S. Lorand. New York; International Universities Press.

GORDON, HIRSCH LOEB (1949). *The Maggid of Caro.* New York; Pardes.

GOSLINER, B. J. (1954). Personal communication.

GREENACRE, P. (1950). "General problems of acting out." *Psychoanal. Q.* **19**, 455.

HIPPOCRATES. *Precepts,* Chapter 6.

ISAACS, S. (1952) "The nature and function of phantasy." *Developments in Psychoanalysis,* p. 90. London; Hogarth.

JAFFE, D. S. (1953). Personal communication.

JANET, PIERRE (1920). *The Major Symptoms of Hysteria,* p. 106. Washington; Armed Forces Medical Library.

— (1931). *L'Etat Mental des Hysteriques; Etudes sur Divers Symptomes Hysteriques,* p. 168. Paris; Alcan.

JENSEN, R. A. and WERT, A. D. (1945). "Conversion hysteria in children. *Lancet,* **65,** 172.

Joint Armed Forces Statistical Classification and Basic Diagnostic Nomenclature, p. 13. Washington; U. S. Government Printing Office.

KARDINER, A. (1948). Chapter in Lorand, S. Ed: *Psychoanalysis Today.* New York, International Universities Press, pp. 187–190.

KARPMAN, B. (1953). "Psychogenic (hysterical) dysphagia: report of a case." *Am. J. Orthopsychiat.,* **23,** 472.

KLEIN, M. (1950). *Contributions to Psychoanalysis,* pp. 98–99. London; Hogarth.

KOLB, L. C., FRANK, L. M., and WATSON, E. J. (1952. "Treatment of the acute painful phantom limb." *Proc. Staff Mayo Clin.,* **27,** 110.

— (1954). Personal communication.

KOURETAS, D. (1962). "La Catharsis d'apres Hippocrates, Aristotle, etc." Breuer-Freud Communication to the Neo-Hippocratic Congress of Montpelier (France).

KRETSCHUNER, E. (1926). *Hysteria.* New York; Nervous and Mental Diseases Publishing Co.

LAUGHLIN, H. P. (1953). "The conversion reactions." *Med. Ann. Distr. Columbia,* **22,** 581.

—, Editor (1955). *A Psychiatric Glossary,* 5th rev. ed. Washington; American Psychiatric Association.

— (1954). "The neuroses following trauma." *Med. Ann. Dist. Columbia,* Part I, **23,** 492; Part II, **23,** 567.

— (1956). *The Neuroses in Clinical Practice.* Philadelphia; Saunders.

— (1963). *Mental Mechanisms.* Washington; Butterworths.

—, Editor (1953). *A Psychiatric Glossary,* 4th rev. ed., p. 15, Washington; American Psychiatric Association.

— (1955). *The Psychoneuroses,* Section V (mimeo). Washington; George Washington Medical School.

— and RUFFIN, M. DEG. (1953). *An Outline of Dynamic Psychiatry,* pp. 128–135, 4th rev. mimeo. Washington; George Washington Medical School.

— (1954). "The obsessive personality." *Med. Ann. Dist. Columbia,* **23,** 212.

— (1953). "Suicide; impulse and remorse." *Q. Rev. Psychiat. Neurol.* **8,** 19.

LEBENSOHN, Z. M. (1954). Personal communication.

LEGAULT, O. (1954): "Denial of operation and certain other post-lobotomy symptoms." *Psychiatry,* **17,** 2.

LIFSCHUTZ, J. E. (1957). "Hysterical stigmatization." *Am. J. Psychiat.,* **114,** 527.

LITTERAL, E. B. (1954). Personal communication.

LOWENSTEIN, R. M. (1945). "A special form of self-punishment." *Psychoanalysis,* **22,** 250.

MARMOR, J. (1954). "Orality in the hysterical personality." *J. Am. Psychoanal. Ass.,* **1,** 656.

MENNINGER, W. C. (1954). Personal communication.

— (1930). *The Human Mind,* p. 134, Garden City; Garden City Publishing.

MUNCIE, WENDELL (1939). *Psychobiology and Psychiatry.* St. Louis; Mosby.

NOBLE, D. (1951). "Hysterical manifestations in schizophrenia illness." *Psychiatry,* **14,** 153.

—, PRICE, D. B., and GILDER, R. (1954). "Psychiatric disturbances following amputation." *Am. J. Psychiat.,* **110,** 609.

OSTLER, W. (1892). *The Principles and Practice of Medicine,* p. 974. New York; Appleton.

PERLEY, M. J. and GUZE, S. B. (1962). "Hysteria—the stability and usefulness of clinical rciteria." *New Engl. J. Med.,* **226,** 421.

ROSS, T. A. (1924). *The Common Neuroses.* London; Arnold.

— (1924). *War Neuroses.* Baltimore; Williams & Wilkins.

SAUL, L. K. (1954). Personal communication.

— (1947). *Bases of Human Behavior,* p. 150. Philadelphia; Lippincott.

SCHULER, E. A. and PAVENTON, U. J. (1943). "A recent epidemic of hysteria in a Louisiana high school." *J. Soc. Psychol.,* **17,** 221.

SHARPE, E. F. (1950). *Collected Papers on Psychoanalysis,* pp. 92–93. London; Hogarth.

SIEGMAN, A. J. (1954). "Emotionality——a hysterical character defense." *Psychoanal. Q.* **23,** 339.

SIMMEL, E. (1918). *Kriegsneurosen und Psychisches Trauma.* Munich and Leipzig; Nemmich.

— (1944). "War Neuroses." In *Psychoanalysis Today,* pp. 227–248. Ed. by S. Lorand. New York; International Universities Press.

SPERLING, M. (1933). "Food allergies and conversion hysteria." *Psychoanal. Q.*, **22**, 525.

STEPHENS, J. H. (1962). "On some aspects of hysteria: a clinical study." *J. Nerv. Ment. Dis.*, **134**, 305.

STEVENS, HAROLD (1958). "Conversion hysteria—the domain of neurology." Wien. Z. NervHeilk., **15**, 307.

SULLIVAN, J. D. (1955). "Psychiatric factors in low back pain." *N. Y. St. J. Med.*, **55**, 227.

WALKER, C. F. (1947). "Hysteria in childhood." *Am. J. Orthopsychiat.*, **17**, 468.

WEISS, E. and ENGLISH, O. S. (1949). *Psychosomatic Medicine*, 2nd ed. Philadelphia; Saunders Co.

WOLBERG, L. R. (1945). "A mechanism of hysteria elucidated during hypnoanalysis." *Psychoanal. Q.* **14**, 528.

ZIEGLER, F. J. and IMBODEN, J. B. (1962). Contemporary reactions." *Archs Gen. Psychiat.* 64, 279.

—— and MEYER, E. (1960). "Contemporary conversion reactions: a clinical study." *Am. J. Psychiat.* **116**, 901.

— and PAUL N. (1954). "Natural history of hysteria in women." *Dis. Nerv. Syst.* **15**, 301.

ZILBOORG, G. and HENRY G. (1941). *A History of Medical Psychology*, p. 374. New York; Norton.

XI. REVIEW QUESTIONS ON THE CONVERSION REACTIONS

1. Why do the Conversion Reactions deserve a certain measure of priority?
2. Define:
   - (a) Conversion
   - (b) Somatic Conversion Reaction
   - (c) Physiologic Conversion Reaction
   - (d) Psychologic Conversion
   - (e) Somatic or "body language"
   - (f) Physiologic language
   - (g) Overdetermination
   - (h) Transparency Theory
   - (i) Psychic Reduplication (of organic pain)
3. Discuss the historical background of the Conversion Reactions. What are the disadvantages of the older term "hysteria"?
4. (a). How is a diagnosis reached on positive grounds? What are the advantages?
   (b). How would you differentiate a Conversion Reaction from Hygeiaphrontis? Is the *Hygeiaphrontic Discrepancy Principle* [p. 443] of use?
5. Why has the Conversion Reaction been called the Great Imitator?
6. What influence have cultural factors had on types of symptoms and incidence?
7. Discuss: (a) The Concept of Secondary Defense, (b) Conversion Pain, (c) Acting Out, and (d) *la belle indifférence.*
8. List the more common symptoms of the Conversion Reactions.
9. (a). What are the psychologic purposes of the Conversion Reaction? (b) What is: The Conversion Endogain?; The Conversion Epigain?; The role of repression in conversion symptomatology?
10. Discuss three of the important factors in symptom choice and location.
11. Name the principle mechanisms in Conversion Reactions.
12. Discuss the role of: (a) Identification, and (b) Suggestion, in the Conversion Reactions. What is: (a) A conversion epidemic? (b) Character analysis?; (c) The Hazard of Symptom-Exchange? (d) The Therapeutic Bargain?
13. Discuss therapeutic measures in the Conversion Reactions. What is the "Flight-to-the-Physical?"
14. What are the challenges in therapy? Discuss the "treatment of choice".
15. What is meant by:
    - (a) The Rhazes Maneuver?,
    - (b) The Method of Progressive-Suggestion?;
    - (c) The Red-Ink Cure?;
    - (d) The Concept of Interpersonal Perpetuation?;
    - (e) The Emergency Analytic-Bridge?;
    - (f) The Rule of Individual Symbolism?;
    - (g) The Doctrine of Scientific Determinism?

CHAPTER 13

THE DISSOCIATIVE REACTIONS

. . . . Dissociation Concepts, Dreams, Somnambulism, Depersonalization, Fainting, Amnesia, Fugue States, Alternating Personality, Automatic Behavior, and Hypnosis

I. DEFENSE CHALLENGES PHYSICIAN AND INTRIGUES PUBLIC

A. Separate Consideration Warranted
1. Useful and Acceptable Development; 2. Dissociation and Dissociative Reactions Cover Broad Range

B. Opportunities for Familiarity Restricted; Psychologic-Flight Avoidance Concept
1. Few Instances Available for Study; 2. Need for Concealment; Secondary Defense Active

C. Public Interest Intrigued
1. Dissociated Purposeful Activity and Amnesias Newsworthy; 2. Many Areas for Dissociation

II. CONCEPTS OF DISSOCIATION IN PSYCHIATRY

A. Segment Split Off
1. Dissociation Defined; 2. Clinical Types Distinguishable; 3. Dissociative Reactions Produced

B. Historical Background
1. Early Beginnings; 2. Janet's Theories; 3. James, Prince, Breuer, and Freud

C. Diagnosis of Dissociative Reaction
1. Diagnosis Indicated; 2. Major Types of Dissociation

D. Incidence

E. Symptoms and Clinical Features

1. Clinical Dissociation; 2. Affect Dissociation; 3. Alternating Dissociation; 4. The Dissociation of Automaticity; 5. B.B.C. Dissociation; Induced Dissociation; 6. Breuer's Dissociation; 7. Fragmental Dissociation; 8. The Janet Dissociation; 9. Physiologic Dissociation; 10. Schizophrenic Dissociation; Bleuler's Dissociation; 11. Side-by-side Dissociation 12. The Dissociative Reactions

F. Psychodynamics and Pathogenesis
1. Ego Function; Mediating and Integrative; 2. Primitive Reaction; 3. Conversion and Dissociation; 4. Dissociative Reactions Reflect Operation of Four Types of Dissociation

III. DREAMS

A. Dream Functions
1. Vital Process; 2. Sleep-Preserving Function; 3. Wishes in Dreams; 4. Fears Expressed

B. Interpreting Dreams
1. Analysis Reveals Unconscious Material; 2. Free Association; Manifest and Latent Content

C. Mechanisms and Concepts in Dreams
1. Fifteen Important Precepts; 2. Nocturnal-Fantasy Concept

D. Added Aspects of Interest
1. Dissociation Within the Dream; 2. Certain Dreams Have Special Significance; 3. Rule of Individual Symbolism

IV. SOMNAMBULISM

A. Definition; Activated-Nocturnal-Fantasy Concept

B. The Significance of Sleep-walking
  1. Symbolism Simple or Involved; 2. Capacity for Dissociation

C. Pathologic Significance Varies
  1. Conflict-Indicator Concept; 2. Usually Well Safeguarded

D. In Summary

V. DEPERSONALIZATION

A. Personal and Environmental Feelings of Unreality
  1. Highly Subjective; 2. Definitions

B. History

C. Diagnosis and Incidence
  1. Common Subjective Experience; 2. Incidence as to Type

D. Clinical Features
  1. Variability; 2. Feelings of Unreality and Estrangement; 3. Relation to Stress and Danger; 4. Many Sources of Depersonalization; 5. Depersonalization Sometimes Alarming

E. Psychodynamics
  1. Incipient Fugue Concept; 2. Psychologic-Flight Avoidance Concept; 3. Depersonalization and Identification

VI. FAINTING

A. Temporary Loss of Consciousness
  1. Fragmental Dissociation; 2. Fainting Defined; A Primitive Defense

B. Variable Threshold; Incidence

C. Range of Stimuli Broad
  1. Many Situations; Meaning Individual; Emotional Contagion Concept; 2. Circumstances Unconsciously Arranged; 3. Helpless Position, As All Perception Surrendered; Ostrich Concept

VII. AMNESIA

A. Memory Loss
  1. Primarily Psychologic; 2. Definition of Amnesia

B. Notes on Diagnosis
  1. Medicolegal Implications; Malingering; 2. Organic Amnesia; 3. Psychologic Amnesia

C. Incidence
  1. Protectively Intended Function of Avoidance; Affective Escape Route; 2. Memories Lost Through Repression; Individual Selectivity; 3. Forgetting Facilitated Via Sleep; Contribution to Respite-of-Sleep Principle

D. Clinical Features
  1. Categories of Amnesia; 2. Psychologic Amnesia; 3. Sequela to Concussion; 4. Traumatic Encephalopathy of Boxers; 5. Amnesia Secondary to Alcohol; 6. Aging; 7. Derepression

E. Psychodynamics
  1. Pathologic Amnesia and Pathologic Forgetting; 2. Antecedent Pattern; 3. Dissociative Reactions Versus Conversion Reactions; 4. Amnesia Versus Psychopathy

F. Amnesia as a Legal Defense

G. Unconscious Falsification of Memory

H. Memory Loss with Electric Shock
  1. Regular Occurrence; Intensive Study Rare; 2. Memory Loss Comes to Light; 3. Principle of Psychic-Selectivity in Post-Electroshock Amnesia; 4. Contributory to Benefits

I. Treatment
  1. Conservative Approach Preferable; 2. Goals of Treatment Broad: Deep Treatment Ideal

VIII. FUGUE STATES

A. Major Personality Dissociation
  1. Flight Both Figurative and Literal; 2. Definition of Fugue State

B. Notes on Diagnosis
  1. Ideal Criteria; 2. Differential Problems; 3. Similarity to Psychotic Reaction

C. Incidence

D. Clinical Features of Fugue States
  1. Past Dissociated: Daytime-Somnambulism Concept; 2. Total Response to Crisis

E. Psychodynamics
  1. Unconscious Meanings; 2. Escape to More Pleasant Area; 3. Self-punitive Aspects; 4. Dissociation Defends Against Anxiety; 5. Overwhelming Stimulus with Pre-existing Diathesis; Peg Concept Applicable

F. Treatment of the Fugue
  1. Work Out Psychodynamics; 2. Conservative Approach; 3. Hypnosis: Reliving the Onset; 4. In Conclusion

IX. THE ALTERNATING OR DOUBLE PERSONALITY

A. Separate Lives
  1. Major Dissociation Allows Alternate Dominance; 2. Definition

B. Diagnosis and Incidence

C. Clinical Instances of Multiple Personality
  1. Dr. Morton Prince and Miss Christine Beauchamp; 2. Recent Cases

D. Note on Psychodynamics

X. AUTOMATIC BEHAVIOR

A. Automatic Writing

B. Old Pattern Takes Over: Automatic Behavior

XI. HYPNOSIS
  A. An Induced Dissociation
     1. Reaction to Suggestion; 2. Definition
  B. Historical Notes on Hypnosis
     1. From Antiquity; 2. Mesmer; 3. Later Contributors
  C. Clinical Features
     1. Induction of and Emergence from Hypnosis; 2. Selectivity for Hypnotist and Subject
  D. Dynamics
     1. Intense Relationship; 2. Suggestibility and the Power of Suggestion
  E. "Truth Serum": Adjunctive Drugs
     1. No Guarantee of Truth; 2. Important Factors in Criminal Interrogation; Psychic Pressures in Confession; 3. Adjuncts to Hypnosis

  F. Antisocial Acts Under Hypnotic Influence
  G. Hypnosis as an Implement of Psychiatric Research
     1. Exploration of Psychodynamics; 2. Post-hypnotic Suggestions; 3. Memory Loss and Recall; 4. Dreams; 5. Time Distortion; 6. Regression; 7. Conflicts, Illusions, and Hallucinations
  H. Comments on Hypnosis in Therapy
     1. Disadvantages; 2. Loss of Interest; 3. Limited Use; 4. Inherent Appeal in Passive Role; 5. Keep Within One's Depth; 6. Built-in Safeguard

XII. SELECTED REFERENCES AND BIBLIOGRAPHY

XIII. REVIEW QUESTIONS FOR THE DISSOCIATIVE REACTIONS

I. DEFENSE CHALLENGES PHYSICIAN AND INTRIGUES PUBLIC

A. SEPARATE CONSIDERATION WARRANTED

1. Useful and Acceptable Development

A. PRIOR DISCUSSION PROVIDES EXCELLENT FOUNDATION.—The consideration of the Dissociative Reactions at this point is a suitable progression from our discussion of the Conversion Reactions in the preceding chapter. An understanding of conversion and of the reactions of Somatic Conversion and Physiologic Conversion provides us with an excellent foundation, and one from which we can far better proceed.

As we shall observe, the psychodynamics of the two groups are related. Authorities have grouped the Dissociative Reactions and the Conversion Reactions together in the past, and undoubtedly a few may continue to do so.

B. DELINEATION OFFICIAL.—It would seem best, however, for the Dissociative Reactions to be considered separately. This has worked out well since this was undertaken in the first edition of this text (1956). It has proved to be a very useful and quite an acceptable development. Further, there is a good scientific basis for their separation.

Finally, they were officially first assigned such a position just four years still earlier, in the classification of the American Psychiatric Association and in the *Standard Nomenclature of Diseases and Operations* of the American Medical Association.

2. Dissociation and Dissociative Reactions Cover Broad Range

The Dissociative Reactions which we review in the present chapter include Dreams, Somnambulism, Depersonalization, Fainting, Amnesia, Fugue States, Alternating Personality, Automatic Behavior, and Hypnosis.

These intriguing clinical reactions are a consequence of the operation of the various types of dissociation. These types of this intriguing process will also shortly be outlined, and later briefly discussed.

The Dissociative Reactions constitute a large group of interesting, uncommon, and sometimes bizarre conditions. These comprise another major attempted route of escape from anxiety by man, in what has earlier been termed our *Age of Anxiety* [*See* references, pp. 18, 477, and Ch.12:VE*1*]. They cover a broad psychopathologic spectrum. They range from the normal (dreams) to the deeply pathologic (Fugue States). Many kinds and combinations of underlying psychodynamic formulations are involved. The psychodynamics and the clinical manifestations of several of the Dissociative Reactions may overlap with another member of the same group.

B. OPPORTUNITIES FOR FAMILIARITY RESTRICTED; PSYCHOLOGIC-FLIGHT AVOIDANCE CONCEPT

1. Few Instances Available for Study

The Dissociative Reactions have tended to remain in a more obscure position clinically and dynamically than have other patterns of defensive reaction. Relatively few cases of some reactions of this group (Amnesia, Fugue States) have been clinically available. This is in contrast to other more familiar groups of emotional reactions. As a consequence, fewer cases have been available for observation and teaching demonstration, or for intensive study, and fewer even of these have been reported in the medical literature. Only a small handful of cases of Alternating Personality, the rarest member of this group, have been written up through the years.

The nature of the precipitating events, together with the personal and clinical consequences of an episode of amnesia or fugue, for example, do not ordinarily lead these persons to seek psychiatric treatment. Patients with amnesic episodes are likely to wind up in a police station or a general hospital, not in the psychotherapist's office. The victim of a Fugue State is more likely to head away from a possible source of study and therapeutic help. The Dissociative Reactions are a defensively intended psychologic kind of flight from crisis and danger. They constitute the most active variety of the attempted *avoidance* of conflict through flight — actual (literal and physical), symbolic (figurative and psychological), or both. This is what we might term the *Concept of Psychologic-Flight Avoidance,* which is basic to the Dissociative Reactions [p. 531]. [*See* discussion of avoidance, pp. 525–530.]

In turn, the flight is itself defended. This is the *secondary defense** of the symptom. Often a most effective defense, it has contributed substantially to our lack of familiarity with this group of emotional reactions.

---

* The symptom, in itself a psychologically intended defense, is in turn defended. Thus the symptom is a major *primary defense,* and the defense *of* the symptom constitutes a *secondary defense.* This interesting and important Concept of Secondary Defense in emotional illness has been considered further. [*See* other references, pp. 144, 267, 359, 445, *Case 101* (pp. 487–9).]

2. Need for Concealment; Secondary Defense Active

A. MEMORY GAPS LOST AND HIDDEN; CONSPIRACY-OF-SILENCE CONCEPT.
—Many patients suffering from somnambulism, or from brief memory lapses, may tend to hide or to deny these phenomena through personal embarrassment or self-critical attitudes, or because of unpleasant social connotations. Family members may actively encourage or urge such concealment when they are aware of the instances. They may participate with the patient in what we might term a *Conspiracy-of-Silence.*

Finally, many minor episodes are also apt to be brief and transient. A small memory gap may hardly seem a handicap to the person concerned. If complete enough, he may be completely unaware of its existence. If it is successful in so far as being the answer to the underlying needs, it is lost. In a fair number of instances, whether or not this is the case, it will pass unnoticed by others. This may also be true even with certain of the more major episodes of fugue.

The memory loss in an emotional amnesia subserves a more-or-less vital intrapsychic purpose for the individual concerned. The protection which the blank area affords leads to a natural resistance to its being dispelled, the secondary defense. In such a setting one would hardly expect the patient to be wholeheartedly eager himself to have the disturbing or painful memories recalled. Not surprisingly, Dissociative Reactions rarely illustrate the Attention-Absorption Concept [pp. 452, 466, and 487–9].

B. CHALLENGE FOR THE PHYSICIAN.—In so far as the general physician is concerned, a person with an amnesic episode or somnambulism, for instance, is apt to represent something troubling, or a puzzle. These persons are a real challenge to his professional acumen. Such a person, however, is likely to represent also quite a problem to him. This kind of situation in a patient constitutes a difficult case for therapeutic resolution. Such a clinical problem is also likely to be beyond those psychiatric areas which may happen to be more familiar to the individual physician.

The physician may therefore, rather understandably, prefer to avoid involvement. Why pursue such a baffling matter with a patient who is himself relatively unconcerned,* if not actively disinterested? Dissociative Reactions are problems for the physician. For the foregoing reasons one might expect that at least minor instances of the Dissociative Reactions are somewhat more frequent than the review of case reports in the literature would lead one to believe. For the various reasons as cited, the opportunities for familiarity with them are limited.

C. PUBLIC INTEREST INTRIGUED

1. Dissociated Purposeful Activity and Amnesias Newsworthy

The reactions which are ordinarily to be included in this group have an inherent interest and appeal to the general public. Their strangeness,

---

* A type of outward attitude toward the Dissociative Reaction may be seen which is very closely akin to *la belle indifférence* of the patient toward his major handicap in a case of Somatic Conversion Reaction [Ch.12:VC3]. This also contributes to the secondary defense of the symptom.

particularly including the phenomenon of semi-automatic, non-conscious behavior, very much intrigues people. A case of claimed or actual amnesia, especially if there are medicolegal implications, is nearly always newsworthy.

At the same time there is likely to be a considerable degree of public and professional skepticism in regard to the publicized details of individual cases. This is hardly surprising since it may be most difficult, if not impossible in some instances, clearly and unequivocally to identify an amnesic state or a fugue as the genuine article. Enough authentic cases have been reported, however, to illustrate the fact that an individual actually may travel about for days, or even months, during his Fugue State. He may undertake various kinds of purposeful activity. The people around him may not even remotely suspect that he is functioning in a state of dissociation of consciousness.

2. Many Areas for Dissociation

In the present chapter we shall first consider the phenomenon and our conceptions of Dissociation generally, after which each of the various Dissociative Reactions will be discussed briefly, in turn. Dissociation is an important psychologic process. As a concept it has many applications in psychiatry.

Classification, definitions, and tabulation of the different types of Dissociation will be offered shortly. We shall learn that Dissociation and the Dissociative Reactions can occur in many areas. We shall shortly consider each of these at some greater length in the appropriate sections of our discussion to follow. The Dissociative Reactions are *symptom neuroses* in distinction from character neuroses, although symptoms as such are not necessarily prominent and the neurotic picture tends to be a reaction-of-the-whole.

II. CONCEPTS OF DISSOCIATION IN PSYCHIATRY

A. SEGMENT SPLIT OFF

1. Dissociation Defined

Association means the joining or connecting of one thing with another. *Dissociation* means the separation of one thing from another. It is a process in which something is broken up into two or more components; a splitting off of constituents. Psychologically, dissociation means disunion, separation, splitting off, or splitting apart.

In emotional dissociation then, there is *an isolation or splitting away from the total personality of some element, which can then be separately conceived, observed, and studied. Through the process of dissociation there is unconsciously secured the separation of an idea, wish, function, greater or lesser segment of attention, behavior, or awareness, and so on, from (the main stream of) consciousness.* The splitting of the personality takes place into (at least temporarily) disunited parts. Personality synthesis is disrupted. Rarely, one of the components is so major and powerful that it takes over for a time.

The concepts of association and dissociation have had wide usage in the description of psychologic phenomena. Obviously, many kinds of things can become associated psychologically. Likewise, many kinds of things can become dissociated psychologically. Our present interest lies particularly in the types of emotional dissociation which occur involuntarily, largely outside of and beyond conscious awareness, and as defined above.

2. Clinical Types Distinguishable

For purposes of description, classification, and communication the author currently recognizes ten major types of dissociation. These will shortly be listed in tabular form and then briefly discussed.

Their operation can often enough be delineated by definition, and distinguished clinically, as well as from the standpoint of their effects. Despite some overlapping they are more or less separable. The major clinical Dissociative Reactions in essence are acute emotional decompensations.

3. Dissociative Reactions Produced

As noted thus, there are a number of important conceptions of dissociation as an unconscious mental process. The consequences and effects of these produce the clinical members of our group of Dissociative Reactions. These are a major group of reactions, each of which can be essentially a clinical entity in itself.

The Dissociative Reactions principally are characterized by a dissociation of a segment of consciousness, as the most prominent feature of the illness. Sometimes the dissociated area even takes over temporary direction and control of the entire personality, during which time the individual may appear to be functioning quite satisfactorily to the casual observer. We shall see this illustrated later in more marked fashion in certain cases of fugue and double personality.

B. HISTORICAL BACKGROUND

1. Early Beginnings

In early times there was some awareness of the existence of the dissociative phenomena. Little was understood, however, about their nature or origin. For instance, such phenomena as trances were spoken of and written about. During the Middle Ages, their nature was cloaked in mysticism or superstition. At other times the results of dissociative processes were associated with magic or "spells" or witchcraft.

In the latter half of the nineteenth century increasing scientific attention was directed toward the interesting phenomenon of hypnosis. The resulting study of hypnotic phenomena inevitably led to more awareness of the interesting human capacity for dissociation. Mesmer popularized and dramatized mesmerism (hypnotic suggestion). Braid used hypnosis in surgical procedures and gave it its name. Further work in using and in understanding this phenomenon was paced by such pioneer workers as Liebault, Bernheim, and Charcot.

2. Janet's Theories

It became increasingly clear that consciousness was not an indivisible stream. Pierre Janet thought in terms of the splitting up of the mind into separate consciousnesses. Each of these might then be displayed as a different aspect or kind of personality. According to this view, a conversion patient, for example, might "abandon" a part of his consciousness, through his being too weak nervously to maintain its integration. Thus Janet developed the concept of the splitting off of a part of consciousness from the main stream; that is, a dissociation of consciousness. He recognized the major importance of this kind of psychologic splitting off, or splitting apart.

This early concept was illustrated particularly by clinical cases of major conversional states, in which the dissociation of memory, behavior, and emotion was marked. Conversion (hysterical) spells, pseudo-epilepsy, and hypnoid syndromes were included by Janet, as were certain delusional or semi-delusional states, which today might be diagnosed as schizophrenia.

Janet, however, assigned to dissociation an all-important role in the etiology of the neuroses. Becoming aware of and developing a highly useful concept, he fell into the always-so-tempting trap of its overvaluation. Attempts were made to fit most, if not all psychologic phenomena into an overall theory of dissociation. Certain aspects of this made a good deal of sense. Good adaptation to daily living, according to Janet, vitally required an integration of the various mental processes. The possession of a normal amount of "mental energy" was a *requisite for the maintenance of this integration.*

When the level of this necessary energy continued high, integration or personality synthesis would be maintained. When it became low, the integration might falter. The personality might then cease to function as a unit and consequently split, or dissociate. The consequence would be emotional illness, of nearly any type.

3. James, Prince, Breuer, and Freud

Janet tended to explain most psychopathology on this kind of basis. While he overapplied his theories of dissociation, he nonetheless made a very significant contribution to psychiatry. William James (1842–1910), scholar, author, and professor of psychology at Harvard University for many years, lectured and wrote about Janet's theories, and reported the interesting case of the Reverend Ansell Bourne. Soon Morton Prince (1854–1929), also in the United States, began a series of important psychopathologic studies and observations of dissociative phenomena.

His professional work, which was mainly concerned with dissociation, did a great deal to stimulate psychiatric interest in this country. He reported the classic case of Multiple Personality of his patient, Miss Christine Beauchamp.

The concept of psychologic dissociation was accepted by Breuer, Freud, and early adherents of the analytic school. Since the turn of the century, conceptions and theories of dissociation have been further evolved, laying the necessary foundations for their continuing development and presentation in our current study. Today they make up an accepted part of the foundations of modern dynamic psychiatry.

C. DIAGNOSIS OF DISSOCIATIVE REACTION

1. Diagnosis Indicated

The diagnosis of a Dissociative Reaction is indicated whenever the manifestations of one of the group of such reactions is the major clinical feature of an emotional illness. As noted earlier, the incidence is highly variable for the different entities among the Dissociative Reactions. Certain phenomena which are considered to be dissociative in nature are practically universal, while others are exceedingly rare.

There are a number of major types of Dissociation. The author has attempted their classification and tabulation, in an effort more clearly to delineate their relative positions, to indicate their interrelationships, as a convenience for their study, and for the interested student's readier reference.

2. Major Types of Dissociation

The following ten types of dissociation are presented alphabetically, in tabular form (*Table 34*). Some are more important; some occur more frequently; some will be more commonly referred to than others. For purposes of identification, seven names have been assigned empirically and on a descriptive basis; three of these are named after professional pioneers in this area, an explanation of which follows each listing.

Table 34

Major Types of Dissociation

1. *Affect Dissociation.* Named for the split-off emotional or affective component. This is the dissociation, or splitting away, of the painful affect, emotion, and emotional association from a psychologically or physically traumatic event.

   This is the principal function of Dissociation as a *mental mechanism* or *dynamism* [comprising our *First Line of Defense*, pp. 25, 343, and 517].

2. *Alternating Dissociation.* Named descriptively. In this kind of dissociation, a large area of consciousness is split off at least temporarily, to more or less completely displace and dominate the remainder.

(*Table continued on next page*)

Table 34—Continued

This dissociation is the type leading to the production of, and to be observed in, instances of the *Fugue States,* and in the very rare case of Double, Multiple, or *Alternating Personality.*

3. *Dissociation of Automaticity.* Named for the automatic nature of the phenomenon. In this type there is the dissociation of a specific activity. Typically, it may be observed in instances of *automatic behavior* or *automatic writing.* Somnambulism may be thought of as illustrating both Fragmental Dissociation and the Dissociation of Automaticity.

4. *B.B.C. Dissociation; Hypnotic or Induced Dissociation.* Named after its origins; or for the three pioneers: *B* (Braid), *B* (Bernheim), and *C* (Charcot). This dissociation is that which is purposely elicited or induced in the hypnotic state [Ch.12:IIA2].

   There are both cogent advantages for and reasons against naming it after one or all of several major pioneers: notably, Mesmer, Braid, Liebault, Bernheim, and Charcot. The B.B.C. designation is a compromise.

5. *Breuer's Dissociation.* This type the author has proposed naming for Joseph Breuer, who discovered around 1880 the significance of "forgotten" painful events in the onset of the major conversion symptoms.

   In Breuer's Dissociation, there is the dissociation from consciousness and/or control (*of the individual mental representation*) of a specific somatic function of a part, such as the loss of sensation, or voluntary activity in a (part of, or an entire) limb. This we have observed through its repeated illustration in the *Somatic Conversion Reactions* in the preceding chapter. Herein the dissociation may be thought of as in conjunction with or as a consequence of, the conversion process [Ch.12:VE*1* and VIB].

6. *Fragmental Dissociation* (Laughlin). Named descriptively. The dissociation of an area, segment, or of a fragment from the main stream, or from the remainder of consciousness. This occurs, for example, in *depersonalization,* in *fainting,* and in *amnesia.*

7. *The Janet Dissociation.* Herein the author includes those instances of the splitting away or dissociation of an area from the stream of consciousness, such as occur in conversion emotionalism, convulsions and pseudo-epilepsy, spells, and other conversion (hysterical) behavioral manifestations [*see also* Ch.12:VIB*2*].

   Naming this group for Pierre Janet would seem most appropriate, as being in keeping with his originally having viewed many conversion manifestations as dissociative phenomena.

8. *Physiologic Dissociation* (Laughlin). Analogous to Breuer's Dissociation, No. 5 above. The similar dissociation of a *physiologic* area. This kind of dissociation occurs in the *Physiologic Conversions,* including the psychosomatic illnesses and somatization reactions.

9. *Schizophrenic Dissociation; Bleuler's Dissociation.* Named for the psychotic reaction in which it is to be observed, or for Bleuler who introduced the term *schizophrenia.* This refers to the dissociation of appropriate affect from ideation [Ch.12:VD*4*]. Not qualitatively different basically from the above. Its distinguishing features are to be found: (1) in degree; (2) in its often ready verbal expression; and (3) in the ease of observation by an observer.

10. *Side-by-Side Dissociation.* Named after the coexistent activities which result.

    This type of dissociation makes possible and facilitates the performing of simultaneous mental and/or physical activities. They are then able to be accomplished at the same time, but at least quasi-independently.

D. INCIDENCE

Dissociation as a clinical phenomenon is very widespread in its incidence. Evidence of dissociative processes can be uncovered in almost every neurosis.

Instances in which a major dissociative process constitutes the single most prominent clinical feature of a neurosis, however, are much rarer. It is estimated that only perhaps 2–4 per cent of the clinical cases of neuroses would warrant a diagnosis and classification within the major category of the Dissociative Reactions. Added comments on incidence will accompany the discussion of the individual reactions (*also see Table 16,* p. 243 for the estimated incidence of other neurotic reactions).

E. SYMPTOMS AND CLINICAL FEATURES

1. Clinical Dissociation

At this point some further clarification, definition, and elaboration of the various applications and concepts of psychologic dissociation is indicated. Let us consider them with numbers corresponding to the order as outlined previously (*Table 34*), and from a clinical point of view.

2. Affect Dissociation

A. CAPACITY FOR EMOTIONAL EXPERIENCING IS SPLIT-OFF.—Affect Dissociation is *the operation of dissociation as a mental mechanism or dynamism; the dissociation of otherwise painful affect or emotion.* As a mental mechanism, Dissociation has been more definitively discussed and defined elsewhere. The protective purpose of this kind of mechanism is readily apparent. If a situation, idea, or event is accompanied by intolerably painful emotion, the dissociation of the emotional charge from conscious awareness is in the service of ego protection. As a mental dynamism, dissociation is part of our psychic *First Line of Defense* [pp. 25, 343, 517].

It is as though the capacity for conscious perception and experiencing of the emotional import is at least temporarily blocked, or split off. This particular function of dissociation is as an intrapsychic mechanism of defense or specific dynamism. The author prefers to delimit its usage as a mental mechanism to this specific area.

B. EMOTIONAL-IMPACT-DEFERMENT (E.I.D.).—This kind of operation may be temporary or semi-permanent. At times it represents what the author proposes we might for purposes of convenience and identification, refer to as an unconscious kind of *emotional-impact-deferment* or postponement [Ch.14:VH3]. This is sometimes reflected in the lay reference to "something having caught up with" one. This common expression is used to indicate that emotional impact previously deferred, is now being experienced. The E.I.D. is an interesting protective operation.

The use of dissociation in the context of a mental mechanism ties in with and tends to overlap our conceptions of blocking and repression. Indeed, to a certain extent all kinds of repression and memory loss are dissociations from the usual or main stream of consciousness, or conscious awareness.

The splitting away of the painful emotions from an event is illustrated in the following instance. This example also illustrates our concept of the defensive process of Emotional-Impact-Deferment (E.I.D.).

Case 150

Emotional-Impact-Deferment; Dissociation in Sudden Death

A thirty-two-year-old married woman had been having her parents, who lived in another city, as guests for a ten-day period. They were scheduled to leave the following morning, and upon retiring appeared in their usual good state of health and spirits. An urgent call from her father at 12:30 a.m. brought the daughter and her husband to the bedside of the mother, just in time to see her draw her last few breaths. A sudden heart attack proved fatal.

This was a tremendous loss and shock to the daughter, especially because of the unexpectedness. An excellent, warm, and close relationship had existed. The daughter consciously felt little grief at the time. She helped to make the necessary arrangements concerning the body and her mother's personal effects. She was even able to return to sleep rather promptly, several hours later. Her Total Individual Response to Trauma included the temporary dissociation of the *emotional* impact, from her *intellectual* recognition of the death. Through the dissociation this was postponed. This illustrates an instance of E.I.D.

The daughter clearly recognized on a conscious, intellectual level the presence of death. Unconsciously, she had "split away" the ordinarily attached affect. In this instance this permitted her to continue to function effectively. It "deferred" the terrific emotional significance and meaning to a later time, when it could be experienced more gradually and with less interference with the practical demands of the immediate present. This was a significant Emotional Deferment.

Less dramatic instances are seen more frequently. Often also the dissociation of affect is more partial than total.

3. Alternating Dissociation

Alternating Dissociation is *the massive kind of dissociation of the personality, in which a major "section" or area splits off from the balance and replaces the entire structure in its control and direction of the individual.* This major type of dissociation is the *alternating* variety, and will be observed in some major amnesic episodes and Fugue States [Ch.13:VIII].

Alternating Dissociation also occurs in the very rare kind of Double or Alternating Personality. This is illustrated by James' case, the Reverend Ansell Bourne, and by Prince's Miss Christine Beauchamp. *Case 142* has sufficient of this type of dissociation present to also be worth reviewing.

4. The Dissociation of Automaticity

In the Dissociation of Automaticity the distinction is largely descriptive. Herein one may observe *the automatic carrying through of some specific type of activity.* This type of dissociation is *exemplified in the phenomenon of automatic writing,* as later described [Ch.13:XA].

This type of dissociation is also so labeled in instances of automatic behavior when one follows, for example, a long established but no longer appropriate habit pattern. This occurred in *Case 173,* and has been observed in a number of similar occurrences. It is closely related to, and can at times overlap with instances of Side-by-Side Dissociation.

The existence of a capacity for the Dissociation of Automaticity may be uncovered through careful history taking, and through its being elicited by actual clinical trials and experimental tests. Its presence demonstrates the individual's capacity to dissociate. It can also indicate ready hypnotizability.

5. B.B.C. Dissociation; Induced Dissociation

The Braid-Bernheim-Charcot Dissociation is that which is *deliberately induced, elicited, or brought on by suggestion and through hypnosis.* Accordingly it might also be appropriately referred to as *Hypnotic Dissociation,* or as *Induced Dissociation.*

A considerable capacity for dissociation and for suggestability must be present for a person to become at all readily hypnotizable. B.B.C. Dissociation is elicited in the induction of hypnosis and is a prerequisite to its operation [*see also* Section XI]. Many interesting clinical phenomena in the hypnotic and post-hypnotic states are thereby possible.

6. Breuer's Dissociation

Breuer's Dissociation refers to *the dissociation from consciousness and control (of the individual representation) of a specific physical function.* This is what occurs psychodynamically in the Somatic Conversion Reactions (Conversion Hysteria) [Ch.12:IIB2]. It is a process that we have seen illustrated in the preceding chapter. As was pointed out in the descriptive studies of conversion as far back as the latter part of the nineteenth century, there is a most important distinction between the actual structural anatomy and its innervation and the conversion area of a loss of motor ability or sensory receptivity, in a given part of the body.

The intrapsychic (unconscious) concept of an arm or leg or other part is entirely individual. It does not necessarily bear any relation to logic, to anatomy, or to the nerve supply. Instead, it follows what the individual concerned "thinks" it to be [Ch.12:VE1]. It is as he represents it to himself consciously, and within his psyche. Therefore it is hardly surprising that the conversion paralysis may not conform to the actual nerve distribution. The unconscious does not know the nerve supply, and cares little about it!

When it occurs, the paralysis follows the patient's own *mental representation* of a physical function or unit. This interesting type of dissociation makes the Somatic Conversion Reaction possible. It also may be thought of as contributing to it, or as being a part of the conversion process. In view of the examples cited in the chapter on Conversion Reactions, another example seems unnecessary here. We shall therefore devote little further consideration to this particular rather technical conception of dissociation, or to the analogous one of Physiologic Dissociation (No. 8).

7. Fragmental Dissociation

Fragmental Dissociation is a major dissociative process which the author has named descriptively. It refers to *the dissociation of a more or less specific fragment or area, of consciousness.* This is one of the principal usages of the concept of dissociation for the purposes of this chapter. Herein is contained the essential dynamic process underlying several of the types of Dissociative Reactions to which we will refer further.

This major type of dissociation is seen in Depersonalization, in Fainting, in most amnesic episodes, and possibly in certain instances of Automatic Behavior. It is this conception of dissociation with the clinical reactions which are produced through its operation, together with the foregoing Alternating Dissociation to which this chapter principally will be devoted. Fragmental Dissociation may circumvent an A.A.A. [p. 89]; thus also the possibility of a *Circular Generation of Fear* [pp. 89 and 518] of a recurrence is negated.

8. The Janet Dissociation

Janet's Dissociation is named for Pierre Janet, because of his recognition and description of the various conversion (hysterical) reaction attacks, and their dissociative nature [Ch.12:IIIA4]. He made excellent clinical studies of these. Typical is his report of the "somnambulistic" (a term and adjective then widely so used) behavior of his patient Irene, who suffered such grossly dissociated, conversion attacks. In these she "acted" over again the very disturbing and tragic events of the time of her mother's death. She had nursed her mother through the latter's terminal illness, and had tried futilely to revive the corpse. On the conscious level, she had forgotten (repressed) the painful scene. Between her attacks she appeared to be "callous and insensible [to her mother's death] . . . and did not remember her attacks . . .".

This type of dissociation might be defined as *the splitting away of an area of consciousness and behavior which is ordinarily repressed, but which becomes evident during the course of conversion (hysterical) attacks.* At times the onset of these may come on in response to hypnotic suggestion.

The Janet Dissociation would also include related types of conversional dissociative states relating to consciousness and behavior. Herein are the now rarer (in the more sophisticated cultural groups) instances of conversion spells, wild emotional attacks, convulsions [Ch.12:VE1], and pseudo-epilepsy. Also to be included might be certain fainting attacks, plus such other behavioral manifestations as would appear appropriately grouped under the heading of Conversion (hysterical) Reactions.

9. Physiologic Dissociation

A. GENERALLY INIMICAL TO HEALTH AND WELL-BEING.—This type of dissociation is analogous to Breuer's Dissociation. Through it there is *the analogous dissociation of a physiologic area.* In this type of dissociative process some kind, part, or aspect of physiologic function, which ordinarily operates efficiently and automatically in the service of the individual as a whole, becomes dissociated. As a consequence it can be converted (and subverted) so as to come to more or less symbolically express consciously disowned drives, emotions, or wishes. The results in disordered physiology are generally inimical to the health and well-being of the person concerned.

One may properly speak of the dissociation of the disturbed and disturbing area of function from the balance of overall function, which remains generally constructively integrated in the healthful service of the biologic unit. Similar factors to those in the dissociation and loss of a specific physical activity or sensation apply, as to the unconsciousness and individuality of the mental representation. This by no means necessarily conforms to actual function, as noted earlier in relation to somatic conversions.

This kind of dissociation occurs in the Physiologic Conversion Reactions, including the Somatization Reactions and psychosomatic illnesses, and so on. [*See Table 31.*]

B. SYMPTOMS EXPRESS FEELINGS DISSOCIATED FROM THEIR INTRA-PSYCHIC CONTEXT.—In the following rather simple instance, symptoms of palpitation, pain, and hyperhydrosis were the established and otherwise unaccountable physiologic expressions of consciously disowned emotions.

Case 151

Palpitation and Hyperhydrosis as the Dissociated Physiologic Expression of Consciously Disowned Emotions

A thirty-nine-year-old single woman sought analytic treatment because of certain recurring problems in her interpersonal relationships. She also reported distressing instances of palpitation, nausea, stomach pain, and increased perspiration. These came on seemingly unaccountably. They bore no relationship to anything she could consciously ascertain. They were an added source of strain and embarrassment since she felt that on occasion they were so marked as to be apparent and possibly offensive to her friends.

During a prolonged period of study we came to learn that the physiologic changes were related to repressed emotions. The palpitation, nausea, pain, and increased perspiration came on when these threatened to break through into conscious awareness. Through their dissociated expression into the symptoms, these were thus divorced from their real emotional basis and context. By their conversion and dissociated expression, her attention was also defensively diverted to the functional changes.

Her once-held view had been that the basis for these manifestations was solely physical. To her, emotions had seemingly played no part. The belief constituted a *secondary defense* of the symptoms. This was also part of her resistance. As the basis for her symptoms became more apparent under psychotherapeutic study, they greatly diminished.

10. Schizophrenic Dissociation; Bleuler's Dissociation

A. EMOTION INAPPROPRIATE.—Dissociation is also used as a descriptive term to describe *the break-off of the normal relationship between thoughts and feelings, as can be most typically and pathologically observed in schizophrenia* [Ch.12:VD4]. In this condition there is an apparent separation of the intellectual and emotional processes, so that the emotional expression is frequently inappropriate and is often diminished.

Sometimes the term has also been used rather loosely to describe the so-called "dissociation" from reality in schizophrenia. In a psychotic episode the patient may split off a greater or lesser area of reality from his perception. This is especially true in so far as the segments which conflict with his abnormal mental content are concerned [*see also* comment in *Table 34*].

B. PSYCHOTIC DISSOCIATION.—This would be an extension of our concepts of Schizophrenic Dissociation. According to this usage, many of the psychotic reactions would be viewed *in toto* as a massive kind of splitting off of emotional and mental aspects of the self, from reality.

11. Side-by-Side Dissociation

A. ONE ACTIVITY SEMIAUTOMATIC.—In this type of dissociation there is *the side-by-side dissociation, that is, from each other, of purposeful mental functions and/or physical activities. As a consequence they can then be carried on more readily, simultaneously.* In this kind of process, one or the other type of activity is at least partially dissociated from conscious awareness and comes to function in an automatic or semiautomatic fashion. The whole process may be in its initiation, a rather conscious one.

Dissociation is thus employed as the name for the psychologic process in which there is a division of the psychic-mental controls into two or more parts, each of which possesses the capacity to function more or less independently. This dissociation may be partial and temporary.

In this particular usage, the process of dissociation may serve a useful purpose. The following examples illustrate Side-by-Side Dissociation.

Case 152

Planning Business Operations While Driving

A businessman made, for a long time, several trips each week from Washington, D. C. to Frederick, Md., and to Hagerstown, Md. He was an excellent driver and had become thoroughly familiar with the route.

He reported that he had been able much of the time to reduce his driving to a semiautomatic process. This left a considerable segment of his attention safely free to plan his current business operations en route. At times he would find himself many miles along the route, with no conscious recollection of what had transpired in so far as the travel was concerned.

In the meantime he had reviewed an important business proposition or so. Still, his driving seemingly had not suffered.

Case 153

A Professional Window-washer Dreamed and Planned

A professional window-washer reported the presence of involved daydreaming kinds of fantasies. He had indulged in these, as well as in constructive personal planning, while performing his usual activities many stories above the street.

His work had become sufficiently routine to allow a segment of his attention to be devoted elsewhere. This was seemingly without untoward effects on his primary occupation, or on his personal safety.

B. PERSONAL USE AND CONVENIENCE.—This kind of dissociation is related to the phenomena of automatic writing and automatic behavior. These have been mentioned (in our Dissociation of Automaticity, No. 3 above) and will be discussed further later in this chapter. When two activities can be usefully and safely carried on simultaneously, the process of dissociation can be helpful and constructive. The following instance is illustrative.

Case 154

A Radio Announcer Filled Several Jobs

An announcer in a small radio station conducted a two-hour weekend program, interspersed with transcriptions, interviews, and various matters of general interest. As a matter of preference, he conducted his program from the transmission station instead of in the downtown studios. This however, involved his necessary assumption of a number of added duties.

On one occasion I watched with interest his facility in simultaneously serving as announcer, engineer, program director, and interviewer. These functions he carried on with efficiency. Some of them, particularly the control of transmission and the broadcasting of recordings, were relegated to a semiautomatic and semi-independent kind of control, in an efficient operation of dissociative character, of the side-by-side variety.

Most of us learn ways of putting some aspect of this to personal use and convenience. We may be already aware of these, or they might become more noticeable upon closer self-observation.

C. DISTURBED BALANCE SELF-DEFEATING AND DANGEROUS.—These foregoing examples are neither pathologic nor harmful. Instances may be observed, however, in which the area requiring primary attention is too completely replaced by the secondary one. The resulting inattention can lead to hurt, loss, or damage, as illustrated in the following case.

Case 155

Dissociated Activity with an Unhappy Consequence

A young college professor was in the habit of carrying on serious discussions with a colleague while driving to his university office. These discussions were often highly technical and involved. One morning the conversation was perhaps particularly animated and engrossing. Turning to his companion to make a specific point, he failed to notice the sudden stop of the car ahead. A fairly serious collision resulted.

He had relegated his driving to a semiautomatic activity. This had worked well heretofore. This time he had allowed it to go too far; or perhaps rather the other side had become too absorbing, engrossing, and demanding. The balance of the side-by-side dissociation of attention and activity in the two simultaneous endeavors was upset. The discussion side gained too much priority, at the expense of the driving side. The result was self-defeating and hazardous.

12. The Dissociative Reactions

We shall shortly take up the various clinical entities and phenomena which might best be considered with the Dissociative Reactions. Some are symptoms, others major syndromes. Some represent our concept of

Table 35

THE DISSOCIATIVE REACTIONS: COMPARATIVE DATA

	Clinical Entity or Symptom	Type of Dissociation	State of Consciousness	Memory
Alternating (or Multiple) Personality	C.E.	Alternating D.	No change apparent; as though the conscious is double or multiple, and the parts completely alternative	Little or no memory by the dominant personality present for the suppressed one
Amnesias	C.E. *or* S.	Fragmental D.; rarely Alternating	May or may not appear impaired	Blank area the distinctive feature
Automatic Writing and Behavior	Neither; a phenomenon which is sometimes useful. Indicates dissociative ability	D. of Automaticity; occasionally Fragmental D.	No apparent change	May not consciously recall
Depersonalization (including *Déjá Vu*)	Nearly always S.	Fragmental D.	No apparent change	Unaffected
Dreams	S., or non-associated with a C.E.	Fragmental D.	Sleeping state	Ability to recall varies; almost never total
Fainting	S.	Fragmental D.	Unconscious	No recall for duration (period) of attack
Fugue States	C.E.	Alternating D.	From no apparent change, to confusion and poor synthesis	Recall absent or spotty
Hypnosis	Neither	B.B.C. or Induced D.	Neither waking nor sleeping, with aspects of both. May appear close to either	Quite variable; depends upon suggestions
Memory Loss (by repression)	S., or neither	Affect D.; none	No effect	Nil
Side-by-Side Dissociation	S.; possibly neither	Side-by-Side D.	No effect	Partial, variable
Somnambulism	S.; very rarely C.E.; or non-associated with a C.E.	Fragmental D.	Dissociated activity while asleep	Nil
Traumatic Encephalopathy of Boxers	S. or C.E.	Usually none	Scattered effects upon cerebral activity, not on consciousness	Scattered defects possible

an "overall language" as expressed in a major dissociation. Some are universal experiences, some terribly rare. In an effort to summarize a few of the features of this diverse group in a comparative fashion for the convenience of the student, several of them have been tabulated in *Table 35.*

Table 35—Continued

Historically Associated With	Response to therapy	Ease of diagnosis	Incidence	Significant clinical features
James; Prince	Potential excellent	Fair, to difficult	Terribly rare	A previously submerged major area of the personality alternates, to become dominant.
	Poor, to excellent	Ranges from readily made, to impossible	Not infrequent	A blank space of memory loss. Psychologic or physical initiation.
	Rarely required. Occasional use as adjunct to treatment	Usually evident	Moderately rare	A dissociated area directs the writing or behavior automatically (outside of consciousness).
Krishaber; Dugas, Janet	Very good	Easy	Common, if not universal	Subjective; person must report. Sometimes accompanies or prodromal to more serious problems.
Freud	Interpretation an excellent adjunct to therapy	One is dependent upon person's reporting	Universal and nightly	Probably vital to health and well-being. Meanings usually distorted, symbolized, hidden, and so on.
	Fair	Usually few problems	Gradually becoming more rare	Lack of injury usual. A significant person or persons likely to witness. Epigain tends to be more apparent.
	Poor to fair. Occasionally good	Problems can be major	Rare	A figurative and literal flight from unbearable conflict. Confusion at times.
Mesmer; Braid; Liebault; Bernheim; Charcot; Breuer	Judiciously employed as an adjunct to treatment	Occasionally uncertain	5–10% or more of people are hypnotizable	See definitions. Contacts limited to operator. Ability to dissociate; suggestibility.
Breuer; Freud	Good	Only recall establishes	Universal	Important in treatment. Associative recall possible.
	Seldom needed	Depends upon history	Fairly common	Useful simultaneous activities may be carried on.
	Fair	Person or family reports	Moderately common especially in childhood	Self-preservation maintained. An unconscious "acting" or "seeking."
Hartland	Nil	Can be difficult; progression is insidious	Occupational hazard for boxers	Major preventative is early retirement from the ring.

F. PSYCHODYNAMICS AND PATHOGENESIS

1. Ego Function; Mediating and Integrative

A. INTEGRATIVE VS. DISSOCIATIVE EVENTS.—In our study of the bases of dissociation, we are essentially dealing with the external and the internal (intrapsychic) factors which result in the splitting off, or the tendency to split off, parts of the ego. The function of the ego is integrative — to secure and to maintain integration. The ego seeks to maintain a reasonable state of balance through its major function as a mediator between the id drives on the one hand, and the demands of the superego, plus the standards and requirements of the outside world on the other. Dissociation is a disintegrative and psychologically disjunctive consequence of certain individually intolerable stresses and trauma. It can be organic, psychologic, or both.

Dissociation is one type of unconscious individual response. It is a psychologic defense. Through it, avoidance is achieved via a form of psychologic flight. It is a segment of the individual Total Reaction to Crisis or to Trauma, the T.R.C. and T.R.T. The defense of dissociation leads to certain clinical states. These can assume psychopathologic implications of major import. At times, a major Dissociative Reaction is seen to be the direct response to trauma. This will be illustrated in *Case 205,* in Chapter 14. Here, a Dissociative Reaction proved to be the major psychologic part of the Total Reaction to Crisis of a young man, after his being the survivor in a struggle with his brother against drowning.

One may think of experiences and events generally as being either integrative *or* dissociative, in their consequences to the individual. This applies especially to the vicissitudes of interpersonal relationships. The possible dissociative and disintegrative effect of these may have important consequences later. This is more marked with the vicissitudes of early life. Here, they contribute to the antecedent emotional conditioning of the individual, and can establish important models for later possible conflicts, and their increased consequences.

Brain injury, hemorrhage, infection, drugs, and toxins, for example, can sometimes produce effects which are manifested by dissociation on a psychologic level. These dissociations, however, are less mysterious than are massive dissociations on a psychologic basis alone, with their widespread alterations in consciousness or of self. To adapt successfully, each of us must function as an integrated unit.

The partial loss or detachment of a segment of the self is a handicap. Such integration is the primary function of an intact ego. Indeed, one might almost say this *is* the ego. Ego function is mediating and integrative.

B. IN PSYCHOSES.—The psychoses may perhaps be viewed as a massively pathologic kind of emotional and mental dissociation from reality. Herein there is a splitting off of the self from the environmental circumstances which have been present, and which have become intolerable for various reasons.

In the development of the psychoses, the ego loses its battle to maintain integration. It is overwhelmed. A psychosis is the result of ego-disintegration.

C. COMPARTMENTALIZATION.—We may have a tendency to understress certain facets of the defensive intent of the dissociative process. How does it tend to operate thus in the more minor uses of its employment? How does it seek to resolve emotional conflict?

The author prefers to regard one of its main functions in this endeavor as what we might term *compartmentalization*. Such a name would appear appropriate, descriptive, and useful. Presumably, if one could isolate separately the opposing elements in an emotional conflict, a greater measure of harmony would result. Thus one might seek to maintain separate compartments for each of such conflicting elements.

To the extent this dissociation of the conflictual components were possible, one might allay or avoid conflict. The conflicting component would be defensively compartmentalized. One might, for example, avoid censure for a disapproved act. The awareness of the act, and one's disapproval of it thus would be maintained in separate compartments. They then would not be in communication. As long as this could be maintained, however nonrationally, "never the twain shall meet!"

From an intuitive standpoint at least, the laity is not unaware of this type of operation, as indicated in the following case:

Case 156

Compartmentalization

A thirty-six-year-old businessman sought to keep his censuring judgment of a personal love affair out of conflict with his more usual and stricter social standards. One day he commented: "You've got to keep parts of your life in separate compartments, so they aren't in conflict!"

To the extent this was successful he could then allay or attenuate his personal censure and his conflicts over the love affair. He had some conscious awareness of what his defensive endeavor was. He had employed just such a process of compartmentalization heretofore, on a far less conscious level.

2. Primitive Reaction

Dissociation in its major forms is a primitive and magical kind of process. As a pathologic phenomenon, it occurs automatically. It is completely beyond any voluntary control, and is deeply buried from conscious awareness. The factors which result in dissociation are very similar to those which occur, for example, in conversion and in repression. In reference to the latter, Brierley commented that the dynamics of dissociation are practically coterminous with the dynamics of repression.

In accordance with this view, pathological dissociation in adults follows the lines of infantile and childhood repressions. Dissociation can vary in its expression from a partial dissociation of the stream of consciousness (which can be constructive), to a nearly complete splitting of the psyche, resulting in the marked pathology of gross personality disorganization.

3. Conversion and Dissociation

A. "PART-REACTION" VS. "REACTION-OF-THE-WHOLE."—This brings us
to the psychologic basis and the close relationship of these two important
concepts. Both conversion and dissociation are primitive kinds of mechanisms. They follow in adulthood the antecedent patterns and capacities
for such responses that have been laid down in infancy. The author has
found it useful to think of the psychogenesis as what we might refer to as
a *Part-Reaction* in conversion [Ch.12:VIB2]. In distinction, we might
refer to a *Reaction-of-the-Whole* in dissociation. This will now be explained.

In Somatic Conversion the conflict is expressed in disguised and distorted form somatically. As described earlier, it constitutes a kind of *body
language* [Ch.12:IB1], which is expressed through a part of the physical
self. In Physiologic Conversion the conflict is expressed in disguised and
distorted form functionally. It is therefore *a physiologic language*
[Ch.12:IB2], which is expressed through a part of the physiologic self.
Thus the Somatic and Physiologic Conversion Reactions may be viewed
as analogous processes.

B. CONFLICT EXPRESSED BY OVERALL ACTIVITY; OVERALL-LANGUAGE
CONCEPT.—In the Dissociative Reactions, particularly in the major ones
(amnesia and fugues), the overall activity of the entire person expresses
the conflict, or parts of it. This is concealed from conscious recognition
and may often be disguised and distorted. It too can be regarded as a
symbolic expression or language — an *overall language* or symbolism.
Instead of the conflict being expressed through a part of the self, as in
conversion, it is expressed by a *reaction of the entire self*. This is the
Concept of an Overall Language, as expressed in amnesia and through
the fugue state. The overall behavior of the person, dissociated from
conscious awareness, thus may come symbolically to express various
unconscious needs and impulses. These have been the source of conflict
and have been repressed.

We shall see cases later in this chapter in which the behavior represents, for example, a seeking of something, a fleeing from something, an
inhibition of action or *rage-equivalent* [Ch.12:VD5], gratification, a denial, self-punitive activity, or some combination of these and others. Here
*the psychologic endeavor (of symbolically expressing the elements of the
underlying conflict through the overall behavior in the Dissociative Reactions), is analogous to that of the symptom in the Conversion Reactions.*

C. DEFENSIVE FLIGHT INTO A DISSOCIATED STATE.—Rarely, dissociation
to a dramatic degree is seen to take place abruptly in a case of neurosis,
in response to a sudden, overwhelming psychologic threat. This can represent psychologic avoidance. The flight is partly both figurative and literal.
It can be a defensively intended escape through psychic flight, into a
Dissociated State. This is in accord with our *Psychologic-Flight Avoidance
Concept,* as noted [Ch.13:IB1].

An example follows in which this took place in early analytic treatment.
The therapist's reaction to this emergency proved effective.

Case 157

A Dissociated State Follows Sudden Reactivation of Conflict

(1) *Source of conflict unexpectedly returns*

A twenty-six-year-old single woman was in intensive therapy. She had a strong but consciously abhorred and rejected attraction toward an actively homosexual girl friend. Following the departure of the latter for a job in Tokyo some eighteen months earlier, however, the intolerable conflict had seemingly been resolved.

One day the patient received a cable announcing the imminent but unexpected return of her friend by air. Accompanying this was a request that she make room for the friend in her apartment.

(2) *Acute onset of Dissociated State*

This served to suddenly reactivate her intense conflict. Her response was to dissociate a large segment of her consciousness from the situation. She became partly disoriented. She could not really carry on a coherent conversation. This was a primitive reaction. It was her unconscious pathway of avoidance through a psychologic flight, that is, *Psychologic-Flight-Avoidance.*

An alarmed friend brought her to her therapist for an emergency consultation. After considerable time and effort on the part of the analyst, her verbal productions continued to make little sense. This was a crucial juncture. The acute Dissociative Reaction threatened to break up the therapy. The therapist's position was fairly helpless. How could he break through the protective curtain of her dissociation? How could communication be reestablished?

(3) *Therapeutic management effective*

Finally, calling in the friend, the physician told her in all seriousness, but also in the patient's hearing, that he had done all he could. The rest was up to the patient. If the friend found her unmanageable, the only recourse would be immediate hospitalization.

This communication was sufficiently poignant to penetrate the protective dissociation. It dramatically fell away, allowing a resumption of communication. During the course of her subsequent treatment, she gradually became able to recognize and to "face" her conflict in in a more constructive fashion. Her therapy was continued ultimately to a successful conclusion.

4. Dissociative Reactions Reflect Operation of Four Types of Dissociation

One may classify the clinical Dissociative Reactions as resulting from the operation of one or more of four of our major types of dissociation: *Fragmental Dissociation* (Depersonalization, Fainting, Amnesia, Dreams, Somnambulism); *Side-by-Side Dissociation* (Simultaneous Activities); *B. B. C. Dissociation* (Hypnosis); and *Alternating Dissociation* (Fugue States, Multiple Personality).

The Side-by-Side type was illustrated in several of our case examples (*Cases 152, 153,* and *154*). Here two or more apparently independent activities took place simultaneously in dissociated fashion. It was as though the stream of consciousness was split into two simultaneously flowing streams. This may occur without untoward effects.

The Alternating type will be illustrated in some instances of amnesia, Fugue States, and in the so-called double personality. Here one part of the personality "takes over" or replaces another. It is as though the flow or stream of consciousness is abruptly halted and replaced by a new one. The alternating and complete dissociation of consciousness is the more drastic and indicates serious psychopathology. We shall consider the clinical varieties of Dissociative Reactions briefly, in turn.

III. DREAMS

A. DREAM FUNCTIONS

1. Vital Process

The inclusion of several points in reference to dreams and to dreaming is appropriate. Dreaming is important as a universal and familiar example of the activity of the unconscious. Further, it is a vital process to the individual, his emotional well-being, integration, ability to function, and happiness. This is far more true than has been generally recognized to date.

From our present point of view, dreaming also illustrates a kind of mental activity which is clearly split off, that is, dissociated from the consciousness, during sleep. A dream is an expression of emotional and mental activity. Since it occurs while sleeping and with relatively no conscious control, it is an activity which is dissociated from the self of the waking state. Dreaming is also not far removed from somnambulism [Ch.13:IV] as a next step. The dream perhaps best illustrates the fragmental type of dissociation and, less well, the Dissociation of Automaticity.

In this discussion fortunately a few pertinent points can be mentioned. We cannot undertake, however, to cover fully the great body of technical data already in the literature about dreams, theories about dreaming, techniques in their interpretation, and their role in therapy.

2. Sleep-Preserving Function

Freud postulated a sleep-protective role of dreams through their illusory gratification of wishes. The *Respite-of-Sleep Principle* stresses the refuge and haven of sleep [p. 38]. Its preservation is thereby important. The sleep-preserving function of dreams is correct so far as it goes, but the author presently regards it as an oversimplification. The preservation of sleep is merely one of a number of possible defensive functions. It is true that one dreams so that one can continue to sleep. Far more significant perhaps, is the reverse, *One sleeps so that one can dream!* This is in accord with the author's earlier (1953) advanced Hypothesis as to the vital *Contribution of the Dream* to the Maintenance of *Emotional Health* [p. 39 and Ch.14:VC6].

The sleep-preserving function is illustrated most readily in certain dreams in which there is a simple kind of physiologic wish fulfillment. The dream content, for example, may provide a drink of water when the sleeper is thirsty, or allow the dreamer to void when his bladder is full. For example, a colleague told the author of an instance of enuresis in his child, accompanied by a dream of going to the bathroom. His six-year-old son's bed was wet, but he was not! This type of simple dream is more common with children. However, it is not uncommon with adults.

There are many similar, rather simple wish-fulfilling dreams. A pregnant mother who longed for the termination of her pregnancy, dreamed happily that she had given birth to a fine baby boy. A would-be mother thus "achieved" her wish. The object-of-desire for a young swain is responsive in his dream.

One dreams he has gone to work, and so can safely continue his slumber. A man dreamed he had closed his windows before an approaching storm, and slept on, oblivious to the rain coming in! Planning to arrive early for an exam, a college student dreamed she had taken it, and slept blissfully through the din of her alarm clock! In the post-traumatic civil or military type dream, a *desensitizing purpose* or function of the dream may become more readily apparent [Ch.14:VC4; VIID*1*].

3. Wishes in Dreams

A. WISH FULFILLMENT.—Many kinds of wishes may be expressed in a dream. Some of them may be much more complex than the above. Some wishes are expressed quite directly and simply.* In the public mind dreams are equated with the expression and/or fulfillment of wishes. This is illustrated over and over again in the many popular references in this direction in poem, story, and song. There are many instances such as "Dreams", "I'll See You in My Dreams", "All I Do is Dream of You . . .", "Mr. Sandman", "Dreams for Sale", "Order it up in a Dream!", "Did You Ever See a Dream Walking?", and so on. The phrase my (or his) "fondest dreams" may be used. This is but one of the many figurative uses of the term *dream,* in everyday parlance, in a similar place and meaning to that of the word *wish*.

The following is an instance, from the song "Wishing":

> "Dreamers tell us dreams come true.
> That's no mistake.
> For wishes are the dreams we dream
> When we're awake!"

B. CONSCIOUSLY UNACCEPTABLE WISHES EXPRESSED IN DISGUISED FORM. —Dreams are also apt to represent in disguised, condensed, and symbolic fashion those wishes † which are consciously unacceptable. As a consequence, these wishes (or the impulses arising from them) were earlier actively pushed into the unconscious. This process of banishment to the unconscious is termed *repression*.

---

* The following personal example occurred during the original endeavor of writing this book. For more than two years a suitable title had been sought for the volume. None seemed precisely to meet the requirements. This had become a considerable problem. One night, after doing some work on the final draft of this chapter, I had a vivid dream in which the proper title came to mind. In my dream I tested it against the various criteria. It suited perfectly. The troublesome problem was solved. I could relax and continue my sleeping. When I awoke I could not for the life of me recall the title! Nor have I yet been able to do so.

† Whether the content is clear and apparent, or disguised and obscure, scholars and writers have long recognized the implicit honesty of what appears in dreams. One may consciously dissimulate. One may adopt a mask which fools one's friends, or perhaps even oneself. One cannot easily be dishonest in his dreams. As William Hazlitt (1778–1803) wrote long ago, "We are not hypocrites in our sleep."

When the repressed data find some expression in the dream content, their expression is in a distorted and disguised form. This is an important tenet in dream psychology.

4. Fears Expressed

The wish-expressing function of dreams has been stressed by many. Scant attention, if any, has been paid to another important expressive function of the dream. Reference is made here to its serving as a similar vehicle for the *expression* (often also in similar symbolic and concealed guise) of fears and concerns.

Often included in dreams are representations of those fears and worries which have been consciously denied, rationalized, and so on. Dreams also similarly express disguised unconscious goals and needs.

B. INTERPRETING DREAMS

1. Analysis Reveals Unconscious Material

People often describe their dreams as "silly" or "senseless", or even in such terms as "crazy" or "irrational". They are senseless only in so far as their meaning remains consciously hidden and obscure to the dreamer. When the meaning can no longer elude the dreamer, when he has mastered the techniques of dream interpretation, dreams can reveal most interesting data from one's unconscious.

Thus, when a dream is successfully analyzed, it makes a great deal of sense indeed to the person concerned. Further, the sense it makes can be so clear (and so consciously unwelcome) that, however accurate it may be, *the interpretation of a dream too early, too completely, or injudiciously, in the course of analytic therapy can cause the patient to shy off both consciously and unconsciously from his therapeutic endeavors.* Treatment can be delayed, retarded, interrupted, or postponed as the consequence. At the least, the Secondary Defensive resistance stiffens for a time.

The author has observed these kinds of unwelcome effects transpire in therapy, to his own dismay, as well as to that of a fair number of his colleagues, as they have so reported. Stiffening of the Secondary Defenses can also have other or additionally handicapping results. The automatic, unconscious, protective response also on occasion can be a cessation of the recall of dreams. Still another alternative consequence is the appearance of impossibly baffling and disguised dream material, in place of the preceding simpler dream content.

In the hands of the expert, the interpretation of dreams can be a major adjunct to therapy. It affords us an occasional window to the unconscious. Freud once described the dream as "the royal road to the unconscious". The author would delete the word *royal*. The dream can serve as a road to the unconscious, but only *comparatively* and relatively so. It is certainly not very direct. There is no royal road. No road is at all easy. This one is simply often a better route among the other often difficult, and possibly still more tortuous routes which may be followed.

2. Free Association; Manifest and Latent Content

There are many dreams that defy the expert, even with the best cooperative efforts of the patient. On the other hand, there are many dreams in some of which the meaning can be at least inferred with little or no special training. In general, however, a fair amount of special training and experience in psychodynamics is a requisite for a reasonable degree of success in unlocking the secret messages which are expressed in dreams.

We owe the development of a systematic method for the unraveling of the hidden meanings of dreams to Freud. He worked out the system of *free association* which is widely used today. Herein the dreamer is asked carefully to note and to report aloud without prior reservation or censorship, all thoughts which come to mind as he relates the dream, and as he thinks of its various components. The dream is considered first as a whole. Subsequently each segment of the *manifest* content is taken as a subject, to which associations are sought.

To the person experienced in dream interpretation, the collective associations may provide important clues to the *latent* content (that is, to the unconscious motivation and meaning) of the dream. The latent content includes the unconscious emotional data which is symbolically expressed. This is expressed outwardly in distorted and disguised form, as the conscious or manifest content of the dream. It includes the forces responsible for the production of the dream.

C. MECHANISMS AND CONCEPTS IN DREAMS

1. Fifteen Important Precepts

A number of concepts are valuable in one's endeavor to study and to understand dreams. The author has also found them most useful in the evaluation of a patient's associations to his dream material. Accordingly he offers in outline form the following fifteen major principles or precepts as a useful guide. For the student and therapist their study and review at reasonable intervals can offer an extra dividend.

(1) *Condensation* (Overdetermination). In dreams, two or more ideas, objects, or concepts can come to be *condensed* in their symbolic representation, so as to be represented by a single item in the dream. The single dream symbol thus may stand for several items, or even for a group of items.

Condensation thereby results in the *overdetermination* of the symbols in dreams. Symbols are thus not merely determined in dreams. Through the process of condensation, they are overdetermined.

(2) *Convergence of Associations*. This is a major tenet of the important principle of *Free Association*. Its meaning is that a number of associative thoughts can be observed at times to converge toward a common meaning.

This is an important precept in the use of the technique of free association in the interpretation of dreams.

A related concept is that of the *Reinforcement of Associations*. This refers to the support to a given interpretation which is provided by later associations, when they prove to be similar to, or like earlier ones. Subsequent dream content, or associations to it, can also reinforce earlier associations, or "educated surmises" which have been based upon them. This follows the *Geometric Principle*. This is at times illustrated in the repetitive dream.

(3) *Displacement.* As part of the protective disguise of the latent and hidden meaning of the dream, displacement of affect can take place to seemingly neutral dream objects.

These objects are dream symbols. This displacement takes place in a somewhat similar process to that which we saw illustrated concerning the operation of displacement in the phobic pattern of defense.

(4) *Routine and Universal; "Fast Time".* Dreaming is universal. Everyone dreams. Further, everyone dreams nightly. Dreams may not be subject to recall. This has a different meaning, however, than the mere, simple indication of their absence. It does not mean that dreaming is absent or even less frequent. It is more likely to mean that the person has less interest, willingness, or ability to recall his dreams, or that there are greater resistances to recall, and so on.

Dreaming tends to have a rhythmic pattern, with intervals or dream periods through the night. As sleeping progresses these become larger and more frequent. Dreams are more frequent when sleep is lighter and when the needs for sleep have been partially satisfied. This is true for night or day sleeping. It helps account for the increased dreaming toward morning. Lighter sleep then, plus more dreams, enters into the more frequent early morning awakening from disturbing dreams; possibly also in more covert fashion in the *Dawn Insomnia* [pp. 142, 145, 156, 163] which can be pathognomonic of depressed states.

There are important individual variations, however. In previously unreported experiments the author has elicited repeated dreams taking place in what we might call *fast time,* that is, in a faster time for the dream than the events would require in real life. Further, dozens of these dreams were elicited seconds after the first onset of sleep for a given night. In the excellent subject sleep would be resumed in a few minutes, sometimes less, and a few seconds later, upon being awakened another dream sequence was reported. This could be repeated from four to ten times in rapid order.

The recall of dreams more generally, however, relates to their meaning and significance and the training of the dreamer to recall. Ordinarily the later dream (that is, the final one or ones prior to spontaneous awakening) during a period of sleep is more readily recalled.

There can be a merging of the last of one's waking thoughts on into dream content. This may be noted at times when the thought content becomes increasingly dream-like, as one gradually sinks into slumber. Being awakened at this point can lead to the recovery of some of the transitional material. This is an interesting experiment, readily enough performed.

(5) *Necessity for Emotional Health.* The author has believed for many years that the process of dreaming was essential for emotional health. Dreams allow the partial (and often, symbolic) discharge of conflictual data. They aid in the maintenance of repression. Dreaming is too regular and routine an aspect of sleeping to have other than important functions. Further, the author has suspected that the enforced absence of dreaming in sleep deprivation was related to the frequent abnormal psychologic effects which are to be observed. Accordingly he devised in conservative terms, an *Hypothesis of the Dream's Contribution to Emotional Health.* The facts doubtless warranted something stronger. Today he regards this hypothesis as being still closer to fact [*see also* illustration of a post-traumatic dream, Ch. 14:VC6].

The author would accordingly venture the statement currently that dreaming is a necessity for emotional health. The individual *needs* to dream. Fisher and Dement, holding similar views, have recently introduced the very useful term of *dream deficit,* to describe the need that builds up for dreaming when dream deprivation is enforced experimentally. Dreams with action in them are accompanied by eye movements which are detectable visually and are accompanied by electroencephalographic changes. These make possible the experimental suppression of a fair proportion of a subject's dreams, through careful observation and repeated enforced awakening. The results suggest that a sufficiently large "dream deficit" will lead to a greater or lesser breakdown of integration, and the possible eruption of psychotic symptoms. This probably has been at least partially borne out in work with experimental sleep deprivation.

The positive contributions of dreaming to stability, synthesis, and emotional health are more readily observable in certain dreams in which more traumatic abreaction takes place. Battle dreams following combat, and repetitive dreams after a traumatic event, most readily illustrate this.

(6) *Disregard for Logic.* The manifest dream content frequently appears illogical and out of context with reality. This is hardly surprising. Dream content is *emotionally determined.* It is not rationally determined. Further, the forces of repression have a large stake in concealing unconscious data. In effect, the dream may thus be regarded as having an attempted conflict-resolving function. This is present, for example, through its compromise kind of partial and usually symbolic expression and gratification of intolerable but otherwise buried (that is, repressed) data, which stem from the unconscious. This includes consciously disowned wishes and impulses. These are expressed in the manifest content of the dream, but in a form which is ordinarily unintelligible.

There is little need for logic in the very personal world of the dreamer. Sleep brings the sleeper to a world all his own. The mental content during sleep does not have to meet the test of reality. As Plutarch (46-120 A.D.) wrote, "All men whilst they are awake are in one common world, but each of them, when he is asleep is in a world of his own."

Despite his somnolent state, the dreamer may simultaneously insert some doubts about his dream situation. Thus the dreamer may feel doubt or incredulity about things that are happening in his dream, while they are transpiring. His dream may seem unreal even during its course. [*See* Section IVD*1* and Section VD*2*: *Case 159.*] This feature can also of course be protective in itself.

(7) *Distortion.* In a dream, distortion in the representation of ideas, wishes, or objects is more the rule than the exception. Often this is true even in regard to that which is apparently direct representation, as well as that which is more clearly symbolic.

Those objects or individuals which are occasionally directly represented, often still have some elements of distortion. They may and often do stand for something or someone completely different, or for something or someone in addition.

(8) *Elaboration.* In rather the converse of the process of condensation in dreams, elaboration of the symbolism may similarly occur. A symbol may be elaborated and become more complex, detailed, and expanded, as part of the distortion and disguise of what it actually represents.

Condensation and elaboration may be operative simultaneously in different areas of the same dream. This can add to the problems of the painstaking detective work involved in dream interpretation. The presence of neither is universal, but rather uneven. Both are erratic as to their presence and extent.

(9) *Latent Content.* The latent content refers to the hidden factors which result in the occurrence of the dream. What is latent underlies what is manifest. It conveys the true meaning; the manifest is the cover. The latent content is unconscious.

On occasion the meaning of the latent material may be correctly surmised through careful, painstaking elicitation and evaluation of the manifest content, and the free associations to the latter. All of these must be carefully evaluated and interpreted in the context of the individual's own environmental setting and personality.

(10) *Manifest Content.* The manifest content of the dream is the actual flowing picture and idea sequence of the dream, as reported. Even this outwardly manifest content tends to slip away very quickly from the dreamer's memory, often in a few seconds following awakening. This is part of the Secondary Defense of the dream, of its contents and functions.

Training of one's power of observation and recall can help in the process of recollection and analysis. Sometimes this may be usefully augmented by keeping a small notebook and pencil by the bed. Their prompt employment upon waking will help to catch dreams perhaps otherwise quickly lost to recollection.

(11) *Multiple Representation of Figures.* A single person who appears in a dream may actually represent two or more persons, or aspects of them. For instance, a dream figure might represent simultaneously a parent, the dreamer, and someone in addition.

The sex of the dream figure tends to follow the sex of the person represented, but not necessarily. When the sex is at variance this can have some important meaning. Thus the sex is more likely to indicate the sexual characteristics of the dream figure, as these are *really* viewed by the dreamer. Animals or objects of all varieties may also serve as dream symbols for persons.

(12) *Overdeterminism* (Convergence). Similarly to the operation of this principle in the formation of symptoms of the Conversion Reactions, dream symbols or events may be the expression of more than one unconscious idea, need, or wish. The dream symbol or action thus tends to be not merely determined but *overdetermined*.

Thus in the dream symbolism, as in other psychic phenomena, several different psychic factors, both conscious and unconscious, operate at the same time in determining a given dream element: symbol, event, action, symptom [*Case 102*, pp. 486–489, and Ch.12:VIIB] or even word. Monroe suggested that the term "multiple determination" might be preferable.

The term "overdeterminism" finds almost identical usage to the earlier presented concept of condensation. Associations thus tend to converge toward a specific meaning or interpretation.

(13) *Reinforcement; Geometric Principle*. The repetition of associations or the occurrence of similar ones serves as an important reinforcement in their evaluation. Considerable added weight should be given in the interpretation of their relative significance. Expressed mathematically, one might say that the progression is geometric. This is in accord with a *Geometric Principle* of the reinforcement of associations. This operates in a number of areas, in addition to dreams. Convergence and overdetermination are more important because of the operation of this principle.

Through the operation of our Geometric Principle, thus a once reinforced association would be possibly four times as important as another one not so reinforced; a twice reinforced one might perhaps warrant receiving nine times the value. This concept is similar to that of convergence [*see also* the *Reinforcement of Association Concept*].

(14) *Symbolism*. This is a basic process through which the continued repression and the disguise of unconscious material are ordinarily insured. Symbolism permits the disguised and concealed manifest expression of what is otherwise closely guarded, unconscious data. A dream symbol may be a similar, a very different, or even a reversed representation. In the personal life of the dreamer there is often a significant connection, although this may not be at all accessible to ordinary awareness. The usual intellectual logic does not prevail in the unconscious selection, or in the automatic adoption of symbolic substitutes.

Symbolism is to be regarded as essentially an emotional process. A symbol is an abstract or general representation of a particular object or idea. It is something which stands externally and consciously in the place of, or represents, something else, the latter usually remaining completely hidden from conscious awareness. [*See* later *Rule of Individual-Symbolism*.]

(15) *Validation*. Hadley stressed the importance of condensation, convergence, and reinforcement in dream interpretation. To these he added

Validation, as another important principle. In its broad sense, validation would refer to any kind of data subsequently secured in validation of the interpretation.

Validation might take place through trial, or by subsequent events. It might be secured in part through reinforcement, from other later personal sources, or one's recollections, and from confirming data secured from other people.

2. Nocturnal-Fantasy Concept

One may regard dreams as fantasies taking place during sleep. This is a view and concept of the dream, through which we might accordingly refer to the dream as a *Nocturnal-Fantasy (N.F.).* During this N.F. most, if not all, of the conscious control has been removed.

In its relation to conscious, purposeful, and more controlled activity, the dream is a dissociation. In other words, a segment of mental activity is thus dissociated in the sleeping state, to function in a rather independent fashion. This dissociated mental and emotional activity comprises the Nocturnal-Fantasy.

D. ADDED ASPECTS OF INTEREST

1. Dissociation Within the Dream

Dissociative trends are sometimes seen *within* the dream itself. Six of the ways in which this may be evident are: (1) The dreamer may be represented by two or more of the figures in the dream. (2) The dreamer may simultaneously recognize (often reassuringly!) that the action taking place is *really part of a dream.* To this extent he becomes detached from what happens. Further, (3) he may even "stand apart" and "watch himself" in the dream action. (4) Parts of the self may be themselves split off within the dream, and may be represented symbolically, or appear in a substitute figure. (5) The dreamer may experience a dissociation (example: feelings of unreality, or *dejá vu,* which can be a marked phenomenon, and so on) during the course of his dream. [*See Case 159.*]

Finally, such a dissociative trend within the dream is also illustrated (6) in the dreamer's doubt or incredulity at the time about the objects which he may see in his dream, or concerning the often unrealistic events that are taking place within it. Reference is made here to the doubts which are sometimes experienced during the actual course of the dream. While he is still dreaming, the material is simultaneously being questioned.

The multiple representation of the dreamer himself illustrates dissociation in that important aspects of the self are split off, to be represented in or by another figure in the dream, who is then seen by the dreamer as though he were another person. At times two or even more figures may appear in this fashion. They are hidden from the ordinary conscious awareness but they may stand for the dreamer or for aspects of him. This kind of multiple representation may also apply to other people or aspects of them. It is roughly the converse of the process by which in turn a single dream figure can simultaneously represent two or more other person's in the dreamer's life.

2. Certain Dreams Have Special Significance

Certain dreams in the course of intensive analytic therapy ordinarily are to be regarded as having special significance. For example, the first dream is often particularly important prognostically. It is important in determining the nature of the basic problems, and at times in gaining some early ideas of the basic attitudes toward the analysis and the physician.

As another example, dreams in which the therapist appears directly can have important prognostic indications, convey implications as to the development of the transference-counter transference situation, and meaning as to the chances of therapeutic success. Dreams at certain crucial junctures in the therapy also can be particularly important.

3. Rule of Individual Symbolism

It may be useful before leaving this all-too-brief discussion of dreams to mention one aspect that young psychiatrists as well as lay persons sometimes find troubling and disappointing. When order and system are highly desirable and often very much sought as an aid to entering such a highly complex and variable field, the student often hopes to find some rules or guides for determining in fixed fashion the meaning of dream symbols. Thus if one found, for instance, that a black horse always stood for death when present in a dream, or for the "dark" aspects of a powerful father, how much easier would be the interpretation and understanding of the next dream in which a black horse appeared! This would still be true even though it were granted that one might encounter an almost limitless number and variety of symbols in the dreams of different people. The physician still might have something definite to begin with, to count on, and to store up in encyclopedic fashion.

Unfortunately for the hopeful student, it simply does not work this way. Symbols are completely individual, and a similar symbol or object in the dreams of two people can, and more often does, have somewhat divergent, if not completely separate meanings. There is a tendency for certain symbols to equate similar meanings in a kind of generic relationship, but this cannot be given too much reliance, especially for the newcomer. With considerable experience, this sort of common meaning can begin to have some practical usefulness. The student is safer, however, simply to *regard every dream and each item of its content as a strictly individual phenomenon.* This follows an important precept mentioned earlier [Ch.12:VID*3*] which refers to the individuality of meaning and symbolism in symptoms, dreams, and indeed in every emotional manifestation. For purposes of identification, communication, convenience, and of stressing its importance, we have named it the *Rule of Individual-Symbolism.*

There has been an exhaustive amount of work done in the study and interpretation of dreams. Several volumes might not suffice to cover thoroughly the amount of theoretical study and clinical investigation which

has been undertaken. It lies within the scope of our present study however, only to outline a number of the important and interesting principles
which perhaps enjoy some general acceptance.

IV. SOMNAMBULISM

A. DEFINITION; ACTIVATED-NOCTURNAL-FANTASY CONCEPT

Somnambulism is the term which is employed to describe walking in one's
sleep. It also has been used to describe certain states of dissociated but
coordinated mental and motor activity during hypnotic trances. Our use
of the term will be limited to sleepwalking unless otherwise stated. Sleepwalking may be regarded as the extension of similar functions to those
of the dream, in which the motor activity of walking about is added. A
dynamic relationship to the Fugue State is also implied in our view of
the latter as sometimes approximating Daytime-Somnambulism [Ch.13:
VIIID1].

Somnambulism is undoubtedly always accompanied by dreams. However, their content is often immediately lost to conscious awareness upon
awakening. On occasion it never gains conscious awareness at all.* The
dream has been regarded as a free-wheeling uncontrolled kind of mental
process, which is split off from the main stream of conscious, waking
mental activity. We can similarly regard sleepwalking as *a more or less
coordinated physical activity during sleep, which has been split off or dissociated from the more usual stream of consciously directed and purposeful
mental and physical functioning.*

Somnambulism is unconsciously purposeful. If we are to regard the
dream as a *Nocturnal-Fantasy* [Ch.13:IIIC2], an analogous view of somnambulism might add the element of "acting out" to this fantasy. Somnambulism thereby can sometimes be conceived as an *Activated Nocturnal
Fantasy.* As with the dream, its latent meaning and motivation are subject
to interpretation. Also as with the dream, and its extension to include
somnambulistic activity, perhaps best illustrated is the fragmental type
of dissociation and, less well, the dissociation of automaticity.

B. THE SIGNIFICANCE OF SLEEPWALKING

1. Symbolism Simple or Involved

Sleepwalking, as we saw with dreams, can be a specific response to
more or less simple internal physiologic needs. On the other hand, it can
represent a highly specific expression of a definite unconscious problem

---

* Contrariwise, according to Jacobson's all-night E.E.G. studies (1965) with nine
subjects, somnambulistic incidents did not occur in association with dreams (and
rapid eye movements). Dream time did not differ from nights with or without incidents. This would suggest an absence of correlation between dreams and somnambulism.

or conflict. The movements of the sleepwalker may be in response to, or may parallel, parts of the manifest dream content. His activity may also be an expression of the latent factors responsible for the dream. The symbolism may be minor or simple.

As with dreams though, sleepwalking may have deep symbolic meaning. One may be symbolically seeking "something". The something sought may cover a wide range of possibilities, from something quite specific and concrete, to a more general goal of life. The walking may represent, as examples, an attempted escape, heading for security, the seeking of a forbidden pleasure, or a way of protection against the latter. The symbolism can cover a wide range of possibilities. Its elucidation is challenging, and its meaning often most interesting.

In nocturnal somnambulism the sleeper arises and behaves somewhat as an automaton. His movements are likely slow, but are more or less directed and seemingly purposeful. In many if not all instances he is carrying out the physical action to some extent as required by an associated dream. Gentle interruption may allow his acquiescent return to bed. This is usually accompanied by amnesia for the entire event. A rude awakening is also likely marked by amnesia, but also sometimes by a period of at least some brief, initial confusion.

2. Capacity for Dissociation

For an individual to be a sleepwalker, he must possess the unconscious capacity for dissociation of his motor activity. Where the capacity exists, sleepwalking can result when the external stimulus is marked, or where the capacity for this kind of dissociation is strong, or from both. Generally, suggestibility tends to accompany a capacity for dissociation. Suggestibility is undoubtedly operative in the somnambulism of "normal" sleep. It can be quite readily demonstrated also in the "somnambules", those excellent subjects of hypnotic states. In the former the source of the suggestion is generally internal although precipitating stimuli can sometimes be identified, whereas in the latter the source of the suggestion is generally external and comes from the hypnotist.

At times one observes the resumption of sleepwalking, after years of its absence. Sometimes these instances, which may be single or the recurrence of a pattern, can be traced to an increase of situational or interpersonal stress. Herein the somnambulism is part of the individual T.R.C., or Total Response to Crisis. It is a part of the effort of a harried ego unconsciously to seek some resolution of disturbing internal conflict. Sometimes it is to be regarded as what we have termed a *compromise formation* [p. 118; Ch.12:VC2 and VIB2].

On occasion an example of sleepwalking is seen in which the strength of the psychologic purpose which is served can be recognized. This may be partially illustrated in the resistances to efforts which are designed to stop the particular instance of somnambulism. These points are apparent in the following case, in which sleepwalking was a major problem.

Case 158

An Example of Sleepwalking

(1) *Somnambulism onset follows return from combat*

The thirty-four-year-old former commander of a PT boat squadron in World War II had returned to the United States after two years of strenuous combat duty in the South Pacific theater of operations. He found all kinds of troubling domestic and situational difficulties at home. He struggled with these with little success.

He had not been back home very long before his wife noticed one night that he was not in bed. After some alarmed minutes, she found him wandering about semiclothed in the vegetable garden. He was sound asleep.

(2) *Pattern not readily interrupted*

That was the first of a long series of such incidents. Husband and wife were mystified and troubled by his nocturnal wanderings. This dissociative activity was carried on with a fair degree of coordination. He usually managed to get up, exchange his pajamas for some clothes, navigate the stairs, the porch, and some part of the garden. It was usually difficult to wake him when he was finally located.

Various methods were tried to "break him of this worrisome and dangerous habit". None was successful. When he was discovered leaving the bedroom, it would take a great deal of effort to wake him, or considerable physical restraint if one tried simply to interfere with his activity.

(3) *Clarification of emotional problems required*

The couple once tried tying a rope from the ankle of the husband to the ankle of the wife. On two occasions she was bodily pulled from her bed before the somnambulistic husband awoke! His resistance to waking helps illustrate the determined nature of the activity of some sleepwalkers, and incidentally the strength of the hidden psychologic need for the act. Strenuous methods and attempted direct interference were of little avail.

Fortunately, it gradually became possible, with a moderate amount of professional assistance and support, for him to clarify and deal more constructively with some of his emotional problems. The episodes of sleepwalking decreased in frequency and finally ceased altogether. The specific psychodynamics of the sleepwalking were not well worked out, although certain inferential meanings were uncovered.

C. PATHOLOGIC SIGNIFICANCE VARIES

1. Conflict-Indicator Concept

Somnambulism is a type of dissociated activity which is a reasonably common experience. While it is by no means easy to understand the "whys" and the "hows" of sleepwalking, people generally accept its existence rather casually. An occasional instance of sleepwalking in itself may have no great significance, but it is nevertheless to be regarded as *indicative of underlying emotional conflict* or personality problems.

This is also true with nail biting, stuttering, A.A.A.s, temper tantrums, and so on. The potentiality exists when one of these phenomena is present for a future increase of emotional difficulty [Ch.13:VC2]. This outlines in essence our important *Concept of Conflict-Indicators* [*see also* p. 406 and Ch.12:VC2]. These are more or less *specific items of activity, behavior, and appearance which can generally be regarded as indicative of underlying conflict.*

Other major and often significant *Conflict-Indicators (C.I.s)* would include persistent thumb sucking, bed wetting, nightmares, sleep-talking and tics [Ch.12:VC2]. Certain mannerisms can be C.I.s, as can be depersonalization [Ch.13:IB2], emotional coughing, hair pulling or twisting, overeating, insomnia, rhythmic rocking ("bucking"), and head banging. Persistent itching, or picking and a host of otherwise isolated psychophysiologic manifestations and physiologic conversion illnesses may be significant C.I.s.

Case 159

Somnambulism Twelve Stories Above the Street

A twenty-two-year-old man was subject to repeated episodes of sleepwalking. One night while asleep he climbed from the window of his apartment, twelve stories above the ground, and walked on a narrow (eighteen-inch wide) outside ledge to another window. He returned to bed without waking.

A horrified roommate awoke in time to watch the latter part of this performance and his friend's return to the room. He had been afraid to move or to comment for fear of awakening the patient, who might have become startled and fallen to the street below.

When the sleepwalker was awakened, he had no recollection of the incident. He refused to believe it as described, until confronted with his sooty feet and, in the morning, by the clear footprints which he had left on the ledge.

One might note in this case the individual's considerable ability, despite his dissociative state, to look out for his own safety, as well as the implicit evidence of his excellently integrated physical activity during the somnambulistic episode.

Most sleepwalking occurs in childhood. It is more significant pathologically when somnambulism persists into adult life, or if it later recurs in adult years. In either case it is usually a Conflict Indicator, as noted earlier. In some instances it can be a most significant C.I.; occasionally is the only such outward evidence of intrapsychic conflicts.

2. Usually Well Safeguarded

It is rather rare that injury is suffered by the sleepwalker. In his dissociated and sleeping state there is usually sufficient of the self-preservative instinct retained to well safeguard him. Even though in the foregoing unusual instance the sleepwalker performed a highly hazardous maneuver, he carried it off quite safely.

Lack of injury is not invariably the case, however. There are potential hazards. Accidents can occur. An instance came to the author's attention not long ago involving a sixty-two-year-old executive who fell down a flight of stairs and cracked several vertebrae. This was his first known somnambulistic episode since childhood. Following this episode he gradually retired from his executive duties. There has been no recurrence. Among the possible determinants as surmised, were guilt, a need to suffer, self-punishment, seeking a retreat, and doubtless others.

D. IN SUMMARY

Somnambulism is the scientific term applied to the dissociative reaction which results in gross and more or less coordinated physical activity while asleep. Somnambulism occurs with a fair amount of frequency in childhood, and, upon occasion, on into adolescence and later life.

Its relative pathologic significance and its importance as an indicator of underlying emotional conflict in these years may vary greatly. It should perhaps be regarded as a symptom of underlying emotional disturbance rather than as a diagnostic entity. Almost invariably it is to be regarded as a C.I., sometimes as one of considerable significance.

V. DEPERSONALIZATION

A. PERSONAL AND ENVIRONMENTAL FEELINGS OF UNREALITY

1. Highly Subjective

Depersonalization is both a fairly common subjective disturbance, and a psychiatric symptom which is dissociative in character. Reflecting the presence of intrapsychic emotional conflict, to the psychiatrist it serves as a *C.I.* and as a "psychic barometer." To *personalize* is to make something personal, to give it more personal significance. To *depersonalize* is to remove the personal significance, to make something less personal.

Psychologically, through depersonalization, attributes of the self (or of the external world—as personally perceived) become strange and unreal. In view of its many manifestations and multiple etiology, it is best regarded as a clinical type of Dissociative Reaction, or as an emotional symptom of dissociation. Feelings of depersonalization are often best described simply as *feelings of unreality,* or as *feelings of estrangement.* Included with this group is the common *dejá vu* (already seen) phenomenon, also the *dejá entendu* (already heard) one. In these interesting personal vignettes one feels that he has already experienced whatever is going on. It has a strange, eerie, and sometimes very frightening quality of familiarity.

The psychopathology of this high subjective manifestation varies greatly. Mild and fleeting feelings of some degree of such a loss of personal identity are not uncommon. These often have little significance. On the other hand, in their most advanced manifestations they form part of the symptomatology of certain of the severe psychotic reactions. In its expression of a figurative meaning, depersonalization can be an instance of a "symptom language" of dissociation.

2. Definitions

There are two major clinical types of depersonalization: (1) the personal, and (2) the environmental. In the *personal* variety of depersonalization there is *a subjective feeling of the loss of personal identity. This may be partial, include various aspects of the self, or it may be massive. The person himself feels estranged, unreal.* Included, for example, are feelings that one is no longer himself, that he has changed, that something about him is different or strange, or even that to a greater or lesser extent he has become someone else.

In the *environmental* type of depersonalization, *the changes seem to be external, in the world about oneself. Some minor or major part of aspect of the environment, or even the entire world about one, seems strange and unreal.* Both types are indicative of anxiety. Since depersonalization may almost directly "replace" anxiety, it can perhaps be regarded as an *anxiety-equivalent.* [*See* pp. 103, 145, 324, 462, and Ch.12:VC3].

Dejá vu is French for already seen. The *dejá vu* phenomenon is probably universal. It is one which nearly everyone has observed. It may be regarded as a specific variant of depersonalization. In it *one feels undue familiarity; as though a person, place, or situation has been seen or experienced before.* As with feelings of unreality this experience can prove quite frightening. Its significance psychopathologically is similar. *Dejá Entendu* is a related and analogous carryover of the already-seen concept, to that of having already heard something. Both phenomena can be regarded as C.Is.

B. HISTORY

Feelings of personal and environmental strangeness and unreality have long been recognized. They have attracted considerable attention because of their wide incidence and because some of them are disturbing. Mental and emotional phenomena were being increasingly studied and described after the year 1850. It was inevitable that this group of subjective sensations was soon to be further delineated and named. Krishaber, in 1872, wrote of a symptom complex which was to some extent a prototype for the later clinical descriptions. Galdston has credited Dugas with introducing the term *depersonalization,* in 1887.

Pierre Janet discussed depersonalization shortly after the turn of the century. He believed that fatigue, exhaustion, and possibly constitutional factors played a role in diminishing what he termed the *mental synthesis,* which was maintained by "mental energy". A strong mental synthesis was implicit to good mental health. If the synthesis diminished, integration might falter or split. Dissociation and depersonalization feelings of unreality were possible consequences.

In the last few decades several investigators have studied feelings of unreality and depersonalization. There has been reasonable concurrence in the clinical findings. Factors which have been reported to operate in the psychodynamics, and in the evaluation of their psychogenesis, have indicated more divergence. This section is an attempted brief, summarized synthesis and organization of the work and research thus far, together with the results of the author's clinical and theoretical studies.

C. DIAGNOSIS AND INCIDENCE

1. Common Subjective Experience

Fleeting feelings of unreality (that is, depersonalization) are not an uncommon experience. They are not necessarily indicative of emotional illness. In their milder form, their incidence approaches the universal in subjective experience, helping to illustrate our thesis that problems are universal, and the *Law of Universality in Emotional Health* [p. 2]. They may occur more often for example, during extreme states of fatigue or boredom, or while going to sleep. They are found also in systemic illness such as pneumonia, in localized neurologic disease of the temporal lobe (the dreamy states of Hughlings Jackson), and in intoxication with alcohol, or with drugs such as cannabis. They may occur with many kinds of emotional stress or tension, which need not be at all available to conscious awareness. Depersonalization frequently occurs as a prominent feature in the beginning phases of schizophrenia. Here it has its most serious prognostic import.

Very seldom are these subjective feelings of sufficient prominence and severity in and of themselves to warrant a separate diagnosis. However, one should be clearly able to recognize such a clinical phenomenon, and to name it as the symptom or emotional reaction. He should be able to estimate its relative pathologic import, and to have some ideas about the situations and conditions in which it appears.

2. Incidence as to Type

Meyer-Gross reported (1935) a series of hospitalized persons in whom the symptom of depersonalization was prominent. The diagnoses of his group of 26 seriously ill patients included: depression, 12; schizophrenia, 6; conversion reaction (hysteria), 3; neurasthenia, 3; and doubtful diagnosis, 2. He divided his findings into the two clinical types. The first was the personal type of depersonalization, that is, the feeling of personal unreality or change. The second was the environmental type of depersonalization; environmental unreality or change.

Meyer-Gross reported that 11 patients had only the first type, four had only the second type, and the remainder (roughly half) had both types of depersonalization. These proportions are not terribly out of line with current clinical experience as to incidence.

D. CLINICAL FEATURES

1. Variability

Clinical manifestations of depersonalization, including *dejá vu,* may vary from those which are almost unnoticed to those which are very severe. They may vary from fleeting and rare, to prolonged and frequent. The complaint is most frequently apt to be that somehow things seem different.

The feelings of unreality may be confined to one portion or area of the body. They are usually rather transient. Sometimes, however, a patient may even consult an ophthalmologist because of his altered perception of the world, which appears to him to be changed, strange, or unreal.

2. Feelings of Unreality and Estrangement

A. INDIVIDUAL AND SUBJECTIVE.—The patient may complain that the world looks two-dimensional, as though it is painted on glass, or that there is an invisible barrier shutting him off from the rest of the world. He may describe subjective feelings that he is in a different world, or even on another planet. In the more severe cases the feelings of unreality further involve the person himself, and he may come to doubt even his own existence. He may feel as though he has become completely detached from his own body, or he may feel like an automaton, as though part of him were a machine.

To the person with feelings of unreality, it may seem that he has become someone else, or that part, or even all, of the external world is unreal. He may feel that a feeling or thought is *not* his own [*see Case 65*], that is, in a defensive endeavor of depersonalizing it (from himself). Lange described the experiencing of marked feelings of depersonalization in the following terms: "the sound of his voice, his face in a mirror may come to seem strange to him; his mental pictures are shadowy, his perceptions do not awaken a feeling of reality. His actions seem to him mechanical, without the feeling of will. Thoughts come or go without personal effort. The patient feels like an apathetic spectator without connection with his own perceiving and doing. . . ." Feelings of unreality are quite individual and are of course completely subjective. The concurrent presence of anxiety is in accord with our *Incomplete Symptom-Defense Concept* [pp. 89, 189, 477 and Ch.12:VIB2]. When present it indicates the failure fully to bind or allay the anxiety through the symptoms.

B. IN DREAM CONTENT.—Feelings of depersonalization and *dejá vu* may occur within dreams. Several interesting instances have been reported to the author. In a recent example, the strange and frightening dream experience was one of prolonged subjective levitation and unreality.

Another disturbing instance is illustrated in the following dream:

Case 160

Depersonalization in a Dream

"I dreamt I was in a crowded place. It was on Fifth Avenue, and it must have been Easter. Crowds always trouble me and make me uneasy . . . Then I found myself in St. Patrick's. I was standing in the aisle. Things began to seem strange. Then the floor started to tilt slowly back and forth. I felt detached from it all, like I was there and yet watching from a distance. Things became very unreal and I hung on to the railing . . .

"I've had feelings like this before when I'm awake, and sometimes they frighten me. I was real scared in the dream . . . After awhile I woke up and was so relieved. It was the strangeness that was frightening in the dream; things around me becoming unreal. . . ."

3. *Relation to Stress and Danger*

A. AFFECTIVE ESCAPE ROUTE.—Feelings of unreality occur at various times. They may come on particularly at times of stress and personal danger. This brings us to their psychologic origin. Depersonalization may be one route for the automatically attempted escape from unbearable or intolerable reality. Naturally this is related to the relative intactness of individual integration. It is also related to the level of stress. Instances occur, however, in which the integrative faculties can be very sound and still respond with feelings of depersonalization in times of considerable stress.

According to what might be referred to as the Concept of an *Affective Escape Route,* the current one under discussion is the depersonalization route. For some individuals it is unwittingly employed with some frequency. Other routes include avoidance, various mental mechanisms, amnesia, neurotic reactions, and so on [Ch.13:VIIC].

These "affective escape routes" then can also be regarded as part of the psychologic component of the individual's Total Reaction to Crisis. Lief offered the following interesting experience of his own which helps to illustrate this.

Case 161

Depersonalization as Part of the Individual Total Reaction to Crisis; the T.R.C.

"I can recall, when I was senior officer in an assault boat, heading for shore on D-Day in Southern France, looking around at my fellow men, all combat engineers, armed to the teeth. I felt detached and unreal, as if I were off in the distance looking at a scene which included myself . . .

"I kept thinking with a kind of amusement how odd it was for a medical officer to be in this situation. There was no anxiety. The depersonalization, the emotional detachment worked. At the same time I was *aware* of the depersonalization, and made a mental note, in an abstract and detached kind of way, to remember it. . . ."

This example also illustrates the defensive dissociation of affect as discussed earlier. This is the mental mechanism effect. It is achieved partly through the depersonalization.

A personal wartime experience is also reminiscent. This took place as follows, while the author was serving as the medical officer aboard a U. S. Navy combat ship in the early days of World War II.

Case 162

Combat Seems a Stage Production

We were lying just off the beach at Lungi Point, Guadalcanal, in the South Pacific. The sun was shining brightly. People aboard the ship, while alert, were performing routine duties rather languidly. Off-duty personnel were occupying themselves in various ways. We seemed for the nonce strangely detached and quite distant from the war. Yet it was underway hot and heavy and close at hand. We could see much of it.

Close ashore artillery was active, planes were strafing, tanks were in action, and men were dying. It seemed quite unreal. The war was going on in the hills just beyond the beach, but it seemed like a stage production, as we watched it from no great distance. As such it had no power to hurt us; we were quite detached and uninvolved!

B. DEPRIVATION OF FAMILIARITY.—Of the process of depersonalization, Federn wrote that "while no object is deprived of its reality, the reality of the object is deprived of familiarity." This useful distinction helps us differentiate what happens in the phenomenon of depersonalization, versus the actual distortion or deprivation of the reality in the perception of objects in schizophrenia. Moderately severe symptoms of depersonalization however, may indicate the presence of latent schizophrenia.

Berman regarded depersonalization as an attempted defense against the experiencing of painful affects and sensations. His view is illustrated in the unconscious defensive employment of depersonalization in the foregoing instances.

C. ON ACHIEVING A SAFE POSITION.—Another situation in which feelings of unreality can occur is when one has reached safety and finds it hard to believe. Here the danger is over. The disturbance of personal identity is as though one says in effect, "I can't believe this is happening to me."

The following personal instances illustrate this. In the first, the achievement of a safe position involved arrival back in the United States from combat duty overseas.

Case 163

Depersonalization Accompanies Safe Arrival

It turned out to be an essentially uneventful trip (during early World War II), via the *S.S. Mormachawk.* She was a freighter-transport. We sailed unescorted across the Pacific from Espiritos Santos in the New Hebrides, and eventually arrived at San Francisco. I spent the day with a friend, walking through the city, riding the trams, seeing the Coit Tower again, visiting the downtown area, the St. Francis, the Top of the Mark, and eating at the Cliff House and Fisherman's Wharf. I vividly recall the events of the day, and the intermittent feelings of unreality that recurred at odd moments. In unrealistic fashion, it all seemed somehow strange.

Here the unreality was in the dissociation of the environment. It was as though my feelings said, "Could this really be San Francisco after all?"

I felt, "Is it actually true that this is the safe and secure mainland again?" When I saw evidence of serious activity going on along the line of civil defense, I felt some rather detached and unsympathetic amusement. This also seemed remote and unreal. In their position of such greater relative safety, how could they be so concerned? Partly I think it was the great contrast. On board ship in combat areas we had at times, when feasible, even shown movies on deck. This had been within easy range of enemy land-based bombers . . . I felt unreal. This was fleeting, but it kept coming back. It appeared off and on during this first day back in the United States, from the initial occasion while we were still aboard ship, as we passed under the Golden Gate Bridge.

In the second instance, similar feelings had been noted also upon completion of the tour of duty in the southwest Pacific. As the author pulled away in the motor launch the last time from the *U. S. S. Strong,* on which he had experienced warm friendships, intermingled with the constant potential for destruction, his identity had briefly seemed unreal, changed, or questionable. There were two aspects. First, was he really headed for safety, after so many months of harrowing and dangerous experiences? Second, what right had he to this good fortune; and how could he so leave behind him all his friends to continue to face the hazards of combat? He belonged with them, in place of having the pleasant and safe prospects of stateside duty.

4. *Many Sources of Depersonalization*

Depersonalization can occur in a wide variety of sufficiently strong emotional situations, and wherever the capacity for this kind of response exists. Feelings of unreality and estrangement may follow the use of drugs, acoustic stimuli, physical changes, and many kinds of meaningful emotional and/or physical stimuli.

The more common sources of depersonalization are summarized in *Table 36.*

Table 36

The Sources and Stimuli of Depersonalization

1. Threatened derepression of intolerable conflicts. (The symptom says in effect, "I couldn't be the person who had such ideas; needs; urges; in such danger" and so on).
2. Defensive denial of the self and one's role in a situation. ("This couldn't be me", "I may not be my [condemned] self at all", and so on).
3. Exposure to a feared but secretly desired temptation or urge. ("Since it's not me, then I would be in no danger of responding.")
4. As an expression of self-doubt. (The "Who?, Me?" sequence).
5. As a retreat from, or denial of, an unsatisfactory segment of one's past, present, or future life. ("Is it the present time or another year?"; "Am I single, or married?"; "Is my wife changed [that is, someone else?]; and so on).
6. Confusion over sexual identity. ("What is my real sex?") *See Faulty Identification Concept* [Ch.13:VE3].
7. Confused identification with another person. ("Who am I?; Am I myself, or am I someone else?").
8. Rejection by a parent, spouse, or another significant person or group. (Wittels cited a case in which an orthodox Jewish woman married a Gentile over stern parental objections. After her unrelenting father had her pronounced dead in the synagogue, her symptoms, including severe depersonalization, began.)
9. As a response to any kind of severe psychologic trauma or threat (*Case 157*).
10. Unexpected relief from danger, rescue, or gaining safety (*Cases 160, 162,* and *163*).
11. Certain drugs, and anesthetic agents upon occasion. These include:
    (*a*) Mescal and the mescaline group.
    (*b*) Marijuana and the cannabis group.
    (*c*) L.S.D. (lysergic acid and its derivatives)

(*d*) Scopolamine.
(*e*) Certain narcotics—heroin and others.
(*f*) The antihistamine group (*Benadryl, Pyribenzamine*).
(*g*) Alcohol, on occasion.
(*h*) Paraldehyde.
(*i*) The amphetamines; also the closely related drug *Actedron,* the hydrophosphate salt of the phenyl-isopropylamines (originally synthesized in eastern Europe and used in brainwashing; *Ephedrine.*
(*j*) (Rarely with) the untoward action of certain barbiturate compounds. Also tranquilizers.
(*k*) Surgical anesthesia, especially the stages of induction and post-anesthesia.
(*l*) *Dramamine.*

12. Certain intense acoustic stimuli:
    (*a*) Continued low tones (20–40 cycles per second).
    (*b*) Continued high tones (15,000–20,000 cycles per second).
    (*c*) Protracted loud sounds. (Close proximity to jet plane operations, for example).
    (*d*) Prolonged total silence, as in the experimental deprivation of all sensory stimuli.
13. (In reference to other people seeming unreal) a change or a retreat, which results from the protective maintenance of distance. This is in support of a fairly common attempted psychologic defense.
14. Very occasionally as a sequela to intracranial organic lesions.
15. The *déjà vu* phenomenon, in which one feels as though a new experience has occurred before, or somehow seems familiar. This interesting and probably universal phenomenon may be regarded as a specific variant of depersonalization.
16. With certain physiologic states, such as faintness, weakness, and hunger.
17. With physical illness. Any severe illness, or infection, especially with high fever.
18. With head exhaustion, sunstroke, or motion sickness.
19. Sudden postural changes. At times upon closing one's eyes to go to sleep. When the eyes are closed at the time of the onset of feelings of depersonalization, opening them will sometimes dispel the sensations.
20. For some individuals, feelings of depersonalization may accompany the false sensations of continued motion, present, for example, after a long sea voyage, prolonged horseback riding, roller skating, and so on.
21. An attempted escape from an intolerable situation; a minor or incipient kind of fugue as a psychologic kind of flight (*Cases 164* and *165*). In occasional instances, the repression of a childhood traumatic event has been reinforced by parental denial. (V. H. Rosen cited a case in which there were prominent symptoms of depersonalization. A mother's attempt to hang herself was witnessed by a son, aged three years. The child had been told subsequently that he imagined it, or had had a bad dream.)
22. Enforced deprivation of and removal from one's usual and familiar surroundings.

5. Depersonalization Sometimes Alarming

A. CONCERN NOT NECESSARILY IRRATIONAL.—Depersonalization can be a very disturbing subjective experience on some occasions and for some people. These feelings of unreality may become very frightening since they can constitute in effect a threat to personal integrity. It may seem as though the very foundations of personality integration are shaken, or that they threaten to split apart.

The subjective apprehension and alarm which is aroused may be much greater than in fugues, despite the usually more serious import of the latter. The dissociative splitting of consciousness of the Fugue State occurs automatically and rapidly. There is likely to be little subjective discomfort since there is probably little enough subjective awareness of what is transpiring psychologically.

Since in very occasional instances the emotional situation may actually progress to a complete psychotic break, the alarm experienced is not entirely irrational. Gutheil noted that these feelings of estrangement are often regarded by the persons concerned as a forerunner, or as an indication of the presence of serious mental illness. The resulting anxiety may lead the patient to seek treatment.

B. IN DEJA VU.—The *deja vu* experience can similarly be disturbing. It can become a source of great worry and anxiety. On occasion it can become frightening enough and frequent enough in itself to lead to the initiation of therapy. In these instances it has the same general significance as do other manifestations of depersonalization.

In a recent instance *dejá vu* was prodromal of the imminent onset of a psychotic reaction. This was a rapidly deteriorating situation, in which only the prompt initiation of intensive analytic therapy fortunately served to abort the rapidly developing psychotic manifestations. On the occasion of an earlier episode this person had been far less fortunate, with a resulting long period of psychosis and hospitalization.

E. PSYCHODYNAMICS

1. Incipient Fugue Concept

A. MAY ACCOMPANY ANY INSTANCE OF PSYCHOPATHOLOGY.—Many of the foregoing comments have related to the dynamic implications of depersonalization. *Table 36* also summarizes the dynamic factors in the psychogenesis of depersonalization.

Depersonalization can be closely related dynamically to the Fugue State. It can at times be regarded as what we might term an incipient or *minor fugue,* in which the personal identity is *partially* lost. This is the *Incipient Fugue Concept* of depersonalization. Depersonalization thus may reflect, as can the Fugue States for example, the self-doubt or rejection which can occur as a consequence of the condemnation or disowning of the self by the conscience. In other words, depersonalization may reflect an automatic kind of ego-disowning, due to superego disapproval.

In our study of dissociative phenomena it is useful for us to stress the *integrative* function of the ego, in serving and preserving the id and the superego. All psychopathology thus is more or less clearly associated with a disturbance of this integrative function of the ego. Depersonalization accordingly can be considered to be a signal of disturbance or a Conflict Indicator, in the integrative functions of the ego. Accordingly it may accompany, and be experienced, in almost any instance or kind of psychopathology. These can vary from the "normal" or quite minor, all the way to the grossly psychotic.

B. SYMBOLIC ESCAPE.—In the instance to follow, the feelings of depersonalization equated a symbolic kind of escape from what had become for the patient an intolerable amount of parental control. The level of illness in this case was not psychotic, although not far removed. As one aspect of the psychodynamics we might refer to depersonalization as a *Symbolic Escape*. This would fit in with our view of the Dissociative Reaction as one of Psychologic-Flight Avoidance [Ch.13:IB]. This avoidance, which is ultimately that of anxiety, is thereby also in conformity with our earlier [pp. 4, 85, and 516] Principle of the Avoidance of Anxiety.

The feelings of unreality which were experienced in the following instance consisted of a kind of detachment from the immediate situation. They often occurred at a time of what was for her, crisis and impending or potential danger, in that she felt threatened and less secure. This is the converse of the situation in *Case 167,* in which the depersonalization occurred on achieving greater security.

Case 164

Depersonalization Equating an Attempted Psychic Escape from Intolerable Parental Control

An eighteen-year-old girl gave birth to an illegitimate child. Her parents gave her very little emotional support in this difficult position. Instead, they unbraided her as a loose and depraved woman. They adamantly refused to allow her to keep the baby, or to marry the child's father. In the course of this experience she became ill with symptoms of fever and pleural effusion, and she was hospitalized for pulmonary tuberculosis. As a result, she was able to get away from her parents and their intolerable control, at least for a time.

Her respite from her mother, however, was brief. Soon the mother was herself hospitalized for tuberculosis. The authorities thought they were doing mother and daughter a great favor by placing the mother in the same room with the patient! Directly the patient developed strong feelings of unreality. She felt that there was an invisible wall separating her from the rest of the world, a wall which came down so that it also separated her mother's bed from hers.

She also developed vertigo, and felt that she could stand aside and watch her head swirling round and round. When she washed, she noticed that her hands did not seem to belong to her. In treatment, these symptoms recurred for a period of time, whenever she discussed her mother and their relationship.

2. *Psychologic-Flight Avoidance Concept*

A. STEP IN THE DIRECTION.—The attempted resolution of conflict by a psychologic kind of escape or retreat can be further illustrated by many clinical cases in which depersonalization has occurred. In some of these instances, one is certainly reminded of the more drastic variety of psychotic retreat into a state of unreality, or the complete dissociative splitting away from certain painful aspects of reality as illustrated in the Fugue States. It is almost as though the feelings of depersonalization represent what we might term an *unconscious step in the direction,* toward this sort of more severe disturbance. This view of them is in accord with our Concept of Psychologic-Flight Avoidance. It is then not surprising to find these feelings not infrequently prominent in early schizophrenia, or as a premonitory feature.

A patient of Gutheil with severe feelings of depersonalization wrote in her diary: "Life can do me no harm; if I do not feel well or things are going badly with me, I retreat into my temple where my better self lives."

This is not to suggest that such a patient voluntarily invokes feelings of unreality. This is generally not possible. Some patients, however, can to some extent consciously encourage such feelings, or fight them off. This patient was rather expressing a conscious parallel, for the unconsciously attempted refuge which she had "sought" through her symptoms.

Case 165

The Psychologic Flight of Depersonalization

A colleague recounted to me the regular subjective experiences of depersonalization which he used to experience while playing football in college. His participation in this sport was largely on the basis of great inner needs for self-esteem and prestige. Because of these very strong motivating factors, he was playing out of his weight class.

He had performed far beyond what one might expect, but he was really very frightened. He felt intense fear and anxiety at the start of each game, although he always managed to avoid serious injury and usually turned in a sparkling performance.

The intense feelings of unreality were part of an attempted automatic Psychologic-Flight Avoidance from the situation, that is, from the nearly intolerable fear and the possible resulting handicap. He felt that his depersonalization in this stress was a conflict-solving attempt which maintained his ability to function effectively in the game. The "solution" was psychologically advantageous. It was in some contrast to that of another football player [Case 97, p. 474], who had to deny completely to conscious awareness one side of his conflict over the game.

In the neurotic patient, depersonalization often serves as a defense against anxiety. In a threatening situation one response may result in a general inhibition of feeling. This may be contributed to by depersonalization. Both are non-voluntary, intended escapes.

B. FEELINGS OF ESTRANGEMENT IN SCHIZOPHRENIA.—Nunberg pointed out that feelings of estrangement are frequent in schizophrenic patients. The author would agree, although they are not always readily uncovered. However, many well adjusted individuals as well have feelings of unreality. Those who suffer from depersonalization report all gradations. These can range from a simple, hardly noticeable estrangement of the external world, to the greatest derangement of self-feeling. At the latter extreme the patient can come to feel that he has lost everything, that he is a nonentity, "no longer a member of the human race" has lost his ego, or is nonexistent, and so on.

In the severe reactions seen in schizophrenia, depersonalization follows withdrawal of the libido from external objects. There can be an investment of the libido onto the patient's own organs, giving rise to all sorts of bizarre sensory and hygeiaphrontic (hypochondriacal) symptoms. The organ-parts so invested, or the entire body, may then be perceived, consciously or unconsciously, as though they belonged to someone else. This terribly uncomfortable state of affairs is countered by attempts to ward off the severe depersonalization.

Symptoms of depersonalization (or *dejá vu* as noted) may greatly increase, when a psychosis approaches, or in an existing psychosis when it takes a turn for the worse. This can illustrate our very important Concept of Defensive-Layering [*See* pp. 367, 465, 486–489 and Ch.12:VC5.]

3. *Depersonalization and Identification*

A. CONCEPT OF FAULTY IDENTIFICATIONS.—In conclusion, a point or so may be noted about the relation of depersonalization to identification. The mechanism of identification and the efficiency and degree of its function can play an important role in the production of feelings of depersonalization and in Fugue States. Faulty Identifications can lay the foundation for later ego disturbances, or can interfere with ego integration. The Faulty Identification Concept (F.I.C.) implies resulting emotional conflict [*see also Case 115* and *Case 143*]. In *Table 36,* among the factors which can result in depersonalization, we noted the relation of this interesting psychologic phenomenon to possible confusions of identification. Incomplete, partial, mixed, or overlapping unconscious identifications can prove quite confusing to the ego. Undoubtedly, in the development of the personality, multiple partial identifications are made. Of these, the most important are those early ones which are made with significant adults in childhood.

In addition, we continue throughout life to have contacts with many people, elements of whom we strive to emulate. This process is intermittently active, and its unconscious aspects are especially important. These elements ordinarily become integrated, that is, assimilated. The degree of success or completeness of such assimilation theoretically can vary considerably. It is the conflictual or partial identification, and the less completely assimilated ones, that may lead to depersonalization.

B. UNCERTAIN SEXUAL IDENTIFICATION.—Oberdorf wrote of the problem of unclear or uncertain sexual identification leading to the onset of feelings of unreality. Here, depersonalization was believed to follow a conflict (or confusion) over the individual's sexual identification, with the result that, feeling temporarily uncertain on an unconscious level as to his true sexual identification he then felt unreal.

Oberdorf observed that, ". . . In these individuals a mixture of masculine and feminine mental tendencies persisted up to the time when the feelings of unreality appeared and seemed to have definite etiologic significance . . .".

C. INTERNAL PHANTOMS.—Wittels worded some of the bases for our Faulty Identification Concept in interesting terms in emphasizing the role of partial conflicting identifications in depersonalization. He spoke of these identifications as constituting multiple internal phantoms: ". . . All the world is a stage not only surrounding us but even more so within us. There are phantoms that we have to live up to; there are others whom we fear, others we hate or secretly love. Some of them we consider to be our real self. Some of them must be punished, others cajoled. It is not always easy for the poor 'ego' to find his way in such a crowd!

"Depersonalization presupposes a considerable number of phantoms in a person and [the] ego is at a loss to decide which one of these phantoms or group of phantoms has to be accepted as his real self . . .". The resulting uncertainty and confusion leads to feelings of unreality and estrangement. It contributes to our Concept of Faulty Identification [*See Table 33* in Chapter 12.]

D. CONCEPT OF UNWANTED IDENTIFICATIONS.—Feelings of estrangement and unreality also may come on when one struggles to avoid what we might refer to as "Unwanted Identification", as with criminals by wartime political prisoners, imprisoned with them. Many sources for such conflictual identifications exist. Being of course also in nature conflictual, this concept is a tenet in that of the Faulty Identification, as outlined.

For example, Jacobson reported the symptom of depersonalization as persistent in a group of female political prisoners in Nazi Germany. Feelings of unreality were prominent: (*a*) for the early weeks after incarceration, (*b*) following severe interrogation, and (*c*) psychologically in combating unwanted identifications as above, and when opposing partial identifications were in conflict.

Any sudden enforced change in one's familiar surroundings is a threat, and to an extent emotionally and psychologically disruptive. It can serve as an S.E.H.C. [p. 34] or, less frequently, as an S.E.H.A. [p. 38], and as such may well bring on symptoms which can include depersonalization.

VI. FAINTING

A. TEMPORARY LOSS OF CONSCIOUSNESS

1. Fragmental Dissociation

The occurrence of a temporary loss of consciousness in response to emotional stimuli is a commonly enough accepted phenomenon. Everyone knows about it. Most people have witnessed it. Until the separation of the Dissociative Reactions was made for purposes of classification, fainting was widely considered as conversion (hysterical) in origin. Fainting may be regarded as an ultimate extension of "selective hearing" and "selective inattention", [Ch.12:VE2]. As such, it would automatically provide complete *Secondary Restriction;* the defensive cutting-off of painful or threatening sensations or associations. The Fainting provides the *primary* restriction, of all sensory perception.

Fainting is to be generally regarded as a completely involuntary reaction. There are occasional instances where it almost appears as if the individual prone to frequent fainting attacks can consciously initiate them. It is more clear in certain other cases that a fainting episode can be fought off or consciously held back by some persons. Fragmental Dissociation [Ch.13:IIE*1*; IIF*3*] is the type which is operative in the reaction of fainting.

2. Fainting Defined; a Primitive Defense

Fainting is *a primitive type of defensive reaction through which one completely surrenders or shuts off outside perception.* In this sense it may be regarded as a temporary nonpsychotic break with reality, or as a complete involuntary surrender of consciousness and perception, in the face of emotionally intolerable stimuli.

Fainting is *the sudden, complete, and involuntary loss of consciousness, in the absence of sufficiently powerful physical trauma, injury, or disease. Fainting is a transient but sometimes repetitive phenomenon, the basis of which is wholly, or always at least in part, psychologic in origin.*

An attack of Fainting is a temporary, rather complete dissociation of the subjective, conscious self from one's surroundings. The responsible stimuli may have all kinds of deeply hidden psychologic implications for the individual concerned. Temporary unconsciousness has become (at least unconsciously) preferable to the emotional stimuli which impinge or which threaten to impinge.

B. VARIABLE THRESHOLD; INCIDENCE

The individual threshold for fainting varies widely. Many people never faint. A fair number of people have fainted occasionally, and a few people faint frequently. The stimulus responsible depends on its individual significance to the person concerned. What may cause fainting for one person will leave another untouched.

In the author's experience, fainting has been slowly declining in frequency. It would seem that it is more frequently associated with the groups which are culturally and socially less well endowed. In earlier medical experience fainting was far more frequent. Its gradual decrease in incidence coincides with a gradual rise in sophistication.

Certain earlier comments about the incidence of conversion, the Changing-Trends Concept, and our Theory of Transparency could apply here. The pattern of emotional symptoms adopted is influenced by the cultural milieu and by the level of sophistication. With the more culturally sophisticated groups, the more "advanced" types of neurotic illness tend to develop, rather than the more primitive ones.

The Profitable Patterns Concept [pp. 447, 539–540, and Ch.12:VE2] can also have some applicability as to incidence. Thus the child can intuitively perceive the psychologic "profit" or lack of it, implicit to the adoption of such a pattern.

C. RANGE OF STIMULI BROAD

1. Many Situations; Meaning Individual; Emotional Contagion Concept

The possible stimuli which are reacted to by a fainting attack cover a broad range. The sight of blood, illness, injury, a broken bone, or a hospital may be reacted to by fainting. This is an interesting aspect of his Total Reaction to Crisis, in the professional study of the person concerned. There are many situations which can lead to the response of fainting. This reaction in each instance, however, is quite individual. So is its meaning and interpretation. The Psychic Reduplication Concept [p. 468; Ch.12:5B*1*] can find some applicability, since earlier fainting with pain, trauma, or illness sometimes will establish an antecedent for later episodes on a psychic base alone.

Injections may cause some to faint. This has been observed in lines of men awaiting inoculations at military establishments, and among high school students. Not infrequently such a reaction tends to be communicated. The sight of others fainting tends to increase the susceptibility of certain individuals, in another possible striking and intriguing instance of what we might term an Emotional Contagion, as noted earlier [pp. 32, 464, 476]. This can occur at military reviews, parades, and patriotic, school, or fraternal exercises. On some of these occasions heat (through heat exhaustion) can play a significant contributory role.

Occasional instances of fainting are reported upon initiation of intercourse or at point of orgasm. Many, many situations of emotional stress or crisis can lead to or contribute to fainting. Rarely, fainting can terminate an A.A.A. [pp. 89*ff.*] or occur at the same moment, as a substitute.

The popular belief that women are far more susceptible to fainting than men tends to be a misconception. Fainting is not infrequent, as noted, among service men. Herein certain physiologic, climatic, and postural circulatory factors also enter.

2. Circumstances Unconsciously Arranged

People who faint seldom hurt themselves. The unconscious protective devices are usually sufficiently preserved. These, together with the unconscious needs to be so subserved, generally quite carefully, albeit unconsciously, manage to "arrange" the time, place, and position in such a way as to prevent injury. This is not an absolute finding, however. In accord with the internal needs, the situation and the audience are also so "arranged", as may be fitting and appropriate. An audience or witnesses are almost a must for a *bona fide* psychologic fainting attack.

Sometimes the unconscious needs or wishes expressed in the attack are quite dramatic. They are often interesting, perhaps transparent, and at times very poignant. A case of the latter was reported to the author in which a widow fainted on the desperately sad and tragic occasion of her husband's funeral, following his unexpected and untimely death. As she was taking her last farewell of the deceased, she fainted and actually fell forward *into* the coffin! Her unconscious wish thus expressed, was both apparent and poignant.

3. Helpless Position, as All Perception Surrendered; Ostrich Concept

In concluding our brief discussion of Fainting, we might note the great potential for self-defeat in this kind of reaction to emotional threat or stress. There is a relation to Denial and the *Ostrich Concept,* as presented in the author's previous monograph, *Mental Mechanisms* (Butterworths, 1963). Fainting is even more ostrich-like.

The ostrich sacrifices mainly his visual perception, but at the least he maintains his other perceptive abilities, plus his powers of motility. The person who has fainted has successfully cut off all his usual areas of perception and motility as well. This may be a vital mode of psychologic defense from the painful perception of stimuli. The individual, however, could hardly be in a greater position of physical and mental helplessness, impotence, and dependence.

VII. AMNESIA

A. MEMORY LOSS

1. Primarily Psychologic

Amnesia is a psychiatric term employed to describe the loss of memory. As such it has been directly carried over from the identical Greek word *amnesia,* meaning forgetfulness. Loss of memory may result from many causes, but is primarily and mainly psychologic. Some amount of memory loss is an occasional sequela to such physical insults as head injury and concussion. Memory loss, however, frequently occurs in the complete absence of injury, or in occasional instances in which there is only very minor injury. In the latter, the injury often serves merely as a precipitating factor. Here, as in so many instances, the amnesia is the result of psychologic factors.

The mental mechanism of *repression* is closely related to memory loss and amnesia. As important introductory material to the understanding of the psychologic factors in amnesia, the section on Repression in the author's monograph *Mental Mechanisms* [pp. 27–76] is worth reading or reviewing. The occurrence of amnesia is illustrative of the operation of Fragmental Dissociation.

2. Definition of Amnesia

Amnesia may be defined as *a loss of memory,* or as *pathologic forgetting.* Instances of amnesia may be sharply circumscribed as to limits in time. Amnesia also may be spotty, irregular, and scattered, or it may be diffuse. Amnesia may be limited to events of the immediate past. It may extend into areas of the remote past, or be confined to scattered areas of the latter. Fourteen types of amnesia will shortly be tabulated (*Table 37*). There are two major categories: the psychologic and the organic.

Amnesia is *a dissociative phenomenon, in which an area of one's experience or recollections is lost or split off and becomes consciously inaccessible.* Technically at least, the area of loss is always recoverable. Even those traumatic amnesias following head trauma can be reduced in area.

B. NOTES ON DIAGNOSIS

1. Medicolegal Implications; Malingering

There is little diagnostic difficulty present in the clearcut case of amnesia in which the individual presents himself so as to report some specific memory loss. On the other hand, determining the presence of true amnesia may be most difficult. This is likely to be the case particularly when there are important medicolegal implications. In certain of these kinds of instances, especially in the more complex of the cases in civil life, the accumulated experience and judgment of many years of work in the field is a minimal requirement. Even the most experienced clinician may find the decision to be equivocal.

The accuracy of diagnosis in occasional instances will require the elimination of the possibility of malingering. Certain aspects of malingering and its distinction have been discussed [*See* pp. 61–62, 494, and Ch. 14: VA2].

Kiersch reported a series of 98 persons admitted to an Army general hospital with reported amnesia, most of whom were young (21–30 years of age) males (92). Of these, 25 later admitted on the conscious level that their "amnesia" was feigned, and 16 additional individuals indicated this under hypnosis. One third of the 98 faced certain or probable legal action, 21 of whom were in the feigned group.

2. Organic Amnesia

In cases in which physical factors (such as senility, trauma, cerebral lesions, and alcohol) are apparent etiologic contributors, the resulting organic amnesia is an expected consequence and therefore less surprising. Diagnosis may offer little trouble. It should be remembered in these cases, however, that underlying psychologic factors still most often form an important part of the foundation for the clinical picture which develops. In hidden and less tangible fashion, they play an important role in determining the pattern, the extent, and the subject of the pathologic forgetting which ensues.

Occasionally amnesias and Fugue States must be differentiated from cases of organic confusion. At times the withdrawn and noncommunicative patient suffering from an acute schizophrenic episode must also be differentiated from the amnesia victim. Clinical experience, careful history (including accessory sources), psychologic testing and observation can each be a significant aid in diagnosis.

Even when the etiology of amnesia is basically organic, it is important to keep in mind that there is still often present a high degree of selectivity as to just *what* is lost. In this fashion, psychologic factors are still operative and important in cases of organic and traumatic amnesia. This helps to illustrate the close relationship which often exists between the organic and the psychologic in the determination of the particular manifestations of an illness [Ch.14:VH].

3. Psychologic Amnesia

More problems in establishing a diagnosis are encountered in the psychologic amnesias. The patient is most likely to be first seen by a general physician, who may have had little prior experience with or limited interest in, this type of case. The emergency services of most large urban hospitals are likely to receive persons suffering from amnesia. Police officers who have had long and varied experience have encountered such individuals.

Amnesia is associated with every case of fugue. In these cases its presence may completely escape casual observation. In some cases, the individual has some awareness of his major memory gap for past events, and feels a personal need to conceal this. There are instances in which the dissociation is alternating and fairly complete, and in which the precipitating factors are entirely or largely psychologic in nature. These often require a careful evaluation and clinical study. The establishment of the diagnosis in some of the more complex instances may require the most experienced and professionally sophisticated judgment.

In probably most examples of memory loss the patient has some awareness that this is the case. There may be relatively little concern in evidence about it. This is not difficult to understand when the amnesia serves such a vital psychologically protective function as it often does. When present to any real degree, this may be regarded as a similar phenomenon to that of *la belle indifférence,* which we have observed to be operative in certain cases of Somatic Conversion [Ch.12:VC3]. The purposes and importance are analogous. One may regard the relative lack of concern as being part of the Secondary Defense of the symptom. [*See* pp. 96, 144, 267, 359, 366, 444, 487, 505; and Ch.12:VA2]. Occasionally our Flight-to-the-Physical Principle is illustrated, as many patients would prefer to ascribe such difficulties to some physical basis or to trauma rather than to something "mental" (actually of course emotional).

In the spotty amnesia frequently observed as an accompaniment of advancing years, there may be considerable personal concern present. There may also be a defensive irritability and denial. This can be especially marked if the attention that is invited to it is unwelcome to the person concerned.

C. INCIDENCE

1. Protectively Intended Function of Avoidance; Affective Escape Route

The incidence of amnesia as a response to trauma, aging, alcoholic overindulgence, and many varied factors, is not rare. On the other hand, marked cases, those which approach the Fugue State or the Alternating Personality in the completeness and extent of dissociation, are much less frequently seen.

Amnesia is always a response to a physical or a psychologic event, or to a combination of both. Psychologic amnesia represents an unconscious way of escape or flight from intolerable emotional conflict. It constitutes another type of psychologic *Affective Escape Route* [Ch.13:VD*3*]. Thus, when a situation or series of events becomes intolerably difficult or painful to the individual who already possesses the predisposing psychologic diathesis for this type of dissociative avoidance and escape, amnesia results. The amnesia attempts to subserve a protective function.* In so doing it may well become the presenting pathologic feature. Well circumscribed psychologic amnesia for a specific area or an event of some moment, and persisting over a span of time, is not common.

2. Memories Lost Through Repression; Individual Selectivity

We must keep in mind that the forgetting of emotionally painful or conflictual events is an almost continual protective psychologic process. This process is particularly active in the early years of life. This is repression. Repression is *the involuntary relegation of emotionally disturbing and painful material to the unconscious.* It is intermittently continuous throughout life. We have studied elsewhere some of the important factors about repression. Indeed, were this process not continually active, the cumulative effect of our individual emotional traumata might soon become overpowering. Repression and defensive memory loss or discard often persist long past the subsiding of the initiating stress or significance. This follows in effect our *Concept of Continued Physiologic Momentum* [pp. 99, 455, and Ch.12: *Table 33*].

Conversely, with most persons, certain "selected" painful experiences in particular appear to be retained. This selectivity of those painful emotional experiences which are "lost" (that is, repressed), as opposed to those which are retained, is a highly individual matter. Its basis in each case might be sought separately.

3. Forgetting Facilitated Via Sleep; Contribution to Respite-of-Sleep Principle

The protective and restorative value of sleep lies partly in its facilitation of the forgetting process. Sleeping probably facilitates repression. Dreams aid in its maintenance. The removal of possible disturbing events to a less immediate and more remote position is thus facilitated. Through sleep, as noted earlier [p. 38 and Ch.13:IIIA*2*], one gains a "psychologic respite".

The stress and tensions of the day, the memories of disturbing events, and the failures and dissatisfactions of the immediately preceding waking hours are dulled or lost. The psychologically restorative purpose of sleep is perhaps at least as important and necessary as is the physically restorative value. As earlier observed [Section III], dreaming also plays an important role.

---

* When fully effective there is no anxiety. *See* Concept of Incomplete Symptom-Defense, pp. 89, 189, 451, and Ch.12:IIIB*2*.

D. CLINICAL FEATURES

1. Categories of Amnesia

The author has found the delineation of some fourteen categories or types to be currently quite sufficient for the classification and description of clinical instances of amnesia. These have proved useful to him personally for purposes of communication and reference. Their employment facilitates descriptive accuracy. Some have enjoyed considerable prior use. Several of the categories are his own.

The names which have been assigned have been so primarily on a descriptive basis, and are largely self-explanatory. As might be expected, there is some overlapping. The types of amnesia, together with their definition, are tabulated in *Table 37* in alphabetical order.

Table 37

Types of Amnesia

1. *Alcoholic Amnesia*

    Amnesia associated with the excessive, episodic or chronic use of alcohol [Ch.13:VIID4]

2. *Anterograde Amnesia*

    Amnesia extending *forward* in time from the precipitating event.

3. *Circumscribed Amnesia*

    Amnesia with sharply delineated limits in time, or as to the events thus lost.

4. *Emotional Amnesia*

    Amnesia which is primarily emotional in origin. This means a dissociated, avoidance kind of "flight" response to the presence of intolerable emotional conflict. *Fugue Amnesia* is classified as emotional and psychologic.

5. *Episodic Amnesia*

    Amnesia for a particular episode or a small area of experience. At times in alcoholic amnesia.

6. *False* or *Feigned Amnesia*

    The "amnesia" which is claimed in malingering.

7. *Organic Amnesia*

    Amnesia in which the origin is primarily organic. Example: amnesia with organic brain disease. Traumatic amnesia is nearly always organic. The *area* for loss, however, may be partially or largely determined on a psychologic basis.

    Amnesias of organic origin, as distinguished from those which are psychologic in origin [Ch.13:VIIB3].

8. *Paramnesia*

    Loss of memory in which there is an accompanying and compensating confabulation, or unconscious filling in of memory gaps. Sometimes encountered in alcoholic amnesia; also in Korsokoff's syndrome.

(*Table continued on next page*)

Table 37—Continued

>   9. *Posthypnotic Amnesia*
>
>   Amnesia following hypnosis. It may be spontaneous, or occur in response to suggestions made during the hypnotic trance. *Induced Amnesia* is that which has been thus suggested or directed.
>
>   10. *Psychologic Amnesia*
>
>   Another term for amnesia of emotional origin. Amnesia of psychologic etiology, as opposed to that of an organic basis [Ch.13:VIIB2]. The presence of amnesia underlines our *Concept of Symptoms as an Implied Preference* [p. 503 and Ch.12:VIB2], to the alternative of painful awareness and recollection.
>
>   11. *Retrograde Amnesia*
>
>   Amnesia extending *backward* in time from the precipitating event, whether this be emotional, organic, or traumatic.
>
>   12. *Shock Amnesia*
>
>   Amnesia which follows electroshock. It is generally also to be classified as retrograde, organic, and in less obvious ways, partly psychologically determined as to areas [Ch.13:VIIH]. [*See* Principle of Psychic Selectivity in post-shock memory loss, Ch.13:VIIH3.]
>
>   13. *Senile Amnesia*
>
>   The amnesia of aging. Tends to be scattered and is more noticeable in relation to the more recent, day-to-day events [Ch.13:VIID6].
>
>   14. *Traumatic Amnesia*
>
>   Amnesia following physical injury. Most often occurs following a blow on the head, with concussion. Includes the Traumatic Encephalopathy [Ch.13VIID3] of boxers [Ch.14:VH2].

There are two major divisions or classes of amnesia: those of emotional (psychologic) origin, and those of organic origin. The emotional ones are dissociative, and the organic ones are apparently due to physical changes in the cerebral cortex. The emotional group results in a dissociative loss of a greater or lesser area which is usually fairly discrete. The loss is of an emotionally determined segment of the individual's experience. The organic amnesia is more often scattered. It mainly involves recent events. These are likely to be those which have a less specific psychologic significance for the person concerned.

The first type of amnesia needs psychologic investigation. The second type needs organic investigation. Often the latter can be the first recognizable sign of organic cerebral disease. It may be in evidence long before other physical or laboratory indications of organic cerebral disease are present. Amnesic E.O.C.s (Emotional-Organic Combinations) of course include contributions from both sources.

2. Psychologic Amnesia

Occasionally a person will complain of memory loss rather promptly after its onset. This may be discovered, or he may report this himself. One might suspect that in at least some of these instances of being discovered the degree of dissociation is possibly less complete and that other deeply hidden psychologic factors unwittingly might aid in bringing about the "discovery", before much of the more prolonged activity occurs which is more characteristic of the fugue.

Identification of the victim in marked cases of amnesia is sometimes similarly facilitated. For example, documents are not infrequently "found" on the person of the victim which aid in the efforts at identification. All of this by no means implies that any of this is conscious or deliberate. The amnesia is genuine, and these events are unconsciously determined. There may be intent in them, but the person concerned is not consciously aware of this.

Episodes of amnesia are clinically very frequently tied up with Fugues. In the more marked Fugue, circumstances are often avoided in unconscious fashion which might lead to discovery or to identification, at least for longer periods.

The following case of amnesia was discovered some six hours after its onset. The amnesia was *emotional* in type, following the increasingly intolerable pressure of psychologic conflicts. Further and descriptively classified, it was *circumscribed* as to time. It was also *retrograde,* attempting the resolution of conflicts through the detachment (that is, the dissociation) from the patient's conscious awareness, of his entire past. This instance also includes elements characteristic of the Fugue, of which it is also a less marked example and from which a clear distinction cannot be made.

Case 166

A Case of Psychologic Amnesia; Dissociation of Memory as the Unconscious Defensive Response to Intolerable Emotional Conflict

(1) *Parental approval vital*

Mr. G. R. was a twenty-four-year-old college student. He was the only son of an extremely ambitious father who was a very successful engineer. His mother was perfectionistic, obsessional, and domineering. The young man was in his third year of university study, struggling to get through a pre-engineering course, in which he was not in the slightest bit interested. However, he felt he had to continue, largely as a result of irresistible parental pressure. He had already failed one year in this course.

His third year was further complicated by the fact that he had made a marriage which had been kept secret, in as far as his parents were concerned. He did not feel that he could possibly tell them of his marriage unless at the same time at least, he could also present them with a successful college record. This was impossible. The parental approval which had always been vital to him appeared forever lost!

(2) *Precipitating event*

The marriage had involved emotional and time demands, which had still further interfered with his college performance. He had become extremely anxious about the probable results of examinations, which were due to begin in a few weeks' time. One Friday afternoon, after classes, he took part in a "bull session" in the college dormitory. This left him thoroughly convinced that he would not be able to pass his examinations. This served as the precipitating event.

He started for home, but did not arrive there. Late that evening he was found wandering in the streets of a city some two hundred miles away from the site of his college.

(3) *Prompt identification and medical care*

He was soon identified by papers in his wallet. There was also a picture of the few people who had been present at his wedding. One of these happened to be recognized by one of the local policemen. This friend had acted as best man at the wedding some six or seven months before. He was called to the police station to identify his friend. This he was quite promptly and positively able to do, athough at this time the patient had no conscious memory of ever having seen this man before.

The patient was admitted to the psychiatric service of a general hospital and treated psychotherapeutically. *Pentothal* interviews were accompanied by strong suggestions that he would gradually recover his memory. By the end of the week, things were pieced together and, with the exception of some of the events of the trip from college, the material was returned to consciousness.

(4) *Amnesia an extension of avoidance pattern of defense.*

Further psychiatric study over a period of time revealed that this man had always been disturbed by his parents' attitudes. His established and usual method of handling these difficulties had been to attempt to ignore them. This was a pattern of avoidance. As he said, "I just pretend they're not there. In this way, I can deal with them. . . ."

His amnesic episode represented an episodic magnification and extension of this established pattern of defensive avoidance. Psychotherapy was able to resolve many of the problems. He accordingly was enabled to make marked improvement, with more realistic evaluation of his assets and future possibilities, and partly through some helpful modifications in certain of the parental attitudes.

3. Sequela to Concussion

A. AMNESIA PROTECTION CONCEPT.—This discussion would not be complete without some consideration of the usual kind of retrograde amnesia which most often follows concussion.

Let us consider an important concept. It is one which has received little attention heretofore. This is the *Concept of Amnesia Protection*. The author refers to the emotionally protective function subserved in a fair number of cases of traumatic amnesia.

Case 167

Traumatic Retrograde Amnesia Incident to Concussion

A mother and father and their two daughters, aged ten and twelve years, were making a motor trip through Pennsylvania. While traveling at about fifty miles an hour, their car collided with a truck. Everyone in the car was injured.

Of the two girls, the younger child was knocked unconscious, suffering a moderate concussion. In fact, the younger child suffered the greatest *physical* injuries of all. However, she retained no memory whatsoever of the collision, or of immediately preceding events. She seemed to have suffered few untoward emotional consequences. A few weeks later she was fully recovered and in excellent shape.

The older girl, however, was relatively less fortunate. Her physical injuries were slight, compared to her younger sister's. However, she remembered in detail all the painful events of the collision. She suffered intermittently from nightmares, tremors, and episodes of palpitation, as well as a number of other indications of gross anxiety. She was afraid to ride in a car for months. Remnants of anxiety were in evidence six months later. These subsided gradually during the course of a short series of psychotherapeutic consultations.

From the foregoing incident, one could conclude that the traumatic amnesia following the accident and the concussion served an emotionally protective kind of function for the younger child. This illustrates rather well our Amnesia Protection Concept. This example also helps point out how upon occasion *the emotional sequelae of trauma can be much more troubling and serious than the* actual physical injuries; *see also* similar *Case 177,* Ch.14:VD*3.* Persons suffering concussion who have no memory loss and who can recall the circumstances of their accidents, not only are likely to suffer emotional sequelae but also are likely to have many physical symptoms and complaints. The contrasting response to a traumatic situation is interesting in the foregoing instance. *See also Cases 178A* and *179* [Ch.14:VD*4*] for another set of contrasting responses to similarly traumatic (psychically) situations.

It might also be noted at this point that amnesia can also be protective in certain psychologic situations in additional ways. On rare occasions, its unconscious onset has interrupted the completion of a sequence of activity with the potential for tragedy, such as murder or suicide.

It might be pointed out again briefly for emphasis that some degree of retrograde amnesia accompanies most head injuries.* This more often spontaneously clears up in time, but it may also partially remain. Confabulations and paramnesias are not uncommon, as the person strives consciously and otherwise to make up for his deficit. The individual with post-concussion amnesia tends to be uncomplaining. Treatment is seldom indicated. In Kiersch's series, in the head injury cases, the retrograde portion of the amnesia could be recalled or significantly reduced.

B. BLOW RARELY RECALLED.—Persons who are knocked unconscious rarely, if ever, can recall the actual instant of the blow responsible. Amnesia, when it follows concussion is highly selective. Weinstein and colleagues, in a study of 200 cases, believed the amnesia became a way in which the person referred to otherwise unverbalized problems and disabilities. They also noted an interesting correlation between the last thing reported as remembered and current personal problems, for which the episode was a symbolic representation.

Occasionally the memory loss following concussion may become more serious. The author recalls the instances of two friends and classmates, each of whom suffered marked traumatic amnesia incident to concussions while playing college football. One fully recovered in three days; the second had made only a moderate and partial recovery after some weeks, and eventually had to leave school.

4. Traumatic Encephalopathy of Boxers

A. MARTLAND'S "PUNCH DRUNK".—The cumulative effects of repeated head blows lead to the onset of an organic syndrome. This is seen commonly in what the author proposes to call the *Traumatic Encephalopathy*

---

* A long recognized fact. Pollock's grandfather, a layman and soldier, active in the Nez Perce campaign of 1877, described an instance of traumatic amnesia in quite matter-of-fact terms.

of prize fighters. This syndrome was first identified and named "Punch Drunk" by Martland, in 1928. Boxers who have absorbed a fair amount of punishment in the ring are likely to show varying evidence of cerebral damage, or "punchiness". This may extend all the way from very minor effects, to obvious ones resulting in gross handicap. Scattered amnesia may be present, although this is not the most prominent feature of the syndrome.

This condition can be attributed to the cumulative traumatic damage to the cerebral cortex. Concussion brings on injury, a single instance usually being minor as to its consequences and effects. In repeated concussions from any cause however, these effects accumulate to produce more marked overall changes and consequences.

B. CLINICAL FEATURES IN MARKED INSTANCE.—Some years ago the author had for a patient a former nationally prominent, heavyweight boxer. He had fought a great many bouts. He had been a major opponent of Joe Louis during the latter's prime. During the declining period of his pugilistic prowess, however, he took some severe beatings. Clinically, all of his mental faculties were slowed, and his mental performance was irregular. Retention and recall were irregular and spotty.

His friends described for the author how, when he became excited or confused — which happened rather readily, for one example, when a streetcar approached and clanged its bell while he was crossing the street — he would crouch and begin to spar protectively against an imaginary opponent. This was a pathetic picture. His was a typical and marked instance of pugilistic encephalopathy. Following his enforced retirement from the ring, the extent of his Traumatic Encephalopathy showed little further progress. On the other hand, neither was there any significant improvement in evidence.

C. PRECEPT OF CUMULATIVE TRAUMA.—This syndrome is well known in professional boxing circles. Fortunately, the extremely marked instances are not terribly common. The only preventive is not to continue boxing past one's prime. When a boxer begins to slow down, he is forced to take more punishment in the ring, and some degree of cumulative encephalopathy is likely to result, and at an increasingly faster rate.

Accordingly, the traumatic cerebral dysfunction leads to further slowing down, and this in turn to more punishment and more cerebral damage. This can become a rapidly progressive vicious circle. Traumatic Encephalopathy is an accumulative process. Its etiology accordingly is based upon what we might call the *Precept of Cumulative Trauma*.

The results of early examinations are often inconclusive. Changes are not easily detected until fairly advanced. This stresses their insidiousness and their cumulative nature. Kaplan and Browder studied and made electroencephalograms of more than one thousand active fighters. Those lower in their ring rating had a greater percentage of disorganized tracings. The top-rated fighters were found most prominently in the group of recordings with low voltage and fast waves. There were no detectable changes, for example, between pre-fight and post-fight tracings. It is the continuing series of bouts that adds up over a period of time, to produce an increasing level of cerebral pathology.

The Traumatic Encephalopathy of boxers may be defined as *a syndrome which can result from the cumulative punishment absorbed in the boxing ring from continued bouts. It is characterized by the general slowing of and interference with mental functions, occasional bouts of confusion, and scattered bits of memory loss.* Traumatic Encephalopathy is an insidious organic syndrome due to progressive cerebral pathology.

5. *Amnesia Secondary to Alcohol*

A. PSYCHOLOGIC CAPACITY PREEXISTS.—Amnesia following alcoholic indulgence is seen with enough regularity to make it a rather accepted development among the laity. With some individuals, memory loss for the events of an alcoholic binge is almost routine. Others demonstrate acute retention of the smallest details of what happens while intoxicated, unless they manage to reach the stage of unconsciousness or somewhere close to it.

For many people alcohol appears to bring about the lessening of inhibitions, hence it is frequently misnomed as a stimulant. Often the behavior which occurs while intoxicated simply indicates that the underlying capacity for such activity has been present all along, although in more covert fashion. This applies likewise to a considerable extent to the individual physiologic and psychologic responses to alcohol. It is not merely the alcohol as such which causes amnesia. It is in addition the hidden psychologic capacity of the personality for the development of such an amnesia, in response to alcohol.

B. ALCOHOLICS ANONYMOUS.—The approach of Alcoholics Anonymous to the problem of alcoholism seeks sobriety and self-control. These somewhat limited goals are sought and sometimes secured through supportive, inspirational, religious, and group methods which encourage suppression and facilitate repression. Many members of AA do not support or encourage psychotherapy. Instead of viewing it as an adjunct or an ally, it is far more often derogated, resisted, attacked, and regarded as a threat. It is of course a threat — but to repression, and to the repressed. It is not a threat to the individual, nor to his well-being and future. Here it can be a Godsend.

The AA work is suppressive, favors repression and memory loss. Analysis is antirepressive, and seeks the recall of lost memories. Sobriety and self-control are wanted here also, in so far as applicable, and in accord with the goal of eliminating recognized, as well as inadvertent, self-defeat. However, much more is wanted psychiatrically. Psychotherapy seeks to learn the how, the why, and the when of problems and their initiation; the general motivation of the individual, and what makes him tick. It is antisuppressive.

6. *Aging*

A certain amount of spotty amnesia is an expected but greatly variable accompaniment of aging. More likely to involve recent (as opposed to remote) events, this retrograde and scattered kind of memory disturbance reaches its greatest pathologic development in certain cases of arteriosclerotic and senile psychoses. This type of memory loss is *Senile Amnesia*.

Memory disturbances can occur with almost any kind of cerebral lesion. This particularly includes vascular changes of all kinds, and occasionally neoplasms (more particularly in the frontal area). For an example of the latter, the author was once called in consultation in the case of a seventy-one-year-old woman. Among her more prominent early symptoms was that of scattered bits of memory loss. These were described by one member of her family as "a kind of absentmindedness, not like her at all." This was *not* psychologic or senile amnesia. There was an organic lesion responsible. The lesion proved to be a right temporal neoplasm, involving the uncinate gyrus.

7. Derepression

As pointed out earlier, scattered areas of memory loss are also a frequent consequence of psychologic trauma. Such trauma may be major or minor. It is common enough, however, for the psychiatrist to hear patients recall "forgotten" memories of painful situations or events from early life [p. 120]. In these instances the scattered and very (automatically) selective amnesia has been, of course, the result of repression. The successful therapeutic endeavor has resulted in the release of the data to conscious recall. This result is termed therapeutic derepression.

E. PSYCHODYNAMICS

1. Pathologic Amnesia and Pathologic Forgetting

Thus far several important points have been made concerning the psychogenesis of emotional amnesia. We have learned for example that an amnesic episode may occur in response to one or a series of intolerable emotional conflicts. In these instances the preexisting psychologic capacity for amnesia already has been present. [*See Peg Concept:* pp. 464, 529, and Ch.10:VIIID2 and Ch.12:VD3.] Clinical amnesia may also be regarded as a giant step in the further extension of repression. In addition it is frequently a kind of psychologic flight. There are several additional points which might be considered.

First, let reference again be made to the relationship between the defense of pathologic *amnesia* for large areas, to the defensive mechanism of pathologic *forgetting* for small, isolated, or scattered areas. The latter process is called repression. It has been discussed elsewhere, and also mentioned earlier in this chapter. Basically, there is little real difference dynamically. Both are defensive. Each is emotionally determined. One is larger and may be massive, in which case it becomes rather rare. The other is universal and at least to some extent occurs almost continuously.

One might conceivably regard emotional amnesia as an instance of massive, sudden repression occurring most often in adult life. Often enough it will to some extent subside spontaneously or in response to therapy in competent hands.

2. Antecedent Pattern

At this point, let us ask if there might not be earlier periods in life when such a massive kind of repression occurs? In the author's monograph *Mental Mechanisms* (Butterworths, 1963) there was a discussion on the important *primary repressions* of the infantile period. In this early stage of personality development, massive repression of whole areas of instinctual feelings, drives, and impulses takes place. Ordinarily the results of this repression are rather permanent. This type of repression does not continue into later life.

However, the reader can see the possible parallel between the infantile kind of massive repression, and what might be a continuing latent capacity present for this in some individuals. Such a capacity can result in an emotional amnesic episode in response to intolerable stress in later adult life. In commenting along these lines, Brierley suggested that the author might make a bit more evident that pathologic dissociation in adults follows the lines of infantile and childhood repressions.

From this viewpoint, the later dissociation of adulthood follows as a pattern of response from a kind of archaic and primal emotional "rest". It is a vestigial carryover of a primitive infantile capacity. This has been surrendered in the more fortunate individual, in favor of other, more mature and constructive emotional responses to crisis.

3. Dissociative Reactions Versus Conversion Reactions

A. SIMILAR PERSONALITY FACTORS COMPRISE THE DISSOCIATIVE DIATHESIS.—Can we distinguish the psychodynamics of the Dissociative Reactions from those of the Conversion Reactions? This can be a difficult matter, but perhaps one which becomes possible in certain instances [*see also* Ch.12:VIB]. On a very basic, deeply unconscious level, the adaptive pattern in the whole group of Dissociative Reactions is quite similar. The Dissociative Diathesis includes common items in the personality makeup of persons destined to develop a Dissociative Reaction.

Essentially, these people are reacting primarily to intense, internal, hidden frustration. This is most often in the area of dependency love and, less frequently, in the sexual area, or in the consequences of hostility and rage. The individual reaches out actively, or even symbolically, to compensate for the frustration in one of these areas.

This results in the intensification of existing hidden emotional conflicts. New ones may be created, and the barriers of repression may be seriously threatened. Intense hostile-aggressive impulses may develop. Large amounts of guilty fear are psychologically generated. This type of personality adaptation seems to be basic for the Dissociative Reactions. At times the dissociation via amnesia or fugue is the last desperate step, taken unconsciously, to avoid acting upon the hostile or sexual impulses.

The foregoing material outlines some basic points in a possible Dissociative type of Personality. [*See* pp. 228, 283–286.] Exaggeration of these trait defenses would accordingly illustrate our *Defense-Hypertrophy*

Principle [pp. 73, 229, 251, and Ch.12:VC5]. As a group they would comprise a character trait *constellation* of the Dissociative type.

B. MASOCHISTIC (SELF-PUNISHING) FEATURES COMPARED.—The dissociative patterns of reaction are also partly invoked on an unconscious level to avoid punishment. As Heath expressed this, the patient's reaction sometimes says in effect, "It is not my fault. It was beyond my control. I can't be brought to task because I am not to blame."

The masochism in the Dissociative Reactions and that in the Conversion Reaction vary considerably, though it is present in both. The classic conversion patient more clearly punishes himself by his symptom, or secures the punishment he unconsciously feels he deserves, in masochistic fashion. In the Dissociative Reaction, this is much less apparent, although reference was made earlier to the frequency with which, in covert fashion, the amnesia victim, or the person with a fugue, unconsciously manages to be "apprehended" by the police, or turns himself over to the authorities. He is reacting here in response to his guilty fear as though he were a criminal, seeking to have the score evened by being punished for his "crimes".

His symptoms are less likely fully to satisfy the demand for punishment, as is the case with conversion patients; hence some of the differences which can be noted in behavior. This kind of unconsciously motivated behavior, such as arranging apprehension, and the like, is, of course, in direct opposition to the patient's psychologic flight into an amnesia or fugue in the first place. The flight was partly the unconscious attempt to escape punishment in response to the hidden feelings of guilt. In other words, the amnesia patient "runs" from his guilty feeling of need for punishment, and, since this is not at the same time satisfied through his symptoms (as it is with the conversion patient), he continues to treat himself as a guilty miscreant. There will be some further comments about the self-punishment inherent in the dissociation when we consider the psychodynamics of the Fugue State.

4. Amnesia Versus Psychopathy

Heath noted the differential in the amnesia patient and the psychopathic individual, in terms of their motivation. Hereby, the person in the dissociative group can be distinguished because the unconscious motivation is primarily to obtain gratification in the sphere of love or dependency. This is in contrast with the psychopathic individual. His more conscious motivation is based upon the securing of realistic tangible gain.

F. AMNESIA AS A LEGAL DEFENSE

Amnesia, at least until recently, had tended to rival the plea of insanity as a defense in certain medicolegal cases. When the presence of amnesia is claimed in a criminal case as a mitigating circumstance, careful evaluation of its genuineness by experts may well be indicated. In these instances there can be a powerful stimulus to conscious secondary gain, or to malingering. While our earlier outlined [Ch.12:VD*3*] *Rhazes Maneuver* can sometimes uncover an instance of simulated amnesia, it is next to impossible to have such an approach prove successful in dispelling a genuine amnesic episode.

The following example illustrates the type of problem which can be encountered.

Case 168

Amnesia Claimed in Mitigation in a Criminal Case

A twenty-six-year-old defendant was positively identified as one of three men participating in a holdup which involved murder. He made no attempt to deny being present. His defense rested largely on a claimed amnesia for the entire event, including the identity of his companions or even for any association with them.

To the extent that this might be accepted by the jury, he was by implication denying all responsibility for any of his alleged participation in the crime. Psychiatric examinations on behalf of the court indicated considerable doubt as to the validity of the defendant's contention. He was ultimately convicted.

G. UNCONSCIOUS FALSIFICATION OF MEMORY

This very interesting manifestation is much more common than one might ordinarily suspect. Unconscious falsification of recollections constitutes a similar intrapsychic defense to that of rationalization. It is not recognized more generally because, when fully successful, the patient has no conscious recognition of its existence, let alone of the many possibilities of unconscious needs which it might subserve.

This kind of unconscious falsification can be grouped most conveniently with the amnesic methods of defense. Brierley recalled the use of this kind of reaction by a patient on several occasions in the transference situation. In one instance the person bitterly complained about the earlier refusal of a request, when the physician in fact had complied as requested. Her need was to be treated badly, that is, the falsification usually served as a masochistic defense against her deeper, dreaded sadism.

H. MEMORY LOSS WITH ELECTRIC SHOCK

1. Regular Occurrence; Intensive Study Rare

Patients who receive electric shock as a part of their therapeutic regimen regularly suffer some degree of memory loss. This tends to be a circumscribed and retrograde type amnesia in relation to events of the preceding day or days, or even longer. In addition, or as an alternative, there may well be scattered, selective bits of memory lost. These are more in relation to recent recollections, and less but still possibly present as regards to more remote ones. There is a tendency for these lapses of memory to show some gradual improvement on a spontaneous basis. Rarely, if ever, does all memory return.

Frequently, the forgetting which occurs is highly scattered, and it may be most difficult to detect. Detailed before-treatment study and after-treatment study and observation may be necessary to detect its presence. There is no certainty even then that it can be disclosed. The author suspects that it often remains quite undetected clinically. Instances of any full or intensive study are rare indeed. There are several reasons for this.

First, it is not certain as to how much of the memory loss results: (*a*) from the shock and the convulsion; (*b*) from the cerebral trauma; (*c*) how much is emotionally (psychologically) determined; and (*d*) how much is a combination of the interaction of these. *Second,* the person who suffers various smaller or larger areas of post-shock forgetting, where their loss to him serves some covert (unconscious) psychologic defensive need, is hardly likely to have much conscious awareness of the loss, let alone much strong interest in securing its recall. *Third,* the busy psychiatrist is not often likely to have the necessary inclination, interest, or time available systematically to locate all such areas.

Further references to electroshock will be found in the section on Treatment in Chapter 4 [pp. 215–218].

2. Memory Loss Comes to Light

Major areas of post-shock memory loss can exist beyond the slightest suspicions of psychiatrist or patient. Sometimes one of these becomes apparent through fortuitous circumstances. In the following instance a large amnesic area, having its onset following shock treatment, and which was previously unsuspected, came to light somewhat by chance.

Case 169

An Area of Post-shock Amnesia Comes to Light

(1) *Electroshock follows offer*
At one point during World War II, the author had co-responsibility for the psychiatric management of a high ranking Allied officer suffering from a serious depression. He had been primarily instrumental in developing what was rapidly becoming one of the most significant advances in modern warfare. One day, early in his hospitalization, he had offered to arrange to have shown some of the films of his work which were then classified as Top Secret. A colleague and I accepted his very sincere offer with thanks. Nothing more was said aloud in reference to it, the arrangements and details being left up to our patient.

Following a continuing period of psychotherapy with rather limited success, he was given three electric shock treatments. These were followed by some further recovery. There was no evidence of confusion or memory loss apparent to the patient, or to us. Some of his areas of great conflict were in reference to his work.

(2) *Professional conflicts significant*
One day as his scheduled time for discharge from treatment was approaching, these conflicts were again under discussion. He happened to mention casually that sometime we might have an interest in seeing some highly secret films of his work. At this point his earlier offer was recalled, and he was asked if he remembered the offer and discussion. He did not remember it at all. Being a person who prided himself on his precision and exactness, he was quite puzzled.

There were some very strong personal reasons which might well enter into a reluctance on his part again to view these films. It did not appear too surprising that he might, as a matter of unconscious convenience, forget the arrangement, with the additional assistance from the shock.

Involved arrangements "wiped out"

What proved rather surprising to all of us, however, was the extent and completeness of the hitherto unsuspected bit of forgetting. Enough people were involved so that it was not difficult to fill in the gap. Unknown to us, this patient had gone to considerable pains to have the films brought to Washington following his rather casual-sounding original offer. Further instructions had been awaited from him, and these of course had not been forthcoming; understandable in the light of the post-shock amnesia.

These plans had included special arrangements to have the films flown to this country — one leg of the trip by a special flight — the services of a courier, the intercession of his country's ambassador, and so on. In these involved arrangements he had played a personal part. The whole complex series of contacts and plans had simply been wiped from all conscious awareness. Completely unsuspectingly, he had "arranged" to avoid what would have been for him an uncomfortable reopening of certain psychologic wounds. The shock had "knocked out" the memory. Neither the patient nor his physicians had had awareness that this particular gap had occurred until this became apparent through fortuitous circumstance.

One might note in this case that there was no determinable loss in professional or technical competence in response to the electroshock. The memory losses which occur are often relatively spotty and scattered. They occur in emotional and *personal* areas, in some degree of preference to *technical* ones. Of course, if the technical ones become personal, or if there is overlapping, losses here can occur as well. However, this example helps to illustrate the selectivity of the loss. It is also possible, of course, that the scientist in the foregoing instance had some added misgivings or conflicts over the showing of the films or concerning other related areas.

3. Principle of Psychic-Selectivity in Post-Electroshock Amnesia

The memory which may be lost with electric shock may be large or small in extent. It may be circumscribed or scattered. Often its detection is not only more difficult than in the foregoing example, but it may be actually impossible. The area lost generally has some emotionally unpleasant or painful connotation to the individual concerned. The existence of these psychologic factors, however, is often by no means easy to ascertain. However, careful observation and study should, when sufficiently thorough and detailed, demonstrate some memory loss in every case treated by electric shock. Since the selectivity of specific areas involves important psychologic factors in its determination, we might term this the *Principle of Psychic-Selectivity,* in post-shock memory losses.

Alexander reported an interesting instance in which a "normal" person was given electroshock. By chance, on the scheduled morning the individual was involved in what was for him an emotionally disturbing but actually minor, traffic accident. The electroconvulsive "therapy" was administered anyway. After this, the patient no longer had any memory of the upsetting experience. After ten days the accident was finally recalled to him. At this time it appeared to have lost all of its emotional significance to him. This interesting report helps point up the selectivity in the effect of electrotherapy upon one's memory for recent disturbing events.

4. Contributory to Benefits

There is no universally accepted explanation for the benefits which may accrue to some of the patients who are treated by electric shock. Some psychiatrists believe the benefits are due to strictly organic changes. Others believe the shock serves to allay unconscious needs for punishment. These and other views do not have to be mutually exclusive. On the basis of the foregoing discussion and as the result of some earlier (pre-1947) years of considerable experience with electric shock, it has seemed to the author that memory loss has also played an important contributory role in the therapeutic effects of electric shock. Certain memories, particularly those of recent painful events which may have been of greater significance in the precipitation of the emotional disorder, were most likely to be the ones eliminated.

If some of these what we might call *"straws that broke the camel's back"* were removed, if certain aspects of the more recent and acute emotional conflicts were thus dimmed, a measure of improvement would follow. This could also enter into the explanation of the relative efficacy of electric shock treatment in some acute cases, as opposed to the indifferent or poor results in many of the more chronic ones. In the latter instances, the originally more acute and traumatic precipitating events would have receded farther from current awareness. They would have refuge in areas less accessible to the possible discard by shock. The areas of recent memory would be more vulnerable to such discard.* Patterns of defensive reactions and adjustment would be more firmly established and "grooved".

I. TREATMENT

1. Conservative Approach Preferable

The presence of amnesia on a psychologic basis is in itself an indication for psychiatric treatment. The author's present personal preference ordi-

---

* Not all would agree with our views and discussion concerning electroshock. The following are verbatim quotes from two strongly dissenting colleagues, offered in 1954.

   1. "I would have some quarrel with the explanation of the efficacy of electro-shock treatment on the memory loss. For twelve years now, I have done a fair amount of electroshock treatment, and it is very definitely my impression that patients with little memory loss do much better than those who have memory loss. I therefore cannot believe that the efficacy of treatment is dependent on memory loss. I also do not believe that electroshock treatment is any more efficacious in acute depressions than it is in chronic cases. I have treated people who have been ill for eight years with a 'rut' depression and had a very satisfactory recovery."

   2. "The benefit of electroshock treatment is certainly unexplained thus far, but I cannot feel that loss of memory for any particular precipitating or causa-tive event could explain it. It has been my experience to see many very acutely disturbed patients quickly relieved by intensive electroshock treat-ment and, actually, without any memory disturbance."

narily is for the more conservative approach of intensive psychotherapy, wherever one has the choice. The use of interviews using *Amytal,* narco-synthesis, and hypnosis can occasionally offer the prospect of a faster and more dramatic route to the recovery of the "lost" areas, but in many hands there are disadvantages to the use of these methods. As in instances of *Conversion Reactions* [Ch.12:VD*1*], the *Principle of Self-Esteem Maintenance* can be very important to follow. This also applies to the Fugue State.

There is apt, for example, to be an unfortunate tendency to focus undue attention on the amnesia as such. Ideally, one should not at all make the mere recovery of the "lost" events the prime goal of treatment. On the other hand, of course, sometimes one perhaps must be content with such very limited therapeutic goals. Further, at times the sudden dissolution of the amnesia [or in *Case 171*], will precipitate great tension and anxiety, an A.A.A. [pp. 89–98], or even a Symptom Barrage [Ch.12:VA2].

2. Goals of Treatment Broad: Deep Treatment Ideal

The ideal treatment of course would also aim at the return to conscious awareness of forgotten memories, regardless of the approach used. However, it would also go considerably farther and deeper, with the additional major aims of recognition, clarification, and resolution of the very important underlying emotional conflicts. In other words, symptom removal ideally ought not to become the end in itself of the therapeutic endeavor. This principle generally applies in the therapy of all emotional problems.

One hopes constructively to influence the basic personality capacity for this kind of massive psychologic flight in accord with our concept of *Deep Treatment* [pp. 209 and 212], which is the ideal. Only in this way will it become possible subsequently for the individual to attempt more constructive solutions upon a more realistic basis. Possible later traumatic experiences in living will be dealt with more suitably. The amnesic diathesis should be dissolved as the individual gains in maturity. The ultimate goals of treatment should be ambitious, broad, and inclusive.

VIII. FUGUE STATES

A. MAJOR PERSONALITY DISSOCIATION

1. Flight Both Figurative and Literal

A. MARKED BY AMNESIA.—A fugue is a major state of personality disso-ciation in which amnesia is present. There is frequently a greater or lesser degree of personality disorganization. The victim thus may appear confused. His activity may be less organized and purposeful than in Double Personality or in certain states of amnesia. On the other hand, the person in a fugue can sometimes carry on rather well in his new role, as we shall see.

The term *fugue* is derived from the Latin *fuga,* meaning wild or confused flight. The type of dissociation in the Fugue State is *Alternating*

Dissociation. The Fugue State is a major clinical entity in the Dissociative Reactions.

B. TYPES OF FLIGHT.—The term *Fugue State* is properly reserved to describe a dramatic and *major psychologic kind of flight from intolerable reality,* as another major variant of the T.R.C. responses to (internal) threat and danger. There are actually two types of flight, both of which are usually present. The first is the *psychologic* flight, via the important and massive dissociative break with prior conscious existence. The second is the usually accompanying *physical* flight, from the actual prior location of living and experience. The flight in the fugue thus is both psychologic and physical; figurative and literal.

A fugue is a wild flight of avoidance, both from consciousness and from the immediate environment as well. The latter has been associated with the emotional conflicts, which have become intolerable. The Fugue State is to Amnesia somewhat as Somnambulism is to the Dream [*earlier footnote dissents*]. In each there is also the characteristic addition of physical activity. In each this is beyond the usual conscious control.

C. INVOLUNTARY ACTION.—The use of the term *flight* by no means implies voluntary action or conscious decision. In the Fugue State the individual flees in forced, involuntary fashion, literally impelled by irresistible, unconscious forces. These are beyond his control. They are outside of his conscious awareness.

Amnesia is always associated with the fugue when the latter transpires. During its course the patient may engage in activities which appear to casual observation to be normal enough. The patient may also wander about rather aimlessly and appear lost and confused. The duration of a fugue may be from days to months. It is to be distinguished from amnesia and from Multiple Personality.

2. Definition of Fugue State

The fugue may be further defined as *a major state of personality dissociation characterized by loss of memory. In a Fugue State the patient "flees" both psychologically and unconsciously, often, in a rather confused fashion.* The flight is from his usual environment and circumstances, figuratively through the development of amnesia, and literally through physical departure. The fugue constitutes *a drastic, involuntary type of avoidance of intolerable conflict through flight. The flight is both psychic, through the amnesia, and actual, through the physical action. Thus it is a combination of the figurative and the literal.*

The victim of the Fugue State may wander about in some strange city, or another section of his own city, in a rather aimless fashion for some time, or on occasion carry on well and unsuspectedly in a new role. Upon recovery, there is ordinarily a subsequent inability consciously to remember the events of the episode. Their recovery to memory is always theoretically possible. This may be sought or secured through psychotherapeutic methods.

B. NOTES ON DIAGNOSIS

1. Ideal Criteria

The diagnosis of a true Fugue State is ideally indicated: (1) when the individual concerned is truly amnesic; (2) when he has traveled or wandered away from his usual environment; and (3) when there is some evidence of a psychologic flight from conflicts, which have become intolerable to him.

In the most favorable circumstances, the diagnosis can be further confirmed by the therapeutic working out of the underlying psychodynamics. This is seldom easy; often not at all feasible; often enough impossibly difficult. The three criteria for establishing the diagnosis conform with the definitions above.

2. Differential Problems

The major problems in differential diagnosis are likely to be: (1) organic confused states, (2) post-alcoholic states or drug intoxications, (3) post-traumatic syndromes, (4) psychotic episodes, and occasionally (5) other psychologic conditions such as Conversion Behavioral States, Amnesia, and Alternating Personality.

The differential diagnosis in certain clinical cases may be difficult to work out. In all of them, however, regardless of the precipitating cause, we have increasingly learned to consider the crucial role of pre-existing personality factors, and underlying emotional conflicts. These can influence the clinical features, even though the precipitating factors themselves are clearly or seemingly largely organic or traumatic.

3. Similarity to Psychotic Reaction

Hallucinatory-like experiences can occur in Fugue States. Since the patient has memory loss, has often lost his awareness of personal identity, and may appear confused, the separation from a psychosis may be very difficult. There is no substitute here for clinical experience and careful observation in problem cases. A paranoid coloring in attitudes and relationships may reflect the projection of consciously intolerable hostility and guilt.

An important differential feature from the psychotic reactions is that the hallucinations (when present), the confusion, and the other psychotic manifestations will be found to disappear upon restoration of memory. This occurs in the Fugue State, but not in the psychosis. In other words, termination of the fugue period in essence can prove its nature. Depressive features are not uncommonly present at the time of onset. These, however, do not ordinarily pose a problem in differential diagnosis.

C. INCIDENCE

Fugue States are not common. The average psychiatrist over a period of some years in active practice generally will not see many cases. Firstly, this is because of their actual relative scarcity. Secondly, this is because of certain factors inherent in the disorder. These factors include: (*a*) the frequent lack of any great interest in securing help, on the part of the patient; (*b*) his possible conscious or unconscious concealment of the circumstances; and, finally (*c*) his not infrequent tendency to "manage" to turn himself over to the authorities. The latter is an external action in response to unconscious attitudes. These are often present toward himself as a guilty person who should be punished. Because of these factors, it becomes apparent that more cases exist than those which come to professional attention.

There is obviously a relation to the intolerable situation. This always antedates the onset of a Fugue State. In a recent series of 37 cases collected by Berrington and colleagues in Ireland, 35 patients were escaping intolerable situations, 14 from justice. Simulation was a feature in 10 patients, 9 of whom were fleeing the law. More of the cases in which the elements of the intolerable situation include the law and justice are likely to come to light, than the ones in which the elements are private and individual. Cases of amnesia and fugue undoubtedly enter into some of the many reports of missing persons.

D. CLINICAL FEATURES OF FUGUE STATES

1. Past Dissociated; Daytime-Somnambulism Concept

A. ONSET AND EFFECTS.—Since amnesia is invariably present in the Fugue State, most of what has been said about amnesia which therefore properly was discussed first, is to a considerable extent applicable to our discussion here. Generally the amnesia is retrograde and is complete to the point at which the psychologic flight of the fugue begins. One may compare the fugue in one concept, to what we might term *Daytime-Som-nambulism,* generally of greater duration, of course, in which however, the patient is not asleep [Ch.13:IV]. Viewing the Fugue State according to this concept may help point out for us that the reactions of sleep and sleep walking and the fugue are related. As distant "cousins" their dynamics have certain similarities. In the Fugue State, in place of sleep, there is Amnesia. The dissociation is complete. The past is completely split away from consciousness and is no longer accessible during the course of the fugue. In turn, upon the dissolution of the fugue, the events of this period are no longer accessible.

The onset is usually sudden, and the maximum effects are almost instantaneously achieved. The rare patient may be able to later describe the onset subjectively, as being accompanied by sensations of loss of consciousness, fainting, a black-out, or even simply going to sleep. He may feel confused, dizzy, or depersonalized, and he may complain of blurred vision, headache, or various uncomfortable somatic sensations. During the period of the fugue he may appear to observers to be confused, and his activity may appear somewhat aimless. A brief fugue following an acute psychically traumatic event is included in the following chapter

[Ch.14:VC2]. He may also appear superficially well integrated and may seem to possess the capacity for a reasonably satisfactory level of function.

B. MARKED FUGUE STATE.—The following instance of a marked fugue state occurred in a young man who managed to join the Army and to function at least satisfactorily for a year of military service. This kind of fugue is practically a case of Double Personality, on the basis of severity, duration, and the apparently well integrated level of activity which was carried on.

The line of distinction in these cases can be a narrow one. This is more apt to be true as the dissociation in the Fugue State progresses to become more marked, more separate, more organized, and more functional. Marked by the same type of Alternating Dissociation, in effect the one can merge into the other.

Case 170

A Young Man Joined the Army and Served for a Year During a Fugue State

(1) *Pre-existing Fugue recognized through its "spontaneous" dissolution*

A young soldier, with one year of military service, was admitted to an Army hospital with a complaint of severe cramp-like abdominal pain. Physical and other examinations were negative. The pain subsided within a few days, and the soldier was discharged to duty. A few nights later, however, he was readmitted to the hospital in a dramatic convulsion-like state. He could not be roused, and for several hours he exhibited intermittently convulsive motor patterns that were semi-purposeful in nature, together with board-like arching of his back. These attacks were judged to be conversion (hysterical) in nature.

The following morning, without additional treatment, the patient had become calm, composed, and mentally clear. A pre-existing but totally unsuspected Fugue State had "spontaneously" dissipated. He was at a loss to explain his surroundings or what had transpired. He asked how he happened to be in the hospital, what town he was in, and who were the people around him. The following story was elicited about his own earlier background, prior to his military service.

(2) *Onset with otherwise insoluble problems*

He had been only fifteen years old, and was attending high school in a town in New York State. He was rather large for his age. He was teased by his fellow students, and was not doing well in his studies. Things had been going increasingly badly socially and at home. He was very upset over his many problems, which had come to appear absolutely insoluble. There was a growing amount of anxiety and of *apprehensive anticipation* [Ch.13:VIIIE1].

He remembered going home one afternoon and throwing his books on the porch. He remembered absolutely nothing more until one year later. The patient's father was called, and he corroborated the earlier history as given by the patient.

(3) *Dissociation thorough; scattered memories recalled*

In the next several weeks, through a series of psychotherapeutic interviews, some scattered memories of the year of Army service were obtained. The dissociation between his earlier life and his Army life however, had been quite thorough. He had been able to carry on rather complex activities during his year of service seemingly without anything being detected as very much out of the ordinary by his associates.

At the father's request, the boy was discharged from the service as under age. Neither had much interest in his having further therapy, and subsequent contact was lost.

C. APPEARANCE TO ASSOCIATES.—As in the foregoing instance, the patient may actually appear quite "normal" to his associates, even though this is not at all true. Comparison with his previous existence, if this were possible, would show variations in his emotional reactions. As with the above patient, the desperate straits at the time of the flight from the intolerable situation are often marked by a depressive mood. Observation at this time would likely disclose some of the more usual manifestations of depression. The impending fugue would not likely cast too much of a shadow, nor a very characteristic one.

The fugue victim may show a wide range of emotional responses. He may appear cheerful, depressed, or confused. Following the dissolution of the fugue he may seem indifferent to the lost background, if awareness of its existence has been uncovered. His attitude to the recall of the events during the fugue may vary from intense interest to indifference, or even opposition, when he regains his former (pre-fugue) state of consciousness.

D. ALTERNATING DISSOCIATION.—The type of dissociation seen in the Fugue State is alternating. It is as though one stream of consciousness more or less completely replaces another. One seemingly independent part of the personality takes over, with the complete submergence of the remainder. When the fugue ceases, the erstwhile submerged part again asserts its dominance and control, with the submergence in turn of the other. This alternating type of dissociation is clinically and dynamically the most severe. It nearly reaches its ultimate development in the Fugue State. It is also seen in the rare instances of Double Personality in which there is some further development and progression.

Table 38

Clinical Types of Fugue States

Currently, at least several more or less distinct clinical types of Fugue State can be described. These we might perhaps attempt to distinguish clinically and descriptively. As a matter of convenience in communication they might also be named, as follows:

(1) *The Incomplete Fugue:*
Fugues which are accompanied and characterized by the retention of *some measure of awareness* of the loss of personal identity during the fugue. These are rare.

(2) *The Identification Fugue:*
Fugues with a *change of personal identity*. Herein the victim identifies himself unconsciously with a favorite, or envied, or an idealized person whose attributes, way of living, or even name, he may assume. This group would also include some cases also classifiable as Alternating or Double Personality.

(3) *The Retrograde Fugue:*
In this variety the underlying motivation leads to the sought-after and more or less symbolic *return* to an earlier, more satisfying era.

(4) *The Mixed Fugue:*
Combination in varying degree of the foregoing, plus those *States not* clearly or *readily* so *categorized.*

2. *Total Response to Crisis*

A. ANTECEDENTS IMPORTANT.—When an individual possesses the basic psychologic capacity for dissociation in response to a personally intolerable situation, a careful history may disclose earlier, antecedent dissociative reactions. These may have been less major or have been manifested in a different form. This response is part of his T.R.C. (total response to crisis). He may, for instance, have suffered from fainting attacks, somnambulism, loss of consciousness, delirium during illnesses, or prior amnesic episodes. This would be in accord with our *Individual Appropriateness of Response Principle* [pp. 14, 84, 477, and Ch.12:VIC2]. This may represent the pattern of response to stress or crisis which he has developed. A dissociative reaction would thus have become part of the psychologic potential of his individual total reaction to crisis, danger, or threat. They are also *Conflict Indicators* of significance.

An antecedent prototype for the fugue type of response may be set up through the sequence of events of an earlier head injury and its possible post-concussion type of amnesia-confusion. A history of an old (or recent) concussion is not infrequent. A bout or bouts of alcoholic overindulgence can also serve in part as such an unwitting model.

B. REPEATED FUGUES A PATTERN OF REACTION.—In the following case, a pattern of response to stress had developed which included repeated brief fugues, in which the person unconsciously sought a better situation.

Case 171

Repeated Brief Fugues as the Defensive Pattern of Response to Stress

(1) *Facade helped conceal dependency needs*

A forty-two-year-old, grossly overweight man was referred to the University Psychiatric Clinic because of several known episodes of amnesia. He was a very unhappy person who was poorly integrated emotionally. He had a most traumatic background. History disclosed that he had been thrown out on the streets at a very early age, literally having to fight for survival. The *Second Tenet of the Parental Role* [pp. 174, 476, and Ch.12:VIC1] pointed out that inordinate dependency needs are not likely to develop when the early environment was satisfactory. This man's background was empty and traumatic.

His resulting tremendous needs to be loved, cared for, and fed were buried under a facade of pseudo-independence. They indirectly revealed themselves in part through his excessive degree of overweight, in his occupational choices, and in his marriage. One after the other, his jobs had to do with restaurants: as a waiter, bus boy, short order cook, manager, or part owner. His choice for a wife had been a large, overweight, maternal figure.

(2) *Pattern of reaction; part of T.R.C.*

When he was overly threatened at home or on the job, he developed a Fugue State. This had happened on a number of occasions. It was a pattern of reaction, as a prominent part of his T.R.C. He would wander around the city for from twelve to twenty-four hours in a dazed condition, but would eventually get back home.

He would never have more than the foggiest notion of where he had been or what he had done. It seemed as though he were searching for something, but didn't know what. The police picked him up a few times, usually when he was sleeping in his car at 4 a.m., or wandering around the streets.

(3) *Three major functions of Fugue endogain*

A graduate of the "school of hard knocks", he was unconsciously looking for a more ideal "alma mater". *His conflict was that he couldn't dare really acknowledge this consciously, for then all the accumulated anxiety of the first years on the street, alone, cold, helpless, and hungry, would hit him with a tremendous and intolerable impact. He had to separate his dependency needs completely from his self-awareness.

The fugues intervened as part of his Total Reaction to Crisis when conscious awareness (and anxiety) threatened. His pattern of dissociative reaction had developed as part of his automatic protection against anxiety. Thus at least three major functions were unwittingly subserved: (1) maintaining repression, (2) averting anxiety, and (3) seeking a better, safer position.

In this case there occurred a whole series of defensive psychologic flights from individually intolerable threats. In each instance some crisis would set off the reaction. Perhaps minor under other circumstances, these acted as precipitating factors in an already prepared and sensitized personality diathesis.

In certain other cases of fugue, various additional kinds of otherwise unacceptable and forbidden wishes or needs are "acted out". This can occur then in a safer milieu, away from the danger of the disapproving remainder of consciousness. A flight is taken in these instances, which is essentially also an escape from the forbidding and punishing superego.

E. PSYCHODYNAMICS

1. Unconscious Meanings

A. SYMBOLIC SEEKING OR ACTING; APPREHENSIVE ANTICIPATION.—As just discussed and as earlier noted in relation to amnesia, we can often also view the fugue in part as a response to guilty fear. In these instances, it is an attempted psychologic flight from punishment and censure by the superego. The victim is attempting to hide from his conscience, that is, from (part of) himself. The *Concept of Defensive Overreaction* [pp. 95, 115, and Ch. 12] is illustrated, as the psychologic flight progresses on into the clinical Fugue State.

The fugue is also a way of magically denying responsibility for what is regarded by the individual concerned as evil and intolerably bad. As in *Case 170*, there may be a symbolic seeking for the long lost (or never really even secured) dependent position, or an acting-out of consciously intolerable wishes. Some would regard the Fugue State as representing the ultimate in *acting-out* [pp. 193, 258, and 355–6, and *Case 144,* Ch. 12: VE*1*].

The fugue always has unconscious meanings. These vary greatly in their accessibility to awareness by the neutral observing therapist. We shall consider several of the more likely ones in some further detail. While

---

* See earlier references to *Vicious Circle of Self-Defeat Concept* in the neuroses [pp. 71, 265, 476, and Ch.12:VA*3*]. Thus the more he might strive in the foregoing fashion, the less he would be likely to receive. This is one of the great tragedies in the neurotic reactions.

anxiety is crucial in the basis of the fugue, a pre-onset buildup of *Apprehensive Anticipation* [p. 17] is not uncommon [*Cases 169* and *171*].

B. RELATION TO DEPRESSION.—A relationship to depression should be noted. This can be of major import. An earlier comment referred to the presence of depression at the outset. The Fugue State can be contributed to by a Depressive Reaction.

The fugue can also be regarded as an escape *from* depression, or as an attempt to ward it off. Berrington's group mostly (29 of 37 cases) had a depressive mood precipitating or accompanying the fugue. Association of a fugue with suicide or a suicidal attempt is not unknown.

2. *Escape to More Pleasant Area*

Abse reported an interesting case from military life that illustrates two of our earlier noted important unconscious meanings such as are often to be encountered in the fugue: flight from a presumably intolerable situation, and the attempt to recapture a more satisfying era from the past. In Abse's example the escape was from military life.

This escape was of course unconsciously achieved, as was the locale to which the patient fled. This proved to be a popular shore resort, the site of annual vacations, his honeymoon, and many pleasant associations. When it becomes possible for the meaning to be fathomed, the flight in the Fugue State may not be as aimless, purposeless, or disorganized as it may have appeared at first blush.

Relations to early childhood antecedents and to parental or other significant interpersonal influences may be more difficult to uncover than in other neurotic reactions. Our *Concept of Interpersonal Perpetuation* [pp. 275, 291, 334, 455, and Ch. 12: VA2, Ch. 13: VA2], finds more tenuous and obscure applicability.

3. *Self-Punitive Aspects*

A. SACRIFICE OF PERSONAL IDENTITY.—Earlier comment was made on the differential between the self-punishment aspects of the symptoms of Conversion Reaction and those of the Dissociative Reaction. The self-punishment inherent in the conversion symptom is certainly more apparent. However, what greater suffering and personal sacrifice might one make than that of one's complete personal identity, as occurs in the fugue?

Still, even this is often insufficient to satisfy the demands of the internal and unconscious needs for self-punishment. This has been noted earlier in this chapter and has also been pointed out by Fisher. One often enough sees the victim of the fugue expressing his guilty fear (including that over his defiance of his superego), *and* his need for punishment, in outward behavior which becomes like that of a hunted person or criminal. He may fancy himself being followed or chased and may turn himself in to the authorities, or "arrange" his apprehension. Occasionally he may make "confessions", which prove to be completely spurious.

As with other emotional symptoms, the fugue and its manifestations are individually motivated and follow the *Principle of Hidden Determinants*.

B. PERSONAL AND SOCIAL EVALUATION.—Sometimes there may be basis enough in fact for an objective social condemnation. This is illustrated in the following instance. In this case the pressures developing from unsuccessful, increasingly involved, semilegitimate or dishonest business machinations built up to a personally intolerable level.

Case 172

A Fugue State in Response to the Increasingly Intolerable Pressures of Legal Complications

(1) *The stage is set*

Mr. M. G., a forty-four-year-old stock promoter, had for two years been involved in the selling of stock in an electronics firm of dubious assets or future. After some $30,000 worth of stock had been sold, a skeleton sort of building was erected. However, before any machinery was purchased or further steps had been taken to develop the business, the building mysteriously burned to the ground.

This event precipitated an investigation into the company. Mr. M. G. found himself in an extremely difficult position. The stockholders and the insurance company soon were both bringing increasing pressure to bear upon him. There was a build-up of *apprehensive anticipation,* that is, tension which is based upon the expectation of external threat, the nature of which is unknown, not necessarily unrealistic, but the character of which can be anticipated [pp. 17–18].

Over the next three or four months, in an effort to keep his head above water financially, he continually "robbed Peter to pay Paul". He managed for a time in this way to ward off his most insistent creditors. Eventually things became still more difficult. His creditors, the stockholders, and the insurance company had finally filed suit for an accounting. A date was set for a showdown court hearing.

(2) *Onset of Fugue at crucial juncture*

A few days before this was to take place, the patient backed out of his driveway as usual one morning. On this occasion he completely overshot the road. To an onlooker, he had seemed dazed for a moment, but apparently no serious damage resulted. He drove off toward the neighboring town, some ten miles away, presumably to discuss the impending court action with his lawyer. He never reached the attorney's office.

A few days later he was picked up wandering in the streets of New York, not knowing how he got there, what his name was, or remembering any of the events of his past life. A letter was found, however, in his pocket which was addressed to his aunt in New York. Through this woman, he was soon identified and returned for treatment to his home province in Canada.

(3) *Recovery of dissociated data leads to onset of Anxiety State*

On his arrival home, he was still completely amnesic. He had no memory for the complex difficulties in which he was embroiled. He stated that he "felt fine, slept well, and had no symptoms of any sort". With *Pentothal* narcosis, the dissociated material was recalled, and within a few days memory of the past had been fully restored to his conscious awareness.

Now, however, he became extremely anxious and had difficulty with his sleep. He woke with anxious dreams of falling, in some of which the symbolism was not too difficult to surmise! These were accompanied by cardiac palpitations* and great fear. Clinically, he now presented the picture of a severe Anxiety State. Further psychotherapy was not possible because of court action, which disposed of his case in a way which prevented further medical study and treatment.

---

* Most of the more common direct manifestations of tension, stress, and anxiety were present [*see Table 1,* p. 20, and *Table 33:* Ch.15:IIIB]. This acute reaction comprised a veritable *Symptom Barrage* [Ch.12:VA3; also pp. 470, 485, and 505].

4. Dissociation Defends Against Anxiety

A. IMPORTANT PRECEPTS: (1) ANXIETY IN INVERSE PROPORTION TO SYMPTOMS; (2) SYMPTOM RESOLUTION-SANS-SEQUELLA; AND (3) INVERSE ANXIETY-PSYCHOSIS RATIO.—The foregoing case illustrates very clearly the vital defensive purpose of the massive amnesic dissociation. As long as the fugue was maintained, the patient was comfortable. He had dissociated his intolerably painful and conflictual situation from all conscious awareness. This was a massive kind of dissociation similar to the repressions of early childhood. Upon the removal of the protective iron curtain of this dissociation, however, he became most intensely anxious. This followed our *Concept of Symptom-Exchange Hazard* [Ch.12:VIIIF4 and Ch.13:VD5].

This reaction clearly indicates the defensive intent of the fugue. Its *forcible* interruption on the one hand may be thus followed by marked anxiety, or by depression, or by other symptoms. Here, as in other emotional syndromes, *the outward manifestations of anxiety are in inverse proportion to the* (other psychologic) *symptoms.* This is the important *Precept of Inverse Anxiety-Symptom Ratio.* This inverse ratio of anxiety to symptom is true generally.

The *spontaneous* dissolution of a fugue, on the other hand, as in *Case 169,* may be followed by a relative absence of other emotional manifestations. The fire of the original intolerable situation has burned down. The fugue has served its defensive purpose. It is no longer necessary. It can lift.

This brings us to another important principle in therapy; the *Principle of Symptom Resolution-Sans-Sequella.* This is a general principle concerning the genuine *unforced* therapeutic resolution, and usually also instances of spontaneous symptom resolution; according to which these welcome developments are followed by *no* anxiety *or* other symptoms.

One sometimes sees similar but reversed reactions to the foregoing, in which marked *diminution* of gross subjective anxiety *follows* the *onset,* especially the acute one, of a psychotic episode. This latter helps illustrate the major defensive purpose, and the more specifically anxiety-countering function of psychotic manifestations. It constitutes an important corollary to our Precept of Inverse Anxiety-Symptom Ratio. It is an *Inverse Anxiety-Psychosis Ratio.*

As in the above case, the onset of anxiety may occur in its most severe form upon the removal of a psychologically vital symptom-defense. One must be prepared for such a possible eventuality. This knowledge should serve as an important caution in the therapy and management of emotional ills. This is true with the fugue, as elsewhere. Too forceful therapeutic intervention in some cases, or the sudden removal of psychologically vital defensive symptoms, should this prove possible, can serve the therapy, the patient, and the therapist, quite adversely.

B. ONSET DEFENDS AGAINST CONSCIOUSLY INTOLERABLE ACTS.—The author has noted how the fugue may allow the opportunity to carry out symbolically, certain otherwise intolerable ideas. Since this gratification is nearly always symbolic, criminal acts actually carried out during dissociative states are fortunately rare enough. Indeed, Fugue States instead may have their onset, or their termination at the point of committing a criminal act, as though to protect against its commission. The avoidance of antisocial or criminal activity during Fugue States and Amnesias indicates how the underlying standards and conscience continue to exert their influence during the dissociated state.

Fugue States indeed have their onset at times as a last-ditch, desperate defense against consciously intolerable murderous impulses. Murder during a fugue is theoretically possible, but actually rare. Menninger once cited a case in which a defendant claimed that he killed his wife while he was "asleep".

C. ANTAGONISTIC AIMS SUBSERVED.—The fugue can have seemingly contradictory defensive intents and effects, both in allowing the symbolic expression (and partial or token gratification) of otherwise consciously disowned urges, and at the same time in defending against their expression.

Despite these seemingly antagonistic aims from an ordinary intellectual or rational level, their simultaneous operation in varying relative strength is entirely possible from an emotional standpoint. Both functions are unconscious endeavors at conflict resolution.

5. Overwhelming Stimulus with Pre-existing Diathesis; Peg Concept Applicable

It is important to note again that the pre-existing psychologic capacity must be present for the development of a fugue. Its development also depends upon an individually appropriate, "overwhelming" stimulus or situation. This stimulus, however, is effective only when added to a foundation already well prepared. This concept is quite analogous to the *Peg Concept,* in the "selection" of the phobic object and elsewhere [p. 464; Ch.14:IVB2]. It applies in the initiation of many emotional symptoms.

At times, elements of the clinical features appear to be determined by the patient's response to certain external "suggestions". In continuing an analogy to phobic dynamics, this recalls the influence which is sometimes exerted by the sensory context at the time of the so-called "critical attack". These kinds of suggestions in the fugue and in other emotional reactions, are present through what might ordinarily be regarded as a normal extraneous event. In the following case, the amnesia was a part of a typical Fugue State in which an air cadet wandered somewhat aimlessly, lost and disorganized.

In the initiation of his illness, he unwittingly utilized what we might name the "initiating suggestion", which he had "obtained" from a newspaper. He developed a major psychologic illness which eventually helped him to resolve a previously insoluble conflict. This was done on an unconscious, involuntary level of awareness. Careful study of this case unraveled the essential psychodynamic factors in the psychogenesis of his fugue. In accord with a useful concept, the Fugue developed in *Favorable Psychologic Soil* [Ch.14:VIA].

Case 173

A Fugue State Follows Intolerable Conflict

(1) Interest in aviation since childhood

A young Air Force cadet disappeared from his base during World War II. Some days later, he turned up many miles away, in Oklahoma City, where he was discovered wandering aimlessly around in the streets, amnesic, and unable to identify himself. When his identity was finally discovered, he was returned to Randolph Field and hospitalized. Here, intensive study revealed the following basis for his intolerable conflicts, and also recovered the *Initiating Suggestion.*

He had been extremely interested in aviation since childhood. He had long wanted to become a pilot, a vocation which was a means to bolster his self-esteem, and through which he could become a hero. He had early idealized and later identified himself with a famous World War I ace.

(2) Inversion of attitudes and interests transpires rapidly

During World War II he had been successful in gaining his admittance to an Air Force training base. However, as an air cadet, to his tremendous disappointment, chagrin, and disillusionment, he rapidly became extremely fearful of flying. As a consequence he soon also developed an intense hatred of it. This was an *inversion** of his entire prior attitude and interests. With each successive training flight he became more anxious, as well as nauseated and sick. After much personal struggle, he finally made efforts to have himself grounded. These were, however, not at all successful. He was still unable to admit to himself consciously, the extent of his underlying conflicts.

He had advanced various of the more socially acceptable reasons why he should give up flying. These were not particularly impressive to his instructors. They paid little attention to him. His difficulties increased. He in turn became increasingly desperate.

(3) The Peg Concept illustrated: An "Initiating Suggestion" secured

It was approximately at this time that the cadet had read by chance an article in a newspaper about the case of an amnesia victim, a woman in Hollywood, California, who was being sued for divorce by her husband because of infidelity. The woman claimed amnesia for the events of her extramarital experiences.

This constituted the *Initiating Suggestion* in the cadet's case. It operated unconsciously. Some days later, the cadet disappeared from his base, to be found as described earlier.

(4) Therapy effective

With psychotherapy, he was gradually able to recognize and to verbalize his fears, his conflicts about flying, and his lifelong insecurity. It became evident that his future career as an aviator was best at an end for all concerned. This was a forcible medical resolution of his conflicts over flying.

Such resolution however, allowed him maintenance of his self-esteem. He subsequently recovered rather rapidly, and eventually was able to recall rather completely the events of the period of amnesia. His release to civilian life terminated his therapy.

F. TREATMENT OF THE FUGUE

1. Work Out Psychodynamics

A. ADJUNCTIVE MEASURES.—The goal of the therapy with the fugue patient is the gaining of sufficient understanding by patient and physician

---

* *See* discussion of the mental dynamism of *inversion* in *Mental Mechanisms*, pp. 168–198, (Butterworths, Washington, 1963).

of what has happened psychodynamically. This should be accomplished as thoroughly as practicable in the individual case. Needless to say, our concept of the *Inverse Ratio of Symptom-Success to Motivation Toward Treatment* [pp. 9, 298, and Ch.12:VG] holds.

Naturally one wishes to restore the lost area of memory. This, of course, is a most limited therapeutic goal. However, on occasion this can be accomplished fairly rapidly, with the adjunctive use of hypnosis or *Sodium Amytal* narcohypnosis [*see also Case 142, Ch.12:VIIIB4,* and Ch.12: *VD3*]. Cautions already noted and referred to later are applicable. The restoration of memory often can be secured, albeit more slowly, with psychotherapy alone. As noted in our discussion of amnesia, there is added merit indeed to the latter approach where feasible. However, one should not completely discard the potential value of emergency adjunctive measures judiciously applied, in selective cases and in expert hands.

Hypnosis offers a valuable therapeutic assist in certain instances. This applies particularly since these patients have already demonstrated clinically their capacity for dissociation. The amnesia is not unrelated to the repressions demonstrable under hypnotic suggestion. On occasion, patients themselves have compared a fugue to a state of hypnosis.

Most of the earlier comments in regard to the treatment of amnesia in Section VII are also applicable to the treatment of Fugue States.

B. DEFINITIVE THERAPY.—Removal of the gross memory defects in the fugue and restoration of the prior personality is a dramatic and important therapeutic endeavor. However, without detracting from its importance, it can also be compared to symptom removal in conversion or the phobias. More definitive or "deep therapy" as we have termed it, would further and ideally lead to the removal of the basic need for psychologic reliance upon such a primitive defensive kind of gross dissociative process.

Basic conflicts should be uncovered, defined, analyzed, and resolved. Internal psychologic drives should be recognized, accepted, and resolved in a more constructive way. The development of more mature defenses, as opposed to the more primitive kinds of dissociative intrapsychic defenses, should be encouraged. The fundamental character structure should become more stable and mature. The degree of constructive gain is in direct proportion to the success of the therapy, and *vice versa.*

In discussing the "imperative challenge" to dispel the amnesia, Fisher and Joseph properly stressed the fact that "no individual abandons the memory of his entire past, [and] his sense of personal identity without pressing cause." This should be kept firmly in mind whenever one considers a direct assault on the amnesic area. One might well seek to resist the challenge! Long-term intensive therapy is far preferable, through which one can secure substantial character realignment.

The foregoing points out the great stress and significance of the psychologic forces required to initiate a fugue. Further indicated is the great level of self defeat risked or engendered. Finally, the *Symptom Defense-Defeat Parallel Concept* may well be borne out, as a significant corollary to our Concept of Secondary Defense. Thus the strength of such defense in the Fugue can approximate the great amount of defeat and masochism produced [pp. 291, 505, and Ch. 12 : VA2].

Case 174

Fugue Treated by Conservative Approach

(1) Retrograde amnesia on admission: developing problems

A thirty-two-year-old housewife was admitted to the hospital appearing depressed and somewhat confused. She had a complete retrograde amnesia for her entire past life. She had no knowledge of her name, or where she came from. She could give no details of her past history. Her identity was fortunately established very soon. However, she was unable to recognize her husband or friends when they came to visit her.

The history, as obtained from her husband, friends, her mother, and later in the course of treatment from the patient herself, was essentially as follows. A year earlier the patient lost a six-months' pregnancy after the fetus had died in utero. The loss of the potential birth was most upsetting to the patient, but she had appeared to recover physically and emotionally. The patient and a new friend began to spend long hours discussing their personal problems. The "friend" had belittled the patient's husband, and made subtle accusations that he was being unfaithful. The patient's husband had sensed the presence of danger in this relationship, and objected to it.

For six months the patient suffered from "heart trouble". About three months prior to admission she began to have an intense fear of her husband. Out of character, he had begun to speak somewhat harshly, was less considerate, and became demanding upon occasion. She began to have episodes of insomnia during which the husband would unsympathetically order her back to bed. In addition to caring for her three children and home, she was attempting to hold down a difficult job. The intense neurotic fear of her husband reached such a degree that the patient was soon unable to think of anything else.

(2) Events reached a climax; typically dissociated, confused, physical and psychological flight ensued

Four nights prior to her admission, the patient had a violent argument with her husband. At this point life had become absolutely intolerable. She got into a taxi with the intention of going to her employer's office. After going several blocks, she got out of the cab and wandered aimlessly for three days; sleeping on park benches; not eating. On the day of admission she was found by some kindly people and eventually brought to the hospital.

The patient's previous personality and character had been exemplary in every way. She was one of seven children. Her entire family had depended upon her because of her unusual perception and judgment. Her intelligence was above average and, despite great handicaps, she had finished high school with high marks. There was no earlier history of any kind of emotional disorder.

(3) Choice of conservative route well vindicated

In the hospital it was soon evident that the patient became very anxious whenever her friends attempted to discuss with her any of the happenings of which she had no memory. All visitors except her husband were restricted from visiting her. She was treated psychotherapeutically. Within three weeks the patient was beginning to remember things spontaneously without the assistance of the therapist. By the end of six weeks she seemed to be completely reconstituted emotionally.

She and her husband had gained considerable awareness of the unfortunate circumstances that had given rise to the Fugue State. The patient was discharged and has since gotten along well, following a period of extramural psychotherapy. The conservative approach proved most rewarding and beneficial. Most of the criteria as outlined earlier, concerning the potential results which favor ones' following this therapeutic route, were secured.

3. Hypnosis: Reliving the Onset

When hypnosis is used therapeutically in seeking to work out what has happened in a Fugue State, a helpful approach is through securing the reliving, under hypnosis, of the events in detail up to the point at which the fugue began. Often the patient can then continue into the events of the fugue. Drugs as well can sometimes aid the therapist in establishing what was earlier termed the therapeutic Emergency Analytic Bridge [Ch.12:VD3].

In working out the psychodynamics of a particular attack, the mental content around the point of onset is vitally important. Fisher stressed that the most important factor in working out the psychodynamics of a fugue is the uncovering of the unconscious fantasies which occur at its onset. This cannot be overstressed in gaining an understanding of the psychogenesis of a given Fugue State. It is absolutely necessary to explore as thoroughly as possible, exactly what was going on in the patient's mind just prior to, during, and immediately after the moment of onset. This is in accord with our earlier outlined Tracing Technique in Therapy [p. 534].

4. In Conclusion

In closing this discussion it is desired to stress the fact that more detailed knowledge is needed about the clinical findings and the psychodynamics of the Fugue States. Additional study and research in this interesting and unusual kind of psychologic flight would constitute a useful contribution. Another related case is summarized in the following Chapter 14, [Section VC2], as noted earlier. This is an instance of a brief dissociative state in response to acute psychologic trauma.

This brief discussion of the Fugue State should always be considered and studied together with the preceding one on Amnesia. In the therapy of both it is important to preserve self-esteem, in accord with our earlier advocated [Ch.12:VD1; and VIIIC2] Principle of Self-Esteem Maintainence.

IX. THE ALTERNATING OR DOUBLE PERSONALITY

A. SEPARATE LIVES

1. Major Dissociation Allows Alternate Dominance

The alternating or double personality type of phenomenon is one of the most spectacular and dramatic of all psychologic reactions. Instances are, however, quite rare in clinical experience. The mere existence of such a potential in human behavior has captured the imagination of many people and has been used as the theme for several famous works of fiction. The classic example of these is perhaps the fictional account of Dr. Jekyll and Mr. Hyde, originally written by Robert Louis Stevenson, around 1885.

Shortly thereafter (1890) Professor William James reported the more intriguing than fiction, real life case of the Reverend Ansell Bourne. Having disappeared from his ministry in Rhode Island, he later "found himself" in a small Pennsylvania town. Here he had rented a confectionery shop some six weeks earlier, under the name of A. J. Brown. He apparently lived a normal enough life, at any rate so as not to arouse undue comment, until one day he suddenly found himself again to be the Reverend Bourne! He could not recall the circumstances since his disappearance, could not explain how he had gotten where he was, nor what had happened. His insistence on his (original) identity mystified his (newer) acquaintances. Identified by relatives, he could not explain the uncanny episode.

2. Definition

The Alternating Personality is *a rare major Dissociative Reaction in which the patient leads two or more lives independently, usually alternately, neither personality being aware of the other.* Each seemingly possesses the ability to function separately and independently in a dominant position, while the other is kept submerged for a time.

This reaction is also known as Double or Dual Personality. It is the ultimate pathologic dissociative progression from clinical amnesia and the Fugue State. Alternating Dissociation is the type which accounts for this unusual clinical syndrome. The terms Alternating Personality and Double or Multiple Personality are used interchangeably. Each is acceptable.

B. DIAGNOSIS AND INCIDENCE

The diagnosis of Alternating Personality can only be made with clear clinical evidence of the presence of separate major aspects of the personality. These must have demonstrated a capacity for their complete dissociative splitting apart, and an ability to function independently of each other.

The incidence is very rare. Only a handful of authenticated cases have been reported.

C. CLINICAL INSTANCES OF MULTIPLE PERSONALITY

1. Dr. Morton Prince and Miss Christine Beauchamp

Dr. Morton Prince was responsible for the introduction of the concept of Alternating Personality into medicine. Prince was a native of Boston, Massachusetts, having been born there in 1854 and graduated from Harvard Medical School in 1879. The next year he took his mother to Charcot's clinic in Paris for treatment. Largely as a result of this experience, he became increasingly interested in psychologic medicine, devoting himself exclusively to work in psychopathology after 1890. Prince introduced the concept of multiple personality, reported the now classic case of Miss

Christine Beauchamp, and stimulated great interest in the study of psychopathology in the United States.

Prince began the study and treatment of Miss Beauchamp, a Radcliffe student, in 1898, and worked with her for six years. At various times she exhibited three separate "personalities". Her "saintly" personality regarded selfishness, rudeness, and suppression of half the truth, as great sins that should be cast out by fasting and prayer. The second personality, Sally, was described as the "devil", and was a childish, impish personality. The third personality, described as the "woman," exhibited ambition and strong self-interest. Prince was early aware of two personalities, the "saint" and the "woman". Under hypnosis, he discovered the "devil", which the patient herself called "Sally". "Sally" was aware of the things that the saintly Miss Beauchamp did, but the saintly personality was unaware of Sally's existence.

Prince used his findings in this case to point out how a part of the personality might remain completely out of the conscious awareness of the patient, but still importantly influence behavior. He reported at some length the conflict between the three "personalities" of his patient which were constantly taking place in her unconscious. He was finally able to secure the resynthesis of the dissociated portions, with a resulting therapeutic integration of the patient.

The case achieved considerable fame in medical circles and with the laity. A successful Broadway play, *The Case of Becky*, was based upon it.

2. Recent Cases

A few excellent case reports of Alternating Personality have been published. One of these was reported by Lipton in 1943, and another by Masserman in 1946. In the latter, a desperately unhappy housewife unconsciously renounced her former life, to live quite successfully for four years in a long-envied dissociated role from her past. She had returned to her college town (the location of her happiest earlier era) where she had adopted the life and the name of a happier and more socially successful college roommate. This had provided a kind of unconsciously-sought *emotional prototype* [*see* pp. 490–4]. This is an instance of a prolonged Fugue State, with sufficiently marked dissociation for it to be regarded as a case of Alternating Personality. Her major Dissociative Reaction had achieved a certain balanced state, illustrating our *Status Quo of Adjustment Concept* [Ch.12:VA2]. When such is achieved through neurotic symptoms, the Secondary Defense is likely stronger and more determined.

In 1957 Thigpen and Cleckley reported at some length the interesting case of Eve White-Eve Black. In this instance of Multiple Personality, the two opposite personalities were in conflict. As therapy progressed Jane, a third, more integrated personality emerged. The two Eves lost their power of dominance, as there developed a more mature level of emotional adjustment and reaction.

Finally *Case 142* [Ch.12:VD3] also satisfies several of our criteria for the Double Personality category.

D. NOTE ON PSYCHODYNAMICS

The dynamics are most readily understood by viewing these rare cases as instances of a more advanced and complete dissociation than is present in the more usual Fugue State. The Alternating Personality is the ultimate expression of the complete, alternating kind of personality dissociation. Each area appears to possess the ability to function independently of the other and usually outside of its conscious awareness.

James' and Prince's cases, and others reported since [*see also Case 142* in Ch.12:VD3], are little less dramatic than Stevenson's characters. In general, the person displaying this alternating type of personality carries on two or more completely separate and distinct existences. For example, the physician might become a factory worker, with no memory of his former state or life. He may even function quite effectively in the new role. Reversion may be precipitated by physical or emotional events individually and specifically important to him. At this juncture the old personality asserts itself, and the victim is amazed to "find himself" in an "unfamiliar" situation. He is at a loss to explain what has occurred, or the meaning of his current activities, dress, and so on.

The psychodynamics involve: (1) the force, significance, and individual acuteness of initiating circumstances, (2) the personality diathesis, and (3) the basic underlying conflicts. Thorough analysis of these will ordinarily lead to a resynthesis of the dissociated parts of the personality. The personality now integrated will be more or less free of the prior serious conflicts, and will be more mature. Opportunities for such therapeutic intervention and study are most rare.

X. AUTOMATIC BEHAVIOR

A. AUTOMATIC WRITING

Many years ago physicians learned that certain individuals possessed an unusual capacity for an interesting kind of dissociation which we might term the *Dissociation of Automaticity* [Ch.13:IIE]. This was demonstrated in the phenomenon which was named *automatic writing*. A pencil could be placed in the hand of a person whose attention was fully occupied elsewhere. He could be induced to write various things, of which he would have no conscious awareness.

In one means of demonstrating this reaction, one distracts the attention of a patient who is writing. In certain patients, the process of automatic writing simply "takes over". The dissociative response results in the eliciting of unconscious material, which is written down. Such data can be investigated, and sometimes proves to be profitable therapeutically, through providing useful data for the treatment process. This phenomenon is an intriguing illustration of the dissociative capacity of some people. It is related to all other dissociative phenomena. Automatic writing, together with narcosis Sodium Amytal and hypnosis have all been used clinically to test the relative dissociative capacity of a patient.

The term "automatic writing" has also been applied to the writing which follows the suggestions made to a patient while he is in a hypnotic trance. Kaplan reported an interesting instance in which a patient under hypnosis responding correctly to the appropriate suggestions, firmly denied vocally the presence or the discomfort of painful stimuli in his left arm, but who also began automatic writing with his right hand. This simultaneously expressed the reverse, stating, "Ouch, damn it, you're hurting me!" This very interestingly illustrated automatic writing and dissociation under hypnosis.

The hypnotic or induced dissociation plus the suggestions, had allowed repression and denial of the painful stimulus. From the content of the automatic writing however, it was clearly evident that the painful sensations were still perceived ("Ouch") and reacted to (by anger: "Damn it") by another aspect of the personality.

B. OLD PATTERN TAKES OVER: AUTOMATIC BEHAVIOR

Various similar kinds of automatic behavior are sometimes to be observed clinically. These are not necessarily pathologic. Many are understandable simply on the basis of the surrounding circumstances.

The following instance is one example, and includes elements of the continuation of an established pattern of activity, preoccupation, plus the expression of an unconscious wish which was not too deeply buried.

Case 175

An Instance of Automatic Behavior

A twenty-four-year-old bachelor broke up with his steady girl friend, after three years of regular courtship. He had dated her routinely on Monday, Wednesday, and Saturday nights. He had resolved that the break was permanent, and declared to himself that he didn't care if he never saw her again.

One Monday evening several weeks later he had been driving along in his car and thinking in serious fashion about his future plans. He parked the car and started to get out. He looked up and found, to his surprise, that he had driven to his ex-girl friend's home in automatic fashion. He had carefully parked his car there, just as his custom had been in the past.

XI. HYPNOSIS

A. AN INDUCED DISSOCIATION

1. Reaction to Suggestion

Hypnosis is a most interesting phenomenon. It has intrigued scholars and the public through the ages. Clinical and experimental hypnosis offer excellent illustrations of purposely induced dissociation. Required is a willing subject, with the requisite dissociative capacity.

Under hypnosis, the selected subject has been induced, more or less voluntarily, to split off or to dissociate a broad area of his usual conscious awareness and perception from the environment. His attention and his perceptions become focused into an increasingly narrow area, subject to the suggestions of the hypnotist.

The type of dissociation which is operative in hypnosis is Induced Dissociation, or Hypnotic Dissociation. The author has also suggested the adoption of the name *B.B.C. Dissociation* after three of the most respected pioneers in its use; namely James Braid, Hippolyte Bernheim, and Jean Charcot.

2. Definition

Hypnosis may be defined as *an altered state of conscious awareness which is induced in a cooperative subject. Through the suggestions of the hypnotist, a passive trance-like state of dissociation is produced. In it the subject more or less pays attention only to that which the hypnotist wishes.*

The term "hypnosis" is derived from the Greek *hypnotikos*, meaning inclined to sleep, or putting to sleep. *Hypnos* in Greek mythology was the god of sleep, often depicted in art as winged; the twin brother of *Thanatos*, death. *Hypnos* is also Sleep, a personification. Hypnosis is *a state often resembling, but differing from normal sleep.* As such *it may be regarded as being somewhere between wakeful consciousness and sleep, being different from, but possessing some of the characteristics of both.* Hypnosis varies in depth. Cataleptic or Somnambulistic hypnosis refers to the deeper and more profound hypnotic trances.

The ability to be an excellent subject for hypnosis depends upon the pre-existing individual capacity for dissociation. This would apply to perhaps less than ten per cent of the general population, in the United States. This percentage would vary somewhat in other countries and in differing cultures.

B. HISTORICAL NOTES ON HYPNOSIS

1. From Antiquity

The history of hypnosis extends into remotest antiquity. Trances and trance-like states are described in ancient history, literature, and folklore. Hypnotic trances have been associated at various times with magic, mysticism, demons, and evil spirits; with theatrics and with religion.

Considerable knowledge has also long existed about suggestibility. This is also true about the occasional considerable ability of one individual to control or influence others. Sometimes this has been to an undue extent. Empirically at least, some aspects of dissociation have been long recognized, if not by this name. However, it is only in relatively recent times that medicine and science have attempted to explore and understand these phenomena.

2. Mesmer

Dr. Franz Anton Mesmer (1733–1815), a physician and native of
Austria, first recognized the tremendous but then scientifically unknown
power of suggestion in therapeutics. From 1775 until a while before his
death, he employed it widely and with notorious success, mainly in Paris.
He was a pioneer, although he did not understand the basis of the forces
he put to such effective and spectacular uses. Partly in an effort to meet
his critics and detractors, he devised a theory of "animal magnetism" to
explain his results. Included were his 27 "propositions" which were advanced, without much further proof, in an 88-page booklet in 1779. Mesmer's clinical and therapeutic results were often little short of tremendous.
For years his personal popularity was very great. Patients came in crowds
to him and to his group of associates.

His efforts to secure wider scientific acceptance of his theories were not
effective. His propositions would not stand the test of scientific scrutiny
and trial [Ch.12:IIA2]. Others could not duplicate his results. His theories eventually resulted in injuring him and depopularizing his method
of treatment. He came under increasing attack.

Mesmer was eventually discredited and lost his popularity. He came
to be regarded by many as a charlatan. This was the final result of a report
by a royal, learned commission headed by Benjamin Franklin (then serving
as U.S. Ambassador to France), which had been appointed by Louis XVI
in March of 1784 for the purpose of evaluating his work and theories.
All but one of the 13 commissioners of the Faculty of Medicine, and the
Academy of Sciences, including Benjamin Franklin, signed the two reports;
one being secret, and the other one of which was widely publicized (20,000
copies), in August 1784. This gradually but effectively discouraged the
acceptance and use of "animal magnetism", or "Mesmerism", as it was
variously called for several decades. After some years of great popularity,
and later increasingly bitter attack, Mesmer had departed from Paris, to
eventually die at 81 years of age in 1815, nearly forgotten. However, it
was not too long before adventuresome physicians in several countries were
again trying to influence people, their emotions, behavior, and symptoms
through hypnotic suggestion. The Medical Renaissance [p. 312] was
under way.

3. Later Contributors

A. BRAID, BERNHEIM, AND CHARCOT.—Hypnosis was given its name in
1841 by James Braid (1795–1861), an Englishman. He had also earlier
used the term "animal magnetism". Braid adopted the term "hypnosis"
from the Greek, having originally regarded the phenomenon as a form of
sleep. Later he came to view it as better characterized by the presence of
a single prevailing idea, and suggested a different name (accordingly,
"monoideism"). The terms "braidism" and "braidist", after him, have
also been used. The term "hypnosis", however, came to prevail in usage
since. An alternative name which he later himself suggested as being
preferable, thus did not survive.

Braid, a surgeon, successfully used hypnosis to perform certain surgical procedures while working in India. Its use in medicine and in surgery has continued at least sporadically ever since. Interest and use increased as more was learned of its nature and dynamics. Hypnosis regained respectability. Prior to the discovery of anesthesia, it was occasionally used quite successfully in surgery. Similar uses are advocated today and employed to a limited extent, by small groups of practitioners in dentistry, obstetrics, medicine, and in certain surgical procedures.

In the latter part of the nineteenth century an increasing number of reputable physicians made use of, or studied hypnosis.* These included Ambroise A. Liebeault (1823–1904) of Nancy, France; the famous neurologist Jean M. Charcot (1825-1893) of Paris, and his associates; Hippolyte Marie Bernheim (1840–1919) of Nancy, Liebeault's famous pupil; as well as Pierre Janet (1859–1947). As earlier noted [Ch.13:IIE*1*] it has been suggested that the hypnotic type of induced dissociation might well be named *B.B.C. Dissociation,* after Braid, Bernheim, and Charcot.

B. MANY SUBSEQUENT CONTRIBUTORS.—Joseph Breuer (1841–1925) and later Sigmund Freud (1856–1939), who was for a time one of Bernheim's and Charcot's observer-students, early used hypnosis as a means to the recall of "forgotten", painful emotional experiences and memories. Freud also used the interesting phenomenon of post-hypnotic suggestion to help prove the existence of the unconscious. Merton M. Gill and Margaret Brenman, Harold Rosen, M. H. Erickson, André M. Weitzenhoffer, Lewis R. Wollberg, and many others have contributed to our present-day concepts of hypnosis. This discussion attempts very briefly to summarize the highlights of the work to date, including some of the author's personal findings and theories.

Although Freud, as have others since, soon largely abandoned the use of hypnosis as an adjunct in psychiatric therapy, the subject has served to intrigue people in widely diverse fields. It has generally failed to provide an easier or faster pathway to the dynamics in most individual cases of emotional illness. Hence it has not earned a place as a major therapeutic tool, or one of really widespread utilization in medicine. Nevertheless, hypnosis, by its very existence as a dramatic procedure, continues sporadically to hold the interest of various physicians and scientists. As we shall also learn, hypnosis has a valid role in our research into psychodynamics.

C. CLINICAL FEATURES

1. Induction of and Emergence from Hypnosis

A. PROGRESSIVELY RESTRICTED FOCUS OF ATTENTION.—Various techniques have been favored in the induction of the hypnotic trance. Most of them have in common the directing of the focus of the subject's attention, usually visual, upon some small object, to the complete elimination of out-

---

* The term "mesmerism" (after Anton Mesmer) is sometimes still heard. Its use may carry an unpleasant connotation, implying undue influence, or questionable ethics.

side influences. This is accompanied by the concurrent and often monotonously repeated suggestion of drowsiness and sleep. Monotonous sensory suggestions in addition to the visual also have included stroking the brow or arms.

The skilled operator can often induce a hypnotic trance of some depth in the willing subject in a matter of minutes or even seconds. The hypnotic state is achieved through a progressive kind of restrictive narrowing of the focus of the person's attention and of his conscious awareness. Following induction, the subject is in a state of hypnotic rapport with the hypnotist, and is responsive to his direction and suggestions.

B. HYPNOTIZABILITY.—Who are good subjects? What determines the ability? Among the general population one out of from five to ten persons is a "good" candidate. Hypnotizability is substantially higher percentagewise among persons with conversion manifestations or diathesis. This is also true among those manifesting the Dissociative Reactions. Accordingly we would expect to find a considerably higher ratio of excellent subjects for hypnosis among those who have had clinical attacks of amnesia, Fugue States, Automatic Behavior, and Alternating Personality.

This relationship is less marked but still applicable for persons subject to nocturnal somnambulism and depersonalization. A higher proportion of susceptible subjects is often found under or following conditions of stress and danger, as under combat conditions. Generally, hypnotizability is in direct proportion to the capacity for dissociation and to responsiveness to suggestion. It is never fully predictable, however, in advance, from the individual standpoint. Any full understanding of the factors of hypnotizability for the specific subject thus continues to remain rather enigmatic. Some added comments on hypnotizability will follow shortly.

With repeated hypnosis and with the addition of previously implanted suggestions of easy hypnotizability, induction can be made progressively easier. In some instances it can be effected almost instantaneously. Here the trance occurs as a prearranged response to a simple stimulus. In this way the subsequent induction of a hypnotic state is aided and facilitated by post-hypnotic suggestion. In this aspect hypnosis has some of the characteristics of a learned response and of a pattern of habit.

C. APPEARANCE, BEHAVIOR, PROBLEMS IN RESYNTHESIS.—The behavior and appearance of the hypnotized individual is subject to variation. The new subject is likely to appear somnolent; his eyes are often closed, pending suggestions to the contrary, while his movements, responses to questions, and speech are slowed and somewhat deliberate. This can change with repeated experience, and in response to suggestions. The behavior and appearance of the person under hypnosis, initially at least, conforms to a considerable extent to his prior impressions of what these will be.

The subject usually emerges from his trance promptly upon suggestion. If the suggestion is not given, the patient will usually come out of hypnosis spontaneously anyway, although this will be a gradual process, and require a varying period of time. Occasionally subjects will "refuse" or be unable, to surrender their state of hypnotic dissociation. Investigation when feasible will usually indicate that the continuation of the trance offers some secret (that is, unconscious) psychologic advantage to the person. This unwillingness to resynthesize is comparable in its basis to the unconscious advantages (both epigain and endogain) afforded by amnesia and the fugue.

This continuation of the trance is a frightening sequela to occasional trances induced by novices. It is not without its possible untoward consequences to the patient.

Hypnosis is not a toy. It should not be treated lightly, or used flippantly. It should best not be employed in the theater or by amateurs in parlor games.

2. Selectivity for Hypnotist and Subject

A. IDEAL SUBJECTS QUITE LIMITED.—An important aspect and a real limitation to the medical use of hypnosis is the considerable amount of selectivity which applies both as to the hypnotist and to his subjects. The ability to become a good hypnotist involves art as well as science or training, although these latter factors can, of course, contribute substantially. A limited number of persons are able to develop great skill in the medical therapeutic use of, or in the research employment of hypnosis.

The number of persons who can become ideal subjects for hypnosis is likewise very limited. Even those who have used hypnosis in the field of theatrics or entertainment have quickly learned empirically that the careful selection of subjects is an absolute prerequisite to successful demonstrations. Authorities differ somewhat in their estimates of the hypnotizability of the public at large. The author estimates that from 10 to 20 per cent of the general public in the United States could be so considered. Of these only a still smaller number are really "good" subjects. Some people have offered higher estimates.

These figures would show some variance around the world, according to the culture, the general level of education and sophistication, and the index of suggestibility of the people of a given culture and country, as noted. In the underdeveloped countries these figures should rise substantially.

Some years ago (1951) the author made a survey of the literature on hypnosis. This included the preparation and item-by-item review of more than 700 contributions to the literature. The repeated references to "good" or "excellent" subjects by a great many of the more experienced clinicians and investigators, particularly in conducting the more complex kinds of experiments, were impressive as regards the requirement for selectivity of subjects.

B. DETERMINING INDIVIDUAL SUSCEPTIBILITY.—Various tests have been devised to determine the individual susceptibility to hypnosis. These vary from the gross tests of suggestibility as used by stage entertainers, to research with complex psychologic testing such as interpreting the results of the Rorschach test. One simple method which has been employed in the theater by entertainers, for example, has been to ask the audience to raise their hands above their heads, clasp them together, and then suggest that there will be difficulty in unclasping them. People who have some obvious difficulty as a result of this simple suggestion are then chosen as subjects. They usually prove to be good ones.

The use of the Rorschach test is a scientific refinement which has been studied and employed by a number of investigators. Favorable signs from this test are those which generally indicate free-floating anxiety and labile affectivity, although these are not to be regarded as absolute.

C. PRINCIPLE OF DIRECT CORRELATION OF YOUTH TO HYPNOTIZABILITY. —In addition to the requirements earlier implied, the subject must have a great deal of trust, faith, and confidence in the operator. He must be submissive, and must possess the underlying ability or capacity to dissociate. Suggestibility is also important, and so is youth. The "best" experiments generally involve willing subjects in the young adult age group.

There appears to be a direct correlation between youth and suggestibility, so that as age increases one's value as a potential subject is very likely to decrease. This is the Principle of the *Direct Correlation of Youth with Hypnotizability*. While there are noteworthy exceptions, in general this correlation tends to hold. To be more technically correct, this correlation might be more accurately stated of course as being between one's *susceptibility to suggestion* and his *relative hypnotizability*.

Resistance associated with stubborn perversity can at times be handled by appropriately phrased reverse suggestions (Example: "I know you can't be hypnotized, so of course you can pull your hands apart", and so on.)

These comments as to the selectivity for operator and subject in hypnosis are also important as further indications of its limitations. On the other hand, sometimes occasional witnesses of a demonstration on hypnosis will prove to be very susceptible. At times they may be seen to fall unwittingly into some degree of trance, even though they themselves are not actually serving as subjects. While this may be observed as an indication of individual suggestibility, nevertheless hypnosis is ordinarily not to be regarded as ever possible against the will of the subject.* Cooperation must be voluntary and complete.

D. DYNAMICS

1. Intense Relationship

In hypnosis an intense relationship is established between two people. As a result, the subject becomes able, under suggestion, to dissociate from his conscious awareness the impingement of influences or perceptions except those which are directed by the hypnotist. To the subject in deep hypnosis, nothing appears to exist except what the hypnotist wishes to exist for him. To be a "good" subject, there must be voluntary complete surrender to the will of the hypnotist. This requires a great amount of trust, faith, confidence, and submissiveness, as well as the basic capacity for dissociation to the extent required. It becomes apparent that successful hypnosis implies an intense kind of interpersonal relationship.

Where might one find an antecedent relationship for that which is induced in hypnosis? Various possibilities occur. Among these are the

---

* Hofman-Bang stated his opinion which is in dissent, that few people can resist hypnotic suggestion by the experienced and clever operator.

blind obedience and compliance of the small child with the authority figure of father or mother. Another is the absorbed and compliant state in relation to the mother, which is sometimes to be observed in the nursing infant.

Young patients who possess conversion personality defenses, those with the basic capacity for massive conversion or dissociation, and those who are rather on the immature and naive side are generally the most suitable subjects for hypnosis. With increasing maturity, the capacity for hypnotic suggestibility and dissociation generally decreases.

2. Suggestibility and the Power of Suggestion

The importance of suggestibility has been referred to a number of times in reference to its requirement for the induction of a hypnotic trance. Mesmer's patients were very subject to suggestion. He could induce simultaneous trances in scores of people. Often they were doubtless conditioned to this before ever seeing him.

The power of suggestion can be strong indeed. Two rather dramatic instances, one factual and the other an oft-told story of rather doubtful veracity, come to mind and are related in an endeavor to illustrate the power of suggestion.

The first instance concerns a high-wire trapeze artist who had been a professional performer for two years. Everything went well until a "friend" commented that his timing looked off. With this, his confidence became shaken. Reassurance by his associates and family had little effect. His performance deteriorated. He had a fall to the net, and had to give up his act temporarily.

The second is an oft-told story about a group of medical students who wanted to test the power of suggestion in the onset of illness. This they proceeded to do in a cruel and sadistic fashion. Accordingly, they undertook a series of suggestive comments to the custodian of their apartment building. First they told him that he did not look too alert, then that he didn't look well. In progressively serious fashion they commented that he appeared ill, and so on. According to the story, the janitor became ill, and died several days later.

E. "TRUTH SERUM": ADJUNCTIVE DRUGS

1. No Guarantee of Truth

In the effort to overcome some of the limitations of hypnosis, various adjunctive drugs have been used in place of, or in conjunction with, the induction of hypnotic states. They also have been used to facilitate interrogation, particularly in criminal cases. The scientifically unfortunate misnomer "truth serum" has been applied to members of this group of drugs, especially to *Sodium Amytal*. Enthusiastic journalistic adoption encouraged the use of this term. It has become popularly acceptable despite its inaccuracy and disadvantages. Certainly it should be very clear that neither *Sodium Amytal* nor *Pentothal* is a serum; neither do they guarantee the truth!

The drugs most frequently used in these endeavors have been *Sodium Amytal, Pentobarbital Sodium,* scopolamine hydrobromide, various other barbiturates, and, less frequently, nitrous oxide and some of the anesthetics. These drugs already to some extent, and even more so in the case of alcohol in its various forms over the ages, have historically been employed in efforts to decrease conscious control, lessen inhibition and censorship, and increase volubility. The use of *Sodium Amytal* has been referred to earlier in connection with amnesia, and will be referred to again later in this volume. In certain of the dissociative states, sometimes including acute psychoses, the judicious employment of *Sodium Amytal* as an adjunct to psychotherapy temporarily, may serve at least to re-effect integration and to allow communication to be re-established. This has been illustrated earlier in our concept of the *Emergency Analytic-Bridge* [Ch.12:VD2].

2. Important Factors in Criminal Interrogation; Psychic Pressures in Confession

Two major factors influence the success of criminal interrogation. These are of considerably greater importance than the use of hypnosis or a drug, which are to be considered as adjuncts only. The first relates to the skill, experience, resources, and judgment of the interrogator.

The second factor relates to the combinations of underlying psychologic factors in the subject, tending to produce a confession. These are in accord with a Concept of *Psychic Pressures in Confession.* Several such major factors are summarized for more convenient reference in the following tabulation.

Table 39

Psychic Pressures in Inducing Confessions

Psychic pressures exist or are sometimes activated, and can serve to aid in inducing confessions. Herein we might include four such important emotional factors.

(1) *Self Punishment:*
The subconscious wish and need for punishment. A masochistic "seeking" to suffer.

(2) *Attention-Seeking:*
A desire to gain attention and notoriety, or a perverse kind of "credit". An underlying seeking for attention can help to account for the multiple confessions which are sometimes reported following a particularly noteworthy crime.

Identification with victim, confederates, other or prior transgressors, and so on. The possession of various similar (to that of the actual criminal thought, urge, and/or act; especially in the false confession) unconscious motivations.

(3) *Relief and Release:*
The resulting release of tension and anxiety, plus the consequently lessened need for constant, tiring, alert defense, caution, and self-preservation.

(4) *Superego Pressures:*
The easing of one's personal conscience — the desire to "square things" with oneself, and/or with the community.

A criminal may sometimes "welcome" narcosis as providing an "excuse". This perhaps may then allow him more readily to accede to already present but hidden (that is, unconscious) psychologic forces which are already urging him to make a confession. It can also provide the basis for his setting up a *Symbolic Authority*. [*See* earlier reference to concept, pp. 195–6.]

3. Adjuncts to Hypnosis

In general, the use of appropriate drugs as adjuncts to hypnosis may be summarized by stating that the susceptibility to hypnosis may be increased. Drugs are occasionally used with refractory patients to secure initial trances, with a subsequent gradual lowering of dependence upon the drug itself to help induce hypnosis on subsequent, repeated occasions.

It may be surmised correctly that the administration of the drug can, of itself, have important psychologic implications. These can contribute to varying results. This has been illustrated in instances in which an inert substance was unwittingly used, and results were still forthcoming.

Narcotics and barbiturates are often totally unsuccessful in helping to elicit otherwise hidden truths, perhaps especially when there are criminal implications. Conscious suppression may continue to be very effective as a barrier. Likely their best medical use is in the judicious elicitation of repressed material. This has some application in acute traumatic cases, as we shall study further in the Chapters to follow.

F. ANTISOCIAL ACTS UNDER HYPNOTIC INFLUENCE

Experiments have been devised purporting to prove the position of many authorities that hypnotized subjects cannot be induced to carry out acts which are injurious to themselves, or which are antisocial in nature. However, Brenman has reported some interesting experiments which have tended to challenge the usually accepted stand in this regard. In these later experiments, various refinements of approach and subtleties of suggestion have been employed. The results tend to raise some doubts about the earlier contentions.

Whenever the production of acts under hypnosis which are contrary to normal conscience is attempted, a measure of success undoubtedly depends upon:

(1) Concealment of the antisocial nature of the act, by implanted suggestions, illusions, or false impressions. The subject may then be unaware of the full implications of what he does. The acts as performed and as experienced by him then tend to become compatible with his usual ethical and moral standards.

(2) The presence in the subject of preexisting, partly or entirely, unconscious drives toward carrying out the suggested act anyway.

(3) The establishment of a very considerable bond of faith, trust, and confidence in the hypnotist, which would help discount any possible inimical consequences, to the subject's judgment.

In a brief review of this question, Weitzenhoffer summarized: "If the situation appears (or is made to appear by illusion or delusion, paramnesias or suggestion of the operator) socially, or in other ways acceptable to the subject, he probably can be induced to commit antisocial acts. If he perceives a situation is contrary to his own ethical system, it is very unlikely that he can be made to carry out criminal acts".

In general it must be borne in mind that this question remains an area of controversy. The suggestion of an act quite clearly contrary to conscience, or to his usual moral or ethical standards, ordinarily results in simple refusal by the hypnotic subject, or in his waking from the trance.

G. HYPNOSIS AS AN IMPLEMENT OF PSYCHIATRIC RESEARCH

1. Exploration of Psychodynamics

Hypnosis has perhaps its best legitimate scientific use currently as an implement of research. The degree of control possible with an excellent subject offers many avenues to the interested investigator for the exploration and verification of psychodynamic principles.

Knowledge of the degree possible of hypnotic control, together with the appreciation of the possible untoward emotional consequences and the misuse of hypnosis, possibly could have some implications as regards the relative infrequency with which hypnotists themselves report undergoing hypnosis. Several of the interesting possible avenues for research and investigation by means of hypnosis follow.

2. Post-hypnotic Suggestions

Post-hypnotic suggestions are those given to a subject under hypnosis for him to later (post-hypnotically) perform some given act. He is instructed to undertake this when a certain word is said or a stimulus is provided. "Recognition" of the stimulus is unconscious. The subject also lacks conscious awareness of why he undertakes such an act.

Many interesting experiments have been devised. As noted previously, Freud early used this instance of obeying a "forgotten" instruction as added proof for the existence of the unconscious. Patten found that suggested responses persisted post-hypnotically at least one month, while others have reported even longer persistence.

In most instances the subject covers up his lack of knowledge for the motivation of what he does in response to the suggestion made under hypnosis. He automatically produces what are quite plausible explanations, or perhaps more accurately, rationalizations.

3. Memory Loss and Recall

Memory loss normally occurs to some extent for the events of the hypnotic session. This can be reinforced through suggestion to the point of securing a vigorous, conscious denial of the hypnotic experience ever having happened. In Brenman's experiments a particular subject following hypnosis thus later vigorously insisted that he was even among the poorer and rejected candidates for hypnosis!

False memories, paramnesias, can be implanted. On the other hand, the recovery of lost memories can be facilitated in many instances. It is an interesting experience to witness the recalling of long-forgotten events from the early years. This kind of experience can forcibly bring home the existence of the unconscious retention of a large body of memories, which are ordinarily well buried from the more usual conscious awareness and ready recall.

Judicious use of hypnosis can be antirepressive. The recall of repressed experiences and the eliciting of unconscious motivations can be far more quickly secured under hypnosis than by more conservative approaches. There are several disadvantages, however. *First,* false data may be forthcoming. *Second,* there is a large gap between hypnotic awareness and conscious awareness. Getting the patient over this can be dangerous and traumatic. It may also prove difficult, or impossible in any reasonable time. *Third,* being so far ahead of his patient and the latter's ability to assimilate such data can become quite frustrating for the therapist. Such advance knowledge gained and held so one-sidedly, is not unequivocally good or an advantage in the long-range therapeutic endeavor.

4. Dreams

Dreams may be induced under hypnosis. Subjects can also sometimes more readily interpret the symbolism of their own dreams as well as the dreams of others while hypnotized. This proves possible as a consequence of a decrease of the inhibitions which are usually present in full consciousness. Research into dreams and dream symbolism offers interesting areas for study.

5. Time Distortion

The more usual appreciation of time and time passage can be greatly affected. By suggestion, time may be made to appear to pass much faster, or more slowly. The day, month, or year may be changed. Anniversaries or important earlier experiences may be recalled and in some instances relived.

There is a close relationship in this phenomenon to that of regression. Time distortion is often readily induced in hypnosis. Its experiencing offers certain analogies to the experiencing of the passage of time in the dream.

6. Regression

By appropriate handling of the "best" subject in hypnosis, temporary artificial regression can be induced. Thus the subject can be carried back to an earlier age level, as suggested for him by the operator. His behavior and responses will more or less approximate the corresponding developmental level. This allows the potential for many interesting kinds of studies.

Figures 1, 2 and *3* as follows, illustrate the phenomenon of regression in response to appropriate suggestion under hypnosis in the case of a man aged twenty-one years. This was one graphic result of the kind of study which proved possible in this instance.

Figure 1.—The subject under deep hypnosis writes his name. He then draws a favorite cartoon character which he originated. His chronologic age is 21 years. Regression has not been suggested.

Figure 2.—Through suggestion the subject has now regressed to the age of 9 years. Note that the name is printed, and the drawing uncertain, and much less detailed. The work is in keeping with low average for a boy of this age.

Figure 3.—Through suggestion the subject has now regressed to the age of 6 years. Having suffered a serious illness with nearly a year's hospitalization, he had missed starting school. Therefore he could not write or print his name. He could only crudely print his initials.

He drew a hypodermic syringe and needle. This was done with visible emotional stress. There were many unpleasant memories associated with the early painful experiences in the hospital.

7. *Conflicts, Illusions, and Hallucinations*

Conflicts may be produced experimentally, as may feelings of guilt and anxiety. Illusions, false perceptions, and both hypnotic and post-hypnotic hallucinations of various kinds can be suggested. However, even the experienced investigator had best explore these areas with great circumspection. The possibility of untoward psychologic consequences is considerable in this kind of experiment.

Instances have been observed in which these kinds of suggestions have led to various inimical psychologic and physiologic consequences. These can be serious. An instance is recalled in which an overenthusiastic resident continued such experiments against advice. There were some increasing hints of emotional disturbance, which should have served him as a P.S.F.* The subject of his experiments one day suddenly developed an acute and drastic exfoliative dermatitis of an emotional basis. Fortunately he recovered, although he became quite acutely ill. The experiments were discontinued.

Even though serious and sometimes dangerous in itself, this kind of inimical iatrogenically-produced Physiologic Conversion is likely to have fewer long-range repercussions than many of the less outwardly apparent emotional ones. These can be accompaniments or occur independently of functional disturbances.

H. COMMENTS ON HYPNOSIS IN THERAPY

1. *Disadvantages*

As a part of the average physician's armamentarium, hypnosis has not proved popular, nor has it secured widespread medical acceptance and use. This has resulted in large part from several factors noted earlier.

These include: (*a*) its limitations; (*b*) its selectivity; (*c*) the inherent dangers in the hands of the less experienced; (*d*) the somewhat unpredictable results; and (*e*) its unfortunate nonprofessional use for purposes of entertainment, or perhaps occasionally for still more questionable purposes. Several earlier comments are also pertinent here.

2. *Loss of Interest*

Although many if not most, psychiatrists become interested in or enthusiastic about hypnosis, usually at some point in their early training or experience, this interest seldom continues. Morse noted that this is often observed to take place during the course of the personal analysis of young psychiatrists.

Freud early worked extensively with hypnosis, but he abandoned it in favor of the free association of psychoanalysis. This had proven to be more uniformly effective in approaching the repressed material of the unconscious. The great majority of analysts ever since agree.

---

* Prognostic Signal Flag (P.S.F.): p. 505 and Ch.12:VA2.

3. Limited Use

Hypnosis enjoys professional use by a very limited number of psychiatrists. Of the more than 550 psychiatrists currently located in the Washington metropolitan area, for example, very few make even occasional use of hypnosis in therapy. Less than one in thirteen (13 of 172) responding to a survey conducted by the Washington Psychiatric Society, occasionally used hypnotism. Only one psychiatrist in six (28 of 172), even knew of another psychiatrist in the Washington area who employed hypnosis in practice. On the other hand, 69 (or two-fifths of the 172 respondents) reported that they had used hypnosis at least at one time.

In a few instances hypnosis has been used to considerable advantage by experts. The hypnotic investigation of dreams (actual, or hypnotically suggested) and of symptom function has appeared to be of value in reported cases. Rosen developed an interesting technique of "intensifying" or of "unmasking" an otherwise latent or hidden emotion while the subject is in a hypnotic trance. Recently he reported using hypnotically induced regression effectively in the treatment of a depressed patient.

Meares discussed the technique of hypnography — painting and drawing under hypnosis. The patient then is asked to produce associations to his work while still hypnotized. These and other techniques are subject to the same limitations and cautions as noted. Automatic writing is another technique sometimes utilized in hypnosis. Symptom substitution is sometimes possible, but has a number of inherent hazards. The encouragement of abreaction in relation to key figures can be useful as a pathway of emotional ventilation. In selected instances hypnotic suggestion can help to relieve pain, secure relaxation, and sometimes to reduce functional tension.

4. Inherent Appeal in Passive Role

Hypnosis has a considerable appeal to some persons because of the passive role required of them. How nice to relax, "sleep" a while, and have someone painlessly search out the pieces of the puzzle and reintegrate them. It would be nice indeed if such an easy pathway were possible, but it is not.

Investigative psychotherapy would be much less difficult and painful if the therapist took over the responsibility for the work, while the patient would be, in effect, anesthetized. Unfortunately, this cannot be.

For psychotherapy to be effective, the patient must be a willing and active collaborator. In effect, he must assist with the painful psychologic surgery which is necessary, without benefit of the anesthesia available in actual surgery. Even in cases in which the therapist can occasionally through hypnosis learn about the dynamics of the case, securing real acceptance and constructive use by the patient may prove no quicker or easier. Indeed, as noted earlier, this circumstance may become intolerably frustrating to the therapist.

5. Keep Within One's Depth

Hypnosis is by no means without its dangers. These cannot be fully covered here. However, the amateur hypnotist or novice invites possible serious psychologic sequelae in delving into mental mechanisms and processes beyond his understanding. Hypnosis is not a plaything. Its use should best be clearly restricted to the experienced and competent professional scientist, working in legitimate areas of therapy or research. *Case 149,* [Ch.12:VIIIB4] illustrates the Concept of the *Hazard of Symptom-Exchange.*

For the interested student there are many references available describing ways in which physicians have endeavored to use hypnosis in psychotherapy, or as an adjunct to various psychotherapeutic approaches. The would-be experimenter is urged to keep within his depth, and to proceed only with due caution and circumspection. The completion of psychiatric training well might be advocated professionally as a minimum prerequisite for attempting hypnotherapy.

6. Built-in Safeguard

It may be noted in closing that even with the most cooperative subject, there is usually retained by him a rather considerable degree of residual unconscious control. This continues to serve a protective function for the hypnotized subject. This is a built-in insurance and safeguard. This also helps to maintain certain limits of effectiveness for the process, and to maintain limits as to the degree of outside control which can be exercised by the operator. It further helps in general to insure the temporary nature of personality changes which are likely to be produced.

It is seldom possible to produce any quick or major changes in orientation, in attitudes, or in behavior which will become permanent. Ordinarily none of the basic personality structure can readily be altered in any substantial fashion through hypnotic suggestion.

XII. SELECTED REFERENCES AND BIBLIOGRAPHY

ABSE, D. W. (1959). "Hysteria." In *American Handbook of Psychiatry,* Vol. I, pp. 273–292. Ed. by S. Arieti. New York; Basic Books.

ADLER, M. H. and SECUNDA, L. (1947). "Indirect Technic to Induce Hypnosis." *J. nerv. ment. Dis.,* **106,** 190.

ALEXANDER, L. (1953). "The Effect of Electroshock on a Normal Person Under Recent Stress." *Am. J. Psychiat.,* **109,** 696.

AMERICAN MEDICAL ASSOCIATION (1952). *Standard Nomenclature of Diseases and Operations,* 4th ed. Philadelphia; Blakiston.

ARLOW, JACOB A. (1959). "The Structure of the *Deja Vu* Experience." *J. Am. psychoanal. Ass.,* **7,** 611.

BARBER, T. X. (1961). "Antisocial and Criminal Acts Induced by Hypnosis." *Hypnosis,* **5,** 301.

BERMAN, L. (1948). "Depersonalization and the Body Ego with Special Reference to Genital Representation." *Psychoanal. Q.,* **17,** 433.

BERNHEIM, H. (1886). *De la Suggestion et ses Applications a la Therapeutique.* Paris; Octave Doin.

BERRINGTON, W. P., LIDDELL, D. W., and FOULDS, G. A. (1956). "A Re-evaluation of the Fugue. *J. ment. Sci.*, **102**, 280.

BRENMAN, M. and GILL, M. M. (1947). *Hypnotherapy.* New York; International Universities Press.

— and REICHARD, S. (1943). "Use of Rorschach Test in Prediction of Hypnotizability." *Bull. Menninger Clin.,* **7**, 182.

— (1942). "Experiments in Hypnotic Production of Antisocial and Self-Injurious Behavior." *Psychiatry,* **5**, 49.

BRIERLEY, M. (1953). Personal communication.

— (1951). *Trends in Psychoanalysis.* London; Hogarth Press.

CANNON, A. (1951). "Some Ancient Methods of Hypnotism." *Med. Wld, Lond.,* **74**, 348.

CHALMERS, R. and LELAND, T. W. (1962). "Amnesia and Memory." In *Traumatic Medicine and Surgery for the Attorney,* Vol. 6 (Laughlin, H. P., Section Editor). Ed. by P. D. Cantor. Washington; Butterworth.

CHRISTENSON, J. A. (1949). "Dynamics in Hypnotic Induction." *Psychiatry,* **12**, 37.

CONN, J. H. (1956). "Medical Hypnosis." *Penn. med. J.,* **59**, 1156.

COOPER, L. R. (1948). "Time Distortion in Hypnosis." *Bull. Georgetown Univ. med. Cent.,* **1**, 214.

— and ERICKSON, M. H. (1950). "Time Distortion in Hypnosis." *Ibid.,* **4**, 50.

— (1955). *Time Distortion in Hypnosis.* Baltimore; Williams and Wilkins.

DeMARTINO, M. E., Ed. (1959). *Dreams and Personality Dynamics.* Springfield, Ill.; Thomas.

Diagnostic and Statistical Nomenclature (1952). Washington; American Psychiatric Association.

DRIBBEN, I. S. (1949). "Psychosis Following Amateur Hypnosis, a Case Report." *Milit. Surg.,* **104**, 136.

ERICKSON, M. H. (1939). "Experimental Investigations of Possible Antisocial Acts." *Psychiatry,* **2**, 391.

— (1932). "Possible Detrimental Effects of Experimental Hypnosis." *J. abnorm. soc. Psychol.,* **27**, 321.

FARBER, L. H. and FISHER, C. (1943). "An Experimental Approach to Dream Psychology Through the Use of Hypnosis." *Psychoanal. Q.,* **12**, 202.

FEDERN, P. (1952). *Ego Psychology and the Psychoses,* pp. 241–261. New York; Basic Books.

FENICHEL, O. (1945). *The Psychoanalytic Theory of Neurosis.* New York; Norton.

FISHER, C. (1945). "Amnesic States in War Neuroses: The Psychogenesis of Fugues." *Psychoanal. Q.,* **14**, 437.

— and JOSEPH, E. D. (1949). "Fugue with Awareness of Loss of Personal Identity." *Ibid.,* **18**, 480.

— and DEMENT, W. C. (1963). "Studies on the Psychopathology of Sleep and Dreams." *Am. J. Psychiat.,* **119**, 1160.

FREUD, S. (1933). *The Interpretation of Dreams.* New York; Macmillan.

— (1950). "A Note on the Unconscious in Psychoanalysis." In *Collected Papers,* Vol. 3, p. 23. London; Hogarth.

— (1950). *Ibid.,* Vol. 1, pp. 22–35, 253.

— (1946). "Hypnotism and Suggestion." *Int. J. Psychoanalysis,* **27**, 59.

GALDSTON, I. (1947). "On the Etiology of Depersonalization." *J. nerv. ment. Dis.,* **105**, 25.

GERSON, H. J. and VICTOROFF, V. M. (1948). Experimental Investigation into Validity of Confessions Obtained Under Sodium Amytal." *J. clin. Psychopath.,* **9**, 354.

GILL, M. M. and BRENMAN, M. (1959). *Hypnosis and Related States.* New York; International Universities Press.

GOSLINER, B. J. (1954). Personal communication.

GUTHEIL, E. (1930). "Depersonalization." *Psychoanal. Rev.,* **17**, 26.

GUTTMANN, E. and MacKAY, W. S. (1936). "Mescaline and Depersonalization." *J. Neurol. Psychopath.,* **16**, 193.

HAZLITT, WILLIAM: *On Dreams.*

HEATH, R. B. (1954). Personal communication.

HOFMAN-BANG, A. (1946). "Complications and Dangers in Use of Hypnotism. Brief Survey." *Acta psychiat. neurol. scand.,* **21**, 365.

JACOBSON, A. *et al.* (1965). "Somnambulism: All-night Electroencephalographic Studies." *Science,* **148**, 975.

JACOBSEN, EDITH (1959). "Depersonalization." *J. Am. psychoanal. Ass.,* **7**, 581.

JAMES, W. (1890). *The Principles of Psychology,* Vol. 1, p. 210. New York; Henry Holt.

JANET, P. (1903). *Les Obsessions et la Psychasthenie.* Paris.

— (1908). *Le Sentiment de Depersonalization*. Paris.

JONES, R. O. (1954). Personal communication.

KAPLAN, EUGENE A. (1960). "Hypnosis and Pain." *Archs gen. Psychiat.*, **2**, 567.

KAPLAN, H. A. and BROWDER, J. (1954). "Observations on the Clinical and Brain Wave Patterns in Professional Boxers." *J. Am. med. Ass.*, **156**, 1138.

KIERSCH, T. A. (1962). "Amnesia: A Clinical Study of Ninety-Eight Cases." *Am. J. Psychiat.*, **119**, 57.

KIRSHABER, M. (1873). *De la Nevropathie Cerebrocardiaque*. Paris.

LANGE, J. (1927). *Kraepelin-Lange, Psychaitrie*, Vol. 1.

LAUGHLIN, H. P., Ed. (1955). *A Psychiatric Glossary*. 5th rev. ed. Washington; American Psychiatric Association.

— (1955). *The Psychoneuroses*. Section 6. Mimeo. Washington, George Washington Medical School.

— (1953). "The Dissociative Reactions." *Med. Ann. Distr. Columbia*, **22**, 541.

— (1953). "Research in Sleep Deprivation and Exhaustion." *Int. Rec. Med.*, **166**, 305.

—. "The Present Status of Hypnosis" (including a review of the literature and bibliography). Unpublished data.

—, Ed. (1953). *Directory of Psychiatrists and Clinical Psychiatric Facilities in the Washington Area*, 4th ed. Washington, Washington Psychiatric Society.

— (1963). *Mental Mechanisms*, pp. 27–75. Washington; Butterworth.

— and RUFFIN, M. DEG. (1953). *An Outline of Dynamic Psychiatry*, 4th rev. mimeo, p. 191. Washington; George Washington University Medical School.

LEBENSOHN, Z. M. (1953). "The Truth About 'Truth Serum'." Editorial. *Med. Ann. Distr. Columbia*, **22**, 194.

LIPTON, S. (1943). "Dissociated Personality: A Case Report." *Psychiat. Q.*, **17**, 35.

MACDONALD, J. M. (1954). "Narcoanalysis and Criminal Law." *Am. J. Psychiat.*, **111**, 283.

LIEF, HAROLD I. (1954). Personal communication.

MARTLAND, H. S. (1928). "Punch Drunk." *J. Am. med. Ass.*, **91**, 1103.

MASSERMAN, J. H. (1946). *Principles of Dynamic Psychiatry*, pp. 33–35. Philadelphia; Saunders.

MATTHEWS, J. H. (1950). "Narco-analysis for Criminal Interrogation. Preliminary Report." *Lancet*, **70**, 283.

MAYER-GROSS, W. (1935). "On Depersonalization." *Br. J. med. Psychol.*, **15**, 103.

MEARES, A. (1954). "Hypnography—a Technique in Hypoanalysis." *J. ment. Sci.*, **100**, 965.

— (1955). "Anxiety Reactions in Hypnosis." *Br. med. J.*, **1**, 1454.

MENNINGER, K. A. (1930). *The Human Mind*, p. 234. Garden City (N.J.); Garden City Publishing Co.

MESMER, F. A. (1779). *Memoire sur la Decouverte du Magnetisme Animal*. Paris; Didot.

MEYER, M. A. (1944). "Dream Mechanisms and Interpretations." In *Psychoanalysis Today*. Ed. by S. Lorand. New York; International Universities Press.

MONROE, RUTH L. (1955). *Schools of Psychoanalytic Thought*, p. 54. New York; Holt, Rinehart, and Winston.

MORGENSTERN, S. (1931). "Psychoanalytic Conception of Depersonalization." *J. nerv. ment. Dis.*, **73**, 164.

MORSE, R. T. (1953). Personal communication.

NUNBERG, H. (1959). *Practice and Theory of Psychoanalysis*, pp. 60–74. New York; Nervous and Mental Disease Monographs.

OBERNDORF, C. P. (1936). "Feeling of Unreality." *Archs Neurol. Psychiat.*, *Chicago*, **36**, 322.

— (1934). "Depersonalization in Relation to Erotization of Thought." *Int. J. Psycho-Analysis*, **15**, 271.

ORNE, M. T. (1962). "Implications for Psychotherapy Derived from Current Research on the Nature of Hypnosis." *Am. J. Psychiat.*, **118**, 1097.

PATTEN, E. R. (1930). "Duration of Post-hypnotic Suggestion." *J. abnorm. Psych.*, **25**, 319.

PLUTARCH: *Of Superstition*.

PRINCE, M. (1905). *The Dissociation of a Personality*. New York; Longmans.

POLLOCK, ROBERT W. (1963). *Grandfather, Chief Joseph, and Psychodynamics*. Baker, Ore.; (private).

ROSEN, H. (1955). "The Reconstruction of a Traumatic Childhood Event in a Case of Depersonalization." *J. Am. psychoana. Ass.*, **3**, 211.

— (1953). *Hypnotherapy in Clinical Psychiatry.* New York; Julian Press.

— (1954). "Dehypnosis and Its Problems." *Br. J. med. Hypnot.,* (Spring).

— (1952). "The Hypnotic and Hypnotherapeutic Unmasking, Intensification and Recognition of an Emotion." *Am. J. Psychiat.,* **109**, 120.

— (1955). "Regression Hypnotherapeutically Induced as an Emergency Measure in a Suicidally Depressed Patient." *J. clin. exp. Hypnosis,* **3**, 58.

— and ERICKSON, M. H. (1954). "The Hypnotic and Hypnotherapeutic Investigation and Determination of Symptom-function." *Ibid.,* **2**, 201.

ROYAL COMMISSIONERS OF THE FACULTY OF MEDICINE AND THE ACADEMY OF SCIENCES (1784). *Examination of Animal Magnetism.* Paris; Bailey.

SARBIN, T. R. and MADOW, L. W. (1942). "Predicting Depth of Hypnosis by Means of Rorschach Test." *Am. J. Orthopsychiat.,* **12**, 268.

SARGANT, W. and FRAZER, R. (1938). "Inducing Light Hypnosis by Hyperventilation." *Lancet,* **2**, 778.

SAVAGE, CHARLES (1954). Personal communication.

— (1955). "Variations in Ego Feeling Induced by D-lysergic Acid Diethylamide (LSD-25)." *Psychoanal. Rev.,* **42**, 1.

SEARLES, H. F. (1932). "Note on Depersonalization." *Int. J. Psycho-Analysis,* **13**, 345.

SEITZ, P. F. D. (1953). "Experiments in the Substitution of Symptoms by Hypnosis." *Psychosom. Med.,* **15**, 405.

THIGPEN, C. H. and CLECKLEY, H. M. (1957). *The Three Faces of Eve.* New York; McGraw-Hill.

TROSRAN, H. (1963). "Dream Research and Psychoanalytic Theory of Dreams." *Archs gen. Psychiat.,* **9**, 27.

WAGNER, F. F. (1951). "Hypnotic Induction by Means of Folding Hands." *Acta psychiat. neurol. scand.,* **26**, 91.

WEINSTEIN, E. A., MARVIN, S. L., and KELLER, N. J. A. (1962). "Amnesia as a Language Pattern." *Archs gen. Psychiat.,* **6**, 259.

WEITZENHOFFER, A. M. (1953). *Hypnotism: An Objective Study in Suggestibility.* New York; Wiley.

— (1950). "A Note on the Persistence of Hypnotic Suggestion." *J. abnorm. Psychol.,* **45**, 160.

— (1957). *General Techniques of Hypnosis.* New York; Grune.

WELLS, W. R. (1941). "Experiments in Hypnotic Production of Crime." *J. Psychol.,* **11**, 63.

WHOLEY, C. A. (1925). "A Case of Multiple Personality." *Psychoanal. Rev.,* **13**, 1.

WITTELS, F. (1940). "Psychology and Treatment of Depersonalization." *Psychoanal. Rev.,* **27**, 57.

XIII. REVIEW QUESTIONS FOR THE DISSOCIATIVE REACTIONS

A. On Dissociation

1. How are opportunities restricted for professional familiarity with the Dissociative Reactions?

2. What is the intent of the "Conspiracy of Silence", in memory gaps?

3. Discuss Fragmental Dissociation.

4. List and outline the significance of four additional major types of dissociation.

5. Explain: (*a*) Emotional Deferment; (*b*) Compartmentalization, and (*c*) their defensive aims.

6. What are the relationships of Conversion and Dissociation? What is meant by *the part reaction* in conversion, *vs. the reaction of the whole* in dissociation?

B. On Dreams and Somnambulism

1. Discuss the functions of the dream and dreaming.

2. What is meant by the *Hypothesis of the Dream's Contribution to Emotional Health?*

3. (*a*) Outline eight of the major precepts operative in dreams;

(b) In relation to dreams, what is meant by:
  (1) "fast time"?
  (2) Geometric Principle of reinforcement of associations?
  (3) Nocturnal Fantasy?

4. What is meant by the Individuality of Symbolism, in dreams?

5. Discuss somnambulism. How does it relate to dreams?

6. A mother consults you about two instances of somnambulism in her twelve-year-old boy. What information would you seek? What could you supply?

7. What is the significance of the *Rule of Individual Symbolism* in Dream Interpretation?

C. On Depersonalization

1. Distinguish personal and environmental depersonalization; *déjà vu*. What is the *Concept of Affective Escape Routes?* How does depersonalization fit in?

2. What is the incidence of depersonalization? Cite three instances.

3. Explain how feelings of unreality can follow both exposure to stress and danger, and achieving a safe position.

4. List ten sources of depersonalization feelings.

5. Discuss a person's alarm in response to experiencing feelings of unreality.

6. What is meant by depersonalization being (a) a "minor fugue"; (b) a "symbolic escape"; (c) a psychologic flight. What are the relationships of depersonalization and identification?

D. On Fainting

1. What is fainting? What is its defensive intent? Why do people faint?

2. What is *emotional contagion?* What is the *Ostrich Concept?*

3. Discuss the factors in the probable decrease in frequency of fainting.

E. On Amnesia

1. Distinguish *Organic Amnesia* from *Psychologic Amnesia*.

2. List and define six types of Amnesia.

3. In Amnesia, what is the role of: (a) concussion; (b) alcohol; (c) age; (d) emotional conflict?

4. What is the intended defense of Amnesia? How is it self-defeating?

5. Discuss memory and electroshock.

6. What is the relation of Amnesia to the Fugue State?

7. What clinical findings might distinguish an instance of *Traumatic Encephalopathy?* What is the *Precept of Cumulative Trauma* in its etiology?

8. What is meant by *psychic selectivity* in post-shock areas of memory loss?

9. What does Deep Treatment infer?

F. On Fugue States

1. How is the Fugue State both a figurative and a literal flight?

2. Why might one refer to the Fugue State as "daytime somnambulism"? Are there advantages in so doing?

3. Delineate two types of Fugue States.

4. How would you distinguish a psychotic reaction from a Fugue State?

5. What is the *Precept of Inverse Anxiety-Symptom Ratio?* the *Inverse Anxiety-Psychosis Ratio?*

6. Discuss the unconscious meanings of the fugue. How can one make an analogy of its onset to the *"Peg Concept"* in the phobia?

G. On Alternating Personality

1. What is Alternating or Multiple Personality.

2. Why are such cases intriguing? Why are they rare?
3. Explain their onset.

H. On the Dissociation of Automaticity and Automatic Behavior

1. What is the *Dissociation of Automaticity?* Illustrate.
2. What are its benefits? Its hazards?
3. What is Automatic Behavior?
4. Discuss the uses of Automatic Writing.

I. On Hypnosis

1. Define Hypnosis.
2. What have been its origins and its role in medicine?
3. Discuss resynthesis following hypnosis.
4. Discuss hypnotizability, and selectivity for the subject. What determines a good subject? What is the *Principle of Correlation of Youth and Hypnotizability?*
5. Additional questions: (*a*) Why is "truth serum" a misnomer? (*b*) What is the *Concept of Psychic Pressures in Confessions?* (*c*) Can a hypnotized person be induced to act against his conscience or society? Explain. (*d*) Outline research possibilities in hypnosis. (*e*) Discuss hypnosis as an adjunct to psychotherapy.
6. Outline: (*a*) The cautions in the use of hypnosis. (*b*) The disadvantages of hypnosis in medical and psychiatric treatment.

CHAPTER 14

THE NEUROSES FOLLOWING TRAUMA

*.... A Group of Neurotic Reactions
the Onset of which Follows Trauma*

I. TRAUMA AND NEUROSIS

A. A Group of Neurotic Reactions

1. Terminology; The Traumatic Reactions; 2. Relation to Trauma; 3. Psychic Trauma Antecedent; Basic Drive Toward Emotional Health Concept

B. All Emotional Illnesses Ultimately Traumatic

1. Consequences Beyond the Physical; 2. Flight-to-the-Physical Principle; Emotional Problems More Painful Than Physical Ones; 3. Specific Traumatic Events with Every Neurosis

C. Definitions

1. Trauma; 2. Neuroses Following Trauma

II. NOTES ON HISTORICAL BACKGROUND

A. Medical Renaissance Begins

1. Doctrine of Cause and Effect Holds out Promise of Solutions; 2. Oppenheim's Theory of Molecular Change

B. Emotions and Physiology

1. William Beaumont; Observations a Medical Milestone; 2. Psychic Origin of Symptoms Established; 3. Ivan P. Pavlov and Walter B. Cannon

C. Increasing Understanding

1. Concepts of Physical Etiology Die Hard; 2. Every Symptom and Every Neurosis a Part of the T.R.C.

III. INCIDENCE AND PREVALENCE

A. Reliance on Estimation

1. Need for Specific Standards; 2. Instances Not Rare; 3. Numerical Estimates

B. Factors Influencing Long-Range Trends in "Popularity" of Neurotic Reactions

1. Cultural Influences on Neurotic Patterns of Reaction; Transparency Theory; 2. Principle of Symptom-Survival: Conflict Resolution Relieves Symptoms

IV. MAKING THE DIAGNOSIS

A. Relation to Traumatic Event

1. Diagnosis Made on Descriptive Basis; 2. Importance of the Outstanding Clinical Feature; 3. Assessing Role of Trauma

B. Important Points in Diagnosis of Neuroses Following Trauma

1. Six Considerations; 2. Principle of Hidden-Determinants; Peg Concept

C. Any Kind of Clinical Picture May Follow Trauma

V. SYMPTOMS AND CLINICAL FEATURES

A. Events in a "Typical Case"

1. The Part Played by Injury; The Traumatic Discrepancy; 2. Concepts of Gain: Epigain and Endogain Versus Malingering

B. Symptoms Legion
   1. Anxiety Reactions Following Trauma; 2. Concept of the Functional-Structural Progression; 3. Anxiety, Hygeia-phrontic, and Conversion Reactions More Frequent

C. Three of the More Rare Post-traumatic Syndromes
   1. Symptoms Out of Proportion to the Injury; 2. The Dissociative Reactions; Concept of Overall Language; 3. The Obsessive Reaction; 4. The Phobic Reaction; 5. Basic Concepts in Neuroses Following Trauma; 6. The Post-traumatic Dream; Desensitizing Purpose Concept

D. Marked Variation in Response to Trauma
   1. Rule of Non-Proportionate Response; 2. Total Individual Response to Crisis and Trauma; the T.R.C. and T.R.T.: Compliant-Resignation-Response to Death; 3. Contrasting Responses to Trauma and Stress; Final Straw Concept; 4. Contrasting Vulnerability to Trauma May Reflect Parental Attitudes

E. The Trauma and Its Effects; Time-Lags; E.I.D.
   1. Effects of Trauma Deferred; 2. Time-Lag in Concussion; 3. Time-Lags in Crisis and Trauma: E.I.D.; 4. Part of Total Reaction to Crisis; 5. Cool Head Versus Panic

F. Physiologic Changes in Stress

VI. PSYCHODYNAMICS AND PATHOGENESIS

A. Favorable Psychologic Soil
   1. Special Individual Significance; 2. Ability to Cope with Trauma; Favorable Psychologic Soil Concept; 3. Freud's Contributions; 4. Need to Suffer; Remission - Following - Trauma

B. Severe Neurosis Follows Psychologically Traumatic Event
   1. Psychogenetic Principles Illustrated; 2. Significant Antecedents Determine Reaction

C. On Gains and Mechanics
   1. Epigain and Endogain; 2. Common Defenses Against Prospect of Danger; 3. Regression

D. In Conclusion
   1. Complex Subject; 2. Many Psychodynamic Components; 3. Broad View of Trauma Useful

VII. COMPENSATION AND NEUROSIS

A. Evaluation of Claims Difficult

B. Industrial Compensation Case
   1. Problems in Management; 2. Compensation Neuroses; 3. Evaluating Emotional Difficulties

C. Unrewarding and Unpopular Work
   1. Sufferer Penalized; 2. Lack of Organic Explanation Frustrating; 3. Psychiatrist's Position

D. Instances of Emotional Disability Following Trauma

E. Notes on Therapy: Principle of Symptom-Longevity
   1. Need for Public Education; 2. Joint-Endeavor Principle in Psychotherapy; 3. Promptness Valuable; 4. Factors in Prognosis and Response to Therapy

VIII. TREATMENT

A. Importance of Promptness
   1. Prognosis Progressively Gloomier with Passage of Time; 2. Dependency Position Secured

B. The Secondary Defense
   1. Guarding the Status Quo of the Neurosis; The "Balanced Neurotic Position"; 2. Resistance Protectively Intended; 3. Understanding and Insight Needed; Phases of "Initial Decline" and "Initial Remission" in Therapy

C. Comments on Prognosis
   1. The Epigain and Prognosis; 2. The Theory of Antecedent Conflicts; 3. Potentials of Thorough, Completed "Deep Treatment"; 4. Treatment in Acute Cases

D. Goals of Psychotherapy

IX. SUMMARY AND CONCLUSIONS

A. Introduction
   1. Trauma and Neurosis; 2. Oppenheim, Beaumont, Charcot, Pavlov, and Cannon; 3. T.R.C. and T.R.T.; 4. Cultural Influences; 5. Distinguished by the Sharpness of the Trauma

B. Clinical Features
   1. Typical Course; 2. Epigain and Endogain; 3. Everyone Has a Breaking Point

C. Psychogenesis
   1. Psychologic Defenses with Trauma; 2. Recapitulation of Antecedent Conflicts; 3. Compensation and Neuroses

D. Therapy
   1. Active Participation Required; 2. Resistance Part of Secondary Defense

X. SELECTED REFERENCES AND BIBLIOGRAPHY

XI. REVIEW QUESTIONS ON THE NEUROSES FOLLOWING TRAUMA

I. TRAUMA AND NEUROSIS

A. A GROUP OF NEUROTIC REACTIONS

1. Terminology; the Traumatic Reactions

THIS chapter is concerned with a rather heterogeneous group of neurotic reactions. These might perhaps be included together for purposes of discussion under the generic classification of Traumatic Neuroses; or perhaps better and more consistent, the *Traumatic Reactions.* The term "traumatic neurosis" is a useful one, which was probably first used by Oppenheim, a German neurologist, only about a hundred years ago. At times it has been fairly well accepted in medicine. There are several reasons, however, why this chapter is entitled instead The Neuroses Following Trauma.

First, this title emphasizes that we are dealing with a *group* of neurotic reactions. *Second,* through the years medical opinion has varied as to just which reactions should be properly considered as traumatic neuroses. Perhaps a specific and limited category will gradually evolve as a generally agreed upon kind of diagnostic entity. Currently this is not the case. *Third,* this latter situation is reflected by the fact that traumatic neurosis has yet to be accorded a separate niche in the official diagnostic and statistical nomenclatures of the American Medical Association and the American Psychiatric Association. *Fourth,* the scientific literature reflects a lack of concurrence of professional views. Authorities use various diagnostic terms for the large group of Neuroses Following Trauma and its members. Different terms are occasionally used to describe similar or overlapping clinical reactions. *Finally,* the clinical pattern of neurotic symptoms which can occur post-traumatically is great. Although some types of emotional symptoms occur rather rarely, actually every kind of neurotic feature can follow trauma. For these reasons, it has seemed preferable for the present to entitle our discussion the Neuroses Following Trauma. The term Traumatic Reactions is proposed for these clinical phenomena, as a category in line with those we employ for the other patterns of neurotic reaction.

2. Relation to Trauma

Some types of neurosis have a closer link with trauma than others, but any type of neurotic reaction may be related to trauma. Anxiety, Hygeiaphrontic (hypochondriacal) and Conversion Reactions are the most frequently encountered specific emotional patterns of reaction to trauma in civilian life. Anxiety Reactions can include occasional A.A.A. [p. 89] or A.T.S. [pp. 98 and 167] and Anxiety Neuroses [pp. 104*ff*]. The trauma can be physical, psychic, or a combination of both. It may be major or minor, and its role can vary widely in the onset of emotional symptoms. Thus the trauma can initiate, precipitate, contribute to, or aggravate a neurosis. The onset of symptoms can follow the trauma immediately or can be delayed for a considerable period. Most Traumatic Neuroses are what we have earlier termed *symptom neuroses.* Some are more primitive and some more advanced in accord with our Concept of Primitive *vs.* More Advanced Defenses and Reactions.

The effect of a given trauma will vary widely from person to person and is largely unpredictable. When the trauma is physical the resulting disability is sometimes seen to be disproportionate to the physical injury. The acuity or repetition, or both, of the trauma are also factors that have to be considered. Occasionally, emotional manifestations may undergo remission after trauma.

3. Psychic Trauma Antecedent; Basic Drive Toward Emotional Health Concept

Psychologic traumas in early childhood can often lay the foundation for later emotional illnesses. As important antecedents, such events can contribute to the vulnerability of the individual to later physical or psychologic stress; though alternatively they may lead to the development of more effective emotional defenses.

This latter alternative is in accord with an important and more optimistic principle of a *Basic Drive Toward Emotional Health.* According to this concept, other factors being equal, the individual's emotional health ordinarily tends to improve (or recover). Of related interest, we earlier noted through the term and conception of constructive anxiety [pp. 12, 41, and 119] that the effects of anxiety can subserve individually and socially useful purposes. They are not necessarily destructive.

The neuroses following trauma may find expression in a wide variety of symptoms which can:

(*a*) be emotionally or physically disabling in varying measure; (*b*) increase the susceptibility of the patient to repeated trauma; (*c*) interfere with one's effectiveness or completely prevent working; and (*d*) limit one's satisfactions in living.

B. ALL EMOTIONAL ILLNESSES ULTIMATELY TRAUMATIC

1. Consequences Beyond the Physical

We have long known that certain relationships existed between the neuroses and trauma. Their exact nature and importance, however, has been far from being universally appreciated. In the course of the last several decades there has been a useful accumulation of data. Not only have we gained more knowledge, but in addition there has been considerable further integration and organization of this knowledge. As a consequence, our present discussion concerning this important area in medicine and in psychiatry can be better synthesized and more authoritative than earlier possible.

It has been widely recognized by most people of course that both physical and psychologic trauma can and do have far-reaching effects upon the human economy. A smaller group perhaps has also recognized that the disability and the consequences which often follow traumatic events are frequently observed to extend far and away beyond any demonstrable physical impairments alone. Such disabilities are on an emotional basis. This, however, makes them no less real. Handicaps and disabilities which are emotionally based are at least as real and as troubling to the hard-pressed and unwitting victim as are physical ones. In some ways they are infinitely more so, since one has less control or understanding; one is thus more helpless and less able to cope with them effectively. Because of this, they are likely to be even more troubling, sometimes far more so. The consequence can be an acute Emotional Decompensation [pp. 48 and 159].

These very basic truths are still not clearly recognized by all physicians. Psychiatrists more commonly recognize them. They also have major implications for legal medicine. Their impact in this important area is beginning to have some effects. One might guess that this impact is likely to increase substantially in the next twenty years or so.

2. Flight-to-the-Physical Principle; Emotional Problems More Painful Than Physical Ones

In accord with the foregoing, when one begins to study the field of emotional problems, he is likely to learn rather quickly and with great weight that emotional problems are apt to be more painful, to be more troubling, and to be more disturbing than physical ones. For example, every physician can report instances in which a patient will try — sometimes with great effort and seemingly endlessly — to discover physical bases for symptoms which are essentially emotional in origin. The uncovering of such more tangible bases and less disturbing ones would appear to him to represent a great gain. The patient-victim would thus be less helpless in having something done, in seeking relief. He could also thereby presumably avoid the exploration of emotional areas which he may well fear as being possibly quite painful.

Emotional problems are also likely to be far more complex in so far as effecting their resolution, than are physical ones. It is indeed rare, on the other hand, to have a patient with physical symptoms seek to assign to them an emotional or psychologic origin. The foregoing discussion is quite in accord with the phenomenon earlier named for convenience the Flight to the Physical [pp. 46, 707].

3. Specific Traumatic Events with Every Neurosis

A. PRINCIPLE OF PREDETERMINED VULNERABILITY.—In the broadest sense, all emotional illnesses are ultimately traumatic in origin. From this viewpoint, the trauma is psychologic, or physical, or both. As noted, early psychic trauma may lay the foundation for later emotional illness. The effects may remain latent, contributing however, to later vulnerability to either physical or psychologic events, which then serve as precipitating factors. Specific traumatic events of a psychologic nature are uncovered with the definitive psychotherapy of every case of neurosis. These may be major or minor. They may be single or multiple. Their contribution to the genesis of a given such illness may be little or great. This vulnerability is usually determined long in advance. This is in accord with what for convenience we might refer to as the *Principle of Predetermined Vulnerability*. It applies to most if not all neurotic reactions. This principle plays a role in our understanding the military and combat reactions, as outlined in the following Chapter 15.

These traumatic events will have contributed in varying degree to the development of the neurosis. On occasion immediate traumatic events may be of major importance. They may have served to precipitate an incipient or latent neurosis. In other instances they may be regarded rather as aggravating an existing emotional situation which was already unstable.

In the ensuing discussion this very broad conception will not, of course, be followed. The margins, however, will be kept fairly broad. In general, all those neurotic situations will be included in which the major significance is attached by the patient, by the physician, or by both, to immediately preceding trauma. Neuroses Following Trauma will therefore be considered to include these kinds of neurotic reactions without regard to their specific clinical manifestations, type, or combination.

B. ROLE OF TRAUMATIC EVENTS EMPHASIZED.—The major factor in common for this group of neurotic reactions accordingly will be that the clinical onset follows trauma. It might be further noted that the actual amount of initiating physical injury or trauma, particularly, can vary all the way from major to minor and, for all practical purposes, almost to the nonexistent. Likewise, the time of onset of symptoms following the trauma can vary from immediately, to a separation by a considerable period of time. It is indeed clear that the role of trauma in a given neurotic reaction can vary widely.

This chapter has been written to help emphasize the role which traumatic events, whether psychic or physical, can play in the initiation of various neurotic patterns of reaction. Perhaps it should be titled to more closely reflect this. Trauma can have a precipitating role in the onset of symptoms. It can also help perpetuate such a pattern once established. We shall first consider some aspects of trauma and its relation to the various patterns of neurosis. A short section on Compensation and Neurosis has been included. Also included as Related Subjects of Importance are some brief comments on the Combat Reactions, and on Prisoner Processing (Brainwashing) in the following chapter. These have been assigned separate chapter consideration in acknowledgment of their importance and to secure them an increased emphasis. Otherwise, however, the two chapters are intended to be considered together, as a unit.

C. DEFINITIONS

1. Trauma

Trauma is *injury*. The origin of the word is by direct carryover from the Greek word *trauma,* meaning wound. Trauma is *physical, or psychologic, or both. It may refer to the injury done, or to the condition which results.* A psychic trauma is *one which leaves some more or less lasting effect upon the individual and his adjustment.* Emotional and psychologic trauma can follow many diverse kinds of physically and psychically injurious events.

Observant people know that physical trauma can have the potential to precipitate disabilities which are essentially emotional and psychologic. As noted, these are often far beyond the amount of strictly physical handicap, which does not have to be present at all. Actually, the severity of these kinds of disabilities is not in direct proportion to the amount of physical impact or injury. Occasionally one can compare the relative severity of the sequella of emotional *versus* physical trauma. The relative severity of the emotional disability can be impressive. This is illustrated in the following instance and in [*Case 128,* p. 621]. The concurrent presence of traumatic *physical* injury with a significant measure of *emotional* symptomatology or overlay comprises an *emotional-organic combination* or E.O.C.

Case 173

Relative Severity of Emotional Disability

An eighteen-year-old boy was on a car trip with his father and a seventeen-year-old cousin. Another car pulled into their path from a side road. In the ensuing serious collision both vehicles were demolished. The driver of the other car was killed. The father was injured seriously, and his son suffered a concussion with unconsciousness * and multiple fractures. The cousin, however, was *physically* unhurt; he "miraculously escaped without a scratch", according to the newspaper accounts.

However, let us look at these people ten or twelve weeks later. The father has recovered. His son's fractures have mended in excellent fashion with expert orthopedic care, and he is fine. The cousin, however, who "escaped without a scratch" seems a different person. He is constantly nervous and apprehensive and has lost weight. He suffers from nightmares and is too restless to read. He has been unable to resume his schoolwork, appears listless, unhappy, and his social adjustment has suffered greatly.

After six months he continues to be quite anxious about traveling or even leaving home. By dint of considerable effort he can sometimes get himself into a car, but is never comfortable. He has suffered several Acute Attacks of Anxiety, or Anxiety-Panic.

Still later — after one year — he continues to be nervous, and is somewhat pale, wan and underweight. The bloom of vigorous physical and emotional health which was present prior to the accident thus far has not returned. This unfortunate boy has developed chronic symptoms of an Anxiety Neurosis, precipitated by the accident.

2. Neuroses Following Trauma

The Neuroses Following Trauma are *a group of emotional illnesses or neurotic reactions having their onset following physical or acute psychic injury, or both.* They are *neurotic reactions which have been attributed to, or which follow a situational traumatic event, or a series of such events. The resulting emotional or physical consequences are highly variable in degree and in time of onset.* They include a wide variety of possible emo-

---

* *See* comments on Traumatic Amnesia, in Chapter 13.

tional responses and neurotic symptoms. These may be transient or permanent, single or multiple, and may appear immediately following a traumatic event or be delayed in their onset.

The principle members of this group when otherwise identified are Anxiety Reactions, Conversion Reactions, and Hygeiaphrontic Reactions. Also included as belonging within this group are a diverse group of entities with varying degrees of acceptance as to their delineation and terminology. These include accident neurosis, industrial neurosis, compensation neurosis and, stress reactions. At times, the military reactions and the consequences of prisoner processing [*see* Chapter 15], may be included as well.

In this large group of the Neuroses Following Trauma, thorough study of the pathogenesis will generally reveal in each case that the traumatic circumstances already have held some prior individually specific significance for the patient. This is in line with our Principle of Predetermined Vulnerability, as cited. In other words, the effect of any given trauma can have wide individual variation. This is due to the inherent personality make-up, and to unconscious factors and personal significances, which are individually specific. This view is also in accord with our Principle of the Individual Specificity of Emotional Defenses [pp. 14, 137, and 574].

II. NOTES ON HISTORICAL BACKGROUND

A. MEDICAL RENAISSANCE BEGINS

1. Doctrine of Cause and Effect Holds Out Promise of Solutions

A. SYMPTOMS IN ABSENCE OF OBVIOUS INJURY PUZZLING.—Dr. Herman Oppenheim (1858–1919), a German neurologist, early evolved a theory concerning the etiology of traumatic neurosis which for a time enjoyed wide acceptance. The onset of severe and disabling "nervous" symptoms following trauma had long been noted. The puzzling feature had been the frequent absence of evidence, or relatively minor extent, of any physical injury. The symptoms were severe and difficult to treat. They responded far more unpredictably and slowly than did those (more strictly physical) symptoms where the injury was physical and obvious. Treatment was sometimes pseudomagical or religious and suggestive, with relative success perhaps dependent upon our earlier [p. 646] identified Principle of Belief.

A broken leg or arm, with its attendant pain, loss of use, and possible subsequent limitations, was not difficult to understand, even though at times complex in nature. The onset, for example, of anesthesia and paralysis in an extremity following an injury in which there was no obvious (or remaining) physical damage, however, was another matter. This was indeed puzzling and troubling.

By the middle part of the nineteenth century science had advanced considerably. Increasing recognition of the relationship of cause and effect was influencing medical thought. What has been referred to earlier as the Medical Renaissance was under way. More was being learned about pathology and its role in the causation of disease. Cause came to be diligently sought after and studied, in order better to understand effect.

B. GOLDEN AGE FOR RESEARCH AND DISCOVERY.—In Neurology as in other medical fields the new science was applicable. These were fascinating and memorable decades, as more discoveries were made and medical knowledge expanded. Pathologic entities for a long time poorly understood, became better known. Doors to etiology never before known were opened wide. It seemed only a matter of time before all illnesses would yield their secrets to the microscope or to the x-ray tube, and so on. This was indeed a golden age in medical research and discovery. The new doctrine of cause and effect on a physical level held out endless promise.

Accordingly, it is hardly surprising that mental and emotional ills should be rather widely regarded and approached in the same ways which were proving so successful in the case of the physical ills. Might it not seem a safe assumption, that the cases of hysteria (conversion), melancholia (depression), and hypochondriasis (hygeiaphrontis) simply needed more study and research to uncover their obscure and puzzling, but certainly *physical* basis? If this did not occur soon, then perhaps one merely needed more careful study, new tests, instruments, or techniques. Just as the solutions as to their cause, pathology (and therefore their indicated treatment) were being successfully worked out for so many illnesses, the optimism engendered by these widespread advances led many of the medical scientists to expect the same kind of resolutions in areas which we include today under various headings such as functional illnesses, neuroses, and psychoses. These aims and hopes were to prove naive. Their lingering possessors were doomed to great disappointment and endless frustrations.

2. Oppenheim's Theory of Molecular Change

Oppenheim theorized that trauma led to nervous symptoms through its direct physical effects upon tissue in the central nervous system. In other words, his theory proposed that actual molecular changes took place in the central nervous system tissue as a consequence of the initiating trauma. Such changes therefore would of course be directly responsible for the symptoms which followed. While at no time could the changes as hypothecated be demonstrated, nevertheless many were understandably willing enough to accept this theory, and did so for at least several decades. It was quite well in keeping with the times and it offered what was then a seemingly credible solution for many otherwise most puzzling and knotty medical problems.

This theory has been discarded for a long time, but some of its adherents surrendered it only gradually and with pained reluctance. With time newer viewpoints have evolved. As researchers and scientists became increasingly able to accept the major role of emotion in illness, the death knell was sounded for the theories of those diehards who had continued to insist that a physical basis accounted for every symptom.

Today we know that emotional factors in and of themselves cause a host of illnesses. In addition, they can and frequently do influence, often substantially, the course of almost any illness, regardless of its basis.

B. EMOTIONS AND PHYSIOLOGY

1. William Beaumont; Observations a Medical Milestone

Sometimes when scientific discoveries are made they are not appreciated for a time, or perhaps their full significance requires a period of years or even decades for adequate recognition. Undoubtedly the present recognition of the role of emotions in health is one of the greatest advances which man has made in his tortuous climb from savagery. The full impact of all this still remains to be appreciated. Nonetheless, the early pioneers already have an historic position.

One of these was a then rather obscure medical officer in the U. S. Army named William Beaumont, who lived from 1785 to 1853. He had an active curiosity and interest which enabled him to make some most important observations on emotions and digestion. Despite a relative lack of interest or encouragement from others, practical difficulties, and a sometimes uncooperative and temperamental subject, Beaumont studied, recorded, and published findings which in retrospect are of ever increasing importance. They constitute a major milestone in medical progress.

In 1822 at a Mackinac Island tavern, a young French Canadian, Alexis St. Martin, was severely wounded by gunshot, accidentally. As a consequence, his chest, lung, and stomach lay open. Miraculously he lived. Upon "recovery" a persistent defect remained in his abdominal wall. This allowed the direct visualization into his stomach and part of its lining. Beaumont quickly recognized this as a most unique opportunity to study the physiology of digestion. He was able to observe changes in gastric activity and secretion under a variety of conditions. He learned that most of the significant environmental changes and emotional stimuli substantially influenced stomach function and digestion. These finds were most important. Published in a modest booklet in 1833, they created little stir at the time, however, in scientific circles. Indeed they received inadequate attention for many years. Herein was the first real demonstration of the vital relationships which exist between emotions and physiology. Medicine needed at least another fifty years to begin to appreciate at all properly the significance of these relationships.

Beaumont received his license to practice medicine in 1812, by apprenticeship in Vermont. In 1833, Columbia College, now George Washington University, in recognition of his professional achievements awarded him, at the age of 48 years, his only medical degree.

2. Psychic Origin of Symptoms Established

By the end of the nineteenth century a number of contributors had worked in related areas. Slowly and gradually, appreciation was increasing among a growing handful of physicians as to the importance of psychologic factors in the etiology of the neuroses and psychoses. Jean M. Charcot, the famous French clinician, was able successfully to reproduce experimentally for the first time conversion symptoms identical to those observed following trauma. Charcot, through suggestion under hypnosis, was able to bring on, and to resolve these symptoms. Thus, he was able to establish for the first time and beyond any doubt the completely psychic origin of various symptoms. This work in the final two decades of the last century was another important milestone in our gaining further knowledge about what could begin to be, with increasing accuracy, referred to as the psychogenic illnesses.

Among the many visitors who observed Charcot's demonstrations was Sigmund Freud, who was much impressed by what he observed. In 1893 Freud wrote that Charcot, together with his pupils, had successfully presented the case for the psychologic origins of hysteria (conversion), from their "research work concerning the nervous diseases following upon traumas — the traumatic neuroses." Freud went on to devote his life to the further unraveling of psychodynamic mysteries, making important contributions to many of our present-day concepts. He early recognized that the important aspect in the onset of emotional symptoms following trauma was that which was on the emotional side. The injury could be trifling from any resulting physical evidence. The emotions which were present around the time of the injury or trauma were the determining feature.

Stated another way, in a traumatic neurosis the psychic part of the trauma is far more important in the etiology of symptoms than is any physical trauma. A man might be riding in a car, be involved in a slight accident and suffer minor or even no physical ill-effects. Nonetheless, if there were enough fright, anxiety, or other unpleasant emotions stirred up by this event — if there was enough psychic trauma (as distinguished from physical trauma) — symptoms of a traumatic neurosis could ensue.

3. Ivan P. Pavlov and Walter B. Cannon

A. EMOTIONS INFLUENCE BODILY FUNCTIONS.—With the classic contributions of men such as Beaumont, Charcot, and Freud setting the pace, more scientists in the field of medicine and related sciences became interested in emotional factors in health and illness. Needless to say, there have been a host of other contributors since.

While it is not possible to include many of them in our current discussion, mention should be made of at least two: Ivan P. Pavlov (1849–1936), a Russian physiologist who introduced the very important concept of conditioning, and his friend Walter B. Cannon (1871–1945), an American who studied the effects of various emotional states such as fear, hunger, pain, and rage, on bodily functions, and produced an important series of papers reporting his work, over some twenty years, beginning in 1909 [p. 388]. Cannon recognized the emergency mobilization which the body undertakes as a preparation for flight or for fight. This is an important segment of one's T.R.C.

B. THE CONDITIONED REFLEX.—Pavlov studied the effects of repeated identical stimuli on animals and their responses. He found that a response which was originally quite appropriate to a given stimulus, could be induced to take place automatically, that is, without conscious volition, in reaction to a new but regularly associated stimulus which was in and of itself no longer necessarily appropriate. A response thus became *conditioned* to occur with the new stimulus alone, and in the absence of the original one with which it had been for a sufficient time associated. The new stimulus thus became quite thoroughly associated with, and equated to, the original one for the subject, through its repetition. In one oft-cited experiment a dog was offered food and at the same time a bell was rung. After sufficient repetition, the same salivary and gastric preparation for digestion occurred when the bell alone sounded. The two stimuli, food and bell, had become thoroughly associated, and in effect equated. Either could now elicit the same reflex responses.

From his experiments it became apparent that physiologic responses ordinarily considered to be of an automatic character could be modified, learned, or as Pavlov termed it, conditioned. This is the concept of the conditioned reflex, an important one for all students of behavior. By extension of this theory and its applications, similar kinds of conditioning can be observed to influence emotional response and patterns in men. Thus, also, one can find evidence of conditioned responses in neuroses. While these are often far more complex, many important and interesting applications exist. Pavlov's work was another pioneering step in our understanding of the importance of non-organic factors in illness. An untoward extension later led to the sinister development of Prisoner Processing, or brainwashing, which we will consider briefly later in Chapter 15.

C. INCREASING UNDERSTANDING

1. Concepts of Physical Etiology Die Hard

Concepts of a physical etiology for the Conversion Reactions and the other neuroses were gradually falling into discard, at least in some quarters. Old accepted theories, however, die hard. This was true despite this being hurried along by cogent observations concerning their underlying psychodynamics on the part of an increasing group of dynamically oriented psychotherapist investigators. These kinds of understandings gradually received wider circulation. This made the discard of earlier theories as to a physical etiology inevitable.

By 1940–1950, belief in the bases of underlying physical changes as accounting for emotional manifestations had largely died out, although there had been long-lingering adherents. These had continued to exert some influence.

2. Every Symptom and Every Neurosis a Part of the T.R.C.

Newer terms in the neuroses have tended to more accurately reflect the psychologic basis of the condition. This is also true with Combat Reactions, as opposed to "shell shock" or "blast syndrome." Their employment, together with the use of other more accurately descriptive terminology in the neuroses, also makes it more likely that we will keep in mind a concept of individual response; of reaction — psychic reaction to stress and trauma.

Accordingly, every neurosis, every Neurosis Following Trauma (or traumatic neurosis), and every psychogenic symptom is part of the total individual response. This is generally best regarded as a response to crisis, stress, or trauma. The sum total of one's responses may be healthy and constructive, or may be destructive, inefficient, and unhealthful, or some more complex combination of these. This brings us again to the useful concepts of the Total Individual Response to Crisis (T.R.C.) and the Total Individual Response to Trauma (T.R.T.) which we shall consider further shortly.

III. INCIDENCE AND PREVALENCE

A. RELIANCE ON ESTIMATION

1. Need for Specific Standards

Currently there are no accurate figures available which would give us reliable detailed information as to the occurrence and frequency of neuroses following trauma. We do not at this time have standards to compute morbidity rates. On the other hand, we do know that the incidence of neurotic reactions more generally is indeed high. A certain proportion of these — perhaps some 2–3 (possibly as many as 6) per cent — variable according to the criteria employed, could be classified as Neuroses Following Trauma.

Earlier it was stated that in the broadest sense all emotional illnesses (that is, all psychogenic mental and nervous disorders) could be considered as ultimately traumatic in origin. Occasionally, specific traumatic events of a physical nature, but more often psychologic, lay the foundations for the development of neurotic reactions. Their role in this regard, however, is far more readily appreciated in the more acute situations. A sudden, acute illness invites attention to the initiating or precipitating bases. In less dramatic situations the role of traumatic events may be just as important, but far less readily appreciated.

2. Instances Not Rare

In recent years more attention has been focused on the neuroses in general by a number of professional groups. While we very much lack precise figures, it would certainly appear that instances of neurosis following trauma are not rare. In addition, there are situations in which the careful observer is likely to encounter this kind of disability more frequently.

Thus, there are few people involved in serious accidents who do not suffer emotional sequelae of one type or another. Sometimes the consequences are slight and transient, sometimes not. Another group develops symptoms following a near accident or a "close shave." Finally, there are special types of emotional reactions following prolonged stress or danger such as are encountered in conditions of war, in which there may or may not be associated physical trauma.

3. Numerical Estimates

A conservative estimate as to the total number of persons with neurotic symptoms or character trait manifestations, or both, of sufficient moment to warrant a diagnosis of neurosis or character neurosis, would include at the very least 5–7 million persons in the United States of America. Estimates as to a percentage breakdown among the various separate categories have been made. According to these, the Conversion Reactions (16–20 per cent) thus very conservatively would number at least 0.85–1.4 million persons. Overconcern-With-Health, numbering perhaps 3–5 per cent, would include a minimum of 150–350 thousand individuals. Anxiety Reactions (12–15 per cent) would include 600–1,050 thousand. Neuroses Following Trauma (some 2–3 per cent of the total) would likely number at least 200–800 thousand, with many more cases, of course, in which traumatic factors have played an aggravating role of varying significance. Other types of neurotic reactions, less commonly related to trauma, make up the remaining percentages. These estimated numerical figures are considered quite conservative.

B. FACTORS INFLUENCING LONG-RANGE TRENDS IN "POPULARITY" OF NEUROTIC REACTIONS

1. Cultural Influences on Neurotic Patterns of Reaction; Transparency Theory

From any long-range perspective we must keep in mind that cultural and social trends influence the types of neuroses that develop and the likely course that they will follow. That is to say that the relative incidence of the various patterns of neurotic reaction are not static, but will tend to change and vary albeit very gradually, so as to reflect the cultural and social setting, the level of general acceptance, the understanding, and the evolving ability better to appreciate the underlying unconscious motivation of given symptoms and complexes [see also related discussion beginning on page 568].

Factors which are of particular importance in a given such setting are those of educational level and sophistication. Also included are general attitudes, beliefs, religious convictions, and prejudices of many kinds. While not widely appreciated, there is a considerable and continuing amount of pressure exerted by the relative amount of social acceptance which may be encountered in response to the possession of a given neurotic symptom or reaction*. Although this kind of influence is subtle and difficult to measure, it can nonetheless exert considerable effect from a long-range perspective on the kinds of symptoms which are more likely to be encountered.

---

* This is the *Theory of Transparency* in the social and cultural influences upon types and prevalence of emotional reactions [see also related discussion, pp. 661 and 707].

Accordingly, certain aspects of the underlying meaning of symptoms cannot be too apparent; *must not become too transparent* to the lay (or even professional) observer.

Elements of secondary gain in symptoms may be completely unconscious (epigain); their too ready appreciation by others further lessens, and downgrades the "usefulness" of the symptoms to their possessor. Among more sophisticated groups of people today the more gross kinds of conversion symptoms have become less common.

Today if one wishes to see examples of major conversion paralysis, blindness, convulsions, and so on, he will most likely seek them among the charity patients in the large municipal hospitals. Even here they are in considerably fewer numbers than a generation or so ago. Accounts from World War I describe wards full of such patients. While these cases were still encountered, and these more commonly among servicemen from the more "backward" rural areas in World War II, there were no such scenes. Indeed, the overall numbers of such cases in relation to emotional and psychiatric casualties generally made them relatively rare. Palpitation, other functional cardiac symptoms, gastrointestinal malfunctions, headaches and backache, for example, became far more frequent. They were also far more personally and socially acceptable.

This has been a brief discussion of a complex subject. It is in accord with the Transparency Theory. Neurotic symptoms are unconsciously determined. Still, they are influenced in many subtle ways as to their onset, form, and incidence, by unconscious, personal, social and other factors. If their bases were not unconscious, they would not evolve and develop as neurotic symptoms. They could not serve their unconsciously intended purposes.

2. Principle of Symptom-Survival: Conflict Resolution Relieves Symptoms

This concept ties in directly with certain important ones concerning treatment. At this point the reader might well surmise, and correctly so, that ordinarily *a given emotional symptom cannot survive the resolution of the underlying conflicts responsible.* This is the *Principle of Symptom-Survival* [*See also* p. 579. I would propose we so name it to invite increasing emphasis to a major principle in therapy].

In other words, working out the unconscious factors lying behind the symptom tends to secure its resolution. In order to survive, a symptom "cannot allow" the underlying motives and mechanisms to gain consciousness. The factors entering into symptom elaboration must remain buried and secret; that is, they must be maintained in the unconscious. It is small wonder that the emotional symptom — a defense in itself — is thereby in turn secondarily defended, in accord with our major *Concept of the Secondary Defense* of established symptoms.

Definitive therapy in psychiatry therefore aims at making the unconscious conscious. This is a direct application of our recognition of the foregoing important *Principle of Symptom-Survival.*

IV. MAKING THE DIAGNOSIS

A. RELATION TO TRAUMATIC EVENT

1. Diagnosis Made on Descriptive Basis

Beginning around the turn of the century, a trend slowly developed in psychiatry for the diagnosis of a given case to be made upon a descriptive basis. This is particularly true for the neuroses and for others of the non-psychotic conditions.

This trend continued and grew, until today the preponderance of diagnostic labels are descriptive. [See Table 3, p. 46]. This has been a useful development.

2. Importance of the Outstanding Clinical Feature

There have been two concurrent major trends in the terms used for diagnosis of the neuroses during the course of the past 60 years, which have also been practical and useful. The first has resulted in the diagnosis being made on the basis of *the single most outstanding clinical feature.*

Thus, a patient with a phobia may also have symptoms of anxiety or obsessive traits, for example. If the phobia is *the* major and/or the outstanding symptom, the proper diagnosis is one of phobic reaction. Should the obsessive manifestations be *the* major manifestation clinically, even though there were some phobic or other neurotic elements present, the diagnosis properly would be Obsessive-Compulsive Reaction.

The second trend referred to has led toward the discard of certain terms of quite hoary origin. Indeed, although based upon completely mistaken ideas of etiology, several of these, such as hypochondriasis [p. 448], hysteria [pp. 258 and 639*ff.*], and melancholia [p. 140] originating in the world of ancient Greece, have been used for so many centuries and so widely that discard has neither been rapid nor complete. It will hardly be surprising therefore if even non-medical people have some acquaintance with them.

3. Assessing Role of Trauma

The diagnosis of a neurosis following trauma is likewise made descriptively. Perhaps it is not so much the form that the neurotic reaction takes, nor the symptoms, which can vary considerably, but the relation of the entire reaction to a traumatic event which is the important criterion. Therefore, we follow the same kind of descriptive rules in labeling this kind of neurotic reaction as in others. The important consideration is the initiating trauma and the significance this has or has been assigned in the onset and course of the illness. Concurrent physical *and* emotional sequellae comprise an E.O.C. (emotional-organic combination).

In assessing these, one needs to give thought as to how they are viewed by the patient. While he may correctly or incorrectly assign too much or too little weight to the role of trauma in so far as his particular symptoms are concerned, nonetheless his view and understanding of the situation is of importance. One needs carefully to assess the role of trauma in arriving at a diagnosis.

B. IMPORTANT POINTS IN DIAGNOSIS OF NEUROSES FOLLOWING TRAUMA

1. Six Considerations

There are several important points to note about the diagnosis of the Neuroses Following Trauma. *First,* symptoms as such are usually non-specific. *Second,* the principles current in diagnosis require that the trauma play a major role, and that the relationship between the symptoms and the trauma be well established. Upon occasion the time sequence alone or other factors may of course provide presumptive evidence of the initiating role of the trauma. In other instances, the decision can extend the skill of the keenest diagnostician.

Third, the more thoroughly one understands emotional problems in general and the neuroses in particular, the better one can make judgments about the role of trauma in a given case. These may include estimations as to its various possible contributions in the initiation, exaggeration, prolongation, contribution, or complication of a given neurotic reaction. *Fourth,* one distinguishing feature in a fair segment of cases of traumatic neurosis is likely to be the acuteness of the situation; that is, the relative speed of onset and the character of symptoms following a given traumatic event. *Fifth,* a differential feature can lie in the acuity of the trauma, in comparison to that in other neurotic reactions. *Sixth,* the reproduction of the traumatic situation in subsequent dreams may be a diagnostic criterion.

2. Principle of Hidden-Determinants; Peg Concept

Added important points relate to the psychopathology, the pre-existing personality structure, the symbolic language which the symptom may express, as well as personal, familial, economic, and social environmental pressures and stresses. Although a traumatic event may initiate a symptom, as we shall learn, pre-existing factors (determinants) help to determine the form, type, and substance of the symptom in each case. This we might refer to as the *Principle of Hidden-Determinants.* [See *Table 33,* p. 697.] As noted, this points up the pre-existence of factors which are major influences in determining the form that symptoms will take. Reference should also be made to the vital Concept of Conflict Indicators [pp. 406 and 671]. Quite an important corallary is the Peg Concept [pp. 581, 588, 594, 681], according to which the peg already exists upon which one hangs his hat (the symptom).

There are special situations, such as combat, where the presence of particular and prolonged stress adds to the number of cases which are diagnosed. Study of these suggests that vulnerability to stress increases symptoms directly, in proportion to the level and strength of the stress. Military and Combat Reactions will be covered briefly in our final chapter.

C. ANY KIND OF CLINICAL PICTURE MAY FOLLOW TRAUMA

Types of neurotic pictures following trauma may illustrate any of the clinical groups we have outlined and studied thus far. These include both the groups in which anxiety and effects are manifested directly, and the ones in which anxiety and its effects are more indirectly manifested. [*See Table 1*, p. 20.] The features of Conversion Reactions (Somatic Conversion and Physiologic Conversion) occur more frequently than those of other groups. *Case 143* [p. 681] is an example. Features of the Anxiety Reactions and probably the Hygeiaphrontic Reactions (hypochondria) are next in order of frequency. Dissociative Reactions may occur. Phobias occasionally have their onset following traumatic experiences. Depressive Reactions and Fatigue States are likely to be more rare. Once in a while, following trauma, Obsessive manifestations first so appear, or undergo an abrupt exaggeration. *Case 90* [p. 454] is an instance of the development of an obsessive kind of Hygeiaphrontic Reaction in response to combat stress. In this type of neurotic evolvement, the Hygeiaphrontic Discrepancy is of importance [pp. 443*ff*.]. *Case 143* [p. 681] is an instance in which conversion symptoms had their onset following a fall and a slight concussion sustained while playing baseball.

V. SYMPTOMS AND CLINICAL FEATURES

A. EVENTS IN A "TYPICAL CASE"

1. The Part Played by Injury; the Traumatic Discrepancy

Let us look at the more typical case of neurosis following trauma. In the more usual clinical instance, a physical trauma will have taken place with from minor to major signs and evidence of injury. Symptoms more or less related to the site of injury may occur immediately. They may also come on in delayed fashion — from days to months later.

Two features are usually of significance at this juncture. *First,* the patient is most likely to assign the full significance to the role of the preceding injury in the onset of his symptoms. He feels — and in essence rightly so — that were it not for the injury he would not have his condition.

The injury may of course play a part all the way from one of initiation, of precipitation, or of merely providing a convenient peg (in accord with our *Peg Concept*) for the development of symptoms on the basis of long-present conflicts and tensions. In other words *the response to trauma is not necessarily proportional to its severity.* This is in line with our later *Non-Proportionate Response Rule* in the Neuroses Following Trauma. This comprises a *Traumatic Discrepancy* when marked, which is analogous to our earlier [p. 443] *Hygeiaphrontic Discrepancy.* In any event, there is still some truth to the patient's views and contentions concerning the role of trauma in his symptoms [*see Case 177*, p. 860].

Second, careful medical study will quickly indicate even initially a discrepancy between the symptoms and resulting interference, handicap, and disability on the one hand, and the actual physical extent of the trauma on the other. Thus, the medical evaluation will determine upon objective assessment that the symptoms and their sequelae are apparently out of proportion to whatever might be ordinarily expected to follow the kind and extent of injury which has been suffered.

The patient assigns a direct cause and effect relationship. The physician is likely to have reservations about this. The psychiatrist finds a complex situation the subtleties of which may defy absolute and exact determinations, but which fit the clinical picture as well as establish the diagnosis. Underlying psychologic conflicts and needs play a significant role, in accord with our *Iceberg Analogy* [p. 444].

2. Concepts of Gain: Epigain and Endogain Versus Malingering

Let us review briefly one source of confusion in our patient's symptoms. Here we refer to the frequent observation that a given symptom gains something for the patient. This is correct. It has been indicated that every neurotic symptom is a defense and thereby does indeed gain something or seeks to gain something for the patient. It may be desperate compromise or resolution for unconscious emotional forces in conflict. It must be remembered that it is effected unconsciously, in contrast to volitionally.

Now in the symptom of a Neurosis-Following-Trauma, certain of these so-called "gains" are likely to be more evident, more transparent to the external observer. Sometimes they are so apparent to the perceptive observer as to suggest that the patient is equally aware, and that the gains are consciously sought. Were this true he would be a malingerer.

Malingering is the deliberate simulation of illness — for whatever reason [Ch.13:VIIB*1*]. Because of the sometimes obviousness of the more externally observable kind of unconscious gain — the *epigain* — of illness, malingering is often suspected. This is more likely to be the case in instances of Conversion Reactions, Hygeiaphrontic Reactions, stress reactions during war, and some of the Neuroses-Following-Trauma. Of course the "gain" in its ultimate net result to the patient is really a loss. Nonetheless, it is vitally necessary as a last ditch defense in his individual psychology. So we have the sad paradox existing: that the vitally and desperately needed internal defense achieves its purpose to some extent, but at a great overall net cost to the person. A required and unwittingly sought "gain" is really a loss.

The *endogain* [p. 68*ff.*] is the primary gain of an emotional illness. Basic to the illness, these gains and the need for them are responsible for its initiation. The symptoms develop in its service. It is always deeply unconscious. The *epigain* [p. 61*ff.*] is more superficial, although still also unconscious. It is secondary, in that gain is thus unwittingly sought from the symptoms which are already present.

Epigain can (secondarily) follow symptoms which are physical, or emotional, or a combination of the two. It must be distinguished from malingering. The latter is the conscious and deliberate simulation of illness. *Epigain* is the unconsciously secured gain from the external environment, through emotional (psychologic) symptoms already existing. Its effects often aid in the perpetuation of a symptom or illness, which thereby gains increased value and significance to the individual concerned, as a consequence.

B. SYMPTOMS LEGION

1. Anxiety Reactions Following Trauma

A. DIRECT MANIFESTATION OF ANXIETY.—[*See Table 1*, p. 20.] So far we have stressed, and correctly so, the individuality in the symptom and the clinical picture in the Neuroses-Following-Trauma. This is true in so far as it applies to: (*a*) the potential for pathology; (*b*) the presence of any resulting limitations; (*c*) the kind of trauma; and (*d*) the types of symptoms to be evolved. The physiologic responses make up an important component in the T.R.C.

All kinds of physiologic or functional changes may follow crisis and stress. These are of particular moment at this juncture as acute manifestations and often fall under the category of Anxiety Reactions. Most frequent are anxiety and nervousness as such. Next are various gastrointestinal symptoms (for example, anorexia, pain, nausea, weight loss), cardiovascular symptoms (for example, palpitation, precordial distress, skipped beats, flushing, increased perspiration), genitourinary symptoms (for example, frequency, urgency), emotional fatigue, weakness, headaches, and backaches.

In a situation of stress and threat the body mobilizes its resources to cope with the danger. It conducts a kind of emergency mobilization, or in Navy terms a "call to general quarters." In other words, the T.R.C. literally includes a great deal of the earlier primitive preparation to fight or to flee, as may be needed. The physiologic changes are a major segment of the T.R.C.

B. EXTERNAL VERSUS INTERNAL DANGER.—Again we may emphasize that such changes are quite automatic and occur non-volitionally. They are mediated via the protectively intended T.R.C. They may overdevelop, with a resulting chronicity or hypertrophy or both, leading to distressing and troubling symptoms of a semipermanent or permanent nature. It is further of importance to us to recognize that physiologic changes occur in response to threat and danger, whether such threat is external and physical, or internal, hidden and psychologic. In response to a physical kind of threat from the external world, the mobilization of the T.R.C. is often most appropriate, and indeed can be life-saving.

When the threat is psychologic, when it is a response instead to internal emotional conflict, many of the T.R.C. changes, and particularly the physiologic ones, are likely to be of little use. More important, they may prove handicapping and harmful. Physical action — fight or flight — is at the least inappropriate in many of the cases of stress and danger, as experienced by modern man. Tensions are built up for which there is no appropriate outlet or discharge. This dammed up tension is destructive.

2. Concept of the Functional-Structural Progression

General patterns of bodily defensive reaction developed by man to cope with external danger may once have been quite appropriate for the more exposed and primitive conditions of our ancestors. They may be no longer so for us. Present day psychologic threats and dangers are often far different from external and physical ones. Physical and physiologic preparations for fight or for flight may be no longer appropriate. They can be handicapping.

When continued in response to many kinds of today's chronic stresses, such defensively intended preparations can progress toward their fixation. Ultimately via functional alterations of response, such chronic patterns may progress still further into structural alterations. Finally, this sequence can lead into a state of irreversibility.

These concepts are what we might term the Functional-Structural Progression [p. 468]. They are most basic in our present day understanding of the relationships of emotions, physiology, and the progression of temporary functional changes into chronic ones, and the further progression of these thence into organic disease.

3. Anxiety, Hygeiaphrontic, and Conversion Reactions More Frequent

A. ANXIETY IN INVERSE PROPORTION TO OTHER SYMPTOMS.—Each group of neurotic symptoms, according to standard nomenclature, provides representatives of Neuroses Following Trauma. Actually, trauma can precipitate any given type of emotional difficulty. Post-traumatic symptoms in psychiatry can run the gamut of clinical manifestations. On the other hand, we also recognize that anxiety, hygeiaphrontic, and conversion reactions are the most frequent ones bearing a relationship to trauma. Phobias, depressions, emotional fatigue, and the obsessive-compulsive reactions are less frequently observed.

The symptoms which may be seen in the various neuroses which may have their onset following trauma are indeed legion. Nervousness, restlessness, tension, insomnia, and other direct manifestations of anxiety are common. The manifestations of Somatic Conversion or Physiologic Conversion, with their physical limitations and functional alterations, are frequently seen. In these there is most likely to be less evidence of overt anxiety. [See earlier Concept of Inverse Ratio of Anxiety to Symptom Success, p. 9.] The anxiety has become allayed or bound, so to speak, as elements of the emotional conflict become converted into these more devious, concealed, and symbolic forms of psychologic and physiologic expression. Generally the presence of anxiety is in inverse proportion to the presence of other emotional symptoms, and to the degree of "symptom-success" they have achieved, in allaying anxiety. This, of course, also is in line with our earlier [pp. 89, 108, 120, and 555] Concept of Incomplete Symptom-Defense.

B. IMPAIRED SEXUAL FUNCTION.—Diminished sexual interest and impaired sexual function are frequent accompaniments of post-traumatic syndromes. See the earlier Concept of Sexual Maladjustment as Effect (rather than cause) of Emotional Problems [p. 269].

At times a major Dissociative Reaction may even occur. Fainting is a primitive kind of total response, aimed at excluding the traumatic stimulus by cutting off perception. Amnesia and rarely a Fugue State may be seen. Symptoms of Depression and of its close relative, Emotional Fatigue and the Fatigue State, may be seen very occasionally.

C. FOLLOWING HEAD INJURY.—The Total Individual Response to Trauma includes all types of symptoms and defenses and combinations of them. Every type or classification of neurosis has been observed to follow some traumatic event as the precipitating cause. In discussing the neurotic symptoms which followed head injuries, Schilder found the most frequent group to be conversion [p. 639], with the hygeiaphrontic-neurasthenic groups [pp. 379, 424, 441] perhaps next. The author's personal experience would confirm this. This is reflected by an earlier definition of Traumatic Neurosis as a special combination of situational Conversion Reaction and Hygeiaphrontis. This definition was an oversimplification. The Anxiety Reactions [p. 81] would perhaps run a close third. Occasionally one sees a Depressive Reaction [p. 135], more rarely a massive Dissociation or Phobic formation.

C. THREE OF THE MORE RARE POST-TRAUMATIC SYNDROMES

1. Symptoms Out of Proportion to the Injury

A physical trauma with from minor to major evidences of injury is followed by the onset of a variety of symptoms. These may include emotional manifestations, functional symptoms, or both. They are most likely to include conversion, anxiety, or hygeiaphrontic elements.

Frequently, medical evaluation will determine that the symptoms are out of proportion to anything which might be objectively and ordinarily expected to follow the kind of injury which has been suffered. The patient is often convinced that a direct cause and effect relationship exists. Elements of traumatic epigain may be prominent and readily seen.

This kind of clinical picture is a rather familiar one to many physicians. Accordingly, three examples of the more rare kinds of response to trauma will be cited. These are in turn dissociation, obsession, and phobia.

2. The Dissociative Reaction; Concept of Overall Language

The following case is an example of a rather rare kind of dissociative, fugue-like state which can occasionally follow an emotionally traumatic event. This reaction comprises an acute instance of what we earlier [p. 644] termed an *overall language*.

Case 174

A Brief Dissociative State Follows a Traumatic Event

(1) *One brother survives*

I had read the local newspaper account of a tragedy in which two young brothers had gone swimming together and had gotten into trouble in the water at the same time. The elder brother had made it to shore with some assistance. The younger brother had drowned. My speculation at the time concerned the possible traumatic effects of such a tragedy upon the survivor. I had no way of knowing then that I would be called upon to see him professionally.

The body of the victim was soon recovered. Shortly thereafter, the surviving brother visited the funeral parlor to view his brother's remains. At this time he became acutely disturbed emotionally. This rapidly progressed into an overactive, fugue-like kind of Dissociative State. He was partially irrational, moving restlessly and aimlessly about, at a pace which varied from moderate to frenzied. There were also conversion elements in his overall responses. This was a not too comprehensible instance of the *overall language* in gross dissociation, as earlier labeled. He remained quite suggestible despite his wild behavior. His motor activity increased whenever relatives happened to be present. An *Emergency Analytic-Bridge* [*Case 142*, p. 679] was needed. A massive amount of sedation was required before the desired calming effect on this nonconstructive overactivity was secured. He had been admitted to a general hospital, where he was shortly seen in consultation.

(2) *Antecedent conflicts reactivated*

Some thirty six hours later, under sedation and supportive psychotherapy, he had calmed down substantially. It was soon possible to secure a fairly adequate history of the immediately precipitating traumatic events. The two brothers had actually struggled together in the water for survival. One can readily appreciate some of the terrible conflicts activated by such a desperate situation and its tragic finale. The survivor suffered unbearable self-doubts, guilt, and recriminations. These were partially reactivations of certain almost inevitable, severe antecedent conflicts in the realm of sibling rivalry and competitiveness. These had been of some considerable strength for him for a number of significant intrafamilial reasons. His route of escape from the intolerable emotions which were aroused had been a psychologic kind of flight into the Dissociative Fugue State which was observed clinically.

The Fugue State was of brief duration in this instance, largely because he had previously been a rather well adjusted person with a number of effective conversion character defenses. He was a person of limited imagination and intellectual resources. He was, however, able to reintegrate his defenses rather quickly, with some outside assistance from therapy. These defenses consisted largely of denial and the assignment of responsibility to fate. While they were operative on a primitive level, their operation was most effective.

The patient was able to attend his brother's funeral in a few days without further apparent untoward effects. He had suffered an acute but short-lived Dissociative State and had then effected some rapid psychologic adjustments, however primitive. He was soon able to carry on with no outwardly apparent ill effects. One may, of course, indulge in some speculation about the possible future significances or emotional effects of such a soul-shaking traumatic experience. He had little interest in the further pursuit of therapeutic self-study and shortly broke off our relationship with thanks.

3. The Obsessive Reaction

Where the predisposition exists, a rare kind of post-traumatic defensive retreat into obsessional preoccupation may be seen. For other data on the obsessive pattern of defense see Chapter 6. The following instance illustrates the post-traumatic onset of this unusual kind of obsessive over-concern with detail. This was observed following an automobile accident.

Case 175

Obsessive Preoccupation Follows an Automobile Accident

Many years ago I observed the immediate aftermath of a serious colli-sion. One of the drivers in a three-car smash-up alone had miracu-lously survived uninjured. We had come upon the wrecked cars shortly after the accident. This man, in torn and soiled clothes, was standing by what was hardly any longer recognizable as a car. His curious response to the disaster was his reciting aloud over and over again how fortunate he was that his right foot had escaped injury. Despite his right shoe being torn off when the motor block was pushed back past the dashboard, his foot was unharmed.

His preoccupation in obsessive fashion with his relatively minor aspect of the tragic event was remarked upon curiously by several people among the crowd which had quickly collected. It was not difficult to recognize part of the evident protective intent in his obsessive pattern of reaction. By focusing his attention upon what was, relatively speak-ing, a trifle,* he avoided other more serious and disturbing thoughts and emotions. These might have arisen for example, from contempla-tion of the lives lost, possible responsibility on his part, and perhaps the genuine, but perhaps more frightening narrowness of the escape of his *entire* self, as opposed to just one small part.

Obsessive preoccupation of a different variety is seen in some industrial and service cases. Often this may concern subjective symptoms. At times it is directed toward various aspects of compensation for the injury.

4. The Phobic Reaction

The third and following instance helps to illustrate the earlier important point that almost any type of illness, including a phobia, can have its initiation through a traumatic event. This case also again illustrates the important psychologic principle that vital factors relating to the onset of an emotional illness are likely to be unconscious. Events are relegated to the unconscious because they are consciously too painful or unbearable. Although they are so assigned, and automatically so, they do not lie dormant. They have their important effects on us through life.

Case 176

A Phobic Reaction Initiated by Trauma

(1) A phobia of snow

A thirty-two-year-old married woman came into therapy because of an unusual type of phobia. Her object of phobia was snow. She also had some emotional problems relating to areas of her family and social adjustment. There were handicapping personality traits, some trouble in sleeping, and intermittent physiologic conversion manifestations of

---

* In discussing the defensive operations of obsessively oriented people, Lewis B. Hill noted appropriately "the regular characteristic of these people to displace their concerns onto trifles." The above instance illustrates this as an acute kind of reaction [*see also* pp. 245*ff.*, and pp. 188, 311*ff.*, 398].

headaches and skin rash, but the most outstanding single manifestation was her phobia of snow. A diagnosis of Phobic Reaction was made and treatment was undertaken.

In her particular illness this phobia was the major presenting feature and had become increasingly handicapping and troublesome. As one consequence of her husband's business success they had taken up suburban living, where there was likely to be even more snow and of longer duration! More travel was required — at times through snow during wintertime — to get to the store or to any other place; further, in the last several winters, there also had been more snow in her particular metropolitan area.

It is hard to picture adequately the extent of fear present. This woman's fear of snow petrified her. She could not stand to go out in it; she could not stand to see it; in winter she could not listen to weather reports because someone might make some reference to snow! The many, many ways in which this phobia could affect her day-to-day living were almost incredible. The effects were pervasive and thereby profound.

(2) Time, effort, and work required for successful therapy

Any reference to snow, or even subjective thoughts about it, would make her uncomfortable, frightened, and tense. One could hardly overestimate her level of limitation and suffering. Of course, as in other instances of this type of symptom, this patient had no conscious explanation for her phobia. Also it is not possible to give an adequate impression here of the hundreds of hours of intensive work that are often required to try and bring about a resolution of symptoms in this, as in most types of emotional difficulties. The resolution of a single manifestation in an emotional illness usually requires a substantial investment of time and energy. One can seldom tell accurately in advance what will be required. Needless to say, however, almost no effort is too great when it can be successful in eliminating a basis for anxiety, a limiting physical symptom, a phobia, or an emotional depression.

Over a period of years, requiring hard work on the part of the patient, plus the assistance of the experienced and trained physician-therapist, the major endeavor of intensive psychotherapy and analysis is to try and learn what makes the patient "tick." Only those perhaps who have had the benefit of some personal experience in psychotherapy may know what a most rewarding experience this can be, as well as how much hard work may be required, and how long one may have to work toward this goal.

In this instance, we were most fortunate eventually to uncover what proved to have been the major precipitating event in the onset of the phobia. This was a traumatic experience dating from when the patient was eleven years old. This experience had lain completely out of sight, hidden in her unconscious, for 21 years — repressed, but hardly dormant. With its acute and dramatic onset, this phobia would be classified as a *Critical-Displacement Phobia* [pp. 547, 575, 578, and 584].

(3) The Precipitating Situation

In the winter of her eleventh year she had accompanied an aunt and uncle to a ski lodge in Vermont. One afternoon she wandered off by herself a short distance, into a small ravine which lay parallel to, but considerably below, an old logging road. She played and gradually waded her way through the snow for several hundred yards down the ravine. Looking up at this point, she could see some people on the road far above her. There was some banter exchanged between them. A few snowballs or stones were thrown in her direction. A large chunk of snow either came loose or was started towards her. To her intense horror it quickly gathered speed and volume. Suddenly she found herself in the path of a miniature avalanche. She was helpless to move out of the way in time and was engulfed. She was literally buried alive, and was unable to move or to extricate herself. Somehow, however, she managed to maintain, or was fortunate enough to have, a channel so that she could continue breathing. The people on the road above simply disappeared, either not knowing what had transpired, or perhaps in a guilty attempt to dissociate themselves from tragedy.

The little girl remained there, absolutely petrified with fear, for an indeterminate period of time, until discovered through most fortuitious circumstances by her worried uncle. It had seemed an eternity.

Her complete repression of this episode was enhanced by its unbearable horror, plus her certainty of death. This may have also been encouraged a bit by her uncle's reluctance and her own fear of having her parents ever learn about the near tragedy. Each felt in some measure responsible and subject to censure. Any possibility of future excursions would in addition become extremely unlikely.

5. Basic Concepts in Neuroses Following Trauma

In such occasional dramatic circumstances, when a specific precipitating cause can be found in an emotional illness, the relief of a particular symptom may take place, as it did in the above case. One must bear in mind, however, that this does not mean that the cure is complete, nor that therapy should be concluded. One must continue the study of finding out more about the pre-phobic personality, and in many instances far less dramatic than this, what it was that has made the person susceptible to the onset of symptoms, even though the traumatic event may have been fairly severe.

In the foregoing discussion are illustrated some of the following basic concepts in the area of Neuroses Following Trauma. *First,* traumatic events can play a most important role in an individual's life for months, years, or a lifetime. *Second,* from the broadest viewpoint all emotional symptoms and illnesses can be regarded as ultimately stemming from trauma, whether the trauma is physical, psychologic, or both. *Third,* certain types of neuroses and neurotic symptoms are more frequently related to trauma. *Fourth,* emotional symptoms and neurotic reactions can follow traumatic events, in which they may be regarded as being caused by or as being precipitated by them. *Finally,* the prior existence of what was earlier termed [p. 574] *favorable psychologic soil* has a considerable bearing upon the relative emotional impact of a given traumatic event.

6. The Post-traumatic Dream; Desensitizing Purpose Concept

One characteristic feature in the acute type of post-traumatic emotional illness which is worthy of our early consideration is the repetitive disturbing dream. These dreams had occurred in the foregoing case, albeit in such guise as to require the usual detective work in their elucidation. Psychiatrists see these illustrated not infrequently.

In combat situations, as in acute civilian traumata, the dream often appears to serve an important kind of *desensitizing purpose.* The actual events may be expressed more or less directly. They may be somewhat, or even quite, disguised. The dream work serves to an extent to modify them rather magically, rendering them less disturbing and less traumatic. From this standpoint the author has regarded some instances of this type of disturbing dream as a subconscious abreaction. This is the *Desensitizing Purpose Concept* of the function of many dreams, especially those which are post-traumatic [*see also* earlier refs, p. 39; Ch.13:IIIA2].

Lowenstein analyzed a post-traumatic dream which followed a dramatic canoe upset. A miraculous rescue had taken place after the patient had traversed some dangerous rapids. In the dream the traumatic event was repeated, but not exactly. Distortions served to conceal and partly to hide the original trauma, to fulfill wishes, and to master what had been almost overwhelmingly threatening reality. The dreams in the snow phobia were similar, but were probably less effective in reducing the emotional impact. In accord with our earlier Hypothesis of the Dream's Contribution to Emotional Health, pointing out the valuable functions of the dream [Ch.13:IIIC*1*], this added concept helps point out how the dream can make an important contribution to maintaining one's healthful equanimity.

D. MARKED VARIATION IN RESPONSE TO TRAUMA

"The web of our life is of a mingled yarn, good and ill together." (Shakespeare, *All's Well That Ends Well*, IV; 3, 83)

1. Rule of Non-Proportionate Response

Experiencing misfortune is universal to human experience. An important circumstance lies in the variable individual capacity to tolerate it. The reaction to trauma is a highly individual matter. Various major stressful events have occurred which have provided an opportunity to observe this. In them, a number of people have been exposed to almost identical stresses. These include such traumatic situations as civilian or war-time sinkings, bombings, other kinds of war experiences, and all manner of civilian disasters.

Highly variable and individual consequences occur, in accord with our earlier [p. 14] formulated Principle of Individual Appropriateness of Response. Many persons are relatively unaffected, or quickly recover from any undue effects. A few develop emotional difficulties. These consequences in turn are likely to vary widely in their extent and degree. It becomes amply clear that *the degree of emotional disturbance is by no means necessarily in direct proportion to the intensity of the traumatic experience.* The pre-existing personality make-up and adjustment are vital in determining what will be the response of any given person. Individual susceptibility and vulnerability run the gamut of possibility. Accordingly, we can formulate a *Rule of Non-Proportionate Response* for the manifestations of the Neuroses-Following-Trauma. It is of course analogous to our earlier Characteristic-Disproportion Principle, in identifying Emotional Fatigue [pp. 381 and 388].

2. Total Individual Response to Crisis and Trauma; the T.R.C. and T.R.T.; Compliant-Resignation-Response to Death

A. DEFENSE AND SURVIVAL.—As mentioned earlier, in studying the individual significance of trauma and its widely variable effects upon different persons, the author has found it convenient and useful to employ certain concepts. These refer to the *total* reactions of the individual concerned, as will now be briefly amplified.

In the presence of crisis or stress, each individual mobilizes his resources to meet the situation. The crisis may be external or internal. It may be conscious or unconscious. It may result from a clearly visualized external danger. It may also result from a deep-seated emotional conflict which is partly or wholly unconscious (that is, out of conscious awareness). It may result from a complex combination of various factors.

In the case of the clear-cut external danger, the emotional component of the individual's total reactions to crisis, his T.R.C., will likely include fear (the emotional response to a clearly recognized external danger). Where the danger is internal and its source lies in emotional conflict, the emotional component of his T.R.C. will likely include anxiety (the emotional response to an internal danger, the nature of which is not known or is unclear). The subjective sensations and the physiologic responses in both fear and anxiety are the same, or quite similar. Anxiety is likely to be more disturbing than fear, since the individual does not know its basis, is less able (or unable) to resolve the underlying conflict which is responsible, and is therefore more helpless. When anxiety is present the person may report his feelings in terms of experiencing "apprehension", "tension", "anxiety", or "fear", or all four, but does not know what it is that he fears.

B. ALL AREAS INCLUDED.—The T.R.C. includes *all* of the components of one's reaction to a given crisis. Thus, we would include all of the *intellectual,* the *physical,* the *emotional,* the *physiologic,* and the *psychologic* responses which are brought into play. This is why we refer to the reaction or response as a *total* one. Each of these is an important area. Various aspects of them might be brought into action automatically in a reflex kind of response, deliberately, or some of each. They can be thought of as defenses or, perhaps better, as attempted defenses.

The T.R.C. thus includes the sum total of the reactions of the individual concerned. When a major or minor crisis impends, the individual responds in the best way he can to meet the threat or danger.

C. ABILITY TO SURVIVE.—The T.R.C. plays a vital role in overall defense, which also of course includes offense. Its relative effectiveness determines the individual's ability to survive. It determines his mode and patterns of self-defense. From the emotional and psychologic viewpoints, therefore, the reaction patterns developed by the evolving T.R.C. will have most important influences on the character defenses and on the personality structure, as these evolve.

One's T.R.C. includes the creation of potential for action, including attack, counterattack, and offensive measures. This concept is intended to help convey the close interrelationships and normally synergistic action of the intellectual, emotional, physical, physiologic, and psychologic areas, all of which are included. Many of the factors which help to determine what the T.R.C. shall be and how it shall operate are called into play automatically or semi-automatically. The T.R.C. and its healthy and efficient operation is a vital part of oneself and one's function. It is therefore often an accurate accessory indicator of the relative level of emotional adjustment.

D. TOTAL INDIVIDUAL REACTION TO TRAUMA.—The T.R.T. is a direct carryover of this interesting and important concept as outlined, to the individual response to actual *trauma*. The trauma may be emotional, physical, or a combination of the two. The total response, as with the T.R.C., includes the intellectual, the emotional, the physical, the psychologic, and the physiologic areas.

In the Neuroses-Following-Trauma or Traumatic Reactions, this carryover becomes more important. From one standpoint, of course, crisis or stress itself might be considered trauma, that is, psychic trauma. From another, *the neurotic symptoms which can follow trauma can be considered part of the individual's total reaction to trauma*. The T.R.C. and the T.R.T. are both conceived as inclusive reactions, without limits as to time. They would accordingly include both immediate, later, and even long-delayed responses.

E. INDIVIDUALITY STRESSED.—It is important to bear in mind the complete individuality of the T.R.C. and the T.R.T. In making any estimation, evaluation, or interpretation of a person's total reaction to crisis or trauma the individual specificity is crucial. No two persons will react exactly in the same situation. In any situation of crisis or danger all the consequences of past training and experience will influence what transpires. This includes reflex activity, conscious control, conditioning, the possible presence of similar antecedent stresses, important unconscious factors, and patterns of defense already evolved to cope with stress.

Further, the individual's response to any given threat must be considered in the light of the individual meaning, including symbolism, of the threat to the person threatened.

In other words, the effect of a crisis or threat on the personal psychologic economy will depend upon the amount of threat which is experienced subjectively, and not necessarily upon any objective evaluation. The trauma may have symbolic meanings and individually important and specific unconscious meanings. The T.R.C. will vary accordingly.

F. COMPLIANT-RESIGNATION-RESPONSE TO DEATH.—If the threat experienced is great, the preparations to meet it will be maximal. In rare instances, when physical dissolution is imminent, however, the threat is simply overwhelming. Instances have been reported, for example, in which the T.R.C. is quite the reverse to that which more usually follows a situation of threat, crisis, or danger. Reference is made here to such rare instances as those in which a person has fallen from a cliff toward certain death, for example, only to have his life miraculously spared.

Feelings of tranquility, resignation, mild surprise, or even a strange exhilaration sometimes may be reported to have been present at such times. In these and perhaps similar instances of what at least appears to be certain demise, the psyche may retreat to what may be a deeper, more primitive level of denial and passive acquiescence. This may represent an implicit acceptance of the futility of standing against the inevitable. These reactions which can accompany seemingly certain death may be termed the *Compliant-Resignation-Response to Death*. See also related concepts in our discussion of the Depressive Reactions [p. 175] and Suicide [pp. 192–3 and 207].

3. Contrasting Responses to Trauma and Stress; Final Straw Concept

A. SEVERE NEUROSIS PRECIPITATED BY MINOR TRAUMA.—Some of the significance of the foregoing can be observed in instances in which we are able to contrast the post-traumatic effects in certain cases where symptoms are maximal following minimal trauma (as assessed by the casual external observer), with others where symptoms are absent or much less when the trauma is actually quite considerable. The presence of underlying (unconscious) significance and symbolic meaning to the patient often determines in most covert fashion if symptoms will occur, together with their form, and their relative severity.

To help point up some of these and other principles, two contrasting case abstracts are presented. In the one instance a severe neurosis followed objectively minor physical trauma. This instance also serves to help illustrate what for purposes of emphasis has been labeled the Final Straw Concept [pp. 162, 399, 713]. In accord with this concept, an otherwise or seemingly minor event, stress, or trauma can prove to be "the final straw" in precipitating a neurotic reactions. In the case to be contrasted (*Case 184* in Chapter 15), a severe neurosis occurred only after prolonged maximal stress. In each instance the pre-existing level of adjustment and personality structure played an important determining role as to the degree of vulnerability.

Case 177

The Onset of a Severe Neurosis Following Minimal Trauma

(1) *Symptoms ascribed to mishap*

A forty-one-year-old mechanical engineer was seen in consultation because of weakness, severe headaches, blurred vision, sleeping disturbances, nervousness, and tremors. These troubling symptoms had progressed to the point that he was unable to work. The clinical picture most nearly fitted into the older descriptive concept of neurasthenia [pp. 424 *ff.*], with hygeiaphrontic overtones [pp. 441*ff.*]. The patient appeared tired, thin, worn-out, apathetic, and discouraged. His speech and manner showed little spontaneity or expression. The patient dated all his symptoms from what he described as a "serious head injury which I suffered when the ceiling fell down on me". His co-workers described the breaking loose of a smallish (approximately 12" x 18") section of ceiling plaster, which fell in a shower of fragments over the patient and his drafting board. The observers made light of the incident. They did not see how *any* physical injury could have possibly resulted. The injury however was not physical. This event had provided a convenient and perhaps even essential peg [p. 58] for the attachment of symptoms already pressuring for expression. Indeed he was psychologically so "ready" for the trauma that we might regard him as having an Emotional Achilles Heel [Ch.14:VF]. This would be in accord with our earlier Principle of Predetermined Vulnerability.

(2) *Inviting attention to the discrepancy serves little purpose*

It is rather readily apparent in such a situation that calling attention to the discrepancy between the severity of the trauma as estimated by the patient, and by others, serves little constructive purpose. Indeed, it can be harmful. Any exaggeration by the patient should be regarded as necessary to fit into his deeply fixed internal needs. These are emotional in origin and are unlikely to respond to logic. Accordingly, it is hardly surprising that direct efforts to convince or persuade often only arouse antagonism and resistance. It is more likely to be defeating to the therapy, and to a potentially constructive therapeutic relationship to pointedly or unduly invite attention to such a Traumatic Discrepancy.

(3) *Final Straw concept*

This patient's symptoms began promptly and progressed rapidly to a severe plateau. Here they had tended to become fixed, for a period of several months prior to the time I saw him.

The external event, from the standpoint of its objective slightness, appeared to serve as a convenient attachment for something which was perhaps all ready to occur. The falling plaster precipitated matters. It was the final straw. This instance thus illustrates the interesting Final Straw Concept, which can sometimes be observed in rather striking form in the neuroses. It is also illustrated as a "more weighty" straw in Case 184.

(4) *Collapse threatened from several quarters*

Background history indicated a poor, passive, dependent adjustment, in a person with an insecure early family environment. His economic and professional achievement had been marginal, especially in view of his long training. Both in his marriage and at work his adjustment had been gradually becoming increasingly precarious. It was as though the accident represented on one level a welcomed way of retreat into a more passive position, from an increasingly intolerable, more active one. In addition to the steady deterioration in his level of security, there was the constant threat of complete collapse from any one of several quarters; that is, marriage, family, professional standing, loss of his position, and so on. The "roof" might well indeed have fallen in on him thus at any time! Accordingly, the actual ceiling collapse understandably had considerable symbolic meaning for him.

He was the impotent, helpless person caught in the web of his own adjustmental and emotional inadequacies. It was as though he had simply been impotently awaiting some area to give way or collapse. This type of neurotic collapse has been observed to follow occasional but similar ceiling collapses, perhaps warranting our foregoing speculation as to part of the underlying symbolism.

This man refused therapy. On last contact he was fitting himself quite thoroughly into an increasingly passive and dependent position, being supported by a small pension and his wife's earnings.

In comparing the foregoing case, with its apparently minimal external stress and trauma, to *Case 184* in the following chapter, one will note the tremendous stress and impact of the *Final Straw* which led to the ultimate emotional breakdown of a four-time naval survivor. The two instances appear to represent nearly opposite poles of resistance to stress and trauma.

4. *Contrasting Vulnerability to Trauma May Reflect Parental Attitudes*

Another pair of contrasting clinical cases will now be considered. In the first instance (*Case 178*) the emotional consequences of what was a very dangerous situation, and one which could have been very traumatic psychologically, were minimal. In the second case a relatively much less severe traumatic experience had far greater emotional impact. One can occasionally see such contrasting examples as the following in private practice.

Years of conditioning by over-cautious parents had determined the unusual vulnerability of the patient in the second example (*Case 179*). These findings can help lend support to the Interpersonal Perpetuation Concept [pp. 291, 323, 334], and to our Principle of Predetermined Vulnerability [Ch.14:1B*3*].

Case 178

A Traumatic Experience with Minimal Sequelae

The history of an experience suffered when he was twelve years old was recently reported to me by a patient. He had been playing alone in the shallow water at the edge of a lake. He was unable to swim. Despite a previous admonition about just such a possibility, he incautiously stepped backward off a ledge into deeper water.

There was no one near to offer help. Most fortunately, and by dint of his desperate efforts, he managed somehow to extricate himself from the perilous situation. All this was, quite realistically, a terrific threat.

Such a close call might have understandably precipitated various types of emotional difficulty in some persons. For this particular individual there was a minimum of emotional disturbance. He had one nightmare and was uneasy about the water for a few days. He went on shortly to learn to swim despite this. He has not been uneasy about water or swimming since.

In this instance his parents were very relaxed about water sports, so much so, indeed, that they might have been severely criticized on this score. In any event, their son's emotional tolerance for this traumatic experience was very great.

Now let us contrast this case with the following instance:

Case 179

Emotional Disturbance Follows a Slight Traumatic Event

A forty-two-year-old man became anxious, sleepless, and had repeated disturbing dreams over a period of many months. This Anxiety Reaction or A.T.S. [p. 98] had had its onset following a visit to the beach and what for many people, would have been a minor mishap. A painfully cautious person around the water, he had a great uneasiness about it. He had never learned to swim. He only went bathing on rare occasions upon his wife's insistence.

On this occasion a wave had pushed him off balance when his attention was directed elsewhere. He was in water that only reached to his knees between waves. His wife, a competent swimmer, and friends, similarly competent, were practically within arm's length of him at the time.

In this instance there was a long history of over-caution and fear which had been protectively induced by his parents. He was one of the younger children in a large farm family. There was a fair-sized creek not too far from the house. His parents were very busy. They also could not swim themselves. Their own best protection was to induce enough cautious feelings in the small boy so he would simply keep a safe distance away from the creek. While this had proved eminently successful, he was left in adult life with a deeply established emotional reaction of fear about water.

In somewhat self-defeating fashion, this had far exceeded its original protective intent. In this instance it is clear that the traumatic event was only of this level of significance to him because of the protectively intended conditioning which had taken place during his early formative years. The A.T.S. [pp. 98 and 167] had resulted.

E. THE TRAUMA AND ITS EFFECTS; TIME-LAGS; E.I.D.

1. Effects of Trauma Deferred

A. A TIME-LAG FOR SYMPTOMS.—It is to be noted that there may be a time-lag of from minutes to months (rarely even years) after a traumatic event, before the onset of symptoms. The patient may likewise delay for some time before he attributes responsibility for the difficulties to the earlier accident. This is sometimes to be observed in industrial cases. *Case 183,* to follow, is an example.

Why does a time lag sometimes occur between trauma and symptoms? The answer to this is always strictly individual and accordingly has to be searched for in each case. However, it may be possible to note some general principles. Many of our human reactions may be viewed in the light of a defensive intent. Thus, even in the case of a physical injury one can sometimes observe the injured person seemingly "defer" the effects of the injury to allow him to continue to function for a time. This can occur when injuries are severe, even fatal.

Soldiers fighting the Moros in the Philippines found these determined opponents sometimes "did not know when they were killed!" Fatally wounded, they could continue to fight. In fact, the U. S. .45-caliber service automatic was developed because of the need to stop them. It is not too uncommon in war for a severely wounded man to continue fighting when by most calculations he should no longer be able to do so. Only after the immediate urgent need is past does he then "accept" the effects of his wounds. These have seemingly been deferred until the emergency subsides. Such "impossible" activity is also often directly reflective of the powerful driving motivation present.

B. UNCONSCIOUS OR AUTOMATIC ACTION.—This kind of effect can be observed during sporting events. On occasions football players complete a play or a sequence after being hit hard, the latter being borne out by the player's subsequent collapse after completing the action. In other instances a player has completed part, or even the balance of the game with no recollection of the events [Ch.13:VIIB2].

These and many other instances of deferment of the effects of trauma can be encountered. One may perhaps think of them as the carryover of a primitive kind of self-preservative deferment in which our earliest ancestors may have thus saved their lives on occasion in struggles with men or beasts.

2. Time-Lag in Concussion

The time lag seen in some instances of concussion is somewhat similar. There are instances in which this type of head injury is followed by a period of time between the blow and its full effects. During this period the boxer, athlete, or traumatic victim may briefly continue or finish some sequence of activity — more likely so if this seems vital to him at the time.

These occurrences can have a clear explanation in physical and physiologic principles. However, it is strongly suspected that there exist added factors of psychologic origin, which in the individual instance can make an important contribution. This can perhaps be supported by the notation that the relative import of the emergency plays a role. The following instance illustrated some of the foregoing points.

Case 180

Effects of Trauma Deferred

Many years ago I was in Ardmore watching a minor league baseball game. It was a hotly contested event, with each player seemingly terribly intent on doing his utmost. In the fifth inning a man got safely on first on a short, line drive. After two strike-outs the next batter suddenly hit a bad pitch almost directly down the first-base line. This struck the previous batter a glancing but still heavy blow on the head. The latter paused momentarily to size up the situation, seemingly deliberately determined that the hit was a fair one, and then streaked to second base.

He arrived there safely and stopped with his foot carefully on the bag. Immediately thereafter he suddenly and abruptly collapsed. He was carried from the field. The effects of trauma had been briefly deferred.

3. Time Lags in Crisis and Trauma: E.I.D.

Similar time lags can be noted in situations of dire threat and danger. The fireman suffering from smoke inhalation manages to complete a rescue before collapsing. The badly injured collision victim manages to extricate himself from a burning vehicle. A slightly built woman recently literally lifted part of an automobile from her child and then collapsed.

Following the death of a beloved mother, the son or daughter may handle himself or herself and all arrangements calmly, to surrender some time later to grief. This is an instance of what we might call the E.I.D., *Emotional-Impact-Deferment* [Ch.13:IIE1]. Through this capacity an emotional reaction is held in abeyance. Such an emergency deferral of severe emotions is protectively intended. It can be ego-sustaining and even vital.

The near victim in drowning may upon occasion emotionally and physically fall apart at the seams but only *after* he is safely ashore. The following instance is illustrative.

Case 181

Collapse Deferred Until Danger Past

I can recall an experience some years ago which took place while serving on the Beach Patrol at Stone Harbor. We had a particular rescue in which a middle-aged man had had a narrow escape from drowning. He appeared to get along very well until *after* we pulled him from the surf and he was quite safe, far up on the beach. Only then did he "fall apart at the seams," emotionally and physically. A complete recovery took place some hours later.

In this instance it was as though the person could collapse only after the real danger situation was over — when the need for emergency mobilization was past. The T.R.C. herein provided enough emergency resources to carry the person through the actual situation. The Emotional-Impact-Deferment here may have prevented hopeless panic, and may have proved to be life-saving.

4. Part of Total Reaction to Crisis

In these and similar instances it is as though the T.R.C. of the individual is such as to enable him more effectively to cope with the threat or danger by the deferral of its full impact, thus allowing him to function at a far more effective level during the time of urgent need. Thus he copes with the situation at hand prior to "giving in" to the trauma. If collapse he must, this occurs only after the real danger situation is past. This is E.I.D. or Emotional-Impact-Deferment.

The T.R.C. thus provides emergency energy and drive to sustain the individual through his emergency. There is a time lag. Deferment of the impact, emotional, physical, traumatic, or whatever may be part of this, allows what may be a life-saving action to be completed. In other words, this part of the T.R.C. results in holding the full impact of the crisis or trauma in abeyance until the situational needs are met. It is clear that this type of T.R.C. component, when operative, can on given occasions be defensive, self-preservative, even life-saving.

5. Cool Head Versus Panic

Let us consider for a moment the segment of this reaction that applies to the emotions. What a difference there is between two possible extremes of emotional response to crisis. On the one hand there is coolness, self-possession, and objectivity. At the other extreme is panic, unreasoning fear, and irrationality. Our concept of deferment of possible self-defeating emotional components refers to some degree of the latter. Its value is evident.

How self-defeating, threatening, dangerous, and perhaps deathly can be the occasional irrational blind state of panic which can ensue. A helpless, frozen, or agitated fear in response to a crisis is not only no asset but can be terribly destructive. Panic can be disruptive, disintegrative, and dangerous. We can better see perhaps how instead the deferment of reaction to crisis — and to trauma — when possible can serve a defensive purpose.

In clinical instances of Neuroses Following Trauma this possible explanation is of course seldom so apparent. However, our understanding of some of the foregoing principles may aid in our recognition and understanding of this phenomenon.

F. PHYSIOLOGIC CHANGES IN STRESS

An important component of the Total Response to Crisis is in the physiologic area. Many changes in this aspect of the human economy ensue. Some are measurable by laboratory study. For example, blood clotting time is accelerated. Another study indicates that blood viscosity increases greatly. All of this is part of the protectively intended physiologic preparation for defense or offense. Such preparations usually are automatic and largely beyond voluntary control. They will occur equally in response to crisis or danger. They usually occur equally whether the threat is physical or psychologic. This brings us to comments made in earlier chapters which might well be underlined. Included is our Concept of Continued Physiologic Momentum [pp. 99; 455 and *Case 20,* p. 100].

In response to physical threats, physiologic changes are often most appropriate and may be life-saving. When the threat is essentially psychologic, however, they may be of little use. They may even prove handicapping and harmful. When continued in response to chronic psychologic stress they can lead to functional alteration.

Ultimately the results can be those of fixed structural change and irreversible organic pathology, as earlier noted in the Concept of Functional-Structural Progression [p. 469]. These are important and basic concepts in the relationships of emotions, physiology, and organic diseases.

VI. PSYCHODYNAMICS AND PATHOGENESIS

A. FAVORABLE PSYCHOLOGIC SOIL

1. Special Individual Significance

A. PROTECTIVE INTENT.—Neuroses develop as protectively intended patterns of psychologic defense. The psychologically uneconomic symptoms are intended defenses which have been adopted outside of conscious awareness and beyond voluntary control. One may think of their development in terms of response to stress, an inadequacy of existing defenses, or both.

A principal distinguishing feature of the Traumatic Neuroses from other types of neuroses has been noted to be the subjectively perceived and evaluated sharpness of the precipitating event. As do we, Grinker and Spiegel regarded these neurotic reactions as similar to all other neuroses. In the Traumatic Neuroses there would be a fusion of the pre-existing emotional conflicts with the situation brought about by the acute reaction to trauma. This viewpoint also stresses the basic and important relation of the acute traumatic event to the individual antecedent conflicts. Thus the precipitating stress and the reaction to it might serve as an extension of the vicissitudes of all prior experience, including the early intrapsychic conflicts. This would be in accord with our Theory of Antecedent Conflicts.

Others have written similarly. Alexander reported that what characterizes the group called "traumatic neuroses" is not the trauma, which is present in every neurosis, but the acuteness of the condition. Smith and

Solomon, in their treatise *Traumatic Neuroses in Court,* colorfully wrote that "traumatic neurosis is the flowering stalk of a previously planted seed, the recurrent breaking open of an old scar . . .". Fenichel noted the artificial distinction between traumatic neurosis and the psychoneuroses.

B. PSYCHIC ASPECTS OF TRAUMA MORE IMPORTANT.—Freud had early compared the initiating experience in Traumatic Neurosis with that of conversion, as referred to earlier. He observed that the active cause of traumatic neurosis is not the bodily injury so much as the effect of fright — the psychic trauma. In essence this conforms to our clinical observations; that is, that there is often no apparent correlation between the seriousness of injury and the extent of the symptomatology which may develop. When present, the *Traumatic Discrepancy* helps illustrate this.

It is rather the hidden meaning and the individual significance of what has happened which is important. Thus the outwardly minor trauma, as seen by an objective observer, may actually be of much more serious import than it may appear. This was illustrated in *Case 177.* The dynamics, when ascertainable, will in nearly every case reveal some special individual significance for the circumstances or event which is already present for, or is gained subsequently by the patient. The psychic part of the trauma is often more important than the physical part, as we have observed in several instances.

C. VARIATIONS IN VULNERABILITY.—Much has been said or implied already about the dynamics in the Neurosis Following Trauma, and in this section some of these points will be amplified. Consideration of the complex problems involved in the development of neuroses following trauma lead us to raise some important questions. Among these is the basic one: Why does a given individual develop neurotic symptoms, when following a similar or even a greater traumatic experience a second person will not develop symptoms?

Any attempt to answer this question concerning the variation in individual vulnerability brings us to a number of very important considerations in individual psychology. These include: (1) the level of personal security, (2) the possible symbolism represented in the event or its circumstances, (3) the conditioning effects of antecedent events, (4) the presence of hidden (unconscious) masochistic needs, (5) the kinds of psychologic defenses which antedate the event, and many other factors.

The total response to crisis (T.R.C.) and the total response to trauma (T.R.T.) are affected by all of these. The endogain of symptoms is always deeply unconscious. The epigain (unconscious secondary gain) of the symptoms which are already established, is often almost as difficult to surmise accurately. [*See* pp. 58–81.]

The individual response is affected also by external factors, including the sharpness of the trauma and its unexpectedness, as well as by its severity. One's psychologic vulnerability can vary from one period of life to another and sometimes is subject to cyclical variations even over short time spans. The effect of the trauma is also variable according to relative individual levels of helplessness and impotence.

Personal security is influenced by all the myriad external and internal factors influencing the individual. These include remote as well as recent events. As we have noted, antecedents play an important role in human psychology. Conflicts have antecedents. These tend to condition the subsequent response. All of these foregoing factors enter into and help explain the Principle of Predetermined Vulnerability as outlined earlier.

D. THE RULE OF IMPRESSION-PRIORITY.—The Rule of Impression-Priority states an important psychologic concept; namely, that first events and first impressions take a kind of historical precedence, giving them a much greater influence than later ones. This is implicit in our seeking to "make a good first impression" upon a new individual or with a new idea, and so on [*see also* pp. 531–541].

Once an impression is established it is harder to modify. This helps us understand how all prior events in a person's life will have bearing in determining the effect of trauma upon him psychologically.

2. *Ability to Cope with Trauma; Favorable Psychologic Soil Concept*

A. MATCHING "SEED" WITH "SOIL."—Reference was made earlier to the concept of "favorable psychologic soil" already being present [*see also* p. 663]. This is the result of a very gradual psychologic process of prior impressions and significant antecedent conflicts. Herein lies the predisposition of the individual to the development of neurotic symptoms.

This predisposition, which already exists at the time of the trauma, is seldom readily observable. Accordingly, however, the weakest seed might thrive in the most receptive soil, while it would take an unusually powerful seed to take root in barren and unreceptive soil.

B. THE PROPER SEED.—We must also consider together with the preceding analogy the "proper kind" of seed. Thus certain kinds of trauma will be far more potent for some individuals. This is because of its special meaning; its symbolic significance.

Reference is made back briefly to *Case 177,* in which a small amount of plaster, largely in flakes, fell on the person. This relatively minor occurrence (from an outside viewpoint) had far greater significance for him for a number of reasons. It seemed to him to be the culmination of a long series of blows and mishaps. It became symbolically an instance of "the roof finally caving in" on him. Fitting so nearly precisely into his psychologic position at the time, it was indeed exactly the "proper seed." Falling in such *favorable psychologic soil,* the result was emotionally disastrous. A long and severe traumatic neurosis was precipitated, as we observed.

C. EGO DEFENSES FAIL.—It has been pointed out that the actual traumatic situation as observed objectively can vary from minimal, as illustrated in *Case 177,* to maximal, as illustrated in our later *Case 184.* In general, traumatic experiences are a regular and inevitable consequence to living, in which a factor of major importance is one's relative ability to cope with them. This is the function which one hopes will be adequately served by the Total Individual Response to Trauma.

From this line of thinking, Neurosis Following Trauma may then also be regarded as a consequence to the failure of the defensive and protective forces of the ego. This view, as noted earlier, has some general applicability to the genesis of the neuroses. Stern offered an opinion partially in support of our thesis, in that neuroses are not the effect of trauma. They are rather the result of a specific failure of the defenses against the kinds of traumata which are normal occurrences in the life of many individuals.

3. Freud's Contributions

Freud made a number of references to the relation of trauma to neurosis. In his *Inhibitions, Symptoms and Anxiety* he discussed the origin of anxiety in relation to danger and traumatic situations. At this juncture in his thinking he had come to regarded anxiety as the signal for the avoidance of a danger situation. This was an automatic phenomenon and a product of helplessness. The infant's emotional helplessness would be a counterpart of biologic helplessness. Whereas the later danger to the child is separation from the very necessary person who gratifies his vital needs, the original (primordial) danger was regarded to be the separation at birth. Later, in the *New Introductory Lectures,* Freud noted the twofold origin of anxiety, "first, as the direct effect of a traumatic factor, and, secondly, that a traumatic factor . . . threatens to recur." Here Freud was using "traumatic" in a wider sense than in the present discussion. In the wider sense, "what is feared, the object of anxiety, is always the emergence of a traumatic factor . . ."

Freud called attention to some important factors concerning Traumatic Neuroses. Principal among these was the patient's emotional fixation to the time of the trauma. He also recognized the reproduction of the traumatic situation in dreams. This occurs following acute traumatic experiences in civilian life. We shall also learn how this frequently (reported in 25 per cent) transpires in the Combat Reactions.

In discussing the unconscious wish and significance of a misstep, Freud commented on the onset of nervous ailments following a fall *without* injury. He noted "that the fall was already a preparation of the neurosis . . ." He also pointed out that conversion attacks may occur in which "the attack constitutes a complete reproduction of [the traumatic] situation."

4. Need to Suffer; Remission-Following-Trauma

A. SYMPTOMS AND DISTRESS GREATER WHEN PHYSICAL CONSEQUENCES ARE SLIGHT.—An unconscious need to suffer or to be punished is present in variable degree in neuroses generally. Such a need develops in response to submerged feelings of guilt. Such guilt may be rational or irrational, realistic or unrealistic. In the unconscious this makes no difference. The assessment is made by the internal psychology and need have no relationship to any objective evaluation as might be made by a neutral observer. At times the suffering of a physical injury, or the resulting pain, handicap, and so on, serves to expiate unconscious feelings of guilt. Psychologic and emotional suffering may do likewise. Accordingly, these may be even greater when the physical elements themselves are less. This basis can unconsciously influence the tendency to suffer accidents, including those of the so-called accident-prone person [p. 196]. Visceral masochism [p. 493] may be present.

This helps us in certain instances to account for the failure of the symptoms which develop, proportionately to reflect the degree of the real physical injury following trauma. As we have earlier noted, the symptomatology and distress which are manifested psychologically are often greater when the trauma is actually slight, or at least when the outward physical consequences are slight.

Recall also our earlier concept which points out the reciprocal relationship between anxiety (and conflict) and pain. Thus each can result in the other being more. *Pain and anxiety have a reciprocal relationship* [pp. 123, 470, and 480].

B. STRESSFUL EVENT SATISFIES NEED.—Thus far we have been thinking in terms of neurotic symptoms having their onset following trauma. Let us briefly consider the interesting reverse of this — that emotional manifestations may undergo what we might invite attention to as a *Remission-Following-Trauma.** After the foregoing discussion we are ready for a few remarks on this seeming paradox. Such instances are occasionally observed.

Indeed, cases are likely to come to the minds of psychiatrists in which remission has occurred in a major psychotic or neurotic reaction following some acute and major stress. These can include major surgery, an accident, a serious intercurrent illness, or a traumatic event. When this occurs it constitutes an instance of Remission Following Trauma.

If we think of emotional or physical suffering as serving unconscious needs, presumably some external event can lead to these results actually or symbolically. Then the same internal purpose of the symptoms — or the suffering aspect of them is no longer so demanding. A symptom in which this satisfaction of unconscious guilt was a major determinant can go into whole or partial remission.

RESULTS FROM ELECTRIC SHOCK.—The success of shock treatment in a given case might be partially explained in similar fashion, on the basis of the gratification of unconscious needs for punishment. Weigert wrote that convulsive therapy is opposed to the main aim of analytic therapy, which strives to mitigate the cruelty of an archaic superego and to help the patient to endure the necessary, but not the unnecessary hardships of reality [*see also* earlier references to shock therapy under *Amnesia,* p. 773, and in the chapter on Depressive Reactions, pp. 215–219].

MANIFESTATIONS GREATER WHEN ORGANIC DAMAGE MINIMAL.—Similarly to what may be observed with certain war casualties, an analogous statement can be made in reference to traumatic neuroses. Here it is also true generally that the more severe cases of injury (physical) often do not show severe neurotic symptomatology.

---

* This interesting sequence is the *reverse* of our present main thesis of Neuroses Following Trauma.

Thus we often find greater severity of emotional manifestations where the organic damage is minimal or absent. One can hypothecate that in many cases sufficient organic damage seems to lessen the chances for serious emotional sequelae. In other words, when inner needs for punishment or suffering are strongly operative and the physical injury or suffering from trauma is minimal, they remain unsatisfied or may be only partly satisfied. It is as though the resulting emotional suffering and deprivation which may occur, attempt then to satisfy them in substitute fashion. Organic damage thus may seem to alleviate anxiety and its defensive derivatives.

B. SEVERE NEUROSIS FOLLOWS PSYCHOLOGICALLY TRAUMATIC EVENT

1. Psychogenetic Principles Illustrated

Some of the principles in the psychogenesis of the Neuroses-Following-Trauma may become clearer through the following illustration. Here a serious psychically traumatic event served as the precipitating factor in the onset of a major neurosis.

Case 182

The Onset of a Severe Neurosis Follows a Psychologically Traumatic Event

(1) *Father's death traumatic*

A thirty-three-year-old associate professor of mathematics was referred for analysis several months after the onset of a very severe neurosis. The manifestations were principally those of anxiety and depression, with some obsessive hygeiaphrontic preoccupation. At the time of the first consultation he was tortured by nervousness, insomnia, and recurring disturbing dreams. Strong feelings of guilt and self-blame were accompanied by nearly constant weeping and an unhealthful, obsessional kind of religiosity. Prior to psychiatric referral he had been studied and treated with little success under a purely medical regimen. This had been carried many weeks past any optimal point of study, with a medical conclusion of essentially negative organic findings. This had been largely because of his strong insistence.

The onset of symptoms had occurred abruptly following his father's sudden death. This tragic event had transpired only several hours following an angry and tense scene between the patient and his father. As a consequence the patient had held himself responsible for his father's death. He felt unworthy and sinful. He felt certain of death from an impending heart attack. He described severe chest pains and difficulty in breathing. He announced his belief that God was causing him this discomfort and suffering as the punishment for his "sin." He was so emotionally distressed that he could provide little detailed factual or historical information.

(2) *Elucidate emotional conflicts*

Here then, on the face of it, was a rather simple example of a most severe neurosis following a very severe emotionally traumatic event. However, if one hopes therapeutically to influence the neurotic process one must uncover, elucidate, and resolve the underlying hidden conflicts. In this case the foregoing information is of course barely even a point of beginning. For the traumatic event to have its precipitating and often devastating effect, we have learned that it very often has a special significance, an individual specificity. Intensive study of the individual concerned will reveal this.* Some of the bases for the "favorable psychologic soil" in the present case can be summarized.

The father had been a successful rancher who had worked very hard. He had steadily increased his acreage while raising a large family. Things had gone increasingly poorly, however, in recent years. The father's capacity to work had decreased. His business and social judgment had also deteriorated. These changes were partly a consequence of the joint onslaught of age and arteriosclerosis. There was some rather alarmingly decreased appreciation of social mores. As a consequence there had been several embarrassing incidents. He had made unwelcome sexual advances toward a number of young women acquaintances of the family. He had already sold off half of his ranch holdings, and was in the process of disposing of another large portion of the shrinking balance, to the great concern of his wife and children. He suffered also from chronic heart failure with several heart attacks, after the most recent two of which he had not been expected to live.

In this setting the patient had made a visit to his Texas ranch home. This is the most outwardly apparent part of the objective situation in which he had angrily upbraided his father for depleting the family security. One, of course, cannot rule out the angry outburst as being a possible precipitating factor in the father's death. However, it is a far cry from the total degree of guilt and responsibility which had been assumed by the patient in neurotic fashion.

(3) *Passive dependent role*

In these circumstances why was the consequence of the father's death the onset of so devastating a neurosis as to effectively cripple the patient's capacity for living? Prolonged work in treatment provided many of the answers.

The patient had been an underdeveloped, malnourished, and sickly child. Partly as a result, and because he was also a younger child, he had been overprotected. As an example, decisions had been regularly made for him, a practice which helped to create a passive, dependent role into which he readily fitted himself. At the same time he sympathetically identified with his mother, who "took many things from Dad she should never have had to." His closeness to his mother became part of the intense dependence which was reflected in repetitive fashion in his own later choice of a wife and his subsequent relationship with her. Part of the picture was also a tremendous protective over-control of hostility.

Characterologically, he had gradually become a mild-mannered person who almost never outwardly expressed any disagreement or difference of opinion. The degree of his restrictions and his fear of his feelings in this regard is perhaps illustrated by his reaction in college following a tragic incident in which one of a pair of classmates was killed in an auto accident. This had followed an angry, rebellious outburst by them toward the dean and their subsequent defiance of college rules. His reaction was a vicarious identification with the rebels. He became terribly distressed following the tragic accident. His ordinarily excellent grades dropped. Somatic complaints developed, and he very nearly had to drop out of school completely.

(4) *Destructive potential of anger realized*

This patient's choice of occupation had also tied in with his unconscious needs. Research in mathematics and teaching were for him a passive and dependent way of adaptation. This represented a more abstract, detached, and therefore safer life. His outburst toward his father had been an unprecedented affair. It took place only after many years of storing up resentment, until finally the "warehouse" was bursting.

---

* As Trawick and Bate aptly wrote, ". . . study is necessary if we are to establish a specific relationship of the psychic situation to the personality of the individual. Just as the typhoid bacillus, specific for typhoid fever, depends upon the susceptibility of the individual, so does specificity of the psychic event depend upon the personality structure of the person."

In partial stringent summary, his worst hidden fears of the destructive potential of his own anger had been realized. How frighteningly potent his anger really was when it gained expression! The results approximated his long-buried infantile apprehensions. In consequence he held himself totally, albeit unrealistically, responsible. The hygeiaphrontis was part of an unconsciously attempted neurotic regressive retreat toward an earlier, even more dependent position. The depth of the illness in this case bordered on the psychotic in several areas. However, this man made excellent progress during several years of analysis.

2. Significant Antecedents Determine Reaction

In the foregoing case there was a definite trauma. Undoubtedly this traumatic event would prove distressing in varying degree to anyone. It became such a crushing blow to this patient as to threaten his very existence.

We see that his entire character structure and past existence were so constituted as to provide significant antecedents. These would greatly multiply the effects of the psychologically traumatic event. This had served to precipitate his neurosis. This man made substantial gains through therapy. He gained considerable ability to analyze his feelings and conflicts. He effected some constructive resolutions and became better able to copy with certain others.

C. ON GAINS AND MECHANICS

1. Epigain and Endogain

A. ENDOGAIN THE RAISON D'ETRE OF ILLNESS.—Repression is an important defensive operation which is automatic. While defensively intended, it almost inevitably leads to the employment of other mental mechanisms. The regressive features in Traumatic Neuroses are part of both the epigain and the endogain. The endogain of the Traumatic Neurosis, as in other neurotic reactions, is the *raison d'etre* — its basis; its justification [p. 69]. This is true since the endogain and the underlying intrapsychic needs for this gain are responsible for initiating the illness.

Symptoms of the Traumatic Neuroses may have many kinds of hidden and symbolic significance. For example, the trauma may be "perceived" unconsciously as having elements of symbolic temptation — satisfaction or gratification, on the one hand; and retribution or punishment on the other.

B. EPIGAIN SEEKS MORE FAVORABLE ENVIRONMENT.—Large elements of epigain, the unconscious secondary gain of the illness, frequently complicate the picture. These can substantially darken the prognosis of emotional illnesses, including those which follow physical trauma. The traumatic epigain, as in other neurotic reactions, refers to the gains secured secondarily in unconscious fashion from symptoms which are already established.

Endeavors in the service of the epigain are directed externally to secure modifications which will result in a more favorable external environment [p. 61*ff.*] Epigain can play a vital role in the propagation of the symptoms of a neurosis which are already established.

A volume might be written alone on the many complex problems and the important psychologic considerations incident to the granting or seeking of compensation and pensions in civilian accidents and in certain industrial and military cases. The importance assigned by some authorities to this aspect of the problem is reflected in their use at times of the term "compensation neuroses." To the author's mind it tends to overemphasize one unfórtunate aspect of a most complex illness. This can operate in a way that hardly invites efforts at study, treatment, or sympathetic medical understanding of a knotty medical problem. [Refer to *Table 4*, p. 65, for an outline summary of the epigain of emotional illness.]

2. *Common Defense Against Prospect of Danger*

A. CONSCIOUS AND UNCONSCIOUS.—Many psychologic defenses are employed by the hard-pressed individual in the face of crisis, threat, or trauma. These are part of his efforts to maintain and protect himself and his position. This is true likewise in response to the impact of stress and trauma. Some of these defenses are conscious and others unconscious. He has control over the former. The latter are called into play automatically and without conscious volition, selectivity, or control.

All mental mechanisms, are so employed. Threat, danger, stress or trauma may result in the automatic mobilization of one or more of these defensive operations. Usually a familiar and previously employed pattern of defense is called into play. All possible conscious and unconscious defenses are mobilized.

B. DENIAL.—One commonly adopted defense is the rather primitive mechanism of denial. In this interesting and widely employed intrapsychic defensive operation, one simply denies the presence of threat or danger, the possibility of something happening to oneself or the existence of possible inimical sequelae to such danger.

C. RATIONALIZATION, PROVERBS, AND OTHER MECHANISMS.—Also quite common are the many conscious rationalizations which are attempted. Some are along similar lines to the above. In addition, many different forms of rationalization are attempted. Some people secure comfort through personal consolation or by making favorable comparisons with those less fortunate.

An example of this is in the proverb which was written several hundred years ago by Aesop. "There is always someone worse off than yourself." Others are such common ones as "Count your blessings", "It's never as bad as it seems", "Every cloud has a silver lining", "It's always darkest before the dawn", "Prosperity (or happiness) is just around the corner", and so on.

Other mental mechanisms are called into operation. Displacement may be encountered. Dissociation is seen in the more massive reactions of amnesia and fugue states. Projection is occasionally employed. As noted earlier [pp. 25, 691], the mental mechanisms comprise our First Line of Psychic Defense.

3. Regression

The neurotic illnesses following trauma are more or less clearly regressive in character. Feelings of impotence and helplessness contribute to the impact of the traumatic event. We have learned that unpreparedness or unexpectedness, exhaustion, and the fatigue from chronic stress can similarly contribute. The regressive nature of the symptoms as a consequence to external stress may be often observed through their implicit dependent appeal. In essence the ego has received a desperate blow in its attempt to cope with the environment. A retreat has in effect ensued to a more comfortable antecedent state. The regression is involuntary and beyond conscious awareness. Its unconscious intent is defensive.

Fenichel described this as a "regression to the more primitive passive-receptive type of mastery of the outside world following . . . failure to succeed in an active way." Similarly, in discussing traumatic symptoms and disturbances, Alexander wrote, "All these reactions can be explained as signs of damage to the ego, which, under the intimidating influence of the trauma, abandons its mastery of coordination and regressively retreats to helplessness." Glover pointed out certain "screening functions" of the memories of traumatic events.

Regression thus is frequent in that there is a regressive aspect to most cases of traumatic neuroses. The endogain goal involved here is the seeking of a more protected and less exposed position — a safer one. Many of the symptoms, once they are elaborated, in this group of neurotic reactions are also thus employed in similar fashion as part of the epigain. Symbolization and undoing may be utilized upon occasion.

D. IN CONCLUSION

1. Complex Subject

If we wish to draw some conclusion from what we know about the Neuroses-Following-Trauma and their psychogenesis, perhaps the most important one is the individuality of each case. Each instance is influenced by many factors in the prior life and adjustment of the person concerned. Symptoms run the gamut of psychiatric manifestations. Clinical pictures are widely diverse. There is no trauma without its emotional repercussions. On the other hand, study of any given act of post-traumatic emotional sequelae alone would not necessarily tell us much about the nature or severity of the trauma. Further, it is not possible to forecast what symptoms may develop were a given individual to suffer trauma.

We are thus dealing with an exceedingly complex subject. While some overall similarities exist, cases will not follow a clearly predictable course. Since the manifestations are legion, one can hardly become a *bona fide* expert in the field of Traumatic Neuroses alone. He must first gain some mastery of all the neuroses, or even better, of the field of psychiatry.

2. Many Psychodynamic Components

In these brief remarks on dynamics it should be noted that the field of psychopathology represented here is so broad that it can include factors which we have considered in our earlier discussions of each type of neurosis. Schilder, in discussing neuroses following head injuries, cited three important psychodynamic components: (1) a threat to integrity (death or deformity), (2) a superior force, and (3) a masochistic gratification. Several important components could be added. One might certainly include the important concept that the traumatic experiences of infancy and early childhood may serve to sensitize or to desensitize the individual in his reaction to subsequent traumatic experiences in later life. Thus, his ability to tolerate and to cope with subsequent traumatic events is influenced by his earlier psychologic conditioning. In accord with our Interpersonal Perpetuation Concept [pp. 328 and 464], attitude-responses to trauma may be "taken over" from parents or other significant adults. We have mentioned other important ones.

The individual's Total Response to Trauma, or T.R.T., is the expression of his assembled potential of personal resources, his strengths and weaknesses as present constitutionally, and as modified and influenced by his experiences and the vicissitudes of living.

3. Broad View of Trauma Useful

Trauma may include every conceivable type of physical or psychologic injury. The latter includes separations, moves, deaths, financial disaster, losses of office, position, prestige, divorce, and many others. Any of the S.E.H.A. [p. 38] can comprise a significant psychic trauma. Traumatic responses on occasion will reduplicate past experience [p. 468].

Neuroses may occur after illness, operation, and combat. Thus, emotional trauma may accompany many events. *Case 46* [p. 202] illustrated the traumatic impact of the sudden appreciation of some of the implications of a serious suicidal attempt. A broad vista of trauma and its role in the psychogenesis of the neuroses is useful.

VII. COMPENSATION AND NEUROSIS

A. EVALUATION OF CLAIMS DIFFICULT

The fact has been stressed that even the abrupt onset of a discrete and severe emotional symptom takes place in the psychologic soil already well prepared. This is in accord with our Favorable Psychologic Soil Concept. This important concept complicates the problems of medico-legal work. In consequence to this, plus many other factors, the evaluation and assessment of claims for emotional damages in court is seldom a simple matter.

Thus, in many cases of neurosis a precipitating event may be regarded as "a convenient peg upon which one hangs a hat." Presumably, if this particular peg did not present itself, another might well come along sooner or later, given suitable circumstances and sufficient trauma. This "Peg Principle," as noted, also emphasizes the complexity in making liability determinations about neurotic disabilities or illnesses in relation to trauma, or otherwise.

In fact, it appears that the resulting disability from nearly any case in which trauma has occurred is subject to legal contest. The determination of the degree of liability, and the determination of a fair and equitable estimation as to the extent of damages, can well tax the judgment of a twentieth-century Solomon.

At the same time, we may have barely scratched the surface of the whole huge subject of the neuroses in medico-legal work. Unquestionably, compensation in the past has been inadequate for emotional disability. Historically, the strictly physical sequellae to trauma have been overstressed, in proportion to the emotional side. The latter have been only too often ignored or at the least undervalued.

B. INDUSTRIAL COMPENSATION CASE

1. Problems in Management

Among the knottiest of medical problems are those involving instances of industrial accidents in which there is a neurotic exaggeration of the symptoms following an injury. At times a neurosis develops in which the actual physical injury is minimal or seemingly nonsignificant. All kinds of chronic aches and pains, together with all varieties of functional limitations, have been observed to develop in these situations. These can be extremely troubling, particularly to the general physician, and also to the industrial physician or surgeon, as well as to the psychiatrist. What has been earlier termed for purposes of identification as a *physical scapegoat* [pp. 393, 461], is often unwittingly evolved.

There are many reasons for the problems engendered in the management of compensation in emotional disabilities. Some principal ones are summarized in tabular form as follows:

Table 40

Compensation and Neuroses; Bases for Problems in Management

(1) The elements of unconscious or conscious compensation seeking. This may be an external substitute in some symbolic fashion for underlying unconscious dependency needs. While invisible and not consciously sought, these still hardly contribute to a kinder attitude toward the patient.

(2) Bafflement and frustration in response to one's failure (which may be regarded unfairly as a lack of ability) especially to find an organic basis, and to get the person back to productive work.

(3) The examiner's inability properly to assess and give due regard to the underlying powerful unconscious needs which account for chronic symptoms, for failure to respond to therapy, and for the person's continuing inability to work.

(Table continued on next page)

Table 40—Continued

 (4) The complex medico-legal problems which often arise.

 (5) The externally often obvious but still quite unconsciously sought epigain [p. 56] of such neuroses. This is related to (1).

 (6) The more deeply concealed endogain; the *raison d'etre* of the illness [pp. 68 ff]. This is difficult to appreciate adequately or to understand, even on the part of the experienced specialist. Difficulty in understanding something about the etiology of the illness, means difficulty in appreciating the hard-pressed position of the patient.

 (7) The gradual evolvement of a non-constructive *attitude-symptom* [p. 328, 450], directed toward compensation and life. This can come to comprise what we might term a Compensation Character; the ultimate in self-defeat and pervasive "balanced neurotic position."

2. Compensation Neuroses

These cases are still referred to in various quarters as Compensation Neuroses. This is an unfortunate term. It focuses attention away from etiology and dynamics. They have been so named because of the frequency of some degree of obsessive concern by the patient with compensation, or with efforts to secure compensation. At times an obsessive level of interest develops in litigation or threatened litigation. [*See* earlier reference to epigain, p. 56.]

There also may be preoccupation of an obsessive nature, with the person's interest and efforts directed at securing damages, compensation, pensions, insurance benefits, or retirement. The physician is likely to find himself involved in such actions. Such involvement can be time-consuming, personally unrewarding, and the ultimate in wisdom might seem insufficient to arrive at an equitable evaluation.

3. Evaluating Emotional Difficulties

The following case is presented as an illustration of the involved, unfortunate, and prognostically nearly hopeless kind of situation seen in far too many industrial compensation cases. It helps make clear the complex relationships of compensation and neurosis.

Case 183

An Industrial Compensation Case

(1) *Discrepancy between level of disability and concern*
A fifty-two-year-old machinist sought a review of his claim for compensation in the hope of securing an increase in his financial benefits. He had been receiving regular disability compensation during a three-year period of inability to work.

Upon consultation, he reported symptoms of nervousness, loss of ability to concentrate, and weight loss. A steady increase in symptoms was also reported. He was now unable to undertake any activity involving physical exercise. He described an increasing diminution of right visual acuity, to the point that he could barely see. All of his many difficulties were now attributed by him to have resulted from an auto accident several years earlier. He described in great detail his many disabling symptoms and the terrific handicap in living they represented. However, all of this was presented in a rather bland way, almost as though he were talking about someone else far distant [*la belle indifférence* of Somatic Conversion, p. 671]. There was a distinct discrepancy between his rather apparent level of handicap and disability, and the amount of concern he manifested about this.

(2) Secondary Defense

Any inquiry which was attempted into family relationships or emotional adjustment was answered curtly, if at all. His attitude in response to such efforts seemed to say, "Why in the world do you ask such silly things? That's got nothing to do with my symptoms! I'm disabled and can't work. After all, I'd be glad to go back to work if only you would fix me up. Of course, if you can't do that, then I guess I'll have to have the compensation."

This, of course, is entirely accurate from one viewpoint. If the doctor could do away with the underlying neurotic needs, the patient would indeed be glad to return to work. Sadly, the patient is disinterested. He staunchly resists any possible approach to his problem via psychotherapeutic inquiry and study. His disinterest and his resistance constitute a most effective *secondary defense* of his symptoms. He is unable to assume the necessary responsibility for cooperation in this direction. Without the patient's active cooperation, the physician is helpless in any attempted psychotherapeutic endeavor. He alone cannot do it for the patient. The forces of secondary defense were indeed powerful. In accord with our important Concept of Secondary Defense in emotional illness, the symptoms — vitally necessary intended defenses in themselves — are in turn thereby secondarily defended, and most effectively.

(3) Dependency needs met

The history of this man's accident was that he had been in a minor collision in a company truck nearly four years earlier. At the time he had not considered it serious enough to report to the police or even to his supervisor. Any slight damage to the truck which might have occurred had passed unnoticed by his fellow employees. Six months later, however, he had developed a right eye infection. This he eventually came to attribute to the accident. The infection, a conjunctivitis, cleared up promptly, but he began to suffer from subjective visual impairment. He gradually became increasingly nervous and unable to concentrate. Several competent examiners had ruled out organic reasons for the visual difficulty. However, it continued to interfere progressively with the patient's work.

Nervous manifestations became so severe that the patient soon was forced to leave employment abruptly. Unbeknown to him, his work efficiency and performance had become so unsatisfactory that he barely succeeded in leaving ahead of involuntary separation proceedings. These were actually in process at the time. Needless to say, efforts to interest this man in any kind of constructive introspection were fruitless. Although he had no conscious awareness of the fact, the illness had become too fixed and his compensation (actually his passive-dependent position) too important to him. His unconscious neurotic needs for dependency were satisfied too well by the self-defeating, psychologically uneconomic, and tragic "gains" of his illness.

C. UNREWARDING AND UNPOPULAR WORK

1. Sufferer Penalized

Sometimes the greatly condensed kind of example which is selected for illustration is rather dramatic. It also may tend to provide an oversimplified picture of the Neuroses-Following-Trauma, as with other patterns of neurotic reactions, the preceding comments notwithstanding.

One can sometimes roughly gauge the knottiness, difficulty in making judgments, and the complexity of some of the problems encountered in industrial compensation cases by the size and the weight of the medical file! Also, its size and weight is somewhat an indication as to the lack of unanimity of medical opinion which is present. The file of papers on the foregoing case was well over two inches thick. There is often enough little overt anxiety. The reaction complex (and attitude-symptom) has been "successful" in its control. This illustrates our precept of the Inverse Anxiety-Symptom Ratio [pp. 103, 145, 324, and 462], according to which the more "successful" the symptom, the less anxiety is experienced.

However, our present system tends to penalize the people who suffer with neurotic disabilities. There are many instances of neurotic disability. For example, an individual suffered a paralyzed leg following an injury — a minor injury. There were no organic findings. The symptom possibly could be regarded as an *anxiety-equivalent* [pp. 19, 102, 111 and 462]. Muscle function was intact, nerve function was intact. However, this patient was unable to use his leg. There was no doubt about the genuineness of his disability. At the time of looking into the case some two years after the accident, this individual had still been unable to use his leg. This is not something he imagined or put on — it was not malingering — this was illness.

2. Lack of Organic Explanation Frustrating

Unfortunately, many people, physicians included, tend to become frustrated in this type of situation if they cannot find an organic reason to explain a disability or a loss of function. [*See* earlier reference to our Flight-to-the-Physical Principle, p. 461]. Persons in this situation may well become angry. Sometimes this tends to be literally but unwittingly taken out on the patient. He may be accused, implicitly if not actually, of malingering or of faking, simply to gain attention, or compensation, or whatever. Thereby the sufferer is penalized, and suffers inevitably further.

Some individuals had rather openly regarded the above patient as a "goldbrick" or as a malingerer. Malingering is considerably less likely to be the case. There are occasional cases of malingering, but these occur more rarely than one might believe. The person who consciously malingers to gain a point, to gain sympathy, or to gain compensation and so on can be regarded as emotionally sick, with this type of attempt as a symptom of his illness. It is hardly an evidence of normal or healthy adjustment to have to resort to such ways to gain one's ends. [*See* further discussion, pp. 494–7.]

3. Psychiatrist's Position

In some cases of this kind, it is as though the administrative (or medical) officials in charge must go "all out" to disprove organic disability. Sometimes a psychiatric consultant is hired, but to the shame of all concerned it seems almost that what is actually wanted is not a genuine assessment of the cause, level and degree of disability, but simply more proof that "nothing is wrong."

In such an atmosphere, particularly with these most difficult of problem cases, few psychiatrists are willing to work. When they have been willing to undertake this most tedious and trying kind of assignment, their observation of something in the cases which others are not willing or able to see may make them quite unpopular. As a result of the foregoing, this work is unpopular in turn, as it is often unrewarding.

D. INSTANCES OF EMOTIONAL DISABILITY FOLLOWING TRAUMA

There are many examples of disabilities following or related to trauma. The following *Table 41* tabulates 15 instances illustrating some of the types of emotional disability following trauma which the author has encountered. These types of cases are the ones which are likely to involve currently or in the future, such problems as those of compensation, disability, retirement, and medico-legal involvement. None of the following group comprises an E.O.C. [pp. 393 and 454], which can occur but is rather rare.

Table 41

Instances of Emotional Disability Following Trauma

(1) A man suffered with limitation of motion of the knee, following an instance in which he had stumbled in getting off a public conveyance.

(2) An instance of sensory loss in the arm had its onset following the last of a series of altercations with the man's supervisor.

(3) A case of stomach cramps and nausea occurred in a secretary after she was required to do some exceedingly distasteful work, during long overtime periods.

(4) The case of a patient was marked by persistent headaches. These had their onset following a minor fall.

(5) A passenger developed symptoms of vertigo and faintness following the collision of a public vehicle.

(6) Continued anxiety, insomnia and nightmares were observed by a patient following his recovery from the physical manifestations of severe body burns.

(7) A patient suffered diminished potency and disturbed sexual function following an elevator accident.

(8) An individual reported tension, restlessness, and tremors which had followed an automobile collision. This type of difficulty is fairly common, varying as to duration and severity.

(9) A dairyman reported symptoms of startle reaction, nervousness, palpitation, and gastric disturbance, which had their onset following a charge and minor injury by a thoroughbred bull.

(10) Anxiety attacks (A.A.A.) with precordial pain, labored breathing, fear of heart failure and death, and impaired capacity for close and satisfactory relationships, had their onset for an individual following a fire in which he leaped to "safety" in a fireman's net.

(11) Symptoms of irritability, nervousness, impaired efficiency at work and a deteriorating marital adjustment occurred in the victim of a plane accident; one of the rare persons who survived and "recovered."

(*Table continued on next page*)

Table 41—Continued

(12) A patient reported the presence of severe (nonorganic) back aches following a "strain" on lifting.

(13) A wife suffered mood changes, with moroseness, loss of interest and depression, in which the onset followed the death of her spouse in an electrical accident.

(14) Another individual reported the gradual onset of nervousness and personality changes, with an increased tendency toward perfectionism, parsimoniousness, and an increasingly restricted willingness to take ordinary business risks. These symptoms were those of an executive, which had their initiation following a traumatic experience, with explosion and fire aboard a colleague's yacht.

(15) A government official's family had noted the gradual and subtle exaggeration of his existing character traits, to a point of limitation of efficiency and interference with his successful functioning, marking the establishment of a character neurosis in a previously very successful fifty-two-year-old man. This development began following an automobile crash.

In offering this tabulated series of instances, the presentation of an increasing level of complexity has been purposeful. Actually, one of the problems that we will probably have in further developing our procedures in the whole matter of neurotic damages and disabilities resulting from or following trauma, necessarily will be the subtle nature that they often take.

Despite their subtle nature, the degree of resulting disability, the consequent interference with function, and the resulting impairment of satisfactions in living are often enormous. In each of the foregoing instances the individuals themselves ascribed full responsibility to the preceding traumatic experience. Where anxiety is present concurrently with other symptoms, our Incomplete Symptom-Defense Concept [pp. 89, 189, and 451] is illustrated.

E. NOTES ON THERAPY: PRINCIPLE OF SYMPTOM-LONGEVITY

1. Need for Public Education

A great deal of public education will likely be needed to gain more understanding about emotional illness. In some cases the relative education and sophistication of the jury will prove a vital factor in the proper appreciation of neurotic disability for purposes of adequate and just compensation. This is also true for many doctors and lawyers, who will need more education and understanding to increase their appreciation, and in making a fair and proper assessment of the effects of these factors.

We may well be missing the more severe kinds of disabilities and the more frequent "emotional half" of traumatic claims. The reasons may be because of their complexity, because we may not be able to see, or want to see, or be able easily to demonstrate the tremendous impact from the many changes in mental and emotional function, or from the many changes in mental and emotional stability, which can follow trauma and which can influence every phase of the person's living.

Solving the complex problems of compensation and neuroses will require a great deal of public education. More public understanding and knowledge would also enhance the prospects for individual therapy.

2. Joint-Endeavor Principle in Psychotherapy

Attitudes and patterns of reaction have developed for each individual because they served best for the person concerned. When one seeks to work therapeutically in these areas it soon becomes amply apparent that they are not likely to undergo modification readily — and indeed never — unless some clear advantage lies in their modification. This is in line with our Therapeutic Bargain Concept [pp. 591, 713].

It is small wonder indeed that treatment so often takes a long time and is a difficult and complex joint endeavor. Small wonder also that therapy requires a great deal of personal commitment and must receive a considerable priority among one's other interests and activities during its course. Psychotherapy is a complex joint endeavor. This is the Joint-Endeavor Principle of Therapy.

3. Promptness Valuable

The importance of promptness must be stressed in the treatment of all cases of Neuroses-Following-Trauma. This is particularly true where problems of compensation are involved. *The longer that symptoms are permitted to exist, the greater the chance for their fixation.* In other words, the longer-lived is a symptom, the more difficult it is to resolve. This fits in with what it is suggested we refer to as the *Principle of Symptom Longevity* in the pattern of neurotic reactions [pp. 503, 709].

Therapy should be instituted promptly following an injury with emotional sequelae. The changes for success diminish as the months go by. Thus, in many cases the prognosis becomes gloomier with the passage of time alone. It becomes increasingly difficult to offer what we have described as a Therapeutic Bargain [pp. 300, 501].

4. Factors in Prognosis and Response to Therapy

A. PENDING LITIGATION.—This can play a role in treatment and in the prognosis. From a medical standpoint, the settlement of any pending or possible pending claims could not take place too early. It would be ideal if all litigation could be settled once and for all the first month. This would remove any possible untoward influence from this source, conscious or unconscious, on the main goal of recovery.

Compensation, whether material or psychologic, can enter into the epigain. Its preservation can become an important S.O. [pp. 351*ff*.], or can comprise a soteria [pp. 607*ff*.]. The more important the epigain becomes, the stronger effect it can exert on the side of perpetuating an illness which is already established. One might perhaps even maintain the argument that the longer a settlement is withheld, the more compensation is required, to make up for the emotional handicaps and suffering, which become more fixed and tougher to cope with!

B. DEPENDENCY NEEDS AND REGRESSION.—A disability pension can fit in with unconscious needs for being cared for. These are referred to as part of the dependency needs. Many patients have such needs, the goal of which is a regressive retreat toward a more passive and protected position.* Regression results in a loss of independence. The individual under stresses he cannot cope with, driven by powerful unconscious forces beyond his control or awareness, retreats from stress, from adult levels of responsibility, into earlier, less mature ones. Compensation also can gain great emotional significance.

In the Neuroses-Following-Trauma it is likely to be the people who have stronger underlying regressive trends who develop symptoms. Often the symptoms will fit into the regressive needs. They can lead to a more protected and "safe" position; a less exposed one. They can interfere with or prevent work; can lead to someone else taking over various responsibilities.

C. CONCEPT OF EMOTIONAL INERTIA.—We learned earlier [p. 213] of the increased difficulty of initiating therapy, over maintaining it. A Mechanical Analogy was drawn to illustrate our concept of overcoming what we termed the Emotional Inertia.

The amount of resistance and inertia to be overcome in getting treatment started in many of these instances is likely to be substantial indeed. This concept is valuable in understanding the substantial problem involved in the therapeutic management of Traumatic Neuroses with compensation features. Therapy must be conducted in accord with our Joint Endeavor Principle [p. 130].

VIII. TREATMENT

A. IMPORTANCE OF PROMPTNESS

1. Prognosis Progressively Gloomier with Passage of Time

A prime factor in the psychologic treatment of the various cases in this large group of the Neuroses-Following-Trauma is the promptness with which such therapy is instituted after the traumatic event. Promptness is even more important in the very acute cases. The prognosis in many cases becomes gloomier in geometric progression as time passes. This is directly in accord with the Symptom-Longevity Principle [Ch.14:VIIIE] which emphasizes that the longer emotional symptoms persist, the more difficult they become to resolve. This principle is particularly true in those cases in which compensation becomes important. Although reference is made

---

* Dependency needs may continue, develop, or can be recreated. They may reflect a continuation of our earlier named Profitable Patterns Concept [pp. 320, 338, 464], which stresses the child's automatic adoption and exploitation of interpersonal adjustments and relationships such as have proved most "profitable," as subjectively evaluated by him.

here primarily to material compensation, this can also apply to psychologic compensation. The latter is represented by the satisfaction of strong, deeply hidden dependency needs and by the achievement of a more passive position.

Treatment often has a discouraging outlook in certain industrial compensation cases and in cases in which litigation impends. This is particularly true when a disability pension fits in with unconscious neurotic needs for dependency and for a regressive retreat into a more passive, less active role, as noted. In speaking of this "external . . . advantage through illness", Freud noted that whenever it "is at all pronounced, and no substitute can be found for it in reality, you need not look forward very hopefully to influencing the neurosis by your therapy." In relation to these sometimes powerful factors of secondary gain and compensation, Wechsler noted the "comparatively bad prognosis." Treatment efforts can sometimes lead to a veritable Symptom Barrage [pp. 486 and 664].

Delayed treatment enables the industrial accident case to become more established and chronic [see Case 183]. The traumatic epigain can assume a major role in determining prognosis. It can become a powerful force in the propagation of the symptoms of an illnes which are already established.

2. Dependency Position Secured

Prompt therapy, when it is feasible and when the patient can be interested, may counteract unhealthy regressive trends. Otherwise these can become increasingly fixed. In many of the cases which have progressed into a seemingly placid and sad kind of chronicity, one may see evidence of the regressive retreat into dependent passivity. A "successful" withdrawal has been made to an earlier, childlike level of adjustment where one is cared for (by society, relatives, pension, or compensation), even though poorly.

For the neurotically sick person, these are actually, from any practical standpoint, often minimal or very marginal and self-defeating compensations for his suffering, limitation, and handicap. Still, on one level, they are worth far more symbolically than the much better living which the constructive investment of the same amount of energy could bring him. In many of these cases the traumatic event seems to have been provided the impetus, or to have precipitated the process, for which the psychologic preparation had long been in progress. The person has unwittingly sought and secured a more dependent position. This can illustrate our Concept of Symptoms as an Implied Preference [p. 503].

B. THE SECONDARY DEFENSE

1. Guarding the Status Quo of the Neurosis; The "Balanced Neurotic Position"

Relatively few patients who are close to the pathetic stage just described, can ever sincerely seek or accept meaningful psychiatric treatment. A cure would result in a loss of their dependent position. Often they have a great need to prove to themselves and to others a physical basis for their symptoms and disability. They may too often regard any implication of psychologic factors in their illness as some kind of an accusation or affront. Thus, they are often unable to accept a beginning step in the consideration of possible emotional factors. They may verbally express a desire for "cure", but it is as though their self-respect required them to have an organic origin for their symptoms.

This becomes, however, more importantly an ironclad defense against the possibility of therapeutic intervention. Only too often one automatically seeks to preserve what we might term the *"Balanced" Neurotic Position* [p. 159]. This endeavor at preservation constitutes part of his secondary defense, an important concept referred to in earlier chapters. In most instances this impedes or bars the way for any fruitful exploration of emotional areas which may be actually playing the major role in the illness. The patient does not want to accept responsibility or to invest the required time or effort for insight-directed therapy. Actually, on a more hidden level he desperately guards the neurotic *status quo* as though this position of sacrifice and defeat (from any objective judgement) was most precious and vital. Emotionally, it is. When this position becomes unbalanced the consequence is an Emotional Decompensation, as noted earlier [p. 159].

Unless psychotherapy clearly can offer something better (a *therapeutic bargain*), these particular patients are only too often refractory to psychiatric investigation and treatment. The T.I. is not infrequently encountered. Their emphasis is unfortunately apt to be upon proving the reality of their disability, rather than upon finding out about possible personal internal factors which may enter into their need to continue a disabled existence with compensation. They are quite satisfied with an adjustment on a relatively nonresponsible and infantile level of dependence. Theirs is often a sad and unrecognized dilemma — a hopeless, unhappy position. They cannot secure help unless they want it, and are willing to risk it, and to work at it. The Teamwork Tenet in Psychotherapy [p. 362] holds.

2. Resistance Protectively Intended

Many factors enter into resistance to therapy. The denial or withholding of awareness can serve a vital protective purpose. It is not surprising that it is a common, if not a universal method of defense. In *Case 46* [p. 202], the young mother managed to conceal from herself the consequences that her suicide would have had upon her children. Conscious recognition was a real shock. This incident also helps point up some of the very real reasons why patients resist therapy. The recognition of previously hidden or partially hidden conflicts can have this kind of painful, traumatic impact. The resistance to treatment is protectively motivated. This particular defensiveness may be misdirected, but it is quite powerful.

Resistance as generated by one's secondary defensive forces by no means ceases when a patient accepts the idea of giving psychotherapy a trial. However, this is a vital first step. The Emotional Inertia has been overcome. Now one can come to grips with the resistances. These are present with every patient. The psychotherapist who becomes an expert in recognizing and in dealing with resistances, and in helping his patients resolve them, has become an expert in treatment. This is not an easy accomplishment. Such a goal is by no means readily achieved.

The secondary defenses must be recognized, faced, and dealt with in effective fashion in treatment. Conflicts must be recognized and resolved. Many people are openly and/or intuitively unwilling to face the requisite anxiety, discomfort, and pain. This is true even though such discomfort is temporary, the result is ultimately constructive, and the work is along the necessary pathway to later emotional equanimity. How can one convince an unwilling person that such is the case?

3. Understanding and Insight Needed; Phases of "Initial Decline" and "Initial Remission" in Therapy

If one can understand a patient's reluctance to see his dentist, one can perhaps more readily appreciate his far greater resistance to facing the much greater discomforts which he may have to bear in psychotherapy. Further, in the latter instance, his reluctances are apt to be obscured and disguised by all kinds of rationalizations, even from himself. Understanding of the patient's position is needed. The person in treatment likewise needs insight into his conflicts and his psyche.

The emotionally sick patient is troubled but he is unaware of the real sources of his difficulty. Investigative therapy and analysis aims at the uncovering, clarification, and resolution of conflicts. Often these have been protectively repressed from conscious awareness. In successful treatment, awareness is increased, gained, or regained. Only thereby can conflicts be recognized and discussed. The successful result will lie in their acceptance, desensitization, resolution, and the banishment of irrational and nonrealistic elements. This will inevitably arouse a recurrence of some of the original distress, which resulted in their having been earlier banished to the unconscious in the first place.

Thus, the seeming anomaly is seen not infrequently of the person who *feels worse during the initial or early phase of treatment.** This phenomenon occurs often enough to perhaps warrant the description of the *Phase of Initial Decline* in therapy. Its converse is sometimes seen as well, that of the *Phase of the Initial Great Improvement,* or seeming remission [*see also* related Favorable-Response Concept, as illustrated in *Case 89,* p. 452].

The neurotic patient is troubled but is unaware of the real reasons, the extent, or the degree until increased awareness is gained through treatment. Increased awareness is vital, necessary, and constructive, regardless of the psychologic pain which is sometimes incident to its being secured.

---

* See earlier references to our concepts of the secondary defense. In *Case 41* [p. 202] was not the young married mother referred to actually far better off to recognize the potential consequence of her suicide, even though the gaining of awareness was a very painful experience?

C. COMMENTS ON PROGNOSIS

1. The Epigain and Prognosis

If the regressive satisfactions gained are substantial, if the epigain is of major importance to the patient in the external advantages secured because of the symptoms, and if no substitute can be found by the patient through the work of therapy, one cannot be very optimistic about favorably influencing the course of the neurosis. A Therapeutic Impasse [p. 446] can impend. The epigain can thus play a major role in the prognosis. It can become a potent force in the continuation of neurotic symptoms.

Treatment should be initiated promptly on an intensive basis. Litigation, if a factor, should be settled as quickly as possible. These measures, when feasible and with the patient's active cooperation, can prevent the fixation of symptoms. It is a sad thing to see the so-called Accident Neurosis progress into a seemingly placid and hapless chronic state.

In this situation the evidence of the regressive retreat that takes place becomes increasingly apparent. The patient has made a "successful" withdrawal in various degrees into a state of dependent passivity. Many of his needs are cared for by family or friends. This is part of the epigain of the post-traumatic symptoms. Other needs are met, albeit often poorly enough, via a disability pension or compensation.

From a practical and objective standpoint, such satisfactions and need-gratifications are minimal enough for the victim of the neurosis. Consciously he does not seek nor want the dependent position he achieves. On the deeper unconscious level he is driven to it. On the deeper level the increasingly dependent position is far more preferable. It is desperately needed. Recall our concept of an Inverse Ratio between Symptom-Success and Motivation Toward Therapy [pp. 298 and 508]. The epigain of the established symptoms secures it. The prognosis is influenced accordingly.

2. The Theory of Antecedent Conflicts

The Theory of Antecedent Conflicts is an important one in our consideration of the Traumatic Neuroses. According to this theory [pp. 490–494] every emotional conflict has its antecedent. Any disturbing event which occurs can have its impact multiplied by antecedent vicissitudes of earlier life which have individual significance.

Thus, the consequences of stressful events in early life can have important conditioning effects upon the susceptibility to given traumatic events in later life. One may perhaps develop more effective defenses. On the other hand, one may develop an increased sensitivity and become far more vulnerable to the impact of the trauma.

The later trauma can actually or symbolically recreate the early situation, which serves as a prototype. This is unconsciously perceived as such, and reacted to by the person concerned. When this takes place the earlier events and their emotional components are in effect reactivated. The overall consequences of the later traumatic event are likely to be much greater.

From the broad viewpoint neuroses develop as part of man's efforts to survive and to adapt himself. Man seeks to avoid pain, to counter threats and danger, whether external and physical, internal and emotional, or a combination of these. Our earlier [p. 4] Principle of Avoidance of Anxiety also applies. Traumatic events activate existing or new defenses or both. Some of these can be constructive and some can be destructive despite their preservative intent, leading to the development of neurotic symptoms. The more insight that can be gained into these processes by patient and therapist the more progress will take place therapeutically.

3. Potentials of Thorough, Completed "Deep Treatment"

In his treatment efforts it will prove important for the psychiatrist to bear in mind that the traumatic event will likely have its prior model and analogy in earlier life. In effect, the later events reactivate the situation and emotions of earlier ones, with their more or less dormant and hidden conflicts and emotional disturbances. When an emotional kind of sensitization has taken place as noted, the psyche appears to react out of proportion. Treatment may require considerable depth to be fully effective. Our tracing technique [pp. 366, 494] can be of value.

Thus, at times, the completion of treatment will require resolution of the earliest accessible antecedent conflicts. This can indeed be a difficult and prolonged process. When completed, however, one accomplishes far more than the immediate and limited goal of mere symptom resolution. When completed in proper and thorough fashion, treatment will result in the individual being not only "cured" from a symptomatic standpoint, but in becoming far better able to cope with life in a constructive and successful fashion and being far less vulnerable to similar stresses in the future. The person becomes better, then well.

4. Treatment in Acute Cases

Traumatic symptoms can occur in relatively stable individuals whose prior adjustment was to all intents and purposes quite excellent. This is more prevalent in instances where trauma was repeated and stress prolonged and in instances where the stress and trauma were particularly acute. These conditions are frequently met in combat situations. What are the treatment prospects in these more acute emotional difficulties following trauma?

In many acute cases of Neuroses-Following-Trauma psychotherapy can be quite beneficial. This is particularly true when prior adjustment has been excellent and applies to cases of acute stress reaction whether of civilian or military origin. It can be useful to bear in mind our Concept of Continued-Physiologic-Momentum [pp. 99, 100, and 455].

D. GOALS OF PSYCHOTHERAPY

As implied in the foregoing discussion, the goals of psychotherapy can be variable according to the individual situation. There are, however, certain overall goals which have a general applicability in psychotherapy. In closing, it may be helpful to list them as in the following table.

Table 42

Goals of Psychotherapy

The following goals of treatment are worthwhile ones, regardless of the types of symptoms or illness.

(1) One seeks to secure *improvement in* the patient's external *environmental adjustments.* These particularly include an improved ability in the initiation and maintenance of constructive relationships.

(2) *Behavioral changes.* Behavior will become modified so as to eliminate any unwittingly personally inimical, or socially destructive patterns of behavior.

(3) An improved *self-acceptance.* Self-respect and esteem will increase, based upon an increasingly objective self-evaluation. The self-picture held by others and oneself will come into closer approximation.

Awareness will increase of disapproved inner wishes and drives, with a greater acceptance of their existence and a greater rather than a lesser ability to control them.

(4) *Improved personal and social functioning* and effectiveness is sought as the consequence of finding one's real goals, and adjusting them so as to be in keeping with one's real potentials.

The achievement of realistic personal aims and realistically adjusted needs will be facilitated. The patient may gain substantially improved work efficiency, initiative, professional achievement, and executive ability.

(5) An *improved internal adjustment;* the recognition of emotional conflict will be followed by its acceptance or resolution or both. A better level of personal integration will result.

(6) The achievement and maintenance of a reasonable level of *emotional equanimity.*

(7) The *resolution of* any *emotional symptoms* of clinical or subclinical level, together with the improvement of any overdeveloped character defensive traits, which are thereby personally or socially handicapping.

(8) Securing an *improved level of emotional maturity,* with all the attendant implications for the personal betterment of the patient's position.

IX. SUMMARY AND CONCLUSIONS

A. INTRODUCTION

1. Trauma and Neurosis

This chapter has been written to stress the relations between trauma and the neuroses. During recent years increased knowledge has paralleled increased awareness concerning these relationships. Disabilities following trauma are sometimes observed to be disproportionate to the accompanying physical injury. Such disproportion provides presumptive evidence of emotional factors. The concept of a *Basic Drive Toward Emotional Health* was mentioned. Applying to most, if not all neurotic reactions is the *Principle of Predetermined Vulnerability.* Trauma, and Neuroses-Following-Trauma were defined.

A reappraisal of our more usual medical — often physical — bases of evaluating disabilities is recommended. Emotional symptoms are often subjective. While the interference with living is no less, and possibly more, these symptoms are not demonstrable nor measurable by x-ray, laboratory tests, or a stethoscope. They need careful objective assessment for any medical or legal purpose.

Neurotic symptoms are widespread, if not universal. Neurotic reactions which most frequently follow trauma include the anxiety, conversion, and hygeiaphrontic groups. However, any type of neurosis can be precipitated by trauma. A number of basic concepts were outlined. The *Transparency Theory* was outlined, in helping to explain the cultural influence upon the incidence of emotional symptoms and types of neurotic reaction. Conflict resolution relieves symptoms, in line with our knowledge of the *Principle of Symptom Survival.* In the broadest sense all emotional illnesses are traumatic in origin.

We are dealing with a group of neurotic reactions and not with a single specific entity. Trauma can be physical, psychic, or a combination of both, and its role can vary widely in the initiation of symptoms.

2. Oppenheim, Beaumont, Charcot, Pavlov, and Cannon

The Neuroses-Following-Trauma have in common their relation to trauma as a causative agent. Oppenheim introduced the concept of traumatic neurosis in the latter part of the nineteenth century, believing (mistakenly) that actual damage to the central nervous tissues during the traumatic event accounted for the symptoms.

As the vital interrelationships between emotions and physiology became better understood, more general acceptance of the major role of psychologic factors in the causation of illness became possible. William Beaumont made observations of historical significance. Jean Charcot experimentally brought on and relieved symptoms identical to those of conversion and traumatic neurosis, previously considered by many to be organic and physical in origin. Pavlov discovered the conditioned reflex, and Cannon performed pioneering studies on emotions and bodily functions. Freud and others since have further advanced our concepts of psychodynamics.

3. T.R.C. and T.R.T.

Human beings react to stress in a defensive and self-preservative fashion. The *total reaction to crisis* (T.R.C.) is the sum total of one's responses. All components — emotional, physical, physiologic, and intellectual — are included. The analogous *total reaction to trauma* is the T.R.T.

These are useful concepts in teaching and study. They are quite individual. Accordingly an assessment may aid in one's estimate of individual stability or relative emotional (mental) health.

4. Cultural Influences

The lack of specific standards impedes statistical studies as to the prevalence of neurotic reactions. Estimates were made as to the number of persons suffering from Neuroses-Following-Trauma (2–3 per cent) and from other groups of neurotic reactions most frequently associated with traumatic factors. Certain cultural influences on the type and symptomatology of neuroses were noted. Conflict resolution through therapy leads to the relief of symptoms.

5. Distinguished by the Sharpness of the Trauma

Diagnoses in the neuroses are made on a descriptive basis today. The most outstanding clinical feature is the important one in selecting the proper diagnostic label. The origin of our present diagnostic terms was earlier traced from the ancient Greek. Important points in making the diagnosis of a Neurosis-Following-Trauma were outlined. Making the diagnosis on positive grounds (versus diagnosis by exclusion) is preferable.

A distinguishing feature from other neuroses is the sharpness of the preceding traumatic event. In its absence, the neurosis presumably would not have occurred. The *Principle of Hidden Determinants* notes the pre-existence of factors exerting important influences on the form and character of symptoms in any type of neurotic manifestation. The *Peg Concept* is an important corollary, pointing out that individually, a peg already exists, upon which a symptom may be hung.

B. CLINICAL FEATURES

1. Typical Course

The clinical features may include those of any neurotic reaction described, although Somatic Conversion, Physiologic Conversion, Hygeiaphrontic Reactions, and the Anxiety Reactions are most frequent.

The typical clinical course is for an injury, with physical sequelae of from minor to major significance, to be followed in a period of from days to months by the onset of one or more of a variety of symptoms which are out of proportion to what one might ordinarily expect from the injury alone. The epigain is not infrequently prominent. The patient is often convinced that a direct cause and effect relationship exists between the injury and his symptoms. This is particularly true in industrial accident cases. In acute traumatic situations the post-traumatic dream is frequently present.

Emotional problems not infrequently result in more pain, suffering, and disability than do physical (organic) ones. An example was cited to contrast the greater disability on an emotional basis which was suffered by the one person in an automobile accident who was relatively "uninjured."

A wide variety of symptoms and clinical findings will be encountered. Their emotional bases are non-tangible and elusive. Physicians generally often have additional problems in coping with them because of the relative and seemingly paradoxical neglect of the "psychiatric half" of medical practice in medical school teaching and in most clinical training. The concept of the *Functional-Structural Progression* stresses the gradual transition which can take place from the emotional to functional changes, to chronic alteration of functions, and gradually and ultimately into fixed and irreversible structural changes and pathology.

2. Epigain and Endogain

The symptom in a neurotic reaction is the external expression of an aspect or aspects of underlying emotional conflicts. The endogain is the basis of an emotional illness. These gains and the need for them are responsible for the initiation of the illness. They constitute its *raison d'etre*. The endogain is deeply unconscious.

The epigain is also unconscious although often more superficial. It is secondary, constituting the gain secured (unconsciously) from symptoms or an illness already established. While we refer to them as "gains", and so they are, and vitally so to the individual concerned, still the net result is always self-defeating and a loss to the patient when it is assessed by an objective and neutral observer. Epigain is also associated in varying degrees with many instances of physical illness. Malingering is to be carefully distinguished. It is in turn the deliberate and conscious simulation of illness. When the Epigain is to be surrendered during therapy, the *Principle of Self-Esteem Maintenance* [p. 676] should be borne in mind.

The effects of trauma can be deferred, often in a defensive, and sometimes in a vital and even life-saving service. This was illustrated in physical and in psychologic types of trauma. Symptoms of the Anxiety Reactions in response to trauma were outlined.

3. Everyone Has a Breaking Point

The individual capacity to tolerate stress and trauma versus the relative lack of capacity, with the accompanying development of symptoms is quite variable. According to the *Rule of Impression Priority*, earlier impressions and events take a kind of emotional priority, and help to determine later attitudes and reactions. Unconscious feelings of guilt can enter importantly into symptom formation. Vulnerability to stress and to trauma is influenced also by unconscious symbolism and other factors, and symptoms are frequently therefore disproportionate to the apparent trauma. Remission of emotional symptoms can also occasionally follow stress and trauma.

The *Theory of Ultimate Vulnerability* was advanced, according to which, when sufficient stress, and/or continued stress are applied over a long enough period of time, everyone has a "breaking point." Related to this are the important roles that the acuity of the trauma and its repetition can play in the emotional effects upon a given person. Clinical instances were cited to illustrate a number of important points. The *Concept of*

Psychic Depletion invites attention to the effect of repeated blows, in wearing down ones basic reserves and defenses. Occurring without sufficient respite to allow for adequate recuperation, they can thereby ultimately lead to complete emotional collapse.

The *Principles of Emotional Sensitization* and *Desensitization* were noted. *Emotional-Impact Deferment* (E.I.D.) allows severe emotional reactions to be held in abeyance until a more "convenient", safer juncture.

C. PSYCHOGENESIS

1. Psychologic Defenses with Trauma

Many psychologic defenses are called into play in the face of stress, danger, and threatened trauma, including most of the mental mechanisms. True mental mechanisms are unconscious endeavors; the defenses employed may be both conscious and unconscious.

Denial is frequently operative, as is the related belief in personal invulnerability. Knowledge about the psychogenesis of Neuroses-Following-Trauma is not easily come by, since this is a very complex subject requiring much training and understanding. It is not possible to forecast accurately which emotional symptoms, if any, will develop should a given individual be subjected to trauma.

2. Recapitulation of Antecedent Conflicts

In certain cases the effects of traumata, when an additional such event occurs prior to recovery from an earlier one, appear to be cumulative. In accord with the *Theory of Antecedent Conflicts,* the trauma may have a greater effect when it actually or symbolically recapitulates antecedent conflicts from earlier years.

The neuroses develop as protectively intended patterns of psychologic defense. A Traumatic Neurosis (as do others) usually develops in psychologic soil which is well prepared. The traumatic experiences of early life can condition or sensitize the individual and his reaction to traumatic experiences in later life. A case was cited in illustration. The Total Reaction to Trauma (T.R.T.) is the total potential of all personal resources, strengths, and weaknesses as present constitutionally, and as modified and influenced by experiences and the vicissitudes of living. The interesting reverse sequence of *Remission-Following-Trauma* was noted, together with some factors in its underlying bases.

3. Compensation and Neuroses

To help clarify the mutual interaction of compensation and neurosis this section was included. Instances were noted where accidents in industry are followed by emotional symptoms. Some of these individuals may develop an obsessive kind of preoccupation about compensation, insurance benefits, or pensions. This has led to the unfortunate designation of Compensation Neurosis being applied to these cases. Emotional symptoms evolve in psychologic soil which is usually well prepared. Trauma may initiate or precipitate an emotional reaction, but the foundations are already present.

The Industrial Compensation Case was discussed briefly and some of the major complexities involved were noted. Fifteen instances of some of the various kinds of symptom development following accidents and trauma were outlined. Public and professional education is needed in the important areas of neurosis, emotional disabilities, and compensation. The *Principle of Symptom Longevity* stresses the increased tendency for symptoms to become fixed, the longer they are permitted to exist.

D. THERAPY

1. Active Participation Required

Therapy, to be successful, requires an actively cooperative patient who participates in collaborative fashion in the work of treatment, in accord with our *Team-Work Tenet in Psychotherapy* [pp. 25, 130, 362]. Psychotherapy is the indicated approach, and must be in the hands of a skilled physician with graduate specialist training and adequate experience in the field of psychiatry. Psychotherapy and analysis are actually an educational process of considerable depth, more personal and meaningful than many other and more usual kinds of educational approaches.

According to the *Treatment Rule,* a patient undertakes to say every thought that comes to mind during his therapy session, without reservations or censorship. The major difference between psychotherapy and other medical therapies lies in the active participation and contributions which the patient must undertake. Patient and therapist thus work together in a complex intensive joint endeavor (in accord with our *Joint-Endeavor Principle*) over a considerable period of time.

2. Resistance Part of Secondary Defense

Promptness in the initiation of treatment is valuable and the sooner any possible or pending litigation is resolved, the more the beneficial effects of treatment will be facilitated. The Concept of the *Balanced Neurotic Position* was offered; a status which only too often is automatically preserved. Disability payments can fit in with the unconscious regressive trends and dependency needs. The *Phase of Initial Decline* and the *Phase of Initial Great Improvement* or seeming remission, as phenomena in response to early treatment were noted. The epigain of Traumatic Neuroses includes the external advantages sought unconsciously through symptoms which are (already) present. Dependency gratifications can be part of the epigain. The *Theory of Antecedent Conflicts* was mentioned and the potentials of thorough and complete psychotherapy noted. Resistance in therapy was discussed as a manifestation of the *Secondary Defense*. Treatment in acute cases is best prompt and active.

X. SELECTED REFERENCES AND BIBLIOGRAPHY

ALEXANDER, F. (1948). *Fundamentals of Psychoanalysis*, pp. 241–245. New York; Norton.

BEAUMONT, W. (1833). *Experiments and Observations on the Gastric Juice and the Physiology of Digestion*. Plattsburg, N. Y.; Allen.

BRILL, A. A., Ed. (1938). *The Basic Writings of Sigmund Freud*, p. 120. New York; Modern Library.

BRONNER, ALFRED (1955). "The Role of Sodium Amytal in Psychotherapy and Diagnosis." *Am. J. Psychother.*, 9, 234.

CANNON, W. B. (1929). *Bodily Changes in Fear, Hunger, Pain and Rage*. 2nd ed. New York; Appleton-Century.

DEUTSCH, H. (1951). *The Psychoanalysis of the Neuroses*, p. 128. London; Hogarth.

DORSEY, J. M. (1953). "Morale." The American Imago, 10, 345.

FENICHEL, O. (1945). *The Psychoanalytic Theory of Neurosis*, pp. 117–128, 541–547. New York; Norton.

FREUD, S. (1950). *Collected Papers*, Vol. I, pp. 21, 25–27. London; Hogarth.

— (1926). *Inhibitions, Symptoms and Anxiety*, pp. 108–109. London; Hogarth.

— (1933). *New Introductory Lectures*, pp. 117, 123. London; Hogarth.

— (1943). *A General Introduction to Psychoanalysis*, pp. 242–243, 333. Garden City, N. Y.; Garden City Publishing Co.

GLOVER, EDWARD (1929). "The Screening Function of Traumatic Memories." *Int. J. Psycho-Anal.*, 10, 162.

HOLMES, T. H. and RIPLEY, H. S. (1955). "Experimental Studies on Anxiety Reactions." *Am. J. Psychiat.*, 111, 921.

LAUGHLIN, H. P. (1954). "The Neuroses Following Trauma." *Med. Ann. D.C.*, Part I: 23, 492; Part II: 23, 567.

— (1953). "The Dissociative Reactions." *ibid.*, 22, 541.

— (1954). "Overconcern with Health: Hypochondriasis." *ibid.*, Part I: 23, 96; Part II: 23, 147.

— and RUFFIN, M. DEG. (1953). *An Outline of Dynamic Psychiatry*. 4th rev. mimeo, pp. 170–171. Washington; George Washington University Medical School.

— (1953). "Research in Sleep Deprivation and Exhaustion." *Int. Rec. Med.*, 166, 305.

— (1962). "Neuroses Following Trauma." In *Traumatic Medicine and Surgery for the Attorney*, Vol. 6, pp. 76–125. Ed. by P. D. Cantor. Washington; Butterworth.

— (1963). *Mental Mechanisms*. Washington; Butterworth.

LEVINE, J., LUBY, E., RAUCH, A., and YESNER, R. (1954). "Blood Viscosity of Psychotics and Nonpsychotics Under Stress." *Psychosom. Med.*, 16, 398.

LOWENSTEIN, R. M. (1949). "A Post-Traumatic Dream." *Psychoanal. Q.*, 18, 449.

MENNINGER, K. A. (1938). *Man Against Himself*. New York; Harcourt, Brace.

PAVLOV, IVAN P. (1927). *Conditioned Reflexes*. London; Oxford University Press.

RIPLEY, H. S. and WOLF, S. (1941). "Studies in Psychopathology." *J. nerv. ment. Dis.*, 114, 234.

SAUL, L. J. (1950). "The Nature of Neurotic Reactions." *Am. J. Psychiat.*, 106, 547.

— (1947). *Emotional Maturity*, p. 265. Philadelphia: Lippincott.

SCHILDER, P. (1943). "Neuroses Following Head and Brain Injuries." In *Injuries of the Skull, Brain and Spinal Cord*, 2nd ed. Ed. by S. Brock. Baltimore: Williams & Wilkins.

SMITH, H. W. and SOLOMON, H. C. (1944). "Traumatic Neuroses in Court." *Ann int. Med.*, 21, 367.

SPERLING, O. E. (1950). "The Interpretation of the Trauma as a Command." *Psychoanal. Q.*, 19, 352.

STERN, M. M. (1953). "Trauma, Projective Technique and Analytic Profile." *Psychoanal. Q.*, 22, 229.

TRAWICK, J. D. and BATE, J. T. (1949). "Traumatic Neurosis." *Am. J. Surg.*, 78, 661.

WECHSLER, I. S. (1952). *A Textbook of Clinical Neurology*, 7th ed., p. 715. Philadelphia; Saunders.

WEIGERT, E. (1930). "Psychoanalytic Notes on Sleep and Convulsion Treatment in Functional Psychoses." *Psychiatry*, 3, 189.

XI. REVIEW QUESTIONS ON THE NEUROSES FOLLOWING TRAUMA

1. All emotional illnesses are ultimately traumatic. Explain.
2. What is: (*a*) the Basic Drive Toward Emotional Health? (*b*) the Principle of Predetermined Vulnerability? (*c*) the Transparency Theory? and (*d*) the Principle of Symptom Survival?
3. What are the Neuroses-Following Trauma?
4. Outline the contributions of Beaumont, Pavlov, and Cannon.
5. List three considerations in diagnosis. What is the importance of the Principle of Hidden Determinants in symptom formation? What is the Peg Concept?
6. What emotional syndromes most commonly have their onset following trauma? What is the Concept of Functional-Structural Progression?
7. Discuss the total individual response to trauma (T.R.T.). What is the Concept of Psychic Depletion?
8. How do antecedent conflicts influence our response to emotional trauma?
9. What is meant by "favorable psychologic soil", in the development of emotional symptoms following trauma?
10. List common psychologic defenses against the prospect of external danger.
11. Discuss the relation of compensation to neurosis. What is the Principle of Symptom Longevity?
12. What is the epigain? What is the endogain? What are they in Neurosis-Following-Trauma? How do they influence therapy?
13. State six goals of psychotherapy.
14. What is the significance of:
    (*a*) Feelings of Omnipotent Responsibility
    (*b*) The Principles of Emotional Sensitization; and Desensitization?
    (*c*) Emotional-Impact Deferment (E.I.D.)?
    (*d*) *Remission* Following Trauma?
    (*e*) The Balanced Neurotic Position
15. Discuss therapy in the Traumatic Reactions.

CHAPTER 15

MILITARY REACTIONS and PRISONER-PROCESSING

Part One: EMOTIONAL REACTIONS ASSOCIATED
WITH MILITARY OPERATIONS

I. INTRODUCTION

 A. Continuing Conflicts Stress
 Importance
 1. Bases for Chapter Recognition; 2. Law of the Three M's.: Disproportional Supply of Psychiatrists

 B. Men Under Stress

II. INCIDENCE AND DIAGNOSIS

 A. Statistics: Change Abruptly in War

 B. Diagnostic Labels for Combat Reactions
 1. Evolving Concepts and Terms; 2. Two Studies of Diagnoses Accorded Operational and Military Casualties

III. SYMPTOMS AND CLINICAL FEATURES

 A. Acute Combat Reactions
 1. One Hundred Consecutive Cases; 2. Direct Anxiety Manifestations Prominent

 B. The Theory of Ultimate-Vulnerability
 1. Severe Neurosis Follows Major Stress. Everyone Has a "Breaking Point"; 2. Geometric Progression; 3. Tolerance to Military Stress Extremely Variable

 C. Two World Wars Provided Differing Clinical Pictures
 1. Somatic Conversion Reactions Frequent in World War I; 2. Anxiety and Physiologic Conversion Manifestations Predominant in World War II and Since; 3 All Neurotic Reactions Represented

IV. PSYCHODYNAMIC FACTORS

 A. Four Interesting Features Characteristic
 1. The Startle Reaction; 2. The Battle Dream: Desensitizing Purpose Concept; 3. Irritability; 4. Tremors; 5. Acute Manifestations Subside; 6. Chronicity of Symptoms

 B. Individual Susceptibility to Combat Stress
 1. Personal-Invulnerability Defense Concept; 2. Many Factors Contribute; 3. Extension to Country of Early, Antecedent Conflicts; 4. Dynamics Complex and Individual

 C. Effects of Repeated Trauma
 1. Concept of Psychic Depletion; 2. Increased Vulnerability; 3. Principles of Emotional-Sensitization and Desensitization

 D. Increased Vulnerability the Consequence of Antecedent Conflicts

 E. Additional Predisposing Factors
 1. Level of Personal Security and the Rule of Impression-Priority; 2. Relative Subjective Impotence and Helplessness; 3. Acuity of Trauma

 F. The Unit-Guilt Reaction
 1. A Close Friend is Killed; 2. Unit-Guilt Feelings Long Repressed; 3. Non-rational Need to Share the Friend's Fate

 G. Wounds and Emotional Symptoms

V. NOTES ON TREATMENT OF COMBAT REACTIONS

    A. In Acute Cases
        1. Provide a More Favorable Climate; 2. "Emotional First-Aid" in Combat Reactions; 3. Psychotherapy

B. Hypnosis and Narcosynthesis
    1. Emotional Catharsis and Abreaction Sought; 2. Successful Treatment After Six Years; 3. Limitations

Part Two: THE PSYCHOLOGIC PROCESSING OF PRISONERS

I. INTRODUCTION
    A. Prisoner Processing (Brainwashing)
        1. Application to Individuals More Effective; 2. Unparalleled Control Secured
    B. Perverse Science
        1. Extension of Pavlovian Theory; 2. Additional Psychologic Factors; 3. Torture Too Crude

II. TECHNIQUES OF PRISONER PROCESSING
    A. Time and Effort Required
        1. Months Needed by Trained Professionals; 2. Individual Processing Irresistible
    B. Bases for Success
        1. Respite and Peace At Any Cost; 2. Individual Factors in Susceptibility; 3. Skilled Operators Required

III. THE CONDITIONING PROCESS
    A. Michael Shipkov
    B. Cardinal Mindszenty
    C. Phases of Processing
    D. Individual Procedure

IV. TREATMENT: RESTORING THE SHATTERED EGO

V. SUMMARY
    A. Combat Reactions
    B. Psychologic Prisoner Processing

VI. SELECTED REFERENCES AND BIBLIOGRAPHY

VII. REVIEW QUESTIONS ON MILITARY REACTIONS AND PRISONER PROCESSING

PART ONE: EMOTIONAL REACTIONS ASSOCIATED WITH MILITARY OPERATIONS

I. INTRODUCTION

A. CONTINUING CONFLICTS STRESS IMPORTANCE

1. Bases for Chapter Recognition

The Korean War and the Viet Nam conflict continue to emphasize the role of military operations in our lives and their effects upon the field of emotional health. These intermittent but continuing involvements of United States forces in military conflicts have been paralleled by many other military and para-military operations in troubled areas throughout the globe. Few nations have escaped involvement of at least some of their citizens either officially or non-officially in such conflagrations. These events continuing through the decades emphasize a need for more recognition of the emotional conflicts, anxieties, and stresses associated with military operations and combat, and for more medical and administrative familiarity with the requirements for their adequate management. They underline the pertinence of our naming this era the Age of Anxiety. Their study is a pertinent lesson concerning the major role of stress in function, in health, and in illness. Finally, there are many tie-ins with the emotional problems and ills of civilian life.

For these reasons it has seemed strongly indicated to accord at least brief but separate chapter recognition to the emotional reactions incident to military operations. It is hoped that such consideration will gain increased attention and study for an area of emotional health which can prove rapidly major to nearly any country, however regrettable and tragic the responsible circumstances may be. As a related subject of interest, an additional Part Two on psychologic Prisoner-Processing has been appended.

This material is not intended to stand alone. The fourteen foregoing chapters together provide an all-important background, are basically contributory, and should serve as an important preliminary to our all-too-limited discussion. *Chapters 1, 3, 9, and 14* in particular comprise an essential preface to this one. Further, frequent reference to concepts as earlier advanced or reformulated preserves familiarity with the text thus far. Finally, several dozen of our case illustrations throughout this work have more-or-less direct applicability, many pertain to servicemen and military settings, are most pertinent to our present discussion, and should be reviewed and considered together with this final chapter.

2. Law of the Three M's.: Disproportional Supply of Psychiatrists

World War II greatly stimulated interest in emotional reactions and in psychiatry; even more so than had the first World War. A large proportion of the military casualties proved to be primarily emotional in origin. Emotional factors in addition also played an important contributory role in many of the other disabilities and illnesses of service men. This was true in U.S. forces as in those of most other nations. Physicians generally gained an increased recognition of the vital role of stress in health and illness.

The medical departments of the U.S. armed services suddenly found themselves quite short of trained psychiatrists. One of the services found for example, that approximately one out of every four hospitalized men (25 per cent) was suffering from an emotionally induced (psychiatric) illness. (Thirty per cent of overseas psychiatric casualties were classed as neuroses.) A far smaller fraction of its medical officers were qualified as psychiatrists. This great numerical disproportion was exaggerated still further by the fact that even the minimum of psychotherapy generally requires the investment of considerably more physician-hours per patient then does treatment of the average medical or surgical patient.

The number of psychiatric patients that can be adequately treated by a properly trained medical officer (psychiatric specialist) is much lower then in other branches of medicine. This prospect as outlined thus far, is so very nearly certain in our expectations as to warrant our referring to what we must anticipate as a "law": *The Law of The Three M's*—Military-Medical-Mobilization. Such a term is suggested to invite much-needed attention, and to further emphasize and stress a vital point. Included in our "law" would be three major tenets, namely: (1) The disproportionate and rapid increase in the number of emotional patients incident to any military build-up for war, or threatened war; (2) The resulting rapid and disproportionate need for psychiatrists and auxiliary personnel; and (3) The rapidly increasing need for more, and far more adequate psychiatric space, facilities, and hospital beds.

As could be well anticipated, the psychiatric situation became rapidly acute in World War II and remained so. Intensive training programs were set up in the United States by both the Army and the Navy to train physicians in the basic principles of psychiatry. The increasingly desperate need for psychiatrists was reflected for example, in one very direct way in the Navy by the progressive shortening of these courses time-wise. From an initial two years in length, they eventually were shortened to six weeks! Medical officers for these courses were recruited and welcomed from every specialty in medicine.

It is of tangential interest and some satisfaction (the author assisted and was a staff member with one of the two postgraduate courses so established) to note that nearly all of these physicians so trained by the U.S. Navy—almost without exception—have since remained in the specialty of psychiatry. They have individually and collectively made a most valuable contribution to medicine and to psychiatry throughout the years.

B. MEN UNDER STRESS

World War II offered unusual opportunities for the first-hand study and observation of men under stress. These observations have continued during the Korean War and Viet Nam conflicts. A great deal has been learned. Great individual variation in the ability to tolerate stress has been demonstrated. While some men would "break down" even at induction or during basic training, others could well tolerate a great deal of operational and combat stress. Actually men became sick at all levels of stress and following exposure to extremely variable degrees of psychic trauma [p. 101]. Some, as illustrated in our following *Case 184*, became ill only after unbelievably severe stress. During six and a half years of active military experience with the U.S. Navy, and many subsequent years of service as a Consultant to the U.S. Army training program in psychiatry, the author came personally to support the theory that every man has a potential breaking point, as outlined earlier in accord with the Theory of Ultimate-Vulnerability [Ch.14:VD3]. *Case 177* was illustrative of this premise.

The following data include in abbreviated form some of the important principles of Combat Exhaustion, Combat Reactions, and the emotional syndromes which are most frequently seen in relation to the stresses of military operations. The earlier tabulation of the More Direct Manifestations of Anxiety [*Table 1,* p. 20], and what was delineated as Apprehensive Anticipation [pp. 17ff] were most frequent. The reader should also refer to the earlier list of Military Stressful Eras [pp. 31, 38, and 67], and should compare this with S.E.H.A. [pp. 38 and 119].

II. INCIDENCE AND DIAGNOSIS

A. STATISTICS: CHANGE ABRUPTLY IN WAR

The high incidence of emotional disorders in wartime has been noted. Their directly proportional relation to stress is apparent in the rather abrupt statistical changes in military medicine which take place with wartime operations. The reader is referred to earlier notes [p. 67] as to areas of particular stress. The increase in psychiatric patients as would be expected is much greater than in other groups. No one escapes anxiety in a combat situation. This is hardly surprising and of course is in accord with our Principle of Universality in anxiety [p. 8]. The amount or degree is variable. Indeed, peacetime military service ordinarily offers certain securities not present in civilian life. Anxieties and insecurities for some are allayed. The incidence of military emotional problems during peacetime tends to be disproportionately low when compared to wartime, or to civilian incidence. Indeed, for a few persons the military establishment provides a soterial retreat. An Obsessive Character Structure [pp. 245–258] is not uncommon and can contribute to a successful career. Some officers become *Black-or-White Persons* [pp. 255 and 451].

There is a fairly constant ratio of certain types of psychiatric problems in peacetime. A dependence can develop upon military routines which become in effect C.S.R.s. [pp. 351 and 461], so that their sudden breakdown or change may render the serviceman emotionally vulnerable. The military incidence of the psychoses, for example, continues at a fairly steady rate of 2.8–3.0 cases per 1,000 soldiers per year. Schizophrenic Reactions are the most common, frequently marked by Bleuler's Dissociation [pp. 683, 735*ff*]. This is an approximate incidence of ⅓ of 1 per cent annually. Of 200,000 soldiers on the English pension lists following World War I, one-fifth was suffering from war neuroses. The foregoing helps explain the tighter personnel situation with psychiatric medical officers in wartime, as compared with other specialties. Consequently, there is an urgent need for a much greater reserve pool in the specialty of psychiatry, as noted. There is a concurrent great need for more advance planning in medicine generally, and in psychiatry in particular. Our top military leaders should by all means urge and insist upon much greater anticipation of these ratio changes rapidly taking place in any future emergency.

B. DIAGNOSTIC LABELS FOR COMBAT REACTIONS

1. Evolving Concepts and Terms

The diagnoses accorded cases of Combat Exhaustion or Combat Neuroses have shown considerable variability and development over the years. The gradual discard of beliefs in an organic basis for Traumatic Neuroses and for neuroses in war had a considerable effect. [*See* preceding chapter.] Such views, however, had continued to exert some influence at least through World War I.

This had been still reflected most strongly, in some of the diagnostic labels which continued to enjoy a certain vogue, particularly in the World War I era (for example: "shell shock", "blast reaction", and "concussion syndrome"). Evidence could not be found to validate scientifically the theories of an organic basis which had been evolved to account for the various kinds of nervous symptoms seen following trauma. As a result, these and other terms reflecting a belief in theoretical organic changes in the nervous system to account for post-traumatic emotional manifestations have largely fallen into disuse. During World War I, such terms were applied quite sincerely by some persons, based on a mistaken belief as to a presumed physical etiology for these traumatic neuroses of military operations. Others used them on occasion as a euphemistic kind of effort, and perhaps still a few more, as part of a kind of conspiracy of silence or of suppression of the true nature of the illness. A new terminology has been evolving, keeping pace with our newer concepts.

Modern military usage has replaced these outmoded terms with newer ones; for example, "combat reaction", "combat or operational fatigue", "physiologic conversion", "anxiety neurosis", "somatization reaction", "acute situational stress", and others [see Table 47]. In addition, a large body of data has been accumulated clearly establishing the basic psychologic origins of the symptoms commonly seen in connection with these reactions. The neuroses constituted the most significant psychiatric problem in World War II. There were more than 700,000 such casualties in the continental U.S. alone, with many additional ones overseas.

The following is a list of some of the various diagnoses which have been employed in classifying Combat Reactions. These partly reflect the existence of varying professional views and indicate the variety of terms so employed.

Table 43

Diagnoses Accorded Combat Reactions

The more common names employed diagnostically since 1914 for naming the emotional reactions incident to combat stress and wartime operation, include the following principal ones:

1. A.A.A.:—Acute Anxiety Attack	14. Gross stress reaction†
2. Acute situational reaction	15. Military Reaction
3. Acute situational stress	16. Operational Fatigue
4. Anxiety Neurosis	17. Operational Stress Reaction
5. Anxiety-Tension State, or A.T.S.	(Non-combat)
5. Battle Exhaustion*	18. Physiologic Conversion
6. Anxiety State	[pp. 642, 655].
7. Blast or Concussion Syndrome	19. Psychoneuroses of various kinds
8. Combat Exhaustion	20. Psychosomatic illnesses
9. Combat Fatigue	21. Shell Shock
10. Combat Neurosis	22. Somatization Reactions
11. Combat Reactions‡	23. Traumatic hysteria
12. Conversion reaction	24. Traumatic Neurosis
13. Effort Syndrome*	25. War Neurosis

* Effort Syndrome was previously employed in diagnosis and classification by the Canadian Army. It has been largely replaced in recent years by the term Battle Exhaustion.
† Currently official, A.P.A.-A.M.A. classification.
‡ Personally preferred.

In addition, many cases have been diagnosed in accordance with the customary, popular, or currently preferred nomenclature for the clinical type of neurosis which was present (according to the most prominent clinical manifestations of the individual case). The following tabulations are small statistical examples from World War II which help to indicate the varying diagnoses required and the scattering of major clinical manifestations, as encountered in general military operations.

2. Two Studies of Diagnoses Accorded Operational and Military Casualties

A. NEUROTIC DESIGNATION GIVEN 50 PER CENT OF 1800 PERSONS HOSPITALIZED OVERSEAS.—Ripley and Wolf selected at random some 1,800 persons out of a total of 5,000 patients hospitalized overseas for psychiatric study. Half of these service people had been in combat. Of the 1,800 selected, 967, or 53.7 per cent, were accorded diagnoses in the neurotic categories. Compare these findings with *Table 16,* [pp. 243–244] estimating the relative percentages of civilian neuroses. Most Military Reactions are *symptom-neuroses,* a distinction made from the *character neuroses.*

In the following table are listed the numbers of persons assigned the various neurotic designations:

Table 44

Diagnoses of Neurotic Reactions (53.7%) Accorded 967 Servicemen Overseas

Mixed psychoneuroses	286
Hysteria (Conversion Reactions)	265
Anxiety States (A.T.S.)	215
Reactive Depression	101
Hypochondriasis (Hygeiaphrontic Reactions)	51
Neurasthenia	47
Obsessive-Compulsive States	2
Total	967

B. COMBAT STRESS DESIGNATION GIVEN 470 SERVICEMEN CONSECUTIVELY HOSPITALIZED FOR TREATMENT STATESIDE.—In 1944–45 the author studied the consecutive admissions made each month to his ward in a U. S. Navy treatment center during World War II. It was an active ward for the reception of Marines and Navy personnel who, having become emotional casualties, had been evacuated promptly from overseas combat. This hospital had been established particularly for the therapy of acute emotional illness occurring in combat.

The diagnoses accorded the cases showed some variation. The use of various diagnostic terms was consistent however with the then currently evolving trends in service policy. The shifts thus reflect: (1) a changing acuteness of both emotional reactions and combat stresses, and the strategic situation, as the war drew to a close; (2) individual professional experience and preference; and (3) shifts in emphasis stemming from official military medical preference. The number of cases is significant, indicating the high psychiatrist/patient ratio possible. In the light of our knowledge of the requirements for adequate therapy time-wise per individual, one can see how pressures can mount on professional personnel.

The consecutive monthly admissions over the course of the calendar year 1945 are tabulated as follows, by diagnosis.

Table 45

The Diagnoses Given 470 Consecutive Combat Reactions

The following is a tabulation of the diagnoses given a group of U. S. Navy and Marine personnel suffering from acute Combat Reactions. This group represents the consecutive monthly admissions to an active ward in a U. S. Naval Hospital treatment center. The time was during World War II and covers the calendar year of 1945.

Diagnosis	*Number of Admissions*												
	Jan.	Feb.	Mar.	Ap.	Ma.*	Jun.	Jul.	Au.	Sep.†	Oc.	Nov.	Dec.	*Tot.*
Combat Fatigue	10	9	8	27	25	18	15	16	10	8	2	1	*149*
Psychoneurosis, Anxiety	4	4	7	4	16	7	11	16	19	19	9	4	*120*
Operational Fatigue	16	23	18	2	10	7	11	10	9	13	20	14	*153*
War Neurosis	2	1	2	2	1	—	—	—	—	—	—	—	*8*
Other (misc.)	2	1	2	5	5	3	2	2	2	5	5	6	*40*
Total Admissions	34	38	37	40	57	35	39	44	40	45	36	25	**470**

* *VE Day,* May 8; † *VJ Day,* September 2.

In the future one can expect that diagnosis in the illnesses which are incident to military stress will depend upon individual judgment as well as upon current military medical policy. There has been present generally a considerable interest in considering combat reactions separately from neuroses as such. This has been because of the special circumstances of their onset following military stress, and also perhaps because of certain past lay and medical feelings in regard to using the label of neurosis. For some psychiatrists the differentiation of malingering has posed problems. See the discussion on pp. 494–497 and 774 and other references in this work for some comments on this particular area. The Rhazes type of Maneuver [pp. 677ff. and 787] is sometimes employed to unveil malingering, but does not have too much basis for being recommended.

III. SYMPTOMS AND CLINICAL FEATURES

A. ACUTE COMBAT REACTIONS

1. One Hundred Consecutive Cases

The manifestations of Combat Reactions are particularly those of anxiety, expressed directly or indirectly, or the effects of anxiety. During some interesting research into the emotional reactions to combat stresses, the author had the fortunate opportunity to study fairly intensively many persons suffering from combat reactions during the war. These were quite acute reactions, all in servicemen with extensive combat experience. All were receiving as much intensive therapy as time and circumstances would permit. The comparative clinical data of their symptomatology from one hundred consecutive persons in this series have been selected for presentation.

This tabulation helps to illustrate the relative frequency of the various functional and physiologic conversion symptoms encountered, and may be of some general interest to some readers. It may also assist us in our study of the symptoms and clinical features of combat reactions. Each person in this group had developed his illness during the stress of combat. The author had seen each patient within at least thirty–sixty days following the (final) initiating combat experience.

2. Direct Anxiety Manifestations Prominent

In more than three-quarters of this group anxiety and tension were readily apparent to external observation. [*See Table 1*. Part A, p. 20.] Their *level of anxiety* [p. 11] can and does vary widely and is a matter for one's individual clinical assessment. Half of the group, some 50 patients, showed tremors, which varied all the way from mild finger tremors to gross bodily shaking. Near half—48—were grossly restless. About half of the group also suffered from a considerable degree of insomnia. At least one-fourth complained strongly of their repetitive disturbing nightmares and battle dreams.

A "startle reaction" to sudden noises was still marked in at least 20 per cent. Almost as many reported some appreciable measure of interference with mental function. A very substantial number exhibited physiologic conversion symptoms of various kinds. A smaller group variously manifested depression, emotional fatigue, weakness, or seclusiveness. Gastrointestinal symptoms were frequent (51 per cent). Recall our Psychic-Distaste Concept [pp. 115, 416, 418, and 473]. The multiple symptomatology for each individual is most evident in the tabulations. Thus, one hundred patients had 617 symptoms. This is slightly more than six manifestations for each person, on the average.

These figures might tend if anything to be on the conservative side. At least some of the time their manifestations were elicited in this group, in distinction to their being freely and gratuitously volunteered. Further, an occasional depressed, withdrawn, taciturn and uncommunicative, uncooperative, or even hostile patient would add to the increased possibility of statistical understatement.

A tabulation of the clinical manifestations of this group of patients is shown in *Table 46*. A comparison with *Table 1* [p. 20] summarizing the direct and indirect manifestation of anxiety, is of interest.

Table 46

The Symptoms of Combat Reactions

The study of 100 consecutive cases of acute emotional illnesses developed during combat in World War II indicated the relative frequency of symptoms and clinical features, as follows:

I. The Direct Manifestations of Anxiety   *Number of Patients*

    A. *Direct Anxiety:*   *(Percentage)**

       1. Reported simply as "nervousness" 77

       2. Anxiety (as subjectively reported, observed, or both).... 73

       3. Tension (as reported, apparent, or both) 57

    B. *The Psychomotor Expression and Direct Effects of Anxiety:*

       1. Tremors†; extending from fine finger tremors to
          gross shaking 50

       2. Sleep disturbances:

          (*a*) Marked insomnia 50

          (*b*) Nightmares and battle dreams † 25

       3. Restlessness 42

       4. Startle reaction † 19

       5. Speech difficulties 6

    C. *Effects upon Mental Function;* including in particular,
    disturbances in concentration, attention, and confusion........ 14

    D. *The Autonomic Expression of Tension and Anxiety:*

       1. Palpitation 22

       2. Hyperhidrosis (increased perspiration) 13

II. The Indirect Manifestations and Consequences of Anxiety

    A. *Physiologic Conversion Symptoms:*

       1. Headache 27

       2. Emotional Fatigue and weakness 20

       3. Backache, leg pains (note Emotionally-Determined
          Visceral Pain Principle, pp 467 *ff.*) 6

       4. Cardiovascular symptoms 4

       5. Gastrointestinal symptoms (anorexia, 34; nausea, 3;
          gastrointestinal-based major weight loss, 5; other
          gastrointestinal symptoms, 9) 51

       6. Genitourinary symptoms 2

    B. *Psychologic Conversion Symptoms:*

       1. Irritability † 35

       2. Depression and guilt feelings 18

       3. Withdrawal, seclusion, and apathy 12

       4. Well marked episodes of amnesia 2

       5. Obsessive manifestations, including hygeiaphrontic
          preoccupation 5

---

* The total number of patients in our study being 100, the figures for each manifestation are also percentages. Thus 50 patients suffering tremors and 22 having palpitation indicates the prevalence of these symptoms to be 50 percent and 22 percent respectively, in this series.

† Manifestations which are fairly characteristic of Combat Reactions, especially in their more acute phases.

Apprehensive Anticipation [pp. 17*ff.* and 800] was not specifically checked. It would have been a not infrequent manifestation. Many instances would not be incorrectly categorized as A.T.S. (Anxiety-Tension States). Compare the foregoing findings with those earlier tabulated for Anxiety Neurosis, *Table 8.*

B. THE THEORY OF ULTIMATE-VULNERABILITY

1. Severe Neurosis Follows Major Stress. Everyone Has a "Breaking Point"

In the preceding Chapter 14 we observed that the level of symptoms did not at all necessarily correspond to the severity of trauma. In several instances as cited, serious disability followed "minor" trauma, as assessed by observers. We noted the Final-Straw Concept.

Let us proceed now to the other end of the scale, where the actual trauma is maximal. In the case to be summarized, the almost constant level of stress to which this particular man was exposed was terrific. Many men indeed would have been more profoundly affected than he was, and considerably sooner. His original acute traumatic experience of being a survivor of a wartime sinking in combat was in itself noteworthy enough. Nonetheless, it was repeated on three separate subsequent occasions, although with varying modifications. The final experience could be regarded also as his particular Final-Straw, in accord with our earlier cited concept; but this experience was not only a most substantial "straw", it was probably thus only after great potentiation from prolonged maximal stress.

This type of instance tends to bear out what the author suggests we might refer to as the *Theory of Ultimate-Vulnerability*. According to this theory, *every person, no matter how stable and emotionally well integrated, will reach a breaking point, given sufficient stress* [Ch.14:VIIA2; VIIB1].

Case 184

Severe Combat Reaction Follows Maximal Stress

(1) *Seeking to illustrate an unfortunate thesis*
A rather unfortunate trend was fashionable for a time during World War II in some medical and psychiatric circles. This was to emphasize what some regarded to be the constitutional and psychologic "weakness, or predisposition" to emotional breakdown of certain service men. Sometimes included were those men who became unable to carry on because of incapacitating emotional difficulties during or following combat. In support of his thesis along these lines, late in the War a colleague with little service experience pointed out to me a passing naval petty officer. "Look at that sad-looking specimen," he said. "Do you think he ever had much stability or could have amounted to much? From the first time I saw him on admission two days ago, it was immediately evident that this is a prime example of the basically inferior and unstable person."

"Get them in the service," he continued, "and expose them to a gunshot or two, and poof! they collapse. Furthermore, he is guilty about his failure. Won't talk much. He admits he saw little action and that there's no reason why he should be nervous! I couldn't get any psychologic determinants at all from him, but I bet a real thorough history would find most of them.* He looks to me to be typical of the weak and inferior type of person who just can't take it."

---

* *Conflict Indicators* [pp. 406, 671, 756] were at times assigned a terribly prominent role in medical circles between 1940 and 1946, as "psychological determinants" of later emotional difficulties and neuroses. This is not to say of course that they have no significance. They do.

(2)   *Stresses produce profound changes*

In disagreement with his thesis, and only half-listening to him, I had noticed something vaguely familiar about the person being discussed. He seemed a washed-out and shadowy caricature of someone I had perhaps once known. I noted his specialty rating — quartermaster — and then it came to me. I knew this man well! He had served with me aboard ship some years earlier. This service had included all kinds of strenuous operational and combat conditions.

Now, however, he was barely recognizable. Physically he had shrunk and aged unbelievably since the time when I had last seen him. On that occasion less than four years earlier, he had been a young, strong, and self-possessed person. He had been one of those not-too-common men who seem imbued with a rock-like quality which invites other men to lean on them, and implicitly to accept them as leaders. He had represented a very strong model and emotional prototype [pp. 490 and 808]. Now he was an aged, palsied, defeated, and pathetic figure, shriveled and shrunken to nearly half· his former weight. What events or stresses could have wrought such profound changes?

How unfortunate an example my colleague had unwittingly picked! He couldn't have been more wrong in his evaluation. A poorer illustration in support of his contention could hardly have been found. His shallow, hasty, moralistic kind of judgment condemned a most worthwhile person. His comments could not have been more unjust.

(3)   *Unfazed by harrowing combat experiences*

Serving as shipmate with this man on a destroyer during the touch-and-go of the early months of the War had provided me with an unequaled opportunity to learn to know him well under all kinds of stressful situations. His T.R.C. had functioned at least as ideally as that of anyone aboard ship. The exigencies of war had led our vessel from North Atlantic convoy duty, through the North African landing operations, and finally to the Pacific for the final phase of Guadalcanal and the Solomons campaign.

We had participated in a number of the first hesitant and tentative advances northward in the Pacific area. We had engaged in night bombardments of enemy shore installations. Enemy air and naval units had been encountered. During every situation, no matter what had impended, this man literally had been a "tower of strength." Our ship finally was sunk during an engagement in Kula Gulf, between New Georgia and Kolambangara Islands, under conditions of great stress for her personnel. Among those who were survivors, a fair number developed Combat Fatigue and various stress reactions. Not so this man. He had promptly returned to duty, by request, on another destroyer. He had appeared outwardly quite unfazed by this harrowing experience, superimposed upon prolonged stressful operations.

I was naturally interested scientifically as well as personally in what had happened. What conceivable stresses could account for such unbelievable changes in a man I knew to have been of such outstanding caliber? Fortunately we were able to spend some time together. Gradually I pieced together his history during the intervening several years since our last prior meeting.

Following the loss of our ship in early July 1943, the tempo of stress for him had not only continued uninterrupted but had, if anything, increased. Briefly, he had continued an unusually extensive combat service on two subsequent destroyers. Each of these had been sunk in turn, he being among the survivors. It was not until after the second such experience that he had his first real nervous symptoms. These had gradually increased during service aboard ship number three, and following its loss.

(4)   *A final, culminating experience*

His culminating acute traumatic experience took place on ship number four a month or so prior to his hospitalization. It had in it all the worst elements of trapped helplessness and had ultimately precipitated his particular final emotional decompensation [pp. 343, 675, and 711]. Scouting enemy shore battery positions believed to have been earlier silenced on Southern Okinawa, his ship ran hard aground on a poorly charted ledge. At this point shore batteries believed silent had suddenly opened up at point-blank range.

Salvo after salvo was fired. Hundreds of rounds of ammunition were poured into the helpless ship. With all attempts to retrieve the situation proved futile, the vessel riddled, dead in the water, and sinking, those still surviving were ordered to abandon ship. My former shipmate finally got off the ship into the water.

At this point he found himself slowly being drawn back by the tide, despite his strongest swimming efforts, toward a large area where the surface was covered by burning oil from the stricken destroyer. He didn't know how long this lasted. It seemed an eternity. He managed, however, to stay clear long enough somehow so that the enemy batteries were eventually really silenced and he was rescued. This prolonged and intensely traumatic situation served as the Final Straw [Ch.14:VD*3*].

2. Geometric Progression

Prolonged stress if of sufficient strength and duration will eventually lead to symptoms. In other words, *everyone* has a breaking point—given sufficiently major stress. This is proposed as a theory, a *Theory of Ultimate-Vulnerability* [Ch.14:VD*3*]. The same conclusion probably applies with less severe, or repeated stress over a sufficiently long period of time. Accordingly, each given traumatic event will predispose to some varying extent the response to a subsequent one. Naming the theory may emphasize the concept and possibly facilitate communication.

The progression as far as its effects are concerned for the individual, often tends to be geometric, in contrast to merely an arithmetic one. Repeated trauma in accord with our theory, will ultimately "break down" the defenses of the strongest personality. The invulnerable will eventually become vulnerable.

3. Tolerance to Military Stress Extremely Variable

Perhaps the reader may gain some idea from the brief sketch in *Case 184* of the tremendous stress to which this man was subjected. The author had observed, of course, many instances in which persons lost their military effectiveness in response to minor, moderate, or severe stress. At the time, this case helped bring home most forcibly the tremendous individual variance in tolerance to stress during combat and stressful military operations. No data is available as to any further possible reinforcement of the impact of the final traumatic event by virtue of hidden symbolism or of other unconscious factors. On the surface of it, however, such contributions would hardly seem necessary.

The usual dynamic position in this regard was expressed by Deutsch in describing the onset of neurotic symptoms following a psychologically traumatic experience: ". . . such traumatic experiences may well be the occasion for the outbreak of a neurosis, but they are extremely seldom the ultimate and only cause of the illness." Until a better possible example is learned of, the author is willing to advance the foregoing instance as a good "candidate" for this "extremely seldom" type of case. This instance also invites attention to our important Concept of Continued Physiologic Momentum [pp. 99 and 776].

Every man has his breaking point. The author's erstwhile shipmate, originally a person of clearly superior integration and stability, unfortunately had reached his.

C. TWO WORLD WARS PROVIDED DIFFERING CLINICAL PICTURES

1. Somatic Conversion Reactions Frequent in World War I

One might be rightly impressed with some of the differences in the kinds of symptoms of the cases described clinically in World War I and in World War II and later wars. Ferenczi, in describing cases in the earlier conflict, reported frequent gross disorders of movement [Janet Dissociations; pp. 648 and 693] and serious degrees of handicap, contractures, spasticities, and the like. *La belle indifference* [pp. 671ff.] was the frequent accompaniment. Camptocormia [p. 670] was more frequent. Many of these reactions were gross Somatic Conversion Reactions [pp. 639–719]. The Somatic Conversions were seen much less frequently in World War II. Not one of the series (*Table 46*) had a Somatic Conversion symptom. In fact, among thousands of persons admitted to our treatment center, these were most rare indeed. They were also relatively rare in the author's experience during several years of duty in other Navy hospitals, and during ten years of Army consultant work. When present however, these as well as certain other symptoms often could be correctly regarded as compromise formations [pp. 118, 671, 693, and 755]. Also of interest is the reference to cultural influences on conversion manifestations [pp. 658–662]. Neurasthenia was a not-infrequent diagnosis in the earlier conflict. Symptoms of Military Reactions can comprise as part of their psychodynamic anatomy, a vital S.O. or Security Operation [pp. 351, 461, and 708].

2. Anxiety and Physiologic Conversion Manifestations Predominant In World War II and Since

In World War II there were far more cases in which the manifestations of anxiety were direct. Physiologic Conversion Symptoms and Reactions (also known as somatization reactions, psychophysiologic or psychosomatic illnesses, and so on) were correspondingly much more frequent. [*See Table 31,* p. 655.] All types of earlier pain and dysfunction can be reproduced on a psychic basis, in accord with our Psychic Reduplication Concept. The S.E.E.R. Concept [p. 422] can have important implications in Combat Exhaustion. Functional symptoms often can bespeak a physiologic language [pp. 467, 644, and 742] which expresses significant messages, however symbolic, oblique, and obscure these may be.

Among the manifestations of acute Combat Reactions in World War II the outstanding clinical feature was usually the tremendous amount of anxiety which was mobilized, and which was often outwardly apparent [*Table 46*]. The Inverse Ratio of Symptom-Success [pp. 9–10] in allaying anxiety, and its adverse effects on motivation towards therapy, may play a less significant role than in civilian neuroses. Thus, in line with our Fuel Analogy [pp. 42, 119, 363], there may be more "anxiety-gasoline" to drive the "therapy-motor". *Cases 7* and *8* also illustrate anxiety manifestations in response to wartime stress. The contagion of anxiety [pp. 10; 464] can be a very real matter in the military setting. *Cases 19, 20,* and *21* note the onset of A.T.S.s in the military setting. Psychologic Conversion symptoms, however, also occurred. These included the manifestations of every type of neurosis we have discussed. *Case 90* illustrates the onset of obsessive hygeiaphrontic preoccupation in response to combat stress. The Hygeiaphrontic Discrepancy [pp. 447*ff.*] is an important finding. Both obsessive or hygeiaphrontic manifestations can provide a basis for, and illustrate, our attention and Interest-Absorption Concept, as outlined earlier [p. 311]. Accentuation of earlier dormant trends can at times help swell the ranks of a military group of Seekers-After-Health [p. 461].

The size of the war or the scope of military operations does not necessarily influence the emotional reaction, which remains essentially individual. Anxiety Reactions of the more direct variety remain frequent, of which the following vividly described instance of an A.A.A. from the Viet Nam era is illustrative. The total loss of security is graphically portrayed. The presence of an A.A.A. in particular (as with anxiety generally) is indicative of the Incomplete Symptom-Defense, as outlined earlier [p. 89] in our similarly named concept.

Case 185

An A.A.A.; Viet Nam

". . . It's the most terrible feeling. I feel like I can't get enough to breathe, and when I try I get dizzy. . . . My whole body tightens up. My face feels like its in a press and infra-red hot . . . I realize what's about to happen [from past A.A.A.'s] and it scares me so much! The harder I try to breathe fast the more tense I get, and the more tense, the harder I must try. It's a vicious circle. I'm afraid I'll pass out; or explode; or die. Then it begins to subside, but it's a long time before I'm really relaxed or calm again and sometimes I think this will never come again. . . . While it's at its peak, I have nothing to hang on to. Everything is empty . . . nothing to care about. An overwhelming sense of hopelessness about the whole military situation, about life in general. Everything got tipped upside down. . . . Everything is gone. It's terrible; like the floor dropped out . . . No place to turn to . . . . . . no way to release the misery. . . . No way for solace."

In the foregoing instance the Circular Generation of Fear [*see Case 16,* p. 93, and p. 529] was illustrated. Not only would physical threats and hazards of combat stress add to tension, but the fear of a recurrence became if anything, even more of a threat. Indeed, this dread in itself can at times partly replace the more usual fears in combat. Anxiety can find expression as anger (and irritability). Anger in turn can secure a variety of expressions. Some of these clinically can represent what have been termed [pp. 683 and 742] rage-equivalents.

The A.T.S. [Anxiety-Tension State, pp. 98–104] is very common indeed in military situations. *Cases 20* and *21* are illustrative. *Case 24* illustrated an Anxiety Neurosis which became exaggerated during combat service in the Korean War.

3. All Neurotic Reactions Represented

Ripley and Wolf's figures indicate the frequency of depression; some 10.6 per cent of their neurotic reactions. As a symptom 18 per cent of the author's group of patients were depressed. There is a relatively greater frequency of Amnesia and Fugue States among servicemen in wartime. Torrie reported Amnesia and Fugue·in 86 of 1,000 cases of emotional casualties in the Middle East. Grinker and Speigel reported the frequency with which they were encountered in the Tunisian campaign. *Cases 170* and *173* illustrate Fugue States in military personnel who were not under combat stress. Major Dissociative Reactions may be regarded as Reactions-of-the-Whole in distinction from Part-Reactions. Schonberger also described states of depersonalization during wartime. He discussed the process of adaption to traumatic circumstances as one in which a new "war ego" comes into existence.

When the person does not already have the ground well prepared for the onset of emotional disturbance. a severely traumatic experience is often well tolerated. Many servicemen suffered exposure to all varieties of traumatic war experiences and showed few appreciable outward effects. Their ability to adjust to war conditions was eminently successful.

By the same token emotional effects are not always outwardly apparent. Their remnants can also persistently linger, in varying degree. A colleague related to the author recently how, many years (25) after his wartime destroyer duty, the discussion and recall of his experiences bring on subjective evidences of anxiety and tension. While these have decreased in degree over the years, they are still quite appreciable. This feature is not uncommon to some extent for many veterans.

Clinical illustrations of every type of emotional reaction to the stresses of military operation and combat experience are to be observed. They are liberally scattered throughout this work. An important precept as outlined earlier [pp. 698 and 753] stresses the complete individuality of meaning and symbolism in *each* symptom. This is the Rule of Individual-Symbolism. *Case 139* illustrated Somatic Conversion in a soldier, and an earlier reference [p. 658] noted the high incidence in World War I of this conversion reaction.

Somatic conversion reactions can provide instances of an obscure, striking, or poignant *body* or *somatic language* [pp. 643 *ff.*] *Case 140* noted a Conversion Reaction in a recruit; *Case 144* described an instance of conversion "drum-major gait"; *Case 147* dealt with the Red-Ink Cure, through progressive suggestion in a seaman [*see also* related *Case 148*]. An earlier caution was noted [p. 677] concerning an undue medical focus on factors of secondary gain. *Case 142* illustrated conversion aphonia and dissociation, as the marked reaction to the kind of intense homosexual conflict which can occur in military service. Selective hearing [p. 688] may become prominent, as an automatic intended-defense. Conversion epidemics can occur among soldiers [p. 703]. These can include fainting [pp. 771 *ff*]. Strecker cited a group of 500 gas casualties "with similar respiratory symptoms who however, had had no gas inhalation." As noted earlier [p. 693], conversion symptoms have been called Janet Dissociations.

Secondary gains were noted in *Case 10*. Depression in the military setting is not infrequent and is often poorly recognized [*see Case 29*]. Note the frequently characteristic Dawn-Insomnia [pp. 142 *ff*. 156, 163, 748]. Accident-Proneness [pp. 196–198] can play a significant role in certain combat and service connected injuries. *Cases 44, 45,* and *49* discuss relationships of suicide. Pain of many varieties is frequent: consult again our Axiom of Inverse Pain-Conflict Ratio as outlined earlier [p. 470]. Most of our clinical and dynamic concepts, as advanced and supported throughout this text, have major applications in service situations. Obsessive-Compulsive Reactions [pp. 244–258 and 307–378] are encountered. Servicemen frequently evolve their own S.O.'s [pp. 351–352 and 621] and C.R.'s [pp. 349–351]. Sleep and Fatigue have an important bearing on stress-tolerance in military operations. In assessing emotional reactions under combat stress and the lurking or partially concealed E.O.C. [Emotional-Organic Combination; pp. 393 and 454] must be borne in mind. In their management, so must our Concept of Functional-Structural Progression [pp. 13, 113, 468, and 642], which constitutes a strong vote in favor of early removal from stress, and prompt therapy. The problems of secondary gain *vs*. epigain [pp. 61–68] *vs*. malingering [pp. 62, 494–7] can require special attention. The presence of concurrent organic illness comprises an E.O.C. The presence of other neurotic reactions (with anxiety) can bear out our Incomplete Symptom-Defense Concept [pp. 89, 189, 477, and 692].

Acute phobias as well as chronic and long-established ones can interfere with military performance. A bombardier with a great phobia of mice (musophobia), recently related a tense and tragihumorous incident when he discovered a mouse "stowaway" in his plane compartment. This caused him far more fear, tension, and panic than the thick flak concurrently being encountered from enemy ground fire. As they approached their bombing run the presence of the mouse was nearly disabling . . . not the flak.

Certain phobias [for example: *atomosophobia, thanatophobia,* and *werrephobia; Table 27*] have their phobic-object source in war. Acute war experiences can provide the basis for instances of what we have sought to distinguish by the name of Critical-Displacement Phobias. Multiple symptoms, and in the acute situation, can comprise a literal Symptom-Barrage.

The soteria and Soterial Reactions often have special significances for people in military situations, as with many persons under stress. Soterial objects are frequently incorporated as components of the individual psychologic defenses and S.O.'s. At times the service itself can come to comprise an important soterial refuge, as a carryover from the home [p. 630].

The combat evacuee not infrequently has a great defensive and ego-saving (unconscious) need to evolve a physical scapegoat * [pp. 392, 461, and 652]. Accordingly, our Surgery-in-Abeyance Rule may need to be invoked. War Neuroses symptoms can on occasion illustrate our Psychic Reduplication Concept.

Following our Psychologic-Flight Avoidance Concept, basic to the Dissociative Reactions, various ones of these may be encountered. As with other, more indirect neurotic manifestations of stress their secondary defense may be very strong. Stress causes or contributes to dissociation where this evolvement is possible. Dissociation is one major form of P.F.A. and as such helps comprise the T.R.C. and T.R.T. for certain individuals. The major Dissociative Reaction as noted are Reactions-of-the-Whole [p. 742] in distinction from certain Part-Reactions [pp. 692, 742]. Amnesia and the Fugue States, for example, are also thought of as expressing what was earlier referred to [p. 742] as an Overall Language Concept.

Depersonalization can serve as a C.I. and can reflect and/or express stress and tension. It can be an anxiety-equivalent [pp. 103, 145, 462]. Actually it can be such a common experience at one time or another for nearly everyone as to bring to mind our earlier stated Law of Universality in Emotional Health. *Déja vu* is one major variant. *Cases 161, 162, and 163* offer examples from service experience. These can help illustrate a concept of the so-called Affective Escape Route. To stress its pathologic potential and its role at times as a significant P.S.F., depersonalization has on occasion been referred to as an Incipient Fugue.

The fugue itself clinically is usually marked by both psychologic and physical flight [p. 792]. A concept has compared the fugue to an extension of a more commonplace activity through its name of Daytime Somnambulism. The fugue is illustrated in servicemen in *Case 170* and *Case 173*. As a response to crisis, the dissociation and even more so the fugue, become a C.I. of some significance [pp. 756–7 and 797].

IV. PSYCHODYNAMIC FACTORS

A. FOUR INTERESTING FEATURES CHARACTERISTIC

1. The Startle Reaction

As observed in World War II, there were four interesting clinical features which tended to be characteristic of many instances of Combat Exhaustion, especially in their more acute stages. These were: (1) the startle reaction, (2) the repetitive battle dreams, (3) the irritability, and (4) the presence of tremors. The rapid onset of a Combat Reaction can be regarded as an emotional decompensation [pp. 48, 159].

---

* A physical scapegoat may die hard (or never!). A patient told me that his most significant realization from three years of psychotherapy (and which alone made the entire endeavor worthwhile) thus far, was the final full recognition that his difficulties were emotional in origin — not physical [*see also* Flight-to-the-Physical Concept].

The Startle Reaction is perhaps best understood on the basis of conditioning to danger. In battle, immediate, that is reflex physical reaction, is vital to survival. The soldier becomes conditioned to so respond. It is part of his T.R.C. or Total Reaction to Crisis, which has seen further development during training and service. It becomes very firmly established. Its efficient functioning is likely to be life-saving under combat conditions. In combat sudden noises or movements actually carry a high probability of personal danger to the soldier. In the alert serviceman, a sudden noise produces instant mobilization for flight or fight. Sometimes this is overdone and the resulting reaction may be inappropriate in extent or time. This is in line with our Concept of Defensive-Over-Reaction [pp. 95, 115, 641]. The startle reaction, especially following removal from the actual danger zone, is an example. It should also be noted that a large potential of energy is made available in both the appropriate, as well as in the later no longer appropriate situation.

Upon occasion this reaction of automatic preparation to meet danger can quickly change into an angry-hostile outburst. It can lead to an assault with swinging fisticuffs. This has happened, for example, when someone has deliberately elicited this reaction by making a sudden noise behind the person, as an ill-begotten attempt at humor.

2. The Battle Dream: Densensitizing Purpose Concept

Repetitive dreams of combat partly serve a protective function. This is gained through a measure of subconscious abreaction and desensitization taking place. There results a more or less symbolic reassertion of mastery over the terribly threatening environment. Earlier reference [p. 745] has been made to the desensitizing purpose of the post-traumatic dream of which the combat dream is an excellent illustration. However, they can be in turn terrifying experiences in themselves. It is not too uncommon for a soldier to fear to go to sleep because of them. See earlier comments on dreams and their functions [pp. 744–754]. Similarly, somnambulism as its occasional extension, might in analogous fashion be regarded as an Activated Nocturnal Fantasy.

3. Irritability

Irritability can be a complex manifestation. Included may be such elements as: (1) resentment toward authority, (2) a response to projected self-disapproval and guilt feelings which may or may not be realistic, and (3) a transition into angry-hostile feelings of the continued anxiety-tension potential. This latter is at times in accord with our concept of anger comprising an Anxiety-Equivalent.

The irritability and its expression can at times also have an unconscious aspect of almost flagrantly seeking retaliatory restriction or punishment. This is particularly true when present in a military situation. Irritability can become a pervasive part of the serviceman's overall attitude, in effect comprising what we have identified as an Attitude-Symptom. It is an aspect which must be recognized in any adequate handling of the many disciplinary problems which are apt to arise in this group of patients. Acting out [pp. 193, 258] can contribute substantially to this problem. A considerable measure of understanding-in-depth may be required in these situations. One needs to look out for the trap implicit to our Anger-Breeds-Anger Concept [pp. 446, 711].

Provocativeness more directly, may be encountered as a related symptom. This can be masochistic. It can also serve as a more or less concealed route for the expression of aggressive feelings. Here the person behaves in such a way as to practically invite punishment. Obviously such reactions often bear a close relationship to antecedent conflicts of an interpersonal nature from earlier life. In some way this behavior may have developed in line with our Profitable-Patterns Concept. In effect, these patterns of relationship may have been reactivated by the stress of combat.

4. Tremors

The tremors in Combat Reactions are a frequent manifestation. They range in severity from fine finger tremors to gross shaking. In frequency their incidence runs from about 50 per cent in the series studied 30 to 60 days post-combat; likely close to if not a full 100 per cent just prior to evacuation from the combat situation. They directly reflect the level of tension and anxiety.

The tremors and shaking (as also the restlessness) are the partial translation into nonconstructive bodily expression of the undischarged energy potential. This is their main physiological basis. It illustrates our Concept of Defensive Overreaction [pp. 95, 115, 798]. Symbolism and other unconscious facets can play a varying role. Hyperhidrosis can upon occasion be quite marked. The author has observed acute cases in which the palmar sweating was so prominent that large drops of perspiration fell steadily from every finger, each soon forming its own small puddle.

5. Acute Manifestations Subside

These very acute reactions generally slowly subside spontaneously, following removal from the danger situation. Resolution of the symptoms can be speeded up considerably by judicious management and by kindly, sympathetic, and understanding therapy, even on a fairly superficial level. In any analysis of the basis of a given combat symptom, the Rule of Individual Symbolism [p. 699] holds. Group therapy can be especially helpful at times, in view of the similarity of experiences and symptoms. It is also useful as a means of helping to meet the expected scarcity of skilled professional help.

6. Chronicity of Symptoms

Recent studies indicate that for certain individuals, some of the more typical symptoms of startle reaction, sleep difficulties, anxiety, irritability, and functional symptoms tend to persist in some measure; they become fixed and chronic. Archibald and colleagues, for example, found this to be true for a number of persons fifteen years after the Second World War. As noted, recurrence of some manifestations can be induced through recall of initiating circumstances.

The reluctance to express feelings, inability to discuss them, avoidance of combat-like situations (movie, T.V., and so on), failure to secure prior abreaction, and social withdrawal, are factors which appear to contribute. Our concept of the Secondary Defense of symptoms [pp. 144, 366, 444] finds applicability in Combat Reaction Symptoms. *Cases 187* and *188* illustrate semichronic symptoms and their successful treatment after some years. Finally, it would hardly be surprising if certain symptoms had developed as what have been termed secondary restrictions — of sensory perceptions which are threatening and frightening.

B. INDIVIDUAL SUSCEPTIBILITY TO COMBAT STRESS

1. Personal-Invulnerability Defense Concept

A related defense and a rather common one is that expressed in our Concept of the Personal Invulnerability Defense. This is seen quite frequently among personnel in combat. Herein the constant idea and emotional feeling is fostered that such and such an event or tragedy "may befall someone else, or even many others — but it will not involve me. I am somehow invulnerable; others, but not me!"

Through this kind of "personal invulnerability" which thus becomes created, one becomes the magical all-powerful master of chance and fate. Any possibility of personal danger or disaster is shoved out of conscious awareness and requires little attention. Threats of death can be at least temporarily dismissed. The protective intent becomes obvious. One could hardly function effectively if he dwelt too steadily on the prospects of death, which lies potentially around many corners. Thereby personal impotence in relation to acts of nature or of man is replaced by feelings of invulnerability or omnipotence. The development and operation of these kinds of defenses is largely automatic and unconscious. The reverse development of this defense, described as "feelings of omnipotent responsibility", was observed earlier.

In accord with our Second Tenet of the Parental Role less susceptibility to stress (including that of military origin) is present when the early background was secure and relationships adequate. The Theory of Antecedent Conflicts can play, as noted, an important role in one's relative vulnerability to combat stress [pp. 490–494]. Nearly any symptom can be evolved by the psyche. Many stress-determinants supplement those earlier outlined in preceding chapters. [For example, see *Table 33*, pp. 697–8, for an outline of some important determinants in symptom choice and location.]

2. Many Factors Contribute

War and combat neuroses demonstrate the vital role of self-preservation in individual psychology. One's relative individual susceptibility to the stress of combat is in accord with our basic Law of Relativity in Emotional Health. It is based upon many factors. These include the following, as tabulated:

Table 47

Individual Factors in Susceptibility to Combat Stress

(1) The prior and basic individual stability and adjustment. The *Peg Concept* has applicability here. So also does our *Iceberg Analogy.*

(2) The sensitization or desensitization *effects of prior trauma.* See Chapter 14. This is in accord with the *Rule of Impression Priority* and our *Theory of Antecedent Conflicts.*

(3) The adequacy of the defenses which have been mobilized and developed during military training and experience, prior to combat experience. These may aid in reducing combat engendered anxieties or one's susceptibility to them. The *Principle of Avoidance of Anxiety* will still hold however, and will exert influences accordingly.

(4) The level of *morale,* and the effectiveness of unit or *group identification.*

(5) The level of *subjective feelings of helplessness,* impotence, vulnerability, or their converse, omnipotence.

(6) The *current* tactical and strategic *military position.* For example, a retreating or a defeated army has a much tougher job maintaining the morale of its men. Our *Emotional Contagion Concept* also has applicability here.

(7) The presence of *undue fatigue, sleeplessness,* and *exhaustion.*

(8) The weakening of defenses through repeated exposure to trauma, and to chronic stress, without the opportunity to recoup one's physical or psychic defenses. The cumulative effects are important; see later *Psychic Depletion Concept.*

(9) *Wounds.* Note earlier concept of *Inverse Relation Between Severity of Wounds and Emotional Symptoms.*

3. Extension to Country of Early, Antecedent Conflicts

Zabriskie and Bush described war neurosis as the outcome of a conflict between fear and the urge to flee on the one hand, and a sense of duty on the other. Sperling wrote that both war neuroses and civilian traumatic neuroses are based on the conflict between love and hatred, transferred from the Oedipus complex to society (the country) as a whole. He believed that war neurosis is based on a conflict between love for, and hatred of one's country. Trauma is one of several factors that mobilize hatred.

One can sometimes predicate an unconscious extension to country of early attitudes (and conflicts) in relation to parents and parental authority. Earlier intrapsychic as well as interpersonal emotional conflict can so extend. Early antecedent conflicts thus may establish models for later ones, which are brought out by the stresses of war.

4. Dynamics Complex and Individual.

In many instances the dynamics of individual cases are rather complex. A number of years of the author's own military experience during the

Second World War, as indicated, were devoted exclusively to the management and treatment of patients who had developed acute emotional casualties during and following combat. From 1947 to 1958 the author also served as civilian consultant to the Surgeon-General of the Army, assisting with the graduate training program in psychiatry at the Walter Reed Army Medical Center. This provided contact with many additional cases, including the combat evacuees from Korea.

Among the many hundreds of persons the author worked with or had contact with through these years either directly, or in a supervisory-therapeutic capacity, it would not seem feasible to very simply categorize the dynamics in many instances. Although patients often have many common features, the management and understanding of each is an individual matter. Many instances would be categorized as belonging with our More Advanced or Less Primitive Neuroses.

The belief has at times existed that one or another of the military services posed less stress and threat than the others. Davidson believed that certain conditions aboard a war vessel tended to mitigate anxiety more than in land fighting in the army. He cited such factors as ability to see what is going on, public address system announcements, every man having a job, and the more questionable one that most sea battles are fought in the daytime. This author is not sure whether he could accept his conclusions. However, it is certainly clear in any event that the stresses of combat are severe regardless of the branch of service.

Functional alterations, such as pain, come into awareness more readily with anxiety and with stress. This particular "source" of added distress was earlier tagged for identification [p. 480] the Lowered-Perception-Threshold Source for symptoms. A Visceral-Masochism Concept [pp. 482, 491] also outlines an added pathway.

Simmel, in the discussion of his experiences and of theory, also stressed the importance of the accumulation of traumatic influences in the onset of war neuroses. Undoubtedly the optimal following of our First Tenet of the Parental Role builds up inner resources and security, lessening one's vulnerability to later stresses.

Kardiner differentiated traumatic reactions from other forms of psychoneuroses. Dreyfuss regarded the shock itself as a "screen" experience. Rosenberg believed that a number of neuroses in World War II were due to separation anxiety. The fear of death might then be due to an unconscious fear of separation as well as to a more conscious dread of physical pain and the unknown. In considering underlying dynamics, our Iceberg Analogy [p. 444] should be borne in mind. Actually, volumes could be written on this fascinating subject of the emotional reactions to combat. It is unfortunate and at first also a bit puzzling that more has not been written by those observers at the time, who had such an excellent first-hand opportunity. On further reflection, perhaps some of the less comfortable factors and personal consequences developing, which might enter into a restriction of writing about (one's experiences in) these areas might well be surmised!

C. EFFECTS OF REPEATED TRAUMA

1. Concept of Psychic Depletion

At times an individual appears to tolerate a single traumatic experience very well. We observed this in *Case 183,* already referred to. Here the more acute traumatic experiences were fairly widely separated in time. They were accompanied during the intervals between them, however, by almost constant external stress. The human organism ordinarily has great powers of recuperation from psychologic as well as physical trauma. Repeated trauma *before* the individual has time to make emotional and psychologic "repairs" however, often seems to find him more vulnerable to each next succeeding traumatic event. This brings us to an important principle which for convenience we might call the *Concept of Psychic Depletion.*

Repeated exposure to trauma (and to prolonged chronic stress) can also undermine confidence in one's continued ability to cope with threats. Tolerance may decrease as "psychic weariness" or depletion increases. Emotional fatigue, disillusionment, and cynicism ensue. It is sometimes as though there is a "wearing down" process which enters into an increased susceptibility to neurosis. Depersonalization can at times become increasingly frequent as a P.S.F. Dynamically this manifestation may be an intended symbolic escape. Upon occasion it appears from almost a quantum kind of view that the psychic energy and resources gradually become depleted, with the result that the earlier elaborated psychic defenses eventually weaken or collapse. A variety of symptoms is ushered in by the final acute (or subacute) emotional decompensation.

This outlines the Concept of Psychic Depletion of one's total potential resources and defenses. It is a psychic debilitation under repeated blows, which can ultimately lead to complete emotional collapse.

2. Increased Vulnerability

Thus, repeated threats may damage the self-protective and the defensive effectiveness of the individual's Total Reaction to Trauma. Its protective ability may be damaged or lost. This more mechanical viewpoint is taken temporarily for convenience only. It is not intended to detract from the important symbolism and conditioning effects which are implicit to our Theory of Antecedent Conflict.

Some of the effects of repeated psychologic trauma upon personal defenses are illustrated in the following case.

Case 186

Cumulative Effect upon Personal Defenses of Repeated Traumatic Misadventures; "Feelings of Omnipotent-Responsibility"

(1) *Five near misses*

A twenty-nine-year-old bombardier in a high state of nervous tension was relieved of his flying duties. He asserted that he could never fly again. He had undergone an acute *emotional decompensation* in response to terrific psychic stress. The precipitating event was his having just missed being aboard a plane which crashed and burned on take-off. All lives had been lost. Shortly before, he had been sent by the pilot to check on some missing gear. Immediate and urgent orders had been then received to take off, slightly ahead of the scheduled time. Accordingly, the take-off was made without getting the missing man aboard.

He had missed a flaming death by minutes, and apparently by pure chance. While this might have had a considerable impact upon him in any event, it was very much more devastating and became for him a *final straw* as the *fifth* more or less similar incident. A series of such near disasters had taken place for him over a rather short space of time. In each something apparently extraneous had transpired so that he had not been aboard a plane which subsequently crashed.

(2) *Omnipotent responsibility assumed*

The significance of the cumulative effect of the traumatic events upon his ego defenses was initially unclear. In view of the acuteness of this situation, and to establish very rapidly an *emergency analytic bridge* for enhanced early communication, several interviews were conducted under *Sodium amytal* narcosis. (See later cautions about the use of this and similar drugs, under Treatment.) The emotional abreaction was massive. It quickly became apparent that each traumatic event had dealt an increasingly effective blow at some of this patient's basic defenses.

This man, under the cumulative effect of the traumatic events, had literally reversed his original omnipotent feelings of "It can't happen to me." Instead, he had become a victim of the reverse, which we might term *"Feelings of Omnipotent Responsibility."* He felt in effect, "This has happened *because* I was there. It was because of *me*. I am the jinx. Therefore I am responsible for the dread accident."

(3) *Unit-Guilt Reaction*

This patient had a considerable burden of guilt. Part of it was on the above rather "magical" basis of responsibility. It was additionally on the "buddy" or *Unit-Guilt Reaction* which is seen not infrequently in combat and occasionally in civilian situations. Unit guilt is an unrealistic kind of neurotic guilty response to the death or injury of one's buddy or comrades from one's military unit or civilian outfit. Large elements of this reaction when present are usually repressed from conscious awareness. As a result, Unit Guilt can substantially contribute to the emotional distress following the stress of combat. [*See* later references to the Unit Guilt Reaction, also *Cases 188* and *189*].

This was an assumption of an objectively irrational position. His presence became unrealistically somehow linked with the disaster. One may notice certain similarities to what has been referred to as the *paranoid position,* with its grandiose assumption of great personal significance. This is accompanied, of course, by what one may regard as the high price paid for such increased significance, that is, subjective suffering *by* the paranoid patient of what then becomes experienced as persecution.*

The foregoing patient made a great deal of improvement under short-term intensive therapy. He became thoroughly and emotionally aware of the lack of realism in his regarding himself as a jinx. He also worked out most of the basis of the Unit-Guilt Reaction. His ego defenses became substantially reconstituted, and he became able to return to duty. He was detailed to another type of assignment, and when last heard from had been doing well.

---

* The paranoid patient thereby achieves at terrible cost the illusory "attention" of people. This, which we might for convenience call the *paranoid position,* includes his being important enough to people to become the "object" of what is to him their hostility, plotting, scheming, and efforts to destroy him.

Actually, his "gain" is usually less apparent than the price in suffering he simultaneously pays for it. This is only one aspect of the complex syndrome. For example, projection also plays an important role in the "paranoid position."

3. Principles of Emotional Sensitization and Desensitization

Some authorities have claimed, especially in the past, that somehow the predisposition to the development of neurotic symptoms was found in some not-too-specific kind of constitutional weakness; an inherent kind of inadequacy or some kind of "second grade protoplasm".

The author does not believe that any predisposition to neurosis is inborn. He does believe that the early events of life and the very early environmental experiences can result in patterns which render the individual more subject to possible later neuroses. This is in accord with our basic and important Concept of Interpersonal Perpetuation.

Sometimes early psychic trauma will lead to the early elaboration of more adequate psychic defenses against later psychic trauma, as with what we might call the *Principle of Emotional Desensitization*. On the other hand, early psychic traumas can result in greater vulnerability, and through conditioning processes of a complex nature, can lead to more specific vulnerabilities to specific kinds of traumatic events. The latter is in line with the converse *Principle of Emotional-Sensitization*.

D. INCREASED VULNERABILITY THE CONSEQUENCE OF ANTECEDENT CONFLICTS

According to the Theory of Antecedent Conflicts, we might well expect to find an increased vulnerability to psychically traumatic situations when these more or less closely follow antecedent patterns of painful significance from early years. It is as though an emotional conditioning has taken place which results in increased susceptibility and vulnerability. Thus, long-past events may result in a vulnerability to certain traumatic events or injuries so as to constitute a veritable Emotional Achilles Heel, as illustrated in *Case 176*. As Fenichel stated in discussing traumatic neurosis, infantile conflicts are reactivated and old infantile threats and anxieties suddenly reappear.

Trauma precedes the illness, may directly precipitate it, and may appear to cause it. Probably in most instances the latter appearance is superficial, and further search, when feasible, will often disclose deeper dynamic roots. Such was the case in the following instance. As stress leads to the elaboration of new defenses, our important Concept of Defensive-Layering may have applicability.

Case 187

The Effects of a Traumatic Relationship Are Reinforced Through Its Early Antecedents

A young sergeant was admitted to the sick list overseas following "a quarrel with the C.O." On examination, he was tremulous, restless, and virtually in a state of panic. Initially he was so upset that he could give little information. From collateral sources it was learned that the major in his outfit had singled him out for a particularly abusive and violent "dressing down." This, it seems, had been the culminating event in a long, unsatisfactory relationship between the two men. Their relations had been punctuated by a series of similar incidents. The "dressing down" had served as a significant trauma for the young sergeant. The emotional disturbance ensued.

The major was a man of violent temper. He was given to bursts of rage in which he was apt to abuse someone he felt had fallen short in the line of duty. He indulged heavily in alcohol, at which times these tendencies were magnified. However, other men had also served as objects of his wrath, but apparently without such an undue effect. Perhaps they had been able to accept it more stoically; to "shrug it off." Not so with the sergeant. It was as though his very vulnerability had contributed to more angry outbursts. These had resulted in the further destructive deterioration of the relationship. It seemed almost as though the sergeant had unwittingly "invited" incidents.

In résumé, the sergeant's father had been an abusive, violent-tempered alcoholically habituated person. He had been given to physical assaults on the patient's mother, and occasional beatings of the son. He had eventually deserted them permanently when the patient was nine years old. During treatment, the parallels between these relationships became increasingly apparent. The patient had seemingly "forgotten" the many conflicts consequent to his early years. They had, however, become reactivated.

Old anxieties were rekindled by what amounted to both actual and symbolic reconstitution of the earlier desperate threats and conflicts. It was to him in effect a repetition of his terribly unfortunate relationship with his father. These and certain other areas were clarified in so far as possible with the patient, during a brief but intensive therapeutic regimen with limited goals. During his therapy he made substantial gains. He was returned to duty with a new outfit where his adjustment was excellent during a number of succeeding months, while contact continued possible.

E. ADDITIONAL PREDISPOSING FACTORS

1. Level of Personal Security and the Rule of Impression-Priority

During our discussion thus far the individuality of one's reaction to stress and trauma has been stressed. One's entire past experience enters into this, predetermining in hidden fashion what reaction will occur following exposure to trauma. Such predetermination even goes so far as to influence the genesis of the trauma itself. This is illustrated in the occurrence of many psychologically determined accidents. It is most marked in instances of the Accident-Prone Individual as noted earlier and about whom the interested student can learn more elsewhere [p. 196].

The relative presence or lack of personal security is also most highly individual. This is an important factor in the T.R.T. (Total Reaction to Trauma). It has developed largely on the basis of prior experience in life, and particularly through the vicissitudes of relationships with various important and significant people. Among these, those with the significant adults of childhood are the most vital because of their primordial position and antecedent role. Any mental mechanism may be evolved, as part of the serviceman's psychic First Line of Defense.

Further, as pointed out in our earlier study of the Hygeiaphrontic Reactions, as elsewhere, the attitudes of parents toward themselves and toward their children play a vital role in the developing attitudes of the children toward themselves. The Concept of Interpersonal Perpetuation is applicable. Thus overprotectiveness, overcaution, and apprehensiveness on the part of the parents often establish important prior impressions. These set up antecedents for later similar attitudes in the child toward himself.

2. Relative Subjective Impotence and Helplessness

Impotence and helplessness can play an important role in influencing the effectiveness of the T.R.T. The final climax, with development of symptoms, will take place in some cases at a time when the subjective feelings of powerlessness and helplessness are very marked. Thus, the presence of relative impotence or helplessness in the face of threat, danger, or feared unknown impending change often greatly increases the person's psychologic vulnerability. These as well as other predisposing factors can contribute to the applicability of our Peg Concept.

This is also true concerning feelings of incapacity to cope with or to influence the threatening situation. This is an important concept in our study of the psychologic concomitants of trauma and the individual T.R.T. The relative individual impotence or helplessness can be contributed to greatly in turn by reinforcement occurring by virtue of hidden symbolism. Can we say that our concept of favorable psychologic soil holds? [p. 802].

Freud, in discussing a traumatic situation, observed that it consisted of the subject's estimation of his own strength, compared with the magnitude of the danger and his admission of helplessness in the face of it. He divided this helplessness into physical, when the danger is objective, and psychologic, when the danger is instinctual. Earlier Freud had offered a general comment about the traumatic experience. Within a very short space of time this subjects one to such a stimulation of assimilation that it can no longer be effected by normal means. Accordingly, lasting disturbances must result. We might include in such stimulations both physical and psychologic factors, including such contributions or reinforcements as might result from their individual symbolic significances. The sum total response in each instance would be the individual Total Reaction to Trauma.

3. Acuity of Trauma

The sharpness, acuity, and strength of the trauma can play an important role as to its effects. The sharper and more acute the trauma, the more unexpected it is. The more unexpected, the less chance the psyche has to call into play its defenses; to mobilize its resources. Certainly in every instance the Individual-Appropriateness-of-Response Principle holds. Although the too-intense experience [p. 694] was outlined first with children in mind, it can well carry over to military situations. A combat experience thus can well constitute such a too-intense stimulus, too intense for psychic mastery and for adequate integration to proceed. Psychic indigestion can result. Morale, pride, unit identification, and even vanity can contribute to the concealment of developing "cracks in the psychic-armor". This can amount to a highly personal Conspiracy-of-Silence [p. 725], which may or may not be shared in to some extent by one's comrades-at-arms. Another defense, a more automatic one, lies in the capacity some have for E.I.D. [Emotional-Impact Deferment; pp. 731–2 and *Case 150*], through which one unconsciously defers the real impact of an acute emotionally traumatic event until a later time, of greater tolerance. [*See also* defense of compartmentalization, as in dissociation, on p. 741.]

The greater and stronger the trauma, especially its psychologic aspects, the more chance that the existing psychologic defenses as developed may prove inadequate or be overwhelmed. In a sense, when stress is prolonged but semiacute or chronic, the psyche has a better chance to adjust, providing of course it is not of too high a level or too prolonged [*see Case 183*].

Stress of operational or combat origin can have its effects upon character [pp. 227 *ff*] and character defenses. While the personality can "change" rather drastically, more common is an overdevelopment or exaggeration — sometimes to be viewed as a speeded-up evolvement — of existing defenses under the added pressures of great stress. At times a considerable change transpires rapidly characterwise. These developments illustrate our *Defense-Hypertrophy Principle*. Rarely one might outline what we could term as a *Stress Character* or *Combat Character* in line with our earlier formulations.

F. THE UNIT-GUILT REACTION

1. A Close Friend is Killed

The presence of an interesting pattern of psychologic reaction which is characterized by objectively untoward guilt is not infrequently seen in certain of these combat-associated emotional disturbances. It is particularly likely to occur in situations in which close friends or a "buddy" are lost or killed. Often the person developing this reaction was a member of the same unit, was a participant in the same action, and/or was in close proximity at the time of his friend's death. This syndrome has been previously referred to as the Unit-Guilt Reaction, or Buddy Guilt. It has been so named in an effort to secure emphasis and to invite further interest in it.

This particular reaction was a feature in *Case 186* as summarized earlier. In a subsequent instance (*Case 189*) we shall see another illustration in which the Unit Guilt Reaction was prominent, the patient unrealistically suffering intense feelings of responsibility in the death of his comrades who had been trapped in a disabled and burning tank.

2. Unit-Guilt Feelings Long Repressed

The following case in stringent summary is an illustration of the powerful and long-lived effects of Unit Guilt.

Case 188

The Unit-Guilt Reaction

A United States warship was hit in the forward boiler room by a Japanese torpedo early during World War II. The communications officer and an assistant received verbal orders to go below into the officers' quarters and destroy the secret communications codes and the keys for them. Any chance that these vital means for the enciphering and deciphering of messages might fall into enemy hands had to be prevented at all costs. Tragically, events topside moved too rapidly and beyond control. The hit had been fatal. Power was totally lost very quickly, and within ten minutes the ship had settled appreciably. In another fifteen minutes it had sunk beneath the surface. Busy behind watertight compartment doors, the two officers never received the word which was passed to abandon ship. They were trapped below when she went down.

Another officer who had been personally close to them subsequently suffered bitter feelings of Unit Guilt. These had been repressed from conscious awareness for some years. Under analysis some five or six years later, access to these buried feelings was regained. During several painful sessions he gained full conscious awareness of them. They were expressed and therapeutically abreacted. At this time the fellow officer had strongly expressed his tearful wish to have been with his comrades; to have suffered with them.

It was as though the sharing of the fate of the lost comrades in this Unit-Guilt Reaction would be the ultimate in loyalty and duty. It would satisfy his guilt for surviving, whereas his comrades had not. This was further unrealistically demanded as penance by an archaic and punitive superego. It would be in retribution for certain hostile, selfish, and aggressive feelings which had been present. These had been adjudged unworthy and intolerable. These feelings were "worked through" in treatment and gradually ceased to be an unconscious and inaccessible source of difficulty.

3. Nonrational Need to Share the Friend's Fate

The author has observed the similar recall of these kinds of painful Unit Guilt feelings, especially during abreaction under narcosis, and in analytic treatment. Evidence of their presence may sometimes also be ascertained in dream content. Deeper unconscious roots may be uncovered, leading into antecedent conflicts of early life. A related phenomenon is the Goal of Lost-Object Reunion sometimes encountered in the depression of the Depressive-Reactions and Suicide [p. 182].

The precipitating situation is the feeling of responsibility and guilt toward the comrade. It is as though the survivor has a guilty and nonrational need to share the fate of the lost buddy, or that of his friends. At times there is also underlying guilt over such pre-combat or combat thoughts as, "If it has to be someone, let it be someone else!", or "I don't care who gets it, just so it isn't me", or "I'd rather even have my best friend Bill get hit than me." For an example of therapeutically useful abreaction, see *Case 189,* under the section on Treatment.

G. WOUNDS AND EMOTIONAL SYMPTOMS

An interesting phenomenon which deserves brief mention is at times encountered by the combat medical officer. Reference is made to the seemingly paradoxical inverse relation between the severity of wounds and the severity of emotional symptoms. Increased psychologic understanding, experience, and sophistication make this more comprehensible. This discrepancy is best illustrated among certain seriously wounded patients in wartime. Thus, they are sometimes less apt to show the intense emotional disturbances seen in some of their unwounded or less seriously wounded comrades. They may also complain less. The E.O.C. [pp. 393 and 454] of course occurs but is less frequent than ordinarily surmised. Emotional disturbances appear to be more frequently encountered in those who are *unwounded,* or only slightly so. This inverse phenomenon is related to masochistic and self-punitive aspects. The serious wound thus would well satisfy such needs. Emotional symptoms occurring independently or together with the trauma and the consequent suffering, would not be "required" by the individual's intrapsychic needs. There can be some relationships psychologically, to our Flight-to-the-Physical Principle [p. 708]. Note also our Amnesia-Protection Concept [p. 781], which has applicability in certain instances of physical trauma.

V. NOTES ON TREATMENT OF COMBAT REACTIONS

A. IN ACUTE CASES

1. Provide a More Favorable Climate

In many acute cases, and particularly in those in which the prior adjustment has been reasonably sound, psychotherapy can be highly beneficial. This is true in many cases of gross stress reactions of both civilian and combat origin. Here limited and temporary gratification of what may be regarded as emergency dependent needs may be helpful. This has been noted in conjunction with Combat Reactions. Thus, rest, reassurance, food, sleep, shelter, and judicious use of sedation can be very effective adjuncts to treatment. They offer a psychologic respite. They provide a more favorable climate temporarily, to allow reintegration of defenses, remobilization of depleted psychologic resources, and the regaining of the sense of personal mastery over a recently overthreatening environment. Although our emotional-inertia concept [pp. 213, 433, 504, and 707] applies, it *may* not be as difficult to overcome in Combat Reactions.

Another valuable adjunct, particularly in these cases, is therapeutically encouraged catharsis and abreaction in skilled hands. The repetitive dreams partly represent one of Nature's attempted steps in this process. Interviews judiciously conducted can be very helpful. Group therapy can be a useful adjunct in management. Fortunately, the acute combat reaction rarely bogs down so as to become an illustration of what we have termed the balanced neurotic position.

2. "Emotional First-Aid" in Combat Reactions

An immediate kind of emotional first aid may be adopted to fit the needs of the case. This can be done in the field, to whatever extent it may be feasible. As outlined, the provision of rest, reassurance, food, sleep, shelter, and supportive psychotherapy can be quite beneficial. See the earlier [pp. 38, 744] Respite-of-Sleep Principle and the Hypothesis of the Dream's Contribution to Emotional Health [pp. 39, 744, 749]. Dreaming, although a not infrequent source of complaint, can also serve its *desensitizing effect,* as noted. Their interpretation should be approached judiciously. The judicious use of sedation on a temporary basis can serve a valuable adjunctive purpose. In all cases one should observe our Principle of Self-Esteem-Maintenance, as indicated.

These measures serve a number of important functions. They help provide a more favorable external environment. A greater measure of external security can, to an extent, promote a greater measure of internal security.* They provide a limited and temporary gratification of dependent needs which may have increased greatly on a short-term basis. Further, a period of respite in such favorable surroundings can aid both the harassed physical self, as well as the overburdened psyche to recoup. The T.R.C. effects of stress tend to continue once mobilized often enough. This is in accord with our useful Concept of Continued Physiologic Momentum [pp. 99 *ff*. and 455]. However, often enough, the emotional defenses can be reintegrated, depleted psychologic resources restored, and one may quickly gain a renewed measure of ability to face the stresses and threats of living. The patient needs to regain his sense of personal intactness and to recover from the feelings and/or conviction of impotence, defeat, helplessness, and the sense of being overwhelmed. These measures together help comprise what we might refer to as *emotional first aid* for the acute Combat Reaction. In the treatment of Conversion Reactions, our Transparency Theory should be borne in mind.

3. Psychotherapy

Psychotherapy in combat situations is likely to be quite different than outlined in our previous chapters for a number of reasons. First, the volume of patients makes it impossible to follow the kinds of definitive therapy which one might prefer. Second, the type of case is different by virtue of the acuteness of the trauma suffered. Finally, the patient is likely to be different also, with an average prior overall adjustment of a more satisfactory level. In understanding his successive elaboration of psychic defenses in response to military and combat stresses, our intriguing Defensive-Layering Concept [pp. 367, 465, and especially *Case 101*] can prove helpful.

Verbal and emotional catharsis is to be encouraged in psychotherapy. The abreaction of painful and emotionally charged events is highly useful. Group therapy can be a useful adjunct in this kind of treatment. The goals are limited in combat cases. The demand is great, the patients are many, the psychiatrists few, and one does the best one can on an emergency basis. Awareness of the Law of the Three M's would help to mitigate these difficulties. Our Surgery-in-Abeyance Rule can have important applications. Electroshock was occasionally advocated in the Second World War, but cannot be recommended at all. *Case 169* illustrates post-shock amnesia in a service officer and the Principle of Psychic-Selectivity in this situation.

---

* Recall also the earlier principle covering the Circular Generation of Fear, which helps point out how the presence of anxiety can in turn contribute to the (circular) generation of fear.

B. HYPNOSIS AND NARCOSYNTHESIS

1. Emotional Catharsis and Abreaction Sought

Other adjunctive measures which have been utilized in acute situations include hypnosis and narcosynthesis. Each has certain limitations, of course, with benefits restricted and results quite variable. The object is to secure emotional catharsis and abreaction of the precipitating traumatic events. The more these are brought out and discussed, the better. Such adjuncts can facilitate the therapist establishing what was earlier termed an emergency-analytic-bridge [see Case 142].

In hypnosis the application is limited, owing to factors of patient response (a limited percentage make good hypnotic subjects), and operator skill [pp. 810–825]. In narcosynthesis one seeks to induce a somewhat similar dissociative state by virtue of using drugs, notably Amytal sodium. Abreaction is at times greatly facilitated through use of this drug and a skillful psychotherapeutic approach, in both of which measures the resulting induced dissociation is of the B.B.C. type. Suggestibility is a requisite. When sufficiently marked it can lead to improvement in response to almost any change, suggestion, or new regimen, illustrating our Favorable-Response-Concept [pp. 392, 453, 472, 709] in the neuroses.

These special methods are best reserved for acute situations. Their place in the more usual chronic type of neurosis encountered in civil life is extremely limited. Accordingly, they are not used by the average psychiatrist in his treatment of the neuroses and indeed their current use at all is rather rare.

Grinker first described the use of what he then aptly termed *narcosynthesis* in the North African theater in World War II. With the adjunctive use of *Pentothal sodium* he learned that treatment in many acute cases could rapidly alleviate severe manifestations. *Sodium Amytal* is currently the most widely used drug for such therapeutic efforts. Its specific use is best reserved for such acute situations, and for occasional selected psychiatric emergencies. It should not be used simply in response to patients' requests, and especially where it is sought as a substitute, easier, and more passive approach to the resolution of problems. Bronner has noted its proper role as an adjunctive agent for symptomatic relief.

2. Successful Treatment After Six Years

With the neuroses which develop following severe, emotionally traumatic war experiences, occasional instances are still encountered in which successful therapy can be conducted after a lapse of some years. The following case is an illustration of therapeutically useful abreaction. It also illustrates the Unit Guilt Reaction, and indicates that the Therapeutic Impasse or T.I. [pp. 446, 713] is less likely to be more enhanced by a time lag in initiating therapy in these cases. Likewise the emotional inertia to be expected in initiating therapy is not too likely of necessity to become more marked through the passage of time alone.

Case 189

Successful Narcosynthesis of a Chronic Post-Combat Neurotic Reaction

(1) *Stable background*

A twenty-eight-year-old sergeant was admitted to a service hospital in 1949 because of nervousness, fatigue, crying spells, irritability, and loss of effectiveness at duty. The history disclosed almost constant emotional difficulties in his military and personal adjustment, dating at least from his re-enlistment in the service about a year previously.

His early background was relatively stable. He had possibly slightly more than the usual early adjustment difficulties with several brothers. He had a tendency to worry and he had always been rather overconscientious. His background, however, was quite stable in his pre-service years. He had enlisted in the Army early in World War II. He had done well in service, and had participated in the North African campaign, as well as in the invasion of Sicily and Italy. He had had no difficulty until after a tank engagement in early 1943. Increasing emotional symptoms developed following that time. The rapid uncovering of this information was important and illustrates another application of our valuable Tracing Technique in Therapy.

He left the service at the close of the war and, after a period of increasing restlessness and dissatisfaction, had re-enlisted. His return to military service was symptomatic and of some significance, in the light of his emotional conflicts.

(2) *Symptoms of combat reaction*

On examination he was tense, anxious, and restless. He was tremulous at times, had trouble sleeping, and still suffered from startle reaction and occasional battle dreams, even after six years. He appeared depressed, and reported crying spells. Despite the length of elapsed time since combat, he still presented many of the earmarks of the acute combat case. The symptoms were those of the typical Combat Reaction. In view of this, the prognosis in treatment was considered good. Psychotherapeutic interviews were begun with adjunctive use of *Sodium Amytal*.

(3) *Emotionally traumatic events re-experienced*

An amazing quantity of dramatic emotional material was produced. Several times he "relived" the precipitating desperate battle scene. In this his tank was hit and set afire, and he alone escaped. While he lay pinned down by intense gunfire near the tank, it burned. He heard the terrified screams for help of his trapped crewmen, whom he was powerless to help.

He had previously "successfully" repressed much of this painful scene, his conflicts, and his soul-tearing irrational feelings of guilt and complete responsibility, from conscious awareness. This did not mean these no longer troubled him. Instead, they were even more destructive, since the material was not available to conscious awareness. Its effects continued.

(4) *Substantial improvement*

This patient had a typical Unit-Guilt Reaction. By bringing his repressed guilt into conscious awareness, he gained an advantage. It now became possible to deal with this terribly disturbing material on a conscious level. Factors were brought out tying back to his early family situation and especially his relations with his siblings, symbolically represented by his tank crew.

Rather rapidly he was able to resynthesize his adjustment and to accept the terrible events on a more objective level. He came to terms with himself and at this delayed date was able to reassert his mastery over the long-past external threats. His depression lifted, he became cheerful, lost his irritability and other acute symptoms, and returned to duty. He achieved substantial improvement. In accord with our concept of Deep Treatment the potential for future difficulty was probably lessened appreciably.

3. Limitations

In general, however, the more promptly this approach is utilized, the better the results. It is also to be noted that despite such occasional note-worthy instances of success as the above, when symptoms have been present for years, narcosynthesis offers relatively little in the more usual and more chronic kind of civilian or military neurosis. Further, its use is to be generally avoided except in expert hands and in judiciously selected cases. One should be cautious in certain instances of the Hazard of Symptom-Exchange [pp. 556, 673, 711].

Civilian patients will often seek such treatment as a hoped-for, painless, and easy kind of cure which would enable them to take a more passive position in the therapy. Generally the therapist had best give such requests little consideration and rule out the possibility politely, but promptly and firmly.

PART TWO: THE PSYCHOLOGIC PROCESSING OF PRISONERS

I. INTRODUCTION

A. PRISONER PROCESSING (BRAINWASHING)

1. Application to Individuals More Effective

During the last several decades certain inhuman and sinister methods of profoundly influencing people in their beliefs, reactions, and behavior have been evolved in the totalitarian countries. These have been developed to secure an almost unbelievable measure of influence and control over certain military and political prisoners. More results along these lines have been achieved than has heretofore generally been considered possible. First termed *brainwashing* in September 1950 by Edward Hunter, it has proved an intriguing subject. Prisoner processing and brainwashing will be used interchangeably in our present discussion.

This process has been applied to groups with considerable success; to societies and nations less so. Its greatest effects, however, have resulted from the coldly calculated application of these methods to individuals. It is these latter applications with which we are primarily concerned. Our knowledge is recent. We in the western world gradually have learned more about this perverse science and its uses. A number of names have been introduced for it. These have been independently arrived at. In addition to the first one, *brainwashing* (Hunter, 1950), they have included: *menticide* (Meerloo, 1951), *prisoner processing* (Laughlin, 1952), and *cortivisceral psychiatry* (Freedom, 1956).

Brief discussion of this topic is included as a final section in this work because of its general interest, its specific relevance to the military and diplomatic fields, and because of its many implications as to personality development and alteration and the neuroses for the student of human behavior. The subject of prisoner processing has tended to be a somewhat mysterious one. As a consequence the amazing end results which are possible in the individual instance have been sometimes regarded with skepticism or disbelief. Actually there is little mystery when one studies the methods which have been used. These methods represent a considerable modern psychologic refinement over the far cruder approaches of physical torture of centuries past. They are far more subtle. Modern psychologic knowledge has been applied in a deliberately traumatic fashion. Prisoner processing is an endeavor that is decidedly antitherapeutic, terribly cruel, and destructive.

2. Unparalleled Control Secured

The processing or conditioning of prisoners as developed in the Communist world is a traumatically induced method of personality alteration and control. The results are disruptive of the pre-existing personality integration. The methods used are deliberately inimical. Some of the most modern psychologic theories have been altered and applied so as to help produce maximum psychologic stress and emotional pressure. This is in sufficient force and focused over a sufficiently prolonged period, to result in the actual remoulding of the prisoner's attitudes and behavior to the desired ends of the operators. Prisoner processing constitutes a destructive assault upon human personality and upon personal integrity on an unbelievable level of cruelty. There have been indications that its employment has fallen in favor if not repudiated officially in the Soviet Union, following Stalin's demise.

Through the processing of the individuals selected, unparalleled control has been secured over political and military victims. For the latter, exposure constitutes a particularly vicious M.S.E. [pp. 31, 38, 67]. As a consequence, seemingly valid "confessions" have been secured, attitudes have been changed, and loyalties altered. Victims of such thorough processing suffer a profound, traumatically induced emotional disorder. This is why some consideration of this important subject is undertaken at this point. There are some relationships of the psychologic processing of prisoners to much of our prior concepts and discussion in earlier chapters, especially to that in Chapters 1, 2, 5, 9 and 13, and particularly in Chapters 14 and 15 thus far. Gaining familiarity with this material will provide a more adequate basis and background for our present summary of this subject.

B. PERVERSE SCIENCE

1. Extension of Pavlovian Theory

The development of what we might term this perverse science actually gives new weight in savage form to the conditioned reflex theories of Pavlov. Here one sees the ultimate development and extension of these original theories into complex applied methods of influencing human behavior and attitudes.

A man may be told he is guilty of something. This is endlessly repeated. During this period he is kept under most exaggerated and prolonged stress and deprivation. With sufficient repetition and length of time, he will eventually begin to believe it. To state it thus is an oversimplification of something highly complex and difficult. Unremitting efforts over a long period of time and by skilled operators are necessary. Needless to say, to induce this kind of response in a man is much more difficult and vastly more complex than in Pavlov's relatively simple early experiments with dogs. Nevertheless, the point is eventually and ultimately reached at which this will take place.

2. Additional Psychologic Factors

In addition to the basic Pavlovian theory, empirically devised factors have been added. These have been developed from the basis of trial and error, and accumulated experience as prisoner processing techniques for individuals have been evolved. The presence of unconscious guilt and the securing of mental, emotional, and physical exhaustion are important factors. Prolonged sleep deprivation is a regular feature in breaking down the conscious will to resist. In the development of the psychologic pressure techniques as applied in brainwashing, one might conclude that an entirely new "profession", a perverse science, has been evolved.

The controlling of people, the securing of the most detailed and incriminating confessions, and the powerfully puppeteered court behavior of accused prisoners, all have borne tragic witness to the effectiveness of this kind of human conditioning in expert hands. A number of accounts offer more of the details for those interested further as to how these results are achieved. Prisoner processing provides us with a pointed example of the tremendous effects which can be wrought on the stability, the adjustment, and the personal integrity of the person of high moral fiber through psychologic trauma — in these instances deliberately cultivated and applied.

3. Torture Too Crude

Physical torture in totalitarian countries in turn has largely been reserved for the less well educated and cultured person, who is lacking in development of a high level of ethical standards and moral fiber. For the highly motivated and sophisticated person, methods of physical torture were far too crude and often simply resulted in death. Accordingly, prisoner processing was developed as a more effective approach. A dead prisoner was worthless. A well-processed one could potently serve a variety of most valuable political ends and propaganda purposes. Prisoner processing or brainwashing is more devastating and is more diabolically effective than the older and cruder forms of physical torture. The methods of the Spanish Inquisition were far less refined.

II. TECHNIQUES OF PRISONER-PROCESSING

A. TIME AND EFFORT REQUIRED

1. Months Needed by Trained Professionals

From the study of the more noteworthy known instances (for example, those of Cardinal Mindszenty, Michael Shipkov, Hans Fritzsche, Robert Vogeler, William Oatis, and others) we learn of the many months of time and constant efforts which were exerted. The most skilled operators worked around the clock in shifts in the "processing" of these unfortunate victims. In the case of Shipkov, a complete detailed "confession" was first secured in thirty-two hours. This was too rapid. As an indication of this, it did not hold up. It was later repudiated.

On the other hand, Cardinal Mindszenty withstood three days and two nights of steady, ceaseless pounding, interrogation, suggestion, and demands before he made even his first tentative capitulation. Months of subsequent steady psychologic battering by the most skilled operators were required before he was, for all practical purposes, molded to their will.

2. Individual Processing Irresistible

For psychologic prisoner processing to have its strongest effects, it must be applied individually. When the political gain is sufficient to justify employment of the requisite effort and time of the most skilled operators, it is indeed most highly doubtful whether anyone can fail eventually to become an abject and pliable victim. When applied in its ultimate terms, individual processing is literally irresistible. Undoubtably some subjects have "escaped" the full treatment, and proved disappointing failures to their operators, through their unwanted death.

The Reverend Fulgence Gross, a Franciscan missionary, underwent six years of imprisonment in Red China prior to his release in March of 1957, and was brought falsely to confess, as others have been, to being an American spy. Having himself experienced what could transpire, he had scant sympathy for those who condemned "confessors". As quoted in the *Washington Post* (A.P., May 6, 1957), he said: ". . . I haven't got much use for . . . people who condemned the American prisoners in Korea for their confessions . . . Let those who condemn . . . experience just three months of interrogation."

B. BASES FOR SUCCESS

1. Respite and Peace At Any Cost

Eventually the victim will come to be willing to say, to write, to do anything that his inquisitors request. Eventually he will *want* to give anything or do anything to try to satisfy the demands of his tormentors. His need is to secure peace and respite; surcease. He becomes actually most anxious to begin whatever punishment which he feels may be meted out, and even to die if this is to be his fate. The wish for death as a way to peace or escape is not uncommonly expressed by the victim, as the ceaseless interrogating and demanding efforts continue.

Complete isolation, the feeling of abandonment, and impotence are strong factors. Threats to relatives, friends, associates, or colleagues are meted out whenever it is felt that these will help. This is usually done in an atmosphere in which the victim has few doubts that any of the threats made could and would be carried through.

Part of the skill of the "professional" interrogator in the field comes from the fine judgment which he is able to exercise on the basis of his prior experience and training, as to just how far and to what given point he can push his victim at any one time. In order to achieve success, of course, he must be able correctly to anticipate the breaking point, and to ease the pressures sufficiently at any indicated juncture to avert a psychotic episode or death. The ends to be achieved are of great potential importance politically. A psychotic or a dead prisoner is less than worthless. Potentially this might become quite a liability.

2. Individual Factors in Susceptibility

In general, the amount of time and effort required to secure the desired degree of control and behavior in the conditioning of a given prisoner will depend on a number of variable individual factors. These may be tabulated as follows:

Table 48

Individual Factors in "Success" of Prisoner Processing

(1) The previous emotional and mental conditioning of the prisoner.

(2) His total psychologic and personality integration (this is important); his T.R.C. and T.R.T.

(3) The treatment, mistreatment, or threats to members of the prisoner's family or friends (and the potential ability to carry them out).

(4) The determination and the morale of the prisoner; stamina and strength of will to resist.

(5) The determination, persistence, skill, and experience of the "examiner" or "interrogator".

(6) The urgency of the need to secure results.

(7) The presence and significance of unconscious guilt feelings.

(8) The relative susceptibility to the sequelae of sleep deprivation and exhaustion.

(9) It is possible that slower methods of wearing down a person's resistance are far more effective in individual cases. These might become a requirement, because of unusual stubbornness or resistance on the part of the prisoner.

(10) In general, the prisoner's educational, social, ethical, and economic background, as well as his moral stamina, patriotism, existing loyalties, and personality stability, are all very important factors.

(11) A variation of our earlier Principle of Belief [pp. 646, 710] can apply, in that results may be facilitated and become more certain when the victim and operator believe in their inevitability.

(12) The *development* of other *disturbing emotional symptoms* in response to the induced stress.

3. Skilled Operators Required

A. LIMITATIONS TO WIDER APPLICATIONS OF PRISONER-PROCESSING.—It is clear that the "operator" must possess a great amount of certain personality attributes in order to achieve the personality disintegrating effects which are sought. It is undoubtedly difficult to find the type of personality even capable of developing skill in brainwashing techniques. Further, there is unquestionably a great amount of training and experience required. Fortunately, these factors, plus the great amount of time and effort required, serve significantly as limitations to the wider application of this perverse science.

As noted earlier, while inhuman to the utmost, the ultimate techniques to be successful are often refined, subtle, and require most careful judgment. The point of demarcation between insanity and the alteration of basic beliefs may become a rather fine line in some cases of prisoner processing. Thus the most meticulous care and the finest judgment are undoubtedly required at times to prevent untoward results. As noted, an insane or a dead subject has no value for propaganda purposes. He becomes a liability rather than a possible great potential asset.

B. BALANCE MAINTAINED BETWEEN MAXIMUM PRESSURES AND DISSOLUTION.—The operators must balance their efforts in bringing the maximum pressures to bear, at the same time conserving the life and sanity of the hapless victim. Undoubtedly few enough people have the necessary personality attributes of callousness, detachment, and obliviousness to human suffering, plus an absence of compathy,* sympathy, empathy, or identification, to enable them to develop the requisite techniques.

There are no doubt various additional pressures in turn, which are also operative to help produce success. The life of the operator who fails with an important case could hardly be of little more import to his masters, in turn, than is the integrity of his intended victim!

III. THE CONDITIONING PROCESS

A. MICHAEL SHIPKOV

Let us consider briefly how a person of high integrity and considerable moral fiber can be brought to apparently sincerely "confess" to things he could not possibly have done. A limited number of rather detailed accounts are available through various circumstances, which enable us to work out some of the details.

In the first stage, the hapless and helpless victim is likely to be constantly bombarded by interrogation, with no rest, with limited food, and with no water. Operators work in shifts, often around the clock. An endless assault is maintained, with ceaseless battering psychologically. The patient's will to resist is slowly beaten down. The burdens of fatigue and loss of sleep

---

* *See* discussion and definition of compathy in the author's *Mental Mechanisms*, pp. 131-133 and 145-146 (Washington; Butterworths, 1963).

are added. Threats and demands alternate with promises of better treatment. The mechanism of Denial, together with operation of the Ostrich Concept [p. 772], can help to conceal the futility of a surrender-in-part, in order to secure it.

Case 190

The Processing of Michael Shipkov

(1) *Processing lacked skill*

Michael Shipkov was a man of intelligence, education, and high ethical standards. Nevertheless, he was induced to accede to the demands of his inquisitors in a relatively brief period of time. It is apparent, if by no other means than the fact that details of the case are in our possession, that the processing in Shipkov's case was not sufficient nor skillful enough. It is of interest to note the rapidity with which such results as indicated were obtained and achieved.

Shipkov referred to emotions created in such unfortunate prisoners as "degradation", "misery", "self-loathing and contempt", and "sense of guilt for all the people I had incriminated." Shipkov had not reached a point beyond that in which he still felt the need to try to undo the wrongs he had been forced to do in incriminating friends, relatives, and officials. Accordingly, he later wrote out a detailed account of what had happened to him. He placed it in safekeeping in the hands of the American Minister in Sofia, in case he was later apprehended, as he was. This is why we have access to his own account. It is quite understandable that in many instances the burden of self-recrimination and guilt would be great enough to retard or absolutely prevent the person from ever making an open admission of what he had done. This would be true despite the means which had been employed to bring this about.

(2) *No chance for respite*

The methods that were used with Shipkov included the use of three alternating teams of two interrogators each, together with a chief interrogator. The teams took turns in their persistent and determined efforts at questions, demands, and securing admissions. The prisoner was never given the slightest chance to rest or to collect his thoughts.

During a considerable part of the time of his particular interrogation he was placed in the following position: He stood away from a wall at a point where he could just touch it with his outstretched fingers; then he was backed away another twelve inches and made to lean forward, balancing and resting his weight on one outstretched index finger from each hand. This position was enforced throughout the many hours of the constant and continuous barrage of questions, demands, and efforts to gain admissions. The fatigue and pain of this position contributed to the more rapid lowering of his resistance and to the speeding up of the processing. One can, of course, note here again the influence of the semihypnotic effects and the loss of reality contact deriving from the situation, and from the psychologic bombardment, as well as from pain, misery, fatigue, thirst, and sleep deprivation.

(3) *Factors contributing to breakdown*

Mr. Shipkov wrote: "they are not overly interested in what you tell them. It would appear that the ultimate purpose of this treatment is to break you down completely, and to deprive you of any will power or private thought or self-esteem, which they achieve remarkably quickly . . . They appear to place importance on the . . . appearance of repentance and self-condemnation that comes up with the breaking down of their prisoner."

In considering the psychologic background for the breakdown of Shipkov, it appears that because of his own certain anticipation of what would happen, that is, the ultimate results, his breakdown was achieved more rapidly. He had long entertained a certainty of apprehension, arrest, and misfortune. As further factors, in his words, "This depression is augmented by a feeling of helplessness and despair, no possibility of evasion, no issue, no real hope for assistance or protection . . ."

(4) *The Interrogator-Operators*

Shipkov makes comments which carry clear implications as to the kinds of people who are employed in such endeavors. He discussed briefly the seven interrogators who were responsible for his grueling thirty-two hour continuous initial session of psychological pounding.

"I really could perceive no personal hatred or enmity for me — contempt certainly, but sooner an academic detached dealing with an annoying problem in order to achieve the goal, and a fanatic rabid obsession of devotion to Communism and hatred for Anglo-American resistance to them — all the newspaper talk [propaganda] is to them gospel truth. And in this respect they are to be taken as disciples and fervent followers of the dogma — undeviating loyalty to their creed, fanatic belief in their own cause, fanatic hatred and mistrust of anything else. No possible contact with them on any intermediary grounds. No fear of possible retaliation, not within the ranks that I met. No conscience, unless that of duty to their creed."

Shipkov disappeared permanently, following the release of this account.

B. CARDINAL MINDSZENTY

The case of Cardinal Mindszenty must have represented an acme of achievement in the perverse science of prisoner-processing. A tremendous amount of planning and effort was devoted to secure the results obtained. Mindszenty was a man of the greatest courage, strongest convictions, marked devotion to his people, country, and creed, and enormous personal integrity and resources. Yet even he was so conditioned as to eventually become almost a puppet during the period desired. This was of tremendous propaganda and political value at the time. The stakes were most high to his captors. Failure could have been costly. The most skilled expert in processing supervised the procedure, which continued for months.

It is apparent that there was a careful predetermination of charges and tactics to be employed. The strategy was carefully adjusted to suit the ends desired, the circumstances involved, and the developing situation of his processing. In the case of the Cardinal, despite his resistance and determination, the work was so successful from the standpoint of the captors that there was little real question in their minds at any given time as to its success. Actually the experts employed were so certain of their success in this case that his "confession" was announced by government spokesmen even before the processing began.

Case 191

Prisoner Processing; Cardinal Mindszenty*

(1) *Elaborate preparations*

The general approach as previously described [*Case 190*] was followed with Cardinal Mindszenty. The pattern, however, was greatly refined, and much more elaborate and complex. It was altered to meet circumstances as the situation changed. In the beginning, there were repeated charges of guilt, accusations, and determined questioning. As in most cases, a detailed and complete autobiography was de-

---

* As modified and summarized from *The Cardinal's Story,* by Swift, by permission of The Macmillan Co., publisher.

manded. Partly from this and partly from accessory and previous information, facts were obtained, distorted, and placed in the light in which the interrogators wished them to appear.

The victim was frequently confronted with implications or admissions of guilt by other people, which, in turn would involve him. Facts and evidence were distorted, in order to achieve or to help to achieve some desired effect. Forgery, fake documents, false confessions, and inaccurate testimony were used *ad lib*. The involved preparation required for these is a small instance of the lengths to which the processors were prepared to go. There were physical confrontations with former associates and intimates. In some cases these had already broken down and had given desired "confessions" which implicated the principal.

(2) *Endless interrogation, with "hope" held forth*

There was endless interrogation, continuation of charges, accusations, and brow-beating by examiners working in three-hour shifts. These were made in an uninvolved, unemotional, and detached, but heartless and cruel fashion. There was little in the way of actual physical abuse. Physical torture was not used. The bastard science of interrogation or processing had learned well that physical torture only depletes the physical reserve and sometimes ends in premature physical dissolution. This would in turn destroy the usefulness of a tool which otherwise might possibly be forged of the victim.

"In some instances the same questions were repeated as many as two hundred times in succession and no answer ever satisfied the examiners. . . . None of the questioners themselves could stand the strain for more than a half-hour at a time. None remained in the room more than three hours. As one of the guards reputedly said, who had to attend just one such a three-hour session inactively, 'My head whirled; my eyes were blinded; and for days I heard the same questions ringing in my ear.'"

A constant technique is the holding out of hope. Hope is held out for whatever is wished for, from food to freedom, from toilet facilities to peace. Respite or more comfortable surroundings were longed for. The possibility of these things being granted was constantly implied or offered in return for answering the questions, that is, *providing the desired answers; ones that would satisfy the inquisitors.*

After sixty-six hours the Cardinal said, "End it all. It is useless! Kill me! I am ready to die!" He was assured in calm tones that no harm would befall him, and that the only thing that was required was the proper answers. To this his response was, "Your questions are no questions. They are suggestions of the Devil." This indicates the impact his experience had already made.

The admonitions were always simple. He was told in effect, "You can end it all by answering certain questions in the way we wish you to." As the wearing-down process continues, the desire to please one's tormentors and interrogators by any way possible as a means of achieving peace and respite grows. It is of course a forlorn hope but a continuing one. The victim feels that by making some admission, that by giving his interrogator what is asked for, the desired peace and solace will be achieved. This is, indeed, a false hope, but it is one which is fostered by the interrogators.

(3) *Beginning doubt and acquiescence*

One might note from the foregoing response that there was already an indication of possible beginning doubt in the Cardinal's mind, and beginning acquiescence to the constant suggestions of guilt and complicity. Perhaps to some extent he was already accepting the implied suggestions and urgings of the inquisitors to admit things which were not actually true. One must also note the appeal to unconscious feelings of guilt. There is also the possible correlation of this with his more or less secret feelings of opposition to the regime.

The implication is directly and indirectly constantly kept before the prisoner that the interrogators will continue until the questions are answered, that is, *until they get what they want*. After three days and two nights of steady, heartless, and ceaseless efforts, the Cardinal still resisted. This was a tremendous resistance. Another twenty-four hours or so later, he had finally lost his composure. Several times he fell from his feet. There was painful swelling of his legs and feet. He maintained balance with difficulty. Only after eighty-four hours did he finally give in and sign the first set of implicating statements.

One might comment here that in view of his ability to withstand his inquisitors, in relation to the success eventually achieved, the results with Cardinal Mindszenty were highly successful. In comparison, the job done with Shipkov was an amateur and bungling affair.

(4) Surrender complete

After signing the "confession" as desired, the Cardinal was allowed two days of physical recovery. Following this he was confronted with the "confession" which he had signed, and the inquisition resumed. He became upset and excited. But after thirteen further hours of the same type of procedure, he finally wrote the "confession" in his own handwriting as directed. One might note that one of the things that happens when the spirit has finally broken is the gradual rather regressive development of an infantile and helpless dependence. This occurs to the point where the victim is eventually forced to obey the slightest suggestion and wish of his interrogators—even as the hypnotized and suggestible person is forced to obey the demands of the operator in hypnosis. This brings us to another technique.

With a regressive kind of dependency developed, attachment is now possible to new sources. Thus it was not long after this that the policy of introducing a "friend" or confidant to the Cardinal was followed. This person stayed with him most of the time henceforwards as an "advisor". By his contrasting attitudes of "friendliness" and sympathy he was able to make further inroads on the Cardinal's personality and weakened integrity. The final complete breakdown was hastened.

Now followed repeated routine sessions as the Cardinal's "re-education" was allowed to progress. During periods of days, there was a distinct change in the Cardinal's personality [which] could be observed from day to day. He practically ceased to act as an individual and seemed to be in a daze. As time progressed, he became more and more dependent on other persons; most of his acts became responses to outside influence or a command. Sessions continued. "The questions during these interrogations now dealt with details of the Cardinal's 'confession.' First his own statements were read to him; then the statements of the other prisoners accused of complicity with him; then again elaborations were read. At times the Cardinal was morose; at others, greatly disturbed and excited. But he answered all questions willingly, repeated all sentences—once, twice, or even three times when he was told to do so.

All this betrays to us only too graphically how complete and abject a surrender had finally been obtained. It is also apparent to us that once this point has been reached one may have doubts as to the ability of a person to ever fully recover from such psychologic assault and the subsequent damage to his integrity and ego.

(5) "No spirit we cannot break"

The interrogators knew where to draw the line. This was undoubtedly based on their extensive prior experience and training. They knew enough to be able to bring their victim repeatedly near the breaking point and still be able to maintain the process and save him so that he could be useful for the purpose of his captors. Of course, had he died or suffered a psychotic break, he would have been of little further use to them. It was important to maintain physical integrity.

"Of those who witnessed his first nineteen days in prison, none believed it possible that any human being could stand the physical and psychological tortures he had to suffer. Later it was rumored . . . that the chiefs in charge of the procedure had stated that the Cardinal had been their most difficult and psychologically most complicated case." Kotlev (a chief) reputedly described it as the outstanding example of the obstinate resistance of the human spirit, but he added, "No obstinacy exists that we cannot overcome. No spirit that we cannot break."

(6) *Forty days*

In the case of the Cardinal, an amphetamine derivative was reputedly used as a stimulant during the first stage. Synthetic derivatives of the mescaline group of drugs are more apt to be used in the later stages of processing. The Russians are also reputed to manufacture a synthetic of this group known as trimethoxyphenylethylamine. The mescaline group of drugs produces a weird psychologic effect, in which there may be hallucinations. One of the subjectively disturbing characteristics is the onset of strong feelings of depersonalization. There may be disturbances of association, blocking of thoughts, and extreme distractibility.

The "processing" of Cardinal Mindszenty was finally complete in about forty days. There are fairly reliable eye-witness accounts of a large part of the first half of the interrogation. At this point probably some leak in security was detected, and measures were applied which make the latter half of the work much less available.

C. PHASES OF PROCESSING

The conditioning of prisoners may be regarded as going through several stages or phases. These are present in the preceding case. The *first phase* was alluded to earlier in this section. In the *second phase* the individual has already made his first "admissions" in the vain hope of being left alone. Now he is conditioned to accept his confession, and to elaborate upon it. His hope of surcease, by having given his interrogators something of what they wanted, has indeed been in vain. If anything, this is encouraging to them, spurring them on to greater efforts, as it presages further surrender. The eventual collapse of will can now be anticipated, on the basis of prior experience.

A *third phase* may begin in which a predetermined relationship is set up with someone who identifies himself rather closely with the prisoner and acts to encourage in subtle and indirect ways the efforts made and the changes desired. As noted earlier, he plays a friendly and sympathetic role to the victim. He helps to hold out hope and the assurance of better treatment as, and if, the victim will more and more fit into the wishes of his captors. This he encourages him to do in various "friendly" ways.

In the *final phase* the victim has now been completely conditioned to accept his own guilt. He is trained in turn to bear false witness against himself and against others. He is prepared for trial. Now he becomes softened completely, is remorseful, and is willing to be sentenced. Desired trial responses are endlessly rehearsed.

One can imagine how complete this treatment has been, from the later appearance of the victims in public and on trial. To parade their subjects thus publicly indicates the great confidence the operators have in the medium-term stability of their results. In most instances there has been little or no indication from the casual outward observation possible as a courtroom attendant that the person is doing other than what he completely and voluntarily wills. It is hardly surprising that many observers have been completely or partially "taken in" in the past, accepting the "confessions" as *bona fide* and the court appearances as genuine.

D. INDIVIDUAL PROCEDURE

The techniques of prisoner processing reach their optimum results in intensive work with individuals. From a study of specific cases, it becomes apparent that for the processing to have its strongest and most sought-after effects it must be applied individually, and on an individual basis. Modified or diluted efforts with groups are much less effective. Some exceptions to this may exist, although in general this is true. It has been borne out in the case of groups of released or escaped prisoners.

One should not, of course, completely discount the effectiveness of the group propaganda and psychologic pressures that have been applied prior to their release, to repatriated former prisoners of war. A systematic large-scale regional kind of brainwashing was apparently carried out on a vast scale in Red China in the early days of the regime. This has continued, modified in various ways.

As an individual procedure, prisoner processing generally has been and will be reserved for highly selected people or for occasions when the propaganda purposes to be subserved are considered very important. Fortunately it has been an infrequent S.E.H.A. for the vast majority. These limiting factors, plus the requirement for skilled operators, actually from one viewpoint constitute a certain safeguard. Mass application of prisoner processing in the ways and to the extent illustrated is simply not feasible. The moral condemnation and loathing of such inhuman methods by free people everywhere is another safeguard. Widespread publicity is still another effective counter-weapon. Few people of any political persuasion or national loyalties could really approve the use of such individually destructive, barbarous and inhuman methods. At least, they are totally counter to the Golden Rule philosophy, some form of which historically has been held in high regard in every culture.

IV. TREATMENT: RESTORING THE SHATTERED EGO

When it is possible to secure the release of a victim, rehabilitation is feasible, although it is doubtful if the deeply ingrained personality-disruptive effects can ever be completely removed. Treatment should aim at the re-creation of personal dignity, integrity, and security, and at counteracting the effects of the long-term weight of terror. It is as though the psyche cannot at times "realize" that it is over and past. There may be a Continuing Psychologic Momentum which is roughly analogous to our Concept of Continued Psychologic Momentum. The level of self-esteem must be restored. This can often help provide an adequate Therapeutic Bargain.

The victim will have suffered shattering self-doubts, guilt, and recriminations, particularly if he has been forced to involve others in his "admissions" and "confessions". His suffering as a victim has been too much already, without the added burden of self-blame and accusations which are unrealistic in the face of the pressures to which he has been subjected.

In instances in which the victim of prisoner-processing techniques is fortunate enough to be repatriated, his subsequent reactions are naturally greatly influenced by his need for self-respect and ego-boosting. Our Self-Esteem-Maintenance Principle can have important applications. Self-respect will very likely tend to require the returned victim of brainwashing to:

(1) Make light of the effectiveness of the psychologic pressures which have been applied to him.

(2) Build up (for himself and for others) a picture of a relative ability to resist. This is in keeping with culturally promoted ideals of moral strength and stamina.

(3) Stress personal loyalty and patriotism. Try and restore a picture of nonsusceptibility and relative invulnerability. Recreate some basic personal defenses.

(4) Point up and enlarge upon the presence of his rebellion toward ideas which were presented, his resistance to the influences which were applied, and toward those who applied them.

V. SUMMARY

A. COMBAT REACTIONS

A short section was devoted to some of the important principles concerning Combat Exhaustion or the *Combat Reactions,* and the emotional reactions incident to military operations. Under conditions of war stress, psychiatric cases increase in numbers rapidly and quite disproportionately to other types of medical cases. The *Law of the three M's* (Military Medical Mobilization) points up the need for increased advance planning in psychiatry for the medical departments of the armed services. In World War II Somatic Conversion Reactions were less frequent than in World War I.

Physiologic Conversion and symptoms and the direct manifestations of anxiety were more frequent in the second conflagration. Some of the psychodynamics of the startle reaction, battle dreams, irritability, and tremors, as frequent and rather characteristic symptoms of Combat Reactions, were briefly mentioned. Factors as to the individual susceptibility to combat stress were listed. The *Unit Guilt Reaction* was discussed.

In combat and war situations a regimen of *emotional first aid* can prove quite efficacious. Following a brief reference to hypnosis and narcosynthesis, the goals of psychotherapy were outlined.

B. PSYCHOLOGIC PRISONER PROCESSING

A brief discussion on the psychologic conditioning of prisoners, earlier named by Hunter as *brainwashing,* was presented. This may be described as an antitherapeutic, traumatically-induced state of dependence and malleability.

Prisoner Processing, as it is also known, is destructive and disintegrating. As a consequence to its use, seemingly valid confessions have been secured, attitudes have been changed, and loyalties altered. Some of the details of the methods employed were presented, and the case of Cardinal Mindszenty as a prime example was summarized. The results and their implications offer food for considerable scientific and philosophical discussion.

VI. SELECTED REFERENCES AND BIBLIOGRAPHY

ARCHIBALD, H. C., LONG, D. M., MILLER, C., and TUDDENHAM, R. D. (1962). "Gross Stress Reaction in Combat— A Fifteen-year Follow-up." *Am. J. Psychiat.*, **119**, 317.

U. S. Department of State (1951). "A. P. Correspondent's Trial Called Travesty of Justice." *U. S. Dept. of State Bulletin*, **25**, 92.

BLAIN, D. and HEATH, R. G. (1944). "The Nature and Treatment of Traumatic War Neuroses in Seamen." *Int. J. Psychoanal.*, **25**, 142.

BRILL, N. Q. and BEEBE, G. W. (1955). *A Follow-Up Study of War Neurosis.* Washington, D. C.; V. A. Monograph.

CHODOFF, P. (1963). "Late Effects of the Concentration Camp Syndrome." *Archs gen. Psychiat.*, **8**, 323.

DAVIDSON, S. (1942). "Anxiety States Arising in Navy Personnel—Afloat and Ashore." *N. Y. State J. Med.*, **42**, 165.

DREYFUSS, D. K. (1949). "Delayed Epileptiform Effects of Traumatic War Neurosis and Freud's Death Instinct Theory." *Int. J. Psychoanal.*, **30**, 759.

FERENCZI, S. (1952). "Two Types of War Neuroses." In *The Theory and Technique of Psycho-Analysis*, pp. 124–141. New York; Basic Books.

GOODFRIEND, ARTHUR (1951). "When the Communists Came to Chuang." *Reader's Digest*, **58**, 77.

GRINKER, R. R. (1946). "The Use of Narcosynthesis in War Neurosis. In *Psychoanalytic Therapy*, pp. 325–337. Ed. by Alexander R. and French, T. M. New York; Ronald Press.

— and SPIEGEL, J. P. (1945). *Men Under Stress.* Philadelphia; Blakiston.

— — (1943). *War Neuroses in North Africa.* New York; Josiah Macy, Jr. Foundation.

HUNTER, EDWARD (1956). *Brainwashing.* New York; Farrar, Straus and Cudahy.

— (1951). *Brain-washing in Red China.* New York; Vanguard.

KARDINER, A. (1941). *The Traumatic Neuroses of War.* New York; Hoeber.

LAUGHLIN, H. P. (1963). *Mental Mechanisms.* Washington; Butterworths.

MEERLOO, J. A. M. (1951). "The Crime of Menticide." *Am. J. Psychiat.*, **107**, 594.

— (1954). "The Psychology of Treason and Loyalty." *Am. J. Psychother.*, **8**, 648.

— (1956). *The Rape of the Mind.* Cleveland; World.

National Research Council (1941). *The Traumatic Neuroses of War.* Washington; N.R.C.

U. S. Dept. of State (1951). "Release of Robert A. Vogeler by the Hungarian Government." *U. S. Dept. of State Bulletin*, **24**, 723.

ROSS, T. A. (1942). *War Neuroses.* Baltimore; Williams and Wilkins.

SARGANT, WILLIAM (1957). *Battle for the Mind.* Garden City, N. Y.; Doubleday.

SCHONBERGER, S. (1948). "Disorders of the Ego in Wartime." *Br. J. med. Psychol.*, **21**, 248.

SEGAL, H. A. (1954). "Initial Psychiatric Findings of Recently Repatriated Prisoners of War." *Am. J. Psychiat.*, **111**, 358.

SIMMEL, E. (1944). "War Neuroses." In *Psychoanalysis Today*, pp. 227–248. Ed. by Loraird, S. New York; International Universities Press.

Staff writers (1951). "Vogeler's Own Story." *Newsweek*, **37**, 23.

U. S. Dept. of State (1951). "Story of the 'Secret' Telephone Line, a Communist Technique at the Oatis Trial." *U. S. Dept. of State Bulletin*, **25**, 489.

U. S. Dept. of State (1950). "The Story of Michael Shipkov's Detention and Interrogation by the Bulgarian Militia." *U. S. Dept. of State Bulletin*, **22**, 387.

SWIFT, S. K. (1949). *The Cardinal's Story: The Life and Work of Joszef Cardinal Mindszenty.* New York; Macmillan.

TORRIE, A. (1944). "Psychosomatic Casualties in the Middle East." *Lancet*, **1**, 139.

U. S. Dept. of State (1951). "Trial of William N. Oatis: With Text of Indictment and Excerpts from Proceedings." *U. S. Dept. of State Bulletin*, **25**, 283.

VOGELER, R. A. (1952). *I Was Stalin's Prisoner.* New York; Harcourt, Brace.

WEST, LOUIS J. (1964). "Psychiatry, 'Brainwashing', and the American

Character." *Am. J. Psychiat.,* **120,** 9.

ZABRISKIE, E. and BUSH, A. L. (1941). "Psychoneurosis in Wartime." *Psychosom. Med.,* **3,** 295.

VII. REVIEW QUESTIONS ON MILITARY REACTIONS AND PRISONER PROCESSING

PART ONE: MILITARY AND COMBAT REACTIONS

1. How can our *Changing-Trends Concept* [pp. 658–661] and our earlier *Cultural Vogue Concept* [p. 568] have applicability to Combat Reactions?
2. What is the rationale for promulgating a *Law of the Three M's.*?
3. Why does the incidence of psychiatric casualties in the armed forces change so abruptly in wartime?
4. What is your preference as to diagnostic labels in Military Reactions? Support your preference.
5. In regard to symptoms of Military and Combat Reactions:
   (*a*) Name the more frequent symptoms.
   (*b*) List four of them which are nearly characteristic.
   (*c*) Why are the "direct" manifestations of anxiety so frequent?
   (*d*) What is meant by the *Theory of Ultimate-Vulnerability?*
   (*e*) Why is tolerance to military stresses variable?
6. What are some of the dynamic implications of:
   (*a*) Startle Reaction?
   (*b*) Battle Dreams?
   (*c*) Irritability?
   (*d*) Tremors?
7. What is meant by:
   (*a*) *Personal-Invulnerability Defense?*
   (*b*) Extension of personal conflicts?
   (*c*) *Feelings of Omnipotent-Responsibility?*
   (*d*) T.R.T.?
   (*e*) *Principle of Emotional-Sensitization?*
8. Discuss the *Unit-Guilt Reaction.*
9. List factors contributing to one's susceptibility to military stresses.
10. Discuss treatment in Military and Combat Reactions.

PART TWO: PSYCHOLOGIC PRISONER PROCESSING

1. Why is knowledge of Prisoner Processing quite important in military medicine and administration?
2. How are the results achieved?
3. What limiting factors mitigate against the wider application of Prisoner Processing techniques?
4. List five factors contributing to Prisoner Processing "success", in individual instances.
5. Discuss principles involved in the reintegration of the victim of Prisoner Processing.

APPENDIX

APPENDIX

Emotional and Mental Illness
An Outline Classification

I. THE PSYCHOLOGICALLY DETERMINED REACTIONS

A. The Neuroses

Diagnosis of a neurotic reaction is to be made on the basis of the most prominent clinical feature. See the appropriate chapter for the criteria for diagnosis in the various neuroses.

1. *The Anxiety Reactions:* The more direct expression of anxiety and its effects; pp. 81–135.
   (a) The Acute Anxiety Attack or A.A.A. (Anxiety Panic); pp. 84–98.
   (b) The Anxiety-Tension State or A.T.S.; pp. 98–104
   (c) Anxiety Neurosis; pp. 104–120

2. *The Dissociative Reactions:* Neurotic reactions which are marked by some measure of personality dissociation or disturbance of organization and synthesis; pp. 721–829.
   (a) Dissociated Personality; pp. 723 ff
   (b) Dreams; pp. 744–754
   (c) Somnambulism; pp. 754–758
   (d) Depersonalization; pp. 758–770
   (e) Fainting; pp. 770–773
   (f) Amnesia; pp. 773–791
      (i) Traumatic Encephalopathy; p. 781
      (ii) Alcoholic A.; p. 783
      (iii) Organic A.; p. 774
      (iv) Paramnesia; p. 777
      (v) Post Hypnotic A.; p. 778
      (vi) Post-Shock A.; p. 788
      (vii) Senile A.; p. 784
      (viii) Traumatic A.; p. 778
   (g) Fugue States; pp. 791–806
   (h) Alternating Personality; pp. 806–809
   (i) Automatic Behavior; p. 809
   (j) Hypnosis pp. 810–825; and Hypnotic States

3. *The Conversion Reactions:* Elements of emotional conflict are converted so as to secure symbolic external expression via somatic and physiologic routes; pp. 639–719.
   (a) Somatic Conversion; p. 642 ff
   (b) Physiologic Conversion; p. 642 ff
   (c) Psychologic Conversion; p. 643
   (d) Conversion epidemic; p. 703
   (e) Phantom-limb syndrome; p. 704

4. *The Phobic Reactions:* Psychic avoidance through displacement and substitution; pp. 515–607
   (a) Critical-Displacement Phobia; p. 515 ff
   (b) Situational Phobia; p. 515 ff
   (c) Gradually Evolving Phobia; p. 515 ff
   (d) Mixed types

5. *The Obsessive Compulsive Reactions:* Defensively elaborated patterns of reaction marked by the intrusion of insistent, repetitive, and unwelcome thoughts or urges; pp. 307–378.
   (a) Obsessive Reactions; pp. 307 ff
   (b) Compulsive Rituals, or C.R.; p. 349
   (c) Neurotic Security Operations (S.O.) and
       Compulsive Security Rituals, or C.S.R.; p. 351

6. *The Depressive Reactions:* Pathologically lowered spirits, sadness, and dejection; pp. 135–226.
    (*a*) Emotional Depression, of neurotic level; pp. 135–184
    (*b*) Grief States; pp. 165–167
    (*c*) Situational (Reactive) Depression; pp. 184
    (*d*) Depressions of Success; Promotion and
        Completion Depressions; pp. 185–189
    (*e*) Anxious Depression; pp. 189–191
    (*f*) One-Day Depression; p. 191
    (*g*) Related Entities:
        (*i*) Suicide and Suicidal Attempts; pp. 192–210
        (*ii*) Accident Proneness; p. 196
        (*iii*) Fracture Proneness; p. 197

7. *The Character Reactions:* Character trait defenses, their constellations and hypertrophy; pp. 227–305.
    (*a*) The Obsessive Personality and Character Reaction; pp. 245–258
    (*b*) The Conversion Personality and Character Reaction; pp. 258–270
    (*c*) The Depressive Personality and Character Reaction; pp. 270–283
    (*d*) The Hygeiaphrontic Personality and Character Reaction; p. 283
    (*e*) Added Constellations of character defenses:
        (*i*) Phobic
        (*ii*) Casual
        (*iii*) Paranoid
        (*iv*) Soterial
        (*v*) Antiseptic
        (*vi*) Anxious
        (*vii*) Impulsive
        (*viii*) Hygeiaphrontic; p. 472

8. *The Fatigue Reactions:* Fatigue incident to emotional stress, tension, and psychic conflict; pp. 379–440.
    (*a*) Emotional Fatigue; p. 381 *ff*
    (*b*) The Fatigue State; pp. 389; 399
    (*c*) Neurosthenia; pp. 385; 424–430
    (*d*) Fatigue Reaction or Neurosis

9. *The Hygeiaphrontic Reactions:* Anxious concern about health, and nonorganic symptomatology (hypochondriasis); pp. 441–514.

10. *The Soterial Reactions:* Emotional security from an illusory external object-source; pp. 607–639.

11. *The Neuroses-Following-Trauma* or Traumatic Neuroses: A group of neurotic reactions the onset of which follows, and which are attributed to, trauma; pp. 831–898.
    (*a*) Traumatic Reactions; p. 831 *ff*
    (*b*) Accident and Occupational Reactions; p. 876 *ff*
    (*c*) Compensation Reaction; pp. 876–884

12. *Military Reactions:* Emotional reactions associated with military operations; pp. 900–933.
    (*a*) Combat Reactions; p. 899 *ff*
    (*b*) Operational Fatigue or Stress Reactions; p. 909–912.
    (*c*) Military Somatization Reaction; Psychophysiologic and Psychosomatic States; p. 912
    (*d*) Prisoner Reactions
        (*i*) Prisoner Processing; pp. 933–945
        (*ii*) Concentration Camp Syndromes
        (*iii*) Repatriation Reactions

B. The Psychophysiologic Reactions

Includes all the alterations, changes, or disorders of function which may take place as a consequence of emotional conflict and stress. Such alterations may ultimately result in structural, organic, tissue, organ, or system changes, in accord with our *Concept of Functional-Structural Progression.*

This group follows three major pathways: (1) as a more or less direct response to prolonged emotional stress and tension; (2) through Physiologic Conversion, i.e., the conversion into a more or less symbolic "physiologic expression or language" of elements of consciously disowned impulses, needs, or wishes, plus elements of the conflict over them, the repressing forces, and self-punitive aspects; and (3) a combination of (1) and (2).

This large group of disorders includes all of the psychopathologic conditions included in the following major categories:

1. *Autonomic and Vegetative Reactions* (Organ and Vegetative Neuroses).
2. *Physiologic Conversions.* Physiologic Conversions may involve any region of the body or system. Ex.: gastrointestinal, genitourinary, circulatory, respiratory, nervous, and endocrine systems, skin, and special sensory organs; pp. 639 *ff.*
3. *Psychosomatic Illnesses.*
4. *Somatization Reactions*

C. The Personality Disorders

1. *Personality Disorders*
   - (*a*) Inadequate personality
   - (*b*) Schizoid personality
   - (*c*) Cyclothymic personality
   - (*d*) Emotionally unstable personality
   - (*e*) Passive-aggressive personality
2. *Sociopathic Personality Disorders*
   - (*a*) Antisocial reactions
   - (*b*) Dyssocial reactions
   - (*c*) Sexual deviations
   - (*d*) Addictions. Ex.: alcoholism, drug addictions

D. The Psychotic Reactions, or Psychoses

1. *The Affective Psychoses*
   - (*a*) Manic-Depressive Reaction, manic type
   - (*b*) Manic-Depressive Reaction, depressive type
   - (*c*) Psychotic Depression
   - (*d*) The Agitated Depression
2. *The Schizophrenic Reactions, or Psychoses*
   - (*a*) Schizophrenic Reaction, simple type
   - (*b*) Schizophrenic Reaction, hebephrenic type
   - (*c*) Schizophrenic Reaction, catatonic type
   - (*d*) Schizophrenic Reaction, paranoid type
   - (*e*) Schizophrenic Reaction, acute undifferentiated type
   - (*f*) Schizophrenic Reaction, chronic undifferentiated type
   - (*g*) Schizo-affective Psychoses
   - (*h*) Childhood Schizophrenia
3. *The Paranoid Reactions*
   - (*a*) Paranoia
   - (*b*) Paranoid State
4. *Psychoses with Special Situational Factors*
   - (*a*) Postpartum Psychoses
   - (*b*) Involutional Psychosis

II. ORGANICALLY DETERMINED DISORDERS

These disorders are those with impairment of brain function due to (or associated with) various organic factors. The disorder may result in defects in function, mental deficiency, or psychosis. The form that they take may be influenced in varying degree by preexisting psychogenetic factors.

A. Circulatory Disturbances

1. *Cerebral Arteriosclerosis*
2. *Cerebral Vascular Accidents*

           (*a*) Embolism
           (*b*) Hermorrhage
           (*c*) Infarction
        3. *Hypertensive Encephalopathy*

B. **Constitutional Deficiences**
        1. *Congenital Anomalies*
        2. *Development Defects (including Hydrocephalus)*
        3. *The Mental Deficiencies*
        4. *Mongolism*

C. **Convulsive Disorders**
        1. *Idiopathic Epilepsy*
        2. *Convulsive States*
        3. *Narcolepsy*

D. **Degenerative Conditions**
        1. *Alzheimer's Disease*
        2. *Pick's Disease*
        3. *Presenile and Senile Psychoses*

E. **Infections**
        1. *Intracranial Infections*
           (*a*) Abscess
           (*b*) Encephalitis
                 (*i*) Afebrile type of viral encephalitis
           (*c*) Meningitis
           (*d*) Paresis
           (*e*) Syphilis (and other types of CNS infections)
        2. *Systemic Infections*
        3. *Postinfectious Sequelae*

F. **Intoxications**
        1. *Drugs and Poisons*
           Carbon monoxide, barbiturates and related drugs, bromides, marihuana, mescal, morphine and derivatives, ACTH, LSD.
        2. *Alcohol*
           (*a*) Acute Intoxication
           (*b*) Alcoholic Hallucinosis
           (*c*) Delirium Tremens
           (*d*) Korsakoff's Psychosis

G. **Intracranial Neoplasms (Brain Tumors)**
        1. *Primary*
        2. *Secondary* (metastatic)

H. **Metabolic and Nutritional Disturbances**
        1. *Endocrine Disorders*
           (*a*) Pituitary
           (*b*) Thyroid
           (*c*) Adrenal
           (*d*) Pancreas (Diabetes)
        2. *Nutritional States*
           (*a*) Avitaminoses
           (*b*) Pellagra

I. **Trauma**
        1. *Accidents, Brain Injuries*
        2. *Birth Trauma*
        3. *Boxer's Encephalopathy;* p. 781
        4. *Electrical Trauma*
        5. *Radiation Injury*
        6. *Postoperative Deficiencies*

J. **Undetermined and Miscellaneous**
        1. *Familial and Hereditary Conditions*
        2. *Huntington's Chorea*
        3. *Multiple Sclerosis*

A GLOSSARY OF PSYCHIATRIC CONCEPTS
AND TERMS

A

AAA. Acute Anxiety Attack (*q.v.*)

A.N.A. American Neurological Association.

A.T.S. Anxiety-Tension state (*q.v.*)

abasia. An inability to walk, which is based upon defective coordination.

abberation. Deviation from the normal, usual, or ordinarily expected.

    emotional a. (1) any emotional response other than that which might ordinarily be expected. (2) An emotional illness, especially one in which the manifestations and symptoms are in themselves directly emotional (as distinguished from physical, behavioral, and physiologic).

ability. The capacity to perform an act. Such capacity may be increased by training. To be distinguished from aptitude. See *aptitude*.

    general a. Any capacity or competence present in varying degree for most persons and influencing the overall performance of the individual.

    special a. Talent, special endowment, or competence in a specialized or particular area of activity.

abnormal. Divergent from the normal.

abnormal psychology. A major branch of psychology in which study is focused primarily upon divergent emotional processes, pathologic mental phenomena and resultant behavior.

Abraham, Karl (1877–1925). Pioneer psychoanalyst; best known for his original work on the psychodynamics of depression and on personality trait development.

abreaction. An emotional release or discharge that results from mentally reliving or recalling to awareness a painful experience which has been forgotten (repressed) because it was intolerable to conscious awareness. Refers particularly to abreactions as they occur in psychiatric treatment.

Abreaction is often effectively induced by drugs, best administered shortly after an acute traumatic emotional experience. An example is the use of Sodium Amytal or Pentothal to help produce abreaction in a soldier following a painful combat experience. The therapeutic effect is through discharge of the painful emotions, and de-sensitization of the disturbing material, often accompanied by increased insight.

Abreaction also occurs in intensive psychotherapy. Herein, a repressed emotion may be released through reliving during therapy the original painful or traumatic experience.

absentmindedness. A state of absorption in thought in which one is in varying degrees oblivious to surroundings, to being spoken to, or other similar stimuli.

absolute. (1) Positive, unqualified. (2) Unmixed, pure.

Absolution. A mental mechanism operating unconsciously, through which one secures a measure of freedom from guilt or penalty, the remission of sins, or forgiveness for an offense. Release from responsibility, consequences, or obligations is achieved or sought.

abstract. (1) Theoretical; an idea or subject considered apart from a material basis or object. Without reference to particular applications. (2) Used as a verb to convey the type of thinking involved. Exs., abstract idea, abstract reasoning, etc.

abstraction. (1) The mental process of forming abstract ideas. (2) A state synonymous with *absentmindedness* (*q.v.*).

    a. experiment. A type of psychologic experiment where the subject is required to respond verbally, or in action, to common features in objects or situations presented serially.

absurdities test. A type of mental test in which the subject is asked to point out what is absurd about a picture, statement or story.

abulia. (1) The lack of or impairment of will power, initiative and drive. (2) Inability to make decisions or to act upon them. Also *aboulia*.

acatamethesia. Inability to comprehend situations as perceived, specific objects, or language.

acataphasia. Inability to connect words in orderly fashion into sentences.

acceptance. (1) Favorable reception of an idea or tangible object offered; (2) the accepting of an idea, judgment or belief offered in hypnosis or suggestive therapy.

accessory. (1) Something additional, often subordinate. (2) Employed especially for those parts of a sensory organ which have the function of making the reception of the stimulus more efficient, *e.g.*, the lens system or the muscles of the eye; in contradistinction to the *essential* parts.

accident prone. Specially susceptible to mishaps. Accident proneness results from the operation of intrapsychic forces which predispose to such misadventures.

accommodation. (1) Adjustment of differences. (2) Adaptation. (3) Reconciliation. (4) Technical senses: (*a*) changes in curvature, and therefore focal length, of the eye. These are effected by the ciliary muscles, with the object of focusing for different distances; (*b*) the effect produced on sense organs by continued and changing stimulation so that ultimately no sensation is experienced.

acedia. Apathy and low spirits.

acrophobia. The morbid fear of heights. See *Phobia.*

acting out. Refers to the unconscious "acting out" of emotional conflicts. Hostile or loving feelings, for example, are thus expressed in some concealed form of action. The person concerned manages to maintain conscious ignorance of his unconscious feelings or impulses or of their having been "acted out." Such "acting out" may or may not escape the observation of the person who happens to be the object, as well as that of other observers.

Acting out is a defense pattern analogous to somatic or physiologic conversion. The patient unconsciously expresses elements of the hidden emotional conflict in various kinds of neurotic behavior. Thus it constitutes a "behavioral conversion" or a "behavioral language."

actual neuroses. Anxiety Neurosis, hypochondriasis, and neurasthenia, according to an early concept of Freud. No longer used.

Acute Anxiety Attack. An acute, uncomfortable, and dramatic burst of anxiety which is usually self-limited. It is accompanied by the changes usually associated with intense fear. The basis of concern lies outside of conscious awareness. Abbreviated *A.A.A.*

acute situational stress reaction. A diagnostic term sometimes employed for certain acute emotional reactions incident to the stress of military operations or civilian disasters.

addiction. A strong emotional and/or physiologic dependence upon alcohol or a drug, which has progressed beyond voluntary control.

adiadochokinesia. Inability to perform or impairment of the performance of fine, rapidly repeated coordinated movements.

adjustment. (1) The relative state of harmony of the personality. (2) The relation between the individual, his inner self, and his environment. (3) The relative degree of resolution of emotional conflicts.

Adler, Alfred (1870–1939). Distinguished Austrian psychiatrist who proposed a system of psychiatric theory and therapy which he named Individual Psychology.

adolescence. (1) Roughly, the "teen age" years. (2) The stage of development from the end of puberty (generally about 13 years of age) to the beginning of adulthood (variously regarded as from 17 to 19 years of age).

adulthood. The stage of relative maturity; from 17 to 19 years to senescence. Also the *Heterosexual Stage.*

Specific Emotional Hazards of Adulthood (S.E.H.A.). Included as such specific hazards are such potentially traumatic and anxiety-provoking events as matriculation, graduation, marriage, separation, divorce, deaths, births, menopause, first sexual experience, traumatic civilian and service situations and so on. Also included herein, are the Military Stressful Eras (M.S.E.s), and that of "passing the peak," as some adults reach a point past which they feel their vigor will henceforth decline.

aerophagia. Air swallowing. Often seen in conjunction with neurotic gastrointestinal manifestations.

affect. (1) Any kind of emotion or feeling, especially that attached to an idea. (2) The emotional feeling-tone of a person. (3) The sum total of the various feelings which are present and acting together. A *strong* affect is an emotion. A *prolonged* affect is a mood. In most usage, affect and emotion are employed interchangeably. See also *Law of Universal Affect.*

affect dissociation. See *Dissociation, affect*

affective psychosis. A psychotic reaction in which there is a severe disorder of mood or emotional feelings. Examples: The elated, excited state as in the manic phase of a manic-depressive psychosis, or the extreme depression of involutional melancholia.

affectivity. The individual capacity to react with emotional feeling.

afferent. Inward, centripetal. An afferent nerve conveys impulses *from* the periphery of the body toward the center. Synonymous with sensory, as distinguished from efferent or motor.

Age of Anxiety. The bases for so naming our present era would include: (1) Attention thus might be better directed toward the special stresses and strains of present-day living. (2) However, of far more importance scientifically is our recently acquired and vastly increased recognition of the tremendous importance of anxiety in the whole scheme of things. (3) Increasing attention has been directed toward the study of anxiety and its important role in human life by professional people of varied orientation. (4) There is for the first time the clear recognition today of its universality as a part of human experience. (5) The problem of anxiety is now recognized as central to the whole concept of the psychogenesis of emotional illness. (6) Finally, there are the most important implications as to the continuing and significant role of anxiety in individual personality development, in character trait formation, and in the destiny of peoples and nations.

aggression. A forceful self-assertive attitude; a forceful attacking action, usually directed toward another; often an unprovoked assault. In psychiatry, considered inseparable from its emotional association.

  constrictive a. Self-protective and preservative aggression, realistically evoked by threats from others. In-

cludes *healthful self-assertiveness* which is necessary to protect one's reasonable rights when they are infringed.

  destructive a. In response to internal hostility; it is not essential for self-preservation or protection and is the type which is injurious to others.

  inward a. Directed inward, or inverted toward the self.

  outward a. Directed outward toward the external world and other people.

agitated depression. A severe emotional disorder in which profound emotional depression is accompanied by gross restlessness, i.e., psychomotor agitation.

agitation. A state of restlessness or continued rather purposeless activity. Agitation is a major kind of psychomotor expression of nervous tension.

agnosia. (1) Loss of the ability to recognize the significance of perceptions via one or more of the special senses (i.e., sight, taste, hearing, smell, and tactile sense). (2) A disturbance of recognition or identification due to cortical lesion. Included may be objects, persons or human parts, and verbal symbols.

agoraphobia. The morbid fear of open spaces. See *Phobia.*

agraphia. A loss of the ability to express thoughts in writing.

ailurophobia. The morbid fear of cats. See *Phobia.*

akinesia. Impairment of motor function.

alalia. The inability to talk.

alcoholic psychoses. A group of severe mental disorders incident to prolonged alcoholic habituation. Includes (1) Acute Hallucinosis, (2) Delirium Tremens, and (3) Korsakoff's syndrome.

Alcoholics Anonymous (A.A.). The name adopted by a group of persons formerly habituated to alcohol whose collective efforts are directed toward assisting alcoholics to throw off their dependence upon and habituation to alcohol.

alcoholism. The overuse of alcohol which usually implies some degree of habituation, dependence, or addiction. Alcoholism is medically significant when one's physical or mental health is impaired or threatened, or when the overuse of alcohol hampers personal relationships and individual effectiveness. May be acute or chronic.

alexia. Roughly, impairment of reading ability. A kind of visual aphasia in which understanding of written words and context is impaired. Sometimes called "word blindness," it is usually due to a cerebral lesion.

alienist. Any psychiatrist who testifies in court as to a person's sanity and mental competence. [obsolescent.]

alloplastic. Pertaining to the direct, open, and unmodified expression of impulses outwardly into the environment. Used in connection with certain antisocial and criminal individuals. This is in contrast to the more typical *autoplastic* manifestation of the neuroses.

Alternating Personality, Double or Dual Personality. A rare major dissociative reaction in which the patient leads two or more lives independently, usually alternately, neither personality being aware of the other.

Alzheimer's disease. A degenerative organic brain disease marked by premature senility and occurring in late middle life. Symptoms are usually rapidly progressive with aphasia, apraxia, intellectual deterioration, explosive emotions, and, occasionally, convulsive seizures.

amaurosis. Blindness following degeneration of the optic nerve, without apparent change or injury to the eye.

amaurotic family idiocy (Tay-Sachs' disease). A hereditary degenerative disease of the brain of children. Characterized generally by blindness, dementia, muscular dystrophy, and early death.

ambivalence (Bleuler). (1) Mixed feelings; usually the simultaneous presence of opposite emotional feelings. These may be conscious, partly hidden from conscious awareness, or one side of the feelings may be unconscious. (2) The presence of two opposing drives, desires, feelings, or emotions toward the same person, object, or goal. Example: the coexistence of love and hate toward the same person.

amentia. Defective mental functioning. Literally, "The absence of intellect." Amentia is usually organic and due to a developmental lack of adequate brain tissue. Not to be confused with dementia.

amnesia. (1) The medical term generally employed to describe pathologic loss of memory; forgetting. Amnesia may be sharply circumscribed in limits of time, spotty or diffuse, and can include recent or remote events. Amnesia is a dissociative phenomenon in which an area of one's experience or recollections is split off and becomes consciously inaccessible. Amnesia may be of psychologic, organic, or mixed origin. (2) A dissociative phenomenon in which an area of one's experience or recollection is lost or split off and becomes consciously inaccessible. The following are the major descriptive categories:

anterograde a. Amnesia extending *forward* in time from the point of onset.

circumscribed a. Amnesia with sharply delineated limits in time or as to events.

emotional a. Amnesia which is primarily emotional in origin. Example: In certain hysterical or dissociative states, following intolerable emotional stress.) Organic injury and damage is not responsible. The name indicates its emotional origin. It may be regarded as a kind of psychologic flight.

episodic a. Amnesia for a particular episode or a small area of experience.

feigned a. The pretense of amnesia; a form of malingering.

organic a. Amnesia secondary to organic defects, damage, or disease.

posthypnotic a. Amnesia following hypnosis. It may be spontaneous or may occur in response to suggestions made during the hypnotic trance.

psychologic a. Another term for amnesia of emotional origin. Amnesia of psychologic etiology as opposed to organic.

retrograde a. Amnesia extending *backward* in time from the precipitating event, whether this be emotional, organic, or traumatic.

traumatic a. Amnesia following physical injury. Most often occurs following a blow to the head (concussion).

anabolism. The building-up phase of metabolism. Includes glycogen storage and the constructive increase of energy potential.

anaclisis. The process of a sexual drive becoming attached to and exploiting various non-essential self-preservative trends such as eating and defecation.

anaclitic depression. An acute and striking impairment of an infant's physical, social, and intellectual development which sometimes occurs following a sudden separation from the mothering person.

anal erotism. (1) The primordial infantile pleasurable part of the experience of anal function. Anal erotism is usually seen in disguised and sublimated forms in later life when present. (2) A psychoanalytic term indicating a fixation of libido at the anal phase of psychosexual development.

anal stage. The stage of development from 9 to 12 months to as late as 36 months.

analgesia. The dulling or loss of pain sense.

analogy. See index references.

analysand. The patient in psychoanalytic treatment.

analysis. An intensive psychotherapeutic approach. Often used as a synonym for psychoanalysis.

analysis, character. The systematic psychotherapeutic investigation or analysis of the personality traits or defenses of an individual.

analytic psychology. The metapsychologic system of Carl Jung.

analtyic rule. A rule for patients to follow in psychoanalysis whereby the unedited and unselected voicing of free associations is undertaken in their order of occurrence.

anamnesis. The development history of an individual and of his illness, usually taken by the examining physician at the time of the initial interview.

anergasia. A behavioral disorder caused by organic lesions of the central nervous system.

anesthesia. The abolition of sensation.

anger as Anxiety-Equivalent. Anger translated into the emotional feeling of anxiety, in place of the experiencing and/or expression of angry feelings.

anhidrosis. Absence of sweating.

anima. The unconscious or inner being, according to Jungian psychology. Dis-

tinguished from the *persona,* the outward attitudes and character.

animism. (1) Endowing inanimate objects with life. (2) A belief that objects in nature possess souls or spirits, becoming their abode.

animus. See *Anima.*

anomia. An aphasic kind of disorder in which objects and persons cannot be associated with their names.

anorexia nervosa. A condition marked by the absence of appetite, accompanying weight loss, and other nervous symptoms on an emotional basis. The appetite loss may progress to an active aversion to food.

anosmia. Loss of the sense of smell.

antecedent conflicts, theory of. Two major corollaries: (1) the effect of an emotionally disturbing event may be multiplied as a consequence of the important effects of various antecedent vicissitudes of early life, which come to serve actually or symbolically as analogous prototypes. (2) Theoretically, every emotional conflict has its earlier antecedent. The memories for any connection between the conflict and its important antecedent are very likely lost to conscious recollection.

anthropology. The study and science of man, in historical and cultural perspective.

anthropophobia. The morbid fear of people. See *Phobia.*

Antiseptic Personality. Overly moralistic, guilt-ridden, and sexually super-inhibited personality constellation.

antisocial. Contrary to or against usual social standards or mores. An antisocial reaction pattern is that which is seen in those individuals who are frequently in conflict with the rules and standards set up by society, seeming neither to profit from experience nor to modify behavior in the face of punishment. See *Psychopathology.*

anxiety. (1) The apprehensive tension or uneasiness which stems from the imminent anticipation of danger, when the source is largely unknown or unrecognized. Anxiety is primarily of intrapsychic origin. *Fear,* in turn, is the emotional response to a consciously recognized and usually external threat or danger. Both anxiety and fear are accompanied by similar physiologic changes. These are part of the individual's T.R.C. (i.e., his total response to crisis). These changes are defensively and protectively intended to help prepare the person for physical activity which may be necessary to cope with the threat. (2) Fear in the absence of an apparently adequate cause. Also called *free-floating anxiety*. Where the apprehension is objectively out of proportion to the apparent cause, it is also sometimes referred to as *neurotic anxiety*.

conditioned a. Anxiety which originates or is increased as a consequence of earlier psychologic and emotional sensitization or conditioning.

absence of a. May interfere with, delay or even prevent therapy.

Anxiety Avoidance-Principle. Man consciously seeks to avoid anxiety and the circumstances in which it arises. Resolution is sought for the underlying intrapsychic emotional conflicts which are individually responsible for the anxiety.

Attempted defenses against anxiety may result in the unconscious employment of various mental mechanisms, the development of character defensive traits, the possible overdevelopment of either or both, with resulting unwitting self-defeat and handicap, and/or ultimately in the more clear-cut symptoms of emotional illness.

anxiety, castration. The anxiety which is theoretically ultimately traceable to the threat of retaliation for forbidden, and thereby dangerous, hostile, aggressive, or sexual impulses. So named for the feared retaliation of castration as fantasied by the infant, but in practice more broadly used.

anxiety, constructive. Anxiety may be a constructive force tending to advance individual personal adjustment and socialization. May play important role in initiating and/or continuing therapy. See also *Constructive Anxiety*.

anxiety, constrictive. Endeavors of the individual to deal with or escape from anxiety may result in an increasingly constrictive effect upon living. A vicious circle may be thus established. See also *Constrictive Spiral*.

Anxiety-Countering Principle. A major principle in the *soterial* pattern of defensive reaction. The soterial object thus becomes an object-source of safety, comfort and security, in varying degree.

Anxiety, Critical Attack of. An attack of anxiety which is of a sufficient level or quantity to be crucial or critical in so far as maintaining the existing pattern of personality defenses and balances is concerned. The critical attack of anxiety results in the mobilization of additional intrapsychic mechanisms of defense.

For example, in the acute onset of some phobias, the initial repression of painful affect from an idea or impulse and its displacement externally take place at the time of a critical attack of anxiety. The level of anxiety had become so critical as to render the previous attachment of the affect unstable. The attachment of the unstable affect externally creates a new *emotional-object amalgam* (*q.v.*).

Anxiety, Depletion Concept of. Anxiety even in persons not considered ill, may exert important restrictive effects on function and may interfere with certain kinds of mental and emotional activity.

anxiety, destructive. Anxiety which interferes to any extent with personal effectiveness or satisfaction.

anxiety, emotional contagion of. The intuitive communication of anxiety from a significant adult to a child.

anxiety-equivalent. Anxiety sometimes finds partial or even greater expression in anger, into which it may be transformed. Anger thus becomes what we might term an anxiety-equivalent. A tense and anxious person also is much more likely to become angry. Herein the anxiety is again translated into a kind of emotional activity; the experiencing or expression of angry feelings, or both.

anxiety, free-floating. Fear with the lack of a consciously recognized source of danger for attachment of the anxious feeling.

anxiety hysteria. A condition particularly marked by the presence of phobias. (See *Phobias*.) Introduced by Freud, it has not become widely accepted, and it has not been included in official terminology. Currently interchangeable with the *Phobic Reactions*.

anxiety, level of. Anxiety and its more direct manifestations vary considerably in level from patient to patient, and from one period of time to another.

anxiety, manifestations of. *Direct:* Subjectively experienced tension; psychomotor expression; autonomic expression; interference with mental function; certain clinical states (the Anxiety Reactions). *Indirect:* Physionogic conversions; somatic conversions; psychologic conversions.

anxiety neurosis. An established and chronic reaction pattern of emotional illness. It is characterized primarily by the direct subjective experiencing of anxiety, which is the most prominent feature of the reaction. Anxiety and its effects are also expressed directly in varying degree via psychomotor, autonomic, and mental pathways. The effects and the consequences of the direct manifestations of anxiety in chronic form are also an important part of the clinical features of Anxiety Neurosis (see Table 8, pp. 114–115).

anxiety, neurotic. Anxiety in which the apprehension is objectively quite out of proportion to any apparent cause.

anxiety panic. See *Acute Anxiety Attack* (the A.A.A.).

anxiety, pathologic. The protectively intended and integrative responses to anxiety are limited, inadequate, nonconstructive, disorganized, inappropriate, exaggerated, or ineffectual. The net overall effect for the person concerned is nonconstructive.

anxiety reactions, major. (1) Acute Anxiety Attack; A.A.A. (2) Anxiety-Tension State; A.T.S. (3) Anxiety Neurosis.

anxiety, reciprocal influences of and pain, Concept of. Pain can produce or increase anxiety, which in turn may lower the threshold to the perception of pain.

anxiety, separation. Apprehension resulting from removal of significant persons or familiar surroundings. Common in infants from 6 to 10 months old, and may recur in later life.

anxiety, situational. Anxiety in response to threats from external sources, such as threats of physical or psychologic injury.

anxiety, sources of. *Primary sources:* Those most responsible in infancy and childhood: helplessness; separation or threat of separation; privation and loss; frustration; "emotional contagion"; disapproval or fear of disapproval; physical threats from external or internal environment or actual physical punishment; specific emotional hazards of childhood; conditioned responses. *Secondary Sources:* Those most closely associated with adulthood: antecedent prototypes; superego conflict; disapproval or fear of disapproval; social conflict; threats to self-preservation; threats to racial preservation; conditioned responses; frustration, hostility, anger; infantile carryovers; apprehensive anticipation; specific emotional hazards of adulthood.

Anxiety-Symptom Success, Concept of Inverse Ratio of. See *Symptom-success; inverse ratio.*

Anxiety-Tension State (A.T.S.). A less established pathologic entity than Anxiety Neurosis, from which the anxiety present is differentiated more quantitatively than qualitatively. The Anxiety-Tension State often has important environmental or situational factors and theoretically will markedly subside or will enter remission upon their removal. In analogy to medical pathology, the Anxiety-Tension State might be regarded as a subacute phase, distinguished from an Anxiety Neurosis as a chronic phase.

Anxiety, Universality Principle of. Anxiety is universally experienced, and efforts at its avoidance are a potent force in the individual personality formation.

anxious depression. See *Depression, Anxious.*

apathy. A state of reactive absence of emotions; want of feeling, or lack of emotion. Such absence of emotional feeling may be more apparent than real in cases of emotional illness.

aphasia. The loss of the ability to pronounce words, or to correctly name common objects or to indicate their use. In *motor aphasia*, understanding remains, but the memory traces necessary to produce a certain sound are lost. In *sensory aphasia,* the power of comprehension is lost; the meaning of words or phrases or the use of objects has been lost. The aphasias are due to cerebral lesions which impair perception and/or expression.

aphonia. The loss of the ability to speak.

aphrodisiac. Any agent, usually a food or drug, which is believed to have powers of sexual stimulation.

apoplexy. A stroke. An acute organic disorder due to hemorrhage or sudden obstruction in a major blood vessel of the brain. Symptoms are likely to include paralysis of the opposite side of the body. Aphasia is frequent.

apperception. Clear perception, in particular where there is recognition or identification.

apprehension. (1) Perception and understanding. (2) Anticipatory fear or anxiety.

apprehensive anticipation. An emotional reaction akin to anxiety and fear in which something unpleasant or dangerous is awaited; as in awaiting attack during a combat alert. The something which is awaited is external and real if it occurs, and its nature can be guessed at although it is not definite. Thus Apprehensive Anticipation lies somewhere between anxiety and fear, having some of the characteristics of each. See *Anxiety* and *Fear.*

Appropriateness of Response, Individual, Principle of. On a *deep* level of meaning and significance, every response is individually appropriate to the stimulus.

apraxia. (1) An impairment or a loss of the power to perform coordinated voluntary movements. (2) Mind blindness; a loss of the mental imagery and understanding of the nature of things that controls and makes such movements possible.

aptitude. Natural ability. The possession of the basic capacity to acquire ability or skills. Tests to determine the presence or level of such natural abilities or skills are called Aptitude Tests.

aptitude test. Any type of test designed to measure the capacity for developing general or specific skills.

aquaphobia. The morbid fear of water. See *Phobia.*

archaic. Very ancient; out-of-date. May be used to refer to the ancestral phylogenetic psyche.

asemasia. Loss of the power of communication by words, gestures, or signals.

asemia. Loss of the power of communication, the use or understanding of speech or signs.

asexual. Without sex, usually without sexual drive or sexual orientation.

assimilation. (1) *Educationally:* absorption of data into one's general fund of knowledge. (2) *Sociologically:* becoming like one's social milieu. (3) *Physiologically:* transformative of food into tissue (the constructive phase of metabolism). (4) *Psychologically:* absorption of new experiences, esp. emotional, into existing psychological make-up.

association. (1) A relation between ideas or emotions by contiguity, continuity, or similarities. An associative thought comes by the normal, unimpeded flow, succession and progression of mental activity from the pre-existing idea. (2) *Neurological:* (*a*) of certain fibers connecting areas within the same hemisphere; (*b*) of certain areas of the cerebral cortex whose functions remain uncertain. (3) Of certain experiments or tests employing controlled, directed or free association in education, learning, psychology and psychiatry. (4) Of ideas; the mental operation by which one impression or idea calls to mind an associated one, frequently from past experience.

a. center. Center of cerebral cortex not itself functionally differentiated but connected with other centers by association fibers or tracts.

controlled a. Associative ideas called into conscious awareness in response to stimulus words provided the subject.

free a. The unimpeded association of ideas and memories in spontaneous succession when consciously unrestricted and uncensored. Especially the verbal reporting of the full and unedited free train of thought in psychotherapy and psychoanalysis.

astasia-abasia. A gross hysterical disturbance of gait and locomotion.

astereognosis. A loss of the ability to recognize objects through the sense of touch.

asthenia. Weakness.

asthenic. Slender. (A body type of Kretschmer.)

astraphobia. The morbid fear of lightning. See *Phobia*.

ataractic. Any agent or drug which induces ataraxy. Has been loosely applied as a class name for a new group of drugs.

ataraxia. (Greek: non-agitation.) Troubled calmness; absence of anxiety. Ataraxy (preferred). See *Ataraxy*.

ataraxy. (1) A state in which there is an absence of anxiety. (2) Complete equanimity, homeostasis, or peace of mind; untroubled calmness.

atavism. The reappearance of inherited traits after a lapse of several generations.

ataxia. Incoordination of voluntary muscular movements.

athetosis. Involuntary, slow, and repeated gross movements.

atony. Lack of normal muscular tone.

atrophy. Wasting.

attention. Mental focusing. Attention may be fleeting or sustained.

attention hypothesis. Attention tends to be selectively, automatically, and unconsciously drawn toward our personal areas of greatest interest and concern.

attitude. Established patterns of mental views which are developed and predetermined by cumulative prior experience.

aura. A premonitory wave of subjective sensation usually preceding some anticipated event. An epileptic aura precedes the attack. It is a prodromal or warning phase preceding the convulsive seizure.

autism; autistic thinking. (1) A form of thinking which is highly subjective and is essentially nonconforming to that generally common to society. (2) Personalized thinking which gratifies unfulfilled personal desires without due regard for the demands of reality. Objective facts are distorted, obscured, or excluded in varying degree. The fantasy is an example of autistic thinking. Daydreaming, when it is of a kind in which thinking is greatly divorced from reality, can become autistic.

early infantile autism. An emotional illness characterized by a very early failure to relate emotionally to parents and others.

auto-erotism. Roughly, self-love. Refers to the stage in emotional development in which sensual gratification is largely secured or attempted through oneself alone. Erotic aims are self-directed and are principally gratified in the self.

automatic behavior. Instances of various kinds of behavior which take place outside of conscious awareness in similar fashion to automatic writing.

autonomic conversion. See *Conversion, Autonomic.*

autonomic nervous system. The non-voluntary part of the nervous system, which controls basic functions, such as heart rate and breathing. It operates outside of the consciousness.

automatic writing. (1) A dissociative phenomenon in which an individual writes material while his attention is distracted. He is consciously unaware of what he writes. Used occasionally for experimental purposes, for testing the relative disassociative capacity of a patient, and (rarely) as a means of access to unconscious data. (2) Also applied to the writing which follows the suggestions made to a patient while he is in a hypnotic trance.

automatism. Automatic, mechanical, and apparently undirected symbolic behavior which is outside of conscious control. Seen in schizophrenia and in the Dissociative Reactions.

autonomic. Autonomous, self-controlling. Usually refers to the autonomic Nervous System, that portion of the nervous system (including the sympathetic and the vagal systems) which is independent of the craniosacral or central nervous system.

autonomic conversion. See *Conversion.*

autoplastic. Pertaining to the indirect modification and adaptation of impulses prior to their outward expression, as found in the neuroses.

965

avoidance. A conscious and/or unconscious human reaction defensively intended to escape anxiety, conflict, danger, fear, and pain. Efforts at avoidance may be physical or psychologic. Many of the mental mechanisms are employed in the service of attempted psychologic avoidance.

B

B.B.C. Dissociation. See *Dissociation, B.B.C.*

Balanced Neurotic Position. A position of neurotic balance of symptoms in which anxiety is minimal or absent. A neurotic *status quo*. Interest in therapy is lacking, resistance to therapy is great and the patient has little motivation toward change. The Secondary Defenses are powerful.

Beard, George Miller (1839–1883). American psychiatrist who introduced the concept of nervous exhaustion, which he named *neurasthenia* in 1869.

Beaumont, William (1785–1853). U. S. Army surgeon who published in 1833 his classic observations of the traumatically exposed gastric mucosae of a French Canadian *voyageur,* Alexis St. Martin.

bedlam. (1) An insane asylum. (2) Pandemonium, confusion. (Derived from "Bedlam" Hospital, the Hospital of St. Mary of Bethlehem, a mental hospital in London, founded in 1402.)

Beers, Clifford W. (1876–1943): Author of *A Mind That Found Itself* and founder (1909) of the *National Association for Mental Health.*

behavior. Deportment or conduct. Any or all of the total activity of a person or persons, especially what can be externally observed.

behaviorism. A school of psychologic thinking concerned with observable, tangible, and measurable data, i.e., largely with behavior and human activities. Ideas and emotions as purely subjective phenomena are largely excluded from consideration.

The Behavioristic School was founded by *John B. Watson* (1878–1958).

Bernheim, H. A. (1840–1919). Physician, hypnotist, and therapist, of Nancy, France.

bestiality. Sexual relations between human and animal.

biodynamics. The study of the dynamic processes manifested in the behavior of organisms.

birth trauma. In Rankian theory, the psychic shock of birth.

bisexual. Literally, two-sexed. Having both active (male) and passive (female) sexual interests or characteristics.

black or white response. An emotionally determined pattern of viewing something as either absolutely true, present, or as desired (i.e., white), or else totally untrue, absent, absolutely undesirable, etc. (i.e., black). Herein the individual has difficulty in seeing something as partially true, or gray.

blast syndrome. The emotional-physiologic syndrome following supposed exposure to an explosion. Now seldom used.

Bleuler, Eugen (1857–1939). Swiss psychiatrist who revised the concept of dementia praecox and introduced the term schizophrenia.

blind spots. See *Psychologic Blind Spots.*

blocking. The inability to recall, difficulty in recalling, or the interruption of a train of thought or speech. It is due to emotional factors which are usually out of conscious awareness.

borderline state (borderline psychosis): A diagnostic term used when it is difficult to determine whether symptoms are predominantly neurotic or psychotic. The symptoms may shift from one type to the other. They often include *acting out* (*q.v.*) and behavior which is suggestive of schizophrenia.

boxer's encephalopathy. See *Punch Drunk.*

brain syndrome, chronic. (May also be acute and/or reversible). A syndrome which results from relatively permanent and more or less irreversible diffuse organic impairment of cerebral tissue function. Disturbances of memory, orientation, comprehension, and affect of greater or lesser degree are characteristically present. Examples: general paresis, cerebral arteriosclerosis, brain trauma, Huntington's chorea, Pick's disease, brain tumor.

brain washing. (1) The emotional and mental processing or conditioning of prisoners which is aimed at securing wishes of the captors. (2) Prisoner-Processing (preferred term). (3) Attitudes which will conform to the systematic, intensive and forced method of political indoctrination.

Breuer's Dissociation. See *Dissociation, Breuer's.*

Breuer, Joseph (1841–1925). Viennese psychiatrist who made important discoveries about hysteria. Discovered the psychologic importance of seemingly "forgotten" memories. Collaborated with Freud for some years.

Brigham, Amariah (1798–1849). Early American psychiatrist who founded the American Journal of Psychiatry in 1844.

Brill, A. A. (1874–1948). First American psychoanalyst. A pupil of Freud. Noted for his translations of Freud's writings.

"buddy" guilt. A neurotic kind of guilt which has been seen in combat situations following the death of a buddy, close associate, or comrade.

bulemia. Morbidly increased hunger.

C

C.R. Character Reaction (*q.v.*).

cachexia. Emaciation, malnutrition, and debility.

camptocormia. Neurotic "bent back." Forwardly flexed, bent posture of the back on a Somatic Conversion basis.

Cannon, Walter B. (1871–1945). American physiologist; for 36 years (1906–1942) professor at Harvard. First adapted X-ray techniques to the study of digestive function. In 1915, his classic book *Bodily Changes in Pain, Hunger, Fear and Rage* gave further scientific reinforcement to recognition of the important influences of emotional forces upon physiology.

carbon dioxide therapy. A treatment approach in which CO_2 is inhaled with the inducing of unconsciousness. A form of *shock therapy* (*q.v.*), less in use today.

carphology. Repetitive picking or plucking movements. May occur in advanced schizophrenia or occasionally in organic psychoses.

castration. Removal of the testicles. Less accurately used to refer to any kind of injury to the genital organs; especially the fantasied loss of the penis. Its more figurative use includes the concept of being "set at naught," in the sense of being rendered impotent, powerless, helpless, and defeated.

castration anxiety. See *Anxiety, Castration.*

castration complex. (1) The fear (usually fantasied) of damage to sexual organs. (2) A series of emotionally invested ideas which are out of awareness, actually or symbolically referring to fear of loss of the genital organs, usually as punishment for forbidden sexual desires or desires with sexual implications. Includes the childhood fantasy that sexual differences have resulted from loss of the penis. Also see *Complex.*

casual personality. Approximately the converse of the *Obsessive Personality.* Characteristic casualness may be an asset, or a liability perhaps to the point of being considered a neurosis.

catabolism. The tearing down phase of metabolism. Includes the utilization of stored glycogen and the discharge of energy potential.

catalepsy. A condition in which the limbs or body of a patient passively remain in any position in which they are placed. This kind of muscular hypertonicity is also called *flexibilitas cerea* (waxy flexibility). Catalepsy is a term which may be sometimes used for any form of sustained immobility.

cataplexy. A momentary loss of skeletal muscular tone with resulting weakness. Cataplexy is usually associated with narcoleptic attacks (i.e., uncontrollable sleeping).

catatonia. A clinical type of schizophrenia characterized by immobility with muscle rigidity or inflexibility (*flexibilitas cerea*). Alternating periods of physical hyperactivity and excitability may occur. In general, inaccessibility to ordinary methods of communication is marked. See *Schizophrenia.*

catharsis. (1) The healthful (therapeutic) release of ideas through a "talking out" of conscious material, accompanied by the appropriate emotional reaction. (2) The release into awareness to some extent of repressed (i.e., "forgotten") material or experiences from the unconscious. Catharsis may be encouraged or welcomed in psychiatric treatment as a kind of emotional purgation. Considerable relief and loss of tension may follow. Catharsis takes place in abreaction which is, however, a more explosive reaction and is more properly limited to the recall and mental reliving of "forgotten" material, usually from a specific emotionally traumatic event, whereas catharsis includes and refers also to the "talking out" of conscious material. Catharsis and abreaction are sometimes used interchangeably.

cathexis. (1) The attachment of emotional feeling and significance to an idea or object. (2) The attachment of libido (i.e., psychic or emotional energy) to an external object. By cathexis, the idea, object, or situation becomes invested with increased psychologic significance. Cathexis can enter into the formation of ideals, devotion, or dedication to a cause, and the emotional significance or importance that an individual attaches to an idea. The degree of cathexis is measured by (1) level and amount of interest in and significance of the object, (2) the frequency with which it comes into awareness (association), and (3) the relative extent or degree of inadvertent influence upon one's thinking and behavior.

causalgia. Burning pain of psychic or organic basis.

censor. A psychoanalytic concept which envisions a part of the unconscious self (i.e., the ego) functioning as a guardian to prevent the emergence into conscious awareness of repressed material.

central nervous system. The brain and spinal cord. The C.N.S.

cephalalgia. Headache, or pain.

cerea flexibilitas. Literally "waxy flexibility." Often present in catatonic schizophrenia, in which the patient's arm or leg for example, remains passively in the position in which it is placed.

cerebellum. The lower back part of the brain, having to do largely with coordination.

character. (1) Roughly equivalent to personality; "what a person is" as we observe him, excepting physical attributes.

(2) The relatively fixed or continuing group of individual personality attributes of a person. (3) The characteristic patterns of behavior of the individual. The social, emotional, and intellectual manifestations of a person's character are called his personality.

character analysis. The systematic psychotherapeutic investigation, study and analysis of the personality traits or defenses, and patterns or *constellations* of defenses, of an individual. This focus of attention, interest, and study on the part of analyst and patient is substituted for the intensive scrutiny in analogous fashion of the dynamics and the defensive purposes of the clinical symptoms of other types of emotional reactions, *e.g. symptom analysis.*

character defense. Character or personality trait. This term conveys the concept of traits serving an unconscious defensive purpose. The defensive endeavor is intrapsychic in origin and is hidden from ordinary observation, as well as from the conscious awareness of the person concerned.

In the *Concept of Character Defenses,* character traits evolve gradually as more or less fixed patterns of attitude and response. Their essential function is defensive; hence the term character defenses.

All character traits are thus believed to develop defensively, in the service of vital internal psychologic needs. Each such trait has an individually specific defensive intent or purpose. The defensive endeavor of the trait is intrapsychic in origin.

character defensive trait. Personality trait or attribute.

character disorder. An unhealthy pattern of behavior and emotional response which is to varying degrees socially unacceptable or disapproved, and which is accompanied by minimal outward evidence of anxiety or symptoms as ordinarily seen in the neuroses.

Character Neurosis. A neurotic reaction in which certain personality traits (i.e., character defenses) have become exaggerated or overdeveloped. The resulting imbalance, while defensively vital to the patient, has elements of self-defeat which are largely hidden from conscious awareness.

The overdeveloped traits are equivalent in the character neurosis to the clinical symptoms in other types of neurosis. To be distinguished from *Symptom Neurosis*. See *Neurosis*.

Character Reaction. (1) The overdevelopment or exaggeration of specific individual character defenses or personality traits, or groups of traits to a level of impairment of some facet of living, so as to constitute a neurotic reaction. (2) A neurotic reaction in which certain personality traits (i.e., character defenses) have become exaggerated or overdeveloped. The overdeveloped traits in the Character Reaction are equivalent to the clinical symptoms in other types of neurosis.

Character defenses tend to develop in association with other similar ones. Such groupings may be referred to as constellations; the Obsessive, the Depressive and the Conversion (or Hysterical) are the major constellations.

Cultural Vogue in C.R.s. The incidence of various patterns of character reactions can vary from one cultural group to another. Cultural influences and social pressures may encourage the development of obsessive, depressive, or hygeiaphrontic traits.

Defense-Hypertrophy, Principle of, in C.R.s. Overdevelopment of a character defense equates neurosis. A defense in its evolvement becomes exaggerated or hypertrophid, to become handicapping and self-defeating in its overall net effect leading to neurosis.

character trait. Personality trait; character-defense.

Charcot, Jean M. (1825–1893). Famous French neurologist and psychiatrist. First reproduced conversion (hysterical) disabilities under hypnotic suggestion, demonstrating their basic psychic origin.

chorea. An organic nervous disorder, usually due to encephalitis. It is marked by variable spasmodic movements which may be accompanied by outbursts of excitement.

Circular Generation of Fear Principle. The presence of anxiety can in itself produce fear. Thus fear of anxiety and an A.A.A. can in turn lead to its (circular) perpetuation. Fear and tension contribute to anxiety, which in turn generates fear of its recurrence.

circumstantiality. Speech marked by rambling and irrelevance in which many unnecessary, essentially unrelated details are included and in which the main goal or idea is delayed, obscured, or remains unexpressed.

claustrophobia. The morbid fear of closed spaces. See *Phobia*.

climacteric. Menopause. Also used to refer to the corresponding age period (40 to 50) in men and women.

clonus. Hyperactive reflex resulting in a number of continued responses in pendulum fashion following an initial stimulus.

coitus. Sexual intercourse.

coitus interruptus. Interruption of the sexual act by withdrawal just prior to emission.

cognitive. Refers to the intellectual processes which pertain to learning and knowing. Includes the mental processes of comprehension, judgment, memory, and reasoning.

collective unconscious (Jung). The portion of the unconscious which is theoretically common to mankind. Also *racial unconscious*.

coma. A state of complete loss of consciousness in which there is no perception or voluntary movement possible.

combat exhaustion. The state of emotional and physical exhaustion occurring during intensive or prolonged combat.

combat fatigue. Disabling physical and emotional fatigue incident to military combat. Also used as another term for combat neurosis during World War II, one of the Neuroses-Following-Trauma (*q.v.*).

commitment. The legal process for mandatory hospitalization of patient in need of treatment for mental disorder.

community psychiatry. A broad term referring to the mobilization of community resources on behalf of the emotionally ill patient in his own area.

Compathy. The close *sharing* of emotional feelings with another person; an affective kind of Identification through which one subjectively experiences the emotions of another. It is semiautomatic and thus practically independent of voluntary control or direction.

compensation. (1) A mental mechanism operating outside of and beyond conscious awareness through which the individual attempts to offset, to make up (i.e., to compensate) for real or fancied deficiences. There may be actual or imagined defects in such areas as physique, performance, or various skills or attributes. (2) A conscious process in which one strives to make up for real or imagined defects in such areas as physique, performance, skills, or psychologic attributes.

Compensation Neurosis. A term applied to certain neurotic reactions, largely following industrial trauma, in which features of secondary gain are prominent. There is often an absorbing interest in securing compensation or pension for an alleged injury.

Completion Depression. See *Depression, Completion.*

complex. A group of associated ideas which have a common strong emotional tone. These may be in part unconscious (i.e., out of awareness) and can help importantly in determining attitudes and association. Four examples of complexes rather frequently referred to are:

castration c. Unconscious but emotionally charged ideas having reference to the fear of losing genital organs, generally as punishment for forbidden sexual desires. Also see *Castration.*

Electra c. The attachment of the female child to the father, and the resulting feelings and fears.

inferiority c. (Adler). Feelings of inferiority stemming from real or unreal physical or social inadequacies. The individual may overcompensate (as well as develop anxiety, or have other adverse reactions) by excessive ambition or by the development of special skills, often in the very field in which he was originally handicapped.

Oedipus c. (Freud). Positive feeling of the child for the parent of the opposite sex, accompanied by envious and aggressive feelings toward the parent of the same sex. These feelings are largely repressed (i.e., made unconscious) because of the fear of displeasure or punishment by the parent of the same sex. In its narrower use, it applies only to the male child.

Compliant Response to Implicit Command, in suicide. The individual acts as he unconsciously feels directed to die, in response to the "implicit-command" of rejection; *i.e.* to be gone, to vanish, or even to die. May be an important component in suicide. See also *suicide.*

compulsion. An insistent, repetitive, intrusive, and unwanted urge to perform an act which is contrary to the patient's ordinary conscious wishes or standards. A compulsion is a defensive substitute for hidden and still more unacceptable ideas and wishes. Anxiety results upon the failure to perform the compulsive act. A compulsion is a command from within.

compulsion neurosis. See *Neurosis, Obsessive-Compulsive.*

compulsive. Conveys a "driven" quality in which certain acts or patterns of behavior must be followed seemingly almost in propitiation against the onset of uncomfortable feelings of anxiety or guilt.

compulsive personality. A personality characterized by excessive adherence to rigid standards. Typically, these people have traits of rigidity, repetitive patterns of behavior, overconscientiousness, overinhibition, and lack of normal capacity for relaxation.

compulsive ritual. A series of acts repetitively carried out in a compulsive manner. As with single compulsions, carrying out of the ritual relieves tension and anxiety.

conative. Pertaining to the basic strivings of an individual, as expressed in his behavior and actions.

concussion. Injury to the brain from a blow, generally accompanied by a loss of consciousness.

concussion syndrome. The emotional-physiologic reaction following supposed exposure to a blast or an explosion. Now seldom used as a diagnostic term.

condensation. Overdetermination. A psychologic process often present in dreams in which two or more concepts are fused or condensed so that a single symbolic representation may serve. Several ideas, thoughts, or experiences may be condensed to become represented by a single word, action, or figure.

conditioned anxiety. When the anxiety occurs or is considerably increased as a consequence of prior sensitization or "conditioning." This concept of conditioned anxiety is in accord with our Theory of Antecedent Conflicts. See also *anxiety*.

conditioned emotional responses. Emotional responses in later life which are greater as a consequence of the conditioning effects of similar ones from early years. Following a sufficiently threatening experience or a series of them, the adult may suffer similar feelings when only part of the sequence or event is later present.

conditioned reflex (Pavlov). An induced reflex developed by training in association with a particular stimulus. Example: A dog is offered food at the same time a bell is rung. After a period of conditioning, the ringing of the bell alone will bring on salivation and the same responses originally present when food alone was presented.

confabulation. The "filling in" of actual memory gaps by often complex but imaginary or fantastic experiences. These are related in a detailed and plausible way as though they were factual. Confabulation is seen principally in certain psychotic reactions, such as Korsakoff's psychosis (*q.v.*). It may be regarded as an outward response to conscious and/or unconscious needs for compensation and rationalization.

conflict. The clash between two opposing emotional forces which may be conscious or unconscious. In the latter, an internal (instinctual) wish or striving is opposed by another internal and contradictory wish. Example: An instinctual wish for gratification comes into conflict with the restrictions of conscience, or with external (social) requirements. A compulsive need for love, for instance, comes into conflict with an opposing strong need to be self-sufficient and independent of the need for love. This conflict might be dealt with by attempted denial of the first need.

  emotional c. The clash which may occur between one's (superego) conscience or moral, social and personal standards on the one hand, versus egocentric and (id.) instinctual strivings on the other; self-preservation, acquisitive, reproductive, aggressive and destructive drives; the personal desires, needs and strivings for love, sex and possession.

  extrapsychic c. Conflict involving external factors. May be used to refer to conflicts between parts of oneself and the external environment.

  intrapsychic c. Internal psychologic-emotional conflict; within the personality.

Conflict Indicator Concept. Various phenomena indicate the presence of emotional tension and underlying intrapsychic conflict. These include nail biting, stuttering, nightmares, mannerisms, tics, insomnia, and many psychologic and psychosomatic symptoms.

confusion. Disturbed orientation in respect to time, place, or person, which is sometimes accompanied by disturbances of consciousness.

congenital. Present upon birth.

conscience. (1) The moral, self-critical part of oneself wherein have developed and reside standards of behavior and performance and judgmental attitudes. (2) The conscious superego.

conscious (1) Pertaining to that of which one is aware. (2) Personal apperception and awareness of oneself and of one's relative position, especially in the immediate environment.

consciousness. The state of awareness of one's internal and external environment.

constitution. The total of the inherent physical and psychologic endowment of a person. Is sometimes used more narrowly to indicate the physical inheritance or potential from birth.

constitutional inadequacy. A loose concept of hereditary inferiority.

constitutional types. Constellations of morphologic, physiologic, and psychologic traits as earlier proposed by various researchers. Galen, Kretschmer, and Sheldon proposed the types which were most often referred to. These are as follows:
  Galen: Sanguine, melancholic, choleric, and phlegmatic types.
  Kretschmer: Pyknic, asthenic, athletic, and dysplastic types.

Sheldon: Ectomorphic, mesomorphic, and endomorphic types.

Constrictive Spiral of Anxiety. See *Anxiety, Constrictive Spiral* of.

Constrictive Spiral Concept. The endeavors of some individuals to deal with or to escape from their anxiety can result in an increasingly constrictive effect upon their living. Sometimes a vicious circle may become established.

For example, a person may experience an Acute Anxiety Attack in a subway. Associating the acute discomfort with the subway, he may subsequently try to avoid subways as a way of preventing a repetition. Perhaps he continues such a policy of avoidance. Subsequent attacks of anxiety may occur, as is only too likely. Other related sites may come to be similarly avoided. The gradual result can be a progressive restriction of his activities, as more and more places, experiences, or situations are avoided in his continued but futile efforts to escape his anxiety.

This type of response with a resulting progressive constriction of living is not uncommon. It may progress very slowly and gradually, or its tempo can become rapid. The vicious circle may begin when the avoidance of the situation (which is feared will result in a repetition of the dreaded anxiety) in turn results in new conflicts.

Constructive Aggression. See *Aggression, Constructive.*

Constructive Anxiety Concept. Anxiety can be the basis of much creative effort, for it is often in response to his anxieties that man looks to the future and seeks to improve things. This may be part of his efforts to make his life more secure, less dangerous, and less anxious.

The drives which impel man to seek security are very compelling ones. Anxiety is the force that moves men to sublimate the natural unfettered expression of their basic desires, which seem so full of dangerous possible consequences, retaliation, or punishment. From this point of view anxiety may be regarded as laying the basis for many socially constructive and civilizing efforts.

Anxiety is an important force in character formation and personality development. From this standpoint also, anxiety can be viewed in a broad sense as exerting a constructive influence (within certain limits). It may counteract apathy and halt tendencies toward the stagnation of self-satisfaction.

Anxiety may be considered as a constructive force tending to advance individual personal adjustment and socialization. Thus, the uneasiness and apprehension (anxiety) aroused by the disapproval of parents, the "significant adults," are emotions which often tend to bring about constructive change in the infant. Thus, to a point, anxiety may be a socializing influence, a promoter of acculturation. See also *anxiety.*

convergence. The name for the phenomenon by which association shows a tendency toward pointing in a similar direction; i.e., they *converge* toward the central problem or meaning as, for example, in the attempted interpretation of dreams in therapy through the study of the free associations produced by the patient as he relates his dream and as he thinks of segments of it.

Conversion. (1) The unconscious process through which intrapsychic conflicts, which would otherwise give rise to anxiety if they gained consciousness, instead secure symbolic external expression. The ideas or impulses which are consciously disowned, plus elements of the psychologic defenses against them, are changed, transmuted, or converted into a variety of physical, physiologic, behavioral and psychologic manifestations. (1) Concept introduced by Breuer and Freud after 1890, but considerably broadened since. (2) A major mental mechanism operating outside of and beyond conscious-awareness which is basic to the evolvement of the Conversion Reaction.

autonomic c. Conversion into an autonomic expression or "language" of the repressed emotional conflict. This expression is principally mediated via the autonomic (or vegetative) nervous system.

behavioral c. The expression in neurotic behavior of elements of intrapsychic conflict in acting-out, or behavioral language.

physiologic c. An emotional illness in which the consciously disowned impulses, and/or other elements of the unconscious conflict over them, are transmuted into symbolic physiologic expression. The functional symptoms which result serve to allay anxiety by maintaining repression and by seeking resolution or some relief of unconscious conflicts.

As hysterical conversion is the expression of the unconscious conflict into somatic "bodily language," with the formation of physical symptoms, in analogous fashion physiologic conversion is the expression of unconscious conflicts into "physiologic language," with the formation of physiologic symptoms. *See p. 655.*

psychologic c. The expression of the unconscious conflict into psychologic language with the formation of psychologic symptoms. A psychogenic manifestation or illness in which the consciously disowned impulses and/or other elements of the unconscious conflict over them are transmuted (converted) into symbolic psychologic expression. The psychologic symptoms which result serve to allay anxiety by maintaining repression, and by seeking resolution or some relief from the pressure of the unconscious conflicts.

somatic c. (Hysteria). An emotional illness in which the consciously disowned impulses and/or other elements of the unconscious conflict over them, are transmuted into (and so as to secure) symbolic somatic expression. The body symptoms which result serve to allay anxiety by maintaining repression and by seeking resolution of unconscious conflicts.

conversion hysteria. See *Neurosis, Conversion hysteria; Conversion Reaction.*

Conversion (or Hysterical) **Personality.** The descriptive term for a type of personality structure in which there is present a pattern of several of the conversion group of personality traits or defenses. Often present are egocentricity, coquetry, appeal, charm, readiness to quick friendships, elasticity, impulsiveness, suggestibility, dependency, and warmth. Sometimes also characterized as being immature, and emotionally labile, with strong dependency needs, and a flair for the dramatic. Seeks attention, and may be impulsive and demanding.

Conversion Reaction. An emotional illness in which consciously intolerable and disowned impulses and/or elements of the conflict over them, are transmuted or "converted" unconsciously so as to secure symbolic external expression in organs or parts of the body, usually those that are mainly under voluntary control. See *Neurosis, Conversion hysteria,* and *Conversion.*

Conversion Reactions as a diagnostic group most properly include those emotional illnesses which are marked by prominent symptoms of physiologic or somatic conversion. Where the major symptoms develop as behavioral or psychologic conversion, the illness is better classified elsewhere.

convulsion. A fit. Major generalized involuntary muscular contractions or spasms.

convulsive disorders. Primarily include grand mal, petit mal, Jacksonian, and psychomotor epilepsy. Also to be included are certain minor or equivalent states: prolonged drowsiness, torpor, stupor, coma, and twilight states. Personality disturbances may be associated with convulsive disorders.

coordination. Harmonious working together.

coprophagia. Eating of filth or feces.

coprophilia. Love of filth or feces, or excessive or morbid interest therein.

coprophobia. The morbid fear or revulsion to feces or dirt See *Phobia.*

cortex. The outer layer. Cerebral cortex, the outer layer of the brain.

countertransference. The (partly unconscious) emotional reaction of the therapist to his patient. Usually is partly in response to the transference of the patient as well as including the therapist's own repressed distortions of the relationship. The nonrational emotional response of the therapist to the patient in the treatment situation. Roughly the converse of transference. See *Transference.*

couvade. In certain cultures, the enactment of the birth process by the male.

cranial nerves. The following twelve pairs of nerves which issue directly from centers in the brain:

973

I. Olfactory	VII. Facial
II. Optic	VIII. Acoustic
III. Oculomotor	IX. Glossopharyngeal
IV. Trochlear	X. Vagus
V. Trigeminal	XI. Accessory
VI. Abducens	XII. Hypoglossal

cretinism. Bodily malformation from thyroid deficiency, often accompanied by mental defectiveness.

critical attack of anxiety. See *Anxiety, Critical Attack.*

culture. The social heritage. Material culture includes all technologic achievements. Nonmaterial culture includes the values, customs, institutions and social organizations.

Cultural Ratio, Direct, Concept of. The greater the cultural pressures, the higher the incidence of Depressive Reactions. See Depressive Reactions, pp. 135-224.

Cultural-Vogue Concept in Character Reactions. See *Character Reactions, Cultural Vogue In Conversion Reactions.*

cunniligus. Stimulation of female genitals by the use of mouth and tongue.

cybernetics. The science of control mechanisms. It covers the entire field of communication and control in machines. Norbert Wiener (1894–1964) pointed out similarities between the human nervous system and electronic control devices. Cybernetics applies to the ways in which mathematical and engineering principles are applied to human thought and communication.

cyclothymic personality. This type of person is characterized by frequently alternating moods of elation and sadness. The mood swings are out of proportion to apparent stimuli. They result from internal (psychologic) causes rather than from external events, although external events may play an important precipitating role.

cynophobia. The morbid fear of dogs. See *Phobia.*

D

Dawn Insomnia. See *Insomnia.*

daydream. A type of fantasy (*q.v.*) in which the individual gives himself over to idle, indulgent and wishful thinking. Overindulgence in this type of fantasy may become so marked as to be a psychotic symptom, as in schizophrenia.

Death, Emotional. See *Emotional Death.*

death instinct. The concept of an individual unconscious drive toward dissolution and death. According to certain theories, its inversion enters into suicide, while its outward expression is aggression and hostility sometimes leading to murder.

decompensation, emotional. Breakdown of an emotional adjustment previously stable, or of a defensive system seemingly adequate.

decussation. The crossing of nerve fibers from one side to the other. Usually occurs simultaneously from each side to the other.

Defense-Hypertrophy, Principle of. A useful defensively-intended character trait, originally elaborated protectively and subserving a useful purpose, develops too far and becomes self-defeating and personally handicapping. See *Character Reactions.*

defense mechanism. (1) A psychologic reaction aimed at protection against a stressful environmental situation. A defense against anxiety. (2) Any one of a number of psychologic techniques adopted by the ego for warding off anxiety. A psychologic protection against inner stress. See *Mental Mechanism.*

Defensive Over-reaction, Concept of. Psychic and physiologic over-reactions, defensively intended, can lead to all manner of emotional and functional symptoms.

defense, primary. See *Primary defense.*

defense, secondary. See *Secondary defense.*

dejá vu. A specific variation of depersonalization in which one feels undue familiarity, as though a person, place, or situation has been seen or experienced before. *Dejá entendu* is a related carryover to that of having already been heard.

delinquency. In general terms is used to indicate socially nonconforming behavior in a minor. May include asocial, antisocial, and illegal conduct.

delirium. A disturbance in mentation and sensorium in which there is disorientation and confusion. May occur in febrile states, with drugs, or in intoxication. Hallucinations may be present. Delirium may be physical, chemical, or psychologic in origin. Examples: the delirium of fever, delirium tremens (alcohol), bromide intoxication.

delirium tremens. An acute and frightening delirium occurring in severe chronic alcoholism upon withdrawal of alcohol.

delusion. A false belief which is out of keeping with the person's level of knowledge. It is maintained against logical argument and despite objectively contradictory evidence. An evaluation must be made in relation to culture. A delusion is a false belief which is not considered tenable by one's associates.

   d. of grandeur. Exaggerated ideas of one's importance or identity.

   d. of persecution. Ideas that one has been singled out for persecution. See *Paranoia*.

   d. of reference. Incorrect assumption that certain casual or unrelated remarks or the behavior of others applies to oneself. See also *Ideas of reference*.

dementia. An older term denoting madness or insanity, being "out of one's mind." It was especially used to convey the presence of intellectual impairment. Generally used to refer to the advanced chronic and established cases of psychotic illness. These may have been organically or psychologically determined. Current use especially infers organic loss of intellectual functioning.

dementia praecox. An older descriptive term for schizophrenia. Now largely obsolete. The term is no longer used officially. See *Schizophrenia*.

dementia, senile. A chronic brain disorder. The responsible organic pathology is a generalized atrophy of the brain. This is accompanied by a "falling out" of nerve cells, increased glia formation, the presence of senile plaques, and neurofibrillary changes. Clinically it is insidious in onset, and is characterized by deterioration in intellectual functions, such as confusion, disorientation, and memory defects. The disease generally begins later in life than arteriosclerotic brain disease, but mixed pathologic pictures are frequent. An older term for *Senile psychosis* (q.v.).

Denial. A primitive, or "lower-order," mental mechanism operating outside of and beyond conscious awareness in the endeavor to resolve emotional conflict and to allay consequent anxiety, by denying one or more of the elements of the conflict.

Dependency Dilemma of Childhood. The infant subconsciously 'recognizes' that the object of its rage is also the cherished love object, upon whom he is also totally dependent and which he cannot attack or destroy. The conflict is of considerable magnitude.

dependency needs. Vital infantile needs for mothering, love, affection, shelter, protection, security, food, and warmth. May continue into subsequent years in overt or hidden forms, or increase as a regressive manifestation. They are not necessarily pathologic.

depersonalization. Feelings of unreality or strangeness. Depersonalization is a dissociative phenomenon. There are two major clinical types of depersonalization: the environmental and the personal.

   environmental d. The changes seem to be external, in the world about oneself. Some minor or major part or aspect of the environment seems strange or unreal.

   personal d. Subjective feelings of the loss of personal identity. These may be partial, include various aspects, or be massive. The person feels unreal. Included, for example, are feelings that one is no longer himself, that he has changed, that something about him is different or strange, or that he has become someone else.

Depletion Concept of Anxiety. See *Anxiety*.

depression. The term used for a widely, if not universally experienced emotional symptom. As employed to describe an emotional feeling or symptom, depression refers to *lowered spirits or a depressed mood. Emotional depression is an affect of undue sadness, dejection, or melancholy. Clinically, the lowered spirits appear out of proportion to the stimuli, as determined by the ordinary means of observation. This is because the origins of the feelings are internal, as opposed to external.*

In contradistinction, the terms of sadness and grief are more usually employed to describe emotional reactions to external loss. These reactions are more or less realistic and proportionate to what has been lost. Sadness and grief are to fear, as depression is to anxiety. In both grief and fear *the stimulus is external and consciously recognized, and the response is proportionate*. In depression, as in anxiety, the real source of the emotion is largely unknown and unrecognized. It is intrapsychic, and it stems from unconscious emotional conflict.

agitated d. Depression accompanied by anxiety, psychomotor activity, and great restlessness or agitation.

anxious d. An emotional reaction in which there is concurrent anxiety and depression. The presence of anxiety denotes the incompleteness of the defense of depression. Clinically, the reaction can vary from a mild one to the other extreme of an Agitated Depression of psychotic depth.

completion d. A variant of Depression of Success, marked by the potential for emotional and physical letdown following the completion of a great time-filling and absorbing undertaking or project.

diffuse retardation in d. Concept of. Retardation of thought, mental activity, and physical-physiologic activity permeates the adjustment and defenses in clinical depression.

Direct Cultural Ratio, Concept of. The greater the cultural pressures, the higher the incidence of Depressive Reactions.

Frozen State of Rage. Depression may sometimes be referred to as a Frozen State of Rage. Frustration and loss, and rage which does not subjectively exist in conscious awareness, may be unconsciously transmuted into depression, Emotional Fatigue, and the Fatigue States.

involutional d. (In older terminology, melancholia.) Frequently accompanying menopause in women, or decline in sexual or vocational activity in men. Usually characterized by agitation or paranoid thinking.

One-Day d. A brief depressive episode marked by a depressive mood and/or physiologic equivalents of depression. sion.

primal d. The early primordial depressive response in infancy to intense frustration denial of needs. It establishes an antecedent pattern for depressive reactions in later life.

promotion d. A type of reactive situational depression which is occasionally seen to follow a promotion in civil or military life.

Psychotic d. (1) The very severe depression in which contact with reality is more or less broken. Other psychotic manifestations may be present. (See psychosis). (2) Any depression of a psychotic level or depth.

reactive d. (1) A depression resulting from such traumatic events as the loss of a loved one or a treasured relationship, or the failure to achieve a highly desired goal. (2) A depressive neurotic reaction which follows a specific traumatic situation, event, or loss. The event which it follows serves an important function in the precipitation of the illness, as opposed to being its cause *per se*.

Recurrence Principle. In the absence of substantial changes in psychologic adjustment, character structure, or both, depression is likely to recur at some future date.

retarded d. Depression accompanied by slowed thinking, speech, and movements.

situational d. Reactive depression.

success d. The seemingly paradoxical depression which sometimes follows the achievement of what appears to ordinary observation to be a considerable success. On a deeper symbolic level, the success or goal achieved unconsciously equates a most vital loss to the individual concerned.

depression à deux. Simultaneous clinical depression in two closely related persons.

depressive personality. The descriptive term for a type of personality structure in which there is present a pattern of several of the depressive group of personality traits or defenses. These may or may not be sufficiently marked to cause interference with living, a loss of efficiency, or a limitation or normal satisfactions or social adjustment. When they are, this constitutes the depressive type of Character Neurosis.

The Depressive Personality is one major constellation of character defenses. The depressive group of character or personality traits includes overseriousness, lowered spirits, increased vulnerability to letdown or disappointment, overconscientiousness, dependability, compliance, subservience, and deliberateness.

depth psychology. Systems of psychology which deal with intrapsychic phenomena, as opposed to those which are primarily concerned with more superficial, i.e., behavioral, phenomena.

dereistic. Mental activity not in accordance with reality, that does not follow logic or experience. Dereistic ideas are not so personalized as autistic ones.

derepression. The coming back of ideas or impulses into conscious awareness which were earlier pushed from such awareness into the unconscious because they were personally intolerable. Derepression threatens when the psychic energy of the repressed material becomes too strong or when the repressing forces prove inadequate. The threat of derepression results in an increase of the strength of existing character defensive traits or symptoms or, should these prove insufficient, in the development of new ones.

descriptive psychiatry. Psychiatry based upon the observation and study of external factors which can be readily seen, felt, or heard, as differentiated from dynamic psychiatry.

Destructive Aggression. See *Aggression, destructive.*

Deterioration. (1) In mental illness, the progressive disintegration of intellectual and/or emotional functions. Is often progressive and may or may not be irreversible. It is also used to refer to functional mental loss accompanying destructive organic brain lesions. (2) Deterioration is also used to describe the chronic progressive downhill course (or the level reached) in a psychic kind of deterioration as seen in the psychoses, especially schizophrenia. The term *emotional deterioration* may be used to describe the clinical picture in psychosis in which the patient appears apathetic, and loses his interest in his appearance, environment, and social adjustment.

determinism. (1) A scientific doctrine by which nothing in the emotional or mental life, as well as in the physical world, happens by chance alone. Every event and everything that happens is the result of specific causes or forces even though they may be deeply hidden from conscious awareness. (2) Used sometimes to refer to predetermination and preordination, the belief that things and events have been already settled by fate.

detumescence. The lessening or subsiding of congestion and swelling. Especially used to refer to erectile tissue of sexual organs.

devaluation. A defensive operation, sometimes a variant of Rationalization, by which one unconsciously endeavors to downgrade the emotional significance of an event in retrospect.

Developmental Influences in Mental Capabilities, Hypothesis of. The level of intelligence may be improved through favorable environmental influences, particularly the interpersonal ones.

diaschisis. Disease in one portion of the nervous system has led to disturbed function in another portion.

diathesis. Strictly speaking, an inherited predisposition to an illness or a disease. Now used more generally to indicate a physical or emotional predisposition to an emotional or physical illness.

dilapidation. Advanced deterioration.

diplegia. Paralysis of both arms or both legs.

diplopia. Double vision.

dipsomania. (1) Periodic episodes of compulsive drinking, frequently associated with behavior disturbances. (2) Periodic behavior disturbances brought on by consumption of alcohol.

disorientation. The loss of awareness of the position of oneself in relation to space, time, or persons.

displacement. (1) A conscious process in which emotion is transferred or "displaced" to a new object. (2) A mental mechanism operating outside of and beyond conscious awareness in which an emotional feeling is transferred from its actual internal object to a substitute and external one. In phobias, by the mechanism of displacement, there is an automatic transfer of fear and threat from its original hidden and internal (unconscious) source to another which is external and apparently completely unrelated in so far as the patient is consciously concerned. Displacement is an important process in the protective distortion of the latent content of dreams.

dissimulation. Pretense, deceit, false behavior or demeanor.

dissociation. A psychologic separation or splitting off. Concepts of psychologic dissociation are used widely in psychiatry. They include the following:
(1) As a *mental mechanism* dissociation may be defined as an intrapsychic defensive process which operates automatically outside of and beyond conscious awareness. Through its operation, the emotional significance and affect is separated and detached (i.e., split off or dissociated) from an idea, situation, or object. This may represent an unconscious deferment or postponement of the emotional impact. (2) *Side-by-side dissociation* of simultaneously conducted mental or physical activities. (3) The dissociation from consciousness and control (of the individual mental representation) of a specific physical function. Illustrated in certain of the Somatic Conversions (Conversion Hysteria). (4) The analogous dissociation of a physiologic area. Illustrated in certain of the Physiologic Conversions. (5) The dissociation of a fragment of an *area of consciousness.* Examples: Depersonalization, fainting, certain episodes of Amnesia, Automatic Behavior, and hypnotic phenomena. (6) The massive kind of *alternating dissociation* in which a major area of the personality splits off and takes over control and direction. Examples: certain amnesias, fugue states, and the very rare alternating personality.

dissociation, alternating. Following the splitting of the stream of consciousness, one part takes over the control and direction of the whole personality.

Dissociation of Automaticity. The automatic carrying through of some specific type of activity. Exemplified in phenomenon of automatic writing.

dissociation, B.B.C. Braid-Berheim-Charcot Dissociation; that which is deliberately induced, elicited, or brought on by suggestion or through hypnosis.

dissociation, Bleuler's (or **schizophrenic dissociation**). See *dissociation, schizophrenic.*

dissociation, Breuer's. Dissociation from consciousness and control (of the individual representation) of a specific physical function.

dissociation, Janet's. The splitting away of an area of consciousness and behavior which is ordinarily repressed, but which becomes evident during the course of conversion (hysterical) attacks.

dissociation, side-by-side. A splitting of the stream of consciousness into simultaneously functioning parts. Separate mental or physical activities are carried on at the same time.

Dissociative Reactions. Include Dissociation, Double Personality, Depersonalization, psychologic Amnesias, Somnambulism, Fugue States, and Hypnotic phenomena.

distortion. (1) A prime mechanism in the dream which, along with condensation, symbolism, and overdetermination, aids in the disguise of unacceptable data and in the maintenance of repression. (2) A perception or conception which is viewed in an inaccurate and changed (i.e., distorted) light by the individual concerned. Psychologically significant distortions are outside of conscious awareness of the patient and serve a defensive purpose. Properly speaking, distortion is an unconscious change. Misrepresentation or perversion of the original intrapsychic affect, drive or aim.

parataxic d. Sullivan's term for certain distortions in judgment and perception, particularly in interpersonal relations. These are based upon the need to perceive objects and relationships in a particular way, in accord with a pattern from earlier experience. Earlier limitations in perception and resulting distortions occurred as part of the attempted defense against anxiety. Current relationships are interpreted according to earlier impressions which were formed as a consequence of the relationships with significant people in early years. From small cues which are extended, the new person or parts of him come to be automatically viewed and reacted to as though he were the earlier one. This is similar to transference in the analytic therapy situation. It has application to many additional relationships.

distractibility. A state in which the stream of thought or talk is readily diverted (i.e., distracted) from its original goal. Almost any chance occurrence in the environment may serve as a stimulus.

distributive analysis. The analysis of the psychobiologic school. Refers to the guided and directed extensive investigation and analysis of the patient's entire past experience and his assets and liabilities. Reliance is not made upon the spontaneous free association techniques of psychoanalysis.

Dix, Dorothea Linde (1802–1887). An American pioneer in the crusade to improve the hospital care of the mentally ill.

dizygotic. Twins from separate ova.

dolicomorphic. A long, thin, asthenic body type.

dominance. Control; overshadowing (i.e., dominating). In heredity, the overshadowing prominence of a particular inherited characteristic. Recessive traits, while they may be simultaneously present, are obscured and not in evidence, or less in evidence, because of overshadowing dominant traits.

Don Juan. A legendary lover and seducer. Occasionally used to denote compulsive or anxiety-driven sexual overactivity.

double personality. A rare, major dissociative reaction in which the patient leads two lives independently, usually alternately, with neither personality aware of the other. Each seemingly possesses the ability to function separately and independently, while the other is kept submerged for a time. It is also known as alternating or dual personality. It is the ultimate pathologic dissociative progression from clinical amnesia and the fugue state. See *Alternating Personality*.

Dream's Contribution to Emotional Health, Hypothesis of. Dreaming is likely a requisite to health, providing among other benefits: (1) partial discharge in symbolic fashion of otherwise forbidden thought or urges, (2) effecting emotional compromises, to this extent, (3) securing this kind of interaction with unconscious data, and (4) aiding in the maintenance of repression.

drive. In psychiatry, a term for motivation; a basic urge.

Durham Decision. A decision of the U.S. Court of Appeals, for the District of Columbia, which found that an individual was not liable for the commission of an unlawful act if such act was the consequence of a psychopathologic state.

In Federal courts it supplants the earlier precedent of the McNaughton Rule. This decision was the result of centering psychiatric testimony on the presence or absence of a psychopathologic process. See *McNaughton Rule*.

dynamic psychiatry (as distinguished from descriptive psychiatry). Particularly related to the study of emotional processes, their origins, and the mental mechanisms. The study of dynamic psychiatry implies the study of the active, energy-laden, and changing factors in human behavior, as opposed to the older, more static and descriptive study of clinical patterns, symptoms, and classification. As an adjective, dynamic indicates energy potential, constant change, mutual interaction, shifting emphasis, and development. Dynamic principles are those which are forceful, driving, and compelling. They convey the concepts of change, of evolution, and of progression or regression.

dynamics. (1) The determination of how an emotional or a behavior pattern comes to be. The mechanisms of the unconscious development of emotional reactions. A noun which refers to the intrapsychic mechanisms of defense, the mental mechanisms. (2) The sequence and relationship of the psychologic factors entering into and producing emotional illness, complexes, mental mechanisms, and behavior disturbances. More properly Psychodynamics.

dynamism. A mental mechanism. See *Mental Mechanism*.

dysarthria. Impaired, usually difficult speech. Usually due to organic disorders of the nervous system. Sometimes applied to emotional speech difficulties, such as stammering and stuttering.

dysbulia. Impaired will power.

dysergasia. A psychobiologic term for a behavior disorder due to toxic organic changes in the nervous system.

dysesthesia. Disturbance of tactile sensation.

dysgeusia. Disturbance of taste.

dyskinesia. Disturbances of coordination and motor activity in the voluntary muscular system. Includes tics, tremors, spasms, and convulsions.

dyslogia. Incoherence.

dyspareunia. Painful intercourse in the female.

dysphagia. A hysterical symptom of difficulty or inability to swallow.

dysplasia. Abnormal development of the body or some special part of the body.

dysplastic. Disproportionate. (A Kretschmer body type).

dystonia. Impaired muscular tonus.

dystrophy. Disturbed development and nutrition of a body part.

E

E.C.T. (or **E.S.T.**). Electroconvulsive or electroshock therapy. See also *Electroshock therapy.*

E.E.G. Electroencephalogram (*q.v.*).

E.O.A. Emotional-object amalgam (*q.v.*).

E.O.C. Emotional-organic combination in a given illness or symptom.

E.P.I. Emotional-physiologic illness (*q.v.*).

E.S.P. Extra-sensory perception (*q.v.*).

echolalia. The automatic repetition by some psychotic patients of phrases or words said in their presence. Echolalia is observed in certain schizophrenic disorders. Implies an automatic, compliant kind of obedience, as opposed to the hostility sometimes implied in mimicry or imitation. It may be employed as one type of psychotic defense, in avoiding more meaningful verbal communication.

echopraxia. An automatic and compliant kind of imitation of movements of others by certain psychotic patients. To be distinguished from a more hostile or defiant kind of imitation or mimicry by non-psychotic persons.

ecology. The branch of science dealing with the geographic distribution of living organisms, especially of humans, and their interrelationship with their environment.

economics. A term sometimes carried over to psychiatry to help convey certain concepts. For example: (1) "Psychologically economic" or "psychologically uneconomic." An assessment made according to the net psychologic return to the individual concerned of certain operations, behavior symptoms, or character traits. It is made following the relative evaluation of all the contributing factors which can be ascertained, and the overall total consequences to the individual. (2) In psychoanalytic theory, it may be employed in assessing the relative distribution of libido and its balance between the pleasure principle, the death instincts, and possibly the repetition-compulsion.

ectoderm. The outer of the three layers of the embryo. From the ectoderm are developed the skin and its appendages, the sensory organs, the brain, and the nervous system.

ectomorph (Sheldon). A type of person characterized by the predominant development of the ectoderm. Accordingly, he would be presumably sensitive and hyperactive.

Edipus complex. See *Complex, Oedipus.*

Effect-over-Cause in sexual maladjustment, Concept of. See *Sexual Maladjustment.*

efferent. Outward; centrifugal. An efferent nerve conveys impulses *from* the interior *to* the exterior.

effort syndrome. A term sometimes used to describe certain syndromes of war in which there is anxiety, lassitude, emotional fatigue, and fatigability.

ego. (1) Roughly, the "I," referring to oneself; the individual; the real or conscious self. (2) The central part of the personality which senses and deals with the reality of the external world and is influenced by social forces. The ego modifies behavior by largely unconscious compromise between the primitive instinctual drives (i.e., id) and the conscience (i.e., superego). The ego serves as the mediator and also as the battleground between the internal (unconscious) impulses on the one hand, and the personal standards plus the demands and standards of society on the other hand.

ego analysis. The intensive therapeutic study and analysis of the ways in which the ego resolves or attempts to deal with intrapsychic conflicts. Deals especially with the evolvement and employment of mental dynamisms or mechanisms which the person unconsciously employs, and with the maturation of capacity for rational thought and action.

egocentric. An adjective referring to an overly self-centered attitude. The ego or self tends to be made the center of things for the person concerned.

ego-dystonic. Having the quality of disrupting or disintegrating the ego or its healthy functions. May be applied to any factor which has a destructive vs. a constructive effect upon the ego or self.

ego ideal. (1) the body of conscious aspirations and goals of the individual; the pattern of what one would like to be. (2) In psychoanalytic theory, an unconscious part of the ego, a result of the development of parental substitutes. It is technically regarded as a later elaboration than the formation of the superego. Through identification and introjection, certain idealized aspects of a significant adult, usually from childhood, are taken over to become aims of the self or ego.

Narcissistic e.i. In psychoanalytic theory, a mental image of perfection early constructed unconsciously of himself by the child. A regression to the narcissistic ego ideal may occur from the ego ideals which are developed later through the unconscious operation of the mental mechanisms of identification, idealization and introjection. May be applied to any factor which has a constructive vs. a destructive effect upon the ego or self.

ego instincts. A group of so-called instincts hypothesized in accord with a concept that certain of the drives in man for power, prestige, position, and acquisition have a basis in instinct.

The relative validity of this concept has been debated.

egoism: A self-seeking for advantage at the expense of others; over-evaluation of the self.

egomania. Pathologic self-centeredness and selfishness.

ego-syntonic. Having the quality of holding together or integrating the ego and its functions. May be applied to any factor which has a constructive vs. a destructive effect upon the ego or self. In the healthy ego there would ordinarily be a preponderance of ego syntonic factors.

eidetic image. (1) An unusually vivid, elaborate, and exact mental image which follows a visual stimulus. An eidetic image may be part of a fantasy. (2) Sometimes used to describe a memory so unusually vivid that an experience or experiences are recalled with almost photographic precision and detail.

ejaculatio praecox. The premature ejaculation by the male in coitus at some point prior to orgasm of the female. Often occurs at the beginning of intercourse or even before.

ejaculation. A sudden and forceful ejection. Sexually, ejaculation is the discharge of semen by the male at the time of orgasm in sexual relations.

elaboration. A psychologic principle of expansion and greater detail. In dreams, for instance, it is somewhat the converse of condensation. A symbol (i.e., part of the *manifest* content of a dream) may be elaborated and become more complex, more inclusive, more detailed, and expanded as part of the distortion and disguise of what it actually represents (i.e., part of the *latent* content of the dream).

Electra complex. The attachment of the female child for her father and resulting feelings. Roughly the female equivalent of the Oedipus complex.

Electroencephalogram (E.E.G.). A recording of minute electrical impulses arising from the activity of cells in the cerebral cortex of the brain.

Electroconvulsive therapy. E.C.T. or E.S.T. See *Electroshock therapy.*

electronarcosis. A form of electroshock treatment. See *Shock treatment.*

electroshock therapy. The administration of a series of low voltage electrical impulses to the brain by means of electrodes placed on the patient's head, usually over each temple. Usually a coma is produced, with convulsions. Has its greatest indication for use in the psychotic depressions, and secondarily in certain other psychotic episodes of acute onset. Various reasons have been advanced for the results which are obtained, none of which has been universally accepted. See also *Shock treatment.*

electrostimulation. A form of electroshock treatment. See *Shock treatment.*

E.M. (W. B. Cannon). The "emergency mobilization" in preparation for fight or flight.

emotion. (1) A subjective feeling (of which one may or may not be aware), such as fear, anger, grief, joy, and love. (2) A strong affect. There are often important concomitant physical and physiologic changes, such as pounding heart, dry mouth, increased perspiration, etc., which may also be more or less in awareness.

emotional amalgam. In symptom formation there is the unconscious attempt to bind, as in an *"emotional amalgam,"* to neutralize, to deny, or to counteract the anxiety.

emotional conflict. The clash which takes place between one's moral, social, and personal standards on the one hand, and one's egocentric and instinctual strivings—self-preservative, acquisitive, reproductive, aggressive, and destructive drives; the personal desires, needs, and strivings for possession, anger, love, and sex—on the other. The underlying presence of intrapsychic conflict with the resulting tension, attempted defenses, and sought-after resolution and its disguised outward expression is to be recognized today as the *central dynamic concept in the origin of the neurotic and the functional psychotic emotional illnesses.* Emotional conflict may be conscious, partly conscious, or beyond conscious awareness.

Emotional Contagion. (1) The intuitive communication of an emotion from a significant adult to an infant or child. (2) The "contagion" of emotional reactions, as in the "conversion epidemic," or contagious tainting.

Emotional Contagion of Anxiety. See *Anxiety.*

Emotional Death, Concept of. Physical collapse and death may follow prolonged, acute and unbearable Anxiety Attack, with no demonstrable organic change or pathology. Unconscious factors can contribute to or lead to death in organic, emotional-organic combinations (E.O.C.), and occasionally perhaps, in emotional situations alone.

Emotional decompensation, Concept of. When character defenses prove inadequate or breakdown, a state of emotional decompensation exists.

Emotional Depression. See *Depression, emotional.*

Emotional dissociation. See *dissociation, emotional.*

Emotional Exploitation, Concept of. The unconscious use of a child by a parent or parent surrogate as a major source of emotional support and gratification. May become extreme enough to be almost a reversal of the usual parent-child relationship. May lay psychologic foundations for later major emotional illness.

emotional fatigue. The fairly common type of tiredness or weariness which is out of proportion to the actual amount of physical or mental activity performed. The sources of this kind of fatigue are traceable to emotional origins. See *Fatigue.*

emotional health. A state of being which is relative rather than absolute. In general, the person who is emotionally healthy has effected a reasonably satisfactory integration of his instinctual drives. He has worked out psychologically harmonious solutions for them which are acceptable to himself, and to his social milieu.

This is reflected in: (1) the satisfactory nature of his personal relationships, (2) his cheerful and willing acceptance of social responsibilities, (3) his level of satisfaction in living, (4) his flexibility in adjusting to new situations, (5) his effectiveness—his actual achievements, in relation to his realistic capacities and endowment, (6) the absence of handicapping and limiting symptoms, or character defense traits, (7) his achievement of a reasonable degree of emotional equanimity, (8) his ability to react constrictively to threat or danger, (9) a reasonably realistic subjective appraisal and judgment of any personal "wrong-doing, and the absence of neurotic needs for self-punishment or penance, and (10) the relative level of maturity which he has achieved.

emotional health, Dream's contribution. See *Dream's contribution to emotion.*

Emotional Health, Law of Relativity of. Everyone has problems and suffers at least at times from disturbed and painful emotions, which vary greatly in quantity and quality. The degree of resulting interference with living is a highly individual matter. Emotional health is relative and a matter of degree or level. It is not merely present or absent.

Emotional Health, Principle of Trend Toward. There is a strong, rather fundamental and steadily operative human drive toward emotional health.

Emotional Illness, Concept of the Origin of. The underlying presence of intrapsychic conflict with resulting tension, attempted defenses, and sought-after resolution and its disguised outward expression is to be recognized as the central dynamic concept in the origin of neurotic and functional psychotic emotional illnesses.

emotional instability. A pattern of overreaction emotionally in response to what appear ordinarily to be rather minor stresses. Usually the result is a decreased level of effectiveness.

emotional-object amalgam. The emotional compound which is formed by the close association and attachment of an emotional charge together with its object. It is the union of emotion or emotional significance which has become firmly joined together with a person, event, object, or circumstance. Example: In phobias, the joining of the free or poorly attached anxiety, often at the time of the critical attack, through displacement to the new and uncon-sciously selected external phobic object. The relative stability of the new union of emotion and object is indicated by the term.

emotional paralysis. (1) A symptom as encountered in Somatic Conversion. (2) The stasis or inaction due to opposing psychic drives of equal strength.

Emotional-Physiologic Illness, E.P.I. An emotional illness, with prominent accompanying physiologic changes as an integral part of the total reaction.

Emotional Recapitulation, Concept of. At times *symptoms which were originally present on an organic basis, recur later or continue in whole or in part, on an emotional basis.* This is an interesting phenomenon. A number of intrapsychic processes may be involved, including: (1) conditioning, (2) auto-suggestion, (3) conversion, and (4) the provision of a more convenient, familiar, and thus easily-adopted (pre-existing) symptom pattern. (Pp. 116–117).

emotional symptoms. See *Symptoms, emotional.*

empatheia. (1) The very close sharing of the experiences or subjective emotional feelings of another person. Such an ability can result in one's subjective emotional feelings approximately *corresponding* with those of the second person. (2) An effective kind of automatic simultaneous, close identification with another. Empatheia is stronger, deeper, and closer than sympathy. (3) Actually *compathy (qv.)*, which is preferred.

empathy. An objective and intellectualized awareness and understanding of the feelings, emotions, and behavior of another person, and/or their meaning and significance. Empathy is a form of intellectual and *projective* identification. *Empatheia* and genuine *sympathy* are forms of *affective* identification, as is *compathy, (q.v.)*

encephalitis. Inflammation of the brain.

encephalomalacia. Softening of the brain.

encephalopathy, boxer's. *Punch Drunk.*

endocrine glands. An important group of glands which produce vital internal regulatory secretions. The endocrine glands are ductless. They secrete hormones which control growth and metabolism.

endoderm. The inner of the three major layers of the embryo. From the endoderm are derived the splachnic structures, most of the viscera, and internal organs.

endogain, of emotional illness. The strictly internal and ordinarily deeply-hidden psychologic gains which are the very basis of the illness. These gains and the need for them are responsible for the initiation of the illness. The endogain can be said to be the avoidance of conflict and anxiety. The symptoms are part of the endogain and develop in its service. Thus, the endogain or primary gain, of a symptom basically, is the defense it provides against anxiety. The secondary gain in turn is the material advantage later secured from the symptom after its establishment. When this advantage is secure outside of conscious awareness it is the epigain.

endogain, of symptoms. On a deeper level, the physical and psychologic restrictions are in part a final desperate safeguard as an unconscious attempt to inhibit action. By this means, control over hidden and feared destructive impulses is continued and reinforced. (As one example: One cannot easily kick another person with a leg which has become paralyzed and useless!)

endogenous. Arising from inside the body.

endomorph (Sheldon). A type of person characterized by the predominant development of the endoderm. Accordingly, he would be presumably characterized by prominent visceral development: stout, pleasure-seeking, interested in food, but subject to mood swings.

engram. The supposed traces which may be left in the nervous system following any experience. A memory trace.

enuresis. Involuntary bedwetting while asleep, continued past the usual age of establishing bladder control.

eonism. Female behavior in a male.

epicritic sensitivity. The ability to sense fine variations in touch. Epicritic sensitivity is tested by determining the relative appreciation of light touch, temperature changes, and point-to-point distances.

epigain. (1) The *unconscious* secondary gain of emotional illness. Epigain is externally directed to secure favorable environmental or situational modifications. These are attempted out of conscious awareness by the symptoms of the emotional illness which are already present. The character defenses or traits as characterologic equivalents of clinical neurotic symptoms likewise may be unconsciously used in the endeavor to secure epigain.

Epigain is primarily secured unconsciously through the influence of established symptoms or traits on the attitudes, responses, and behavior of significant people. It is largely in the service of deeply repressed dependency needs. *Secondary* gain is a broader and more inclusive term which may also include any consciously or partly consciously secured gains of an illness.

Epigain refers to the clearly unconscious gains or attempts to gain, through emotional illness after it is present. It is secured via the control or manipulation of the external environment, especially the interpersonal. (2) The external situational or material advantage which is derived from a symptom or illness; the value which the symptom or illness gains subsequent to its onset. It is entirely out of conscious awareness.

Epigain is often more apparent in the neuroses. The epigain is apt to be particularly apparent in instances of: (1) Somatic Conversion or Conversion Reactions; (2) Hygeiaphrontis (Overconcern with Health; Somatic and Physiologic Preoccupation); (3) Fatigue Reactions; and (4) in certain of the Neuroses-Following-Trauma. In these cases it is often apparent that some measure of escape or relief from intolerable responsibilities or unbearable situations may unconsciously be secured by the symptoms.

epigain, suicidal. See *suicidal epigain*.

epilepsy. A disorder characterized by periodic convulsive seizures accompanied by a loss of consciousness, or by certain equivalent manifestations.

jacksonian e. Recurrent episodes of localized convulsive seizures or spasms limited to a single part or region of the body. Unconsciousness is absent. The localized convulsion is due to cerebral motor discharge. Accordingly, there may be subsequent weakness of the affected part. This may be conceived to be a consequence of the exhaustion of the responsible motor cells of the cerebral cortex and their lowered potential for further discharge. Named for Hughlings Jackson (1835–1911).

major e. Epilepsy characterized by gross convulsive seizures with loss of consciousness; *grand mal.*

minor e. Lesser epileptic seizures or equivalents; *petit mal.* May be limited to only momentary lapses of consciousness. These may or may not be discernible to the external observer, or to the subjective awareness of the patient.

psychomotor e. Seizure characterized by automations or temper outbursts. (Regarded by Alpers as a type of minor attack or *petit mal.*)

epileptic equivalent. A manifestation or symptom appearing in place of an epileptic attack, as its equivalent.

epinosic gain (Freud). Secondary gain. See *Epigain,* and *Secondary gain.*

Equanimity, Concept of Goal of. The goal of mankind is the attainment of a state of emotional satisfaction, peace of mind, or equanimity.

equinophobia. The morbid fear of horses. See *Phobia.*

equivalents, physical. See *Depression,* physical equivalents.

equivalents, psychologic. See *Depression,* psychological equiv.

ergasia (Meyer). The total of an individual's functions and behavior.

erogenicity. According to Freud, the "activity of a given bodily area in conveying sexually exciting stimuli to the mind."

erogenous zone. An area of the body which is particularly sensitive to erotic (i.e., sensual) arousal. Especially oral, anal, and genital areas. Sometimes used as synonymous with erotogenic zone.

Eros. The Greek god of love and play.

erotic. (1) Sensual. Refers to love and libido. (2) Consciously or unconsciously invested with sexual feeling. May be used broadly to refer to all kinds of love and warm, affectionate or loving feelings.

erotize. To attach sexual meaning or significance.

erotogenic zones. According to Freud, "certain areas of the body—the erotogenic zones—may act as substitutes for the genitals and behave analogously to them." Sometimes used as synonymous with erogenous zones.

erotomania. Pathologic preoccupation with genital sexuality.

esoteric. Hidden, unusual, infrequent, secret; for the initiated only.

E.S.P. Extrasensory perception. See *Extrasensory perception.*

Esquirol, Jean E. (1772–1840). Early French psychiatrist. He introduced the term hallucination and *la folie du doute.* He applied statistical methods to clinical studies.

E.S.T. Electroshock therapy. Also. E.C.T. See *Electroshock therapy.*

etiology. The basis for, or causative factors, in an illness.

ethnic. Pertaining to human races.

ethology. The study of comparative animal behavior.

eugenics. A branch of science devoted to study of ways of improvement of the race through inheritance and heredity.

eunuch. A male castrated before puberty.

euphoria. An exaggerated feeling of physical and emotional well-being. Usually of psychologic origin. A response out of keeping with apparent (external) stimuli or events. Euphoria can also occasionally be found in organic brain disease and in toxic states.

euthanasia. Induced rapid and painless death for the incurable. Has been advocated by some as an optional choice for the patient with a hopeless illness.

exhibitionism. (1) A kind of "showing off" behavior. (2) Bodily exposure, often involving the display of the sexual organs to a member of the opposite sex. Socially perverse sexual stimulation and/or gratification usually accompanies exhibitionism. (3) The sublimated form of exhibitionism may include such things as the exhibition of talent, clothes, physical attributes, or intellect.

Existential psychiatry. A school of thought based on the existential views of Kierkegaard and Sartre. See *Psychiatry*.

exogenic. Arising from outside of the body or self. Adjective, exogenous.

expansiveness. Behavior of a marked extrovertive type often characterized by overgenerosity, great tolerance, friendliness, and talkativeness. It is sometimes regarded as a lesser degree of euphoria and grandiosity.

Extension. A mental mechanism operating outside of and beyond conscious awareness, through which the scope or boundaries of existing defenses are enlarged (that is, extended) to include areas which are adjacent or continuous; physically or through their emotional association.

Extension, Principle of, in Emotional Illness. The later secondary effects of Acute Anxiety Attacks for example, *can* become considerably more important and influential than the attacks themselves. This occurs through their extension. The *Circular Generation of Fear Principle* (*q.v.*) can apply. See also A.A.A. (the Acute Anxiety Attack).

Various symptoms and emotional ills thus tend to have further *emotional repercussions*. Like a stone cast into a pool, these *can progress in ever-spreading fashion to influence many if not all aspects of the .patient's life.* This is in accord with the Principle of Extension.

Through extension, various places, situations, activities, objects and people thus can come to be associated with the anxiety, or other manifestations, and thereby come to be feared and avoided in turn.

exteriorization. The turning of interests and drives outwardly into work, recreation, and social pursuits.

externalization. A mental mechanism operating outside of and beyond conscious awareness in which the emotion of an internal conflict is directed outwardly. Example: In a phobia the affect of the unbearable idea is directed externally and attached to a previously apparently neutral object or area. See *Displacement.*

extrapyramidal system. That part of the brain and C.N.S. mediating nonvoluntary, skeletal and muscular posture, attitude balance and control.

extrasensory perception. E.S.P. The knowing or perceiving of an external event without the apparent intervention of the five physical senses.

extroversion. A state in which attention and energies are largely directed outward from oneself. Interest is mainly in external activities and social activity, as opposed to interest being primarily directed internally toward oneself, as in introversion.

F

fabrication. A made-up story.

facies. Facial expression or appearance.

fainting. The sudden complete loss of consciousness in the absence of sufficient physical trauma, injury, or disease. It is a transient but sometimes repetitive phenomenon the basis of which is wholly, or (nearly always) at least in some part, psychologic in origin. Fainting is a primitive type of defensive reaction by which the person concerned completely surrenders or shuts off outside perception. It might be regarded as a dissociative blocking of perception, occurring when perception becomes too emotionally painful.

Fairet, Jean-Pierre (1794–1870). French psychiatrist who named obsessive doubting (*la maladie du doute;* the illness of the doubt).

falsification, retrospective. See *Retrospective Falsification.*

fantasy. An imaginary sequence of events or mental images, often normal in children, fantasies in adults. They may represent attempts to resolve emotional conflict by affording unreal substitutive satisfactions. A fantasy is a vivid kind of daydream which is emotionally significant to the individual and which is usually regarded as nonconstructive and psychologically unhealthy. Fantasies occur during consciousness, at any time of the day or night. While superficially they appear to be under conscious control and direction, their outward or manifest content "covers over" a hidden, latent content which is unconscious. Unconscious fantasies also exist.

fatigue. Tiredness or weariness.

combat f. See under *Combat fatigue.*

emotional f. Weariness of spirit. Emotional fatigue is the tiredness or weariness which arises from emotional sources. Presumptive evidence of its presence consists of a discrepancy between the subjective feelings of fatigue which are experienced and the actual amount of mental or physical effort which has been expended.

mental f. Fatigue arising in consequence of sufficiently prolonged mental effort. The fatigue experienced is proportionate to the effort expended.

organic f. The rather rare type of fatigue which is occasionally incident to several physical (organic) diseases, as a post-surgical manifestation, and following severe physical trauma.

physical f. Fatigue which comes on following sufficiently prolonged physical labor. The fatigue experienced is proportionate to the effort expended.

fatigue state. A neurotic reaction in which the most prominent clinical feature present is that of emotional fatigue. The emotional fatigue which is present is more or less chronic. See *Fatigue, Emotional.*

fear. The emotional response to consciously recognized and external sources of danger. An uncomfortable state of apprehension and uneasiness. Lay usage often makes no distinction from anxiety. See *Anxiety* and *Phobia* for important distinctions. (Under Phobia is a list of the more common pathologic fears.)

Circular Generation Principle. The presence of fear can in itself produce fear.

feeblemindedness. Intelligence and mental capacity of a level considerably lower than average. Usually refers to cases of moron level (I.Q. 50 to 69 [Normal 100]), or lower. See *mental deficiency.*

fellatio. The sexual stimulation of the penis by oral contact.

Ferenczi, Sandor (1873–1933). Hungarian psychiatrist.

fertilization. Union of sperm cell with ovum.

festination. Involuntary increase in tempo of movements, especially in gait.

fetish. (1) An object endowed with special power or meaning; often "magical." A fetish may be a soteria. (2) A symbol or article standing for a person, part of a person, or feeling, sometimes with sensual connotations.

fetishism. (1) The process of attachment of emotional significance or special meaning to an inanimate object (or fetish) which serves, usually unconsciously, as a substitute for the original object or person. The fetish may be a soteria. It often serves as a neurotic source of sexual stimulation.

fire drill. A minor mental mechanism through which the individual concerned urgently mobilizes his emotional resources in preparing for an anticipated crisis or emergency.

First Line of Psychic Defense Concept. The internal defenses, called mental dynamisms or mechanisms, automatically and unconsciously employed by the individual in attempts to cope with emotional conflict and the resulting anxiety. They comprise one's so-called first line of psychic defense.

fixation. The arrest or cessation of psycho-sexual development at some given point in the maturing process. Fixation may be a transient, temporary, and nonpathologic block in maturation, or it may become more permanent and pathologic.

flagellantism. A masochistic or sadistic act in which one or both participants derive stimulation or gratification, usually erotic, from whipping or being whipped.

flexibilitas cerea. Waxy flexibility. The passive maintenance of suggested or imposed bodily position. Seen especially in catatonic schizophrenia.

flight of ideas. The rapid mental jumping from one topic to another prior to thorough consideration of the first one. The stream of talk is produced under pressure, reflecting the rapid skipping from one idea to another. Marked by distractibility, it tends to be continuous but fragmentary, with subject changes being determined by chance associations or even by very minor external events or stimuli.

folie à deux. Mania of two. A psychotic reaction in which two closely related persons, usually familial, mutually share delusions.

folie du doute. The obsessional doubting mania. The original term for obsessive states, introduced by Esquirol in 1838.

foreconscious. Preconscious; material not ordinarily in consciousness but subject to voluntary recall.

Forensic psychiatry. See *Psychiatry*.

forepleasure. Sexual play preceding intercourse.

formication. A disturbing subjective sensation as if insects were crawling over one.

fornication. Sexual intercourse on the part of an unmarried person.

fragmental dissociation. See *dissociation, fragmental*.

free association. The unedited and unselected production of thoughts verbally and in sequence as they occur to conscious awareness. The basic contribution of the patient in psychoanalytic therapy. Also used in less technical psychotherapeutic approaches.

free-floating anxiety. Fear in the absence of known cause. See *Anxiety*.

Freud, Sigmund (1856–1939). A psychiatrist of Vienna and later London, who formulated many of the basic tenets of dynamic psychiatry. He founded psychoanalysis.

frigidity. Coldness. Sexual frigidity indicates a relative sexual disinterest, sometimes to the point of complete aversion. Usually applied to the female.

Frozen State of Rage. See *Depression*.

frustration. The blocking of sought-after gratifications or satisfactions, by external or by internal (intra-psychic) forces.

Fuel Analogy. In which anxiety can be viewed as a driving force in treatment, the "gasoline" that fuels the "motor." Severe neuroses thus are sometimes to be encountered in which the relative absence of anxiety interferes with, delays, or even prevents therapy.

fugue. A major state of personality dissociation characterized by loss of memory and actual physical flight from an intolerable situation. It results from the unconscious need to escape from otherwise intolerable conflict. In a Fugue State, the patient "flees" psychologically and unconsciously, sometimes in a rather confused fashion. The flight is from his usual environment and circumstances through the development of amnesia, and through physical departure. A fugue lasts from days to months, during which time the patient loses his identity. He may wander about in some strange city (or his own) in a rather aimless fashion for some time, or, on occasion, he may carry on well and unsuspectedly in a new role. Upon recovery, there is ordinarily a subsequent inability to consciously remember the events of the episode.

functional. Referring to the physiology or the action and purpose (i.e., function) of an organ or area of the body, as opposed to its *structure*.

functional illness. (1) An illness of emotional origin in which changes are present in the function of an organ or system. Organic or structural changes are absent or may occur secondarily to longstanding emotional stress. (2) Psychogenic origin or basis of the illness, as opposed to a physical basis. (3) Morbid physiologic response to emotions.

Functional-Structural Progression Principle. Physiologic accompaniments of anxiety may lead to emotionally determined (psychosomatic) disorders, in which ultimately irreversible organic structural changes may result.

G

Galen (142–200). An influential Greek physician-author who practiced in Rome and who contributed to descriptive anatomy of the brain and nervous system. He believed dryness of the brain aided intelligence and wetness led to dementia.

Ganser syndrome. A reaction in which objects are misnamed and answers are partly senseless. Regarded by some investigators as a hysterical phenomenon, it has been particularly observed in prisoners. Sometimes called "nonsense syndrome," or Prison Psychosis. It is also used to refer to malingered neurotic and psychotic manifestations among prisoners.

gelasmus. Hysterical laughter.

gene. A minute but important unit of inheritance which is located on and transmitted by the chromosome from a cell nucleus. Inherited characteristics are conveyed by genes.

general paresis. An organic disease of the central nervous system resulting from chronic syphilis. Pathologically, it is characterized by diffuse inflammation and degeneration in the cerebral cortex. The symptoms include slurring speech, Argyll Robertson pupils, tremor, paralytic attacks, and impairment of memory and judgment.

generalization. A mental mechanism operating outside of and beyond conscious awareness by which an emotional process extends to include additional areas. Example: In a phobia, the extension of the original phobia more generally to include other areas. A phobia of bridges may, by progression or generalization, come also to include tall buildings, mountains, or any high place. See *Extension.*

genesis. Origin.

genetic. An adjective pertaining to early origin or genesis. Roughly synonymous with hereditary.

genic. Arising from a gene or genes. Refers to endowment as conveyed in hereditary transmission by specific genes, or by genes generally.

genital. Referring to the sexual organs or to reproductive function.

geriatrics. The medical study and handling of the processes and diseases of aging.

gestalt. A whole perceptual configuration. Gestalt is the German word denoting the total structure of an organization and the interrelations of its component parts.

gestalt psychology. A school of psychology noteworthy for its shift from the older traditional direction of attention to single elements of behavior, to the study of larger areas and totality of function.

globus hystericus. An hysterical symptom in which there is a disturbing sensation of a lump in the throat.

gonads. The sex glands: ovaries and testicles.

grand mal. Literally, "great sickness." Epilepsy in which there are typical major convulsions. See *epilepsy.* Synonym: Epilepsy major.

grandiosity. Convictions of a delusional nature concerning the possession of wealth, fame, power, or omnipotence.

grief. The normal and appropriate emotional response to an external and consciously recognized loss. It is realistically proportionate to loss sustained. It is self-limited, and gradually subsides within a reasonable time. To be distinguished from depression. See *Depression.*

grief reaction. An overintense and/or prolonged reaction to loss, particularly the death of someone close. See *Depression* and *Mourning.*

grief state. The prolongation of feelings of bereavement beyond what might ordinarily be expected. The grief state is for practical purposes synonymous with the grief reaction. Both tend to merge in diagnostic, psychopathologic progression into the more established and clinically recognizable cases of *Depression* (*q.v.*).

group analysis. The methods of intensive therapeutic study and analysis as applied to groups.

group therapy. Psychotherapy carried out with groups of patients; used increasingly in recent years in hospitals. The advantages of group therapy can include the opportunity to make realistic comparisons with the emotional responses and behavior of others, participation in making therapy productive as a group project, losing feelings of isolation or uniqueness, and securing a sense of belonging. In the successful group, insights are developed, a personal sense of freedom is enhanced, and group members learn to assume a greater measure of responsibility for themselves and for others.

guilt. The subjective feeling of having committed an error, offense, or sin. Unpleasant feelings of self-criticism. These result from acts, impulses, or thoughts contrary to one's personal conscience. The amount of guilt present does not necessarily correspond to the real amount of injury or hurt produced, as might be assessed by an objective observer. Psychopathologic feelings of guilt stem from unconscious conflicts.

gumma. An organic lesion of syphilitic origin.

H

habit. A characteristic mode of action. It becomes developed by repetition, and it shows itself in facility of performance.

habituation. Emotional dependence without physiologic dependence. There is an absence of withdrawal symptoms as in addiction, which is both emotional and physiological dependence.

Halfway House. A specialized place of residence for mental patients who need intermediate care and protection before returning to fully normal living.

hallucination. A subjectively experienced perception in the absence of an actual external stimulus, but which is regarded by the individual as real. Hallucinations may occur in any of the five senses. They are usually of emotional origin. Very occasionally they are the result of organic brain changes, or may occur following certain drugs, such as mescaline, lysergic acid diethylamide, and alcohol.

hallucinogen. Any agent, usually a drug or chemical, which produces an hallucination.

hallucinosis. A state in which the patient is actively hallucinating. Example: *Alcoholic Hallucinosis.*

hebephrenia. See *Schizophrenia.*

hedonism. The pursuit of pleasure as the major goal.

hemianopsia. Impairment of sight in either half of the field of vision.

hemichorea. Chorea confined to one side of the body.

hemicrania. Headache confined to one side of the head.

hemiparesis. Impairment of muscular strength and activity confined to one side of the body.

hemiplegia. Paralysis of one half of the body, longitudinally divided.

Herd Instinct. (1) Social instinct. A concept by which the forces responsible for man's need to congregate in groups (i.e., gregariousness) and to fit into his social milieu have an ultimate basis in instinct. The validity of this concept has been debated. (2) The supposed innate need of man to belong to a group and to conform to its standards. Gregariousness.

hermaphrodite. Marked by the possession of both male and female sexual parts; almost invariably one sex is predominant. The term 'hermaphrodite' has been loosely, broadly, and inaccurately applied to male, homosexually-oriented persons.

herpetophobia. The morbid fear of lizards or reptiles. See *Phobia.*

heterosexuality. (1) The normal and usual sexual relationships or adjustment between male and female. (2) The normal sexual attraction and interest between members of opposite sexes.

Hippocrates (circa 400 B.C.). The "father" of medicine. He describes several types of mental illness, including *mania* and *melancholia.*

holistic. Pertaining to the whole or totality.

homeostasis. (1) The maintenance of self-regulatory metabolic or psychologic processes within limits which are optimal for individual and racial survival. (2) Equanimity and tranquillity of emotional status.

homogamy. Inbreeding.

Homosexual Panic. An acute and dramatic panic attack or A.A.A. In essence, it is a severe attack of acute anxiety based upon unconscious conflicts of a homosexual nature. See *Acute Anxiety Attack.*

homosexuality. Sexual attraction or relationship between members of the same sex. May be conscious or unconscious. Homosexuality is a condition of inversion of the usual sexual orientation of heterosexuality.

Active h. Marked by overt activity.

Latent h. Homosexual interests or tendencies which are hidden, often from the individual himself. There is no outward expression of them.

Overt h. Open, outward, active homosexuality.

Passive h. Homosexual activity in which a passive role is taken.

homunculus. An imaginary little man of fiction and fantasy.

hormone. The secretion of an endocrine gland. Hormones have vital regulatory functions in body growth, metabolism, or physiology.

Horney, Karen (1885–1952). Psychiatrist and psychoanalyst who founded the American Institute of Psychoanalysis. She proposed a theory of neurosis based on an optimistic philosophy of human nature which emphasized the urge toward self-realization. Neurosis was seen as a process developing from inner conflicts, originating in basic anxiety of childhood, and depending on the interaction of cultural, interpersonal, and intrapsychic factors.

hospitalitis. The term "hospitalitis" has been used (sometimes in not too kindly a fashion) to describe the reaction of certain persons to their hospitalization. Hospital life for them can come to provide emotionally-important comfort, security, and protection. The emotional significance which approaches the soterial, lies in the unconscious gratification of their inner dependency needs. See also *Soterial Reaction*.

hydrocephalus. State marked by an enlarged head due to increased pressure of the cerebrospinal fluid.

hydrotherapy. Treatment by baths, sprays, and wet packs of various kinds and temperatures.

hypalgesia. Decreased pain sensation.

hyperacusis. Unusually acute hearing.

hyperhidrosis. Increased perspiration.

hyperplasia. Tissue overgrowth.

hyperpnea. Increased depth of breathing.

hyperpyrexia. Greatly increased bodily temperature.

hypertonus. Increased tonus or muscle tension.

hypesthesia. Decreased touch sensation.

Hygeiaphrontic Discrepancy. The discrepancy between the actual level of anxious bodily concerns and discomforts on the one hand, and that which would appear indicated following an objective appraisal as to the real need for them on the other hand. It includes the discrepancy between the hygeiaphrontic discomforts, and any physical bases for them.

Hygeiaphrontic Personality. Characterized by narcissism, the development of interests and concerns on a somatic level to excuse shortcomings and failures, thinking in somatic, visceral or physiologic terms, and trends toward regression and seclusiveness.

Hygeiaphrontic Reaction. A state in which there is a more or less persistent anxious overconcern about the state of health and/or the possible presence of illness. This reaction is marked by either somatic or physiologic preoccupation (or both), symptoms, and bodily concerns. These symptoms and concerns are out of proportion to any possible underlying and strictly physical organic difficulty which may be present, and which often enough is totally absent.

Various and sometimes shifting symptoms often develop which may affect any region or area of the body. This lack of organic basis makes them no less real or troubling to the patient, of course; indeed, rather the reverse, since the finding of a more tangible and definite organic basis would provide something usually far easier for him to cope with.

Hygeiaphrontis. (1) An obsessive kind of preoccupation with physical functions and body processes, which is often accompanied by the development of various and often shifting somatic complaints. (2) A more descriptive term for hypochondriasis, (*q.v.*).

hypnagogic fantasy. Fantasy intermediate between a dream and a daydream.

hypnagogic state. An intermediate state between sleeping and waking.

hypnosis (Braid). An altered state of conscious awareness which is induced in a suggestible subject. Through the suggestions of the hypnotist, a passive trance-like state of dissociation is produced. In it the subject more or less pays attention only to that which the hypnotist wishes, manifesting increased receptivity to suggestion and direction.

May be regarded as being somewhere between wakeful consciousness and sleep, being different from, but possessing some of the characteristics of both.

Hypnotic Dissociation. See *Dissociation, hypnotic.*

hypochondriacal personality. See *Hygeia-phrontic Personality.*

hypochondriasis; also **hygeiaphrontis** (preferred). Somatic and/or physiologic preoccupation. (1) Hypochondriasis is a state in which there is persistent, anxious, overconcern in regard to the possible presence of physical illness or the state of health. (2) An obsessive kind of preoccupation with physical functions and body processes which is often accompanied by the development of various and often shifting somatic complaints. Organic changes are usually minimal or absent. These may affect any body region, organ, or system, and their organic basis alone is insufficient to account for the discomfort which is experienced, or the concern which is present.

Many different organs or organ systems may be brought in turn into the focus of attention. Hypochondriasis may occur alone or in association with different types of emotional illness. Picking a frequent locale of such symptoms, the *hypochondrium,* and believing this the area of pathology, the ancient Greeks derived their name of hypochondriasis. They believed the symptoms were due to disorders of the spleen and the region of the hypochondrium. Also see *Hygeiaphrontis* and *Neurosis.*

hypoglycemia. Decreased blood sugar level.

hypomania. (1) A hyperactive state of mild mania. (2) The manic phase of manic-depressive psychoses. (3) A moderately elated hyperactive emotional state which is usually a mild or beginning form of manic-depressive psychosis.

hypoplasia. Undergrowth, or underdevelopment.

Hypothesis, Attention. See *Attention Hypothesis.*

Hypothesis of the Oral Conflict. A hypothesis by which the earliest antecedents of later emotional conflict are found in the early oral conflict of infancy.

hypotonus. Decreased tonus or muscle tension.

hysteria. (1) An illness resulting from emotional conflict. The outward expressions may be seen as dramatic physical symptoms often involving voluntary muscles or organs of special sense, or emotional outbursts, not accompanied by proportionate anxiety. (2) A state generally characterized by immaturity, impulsiveness, attention-seeking, dependency, and possessing a particular capacity for the employment of the menial mechanisms of conversion and dissociation. Classically manifested by dramatic "physical" symptoms involving the voluntary muscles, or the organs of special sense. Synonym: *Somatic Conversion.* See *Conversion, dissociation* and *Neurosis, Conversion R.*

This is an illness which we understand today as resulting from emotional conflict. This knowledge as to its basis is impressively recent in origin from any historical perspective, dating only from the past 80 years or so.

While various explanations were offered prior to this time, the name hysteria derives from the Greek word *hyster,* for the uterus. It was the ancients' belief that the manifestations derived from this organ, wandering through the body, producing symptoms at each location. Outward expressions of hysteria may be evidenced by major and dramatic symptoms such as paralyses, loss of sensation, hearing, speech, and even sight, convulsive-like seizures and emotional outbursts. The correct name today is *Conversion Reaction.*

conversion h. "Solution" to conflict takes place unconsciously (i.e., out of awareness) by symptom formation, consisting of alteration or suspension of a normal function. Example: A combat-evacuated soldier with a paralyzed leg. The paralysis is an unconscious, disguised expression of intrapsychic conflict in response to intolerable fear, and serves as a "solution" by requiring his removal from combat. Synonyms: Somatic Conversion, Hysteria. *Conversion Reaction* preferred.

hysterical personality. The descriptive term for a type of personality structure in which there is present a pattern of several of the hysterical group of personality traits or defenses. These may or may not be sufficiently marked to cause interference with living, a loss of efficiency, or a limitation of normal satisfactions or social adjustment. When they are, this constitutes the hysterical type of Character Neurosis. The hysterical personality is one major constellation of character defenses. The hysterical group of character or personality traits includes strong but shifting emotional feelings, susceptibility to suggestion, impulsive behavior, attention-seeking, immaturity, and self-absorption. *Conversion Personality* is preferred.

hysterics. The lay term for certain more or less uncontrollable emotional outbursts.

I

I.Q. Intelligence Quotient, (*q.v.*).

iatrogenic illness. A medically induced illness, particularly an emotional illness in which the physician's attitude, examination, or comments unwittingly precipitate or contribute to the illness.

id. (1) That part of the personality which harbors the unconscious instinctive desires and strivings of the individual. (2) The largely unconscious part of the personality having to do with the instincts. It is deeply internal and completely hidden. The id serves as a reservoir for psychic energy.

idealization. (1) A mental mechanism operating outside of and beyond conscious awareness in which an object, or a person, is overvalued and emotionally aggrandized. Other attributes may be then also seen in a favorable light. (2) The concentration upon and exaggeration of the liked attributes of an individual so that everything about the "idealized" person comes to be seen in a fine light. Negative aspects may be unseen or forgotten. (3) The conscious or partly conscious process of building a person, a principle, or a system into the position of becoming a standard of excellence, or the ultimate (i.e., an ideal). The position thus achieved has in it a varying degree of unreality when judged objectively. (4) When idealization of self occurs, an *idealized image* is created, aspects of which may be projected to others.

ideas of influence. The delusion that one's feelings, thoughts, or actions are under the control of external forces or persons. The patient may regard such influences as benevolent or inimical.

ideas of persecution. The more or less fixed belief that one is being discriminated against, mistreated, or persecuted.

ideas of reference. The interpretation by an individual of casual incidents and external events as having some direct reference to himself. In paranoid states or psychoses, these can become fixed irrational beliefs in which the patient is firmly convinced (in error) that he is the object of certain thoughts, talk, or actions on the part of others. May be of sufficient strength to constitute delusions. Has also been used loosely to describe an obsessive idea, a compulsive drive or a delusion.

idée fixe. A psychopathologically fixed idea or belief, of a delusional character.

Identification. A mental mechanism operating outside of and beyond conscious awareness through which an individual, in varying degree, makes himself like someone else; he identifies himself with another person. This results in the unconscious taking over and transfer to oneself of various elements of another.

identification, affective. Sympathy, empatheia.

identification, projective. Empathy (*q.v.*).

idiopathic. Of primary or spontaneous origin. Ordinarily used to connote unknown origin or basis pathologically, of obscure etiology.

idiosyncracy. A minor individual trait which is usually to some extent nonconforming and may be regarded as a peculiarity.

idiot. A person with the lowest order of intellectual potential. A level below *moron* (*I.Q.* 50–69) and *imbecile* (I.Q. 20–49).

illusion. The misinterpretation of a real, external sensory experience. A false perception.

imago. An unconscious mental image of important persons in the early history of the individual. The childhood memory-picture of a loved person which remains, often in a more or less idealized version, in adult life.

imbecile. A person with a low order of

intellectual potential. Intermediate between *idiot* (I.Q. 0–20), and *moron* (I.Q. 50–69).

Implicit-Command. See *Suicide,* Compliant Response to Implicit Command.

impotence. Powerlessness. Sexual impotence is the lack of sexual power, vigor, or, more specifically, an inability to perform the sexual act. More frequently used to name this condition in the male. The basis is psychologic in the vast majority of cases.

Impression Priority Rule. The thesis that first impressions ordinarily tend to take an emotional priority.

impulse. A psychic striving. Impulse usually refers to instinctual urges.

Impulsion. An emotional disorder characterized by repetitive compulsions to commit, and the carrying out of various unlawful or socially disapproved series of similar, related or identical actions. They are compulsive repetitive acts. Example: *Kleptomania* and *Pyromania.*

Impulsive Personality. Characterized by tendency toward impulsive acts, usually diffuse and multiple. A pervasive and overall impulsive overtone to actions and behavior.

Inadequate Personality. A person who is characterized by an inadequate response to intellectual, emotional, social, and physical stress. Such persons are apt to be poorly adaptable, inept, with poor judgment, social incompatibility, and a lack of physical and emotional stamina.

Inadvertent Defeat Principle. In the neuroses one tends to lose the very thing which is desperately and urgently sought.

incest. Sexual intercourse between persons so related that marriage cannot legally take place between them.

incoherent. Not understandable.

incompetent. A legal term for a person who cannot be held responsible for his actions, usually because of a severe emotional disorder (i.e., a psychosis), or mental deficiency.

Incomplete Symptom-Defense Concept. Relates to the lack of symptom-success in allaying or preventing anxiety. Presumptive evidence of this is to be found

in any instance in which there is the presence of concurrent anxiety or an A.A.A. accompanying other neurotic symptoms.

Incorporation. A primitive mental mechanism operating outside of and beyond conscious awareness in which another person, parts of another person, or other significant non-material elements, are in symbolic fashion taken within oneself (symbolically ingested and assimilated).

Individual Appropriateness of Response Principle. Refers to our findings that although outwardly, anxiety or an emotional response may not seem appropriate, on a deeper level it always proves to be individually so.

Individual Psychology. The name for the system of psychiatric theory, research, and therapy of Alfred Adler and his followers. Stresses compensation and overcompensation for inferiority feelings.

Induced Dissociation. See *Dissociation, Induced.*

infantile. An adjective applied to early childhood traits and behavior as also seen pathologically in later life.

infatuation. Sudden, strong emotional attachment; the overevaluation of another.

inferiority complex. A term largely in lay usage to describe a condition of self-doubt with feelings of inferiority. See *Complex.*

inferiority, constitutional. Refers to an outmoded concept in which emotional disorders were believed to be caused by hereditary or congenital inferiority of some organ or system of the body. Often the individual then strove to compensate for the inferiority.

inhibit. To retard, hold back, prevent.

inhibition. (1) The restraint of thought, feeling, or action. (2) The unconscious (i.e., out of awareness) interference with or restriction of instinctual drives. Inhibition occurs as the consequence of activity of the superego (i.e., conscience), resulting in the inhibited or shy person.

inhibition-action balance. The relative balance maintained in every individual between his subjective experiencing of emotional feelings and his outward behavior in response to them. This concept also includes the relative balance maintained between one's individual, unconscious aggressive drives on the one hand, and loving drives, and related impulses, on the other; the assessment of the inhibition-action balance and its relative stability can be used as one index to an appraisal of the level of emotional health.

insanity. (1) The legal term still currently used for serious psychologic illnesses, except mental deficiency, through which a person is to be considered irresponsible for his acts, and for which commitment to a mental institution is warranted. The preferable medical term is psychosis. (2) An older, rather vague, legal term for the psychotic state. Generally connotes: (a) mental incompetence, (b) an inability to distinguish right from wrong, and/or (c) the presence of a serious mental disorder which interferes with the individual's ability to care for himself, or as a result of which he constitutes a danger to himself or to others.

insight. (1) Self-understanding; a major goal of psychotherapy. Insight is a matter of degree and may be used to refer to the extent of the individual's understanding of the origin, nature and mechanisms of his attitudes and behavior. (2) On a more superficial and general level, the recognition by the patient, in a varying degree, that his emotional and mental symptoms are abnormal or morbid.

insomnia. Inability to sleep.

   Dawn i. Insomnia characterized by early morning awakening. Pathegnomic of depression.

instinct. (1) An urgent, innate impulse or stimulus. (2) An inborn trait, drive, ability, or potential (as contrasted with behavior or ability acquired through environmental experience). The human instincts are those of self-preservation, *sexuality,* and for some, the *ego instincts,* and the *herd* or *social instincts.* Freud also described a *death instinct.*

insulin treatment. See *Shock Treatment.*

integration. (1) The useful organization of both new and old data, experience, and emotional capacities into the personality. Individual ability to integrate is quite variable, but when successful results in a harmonious personality structure, with resulting greater potential for social adaptation. (2) Integration also refers to the organization and amalgamation of functions at various levels of psychosexual (personality) development.

intellectual functions. The mental faculties of perception, recognition, knowing, reasoning, judging, comprehension, thinking, and understanding. These make possible organized, integrated, and directed thinking.

intellectual identification. Empathy.

intellectualization. (1) Similar to rationalization in the latter's more conscious usage. One attempts defensively to divorce some of the disturbing emotional significance by an intellectual kind of approach. (2) It may be an unconscious process, and as such may be regarded as a mental mechanism. (3) A kind of verbal exercise or gymnastics: (a) The basic meaning is obscured. (b) The subject or opponent is "smothered by words" and/or (c) The point is avoided.

intelligence. (1) The potential ability of an individual to understand what is needed, to recall, to mobilize, and to integrate constructively previous learning and experience in meeting new situations. Implies ability to think clearly and to exercise good judgment. (2) The ability to apply the mind effectively to a situation or problem and to appropriately vary the method of approach to the problem.

intelligence quotient. An arithmetic figure, determined through psychologic testing, which indicates the relation of a subject's intellectual achievement in a series of tests to the statistical norm of his age group. The I.Q. is determined by dividing the mental age (as determined by various standard tests) by the chronologic age (to age 15), and multiplying by 100. The "normal" I.Q. is roughly 100, with limits from 90 to 110. The average I.Q. for college students is 110. See *mental deficiency.*

intention tremor. A tremor which begins upon attempting a voluntary or purposeful movement. Seen in multiple sclerosis.

internalization. A mental mechanism operating outside of and beyond conscious awareness by which certain external attributes, attitudes, or standards are taken within oneself (i.e., internalized). Internalization is very similar to but is not precisely identical with Incorporation and Introjection.

Interpersonal Perpetuation Concept. Parents may tend to encourage the development of their own traits in their children.

Intrapsychic. Taking place within the mind.

Introject. In Introjection, the object which has been figuratively taken in. It remains more or less discrete psychologically, and is not assimilated.

introjection. A mental mechanism operating outside of and beyond conscious awareness whereby loved or hated external objects are taken within oneself symbolically. It is the converse of projection. Parts of a person or the entire person may become a symbolically introjected object. Introjection is less regressive, and is a less primitive mechanism than is incorporation, to which it is closely related and very similar. The process of introjection may serve as a defense against conscious recognition of intolerable hostile impulses. This is illustrated, for example, in depression, in which the individual may unconsciously direct unacceptable hatred or aggression toward (the introjected object within) himself, in place of the original external object. Murderous impulses play an unconscious role in some suicides.

intromission. Insertion of the penis in intercourse.

introspection. Self-study and observation. Introspection can be healthful and constructive, or it may become unhealthfully absorbing and nonconstructive.

introversion. (1) Preoccupation with oneself with accompanying reduction of interest in the outside world. Roughly the reverse of Extroversion (*q.v.*). (2) Turning one's interests inward.

intuition. Knowledge of something without the usual employment of conscious reasoning. A sudden understanding.

Inverse Ratio of Symptom-Success (in the allaying or preventing of anxiety), *with Motivation Toward Therapy.* The greater the symptom-success, *the less motivation toward treatment.*

Inverse Anxiety-Symptom Ratio. The amount of anxiety which is experience tends to vary inversely with the "success" of the symptom.

inversion. (1) A mental mechanism operating outside of and beyond conscious awareness in which a specific unacceptable and disowned wish, impulse, affect, or drive is directly reversed. The emotion has been inverted. (2) The turning inward of affects from an external object toward oneself, usually in conjunction with Introjection. (3) Sexual inversion. Sometimes used to describe the reversal (i.e., the inversion) of heterosexual patterns of drive and behavior into homosexual ones. (4) Inversion of sleep habits: the turning around of the usual nocturnal time for sleeping into a less frequent daytime pattern.

sexual i. Homosexuality.

investment, emotional. The attachment of significance to an object. The object becomes invested with emotional meaning or significance.

involution. The period of life following the climacterium.

involutional psychosis. A psychotic reaction taking place during the involutional period (i.e., the climacterium— 40 to 55 years), and characterized most commonly by depression. The course tends to be prolonged, and the condition may be manifested by guilt, anxiety, agitation, delusional ideas, insomnia, and somatic preoccupation.

Inward Aggression. See *aggression, inward.*

irresistible impulse. A court decision supplementing the McNaughton Rule which held that although a person could distinguish between right and wrong at the time of the commission of an unlawful act, the presence of an irresistible impulse freed him from the usual legal consequence of such action. See *McNaughton Rule,* and *Durham Decision.*

Isolation. A mental mechanism operating outside of and beyond conscious awareness, through which an idea or object is isolated from its emotional connotation. The emotional side of the emotional-object amalgam (*q.v.*) has been detached.

J

Jacksonian convulsion or **epilepsy.** See *Epilepsy, jacksonian.*

Janet dissociation. See *dissociation, Janet.*

Janet, Pierre (1859–1947). Distinguished French psychiatrist, student of Charcot, who introduced concepts of dissociation and psychasthenia.

Joint-Endeavor Principle in Psychotherapy. For psychotherapy to be successful, the patient must not only want to get well but he must give *his genuine and whole-hearted cooperation to his therapist.* His role must be *one of active collaboration.* In psychiatry, treatment requires a collaborative endeavor by doctor and patient such as is seldom to be encountered in any other kind of medical treatment. The result is a unique relationship with the application of the Joint-Endeavor Principle in psychotherapy. See *Psychotherapy.*

Jones, Ernest (1879–1958). A pupil of Freud, and an early pioneer in introducing psychoanalysis. Principal biographer of Freud.

Jung, Carl Gustav (1875–1961). Swiss psychiatrist; founder of the school of *Analytic Psychology.*

juvenile. Adolescent.

K

keraunophobia. Morbid fear of lightning. See *Phobia.*

kinetic. Relating to motion.

King David Reaction. A complex intrapsychic defensive operation. Involving the cooperative and mutual interaction of Repression, Projection and Identification, it is usually supported in some measure by Rationalization and at times relates to Denial and other dynamisms.

Consciously unrecognized and often disowned elements of the self-appraisal are originally present in the other person, or are ascribed to him in part or *in toto* through their Projection to him. These in turn evoke the otherwise un-explained feelings which are experienced toward the other person.

The negative type of King David Reaction is the reaction of *King David's Anger,* or *Royal Anger.*

This complex process can work conversely, with approved portions of the self-appraisal similarly coming to be experienced as affection or love for the second person. Thus the King David Reaction may be the basis for otherwise unexplained positive *or* negative feelings toward another person. It is facilitated by consciously unrecognized physical, behavioral, and/or characterologic resemblances.

Kirkbride, Thomas S. (1809–1883). A pioneer American psychiatrist. Designed a number of mental hospitals.

kleptomania. Compulsive stealing, largely without regard to an outwardly apparent personal need for the stolen object.

Korsakoff's syndrome; Korsakoff's psychosis. A disorder marked by disturbance of attention and memory, and by polyneuritis. Prominent with the loss of retention is *confabulation.* There is general deterioration of character and judgment, in varying degrees. May be due to alcohol, or certain poisons, and infections.

Kraepelin, Emil (1856–1926). A German psychiatrist who contributed to the classification of mental disorders.

L

L.S.D. (lysergic acid diethylamide). An hallucinogenic drug. Produces a psychotic-like state. Hallucinations, delusions and time-space distortions are included. Should be used under careful medical supervision only.

la belle indifférence. Literally, "the beautiful" or "grand indifference." Typically seen in certain patients with Somatic Conversion. This phrase is used to describe their indifferent attitude toward the major physical disability resulting from their symptoms.

labile. Rapidly or readily shifting emotions; changeable; unstable.

lability. The emotional quality of readily shifting, free, and uncontrolled expression of emotions.

lapsis linguae. A slip of the tongue. Due to unconscious factors.

latency period. In psychoanalytic theory, an asexual phase between the infantile and adolescent psychosexual periods of development in which there is normally a preference for companions of the same sex. In normal development sublimations and reaction formations replace the more primitive internal defense mechanisms. The phase extends from about 6 to 10 or 11 years.

latent content. The hidden (unconscious) meaning of a dream, fantasy, or of ordinary thoughts and emotions. It is not accessible to conscious awareness by ordinary avenues. It is often expressed in distorted, disguised, and symbolic form as the *manifest* content.

latent homosexuality. See *homosexuality*.

latent stimulus. The unconscious basis for a symptom, or for an external behavioral manifestation. Example: In the phobia the *latent* stimulus is the unconscious complex underlying the formation of the phobia. This is represented externally, and usually to some extent symbolically, by the *phobic object*. The latter is the *manifest* stimulus of anxiety, fear, and dread.

Law of Retaliation. The principle of retribution in kind, i.e., "an eye for an eye," or "a tooth for a tooth." The Talion Law.

Law of Universal Affect. The basic psychologic premise that every idea, thought, or object, no matter how apparently minor or neutral, possesses a distinct quantum of affect.

learning. The acquisition of knowledge or skill.

lesbian. An overtly homosexual woman.

lethal. Leading to or producing death.

libido. (1) Sexual desire and energy. (2) The psychic drive or energy usually associated with the sexual instinct. (Sexual is to be interpreted in a very broad sense, including pleasure and love-object seeking.) May also be used in a broader sense to connote the psychic energy associated with instincts in general.

Liebault, A. A. (1823–1904). Psychiatrist of Nancy, France, who quietly began again the medical use of hypnosis which had been largely abandoned after Mesmer. The teacher of Bernheim.

lobotomy. See *Psychosurgery*.

locomotor ataxia. An organic disease due to syphilitic changes in the spinal cord.

logorrhea. Excessive talking or chatter.

Longevity, Principle of Symptom-. See *Symptom-Longevity Principle*.

lues. Syphilis.

lumen. The inside space enclosed by a tube, especially a transverse section of this space. Ex., the *lumen* of an artery; or the intestine.

lunacy. A largely obsolete legal term for insanity.

lunatic. An obsolete legal term for a psychiatrically seriously ill individual; a psychotic patient.

M

M.S.E. Military Stressful Era(s). Included are the experiences of: (1) induction, (2) basic training, and (3) situationally-stressful positions, including combat. Also to be included on occasion as M.S.E.s of significance are (4) separation, (5) discharge, and (6) retirement, especially when these are involuntary. (*See also* the related S.E.H.A concept.

maladie du doute. (Falret). The condition of obsessive doubting.

malingerer. One who engages in malingering.

malingering. The deliberate simulation of illness, for whatever purpose. Attempts to malinger are undertaken in full conscious awareness in order to secure for the person concerned what appears to him to be an advantage to be gained from the presence of illness. This can include the avoidance of a personally unpleasant or intolerable alternative.

mania. (1) An emotional illness marked by heightened excitability, an acceleration of thought, speech, and bodily motion, and by elation or grandiosity of mood. Attacks of mania may alternate with depressive attacks. (2) A morbid state of agitation and excitement.

manic-depressive psychosis. A major emotional illness (i.e., psychosis) marked by severe mood swings (elation-depression) and a tendency to remission and recurrence.

depressed type. The depressed type is characterized by depression of mood with retardation and inhibition of thinking (i.e., mental activity) and of physical activity.

manic type. The manic type is characterized by elation with overtalkativeness, extremely rapid ideas, and increased motor activity.

manifest content. The outward, remembered content of a dream, a fantasy, or ordinary thoughts and feelings, as opposed to the latent content which it may help conceal.

manifest stimulus. See *Latent stimulus.*

mannerism. Any one of a number of kinds of activity or expression which is individual and distinctive. A mannerism may be something quite peculiar to one person. It may be odd or bizarre and, in certain serious psychiatric conditions, may be repeated over and over. In psychiatry a distinctive mannerism may be helpful in revealing the unconscious psychodynamics.

masochism. (1) Pleasure derived from the suffering of physical or psychologic pain. The "pleasure" often has a sexual basis which may be apparent or concealed. The suffering may be inflicted by one's self or by others, and is usually "arranged" inadvertently (i.e., (unconsciously) in all kinds of devious and concealed fashion.) (2) A state in which sexual satisfaction is dependent upon suffering (physical and/or psychologic) pain, humiliation, illtreatment, etc. When conscious and related to sexual activity, it constitutes sexual perversion. It is the converse of *sadism,* and the two may be mixed (sado-masochism).

masturbation. Sexual stimulation or gratification of the self.

McNaughton rule also **M'Naughton.** A legal precedent carried over from English law (1843, the trial of Daniel McNaughton for murder) into the statutes of twenty-nine states of the United States, concerning the handling of criminal acts by insane persons. According to this rule, such persons cannot be tried and punished by criminal procedure if they were not aware at the time of the crime, of the nature or the wrongness of the act.

Mechanical Analogy. See *Psychotherapy.*

mechanism of defense. See *Defense Mechanism* and *Mental Mechanism.*

megacephaly. Large-sized head.

megalomania. A symptom-complex which is marked by delusions of great self-importance, wealth, or power. A false belief (i.e., delusion) of personal importance, greatness, wealth, or power.

melancholia. An emotional state of pathologic dejection of spirits. Melancholia is most accurately applied to those cases of emotional depression which are of psychotic depth. Recently deleted from official nomenclature.

memory. The mental recollection or trace of a past event. Memory is used also to describe all the data which are individually subject to recall and to recollection.

menarche. The onset of menstruation in the female life cycle.

Mendelian principles on law. The biologic principles governing inheritance of certain basic physical characteristics and mental capacity.

meninges. The membranes covering the brain. From without, inward, they are the *dura,* the *arachnoid,* and the *pia.*

meningitis. Inflammation, usually infection of the meninges.

mental age. The age level of mental ability as determined by any of several standard intelligence tests, as distinguished from the chronologic age.

mental deficiency or retardation. A term which is used to differentiate conditions resulting from inadequate initial endowment at birth (i.e., a small number of brain cells or a brain which suffered early injury), from distortions and illnesses of the mind from whatever other cause. The patient is, to a degree, lacking in intelligence so that he is ordinarily regarded as being unable to make an "average" or "normal" adjustment to life. In *borderline* cases, there may exist vocational impairment (I.Q. 70–85). In moderately severe cases, patients usually require special training, guidance, and supervision (I.Q. 50–69). Such cases are commonly referred to as *morons.* In severe cases, custodial and complete protective care is required (I.Q. 20–49). Such cases are commonly referred to as *imbeciles*. In the most severe cases, which are referred to as *idiots* (I.Q. 20 and below), severe neurologic and endocrine disturbances generally complicate the picture. The need for institutionalization is usually proportionate to the degree of impairment and the level of emotional adjustment.

mental disorder. Any psychiatric illness or disease officially defined in the *Diagnostic and Statistical Manual for Mental Diseases*. (Am. Psychiatric Assn., 1952), or so regarded through usage.

mental dynamism. Mental mechanism (*q.v.*).

mental fatigue. See *Fatigue, mental*.

mental health. See *Emotional health*.

mental hygiene. The effort to reduce the incidence of mental illness through prevention and early treatment.

mental mechanism. (1) A specific intrapsychic defensive process. It operates outside of and beyond conscious awareness. Through its employment, resolution of emotional conflict and freedom from anxiety is sought. (2) An unconscious attempt at resolution of an emotional conflict. The unconscious mechanism for attempting to resolve anxiety or to reinforce repression. (3) A mental process which takes place out of awareness as an attempted way of securing relief from emotional tension or avoiding the pain of uncomfortable emotions. Conscious efforts in similar directions are not infrequent and may be given the same name. The process to be a "true" mental mechanism, however, must be unconscious (i.e., out of awareness).

The following is a list of the more commonly described mental mechanisms (for which definitions may be found in this Glossary):

Mental Mechanisms, Major

1. Compensation
2. Conversion
3. Denial
4. Displacement
5. Dissociation
6. Fantasy
7. Idealization
8. Identification
9. Incorporation
10. Internalization
11. Introjection
12. Inversion
13. Projection
14. Rationalization
15. Reaction formation
16. Regression
17. Repression
18. Restitution
19. Sublimation (rechannelization)
20. Substitution
21. Symbolization
22. Undoing

Mental Mechanisms, Minor

1. Absolution
2. Atonement and penance
3. Compartmentalization
4. Compromise Formation
5. Condensation
6. Convergence
7. Deferment
8. Devaluation
9. Distortion
10. Diversion
11. Extension
12. Externalization
13. Fainting
14. Fire Drill
15. Generalization
16. Intellectualization
17. Isolation
18. Overdeterminism
19. Personal Invulnerability
20. Replacement
21. Retribution
22. Retrospective devaluation
23. Reversal
24. Splitting
25. Unwitting Ignorance
26. Withdrawal

menticide (Meerloo). A term recently introduced for the "processing" of prisoners, so as to have them present desired behavior at trial or otherwise. Also called "brain washing."

Mesmer, Anton (1733–1815). An Austrian who used hypnosis in treatment in the early nineteenth century, in Paris.

mesmerism. After Anton Mesmer, an early term for hypnosis. See *Hypnosis*.

mesoderm. The middle of the three major layers of the embryo.

mesomorph (Sheldon). A type of person characterized by the predominant development of the mesoderm. He would presumably be characterized by prominent muscular and skeletal development, and would be active and energetic.

metrazol therapy. A type of shock treatment by intravenous administration of Metrazol, now seldom used. Originally introduced by von Meduna, Metrazol produces generalized convulsions.

Meyer, Adolf (1866–1945). Distinguished American psychiatrist who formulated and introduced his concepts of psychobiology as a unitary approach to mental disorders. He was a longtime professor at Johns Hopkins University. See *Psychobiology*.

micron. One one-thousandth (.001) part of a millimeter.

migraine. An illness characterized by recurrent severe headaches. These are often limited to one area and are often associated with visual phenomena, and nausea or vomiting. Frequently due to unconscious emotional conflicts.

milieu. Environment.

Military Stressful Eras, M.S.E. (see *M.S.E.*).

miosis. Contracted pupil.

misanthropy. Hatred of mankind.

misogamy. Aversion to marriage.

misogyny. Aversion to women.

Mitchell, S. Weir (1830–1914). A distinguished early American psychiatrist who developed and used a once popular "rest cure" type of treatment for certain neuroses.

Mongolism. A variety of congenital mental deficiency, so-called because of a superficial resemblance to oriental facial characteristics.

mood. The state of emotions; a prolonged affect.

morbid. Diseased, sick, unhealthy, pathologic; pertaining to illness.

Morel, B. A. (1809–1873). French psychiatrist who first used the term *obsession* (in 1861), and introduced the term *dementia praecox.*

mores. The traditional standard of a social or ethnic group.

moron: A person who is mentally deficient. The I.Q. is 50 to 69. (Normal 100.)

motility. The power of movement. In psychiatry it may include all forms of movement, such as speech, gestures, writing, and locomotion. In mental disease, motility may be disturbed quantitatively, as in restlessness, agitation, motor retardation, and waxy flexibility. It may also be qualitatively disturbed, as in convulsive disorders.

mourning. Grief and sadness over loss. In contradistinction to depression, the reaction is apparently appropriate to the loss, which is external and realistic.

mutism. The absence of speech. May be organic in origin, or the result of negativism or perverseness.

myasthenia. Muscular weakness.

myelitis. Inflammation (usually infection) of the spinal cord. (*Transverse myelitis* is sometimes used to indicate the organic lesion of a cord severance.)

myoclonus. Muscular spasm.

mysophobia. The morbid fear of dirt, germs, or contamination. See *Phobia.*

N

narcissism (also **narcism**). Self-love. In a broader sense indicates a level of self-interest which is normal in early childhood and pathologic in adulthood. Narcissism indicates the presence of a dominant interest in the self.

narcoanalysis. A term similar to narcosynthesis in which psychotherapeutic techniques are employed under the influence of drugs, in certain selected acute cases.

narcolepsy. Brief uncontrollable episodes of sleeping.

narcomania. Over-interest in or preoccupation with sleep and sleeping.

narcosis. The sleep-like state induced by a narcotic drug.

narcosis therapy. Prolonged sleep used as a treatment for certain types of anxieties and excitements. Usually sleep is induced by giving drugs of the barbiturate group.

narcosynthesis (Grinker). Psychotherapeutic treatment of acute combat cases under Sodium Amytal or Pentothal. Abreaction can play an important role in the therapeutic results. Has since had wider applications.

necrophilia. The pathologic sexual use of dead bodies.

necrophobia. The pathologic or morbid fear of the dead.

negative feeling. (1) Hate, dislike, unfriendliness, and "cold" feelings, as opposed to "positive" or "warm" feelings. (2) Destructive, antagonistic, and/or hostile feelings.

negativism. (1) A perverse kind of opposition and resistance to suggestions or advice. Contrariness. Negativism is a psychologic defense, e.g., as automatic ego-preservation seen with people who subjectively feel "pushed around." (2) The opposite behavior to what is ordinarily called for in a given situation.

neologism. In psychiatry a new word, word-symbol, or condensed combination of several words, most often coined by a psychotic patient which expresses a meaning, sometimes a highly complex meaning, usually known only to him. Seen particularly in schizophrenia.

neonate. Newly born.

nervous. Uneasy, apprehensive, jittery, anxious feelings. A lay term for anxiety and tension.

nervous breakdown. A general, nonspecific term for emotional illness. Primarily a lay term. Sometimes employed as a euphemism for insanity, mental disease, or psychosis.

neuralgia. (1) A nonspecific lay term used rather inaccurately and vaguely to refer to various kinds of general aches and pains. (2) Pain along a nerve trunk or in its area of distribution.

neurasthenia. An emotional reaction of neurotic level, usually marked by symptoms of emotional fatigue and fatigability, weakness, feelings of inadequacy, irritability, poor concentration, and various other psychologic, emotional, and physical features. As a diagnostic label, it has tended to become obsolete. Neurasthenia was originally regarded as due to weakness or "exhaustion" of the nervous system.

Neurasthenia is the only major diagnostic term introduced by an American (George Miller Beard, 1869). It was widely used for many decades. This term and concept was predicated on the mistaken belief that the major symptoms, such as fatigue, anxiety, weakness, and sexual malfunctions, were due to weakness (*asthenia*) of the nerves (*neuro*).

Currently this concept and term are falling out of use.

neuritis. Inflammation of a nerve. Also tends to be used rather loosely in lay parlance to describe various aches and pains, more frequently in the extremities, but also generally.

neurologist. A physician with special postgraduate training and experience in the field of organic disorders and diseases of the nervous system, and whose professional endeavors are primarily directed in this area.

neurology. The branch of medical science devoted to the anatomy, physiology, and pathology of the nervous system, its functions and disorders.

neuropsychiatry (NP). A term used to indicate the combination of the specialties of neurology and psychiatry.

neuroses

　actual n. Anxiety Neurosis, Hygeiaphrontis (hypochondriasis), and Neurasthenia.

　Narcissistic n. Manic depressive psychosis, schizophrenia, and the psychogenic psychoses. See also *Neurosis, narcissistic.*

　transferences n. Anxiety Neurosis, Somatic Conversion, (Hysteria), and the Phobic Reactions. See *Neurosis, Transference.*

neurosis (also **psychoneurosis**). The neuroses are one of the two major categories of emotional illness, the other being the psychoses. (1) A neurosis is an emotional illness with minimal loss of contact with reality in thinking and judgment. (2) A disturbance of emotional adaptation due to unresolved internal (i.e., unconscious) conflict. Usually less severe than a psychosis. The patient often recognizes that his emotional feelings are out of keeping with the apparent external stimulus. (3) A neurosis represents the attempted resolution of unconscious emotional conflicts in a manner that handicaps, to varying degrees, the effectiveness of a person in living. The neurosis always affects the personality structure as a whole. It is an unconsciously elaborated psychic mode of response, which is defensively intended and motivated.

The different types of neurosis are described according to the particular symptoms which predominate, as follows:

accident n. One of the neuroses following trauma.

anxiety n. An established and chronic emotional illness. It is characterized primarily by the direct subjective experiencing of anxiety. Anxiety is also expressed directly in varying degree by psychomotor, autonomic, and mental pathways. The effects and consequences of the direct manifestations of anxiety in chronic form are also an important part of the clinical features of Anxiety Neurosis.

Symptoms include subjective uneasiness, apprehension, or anxious expectation. In this condition, the anxiety is not controlled. The various specific defense mechanisms, as seen to be operative in other neuroses, are minor. It is a state of apprehension in which the anxiety present is out of proportion to any apparent external causes.

An established chronic reaction, in which anxiety and its effects are expressed more or less directly, as the most prominent manifestation. See pp. 104*ff*.

character n. The manifestations of the Character Neuroses (preferably Character Reactions), are found in the defensive character and personality traits of the person, and are expressed in patterns of his adjustment and behavior.

The formation of specific symptoms, as seen in other neuroses, is absent. Instead, the defensive character traits become exaggerated. More or less specific constellations of traits are seen, for example, in (1) the Hysterical Personality, (2) the Depressive Personality, and (3) the Obsessive Personality. See *Character Neurosis.*

conversion hysteria; somatic conversion. An emotional illness in which the consciously disowned impulses are transmuted into symbolic somatic expression. The body symptoms which result serve to allay anxiety by maintaining repression and by seeking resolution of unconscious conflicts. The latter is sought through the symbolic expression and gratification of the disowned impulses. Some symbolic expression of the defenses against them is usually also present.

Instead of being experienced consciously, the emotional conflict is converted and expressed in physical symptoms in various parts of the body, especially those which are mainly under voluntary control. The principal mechanism is that of conversion. In a broad sense all neurotic reactions may be regarded as "conversions." They can be classified as Somatic Physiologic, and Psychologic Conversions. See *Conversion Reaction.*

depressive reaction. The presence of low spirits (i.e., depressed mood) is the prominent feature. In neurotic depression these do not reach the proportions of a psychotic depression which may be thought of as being of a lower depth. See also *Depression, Anxious Depression* and *Reactive Depression.*

dissociative reaction. An emotional illness characterized by personality disorganization with various dissociative reactions, such as depersonalization, dissociated personality, fugues, amnesia, or somnambulism. See *Dissociation.*

fatigue reactions. Emotional Fatigue, the Fatigue State, and sometimes Neurasthenia. Psychoneurotic reactions in which the fatigue resulting from emotional stress is the prominent feature. Neurasthenia and asthenia are older terms which continue to enjoy some use. See *Fatigue, Emotional;* and *Fatigue State.*

Hygeiaphrontis (hypochondriasis). Overconcern with Health; Somatic and Physiologic Preoccupation. A neurosis in which there is an obsessive kind of persistent overconcern with the state of physical or emotional health. It is accompanied by the development of various somatic complaints and symptoms without responsible organic pathology. See also *hypochondriasis.*

narcissistic n. A term used by Freud for the reactions in which the capacity for transference of feelings to another person was believed not to be present. Included the psychogenic psychoses, manic-depressive psychosis, and schizophrenia.

neurasthenia (Beard). An emotional reaction of neurotic level, usually marked by symptoms of emotional fatigue and fatigability, weakness, feeling of inadequacy, irritability, poor concentration, and various other psychologic, emotional, and physical features. As a diagnostic term, it has tended to become obsolete. It was originally regarded as due to exhaustion or weakness of the nervous system.

Neuroses-Following-Trauma. A group of emotional illnesses having their onset following physical or acute psychic injury. Includes combat neuroses, industrial neuroses, and compensation neuroses. These are neurotic reactions which have been attributed to or which follow a situational traumatic event, or a series of such events, which may be physical, acute emotional, or both. The dynamics will usually reveal that the circumstance or event already has some specific and special individual significance for the patient.

The resulting emotional or physical consequences are highly variable in degree and in time of onset. See pp. 831–898.

organ n. (Fenichel). An emotional illness with functional and even anatomic alterations. Physiologic changes are caused by the inappropriate use of the function in question.

obsessive-compulsive n. Emotional patterns of reaction associated with the intrusion of insistent repetitive unwanted ideas, or of repetitive, unwelcome impulses to perform certain acts. The patient may regard his ideas and behavior as being either logical or unreasonable. He may feel compelled to carry out certain rituals which may include, for example, repetitive handwashing, touching, or counting, etc.

phobic reactions. Neuroses in which the most prominent feature is the presence of a specific irrational fear which is out of proportion to the apparent stimulus. Commonly observed forms of phobic reactions include fear of dirt, closed spaces, heights, open spaces, animals, syphilis, and other illness. See *Phobia*.

Soterial R. Neurotic Reaction in which security is sought or received from an external object-source. The converse of the *Phobic Reaction* (*q.v.*). *See* pp. 607–639.

symptom n. Any neurosis marked by the development of neurotic symptoms, as distinguished from the overdeveloped and handicapping traits which are present as symptom-equivalents in the Character Neuroses. See *Character Neurosis*.

transference n. Anxiety Neurosis, Obsessive Neurosis, the Phobias, and Somatic Conversion (hysteria). Grouped together by Freud as the neuroses most amenable to analytic therapy, because of their basic capacity for developing transference.

traumatic n. See *Neuroses following Trauma*.

vegetative n. (Alexander). Psychogenic dysfunction of a vegetative organ. The physiologic accompaniment of constant or periodically recurring emotional states.

neurotic. Adjective. Not properly used as a noun.

neurotic anxiety. Fear objectively out of proportion to the apparent cause. See *Anxiety*.

Neurotic Reactions

Higher and more advanced: Depression Reactions, Fatigue Reactions. Overconcern with Health or Hygeiaphrontic Reactions, and Obsessive-Compulsive Reactions.

Primitive and massive: Somatic Conversions, Dissociative Reactions, Soterial Reactions, certain Neuroses Following Trauma, and possibly the Phobic Reactions.

neurogenic. Bringing on or favoring the development of a neurosis.

nihilism. (1) A doctrine of meaninglessness or nothingness. (2) A delusion of nonexistence of the self or part of the self.

nosology. The naming and classification of pathologic conditions.

nostalgia. Homesickness.

numerophobia. The morbid fear of a number or of numbers. See *Phobia*.

nyctophobia. The morbid fear of darkness or night. See *Phobia*.

nymphomania. The presence of a pathologic amount of sexual drive or excitement in the female. The female counterpart of *satyriasis* in the male. *Inverted nymphomania* is the active homosexual state in the female.

O

object libido. The focus of libido upon persons, objects, or things external to the self.

obsession. An unwanted but repetitive

thought which intrudes rather imperatively into conscious awareness. Highly charged with unconscious emotional significance, it recurs against conscious wishes. Unconsciously elaborated, it is a defensively intended endeavor. Characteristically, an obsessive thought is insistent, recurrent, and intrusive.

Obsessive-Compulsive Reaction or **Neurosis.** See *Neurosis.*

Obsessive Personality. The descriptive term for a type of personality structure in which there is present a pattern of several of the obsessive group of personality traits or defenses. These may or may not be sufficiently marked to cause interference with living, a loss of efficiency, or a limitation of normal satisfactions or social adjustment. When they are, this constitutes the obsessive type of Character Neurosis. The Obsessive Personality is one major constellation of character defenses. The obsessive group of character or personality traits includes orderliness, inhibition of emotions and reactions, obstinacy, meticulousness, overconscientiousness, worry over trifles, hidden feelings of inadequacy and self-doubt, indecisiveness, preciseness, procrastination, pessimism, parsimoniousness, and perfectionism.

Obsessive Personality.

   Outward Reversal of Appearance Concept. An individual's outward appearance may be the reverse of his inner feelings. An obsessively oriented person may appear confident, courageous and self-possessed, while he may actually feel inadequate, self-doubting and timorous. Also referred to as *Outward Obsessive Facade.*

occupational therapy. A useful adjunctive type of therapy especially used in mental hospitals. The patient's interests are partly stimulated and occupied in supervised, constructive handicrafts, manual pursuits, and certain sports and recreational activities.

   Occupational therapy or O.T. provides an opportunity for partial sublimation and/or *acting out* of a patient's unconscious emotional conflicts. Similar therapies include music t., recreation t., drama t., dance t., and bibliotherapy.

oedipal period. The stage of development from 3 to 6 or 7 years of age. Also known as the *genital* or *phallic stage,* or early childhood.

oedipus complex. The early childhood emotional constellation in which there is emotional attachment by the boy to his mother, and hostility toward his father. See *Complex.*

oligophrenia. Mental deficiency.

omnipotent. All-powerful; God-like.

onanism. Incomplete sexual relations with withdrawal just prior to emission. Coitus interruptus. Sometimes used incorrectly as a synonym for masturbation.

onomatomania. A pathologic preoccupation with words, names, and terms.

ontogeny. The normal developmental sequence of the individual from the fertilized ovum onward.

onychophagia. Nail biting.

ophidiophobia. The morbid fear of snakes. See *Phobia.*

opisthotonus. A spastic arched back, as seen for example in the tonic phase of generalized convulsions.

Oppenheim, Hermann (1876–1949). German neurologist who devised a theory of molecular, organic change as a possible basis for the Traumatic Neuroses.

optic atrophy. Degeneration of the optic nerve or nerves.

oral conflict. See *Hypothesis of the oral conflict.*

oral erotic phase. The loving (nursing) phase of the oral stage of psychosexual development, usually from birth to 12 months, continuing to as much as 24 months of age.

oral erotism. The primordial pleasurable experience of nursing. Oral erotism is seen in usually disguised and sublimated form in later life.

oral sadistic phase. The aggressive biting phase of the oral stage of psychosexual development.

   Both *oral erotism* and *oral sadism* continue into later life in disguised and sublimated forms.

oral stage. The first stage of the infantile period in psychosexual development, lasting from birth to 12 months, or even to 24 months of age.

Includes both the *oral erotic* and the *oral sadistic* phases (*q.v.*).

organ erotism. In analytic theory, the investment (i.e., overevaluation) of some organ with libido. In this way it comes to be particularly cherished or to have special significance.

organ language. (1) The distorted expression of intrapsychic conflict via change in organ function, as in Physiologic Conversion. (2) Physiologic language, analogous to somatic language of Somatic Conversion (Hysteria).

organ neurosis (Fenichel). An emotional illness with functional and even anatomic alterations. Physiologic changes are caused by the inappropriate use of the function in question. See *Neurosis, organ.*

organic disease. (1) Disease based on physical causes and structural changes, as opposed to functional or psychogenic illness. Examples: infections, cancer, degenerative changes. (2) Illness characterized by structural changes in the tissues and organs of the body. Basic causes are generally physical, as opposed to emotional.

Organic fatigue. See *fatigue, organic.*

organic psychosis. A psychosis of organic etiology, as distinguished from a psychosis of emotional and conflictual origin. An illness of psychotic depth resulting from organic factors, as opposed to emotional or functional. A major mental illness resulting from defect, damage, infection, tumor, or other organic pathology of the brain.

organicist. In psychiatry, one who believes that emotional disorders are based upon organic change or disease.

orgasm. The climax in sexual relations.

orientation. Awareness of oneself in relation to one's spatial, temporal, and interpersonal situations. Orientation is accordingly spoken of in terms of time, place, and person. Time and space appreciation, as well as an appreciation of one's own identity and that of others, is necessary to relate oneself accurately and relatively to his surroundings.

orthopsychiatry. Preventive psychiatry, especially the study of the intrapsychic factors in the development of the normal personality in children.

An emphasis is placed upon preventive techniques which are designed to promote normal healthy emotional growth and development.

Ostrich Concept. The ostrich reputedly buries his head in the sand when danger appears. The Ostrich Concept is especially used in conjunction with, or in reference to the mental mechanism of Denial.

outward aggression. See *aggression, outward.*

Outward Obsessive Façade. See *Obsessive Personality, Outward Reversal of Appearance.*

overcompensation. A mental process of compensation taking place in which a real or fancied deficit inspires an exaggerated effort which results in overcorrection. The handicap may be physical or psychologic. Instead of being handicapped, the individual may become very adept in the area of the original handicap. He may also develop an emotional or characterologic hypertrophy.

Overconcern with Health. See *Hygeiaphrontis; hypochondriasis.*

overdeterminism. In overdeterminism the bases of psychic and emotional phenomena are not merely determined. In accord with the doctrine of scientific determinism, they are overdetermined, and the occurrence of a given emotional reaction, symptom, dream-symbol, and so on, is ensured.

overlay. Medically, an increment; a later addition superimposed upon an existing state or condition. See *Psychogenic overlay.*

overvalued ideas. Overvalued ideas obtrude themselves into the foreground, are remembrances of significant experiences, and are not felt as incorrect or strange.

P

pack. A sedative measure in hydrotherapy for calming overexcited or agitated patients. The "pack" consists of several sheets wrung out in cold or hot water and wrapped snugly around the patient who lies in them for varying periods of time. Cold packs (approximately 60°F.) and hot packs (approximately 120–130°F.) are employed.

Pain, Reciprocal Influences of Anxiety and. See *Anxiety*.

panic. An attack of acute anxiety; the so-called Acute Anxiety Attack or Anxiety Panic.

panphobia. Multiple pervasive phobias.

papilledema. Swelling of the head of the optic nerve or disc. May be seen with the ophthalmoscope. Generally indicates increased intracranial pressure.

Paracelsus (1493–1541). A Swiss German physician who rejected demonology in mental disorders.

parageusia. Distortion of the taste sense.

paralysis. The loss of the power of voluntary motion in some part or parts of the body.

paralysis agitans. A progressive degenerative disease of middle or later life characterized by tremors and increasing interference with voluntary motion. Parkinson's disease.

paramnesia. An unconsciously false memory, or recollection.

paranoia. (1) A rare type of serious emotional disorder of psychotic depth, characterized by an internally logical, intricate, gradually developing system of delusions (i.e., false beliefs), usually of a persecutory variety. These may serve to endow the patient with apparent (i.e., imagined) superior ability, power, or position. In general, the remainder of the personality is left intact. The pure form of paranoia is very rare.

paranoia litigans. A paranoid state marked by legal activity or preoccupation on the part of the patient.

paranoid. The adjective for paranoia. It is also used to indicate a diminutive form of paranoia, i.e., "paranoia-like"; close to, resembling, partially, or like paranoia. The pure form of paranoia is very rare.

paranoid condition or **state.** An emotional condition marked by paranoid trends or paranoid character defenses.

Paranoid Personality. Characterized by a protectively-intended distance-maintaining, distrustfulness, suspiciousness, hostility, and use of the mechanism of *Projection* (*q.v.*).

paranosic gain (Freud). See *Primary Gain* and *Endogain*.

paraplegia. Paralysis of the lower half of the body, including the legs. Upper or superior paraplegia is the paralysis of the arms, shoulders, and usually the upper trunk.

parapsychology. The study of psychic (also called Psi) phenomena; namely, those relationships between persons and events which apparently occur extraphysically, without the apparent intervention of the five human senses. Divided into *psychokinesis,* where the action part of the event predominates, and *extrasensory perception,* where the sensation part predominates.

parasympathetic nervous system. The cranio-sacral, or "extended vagus" system. The sympathetic nervous system and the parasympathetic nervous system together make up the autonomic or vegetative nervous system. The parasympathetic system is cholinergic and generally anabolic and inhibitory.

parataxic distortion (Sullivan). See *Distortion*.

parenchyma. The distinctive and essential tissue of an organ.

Parental Role, First Tenet of. In its broadest aspects, the healthy and constructive facilitation of the process of acculturation and maturation of the child, in an atmosphere of affection and security. This is the fundamental and most important responsibility of parenthood; the *first tenet* of the parental role.

paresis. A psychosis resulting from syphilitic infection of the brain, frequently characterized by the release of previously inhibited but grossly personality characteristics.

Parkinson's disease. An organic syndrome synonymous with paralysis agitans.

paroxysm. A spasmodic attack.

passive-aggressive personality. An immaturity reaction of adulthood characterized by aggression being exhibited in passive ways. Typical is the use of childish behavior such as pouting, stubbornness, procrastination, and passive obstructionism. A neurotic pattern of adjustment and relating to others.

passive-dependent personality. An immaturity reaction of adulthood characterized by helplessness, lack of self-reliance, lack of self-confidence, compliance, indecisiveness, and emotional dependency. A neurotic pattern of adjustment and relating to others.

pathognomonic. Distinctive, specific, diagnostic.

Pavlov, Ivan Petrovich (1849–1936). A Russian neurophysiologist who did early experimental work in conditioned reflexes. Awarded Nobel Prize in Medicine for work on the physiology of digestion.

pavor diurnus. Daytime attacks of terror or anxiety, especially in children.

pavor nocturnus. Night terrors. Attacks of anxiety during sleep.

pederasty. Sexual intercourse with a boy, by anus. To be distinguished from *sodomy, (q.v.).*

pedophilia. A love of children, particularly the sexual love of children by an adult.

penis envy. Literally, envy on the part of the female of the possession of a penis. More generally, the female wish for male attributes, position, or advantages. These may be real, or fancied and neurotic. Such feelings are seen by some to enter importantly into the development of certain character attributes or traits in the female.

pentothal interview. The use of Pentothal sodium as an aid to interview and therapy; narcoanalysis; or narcosynthesis.

perception. Awareness. Incoming stimuli are recorded by the sensory end-organs, transformed into nervous impulses, so that in turn the nature of objects, persons, and animals, and the self can be recognized. Perception involves the combination of different sensations and the utilization of past experiences for the purpose of recognition.

perseveration. The persistent, rather aimless repetition of an activity, words, or phrases.

persona. In Jungian psychology, the personality "mask" or facade which each person presents to the outside world.

personal yardstick. See *Yardstick, personal.*

personality. The sum total of one's character traits, especially as these enter into his internal and external patterns of adjustment to life. The dynamic organization of all those factors within the individual which determine his adjustment to life. These include attributes, drives, aspirations, inhibitions, strengths, weaknesses, and the sum total of the individually varying patterns of reaction.

personality, multiple. The very rare type of major dissociative reaction in which the individual at one time or another will adopt one of two or more different personalities. These are separate and compartmentalized, with total amnesia for the one, or ones, not in use.

personality disorder. A term used diagnostically to include a number of types of disturbances of personality integration.

personality trait. Character attribute or defense. See *Character Defense.*

Personality Types
Conversion (or hysterical) personality, *(q.v.).*
Depressive personality, *(q.v.).*
Obsessive personality, *(q.v.).*
See also *Chapter 5.*

personalize. Making something personal, giving it more personal significance.

persuasion. A largely intellectual kind of therapeutic approach directed toward influencing the patient, his attitudes, behavior, or goals.

perversion. (1) Sexual deviation. See *Perversion, Sexual.* (2) The misdirection of instinctual sexual strivings, usually in a way contrary to the social mores. Often used in reference to homosexuality.

perversion, sexual. The direction of sexual interests, aims, or activity in other than the more usual heterosexual direction.

Pessimism Defense Concept. The Obsessive Personality, seeking protection, anticipates the worst; whatever happens will be less than expected. Related to *"Be Prepared" Concept.*

petit mal. Literally, "little sickness." A slight or partial type of epileptic seizure, as opposed to the gross convulsion of the grand mal.

phallic stage. See *Oedipal period.*

phallus. Penis.

phantasm. Apparition or phantom. In

psychiatry, the phantom of the illusion or hallucination of the psychotic patient.

phantasmagoria. A host of spirits or phantoms; the raising of the spirits of the dead.

phantasy. See *Fantasy*.

phlegmatic. Slow, stable, unemotional, calm, unexcitable.

phobia. A pathologic fear. An obsessively persistent unrealistic fear which is inappropriate and unreasoning; a specific pathologic fear which is apparently out of proportion to the stimulus and which has been unconsciously attached to a specific external object on situation. Displacement of the painful affect has been effected out of conscious awareness from the actual but hidden and internal object to an external one. Example: Fear of heights, fear of closed spaces. A phobia is the converse of a *soteria*.

The following is a list of the more common phobias (or pathologic fears) by their technical names, with the phobic object indicated:

acrophobia. Heights. (Gr. *acro,* height or summit.)

agoraphobia. Open spaces (Gr. *agora,* marketplace, place of assembly.)

ailurophobia. Cats. (Gr. *ailouros,* cat.)

anthophobia. Flowers. (Gr. *anthos,* flowers.)

anthropophobia. People. (Gr. *anthropos,* man, genetically.)

aquaphobia. Water. (Lat. *aqua,* water.)

astraphobia. Lightning. (Gr. *astrape,* lightning.)

orontophobia. Thunder. (Gr. *bronte,* thunder.)

claustrophobia. Closed spaces. (Lat. *claustrum,* bar, bolt, lock. By metonymy, means barrier or bounds.)

cynophobia. Dogs. (Gr. *cynas,* dog.)

equinophobia. Horses. (Lat. *equinis,* horse.)

herpetophobia. Lizards or reptiles. (Gr. *herpetos,* a creeping or crawling thing.)

keraunophobia. Thunder. (Gr. *ceraunos,* thunderbolt.)

mysophobia. Dirt, germs, contamination. (Gr. *mysos,* uncleanliness of body or mind; abomination or defilement.)

necrophobia. Dead bodies. (Gr. *nekros,* a dead body.)

numerophobia. A number, or numbers. (Lat. *numero,* number.)

nyctophobia. Darkness, or night. (Gr. *nyx,* night.)

ophidiophobia. Snakes. (Gr. *ophis,* snake or serpent.)

pyrophobia. Fire. (Gr. *pyr,* fire.)

self-confining phobia. Phobically imposed area or spatial restrictions.

zoophobia. Animals. (Gr. *zoos,* animal.)

phobic avoidance. The modern "magical" adaptation of the "flight" from the primitive "fight or flight" response to danger. The avoidance of the external phobic object.

phobic endogain. The basic primary gain in denying, concealing, or controlling anxiety which is sought through the operation of the various mental mechanisms involved in the development of the phobia, out of conscious awareness.

phobic object. The objectively neutral object which is threatening and feared in a phobia.

Phobic Personality. Characterized by tendency to employ phobic patterns of defense and to develop the manifestations of a *Phobic Reaction* under sufficient stress. Employs techniques of avoidance in response to stress and anxiety.

Phobic Reaction. An unconscious neurotic pattern of attempted defense, characterized clinically by the presence of a phobia or phobias as the most prominent feature of the neurotic reaction and by the predilection to develop phobic manifestations under appropriate conditions of psychic stress. Displacement from the original internal source of threat and danger has taken place to an external object-source. Converse: *Soterial Reaction (q.v.)*

phrenology. The supposed determination of the faculties of the mind by external examination of the bony structure of the skull.

phylogenic. Referring to the history or development of the human race over the ages.

physiologic conversion. An expression into physiologic language of the repressed emotional conflict, with symptom formation of a physiologic nature. This concept is analogous to Hysterical Conversion as the expression into bodily language of the repressed emotional conflict with its symptom formation of a physical nature. See *Conversion*.

physique. Body structure.

Pick's disease. A presenile degenerative disease of the brain. The process affects the cerebral cortex, particularly the frontal lobes. Symptoms may include aphasia, intellectual deterioration, irritability, emotional instability, and progressive loss of social abilities.

Pinel, Phillipe (1745–1826). A French physician who reformed practices in the care of the mentally sick. He removed patients from dungeons and unchained them.

play therapy. A psychotherapeutic approach to children's emotional disorders in which the observation and interpretation of the child's use of his toys, clay, and paints, and his fantasy in his games and in his play, form an important part of the therapy.

pleasure principle. The biologic principle by which man ordinarily and automatically seeks to avoid pain and discomfort, and strives for gratification and pleasure.

poikilothermia. Temperature change in response to external change. A rare neurologic symptom seen in lesions of the hypothalamus of the brain.

polydypsia. Excessive thirst.

polyneuritis. A disorder of the peripheral nerves.

polyphagia. The symptom of excessive eating.

porencephaly. A cavity or cavities within the brain.

positive feeling. (1) Warm, friendly feelings: liking, fondness, friendliness, love. (As opposed to "negative" feelings.) (2) Constructive feelings.

potency. Sexual adequacy, especially in the male.

power struggle. A psychologic contest for dominence or control between two or more people.

pragmatic. Based upon practical observations or experiments.

preconscious. Referring to thoughts which are not in immediate awareness, but which can be recalled at will or by some conscious effort.

prefrontal lobotomy. See *Psychosurgery*.

pregenital. Developmental phase or stage of personality development before the emergency of genital interests.

prenatal. Prior to birth.

presbyophrenia. Early senile dementia. A syndrome of senile psychosis with confabulation and disorientation.

priapism. Persistent, pathologic, and usually painful erection of the penis. An organic condition. The term may be inaccurately used in a psychologic sense.

primal scene. Sexual intercourse, especially by the parents as early witnessed (in actuality or in fantasy) by their young child.

primary defense. The psychogenic symptom in emotional illness. The symptom, a psychologically intended defense, is primary, as opposed to the defense *of* the symptom which constitutes a *secondary defense*.

primary gain, endogain. The deeply buried and hidden psychologic basis of the emotional illness. It is more concealed and is not apparent to the external observer, although it may become so through intensive study. In contrast to the *epigain* (*q.v.*), the endogain is directed internally and aims at preserving ego integrity.

The primary gain is in the service of denial, containment, inhibition, repression, and symbolic gratification of repressed intolerable impulses, self-punishment for having had them, and the diversion and absorption of psychic energy. The internal conflicts concerned largely relate to forbidden and disowned aggressive-hostile and/or sexual drives, wishes and impulses. The gain aims to allay or to prevent anxiety through resolution of intrapsychic conflicts.

The primary gain is basic to the psychogenesis of every emotional illness. Epigain is often responsible in turn for its perpetuation, and contributes to the patient's resistance to therapeutic help.

Both types of gain are present in every emotional illness.

primary process. The free discharge of psychic energy and excitation. Seeks to take place from the unconscious without regard to the demands of the environment, reality, time, order, or logic, refers to that type of mental activity and thought process which is characteristic of unconscious mental life at all times and which in infancy often characterizes conscious mental life as well.

prison psychosis. Refers to severe emotional reactions of psychotic depth which are precipitated, by actual or anticipated incarceration. See *Ganser's syndrome.*

Prince, Morton (1854–1929). American psychiatrist who stimulated interest in psychopathology. Studied dissociative phenomena and described alternating personality.

Process schizophrenia. See *Schizophrenia, process.*

prodromata. Preliminary signs and/or symptoms generally preceding an illness.

progression. See *Generalization.*

projection. A mental mechanism operating outside of and beyond conscious awareness whereby the consciously disowned aspects of the self are rejected or disowned and thrown outward to become imputed to others. The individual attributes his own consciously unwanted and disapproved wishes, motivations, or emotional feelings to another. The attributes which he so assigns to another are real to him and he reacts in response to them accordingly. Sometimes loosely used to indicate the outward direction of affect from internal conflicts (a process which is more properly referred to as externalization).

Promotion depression. See *depression, promotion.*

protopathic sense. Perception of deep pain and temperature, as opposed to epicritic sensitivity. See *Epicritic sensitivity.*

pseudocyesis. False, often neurotically experienced pregnancy. Signs and symptoms of actual pregnancy may appear in support of the strong underlying wish for motherhood.

psychalgia. Psychic or emotional pain and distress.

psychasthenia. The term and concept of psychasthenia was introduced by Pierre Janet, in accord with his etiologic views of weakness (*asthenia*) of the psyche or mind underlying the symptoms. A number of our current neurotic diagnoses were included within this concept and diagnostic category. The term was widely adopted and used for many years.

People gradually became increasingly disenchanted with the concept however, and with the term as well. Accordingly, the use of psychasthenia as a diagnosis has almost completely died out.

psyche. The mind.

psychiatrist. A physician with special postgraduate training and experience in the field of emotional illness and mental disorders, whose professional endeavors are confined to this area. The psychiatrist has an M.D. degree, and specializes in the practice, research, teaching, and administration of psychiatry.

psychiatry. A basic medical science which deals with the genesis, diagnosis, prevention, and treatment of emotional illness and socially unsatisfactory behavior. Also included are special fields of interest such as mental deficiency, physical disorders with associated emotional components or sequelae, psychiatric research, teaching, and administration. Psychiatry is largely concerned with those mental processes which result in abnormal thought, behavior, and symptoms.

Existential p. Based on existential philosophy of Kierkegaard, Sartre, *et al.*

Forensic p. Psychiatry which deals with the legal aspects of mental disorders.

psychic determinism. See *Determinism.*

Psychic Distaste Concept. Anxiety and emotional conflict may lead to emotional and figurative distaste for a person, situation, job, etc.

psychic trauma. See *trauma, psychic.*

psychoanalysis: (1) A psychologic theory of human development and behavior, a method of research, and a system of psychotherapy, the original outlines and foundations for which were largely laid down by Sigmund Freud. In psychoanalysis, by the use of techniques such as free association and dream interpretation, emotions and behavior are traced to repressed instinctual drives in the unconscious. Treatment seeks to modify emotions and behavior by bringing into awareness the origin and effects of the hidden (i.e., unconscious) emotional conflicts, resulting in an increased understanding of the feelings associated with them. (2) A system of insight therapy based upon the works of Freud and subsequent contributors. Cardinal tenets include the concepts of determinism, repression, unconscious resistance, and the interpretation of the psychologic efforts to resolve conflict and to avoid anxiety. Use is made of free association and dream interpretation in the collaborative work of therapy.

psychoanalyst. A psychiatrist with special additional postgraduate training in psychoanalysis, who employs the techniques of psychoanalytic therapy to secure awareness and resolution of unconscious emotional conflicts. (A very few nonphysicians are recognized as psychoanalysts in the United States; a few more, in England.)

psychobiology (Adolf Meyer). The concept of the individual as a total biologic unit. Personality development and functioning of the individual from birth is studied as part of the total organism. The *distributive analysis* of the psychobiologist is the study of the complete longitudinal history, including all the mental and physical factors associated with the growth, development, and status of the individual. Through the therapeutic processes of distributive analysis and synthesis the psychiatrist undertakes to help his patient effect better utilization of the assets of his personality and minimize the effects of the liabilities.

psychodrama. A technique of group psychotherapy, developed by J. L. Moreno, in which individuals dramatize their emotional problems through playing assigned roles. The members of the audience also participate in and profit by the dramatization.

psychodynamics. The predictive science of human behavior and motivation. Through the successful application of psychodynamic principles, the individual's personality make-up and many of his reactions at any given time can theoretically be traced to past interactions between the individual and his environment (including the interpersonal) from birth onward. Psychodynamics is based upon the study and knowledge of mental mechanisms and other basic concepts and principles of modern psychiatry. The important role of unconscious motivation in human behavior, interaction, and reaction is recognized and forms an important part of the science.

psychogenesis. The emotional or interpersonal origin and development of an emotional illness.

psychogenic. Of intrapsychic origin. Psychogenic is an adjective referring to the emotional or psychologic origin of a condition, as opposed to an organic origin.

psychogenic overlay. The emotionally determined increment to an existing symptom or disability which has been of an organic or physically traumatic origin. Psychogenic overlay may be used somewhat inaccurately to refer to the psychologic exploitation by the patient of the illness or its symptoms. This is then secondary gain which may be consciously and/or unconsciously secured. See *Secondary gain,* and *Epigain.*

psychokinesis. The supposed production of an external event by a person without his actual physical intervention. Example: The supposed influencing of what number will appear when the dice are tossed, or which card will appear when a deck is cut, through the exertion of will power or mental effort.

psychologic "blind spots." Those aspects of oneself or of one's relationships with others for which one lacks conscious perceptive ability. The perceptive ability is *blocked.* This is often despite clear recognition by another person. Also sometimes referred to as psychologic blocks.

psychologist. One who specializes in the practice or teaching of psychology. The psychologist generally holds an academic degree (B.A.) or a graduate degree (M.A. or Ph.D.). Ordinarily not having medical training or a medical degree (M.D.), he is not licensed to practice medicine. (*Cf. psychiatrist.*)

psychology. The branch of science devoted to the study of mental processes and behavior.

psychology, analytic. The system of Carl Jung in psychiatric theory, research, and treatment.

psychology, individual. The system of Alfred Adler in psychiatric theory, research, and therapy. Individual psychology stresses concepts of organ inferiority, the inferiority complex, and overcompensation.

psychometrics. The branch of science devoted to the testing and measuring of mental and psychologic ability, efficiency, potentials, and functioning. This is undertaken by the administration of the many tests which have been developed to test and measure various functions.

psychometry. Measurement of the psyche or mind. Especially refers to the administration of standard tests designed to measure intelligence.

psychomotor epilepsy. Epileptic seizure characterized by automations or temper outbursts. (Regarded by Alpers as a type of minor attack or petit mal.)

psychomotor excitement. Generalized physical and emotional overactivity in response to an internal push or pressure and/or external stimuli. Example: A hypomanic state.

psychomotor retardation. A general reduction in activity with a slowing of the drive and initiative. May include physical, mental, emotional, physiologic, and mental areas.

psychoneurosis. A nervous disorder arising largely from unconscious conflicts, marked by symptoms of an emotional character, and resulting in an impairment in one or more spheres of adjustment without loss of reality relationships. See *Neurosis.*

psychopath. A person suffering from a character neurosis of an asocial and antisocial type. Behavior is more or less amoral and/or antisocial and is marked by impulsive irresponsible acts. These satisfy immediate selfish ends or needs, and the individual appears to be narcissistically oriented, without the usual level of concern for the interests of others, nor for possible social consequences.

More properly used as the adjective psychopathic (rather than as a noun). See also *Psychopathic Personality.*

Psychopathic Personality. (1) A personality in which the behavior is impulsive, irresponsible, and calculated to satisfy only selfish interests, with unstable emotional and social adaptation. (2) An individual who is seemingly unable to anticipate the social consequences of his acts, or seemingly cares little about them. He has strong antisocial drives which he is unable to control. (3) One who does not "learn" by experience and who appears undeterred by the prospect of punishment. (Now included for diagnosis under *Sociopathic Personality Disturbances* and classified as the antisocial reactions. These persons are not psychotic, nor is their antisocial behavior dependent upon any actual intellectual deficit.) See also *Psychopath.*

psychopathology. The branch of science dealing with emotional and psychologic pathology. The disorder of mental and emotional processes and their development or psychogenesis. Morbid processes of the psyche or mind.

Psychophysiologic Disorder. A term adopted in 1952 to describe a type of reaction which represents the morbid (i.e., sick) physiologic expression of emotions. (The term was adopted in preference to "psychosomatic disorders" or "somatization reactions.") See also *Physiologic Conversion and Conversion.*

psychosexual development. The sequence of stages through which the infant and child pass in their growth and maturation, especially the stages of personality maturation.

psychosis. (1) A serious and generally prolonged pathologic emotional reaction, in which there is a departure from normal patterns of thinking, feeling, and acting. A severe disorder in the emotional life and personality integration which is accompanied by one or more of the following:

    A. Loss of contact with reality.

    B. Distortion of and inappropriateness of emotions.

    C. Regressive behavior or attitudes

in whole or in some part to an earlier, subjectively more satisfying period in the development of the individual. (See *Regression.*)

D. Loss of control of elementary (i.e., more primitive) impulses and desires.

E. Deterioration. Some deterioration of intelligence may occur in certain psychotic processes, especially those incident to organic disease. Emotional deterioration may also occur, especially with psychotic processes of psychologic origin.

F. Abnormal mental content, including delusions, hallucinations, or illusions.

G. Defective insight, self-evaluation, and awareness of aberrations in thinking, feeling, or behavior which may be present.

(2) A severe emotional illness with mild to complete interference in the ability to adjust socially. (3) Mental or emotional illness to a degree of severity that the patient often requires commitment to a mental hospital. He may be adjudged legally incompetent. See *Insanity.*

psychosomatic. (1) A term indicating the coequal importance, the mutual interactions, and the inseparable interdependency of the physical (or somatic) and the emotional (or psychologic) aspects of the individual. (2) An adjective used in describing serious emotional disorders which are manifested primarily in terms of physical illness. Examples: Asthma, chronic ulcerative colitis, urticaria.

Psychosomatic Illness (Weiss and English, Alexander, Dunbar, *et al.*)

Points out the inseparable nature of the psyche (mind) and the soma (body), their mutual interaction, and their coequal importance.

psychosomatic medicine. The consideration and study of a patient as an integrated organism consisting of body, mind, and emotions. The combination of physical and emotional factors is to be studied, regarded, and treated as an interacting whole.

psychosurgery. The treatment of functional psychotic disorders by means of brain surgery. The most commonly used operation is *prefrontal lobotomy* or *leukotomy,* in which certain nerve fiber tracts of the brain are cut. These are the fibers between the frontal lobes and thalamus. The object of the operation is to reduce emotional tension and distress associated with the individual's disturbed ideation and psychotic ideas. Lobotomy has a useful function in the relief of pain in certain cases of terminal cancer. Modifications of prefrontal lobotomy are *transorbital lobotomy* in which the cutting instrument is inserted through the bony part of the eye socket, and *topectomy* in which certain parts of the frontal lobes are removed. Lobotomy was originally performed by Moniz in Lisbon in 1936.

psychotherapy. (1) The treatment of emotional illnesses through various psychologic techniques. Psychotherapy is the general term for any type of treatment which is based primarily upon communication with the patient in the interview, in distinction to the use of drugs, physical measures, or surgery. Psychotherapy is properly reserved to adequately trained medical specialists or, in certain cases, under medical supervision. (2) The science and art of modifying behavior so as to make it more satisfactory to the patient and more compatible with social living. Most physicians regard psychotherapy as a medical responsibility. (3) A joint endeavor with patient and therapist together seeking greater understanding of the former's emotional processes in order to relieve symptoms. (4) The psychologic approach to emotional (neuroses, psychoses and character) disorders, as opposed to drug, shock and physical measures.

Psychotherapy:

Absence-of-Anxiety Concept. The absence of anxiety may interfere with, delay, or even prevent therapy.

Constructive anxiety. May play important role in initiating and or/continuing therapy.

Joint-Endeavor Principle. Collaborative endeavor by doctor and patient required for the increase in self-understanding, which is the goal of psychotherapy.

Mechanical Analogy. More effort and energy are required to initiate psychotherapy than is required to continue it.

Resistance in Psychotherapy. The patient's conscious or unconscious reluctance to relinquish old and established patterns of behavior; his opposition to allowing associations concerning, or to studying, emotionally painful material; his reluctant opposition to change.

Supportive p. A technique aiming to reinforce a patient's defenses and help suppress disturbing psychological material. It avoids depth probing of patient's emotional conflicts. Used when symptoms are insufficient to warrant intensive psychotherapy.

Treatment Rule. The patient undertakes to say every thought which comes to mind while he is with the psychiatrist, without reservation or censorship.

Psychotic dissociation. *See Dissociation, psychotic.*

puberty. The stage of development between 10 to 13 or 14 years.

pudendum. Genitals; the private parts.

puerile. Childish.

puerperal psychosis. A psychotic episode having its onset in the puerperal period.

puerperium. The period of childbirth.

punch drunk (Martland). The traumatic encephalopathy of prizefighters. A syndrome which can result from the cumulative punishment absorbed in the boxing ring. Characterized by the general slowing of mental functions, occasional bouts of confusion, and scattered bits of memory loss.

pupillary reflex. An automatic reaction of the pupil to light or to accommodation.

Putnam, James J. (1846-1918). American psychiatrist.

pyknic. Stocky. (A Kretschmer body type.)

pyromania. The morbid compulsion to set fires.

pyrophobia. The morbid fear of fire. See *Phobia.*

Q

quadriplegia. Paralysis involving all extremities.

quotient, intelligence. See *Intelligence Quotient,* and *Mental Deficiency.*

R

race. A people or nation of the same stock.

radiculitis. Inflammation of spinal nerve roots.

Rank, Otto (1844-1939) related his theories of anxiety neurosis to the shock at being born (birth trauma).

rapport. A state of mutual understanding. Rapport conveys the presence of a considerate level of harmony and agreement in a relationship.

rational. Sensible, arrived at through reasoning, especially sound reasoning.

rationalization (Jones). (1) a term commonly employed in everyday lay usage to indicate a clearly conscious attempt to explain away or to justify something which is unacceptable to oneself. This often relates to one's own disapproved motives, behavior, and desires, although it may be applied to others as well. Commonly referred to as "sour grapes" when used to devalue an unobtained goal. (2) A mental mechanism operating outside of and beyond conscious awareness in which one justifies or attempts to make intolerable, impulses, needs, feelings, behavior, and motives into one which are consciously tolerable and acceptable. (3) The unconscious substitution of a false but plausible motive for the real but consciously unacceptable one.

Rationalization, Eleemosynary. The relaxation or suspension of one's usual ethical standards, being thus justified on the basis of the worthwhileness of a group, organization, or cause, and so on, and in view of the supposed lack of personal selfish gain to be so derived.

Rationalization, Familial. Rationalization employed to maintain one's picture of the ideal of equality being present in parental affection and regard for each of one's children.

Rationalization, Social. The collective justification by a national group, a class of people, a party, etc., for the shared rationalization of behavior, motives, or guilt.

Ray, Isaac (1807-1881). Early American

psychiatrist who was a longtime superintendent of Butler Hospital, a founder of the American Psychiatric Association, and interested in the legal aspects of psychiatry.

His "Treatise on the Medical Jurisprudence of Insanity" was the pioneering American work in this field.

Reaction Formation. A mental mechanism operating outside of and beyond conscious awareness through which major attitudes, complexes, motives, and needs develop outwardly, which are the opposites of consciously disowned ones. These include large areas of the personality. A conscious reaction is thereby developed, reversing disowned inner drive, against which it thereby defends.

Reactive depression. See *Depression, reactive*.

reality principle. A principle which recognizes the need for modification according to the requirements of external reality. During personality development the original and infantile *pleasure principle* becomes gradually modified by the inescapable demands and requirements of external reality. The process by which this modification and compromise is effected is known as *reality testing* (*q.v.*). Example: Instinctual strivings may be modified in their expression according to the reality principle. Comes into conflict with the *pleasure principle* (*q.v.*)

reality testing. A process which is normally active in personality development and/or in psychiatric treatment. Through it the primordial *pleasure principle* becomes gradually modified in order to effect satisfactory compromises between it and the demands and requirements of external reality.

recessive. Latent or dormant. With reference to principles of inheritance, certain traits are recessive and are overshadowed and effaced by dominant traits.

Rechannelization. See *Sublimation* (rechannelization-preferred).

recidivism. The repetition of criminal and antisocial acts. A *recidivist* is a repeated offender.

Recurrence, Principle of. See *Depression*.

reefers. Slang term for marihuana cigarettes.

reference, delusion of, or idea of. See *delusion of reference*, and *ideas of reference*.

reflex. The automatic response to stimulus.

reflex, conditioned (Pavlov). An induced reflex response to a stimulus different in quality or quantity from the one originally required. The process of developing this kind of response is called conditioning.

regression. (1) The psychic process of returning in a more or less symbolic fashion to an earlier and subjectively more satisfactory (but actually more infantile and immature) level of adjustment. (2) The readoption of infantile ways of gratification. (3) Regression in psychosis may be accompanied by an actual relative return to certain infantile modes of behavior and living.

Regressive Therapy. The therapeutically encouraged and induced surrender by the personality of some level or part of the level of integration, adjustment and maturity already achieved. The aim is new and sounder progression, and a better base from which to begin.

reinforcement. A principle used particularly in dream interpretation which is similar and related to *convergence*. Refers to the support of later associations when they are similar to or like earlier ones. Subsequent dream content or the associations to it can also reinforce earlier associations.

relapse. A recurrence or exacerbation in the course of illness.

Relationship-Improvement Precept. In the improvement of any relationship, *both* parties must want to and must work at it, for successful results.

remission. The abatement of an illness, which may be temporary or permanent.

repetition compulsion. The unconscious need to repeat earlier experiences, relationships, or patterns of reaction, despite inherent disadvantages or self-defeat for the person concerned. The repetition which takes place outside of the conscious awareness of the inindividual, may constitute a recurrent and complex pattern of reaction.

replacement. A mental mechanism operating outside of and beyond conscious awareness in which the real object or feeling is replaced by another. Example: In phobias, the actual internal but hidden object of fear and dread is replaced by a substitute external one. As a mental mechanism, replacement is very similar to *substitution*.

Repression. The automatic, effortless and involuntary relegation of consciously repugnant or intolerable ideas, impulses and feelings into the unconscious. Such material is not ordinarily subject to voluntary conscious recall. Anxiety and the threat of anxiety is the active force which brings about Repression.

primary r. A primal kind of repression which is very early and concerns data which has never really entered into conscious awareness. This kind of repression relates to instinctual feelings, drives, and impulses of most early origin. Also called *primal* or *archaic repression*.

secondary r. Repression of something intolerable that has once been conscious.

resistance. (1) In psychotherapy the patient's conscious or unconscious reluctance to relinquish old and established patterns of behavior; his opposition to allowing associations concerning, or to studying, emotionally painful material; his opposition and reluctance to change. Resistance occurs as part of both conscious and unconscious efforts and endeavors to avoid anxiety. (2) In free association, the forces tending to restrict the free verbal expression of thoughts in unedited form and in unrestricted sequence. (3) The instinctual opposition to bringing repressed (unconscious) data into awareness. Resistance aims at the avoidance of anxiety.

resolution. In psychiatry, the bringing together or compromise of opposing views, as in the resolution of emotional conflict.

Respite-of-Sleep Principle. See *Sleep, Principle of Respite*.

Restitution. A mental mechanism operating outside of and beyond conscious awareness, through which the ego seeks to make amends and reparation to a person or group for losses which have been inflicted, or for injuries and damages for which responsibility is as-

sumed, as these are subjectively assessed by the perpetrator.

retardation. (1) Slowing down of mental and physical activity. Most frequently seen in severe depressions which are sometimes spoken of as *retarded depressions*. (2) A synonym for (mental) deficiency.

Retardation in Depression. See *Depression, Diffuse Retardation*.

Retribution. The unconscious granting or inflicting of one's desserts as requital for good or for evil, but perhaps more especially for evil. Objects for such requital are assessed according to their merit as subjectively evaluated.

retrograde amnesia. See *Amnesia*.

retrospective devaluation. An unconscious defensive endeavor in which one "downgrades" the level and seriousness of emotional significance for an event, in retrospect.

Retrospective Falsification. Unconscious distortion of past experiences to conform to present needs. Details are automatically added or subtracted in remembering an actual past event in order to conform to the existing pattern of thinking. Example: In delusions, events which originally took place before the delusion began are still explained and interpreted in keeping with the delusion.

Reversal. A mental mechanism in which there is an alteration to the opposite. It can refer to position, direction, order, sequence, relation and bearing. A more general term than *Inversion* (*q.v.*), from which distinction may be difficult.

rigidity. (1) Stiffness of muscles, position, posture, or bearing. (2) Psychologic rigidity, used to imply a great resistance and reluctance to change.

rivalry, sibling. Competition between siblings.

Rorschach, Hermann (1884-1922). A Swiss psychiatrist who developed the personality assessment test which bears his name.

Rorschach test. A psychologic test which has been designed to disclose conscious and unconscious personality traits and emotional conflicts through eliciting the patient's association and fantasy responses to a standard set of ink-blots.

Royal Anger. The negative angry and hostile feelings of the *King David Reaction* (*q.v.*).

Rule of Impression Priority. This rule is based upon the thesis that first impressions ordinarily tend to take an emotional priority. This applies to the coloring and influencing of the individual's subsequent attitudes and patterns of reaction to the subject of the impression, or to repetitions of the first experience. It is a corollary to the Theory of Antecedent Conflicts, and has important implications as to psychologic conditioning.

Rush, Benjamin (1745–1813). Early American physician, and signer of the Declaration of Independence, who wrote the first American text on psychiatry, in 1812. He has been referred to as the "father" of American psychiatry.

S

S.E.H.A. Specific Emotional Hazards of Adulthood (*q.v.*).

S.E.H.C. Specific Emotional Hazards of Childhood (*q.v.*).

sadism. A condition in which there is a derivation of pleasure, often sexually tinged, from inflicting pain, discomfort, or humiliation on another person or persons. Conscious awareness of the process and the underlying needs, or of the resulting gratification, may be relatively present or totally absent. The ill-treatment may be psychologic or physical. Sadism is the reverse of *masochism* (*q.v.*).

sapphism. Active female homosexuality.

satyriasis. Pathologically excessive sexual drive or activity in a male. May be of psychologic or organic etiology. Analogous to the term *nymphomania* for the female (*q.v.*).

Scientific Determinism, Doctrine of. Nothing in the emotional or mental life (as well as in the physical world) happens by chance alone. Everything thus that happens is the result of specific forces, motives, or causes, even though these may elude scrutiny or observation, and even though they may be deeply hidden or buried from conscious awareness.

schizoid. Characterized by traits of shyness, withdrawal, introspection, and introversion. Is used as an adjective to refer to mild schizophrenic or schizophrenic-like traits and reactions.

Schizophrenia. A group of severe emotional disorders (i.e., psychoses) most frequently occurring in late adolescence and young adulthood. It is marked by a retreat from reality, by emotional disharmony, by regressive behavior, and by affective deterioration. It is roughly synonymous with the older term "dementia praecox."

According to newer classifications, types of schizophrenia are distinguished as follows:

catatonic type. Disturbances in activity are marked, with either generalized inhibition or excessive activity. See *Catatonia*.

hebephrenic type. A type of schizophrenia with shallow, inappropriate emotions, silly behavior and mannerisms, and unpredictable giggling. There is often progressive deterioration of personal and social habits.

latent type. The preexistence of the capacity for developing overt schizophrenia under sufficient stress.

paranoid type. Unrealistic thinking is prominent, and delusions of persecution are present. Behavior is apt to be unpredictable, reflecting hostility and aggression. Delusions may be prominent.

simple type. Characterized by withdrawal, apathy, indifference, and impoverishment of human relationships, but rarely by conspicuous delusions or hallucinations. It is slowly and insidiously progressive. Emotional deterioration is present, in contrast to the schizoid personality in which there is essentially none.

Schizophrenic Reactions. Acute and chronic, undifferentiated types. These reactions exhibit a wide variety of schizophrenic symptoms with manifestations that are primarily acute or that have become chronic.

1. **Ambulatory s.** (Zilboorg). Schizophrenia in which the patient succeeds for the most part in avoiding institutionalization.

2. **Childhood Schizophrenia.** The somewhat rare onset of schizophrenic reactions in childhood.

3. **Incipient s.** Latent illness or s. psychotic reaction in abeyance. Also a temporary respite in progression to clinical state, or one in which without prompt adequate therapy one would anticipate the progression into clinical manifestations.

4. **Latent type.** A term sometimes used when schizophrenic tendencies are present but find overt expression only under particular stress.

5. **process s.** Schizophrenia in which organic brain changes are considered to be the primary cause.

6. **Pseudoneurotic type.** (1) A form of schizophrenia in which the underlying psychotic process is masked by complaints ordinarily regarded as neurotic. (2) Schizophrenia in which the illness is largely expressed by bodily complaints. These complaints are often on the level of delusions (i.e., false beliefs, unresponsive to logic).

7. **Schizo-affective type.** Cases in this category show significant admixtures of schizophrenic and affective reactions.

8. See also foregoing types (under *Schizophrenia*).

Schizophrenic dissociation (or Bleuler's dissociation). See *dissociation, schizophrenic*.

scotoma. A blind spot.

screen memory. A consciously acceptable and tolerable memory which unwittingly serves as a cover or a "screen" for another one. The latter would prove more disturbing and emotionally painful should it be recalled.

secondary defense. A concept of the defense of an emotional symptom in such ways as (1) the denial of any possible emotional contributions, or (2) by the belief or the insistence in error upon the existence of an organic basis. The symptom, a psychologically intended defense in itself, is in turn accordingly defended.

secondary gain. (1) The external situational gain which is derived from any illness. Has been used somewhat loosely to include the gain from the conscious, partly conscious, and unconscious use of emotional symptoms and character defenses. The term *epigain* has been reserved for the narrower, definitely unconscious part of the secondary gain. Synonym: *epinosic gain*. (2) *The external situational gain or material advantage which is derived from a symptom or an illness. The secondary gain constitutes the "achievements" of an illness in favorably influencing the external environment, particularly its interpersonal aspects. Secondary gain may be secured in conscious awareness, or quite unwillingly.* The secondary gain may be regarded as *the value which the symptom or illness gains* subsequent to its onset. The unconscious part of the secondary gain is the *epigain* (*q.v.*).

Secure Base of Operations Concept. The home becomes a secure base of operations in the adequate developmental situation for the child. With such an antecedent he can venture forth with more confidence and security. Such an ideal base also establishes a precedent for later actual and more figurative bases.

self-abuse. A moralistic lay term for masturbation.

self-confining phobia. The state of morbidly self-imposed area or spatial restrictions on a phobic basis. See *Phobia*.

Self-Defeat Concept, Vicious Circle of, in the Neuroses. The illness ostensibly secure "gains," and is clung to blindly and desperately. It actually loses for the patient the very thing which is sought.

This is a vicious circle. Thus, the more affection which is demanded, the less genuine affection is available. This in turn is followed by increased demands, and so on.

senescence. The period of life past the prime.

senile dementia. See *Dementia, senile*.

senile psychosis. A mental illness of old age characterized by personality deterioration, progressive loss of recent memory, and increasing eccentricity and irritability. Sometimes called by the older term senile dementia (*q.v.*).

sensation. The reception of stimuli via the sensory organs.

sensorium. Roughly approximates consciousness. Includes the special sensory perceptive powers and their central correlation and integration in the brain. A *clear sensorium* conveys the presence of a reasonably accurate memory together with a correct orientation for time, places, and persons.

sentiment. A feeling or emotional attitude.

Separation anxiety. See *anxiety*.

sexology. The scientific study of sex, sexual behavior, and sexual relationships.

sexual deviation. Applies to sexual behavior at variance with a wide variation of more or less accepted normal sexual activities. Includes such pathologic sexual behavior patterns as homosexuality, transvestitism, sexual sadism, and sexually criminal acts.

Sexual Maladjustment

Effect-Over-Cause in s.m., Concept of. Since the sexual relationship represents an interpersonal adjustment of maximum intensity and complexity, it is often the first function to break down when personality adjustment is threatened. Sexual maladjustment is thus often likely to represent the *effect* (rather than the cause) of emotional illness.

shell shock. A nonspecific term especially employed during World War I to include a variety of acute and chronic emotional disorders of a neurotic level. Many of these were Somatic Conversion types of Neuroses-following-Trauma. Obsolete.

shock treatment. Therapeutically directed endeavors in which the patient is given convulsive amounts of Metrazol, insulin, carbon dioxide, or electric current.

carbon dioxide therapy. Shock treatment in which carbon dioxide is administered in inhalation to produce physiological and emotional abreactions.

convulsive shock treatment. Usually carried out by stimulation with an electric current, and hence called *electroshock treatment*. This form of treatment is often used in depressive

reactions and is most effective in this form of illness. Modifications of electroshock therapy are *Electronarcosis* which is used in much the same type of case, and *Electrostimulation* which is a type of treatment in which a convulsion is not produced. Electroshock therapy is also used in various acute psychoses, especially acute schizophrenia. It is not recommended for the neuroses. See also *Electroshock therapy*.

insulin shock treatment. This treatment is carried out by injection of insulin. It is used especially in schizophrenic reactions. Insulin is administered in high enough doses to produce a hypoglycemic reaction, four to five hours in duration, with a "deep" coma of twenty to thirty minutes' duration, although the patient may be "out of contact" for as long as two hours. Introduced by Sakel in Vienna in 1933 and first used in the United States in 1936.

metrazol shock. A form of convulsive therapy induced by intravenous metrazol. Introduced by von Meduna in Budapest in 1935. No longer used.

subshock insulin treatment. A form of treatment in which drowsiness or somnolence (short of coma) is produced. It is used with rest, supportive measures, usually a high caloric diet, and often with psychotherapy, in a variety of emotional illnesses.

sibling. Brother or sister.

side-by-side dissociation. See *dissociation, side by side*.

situational anxiety. See *anxiety, situational*.

situational depression. See *Depression, reactive*.

sixty-nine. Mutual fellatio, as graphically represented by the figures 69.

Sleep-Respite Principle

Sleep refurbishes our psychologic armamentarium for the coming day. Sleep also is a refuge from care and stress. Going to sleep can be a respite, a comfort, and a retreat from the troubles that have beset one during the day.

The restorative value of sleep is of great importance in helping to counteract such possible cumulative effects. Sleep is not only important from the standpoint of physical fatigue, but perhaps even more so from the standpoint of the *emo-*

tional fatigue which results from the effects of tension and stress. According to the *Respite-of-Sleep Principle,* sleep helps counteract the effects of physical and emotional fatigue, and increases individual's tolerance of daily stresses and strains.

Sleepwalking. See *somnambulism.*

social case work. A discipline with training in the application and use of community resources and manipulation of the external social environment in helping to better the total condition, adaptation, and adjustment of the patient. A psychiatric social worker is one who has special training and works in the field of social case work with psychiatric patients. Utilizes social work techniques in a psychiatric setting under medical supervision.

society. Community life or living. A group of people sharing similar social standards, mores, and views. A gradually evolved system of social relations to which the members (of the society) in general conform.

sodomy. Anal intercourse between men. The ordinary legal use of this term is broader and may include other types of perversions.

soma. Body.

somatic. Referring to the body.

Somatic Conversion. See *Neurosis; conversion, somatic; conversion hysteria.*

Somatization Reaction (W. C. Menninger). The formation of functional and physiologic symptoms as the unconscious expression of emotional conflict. Psychosomatic Reaction and Physiologic Conversion may be so named.

somatotherapy. The use of such approaches in treatment as electric shock, drugs, carbon dioxide, nitrogen inhalation, and physical means.

somnambule. One who sleepwalks. Especially in hypnosis, the excellently cooperative and suggestible subject who readily follows directions. These often involve complex and coordinated motor activity which is undertaken in a hypnotic trance.

somnambulism. Sleepwalking. Also employed to name states of deep hypnosis. Coordinated physical activity not under voluntary control which has been split off or dissociated from the more usual stream of consciously directed and purposeful physical activity.

somnifacient. Sleep-inducing.

somnolence. Drowsiness.

soporific. Sleep-producing somnifacient.

Soteria. (1) The converse of a phobia. A reaction through which security and protection which are apparently out of proportion to the stimulus are experienced as coming from an external object. The external object becomes a neurotic object-source of comfort and security. (2) The name for a certain kind of psychologically defensive security operation in which a soterial object is established. (3) A symbolic object which holds for the individual concerned special and apparently undue emotional significance and meaning in the direction of protection, security, and love. Whereas the phobic object is neurotically feared and dreaded, the soterial object is a neurotic source of love, comfort, protection or security. (4) A specific intrapsychic process in which an external object situation, person, habit, ritual, or circumstance, and so on, has come to be the source of feelings of comfort, security and well-being. Such feelings are objectively and intellectually out of proportion to the apparent stimulus.

The external object becomes a neurotic object-source of comfort and security. It is the converse of a *phobia* (*q.v.*).

soterial object. (1) The object of the soteria. That which holds special significance and meaning for the person concerned, in the direction of protection, security, or comfort. The soterial object is roughly the converse of the phobic object. Also called a soteria (*q.v.*). (2) The protective and satisfying persons, object or situation in a *Soterial Reaction.*

Soterial Personality. In the Soterial Reaction objects become an emotional source of comfort, security, and protection. The soterial object is the converse of the phobic object. The Soterial Personality is marked by character traits which are dependent upon soterial mechanisms for adjustment and security in varying degree. See *Soteria.*

Soterial Reaction. An unconscious neurotic pattern of attemped defense, characterized clinically by the presence of a soteria, or soterias, as the most prominent feature. Through this defensive reaction pattern, the easing or resolution of internal emotional conflicts is sought, as is the subjective experiencing of reassurance, and personal feelings of safety, protection and security.

spasticity. Increased muscle tonus or tension. Is generally used to name a symptom of illness.

Specific Emotional Hazards of Adulthood, S.E.H.A. Included are such events as matriculation, graduation, marriage, separation, divorce, deaths, births, menopause, first sexual experience, military stressful eras (M.S.E.s), "passing the peak," etc.

Specific Emotional Hazards of Childhood, S.E.H.C. Included are death of a parent, sibling or close playmate; moving to new home; changing schools; beginning menstruation, frights, certain accidents or a sexual assault, etc.

sperm. The male cell of reproduction. It enters the ovum, or female cell, which is then fertilized.

split personality. A lay term sometimes employed for schizophrenia.

Splitting. A "minor" mental mechanism, through which components of emotional states are "split off" for purposes of their more ready defensive management, denial, isolation, or so as to achieve more protection.

Stahl, George Ernst (1660–1734). Early German psychiatrist who noted the effect of passion on the body and advocated the study of body and mind together.

stammer. Stutter.

Startle Reaction. A conditioned type of protectively intended automatic response to sudden noise or movement. Seen particularly in Combat Fatigue, where the "startle" continues long past the time that sudden noise means danger.

Status Epilepticus. A serious state of more or less continuous epileptic seizures.

stereognosis. Recognition by touch.

sterotypy. Perserveration. The persistent, rather aimless repetition of an activity.

stigma. Distinguishing mark.

strabismus. Deviation of one eye so that both eyes cannot focus simultaneously on the same object.

Stress Reaction. A. Acute Massive Situational. B. Chronic emotional and/or situational stress, and the total individual (sum of) responses.

stridor dentium. Grinding of the teeth, especially during sleep.

stupor. A state in which the sensorium is clouded and the individual has little or no appreciation of his surroundings. In catatonic stupor, the patient may be aware of his surroundings.

stuttering. A spasmodic way of speaking in which there are involuntary halts, breaks, and repetitions. Usually of psychogenic origin.

subconscious. Refers to the level of the mind which is accessible to more or less ready voluntary recall. Also called *presconscious* or *foreconscious*.

Sublimation (Rechannelization). A major mental mechanism operating outside of and beyond conscious awareness, through which instinctual drives which are consciously unacceptable, or are blocked and unobtainable, are diverted so as to secure their disguised external expression and utilization in channels of personal and social acceptability.

In successful Sublimation the direction and aim of the repressed drives has been deflected into new pathways of creative endeavor. The term of *Rechannelization* is preferred.

substitution. (1) The conscious process of the replacement of one object or emotion by another. (2) The mental mechanism operating outside of and beyond conscious awareness, through which an unacceptable or unobtainable goal, emotion, drive, attitude, impulse, interest, or need, consciously intolerable and repugnant, is displaced by a more acceptable one.

Success Depression. See *Depression.*

suggestibility. Ready change of mind, attitude, or behavior in accord with what another person suggests.

suicidal epigain. Epigain in conjunction with a suicidal attempt or act. May be an endeavor to extract some unconscious, vitally necessary concession from the environment, or influence the attitude of others.

suicide. (1) The act of self-destruction.

(2) The ultimate combined destructive expression or "acting out" of the unconscious, self-punitive drives and the unconscious sadistic drives in depression.

Complaint-Response to Implicit-Command in Suicide. The individual acts as he unconsciously feels directed to do, in response to the Implicit Command of rejection; *i.e., to* "be gone," to vanish, or even to die. May be an important component in suicide dynamics.

Partial s. Including all kinds of physical, functional and mental sacrifices which are unconsciously made.

Sullivan, Harry Stack (1892–1949). American psychiatrist best known for his contribution of the Interpersonal Theory of Psychiatry. Human behavior, personality organization, and development are seen to be based upon the relationships of the individual concerned.

superego. (1) Frequently used synonymously with the conscience. (2) In psychoanalytic terminology, that part of the mind which has unconsciously identified itself with important and esteemed persons from early life, particularly the parents. The supposed or actual wishes of these significant persons are taken over as part of one's own personal standards to help form the "conscience." They may remain anachronistic and overpunitive, especially in psychoneurotic patients.

superstition. (1) An unreasoning kind of belief often accompanied by some fear or uneasiness. Often present in regard to facts of nature, chance happenings, supposedly supernatural events, magic, or divine intervention. (2) An act or belief which develops from such fear or uneasiness.

supportive psychotherapy. See *Psychotherapy.*

suppression. (1) The conscious effort to subjugate unacceptatble thoughts and desires. One is clearly aware of the attempt. By suppression, one directs his attention away from undesirable thoughts, objects, or feelings. (2) The process in which one makes or has made deliberate and conscious efforts to forget, control and restrain; one thus actively seeks to subjugate unacceptable thoughts or desires, with the individual concerned being clearly aware of the attempt.

Surgery-in-Abeyance Rule. *Avoid any kind of surgical procedure in cases of emotional illness unless very clearly and urgently indicated.*

surrogate. A substitute person.

sycophancy. Dependency.

symbiosis. The living together or in close association of two organisms, ordinarily dissimilar.

symbol. (1) An abstract or general representation of a particular object or idea. Something which stands consciously and externally in the place of or represents something else. The latter may remain completely hidden from conscious awareness. (2) An object to which emotional feelings are attached.

Symbolic Authority Concept. The setting up of a "symbolic authority," which may be unwittingly undertaken for various psychologic purposes.

symbolization. A widely used mental process operating outside of and beyond conscious awareness by which an object, usually external, becomes the disguised outward representation for another internal and hidden object, idea, complex, or even a number of objects. The symbol is a neutral item set up to stand for or to represent something. As a result, emotional significance is attached to the symbol, and it may come to have what is an apparently undue degree of emotional meaning.

sympathetic nervous system. A chain of ganglia lying outside the spinal cord. Nerve fibers join the spinal nerves to supply the blood vessels, sweat glands, and smooth muscle of the skin. The sympathetic nervous system (thoracolumbar) and the parasympathetic system (*q.v.*) together comprise the autonomic or vegetative nervous system.

sympathy. (1) A harmony of feelings. The partial sharing of another's feelings of sorrow, loss, or misfortune. Sympathy and compathy (*q.v.*) are forms of *affective* identification. (2) An expression of sorrow, pity, or compassion for another's grief or loss. Sympathy is to be distinguished from empathy (*q.v.*)—a form of *projective* identification, in that it is primarily emotional and is likely to be non-objective.

symptom. (1) A physical or emotional manifestation of illness. It may be objective, subjective, or both. In emotional illness, symptoms are often entirely subjective and represent efforts of the individual to make an adjustment. They are also sometimes regarded as defenses or to be the result of defensive efforts. (2) In psychiatry, an emotional symptom is the unhealthy attempted resolution of internal conflict through its disguised external expression. Symptoms are also mental and physical. (3) Emotional s. may represent "unconscious compromises." Intense anxiety may produce repression of conflict and symptom formation.

emotional s. Represent the distorted and symbolic expression of hidden and internal (*i.e.*, unconscious) conflicts.

Symptom Defense.

Incomplete s-d. Concept. Lack of "symptom-success" prevents allaying of anxiety. Anxiety indicates relative lacks of symptom-success and that the symptom provides an "incomplete defense."

Symptom Defense-Defeat Parallel, Concept of. The level of *secondary defense* (of a symptom or trait (*q.v.*), parallels the level of self-defeat which it engenders.

Symptom-Longevity Principle. The longer an emotional symptom persists, the more involved and difficult its therapeutic resolution is likely to be.

Symptom Neurosis. Any neurosis marked by the development of neurotic *symptoms,* as distinguished from the overdeveloped and handicapping traits which are present as symptom-equivalents in the Character Neuroses. See *Character Neurosis.*

Symptom-Success, Inverse ratio of.

(1) The amount of anxiety which is experienced tends to vary inversely with the "success" of the symptom.

(2) The person who has "successfully" established symptoms—physiologic or psychologic—to overcome anxiety is less apt to seek therapeutic help.

Symptom-Survival Principle. Emotional symptoms ordinarily cannot survive the resolution of their underlying conflicts.

syncope. A brief loss of consciousness; fainting.

syndrome. A group of symptoms which are usually associated and which often together constitute a recognizable pathologic illness.

synergy. The correlated (*i.e.*, synergistic) action of two or more functions, processes, muscles, or drugs.

synthesis, distributive. The psychobiologic term for the guided integration of the patient's total self and reactions.

syntonic (Bleuler). The personality reacting appropriately as a stable and integrated organism. Synonym: harmonious.

syntropy (Meyer). The state of felicitous and mutually satisfactory relationship.

T

T.R.C. Total Individual Response to Crisis (*q.v.*).

T.R.T. *See Total Individual Response to Trauma* (*q.v.*)

tabes. Locomotor ataxia. Syphilis of the central nervous system, especially affecting the spinal cord. Symptoms and signs include loss of deep sensibility (*i.e.*, vibration sense), incoordination of movements, painful surface sensations (*i.e.*, paresthesias), and acute visceral pain or functional disturbance (*tabetic crises*). Deep reflexes are usually diminished or absent.

taboo. Forbidden. The basis for prohibition is generally religious, magical, or superstitious.

tachycardia. Rapid heart beat. A common manifestation accompanying many emotions.

Talion Law or Principle. In psychiatry, the primitive unrealistic belief (which is often unconscious) that retaliation in kind is the inevitable result of hostile thoughts or words. Therefore, the expectation of sometimes even the unconscious production of self-punishment is a frequent consequence of such thoughts. It is the Biblical, "An eye for an eye," and "a tooth for a tooth."

tantrum. An angry outburst, especially of children.

taxonomy. The science of naming and classification.

teleology. The doctrine of final causes; study directed according to the adaptation to a definite purpose or purposes.

telepathy. The communication of thoughts from one person to another without the intervention of tangible or physical means.

temperament. (1) A pattern of emotional response. (2) The set frame of mind or mental and emotional character of an individual.

tetany. Sustained rigid muscular contractions.

Theory of Antecedent Conflicts. A theory which points out that the effect of an emotionally disturbing event in adult life may be greatly multiplied through the conditioning or sensitization effects of the antecedent vicissitudes of early life. The early conflicts serve actually or symbolically as analogous prototypes. They are in effect reactivated by the adult conflicts of trauma. Theoretically, every adult emotional conflict has its earlier antecedent.

Therapeutic Bargain Concept. In therapy, the patient must have a choice of something better, before a symptom or trait can be modified or surrendered.

Theory of Antecedent Conflicts. See *Antecedent Conflicts.*

thinking. In psychiatry, the process of logic and reasoning assumed to exist inside the individual and accessible through a study of the verbalized associations and actions. *Archaic* or *primitive thinking* is characterized by impairment or deficiency of abstraction and generalization, with a tendency toward concrete rather than abstract thinking. In Western speech, the subject of discourse has to be stated while the predicate qualifies the state or activity expressed in the subject. In certain cases of schizophrenia, thinking is organized around adjectives, adverbs, and verbs, rather than around nouns. This is called *predicate thinking*.

tic. An intermittent spasmodic movement. As a symptom, a tic is the outward disguised expression of a hidden emotional conflict.

tic douloureux. Severe facial pain stemming from the sensory division of the fifth (facial) cranial nerve.

tonus. The usual tension in a structure maintained by partially contracted fine muscle elements.

topectomy. A type of psychosurgery (*q.v.*).

torticollis. Stiff neck.

Total Individual Response to Crisis. The total individual response to crisis, threat, or danger includes all the changes which occur. Important areas of response include the psychologic, the emotional, the physical, the intellectual, and the physiologic. The T.R.C. is the sum total of the individual's defensive reaction. It includes all those endeavors which are intended to help him prepare for any physical or emotional activity which may seem necessary to cope with the threat.

total individual response to trauma. The total individual response to trauma includes all the changes which occur following injury or shock. The important areas of response include the psychologic, the emotional, the physical, the intellectual, and the physiologic. The T.R.T. is the sum total of the individual's defensive reactions in response to the injury or damage. It includes all those reactions which are intended to cope with the consequences, and with the resulting changed situation.

Both the T.R.C. and the T.R.T. are a reflection of the total personal resources and potential for meeting stress. They reflect the strengths and weaknesses of *all* personal areas as present constitutionally and as modified and influenced by the experience and vicissitudes of living.

total push therapy (Myerson). The simultaneous utilization of all applicable therapeutic measures.

totem. An object or figure usually in less civilized groups to which unusual significance has been attached by the tribe or culture. The totem becomes an important symbol.

toxic psychosis. A psychosis resulting from the effect of various toxic agents, such as drugs, chemicals, and the organic sequelae of fever or illness, etc.

toxin. A noxious or poisonous agent.

trait. A characteristic.

trance. A sleep-like state in which consciousness is partially or entirely suspended. Example: a hypnotic trance.

tranquilizing drugs. A group of drugs used in psychoses, in hypertension and other conditions for their sedative and anxiety-relieving effects. Includes the chlorpromazine and rauwolfia drugs and others.

Transference. The unconscious transfer to new persons of feelings which were originally experienced toward important persons in early life. The entire relationship, or parts of it, then tends to be conceived as following the earlier antecedent pattern of its prototype.

counter t. The (partly or totally unconscious) emotional reaction of the doctor to his patient.

negative t. A transference in which the patient largely experiences feelings of hate, jealousy, or fear, usually toward the therapist.

positive t. A transference in which the patient largely experiences feelings of warmth, fondness, affection, or love.

transference neuroses (Freud). Hysteria, anxiety neurosis, the phobias, and obsessive-compulsive neurosis. See *Neurosis*.

transference situation. The emotional situation in psychoanalytic treatment in which the patient *transfers* various emotional feelings to the therapist. Identification of the latter with various important persons from the past occurs out of conscious awareness to account for the "unreal" feelings directed toward the physician.

transorbital lobotomy. See *Psychosurgery*.

Transparency Theory. The underlying significance of continued symptoms must not be apparent, and cannot become too transparent, if they are to serve their originally intended purposes.

transvestism. A clinical state in which satisfaction is secured through dressing and often masquerading in the clothes of a person of the opposite sex. The satisfactions have a sexual basis which may be denied by the individual and which may be hidden from his conscious awareness.

trauma. Physical or psychologic injury, or both. It may refer to the injury done, or to the condition which results.

Trauma, birth. *Otto Rank* (1844-1939). Related his theories of anxiety and neurosis to the psychic shock of being born.

Traumatic Neurosis. Any of a number of what are usually acute neurotic reactions following physical or acute psychic trauma. See *Neurosis following trauma,* under *Neurosis.*

Trauma, Psychic. Trauma which leaves some more or less lasting effect upon the individual and his adjustment.

Traumatic Encephalopathy. A syndrome which can result from the cumulative punishment absorbed in the boxing ring from continued bouts. Characterized by the general slowing of and interference with mental functions, occasional bouts of confusion, and scattered bits of memory loss.

Traumatic Psychosis. Psychosis following organic head injuries or, very occasionally, following a severe emotional (*i.e.,* psychologic) trauma.

Treatment Rule. According to this Rule, *the patient undertakes to say every thought which comes to mind while he is with the psychiatrist, without reservation or censorship.* This is an important rule. It is more stringent for some than others. Adherence to it speeds and shortens the treatment.

tremor. Fine trembling, quivering, or shaking.

Trend Toward Emotional Health Principle. See *emotional health.*

tribade. A female who takes the male role in homosexual acts.

triolism. A sexual trinity. Sexual interests or practices involving three persons of both sexes. Generally includes bipolar sexual activity.

truth serum. A popular misnomer for the drugs sometimes employed to facilitate interviews. Especially applied to Sodium Amytal and Pentothal sodium when used in criminal interrogation. The agent used is not a serum and its use does not guarantee truthfulness.

Tuke, D. H. (1827–1895). British psychiatrist and author, descendant of William Tuke.

Tuke, William (1772–1822). An early English layman, the founder of York Retreat, who in 1792 tried the management of patients without the physical restraints which were then generally believed necessary.

tumescence. Congestion and swelling. Especially used in reference to sexual organs. The reverse is *detumescence.* Tumescence is the building up phase, while detumescence is the subsiding phase.

twilight sleep. (1) A semiconscious state usually induced by hypnosis or drugs. (2) Rarely of psychologic origin as one of the Dissociative Reactions.

twilight state. A Dissociative Reaction. A transitory disturbance of consciousness during which certain acts may be sometime performed without the individual's conscious volition and without his retaining any remembrance of them.

U

unc. The unconscious.

uncinate fit. The name for certain organically produced hallucinations of taste and smell. So named because of the underlying pathology in lesions of the uncinate gyrus of the brain.

unconscious. (1) Those forces and content of the mind which are not ordinarily available to conscious awareness or to immediate recall. (2) The unconscious area of the mind is the repository for data which have never been conscious (*primary repression*), or which became conscious at least briefly and were subsequently repressed (*secondary repression*) from awareness as too personally painful or intolerable.

Unconscious Compromises. Symptoms often represent the outward but concealed expression of what we might refer to as *unconscious compromises,* between the consciously-disowned drives and the elements seeking their control and containment.

Undoing. An intrapsychic defense mechanism operating outside of and beyond conscious awareness in the endeavor to actually or symbolically undo something which has already been done, including a thought, wish, impulse, or act, the commission or experience of which has proven consciously intolerable.

Unit Guilt. The response seen in certain combat situations whereby an unrealistic kind of neurotic guilt follows the death or injury of a friend or comrades. Identical with *"buddy guilt."*

Universal Affect, Law of. The basic psychologic premise that every idea, thought or object, no matter how minor, seemingly trivial, or apparently neutral, possesses a distinct quantum of affect.

unlust. The reverse of pleasure.

unreality. Often refers to the distorted picture which a patient may have of a situation or event of life. What he sees is not in keeping with an interpretation of the same facts by an independent observer and is often influenced by emotional bias or preconception. See *depersonalization.*

uremic hallucinosis. A hallucinatory state in certain rare cases of advanced kidney disease with uremia.

V

vaginismus. Painful vaginal spasm, usually upon attempted intercourse.

vagueness. Vagueness and tentativeness may be "sought" to subserve an important defensive purpose.

vapors. An older lay term for certain nervous disorders; hysteria, and hypochondriasis.

variant. Differing in structure, function, or behavior from others in one's class or race.

Vegetative Nervous System. The autonomic nervous system. The vegetative nervous system is essentially independent of volitional control.

vegetate neurosis (Alexander). The psychogenic dysfunction of a vegetative organ. A vegetative neurosis is the physiologic accompaniment of constant or periodically recurring emotional states. See *Neurosis, vegetative.*

verbalize. To express in words.

verbigeration. A repetition of rather meaningless phrases or words in which no coherent thought is expressed.

verbose. Overtalkative; overproductive of speech.

vertigo. Dizziness.

vestige. A rudimentary structure which is believed to have once been fully developed and functioning in an earlier stage of evolutionary development.

virgin. Chaste, without sexual experience.

virile. Manly. Especially connotes manly potential.

viscera. Internal organs.

vision. A visual false perception or hallucination. A visual image without corporeal existence, the product of fantasy, imagination, drugs, toxins, or psychosis.

vita sexualis. Sexual life.

Vives, Juan Luis (1492–1540). Learned Spanish philosopher and psychologist who wrote about psychologic associations and emotional influences on memory.

volition. The act or power of making one's own free choice or decision.

voyeurism. Sexually motivated, often compulsive interest in watching or looking at others. Roughly synonymous with the lay concept of the activities of a "peeping Tom."

W

W.A.I.S. Wechsler Adult Intelligence Scale (*q.v.*).

wanderlust. The need and desire to roam.

war neurosis. The name sometimes applied to certain neurotic reactions incident to war. One of the Neuroses following Trauma.

Westphal, Carl Friedrich (1833–1890). German neurologist who early (1878) defined obsessions. In 1871 he introduced the term and described agorophobia.

Wechsler Adult Intelligance Scale (W.A.I.S.) A test, verbal and performance, designed to measure adult intelligence.

wet dream. A slang term for nocturnal seminal emission.

Weyer, Johann (1515–1588). A German physician who was one of the first medical scientists to devote his major interests to mental disease. He is regarded by some as the founder of modern psychiatry. He dared to attack the basis of the Inquisition, protested against the *Mallews Maleficatimas* and sought to divorce theology from concepts of mental illness.

White, William Alanson (1870–1937). American psychiatrist, longtime superintendent of St. Elizabeths Hospital.

Withdrawal. The unconsciously and protectively motivated retreat from external reality. Through it, one withdraws to a greater or lesser extent from contacts, relationships, social situations and painful conflicts.

word salad. A mixture of words and phrases which lack any comprehensive meaning or logical coherence to the listener.

wry neck. Twisted or contorted neck.

X

xenophobia. A morbid fear of strangers.

Y

yardstick, personal. The use of oneself as a yardstick in the estimation and evaluation of other people's feelings and attitudes, and in the attempt to predict their responses and behavior.

Z

zoophobia. The morbid fear of animals. See *Phobia*.

zygote. The fertilized egg produced by the union of a sperm cell with an ovum.

INDEX

INDEX

The more substantive concepts and reformulations of the author are indicated by *italic* type in order to facilitate their identification. Subjects of major importance are indicated by **boldface** type.

A

A.A.A., see ACUTE ANXIETY ATTACK
A.T.S., see ANXIETY-TENSION STATE
Abandonment
  anxiety, as source of, 30
  goals, of, due to anxiety, 24
Abraham, K. (1877-1925)
  anal characteristics, on, 292-293
  anxiety and depression, on, 165
  depressive reaction, on, 141, 170
  obsessive personality traits, on, 234-235
Abreaction, 649, 931
Absolutism in the obsessive personality, 255-256
Absorption of Interest Concept, 311, 332, 462, 708
Abuse as source of anxiety, 30
Acceptance, Deprivation of, 309-310
Accident-Proneness Concept, 197-198
        (*see also* EMOTIONAL DEATH CONCEPT)
Accident-prone families, 198
Accidents as source of anxiety, 30
Acculturation in childhood, 23
Accumulation as Soterial Reaction, 620
Achille's Heel, Emotional, 581, 860, 924
Acrophobia, 553
Acting Out, 193, 258, 318, 355, 670, 684, 798, 918
Activated-Nocturnal-Fantasy Concept, 754
Actual Neuroses, 386
Acute Anxiety Attack, 89-98, 791, 881, 913
  anxiety, manifesting, 20
  Anxiety Neurosis, in relation to, 111
  Anxiety-Tension State, compared with, 98, 104
  cerebral vs. mid-brain origin of, 98
  childhood, in, 33-34 (*see also* SPECIFIC EMOTIONAL HAZARDS OF CHILDHOOD)
  clinical aspects, 89-90, 91-95

Acute Anxiety Attack—*Contd.*
  death resulting from, 94-95 (*see also* EMOTIONAL DEATH CONCEPT)
  defensive denial of, 91
  diagnosis of, 90-91
  duration of, 91
  dynamics of, 95-98
  extension principle, 96
  fear generated by, 89-90, 94 (*see also* CIRCULAR GENERATION OF FEAR PRINCIPLE)
  functional changes accompanying, 89
  general physician, evaluation by, 126
  geriatric instances, 93-94
  heart attacks, confused with, 96, 97
  instances of, 91-95
  military, 913
  morning attack, 93
  old age, in, 93-94
  organic basis for, 96-97
  organic illness used to explain, 91
  origin of, 98
  overreaction to, 95-98 (*see also* DEFENSIVE-OVERREACTION CONCEPT)
  prognosis, 90-91
  psychotherapy for, 90-91
  secondary effects of, 96
  terminology, 45, 46
  tranquilizers used for, 93-94, 129
Adult disapproval as source of anxiety, 29, 30
Adulthood
  anxiety in, 32-33, 119 (*see also* SECONDARY SOURCES OF ANXIETY)
  emotional conflicts in, 119
  emotional hazards of, *see* SPECIFIC EMOTIONAL HAZARDS OF ADULTHOOD
Advanced Defenses, see HIGHER ORDER DEFENSIVE REACTIONS
Advanced Neuroses, see HIGHER ORDER NEUROSES
Advanced-Organicity Concept in Fatigue Reactions, 390-391

Aerophagia, 677
Affect Dissociation
  definition, 729
  emotional deferment through, 732-733
  symptoms, 731
Affection (*see also* LOVE)
  deprivation of, 309-310
  Hygeiaphrontic Reactions, in, 485
  inhibition of, 328
  lessened capacity for, 328-330
  Obsessive Reactions, and, 309-310, 328-330
Affective Escape Route Concept, 762, 775-776
Age of Anxiety, 59, 82-83, 131, 477, 685, 724, 900
Aggression (*see also* HOSTILITY)
  anxiety, manifesting, 20
  categories of, 321-322
  Constructive, 321
  definition, 322
  depression of, 22-23
  Destructive, 321-322
  emotional conflict due to, 22-23
  Inward, 321
  obsession and, 314, 320-322
  Outward, 321
  parent-child relationships, in, 322
  sexual inhibition, parallels to, 296-297
Agitated Depression, 168
  electroshock therapy for, 216
Agitation
  anxiety, manifesting, 20
  tranquilizers used for, 40
Agitation Gauge Concept, 189
Agoraphobia, 553
  S. Freud, of, 552
Ailurophobia, 553, 573
Alarm Reaction, 11
Alcoholics Anonymous, 783
Alcoholism
  Depressive Personality, in, 281
  suicide, and, 208-209
Alcoholic amnesia, 777, 783
Allochiria, 652
All-or-None Person, and Response, 248, 255
Alternating Dissociations
  Alternating Personality resulting from, 807
  amnesia, in, 743
  definition, 729
  Fugue states as, 796
  symptoms of, 732, 773, 791
Alternating Personality
  clinical instances, 807-808
  definition, 807

Alternating Personality—*Contd.*
  diagnosis of, 807
  Dissociative Reaction, as, 806-809
  incidence, 807
  psychodynamics of, 809
  separate lives characteristic of, 806-807
Amalgam, Emotional-Object, Concept of, 585 (*see also* E.O.A.)
Ambivalence
  Obsessive Personality, in, 249-252
  Phobic, 570
  Primal, 562
  Primordial, 562, 598
Amnesia, 773-791
  alcoholic, 777, 783
  Alternating Dissociation, in, 743
  antecedent patterns in, 785
  Anterograde, 777
  boxers, in, 781-783
  categories of, 777-778
  Circumscribed, 777
  clinical features, 777-784
  clinical types of, *Table 42,* 796
  concussion, following, 780
  confabulation, accompanied by, 777 (*see also* PARAMNESIA)
  definition, 773
  diagnosis, 774-775
  Dissociative Reaction, as, 773-791
  electroshock, following, 778, 787-790 (*see also* SHOCK AMNESIA)
  Emotional, 777
  encephalopathy, traumatic, in, 781-783
  Episodic, 777
  escape route, as, 775
  False, 777
  Feigned, 777
  Fugue States
    differentiated from, 774
    in, 791, 795-806
  hypnosis, following, 778 (*see also* POST-HYPNOTIC AMNESIA)
  incidence, 775-776
  legal defense, as, 786-787
  malingering, and, 774
  medicolegal implications, 774, 786-787
  organic, 774, 777
  pathologic aspects, 784
  posthypnotic, 778
  psychodynamics of, 784-786
  Psychologic, 553, 773, 775, 778-780
  psychopathy, differentiated from, 786
  punch drunk, 781-783
  repression operative in, 776
  Retrograde, 778
  Senile, 778, 783-784
  sleep, in relation to, 776
  traumatic, 778

Amnesia—*Contd.*
  treatment of, 790-791
  types of, *Table 41,* 777-778
Amnesia Protection Concept, 780
Anaclitic Depressive Reaction, 170
Anal characteristics in character reactions, 292-293
Analytic Bridge Concept, 677, 818, 931, 923
Anatomy of emotional illness, 56
Anesthesias, 683-688
Anger (*see also* RAGE; *also* HOSTILITY)
  anxiety, as source of, 31
  Anxiety Equivalent, as, 18, 19, 111
  boredom as equivalent for, 416
  Breeds Anger Concept, 446, 711, 918
  Equivalents Concept, 416
  frustration related to, 32
  royal, *see* KING DAVID REACTION
Animal magnetism, *see* MESMERISM
Antecedent Conflict Theory, 29, 120, 132, 161, 490-494, 694, 866, 888
  anxiety, related to, 30, 34
  Anxiety Reactions and, 120-121
  conditioned anxiety related to, 34
  definition, 29, 132
  Depressive Reactions, in relation to, 161-163
    psychogenesis of, as, 169-175
  extension to country of, 920
  fear, in relation to, 519
  Grief State, in relation to, 167
  Hygeiaphrontic Reactions, in relation to, 490-494
  infant dependency, in relation to, 169 (*see also* DEPENDENCY)
  Neuroses Following Trauma, in relation to, 888
  Obsessive Reactions, in relation to, 339
  Oedipal Conflicts and, 490
  Oral Conflicts, and, 490
  Primal Depression in relation to, 169-171
  psychic trauma of birth, and, 492
Anterograde amnesia, 777
Anthophobia, 553, 571
Anthropophobia, 553, 557
Anticipation in anxiety, 13, 795 (*see also* APPREHENSIVE ANTICIPATION)
Antiseptic Personality, 233, 285
Antisocial behavior (*see also* DELINQUENT BEHAVIOR)
  drinking, due to, 26-27
  hypnotic influence, under, 819
  Impulsions, as, 354-355
  psychotherapy for, 26-27

Anxiety
  abnormal, 11
  abnormal functions of, 41
  Absence of Anxiety concept in therapy, 1-53, 123
  acute, 89-98 (*see also* ACUTE ANXIETY ATTACK)
  adult disapproval related to, 29
  adult origins of, 21
  adults, in, *see* Secondary sources of anxiety
  advancement, over, 35
  Age of, 59, 82-83, 131, 477, 685, 724, 900
  aggressive behavior manifesting, 20
  agitation manifesting, 20
  alarm reaction, as, 11
  amount, determination of, 84-85
  anger, expressed as, 19 (*see also* ANXIETY EQUIVALENT CONCEPT)
  Anxiety Equivalent Concept, 19, 102, 111, 145, 324, 462, 880, 917
  Anxiety Exchange Concept, 707
  anticipation featured in, 13
  appetite affected by, 115
  apprehension and, 11, 14, 17, 24, 84 (*see also* APPREHENSIVE ANTICIPATION)
  Appropriateness of Response, 11
  approval vs. independence, causing, 29
  attacks of, 89-98 (*see also* ACUTE ANXIETY ATTACK)
  attention impairment manifesting, 20
  authority, due to, 16-17
  autonomic expression manifesting, 20
  Avoidance of Anxiety Concept, 4-5, 24, 85, 516, 525, 527
  birth experience as prototype of, 28
  castration fears causing, 31, 33
  character defenses arising from, 20, 21
  childhood, in, 21, 29, 30
  classification of, 43-47
  clinical states manifesting, 20
  combat, manifested in, 907 (*see also* COMBAT REACTIONS)
  communication of, *see* EMOTIONAL CONTAGION
  Compulsions manifesting, 20
  concentration impairment manifesting, 20
  conditioned, 12, 13
  confusion manifesting, 20
  conscience, arising from, 21
  conscious awareness of, 24
  consequences of, 20, 87-88, 908
  Constrictive Spiral of, 121-122
  Constructive Anxiety Concept, 132
  constructive aspects, 12, 41-42, 119-120, 132

Anxiety—*Contd.*

Contagion of, 10

continuous, 98 (*see also* ANXIETY TEN-
SION STATE)

Conversion Reactions manifesting, 20

Countering Principle, 66

Critical Attack of, 581-584

crucial role of, 2-8

defenses against, 8, 16, 25, 117-118

definition 11-13

Depletion Concept, 41

depression, in relation to, 20, 28, 137,
145, 165, 189-191

Depressive-Equivalent, as, 144-145

derepression, resulting from, 21, 24

diagnosis of, 43-47

differentiation between normal and
pathologic, 10-11

Direct Manifestations, (*Table 1*) 19-21,
907, (*Table 50*) 908

displacement causing phobic reaction,
571

disruptive functions of, 41

Dissociative Reactions manifesting,
(*Table 1*) 20

dreams manifesting, 20, 40

early studies, 10

emotional conflict related to 20, 21-27

Emotional Contagion, arising from, 13

emotional manifestations of, 20-21

emotional symptoms, responsible for, 5

expressions of, 20

fatigue due to, 20, 408 (*see also* FA-
TIGUE STATES)

fear and, 4, 11-17, 104, 517

Fight or Flight response to, 16, 24

free-floating, 12

Freud's theory of, 10, 28

Fuel Analogy in, 42

Fugue States in relation to, 801-802

*Functional-Structural Progression Re-
sulting from,* 14

functions of, 41-42

goal abandonment in reaction to, 24

Goal of Equanimity Concept related to,
22

hostile impulse repression related to,
15, 28, 29

hostile outbursts manifesting, 20, 917

human existence, in, 4

Hygeiaphrontic Reactions, in, 20, 462

Hygeiaphrontis as defense against, 477

illnesses resulting from, 87-88

*Incomplete Symptom-Defense Concept,
manifested by,* 89, 189, 477

Indirect Manifestations, (*Table 1*) 19-
21

individual response to, 11

infantile origins of, 21

Anxiety—*Contd.*

insomnia due to, 20, 115

internal threat, as, 13, 83, 84

Intuitive Communication of, 13, 32,
404, 464, 568 (*see also* EMO-
TIONAL CONTAGION CONCEPT)

*Inverse Proportion to Symptoms Con-
cept,* 103, 145, 342, 801 (*see
also* INVERSE ANXIETY-SYMPTOM
RATIO)

level of, 11, 86, 110-111

loss of position and regard, over, 14

Manifestations of, 5, (*Table 1*) 20, 21

maturity level related to, 8, 34

mental function impairment manifesting, 20

mental mechanisms employed against,
16, 25 (*see also* FIRST LINE OF
DEFENSE CONCEPT)

nature of, 1-52

net effect of, 11

neurasthenia manifesting, 20

*Neuroses Following Trauma, as symp-
tom of,* 20, 850, 851

neuroses resulting from, *see* ANXIETY
NEUROSES

neurotic, 12, 27

new concept, as, 5

normal, 10-11

obesity due to, 115

obsessions manifesting, 20

obsessive persons susceptible to, 309-
310

Oedipus problem, originating in, 28

old age, in, 93-94

organic basis for, 96-97

origins of, 27-38

oversleeping as response to, 40-41

overwhelming, 89-90

Pain, and, Reciprocal Relationship to,
123

palpitation manifesting, 20

panic, alerting against, 13

parental, 32-33

pathologic, 10-11, 41, 84-86

perspiration manifesting, 20

phobias and, 16, 20, 37, 546-548, 569

physical activity, relieved by, 17, 18-19

physiologic changes accompanying, 12,
13

physiologic conversions manifesting, 20

prestige, over, 35

Primary Sources, (*Table 2*) 30

projection employed in, 14

protective function of, 13, 41-42

psychogenesis of, 20-21

psychogenic symptoms due to, 5

psychologic manifestations of, 5, 20

psychomotor expressions of, 20

Anxiety—*Contd.*

psychopathology, as motive force toward, 20

Psychosis Ratio, Inverse, 801

psychosomatic disorders due to 20, 13-14, 522

psychotherapy for, 25-27, 85

pupil dilation manifesting, 20

quantitative determination of, 84-85

rationalization in reaction to, 24

reactions to, 24

Reciprocal Influences of, Pain Concept and, 123, 470, 480, 870 (*see also* PAIN)

regression in reaction to, 24

repression resulting from, 5, 23

resignation in reaction to, 24

restlessness manifesting, 20

retaliatory attacks, over, 491

role in history and development of man, 8-10

"second theory of", Freud's, 28

Secondary Sources of, 28, 29, 30, 34 (*see also* SECONDARY SOURCES OF ANXIETY)

sedatives and, 39-40

self-esteem, and, 35

self-preservation, and *see* situational anxiety

separation as source of, 28

sexual maladjustment due to, 116 (*see also* SEXUAL MALADJUSTMENT)

sexual satisfaction, and, 10

sleep and, 20, 38-41

Socializing Functions of, 41-42

Somatic Conversions manifesting, 20

Soterial Reactions manifesting, 20

Sources of, 27-38

speech difficulties manifesting, 16-17, 20

Startle Reaction manifesting, 20 (*see also* STARTLE REACTION)

subjective experience, as, 15, 86

sublimation in reaction to, 24

superego as source of, 21

symptom formation resulting from, 28

Symptom Ratio Precept and, 103, 145, 324, 462

Symptom-Success Concept and, 103, 145, 324, 462

tension, due to, 17-18 (*see also* ANXIETY-TENSION STATE)

Total Individual Response to Crisis, in relation to, 12, 16, 18, 19, 28

tranquilizers and, 39-40

tremors manifesting, 20

underweight due to, 115

uneasiness in, 11

Universality Principle of, 8, 131, 903

Anxiety—*Contd.*

unknown danger in, 11

warning function of, 13

weakness manifesting, 20

weight, affecting, 115

Anxiety-Avoidance Principle, 4-5, 24, 85, 516

Anxiety-Countering Principle, 66

Anxiety-Equivalent Concept, 18, 19, 111

depersonalization as, 759

irritability as, 917

Anxiety-Hysteria, 108

Anxiety Neurosis, 104-120, 131-132

adulthood, in, 119

anxiety defenses and, 117-118

anxiety hysteria confused with, 108

anxiety, manifesting, 20

Anxiety-Tension State, differentiated from, 98-99, 104

childhood, in, 119

clinical features of, 106, 110-117 (*Table 8*) 113-114

Constructive Anxiety Concept and, 119-120

definition, 45, 105

Depressive Reaction, analogous to, 167

diagnosis, 106-109

dynamics of, 117-120

early life, in, 119

emotional features, 111, 114

emotional illness, position in, 108

Emotional Perpetuation Concept and, 116-117

Epigain in, 65

events commonly producing, 119

fear, in relation to, 120

free discussion therapy for, 106-107

general physician, evaluation by, 126

headaches and, 115

historical background, 104-105

incidence, 109-110

masochism in, 112

mental manifestations, (*Table 8*) 113, 114

mixed reactions in, 106-107

organic symptoms perpetuated by, 116-117 (*see also* EMOTIONAL PERPETUATION CONCEPT)

pathogenesis of, 117-120

Phobic Reactions, in relation to, 108, 120

physiologic features, 113, 114, 116-117

prevalence of, 110

psychomotor features, 112, 114

sex differences, 109

subjective manifestations of, 111, 114

symbolism in, 118

symptoms, 110-117, 118

Anxiety Neurosis—*Contd.*
terminology, 45, 46
typical findings in diagnosis, 106
Anxiety-Pain Vicious Circle Concept, 123,
480, 706
Anxiety-Panic Reaction, 89, 91 (*see also*
ACUTE ANXIETY ATTACK)
overreaction to, 95
Anxiety Reactions, 81-132
Acute Anxiety Attack, 89-98
Anxiety Neurosis, 104-120
Anxiety-Tension State, 98-104
childhood, in, 120-121 (*see also* ANTE-
CEDENT CONFLICT THEORY of)
classification of, 86-88
clinical types, 81-132
definition, 45
derepression and, 120
diagnosis of, 124
early patterns of, 121
general physician, evaluation by, 125-
126
Hygeiaphrontis manifested in, 450
incidence of, 86, 109, 244
nomenclature, 104-105
organic basis of, 104-105
prognosis for, 125-126
psychogenesis of, 120-121
psychotherapy for
anxiety generated by, 126
early initiation of, 127
imagined symptoms and, 128-129
indications for, 125
patient collaboration in, 130 (*see
also* JOINT-ENDEAVOR PRINCIPLE)
relocation, 130
resistance to, 126
response to, 123-124
surgery and, 127-128
*Symptom-Longevity Principle, in rela-
tion to,* 127
tranquilizers used in, 129-130
subacute, 98-99 (*see also* ANXIETY-TEN-
SION STATE)
terminology 45, 46
tranquilizers as therapy for, 129-130
trauma, following, 850
treatment for, 123-131
types of, 86-88
*Anxiety-Symptom Ratio, Inverse, Concept
of,* 103, 145, 324, 462, 880 (*see
also* INVERSE ANXIETY-SYMPTOM
RATIO)
Anxiety-tension state, 98-104, 131, 167,
862 (*see also* FATIGUE STATE)
*Acute Anxiety Attack (A.A.A.), differ-
entiated from,* 104
anxiety as major clinical feature, 20, 99

Anxiety-tension state—*Contd.*
clinical features, 99-102
combat stress, in relation to, 100-101
complexity of reactions in, 102-103
continuous aspect, 98
definition, 98-99
diagnosis, 98-99
emotional reaction and, 103
Fugue State following dissolution of,
800
Grief State analogous to, 167
Military Reactions, in, 899
psychodynamics of, 102-104
Physiologic Momentum Concept in, 99
(*see also* PHYSIOLOGIC MOMEN-
TUM CONTINUED CONCEPT)
stress, in relation to, 100-102
subacute clinical reaction, as, 98-99
symptoms of, 99-102
Symptom Success, in relation to, 103,
145, 324, 462
terminology, 45, 46
traumatic, 862
Anxious depression, 145, 189-191
Anxious Personality, 285-286
*Anything-Else Technique in Psychother-
apy,* 596
Apathy, 174
Appearance Outwardly Reversed Concept,
240
Appetite, 115
Apprehensive Anticipation, 11-18, 31, 38,
795-801, 902
aboard ship, 17-18
anxiety, and, 11, 14, 17, 31, 38
Concept of, 7, 17-18
crisis, in response to, 18
fear, and, 17
Fugue State, in, 795, 798-799
protective aspect, 18
tension due to, 17-18 (*see also* APPRE-
HENSIVE TENSION)
Apprehensive tension
anxiety, in, 11, 24
Central Dynamic Concept related to,
24-25
emotional conflict, arising from, 24
*Appropriateness of Individual Response
Concept,* 14, 84, 111, 131, 477,
547, 610, 694, 797
Aquaphobia, 553
Armor, Character, 229
Associations Reinforcement Concept, 748
(*see also* GEOMETRIC PRINCIPLE)
Associations, 726, 747-748
Astraphobia, 554
A.T.S., see ANXIETY-TENSION STATE

Attacks, Phobic, 121-122, 159
Attention-Absorption Concept, 188, 311-313, 452, 466, 481-482, 487-489, 657
    Conversion Reactions, in relation to, 657
    Hygeiaphrontic Reactions, in relation to, 481
Attention Hypothesis, 279-280, 349, 586-589
Attention impairment, 20
Attention-seeking, 262, 818
Attitude-Symptoms, 138, 144, 451, 328, 710
Authority, Concept of Symbolic, 220
Automobile accidents and accident-proneness, 198
Automatic Behavior, 809-810 (*see also* DISSOCIATION OF AUTOMATICITY)
Automatic Recoil Principle in therapy, 531 (*see also* THERAPY)
Automatic Writing, 809
Automaticity Dissociation, 732 (*see also* Dissociation)
Autonomic Conversion Reaction, 655
Autonomic expression of anxiety, 20
Avoidance-of-Anxiety Concept, 525, 527, 4-5, 24, 85
Avoidance, Psychologic-Flight, 531, 824
Awakening, Dawn, 142, 156

B

Bacteriophobia, 554
Balanced Neurotic Position Concept, 48, 159, 482, 502, 508, 715, 885-886
    Emotional Decompensation Concept, in relation to, 159
Bargain, Concept of Therapeutic, 509, 591, 713, 883, 707, 300, 883
Barrage of Symptoms Concept, 664-665, 791, 800-801, 470-471, 485-486, 405
Basic Drive Toward Emotional Health Concept, 38, 834
Battle Dream, 917
B.B.C. Dissociation, 647, 730-733, 813
    definition, 730
    symptoms, 733
Be Prepared Concept, 252
Be Prepared Concept of defense, 487
Beard, George Miller (1840-1883), 45, 385
Beaumont, William (1785-1853), 840

Bed-wetting, 23
Behavior, Overall, 742
Behavioral Symptom, 555
Belief-Principle, 646, 838
Biologic Function Concept, 179
Birth experience, 28
Birth Trauma, 28
Black-or-White Person and Response, 248, 255, 451, 903
Bleuler, Engen, 1857-1934), 140
Bleuler's Dissociation, 682 (*see also* SCHIZOPHRENIC DISSOCIATION)
    definition, 730
    symptoms, 735-736, 903
Body Language, 643 715 914 (*see also* LANGUAGE)
Bodily Expression of conflicts, 481
Boredom
    Anger-Equivalent, as, 416
    dynamic features, 415
    escape from, 416
    fatigue, and, 415-417
    reactions to, 415
Bowel training, 292
    obsessive reactions, and, 339-340
Boxer's Encephalopathy, 781-783
Braid, James (1795-1861), 812, 733
Braid-Bernheim-Charcot Dissociation, *see* B.E.C. DISSOCIATION
Braidism, *see* HYPNOSIS
Brainwashing, 933-946 (*see also* PRISONER PROCESSING)
Breuer, Joseph (1841-1925), 648, 813, 733
Breuer's Dissociation, 648, 730-733
    definition, 730
    symptoms, 733
Brontophobia, 554
Buddy Guilt, 927

C

C.I., see CONFLICT INDICATORS
C.R., see COMPULSIVE RITUAL
C.S.R., see COMPULSIVE SECURITY RITUAL
Camptocormia, 670, 912
Cannon, Walter B. (1871-1945), 116, 841
Castration anxiety, 31, 33
Castration Complex, 551-552
Casual Personality, 232, 284
Catharsis, 649
Cathexis, 585
Central Dynamic Concept, 24-25

Changing Trends Concept, 771, 658 (*see also* CULTURAL VOGUE CONCEPT)
Character Analysis
  definition, 231
  treatment of choice, as, 298-299
Character Defenses, 228-229, 298
  anxiety, arising from, 21
  attention-seeking, as, 262
  Concept of, 228, 286, 298-299
  Constellations of, 228-229
  Conversion Personality, in, 241-242, 259-262
  cultural influences on, 244-245
  definition, 230
  depressive, 167-168, 242
  equivalents, 229, 245
  egocentricity as, 262
  gains of, 72-73, 288
  Hygeiaphrontic, 472
  hypertrophy of, 72-73, 78
  hysterical, 241-242
  intrapsychic conflict, reflecting, 58-59
  major groups, 239
  mental mechanisms, and, 288
  obsessive, 72-73, 238-241, 319
  parental influence, on 291-293
  Symptom Neurosis related to, 60 (*see also* SYMPOSIUM NEUROSES)
  terminology, 46
  vagueness as, 287
Character Equivalents, 229, 245
Character Neurosis, 227-305 (*see also* CHARACTER REACTIONS)
  Defense-Hypertrophy Principle related to, 229
  definition, 7
  development of, 88
  emotional illness, in, 59-60
  epigain in, 65
  incidence of, 244
  Symptom Neurosis related to, 60 (*see also* SYMPTOM NEUROSES)
  terminology, 47
Character Reactions, 227-303 (*see also* CHARACTER NEUROSES)
  anxiety, in relation to, 20, 88
  Character Analysis as treatment of choice in, 298-299
  character defenses, and, 228-229
  childhood, in, 21
  clinical features, 245-286
  Conversion type, 232
  cultural vogue concept in—*see* CULTURAL VOGUE CONCEPT
  definition, 230-231
  Defense-Hypertrophy Principle related to, 229-230
  Depressive type, 232

Character Reactions—*Contd.*
  diagnosis of, 236-243
    descriptive system, 236-238
    major patterns in, 238-243
  habit patterns of, 291-292
  historical background, 234-236
  incidence of, 243-245
  Obsessive type, 232
  overeating, compulsive, as, 297-298
  pathogenesis of, 286-295
  personality, and, 228-229
  psychodynamics of, 286-295
  symptom formation in, 286-295
  terminology, 46, 47
  trait development in, 286-295
  treatment for, 298-301
    Character Analysis as, 298-299
    indications, 300
    physician referral, 299-300
    precautions, 300-301
    Relationship-Improvement Precept, 299
    Therapeutic Bargain Concept, 300
Character traits
  Conversion Reactions, in, 645 (*see also* CONVERSION CHARACTER)
  depression, in, 158-159
  development of, 87-88
  emotional response, in, 59-60
  obsessive groups of, 158-159
  Psychologic Equivalents, as, 158-159
  types of, 87-88
Characteristic Disproportion Principle, 381, 389, 857
Charcot, Jean Martin (1825-1893), 647, 733, 840-841
Child, Emotional Exploitation by Parent Concept, 220
Childhood
  acculturation in, 23
  anger in, 340-341
  anxiety in, 21, 29, 119
  Character Reactions in, 21
  Compulsive Rituals in, 350
  Conversion Reactions in, 21
  defenses against anxiety in, 21
  Dependency-Dilemma of Infancy in, 169
  deprivation and rejection in, 174
  Emotional Exploitation by Parent, 220
  emotional hazards of *see* SPECIFIC EMOTIONAL HAZARDS OF CHILDHOOD
  fatigue in, 403
  Hygeiaphrontis in, 463
  instinctual drives in, 23
  needs in, 174
  neuroses developing in, 21

Childhood—*Contd.*
Obsessive Reactions manifested in, 21, 333
Oral Conflict in, 169 (*see also* ORAL CONFLICT *and* DEPENDENCY DILEMMA)
parental emotions, role in, 32-33 (*see also* EMOTIONAL CONTAGION)
parental role in, 23, 32-33, 337-343 (*see also* PARENT-CHILD RELATIONSHIP *and* PARENTAL ROLE, first tenet of *and* second tenet of)
Phobias in, 21, 564
rage toward object of dependency in, 169
Rituals, 350
Circular generation of fear principle, 89-96, 122, 529, 913 (*see also* ANXIETY)
Acute Anxiety Attack, in relation to, 94, 96
anxiety, in relation to, 89-90
definition, 131
phobic response in relation to, 518
Circumscribed Amnesia, 777
Civil disorder originating in anxiety, 30
Classification relativity, 3
Claustrophobia, 554
Clavus, 670
Climate, Proper Emotional, Concept of, 309
Cold Depression, 155, 219
Collecting as Soterial Reaction, 620
Combat
emotional illness in, 900-933 (*see also* COMBAT REACTIONS)
stress in, 101, 902, 909-912, 919-921
Combat Reactions, 899-947 (*see also* MILITARY REACTIONS)
acute, 906-908
Antecedent Conflicts, in relation to, 920
anxiety manifested in, 907
Anxiety-Tension State related to, 99, 101
battle dream as, 917
clinical features, 906-917
Conflict Indicators in, 909
diagnosis, 903-906
Direct and Indirect Manifestations in, 908
Emotional First-Aid for, 929
hypnosis in therapy for, 931-933
incidence, 903-906
Individual Factors in Susceptibility, 920
irritability as factor in, 917
Personal Invulnerability Feelings in Relation to, 919

Combat Reactions—*Contd.*
Psychic Depletion Concept in, 41, 408, 922
psychodynamic factors in, 916-929
psychotherapy for, 930 (*see also* THERAPY)
Rhazes Maneuver, 677, 787, 906
Startle Reaction in, 916-917
stress, in relation to, 101, 902, 909-912, 919-921
symptoms, 906-916
trauma, repeated, in relation to, 922-924
treatment of, 929-933
tremors manifested in, 918
Ultimate-Vulnerability Theory in, 909-912
Unit-Guilt Reaction, 927-928
wounds, in relation to, 928-929
Combat stress, 100-101, 902, 909-912, 919-921
Common cold as a Depressive-Equivalent, 191-192
Communicability
depression, during, 157
suicide, in relation to, 164
Conflicts, *see* EMOTIONAL CONFLICT
Compartmentalization, 741
Compensation (*see also* EPIGAIN)
emotional illness propagated by, 66
epigain, in relation to, 64, 65, 878
Management of Problems, 877-878
neurosis and, 876-884
Compensation neuroses, 703, 876-844 (*see also* NEUROSES-FOLLOWING-TRAUMA)
Conversion Reaction, as, 703-704
Competitiveness as obsession, 332-333
Completion Depression, 187-188
Compliance with Implicit Command Concept, 176, 207
Compliant-Response Concept, 175-177, 192-193, 207, 857-858
Compromise Formation, 118, 671, 755, 693, 912
Compromise, symbolic, 118, 693
Compromise, unconscious, 118, 671
Compulsions
anxiety, manifesting, 20
definition, 310
Impulsion, differentiated from, 355
Compulsive overeating, 297-298
Compulsive Reactions, 307-375 (*see also* OBSESSIVE-COMPULSIVE REACTIONS)
Compulsive Rituals, 310, 349-354 (*see also* OBSESSIVE-COMPULSIVE REACTIONS)

Compulsive Rituals—Contd.
  childhood, in, 350
  Compulsive Security Ritual as, 354
  definition, 350
  handwashing as, 351
  health, obsessive preoccupation with, 352
  Making-Sure Routines, 310, 354
  neurotic, 350-351
  religion, obsessive preoccupation with, 352
  religious rites as, 351
  repetitiveness in, 349-350
  Security Operations as, 351-354
  Soterial Reactions differentiated from, 616
  sterotypy in stories as, 352
Compulsive Security Ritual, 310, 354, 461, 903 (*see also* COMPULSIVE RITUALS)
Concentration impairment manifesting anxiety, 20
Concept of Psychic-Depletion, 922
Concepts, *see* under individual heading
Concussion, 864 (*see also* AMNESIA; *also* TRAUMATIC ENCEPHALOPATHY
Condensation, 747, 691 (*see also* OVER-DETERMINATION)
Conditioned anxiety, 12, 34
Conditioned Responses
  anxiety, in relation to, 13, 30-31, 34, 37
  conditioned anxiety, 34
  Depressive Reactions, in relation to, 171
  Theory of Antecedent Conflicts, related to, 34
Conditioning process, the, 938-944 (*see also* PRISONER PROCESSING)
Confession, psychic pressures in, 818 (*see also* PRISONER PROCESSING)
Conflict
  Antecedent, Theory of, see Antecedent Conflict Theory
  Conflict-Anxiety-Avoidance Circle, 122
  emotional, *see* EMOTIONAL CONFLICT
  Hypothesis of Oral, 579
  intrapsychic, *see* INTRAPSYCHIC CONFLICT
  Pain, Ratio of, 510 (*see also* PAIN)
  social, *see* SOCIAL CONFLICT
  Conflict-Anxiety-Avoidance Circle, 122 (*see also* CONSTRICTIVE-SPIRAL CONCEPT)
Conflict Indicators, 23, 406, 671, 756, 797, 847, 909
  Depersonalization as, 766
  enuresis, 23

Conflict Indicators—Contd.
  Fugue States as, 797
  nail biting, 23
  repression, resulting from, 23
  stuttering, 23
  somnambulism, 756
Conflict-Pain Ratio, Axiom of Inverse, 470, 510, 703
Confusion manifesting anxiety, 20
Conscience, 21 (*see also* SUPEREGO)
Consciousness, loss of, 770-771 (*see also* FAINTING)
Conspiracy-of-Silence Concept, 725
Constellations of Character Defenses, 228-229, 675
Constipation of Grief, 167
Constrictive-Spiral Concept, 121-122
Constrictive Aggression Concept, 322, 373 (*see also* AGGRESSION)
Constrictive Anxiety Concept, 12, 41, 119, 132, 834
  Anxiety Neuroses, and, 119-120
  definition, 12, 41-42
Contagion, Emotional, Concept of, 32, 404, 464, 476, 568, 703
Contagion of Anxiety, 13, 32, 913
Continued Physiologic Momentum Concept, 99, 101, 455, 776, 866, 889, 904-912
Convergence of Associations, 747
Conversion allochiria, 652
Conversion aphonia, 677-682
Conversion Attack, 660
Conversion, Autonomic, 655
Conversion, Behavioral, 193, 258, 318, 355, 670
Conversion Character, 645, 674-675, 701 (*see also* CONVERSION PERSONALITY)
Conversion Epigain, 693, 716
Conversion character defenses, 241-242
Conversion epidemics, 703
Conversion pain
  antecedent prototypes, 667
  camptocormia, 670
  clavus, 670
  Conversion Reaction diagnosis, in, 654
  Fenichel's pathways for, 702
  frequent clinical feature, as, 667
  recapitulating characteristics, 702
  sites of, 670
  surgery contraindicated by, 654, 668-670
  surgical emergency, simulating, 667
  symptomatic features, 667-670

Conversion Personality, 258-270, 674
  appealing aspects, 263
  artistic expression in, 264
  attention-seeking in, 262
  buoyant spirits in, 263
  case studies of, 265
  character defenses associated with, 259-
    260
  charming aspects, 263
  clinical features of, 258-270
  defensive purpose, 260-261
  definition, 232
  diagnosis, 241-242
  egocentricity in, 262
  expressiveness of, 263
  hostility in, 266-267
  personal relationships, and, 262-264
  *Secondary Defense Concept, in relation
    to,* 266-267
  sexuality in, 268, 269-270
  suggestibility in, 268-269
  Traits of, 258-260
  uncooperativeness in, 266-267
Conversion Reactions, 639-719
  anxiety, manifesting, 20
  Autonomic Conversion, 655
  character traits, 645, 674-675, 701 (*see
    also* CONVERSION PERSONALITY)
  childhood, in, 21
  clinical features of, 662-689
    aerophagia, 677
    aphonia, 677-682
    dissociation, 682
    globus hystericus, 677
    I. Q. level, 676
    pseudocyesis, 677
    psychotic progression, 683
    Schizophrenia, 682-683
  Compensation Neurosis, 703-704
  convulsions originated by, 652
  Defensive Overreaction Concept in, 95,
    115, 641
  definition, 7, 641
  development of, 693-697
  diagnosis of, 650-658
    anatomic comparisons useful in, 652
    careful study indicated in, 653
    exclusion, by, 651
    Hygeiaphrontic Reactions, differen-
      tial, 657
    hysterogenic areas, by, 650-651
    I. Q. as a factor in, 653
    pain, by, 654 (*see also* CONVERSION
      PAIN)
    Phobic Reactions, differential, 657
    positive grounds, on, 650-654
    stigmata, by, 650-651
    terminology, 654-658
    when warranted, 656

Conversion Reactions—*Contd.*
  Dissociative Reactions, and, 742, 785-
    786
  dynamics of, 689-700
  elective surgery and, 599
  Emotional-Organic Combinations, 393,
    454, 657
  Emotional-Physiologic Illness, as, 655
  endogain in, 70-72, 671, 689-691, 700
  epidemics of, 703 (*see also* CONTAGION,
    EMOTIONAL)
  epigain in, 57, 64, 70-72, 672
  fits originated by, 652
  functional illness, as, 655
  Functional-Structural Progression in,
    642
  hearing loss originated by, 653
  historical background, 645-650
  hysteria, 641 (*see also* SOMATIC CON-
    VERSION REACTIONS)
  identification as mental mechanism in,
    701
  "imitator, great," as the, 656
  incidence of, 244, 658-662
    sophistication, in relation to, 661
  I. Q., in relation to, 653
  mechanisms in, 691-693
  *Neuroses Following Trauma, as symp-
    toms of,* 851
  Oral Conflict in, 700
  organ neurosis, 655
  overdetermination in, 701-702
  pain originated by, 654 (*see also* CON-
    VERSION PAIN)
  pathogenesis of, 689-700
  phobias and, 556
  physiologic, 642 (*see also* PHYSIOLOGIC
    CONVERSION REACTIONS)
  prescientific views of, 645-647
  Principle of Belief in, 646
  pseudo-epilepsy manifested in, 652
  psychoanalysis as treatment of choice,
    706
  psychologic, 643 (*see also* PSYCHOLOGIC
    CONVERSION REACTIONS)
  psychophysiologic disorder, 656
  psychoses evolving from, 683
  psychosomatic illness, 656, 688
  psychotherapy for, 706 (*see also* THER-
    APY)
  schizophrenia, and, 682-683
  sequence of, 650
  somatic, 641
  Somatization Reactions, 656
  speech loss originated by, 653, 677-682
  symptoms of, 662-689
    Acting Out, 670
    anesthesias, 683-688

Conversion Reactions—*Cont'd.*
   aphonia, 677
   appearance of, 670-675
   behavior toward, 670-675
   character traits, 674-675
   choice and location factors, 697-700
   cramps, 671
   defensive, 663-665
   dyskenesias, 683-688
   emotionalism, 674
   emotion-equivalents, as, 696
   endogain of, 671
   epigain of, 672
   histrionics, 674
   iatrogenic factors, 663
   inhibiting function, 671
   la belle indifférence, 671- 674
   motor and sensory manifestations, 643
   pain, 667-670 (*see also* CONVERSION PAIN)
   pattern perpetuation, 666
   physical, 662
   psychologic concepts, 662-666
   psychosomatic illness, 688
   rage-equivalents, as, 683
   repression maintenance, 665, 690
   self-punitive aspects, 683
   spasms, 671
   surface anesthesias, 699
   symbolic meanings, 643-645, 662, 699, 700
   tics, 671
   unconscious simulation of, 662
   variety of, 677
   terminology, 47
   "the great imitator", as, 656
Somatic Conversion, 641
   treatment of, 706-715
   Anxiety-Symptom Exchange in, 707
   attributes required, 714
   character analysis, 707
   educative measures, 711
   hypnosis, by, 711-712
   interpretive measures, 711
   Mesmerism, 646-647 (*see also* HYPNOSIS)
   Principle of Self-Esteem Maintenance, 677
   Progressive-Suggestion Technique, 709
   psychoanalysis, 706
   psychotherapy, 706
   Red Ink Method, 709 (*see also* THEORY)
Rhazes Maneuver, 677-678

Conversion Reactions—*Cont'd.*
   symptomatic, 708
   Therapeutic Bargain Concept in Therapy, 713
   Tracing Technique, 713
   unconscious simulation of symptoms, 662
   Vegetative Neurosis, 656
   visual loss originated by, 653
Convulsions of conversion origin, 652, 685
Coronary occlusion differentiated from Acute Anxiety Attack, 97
Counter-phobic, 585 (*see also* SOTERIAL REACTION)
Cover Reasons in suicide, 151, 220
Cramps as conversion symptoms, 671
Criminality as source of anxiety, 30
Crisis, *see* TOTAL INDIVIDUAL RESPONSE TO CRISIS
Critical Attack of Anxiety Concept, 464, 581, 802
Critical-Displacement Phobia, 547, 575, 578, 584, 854-856
Cultural Ratio, Direct, Concept of in depression, 135, 161, 219
Cultural Vogue Concept, 244, 316, 715, 844, 568, 601
Cumulative Trauma Concept (and Precept), 782
Cyclic Swings of Energy, 413
Cynophobia, 554

D

D.D.D. or Three D's of Suicide, 194
Danger
   avoidance of, 525-531
   Depersonalization in relation to, 762
   displacement causing Phobic Reaction, 572
   fear as defense against, 516, 525-531
   response to, *see* TOTAL INDIVIDUAL RESPONSE TO CRISIS
Dawn Insomnia, 218, 278
   definition, 142
   Depressive Reactions, as symptom of, 145-146, 156-157
   dreams, in relation to, 748
   suicide, in relation to, 163
Daytime-Somnambulism Concept, 794
Death, Acute Anxiety Attack, from, 94-95
Death wish, 208

Decompensation, Emotional, 48, 159, 317, 343, 367, 675, 835, 886, 910, 922

Deconditioning in Phobias, 596 (*see also* THERAPY)

Deep-Treatment Concept, 791, 889
Depressive Reactions, in, 212
suicide, in relation to, 209

Defense-Defeat Parallel Concept, 291, 505, 804

Defense, First Line of, 25, 578

Defense-Hypertrophy Principle, 72-73, 78, 229-230, 231, 675
Conversion character, in relation to, 675
Functional-Structural Progression Concept, 14, 468-469, 851
Hygeiaphrontic Reactions, in relation to, 473
Obsessive Personality, related to, 238-240
Phobic Reactions, in relation to, 578

Defense, Incomplete Symptom, Concept, 89, 189, 451, 882

Defense, Onion, 367, 465, 486-489

Defense, Personal Invulnerability Concept, 919

Defense, Secondary, Concept of, 144, 267, 354, 445, 487-489, 724
First Line of Psychic, 25
Defense, Primary, 724

Defenses of Higher and Lower Order, 25

Defensive endeavor, symptoms, 48

Defensive-Layering Concept
Conversion character, in relation to, 675
Hygeiaphrontic Reactions, in relation to, 465, 486, 489, 490
Obsessive Reaction therapy, in relation to, 367

Defensive-Overreaction Concept, 95, 115, 641, 798, 918
Acute Anxiety Attack, in relation to, 95-98
Conversion Reactions, illustrated in, 641
Fugue States, in relation to, 798

Defiance, Social, 356 (*see also* IMPULSIONS)

Déjá entendu, 759

Déjá vu
definition, 759
frightening experience, as, 766

Dejection, *see* DEPRESSIVE REACTIONS

Delinquent behavior, emotional gains of, 73-75

Dementia, *see Psychosis*

Demonophobia, 554

Denial, 874

Dependency (*see also* HELPLESSNESS), 885
anxiety, in relation to, 30-32
Conflict, Oral, 598
Fugue States, in, 797
Hygeiaphrontic reactions, in 476
Needs, 879, 884
Position, 885
Role, 872

Dependency-Dilemma of Infancy (and Childhood)
Depressive Reactions, as pathogenesis for, 169
Fatigue Reactions, in relation to, 410-412
hostile aggression related to, 410-411
Obsessive Reactions, in relation to, 341
Phobic Reactions, in relation to, 579

Dependency-satisfaction of drugs (*see* PRINCIPLE-OF-BELIEF; *also* FAVORABLE RESPONSE CONCEPT)

Dependent Appeal, 409

Depersonalization, 758-770
Anxiety-Equivalent, as, 759
clinical features, 760-766
Conflict Indicator, as, 766
crisis, during, 762
danger, in relation to, 762
definition, 758-759
déjá entendu, 759
déjá vu, 759, 766
diagnosis of, 760
dreams, in, 761
environmental, 758-759
escape route, as, 762
frightening characteristics, 765-766
Fugue State, in relation to, 766
historical background, 759
identification faulty in
incidence of, 760
Incipient Fugue Concept of, 766
personal, 758-759
Prognostic Signal Flag, as a, 922
psychodynamics of, 766
Schizophrenia, featured in, 760, 768
sexual identification uncertain in, 769
sources of, 764-765
stimuli for, 764-765
stress, in relation to, 762
subjective disturbance, as, 758
symbolic escape, as, 767
Symptom Language, 759
types of, 758

Depletion Concept of Anxiety
definition, 41
fatigue, in relation to, 408

Depletion, Psychic, 41, 408, 894, 922

Depression (*see also* DEPRESSIVE REAC-
TIONS)
  A deux, 167-168
  aggressive drives, of, 22-23
  agitated, 168
  anxiety, in relation to, 28, 137, 145,
    189-191
  anxiety resulting from, 22-23, 24, 120
  anxious, 145, 189-191
  coldness as clinical feature, 155
  common cold, and, 192
  common feature in emotional illness,
    as, 140
  Completion, 187-188
  constructive, 26
  Dawn Insomnia in, 145, 168
  definition, 19, 137
  Diffuse Retardation Concept, 157
  Direct Cultural Ratio Concept, 161
  emotional conflict, of, 22-23
  emotional fatigue, and, 384, 390, 405-
    408 (*see also* FATIGUE STATES)
  fear, in relation to, 137
  Fugue states, in relation to, 799
  hostile expression and, 159-161
  hygeiaphrontis and, 498-500
  level of, 275-277
  major psychologic conversion, as, 138-
    139
  melancholia, as successor to, 142
  neurotic manifestations of, 154-158
  neurotic vs. *psychotic,* 146-148
  obsession and, 349
  obsessive reactions, as treatment for,
    360
  One Day, 191-192
  Passing-the-Peak, 158
  pathologic, 277
  Physical Equivalents of, 143
  predisposition to, 282-283
  primal, 169-171, 174
  promotion, due to, 186-187
  Prototype, as Antecedent Conflict, 170
  reactive, 184-185
  Recurrence Principle in, 146
  severity, progression of, 146
  sexual drives of, 22-23
  situational, 184-185
  success, due to, 185-189
  sudden improvement, dangers of, 164
  terminology, 46
  therapy hampered by, 10
  work as escape from, 188
Depressive character defenses, 242
Depressive endogain, 178-180
Depressive equivalents, 158, 191
  Attitude symptoms, as, 144
  definition, 144-145
  Hygeiaphrontic, 499

Depressive equivalents—*Contd.*
  physical, 143
  symptoms obscured by, 154-155
Depressive Personality
  alcoholism in, 281
  assets of, 278-279
  Attention Hypothesis related to, 279-
    280
  clinical features of, 270-283
  constrictions of, 278-279
  constructive aspects, 273-275
  criticism, vulnerability to, 279-280
  cultural factors, 277
  .definition, 167-168, 232
  depression, predisposition to, in, 282-
    283
  diagnosis of, 242
  hostility in, 271
  hypomantic activity in, 282
  obsessive traits, 271-272
  old age, related to, 281
  overseriousness in, 270-271
  personal relationships in, 272-273
  reaction formation in, 280-281
  sexuality in, 282
  sombreness in, 270-271
  traits of, 239, 270-272
Depressive Reactions, 135-221
  Accident-Proneness, in relation to, 196-
    198
  Anaclitic, 170
  *Antecedent Conflict Theory, in relation
    to,* 161-163, 169-175
  anxiety, in relation to, 20, 144-145,
    189-191 (*see also* ANXIOUS DE-
    PRESSION)
  Anxiety Neurosis, analogous to, 167
  character traits in, 158-159
  childhood pathogenesis of, 169 (*see
    also* ANTECEDENT CONFLICT THE-
    ORY)
  clinical features of, 154-168
    character traits, 158-159
    communicability, 157
    cultural aspects, 161
    hostility, 159-161
    vasomotor changes, 155
  Cold Depression, 155
  Completion Depression, 187-188
  Dawn Insomnia, 142, 145-146
  Deep Treatment Concept in relation to,
    212
  definition, 137-138
  Depression á Deux, 167-168
  diagnosis, 142-148
    clear-cut, 142-143
    Dawn Insomnia and, 142, 145-146
    Dress Indicators Concept, 156
    positive, 142-144

d.

bscuring, 154-

ncy, 171

uragement, disillu-
isappointment), 194
eatment for, 214-215
ed by, 184-185 (see
ATIONAL DEPRESSION
TIVE DEPRESSION)
10-218 (see also
)
f, 212-213
215
t, 211
ck therapy, 215-218
l Inertia Concept, 213
tion, optimal time for, 211-

herapy, intensive, 210-211
on, 215
nce to, 213
n length and frequency, 213-
214
quilizers, 214-215
tment of choice, 210-214
ep Treatment Concept, 212
esensitizing-Purpose Concept, 39,
856, 917, 945
omotor changes in, 155
thdrawal in, 154, 155
epression, 120, 784
structive Aggression, 322
eterminants,
Psychologic, 90-99 (see also CONFLICT
INDICATORS)
Principle of Hidden, 696, 799, 847
Symptom Choice & Location, in, Table 37, 697
D's, Three, of Depression, 194
Developmental influences on mental capabilities, 254
Diagnoses, euphemistically-intended (in suicide), 150
iffuse Retardation Concept, 157
emma, Obsessive, 169, 341, 579, 601
ependency of Infancy, 169, 341, 410-412, 579
vasive-Ambivalence Concept, 579
obic, 569, 579, 601
nia, 357

Direct Cultural-Ratio Concept, 161 (s
also CULTURAL VOGUE CONCEPT
Disapproval
advancement affected by, 35
anxiety, as source of, 30, 33, 35
position affected by, 35
prestige affected by, 35
status, social, affected by, 35
Discipline conflicts as source of anxiety,
30
Discomfort as source of anxiety, 30
Discrepancy, Hygeiaphrontic, 461 (see
also HYGEIAPHRONTIC REACTIONS)
Dishonesty in the Obsessive Personality,
255
Displacement in Obsessive Reactions, 313,
344-345
Displacement, Critical, in Phobias, 601,
691
Disproportion, Principle of Characteristic
in Fatigue, 381
Dissociation, 726, 805
Affect, 25, 343, 517, 729, 731
Alternating, 729
B.B.C., 729
Breuer's, 729, 648
Fragmental, 729
Janet's, 653, 729
Physiologic, 526
Schizophrenic, 729, 682
Side-by-Side, 729
Dissociation of Automaticity
Automatic Behavior resulting from,
809-810
definition, 730
symptoms, 732
Dissociative Personality, 228, 283-286, 785
Dissociative Reactions, 721-830
affect splitting-away as, 729 (see also
AFFECT DISSOCIATION)
Alternating, 729 (see also ALTERNATING
DISSOCIATION)
Alternating Personality, 806-809
amnesia, 773-791
anxiety, manifesting, 20
automatic, 730 (see also DISSOCIATION
OF AUTOMATICITY)
Automatic Behavior, 809-810
availability for study, 724-725
challenging aspects, 723-726
clinical features of, 731-739
coexistent with other activities, 730
(see also SIDE-BY-SIDE DISSOCIA-
TION)
comparative data, 738-739
compartmentalization in, 741
concept of, 726-744
conversion aspects, 742

Depressive Reactions—C

  problems in, 14

  protean for

  spirits,

Diffuse R

  tion

Direct Cultu

  (*see als*

  CEPT)

Dress Indicators

drugs as treatment

ego support in, 211

elective surgery co

  599-600 (*see a*

  ABEYANCE RULE)

electroshock therapy for,

Emotional Decompensatio.

  in relation to, 159

endogain in, 178-180

epigain in, 57, 65, 181-182

Equivalents, Concept of—*see* D.

  SIVE EQUIVALENTS)

Evening Flood-Tide of Spirits in, 1

frozen state of rage, and, 175-177

Grief States in relation to, 165-167

guilt feelings in, 169

Higher Order Defensive Reaction, as,
  148-149

historical background, 140-142

hostility in, 159-161

Hygeiaphrontic Equivalents, 499

Hygeiaphrontis manifested in, 450

incidence of, 244, 148-154

  cultural groups, in, 148-149

  middle-aged groups, in, 149

  private practice, in, 154

  psychotic depth, of, 149-150

Inverse-Ratio Concept of Hostile Ex-
  pression to Depression, 219

masochism in, 177-178

medical management of, 139-140

melancholia, 140-141

mental retardation as manifestation of,
  157

middle-age, incidence in, 149

Morning Ebb-Tide of Spirits in, 164

neurotic depression, 154-158

One-Day Depression, 191-192

Oral Conflict and, 169

pathogenesis of, 168-184

  apathy in childhood, 174

  Antecedent Conflict Theory, 169-175

  childhood dependency, 169

  conditioned emotional responses, 171-
    172

  deprivation in childhood, 174

  early events, significance of, 171

Index

Depressive Reactions—*Cont*

Physical Equivalents o

  155

speech, in, 157

stress, 158

typical, 156-157, 154-15

withdrawal, 46, 4

terminology,

Theory of Transpare

therapy for, 212-21

Three D's in (disc

  sionment,

tranquilizers as tr

trauma, precipita

  also SIT

  and REA

treatment for, 2

  THERAP

  difficulties

  drugs, 214-

  ego suppo

  electrosho

  Emotiona

  interpret

  212

  psychot

  remissi

  resista

  sessio

ps

psych

  inci

  neuro

rage and,

  childhoo

  frozen sta

recurrence, p

repetition of pa

Retardation, Dif

sadism in, 177-17

Secondary Defense
  144 (*see als*
  FENSE CONCEPT.

simultaneous occurrence
  uals, 167-168

stress and, 158

success, due to, 185-189, (*se*
  CESS DEPRESSION)

suffering in relation to, 168

suicide, in relation to, 149, 15
  163-165, 192-210

symptoms of, 154-168

  coldness, 155

  decreased interests, 154-155

  insomnia, 156-157 (*see als*
  INSOMNIA)

tran

trea

De

D

va

w

De

De

D

Dissociative Reactions—*Contd.*
Conversion Reactions, and, 785-786
Conversion-type, 730 (*see also* JANET DISSOCIATIONS)
defensive characteristics, 723-726
definition, 726-727
Depersonalization, 758-770
diagnosis of, 729-730
Double Personality, 806-809 (*see also* ALTERNATING PERSONALITY)
dreams as, 744-754
ego function in, 740-741
fainting, 770-773
fragmental, 730
Fugue States, 791-806
historical background, 727-729
hypnosis in relation to, 730, 810-825
hypnotic or induced, 730 (*see also* B.B.C. DISSOCIATION)
incidence of, 244, 731
Janet's theories, 728 (*see also* JANET DISSOCIATIONS)
major types, 729-730
masochism in, 786
memory loss, 773-791 (*see also* AMNESIA)
Neuroses Following Trauma, as syndrome in, 852-853
Overall Language Concept, 740-744
pathogenesis, 740-744
physiologic, 730 (*see also* PHYSIOLOGIC DISSOCIATION)
primitive reaction, as, 741
psychodynamics, 740-744
Schizophrenic, 730 (*see also* SCHIZOPHRENIC DISSOCIATION; *also* BLEULER'S DISSOCIATION)
somatic type, 730 (*see also* BREUER'S DISSOCIATION)
Somnambulism, 754-758
split personality, 806-809 (*see also* ALTERNATING PERSONALITY)
symptoms of, 731-739
terminology, 46
types, major, 729
trauma, following, 853
unreality, feeling of, 758-770 (*see also* DEPERSONALIZATION)
Distance-Maintenance, 691
Distaste, Psychic, 115, 416, 418, 473, 907
Doctor-patient relationship in psychotherapy, 25-27, 130
Double Personality, 730-732, 809-810, (*see also* ALTERNATING PERSONALITY)
Dreams, 744-754 (*see also* SLEEP)
activated fantasy, see SOMNAMBULISM
anxiety, in relation to, 20, 40
Dissociative Reaction, as, 806-809

Dreams—*Contd.*
Fugue States and, 795
association convergence in, 747 (*see also* OVERDETERMINATION)
battle dream, 917, 744-754
concepts in, 747-752
condensation in, 747
Contribution to Emotional Health Concept and Hypothesis, 39, 749, 856
convergence characteristics, 751
Dawn-Insomnia, in relation to, 748
deficit, 749
Depersonalization in, 761
Desensitizing Purpose Concept, 39, 856, 917, 945
displacement function, 748
Dissociation within, 752
Dissociative Reaction, as, 744-754
distortion characteristics, 750
elaboration characteristics, 750
emotional health, as contribution to, 39, 749
emotionally determined, 749
evaluation reinforced through repetition, 751
fantasies, as, 752
'Fast Time' aspects, 748
fear expressing function, 746
free association used to interpret, 747
functions of, 744-746
hypnosis, induced by, 821
Hypothesis of Contribution to Emotional Health, 749
individual symbolism in, 753
interpretation of, 746-747
latent content, 750
logic disregarded in, 749
manifest content, 747, 750
mechanisms in, 747-752
multiple representation characteristics, 750
Neuroses Following Trauma, in, 856
overdetermination in, 747, 751
Phobic Reactions, in relation to, 597
post-traumatic, 39, 856, 917, 945
routine aspects, 748
Sleep-Preserving Function, 744
specially significant, 753
symbolism in, 751
universal characteristics, 748
validation aspects, 751-752
vital process, as, 744
wish-fulfillment function, 745
Drinking (*see also* ALCOHOLISM)
antisocial behavior due to, 26-27
Dipsomania, 357
psychotherapy for, 26-27
suicide and, 208-209

Drugs (*see also* SEDATIVES; *also* TRAN-QUILIZERS)
Depressive Reactions, as treatment for, 214-215
D's, Three, 194
Hygeiaphrontis, and, 471
hypnosis, used in, 817-819
psychotherapy, used in, 129-130
Soterial objects, as, 623
truth serum, 817-819
Duplication, Psychic, Concept of, 468, 667, 914
Dynamic psychiatry, fundamental concepts of, 4
Dyskenesias, 683-688
Dysphagia, 677

E

E.I.C., see EMOTIONAL INERTIA CONCEPT
E.I.D., see EMOTIONAL IMPACT-DEFER-MENT CONCEPT
E.O.A., see EMOTIONAL-OBJECT AMALGAM
E.O.C., see EMOTIONAL-ORGANIC COMBINATIONS
E.P.I., see EMOTIONAL-PHYSIOLOGIC ILL-NESS
Ebb-Tide of Spirits Concept, 151
Effect-Over-Cause Concept in sexual maladjustments, 330 (*see also* SEXUAL MALADJUSTMENT)
Ego
defenses and defensive routes, 24
Dissociative Reactions, function in, 740-741
Failure, 868-869
First Line of Psychic Defense Concept, 25
function, 740
psychoses, function in, 740-741
shattered, aim to restore in Prisoner-Processing victims, 944
support in Depressive Reactions, 211
Egocentricity
Conversion Personality, in, 262
Obsessive Reactions, in, 332
Ejaculatio praecox, 9
Elaboration, 750
Electroshock therapy
Amnesia following, 773, 778, 870 (*see also* SHOCK AMNESIA)
Depressive Reactions, as treatment for, 215-218

Electroshock therapy—*Contd.*
disadvantages of, 217
indications for, 216
memory affected by, 218, 778 (*see also* SHOCK AMNESIA)
opinions on, 215-216
Principle of Psychic Selectivity, 789
psychodynamic factors of, 217-218
Emergency-Analytic Bridge in Conversion Reactions, 678-679
Emotion and physiology in Dissociative State, 853
Emotional Achille's Heel Concept, 581, 860 (*see also* ACHILLE'S HEEL CONCEPT)
Emotional-Amalgam Concept, 27
Emotional Amnesia, 777
Emotional blocks, major and minor, 688
Emotional conflict
adulthood, in, 119
aggressive drives, due to, 22-23
antecedents of, 29 (*see also* ANTECEDENT CONFLICT THEORY)
anxiety, related to, 21-27
apprehensive tension arising from, 24
clash between two opposing emotional forces, as, 21-22
conscious awareness of, 22
definition, 21, 23
derepression of, 22-23
Emotional Paralysis resulting from, 25
external symptoms of, 47-48
fatigue, and, 406 (*see also* FATIGUE STATES)
"Fight or Flight" response to, 24-25
frustration related to, 32
Goal of Equanimity Concept, related to, 22
hypnosis, produced by, 823
id vs. superego, arising from, 21
illnesses resulting from, 87-88
indicators of, 23 (*see also* CONFLICT INDICATORS)
instinctual drives vs. conscience, arising from, 21-22
mental mechanisms used in, 25
psychologic responses to, 24
psychotherapy for, 25-27 (*see also* THERAPY)
repression of, 22-23
resolution of, 48
anxiety, through, 20
sexual drives, due to, 22-23
symptom formation, sequence of events leading to, 23
treatment of, 47-51

Emotional Contagion Concept
anxiety and, 13, 30, 31, 32-33, 37
Fainting, in relation to, 771-772
Hygeiaphrontic Reactions, in relation
to, 464, 476
military life, in, 37
parents and children, between, 32-33
Emotional Death, Concept of
Acute Anxiety Attack, in relation to,
94-95
definition, 131
Emotional Decompensation Concept, 48,
159, 317, 343, 367, 476, 675,
711, 910
Conversion Reactions, 675
definition, 48, 159
Hygeiaphrontic Reactions, in relation
to, 476
Emotional-Desensitization Principle, 924
Emotional Determinants, 636
Emotional development, 6
Emotional Equanimity, 22, 890
Emotional Equivalents, 696
Emotional Exploitation Concept, 172-174
Emotional Fatigue
anxiety, manifesting, 20
Characteristic-Disproportion Principle,
381, 389, 857
Concept of, 381, 382
definition, 382
diagnosis, of, 388-389
emotional depression, in relation to,
384, 405-408
Emotional-Organic Conflicts in, 393
endogain in, 408
epigain in, 57, 398, 409-410
Fatigue Discrepancy Principle, 381
Fatigue State, in, 389
neurasthenia, 424-426
organic fatigue, in combination with,
393
oversleeping due to, 40-41
psychodynamic considerations, 405-408
sleep related to, 38, 40-41
supportive therapy for, 431
symptoms in, 397-398
terminology, 46
treatment for, 430-436 (*see also* THER-
APY)
Emotional Habit-Pattern Concept, 540
Emotional hazards
adulthood, of, *see* SPECIFIC EMOTIONAL
HAZARDS OF ADULTHOOD
childhood, of, *see* SPECIFIC EMOTIONAL
HAZARDS OF CHILDHOOD
Emotional Health
anxiety in, 2-4
Basic Drive Toward, Concept of, 38,
834

Emotional Health—*Contd.*
definition, 6
dream contribution to, 39, 749
maturity as measurement of, 6
personal relationships as measurement,
6
Relativity Law in, 2-4
satisfaction in living as measurement
of, 6
sleep, role of, 38-39 (*see also* EMO-
TIONAL FATIGUE; *also* DREAMS)
Trend Toward Principle, 38
universal problems in, 2-3
yardstick for measuring, 6 7
Emotional illness (*see also* EMOTIONAL
CONFLICT)
anatomy of, 56
assessment of gain or loss in, 60
Character Neuroses in, 59-60
compensation propagating, 66
death resulting from, 94-95
endogain in, 56-79
epigain, compared with, 76-78
features of, 76-78
initiated by, 56
initiating, 68-69
paradoxical aspects, 58-59
raison d'etre in psychogenesis of, 69,
70
role of, 67-68
epigain in, 56-79
endogain, compared with, 76-78
features of, 76-78
paradoxical aspects, 58-59
perpetuated by, 56-57
propagating, 66
role of, 57-58
gains, illusory, in, 55-79 (*see also* ENDO-
GAIN; *also* EPIGAIN)
Habit-Patterns in, 59
initiation of, 56, 68-69
marital relationships and, 297
overreaction to, 95-98 (*see also* DEFEN-
SIVE-OVERREACTION CONCEPT)
perpetuation of, 56
relativity in diagnosis and classification,
3
self-defeating aspects of, 59
simulated, 62 (*see also* MALINGERING)
Symptom Neurosis in, 60
traumatic characteristics, 834-836
types of, 87-88
unconscious escape, used as, 58
wounds and, 928-929
Emotional-Impact-Deferment (*E.I.D.*)
Concept, 863, 927
Dissociative Reactions, in relation to,
731

Neuroses-Following-Trauma, in relation to, 864

Emotional Indigestion, 694 (*see also* PSYCHIC DISTASTE CONCEPT)

Emotional Inertia Concept, 213, 433, 504, 707, 886, 929

Emotional manifestations of anxiety, 20-21

Emotional-Object Amalgam (E.O.A.) Concept, 393, 453-454, 568, 837, 846 (*see also* AMALGAM, EMOTIONAL-OBJECT, CONCEPT OF)
  definition, 584-585
  phobic, 585
  soterial objects, in relation to, 624

Emotional-Organic Combinations (E.O.C.), 393, 443, 454, 468, 837, 846
  Conversion, 393, 443, 454, 652, 667
  fatigue, in, 393
  Hygeiaphrontic Reactions, in, 454
  phobic, 585
  soterial, 585

Emotional pain, *see* PAIN

Emotional paralysis, 25

Emotional Perpetuation Concept, 116-117

Emotional-Physiologic Illness, 655

Emotional Priority Concept, 531-541 (*see also* IMPRESSION-PRIORITY RULE)

Emotional Prototypes, 490, 494, 694, 808, 910

Emotional Recapitulation Concept, 117

Emotional-Relearning-Tougher Principle, 535

Emotional response character traits, 59-60

Emotional satisfaction, *see* GOAL OF EQUANIMITY CONCEPT

Emotional Sensitization Principle, 924

Emotional Symptoms, 5

Emotionalism in Conversion Reactions, 674

Emotionally-Determined Visceral Pain Principle, 467, 654

Encephalopathy, Traumatic, 781-783

Endogain
  assessment of, 60
  character defenses, in, 72-73
  Conversion Reactions, in, 70-72, 671, 689-691
  defensive motivation in, 56
  definition, 68, 69
  delinquent behavior, in relation to, 73-75
  depressive, 178-180

Endogain—*Contd.*
  emotional illness, in, 56-79
    initiated by, 68-69
    initiating, 56
    operative factor, as, 57-58
  epigain, compared with, 76-78
  fatigue, in, 408
  Fugue State, in, 798
  Hygeiaphrontic Reactions, in, 481-484
  illusory aspects of, 58-59
  King David Reaction, in, 75-76
  neuroses, in, 70-72
  Neuroses Following Trauma, in, 849, 873-875
  Obsessive Neuroses, in relation to, 73-75
  Obsessive Personality, in, 72-73
  paradoxical aspects, 58-59
  Phobic, 548, 578
  principle features of, 76-78
  raison d'etre in psychogenesis, as, 69-70
  resolution of internal conflicts, in relation to, 70
  self-defeating aspects of, 59
  Success Depression, in, 186-187
  suicide, in relation to, 73-75
  types of, 69-70
  universality of, 73-74

Energy
  cyclic swings of, 413
  loss of, 413, 417-422 (*see also* FATIGUE; *also* FATIGUE STATES)
  physiology of, 417-422
  psychic, 417
  Reservoir Concept, 417
  sleep, replenished by, 422

Enuresis, 23

Environmental Depersonalization, 759

Environment, external
  anxiety, as source of, 30, 33
  epigain, in relation to, 62, 68
  manipulation of, 68

Environment, internal, as source of anxiety, 30, 33

Environmental Modification Concept of Symptom Utilization, 61, 873, 849

Epidemics
  Anxiety, 10
  Conversion, 32, 464, 476, 703
  Emotional, 32, 464, 476

Epigain
  anxiety related to, 65
  apparency of, 63-64
  assessment of, 60
  attention related to, 65

Epigain—*Contd.*
avoidance of unpleasant situations related to, 65
character defenses, in, 72-73
compensation as, 64-66, 878
conflict resolution related to, 65
conscious secondary gain, differentiated
from, 61-62
Conversion Reactions, in, 70-72, 672,
693
defensive motivation in, 56
definition, 61, 62-63, 65
delinquent behavior, in relation to, 73-
75
dependency needs gratified by, 64-65
depressive, 181-182
disproportionate significance of, 66
emotional fatigue, in, 398
emotional illness, in, 56-79
operative factor, as, 57-58
perpetuating, 56-57
propagated by, 66
endogain, compared with, 76-78
extent of, 63-64
external environment, influencing, 62,
63, 68
fatigue, in, 409-410
features of, 76-78
hospital life, in, 66
Hygeiaphrontic Reactions, in, 64, 484-
489
illusory aspects, 58-59
insecurity related to, 65
King David reaction, in, 76
malingering, differentiated from, 61,
494-495, 849
manipulation of people and environment related to, 65
material advantages of, 61-68
military aspects, 67-68
neuroses, in, 63-68, 70-72
Neuroses Following Trauma, in, 849,
873-875, **888-889**
Obsessive Personality, in, 72-75, 365
paradoxical aspects, 58-59
Paranoid Personality, in, 74-75
physical illness, in, 63
responsibility avoidance related to, 65
self-defeating aspects of, 59
self-preservation related to, 65
sexual immaturity related to, 65
soterial securities related to, 66
suicide, in relation to, 73-75
sympathy, in relation to, 65
types of, 65
universality of, 73-74
Epilepsy, false, 652
Episodic amnesia, 777

Episodic Hygeiaphrontis, 482-484
Equanimity Goal Concept, 22, 890
Equinophobia, 554
Equivalents
affect, 686
anxiety, 19, 103, 111, 145, 324, 462,
672, 880
depressive, 144, 155, 158, 191, 218, 499
emotional, 696
physical, 143
physiologic, 191
psychologic, 158-159
rage, 683, 742, 913
symptoms, 228-304
Equivocal suicide, 196
Euphemistic Diagnoses, 150
Euphemistic Disguises, 150
Evening Full Tide of Spirits, 164, 145
Exhaustion (*see also* FATIGUE REACTIONS)
combat, *see* COMBAT REACTIONS *and*
MILITARY REACTIONS
definition, 382
organic bases for, 391 (*see also* OR-
GANIC FATIGUE)
Exhibitionism, 357
Exploitation, Emotional Concept, 172
Extension, Principle of, 96, 131 (*see also*
CIRCULAR GENERATION OF FEAR
PRINCIPLE)

F

F.I.C., see FAULTY IDENTIFICATION CON-
CEPT
Facade, Obsessive, 248, 348
Fainting
definition, 771
Dissociative Reaction, as, 770-773
Fragmental Dissociation, as, 770
incidence of, 771
primitive defensive reaction, as, 771
situations causing, 771-772
Falling, fear of, 30
False amnesia, 777 (*see also* MALINGER-
ING)
Fantasies, Nocturnal, 754 (*see also* SOM-
NAMBULISM; *also* DREAMS)
Fast Time, 748
Fatigue
anxiety, due to, 408
childhood, in, 403
emotional conflict and, 406 (*see also*
EMOTIONAL FATIGUE)
energy and, 413, 417-422
endogain in, 408

Fatigue—*Contd.*
factors influencing, 401-403
frequent symptom, as, 393
hypomanic activity and, 413
Indicator, 434
insulin tolerance test in, 419
intellectual pursuits, in, 402
Inverse Incentive Principle in, 412
organic bases for, 382, 391 (*see also*
    ORGANIC FATIGUE)
performance potential related to, 412
physical, 382 (*see also* PHYSICAL FA-
    TIGUE)
rationalization, as, 403
relative nature of, 402
sleep, and, 422-423
types of, 319-440
Fatigue Reactions, 379-440 (*see also* EMO-
    TIONAL FATIGUE; PHYSICAL FA-
    TIGUE; MENTAL FATIGUE; OR-
    GANIC FATIGUE)
Advanced-Organicity Concept in, 390-
    391
body chemistry and, 420-422
boredom and, 415-417
clinical features, 397-403
defensive purposes, 408-410
definition, 383
diagnosis, 388-393
diet regimen as therapy for, 431
Disproportion, Characteristic, 381
drug therapy for, 431-432
endocrine activity in, 421
environmental changes as therapy for,
    431
epigain in, 64, 409-410
Fatigue Indicator, 434
historical background, 384-388
incentive in, 412-413
incidence of, 244, 393-397
infantile need frustrations, and, 410-412
intensive psychotherapy considerations,
    433-436
interest level in, 412-415
monotony and, 415-417
motivation level in, 412-415
neurasthenia, 385, 424-430
oversleeping due to, 41
parental conditioning effect in, 403
physical modalities as therapy for,
    431-432
physiology of, 417-422
psychodynamic considerations, 403-412
psychotherapy for, 430 (*see also*
    THERAPY)
rest therapy, 432
social attitude toward, 401
symptoms, 397-403

Fatigue Reactions—*Contd.*
supportive therapy, 431-433
stimulants as therapy, 432
terminology, 45, 46
treatment for, 430-436
World War I and II observations, 387
Fatigue State (*see also* ANXIETY TENSION
    STATE)
anxiety, manifesting, 20
definition, 383
Depression, and, 390
emotional conflicts, as product of, 389,
    399 (*see also* EMOTIONAL FA-
    TIGUE)
hostile aggression in, 410
Hygeiaphrontis manifested in, 450
increased responsibility, following, 400
neurasthenia, 425-426
psychodynamic considerations, 410-412
regression of, 410
symptoms in, 399-401
terminology, 46
Faulty Identification Concept, 681, 769
Favorable Psychologic Soil Concept, 574,
    663, 802, 856, 866-871
Favorable-Response Concept, 392, 451-
    453, 472, 709 (*see also* BELIEF-
    PRINCIPLE)
Fear (*see also* ANXIETY, *also* PHOBIAS;
    PHOBIC REACTIONS)
*academic absorption, avoidance
    through,* 523
anxiety, and, 89-90, 94, 517
anxiety differentiated from, 4, 12-17,
    104
Anxiety Neurosis, in relation to, 120
Apprehensive Anticipation and, 17
authority, of, 16-17
avoidance of, 515-544
basic biological response, as, 525-527
Circular Generation Principle, 93, 518,
    529, 913
civilizing influences on, 520-523
close relationships avoided due to, 524
conformity influencing, 520
defense against danger, as, 516, 525-
    531
definition, 11
dreams, expressed in, 746
emergency action, as, 520
falling, of, 30
generation of, 89-90 (*see also* CIRCULAR
    GENERATION OF FEAR PRIN-
    CIPLE)
grief, in relation to, 165
*Impression Priority Rule, in relation
    to,* 531-541
individual assessment of, 518-519

Fear—*Contd.*
origins of, 12
pain, in avoidance of, 525-531
pathologic, 517, 519
phobic response, as 517-518, 546-548, 569
psychosomatic pathology, role in, 522
quality of immediacy in, 13
recognition of danger in, 12
reflex action, as, 520-522
response to, 516 (*see also* TOTAL RE-SPONSE TO CRISIS)
  academic absorption, 523
  clinical, 523-525
  complexity of, 516-518
  external danger, to, 15-16
  phobic, 517, 546-548
  psychologic flight, 524
  varieties of, 518-525
sadness, in relation to, 137
social pressures influencing, 520
speechlessness caused by, 16-17
vital role of, 516
Fear in the absence of a known cause, 1-52 (*see also* ANXIETY)
Feelings of Omnipotent Responsibility, 922
Feigned amnesia, 777
Fenichel's pathways for conversion pain, 702
"Fight or Flight" response
anxiety, resulting from, 24
emotional conflict, to, 24-25
physiologic preparation for, 16
psychologic, 24-25
symbolic response, as, 16
Final Straw Concept, 162, 399, 713, 860-862, 911, 923
First Aid, Emotional, 929
First Line of Psychic Defense Concept, 25, 343, 691, 874
definition, 25, 68
obsessive reactions, in, 343
First Tenet of the Parental Role, 23, 309, 479
Fits in Conversion Reactions, 652
Fixation in hygeiaphrontic reactions, 467
Flight, Fugue, 792
Flight-to-the-Physical Principle, 46, 461, 707, 835, 877, 880, 916 (*see also* PHYSICAL SCAPEGOAT CONCEPT)
  Acute Anxiety Attack, in relation to, 91, 97
  Conversion, in, 672, 708
  fatigue, in relation to, 392
  Hygeiaphrontic Reactions, in, 461, 478
  trauma, in relation to, 835

Flight, Psychologic, 58, 792
Forgetfulness pathologic, see AMNESIA
Fracture-Proneness, 197-198
Fragmental Dissociation, 730-734, 770
  definition, 730
  fainting as, 770
  symptoms, 734
Free association for dream interpretation, 747
Free discussion therapy, 107-108
Free-floating anxiety, 12
Freud, S. (1856-1939), 83, 550, 841, 869
  anxiety, on, 83
  Depressive Reactions, on, 141
  gain, comments on, 62, 69
  grief, on, 165
  masochism, on, 177-178
  Repetition Compulsion, Concept of, 171
Frozen State of Rage, 175-177
Frustration
  anger, related to, 32
  anxiety, as source of, 30-32, 37
  emotional conflict, related to, 32
  helplessness, related to, 32
  hostility, related to, 32
  repression, related to, 32
  symptom formation, related to, 32
Fuel Analogy, 42, 119, 140, 363, 913
Fugue States
  Acting Out, 193, 258, 355-356, 798-799
  Alternating Dissociation, as, 796
  amnesia differentiated from, 774
  amnesia, in, 791
  antagonistic aims subserved by, 802
  antecedent patterns in, 797
  anxiety, in relation to, 801-802
  appearance of, 796
  clinical features, 794-798
  clinical types of, 796
  Conflict Indicator, as, 797
  crisis, in relation to, 797
  definition, 792
  definitive therapy for, 804
  Depersonalization in relation to, 766
  depression in relation to, 799
  diagnosis of, 793
  dissociative reactions, as, 791-806
  effects of, 794
  endogain and, 798
  escape route, as, 799-800
  flight in, types, 792
  hallucinations in, 793
  hypnosis as therapy for, 806
  Identification Fugue, the, 796
  incidence, 793-794
  Incomplete Fugue, the, 796

Fugue States—*Contd.*
  major personality dissociation, as, 791-792
  marked, 795
  Mixed Fugue, the, 796
  onset of, 794
  pre-existing diathesis required in, 802
  psychodynamics of, 798-803
  psychoses, differentiated from, 793
  repeated, 797
  Retrograde Fugue, the, 796
  somnambulism, compared with, 794
  stimuli for, 803
  symbolic aspects, 798
  trauma, following, 853
  treatment of, 803-806
  types of, 722, 796
Functional Equivalent, 191
Functional illness, 655
Functional psychoses, 87
Functional-Structural Progression Concept, 72-73, 78, 113, 229-231, 409 (*see also* DEFENSE-HYPERTROPHY PRINCIPLE)
  Conversion, in, 642
  definition, 14, 113, 468, 851
  Hygeiaphrontic Reactions, in relation to, 469
  Traumatic Reactions, in, 866

G

Gains of Emotional Illness Concepts, 55-79
Gains, illusory, *see Endogain; also Epigain*
Genocide as anxiety source, 30, 36
Geometric Principle, 748
Geometric Progression, 911 (*see also* ULTIMATE-VULNERABILITY, THEORY OF)
Globus hystericus, 677, 695-696
Goal of Equanimity Concept, 22, 25
Graduate Course of Study Concept, 234, 436
Grief State, 165-167
  Anxiety Tension State, analogous to, 98, 167
  constructive aspects, 167
  cultural influences on, 165-166
  definition, 165
  Depressive Reactions, in relation to, 165-167
  destructive aspects, 167
  expression of, 167
  grieving time in relation to, 166

Grieving Time, 116
Guilt
  combat, experienced in, 927-928
  Depressive Reactions, in, 169
  Hygeiaphrontic Reactions, and 482-484
  Unit, Concept of, 923, 927-928

H

Habit patterns, 59
Hallucinations
  Fugue States, in, 793
  hypnosis, produced by, 823
Hand-in-Glove Analogy, 280, 348-349, 485
  Obsessive Reactions, in, 348-349
  Hygeiaphrontic Reactions, in relation to, 485
Hand-in-Hand Concept in Psychotherapy, 634
Hazard of Symptom-Exchange, 683, 711, 801, 825
Head injury causing traumatic neuroses, 852
Headache in Anxiety Neurosis, 115
Health, overconcern with, *see* HYGEIAPHRONTIS, 441 *ff.*
  obsessive nature, of, 352
Hearing loss of conversion origin, 653
Hearing, Selective, 688
Heart attacks confused with Acute Anxiety Attacks, 96, 97
Helplessness
  anxiety, as source of, 30-32, 37
  frustration due to, 32
Herpetophobia, 554
Hidden Determinants Principle in symptom evolvement, 697, 799, 847
Higher Order Defensive Reactions
  definition, 25
  Depressive Reactions as, 148-149
Higher Order Neuroses, 104-120 (*see also* ANXIETY REACTIONS)
Histrionics in Conversion Reactions, 674
Hoarding as Soterial Reaction, 620, 630
Homosexuality causing conversion aphonia, 679-680
Hospitalitis, 66
Hostile Expression, Individual Inverse-Ratio Concept of, 159-161
Hostility
  anxiety, and
    impulses covered by, 15
    manifesting, 20

Hostility—*Contd.*
    repression caused by, 28
    source of, as, 31, 37
    Conversion Personality, in, 266-267
    Depressive Personality, in, 159-161, 271
    Fatigue State, in, 410
    frustration due to, 32
    Impulsions, in, 355-356
    inverted, 206
    Obsessive Reactions, in, 320-322
    parent-child relationships, in, 322
    repression of, anxiety, due to, 28, 29
    suicide, in relation to, 206
Hunger causing anxiety, 30
Hygeiaphrontic Attack, 483, 660
Hygeiaphrontic character defenses, 283
Hygeiaphrontic Discrepancy Concept,
    443, 447, 451, 913 (*see also*
    TRAUMATIC DISCREPANCY)
    definition, 447
    diagnosis, importance in, 451
Hygeiaphrontic Personality, 283-284
Hygeiaphrontic Reactions, 441-514
    acceptance sought in, 485
    affection and, 485
    Antecedent Conflicts role in, 490-492
    anxiety, as defense against, 462, 477,
    491
    character defenses, as, 472
    clinical features, 461-473
    conflicts expressed on visceral plane,
    as, 498-499
    conversion pain in, 469
    definition, 446
    dependency in, 476
    diagnosis, 450-457
        Discrepancy Concept and Principle,
        447, 451
        elimination, by, 451
        Favorable-Response Concept in, 451
        organic disease concurrently present,
        453-454
        overstudy vs. understudy, 451-453
        special conditions of onset, 454-457
    distinguishing features, 450-454
    drugs and, 471
    early environmental factors initiating,
    479
    elective surgery contraindicated by,
    599-600 (*see also* SURGERY-IN-
    ABEYANCE RULE)
    Emotional-Organic Combinations in,
    454
    Emotional Prototype for, 490
    emotional role in, 480
    endogain in, 481-484
    epigain in, 484-489

Hygeiaphrontic Reactions—*Contd.*
    exaggerated, 472
    figurative vs. literal meanings in, 473
    figures of speech, recognized in, 473
    fixation in, 467
    functional pain in, 469
    guilt, and, 482-484
    incidence of, 244, 457-461
    increased awareness of normal func-
    tion in, 464
    indications for treatment, 502
    initiation of, factors in, 476-481
    intensive psychotherapy for, 503-506
    Interest Absorption Defense, 311, 332,
    462, 708, 913
    interpersonal environment and, 484
    introspection, and, 504
    malingering differentiated from, 494-
    497
    Neuroses Following Trauma, as symp-
    tom of, 851
    neurotic reaction patterns in, 497
    Obsessive Neuroses, and, 456
    Oedipal conflicts related to, 490
    old age, in relation to, 471
    onset of, 454-457
    Oral Conflicts related to, 490
    organic disease and, 453-454, 478
    overattention to function in, 461
    pain in
        anxiety caused by, 480
        location and susceptibility, 469-470
        Perception Intensification Concept,
        503
        stress, following, 469
        threshold of, 470
        visceral, 467-470
    pathogenesis of, 473-489
    patient, the, 461-462
    parental role in, 463, 476
    perception threshold lowered in, 479-
    480
    personality and, 283-284
    physician's attitude toward, 500-503
    physiologic preoccupation and, 443-447
        (*see also* INTEREST-ABSORPTION
        CONCEPT)
    physiology and, 480
    precipitating events, 476
    Primitive vs. Highly Developed De-
    fenses, in relation to, 597-598
    Psychic Reduplication Concept in, 468
    psychic trauma of birth, resulting from,
    492
    psychodynamics of, 473-489
    psychopathology criteria, 462
    psychoses, and, 455-456
    punishment and, 482-484

Hygeiaphrontic Reactions—*Contd.*
regression in, 467, 476
response pattern precedents in, 490
schizophrenia, and, 455, 472
Seekers-After-Health, 460, 708, 913
self-punitive factors in, 481
serious portent of, 472
severe pathologic retreat in, 466
somatic preoccupation and, 443-447
Soterial Reactions and, 491, 617
stomach pain in, 468
stress
following, 454
pain due to, 469
stressful living periods, during, 457
sudden dissolution of, consequences of,
477
suffering and, 482-484
surgery, following, 470
symbolic gratification and control in,
481
symptoms, 457-458, 461-473
children in, 463
increased awareness of normal function, 464
overdetermined, 489
varieties of, 462-467
visceral pain, 467-470
*Theory of Antecedent Conflict related
to,* 490-494
treatment for, 500-509
anxiety arousal, 506
concern increased during, 504-505
indications for, 502
intensive psychotherapy, 503-506
introspection constructive in, 504
physician's attitude, 500-502
Therapeutic Bargain Concept, 300,
713, 591
withdrawal from interpersonal relationships due to, 506
underlying conflicts, as expression of,
481-482
Hygeiaphrontic State, 167, 446
Hygeiaphrontic System, 446, 508
Hygeiaphrontic Vicious Circle, 284
Hygeiaphrontis, 443-446
anxiety, manifested in, 20, 450
Constrictive-Spiral Concept in, 284,
463
definition, 44, 446
denial, consequences of, 475
depression, and, 450, 498-500
drugs, and, 471
dynamic implications, 486
epigain in, 57, 64
episodic, 482-484
Fatigue State, manifested in, 450
historical background, 448-450

Hygeiaphrontis—*Contd.*
love and, 485
neurasthenia, manifested in, 450
obsessive preoccupation, as, 466
Obsessive Reactions in relation to, 318
precedents in, 490
terminological development of, 43-44,
46
thyroid deficiency, mistakenly diagnosed as, 478
traumatic reactions, in, 831, 860
Hypertrophy
Character Trait Hypertrophy Concept,
295
Defense Hypertrophy Principle, 473
Hypno-narcosis as conversion therapy,
711-712
Hypnosis
adjuncts to, 804, 819
amnesia following, 778 (*see also* POST-
HYPNOTIC AMNESIA)
antisocial acts under, 819
appearance under, 814
behavior under, 814
clinical features, 813-816
combat reactions, as therapy for, 931-
933
conversion therapy, as, 711-712
criminal interrogation, used in, 818
definition, 811
*Direct Correlation of Youth Principle
and,* 814-816
disadvantages in therapy, 823
Dissociative Reaction, as, 810-825
dreams induced by, 821
drugs used in, 817-819
dynamics of, 816-817
emergence from, 813-815
emotional conflicts produced by, 823
focus of attention in, 813
Fugue States, as therapy for, 806
hallucinations produced by, 823
historical background, 811
hypnotist selection, 815-816
illusions produced by, 823
induction of 813-815
memory loss, used for, 820
Mesmerism, and, 812
*post-hypnotic suggestion used in psy-
chiatric research,* 820
power of suggestion in, 817
problems in resynthesis, 814
psychiatric research, use in, 820-823
psychodynamic exploration by, 820
regression induced by, 821
subject selection, 815-816
suggestibility in, 817-822
susceptibility to, 814, 815-816

Hypnosis—*Contd.*
    therapeutic value, 823-825
    time distortion induced by, 821
    "truth serum" and, 817-819
    youth, in relation to, 816
Hypnotic dissociation, 810-825
Hypnotizability, 814-816
Hypochondriasis, 43-44, 46 (*see also* HY-
    GEIAPHRONTIS)
Hypomania
    Depressive Personality, in, 282
    fatigue and, 413
Hypothesis (*see also* PRINCIPLES)
    Attention, 602
    Oral Conflict, of, 579
    *Developmental Influences in Mental
    Capabilities, of,* 254
Hysteria (*see also* SOMATIC CONVERSION
    REACTIONS)
    anxiety, and, 108
    definition, 44, 641, 645
    terminology, 46, 47
Hysterogenic areas, 650

I

I.D., see IMPACT-DEFERMENT, EMOTIONAL
Id (*see also* INSTINCTUAL DRIVES)
    childhood, in, 23
    emotional conflict related to, 21-22
    superego, clash with, 21
Iceberg Analogy, 444, 685, 921
Identification, 698
    Conversion Reactions, in, 701
    Depersonalization and, 769
    dependency, needs, and, 694
    Depersonalization, Faulty, in, 769
    Faulty, Concept of, 563, 681, 769
    hostile, 701
    multiple, 692, 698
    Uncertain Sexual, 769
    Unwanted, Concept of, 770
Identification Fugue, the, 796
Identity, sacrificed, 799
Illness
    anxiety, as source of, 30
    emotional, *see* EMOTIONAL ILLNESS
Illusions, hypnosis, produced by, 823 (*see
    also* HALLUCINATIONS)
*Illusory Gains Concept in Emotional Ill-
    ness,* 230 (*see also* GAINS)
Imitator, Great, 656
Impact-Deferment, Emotional, 732, 865

Implicit Command Concept (in suicide),
    175, 193, 207-208, 221
*Implied Preference, Concept of Symp-
    toms as an,* 503, 692, 885
Impression-Priority, Rule of, 369, 531-
    541, 868, 925
    Depressive reactions, in relation to,
    171
    Obsessive Reaction therapy, in rela-
    tion to, 368
Impulsions, 354-359 (*see also* OBSESSIVE-
    COMPULSIVE REACTIONS)
    anti-social acts, as, 354-355
    common types, 357
    compulsions, differentiated from, 355
    definition, 354-357
    hostility expressions as, 355-356
    irresistible acts, as, 354-355
    management of, 358-359
    personality traits, 286
    principles of, 358-359
    punishment affecting, 356-357
    remorse affecting, 356-357
    Secondary Defense of, 359
    sexual expressions of, 355-356
    Social-Defiance as, 355-356
    therapy for, 359-359
Impulsive Act, the, 355
Impulsive Character, the, 286
Impulsive Personality, 286
Inadvertent Defeat Principle, 70-72, 75,
    78
Inattention, selective, 688
Incipient Fugue concept, 766
Incentive-Fatigue Ratio, 412-413
Incomplete Fugue, the, 796
Incomplete Symptom-Defense Concept,
    89, 189, 451, 555, 657, 692, 761,
    776, 852, 882
    anxiety, in relation to, 89, 913
    Conversion Reactions, in relation to,
    656
    Hygeiaphrontic Reactions, in relation
    to, 451, 477
    Phobic Reactions, in relation to, 555
Index of Suicide Potential, 163, 203
Indifference, Conversion, 660
Indigestion, Psychic, 542, 573
*Individual Appropriateness-of-Response
    Concept,* 477, 694, 747
    anxiety, in relation to, 14, 84, 111, 131
    Soterial Reactions, in relation to, 610
*Individual Inverse Ratio Concept of Hos-
    tile Expression,* 159
*Individual-Specificity of Emotional De-
    fenses, Principle of,* 14, 137,
    574, 838

Individual Symbolism, Rule of, 698, 753, 914
    Conversion Reactions, in relation to, 699
    dreams, in relation to, 753
Induced Dissociation, 733, 810-825 (*see also* B.B.C. DISSOCIATION; *also* HYPNOSIS)
Inertia Emotional Concept, 26, 213, 433, 504, 707, 884, 886, 929
Infancy, Dependency-Dilemma of, 219, 579 (*see also* CHILDHOOD)
Infanticide as Obsessive Reaction, 324-326
Inhibition, Principle of, 322, 328
Initiating Suggestion, 803
Insight in psychotherapy, 26, 27
Insomnia
    anxiety, due to, 20, 115
    early morning, 218, 278 (*see also* DAWN INSOMNIA)
Instinctual drives
    childhood, in, 23
    conscience, clash with, 21
    emotional conflict arising from, 21-22
Intellect in Obsessive Personality, 253-254
Intellectual fatigue, 402
Interest-Absorption Concept, 311, 332, 462, 708, 913 (*see also* PREOCCUPATION DEFENSE CONCEPT)
Interest, lack of, *see* BOREDOM
Internal Phantoms, 769
Interpersonal Perpetuation Concept, 275, 291, 302, 334, 455, 479, 666, 695, 799, 862, 876, 924
    Conversion Reactions, in relation to, 665-666
    definition, 291
    Fatigue Reactions, in relation to, 403-405
    Hygeiaphrontic Reactions, in relation to, 464, 479, 489
    Obsessive Reactions, in relation to, 323, 328
Intoxication and suicide, 208-209
Intrapsychic conflict, 58-59 (*see also* EMOTIONAL CONFLICT)
Intrapsychic transit, 533
Intuitive communication of anxiety, *see* EMOTIONAL CONTAGION CONCEPT
Inverse Anxiety-Psychosis Ratio, 801
Inverse Anxiety-Symptom Ratio, Concept and Precept, 103, 145, 324, 462, 707, 801, 880
    Anxiety-Tension State, related to, 103

Inverse Anxiety-Symptom, etc.—*Contd.*
    conversion therapy, in relation to, 707
    Depressive Equivalents, in relation to, 145
    Fugue States, in relation to, 801
    Obsessive Reactions, in relation to, 343
    Precept of, 132
Inverse Incentive-Fatigue Ratio, 412
Inverse Ratio of Symptom-Success Concept, 9-10, 298, 508, 689, 707, 851, 888, 912-913
Inversion, 803
    Conversion Reaction diagnosis, as a factor in, 653
    Somatic Conversion, in relation to, 676
Irritability, 917
I-Should Person, 326

J

James, William (1842-1910), 728
Janet Dissociations
    Conversion Reactions, in relation to, 648, 653, 674, 685, 693
    definition, 730
    symptoms, 734
Janet, Pierre (1859-1947), 550, 648, 693, 728, 734
Joint Endeavor Principle in psychotherapy, 25-27, 130, 714, 884
Justification in Obsessive Personality, 254-255
Just-in-Case Phenomena, 611
Just-So Defense Concept in Obsessive Reactions, 355

K

Keraunophobia, 554
King David Reaction
    case illustration, 75-76
    obsessive reactions, in relation to, 345
Kleptomania, 357, 358
Kraepelin, Emil (1856-1926), 140, 550

L

La belle indifférence, 671-674, 912
    amnesia, in relation to, 775
Language
    body, 643, 742

Language—*Contd.*
Overall, 644, 740-744, 852
Physiologic, 467, 642-660, 742, 912
Psychologic, 643
Somatic, 642-720, 690, 692
Symptom, 643, 759
Latent Content, 750
Law of Relativity in Emotional Health Concept
definition, 2-4, 51
diagnosis and classification, in, 3
yardstick for measuring, 6
Layering, Concept of Defensive, *see* DE-FENSIVE-LAYERING CONCEPT
Level of Anxiety, 907
Level of Operations Concept in Hygeia-phrontic Reactions, 497
Literal-Symbolic Expression, 696
Locale-Avoidance, 527, 541
Locke, John (1632-1704), 532, 549
Longevity, Principle of, 48, 503, 709, 883
Loss as source of anxiety, 30, 31-32
Lost Object Reunion, Concept of, 182-183, 206, 928
Love
deprivation of, 309-310
Hygeiaphrontic Reactions, in, 485
inhibition of, 328
lessened capacity for, 328-330
Obsessive Reactions, and, 309-310, 328, 330
Soterial Reactions in, 626
Lowered-Perception Threshold Concept in Conversion, 703
Lower Order Defense Reactions, 25, 834, 104, 148

M

M.M.M., see MILITARY MEDICAL MOBILI-ZATION LAW
M.S.E., see MILITARY STRESSFUL ERAS
Maladie du doute, la, 312
Malingering
amnesia and, 774
clinical relationships, 495-497
distinguishing features, 495-497
epigain differentiated from, 62, 494-495, 849
Hygeiaphrontic Reactions, differenti-ated from, 494-497
Illness, as indication of, 496
Neuroses Following Trauma, and, 496, 849
placebos and, 495
rarity of, 495

Manifest content of the dream, 750
Marital relationships and emotional ill-ness, 297
Masochism
Anxiety Neurosis, in, 112
Depressive Reactions, in, 177-178
Dissociative Reactions, in, 786
suicide, 192-193
visceral, 482, 491, 921
Masturbation in relation to neurasthenia, 425
Maturity level
anxiety influencing development of, 8, 34
defense gradation in, 498
emotional health measured by, 6
neurosis, and, 6
parental responsibility, 23
social adjustment indicating, 6
Mechanical Analogy, 213, 884
Medical Renaissance Concept, 312, 647, 812, 838, 840
Melancholia (*see also* DEPRESSION)
definition, 44, 140
Depressive Reaction, as, 140-141
terminology, 46, 47
Memory loss (*see also* AMNESIA)
Dissociative Reaction, as, 773-791
electroshock therapy, due to, 218
hypnosis used for, 820
Mental fatigue, 383 (*see also* FATIGUE REACTIONS)
Mental mechanisms (*see also* specific types), 25, 343, 541, 691
anxiety, employed against, 8, 16, 25
character traits and, 288
Conversion Reactions, in, 691
emotional conflict, used in, 25
First Line of Psychic Defense, as, 25, 343, 691
Goal of Equanimity Concept related to, 25
major, 25
Mental synthesis, 759 (*see also* JANET)
Mesmer, Anton (1733-1815), 646-647, 812
Mesmerism, 646-646, 812
Middle-age incidence of neuroses, 149
Military life
Emotional Contagion in, 37
emotional reactions associated with, 900-933 (*see also* MILITARY RE-ACTIONS)
Military Medical Mobilization, Law of, 901

Military Reactions, 899-933
  clinical features of, 906-916
  combat, during, *see* COMBAT REACTIONS
  Desensitizing Purpose Concept, of Battle Dream, 917
  direct manifestations of anxiety, 907
  diagnoses of, 903-906
  incidence, 903-906
  irritability as factor in, 917
  Omnipotent-Responsibility Feelings, 922
  Personal-Invulnerability Defense Concept, 919
  psychodynamic factors in, 916-929
  Somatic Conversion Reactions in, 912
  Startle Reaction, 916-918
  stress in relation to, 902 (*see also* MILITARY STRESSFUL ERAS)
  Susceptibility, Factors in, 920
  symptoms of, 906-916
  Ultimate-Vulnerability Theory, 909-912
Military Stressful Eras, 31, 38, 67, 902, 934
  anxiety, as source of, 31, 38
  epigain related to, 67-68
  morale, 37
Mitchell, S. Weir (1828-1914), 386
Mixed Fugue, the, 796
M.M.M., see MILITARY MEDICAL MOBILIZATION, LAW OF
Molecular change, 839
Momentum, Continued Physiologic, Concept of, 49, 101, 455, 776, 866, 889, 909-912
Monotony, 415-417 (*see also* BOREDOM)
Morel, B. A. (1809-1873), 312
Morning Ebb-Tide of Spirits in relation to suicide, 145, 151, 164
Motivation
  defensive, 56
  fatigue, in relation to, 412-415
  Motivation Toward Therapy Concept, 10
  neurotic factors in, 412
  performance potential and, 412
  therapy, toward, 10
Multiple Personality, *see* ALTERNATING PERSONALITY
Mysophobia, 554

N

Nail biting, 23
Narcissism and neurasthenia, 429
Nervous exhaustion, 385 (*see also* FATIGUE REACTIONS)

Neurasthenia, 424-434
  Actual Neuroses Concept, 489
  anxiety, manifesting, 20
  clinical features, 427-429
  definition, 45, 424
  diagnosis of, 426
  etiology of, 425
  fatigue reaction, as, 385-387
  Fatigue State, as a, 425-426
  historical background, 424-426
  Hygeiaphrontis manifested in, 450
  incidence of, 426
  masturbation, in relation to, 425
  narcissism, and, 429
  "One-Day", 430
  parent-child relationship, and, 429
  physical makeup and, 427-428
  psychotherapy for, 430
  supportive therapy for, 431-433
  symptoms of, 427-429
  terminology, 46
  therapeutic results, 429-430
  treatment for, 430-436
Neuroses (*see also* specific neurotic reactions)
  Actual, Concept of, 489
  advantages in classification of, 3-4
  anxiety, due to—*see* ANXIETY NEUROSIS
  categorization, value of, 3-4
  Character, 7 (*see also* CHARACTER NEUROSES)
  childhood, developing in, 21
  criteria for classification of, 3
  diagnostic classification of, 3-4
  diagnostic trends in, 46
  endogain in, 70-72
  epigain in, 63-68, 70-72
  incidence in private practice, 7-8
  list of, 7
  maturity level and, 6
  Obsessive-Compulsive, 311, 314
  pathologically-defensive reactions, as, 3
  Rule of Non-Proportional Response in, 857
  social adjustment failure indicated by, 6
  symptoms of, 7, 60, 237, 286, 383, 446, 833
  terminology of, 43-47
  traumatic—*see* TRAUMA *also* NEUROSES-FOLLOWING-TRAUMA
  types of, 87-88
  Vicious Circle of Self Defeat Concept in, 71-74, 348
Neuroses-Following-Trauma, 831, 897
  anxiety as symptom of, 850, 851
  anxiety, manifesting, 20

Neuroses-Following-Trauma—*Contd.*
childhood antecedents, 834
clinical features, 848-866
compensation and, 66, 876-884
Conversion Reactions as symptoms of, 851
definition, 45, 833, 837
diagnosis, 846-848
Dissociative Reaction syndrome in, 852-853
dreams in, 856
elective surgery and, 599
endogain in, 849, 873-875
epigain in, 45, 57, 64, 66, 833, 849, 873-875, 888-889
goals of psychotherapy for, 889-890
group characteristics, 833-834
head injury, resulting from, 852
historical background, 838-843
Hygeiaphrontic Reactions as symptoms of, 851
incidence, 244, 843-845
malingering differentiated from 496, 849
mechanics of, 873-875
Non-Proportionate Response Rule, 848, 857
Obsessive Reaction syndrome in, 853-854
pathogenesis of, 866-876
Phobic Reaction syndrome in, 854-856
prognosis for, 884, 888-889
psychodynamics of, 866-876
regression in, 875
response variations in, 857-863
severe case of, 871-873
sexual function impaired by, 852
suicidal attempt impact, 876
symptoms, 848-866
terminology, 46, 47, 833
time lag in, 863-865
treatment of, 884-890
typical case, 848
Neurosis
Compensation *see* COMPENSATION NEUROSIS
Organ, 655
Symptoms, 60
Vegetative, 656
Neurotic anxiety, 12
Neurotic defenses, 27
Neurotic Position, Balanced Concept of, 159, 482, 502, 508, 715, 886
Neurotic Reactions, general
defensively motivated, 56
incidence of, 243-244
popularity of, 844
types of, 7

Nocturnal-Fantasy Concept, 752
Now-Proportrinate Response Rule, 857
(*see also* HYGEIAPHRONTIC DISCREPANCY CONCEPT)
Numerophobia, 554
Nyctophobia, 554

O

Object Amalgam, Emotional- see EMOTIONAL-OBJECT AMALGAM
Object, Phobic, 608
Obesity, 115
Obsession (*see also* OBSESSIVE PERSONALITY)
aggressive impulses and, 314
anxiety and, 20, 309-310
definition, 310
depression, and, 349
displacement and, 313
harming family member, of, 324-326
Hygeiaphrontis, in relation to, 318
Phobias, relation to, 318
repression and, 313
sexual impulses and, 314
transference and, 314
Obsessive character defenses, 247
development of, 342-343
military career, useful in, 903
sex and, 345-346
Obsessive-Compulsive Reactions, 307-375 (*see also* IMPULSIONS)
anxiety, manifesting, 20
clinical features, 319-336
definition, 311
diagnosis of, 315-319
elective surgery and, 599
endogain in, 73-75
epigain in, 57, 65, 73-75
historical background, 312-315
Hygeiaphrontic Reactions and, 456
incidence, 244, 315-319
Neuroses-Following-Trauma, as syndrome in, 853-854
personality traits in, *see* OBSESSIVE PERSONALITY
phobias and, 557
Soterial Reactions differentiated from, 616
substitution in, 311
symptoms, 319-336
terminology, 46
traumatic, 854
treatment, 360-373
Obsessive Dilemma, 341-342
Obsessive doubting, 347-348

Obsessive Façade, 248-249, 348
Obsessive Personality
  absolutism in, 255-256
  advantages of, 256-258
  ambivalence in, 249-252
  anal characteristics in, 292-293
  anxiety manifestations in, 72-73
  Black-or-White Persons, 248, 255, 451,
    903
  bowel-habit training related to, 292
  character traits in, 288-290
  characteristics of, 247
  clinical features, 245-258
  definition, 231
  diagnosis of, 238-240
  discomfort in, 240-241
  dishonesty in, 255
  intellectual prowess of, 253-254
  justification in, 254-255
  marital relationships in, 297
  Obsessive Façade, and, 248-249
  overcompliance in, 255-256
  pessimism in, 252
  rationalization in, 254-255
  religious overconcern in, 255
  Reversal of Appearance Conception,
    248
  R.I.G.I.D. Person Concept, 374
  sanctimoniousness in, 255-256
  scrupulousness in, 255
  sexual inhibition, and, 295-296
  soterial implications in, 257-258
  treatment precautions for, 300-301
Obsessive Reactions, 307-375 (*see also*
    OBSESSIVE-COMPULSIVE
    REACTIONS)
  acceptance and, 309-310
  affection and
    deprivation of, 309-310
    inhibition of, 328
    lessened capacity for, 328-330
  aggressiveness in, 320-322
  anger toward parent in, 340-341
  Antecedent Conflict Theory related to,
    339
  Black-or-White Persons, 248, 255, 451,
    903
  bowel training, and, 339-340
  Brill's illustration, 346
  childhood, in, 21, 333
  clinical features, 326-328
  comparison process in, 332-333
  competitiveness in, 332-333
  Compulsive Rituals in, 349-354
  control of, 322-326
  counter-transference in treatment, 365
  derepression in treatment for, 360
  detail, importance of, 334-335

Obsessive Reactions—*Contd.*
  diagnosis of, 317-319
  displacement in, 344-345
  distance-promoting features of, 330-332
  doubting in, 347-348
  early therapy, advantages of, 363
  egocentricity in, 332
  emotional understanding during treat-
    ment for, 362
  epigain in, 365
  First Line of Defense Concept in, 343
  frequency of, 315
  frozen state, 370
  Hand-in-Glove Analogy, 348-349
  hostility in, 320-322
  inhibition in, 322-326
  Interest Absorbtion Defense Concept,
    311, 332, 462, 708, 913
  "I-Should Person" manifesting, 326-327
  "Just-So" Defense Concept in, 335
  kindliness in treatment, 364
  King David Reaction related to, 345
  la maladie du doute, 312
  love and
    deprivations of, 309-310
    inhibition of, 328
    lessened capacity for, 328-330
  mastery, struggle for, in relation to,
    338
  mechanisms in, 343-345
  outward appearance of, 323-324
  parent-child relationship, 337-340
  parental attitudes governing, 334, 340
  perfectionism in, 335
  personal relationships in, 330-331
  personality development in, 338 (*see*
    also OBSESSIVE PERSONALITY)
  precedent established in, 337-338
  Profitable-Patterns Concept in, 338-
    340
  psychodynamic considerations, 337-349
  psychotic manifestations in relation to,
    320
  recognition of, 363
  referral of cases of, 363
  rejection in, 341
  religious counsel in, 371-373
  repetitive compulsions in, 349-350
  R.I.G.I.D. Person Concept, in Relation
    to, 328
  self-absorption in, 332
  self-appraisal in treatment for, 360-362
  self-esteem in, 332-333
  sexual relationships and, 329, 330
  spontaneity, lack of, and, 332
  substitution in, 344-345
  superiority feelings in, 332
  symptomatology of, 327-328

Obsessive Reactions—*Contd.*
symptom onset, 337
tolerance in treatment, 364
transference in treatment, 365
treatment for, 360-373
premature interpretations in, 368
problems encountered in, 364-366
results of, 371
therapeutic problem, 369-370
Tracing-Technique, 366-368
treatment of choice, 363-369
Vicious Circle in Relationships Concept, in relation to, 331
vulnerability in, 330-332, 348
character defenses and, 319
Obsessively Tinted Glasses, 254
Oedipal conflicts
anxiety originating in, 28
Hygeiaphrontic Reactions, in relation to, 490
Oral Conflict, antecedent to, 579
Old age
amnesia in, 778, 783-784
Hygeiaphrontic Reactions in, 471
Omnipotent-Responsibility Feelings, 922-923
One-day Depression, 191-192
Onion Defense, 466 (*see also* DEFENSIVE-LAYERING CONCEPT)
Oppenheim, Herman (1858-1919), 838
Ophidiophobia, 554
Oral Conflict
anxiety, and, 169
basic position, 685
Conversion Reactions, in, 700
Hygeiaphrontic Reactions in relation to, 490
Hypothesis of, 579, 602
oedipal situation, antecedent to, 579
Phobic Reactions, in relation to, 579
Oral Phase, 602
Organ neurosis, 655
Organic amnesia, 774, 777
Organic Fatigue
definition, 382
diagnosis of, 390-391
Emotional Fatigue in combination with, 393
Primary, 390-391
Secondary, 390-391
Organicity, Concept of Advanced, 391
Ostrich Concept, 772
Outward Reversal of Appearance Concept, 240
Overall Language, 644, 740-744, 852
Overreaction, Concept of Defensive, 95-98, 115, 641, 798, 917-918

Overcompliance in Obsessive Personality, 255-256
Overconcern with Health, 460
Overdetermination
Conversion, in, 702
dreams, in, 747, 751 (*see also* CONVERGENCE OF ASSOCIATIONS)
Overseriousness in Depressive Personality, 270-271
Oversleeping, 40-41 (*see also* FATIGUE REACTIONS)

P

P.F.A. see PSYCHOLOGIC-FLIGHT AVOIDANCE CONCEPT
P.S.F., see PROGNOSTIC SIGNAL FLAG
Pain
anxiety and, 30, 123, 470, 480, 870
Anxiety-Vicious Circle Concept, 123, 480, 706
avoidance of, 525, 531, 530
Conflict Ratio, Inverse, Concept of, 470, 703
Conversion Reactions, originating in, 654, 667 (*see also* CONVERSION PAIN)
Hygeiaphrontic Reaction as, 469
fear as avoidance of, 525-531
functional, as Hygeiaphrontic Reaction, 469
Hygeiaphrontic Reactions, in, 467-470, 480
location and susceptibility in Hygeiaphrontic Reactions, 469-470
Lowered-Perception Threshold, source of, 480
phantom limb, in, 704-706
Psychic, 533
Psychologic, Avoidance of, 530
Reciprocal Relationship to Anxiety, 123, 470, 480, 870
stomach, in, as Hygeiaphrontic Reaction, 469
Threshold, in Hygeiaphrontic Reaction, 470
visceral, in Hygeiaphrontic Reactions, 467-470
Palpitations in anxiety, 20
Panic, 13, 89-98 (*see also* ACUTE ANXIETY ATTACK)
Paramnesia, 777
Paranoid Personality
clinical features, 284-285
definition, 233
epigain in, 74-75
Paranoid Position, 74-75, 923

Parent-child relationship
anger in, 340-341
control, parental, in, 340
neurasthenia, and, 429
Obsessive Reactions, in relation to, 337, 341
rejection in, 341
Parental anxiety, 32-33
Parental disharmony as source of anxiety, 30
Parental role
fatigue conditioning, in, 403
First Tenet of, 23, 172, 174, 309, 479, 630, 714
Hygeiaphrontic Reactions, in relation to, 463
Obsessive Reactions, in, 337-341
Secure Base of Operations Concept Related to, 23
trauma, in relation to, 861-863
Parental Role, First Tenet of, 174, 714
anxiety, in relation to, 23
Depressive Reactions, in relation to, 172
Hygeiaphrontic Reactions, in relation to, 479
love deprivation, related to, 309
Soterial Reactions, in relation to, 630
Parental Role, Second Tenet of, 496, 797, 919
conversion development, in relation to, 693
Depressive Reactions, in relation to, 174
Hygeiaphrontic Reactions, in relation to, 476
Part-Reaction Concept, 692, 742
Passing-the-Peak in Depressive Reactions, 158
Pathologic amnesia, 784
Pathologically-defensive reactions, 3-4
Patient's role in psychotherapy, 25-27
Patterns, Profitable, 320, 477, 680
Pavlov, Ivan P. (1849-1936), 341, 841, 935
Peace of mind, *see* GOAL OF EQUANIMITY CONCEPT
Peg Concept, 876
conversion aphonia, in relation to, 681
Fugue States, in relation to, 802, 803
Hygeiaphrontic Reactions, in relation to, 457, 464
Neuroses-Following-Trauma, in relation to, 847, 877
phobic object selection, in relation to, 581
Phobic Reactions, in relation to, 594

"Pension-seeking", 64
Pentobarbital Sodium used in hypnosis, 817
Perception Threshold Source, Lowered, Concept of, 480, 703
Perfectionism in obsessive reactions, 335
Perpetuation, Interpersonal Concept of, 275, 334, 455, 479-489, 695, 799, 862
Personal Depersonalization, 759
Personal Invulnerability Defense Concept, 919
Personal Yardstick Concept, 249, 331
Personality (*see also* CHARACTER DEFENSES)
Alternating, 806-809
Antiseptic, 233
Casual, 232
character defenses comprising, 228
clinical features, 245-286
conversion, *see* CONVERSION PERSONALITY
depressed, *see* DEPRESSIVE PERSONALITY
double, *see* DOUBLE PERSONALITY
hysterical, *see* CONVERSION PERSONALITY
multiple, *see* ALTERNATING PERSONALITY
obsessive, *see* OBSESSIVE PERSONALITY
paranoid, 74-75, 233, 284-285
phobic, 284
terminology, 46
types, 228-229, 231-233
split, 806-809 (*see also* ALTERNATING PERSONALITY)
Perspiration manifesting anxiety, 20
Pessimism in Obsessive Personality, 252, 487
Phantom limb, 704-706
Phobias (*see also* specific nouns *and* classifications)
anxiety and, 546-548
bases of, 574
Conversion Reactions, and, 556
Critical-Displacement, 547, 578, 584, 854-856
definition, 518, 547
dynamics of, 575-580
epigain in, 65
fear and, 517
gradually-evolving, 548, 575
list of, 554
object of, 580-585 (*see also* PHOBIC OBJECT)
Obsessive-Compulsive Reactions, and, 557
organic disease, and, 555
Situational, 547
Soteria differentiated from, 628

Phobic Attack, 548
Phobic Avoidance, 546
Phobic Dilemma Concept, 562
Phobic Ambivalence Concept, 562, 569, 572, 579
Phobic Object
    Attention Hypothesis, in relation to, 586-589
    automatically and selectively determined, 587
    Critical Attack of Anxiety, in relation to, 581-584
    Emotional-Object Amalgam, in relation to, 584-585
    list of, 553-554
    locale, determined by, 580
    selection of, 580-585, 588
    sexual characteristics, 580
    situation, determined by, 580
    Soterial Object, and, 588, 628
    symbolic characteristics, 580
    unconscious seeking out of, 586
Phobic Pegs, 594-602
Phobic Personality, 284
Phobic Reactions, 545-606
    adulthood, in, 566
    ambivalent features, 569
    anxiety, in relation to, 16, 20, 37, 569, 571
    Anxiety Neurosis, in relation to, 108, 120
    Attention Hypothesis, in relation to, 586-589
    castration complex as, 551-552
    childhood, in, 21, 564
    clinical features, 558-563, 569-574, 618-626
    common types, 553-555
    converse of, *see* SOTERIAL REACTIONS
    counter reactions, 585
    Critical-Displacement, 547, 575, 578, 854-856
    cultural influences upon, 568
    danger, displacement of causing, 572
    definition, 547
    defensive pattern of, 546-549
    diagnosis of, 553-564
    differential diagnosis of, 558-563
    dread as symptom of, 569
    dynamic principles of, 551-552
    elective surgery contraindicated by, 599-600 (*see also* SURGERY-IN-ABEYANCE RULE)
    endogain in, 548, 578
    fear as symptom of, 569
    fear avoidance, as, 517, 546-548
    S. Freud, of, 589-590
    historical background, 549-552

Phobic Reactions—*Contd.*
    incidence, 244, 564-569
    individually determined, 574
    inversion of unconscious wish, as, 569
    mental consequences of, 569
    nature and purpose of, 548-549
    Neuroses-Following-Trauma, as syndrome in, 854-856
    object of, 580-585 (*see also* PHOBIC OBJECT)
    Obsessive Reactions, in relation to, 318
    Oedipal situation, in relation to, 579
    oral conflict, in relation to, 579
    pathogenesis of, 574-580
    physical consequences of, 569
    physiologic consequences of, 569
    psychodynamics of, 574, 580
    psychologic consequences of, 569
    Psychologic Conversion, 643
    Psychologic Language, 643
    psychotherapy for
        dream study, 597
        goals of, 592
        important considerations in, 590-593
        indirect approach, 598
    physician's attitude, 592
        prognosis, 601
        techniques of, 593-599
        unskilled, dangers of, 591
        sensory context of, 580
        Soterial Reactions differentiated from, 628
        stimuli for, 548
        symptoms, 569-574
    tenacity of, 590-591
    terminology, 46
    traumatic, 854-856
    treatment for, 590-601
Physical Equivalents Concept, 143
Physical fatigue (*see also* FATIGUE REACTIONS)
    definition, 382
    sleep related to, 38
Physical flight, 461, 463, 478, 792
Physical Scapegoat Concept, 392, 461, 652, 877
Physical threats as source of anxiety, 30 33
Physical Translation Concept, 660
Physiologic changes accompanying anxiety, 12, 13
Physiologic Conversion Reactions, 642, 655, 656, 823
    anxiety, in relation to, 7, 20, 88
    definition, 642
    diagnostic terminology, 655-656
    incidence of, 244
    I. Q., in relation to, 654

Physiologic Conversion Reactions, Contd.
  Military Reactions, in, 912
  symptoms of, 644
  terms used, 655
Physiologic Dissociation
  definition, 730
  symptoms, 734-735
Physiologic Language, 467, 644, 742, 912
Physiologic Momentum Continued, Concept of, 99, 100, 101, 455, 776, 866, 889, 909-912
Physiologic needs as source of anxiety, 30
Placebos, 495
Popularity Concept in Emotional Symptoms, 569 (*see also* CULTURAL VOGUE CONCEPT)
Position changes as source of anxiety, 30
Post-Graduate Course of Study, Concept of Therapy as, 504
Post-Shock Memory Loss, 789
Post-Traumatic Dream, 39, 856, 917, 945
Post-Trough Period of Hazard Concept, 209-210
Posthypnotic amnesia, 778
Posthypnotic suggestions, 820
Potential for Suicide Index, 163
Power of suggestions in hypnosis, 817
Precept of Inverse-Anxiety Symptom Ratio, 132
Predetermined Vulnerability Principle, 836, 860-862
Preoccupation-Defense Concept, 311-312, (*see also* ATTENTION ABSORPTION DEFENSE)
Prestige anxiety, 35
Primal Antecedent Oral Conflict, 169
Primal Depression, 169-171, 174
Primal Threat, 493
Primary Defense, 96, 144, 267, 663, 724 (*see also* SECONDARY DEFENSE CONCEPT)
Primary restriction, 770
Primary and Secondary Emotional-Endocrine Reactions, 422
Primary sources of anxiety, 28-34 (*see also* SECONDARY SOURCES OF ANXIETY)
Primitive defenses, 25, 104, 148, 864 (*see also* LOWER ORDER DEFENSES)
Prince, Morton (1854-1929), 728
Principle-of-Belief, 646, 383
Principle of Symptom-Longevity, 503, 704, 883
Principles—(*see also* HYPOTHESIS)
  Anxiety-Countering, 585, 628
  Circular Generation of Fear, 131
  Defense-Hypertrophy, 73, 229, 238, 251, 301, 675

Principles—*Contd.*
  Flight-to-the-Physical, 91, 97, 392, 663, 672-673, 961
  Hygeiaphrontic-Discrepancy, 443, 467, 509
  Joint-Endeavor, 895
  Recurrence, of, 277
  Symptom-Survival, 334, 579
  Universality, of, 51
  Universality, of Anxiety, 131
Priority, Emotional, 542
Priority of Impressions Rule, 141, 368, 531-541, 643, 868
Prisoner-Processing, 842, 933-946
  conditioning process, 938-944
  factors in success, 937
  phases, 943
  restorative treatment following, 944-945
  techniques for, 936-938
Privation as source of anxiety, 31
Process of Domestication, 6
Profitable Patterns Concept, 447, 464, 539, 771, 884, 918
  Hygeiaphrontic Reactions, in relation to, 464, 477, 688
  Obsessive-Compulsive Reactions, in relation to, 320, 338
Prognostic Signal Flag, 504, 505, 664, 823, 916
Progression, Concept of Functional-Structural, 468, 893
Proper Seed, 868
Prototype, Emotional, 511
Psychic-Selectivity Principle, 789
Psychologic Flight Avoidance, 724-725, 767, 916
Psychologic Soil Concept, 574, 663, 802, 856, 866-871
Psychosomatic illnesses, 688 (*see also* PHYSIOLOGIC CONVERSION REACTIONS)
Punch Drunk, 781-783
Punishment
  anxiety, as source of, 30, 31, 33
  Hygeiaphrontic Reactions, and, 482-484
  Impulsions affected by, 356-357
Pseudocyesis, 677
Pseudo-epilepsy, 652
Psychasthenia, 45, 46, 387
Psychic Defense, First Line of, 25, 65 (*see also* MENTAL MECHANISMS)
Psychic Depletion, 41, 408, 418, 696, 907, 922
Psychic Distaste, Concept of
  anxiety, in relation to, 115

Psychic Distaste, Concept of—Contd.
  hygeiaphrontic reactions, in relation to, 473
Psychic Indigestion, 542, 573
Psychic Pain, 541
Psychic-Reduplication Concept, 698, 702, 772
  conversion pain, in relation to, 667
  Hygeiaphrontic Reactions, in, 468
Psychic trauma
  antecedent of, 834
  definition, 836
  personal relationships causing, 6
Psychogenic symptoms due to anxiety, 5
Psychologic amnesia, 778-780
Psychologic Conversion Reactions
  anxiety, in relation to, 20, 88
  depressive variety, 176
  definition, 643
Psychologic Determinants, 909 (*see also* CONFLICT INDICATORS)
Psychologic Equivalents in Depressive Reactions, 158-159
Psychologic flight, 58, 792 (*see also* "FIGHT OR FLIGHT" RESPONSE)
Psychologic-Flight Avoidance Concept, 530, 742, 916
  Depersonalization, in relation to, 767
  Dissociative Reactions, in relation to, 724-725
Psychologic injury causing anxiety, 30
Psychologic processing of prisoners, 933-946
Psychomotor expressions of anxiety, 20
Psychopathology, anxiety as motive force toward, 20
Psychopathy differentiated from amnesia, 786
Psychophysiologic disorders, 656
Psychoses (*see also* specific nouns *and* classifications)
  anxiety, in relation to, 801
  Conversion Reactions, evolving from, 683
  defense graduation in, 498
  ego function in, 740-741
  Fugue States differentiated from, 793
  functional, 87
  Hygeiaphrontic Reactions and, 455-456
Psychosis, Inverse Anxiety, Ratio of, 801
Psychosomatic disorders due to anxiety, 13-14
Psychosomatic illnesses
  anxiety, in relation to, 7, 20
  Physiologic Conversion Reactions, in, 656, 688

Psychotherapy (*see also* THERAPY)
  anxiety, in relation to, 25-27
  Deep Treatment Concept, 209, 212, 791, 889
  derepression constructive, in, 26
  doctor-patient relationship, 25-27
  educational process, as, 49-50
  emotional conflict, for, 25-27
  emotional equanimity as goal of, 35
  goals of, 890
  individual use of, 85
  Inertia Concept in, 26
  Joint Endeavor Principle in, 25-26
  patient's role in, 25-27, 49
  resistances encountered in, 26-27
  Rule of Treatment in, 50
  status quo resistance against, 27
  symptom meaning sought in, 27
  Team-Work Tenet in, 362
  techniques, 49-51, 366-368
  Tracing Technique, 366-368, 494, 889
Psychotic manifestations in obsessive reactions, 320
Pyromania, 357
Pyrophobia, 554

R

Rage (*see also* ANGER; *also* HOSTILITY)
  anxiety, as source of, 31
  childhood dependency, resulting from, 169
  Equivalents, Conversion symptoms as, 683, 742
  frozen state of, 175-177
  infantile needs, in relation to, 169, 174
Rage-Equivalents, 683, 742, 913
Ratio, Inverse Anxiety-Symptom, 103, 145, 324, 462, 880
Rationalization, 874
  anxiety, in reaction to, 24
  Obsessive Personality, in, 254-255
Reaction formation, 35
Reactions-of-the-Whole, 693, 742
Recapitulation, Emotional, 117, 468
Rechannelization, 24
Reciprocal Relationship of Anxiety and Pain, 123, 470, 480, 870
Recurrence, Principle of
  Depressive Reactions, in, 146
  suicide, in relation to, 164-165
Reduplication, Psychic, Concept of, 468, 667, 697, 914
Reinforcement-of-Associations Concept, 697, 748, 914 (*see also* GEOMETRIC PRINCIPLE)

Refuge, Soterial, 630, 636

Regression
  anxiety, in reaction to, 24
  Hygeiaphrontic Reactions, in, 467, 476
  hypnosis, induced by, 821
  Neuroses-Following-Trauma, in, 875, 884

Rejection
  Compliant-Response, and, 175
  Depressive Reactions, as pathogenesis for, 174, 175
  Implicit-Command in suicides, and, 175

Relationship-Distance Defense Concept, 330, 348, 398, 506, 525, 691

Relationship-Improvement Precept, 299, 473, 714

Relationship, Objects, 627

Relationship-Obsessive, Vicious Circle in, 328

Relativity Law in Emotional Health, 2, 457, 465, 660

Relativity-of-Fatigue Principle, 402

Relearning-Tougher, Emotional, Principle of, 597

Religious overconcern in Obsessive Personality, 255, 352

Remission Following Trauma Concept, 869-871

Remorse
  Impulsions affected by, 356-357
  suicide, in relation to, 164, 199-203

Renaissance, medical, 312, 646, 812

Repetition compulsion, Freud's concept of, 171

Repression
  anxiety, resulting from, 5, 23
  Continued-Physiologic-Momentum Concept in, 99, 455, 776
  definition, 17
  emotional conflict, of, 22-23
  frustration, related to, 32
  obsession and, 313

Reservoir Concept of Energy, 417

Resignation in anxiety, 24

Resignation, Compliant, Response to Death, 177, 857-858

Resistance
  Protective Intent, 886, 202
  Secondary Defense as, 54, 144, 226, 267, 445, 487, 505, 664

Respite-of-Sleep Principle
  amnesia, in relation to, 776
  anxiety, role in, 38, 422

Restlessness manifesting anxiety, 20

Restriction, Primary and Secondary, 770

Retaliation as source of anxiety, 30, 31

Retardation, Concept of Diffuse, 157

Retreat, Soterial, 162, 630

Retrograde amnesia, 778

Retrograde Fugue, the, 796

Rhazes Maneuver, 677-678, 787, 906

R.I.G.I.D. Person Concept, 328-329

Rituals, compulsive, 374

Royal Anger, see KING DAVID REACTION

Rule of Impression Priority, 141, 368, 531-541, 643, 868, 893

S

S.B.O., see SECURE BASE OF OPERATIONS CONCEPT

S.E.E.R., see SECONDARY EMOTIONAL-EN-DOCTRINE REACTION

S.E.H.A., see SPECIFIC EMOTIONAL HAZ-ARDS OF ADULTHOOD

S.E.H.C., see SPECIFIC EMOTIONAL HAZ-ARDS OF CHILDHOOD

S.O., see SECURITY OPERATIONS

Sadism
  Depressive Reactions, in, 177-178
  suicide, in relation to, 192-193, 205-206

Sadness, fear, in relation to, 137 (*see also* DEPRESSIVE REACTIONS)

Sanctimoniousness in Obsessive Personality, 255-256

Saving as Soterial Reaction, 620

Scapegoat, Physical, Concept of, 392, 461, 652, 877, 916 (*see also* FLIGHT-TO-THE-PHYSICAL CONCEPT)

Schizophrenia
  Conversion Reactions, symptomatic of, 682-683
  Depersonalization featured in, 760, 768
  Dissociative Characteristics, 730, 735-736, 903
  electroshock therapy for, 216
  Hygeiaphrontic Reactions and, 455, 472

Schizophrenic Dissociation, 682, 683, 903
  definition, 730
  symptoms, 735-736

Scientific Determinism Doctrine, 701, 719

Scrupulousness in Obsessive Personality, 225

Secondary Defense Concept, 96, 97, 144, 267, 359, 366, 444, 487-489, 505, 623, 663, 665, 724, 845, 879, 887, 919 (*see also* PRI-MARY DEFENSE CONCEPT)

Secondary Defense Concept—*Contd.*

Acute Anxiety Attack, in relation to, 97

Character Reactions, related to, 290-291

Conversion Reactions, in relation to, 266-267, 663, 672

definition, 131

Emotional Fatigue, in relation to, 397

Soterial Reactions, in relation to, 612, 623

Status Quo of Adjustment Concept, 665

(*see also* BALANCED NEUROTIC POSITION CONCEPT)

Secondary Emotional-Endocrine Reaction, 422, 912

Secondary Restrictions, 688, 700

Secondary sources of anxiety (*see also* PRIMARY SOURCES OF ANXIETY)

Antecedent Prototypes, influences of, 34

Apprehensive Anticipation, 31, 38

castration, 31

civil disorder, 30

communication of, intuitive, 31

conditioned responses, 31, 34, 37

criminality, 30

definition, 28-29

disapproval, 30, 33, 35

Emotional Contagion, 32-33, 37

frustration, 31, 32, 37

helplessness, 31, 37

hostility, 31, 37

illness, 30

infantile carry-overs, 31, 37

loss, 30, 32

maturity level related to, 34

Military Stressful Eras, 31, 38, 67, 902, 934

natural catastrophe, 30

nuclear catastrophe, 30

physical danger, 30

pregnancy, 30

privation, 30, 31

psychologic injury, 30

punishment, 31

racial preservation, threats to, 30, 36

rage, 31

retaliation, 31

satisfaction sources, interference with, 30

self-esteem, low, as source of, 30

self-preservation, threats to, 30, 36

separation, 31, 37

situational anxiety, 30, 36

social conflict, 30, 35

Secondary sources of anxiety—*Contd.*

Specific Emotional Hazards of Adulthood, 38

superego conflict, 30

surgical procedures, 30

Theory of Antecedent Conflicts related to, 30, 34

war threats, 30

Second Tenet of Parental Role, 174, 476, 693, 797, 919

"Second theory of anxiey", Freud's, 28

Secure Base of Operations Concept

anxiety, in relation to, 23

Depressive Reactions, in relation to, 174

Soterial Reactions, in relation to, 629-630

Security Operations, 311, 332, 351, 461, 462, 617, 620, 708, 883, 912

Security reaction, *see* SOTERIAL REACTIONS

Security Ritual, Compulsive, 351

Sedatives, 39-40 (*see also* TRANQUILIZERS; *also* DRUGS)

Seed, Proper, 663, 868

Seekers-After-Health, 460, 461, 708, 913

Selective Hearing, 688

Selective Inattention, 688

Self-absorption in Obsessive Reactions, 332

Self-Defeat, Vicious Circle of Concept in the Neuroses, 71, 265, 476, 666, 798

Self-esteem

anxiety, as source of, 30, 35

Maintenance Principle, 676-677, 691, 694, 713, 806, 893, 930

Obsessive Reactions, in, 332-333

symptom formation related to level of, 35

Self-preservation threats as source of anxiety, 30, 36

Senile amnesia, 778, 783-784

Separation as source of anxiety, 28, 30, 31, 37

Separation Reaction, 619

Sex-

Acting Out of, 684

Depressive Personality, in, 282

Displacement of, 685

obsessive defenses, and, 345-346

phobic object, determining, 580

Sexual drives, 22-23

Sexual exhibitionism, 357

Sexual expression, unconscious, 684

Sexual function, impaired by Neuroses-Following-Trauma, 852

Sexual identification in Depersonalization, 769
Sexual immaturity, 65
Sexual Impulses, 314, 355-356
Sexual inhibition
  aggression parallels, 296
  defensive aspects, 295-296
  Obsessive Personality, in 295-297, 314
Sexual maladjustment
  anxiety, due to, 116
  Effect-Over-Cause Concept in, 269-270, 330, 852
  Obsessive Reactions, in, 314, 329-330
Sexual relations
  anxiety, and, 116
  maladjustment in, *see* SEXUAL MALAD-JUSTMENT
  Obsessive Reactions, and, 329
Sexual Smorgasbord, 680
Sexuality
  Conversion Personality, in 268, 269-270
  Depressive Personality, in, 282
  Obsessive Personality, in, 295-297, 314
Shell Shock, 658
Shock amnesia, 778, 787-790
Side-by-Side Dissociation
  definition, 730
  symptoms, 736, 742
Silence, Conspiracy of Concept, 725
Simulation Unconscious Concept, 662
Situational anxiety, 30, 36
Situational depression, 184-185
Situational Phobia, 582, 602
Sleep (*see also* DREAMS)
  amnesia in relation to, 776
  amount needed, 422-423
  anxiety and, 20,38-41
  artificial inducement of, 39-40
  deprivation of, 40, 423
  dreams, preserved by, 744
  Emotional Fatigue, related to, 38
  Emotional Health, role in, 38-39
  energy replenished by, 422
  excessive, 40-41
  fatigue and, 38, 422-423
  loss of, *see* INSOMNIA
  recognition of, general, 39
  recovery from deprivation of, 40, 423
  requirements for, 422-423
  Respite, Principle, 38, 624, 744, 766, 929
  restorative value, 38
Sleep-walking, 754-758 (*see also* SOM-NAMBULISM)
Smorgasbord, Sexual, 680

Social adjustment, 6
Social conflict as source of anxiety, 30, 35
Social Defiance Impulses, 355-356
Social mores causing emotional conflict, 21-27
Social status anxiety, 35
Sodium Amytal
  Conversion Aphonia, used for, 678-680
  dissociation, use in, 809
  hypnosis, used for, 804, 817
Sodium Pentothal used for hypnosis, 817
Soil, Favorable Psychologic, Concept of, 574, 663, 802, 856, 866-87?
Somatic Conversion Reactions
  anxiety, manifesting, 20-88
  definition, 641-642
  epigain in, 64
  incidence of, 244
  I. Q., in relation to, 653, 676
  la belle indifférence as classic feature, 671-674, 879
  Military Reactions, in, 912
  phantom limb, 794-706
  Physical Scapegoat in, 912
  symbolic symptom expression, as 643
    (*see also* SOMATIC LANGUAGE)
Somatic Language, 643, 692
Somatization Reactions, 7, 20, 656
Somberness in Depressive Personality, 270-271
Somnambulism, 754-758
  Activated Nocturnal Fantasy Concept, 754
  Conflict-Indicating Aspects, 756-757
  daytime, in 794 (*see also* FUGUE STATES)
  definition, 754
  dissociative aspects, 755
  Fugue States compared with, 794
  injury suffered during, 757
  pathologic significance, 756-757
  significance of, 754-756
  symbolic aspects, 754-755
Soteria, 607, 883
  definition, 602, 609
  phobias, differentiated from, 628
Soterial defense pattern, 608-613
Soterial objects
  accustomed and familiar characteristics, 619
  adeia, 618
  counter-phobic, 585
  Emotional-Object Amalgam Concept, in relation to, 624

Soterial objects—*Contd.*
emotional significance, 618-623
external protection of, 626
fear and anxiety, as counter to, 608
havens as, 625
home as, 630
individual prototypes, 618-619
marriage as, 630
medical treatment, in, 623
phobic object, differentiated from, 588, 628
phylactory, 618
refuge as, 625
religious, 622
self-defeating aspects, 627
Soterial Personality, 285
accumulation as, 620
Soterial Reactions, 607-638
accumulation as, 620
Anxiety-Countering Effect, Principle of, 66, 608
anxiety, manifesting, 20
art forms, in, 622
business affairs, in, 625
collecting as, 620
common types, 615
compensation as, 624
Compulsive Rituals, differentiated from, 616
converse of, *see* PHOBIC REACTIONS
defensive patterns of, 608-613
definition, 609
diagnosis of, 615-617
differential diagnosis of, 616
Emotional-Object Amalgam in, 624-625
family safety, in relation to, 608-610
historical background, 613-615
hoarding as, 620
Hygeiaphrontic Reactions and, 491, 617
incidence of 244, 617-618
"Just-in-Case" aspects, 611
love, in, 626
maternal comfort, in relation to, 608-610
medical, 624
nature and purpose of, 610-612
object of, *see* SOTERIAL OBJECT
object protection, in relation to, 608-610
Obsessive-Compulsive Reactions, differentiated from, 616
organic disease, confused with, 617
overeating as, 631
personality traits in, 285
Phobic Reactions, differentiated from, 628
psychodynamics of, 626-629

Soterial Reactions—*Contd.*
saving as, 620
Secondary Defense Concept in, 612
Secure Base of Operations Concept, in relation to, 629-630
Security Operations, as, 620
security provided by, 608
Separation Reaction, 619
sinister potential of, 621
symbolic possession, indicating, 626
symptoms of, 618-626
terminology, 46
treatment for, 632-635
universal aspects of 617-618
Soterial Retreat, 903
Sources of anxiety
adult disapproval as, 29
adulthood, in, *see* SECONDARY SOURCES OF ANXIETY
approval vs. independence, conflict as, 29
birth experience as, 28
childhood, in, *see* PRIMARY SOURCES OF ANXIETY
hostility, repressed, 29
Oedipus problem as, 28
Primary, 28, 29
"second theory of anxiety", in explanation of, 28
Secondary, 28, 29, 30, 34 (*see also* SECONDARY SOURCES OF ANXIETY)
separation as, 28
theory, development of, 27-29
Spasms in conversion reactions, 671
Spatiophobia, 122, 554
Specific Emotional Hazards of Adulthood
anxiety, as source of, 38
Anxiety Neurosis and, 119
Depressive Reactions, in relation to, 158
Hygeiaphrontic Reactions related to, 457
Neuroses-Following-Trauma, in relation to, 876
stress and, 158
Specific Emotional Hazards of Childhood, 30, 33-34, 695, 876
Specificity of Emotional Defenses Individual, Principle of, 14, 137, 574, 838
Speech difficulties manifesting anxiety, 20
Speech loss of conversion origin, 653, 677-682
Speechlessness in the presence of authority, 16-17

Spirits, level of, 145

Split personality, 806-809 (*see also* ALTER-
NATING PERSONALITY)

Spontaneity in Obsessive Reactions, 332

Startle reaction, 20, 95, 115, 641, 916-
917

Status Quo of Adjustment Concept, 275,
665, 808

Status Quo of the Neurosis, see BALANCED
NEUROTIC POSITION

Stigmata, 650-651

Straw, Final, Concept of, 162, 399, 713,
860-861

Stress

    Anxiety Tension State, related to, 100-
102

    combat in, 909-912, 919-921 (*see also*
COMBAT REACTIONS; COMBAT STRESS)

    Depersonalization, in relation to, 762

    Depressive Reactions, and, 158

    Hygeiaphrontic Reactions, and, 454,
469

    individual reactions to, 101-102

    military operations, in relation to, 902
        (*see also* COMBAT REACTIONS;
        COMBAT STRESS)

    pain following as Hygeiaphrontic Re-
action, 469

    physiologic changes in, 866

    psychosomatic pathology, role in, 522

    tolerances to, 101-102

    trauma and, 860

STRUCTURAL PROGRESSION, CONCEPT OF
FUNCTIONAL, *see* FUNCTIONAL-
STRUCTURAL PROGRESSION CON-
CEPT

Stuttering, 23

Styles, Concept of Emotional, 568 (*see
also* CULTURAL VOGUE)

Sublimation, 24

Submission-defiance conflict, 321, 341,
356

Substitution, Obsessive Reactions, 344-
345

Success-Depression

    definition, 185-186

    guilt and, 187

    promotion, in relation to, 186-187

    psychodynamics of, 186

Suffering, 168 (*see also* DEPRESSION)

    Hygeiaphrontic Reactions, and, 482-
484

Suggestibility in conversion personality,
268-269, 709

Suggestion, 692

    post-hypnotic, 820

Suggestion—*Contd.*

    Progressive, 914

Suicide

    absolution in, 207

    accident-proneness in relation to, 196-
197

    alcohol and, 208-209

    attempts at, 199-205

        management after, 204-205

    clinical features of, 195-196

    *Compliant Response to Implicit Com-
mand Concept,* 175-177, 192-
193, 207-208, 857-858

    Cover Reasons advanced for, 151

    Death Wish in relation to, 208

    defensive family attitude toward, 205

    Depressive Reactions, in relation to,
149, 150-153, 163-165, 192-210

    endogain related to, 73-75

    epigain related to, 73-75, 199

    Equivalent, 196

    Equivocal Aspects, 196

    Euphemistic Diagnoses for, 150, 196

    ever-present danger of, 163

    Fracture-Proneness in relation to, 197-
198

    hazardous periods following attempts,
209-210

    Hostility, Inverted, and, 206

    *Implicit Command Concept in relation
to,* 175, 192-193, 207-208, 857-
858

    impulse and, 199-203

    incidence of, 150-153, 193-194

    management after attempts at, 204-205

    masochism and, 192-193

    methods of, 151

    middle-age, in, 149

    Overdetermination in, 208

    partial, 196-198

    Post-Trough Period of Hazard in, 209-
210

    potential for, 163-164

    psychodynamics of, 205-209

        absolution, 207

        alcoholic influence, 208-209

        antecedent bases, 206

        death wish, 208

        expiation, 207

        Implicit Command Concept, 207-208

        Inverted Hostility, 206

        Lost-Object Reunion, 206-207

        precipitating bases, 206

        retribution, 207

        sadism, inverted, 205-206

    rates of, 150-151

    Recurrence, Principle of, 164-165

Suicide—*Contd.*
rejection and, 175
remorse and, 199-203
responsibility of therapist, 205
retribution in, 207
sadism and, 192-193
statistics of, 150-151
Symbolic-Authority Concept in relation to, 195-196
tendencies toward, 151-153
thoughts of, 194-195
threats of, 203-204
time for, 151
Traumatic Impact of Awareness, 208, 876
treatment for
potential success of, 209-210
prognosis after, 210
Superego
anxiety, as source of, 21, 30, 35
approval disapproval function, 35
childhood, evolution in, 21
id, clash with, 21
conflicts with, 35
development of, 33
function of, 35
pressures in confession, 43, 818
Reaction formation, related to, 35
Superiority feelings in Obsessive Reactions, 332
Surface anesthesia, 699
Surgery
anxiety, as source of, 30
Conversion pain contraindicating, 654, 668-670
emotional needs for, 599
Hygeiaphrontis following, 470
psychologic contraindications, 599-600, 654, 668-670
Surgery-in-Abeyance Rule
Conversion pain, in relation to, 654, 668-670
definition, 127
Hygeiaphrontic Reactions, in relation to, 470
Phobic Reactions, in relation to, 599, 600, 602
Symbolic-Authority Concept, 195-196, 818-819
Symbolic Escape, 767
Symbolic Gratification, 692-693
Symbolism, 697-751
Symbolism, Rule of Individual, 699, 753
Symptom, Anxiety, Precept of Inverse Ratio, 103, 218, 323, 373, 801
Symptom-Barrage, 470-471, 485-486, 505, 664, 791, 800, 885

Symptom Defense, Concept of Incomplete, 89, 189, 291, 451, 477, 692, 915
Symptom Defense-Defeat Parallel Concept, 291, 505, 664, 804
Symptom Emotional-Organic Combinations, 393, 454, 468, 837, 846
symptom, endogain of, 893
Symptom Equivalents, 231
Symptom-Exchange Hazard, 556, 683, 711, 801, 825
Symptom formation
anxiety, resulting from, 28
Emotional amalgam related to, 27
emotional conflict, resulting from, 23
frustration related to, 32
self-esteem level related to, 35
unconscious defenses, as, 118
Symptom-Longevity Principle
Neuroses-Following-Trauma, in relation to, 882-884
psychotherapy, in relation to, 127
Symptom Neuroses
Character Neuroses, in relation to, 60, 237
Conversion Reactions, as, 675
definition, 7
emotional illness, in, 60
Fatigue Reactions, as, 383
Symptom-Pegs, Concept of, 594, 892
Symptom, Principle of Hidden Determinants, 892
Symptom and Resolution-Sans-Sequella Precept, 801
Symptom Rash, 504
Symptoms
Affect Equivalents, 696
defensive endeavor, as, 48
duration of, 48
emotional bases of, 48
emotional conflict, as external expression of, 47-48
Implied Preferences, as, Concept of, 503, 692, 885
meanings sought through psychotherapy, 27
Post-Trough Period of Hazard, 209
resolution of, 27, (*see also* SYMPTOM-SURVIVAL PRINCIPLE)
resolution of conflict, relieved by, 48
Transparency Theory of, 661, 691, 707, 771, 844-845, 495
treatment of, 47-51
Symptom-Success, Concept of, 144, 804, 851

Symptom-Success, Ratio to Motivation Toward Treatment, 9-10, 298, 508, 689, 888

Symptom-Survival Principle, 27, 324-326, 495, 502, 707, 845

definition, 27, 48

Neuroses-Following-Trauma, in relation to, 845

Phobic Reactions, in relation to, 579

T

T.I., see THERAPEUTIC IMPASSE

T.R.C., see TOTAL INDIVIDUAL RESPONSE TO CRISIS

T.R.T., see TOTAL INDIVIDUAL REACTION TO TRAUMA

Talisman, 585

Tea-Kettle, Boiling Analogy of, 407

Team-Work Tenet in Psychotherapy, 362

Temperature changes as source of anxiety, 30

Tension, 17-18 (*see also* ANXIETY-TENSION STATES

Theory of Antecedent Conflicts, 490-494, 694, 866, 888

Theory of Ultimate Vulnerability, 909

Therapeutic Attitude, Proper, 367, 501, 707

Therapeutic Bargain Concept, 300, 501, 713, 883, 886

conversion therapy, illustrated in, 713, 707

definition, 300

Phobic Reactions, in relation to, 591

Therapeutic Impasse, 446, 714, 886, 888

Therapy (*see also* PSYCHOTHERAPY)

Alliance, Concept of, 435

Attention Absorption, Concept in, 488

Constructive Introspection in, 504

Deep-Treatment in, 209, 212, 221, 594, 791, 889

Defensive-Layering Concept in, 367, 465

Definitive, 804

Emergency Analytic Bridge, 923

Emotional First Aid, 930

Emotional Inertia Concept, 213, 433, 504, 707, 929

Emotional Priority, 534

Evaluation in Depression, 215

Favorable-Response Concept, 392, 451-453, 472, 709

Free Association in, 435

Therapy—*Contd.*

goals of, 890

Hand-in-Hand Concept, 637

Hazard of Symptom Exchange in, 712

Impression Priority, Rule of, 534

Initial Decline Phase, 887

Initial Remission Phase, 887

Inverse Ratio Concept of Symptom-Success, and Motivation toward Therapy, 298, 508

Joint Endeavor Principle in, 25-27, 130, 501, 714, 883

Symptom Survival, Principle of, 891

Team-Work Tenet, 25, 130, 362, 886, 895

Therapeutic Bargain Concept, 300, 501

Transference, 623

Thirst as source of anxiety, 30

Three D's of Depression, 194

Tics in conversion reactions, 671

Time-Lags, 709, 914

Too Intense Experience Concept, 694-695, 926

Total Individual Reaction to Trauma, 740, 876

Total Individual Response to Crisis

anxiety, in, 16, 18, 19, 28, 85, 95

Anxiety Neurosis, in relation to, 116

Anxiety-Tension State, in, 101

Apprehensive Anticipation, in reaction to, 18

Compliant Resignation, Response to, 859

concept, 12

Depersonalization as part of, 762

Dissociative Reactions, in relation to, 740

energy potential mobilized during, 19

externalized danger as reaction in, 16

fear, in relation to, 12, 13, 516

Fugue States, in, 797

Military Reactions, in, 917

Neuroses-Following-Trauma, in relation to, 857-860, 865

protective aspect, 17-18

stress, and, 866

Total Individual Response to Trauma, 859, (*see also* NEUROSES-FOLLOWING-TRAUMA)

Anxiety Neurosis, in relation to, 116

Dissociative Reactions, in relation to, 740

Tracing Technique in Therapy, 366-367, 465, 494, 534, 593, 602, 713, 806, 889

conversion therapy, as, 713

definition, 366-368

Phobic Reactions, for 593